PENGUIN B

REFORMA

'MacCulloch is a wonderful storyte... ...p.. ..
the heart of historical change . . . astonishingly learned and rich'
Daniel Swift, *Spectator*

'Deserves to become the standard history of early modern
Europe religion and its legacy, synthesizing and assessing a
quarter-century of international scholarship . . . Like the best of
historians, he helps us to understand why we are; and why we
need not be so' Ronald Hutton, *Independent*

'We are all children of the Reformation and this magisterial
study shows us why in its remarkable scope, both of width and
depth . . . an astonishing delight' Bernard Green, *The Tablet*,
Books of the Year

'Once embarked upon it, I found it impossible to put down'
Richard Chartres, *Church Times*

'A masterly synthesis . . . Rich, arresting, frequently provocative
and always interesting . . . This compelling and thought-
provoking account is not just for those interested in Reformation
history. Anyone interested in what humanity can do with a
religious creed should read it' Lucy Wooding, *The Tablet*

'Magisterial . . . What is particularly impressive about
MacCulloch's book is its freshness, and the skill with which it
manoeuvres through sometimes complex and arcane
ideas' *Sunday Times*, Books of the Year

'It is difficult to imagine anybody writing a better book about the Reformation. It is even handed, learned and profound. A serious work of scholarship, it is admirably accessible. With great skill, MacCulloch enables his readers to enter an intellectual world that seems light years from our own, and helps us to appreciate the complexity of theological controversies that might seem abstruse but which were at that time a matter of life and death'
Karen Armstrong, *Los Angeles Times*

'This is a big, bold book. The author has woven his own research, and the researches of many others, into a synoptic panorama, strong in human interest. MacCulloch's *Reformation* looks set to become a book like Carlyle's French Revolution, necessary and unavoidable to anyone interested; and it is, additionally, the work of an historian's historian, splendidly accessible' C. W. Kemp, *Prayer Book Society Journal*

ABOUT THE AUTHOR

Diarmaid MacCulloch was brought up in a country rectory in East Anglia and studied in Cambridge, doing his doctoral research with Sir Geoffrey Elton. He is a Fellow of St Cross College, Oxford, and Professor of the History of the Church at Oxford University. He is also a Fellow of the British Academy, of the Royal Historical Society and of the Society of Antiquaries of London. His books include *Suffolk and the Tudors* (1986; winner of the Royal Historical Society's Whitfield Prize), *The Later Reformation in England 1547–1603* (1990), Henry VIII: Politics, Policy and Piety (1995), Thomas Cranmer: A Life (1996; winner of the Whitbread Biography Prize, the James Tait Black Prize and the Duff Cooper Prize), and *Tudor Church Militant: Edward VI and the Protestant Reformation* (2000).

DIARMAID MacCULLOCH

Reformation

EUROPE'S HOUSE DIVIDED
1490–1700

NICHOLAS S. TYRRAS

PENGUIN BOOKS

PENGUIN BOOKS

Penguin Books Ltd, 80 Strand, London WC2R ORL, England
Penguin Group (USA) Inc., 375 Hudson Street, New York, New York 10014, USA
Penguin Group (Canada), 10 Alcorn Avenue, Toronto, Ontario, Canada M4V 3B2
(a division of Pearson Penguin Canada Inc.)
Penguin Ireland, 25 St Stephen's Green, Dublin 2, Ireland
(a division of Penguin Books Ltd)
Penguin Group (Australia), 250 Camberwell Road, Camberwell, Victoria 3124, Australia
(a division of Pearson Australia Group Pty Ltd)
Penguin Books India Pvt Ltd, 11 Community Centre, Panchsheel Park, New Delhi – 110 017, India
Penguin Group (NZ), cnr Airborne and Rosedale Roads, Albany, Auckland 1310, New Zealand
(a division of Pearson New Zealand Ltd)
Penguin Books (South Africa) (Pty) Ltd, 24 Sturdee Avenue, Rosebank 2196, South Africa

Penguin Books Ltd, Registered Offices: 80 Strand, London WC2R ORL, England

www.penguin.com

Published by Allen Lane 2003
Published in Penguin Books 2004
14

Typeset by Rowland Phototypesetting Ltd, Bury St Edmunds, Suffolk
Printed in England by Clays Ltd, St Ives plc

ISBN-13: 978–0–140–28534–5

www.greenpenguin.co.uk

For Simon Yarrow
with whom I discovered Preston Bissett

Contents

PART II EUROPE DIVIDED: 1570–1619

PART III   PATTERNS OF LIFE

List of Illustrations and Maps

PLATES

ILLUSTRATIONS IN THE TEXT

MAPS

Preface and Acknowledgements

I am very grateful to the Arts and Humanities Research Board of the United Kingdom for providing me with the opportunity for extra study leave which was enormously helpful in writing this book. Their generosity was equalled by that of my colleagues in the Oxford Theology Faculty, who with their habitual grace took on administrative and teaching burdens, making it possible for me to enjoy a year of uninterrupted reading and writing. My German teacher, Mathilde Willi, and my fellows in our class during my sabbatical genially put up with my slow progress in the language. I am sorry that Lord Runcie, former Primate of All England, did not live to read this volume, because our conversations over more than a decade did much to widen my horizons and order my thoughts; he remains in my memory the model of what a prince of the Church should be. My thanks go to Stuart Proffitt for his friendly encouragement and unerring publisher's eye for pedantic assumptions, obscurities and clumsy or redundant prose. My literary agent Felicity Bryan, equally eagle-eyed in scanning my text, deserves especial thanks for the wise and creative advice that directly led to my beginning this project. Any remaining infelicities are of course my responsibility and not theirs. Many professional colleagues have shown friendship in their conversation and replies to many importunacies as I have been constructing the book: some of them have even taken on the penitential task of reading drafts of the text. I am indebted to them all, but particularly to Simon Adams, Margaret Bent, Francis Bremer, Owen Chadwick, Michael Chisholm, John Cooper, Maria Crăciun, Maria Dowling, John Edwards, Stefan Ehrenpreis, Elizabeth Eisenstein, Mary Fissell, Thomas Freeman, Malcolm Gaskill, Olwen Hufton, Ronald Hutton, Philip Kennedy, Ian Maclean, Judith Maltby, Peter McCullough, Graeme Murdock, Bill Naphy, Alec Ryrie, Peter Sherlock, Andrew Spicer, David Starkey, Ronald Truman and Katherine Whale. I am grateful to Craig D'Alton, Gregory Graybill, Stephen Hampton and William Wizeman for permission to cite their unpublished dissertations. I must also salute the librarians of Oxford University, who so heroically transcend their chaotic inheritance of inappropriate build-ings to provide a superb service for their readers. I thank all those who helped me with pictures, especially Susan Harris, Alex Newson and Ian Campbell and his colleagues. Lastly, after many past expressions of thanks to Mark Achurch, I now look back over nearly two decades of his loving support of my obsessions in history.

Diarmaid MacCulloch, 2003

Introduction

Who or what is a Catholic? This Greek word has become one of the chief battlegrounds in western Latin Christianity, for it is used in different ways which outside observers of Christian foibles find thoroughly confusing. The word 'Catholic' is the linguistic equivalent of a Russian doll. It may describe the whole Christian Church founded two thousand years ago in Palestine, or the western half of the Church which split from mainstream eastern Christianity a thousand years ago, or that part of the western half which remained loyal to the Bishop of Rome (the Pope) after the sixteenth century, or a Protestant European Christian who thought that the Bishop of Rome was Antichrist, or a modern 'Anglo-Catholic' faction within the Anglican Communion. How can the word describe all of these things and still have any meaning? I have written this book about the sixteenth-century Reformation in part to answer that question. The Reformation introduced many more complications to the word; in fact there were very many different Reformations, nearly all of which would have said that they were simply aimed at recreating authentic Catholic Christianity. For simplicity's sake I will take for granted that this book examines multiple Reformations, some of which were directed by the Pope. From now on I will continue to use the shorthand term 'Reformation', but readers should therefore note that this is often intended to embrace both Protestantism and the religious movements commonly known as Tridentine Catholicism, the Catholic Reformation or Counter-Reformation: the revitalized part of the old Church which remained loyal to the Pope.

'Catholic' is clearly a word which a lot of people want to possess. By contrast, it is remarkable how many religious labels started life as a sneer: the Reformation was full of angry words. 'Calvinist' was at first a term of abuse to describe those who believed more or less what John Calvin believed; the nickname gradually forced out the rival contemptuous term 'Picard', which referred to Calvin's birthplace in Noyon in Picardy.[1] No Anabaptists ever described themselves as Anabaptist, since 'Anabaptist' means 'rebaptizer', and these radical folk believed that their adult baptism was the only authentic Christian initiation, with infant baptism signifying nothing. Even that slippery term 'Anglican' appears to have been first spoken with disapproval by King James VI of Scotland, when in 1598 he was trying to convince the Church of Scotland how unenthusiastic he was for the Church of England.[2]

One of the most curious usages is the growth of the word 'Protestant'. It originally related to a specific occasion, in 1529, when at the Holy Roman Empire's Diet (imperial assembly) held in the city of Speyer, the group of princes and cities who supported the programmes of reformation promoted by Martin Luther and Huldrych Zwingli found themselves in a voting minority: to keep their solidarity, they issued a 'Protestatio', affirming the reforming beliefs that they shared. The label 'Protestant' thereafter was part of German or imperial politics for decades, and did not have a wider reference than that. When the coronation of little King Edward VI was being organized in London in 1547, the planners putting in order the procession of dignitaries through the city appointed a place for 'the Protestants', by whom they meant the diplomatic representatives of these reforming Germans who were staying in the capital.[3] Only rather later did the word gain a broader reference. It is therefore problematic to use 'Protestant' as a simple description for sympathizers with reform in the first half of the sixteenth century, and the reader will find that often in this book I use a different word, 'evangelical'. That word has the advantage that it was widely used and recognized at the time, and it also encapsulates what was most important to this collection of activists: the good news of the Gospel, in Latinized Greek, the *evangelium*.

Reformation disputes were passionate about words because words were myriad refractions of a God one of whose names was Word: a God encountered in a library of books itself simply called 'Book' – the Bible. It is impossible to understand modern Europe without understanding these sixteenth-century upheavals in Latin Christianity. They represented the greatest fault-line to appear in Christian culture since the Latin and Greek halves of the Roman empire went their separate ways a thousand years before; they produced a house divided. The fault-line is the business of this book. It is not a study of Europe as a whole: it largely neglects Orthodox Europe, the half or more of the continent that stretches from Greece, Serbia, Romania and the Ukraine through the lands of Russia as far east as the Urals. I will not deal with these except when the Orthodox story touches on or is intertwined with that of the Latin West. There is a simple reason for this: so far, the Orthodox churches have not experienced a Reformation.

Back in the eighth and ninth centuries many of them were convulsed by an 'iconoclastic controversy', which hinged on one of the great issues to reappear in the sixteenth-century Reformation. But in the case of the Orthodox, the status quo was restored and not partially overthrown as it was in the West. We will return to this issue of images frequently in the course of this book.

My subject, then, is the Church which, when united, might most accurately be described (though clumsily and in narrow technical ecclesiological jargon) as the Western Church of the Latin Rite; I shall more commonly call it the western Church or the Latin Church, and refer to the culture which it sustained as Latin or western Christendom. Latin was inherited from the western Roman Empire formally dismantled in 476; Latin remained the language which united the peoples of this society, and in which they made their official approaches to God. During the sixteenth century this western society, previously unified by the Pope's symbolic leadership and by possession of that common Latin culture, was torn apart by deep disagreements about how human beings should exercise the power of God in the world, arguments even about what it was to be human. It was a process of extreme physical and mental violence. The historian of the German Reformation Peter Matheson compares the effect to the strategy of Berthold Brecht in his plays: Brecht talked of 'alienation', *Verfremdung*, a process of making the familiar unfamiliar in order to shock his theatre audiences into taking control of their perceptions of what was going on in the drama. The reformers, suddenly finding the Pope to be the devil's agent and the miracle of the Mass the most evil moment in their earthly experience, would have known exactly what Brecht was trying to say.[4]

The resulting division between Catholic and Protestant still marks Europe west of the lands of Orthodox (Greek, Russian and oriental) Christianity, in a host of attitudes, assumptions and habits of life which distinguish, for instance, the remaining territories of Protestant Prussia from neighbouring Catholic Poland, or the Protestant Netherlands from the Catholicism of the modern kingdom of Belgium. Sometimes the two communities nurse ancient grievances side by side, as in Northern Ireland. The Protestant communities, which for a variety of reasons and motives cut themselves off from Rome, also cut themselves off from many possible devotional roads to God, because they saw such routes as part of Roman corruption. In one sense, therefore, the Reformation conflicts stifled diversity. Rome closed down options by the decisions of the Council of Trent: Protestants too were anxious to weed out rival versions of Protestantism where princes and magistrates gave them the chance, and they also rejected many alternatives suggested by more radical spirits. Yet that very cutting-down of options heightens the sense of difference between Catholic and Protestant Europe, because of the rival tidinesses which this process of sifting created. The decay of actual religious practice in Europe during the last century makes it all the more urgent a task to explain the reasons for Europe's continuing diversity. The common Latin inheritance of Catholic and Protestant, besides and beyond their sixteenth-century quarrels, is the shaping fact of European identity, but it has become a divided inheritance.

Both the division and the original inheritance continue to shape Europe's effect on the rest of the modern world. For the story of the sixteenth-century Reformation is not only relevant to the little continent of Europe. At the same time as Latin Christian Europe's common culture was falling apart, Europeans were establishing their power in the Americas and on the coasts of Asia and Africa; so all their religious divisions were reproduced there. Because the two first great powers to embark on this enterprise remained loyal to the Pope, the early story of Europe's religious expansion is more about Catholics than Protestants – with one huge exception. In the United States of America, Protestantism stemming from England and Scotland set the original patterns of identity, and the diversity within English Protestantism achieved a new synthesis. American life is fired by a continuing energy of Protestant religious practice derived from the sixteenth century. So the Reformation, particularly in its English Protestant form, has created the ideology dominant in the world's one remaining superpower, and Reformation and Counter-Reformation ways of thought remain (often alarmingly) alive and central in American culture and in African and Asian Christianity, even when they have largely become part of history in their European homeland.

This book has no room to describe the ways in which European religion was transformed in these new settings, but it seeks to alert the reader to the different sources of the modern worldwide religious mixture, and how western Europe began exporting its ways of worshipping God to other continents. It will tell a story, to begin with, as far as possible as an interwoven narrative, because that is how people experienced events. Doing this also minimizes the unfortunate tendency to present the Reformation solely in terms of a handful of significant males, principally Luther, Zwingli, Calvin, Loyola, Cranmer, Henry VIII and a number of popes. These figures are only part of a story which also involves the movements of popular feeling, the slowly changing lifestyles of ordinary people and the political and dynastic concerns of landed elites. This is far from saying that the theologians of the Reformation are unimportant, or that they should be ignored. One conclusion to be drawn from the accumulation of recent research on the Latin Church before the upheaval was that it was not as corrupt and ineffective as Protestants have tended to portray it, and that it generally satisfied the spiritual needs of late medieval people.

That recovered perspective only serves to emphasize the importance of the ideas which the reformers put forward. They were not attacking a moribund Church which was an easy target, ripe for change, but despite this, their message could still seize the imaginations of enough people to overcome the power and success of the old church structures. Ideas mattered profoundly; they had an independent power of their own, and they could be corrosive and destructive. The most corrosive ideas of all were to be found in the Bible, an explosive, unpredictable force in every age. It will do no harm for the reader trying to make sense of these tangled events to have a Christian Bible ready to hand, or at least to have some mental picture of how the Old and New Testaments of the Bible are arranged. It will also help to read through the various key statements of Christianity provided at the end of this book: two creeds, the Ten Commandments in two significantly different arrangements, and the Lord's Prayer. This is the minimum kit which those caught up in the Reformation would have had at their disposal.

The Reformation is contained within the period which historians customarily describe as early modern. Outsiders to historical shoptalk may find this a rather confusing usage, but it is less clumsy than some of the alternatives, and so is a useful label which will appear from time to time in this book. The early modern era is generally reckoned to run from the late fifteenth to the eighteenth centuries, and my survey, after setting the medieval background, runs from around 1490 to around 1700. The 1490s are an appropriate place to start because the new fact about European politics was the shift of warfare to Italy, as the ruling families of France, Spain and the Holy Roman Empire (Valois, Trastamara and Habsburg) contended for a leading position in Europe. It was as decisive a change as that later convulsion centring on the Habsburgs, the Thirty Years War.

The power of ideas explains why the Reformation was such a continent-wide event: using the common language of Latin, which all educated people spoke and wrote, religious revolutionaries could spread their message across smaller-scale culture and language barriers. So this continent-wide narrative, the first third of the book, is shaped by crisis points. Such moments are 1517, when the Church's supposedly reforming Lateran Council ended without achieving much, and when Luther caught the imagination of central Europe as a symbol of social transformation; 1525, the culmination of seven years of popular excitement in which anything seemed possible, ending in the defeat of the German peasants' rebellion and widespread popular disillusion; 1541–2, a moment when prospects for reunion and a civilized settlement of religious arguments were real, only to end in disappointment and futility; 1570–2, when a clutch of separate political crises shifted the balance in favour of Protestants in the north, and of Catholics in the south. Throughout these narratives, when England appears in the story, the aim is to escape the complacent insularity that has particularly afflicted the historiography of the Church of England – to show how a kaleidoscope of religious loyalties in offshore islands interacted with changes in mainland Europe, both Protestant and Roman Catholic.

As religious divisions become ever greater, it becomes necessary to split the narrative, so that Part II consists of a series of regional narratives from 1570, between northern, southern and central Europe. This post-1570 era also witnessed a process to which historians have given the unlovely but perhaps necessary jargon label 'confessionalization': the creation of fixed identities and systems of beliefs for separate churches which had previously been more fluid in their self-understanding, and which had not begun by seeking separate identities for themselves – they had wanted to be truly Catholic and reformed. Confessionalization represents the defeat of attempts to rebuild the unified Latin and Catholic Church. In 1618 the outbreak of the most widespread warfare so far in the Reformation, the Thirty Years War, sealed that defeat. A fragile fifty-year balance between confessional groupings in central Europe was overturned by a political crisis in the kingdom of Bohemia, which sought to throw off Catholic Habsburg rule by electing a German Calvinist monarch; in 1619 this effort was crushed. The resulting war destroyed much of the religious diversity of Reformation Europe, so that the exhausted and polarized society which emerged in 1648 looked very different from that of 1618. Separate from the short treatment of the Thirty Years War is the section on the Atlantic Isles – England, Ireland, Scotland, Wales. This exception is not just a revival of British insularity: it deals with the British political and religious crisis which ran through three decades from the 1620s, and produced one of the most important consequences of the European Reformation, the export of a militant form of English Protestantism to north America.

Once this chronological narrative is complete, the third section takes up social and intellectual themes which do not lend themselves so readily to chronological treatment. Much of this story has traditionally been left on the sidelines. I examine the experience of the Reformation, not merely everyday life, but changing ideas about time and about how the tangible life of this world might relate to the world beyond death. I explore the place of women and children in the newly created societies, together with what it was to be deviant amid these changing certainties, and what happened to deviants. Finally, we may gain some clues as to why, uniquely among world cultures, the descendants of Latin Christianity have begun to reject belief-systems sanctioned by a sacred book – or at least, who hinted to them that they might do so.

My own viewpoint is neither confessional nor dogmatically Christian. My religious background is in the Anglican Communion, coming as I do from a line of Scottish Episcopalian clergy who have merited an entry in *Crockford's Clerical Directory* continuously from the 1890s. I retain a warm sympathy for Anglicanism at its best: its distinctive, low-temperature culture and art, its ability and readiness to question itself, and an attitude to the exploration of truth which is both reverently cynical and patiently serious. I do not now personally subscribe to any form of religious dogma (although I do remember with some affection what it was like to do so). In trying to describe the Reformation to a world which has largely forgotten or half-understood what it was about, I regard that as an advantage. 'Blind unbelief is sure to err', sang the Christian hymn-writer William Cowper in Georgian England. Historians are likely to retort that blind belief has a record even more abysmal: historical narratives told with a confessional viewpoint lurking in the background are very likely to bend the story to fit irrelevant preconceptions.

Over the last few years I have been co-editor, first with Martin Brett and now with James Carleton Paget, of the *Journal of Ecclesiastical History*, which for more than half a century has been a chief forum for its subject. Even though the task has necessarily involved administrative and editorial drudgery, it has also been an exciting privilege: an unrivalled chance to see the extent of research and the emergence of original thought across the whole field of Christian history. Frequently much of this knowledge remains locked inside the world of specialists. If this book can help to liberate such research for wider enjoyment and understanding, then I will feel that it has done a good job.

NOTE ON USAGES AND PROPER NAMES

All primary-source quotations are in modern spelling. I am more of a devotee of capital letters than is common today; in English usage, they are symbols of what is special, different and in the context of this book, of what links the profane and the sacred world. The body of the faithful, the worldwide organization called the Church, deserves a capital, although a building called a church does not. The Mass and the Rood need capitals; both their devotees and those who hated them would agree on that. So do the Bible, the Eucharist, Saviour, the Blessed Virgin, and the persons of the Trinity. My decisions on this have been arbitrary, but I hope that they are at least internally consistent.

My general practice with place-names has been to give the modern usage (sometimes with the contemporary usage in brackets) – so Regensburg not Ratisbon, Leuven not Louvain, Timişoara not Temesvár – except where, in context, the sixteenth-century usage better reflects the general population of that time: so Danzig not Gdansk, Königsberg not Kaliningrad, Strassburg not Strasbourg, and Nikolsburg not Mikulov (such variants are cross-referenced in the index). The common English versions of overseas place-names (such as Brunswick, Hesse, Milan or Munich) are also used. Readers will be aware that the collection of islands which embraces England, Ireland, Scotland and Wales has commonly been known as the British Isles. This title no longer pleases all the inhabitants of the islands, and a more neutral as well as more accurate description is 'the Atlantic Isles', which will be used throughout the book.

Personal names of individuals are generally given in the birth-language which they would have spoken, except in the case of certain major figures in Europe, such as rulers or clergy (like the Emperor Charles V, the Kings of the Polish-Lithuanian Commonwealth or John Calvin), who were addressed in several languages by various groups among their subjects or colleagues. Scholarly clerics and academics at the time often adopted Latinized or cod-Greek names from their place of origin, like Johannes Pomeranus ('the Pomeranian') for Johann Bugenhagen, or as translations of their ordinary surname, like Johannes Oecolampadius for Johann Hussgen ('John House-Lamp'!). Although to some extent an affectation, such names also served to emphasize the international nature of European culture and the pan-European applicability of ideas. I use them where they are more customary than other forms – again with a cross-reference in the index. Many readers will be aware of the Dutch convention of writing down names such as 'Pieterszoon' as 'Pietersz': I hope that they will forgive me if I extend these, to avoid confusion for others. Similarly in regard to Hungarian names, I am not using the Hungarian convention of putting first name after surname: so I will speak of Gábor Bethlen, not Bethlen Gábor. The family name of the Scottish royal family perhaps deserves its own footnote: its spelling in a Scots context is normally Stewart, but when it is transplanted to England to preside over a dual (in fact triple) monarchy after 1603, in an English context it becomes Stuart. This may seem arbitrary, but that is how it is.

I have tried to avoid cluttering the main text with birth and death dates for people mentioned; the reader will find them in the index. I employ the 'Common Era' usage in dating, since it avoids value-judgements about the status of Christianity relative to other systems of faith. Dates unless otherwise stated are 'Common Era' (CE), the system which Christians have customarily called 'Anno Domini' or AD. Dates before 1 CE are given as BCE ('Before Common Era'), which is equivalent to BC. I hope, however, that non-Christian readers will forgive me if, for simplicity's sake, I generally call the Hebrew Scripture the Old Testament, in parallel to the Christian New Testament.

PART I

A COMMON CULTURE

I

The Old Church 1490–1517

SEEING SALVATION IN CHURCH

Lurking in a little English country church, at Preston Bissett in Buckinghamshire, is an object lesson in the difficulty of understanding the religious outlook of past generations. Holding up the arch at the entrance to the chancel, the most sacred part of the church building, are two carved stone figures, sculpted sometime in the early fourteenth century. The figure on the north side, crouched on all fours under the weight of the arch, is displaying his ample buttocks towards the high altar, the place where, day by day before the Reformation, the priest of Preston presided at the Mass, transforming bread and wine into the flesh and blood of the crucified Christ. Some later vandal has knocked the head off the carving, as with countless other carvings in Protestant Europe, but the buttocks are unscathed (see Plate 1a).

It is easier to understand a Protestant sparing the buttocks – which would admirably convey what he or she thought of the miracle of the Mass – than to understand why they were carved in the first place. Preston Bissett's priest could hardly have avoided staring at them as he blessed the people at the end of Mass, before processing down the altar steps and out through the wooden screen which filled the chancel arch and hid the sculpture from his parishioners' eyes. The buttocks are too early to have been carved by a craftsman who was a Lollard, one of those religious dissidents who formed discreet communities in this part of England in the fifteenth century. Did the carving express the impatience which many devout people felt with their clergy when they did not perform their sacred task to public satisfaction? Was it meant to be a warning to a lazy or incompetent priest, or was it a private joke? Was it a symbol of Satan who sought to destroy the Church's proclamation of good news at God's altar?

Otherwise the meaning of the figure is now irrecoverable from a belief system where the physical and the spiritual were much more intimately,

1. *Europe's political units, c. 1500*

unexpectedly and exuberantly fused than they became in the Reformation and Counter-Reformation. This was a religion where shouts of laughter as well as roars of rage were common in church, where the clergy waged a constant if perhaps sometimes half-hearted battle against the invasion of fun, entertainment and commerce into their church building. It was also a religion where death, and the cheating of death, mattered desperately. Preston Bissett's cheeky chancel arch sculpture was only one component in a spectacular and elaborate piece of church furniture at the chancel entrance that celebrated the mystery of the conquest of death: the Rood (the crucified figure of Christ), the screen on which it stood, and its Doom.

Another English parish church, Wenhaston in Suffolk, preserves a fine early sixteenth-century example of this Doom or last judgement by God, painted on boards that once filled the arch above the Rood screen (see Plate 3). As the parishioners listened to the Latin of the Mass in the nave of their church, they would stare up at these pictures, but they would experience them as the backdrop to the most dramatic sculpture in their church, the body of Jesus Christ nailed to the cross, flanked by the grief-stricken standing figures of his mother Mary and his beloved disciple John, to whom the dying Jesus had entrusted his mother. Wenhaston's crowded composition is unbalanced now because image-hating Protestants have ripped away the Rood group and destroyed it, leaving only blank outlines against the painted boards, but around these ghosts of wood-carving the boards are crowded with naked figures, an array of graphically nude flesh that would be considered tasteless or improper if it appeared in the art of modern Western Christianity.

The naked were the souls of dead humanity, in the process of their judgement at the end of time. Some were marching into heaven, newly released from purging their sins in the trials of Purgatory, to enjoy eternal bliss. Others had been excluded by the grossness of their sin even from Purgatory pain, and were already suffering the unending torments of hell, tortured and terrified by demons. The vivid nakedness of these saved and damned souls may have prompted some in the congregation to lustful thoughts, whose foulness would have been a timely personal reminder of why that broken, almost-nude figure of a God made flesh was hanging there on the Cross. A fifteenth-century Buckinghamshire wall painting at Broughton, near enough Preston Bissett for people there to have seen it quite often, makes the same point in a different way: pictures of blasphemers, drunkards and gamblers surround the Virgin, cradling her dead son in her arms, each sin inflicting a fresh wound on the body of Jesus.[1]

Jesus, the Christ or Messiah, son of God and son of Mary, had died in

Palestine for human sin, in order to retrieve something from the wreckage of humanity's failure when Adam and Eve had disobeyed God in the Garden of Eden in the dawn of creation. At the Last Judgement, Christ risen from the dead, fully God and fully Word made human, still gloriously bearing the wounds of his crucifixion, decided the fates of all people: heaven or hell. The Church told the story without ceasing – in Wenhaston, in Preston Bissett, and throughout the churches of western Christendom. The whole drama of the Christian faith was built into this floor-to-ceiling ensemble of the Rood and Doom, extending from the jostle of the living worshippers in the nave of the church, through the array of the Church's saints in heaven painted on the rood-screen, up to the sacrifice of the dying Saviour, then finally to the life everlasting. Beyond it all, through what people called the chancel door of the screen, the priest busied himself with bringing the Saviour in physical form into the church at the high altar. The Rood figure of Christ showed the people the real, bodily presence of God, for it represented the broken body which lay in the round white wafer of bread in the priest's hands. As he held up the consecrated wafer and chalice of wine for the people to see, his assistant rang the church bell to tell the people outside the church building throughout his parish that the Church's work of representing them before God was done once more.

The people of Preston Bissett and Wenhaston knew (because their parish priest told them) that Christ had been nailed to the Rood in Palestine because the Jews hated him. Some of the more sceptical or reflective might have found it strange that their Saviour was also born a Jew, although the problem would hardly affect them personally. They had never seen a Jew, for back in 1290 King Edward I had expelled all the Jews from England, the first monarch in all Christian Europe to do so. The nearest contact they would have with a Jew would be in the caricature villains played on stage when their parish or a nearby town performed a play about the life and death of Christ. They had no chance of knowing the strange tangled history of the Christian Church: a small Jewish sect had separated out from all the other Jewish identities of first century Palestine after it proclaimed its founder Jesus to be the Messiah whom all Jews sought. Over four centuries the little sect had grown into the Mediterranean-wide community which was Christianity, and after 312 CE it had grown powerful when it allied with the emperors of Rome. Judaism and Christianity were fully distinct from the end of the first century CE, and their relationship thereafter was tangled and often bitter: they shared a sacred book of Hebrew Scripture which Christians called their Old Testament. Christians could never forget their debt to the Jews, though they frequently resented it and turned their resentment into condemnation of the parent religion. They borrowed from the law contained in the Hebrew Scripture to suit themselves: they invented a distinction between moral, judicial and ceremonial law which was wholly absent from the intentions of the writers, labelling what they wanted to use as moral law, selecting at will from what they defined as judicial law, and relegating ceremonial law to Jewish history.

The greatest theologian of the western Church was a Roman intellectual born in the fourth century CE, Augustine of Hippo: we will be meeting him very often, for his thoughts decided much in the future thinking of Latin-speaking Christianity (see especially chapter 3, pp. 106–13). Augustine puzzled about what Christians ought to think about Jews. Against Christian extremists, some of whom wanted to reject all the Hebrew Scripture, he strongly reaffirmed that God had chosen the Jews to be a special people; against Jews themselves, he thundered that they were blind in rejecting Christ as their Messiah. Augustine's generation of Christians was one of the first to enjoy the luxury of backing up its opinions with Roman military force. Should this force be directed against obstinate and offensive Jews in the same way as Augustine recommended that Christian rulers ought to put down obstinate and offensive Christian heretics? Augustine thought not. He decided that God had allowed the Jews to survive all the disasters in their history to act as a sign and a warning to Christians. Therefore they ought to be allowed to continue their community life, although without the full privileges of citizenship that Christians enjoyed: God only intended them to be converted en masse when he chose to bring the world to an end.[2]

Accordingly, the Christian Church allowed Jewish communities to survive, while over centuries it destroyed all other religious competitors. Jews kept their own places of worship (synagogues) and they generally spoke the language of the people around them, particularly whatever language was spoken by the wealthy and powerful, reserving their ancestral Hebrew solely for worship and reading their sacred books. Although they thus sought to avoid standing out from the wider population, they were generally excluded from positions of power, which forced them to turn towards other ways of making a living, especially lending money. Most Christians understood the Old Testament to forbid taking of interest on money, and so generally kept away from this activity: Jews had a rather clearer grasp of the nuanced discussion of this subject in their sacred Scripture, and they stepped into the gap.[3] This specialization in money-lending and credit made Jews useful to Christian rulers, yet constantly vulnerable to debtors turning on them: the consequences could be very serious for them if the ruler himself was a bad debtor, or saw a way of courting cheap popularity from his subjects. Hence the Jews' expulsion by Edward I of England, which was followed by similar action from the king of France in 1394.

Other rulers, including the Pope, were more steadfast observers of Augustine's rules in protecting the Jewish community, but there were constant outbursts of anti-Jewish feeling among Christians, often encouraged by local Church authorities. The most serious consequence was the growth in the twelfth century of an anti-Jewish 'blood-libel': a legend that from time to time groups of Jews kidnapped Christian children (usually male) and sadistically murdered them for use in their rituals; characteristically crucifixion was involved. Probably these stories reflected real incidents in which someone had indeed abused and murdered a child: when a local community could not face the horror of what had happened, they deflected the guilt on to the alien community in their midst. Sometimes the Church patently tried to profit from such incidents: the Benedictine monks of Norwich Cathedral in England, encouraged by their bishop, were pioneers in the blood-libel business when in the 1140s they tried to foster in their own church a cult of an alleged young victim of the Jews called William. Unfortunately for the monks, the good folk of Norwich loathed their cathedral more than they did the Jews, and the pilgrimage to little St William never amounted to much. Other cults were more successful (see chapter 2, p. 59), and the blood-libel has remained a recurring motif in the worst atrocities against the Jews.[4]

Other Christian developments added to Jewish troubles. Francis of Assisi, that generous-hearted and anarchic preacher of God's love, started a great renewal movement in the thirteenth-century Church; in part it was institutionalized as the Franciscan Order of friars, who did much to revive preaching in the western Church (see below, pp. 31–2). Franciscan preachers urged the crowds who came to hear them to meditate devotionally on the earthly life of Christ (p. 20). That had the logical consequence of making the faithful also think about the death of Christ on the Cross, and often this led directly to deep hatred of Jews. Franciscans thus ironically became major exponents of anti-Semitism in medieval western Europe and were deeply involved in some of the worst violence against Jewish communities; their fellow friars and rivals, the Dominicans, were not far behind.[5] Not surprisingly, Jews tended to live together for safety, a trend which Christian rulers increasingly turned into an obligation: this developed early in Italy and the word 'ghetto' to describe such enclosed areas is of Italian origin, although there is more than one explanation of what it might originally have meant. Jewish physical isolation made matters worse, and bred new legends among a suspicious population: that the Jews were ready to poison Christian wells, for instance, steal consecrated eucharistic wafers to do them terrible indignities, or collaborate with the Muslim powers which threatened the borders of Christendom.

Already the meeting of art, drama, human fears and hopes in the unpretentious village churches of Preston Bissett and Wenhaston has sent us many hundreds of miles across Europe. That may help us understand the power and European-wide scope of the organization which tore itself apart in the sixteenth-century Reformation. Nicholas Ridley, one of the talented scholarly clergy who rebelled in England against the old Church, wrote about this to one of his fellow rebels John Bradford in 1554, while they both lay in prisons waiting for the old Church to burn them for heresy. As Bishop Ridley reflected on the strength of their deadly enemy, which now he saw as the power of the devil himself, he said that Satan's old world of false religion stood on two 'most massy posts and mighty pillars . . . These two, sir, are they in my judgement: the one his false doctrine and idolatrical use of the Lord's supper; and the other, the wicked and abominable usurpation of the primacy of the see of Rome.' So just as Preston Bissett's chancel arch was supported by its two grotesque stone figures, the whole system of the medieval western Church was built on the Mass and on the central role of the Pope.[6] Without the Mass, indeed, the Pope in Rome and the clergy of the Western Church would have had no power for the Protestant reformers to challenge, for the Mass was the centrepiece around which all the complex devotional life of the Church revolved. We must examine its significance at length, and in particular the doctrine of Purgatory; for Ridley, this would have been at the heart of the 'false doctrine' which distorted the Mass from its origins in the eucharistic meal.

THE FIRST PILLAR: THE MASS AND PURGATORY

The word 'Mass' is a western nickname for the Christian Church's central act, the service of Eucharist. It comes from a curiously inexplicable dismissal at the end of the Latin eucharistic liturgy – 'ite missa est' ('go, it is sent'). To appreciate the importance of the Mass an explanation of what Christians believe about the Christian Eucharist is needed. They see it as a representation, or perhaps dramatic re-creation, of the last supper which Jesus Christ ate with his disciples before his arrest and death. From the Church's earliest days it has been a way to break down the barrier between the physical and the spiritual, between earth and heaven, death and life. It involves objects made by human beings and therefore part of everyday society: bread and wine, food and drink, which bring earthly joy, and which indeed are fraught with danger because they can be enjoyed too much. That is what makes the Eucharist such a potent symbol of offering for what human beings bring to God; yet it is also associated with what Christ offers to humanity through his unique, costly and painful offering to God: life and joy, which are much more than a full belly and a head full of alcohol.

The Eucharist became a drama linking Christ to his followers, pulling them back to his mysterious union with the physical world and his conquest of the decay and dissolution of the physical in death. It was such a sacred and powerful thing that by the twelfth century in the Western Church, the laity dared approach the Lord's table only very infrequently, perhaps once a year at Easter, otherwise leaving their priest to take the bread and wine while they watched in reverence. Even when laypeople did come up to the altar, they received only the bread and not the wine, a custom which has never received any better explanation than that there was worry that the Lord's blood might stick in the moustaches and beards of the male faithful. But the particular power of the Mass in the medieval West comes from its association with another idea peculiar to the Western Church: this most powerful form of public liturgical prayer may be concentrated and directed to steer individuals through the perils of death to God's bliss in the afterlife.

Already by the ninth century, western church buildings (unlike those in the east) were being designed or adapted for a large number of altars so that priests could say as many Masses as possible for the sake of dead benefactors, or for benefactors with an eye on their coming death – the more Masses the better. Even remote little Preston Bissett and Wenhaston would have boasted one or two more altars in other parts of the building apart from their main high altar in the chancel. By the twelfth century, western Christians were taking further this idea of intercession for the dead in the Mass; they developed a more sophisticated geography of the afterlife than was presented in their biblical foundation documents. The New Testament picture of life after death is of a stark choice: heaven or hell. Humanity's general experience is that such finality ill-matches the grimy mixture of good and bad which makes up most human life.

It was natural therefore for creative Christian thinkers to speculate about some middle state, in which those whom God loved would have a chance to perfect the hard slog towards holiness that they had begun so imperfectly in their brief earthly life. Although the first thoughts along these lines came from eastern Greek-speakers in Alexandria, the idea blossomed in the West, and this place of purging in wise fire, with its promise of an eventual entrance to heaven, was by the twelfth century given a name – Purgatory.[7] Further refining of the system added a 'Limbus infantium' for infants who had not been baptized but who had no actual sins to send them to hell, and a 'limbus Patrum' for the Old Testament patriarchs who had had the misfortune to die before the coming in flesh of Jesus Christ, but these two states of limbo were subordinate to what had become a threefold scheme of the afterlife. Such theological tidy-mindedness suggests that there is something to be said for the view that when the Latin-speaking Roman Empire collapsed in the West in the fifth century, its civil servants promptly transferred to the payroll of the Western Church.

Latin is a precise language, ideal for bureaucrats; moreover, bureaucrats appreciate numbers as well as neatness. Unlike Heaven and Hell, Purgatory was a place with a time limit: its swansong, when it would finally be emptied of the triumphantly cleansed, was to come at the Last Judgement, but meanwhile it might also encompass individual time limits appropriate to those who had various quantities of sins to purge. If the prayer of the Mass was able to prompt the mercy of God, might not the degree of that mercy be calibrated in precise numbers of years deducted from Purgatory pain? And could this be linked to numbers of Masses performed? So the medieval West developed a legally founded and endowed institution intended to regularize the prayer of Masses in saving an individual, a family, or a group of associates: this was the chantry (an English word manufactured from 'cantaria', a place for singing, so-called from the convention that all Masses are sung). Some chantry foundations might be temporary and modest, borrowing the services of one priest for a lump sum of money or time-limited wage (an *obit*); others could employ a staff of priests, who needed an elaborate permanent organization, and so formed an endowed associa-tion – in Latin, *collegium*. Oxford, Cambridge and some other medieval universities have preserved a number of de luxe chantry colleges through the Reformation upheavals and expanded their teaching functions at the expense of their original primary purpose.

But while the Mass was at the centre of this burgeoning industry of intercession, plenty of other commodities could be traded for years in Purgatory – literally traded in the case of indulgence grants (see chapter 3, pp. 121–2). Many theologians, particularly the 'nominalist' philosophers who dominated northern European universities from the fourteenth century, cautioned that human virtues were no more than token commodities, which God in his mercy made a free decision to accept from an otherwise worth-less humanity, but many ordinary people may not have appreciated that subtlety (on nominalism, see pp. 25–6). The Church told them that there was a great deal of merit available, if only it was drawn on with reverence and using the means provided by the Church. Human beings could construct their own humble imitations of the mercy of God in good works. Some of these were works of mercy, such as giving to beggars or contributing to the upkeep of the hospitals which looked after the chronically sick or elderly. If someone did the community good with an act of public-spiritedness, that too was a work of mercy: building or repairing a bridge, for instance (bridges tending by their nature to be built on boundaries, ended up as no one's official responsibility). Some people even left money in their wills to pay their village's tax bill to the king, a work of mercy that perhaps deserves revival.

Works such as these could then form part of a spiritual trade within the community of the living for another form of good work – prayer. So the beggar was expected to pray for the future welfare of the soul of the good wife who gave him a coin, the inmates of the hospitals must lie in their beds praying for their benefactors, those who trudged over the bridge must pray for the donor – suitably reminded by an inscription on the bridge soliciting these prayers for the donor by name. Every soul-prayer could bear on one's time in Purgatory. Better still, to pray for the souls of the dead was also mutually beneficial, because the dead in Purgatory, with a good deal of time on their hands, could be expected to reciprocate with their own prayers. Tomb inscriptions in churches reminded the passer-by to 'pray for the soul' of the person commemorated, tugging at the sleeve of the churchgoer as urgently as any beggar in the street wheedled for alms. It was a marvellous way of uniting the dead and the living in mutual aid, to make the barrier seem no wider than that between a congregation and the carved figures in the roodloft, as well as giving the community of the living a sense of mutual responsibility and concern. It gave people a sense that they had some control over death, before which humanity has always stood baffled and powerless.

No wonder Purgatory was one of the most successful and long-lasting theological ideas in the Western Church, or bred an intricate industry of prayer. There is no doubt that this was much encouraged by the trauma of the Black Death in 1348–9, that exceptional pandemic of plague in which perhaps a third of western Europe's population died. With so many dying, including swathes of clergy trying to keep up with the torrent of burials, it was not surprising that the disposal of the dead was often obscenely hurried and perfunctory during that nightmarish couple of years. This was a powerful incentive to later medieval westerners to make elaborate arrangements to make sure that it did not happen again. Nevertheless, the development of an obsession with Purgatory was not uniform within Europe. Increasingly historians are finding that it was the north rather than the Mediterranean area, and perhaps most intensively the Atlantic fringe from Galicia on the Spanish Atlantic seaboard round as far as Denmark and north Germany, which was most intensively concerned with prayer as a ticket out of Purgatory.

The reasons for this are obscure; it may represent an inheritance of special concern for the dead from pre-Christian religion in these Atlantic cultures, and possibly it is a by-product of the culture of mutual gifts that underpinned early medieval Germanic society: the prayer of the clergy became part of a system of exchange of 'necessary generosity'.[8] Whatever explanations make sense, there is hard evidence for the contrast. Dante Alighieri's detailed descriptions of Purgatory in his fourteenth-century masterwork the *Divina Commedia* might suggest that southerners were indeed concerned with Purgatory, but his Italian readers do not seem to have transformed their delight in his great poem into practical action or hard cash. This action can be monitored through the contents of late medieval wills – one of the rare ways in which we can meet thousands of individuals facing death across the centuries and hear echoes of what they made of the experience. In the north, will-makers put a great deal of investment into such components of the Purgatory industry as Masses for the dead. In Germany there was a phenomenal surge in the endowment of Masses from around 1450, with no signs of any slackening until the whole system imploded under the impact of Luther's message in the 1520s.[9] Samplings from Spain and Italy do not reveal the same level of concern; indeed there are several local studies which suggest that such activity was imported by reforming 'Counter-Reformation' Catholic clergy in the late sixteenth century, only then creating a piety reminiscent of that which the Protestants were destroying in much of northern Europe.[10]

Another important symptom of a north–south difference has been noted in research into the many books published to provide clergy with models for sermons about penitence. These books sold well throughout Europe in the fifteenth century, because the faithful particularly demanded sermons during the penitential season of Lent, and they expected their clergy to urge them to use the confessional properly at that time. However, different books sold well in northern and in southern Europe, and they contrast in emphasis in what they say about penance. In the north, the preacher throws the spotlight on the penitents themselves, on the continual need for penance in their everyday lives and on the importance of true contrition and satisfaction when they come to confession; the priest in confession is cast in the role of judge, assessing the sincerity of all this busy work. In the south, the sermons pay more attention to the role of the priest, who is seen as doctor or mediator of grace in absolution of sin; the preacher is not so concerned to urge the layperson on to activity.[11]

The significance of this contrast is that the Purgatory-centred faith of the north encouraged an attitude to salvation in which the sinner piled up reparations for sin: action was added to action in order to merit years off Purgatory. It was possible to do something about one's salvation – this was precisely the doctrine which Martin Luther was to make his particular target after 1517. So the difference between attitudes to salvation in northern and southern Europe may explain why Luther's first attack on some of the more outrageous outcrops of the soul-prayer industry had so much more effect in the north than in the south. He was telling northern Europeans that some of the devotions which most deeply satisfied them, and convinced them that they were investing in an easier passage to salvation, were nothing but clerical confidence tricks. This message was of much less interest or relevance in the Mediterranean lands, which had not paid so much attention to the Purgatory industry.

Even within northern Europe, devotional life was far from uniform; different areas revealed different intensities of emotional and devotional investment in the system. Ralph Houlbrooke has examined hundreds of late medieval English wills and found that a majority of will-makers in Norfolk left money to the gilds or confraternities which sustained prayers and Masses for the dead; by contrast, far fewer did so in Buckinghamshire or Berkshire (where concentrations of Lollard sympathizers may quietly have induced a mood of local scepticism about the whole Purgatory industry). It is also possible that some people may have felt a real weariness about the old system in northern Europe and its labour-intensive devotion, and were ready to hear a message which involved reform of the system. Various English local studies in areas as widely separated as York, Salisbury and East Anglia (Norfolk and Suffolk) have found signs of a decline in the numbers of gilds in the 1510s and 1520s, and in East Anglia, possibly the most intense area of traditional practice in England, most major church-building projects seem to have been over by 1500.[12]

We should not underestimate European laypeople. They were perfectly capable of thinking for themselves, particularly about death, a religious theme in which everyone had an investment and about which everyone was likely to have an opinion. There is no need to invoke the idea of systematic pagan survival to account for this: Europe's mass Christianization had been a steady if piecemeal process from the sixth century through to the fourteenth. Outside the extreme east of Europe in Lithuania, where officially supported non-Christian religion had come to an end only in 1386, the most judicious recent survey of folk belief and devotional custom suggests that its pre-Christian content is very fragmentary: the most widespread and persistent practices in northern Europe, like the lighting of fires with rowan branches on May Day, had no perceptible connection with beliefs about the afterlife.[13] Ordinary people simply drew their own conclusions about the world of the dead, so, as we will see again in chapter 13 (pp. 580–81), religion as practised even by the self-consciously orthodox was not necessarily the same as religion that was officially recommended.

LAYFOLK AT PRAYER

Despite all these qualifications and complications, the great unifying theme of late medieval religion was prayer, of which the Mass was the highest and most powerful form. Prayer was the duty of laypeople as much as the clergy who presided at Mass. It was the way to come close to God and if possible to make him change his mind (although the official Church would have been appalled at too open a statement of this idea) – in the same way that a petition to a monarch or ecclesiastical ruler might produce results. The main institutions designed for this, both in the south and in death-obsessed northern Europe, were called gilds, brotherhoods, sisterhoods or confraternities: a variety of descriptions for the same basic institution. These were voluntary organizations, bound by oath and membership levy, with common activities and purposes; for some, these purposes might involve a common trade or commercial activity, but virtually all had some concern with prayer for the membership. In northern Europe especially, a gild might create a chantry, with its own altars for gild Masses in a chapel building, possibly forming part of a parish church. An important aspect of these essential vehicles of late medieval religion was that they were run by the laity, who paid the gild clergy – giving the lie to the later misrepresentation of the medieval Church by Protestants that it was entirely at the disposal of its priests. Indeed, the wholesale dissolution of the gilds in Protestant countries was one way in which ordinary laypeople lost control of what went on in their churches because of the Reformation.

Because the gilds reflected the needs and preoccupations of laypeople rather than the church hierarchy, they reflected the devotions which appealed to laypeople, sometimes alarming the clergy by their practices. Many gilds were linked with the flagellant movement, whereby, especially after the Black Death, western Europeans sought to appease God by solemnly and publicly beating themselves and each other. At times of the greatest excitement in flagellant processions, another form of purification emerged: murderous popular attacks on the Jews who might be presumed to have attracted divine wrath by their polluting and blasphemous presence in Christendom. More obviously constructive was a frequent association between gilds and communal good works, particularly noticeable in the increasingly powerful and wealthy confraternities of north and central Italy. Here, from the late fifteenth century, charitable and welfare activities became a major concern, although the former communal devotion did not diminish and different groups were tailor-made for different concerns. In Bologna, for instance, a system of hospitals was sustained by a vigorous structure of gilds and two varieties of confraternity developed during the fifteenth century: 'praising confraternities' (*Laudesi*), which drew their membership from particular areas within the city, and more widely based *Disciplinati* or *Battuti*, which carried on the flagellant tradition. Besides these, small and reticent groups called *Stretta* catered for private spiritual self-examination and contemplation, but it was perfectly possible and indeed common for an individual to belong to more than one of these groups for different purposes.[14]

The confraternity system in Italy was also notable for crossing the lay–clerical divide. Italy showed little of the rhetoric of lay dissatisfaction with the clergy which was common in northern Europe, and distinctive Italian developments in the confraternity system have a significant role in this. At Genoa in 1497, a devotional confraternity called an Oratory was founded by a layman, Ettore Vernazza, much influenced by his spiritual contacts with a mystic noblewoman Caterina Adorno, who was preoccupied both with an intense devotion to the Eucharist and with comforting and helping the sick. The Oratory reflected these twin concerns; its clergy and laity combined communal devotions and care for the sick, particularly those suffering the terrifying affliction of syphilis, which appeared for the first time in the 1490s (chapter, 15, pp. 630–33). Not unconnected with this latter work was provision for the sufferings of gentlefolk in financial or other distress, a distinctively Italian charitable concern which became a prominent feature in various foundations of Oratories in other cities, copying the Genoan Oratory; a late but very important example being the Oratory of the Divine Love founded in Rome around 1517. Several leaders prominent in the Italian Church's later recovery of nerve in the face of the Reformation onslaught formed their intense activist piety in the Oratories, and they were also to become associated with the renewal of various religious orders (see chapter 5, p. 217).

Another way in which the laity expressed their yearning to break through the barrier separating them from the divine was to journey in pilgrimage to sacred places or shrines, so that they might offer their prayers in an especially powerful and effective setting. This was a devotion in which a layperson's shoeleather was as good as that of any priest. Like the Mass, the cult of the saints and their shrines was a potent meeting of spiritual and physical: a human being who could be guaranteed as having entered heaven had kept a particularly intense relationship with a place on earth and thus rendered it sacred: sometimes through a relic, perhaps the saint's skeleton or a possession, or simply through association with a holy well or past miracle. A special case was Mary, the Mother of God, for whom there could be no bodily relics, since quite early on, both eastern and western Churches had decided that she had entered heaven in a specially privileged way, with a body that had not experienced the normal pains of death. Characteristically, the West had made sure that this devotional concept was turned into a precise doctrine, that of Mary's bodily Assumption. So although Marian shrines were common throughout Europe, particularly in regions which had bred few native saints, they centred not on a bodily relic (apart from various items of clothing and a remarkably generous number of examples of mother's milk), but instead on a representation of the Virgin's body in the form of a statue. In two famous cases, at Walsingham in England and Loreto in Italy, they went further in exhibiting a replica or transmigrated reconstruction of the Holy House in which the Christ-child had grown up in Nazareth; both these Marian shrines enjoyed an unprecedented boom in the fifteenth century, perhaps reflecting a new interest in seeing family life in the context of the life of the Church.

The pilgrimage routes which had become famous in the eleventh and twelfth centuries continued to unite Europe by sea and land. In West Country England, Bristol was the national departure point for the Apostle James's shrine of Compostela not too far from the Spanish Atlantic coast; Bristol ships made the journey in only five days, at half the price of a fortnight's land journey from England, and pilgrims setting off from the port would be able to enjoy the particular devotion to St James maintained in one Bristol city-centre parish church, or the liturgy in a Benedictine monastery of St James in the city suburbs.[15] But much less well-known saints could also reach across Europe. In 1488, the communal council of the town of Zug, just over the mountains from Zürich, knew where to write to when they wanted a relic of the Anglo-Saxon Oswald for their new St Oswald's church – far-off Peterborough in eastern England.[16]

While some shrines like Compostela were perennial favourites, the public was discriminating and enthusiastic for new fashions to suit its needs or preoccupations, as the growth of Walsingham and Loreto testifies. In fifteenth-century Ireland, certain sacred wells lost much custom while others came to prominence; at the same time in Wales, the increase in pilgrimage traffic may have been swelled by people seeking comfort amid the troubles and disruption of the country's unsuccessful rebellions against the English.[17] Shrines were not uncontested: the relic-cult of Jesus's Holy Blood miraculously preserved was particularly controversial, and several such relics aroused fierce argument between sceptics and believers, among clergy and devout laypeople alike. Consumer demand decided whether such cults would succeed or fail: in thirteenth-century England, Henry III's effort to boost his Plantagenet dynasty by establishing one such blood-relic at Westminster Abbey quickly proved an ignominious flop. By contrast at Wilsnack in Saxony, crowds of pilgrims to the shrine of the Blood ignored the scepticism expressed by a number of leading churchmen, including the investigative commission established by Archbishop Zbinko of Prague in 1405; believers were bolstered in their faith by votes of confidence in the relic from the papacy and other bishops. At Hailes Abbey in England, the fifteenth- and sixteenth-century monk-guardians of another blood-capsule published tales of the miraculous punishment of parish clergy and ordinary laypeople who disbelieved in their relic – a sure indication that there were plenty of such folk.[18]

In such a competitive market for devotion, a cult might flare up after years of obscurity, inspired by some event or charismatic figure. A particularly spectacular example occurred in 1476 at Niklashausen in Franconia, where Hans Behem, a shepherd who was also a talented drummer and a natural showman, found a sense of messianic mission and raised a great crowd to go to the Marian shrine. It was a time of great social and political disruption in Germany; Behem used his charismatic skills to preach a message of social transformation, which was an extreme example of the way in which lay piety might escape the mould which the official Church prepared for it. Naturally he ended up burned at the stake by his local bishop, despite his devotion to Our Lady. A similar outbreak of mass religious hysteria in 1519 in the city of Regensburg was tied to a vicious bout of anti-Semitism: the cathedral preacher (ironically a future radical, Balthasar Hubmaier, whom we will meet again in other circumstances) inspired mobs to pull down the city synagogue, and Our Lady cured a workman badly injured in the demolition. The cult of this 'Beautiful Mary' is reputed to have drawn 50,000 pilgrims within a month of a makeshift shrine chapel going up; as we will see later, it also infuriated Martin Luther (chapter 3, p. 142).

The faithful saw Heaven as being as closely stratified as their own society.

There were ranks of power among God's heavenly servants, the angels, and among the saints too there were degrees of worshipfulness (a phrase which secular society equally employed for its worthies). Local saints were useful symbols of a community's patriotism, so the good folk of Norfolk paid for East Anglian saints to be painted on the rood screens of their parish churches: however, when they made their wills, they hardly mentioned these local figures, looking to more cosmopolitan inhabitants of heaven to act as their intercessor to God. The same absence of local saints has been noted in the wills of Kingston on Hull, a port much further up the eastern English coastline.[19] Mary, Christ's mother, was becoming such a powerful figure in the minds of fifteenth-century people that many felt that this prime intercessor of Christ needed to be approached in turn by someone who would intercede with her: and who better than her mother, a lady named (without reference to the biblical text) Anna? So the cult of St Anne grew as an outcrop of Mary's cult, producing a harvest of new church and chapel dedications during the late medieval period, and we will meet her playing a crucial role in the life of Martin Luther (chapter 3, p. 115).[20]

For many, the Passion (the sufferings and death) of Christ was becoming central to their devotional life, but this concentration on Christ still did not hinder the creation of appropriate holy places. Queen Catherine of Aragon built a 'mount' of Christ's place of crucifixion (the hill of Golgotha) to the north of London to encourage popular devotion to the Passion, although her husband King Henry's general destruction of English shrines soon swept away the Queen's initiative with its rapidly prospering cult, and replaced it with a windmill.[21] This emphasis on the suffering Christ was part of a new exploration of his true humanity: he endured the worst possible physical and emotional pains to atone for human sin. From the time of its foundation in the thirteenth century, the Franciscan Order of Friars emphasized this humanness of Jesus when they preached about him. St Bonaventure, one of their most celebrated early theologians, preachers and mystics, wrote passionately about his vision of sleeping beside the crucified Christ: the image of divine empathy with human suffering much comforted the generation traumatized by the Black Death and left a lasting impression on late medieval spirituality. Earlier medieval art emphasized Christ's divinity: he was a victorious king, so even when on the Cross he was shown as a crowned figure who 'reigns and triumphs from the tree', in words of the sixth-century hymn *Vexilla Regis prodeunt* ('The royal banners forward go'). Now he became a crucified man, who was broken and tortured.

A stunning image of this extreme agony is the Christ on the Cross at the centre of an altarpiece painted in 1512 by the German painter Matthias

Grünewald for Antonian monks at Isenheim. The pockmarked, blood-stained Isenheim figure would have spoken especially poignantly to the similarly disfigured inmates of the monastery's attached hospital, many of them victims of Europe's new and visually harrowing scourge, syphilis. As the faithful meditated on such images, which showed their God in solidarity with their worst sufferings, new Christ-centred devotions sprang up, for instance to the wounds of Jesus, or simply to his name. This was promoted from the 1420s by the hugely popular Italian Franciscan preacher Bernardino of Siena, but it soon spread to northern Europe and became a favourite of Henry VII's mother Lady Margaret Beaufort, who prevailed on the Pope to make her patroness of the Name of Jesus devotion within England; when she lavished money on collegiate foundations at Cambridge she made sure that two of them were called Jesus and Christ's. Following this royal lead, late medieval English churches are often spattered in their decoration with the letters 'IHS', abbreviating the name of Jesus. This concentration on Christ, an outpouring of late medieval piety, was also to become central to the Protestant religious revolution.[22]

A human Christ must have a human mother, from whose flesh he had been 'cut' in his birth – an arresting image from the fifteenth-century Bernardino of Siena. To speak of raw, physical humanity was nevertheless also to emphasize the wonder of the sacrament of the Mass, for it was in the Virgin Mary's flesh, said Bernardino, that 'the whole glory and weight of the sacraments of the Church of God consists'. His preaching on Mary set the tone for a genre of sermons which were an extravagant celebration of womanliness in all its fascination and dangerous power. Mary was a scheming adventuress for humanity's salvation, who (in Bernardino's startling adaption of the biblical Song of Songs) 'seduced, deceived, and I might even say wounded God, with I do not know what caresses and promises'. Approaching Mary from another angle, a contemporary Dominican friar Guillaume Pepin made her into a skilled lawyer, who roundly humiliated the Devil in his lawsuit brought against humanity.[23]

Yet this realistic depiction of a resourceful, activist female went hand in hand with a celebration of Mary's cosmic role: at the moment that Christ died on the cross, said preachers, the whole remaining faith of humanity was concentrated in her unwavering faith alone, while others fitted her into the Apostle Paul's image of Christ as head and Christians as body to describe her as the neck of the Church.[24] Such duality between Mary's earthliness and her role in the drama of redemption sparked a fierce debate as to whether (unlike the rest of humanity) she had been conceived without sin, or whether, after a conception in the ordinary sin of human flesh, she had been immediately granted the grace to avoid committing actual sin. The distinction may seem a fine one, but it meant a great deal to bitterly opposed parties who both wanted to do her honour in their own way while remaining true to a consistent view of human sin. Most Franciscans (Bonaventure being a notable exception) championed the idea of Immaculate Conception; most Dominican friars scorned this idea of their rivals, taking their cue from their greatest theologian, Thomas Aquinas, and the medieval Church never resolved the problem, despite the intervention of Sixtus IV, a fifteenth-century Pope who had been a Franciscan, and who weighted the scales in favour of the Immaculists in his official statements.

In such debates we see a fascinating mixture of scholarly arguments and popular hunger for the certainty of salvation; sometimes the sophisticated language of the university set the pace, at other times scholars were put under pressure by non-professional Christians, who simply wanted to express their longing for divine grace and their desperate search for God's love – through the Mass, the Cross, the Mother nursing her son at her breast or passionately weeping over his crucified corpse. Some laity from around 1400 started receiving the consecrated bread of the Mass more frequently than had been customary for a thousand years, encouraged in particular by the writings of the great French theologian and leading academic Jean Gerson. Others felt that such frequent communion was a threat to reverence and preferred to go on receiving only once a year. Above all, they went on seeking new ways of reaching out for God's mercy in public and private devotion. As far as public liturgy is concerned, it has been suggested that in the half century after 1450, the average major church in England would have added three new feasts to its public round of worship.[25] Laypeople crowded in on their clergy, demanding to know as much as possible about their Saviour and his Mother, who is not served especially well by the biblical record – as we have noted, even her mother's name has to be supplied from other sources. The clergy did their best to fill the gap by their preaching, with the aid of much edifying legend which fleshed out the biblical narratives, but they also encouraged ordinary people to use their imagination privately within the framework of controlled prayer.

The dominant style of piety in the fifteenth century, which helped the laity to do this, was an intense, introspective and creatively imaginative mode of reaching out to God known as the 'modern devotion' (*Devotio Moderna*). The great characteristic of the *Devotio* was that, as with the activity of pilgrimage, laity as well as clergy, women as well as men, could aspire to the heights and depths of experience within it. Its earliest great name, the fourteenth-century Dutch theologian Geert Groote, was never ordained beyond the order of deacon; after spending some time in a Carthusian monastery near Arnhem, he went on to conduct a roving ministry of preaching in the Netherlands and to found his own informal community of friends in his native Deventer. After Groote's death this group did take on the character of a formal religious order, the Brethren of the Common Life, spread widely through central Europe and enrolled members of the calibre of the mystical writer Thomas à Kempis, the philosopher and theologian Gabriel Biel and the future Pope Adrian VI.

However, the *Devotio Moderna* was never a purely clerical movement; even the formally organized Brethren discouraged members from becoming ordained clergy, and they put their houses of Sisters and some of their own communities under the control of local urban corporations rather than the Church authorities.[26] Notably married couples and of course their children might be involved on an equal basis in this deeply devotional lifestyle. The *Devotio* ethos was diffused widely among the serious-minded. Its promise was that laity could aspire to the high personal standards that had previously been thought more easily attainable by the clergy: a programme of practical action and organization of one's thoughts and life that was summed up in the title of Kempis's famous devotional treatise *The Imitation of Christ*. That might sound a daunting agenda, but all sorts of expressions of pious activism might contribute to this earnest quest to come closer to Christ: it was not a faith only for the clever or the articulate.

Consider an example. The monastic Order of St Bridget was founded by a fourteenth-century Swedish noblewoman who was also an outstanding mystic. It was much favoured by Bridget's fellow nobility all over northern Europe and came to represent late medieval piety at its most lavishly funded, intense and sophisticated; its spirituality fused with that of the *Devotio Moderna* movement. However, in the Order's quest to enrich the faith of Christendom it was mindful of the whole range of lay aspirations in prayer, of rich and poor, sophisticated and simple. Accordingly, the de luxe Bridgettine Abbey of Syon, founded by Henry V near a chief palace of the English monarchy, devised the Fifteen Oes of St Bridget for the use of the general public. This devotion (with its characteristic late medieval exclamation of 'O Jesu') unites many of the themes already examined: a yearning for contact with the suffering Christ, a delight in exact and complex numbers, and a confidence in a concrete outcome from personal action in prayer. It was based on a systematic use of a physical object, a set of five beads, the ancestor of the later rosary (see chapter 7, 329). Each bead recalled an aspect of the Passion, which was linked to an English poem of thirty-three words (the number of years Jesus spent on earth). The user would meditate on the passion mysteries, but would also have to repeat every day for a year the Lord's Prayer fifteen times and the Hail Mary fifteen times. That would ensure 5,475 years off one's time in Purgatory, since 15 times 365 days of the year adds up to 5,475. Some advertising blurbs attached to the prayer promised that this action would also liberate fifteen deceased relatives from Purgatory, convert fifteen living sinners to a good life and sustain fifteen other relatives in virtue: altogether value for effort. Here was a satisfying mixture of devotional repetition, soothing physical activity in manipulating the beads, altruism and free-ranging meditation, in whatever proportions suited the worshipper's capacity.[27]

Throughout this rich devotional world there was an interplay of official and extra ritual, official and unofficial theology, all united by the central holy theatre of the Mass. No wonder that Nicholas Ridley saw the Mass as such a strong pillar of the old order. The liturgy of which the Mass was the centrepiece was not only good for the soul, it was fun. German Christians, for instance, looked forward on Easter morning to a good time celebrating Christ's harrowing of hell – his cosmic hooliganism when he triumphantly descended to the Devil's kingdom after dying on the Cross. At Hof in Upper Franconia a solemn procession with crucifix customarily tried to make its way out of the church, only to find its path barred by a crowd of local youths dressed as devils. After a series of ritual challenges and a vigorous mock fight with plenty of noise and slamming of doors, the devils fled the scene, throwing down their flaming torches, representing hellfire, in front of the victorious cross-bearers. At the Holy Spirit's festival of Whitsuntide in the Bavarian diocese of Eichstätt, a carved wooden dove of the Spirit was lowered down on the congregation through a hole in the church roof-vaulting (this hole was a common extra architectural amenity in large German churches); the dove was closely followed by bucketfuls of water, and the member of the congregation most thoroughly soaked became the town's *Pfingstvogel* (Whitsun bird) for the coming year.[28] Clergy might grumble about some of this excess and try to stop it, but in fact it was proof of a huge stability in the old religion: the apparent irreverence was itself a symptom of how strongly the vast majority of people felt faith in the system, and how much they could relax within it. A problem would only arise if the faithful began listening to a question: was the Mass, the linchpin of it all, in fact what it claimed to be?

This question could be asked because the western Church, in its character-istic tidy-minded fashion, tried to find a comprehensible explanation of a miracle: how in the Mass, the bread lying on the paten and the wine in the chalice turned into the body and blood of Christ, making him as corporeally (bodily) present as he had been in Palestine. A variety of answers had been proposed. Such an intricate problem naturally concerned those who taught and developed ideas in the universities, those new institutions of higher education which Europe developed from the twelfth century. The formal university method of academic investigation, by a logical system of questioning and listing data from the authorities, was called scholasticism, as universities were *scholae*. The dominant philosophical system within scholasticism, and so the best analysis of the Mass available in the twelfth and thirteenth centuries, adapted the scientific method of the pre-Christian Greek philosopher Aristotle for Christian theological purposes. This adaptation reached its highest level in the works of the thirteenth-century Dominican genius, Thomas Aquinas (the basis of the intellectual system known as Thomism). Aquinas was determined to show that human reason was a gift of God designed to give human beings as much understanding of divine mysteries as they needed. He formalized and systematized earlier discussion of the miracle of the Mass, and adopted a term which had become increasingly popular in explanations of what happened in this miracle: transubstantiation.[29]

This theory of transubstantiation was never made official in the medieval Church, but got weighty backing even before Aquinas's time when it was used in documents of the Lateran Council of the Church in 1215. It was based on Aristotle's discussion of the nature of existence. Aristotle divided the being of a particular object into substance and accidents. Take a sheep, for instance: its substance, which is its reality, its participation in the universal quality of being a sheep, is manifested in its gambolling on the hills, munching grass and baaing. Its accidents are things particular to the individual sheep at which we are looking: the statistics of its weight, the curliness of its wool, or the timbre of its baa. When the sheep dies, it ceases to gambol on the hills, munch grass and baa: its substance, its 'sheepiness', is instantly extinguished, and only the accidents remain – its corpse, including its weight, curly wool or voice-box – and they will gradually decay. They are not significant to its former sheepiness, which has ended with the extinguishing of its substance in death. It is no longer a sheep.

How, as scholastics following Aquinas's method, might we apply what is true of a sheep to the miracle of the Mass? We start with bread (we could equally start with wine). Bread consists of substance and accidents: its substance is its participation in the universal quality of 'breadness', while its accidents are the particular appearance of this piece of bread (being round, white and wafer-like, for instance). In the Mass, substance changes, accidents do not – why should they? They are not significant for being.

Through the grace of God, the substance of bread is replaced by the substance of the Body of Christ. It is a satisfying and reverent analysis: as long, that is, as one accepts Thomas's scientific or philosophical premises of the language of substance and accidents, affirming the conception of universal realities which are greater than individual instances, such as the reality of being a sheep or being bread, rather than particular instances of sheep or bread.

From the fourteenth century, most philosophers and theologians, particularly in northern Europe, did not in fact believe this. They were nominalists, who rejected Aristotle's categories and thought that words like 'sheep' or 'bread' are simply *nomina* (names), which we choose in an arbitrary fashion to use as labels for collections of objects which we have decided to say are like each other. Nominalists could only say of transubstantiation as a theory of the Mass that it was supported by the weight of opinion among very many holy men in the Church, and therefore it ought not be approached through the Thomist paths of reason, but must be accepted as a matter of faith. Once that faith in the Church's medieval authorities was challenged, as it was in the sixteenth century, the basis for belief in transubstantiation was gone, unless one returned to Thomism, the thought of Aquinas. Those who remained in the Roman obedience generally did this; but in sixteenth-century Europe, thousands of Protestants were burnt at the stake for denying an idea of Aristotle, who had never heard of Jesus Christ.

THE SECOND PILLAR: PAPAL PRIMACY

Bishop Ridley's second pillar of the old system, the Bishop of Rome's active power and claim to supremacy in the Western Church, emphasizes that one of the most striking features of medieval western Christendom was its unity. This unity, which the Reformation decisively ruptured, had been constructed in a period of intensive Church reorganization and centralization in the eleventh and twelfth centuries. This was spearheaded by Gregory VII, Pope from 1073 to 1085 and a major force in papal administration for decades before that. In a previous book I called the resulting changes 'the first Reformation'; the medieval historian R. I. Moore prefers to call his survey of the period 'the first European Revolution', or in the title of one of his earlier works, with a more challenging edge, 'the formation of a persecuting society': a world in which heresy was newly defined and punished and sexuality was regulated with a new tidy-minded ferocity.[30] Not all medievalists choose to highlight the negative side of the revolution, but undeniably there was an attempt to use Europe's clergy to spearhead an intensive and unprecedented regulation of the whole of society. By 1300, this created a shared Latin-speaking culture which had not been in place in 1100: it had been done under the guidance of bishops of Rome who expanded Gregory's project by claiming a God-given universal monarchy in the world as the Vicar (substitute) of Christ on earth. It was never clear how the ambitions of the Pope related to the ninth-century title of the Holy Roman Emperor, who was equally a potential ruler over the Latin West – never clear, either, how the Pope divided jurisdiction with the host of European rulers who, in imitation of the Emperor, were crowned in liturgical ceremonies which suggested that they too enjoyed a sacred status in their lands. Much blood was spilt over two centuries trying to find an answer to these problems: these wars succeeded in weakening the Emperor's power without advancing the papacy's authority.

Although the Popes thus never made a practical reality out of their dream of world domination designed for the greater glory of God, they did succeed in elaborating an ecclesiastical organization whose complexity needs to be described from summit to base before we see how it was ruptured in the sixteenth century. After the eleventh-century papal revolution it makes sense to use a specialized meaning of the word 'Church' to describe the ordained clergy of western Christianity: they were professional Christians, supported by endowments and levies in money and goods from the laity. Their professionalism was expressed by their possession of an information technology – literacy (the ability to read and write). It was not necessarily much use to laypeople: for clergy at least some knowledge of it was vital both so that they could effectively conduct the Church's elaborate liturgy, which was contained in a rationally organized series of books, and also to give them some access to the large amount of written commentary on the Church's central sacred text, the Bible. Not all clergy did very well in reading and writing, but it was considered deplorable if they did not. Another vital mark of clerical status was developing. Clergy were increasingly differentiated from the laity by the official attempt to make all clergy celibate for the whole of their careers, thus separating them from the sexuality which is the most intimate mark of an ordinary human being. This was a requirement borrowed by the clergy from a separate and distinctive section of the Church's life – monasticism.

Celibacy had formerly been a requirement only for specialists in prayer who withdrew from the world to live either alone or in community, and who were therefore called regulars (because they lived under a rule, *regulum*), or monks (from the Latinized Greek word *monachus*, a solitary). This religious life, separate from ordinary society, began to develop in Christianity in the third century CE, at a time when the Church first attracted very large numbers of converts in ordinary society; solitary individuals (hermits) and then groups of men and women took the decision to defy what they saw as an increasingly compromising involvement in the life of the Roman Empire. They spent their time in prayer, keeping up lines of communication to God that were not possible for Christians distracted by worldly affairs. During the fourth century, the first rules of life emerged to keep monastic communities faithful to their aspirations, and during the great administrative revolution of the eleventh and twelfth centuries, monks or nuns acknowledging one particular form of rule had increasingly seen themselves as belonging to a common 'Order'.

Another important change occurred in that era: monks became identified more closely with the ordained clergy. Previously, most monks were not ordained either as deacons or priests, and were therefore peculiar beings: laypeople who were more holy in their lifestyle than the non-monastic clergy who lived in the world (in Latin, *seculum*, so these clergy are called 'seculars'). Monks therefore related slightly untidily to the Church's organization of secular clergy. Nuns, of course, could not become ordained to the priesthood at all, given the assumptions of the day, although some of the leaders of their communities, abbesses, were powerful individuals, who customarily wore mitres on formal occasions like a bishop or an abbot. However, from the twelfth century more and more monks were ordained as priests, so that they could unite their prayers with the increasingly important task of saying as many Masses as was devotionally possible. So now there was an increasing component of 'regular' clergy in the Church alongside the seculars (and significantly, at this time, the nunneries of Europe lost much of their previous power and intellectual importance). At the same time the monastic celibacy rule was extended to the rest of the non-monastic secular priesthood. Celibacy became officially universal in the West for secular as well as regular clergy after the second general Church Council to be held at the Pope's Lateran Palace in Rome in 1139.

After the twelfth century, the secular and regular clergy were not only much more distinct from the laity, but in general they were the best organized part of society; indeed they created forms of administration and archival procedure which lay rulers then imitated. At the centre of it all in Rome was a permanent staff of assistant clergy for the Pope, who shared in his growing power and who from the twelfth century had the privilege of electing a new Pope – the Cardinals – so-called from the Latin *cardo* meaning a wedge rammed between timbers, for 'cardinals' were originally exceptionally able or useful priests thrust into a church from outside. Their appointment breached the early Church's convention that clergy should stick to the same place for life.[31] The Cardinals then grew too powerful for the Pope's convenience; like every other European monarch, he needed a court (or *Curia*) to provide him with more personal and less independent attendants than the Cardinals had become.

This Curia took on much administration, so it became a law court with a scope as wide as Europe itself; it developed a new legal system, canon law, as part of the papal project for bringing the administrative perfection of the kingdom of heaven to a sinful world. Canon law increasingly embraced all western Christendom, all the more successfully because it usefully got things done for people and acted as an external authority to help them sort out major conflicts and personal problems. It was a universal code at a time when other legal systems in Europe were generally fragmented and under-developed; it dealt with the intimate details of people's lives, habits and moral conduct, which were not the concern of secular judges. No wonder that Protestant reformers came to see it as the chief cornerstone of the Pope's power, and a necessary first point for Martin Luther to attack as his clash with traditional Church structures veered into open rebellion.

The internationalism of canon law was echoed by the internationalism of the religious Orders under which monks and nuns lived. Those Orders which had emerged during the eleventh- and twelfth-century administrative revolution usually had some sort of centralized federal structure, nearly all in the cradle of that new wave of monasticism, France. The wealthy and powerful but Puritan-minded Cistercian Order, for instance, took its name from its French mother-house Cîteaux (*Cistercium*), the equally austere Premonstratensians from the abbey at Prémontré; the Carthusian hermit-monks had their mother-house at *Carthusium* (La Grande Chartreuse); and the Cluniacs looked to the glorious performance of the liturgy in the massive abbey church at Cluny. However, even the many older Benedictine houses of monks, which were careful to avoid imitating this formal setting-up of central institutions, shared a common ethos through their observance of the Rule of St Benedict, and they kept up friendly contacts from one end of the continent to the other. Remarkably few Orders were restricted to only one part of Europe, wherever they might have been founded, such was the international hunger to experience the benefits of some new and distinctive departure in monastic life.

Such centralization also made obvious sense for the military Orders of celibate knights, who fought to extend Christendom against non-Christians and defend these conquests. The two main Orders who operated in the

Middle East took their name from the headquarters that they established in Jerusalem until expelled by Muslim counter-attacks: the Templars were particularly proud that their headquarters was founded on the site of Solomon's Temple, and all over Europe (for instance at the Temple in the western fringes of London) they built circular churches in imitation of a building which ironically was actually one of Islam's earliest masterpieces of architecture, the Dome of the Rock. The Knights Hospitallers of St John likewise took their name from the Hospital (in the modern sense of hostel) which they established for western pilgrims in Jerusalem, and which in an effort to upstage the Templars, they often claimed had pre-Christian origins. A northern European Order called the Teutonic Knights relocated itself after thirteenth-century eastern crusading defeats, recreating its Jerusalem hospital in great style not far from the Baltic coast at Marienburg on a branch of the river Vistula (see chapter 2, p. 55). All these Orders financed their crusading campaigns by carefully controlled networks of estates located all over Europe, as far away as Scotland and Scandinavia. Centralization was likewise a wise move for the succeeding wave of foundations of Orders of friars (principally the Franciscans and Dominicans, who took their name respectively from their charismatic twelfth-century founders Francis and Dominic). Firm discipline became necessary for these new Orders because their particular calling was to work among the temptations of the outside world, while still maintaining their community life ('friar' is derived from *frater*, a brother).

Beyond Curia and monastic Orders was an increasingly complex system of pastoral care for the laity, provided by secular clergy organized in dioceses under the authority of bishops. European dioceses were generally very large outside the Mediterranean area, and bishops became great magnates, with huge estates to support their work; in central Europe they were often as powerful as a count, a duke or a prince. Typically a diocese was made up of scores or even hundreds of much smaller and more intimate territorial units called parishes. These were designed to provide the laity with pastoral care from a priest who would be capable of walking around his parish and meeting all his people in no more than a day or two. Parishes were also called benefices or livings, because they were endowed to provide a workable income to support the priest in his job. The bishops' chief churches, the cathedrals (so-called because they contained the bishop's *cathedra* or throne), were rich and powerful corporations in their own right, staffed by a fleet of secular clergy led by an elite group of canons or prebendaries. These well-paid (and often absentee) high-flyers formed the cathedral chapter; they usually worked their way to becoming a corporation virtually independent of their theoretical master, the bishop. Several English cathedrals had a peculiarity seldom found elsewhere, doubling up as monasteries, so their clerical staff were regular rather than secular priests.

A parish priest theoretically had the possession of land (called glebe) and was entitled to receive a tenth (tithe) of his parishioners' agricultural produce; however, other components in the Church's system, particularly monasteries and the greater chantry colleges, diverted much of this revenue to support their specialist duties of prayer, and often became as large and wealthy as any cathedral chapter on the strength of it. This did not go unnoticed among Europe's tithe-payers, who often felt that they were taxed for a far-away religious institution which did them little direct good. But the parish system was designed to provide pastoral care for the entire lay population of Europe, and in great measure it could. Most confraternities, which we have seen become a vital vehicle for Europe's search for salvation, were associated with parish churches. People came to their parish church for the Mass; they also sought comfort from their parish priest when they confessed their sins, and expected to receive penances which were part of the great cycle of building up merit for passage through Purgatory.

Clergy were not just there to dole out a mechanical cycle of forgiveness. By the fifteenth century, congregations increasingly also expected regular teaching to feed their faith and tell them about the Bible, which most of them would never read for themselves. For the first time the humblest churches aspired to building a pulpit, although this was a dual-purpose piece of furniture which the clergy also used to lead informal prayer (especially prayer for the souls of long lists of the faithful, and generous, departed). Townsfolk were more likely to have the opportunity of hearing sermons than people in remote villages, perhaps as many as eight hundred sermons during an average lifespan, according to one modern estimate for late medieval urban France.[32] Surviving sermon texts suggest that sermons were long, and since there was then little seating in church, there must have been a popular appetite for absorbing ideas and biblical stories which overcame physical discomfort. Frequent official prohibitions against excessively dramatic styles of preaching also suggest that preachers were well aware of the tricks which public speakers needed to keep the attention of a varied audience. We have already noted the extravagant language of Bernardino of Siena and Guillaume Pepin (above, p. 21); these were among the masters of the pulpit in Italy and France respectively.

It is worth noting, however, that both Bernardino and Pepin were not parish clergy, but friars, and if they were using a parish church pulpit, they were doing so as guests. The Orders of friars had been created to remedy

A COMMON CULTURE

what their early activists perceived as the faults in existing Church organization, both the older monastic Orders and the secular clergy. At that time,
the early thirteenth century, the newly centralized Church was trying to
provide more intensive pastoral care for the people of Europe by giving
them better advice in the confessional and more detailed teaching of the
faith in sermons, but most parish clergy were seen as incapable of performing
effectively in these roles – hence the specializations of the friars. They
deliberately avoided large endowments for their communities ('friaries'),
because they felt that excessive landed wealth had undermined the missionary zeal and austere spirituality of the Orders of monks and nuns. This
meant that they had to support themselves by continual gifts from the laity,
which had the useful effect of forcing the friars to remain close to the
everyday life of ordinary people. In return for lay charity, they offered a
package of spiritual services within geographical regions carefully demarcated by agreement between different communities of friars (hence the friars'
alternative name of 'limiters'); so on this system even remote areas could
expect a visit from a friar. The friars could provide both preaching and a
special expertise in hearing confessions. Confessing sins to a travelling friar
offered the chance of absolution and spiritual and practical advice from a
cleric who might be more worldly-wise than one's parish priest, and who
would be less embarrassingly near to hand in subsequent everyday encounters. Many friars were highly educated, and they made a special point of
building friaries in university towns and contributing to university teaching.
Their mission thus extended from the humblest parts of society to those
who formed the ideas which held society together.

By the fifteenth century, the parish clergy and their assistants had generally
become much more effective than two hundred years before, both in terms
of education and commitment to their pastoral charges. Particularly in
eastern Europe, parishioners were much less likely to have to complain that
their priest was not living in his parish and providing pastoral care for them.
A third to a half of all clergy in southern Germany now had some experience
of university education, although many had not invested in a formal degree,
and much the same impressive proportion would be found in the scores of
parishes in the city of London.[33] Secular clergy educated to this level were
much more likely to be preachers than before. Notably, when preacherships
were founded in wealthy urban parish churches, royal chapels or cathedrals,
many were now specifically reserved for secular clergy rather than friars –
it was in one such preachership that Huldrych Zwingli first established
himself as an important figure in the city of Zürich (see chapter 3, p. 138).
A rich new crop of textbooks on preaching, specifically designed for secular

clergy, witnesses to this new interest and activity. These were not just written for high-flying graduates or the effortlessly literate, for they included a class of illustrated textbooks for preaching that consisted of the Bible in pictures, produced first in manuscript and later much more cheaply in woodblock form. These were called *Biblia pauperum praedicatorum*, which might be translated as 'Bibles for beginner preachers', because they were intended not for laypeople to read, but for barely literate clergy to get some sense of what they could say about the Bible if they took their courage in both hands and mounted the pulpit steps to preach.

The secular clergy had thus become more effective pastors, confessors and preachers. This brought tensions with the friars, who were still competing with them in all these roles, and also still dominating much of Europe's university education – no doubt often assuming an intellectual superiority not unknown among dons even now. Not surprisingly, secular clergy and friars did not always get on well. By contrast, rivalry between parish priests and members of the older religious Orders was less acute simply because they were not operating in the same market: the older Orders tended to concentrate on praying for the generally elite families who had provided them with their endowments. Friars and secular clergy were competing not just for the esteem of the laity but also for their money, at a time when many clergy all over Europe were finding it difficult to make inflexible sources of income meet changing economic conditions. When the Reformation in the 1520s created a literature of abuse against the Orders of friars and portrayed them as prime representatives of the old corruption, one of the reasons that these bilious pamphlets were so effective was that the mass readership found much that was familiar in the insults on the page.

So it is important to realize that much of the anticlerical rhetoric which became an integral part of the Reformation was actually the product of long-standing disputes among the clergy, rather than spontaneous lay criticism of their faults. Friars sneered at parish priests for being lazy and ignorant: parish priests sneered at friars for being egotistical showmen who tried to seduce women in the confessional; friars sneered at monks for being useless and idle consumers of landed wealth. Even friars sneered at friars, because there were several refoundations of Orders trying to return to early simplicity, particularly among the Franciscans, and the reformers had every reason to denigrate those colleagues of their own Order who opposed such reforms. Some of this bilious comment simply reflected human frailty and tribalism, but it would not have impressed the laity if it did not also reflect the very high standards which the clergy were now setting for themselves. A prime example is provided by John Colet, Dean of St Paul's Cathedral,

London for the first two decades of the sixteenth century: a famous reform-minded scholar and much-admired friend of Erasmus and Sir Thomas More. Colet frequently preached passionately about the faults of the clergy, their worldliness and their neglect of their duties, and his words are often quoted as witnesses to the corruption of the late medieval Church. But the passion which fired the Dean of Paul's was not disgust with the Church structures of his day; it sprang from his fascination with mystical writings from an anonymous sixth-century theologian, which in Colet's time were thought much older, and to have been written by a convert of St Paul, Dionysius the Areopagite. 'Pseudo-Dionysius' had written in ecstatic detail about the hierarchical ordering of heaven, but he had gone on to emphasize that the hierarchy of the clergy on earth was a direct reflection of the orders of angels, and its divine purpose was to reunite fallen humanity with God. For Colet, this meant that clergy had a solemn and inescapable duty to be as pure and effective ministers of God as the angels themselves. His apparently anti-clerical outpourings are in fact the highest form of clericalism.

The structure created by Gregory VII's First Reformation was a marvellous way of containing the teeming variety of Western Christendom's religious needs. A devout Christian hungering to reach out and touch the world beyond death could do so in a rich variety of different settings: in the savage austerity of the monasteries of contemplative hermits, the Carthusians; in the deliberately and exuberantly extravagant liturgy of the most ceremonial version of the Benedictine Rule, the Cluniacs; in the dramatic preaching of the friars or the clerical stars of the secular pulpit chaplaincies; in lighting a single candle at a lonely wayside statue of God's Mother; in craning forward in a crowded parish church to see the elevation of the consecrated bread and wine in the Mass at some cheerfully decorated side altar. The people most withdrawn from the concerns of the world might be especially esteemed by those right in its centre: so in fifteenth-century England, Carthusian hermit-monks dominated the production and distribution of devotional literature, eagerly and perhaps wistfully read by kings and noblemen amid the squalid and often brutal jostles for power which passed for government in England at the time. The Church was everywhere in society. The three most complicated machines which most people would ever see in this world were the pipe-organ, the clock and the windmill: the first two were almost exclusively to be found in churches. What better proof that the Church was in command of humankind's most adventurous and innovative thinking? What better organization than the Church to give western Europe a sense of its common identity?

A PILLAR CRACKS: POLITICS AND THE PAPACY

Nevertheless, the project of uniting the world under papal leadership faltered in the thirteenth century and faced disaster in the fourteenth. First, the French archbishop who became Pope Clement V decided on his election not to base himself in Rome, the city which had encouraged his predecessors to assume their central place in the Church because of its association with imperial power and with the burial places of the Apostles Peter and Paul. In 1309 Clement took up residence far to the north of Rome in what is now south-eastern France, at Avignon. There were good reasons for doing so: the chaos of Rome was a dangerous place for a Frenchman, while Avignon was not only strategically placed to make access to the papacy easier for northern Europeans, but was a territory outside the control of the King of France (the papacy eventually bought it outright from its ruler the Countess of Provence). Yet scandalized Italians saw the move as being as great a catastrophe as the Israelite exile to Babylon, and called it the Babylonian Captivity. Worse was to come: from 1378 there were two popes recognized by different parts of Europe, a 'Great Schism' which made a nonsense of the ideal of unity under the papacy. At the same time, movements of dissent arose which directly challenged all the assumptions which had given the Pope his central role in Christ's Church.

Curiously enough, the first challenge appeared in one of the best-regulated parts of western Christendom, the kingdom of England; it arose out of the thinking of an Oxford don, John Wyclif. Wyclif was a philosopher in a tradition which saw invisible, eternal realities as more representative of reality than the experiences of the everyday world. He drew on this assumption to make a damning contrast between the material, powerful and wealthy Church over which the bishops and the Pope presided, and the eternally existing Church beyond materiality: this latter true Church was a mystical source of grace which the Bible revealed not simply to clergy but to all God's chosen faithful. Wyclif's supporters were harried out of Oxford University in a generation after the 1380s, but they inspired a wider following who created a Bible in English for everyone to understand, fired by Wyclif's insistence that all the Church's teaching and institutions should be tested rigorously against the record of God's purposes in scripture. Sympathizers included some noblemen and gentry who liked the sound of doctrines which might lead to the Church surrendering its huge landed wealth. Their enemies contemptuously called them Lollards, in other words mumblers who talked nonsense.

In the political struggles of early fifteenth-century England, the gentry who sympathized with the Lollards backed the losing side, and the English Church authorities took advantage of this to assert strict orthodoxy, including a step unparalleled in Europe at the time: banning all existing versions of the Bible in English or any further unauthorized efforts at translation. All successive English dynasties of the century – Lancaster, York and Tudor – conscious of their shaky claims to the throne, bolstered their position by fierce continued loyalty to the traditional Church, and the English bishops and senior clergy concentrated on upholding the English Church's reputation as an example of good order to the rest of Europe – with some success, as we will repeatedly notice. Lollards retreated from the mainstream of political power in the kingdom as well as from the universities. In this respect their story immediately contrasts with that of later Protestantism, which started in the same way with the agitations of a university lecturer, Martin Luther.

The Lollards can hardly be blamed for not enjoying Luther's access to printing, for that revolution in information technology was yet to arrive in Europe in their days of open activity, but they did fail (unlike Luther and the Protestants) to gain a significant foothold among the Church's leading popular communicators, the friars – and it seems that they also missed the secret weapon of the sixteenth-century Reformation, popular music and hymn-writing.[34] The remaining Lollards occasionally faced investigation and persecution from the official Church, but more often they made their own quiet compromises with its local life in order to maintain their quest for God in their own way. They produced little new literature to express their defiance after about 1450, but went on treasuring their tattered manuscript pamphlets and sections of the Bible in English, facing only occasional outbursts of harassment from the authorities. Sometimes more prosperous Lollards, who were the natural leaders of their village, took on duties of parish officials such as being churchwarden, responsible for the daily round of mainstream devotion like keeping up the church fabric and paying for liturgical necessities – hardly the stuff of John Wyclif's proposed revolution.

The Lollard defeat in England came at the same time that an allied dissenting movement triumphed against Rome in central Europe. An accident of royal matchmaking in the late fourteenth century linked England to the far-off kingdom of Bohemia (roughly equivalent to the modern Czech Republic), and the resulting contacts between English and Czech nobility and universities brought the writings of Wyclif to Prague, the Bohemian capital. For Jan Hus, Dean of the Philosophical Faculty in Prague University, Wyclif's message shaped his growing dissatisfaction with existing Church institutions, which mirrored the discontents of other leading Czech church-men. In his sermons, soon hugely popular in the city, he took up the theme of Church reform, and his enthusiastic backing by Czech noblemen contrasted with the Lollards' loss of political support in England. Hus's movement became an assertion of Czech identity against German-speakers in the Bohemian Church and commonwealth, and unlike Lollardy, it remained supported in all sections of society from the university to the village. When Hus was summoned to the Church's general council at Konstanz in 1414 to explain his acts of rebellion, it was under a safe-conduct from the Holy Roman Emperor Sigismund, but the Council ignored this, and put him on trial for heresy.

Hus was burned at the stake in 1415 by decision of the Council and of the Emperor. It caused an explosion of anger in Bohemia, and within five years a Czech rebellion established a Hussite Church in Bohemia independent of Rome. In the way of revolutions, it slipped the control of its leaders, and its more radical elements began challenging the status quo in secular hierarchy as well as in the old Church. But after decades of vicious civil war and the defeat of outside attempts to destroy the revolution, an independent Hussite Church structure still survived, grudgingly and incompletely recognized by Rome. It was proud of two points of difference from the Pope's Church: its use in worship of Czech, the language of the people, rather than Latin, and its insistence that the people received wine as well as bread at the Eucharist. From this reception in both kinds or species (*sub utraque specie*), the mainstream Hussite movement gained its name: Utraquism. Hussites regarded it as vital because just as much as the old Church, they were passionately devoted to the Mass (unlike John Wyclif, who saw it as a devilish perversion of a spiritual gift of God) and they wanted to extend its benefits in full to all the faithful, insisting on frequent communion even for infants; the eucharistic chalice containing the wine became a cherished symbol of their movement. From 1471 the Utraquists had no archbishop of their own, and in a curious compromise with the rest of the Catholic world, they sent prospective priests off to Venice for ordination by bishops in that independent-minded republic. In default of a native episcopate, effective power in their Church was firmly in the hands of noblemen and the leaders of the major towns and cities: a transfer which we will meet elsewhere in Europe, and which became a major feature of the official 'magisterial' Reformations in the following century.

Formally separate from the Utraquists after 1457 were remnants of the more radical Hussites, the Union of Bohemian Brethren (*Unitas Fratrum*). What survived of their religious radicalism had major social implications.

Inspired by the south Bohemian writer Petr Chelcický and in the name of New Testament Christianity, they condemned all types of violence, including political repression, capital punishment, service in war or the swearing of oaths to earthly authorities. They rejected the idea of a separate priesthood, and the belief (still so dear to the Utraquists) that the Eucharist was a miracle in which bread and wine became the body and blood of Jesus. All these doctrines would re-emerge in the sixteenth-century Reformation. So between the Utraquists and the *Unitas Fratrum*, Bohemia became the first part of western Europe to slip out of its twelfth-century papal obedience. Only a few German-speaking areas and a few royal free cities within the Bohemian kingdom retained their papal loyalty.

These lonely outposts of obedience to Rome in Bohemia are worth noting because they represented the only part of medieval western Europe to which the description 'Roman Catholic' can be applied with any meaning. It may at first sight seem surprising that this familiar term makes no sense before the Reformation, but it is clearly redundant when everyone consciously or unconsciously formed part of the same Catholic church structure, tied in so many complex ways to the heart and head of the whole organization in Rome. Whatever the Pope's troubles, he could be assured of that, everywhere except Bohemia. England's Lollards bought their survival by abandoning aggressively open challenge to the Church's hierarchy, and making their own prickly contribution to its devotional life. The same was true of the Waldensians, a group concentrated in the remoter mountainous areas of south-eastern France, which represented the last fragment of various movements of dissent which had confronted the centralizing Church in the twelfth century. The Waldensians, who kept up links with small groups of sympathizers in central Europe, did take some interest in what the Hussites were now saying, translating some Hussite writings into Provençal, and they did maintain their own preachers. However, for the most part they received the mainstream Church's sacraments, and were even prepared to complain to the King of France in 1502 when they were exceptionally harassed by the Church authorities.[35] The sermons of some fifteenth-century preachers in central Europe seem obsessed with the problem of heresy and sectarianism, but much of this hysteria probably had as tenuous a connection with reality as the work of Senator McCarthy and the House Un-American Activities Committee in the 1950s.[36] The Pope's continuing problems of authority sprang not so much from the Church's enemies as from its friends.

This challenge to the pillar of papal primacy arose from the widespread belief among senior churchmen that the Western Church's unity was best served by collective authority rather than the single primacy of the Bishop of Rome. There was never a unified movement expressing this idea and there was indeed a great variety in understanding its implications, but collectively this mood can be labelled conciliarism: the proposition that ultimate authority in the Church should lie in a General Council of its bishops – or perhaps in a Council which was even more widely representative of the clergy. From the thirteenth century theologians had speculated on what should be done if a Pope turned heretic, but the situation at the end of the fourteenth century, with the scandal of rival popes and the challenge from Lollardy and Hussitism, transformed academic debates about authority into urgent reality. There was eventual agreement that the only way to end the schism was to call a Council, and at the dire moment in 1414 where there were not just two but three men calling themselves Pope, one of them, John XXIII, took action in conjunction with the Emperor Sigismund.

The resulting Council at the city of Konstanz was that which betrayed Jan Hus, but besides that discreditable decision, the Council finally ended four decades of schism when in 1417 it recognized the election of a new Pope acknowledged by all factions, Martin V. In the midst of the prolonged and complex wrangles which produced this result, the Council produced a decree 'Sacrosancta' proclaiming itself to hold its authority 'immediately from Christ; everyone, of every rank and condition, including the Pope himself, is bound to obey it in matters concerning the faith, the abolition of the schism, and the Reformation of the Church of God in its head and its members'.[37] There could be no clearer statement that papal primacy was to be put firmly in its place in favour of a general Council, but Konstanz added a further idea in its decree of 1417, ordering that a Council should henceforth meet every ten years: in other words, a Council was to become an essential and permanent component of continued reform and reconstruction in the Church.

However, the next few years saw increasing tension between those wishing to develop this conciliar mechanism and successive Popes who wished to build on the papacy's newly restored integrity. The eighteen-year session of a Council at Basel from 1431 helped to discredit the conciliar option because, despite much constructive work, it culminated in a fresh schism. In 1460 a former conciliarist sympathizer, now Pope Pius II, formally forbade appeals from a decision of the papacy to a general Council, in a bull (the most solemn form of papal pronouncement, customarily described by their opening phrase) entitled *Execrabilis*. Seven years before that, Constantinople, last remnant of the Byzantine Empire and mother of eastern Christianity, had fallen to the Ottoman Turks, its Emperor cut down, fighting to the last.

For a Pope contemplating this disaster with horror, now was not the time to risk the future of the West by collective leadership that might be divided and uncertain.

Pius II's change of heart was understandable: there was much that was incoherent or unresolved in the bundle of ideas which carried the conciliarist label. Conciliarists never achieved consensus as to how to define the Church or how to account for the authority of a Council. Was it a representation of all the people of God, in which case its authority rose up or ascended from the whole body of the faithful? Or was it an assembly of God's ordained representatives, the clergy, in which case its power descended from God through the Church's hierarchy? Who precisely among the clergy were to be represented? Konstanz had been an assembly of bishops and cardinals; Basel widened its membership so that lower clergy were given delegates as well, even with a voting majority over the bishops. Conciliarists tended to be clergy and were naturally clericalist in their outlook; this was not a movement which viewed lay participation with much sympathy. Moreover, if conciliarists were drastically limiting the pope's power, how did that affect the centuries-long disputes between the pope and secular rulers? It was unlikely that a major opponent of papal absolutism like the King of France was going to accept a new rival for power in an effective and permanent General Council of the Church, at least not without a good deal of careful explanation from sure-footed theologians that his own power was not affected by the special sacred status of the Council.

Yet the problem which conciliarism had originally raised – how to deal with a Pope who cannot lead the Church as God wishes – would not go away. In the end Martin Luther was forced to give the drastic answer that if the Pope turned out to be the Devil masquerading as the Saviour (Antichrist), then one must walk out of the Pope's false Church and recreate the true body of Christ. Even though in practical and political terms conciliarism faced eclipse from the mid-fifteenth century, plenty of leading churchmen and academics (particularly canon lawyers) continued to believe that conciliar action to solve the Church's problems would be preferable to the rapid rebuilding of centralized papal power that was now taking place. The work of the greatest conciliarists was too fertile to ignore: it raised too many questions about how the faithful acted to fulfil the will of God.

When Jean Gerson (one of the most prominent activists in the Council of Konstanz) struggled to find a way of reconciling conciliarism with the traditional claims of the French monarchy, he developed a view of the Church's history that became of great importance to Reformation leaders seeking to make the same balance between Church and secular commonwealth against more radical Christian thinkers. Gerson saw a threefold development in the Church: a first, primitive heroic era in which it was still unacknowledged and often persecuted by the Roman Empire; a second period after the Emperor Constantine I had allied with it, when Church leaders had justifiably and responsibly accepted power and wealth; but then a third era of decay after the time of Gregory VII, when this process had been taken to excess, so that it must now be curbed. Gerson, like Colet (above, p. 34), was an enthusiast for Dionysius the Areopagite, and set the highest standards possible for the clerical order; so he was not seeking to destroy Church structures, simply to recall them to purity. He was also a strong defender of parish clergy against the pretensions of monks and friars, pointing out that there had been no monastic vows in the Church in the time of Christ, Mary and the apostles. The Reformers and the princes who supported them later took note of what he had said.[38]

Meanwhile, the papacy consolidated its recovery. From 1446 it was once more permanently based in Rome, never again willingly to desert this symbol of its supremacy in the Church. Soon after, in 1460, came a remarkable piece of accidental good fortune for the Pope when large deposits of alum were discovered at Tolfa in the papal territories north-west of Rome: this mineral was highly valuable because of its use in dyes, and before that it could only be imported at great expense from the Middle East. The new source of income (which the Popes were careful to ensure became a monopoly supply of alum in Europe) began benefiting the papacy just when *Execrabilis* reasserted its central power and it began expressing this power in practical ways, such as a grant made by Pope Nicholas V in 1455 to the Portuguese monarchy of the right to rule in certain regions of Africa. Now that Popes were back in Italy, it was unsurprising that they took a particular interest in Italian politics like the other Italian princes around them, and it was no fault of theirs that suddenly in the 1490s Italy became the cockpit of war and the obsessive concern of the great dynastic powers of Europe. The process was begun by the Valois dynasty of France, when in 1494–5 Charles VIII intervened in the quarrels of Italian princes with a major military invasion; this gained France little but threw the various major states of Italy into chaos, war and misery for more than half a century.

Amid this suddenly unbalanced high politics, it was a natural protective strategy for the papacy, stranded in the middle of the situation, to redouble its self-assertion, a mood which in any case came naturally to the successive Popes Alexander VI (1492–1503) and Julius II (1503–13). Alexander followed the example of Nicholas V with an adjudication in 1493–4 between the claims of the two European powers which were now exploring and making conquests overseas, Portugal and Spain; he divided the map of the world beyond Europe between them, commissioning them to preach the Gospel to the non-Christians whom they encountered, in an action which had all the ambition of the twelfth-century papacy (see chapter 2, p. 67). Likewise, fifteenth-century Popes began trying to restore the architectural splendour of their sadly ramshackle city; display was an essential aspect of power for secular rulers, and surely it was all the more important for Christ's representative on earth. The most important – and certainly, as we shall see, the most fateful – project was the demolition of the monumental basilica of St Peter, which the Emperor Constantine had built on the reputed site of Peter's crucifixion, so that it could be replaced with something even more spectacular (see chapter 3, pp. 120–21): this was a particular enthusiasm of Julius II, one of the most discriminating but also one of the most extravagant patrons of art and architecture in the papacy's history.

Yet the two Popes who between them occupied St Peter's throne for two decades (and who deeply detested each other) had a very selective understanding of what might glorify the papacy. Alexander VI, from the Valencian noble family of Borja (Borgia), shielded his vulnerability as an outsider against his many Italian enemies by ruthlessly exploiting the Church's most profitable offices to promote his Borja relatives, including his own children by his several mistresses – a scandalous flouting of the clerical celibacy imposed by the twelfth-century Reformation, even if the Pope's most notorious children Lucrezia and Cesare had not provided extreme examples of aristocratic self-indulgence. Julius II relished being his own general when he plunged into the Italian wars which proliferated after the French invasion, and he was especially proud when in 1506 he recaptured Bologna, second city of the Papal States after Rome and lost to the papacy seventy years before. The contemporary Italian historian Francesco Guicciardini commented with delicate sarcasm that Julius was 'certainly worthy of great glory, if he had been a secular prince'.[39] The Popes' ludicrously obvious failings in their pretensions as leaders of the universal Church made a mockery of their defeat of the conciliarists, and did nothing to end continuing criticism of papal primacy. That made the papal machine all the more sensitive to any new challenge to its authority, or to any attempt to resurrect language and ideas which had been used against it before, as Luther discovered in the years after 1517.

CHURCH VERSUS COMMONWEALTH?

We have seen how the word 'Church' had commonly come to signify the vast European-wide trade union which was the clergy: a trade union large enough to include something like a tenth of the entire population in some of the cities of the late medieval Holy Roman Empire.[40] Alongside this authority of the Church was a kaleidoscopic hierarchy of secular jurisdictions varying in size and scope, from the vast territories and assorted jurisdictional rights of the Holy Roman Emperor to some tiny but effectively independent territory belonging to a free city or a count or a knight. Europe was not then made up of nation-states, which has an important consequence. While I use Jeremy Bentham's eighteenth-century neologism 'international' a good deal in this book in default of anything more convenient, I doubt whether one can use the word 'nationalism' to any great purpose in the fifteenth to seventeenth centuries. Often nationalism has been associated with the coming of the Protestant Reformation, but the link is full of problems. Nationalism is a phenomenon of the world after the 1789 French Revolution; it implies a common consciousness created within a consolidated territory, usually involving a single language and shared culture, producing a public rhetoric of a single national will, and with the agenda of creating or reinforcing a unitary state.

Fifteenth- and sixteenth-century Europe did indeed recognize regions and jurisdictions where people were conscious of a common heritage, usually because they nursed a longstanding hatred against some nearby region. The kingdom of England was perhaps the most exceptionally developed example: it was much older, more united and self-conscious than most European secular jurisdictions. This in turn gave the very diverse Gaelic and English-speaking peoples in the neighbouring northern kingdom of Scotland a vigorous common consciousness of not being English, particularly because of past inept English interference, and one might mistake that for Scottish nationalism. Yet even in the realm of England, five different living languages were spoken in the fifteenth century (English, Welsh, Cornish, Manx and French), making the idea of a common culture in a nationalist sense very problematic. Conversely the common link was often one of language rather than simply region. German-speakers were notorious both for prejudice against Italians and for their colonizing enterprises in eastern Europe. One might see a sense of 'national' consciousness in Spain, with the significant rider that there it did not correspond to a single Spanish kingdom, because there was no such thing, and even more than in the single kingdom of

England, the peninsula was home to several languages. Rather, Spanish consciousness was an obsession with racial and religious identity, based on a hatred of Jews and Muslims to the point of seeing anciently descended Christian Spaniards as a new chosen race (see chapter 2, pp. 58–64). In any case, if this was a 'nationalism', it led not to Reformation but Catholic Counter-Reformation.

The most prominent mark of secular identity in Europe was a shared loyalty either to a dynasty (that is a family of rulers like the Tudors of England and Wales, the Valois of France, the Jagiellons of Poland-Lithuania or the Habsburgs in central Europe), or on the other hand to a particular local corporation with ancient rights and privileges. These contrasting loyalties were not necessarily exclusive, but any individual who owed loyalty to both might feel drawn in either direction depending on circumstances. When the conflicts of the Reformation broke out and the Church's power was challenged, many variations on such loyalties came into play, but dynasty and locality usually counted for more than any chimera of nationalism. Equally, the concept of a secular 'state' is not necessarily the most natural to apply to the secular jurisdictions of early modern Europe, since they were normally tied to the fortunes and personalities of a great family, and also had pretensions to have been created by the providence of God.

The idea of a state designed to fit particular human circumstances, rather than being part of a God-given created order, was given currency in political discourse from the beginning of the sixteenth century by the writings of the Florentine politician Niccolò Machiavelli. Machiavelli's open cynicism and his apparently abstract analysis of an amoral method of conducting government shocked European proprieties, and most people felt it wise to speak of him with disapproval, at least in public. Senior English politicians did begin using the word 'state' unselfconsciously in the 1590s, and around that time the more powerful rulers of Europe were evolving the more centralized, bureaucratic systems of government geared towards sustaining war economies, which may be described as states. However a more flexible word is needed to describe the enormous variety of secular government, in contrast to the forms of government evolved by the Church, which we will meet with in the Reformation era. Throughout this book, I will be repeatedly using one which now has a slightly archaic or specialized meaning: Commonwealth. In various cognates (such as the Latin *Respublica*, which did not normally then mean 'Republic'), it was a familiar idea to people in Reformation Europe.

A contest between Church and Commonwealth might be a fairly straightforward competition between the Pope and a monarch in situations where there was overlap in their claims to jurisdiction. Such quarrels had centuries of history behind them, but they became more likely in the fifteenth century because many secular rulers were now increasing and consolidating their power: they were expanding their ability to collect revenues and to make more decisions of greater complexity within their territories. A major motivation was the increasing expense of the technology of war: guns and the fortifications designed to counter them were becoming more complex, and monarchs were maintaining permanent standing armies (pioneered by the French King Charles VII in the mid-fifteenth century). Such huge drains on revenue favoured and indeed demanded larger units of power. The papacy recognized this changing aspect of political life by a development in its bureaucracy: from the 1490s, it created a system of local representatives, nuncios, out of an earlier system of collectors of papal taxation, in order to represent its interests at the major secular courts of Europe. These paralleled the increased employment by secular rulers of more professional and long-term ambassadors to other rulers, but the nuncios were ambassadors with a difference: they had their own ecclesiastical jurisdiction in the places to which they were sent. Even in the haughty Republic of Venice, which treasured its independence, the papal nuncio Girolamo Aleandro was able in 1533 to sentence a carpenter to life imprisonment for heresy, without consulting the Venetian authorities or indeed getting leave from his superiors back in Rome.[41]

It was therefore only natural that monarchs were concerned about papal intervention and the power of the Church, however personally devout they might be. In view of modern religious politics, it may seem surprising to learn that the Polish monarchy and nobility were wary of and hostile to the papacy, but there was good reason: Popes habitually gave support to the kingdom's long-term enemies, the Teutonic Order of Knights. One leading nobleman, Jan Ostroróg, Castellan of Poznán, spoke for many of Poland's elite when in his *Monumentum pro Reipublicae ordinatione congestum* ('Memorandum compiled for the ordering of the Commonwealth', written around 1475), he insisted that annates (papal taxation of clerical benefices) and legal appeals to Rome should be abolished, and the clergy should be taxed by the Polish crown just like laypeople. This was the programme that Henry VIII of England put into effect in the 1530s. Yet Poland's quarrel was with Rome, not with the Church, whose leaders within the Polish-Lithuanian kingdoms were mostly just as uncompromisingly conciliarist in sympathy as the secular nobility. Poland stood notably firm against any overtures from the Bohemian Hussites, who might have helped them against their common foe, the Teutonic Knights, but only in return for leading the Poles away from the united Western Church.[42]

Some monarchs did their own deals with Rome to neutralize or minimize its interference in territories under their control. In 1448 the Holy Roman Emperor Frederick III agreed with Pope Eugenius IV on the Concordat of Vienna: within the Empire, cathedral chapters rather than the Pope would continue to choose a new bishop for their diocese, while the papacy was still able to collect annates. It was a settlement whose distinctiveness survived to have important consequences for the Counter-Reformation in Germany (see chapter 10, p. 447), but it also meant more money haemorrhaging from the imperial German lands to Rome than from Spain or France, a difference which became a real grievance among the rulers of German territories. Ten years before, the Valois monarchy had encouraged a council of the clergy of France, still in aggressively conciliarist mood, to issue at Bourges a Pragmatic Sanction (a definition of jurisdiction): it forbade Rome to interfere in matters of French church property or appoint to vacant French benefices. This became the cornerstone of an attitude of sturdy independence in France towards Rome which came to be labelled Gallicanism. Gallicanism was not identical in its interests with conciliarism, since it stressed the role of the monarchy in the Church, and most conciliarists wanted to stress the communal independence of the Church – but both sides feared a growth in the power of the papacy. In 1516 François I met longstanding papal objections to the Pragmatic Sanction of Bourges with a new deal, a Concordat signed at Bologna. To the dismay of many conciliar-minded and Gallican French lawyers and theologians, this overturned the Sanction and gave the Pope certain rights in nominating clergy, while still reserving a great deal of freedom of action to the French monarchy.

By contrast, a monarch who did not conclude an agreement with Rome might be a constant source of trouble to the Church: for instance, Henry VII of England after his capture of the throne in 1485. He came from a demonstratively pious family: as we have seen (above, p. 21), his formidable mother Lady Margaret Beaufort was by papal grant patroness of the devotion of the Name of Jesus, and he himself built a family chantry of megalomaniac ambition attached to Westminster Abbey. Yet this did not stop Henry trying to bully the Church – in this case, the English church authorities rather than Rome itself. He encouraged his leading secular lawyers to harass and circumscribe the church courts with prohibitions on their proceeding in legal cases, and he infuriated leading English monasteries with a ten-year campaign in the Roman Curia to end their privileges of exempt jurisdictions. For the time being he lost that latter battle, but forty years later his son Henry VIII picked up many of the threads of these earlier conflicts in the earliest stage of the official English Reformation.

Church and commonwealth were equally liable to clash in towns and cities which (usually with great struggle and effort) had obtained privileges and exemptions from a superior secular ruler. The greatest likelihood for trouble came where a particular local history led to the Church authorities enjoying an unusual concentration of resources or privileges within such places, so they might justly be regarded as parasites within the body politic. In the kingdom of Denmark, either side of the Sound leading into the Baltic, the city leaders of Copenhagen and Malmø were bitterly aware that within their city walls, which prevented any geographical expansion of their community, around a third of all land and houses were owned by the Church and so paid no taxes.[43] Within the Empire, in Würzburg, the bishop was also duke: clergy owned most landed property, and the secular authorities failed to assert their independence, despite struggles that included five serious destructive mass rampages through Church property in the 150 years before the Reformation.[44] Perhaps the saddest and most extreme case is the cathedral city of Mainz where, until the late fifteenth century, up to a quarter of the male population were clergy. A long history of mutual ill-will left the secular citizens faced with savage financial punishment for the wreckage they had wrought in city monasteries: efforts over the next century to pay this off created a burden of taxation which made prosperous inhabitants leave Mainz in despair. The clergy were unmoved by the city's decline, in contrast to neighbouring Frankfurt-am-Main, where the church authorities were prepared to compromise on punishment after similar incidents, and fifteenth-century Frankfurt prospered accordingly.[45]

Not all situations were so dire, and reactions to them were in any case not simple. Certainly the leading councillors in Copenhagen and Malmø were noticeably ready to listen to the Reformation message about a corrupt Church when it came along. But a devout laity might hate certain churchmen while still wanting to love the Church; so they ended up boycotting the offending privileged clergy and looking elsewhere for pastoral care. An obvious alternative was the ministry of the friars, who had a strong rhetoric of denouncing clerical privilege, and who might be only too happy to serve as allies against their own rivals among the clergy. This happened in both Würzburg and Mainz, and we have already noted similar tensions in the English city of Norwich (see above, p. 9). Here the centuries-long and sometimes murderous feud between the Benedictine Cathedral Priory and the city corporation led the city to ignore the Cathedral when it arranged its principal civic religious ceremony, the Corpus Christi procession; at one stage city councillors angrily ended their official attendance at sermons from the Cathedral and went instead to the popular Carmelite friary in the city.

Moreover, when Henry VIII dissolved all English monasteries and friaries in the 1530s, the city bought up the Dominican friary and used part of it as a private corporation chapel; the church is still a proud feature of the city landscape.[46] An extreme case can be found in the southern French cathedral city of Aix-en-Provence, where the cathedral chapter, dominated by landed families from outside the city, sucked revenues out of the two parish churches, paid starvation wages to the parish clergy and barred the creation of any new parishes. The people's answer was to use the friary churches in the city for their parish churches, rather than pay more than token attention to the churches controlled by the cathedral.[47]

The example of the selfish chapter of Aix is a reminder of a major complicating factor for the late medieval Church from Spain to the Baltic: those parts of the Church with most power and landed wealth, bishoprics, cathedrals and older monastic Orders, tended to be invaded by secular landed noble families, who filled them with family members to the exclusion of anybody else. In 1421 the Polish bishops barred membership of their cathedral chapters to everyone except members of the nobility, with the exception of two prebends in each cathedral reserved for professionals who might be useful to the chapter: a Doctor of Law or a Doctor of Medicine.[48] Astonishingly, in a city of the Holy Roman Empire as important as Magdeburg (which its archbishop prevented from becoming a free imperial city), members of the proud and wealthy elite city families were excluded by noblemen from holding office in the city's major churches and cathedral. Such snobbery could reach exquisite levels of refinement; in the cathedral of Eichstätt, the chapter was the preserve of members of the imperial nobility, who haughtily excluded even members of the territorial nobility.[49]

Wealthy monasteries were also very vulnerable to the interest of noble families. Even Pope Pius II, a bitter critic of social exclusiveness in the Church, made no objection in 1458 to confirming the charter of the great Swiss pilgrimage monastery of Einsiedeln, which contained a clause stating baldly that 'no monks shall be received except from noble families, provided that there are enough monks in the monastery'.[50] Very often the head of house would no longer be an abbot, that is a monk drawn from the Order, but instead a powerful layman, who would hold monastic estates in trust (*in commendam*) for the abbey; hence he was known as a commendator. This commendatory system could be found in abbeys right across Europe. Similarly, most bishops would be chosen from among the canons or prebendaries of cathedrals, particularly in regions governed by the Concordat of Vienna; so the great dioceses of Europe became noble preserves. An odd exception was England, where although the dioceses were large and said to be wealthier than anywhere else except Hungary, bishops tended to be sons of lesser gentry or even humbler folk who had come up the hard way by studying at Oxford or Cambridge universities. In the same way, lay commendators were unknown in the wealthy monasteries of England. The exceptional good order of the medieval English Church might be related to these peculiarities.

It is therefore over-simple to see conflicts involving great churches as pure clashes between the laity and the clergy; they might really be struggles between cities and the nobility beyond their walls, or between different interest-groups within the ruling caste. Much was about family power. Within the bounds of the Empire, wealth and territorial jurisdictions provided by the Church could be used as weapons for princely dynasties against the power of the Holy Roman Emperor, who had been a Habsburg since the beginning of the fifteenth century. The Wittelsbach family, one of Germany's most successful dynastic enterprises and the Habsburgs' long-term rivals, was assiduous in collecting bishoprics in its territories of Bavaria and the Palatinate, filling them with trusted officials or junior family members. These included a series of Wittelsbach bishops in the Bavarian diocese of Passau, which happened to hold jurisdiction over the majority of the Habsburgs' hereditary core territories in Austria, and thus provided a useful basis for Wittelsbach interference beyond their borders.[51] Another great German dynasty was the Hohenzollern (who much later proved to be the nemesis of the Habsburgs). During his late fifteenth-century expansion of the Hohenzollern family territories, Albrecht Achilles of Brandenburg remarked about one of the smaller dioceses in Hohenzollern lands: 'What does it matter to us that there is a Bishop of Lebus or who he is, so long as he is a good honest man who is useful to the lordship and its territories? For in any case, whether he likes it or not, he must do whatever a Margrave of Brandenburg pleases in reasonable concerns affecting the Margrave and his territory.' So the Bishop of Lebus must be aware that loyalty to Brandenburg pre-empted any other loyalty, including to the meddling Emperor – perhaps even to the Pope.[52]

Imperial free cities did well to look at the awful example of Mainz, Würzburg or Magdeburg and then take steps to ensure that they were not dominated by any noble-born churchman. Nuremberg was particularly assiduous in cutting the links with its bishop (who luckily for the city had his cathedral church elsewhere, in Bamberg): it secured legal exemptions from his court and by the 1480s was generally acting in ways that provoked him to complain that the city no longer wanted to be subject to him and his chapter in spiritual matters. The city council was unabashed: it placed its own guardians over the monasteries and nunneries in the city, and acquired the patronage of the two main parish churches for itself. This cost a very great deal, and it was celebrated with further extravagant adornment of the churches (see Plate 6), but all was money well spent: before there was any hint of the Lutheran explosion, Nuremberg was in charge of its own ecclesiastical institutions.[53] In Augsburg, despite the ancient presence of the cathedral, the city authorities used their huge late medieval wealth, based on their pivotal position in central European trade, to exclude the bishop from extensive privilege or jurisdiction. By the fifteenth century, successive bishops realized that their position was hopeless and set about establishing an alternative headquarters in the little town of Dillingen twenty miles to the west on the Danube.[54]

Swiss cities had cast off any real ties with the Emperor by the end of the fifteenth century, so they could not exploit imperial privileges as did Nuremberg or Augsburg, but they too used their increasing wealth to buy their way into control of their local churches. In Zürich, the diocesan bishop was conveniently far away in Konstanz. Power in the city passed into the hands of rich gilds who were not prepared to allow church authorities to interfere with their lives: they remorselessly chipped away at the jurisdiction enjoyed by the noble ladies of the once-mighty imperial Benedictine nunnery, the *Fraumünster*, until the nunnery's dominance in the city withered away. Meanwhile the gilds lavished triumphant attention on the city's major collegiate church, their 'Great Minster' (*Grossmünster*) of SS Felix and Regula. Not for nothing did a giant statue of the Emperor Charlemagne leer from the south tower of the Grossmünster towards the slender Fraumünster spire, directly across the waters of the river Limmat: commercial Commonwealth in Zürich had decisively upstaged the aristocratic imperial Church (see Plate 4).

There is a tendency among medieval historians to see such annexations of Church by Commonwealth, either by cities or noble families, as abuses within the system, and certainly we have already noted abuses in plenty. However, these interventions were not necessarily used to promote selfish power. Secular rulers could show genuine idealism; they used their new power in the Church to further their own notions of public godliness. In 1452, the charismatic Observant Franciscan preacher Giovanni di Capistrano toured Thuringia as part of a sustained campaign to arouse central Europe to fight the Hussites. In this effort he was largely unsuccessful, but the local ruler, Duke Wilhelm III, used the excitement provoked by Capistrano's efforts to issue his own orders about morality in his territory and to reform the region's Augustinian friars, restoring them to their vows of strict poverty; he did not simply pocket the resulting revenues, but used them for the benefit of church services and communities of regulars who genuinely needed the money.[55] We have already noted above (p. 23) how the Brethren and Sisters of the Common Life saw to it that their communities were the responsibility of urban governors rather than the Church; that was a vote of confidence from some of the most religiously committed people in European society. Action to take over the running of hospitals or schools from church authority, or the founding of church preacherships paid for by civic funds, was common in energetic and prosperous central European cities like Nuremberg or the major cities of Switzerland, but equally in remote rural areas where peculiar local circumstances gave opportunity, people were prepared to use and extend their control over the Church in order to further its work. In the remote mountain valleys of the Grisons or Graubünden, in the poverty-stricken easternmost part of Switzerland, local communities were exceptionally free from interference by Church authorities or nobility, so they felt it worth spending their scarce resources lavishly on the salaries of clergy and on endowing new parishes and church buildings. Naturally they kept control of these new community assets, and when the Reformation came along, they made a variety of local decisions about where to place their loyalties.[56]

All this means that in many areas of central Europe, well before the Reformation upheavals, *Landeskirchen* or locally run churches were quietly emerging. The development was backed by the assumption that the local magistrate had a responsibility to play the leading part in Church life, an assumption readily to be found in the catechisms (simple summaries of doctrine) which people were taught in their churches, so that they would absorb the idea from the text without thinking too much about it. The result was a local version of conciliarism; or one could view it as a steady return to the balance of power in the Church that had existed before the eleventh- and twelfth-century Gregorian revolution. Princes and city councils boasted of being pope in their own jurisdictions: the prince was after all the father of his territory (*Landesvater*).[57] With the trend in late medieval central Europe for local secular rulers to take more and more power and responsibility away from leading churchmen, it was not surprising that the first reformers in the 1520s looked to princes rather than bishops or abbots to undertake a new round of reforms in the Church, or that much of the Reformation continued to develop with the assumption that the godly prince was the natural agent of religious revolution.

Yet it must be remembered that this takeover was in no way a conscious act of defiance against the Pope. Not all such public-spirited rulers turned away from Roman obedience in the Reformation, even when their concern for the Church had previously led them to clash with members of its hierarchy. So in 1513 Duke Georg of Saxony bluntly described the Church as no longer the Bride of Christ but 'a stinking decayed corpse', and he was ready to bring forward traditional lists of grievances about church officials to the imperial assembly (the Diet) at Worms in 1521.[58] Yet Georg was also deeply shocked at Martin Luther's conduct at that same Diet of Worms (see chapter 3, pp. 131–2), and he went on to be one of Luther's most bitter conservative opponents. The Reformation was not merely about jurisdictions, or even about the best way to reform the Church: such quarrels had happened before, had caused mayhem, and then the wounds had been healed. Far more profound ideas were involved, which made the dispute more lasting than anything that had happened since the Gregorian Revolution. To understand these, we must examine the new hopes and fears dominating the Christendom which Duke Georg would have known as a young man at the turn of the fifteenth and sixteenth centuries.

2

Hopes and Fears 1490–1517

SHIFTING BOUNDARIES

The biggest fear for western Christendom around 1500 was the prospect that it might disappear altogether. Except for Iceland and the barely populated far north of Scandinavia, none of its boundaries were stable or uncontested in 1500, and some were in retreat. At both extremes were decay and failure. Over the Atlantic Ocean in the north-west, the Scandinavian colonies founded in Greenland in earlier centuries had finally died out, cut off from their homelands in Europe, the population malnourished, inbred and sick, and curiously unable to follow the strategies for survival of the nomadic Inuits who lived and flourished around them. To the south-east, the most surprising frontier of Latin Christianity lay in the Mediterranean Sea, six hundred miles further east than Greece: the major island of Cyprus, obstinate survivor from the western crusading exploits of the twelfth and thirteenth centuries. As late as the 1480s, the throne of Cyprus was held by a Lusignan descendant of carpet-bagging Crusader noblemen from western France, until the Venetians pressured the widow of the last king into surrendering the island to Venice, to act as its forward post against Islam.

Under Venetian rule, the Latin Christians of Cyprus continued to lord it over resentful eastern Orthodox Christians, whom they had persecuted and marginalized since their arrival. In Cypriot villages, Orthodoxy was making a creeping comeback, so that village churches were increasingly built with a modest Latin side-aisle tacked on to church buildings where the Orthodox liturgy attracted the lion's share of village devotion. But the cathedrals in Nicosia, Famagusta and Paphos were soaring, pinnacled Gothic structures which would have looked at home in northern France; they still resounded to the chant of the Latin Mass, their stained glass resolutely filtering out the unsympathetic eastern Mediterranean sun. The Cypriot governing elite had its eyes firmly fixed westwards. A bishop of Paphos around 1500, Jacopo Pesaro, was a Venetian nobleman who became not just a major military campaigner against the Turks for Pope Alexander VI but also a patron of Titian, one of whose most famous altarpieces can be seen near Pesaro's tomb in Venice. In Paphos itself, Latin Christian contemporaries of Pesaro asserted their continuing commitment to capturing the alien worlds of Orthodoxy and Islam with their gifts of fashionable Renaissance art to the city churches.[1] Yet the increasingly ramshackle air of the surrounding city cast a large question-mark over their efforts, and over the destiny of Cyprus.

By the sixteenth century that destiny lay with the Ottoman Turks. The Ottoman Sultans had created an Islamic empire-building enterprise designed for conquest. They had advanced inexorably out of Asia Minor, completing their absorption of the Byzantine Empire when they captured Constantinople in 1453, and in a decade from the late 1510s they hugely expanded their territories under the leadership of Sultan Suleyman, who came to be known to western Europeans in a tribute of reluctant admiration as 'the Magnificent'. While far away in north Germany in 1516–17 Luther brooded on his campaign against indulgences, the Sultan overran the territories of fellow Muslims in Egypt and Syria (Venice only preserved Cyprus for the time being by switching its long-established tribute payment from the rulers of Egypt to Suleyman). Then it was the turn of the Latins.

The Knights of St John or Hospitallers were the supposed defenders of Christendom against Islam, but they had long been in permanent exile from the Holy Land in the heavily fortified island of Rhodes off the coast of Asia Minor. In 1522 the Ottoman Turks expelled them from Rhodes after an epic siege. Only reluctantly did the Knights relocate their headquarters far to the west in a barren but equally strategic island, Malta, a virtual gift to them from the Emperor Charles V, which eventually turned out to be a very shrewd investment for the survival of Christendom (see chapter 7, p. 330). But a far greater trauma was to come for the West: the Ottomans advanced from their conquest of eastern Orthodox lands into Latin territory and totally destroyed the kingdom of Hungary, which had long prided itself on being Europe's '*Antemurale*' – its bulwark – against Muslim advance. Sultan Selim I first captured a range of Hungarian-held forts in Bosnia in 1512, his son Süleyman won Belgrade from the kingdom in 1521. The final disaster came in August 1526 at the battle of Mohács, when the Holy Roman Emperor's twenty-year-old Jagiellon brother-in-law King Louis II of Hungary and Bohemia was killed, along with a large proportion of his nobility, five bishops, two archbishops, and 16,000 of his soldiers. The Turks occupied and wrecked the royal capital Buda, whose palace castle was a show-piece of Renaissance art as spectacular as anything in Italy, and home to one of Europe's most distinguished and up-to-date libraries. This was the first loss in the heartland of Latin Christendom: might the Turks overrun everything? By 1529 they had moved west to besiege Vienna and were repulsed only with much heroism and after much destruction.

The trail of catastrophe signalled the failure of the crusading enterprise on Europe's southern and eastern flanks, where crusades had once achieved so many military advances and annexation of territory against Islam. Part of the reason for failure lay in the persistent arrogance of western Christendom not merely to Muslims but to eastern Christians, as we have already observed in Cyprus. The East had not forgotten the scandal of the Fourth Crusade of 1204, which had turned into a Venetian expedition to wreck and exploit Constantinople, a disaster from which the eastern Empire never fully recovered. Subsequent attempts to reunite Christianity foundered on a combination of the Western Church's doctrinal intransigence with understandable anger and suspicion from ordinary Orthodox Christians when eastern negotiators occasionally did manage to secure some not very favourable deal, as at the Council of Florence in 1439. By comparison the Turks were remarkably tolerant of non-Muslim faith communities; once they had taken Constantinople and adapted its greatest church of Hagia Sophia as a magnificent mosque, they did much to enhance the Patriarch of Constantinople's position against his various rivals in the eastern Churches, considering this a good way of controlling their Christian subjects. When eastern scholars fled west after Constantinople's fall, western Christians showed a notable lack of interest in finding out about Orthodox theology and liturgy; they really only esteemed these refugees for the hitherto unknown classical manuscripts that they might bring. It was not surprising that many eastern Christians were more willing to acquiesce in Ottoman rule and preserve their faith intact than to accept help on very unequal terms from western Europeans.

Westerners were still obsessed by the need for crusades, but the results were unimpressive and even bizarre. The Military Order of the Teutonic Knights remained on Europe's north-eastern frontier; after the thirteenth century they had retreated from their unsuccessful efforts to save the Holy Land and instead waged war against Lithuania, the last major pagan power in Europe. The Lithuanians' conversion to Latin Christianity under the sovereignty of the kings of Poland in 1386 discomfited the Order, robbing it of any purpose, but it went on fighting against both the Poles and the Lithuanians for its very considerable economic and political interests, representing a constant enterprise of enlarging German-speaking areas in eastern Europe. The effort earned it a crushing defeat from Polish-Lithuanian armies at Tannenberg in 1410. It was not surprising that one

of the decisions of the Council of Konstanz in 1415 was to transfer responsibility for converting Lithuania from the Knights to the kingdom of
Poland, or that Polish-Lithuanian church leaders loathed the Teutonic
Knights even more than they loathed Orthodox Christians. Power politics
equally compromised the efforts of Italians to unite against the Turkish
menace: Venice was the power most vulnerable to the Ottomans because of
its extensive Mediterranean possessions, and so it was always urging
renewed crusades, but equally it was determined to keep these enterprises
under its own control. Since Venice was the power which other fifteenth-
century Italian rulers feared the most, this was a sure way to limit their
crusading zeal.

In south-eastern Europe, where the Turks were a real and present source
of terror to all ranks in society, the crusading ideal was transformed from
the concern of knights and leaders of the commonwealth to something
more popular. This brought its own problems. We have already encountered
the charismatic Franciscan Giovanni di Capistrano (chapter 1, p. 50); when
the Turks first tried to capture Belgrade in 1456, Capistrano's preaching
stirred thousands of humble crusaders from central Europe in a successful
effort to beat them off. The Magyar *vojvoda* (military prince) János Hun-
yadi, whose personal army was also prominent in relieving Belgrade, was
uneasy about these hordes, and dismissed them as soon as victory was won,
preventing a full follow-up of the Turks' defeat. Popular suspicion grew
that the nobility did not have their hearts in the task of defending Europe,
particularly as the Ottomans went on consolidating themselves in the
Balkans.

The pattern was repeated much more disastrously in Hungary in the
1510s, after the monarchy's efforts to defend the kingdom with a standing
army had produced ruinous taxation and increased social tension. In 1514,
Pope Leo X was prevailed on to announce a crusade; another generation of
Franciscans whipped popular excitement to fever-point in Hungary. Soon
the Hungarian nobility panicked at the mass movement which had resulted,
and they desperately tried to halt the crusade. Its commander György Dószsa
Székely, a minor nobleman, turned his furious peasant forces on them rather
than on the Turks; on his defeat, Dószsa and his troops were punished with
sadistic cruelty. Within a dozen years this riven and chaotic kingdom was
annihilated by the Turks at Mohács.[2]

In the aftermath of Hungary's fall, the Emperor Charles V tried hard to
get the rulers of western Europe to finance more traditional crusades. Even
as late as 1543 Henry VIII far away in England was prepared to sponsor a
nationwide campaign to raise money for his brother-monarch's effort

(despite their being on opposite sides in the Church's schism), but the general political will had gone amid the bitterness of the Reformation.[3] Martin Luther went so far as to consider Charles's effort futile, because he considered that the Turks were agents of God's anger against sinful Christendom – and no one could resist God. Indeed, the Turkish invasions were, paradoxically, good news for Luther. If Charles V had not been so distracted in his efforts to save Europe's south-eastern frontier, he would perhaps have had the will and the resources to crush the Protestant revolt in its infancy in the 1520s and 1530s. When Charles did strike, it was too late.

On the eastern and southern rim of Europe, Islam remained a threat until the end of the seventeenth century. Even when the activities of the Ottoman fleet were curbed after the battle of Lepanto in 1571 (chapter 7, p. 331), north African corsairs systematically raided the Mediterranean coasts of Europe to acquire slave labour; in fact they ranged as far as Ireland and even Iceland, kidnapping men, women and children. Modern historians examining contemporary comment produce reliable estimates that Islamic raiders enslaved around a million western Christian Europeans between 1530 and 1640; this dwarfs the contemporary slave traffic in the other direction, and is about equivalent to the numbers of west Africans taken by Christian Europeans across the Atlantic at the same time. Two religious Orders, the Trinitarians and Mercedarians, specialized in ransoming Christian slaves, and over centuries honed diplomatic expertise and varied local knowledge to maximize the effectiveness of this specialized work. Large areas of Mediterranean coastline were abandoned for safer inland regions, or their people lived in perpetual dread of what might appear on the horizon; this may well explain, for instance, why Italians lost their medieval zest for adventurous trade overseas.[4] The fear which this Islamic aggression engendered in Europe was an essential background to the Reformation, convincing many on both sides that God's anger was poised to strike down the Christian world, and so making it all the more essential to please God by affirming the right form of Christian belief against other Christians. It is impossible to understand the mood of sixteenth-century Europe without bearing in mind the deep anxiety inspired by the Ottoman Empire (for further discussion of the consequences, see chapter 13, pp. 550–55).

THE IBERIAN EXCEPTION

In one area of Europe only did the crusading ideal win striking success: on the south-western frontier of the continent in Iberia (Spain and Portugal). Here that different outcome was hugely significant for the future not merely of western Christianity but of the world. From the eighth century, Arab Islamic conquests had established long-lasting Moorish principalities and kingdoms in the Iberian peninsula. These became centres of a highly developed Islamic culture which, with a tolerance imitated by the Ottomans and not by Christians, also allowed Jewish culture and thought to flourish in its midst. However, the fifteenth century saw the culmination of centuries of gradual Christian reclamations from the Moors with the capture in 1492 of the Islamic kingdom of Granada, in the extreme south of the peninsula. The news was celebrated all over Christian Europe as a rare reversal of Muslim advance: Henry VII of England ordered a service of thanksgiving in St Paul's Cathedral, London.

The victorious troops were in the service of joint monarchs, Fernando of the eastern Spanish kingdoms of Aragon, Valencia and the principality of Catalonia, and Isabel of Castile, a much larger though mostly more thinly populated kingdom which ran from north to south in the peninsula. Aragon and Castile, precariously united by the joint accession of Fernando and Isabel as a married couple in 1474, remained separate political entities, and there was no reason for them to remain linked when Isabel died. However, the death of her successor Philip of Burgundy after only two years resulted in a new union of the crowns under Fernando; henceforth they were never again divided, and Aragon and Castile could be regarded for external purposes as a single Spanish monarchy. To the west, the kingdom of Portugal, at the remote edge of Europe on the Atlantic seaboard, had long before this won its struggles against the Muslims; it had also secured its independence against Castile, and it kept that independence until 1580 (chapter 9, p. 417).

The constant medieval warfare against the rival cultures of Islam and Judaism gave Spanish Catholicism a militant edge not found elsewhere in western Europe. This is symbolized by a form of popular dramatic spectacle unique to Spanish culture, elaborate staged mock-battles between Moors and Christians (therefore called *moros y cristianos*): this developed in the twelfth century, persists into modern times and was even exported to the new Spanish lands across the Atlantic to celebrate the triumph of Catholic Christianity there.[5] Even after the sequence of medieval reconquest (*Recon-*

quista), Iberian Christian culture showed a frequently obsessive suspicion of former members of the rival cultures. In 1391, a particularly vicious wave of anti-Jewish preaching provoked the massacres of around a third of the Jews in Christian Spain and forced the conversion of another third. Such Jewish converts ('New Christians' or *conversos*: former Muslims were known as *Moriscos*) remained a perennial object of worry, to be scrutinized for doubtful loyalty in any time of heightened tension. Even when they were long-established Christians and had rejected all connection with Judaism, 'Old Christians' found a new reason for hating them, because they were now eligible for positions of power in Church and Commonwealth. They developed a myth that the Jews had provided a fifth column when the Muslim conquests had overwhelmed the ancient Christian kingdoms, so therefore no one of Jewish descent could be trusted. In return 'New Christians' were furious that their genuinely held faith and loyalty to the Crown should be questioned, and their fury occasionally erupted into violence. Such tensions remained particularly lively after 1492 in Castile, the area most recently on the front line.[6]

It might have been possible for the Crown to ride out these tensions or act as a referee to the two communities as it had done so often in the past, but the tragic events of the 1490s, which led to the destruction of Jewish as well as Islamic civilization in Spain, were intimately entangled with a complex struggle for control of the Spanish kingdoms within the royal family of Castile. Isabel had married Fernando of Aragon in 1469. Her own claim to the throne of Castile on the death of her half-brother Enrique IV in 1474 was shaky, for it was contested by the old king's daughter Juana, who had at least as good a claim as Isabel. The greatest dissidence that Isabel faced as she consolidated her power came from the south of her new dominions, Andalusia, where tensions between New and Old Christians were at their height: there had recently been widespread violence following an accusation that Jews had murdered a Christian boy for ritual purposes (that blood-libel myth all too frequently activated in medieval Europe). Isabel decided in alliance with local Dominicans to secure the dubious loyalty of the Andalusian nobility by emphasizing the fight against Judaism in her new realm.[7]

This set of political accidents and calculations established the tone for the rest of Isabel's long reign: first there would be an assault on Judaism, and later, after the fall of Granada in 1492, a parallel assault on Islam. The agent of her campaign would be a newly constituted version of an Inquisition, something that had not previously existed in Castile. It was an imitation of the many local inquisitions of the Church, which under Dominican leadership had investigated heresy in Europe since the thirteenth century, but now it was organized by the monarchy, and after complicated royal haggling with Pope Sixtus IV between 1478 and 1480 to create its legal framework, it settled down to work against 'Judaizers' in the kingdom of Castile, burning alive around 700 of them between 1481 and 1488. In the middle of this there came another momentous stage in the Inquisition's development: Pope Sixtus finally yielded to royal pressure in 1483 and appointed the Dominican friar Tomás de Torquemada as Inquisitor-General of all Fernando and Isabel's peninsular dominions. The newly constituted Inquisition was the only institution which united their various kingdoms: as such it attracted a good deal of suspicion and opposition from traditionalist-minded governors and local councils, who rightly saw it as an assault on their privileges on behalf of the monarchy.

When Granada fell, Isabel gave all Jews in Castile the choice of expulsion or conversion to Christianity: the excuse was yet another blood-libel accusation, this time from Toledo in 1490, that Jews had murdered a Christian boy, who has become known to his devotees as the Holy Child of La Guardia and was later attributed the significant name Cristóbal – Christ-bearer. Perhaps 70,000 to 100,000 Jews chose to become refugees abroad rather than abandon their faith, forming a European-wide dispersal which has been called Sephardic Judaism (since the Jews had applied the Hebrew word *Sefarad* to Spain). More Jews chose to convert rather than leave their homes, and the authorities were determined that their conversion should not be a token one.[8] At first there was an official agreement to allow the continued practice of Islam in Granada, but harassment by the Church authorities led to rebellion, which in 1500 provided the excuse for Isabel to insist on conversion of all Granada's Muslims to Christianity; she extended this requirement throughout Castile two years later. For the time being, King Fernando stood faithful to his coronation oath to preserve the liberties of his remaining Islamic subjects (*mudéjares*), who still comprised around 30 per cent of the population in his kingdom of Valencia in the early sixteenth century, but it was to be the attitudes fostered by Isabel in Castile that set the pace for the future. Her expulsions of Jews were imitated in Portugal, when in 1497 King Manoel (who was hoping to marry her daughter) ordered mass conversion of the Jewish population, many of whom had only just fled from Spain.[9]

So Latin Christianity, in an especially self-conscious version of its traditional form, became the central symbol of identity for the peninsula's kingdoms, and from the beginning Protestantism stood little chance of making any headway there against Spain and Portugal's project of building a monolithic Christian culture. Indeed, it is possible to talk of an Iberian

Reformation before the Reformation: well in advance of the general Protestant Reformation in Europe, Spain had tackled many of the structural abuses which elsewhere gave Protestant reformers much ammunition against the old Church. The energy of this Reformation was not merely home-grown, it was promoted by the monarchy, which increasingly excluded any real possibility of interference in the Church from the Pope. A series of concessions by the papacy allowed the Crown to appoint bishops, and by 1600 a third or more of the yearly income of the Castilian Church disappeared into the royal treasury.[10] The Pope tolerated being thus kept at arm's length partly because he had little choice, but partly because Spanish royal power was consistently exercised to create a 'purified' and strong Latin Christianity free from heresy or non-Christian deviation. Equally such a satisfactory deal for the Iberian monarchies meant that they had no reason to sympathize with any other challenge to papal authority.

The chief agent of the royal programme in the Church was Francisco Ximénes de Cisneros, a Castilian who gave up a distinguished career in church administration to join one of the most rigorous religious Orders, the Observant Franciscans, within which he sought to escape the world as a hermit. Yet the fame of his single-minded spiritual activism forced him back into the centre of power: agreeing against his better judgement to become confessor to Queen Isabel in 1492, he found himself in the highest offices in Church and Commonwealth in Castile, Archbishop of Toledo and eventually Regent of the kingdom during the minority of Charles Habsburg. In his austere, focused piety and his determination to proclaim his vision of Christian faith to the peoples of the Spanish kingdoms, he was much more like Luther, Zwingli or Calvin than his Spanish contemporary Pope Alexander VI, yet many of his reforms anticipate what the Council of Trent was to decree many decades later. He used his unequalled opportunities for action energetically and in ways which do not now seem entirely consistent, but which sum up the main themes of the Spanish religious revolution over which Fernando and Isabel presided. He ruthlessly promoted the agenda of his own Observant Franciscans among the more relaxed friaries of Franciscans, provoking much opposition. Yet this advocate of apostolic poverty was also the premier statesman in Spain, and he spent money lavishly as a major patron of the most advanced scholarship of his day: he founded the university of Alcalá out of his own resources, and funded the printing of a great number of books, particularly aimed at introducing the writings of his favourite mystics to a literate public. At the same time as promoting scholarly research, he was also responsible for burning thousands of non-Christian books and manuscripts, and he was central in the work of the Spanish Inquisition; he became Inquisitor General in the same year, 1507, that he was made a Cardinal.

In the aftermath of the fall of Granada (where from 1499 Francisco Ximénes took a personal and disruptively active role in the campaign of forced conversion) the Inquisition became central to the programme of eliminating the rival civilizations of the peninsula. It was not going to let up on the *converso* population, either pre- or post-1492 in Christian convert status, just because *conversos* now claimed to be Christian. This illogicality was aided by a new and sinister feature of the supposed martyrdom of the 'Holy Child of La Guardia' in 1490: the alleged perpetrators had been a mixed group of professed Jews and New Christians.[11] The Inquisition did not merely seek out evidence of continued secret practice of Islam or Judaism, but it reinforced an existing tendency in Spanish society to regard heresy and deviation as hereditary: so it became increasingly necessary for loyal Spanish Catholics to prove their *limpieza de sangre* (purity of blood), free of all *mudéjar* or Jewish taint. Any evidence of *converso* descent ended one's chances of (for instance) becoming a member of the chapter of Spain's premier cathedral, Toledo. The main religious Orders began insisting on *limpieza de sangre*, starting in 1486 with the influential native Order much patronized by the nobility, the Jeronimites, who were closely followed by the Franciscans and Dominicans as well as the secular clergy – in the end the Inquisition even required this assurance for its 'familiars', its network of spies and helpers. There were ironies in this ideological use of genealogy: few of the higher Spanish nobility could claim such purity of blood, and they found themselves excluded from high office in the Church in favour of social inferiors who could prove their lack of taint.[12]

The Inquisition's work was justified in the eyes of the reliably Catholic population, despite many constitutional worries, because there were real continuing challenges to Christian Spain, both internal and external. The general perception of Spain in the rest of Europe was that it remained an exotic place, full of Moors and Jews: an extremely mortifying image for hypersensitive Catholic Spaniards (and so for the many people in Europe who came to loathe Spanish power, it was also a useful theme with which to annoy them). Catholic Spain knew itself to be under continuing threat. As late as 1566, Islamic corsairs raided Granada and marched inland twenty miles, carrying off a reputed 4,000 of the barely converted population of Moriscos to Algeria, just at a time when the future of the whole Mediterranean world seemed in the balance in the aftermath of the great siege of Malta (chapter 7, p. 330).[13] Rebellions by sections of the Morisco population continued well into the sixteenth century, and the fear which they inspired in the majority population was powerful enough to result in a general expulsion order against Moriscos in 1609, more than a century after the fall of Granada. The situation was the same with the Jewish *converso* community. As late as 1600 a substantial community of 'Judaizers' was detected in the central Castilian region of La Mancha around Alcázar de San Juan, and after 1492, the Christianity of much of the newly converted Jewish population was at best confused and at worst a defensive cloak for their older faith. One of them described their unhappy situation as floating aimlessly 'like a cork on the water'.[14]

Thus disoriented, leaderless, and caught between the enthusiasms of two conflicting religions while trying to deal with their crisis, the *conversos* were easy prey around 1500 for prophets proclaiming that the Last Days were coming. Such uncontrolled religious energy spilled over into the population at large, itself disturbed by the sudden change in the peninsula's religious balance; Spain around 1500 was in a ferment of expectation of a universal monarchy, and avid for any dramatic manifestation of God's plan for the future. All this was deeply alarming for a society whose frontier was so recently secured, so the Inquisition could rely to a large extent on self-conscious good Catholics coming forward to let it know of evidence of deviation. By the second quarter of the sixteenth century, the Inquisition was spelling out to the population that sudden conversions, sightings of messengers from heaven or reports of statues that bled were no longer to be treated with respect, and it was bringing a new discipline to Spanish religion.[15]

Yet there were always bounds to the tolerance shown either by secular governors or ordinary people towards the Spanish Inquisition's activities. It was not difficult for the laity to perceive that one motive for the Inquisition's keeping itself in regular business was that its main sources of revenue were the confiscated goods of those it successfully prosecuted. After one of the chief outbreaks of millenarianism in the region of Córdoba in 1499, the Inquisition reacted with violence exceptional even by its own standards: in a series of *autos-da-fé* (ceremonial deliverings of an Inquisitorial legal sentence) in Córdoba, it burned nearly 400 people, and even tried to arrest the eighty-year-old Archbishop of Granada, who sensibly fled the region (though the shock probably hastened his death soon afterwards). It was not surprising that in this case King Philip of Castile intervened to stop the burnings and Cardinal Ximénes himself arrested and then quietly retired the local Inquisitor.[16] Far away to the north-east, in the Aragonese principality of Catalonia, the war with Islam and Judaism was long over by 1500, and people could not see the usefulness of continuing to tolerate the Inquisition's interference in their lives; it never established the hold in Catalonia which it certainly did further south.[17] But even in Castile, the Inquisition was one of the targets for popular violence when there were widespread *Comunero* rebellions in 1520–1; it had done its work too well in combating the menace of Judaism and Islam, and the population was growing restive. The appearance of Protestantism in Europe then luckily provided a new target for the Inquisition's energy, and a way of showing that it did have a useful purpose.

The Spanish version of Catholicism thus presents a complex set of features: it fostered deeply personal yearnings for closeness to God, which were linked to the spirituality of Judaism and Islam and which bore rich fruit in the experience of Teresa of Ávila and John of the Cross (chapter 9, pp. 423–7); it also witnessed official and unofficial moves to remove corruption from the Church's institutions. Alongside this, churchmen revealed a paranoid suspicion of any rival culture, a suspicion which, although many resisted it, found increasing support from the secular authorities in the Spanish commonwealths. After official Spain decisively rejected the peninsula's multicultural past, it is not unfair to see Spanish Christianity as a major exponent and practitioner of ethnic cleansing. The complication and moral ambiguity can be seen if one considers the undoubted renewal of Spanish monastic life: Ximénes as an Observant Franciscan was energetic in promoting renewal, but some of the Observant monks and friars most enthusiastic for reform came from *converso* circles, and their tendency to draw their spiritual intensity from the defeated religious cultures in the Peninsula provoked much suspicion from the Inquisition and led to repressive investigations. These independent forces in Spanish Christianity around 1500 produced a movement of mystical and spiritual enthusiasm in which friars, *conversos* and pious women (*beatas*) came to be styled by their admirers as *alumbrados* ('enlightened ones').

The Inquisition took up this name without the accompanying admiration, and set to work looking for heresy among the *alumbrados*. It found a movement that drew much of its inspiration from reading those parts of the Bible that were available in Spanish, and also northern European works like that classic of the *Devotio Moderna*, Kempis's *Imitation of Christ*. Total condemnation of such orthodox sources was difficult, so the authorities tried to make a distinction between those who practised a disciplined form of meditation or 'recollection' (*recogidos*), and those mystics who 'abandoned' themselves to the love of God (*dexados*); the latter were felt to be dangerous, and were rooted out. Exactly what the movement believed, or how much unity it had, is now difficult to recover, for the *alumbrados* never had the chance to express themselves publicly in complete freedom, either in surviving manuscript or in print, and their fate was sealed when some of them began taking an interest in a new import of northern European spirituality, the writings of Martin Luther. As a result, the whole movement suffered a formal condemnation in September 1525. Yet their legacy fed into some of the extraordinary expressions of spirituality which managed to flourish in later sixteenth-century Spain, despite the straitjacket which church authorities were seeking to impose on the peninsula; and as the *alumbrados* were dispersed by the Inquisition, they had an impact spread still more widely first through the *Spirituali* of Italy and then throughout Europe, as we will see (chapter 5, pp. 213–15, 8, pp. 359–60, and 9, pp. 423–4).

THE IBERIAN ACHIEVEMENT: THE WESTERN CHURCH EXPORTED

The distinctive brand of Christianity formed in Iberia not only destroyed the only non-Christian societies left in western Europe, it also began extending the reach of western Christendom beyond its natural frontiers, in sharp contrast to the defeats and contraction in the east. The initiative in military and commercial conquests across the sea was taken not by Spaniards but by the Portuguese. Their seafaring expertise was forced on them by their exposed and isolated position on the Atlantic seaboard and by their homeland's agricultural poverty, but they also had a tradition of successful crusading against Islam. They began their adventuring in north Africa, capturing the Moroccan commercial centre of Ceuta in 1415, and they went on to contest with Muslims for dominance in African trade through ever more bold exploration, seeing their efforts as a fight for Christianity as well a quest for wealth. From as early as 1443, they were actively involved in the slave trade, which had previously been a Muslim monopoly: they created the first extensive intercontinental slave-trading route, shipping African slaves back home as labour to such an extent that soon a tenth of the population was black in Portugal's southernmost region, the Algarve, a foretaste of later enforced mass movements of population to north and south America.[18]

By the end of the century, Portuguese ships had become much more ambitious. They were fuelled in their adventures by an optimistic myth or quarter-truth, that there was a distant, powerful Christian kingdom ruled over by 'Prester John', who would be an unbeatable ally against Islam – probably an echo of the real existence of a Christian kingdom in Ethiopia.

Although Prester John never fulfilled European hopes, the galvanizing effect of the myth was enough. The Portuguese explored down the western flank of Africa, eventually rounding the Cape of Good Hope, reaching India by 1498 and sailing around the Chinese coast by 1513. In 1500 they made their first landing on the east coast of South America, in what later became their colony of Brazil, and everywhere they established footholds, forming the basis of a maritime empire which to some extent came to justify the pretentious title confirmed by Pope Alexander VI for King Manoel of Portugal in 1502: 'Lord of the conquest, navigation and commerce of India, Ethiopia, Arabia and Persia'. Latin Europe marvelled at their achievement, gradually swallowed its disappointment at the non-appearance of Prester John, and turned from the wretched situation in the Balkans to take new hope for survival. In 1507, Pope Julius II held a thanksgiving service in Rome for all the Portuguese achievements in Asia, on the feast of St Thomas the Apostle (who was supposed to have travelled as a missionary to India): the Italian Augustinian friar Egidio of Viterbo, one of the most celebrated preachers of his day, published the sermon which he gave on this occasion as 'the fulfilment of the Golden Age'. Julius's successor Leo X was delighted to receive a performing albino Indian elephant from King Manoel in 1514. Alas, though much loved, it lived only two years; its tusks can still be seen in the Vatican.[19]

Despite such enthusiasm, it must be said that the Portuguese Church as a potential missionary organization combined most of Spanish Catholicism's drawbacks with few of its signs of rigorous reorganization or renewal. At home, despite the fervent devotion of Portuguese kings and their proclaimed intentions of promoting reform, the nobility and royal family diverted church offices and revenues for their own benefit more outrageously even than in central Europe, and no action followed to match the structural reforms carried out in Spain. Once abroad, the Portuguese turned their crusading ethos to a degree of religious intolerance as extreme as anywhere in western Europe: in the course of establishing themselves in a secure Indian base in Goa from 1510, they were not slow to perpetrate a massacre of the 6,000 Muslims there, and in mid-century they also forbade the practice of Hinduism in Portuguese royal dominions; for good measure they despised the Syrian or Nestorian Christians whom they encountered in India. It was entirely accidental that later Christian mission based on the worldwide Portuguese empire had to show a certain humility and caution in its operations, for the simple reason that the Portuguese never overcame the poverty of their home country. Their empire was run on a shoestring and consisted mainly of a motley collection of fortified but under-garrisoned coastal trading-posts. By the mid-sixteenth century it was in such a mess that the diplomatic historian Garrett Mattingly once unkindly but accurately commented that the King of Portugal had become the proprietor of 'a bankrupt wholesale grocery business'.[20] Consequently the Portuguese usually lacked the military power to impose Christianity by force over widespread territories or on their African or Asian neighbours, with consequences which we will examine (in chapter 9, pp. 427–41).

The frayed texture of Portuguese empire-building contrasted with spectacular parallel achievements under the Spanish monarchy. In 1492, the same year that Granada fell, the adventurer Christopher Columbus rewarded Fernando and Isabel's trust by making landfall across the Atlantic on islands of the Caribbean. His achievement caused tension with the Portuguese, and this prompted Pope Alexander VI (a former subject of King Fernando) to partition the map of the world vertically between the two powers in 1493: the kingdoms confirmed this agreement in 1494 by the Treaty of Tordesillas. Although the uncertain conditions of map-making meant that the line was not as clear a division through the Atlantic as it was intended to be, and the Portuguese were later able successfully to appeal to Tordesillas when they established their American colony of Brazil, the bulk of transatlantic activity would be Spanish (technically the new dominions became part of the Kingdom of Castile). Over the next three decades the Spaniards realized the vast scale of what they were now invading, as they moved beyond the Caribbean into Mexico and Peru, and saw that they had reached not merely Columbus's scattering of islands, but a whole continent.

An important part of this militantly Latin Christian culture was inevitably the promotion of its faith among the peoples now encountered, although Fernando and Isabel had originally envisaged evangelizing the peoples of Asia rather than a new continent; hence the Spanish named the native peoples 'Indios', in allusion to Columbus's original belief that he had reached Asia in his voyages (see Plate 1b). Besides papal mediation over Iberian exploration, the Pope also granted the Spanish monarchy the *Patronato*, the exclusive right to preach the Gospel in its new territories: a major step in the gradual papal abdication of real authority within Spanish dominions (he granted the Portuguese a similar right in their empire, the *Padroado*). Now good intentions clashed with naked greed and brutality. There was in fact an encouraging Spanish precedent: the earliest western missionary work outside continental Europe had taken place in the Atlantic Canary Islands off the African coast, after Castilians established a presence there from the end of the fourteenth century. The missionaries who arrived in the Canaries were mostly Franciscans from Castile's southernmost province, Andalusia:

their behaviour contrasted with that of later Portuguese missions in Africa. They spoke out strongly against enslaving native people who had converted to Christianity, and sometimes they made the leap of imagination also to oppose the enslavement of those who had not so converted. They also persuaded the authorities in Rome to allow the ordination of natives.[21] All this offered precedents for what might happen in what Europe now came to call 'the New World'.

The problem with further implementing a Canary Islands model was the contrasting and appalling record of those military adventurers who undertook Spain's forward movement in America: the encounters of Hernando Cortés with the Aztecs in central America and of Francisco Pizarro with the Inkas of Peru are stories of unprovoked aggression, treachery, theft and genocide. Yet many who took part in these unsavoury feats of conquest saw themselves as agents of the crusade begun back in Spain with the *Reconquista* and the destruction of Spanish Islam and Judaism. Jerzy Kłoczowski, thinking of the clashes in eastern Europe between the Teutonic Knights and the Catholics of Poland-Lithuania, has suggested that one can identify two types of Christianity produced by two different styles of missionary effort: a militant, dogmatic faith stemming from armed Crusades, and a more gentle, flexible creed which was exemplified in the work of missionary Orders of friars.[22] Whether or not his thesis works for eastern Europe, the analysis would be worth applying to the case of Spanish America. Crusading rhetoric there was in plenty, but there was also a Franciscan presence from 1500, and within a decade Dominicans had also arrived. Very soon the Dominicans began protesting against the colonial enterprise's vicious treatment of the native population of 'Indios'. The authorities at home did go some way to responding to such appeals to their conscience. As early as 1500 Fernando and Isabel formally forbade the enslavement of those who were their subjects in America and the Canaries. The Laws of Burgos tried in 1512 to lay down guidelines for relations with the Indios, and even created a set of 'rules of engagement' for further conquests: newly contacted peoples were to be publicly read (in Spanish!) a Requirement, a formal memorandum which explained the bulls of Alexander VI granting Spain its overlordship of their territory. If they co-operated and agreed that Christianity could freely be taught among them, then no force would be used against them.

The Laws of Burgos might have been intended as a concession, but they were an unmistakable example of the crusading approach to mission, and the atrocious exploits of both Cortés and Pizarro post-dated them. The friars' fury at the continuing injustice was therefore unabated. Their most eloquent spokesman was a former colonial official and plantation-owner, Bartolomé de las Casas, who was galvanized out of his profitable activity by hearing a Dominican sermon about the wickedness of what he and his fellow colonists were doing: the shock turned him to ordination as a priest, and he made it his especial task for half a century from 1514 to defend the Indios – he became a Dominican himself in 1522. He won sympathy from the aged Cardinal Ximénes; later his impassioned insistence that the Indios were as rational beings as Spaniards, rather than inferior versions of humanity, naturally fitted for slavery, sufficiently impressed the Emperor Charles V that debates were staged at the imperial Spanish capital at Valladolid on the morality of colonization (it must be said, with inconclusive results).

The writings of Las Casas about Spanish barbarity in America were so angry and eloquent that they became part of the general Protestant stereotype of Spaniards as a naturally cruel race. Alas, part of his remedy for the exploitation of Indio labour was a recommendation that African slaves should be imported to replace them on plantations, radically extending the slave trade which the Portuguese had pioneered in the previous century. Las Casas eventually realized his mistake, but it was too late. Here idealism trying to end one injustice blundered unhappily into colluding with a genocidal crime of three centuries' duration, whose consequences are still built into the politics of both Americas. Rather more equivocally expressed than the passion of Las Casas, but equally important for Latin Europe's future relations with other world civilizations, was the work of a Dominican who never saw the 'New World', Francisco de Vitoria, who for the last two decades of his life was highly influential as the leading theologian of Salamanca University.

Vitoria built on the thought of earlier Dominican theologians to consider what was happening in America in the light of the theory of a 'just war'. Conventional Christian legal wisdom said that there was nothing wrong in enslaving non-Christians who were captured in a just war, but there seemed to Vitoria little that was just in the idea of a crusade, particularly in the way that the idea had been exploited in America. War was justified only if it was a response to infliction of a wrong, and the various peoples of America had offered no wrong to Spaniards before the Spaniards decided to move in on their territory. The Aztec practice of human sacrifice did offer a different justification for Spanish action in central America, since it was a clear wrong, an offence against universal natural law. There were other possible interpretations of wrong: resistance to the preaching of the Gospel, for instance, once the intention to do so had been proclaimed in the Requirement. Vitoria also considered the issue of authority within commonwealths.

He discussed it in terms of sovereignty, that is a ruler's untrammelled power within the boundaries of a commonwealth or state. Such sovereign commonwealths need not be Christian: the Aztecs or the Ottomans were as sovereign as Fernando and Isabel. If that was so, then Pope Alexander had possessed no right to grant sovereignty in America to the Spaniards in 1493, at the same time as he perfectly legimately granted them the exclusive right to preach the Gospel. Such a treatment of sovereignty (coming from within an Iberian Catholic tradition which had already put the Pope firmly in his place) was a clear denial of the idea of universal papal monarchy that had originally fuelled the unity of western Christendom in the twelfth century.

Vitoria's discussion of such questions also had a wider application. He was pioneering a concept of a system of international law, based on the older idea of a 'ius gentium', a natural law applicable to all people everywhere, even Aztecs or Ottomans. His assertions heralded the end of belief in the crusade as a means of extending the boundaries of western Christendom, just at the moment when Europe began a wider mission to spread its particular brand of Christianity throughout the world. The question would soon arise as to whether western Christianity was completely identical with authentic Christianity, an assumption which had been common to most thinking western Christians during the medieval period. But there was more to the development of international law than this. Western European political thought was to develop a relativistic concept of dealing with other cultures and other political units – eventually without reference to their religious beliefs or any sense that one religion was superior to another. Vitoria would have profoundly disapproved of this development, but it emerged as a consequence of the Iberian adventures in the world beyond Europe.

NEW POSSIBILITIES: PAPER AND PRINTING

The Portuguese astronomer and cosmographer Pedro Nunes looked back in 1537 on what his countrymen had achieved in their voyages and trumpeted deep patriotic pride and optimism: 'The Portuguese ... discovered new islands, new lands, new peoples; and, what is more new stars and a new heaven. They freed us from many false impressions and showed us that there are antipodes, about which even the saints had doubts; that there is no region that is uninhabitable because of heat or cold.'[23] Nunes' delight in the new discoveries, his revelling in the enlarged state of the world, is actually quite surprising. For centuries, the general instinct in most branches of learning was that the world and humanity were in decay: present-day people knew less than people in the past, and that true wisdom lay in what had been known a long time. Authority was to be respected, and it usually gave all the answers which were necessary; this was particularly the case with the greatest authoritative text of all, the Christian Bible. Yet far from being intellectually disoriented by the discovery of new continents and new peoples unmentioned in the Bible, with an antipodes or southern hemisphere which confounded all the opinions of the authorities ('even the saints had doubts'), fifteenth-century Europe seemed to welcome the novelty of being 'freed from false impressions' – even those in positions of traditional authority. We have witnessed a Pope taking his pen to the newly enlarged globe to divide it for the Iberians, and his successor Pope holding a jamboree in 1507 to celebrate what the Portuguese had achieved. Clearly this was not a society frightened of novelty; moreover, it could recognize parallels to the voyages across the oceans in other spheres of experience.

Two recent technical innovations were recognized even during the fifteenth century as a radical improvement on the past; together they revolutionized the speed of communicating information and ideas. The first was a writing material in increasingly widespread use in Europe since the thirteenth century: paper manufactured from rags. Europe had not invented this process; it had been known in China for centuries. Paper was much more easily and cheaply manufactured than reed-based papyrus or animal-skin bases for text (vellum or parchment), and by the end of the fourteenth century, Christian Europe far outstripped the Muslim world in production. In the early fifteenth century came the second technological revolution, printing with movable type: again, this was a much older invention of the Chinese, but once it was introduced Europeans rapidly took it up with enthusiasm. It was immediately clear that printing like this was much more flexible and useful as a technology of reproducing information than the existing use of carved woodblocks, which usually rather crudely reproduced mass copies of a design, but only at the size of a single page. The superiority of printing to handwritten texts (manuscripts) was less obvious, for manuscripts could present more directly the work of their author in a format which the author wanted, and they continued to be an important medium of circulating information when only a few people needed to see it, particularly in elite scholarly circles. Niccolò Machiavelli preferred manuscript to print in publicizing his controversial ideas on government to an audience of powerful people. The German Benedictine Abbot Johannes Trithemius, an eccentric but influential scholar, said sniffily in 1492 that writing on parchment would last a thousand years, while printing on paper would probably only survive for a couple of centuries: though he had borrowed this remark from the early Christian scholar Jerome dismissing papyrus a millennium earlier, he had a point.[24]

Although an individual text on parchment might indeed last for a thousand years, once destroyed, it was gone for ever, and it might represent the only copy of the text that it contained. Multiplication was a sure way to preserve information. For texts which required very many copies, printing was soon indispensable. Movable-type text on paper (de luxe copies might still use parchment) was radically cheaper than a manuscript to produce and once the rather laborious process of setting up the pages was completed, it was exhilaratingly easy to reproduce large print-runs, on the same scale as many present-day editions. The commercial ordinances of Geneva in the 1540s assumed that in a day a skilled craftsman could produce 1,300 copies of a single sheet (for the average-sized book, eight pages of the finished product): so editions tended to be in multiples of 700 copies, half a day's work. Larger books, which would be labour-intensive to re-create once their typeface had been broken up and reused, produced the largest runs, and they could appear in an edition of three or four thousand copies.[25] The resulting product was not necessarily cheap to buy, but for that reason, printing could be extremely profitable and was an attractive trade to enter. In England in 1537, a big Bible for churches to buy (as they were soon forced to do by royal command) cost its printer 6s 8d, a third of a pound sterling, in a run of 1,500 copies; in 1539, a similar Bible retailed to the customer at between 10s and 13s 4d (a half to two-thirds of a pound). So Protestantism, when it established itself, would prove to be good business for printers.[26]

Conversely, printing also turned out to be good for Protestantism, for a religion of the book needs books. An English reforming sympathizer celebrated this early in the brief mid-sixteenth-century reign of King Edward VI, when evangelicals in England were at last free openly to print their propaganda: he contrasted his own age with that of the Early Church and the Emperor Constantine. '[B]ut thanks be to the Lord, our King's Majesty may go further with hundred pound in printing, than Constantine might have done with three thousand pound in writing. For the lack of books caused the Bishops of Rome and his [sic] aiders to prevail in all Councils [i.e. General Councils of the Church] since the first.'[27] One of the reasons that the Lollards (chapter 1, p. 35) had failed to consolidate widespread support while a century and a half later their evangelical successors did, was the fact that they could not produce enough copies of their literature to distribute.

Even if the events of the 1520s had never happened and there had been no evangelical challenge to the Church, the coming of printing would have changed the shape of religion. It is true that early printers hastened to supply the safe market which would make an assured profit, and naturally that meant supplying what conventional religion wanted. The earliest surviving dated piece of English printing, from 1476, illustrates this, because it is an indulgence, printed ready for the purchaser's name to be filled in in ink: the Church's exploitation of indulgences was precisely the issue which sparked Luther's fury in 1517 (see chapter 3, pp. 121-3).[28] Yet within conventional religion, with no sense that the impulse was unorthodox, there was a great popular hunger to encounter the book on which the faith and worship of the Church was based – the Bible. The earliest surviving datable printed book of all, published at Mainz in 1457, is a Latin edition of the Book of Psalms (the Psalter).

Bernard Cottret, Calvin's biographer, has observed that the increase in Bibles created the Reformation rather than being created by it, and it is notable how many of these Bibles were translations from Latin into local languages. Not all churchmen approved of this development. Even the great Jean Gerson, who as we have seen wanted to clip the Pope's wings and to encourage laypeople to receive communion more often (see chapter 1, pp. 22, 40), proposed a ban on Bible translations to the Council of Konstanz – but it was not implemented, unlike the drastic and exceptional action taken in England in the previous decade. Gerson's fear was not merely clerical selfishness but reflected the newly flourishing state of preaching in the fifteenth century: the worry was that the laity would spend too much time reading and not listen to sermons. Regardless of such fears, the printers followed the market. Between 1466 and 1522 there were twenty-two editions of the Bible in High or Low German; it reached Italian in 1471, Dutch in 1477, Spanish in 1478, Czech around the same time and Catalan in 1492. In 1473-4 French publishers opened up a market in abridged bibles, concentrating on the exciting stories and leaving out the more knotty doctrinal passages, and this remained a profitable enterprise until the mid-sixteenth century.[29]

The effect of printing was more profound than simply making more books available more quickly. It affected western Europe's assumptions about knowledge and originality of thought. Before the invention of printing, a major part of a scholar's life was spent copying existing texts by hand, simply in order to have access to them. Now that printed copies of texts were increasingly available, there was less copying to do, and so there was more time to devote to thinking for oneself: that had implications for scholarly respect for what previous generations had said. Copying had been such a significant activity that in previous centuries of Christian culture, it had been given a privileged place against original thought. The thirteenth-century Franciscan scholar and devotional writer Bonaventure discussed various categories which might be described as writing: of his four variants, none included pure authorship of a new book as we would understand it today. He spoke of the writer as scribe (that is, a copyist), as compiler of anthologies, as commentator on older texts, and finally as 'auctor' – but even then, that meant someone who produced 'his own work in principal place adding others for purposes of confirmation'. Such a hierarchy of functions would seem bizarrely out of proportion after the fifteenth century.[30]

There were further consequences to basic assumptions about authority, none of which were good news for a Church hierarchy which claimed to have proprietorial rights over what to believe. Printing which produced multiple identical copies of a text encouraged a familiarity with uniformity, very different from the individuality of a manuscript. That in turn was liable to produce a sense of how significant it was when difference appeared: uniformity paradoxically put a premium on individuality. A culture based on manuscripts is conscious of the fragility of knowledge, and the need to preserve it: a priority must be to keep it secure, simply to avoid the physical destruction of a single precious source, and that fosters an attitude which guards rather than spreads knowledge. Print culture multiplies copies, and the printer has a vested interest in as much multiplication as possible, to sell his wares. Similarly, a manuscript culture is going to believe very readily in decay, in knowledge as in everything else, because copying knowledge from one manuscript to another is a very literal source of corruption. This is much less obvious in the print medium: optimism may be the mood rather than pessimism.[31]

Even the larger number of books in circulation had its own effect. Because printing generated so much more to read, reading became a skill much more worth acquiring. It is worth noting that although in our society reading and writing are generally taught in the same educational timescale, there is no particular reason for this, and of the two skills, reading is probably the easier to acquire. In medieval and early modern Europe, many more people could read than could write. This spread of reading skills had consequences which began to be felt in Europe even before printing appeared, but which it then powerfully encouraged. Reading is a passive experience physically but an active one mentally; it is also a solo activity. There are ways of bringing physical activity to it, like mouthing the words to oneself or reading the text aloud as a performance to a group of listeners, but these are peripheral to the central experience of sitting quietly with the text, forming one's own relationship with the writer, and deciding for oneself what he or she is trying to say. Other people are only a distraction, unless they are in turn a passive audience for the reading of the text. Only when the text has been read can it begin to be discussed.

As reading became a more prominent part of religion for the laity (as it had long been for the clergy), the shift in priorities encouraged the more inward-looking, personalized devotion which we have already begun noting in a number of spheres in the fifteenth century: lay enthusiasm for the writings of the mystics, meditation on aspects of the life of Jesus, the ethos of the *Devotio Moderna*. For someone who really delighted in reading, religion might retreat out of the sphere of public ritual into the world of the mind and the imagination. Reading privileges sight among the other human senses, and it further privileges reading text among other uses of the eye; it relies not at all on gesture, which is so important a part of communicating in liturgy or in preaching. So without any hint of doctrinal deviation, a new style of piety arose in that increasingly large section of society which valued book-learning for both profit and pleasure. Even if such people were in the crowd at the parish Mass, they were likely be absorbed in their printed layfolk's companion to the Mass, or a Book of Hours – books commonly known as primers. The wealthier folk among them might build themselves an enclosed private pew in their church to cut themselves off from the distractions provided by their fellow worshippers.[32]

This new emphasis in devotion tended to be urban in its perspectives, for there were more books (and soon very many more printing-presses and schools) in towns than in the country. It was likely to associate the more demonstrative, physical side of religion with rusticity and lack of education, and treat such religion with condescension or even distaste, seeing rituals and relics as less important than what texts can tell the believer seeking salvation. Historians of the twelfth century are familiar with an earlier expression of this sort of view, because that period had likewise seen a sudden upsurge in excitement about classical literature and a hunt for ancient manuscripts – but readers were then so much smaller a proportion of the population, and virtually all of them were clergy.[33] In the fifteenth century, the attitude spread to a much larger group of prosperous and well-educated laypeople: merchants, gentry, lawyers, people who would form a ready audience for the Protestant message, with its contempt for so much of the old ritual of worship and devotion. Yet although this mood certainly found forthright expression in the Protestant Reformations, it was already flourishing in the thought of the major new departure in late medieval Europe's intellectual life, the movement known as humanism.

HUMANISM: A NEW WORLD FROM BOOKS

Humanism can seem a difficult phenomenon to pin down and define, not least because no one used the word in the first age of humanism. Early nineteenth-century historians newly coined it from words which had indeed been in use in the late fifteenth century, when it became common to talk about the liberal/non-theological arts subjects in a university curriculum as 'humanae litterae' (literature which was human rather than divine in focus), and a scholar who had a particular enthusiasm for these subjects was called a 'humanista'.[34] A further complication is that 'humanist' has come to be used in modern times for someone who rejects the claims of revealed religion; this was not a feature of the movement we are considering. Even if some fifteenth- and sixteenth-century humanists might privately have toyed with such an idea, it would have been suicide for them openly to express it. One or two eccentric spirits, like the aristocratic Italian Platonist scholar Giovanni Pico della Mirandola, might privately have preferred the gods of ancient Greece and Rome to Christianity, but again that was not something safe to say. In any case, the vast majority of humanists were patently sincere Christians who wished to apply their enthusiasm to the exploration and proclamation of their faith.

I make no apology for thus grubbing around in words and definitions, because humanists were obsessed with words and how to use them. If we pursue this pedantry further, we will learn to avoid a phrase now frequently used as a synonym for humanism: 'the New Learning'. This is very misleading, because it actually was used in the sixteenth century, but to describe something different: it was an abusive Catholic term for Protestant or evangelical theology, and that is by no means the same as humanism, as we will see in chapter 3.[35] By contrast, a term usefully associated with humanism is 'Renaissance': this conveys the right nuance that while something new was happening in Europe between the fourteenth and sixteenth centuries, it was seen as a rediscovery of something very old. The fourteenth-century Italian humanist poet Petrarch so admired the poetic achievements of his older contemporary Dante Alighieri that he proclaimed that they represented a 'rebirth' ('renascita') of poetry as good as anything which had been written in ancient Rome; nineteenth-century scholars then used this word in its French form (*Renaissance*) to describe the cultural phenomenon which the humanists represented.

Another phrase worth using is 'civic humanism'. This is intended to describe the thought of those humanists who paid particular attention to ancient society, in order to see how their own society and government might be restructured for the general good. They generally sought to construct a republican form of government that owed something to ancient Athens or Rome, although others, 'princely humanists', decided that government was best concentrated in the hands of one man (it is worth pointing out that princes might give very generous financial backing to humanist learning). The modern German scholar Hans Baron pioneered discussion of civic humanism: he considered why it had first appeared in fourteenth- and fifteenth-century Italy and highlighted the special political conditions there – greater contrasts in forms of government than elsewhere in Europe, as well as great political confusion and conflict. There was therefore a particular incentive for citizens of the great cities and the principalities of Italy to consider the nature of government, and when they tried to justify republican or monarchical rule to enemies or potential sympathizers, they looked for precedents in the most impressive and successful commonwealths they could find in the history-books, the cities of classical Greece and republican or imperial Rome.[36] Moreover Italy, more spectacularly than anywhere else in Europe, had the advantage of 'the encyclopaedia of antiquity buried beneath it': a physical legacy of art and architecture that had survived from the heart of the Roman Empire poked out of the soil, or loomed over town and countryside in vast hulks of buildings which might be seen as mocking the achievement of medieval Italians.[37]

Emerging from this welter of definitions, we can now piece together a picture of humanist identity. Far from being 'New Learning', it represented a refocusing of old learning. It brought a new concentration on and a new respect for sections of traditional scholarship which medieval universities considered of secondary importance: the non-theological parts of their arts curriculum, especially poetry, oratory and rhetoric (the arts of political persuasion by speaking and writing). Humanists were lovers and connoisseurs of words. They saw them as containing power which could be used actively to change human society for the better. The words which inspired such excitement were found in ancient texts from long-vanished societies with the same belief in the transforming power of poetry, oratory and rhetoric – ancient Greece and Rome. Part of the project of transforming the world must be to get as clear a picture as possible of these ancient societies, and that meant getting the best possible version of the texts which were the main records of how those societies had thought and operated. One crude but serviceable definition of humanism, therefore, would be to say that it consisted of a realization that there was more to life than the Middle Ages. Another would be to describe a humanist as an editor of texts.

These ancient texts had inspired similar excitement before; so historians talk of the sudden effect of manuscripts on intellectual life in ninth- and twelfth-century Europe equally as two Renaissances. But in this new age of Renaissance, the impact was far more widely spread through society, because the technology of printing on paper opened up far more rapid possibilities of distributing copies of the texts, and gave much greater incentives for the spread of literacy associated with these innovations; this in turn produced a far more intense search for ancient manuscripts often lying neglected in cathedral or monastery libraries since earlier bursts of enthusiasm for the past. Moreover, many more Greek manuscripts re-emerged from this latest treasure-hunt. Medieval western Europe had access to remarkably little Greek literature; the text of such central works of literature as Homer's epics, for instance, was hardly known until the fifteenth century. In fact until then, very few scholars had any more than the vaguest knowledge of the Greek language. If they knew a learned language other than Latin, it was likely to be Hebrew, for the good reason that while there were virtually no Greeks of any significance in the West, there were plenty of argumentative and ingenious Jewish rabbis, who had an awkward ability to question Christianity and so needed to be refuted by reference to their own Hebrew literature. Now, however, western humanists would be forced to acquire skills in a new language if they were to make use of the texts suddenly available.

Paradoxically, the trauma of the Ottoman conquests that so terrorized western Europe tipped the balance in the supply of manuscripts and brought Greek culture west. Many Greek manuscripts came in the baggage of scholars fleeing from the wreckage of Christian commonwealths in the East, or they were snapped up by western entrepreneurs profiting from the catastrophe. For instance, from a single prolonged expedition to Constantin-ople thirty years before its fall to the Turks in 1453, the Sicilian manuscript dealer and collector Giovanni Aurispa brought back no fewer than 238 Greek manuscripts, introducing westerners for the first time to major texts of drama from Aeschylus, Sophocles, and hitherto unknown philosophical works of Plato. The reappearance of Plato was especially significant, because twelfth- and thirteenth-century western scholasticism had been shaped by rediscovering his very different pupil Aristotle, the philosopher whose work was characterized by the creation of lists, syntheses and systems. Now Plato's attitude to the ultimate problems of philosophy, his sense that the greatest reality lay beyond visible and quantifiable reality, cast a question-mark for humanists over the whole style of scholastic learning, its careful distinctions and definitions. More than that, Plato's thought lay behind so many of the assumptions of ancient society; now scholars could begin to explore and understand this, and in the course of time they could also begin to see what a profound impact Plato's writings had made on the thinkers of early Christianity.

Alongside the exhilarating rediscovery of Greek, the humanists also gained new perspectives on the Latin language and culture. They developed a great enthusiasm for the first-century BCE politician turned philosopher Marcus Tullius Cicero ('Tully' to his English-speaking admirers). Civic humanists appreciated Cicero's detailed discussion of government, disre-garding the inconvenient fact that he had been a very unsuccessful politi-cian, and when in 1421 his treatise on oratory was rediscovered in the cathedral library at Lodi in northern Italy, the new book sealed his repu-tation as the ideal model for powerful and persuasive Latin prose. It became the ambition of every cultivated young scholar to write just like Cicero, given inevitable adjustments like newly coined words for printing, gunpowder and cannon-fire.[38]

This humanist literary style, which also resulted in humanists reviving the conventions and metrical forms of ancient poetry, was very different from the Latin which scholastic philosophers and theologians had used over the previous few centuries. One can tell a humanist prose composition from a scholastic text merely by seeing how the sentences are constructed. The contrast became even more obvious when humanist manuscript writers painstakingly mimicked the 'italic' characteristics of what they took to be ancient script; printers then imitated their italic script, producing a typeface very similar to the one which you are reading in this book, and very different to the Gothic type which other printers used in imitation of medieval manuscript 'bookhand'. This was parallel to the Renaissance's architectural and artistic revolution, which began in Italy in the fifteenth century and gradually spread northwards over the next two centuries: the visual forms of ancient buildings, sculpture, paintings and gardens were more and more accurately imitated as part of the effort to bring back to life the lost world of Greece and Rome.

One of the consequences of the reappearance of manuscripts was a flood of new and strange material from the ancient world, which might or might not be valuable if put to use in society. Among much else emerging from the manuscripts was a set of writings about religion and philosophy that claimed to have been written by a divine figure from ancient Egypt, Hermes Trismegistus. In fact they had been compiled in the first to third centuries CE, at much the same time as early Christianity was emerging; some of this material was then codified in Greek in a work now known as the *Corpus Hermeticum*, and much else was later translated into Latin and Arabic. Some of the subjects of these treatises were forms of magic, medicine or astrology to sort out the problems of everyday life, but some appealed to the same fascination with secret wisdom about the cosmos and the nature of knowledge that had influenced Christianity in its first three centuries, among groups collectively labelled as 'gnostics'. Gnosticism tried to assimilate Platonic philosophy to the Bible, just as much hermetic literature was trying to do with Hellenistic mythology. The Christianity that survived as the Catholic Church shouldered aside gnosticism and labelled it as heresy, but the more adventurous minds within Christian scholarship, particularly in the eastern Churches, had never lost a fascination with gnostic speculation, despite official disapproval. Ordinary folk appreciated the further pleasing and pious details about Christ's birth and early life that some surviving gnostic sacred texts helpfully provided. Plenty of these details feature regularly in Byzantine church art, and they include the name of Jesus's grandmother, Anna or St Anne (see chapter 1, p. 22).

So 'hermetic' literature chimed in with many traditional Christian preoccupations, and it became newly accessible after the brilliant Florentine Platonist scholar Marsilio Ficino was commissioned to translate into Latin the available sections of the *Corpus Hermeticum*.[39] It suggested to humanists the exciting prospect of finding a bonanza of fragments from a lost ancient wisdom; with more investigation, hard work and possibly supernatural aid, more might be more fully recovered. Equally exciting were the possibilities opened up by Cabbala, the body of Jewish literature that had started out as commentary on the Hebrew Scripture, but which by the medieval period had created its own intricate network of rabbinic speculation, drawing on sub-Platonic mysticism like the gnostics or the hermeticists. Central to Cabbala was the work known as the *Sefer ha-Zohar* ('Book of Splendour'), a product of thirteenth-century Spanish Judaism, although its readers generally saw it as much older. This offered a majestic vision of the beings who were intermediaries between God and the world, suggested myriad ways of finding wisdom in even the most apparently unrewarding passages of the Bible, and provided more information as to how God was proposing to bring his plans for creation to a final resolution.

Many humanists were impressed by the enormous body of potentially useful data apparently contained in such writings, and they were gratified to find reinforcement for their own optimistic sense of infinite possibilities in humankind. Cabbala embraced a vision of humanity as potentially divine and indwelt by divine spirit. It suggested new approaches to the sudden encounters with world cultures brought about by the Iberian voyages: Cabbala might provide a basis for presenting Christian wisdom to those who found conventional western Christianity unsympathetic. Perhaps, as Ficino hoped, cabbalistic and hermetic ideas together might complete God's purpose in the Christian message by broadening and enriching it. These themes were to play a great part in intellectual life and discussion throughout the sixteenth and seventeenth centuries, while also attracting derision and hostility from many theologians in both Catholic and Protestant camps. We will find that in the end, they helped to bring the Reformation era to a close (chapters 11, pp. 491–2 and 17, pp. 680–84).

How might one establish authenticity amid this intoxicating but unsorted flow of information? One criterion must be to assess a text in every respect – its content, date, origins, motives, even its appearance. So much depended on texts being accurate. This meant developing ways of telling a good text from a corrupt text: looking at the way in which it was written and whether it sounded like texts reliably datable to the same historical period. Historical authenticity gained a new importance: it now became the chief criterion for authority. In earlier centuries, monks cheerfully forged documents on a huge scale for the greater glory of God, particularly charters proving their monastery's claim to lands and privileges. They lived in a world where there were too few documents, and so they needed to manufacture the authority to prove things which they knew in their hearts to be true. That attitude would no longer do. A 'source' for authority, or *fons*, now outweighed the unchallenged reputation of an *auctoritas*. *Ad fontes*, back to the sources, was the battle-cry of the humanists, and Protestants would take it over from them. Hence the relevance of our earlier definition of a humanist as a textual editor: an individual, equipped with the right intellectual skills, could outface centuries of authority, even the greatest authority in medieval Europe, the Church.

A particularly notorious example of a revered text demolished by fifteenth-century scholarship was an eighth-century forgery claiming to be a grant by the fourth-century convert Emperor Constantine I, giving the Pope sweeping powers throughout the Christian world. It is significant that three different scholars working independently – the future German Cardinal Nicholas of Cusa in 1432–3, the Italian Lorenzo Valla in 1440, and the English bishop Reginald Pecock in 1450 – all came to the conclusion that the style of this 'Donation of Constantine' was radically wrong for the fourth century; instantly they demolished a prop of papal authority. Humanists delighted in imitating Valla's method when they tried to sift legend from fact in the lives of the Church's saints. The Valencian humanist Juan Luis Vives, much-respected tutor of the later ultra-devout English Queen Mary I, breezily expressed his contempt for the popular standard Dominican collection of saints' lives, which had been a central text for lovers of pilgrimage for three centuries: 'How unworthy of God and Christian man is that account of saints called the *Golden Legend*. I do not know why it is called "Golden" since it appears to have been written by men with mouths of iron and hearts of lead.'[40]

Eventually the central document of the Christian Church, its ultimate *fons* the Bible, must come under the same scrutiny. Now the humanist preoccupation with words was crucial, because the Bible's words were translations at various different levels. Christians saw them as interpretations of the mind of God to humanity, but beyond this ultimate translation from the perfect to the imperfect, the biblical texts were experienced at different removes from their original human writers. Medieval western Christianity knew the Bible almost exclusively through the fourth-century Latin translation made by Jerome, the Vulgate (that is, 'common') version (see Plate 2). When the Vulgate's printed form was standardized from the 1450s, some persistent copyists' errors were identified in various strands of the manuscript versions, but they were easily dealt with. Humanist excavation then went behind the Vulgate text. Before it reached Latin, the Hebrew Scripture (the Christian Old Testament) had been translated into Greek, principally a version completed in the second century BCE known as the Septuagint. The Septuagint itself contained a number of detectable mistranslations from Hebrew; such deviations interested humanist scholars just as they had long fascinated Jewish scriptural commentators, but they were not going to threaten Christian understanding of faith. Jerome had done his considerable best to re-examine the Hebrew text behind the Septuagint; nevertheless, faults remained.

Some of Jerome's mistranslations in the Old Testament were more comic than important. One of the most curious was at Exodus 34, where the Hebrew describes Moses' face as shining when he came down from Mount Sinai with the tablets of the Ten Commandments. Jerome, mistaking particles of Hebrew, had turned this into a description of Moses wearing a pair of horns – and so the Lawgiver is frequently depicted in the art of the Western Church, even after humanists had gleefully removed the horns from the text of Exodus.[41] An examination of the New Testament had more profound consequences: Jerome had chosen certain Latin words in his translation of the original Greek, which formed a rather shaky foundation for very considerable theological constructions by the later Western Church. We will examine some important examples when we meet the most influential humanist biblical translator and critic, Desiderius Erasmus (see below, pp. 99–101).

It was not simply that Jerome gave misleading impressions of the Greek text: the mere fact that for a thousand years the Latin Church had based its authority on a translation was significant when scholars heard for the first time the unmediated urgency of the angular street-Greek poured out by Jesus's post-Resurrection convert Paul of Tarsus as he wrestled with the problem of how Jesus represented God. The struggle sounded so much less decorous in the original than in Latin: the shock was bound to stir up new movements in the Church and suggest that it was not so authoritative or normative an interpreter of scripture as it claimed. If there is any one explanation why the Latin West experienced a Reformation and the Greek-speaking lands to the east did not, it lies in this experience of listening to a new voice in the New Testament text.

It is perfectly possible that the western Church could have survived the shock intact. The Reformations that took place were not what the humanists sought; they had no intention of overthrowing the old ecclesiastical system. One of the most talented early Italian humanists, Enea (Aeneas) Silvio de' Piccolomini, became Pope Pius II (we have already met him repudiating his earlier conciliarism, in chapter 1, p. 39). Even though Pius was rather embarrassed by the literary efforts of his earlier life, which included a highly popular love story, *Euryalus and Lucretia*, he was generally considered one of the most effective popes of the fifteenth century, and his prestige was a major factor in making humanism respectable in northern Europe, where he had enjoyed a distinguished diplomatic career. Thereafter, bishops and cardinals hastened to be the patrons of humanists, and they were prominent in widening university curricula by founding colleges whose statutes specifically promoted humanist studies, with the particular aim of creating a pool of experts in Greek and Hebrew to aid biblical scholarship. In England, for instance, souvenirs of this lavish funding of humanism form a major and enjoyable part of university architecture. At Oxford, Bishop Fox of Winchester founded Corpus Christi College, and Cardinal Wolsey established a de luxe memorial to himself, rather scaled down by Henry VIII as Christ Church but still exceptionally splendid; in Cambridge, Bishop Alcock of Ely and Bishop Fisher of Rochester coaxed streams of cash and estates out of Henry VII's generous mother Lady Margaret Beaufort for the foundation of Jesus, Christ's and St John's.

Another prince of the Church to become such a benefactor was that intimidating spearhead of the Iberian Catholic Reformation, Cardinal Ximénes. We have already mentioned his university foundation at Alcalá (see above, p. 61); its *Collegium trilinguale* ('College of the three languages', that is Latin, Greek and Hebrew) bore witness to the central place humanism now claimed in the Church. For central to Ximénes' sponsorship of scholars at Alcalá was the ultimate Christian humanist enterprise, a publication of the Bible in its original languages. This Complutensian Polyglot – the Latin name of Alcalá is *Complutum* – was a six-volume text of the Vulgate Bible accompanied in parallel columns by the Hebrew and Greek texts and new Latin interpretations of them; the last volume was published in 1517, just as the Reformation was breaking in northern Europe. Desiderius Erasmus's Greek New Testament of 1516, which went on to corner the market in biblical scholarship and become a major influence on Protestantism, has rather unjustly overshadowed this major collaborative scholarly achievement of Spanish Catholicism. The Polyglot predated Erasmus's work and was more meticulous in its scholarship than his; it was an impressive testimony to the conviction that humanism could help rather than harm the Church's mission.

Not surprisingly some humanists, excited at the novelty of what they were doing, sounded what might seem a call to revolution when they trumpeted their achievement at the expense of older scholarship. At its crudest, this was adolescent self-assertion from a new type of intellectual discipline which previously had a subordinate place to theology in the universities, and (as usual with adolescent self-assertion) it annoyed older professionals who had good reason to be proud of their traditional learning, and resented non-professionals giving themselves airs. So university theologians attacked Lorenzo Valla for his presumption in undertaking textual criticism of the Bible, which they likened to 'putting one's sickle into another man's crop'; that became a common charge against humanists.[42] Many humanists chose not to enter the traditional university system at all; they worked to produce their scholarly editions in close co-operation with printers, who were inclined to set up workshops in big commercial centres from where their books could be widely distributed, rather than in university towns. Many humanists also saw the value of entering the service of powerful and wealthy people who would pay for their services as wordsmiths, employing them to produce official documents in sophisticated Ciceronian Latin to maintain courtly prestige among other powerful people.

Humanist scholars could therefore easily portray themselves as practically minded men of ideas closely involved with ordinary life and the business of government, rather than isolated ivory-tower academics, who wasted their time arguing about how many angels could dance on the head of a pin (this famous caricature of scholasticism was invented by humanists). A less frivolous way of looking at this contrast would be to see it as a dispute about the best road to discovering truth: was it best done through the persuasive word-skills of rhetoric, which the humanists valued, or through formal analysis and enquiry in argument for and against a proposition, the refinement of dialectic which scholastic theologians had perfected? One classic row, where such clashes of principle became entangled with clashes of personality, centred on the lawyer and humanist Greek and Hebrew scholar Johannes Reuchlin and his struggle with Johannes Pfefferkorn of Cologne.

Pfefferkorn was a converted Jew whose zeal for converting his people to Christianity had a destructive agenda. He was disturbed by the current humanist enthusiasm for cabbalistic mystical Jewish literature, regarding such works (quite rightly) as a threat to Christian orthodoxy. He demanded that the Holy Roman Emperor sponsor a campaign of mass destruction of Hebrew religious books. All the theological faculties of the universities whom the Emperor consulted supported Pfefferkorn, but Reuchlin, brought in to give a legal opinion in 1509, was the lone voice in disagreement: he did not mind the confiscations, but wanted the books preserved. Thereafter Reuchlin's noisy protests against the united academic front supporting the Emperor's command for confiscating and destroying Jewish writings escalated, until he was put on trial and was eventually sent to Rome to be fined for heresy. Humanists were furious and interpreted this messy feud as being about freedom of thought: a consortium of them produced a biting satire on Reuchlin's opponents, *Letters of obscure men* (1515, expanded in the significant year 1517).[43]

Some involved in producing the satire later became Protestant reformers, although notably Reuchlin himself did not: this encouraged the idea that there was a natural affinity between humanism and the Reformation. It was more that there was a coincidence of interests: both humanists and reformers were attacking the same professional group, scholastic theologians.[44] So we should be careful about taking the Reuchlin affair, or some of the other rather stagey academic conflicts of the same date, as illustrating a clear-cut fight between obscurantist scholastics and enlightened humanist scholars. Enlightenment is relative. In our terms, Reuchlin was far from enlightened about Jews: like his pioneering mentor in Hebrew studies, the future Prot- estant Reformer Conrad Pellikan (possibly the most learned Christian Heb- raist of sixteenth-century Europe), he was only interested in what Christian culture could extract from their literature. Neither man had any kindly feelings towards the Jewish people themselves, whom they felt shouldered a collective guilt for the death of Christ and deserved all the misery that they suffered in Christian Europe.[45]

In reality the worlds of humanism and scholasticism did not need to be in conflict. Some universities early on became centres of humanist learning, like Vienna, but still went on valuing their medieval heritage; German humanists were especially likely to be proud of the centuries of history of the Holy Roman Empire as a reincarnation of the ancient Roman Empire, and to sneer at Italians, whether they were humanists or not. Scholars might be fascinated by several branches of learning simultaneously. So in early Tudor Oxford, a cultivated Benedictine monk called Robert Joseph wrote reproachfully to a fellow monk who complained about the old-fashioned barbarity of the scholastic curriculum he was studying: 'I always consider Scotus and his followers, in order to take ideas from them, but I find my pure Latin from other more cultured works.' So Joseph was prepared to think like a scholastic but write like a Ciceronian humanist, as the style of his letters testifies – and uniting a farflung society of scholars in a network of correspondence was itself a characteristic humanist activity.[46]

Moreover, around 1500 humanism was not the only body of scholarship seeing itself as a force for change. Medical doctors had for centuries provided a discordant voice against scholastic method, the more adventurous of them being notoriously inclined to believe the evidence of their own eyes rather than that of properly constituted ancient authority. Pietro Pomponazzi, a great Italian medical teacher at the University of Padua, had almost as little time for Christian humanism as for the scholasticism in which he had been trained, and he also had a notorious sense of humour. He cheerfully commented in lectures of the early 1520s that Aristotle's somewhat erratic analysis of animals was based on belief and faith rather than knowledge, since Aristotle had accepted what other people had told him at second-hand, rather as Christians believed in Christ: a comment which was not calculated to please either Church leaders or admirers of Aristotle.[47] But then no devout churchmen would trust a doctor or regard his sceptical opinions as a tool with which to strip away decay from the Church.

Much more significant was the fact that many professional theologians, who wished to keep their primary loyalty to scholasticism, felt as dissatisfied as the humanists with the nominalist scholasticism which had dominated university theology faculties over the previous century and a half. Prominent among them was an Italian Dominican, Tommaso de Vio, who is usually known as Gaetano or Cajetan from his Italian home town, Gaeta; he returned to the philosophical and theological achievement of his own Order's most celebrated product, Thomas Aquinas. He was determined to restore Thomism to its central place in the Church, to promote Thomas's careful balance of human reason and divine revelation in Scripture, his creative appropriation of Aristotle in order to discuss Christianity, from the most profound divine mysteries to the everyday practicalities of the Church's ministry in the world. Between 1507 and 1522 Cajetan published a commentary on the *Summa Theologiae*, Thomas's greatest work (which he was reputed to be able to recite by heart). His volumes proved to be a centrepiece of a major revival of interest in Aquinas's thought, which in the Reformation turmoil seemed the perfect weapon against Protestantism's radical pessimism about the human mind's capacity to know God unaided. Cajetan was established in his turn as one of the Church's major theologians (even before the Reformation had emerged as a threat, he was made a Cardinal in 1517). His fellow Dominican Francisco de Vitoria (see above, p. 69) was a great admirer, and was instrumental in spreading the Thomist revival to Spain; significantly, it was Thomism and not humanism that inspired the Dominican outrage against Spanish atrocities in the Americas.

Renewed Thomist scholarship thus became of great significance in the recovery of the Roman Catholic Church from the shock of the Reformation. Thomists were as ready to exploit the new possibilities of the printing press as any humanist, and in their austere systematizing of theology they were equally suspicious of some of the excesses of late medieval devotion. One of Cajetan's achievements was to prevent Pope Julius II establishing a new feast of the sufferings of the Blessed Virgin Mary. Commissioned to investigate the possibility, de Vio reported back in 1506 that the popular devotion to her swooning away out of grief at Christ's death on the Cross was an unscriptural idea. He craggily commented that in any case swooning was a 'morbid state' which implied that Mary had suffered some bodily defect. This was irreverent, he said: the Queen of Heaven could suffer only mental anguish on behalf of her son. No more was heard of the proposed feast, and Cajetan's intervention began a long process of official restraint on the physical exuberance of western piety, a restraint which was not just a feature of the Protestant Reformation but which affected the Counter-Reformation Church as well.[48]

PUTTING RENEWAL INTO PRACTICE

The varied agendas of renewal did not stay as mere talk, but were put to work in tackling the faults of the Church. Reform at the top turned out to have little momentum. There were still plenty of conciliarists in positions of authority, especially in universities, who might have exploited the mood of reform if an effective General Council had been called, but memories of the fifteenth-century traumas made the papacy nervous about giving any council too much freedom of initiative, and this combined with contemporary politics to cheat widespread hopes. The King of France first engineered a group of cardinals into assembling a council to Pisa in 1511; this talked a great deal in traditional conciliarist terms about Church reform but it was really designed to bring pressure on the Pope in the interests of the French monarchy. In angry retaliation, the Pope called a council to his palace of the Lateran in Rome in 1512.

The opening of a fifth Lateran Council caused much excitement in Europe. In England, the bishops believed that their own careful and tidy administration of the English Church might at last be duplicated elsewhere. Two days after King Henry VIII had formally commissioned English delegates to set off for Rome, Archbishop Warham and his colleagues sat back in their meeting of Convocation to listen in gloomy satisfaction as Dean Colet used all his considerable eloquence to lambast the assembled English clergy for their faults. This penitential version of a school speech day was the culmination of a year-long initiative by the English bishops to search out, discipline and re-educate Lollard heretics, using some of their most talented humanist-educated clergy to lead their campaign, conducted on a scale unprecedented for a hundred years.[49] Yet though the Lateran Council went on to sit for five years, it failed to achieve anything important. It listened to well-argued memoranda on reform, it gave Pope Julius useful support in his haggling over jurisdiction with the King of France, it made clear its disapproval of scholars like Pietro Pomponazzi, who were reviving ancient scepticism about the immortality of the soul, it forbade wild preaching about the Last Days, and it expressed the emphatic opinion that bishops ought to exercise more control over monks in their dioceses. But even that last item raised a problem which would return to complicate Church reform in the Council of Trent: how did the power of the bishops relate to the power of the Pope? No one was prepared to offend vested interests by enacting concrete proposals which would significantly change anything. The Council was dissolved in the same year, 1517, that saw the spark of Luther's Reformation.[50]

The greatest contemporary successes in renewal were various efforts undertaken among the Orders of monks, nuns and friars to reform themselves. There are good reasons for this: in every age, the austerity which monastic societies seek in their community life is in danger of falling away into disorder or comfortable complacency, while conversely, the regular religious life by definition possesses clear rules that can be implemented afresh against laxity. It was easier to call for reforms in communities which were already at least nominally committed to them than to bring new life to the parish and diocesan system. So there is hardly a century of Christian life since monasteries appeared that has not seen attempts to reform them. Humanism was not the only force for renewal working within the structures of the late medieval Church.

The Orders of friars, in particular the Franciscans, indulged in agonies of self-examination almost from the moment that they were founded, and there were repeated waves of attempts to observe their Rules more strictly, usually involving the foundation of a newly independent branch of the movement. Cardinal Ximénes' efforts to promote his own Order, the Observant Franciscans, in the Spanish kingdoms were only one episode in this process, which continued into the sixteenth century with such foundations as the Franciscan Minims in Spain and France (Rule finalized in 1507), the Franciscan Capuchins in Italy (Rule drawn up in 1529) and later in Spain, Teresa of Ávila's Discalced or barefoot Carmelites. One of the most remarkable spheres for revival among the friars was in the far west of Europe, in the Gaelic-speaking lordships of western Ireland. Here an upsurge in the fifteenth century of preaching and pastoral activity was led by Observant Franciscans and Dominicans, and travelled eastwards to galvanize the English-dominated eastern regions of the island. The ruins of these newly founded friaries still form a poignant witness in the Irish landscape to a religious fervour which (in contrast to the rest of the Atlantic Isles) was not diverted on to Protestant paths, and which played a major part in sustaining Irish resistance to the Reformation (see chapter 8, p. 397).

The older monastic Orders found it more difficult to tackle their shortcomings, mainly because their much greater lands and wealth had attracted the interest and involvement of the secular nobility, especially in *commendams* (see chapter 1, p. 48). Generally throughout the continent, the commendatory system for heads of houses was spreading rather than diminishing in the early sixteenth century, despite general pressure from the Observant movement to bring it to an end. Although a minority of commendators were agents of reform in individual houses, generally wherever there was large-scale interference from noble or royal families the monastic

Orders were likely to experience steady decay. The situation was acute equally in Scandinavia and Portugal, despite the very different outcomes of the Reformation in these extremities of Europe. King François I much extended the *commende* in French monasteries after the Concordat of Bologna, dealing a decisive blow to twenty years of effort by the energetic Cardinal-Minister Georges d'Amboise to extend Ximénes' monastic reforms to France. The kingdom of Scotland, always inclined to follow French models, followed suit, and Scottish monasteries also imitated the French in turning monastic endowments into individual financial holdings for particular monks, drastically negating the spirit of community. Paradoxically, such entanglement with the nobility slowed down the process of monastic dissolution in the Scottish Reformation and helped to defend French monasteries against dissolutions in the Reformation years, yet the *commende* also went on proving a hindrance to real restructuring by French Catholic reformers right into the seventeenth century (see chapter 10, p. 475).[51]

Elsewhere there were more promising signs in monastic life. In the fourteenth century English Benedictine monasteries had chosen to make a thoroughgoing adoption of papal proposals for monastic reform which other parts of Europe ignored; they supervised their affairs as a community with a single general chapter and regular visitations, and avoided excessive interference from the English nobility such as the introduction of the *commendam* system. Other older Orders in England imitated the Benedictines in tightening up their community life. The consequences for late medieval English monasteries were financial stability, rising recruitment particularly noticeable from the 1480s, and every sign of a lively intellectual life, with greater numbers of monks going to university, particularly Oxford, and monasteries sustaining the only English printing presses outside London (at Syon, Abingdon, Canterbury and St Albans).[52]

A different reforming initiative took place among the Italian Benedictines, unusually taking its lead from a young commendator nobleman, Ludovico Barbo, who reversed the trend among commendators and himself became a monk. He sought an association of Italian Benedictine monasteries, as the English Benedictines had done earlier, and gathered a number of houses into a Congregation which, after the ancient abbey of Monte Cassino joined it in 1505, became known as the Cassinese. The Cassinese Congregation developed its own approach to the life of prayer, founded on meditation, mysticism and scholarship. It took an interest in the spirituality of the *Devotio Moderna*, but from the 1480s the Cassinese also undertook their own studies of the Bible and writers of the early Church, showing an enthusiasm (unusual for western Christians at the time) for early Greek theologians of the Church of Antioch, especially John Chrysostom. Cassinese organization much impressed Fernando and Isabel in Spain and led to the foundation of a parallel Benedictine congregation there.

The personalities of two individual monastic leaders illustrate the complexities and byways of being a reformer in an age of assorted hopes and fears. Egidio (Giles) of Viterbo was energetic in a series of leading roles in the Church, as prior-general of the Augustinian Canons for more than a decade from 1507, cardinal from 1517, and Bishop of Viterbo from 1523; he was a prominent figure in the rather rarefied debates of the fifth Lateran Council, delivering the opening call for reform and thereafter remaining one of the Council's loudest voices, for instance condemning the 'godless' views of the Paduan academics who speculated on whether the soul was immortal. His zeal for reform and his diplomacy amid the quarrels of the Augustinians impressed the young Martin Luther on the future Reformer's visit to Rome in 1511. Egidio was also a humanist scholar who was a passionate admirer of Jewish Cabbala and fascinated by the rediscovered hermetic tradition. A warm defender of Johannes Reuchlin in his troubles, he insisted that Hebrew was the only truly sacred language in which one could meet God, and that even Greek had distorted the divine message; in his study of scripture, he searched in a fashion reminiscent of gnosticism for a secret meaning which only the chosen few would understand.

This was a very different vision of Christian humanist enlightenment from Erasmus's call for ordinary people to read the Bible at the ploughtail, which Protestants took up with such enthusiasm. Egidio's thinking was full of contradictions. Like a good humanist, he saw the Emperor Constantine's alliance with the Church as the beginning of corruption and worldliness in Christianity, yet he also revelled in splendour and pomp in his own Order. Likewise, he was furious at the idea that bishops should interfere with the Augustinians, even though episcopal oversight was one of the main preoccupations of the Lateran Council. Perhaps the most lasting consequence of his constant publicity for reform of the Church was paradoxical: it made many members of his Order less afraid of the idea when Protestant Reformers brought their own agenda of change.[53]

With Johannes Trithemius (Johann Zeller from Trittenheim) we meet a humanist who took even further Egidio's fascination with the esoteric. When in 1483 Zeller was made Abbot of the Rhineland Benedictine house of Sponheim at the improbable age of twenty-one, he became an energetic administrator in the recently formed German Benedictine Congregation of Bursfeld. He voraciously devoured all the assorted strands of wisdom and esoteric lore which the rediscovery of ancient texts provided, and set about making his own abbey a prototype for his distinctive dream that monasteries could regain their ancient scholarly role, become centres of humanist study, and thus once more lead the world of learning. Under his guidance the library at Sponheim expanded from 48 to around 2,000 volumes. It was a vision of reform to rival the achievements of the Cassinese Benedictines, but it did not inspire the monks of Sponheim. When Trithemius's secular patron, Philipp the Elector Palatine, suffered a disastrous political reverse, the Abbot was deposed in his turn. He spent the last decade of his life at a monastery in Würzburg, dabbling in the occult and otherwise using his great learning and skill as a humanist textual critic to create shameless historical forgeries, enlivening the story of early German Christianity with the aid of hitherto unknown chroniclers such as Hunibald and Meginfrid of Fulda. Trithemius was always hard put to it to explain how his claims for his own scholarly magic made it differ from the sorcery of demons. While his efforts to become a pioneer of steganography (the art of long-distance communication, employing angels as a postal service) did not meet with success, his prospectus for that scheme is now recognized as one of the first studies of codes and code-breaking.[54]

Out beyond monastic precincts in the varied and complex conditions of Europe's dioceses, it was up to individual enlightened bishops to give leadership to clergy and laity as best they could. Bishop Christoph von Utenheim of Basel was inspired by his interest in humanist scholarship and the *Devotio Moderna* to promote reform of the Church's liturgy in Switzerland and around the upper Rhine. He could enjoy the co-operation of varied but distinguished churchmen including Jacob Wimpfeling, prolific humanist author and literary scourge of clerical shortcomings, and the great preacher of Strassburg Johannes Geiler von Kaysersberg (not a humanist, but a nominalist theologian), while Johann Ulrich Surgant's *Manuale Curatorum* clearly supplied a demand for guidelines for the clergy's conduct of worship, finding multiple editions after its publication at Basel in 1503. Surgant stressed the importance of sermons, and also prompted preachers to lead devotions in German as they thought fit within the framework of the Mass. This free form of service was called the prône: taking its name from the screen at the chancel entrance where the priest customarily stood to lead it, the prône could include prayers or teaching about the liturgy or forthcoming feasts. It was an important form of late medieval liturgy that has often been ignored because its very informality has left few traces in the records, but it is clear that except in Italy, it became common all over late medieval Europe. Not only did the prône anticipate the much more thoroughgoing use of vernacular language that Protestants made in services (and perhaps blunted the shock when that happened), but it went on being a customary feature of Catholic worship with official approval in many areas well after the Council of Trent.[55]

One of the most sustained efforts at diocesan reform was in France: it illustrated the difficulties involved, even when the initiative enjoyed powerful support. Guillaume Briçonnet was the son of a cardinal, from a wealthy mercantile family of Tours that took pride in its array of senior churchmen and royal administrators; Briçonnet followed them into royal service. During his diplomatic mission to Rome in 1507 he had been impressed by his observation of the combination of mystical piety and practical charity practised by the Oratory of Divine Love (see chapter 1, p. 17); and when he returned to take up an agreeable and well-funded position in Paris as Abbot of St Germain des Prés, he made his wealthy abbey the centre of Christian humanist scholarship in France, as well as a place to explore the inward-looking, Christ-centred piety of the *Devotio Moderna*. He appointed as abbey librarian the much-admired Jacques Lefèvre d'Etaples (Jacobus Faber), France's outstanding humanist scholar. Lefèvre's 1509 commentary on the Psalms was the first thoroughgoing humanist examination of the biblical text to appear in print, and in his commentaries on Paul's Epistles in 1512, Lefèvre said many things about the text that Luther said later in the same decade (chapter 3, p. 111).

Briçonnet's chance to extend his efforts at reform beyond the abbey came when in 1516 he was appointed Bishop of Meaux, not far to the north-east of Paris. Increasingly excluded from national politics, he determined to put Christian humanism to pastoral use in his diocese. Inviting the help of Lefèvre and other scholars, who included John Calvin's future colleague in Geneva, Guillaume Farel, he set up centres of preaching in his parishes to present instruction for ordinary people based on regular exposition of the good news of Scripture, and he issued detailed orders about public morality. This vision of an informed evangelical Catholicism gained warm support from King François's pious and highly educated sister, Marguerite d'Angoulême, Queen of Navarre, and over the next few decades it inspired many French sympathizers with humanism who also wanted to remain loyal to the Church. However, 1516 proved the worst possible time to launch such a programme: it soon became fatally tangled with the variety of humanism that despaired of Roman obedience and turned to Luther. Anyone annoyed at the Bishop's energy could easily play the heresy card in the 1520s; the initiative was taken by Franciscan friars in his diocese, who saw themselves as the prime exponents of preaching and were furious at his efforts to bring them under his control. Lefèvre's humanist commentaries on the biblical text had already brought him condemnation for heresy by the vigilant Paris theologians of the Sorbonne in 1521, and Briçonnet himself escaped heresy charges in 1525 only by pulling strings at Court. His last decade of life was spent more discreetly promoting what he still could of his agenda, in a state of increasing depression at the growing chaos in the Church.[56]

REFORM OR THE LAST DAYS?

Part of the authorities' suspicion of such local attempts at reform lay in memories of what actually happened in Florence in the years after 1494, in the revolution inspired by a charismatic Dominican friar, Girolamo Savonarola. First brought by his Order to Florence in 1482, in the early 1490s Savonarola began to preach in the church of San Marco about the Last Days, and his preaching was soon accompanied by visions and announcements of direct communications from God. Such prophetic announcements were not unusual at the time, but it was one of those moments when circumstances conspire to catapult a personality and a message to sudden and horrifying success. The Medici family's grip on the former republic was faltering, and the extraordinary flowering of art and culture that they had fostered in Florence seemed mocked by the growing misery of the situation throughout Italy.

The first disaster to give a new credibility to Savonarola's message was a sudden convulsion in the politics of Italy. French armies invaded, sparking military and political miseries which disrupted the peninsula for half a century. A terrifying and hitherto unknown disease also broke out. Apparently as fatal as the plague, unlike that disease it played with its victims for months or years, destroying their looks, their flesh and sometimes their minds, producing sores and scabs that stank and made the sufferers loathsome. Equally seriously it brought public shame, because very quickly people realized that it had an association with sexual activity. The disease rapidly set off on its travels, aided by the movements of armies, but in any case reaching as far away as Aberdeen by spring 1497. Naturally the Italians in their double affliction called the new scourge the French pox, a name that soon caught all Europe's imagination, much to French annoyance: France's attempt to relabel the pox as the Neapolitan disease was not an especially successful piece of spin-doctoring. We now call the modern descendant of this pox syphilis, thanks to a poem published in 1531 by Girolamo Fracastoro, a sixteenth-century Italian doctor; the poem's title gave syphilis its modern name. It is still not certain whether the arrival of syphilis represented a sudden wanderlust in an ancient European spirochete, or whether it was a novel import from America, the New World's revenge on the Old for Columbus's invasion and all the killer European diseases which he and his successors brought with him.[57]

There was thus every sign that the Last Days were indeed arriving: perfect, indeed logical conditions in which Savonarola could call for radical political and moral reform in the name of God. To the existing Florentine secular republican resentments against tyranny was added the dangerously potent idea that divine action would bring a total transformation in existing society: it was to be a theme of militant religious radicalism in Europe over the next two centuries. Accordingly the Medici, militarily humiliated by Charles, were expelled from Florence and a rigorously regulated republic proclaimed, in which Savonarola's prestige rose to the point where the self-consciously orthodox friar was able to defy Pope Alexander's order to cease preaching, and could scorn the papal excommunication which followed. The 1497 city carnival was a high point of Savonarola's charismatic dominance, centring on a 'bonfire of the vanities', which burned anything from carnival masks to some of the finest products of Florentine Renaissance art. Thereafter, his prestige was dented by the continuing political and economic miseries of the city, which did not suggest any imminent intervention by an approving God, and his enemies were able to overwhelm the political faction which supported him.

In 1498 the friar's power came to an end: he was tortured and burned at the stake with his chief lieutenants. Had he been a tyrant or a saintly reformer? Machiavelli, who knew him well, pointed out that he was an 'unarmed prophet', and his last words had the serene dignity of a martyr.[58] He left many admirers: throughout Europe, pious humanists valued the deep spirituality of his writings and overlooked the nightmare years of his republic – far away in the kingdom of that would-be Medici Henry VIII, Savonarola's meditations continued to be much read, and two of his meditations were incorporated in an officially approved English primer in 1534. Ignatius Loyola felt constrained to ban members of the Society of Jesus from reading his writings, despite seeing a lot of good in them, simply because his fate still stimulated unseemly disagreement between supporters and detractors.[59]

In Savonarola's own land this ambiguous legacy remained alarming to the powerful. A group known as the Piagnoni sprang up in Florence to preserve his memory; their organization might be seen as a gild with something of the qualities of the contemporary Oratory of Divine Love, emphasizing mystical meditation and missionary work, and promoting such *Devotio Moderna* classics as the *Imitation of Christ*. Friars continued to be prominent among the Piagnoni (although the Dominican Order throughout Italy was very wary of stepping out of line after the Savonarola débâcle), and the sizeable group of considerable scholars who were adherents were in later years firm against Luther, while still continuing to advocate reform in the Church. However, the Piagnoni also nursed the same combination of political and theological republicanism which had shaped the Savonarolan years, and when they got the chance to overthrow the Medici afresh in 1527–30, their rule became a sadistic tyranny which did much finally to kill off Florentine republicanism and ensure the future of the Medici in power.[60]

The Piagnoni movement was only one symptom of a chronic neurosis and sense of apocalyptic expectation that disturbed the Italian peninsula for decades after Savonarola was burned to ashes. As many noted, 1500 was a half-millennium – surely that was not simply an arbitrary number. The mood was reminiscent of the feverish popular religion in Spain at the same time, and had parallel roots in the military, political, medical and social traumas of the 1490s. It affected high and low, powerful and destitute; female 'living saints' got a respectful hearing when they turned up to proclaim their message of imminent judgement in Italian princely courts. As so often, troubled times spawned a literature of prophecy that tried to make sense of what was happening; accounts of monstrous births and wondrous signs became sure-fire money-spinners for the printing-presses. In 1502 came a publishing sensation: the *Apocalypsis Nova* ('New account of the Last Days'). It claimed to have been written some time before by a Portuguese Franciscan friar, Amadeus Menezes da Silva, and certainly it built on earlier monastic or Franciscan literature with the same apocalyptic theme, such as that of the twelfth-century Cistercian Abbot Joachim of Fiore or his later admirers (see chapter 13, p. 552). This 'Amadeist' book, which still has its devotees and is much quoted in the wilder corners of the Internet, predicted the coming of an Angelic Pastor or Pope, who would be heralded by Spiritual Men; the crucial task was correctly to identify these import-ant characters. Plenty of candidates were lined up or fearlessly stepped forward: the Imperial Chancellor Cardinal Mercurino di Gattinara saw his master Charles V as one of the heralds, while Egidio of Viterbo, with in-extinguishable optimism, successively pointed to Popes Julius II, Leo X and Clement VII. Cardinal Sauli in the time of Leo X found that it was not a good idea to employ the talents of the great painter Sebastiano del Piombo with instructions to portray him in the guise of the coming Angelic Pastor; the Cardinal was promptly arrested, and he died in prison.[61]

It was not surprising that the Lateran Council forbade preaching on apocalyptic subjects in 1513, or that from the 1530s the Spaniards who took over as the major power in Italy made sure that the Italian peninsula became as well-disciplined on the subject of signs, wonders and the Last Days as the Inquisition had now made Spain. In the meantime, over three decades from the 1490s, much of Europe was in high excitement about the future, ranging in expression from decorous humanist editing of hermetic and cabbalistic texts to the prophecies of wild-eyed women in Spanish or Italian villages and angry sermons of respected clergy. A perfect industry emerged, imagining ideal societies and how they might work. Thomas More, the English humanist with a smile more enigmatic than that of the Mona Lisa, invented a word to describe them all in the title of his supposedly serious description of such a place: Utopia – in cod-Greek that means 'nowhere'. More's sense of perspective on the utopian mood was not typical. Who would harness the energies of these varied discontents, hopes and joys, and turn them towards creating a disciplined and a better society for all Catholic Europe? Might it be the internationally revered scholar from the Low Countries, Desiderius Erasmus?

ERASMUS: HOPES FULFILLED, FEARS STILLED?

Erasmus's life and achievements combine so many themes of European renewal in the early 1500s. He came from the land of the *Devotio Moderna* and was destined to become the supreme humanist scholar. He was a friend not merely to princes and bishops but to anyone who shared his passion for learned wisdom. In 1518 he happened to meet a well-read tax-collector on the River Rhine at Boppard, Christopher Eschenfelder, who was thrilled to meet the great man and talk to him about his work. They kept in touch until the end of Erasmus's life.[62] All Europe wanted Erasmus as its property: Cardinal Ximénes made vain overtures to get him to Spain, and the cultivated humanist Bishop of Cracow Pietr Tomicki had just as little success with his invitation to Poland – curiously superstitious, Erasmus would never travel very far east of the Rhine, although he was frequently prepared to risk the English Channel.

Instead, people came to Erasmus as devotees. A quarter century after Erasmus's death, Bishop Andrzej Zebrzydowski (Tomicki's great-nephew) proudly described himself on his tomb in Cracow as *magni illius Erasmi Rotherodami discipulus et auditor* ('a follower and scholar of that great man Erasmus of Rotterdam'), while yet another wealthy young Polish nobleman who was to become a leading Protestant reformer, Jan Łaski, became his major benefactor (chapter 5, pp. 254–8). Erasmus constructed a salon of the imagination, which embraced the entire continent in a constant flow of letters to hundreds of correspondents, some of whom he never met face to face. In the later days of division, this proved a precedent for the letter-writing empires of many Protestant leaders of humanist inclinations, like Philipp Melanchthon, Heinrich Bullinger, John Calvin and Theodore Beza, but also for the 30,000 letters surviving from that phenomenal correspondent of the Counter-Reformation, Archbishop Carlo Borromeo. Erasmus should be declared the patron saint of networkers.

It is interesting that we habitually refer to Erasmus as 'of Rotterdam': in reality, he was indifferent to where he lived, as long as there was a good fire, a good dinner, a pile of amusing correspondence and a handsome research grant. Erasmus himself created this misleading use of the place-name, and he also added the 'Desiderius' as a supposed Greek synonym for 'Erasmus'. His crafting of his name is only one aspect of the great humanist's careful construction of his own image: he perfectly exemplified the humanist theme of building new possibilities, for he invented himself out of his own imaginative resources. He needed to do this because when he was born as Herasmus Gerritszoon in a small Dutch town (it may have been either Rotterdam or Gouda): he was that ultimate non-person in medieval Europe, the son of a priest. His family therefore put him on the customary road to building a self from nothing by preparing him for office in the Church.

After a *Devotio Moderna*-inspired education, the young man was persuaded to enter a local Augustinian monastery at Steyn, but he did so with great reluctance. He hated monastic life, making himself in addition wretchedly miserable when he fell in love with Servatius Rogerus, a fellow monk, but then he identified an escape-route: his passion and talent for humanist scholarship.[63] The Bishop of Cambrai, conveniently far to the south in the Low Countries, needed a secretary to give his correspondence the fashionable humanist polish appropriate to such an important Church dignitary, and Erasmus persuaded his superiors to let him take the post, which he held just long enough to make sure that Steyn was well behind him and that there would be no serious recriminations when he moved on.

Erasmus never returned to the monastic life (the authorities in Rome eventually regularized this unilateral declaration of independence in 1517, after he had become a celebrity). Although he had been ordained priest in 1492, he never took the conventional opportunities for high office in church or university which someone of his talent could have had for the asking. Instead of being pinned down to a specific place and a round of duties, he virtually created a new category of career: the roving international man of letters who lived off the proceeds of his writings and from money provided by his admirers. He craved friendship and affection now that he had rejected human passion, and he found it by becoming the brilliant, entertaining scholar whom every clever, wealthy or attractive, well-educated European wanted to befriend. He created the first bestseller in the (then very brief) history of printing after a stroke of bad luck: desperate for cash after English customs officials had confiscated the sterling money in his luggage, he compiled a collection of proverbs with detailed commentary about their use in the classics and in scripture. This work, the *Adagia* (1500), was a huge commercial success since it offered the browsing reader the perfect shortcut to being a well-educated humanist, and Erasmus much expanded it in successive editions.

At much the same time Erasmus changed the direction of his scholarly enthusiasms, with momentous consequences for the history of European religion: he moved from a preoccupation with secular literature to apply his humanist learning to Christian texts. On one of his visits to England he was inspired to tackle the painful task of acquiring the specialist skill of Greek by his admiration for his friend John Colet's biblical learning; Greek would open up to him the writings of the little-known early Fathers of the Church, together with the ultimate source of Christian wisdom, the New Testament. He produced new critical editions of a range of key early Christian texts, the centrepiece of which was his 1516 edition of the New Testament, accompanied by an expanding range of commentaries on the biblical text. The effect of his superbly presented editions was much enhanced by his collaboration from 1516 with one of the most brilliant and artistically sensitive publishers of his day, Johann Froben of Basel.

Erasmus's New Testament was an inspiration to many future Protestant reformers, because he provided not only the Greek original but also an easy way of puzzling out what this difficult text might mean with the aid of a parallel new Latin translation, tacitly designed to supersede the Vulgate and the commentary that Jerome had created around it. Erasmus hugely admired Jerome's industry and energy, but his work of retranslation and commentary amounted to a thoroughgoing onslaught on what Jerome had achieved a millennium before; that is what made it so much more a sensation than the monumental work of Ximénes' scholars in the Complutensian Polyglot (see above, p. 84). To attack Jerome was to attack the structure of understanding of the Bible which the western Church took for granted. Most notorious was Erasmus's retranslation of Gospel passages (especially Matthew 3:2) where John the Baptist is presented in the Greek as crying out to his listeners in the wilderness: '*metanoeite*'. Jerome had translated this as *poenitentiam agite*, 'do penance', and the medieval Church had pointed to the Baptist's cry as biblical support for its theology of the sacrament of penance. Erasmus said that what John had told his listeners to do was to come to their senses, or repent, and he translated the command into Latin as *resipiscite*. Much turned on one word.

A characteristic medieval way of making sense of the frequently puzzling or apparently irrelevant contents of the Bible was to allegorize them: to find layers of meaning and greater truth behind what superficially appeared to be the literal meaning of the words. Commentators found justification for their allegorizing by quoting a biblical text, John 6:63: 'The Spirit gives life, but the flesh is of no use' – allegory was the spiritual meaning, the literal meaning the fleshly. This text became a favourite of Erasmus too, but he was irritated that it should be used as a support for allegory. If readers of the Bible were correct to note allegory in its text, they should do so with due caution, and direct their interpretation properly. This principle was particularly significant in the cult of Mary, the Mother of God; the cult had become important and elaborate in the Church on a rather slim basis of references to Mary in the Bible, and it was a natural impulse for commentators to try to expand their database on the Queen of Heaven through allegory. Erasmus came to deplore the redirection on to Mary of Old Testament texts; if there was indeed an allegorical meaning in the figure of the beautiful bride in the Song of Songs or the female personification of Wisdom in the Book of Sirach (Wisdom), this should refer to the Church and its relation with Jesus the saviour, not to Mary. Protestant Bible commentaries rammed home this message later.[64]

Other insights of Erasmus proved crucial to the Protestant revolution which was to come. In his 1519 revision of his New Testament edition, he rewrote the Latin version of the Angel Gabriel's greeting to Mary which told her of her sacred destiny, and which was quoted devotionally in the recitation of the Hail Mary; now Erasmus's Virgin became 'gratiosa' ('gracious') rather than 'gratia plena' ('full of grace', in other words full of merits in the sight of God), and so she became less available as a prop for the theology of merit and good works as part of God's scheme of salvation. Erasmus sneered at the misguided Marian devotion which hung on Luke 2:51: 'And [Jesus] went down with [his parents], and came to Nazareth, and was obedient to them'. Some said that this meant that Jesus still owed obedience to his mother and so would act on what she chose to ask. Erasmus's outbreak of common sense on this issue might sound trivial, but it was of huge importance, since it was a wedge to split apart the edifice of intercession by Mary to her Son, which (as we have seen in chapter 1, pp. 18–22) had become all-pervasive in western popular devotion. Hence it threatened one of the great principles of medieval western piety – that God could and should be approached through his courtiers the saints.[65]

Erasmus faced up to one theological issue dependent on the use of allegory which later proved as troublesome to Protestants as to Catholics; this was the universally held belief in Mary's perpetual virginity – that she had remained a virgin all her life. Much of the traditional case for this belief, which has no direct justification in Scripture, was based on an allegorical use of Ezekiel 44:2, which talks about the shutting of a gate which only the Lord could enter, and this was then bolstered by a forced Greek and Latin reading of Isaiah's original Hebrew prophecy that a young woman (not 'a virgin' in the Hebrew) would conceive a son Immanuel (Isaiah 7:14). Erasmus could not read these texts as Jerome had done. In response to shocked complaints about his comments, he set out a precise position: 'We believe in the perpetual virginity of Mary, although it is not expounded in the sacred books.' In other words, Erasmus acknowledged the ancient claim that there were matters of some importance which had to be taken on faith, because the Church said that they were true, rather than because they were found in the Bible. Erasmus had begun to discover a problem which would become one of the major issues of the Reformation and which faced all those who called for Christianity to go back 'ad fontes'. Did the Bible contain all sacred truth? Or was there a tradition which the Church guarded, independent of it? The issue of Scripture versus tradition became a vital area of debate, which had no straightforward outcome for either side, whatever they might claim.[66]

After such rethinking of fundamental matters, it was inevitable that the actual cults of Mary and the saints came into Erasmus's sights. In a set of dialogues which he published as Colloquies, he transformed the pilgrimage journeys he had made to the English shrines at Walsingham and Canterbury into light comedy for his reading public. This was part of his vigorous debunking of the physicality and tactility of late medieval popular piety: a perfect example of the ambiguities in the humanist attitude to how most western Christians approached God. When Erasmus published his New Testament, he wrote movingly and sincerely in its Prologue about his wish to see the countryman chant the Bible at his plough, the weaver at his loom, the traveller on his journey – even women should read the text. He wanted to end the excesses of clerical privilege, particularly the clergy's pretensions to special knowledge, and he was always ready to show contempt both for incompetent and unlearned clergy and for what he saw as the pompous obscurity of professional theologians. But lay piety would have to be recon-structed on Erasmus's own terms; physical passion was not appropriate. Now that he had grimly disciplined himself never again to lose control of his emotions, as had happened at Steyn with Servatius Rogerus, his passions were to remain as abstractions of the intellect. He was profoundly repelled when he observed the everyday reality of layfolk grasping at the sacred. For him that was fleshly religion, ignoring the inner work of the spirit that comes to the faithful through the mind and through pure use of the emotions: 'The Spirit gives life, but the flesh is of no use'!

Erasmus would have understood what C. S. Lewis meant four centuries later by his book title *Mere Christianity*. His own planed-down, white-washed version of medieval western faith was set out in 1504 in his best-selling *Enchiridion Militis Christiani* ('Dagger for a Christian Soldier' – a dagger in the sense of an all-purpose tool, the spiritual equivalent of a Swiss army knife.) This sets out his vision of a purified, Christ-centred faith – something to appeal to pious readers who had previously devoured literature of the *Devotio Moderna*. Outward ceremonies and ritual mattered much less than quiet, austere devotion springing from inner contemplation – although flights of ecstatic mysticism were not for Erasmus, and he never went down the humanist road that delighted in cabbalism or any of the ancient magical variants on the thought of Plato. He later borrowed a phrase from the Dutch humanist abbot Rudolf Agricola to describe this vision of a cerebral, disciplined, biblically based Christianity, cast in a humanist mould to echo the timbre of classical philosophers: the 'philosophia Christi', the learned wisdom of Christ.[67]

Erasmus's nausea at less abstract and more physical forms of Christian devotion found a later home in Protestantism, particularly in its Reformed or Calvinist variety. He attacked the excesses of the cult of relics, devoting particular wit to the easy target of relics of breast-milk from the Virgin: a particularly heavy-handed (not to say offensive) version of this can be found in a much-circulated anti-relic tract of John Calvin's from 1544.[68] Erasmus was sarcastic at length about the saints having replaced pagan deities: St Anthony had taken over from the Greek healing god Aesculapius and the Virgin Mary had staged a *coup d'état* against the Queen of the Underworld Proserpine. In the *Colloquies* and elsewhere he sneered at sailors in distress, who used titles for Mary like 'Star of the Sea, Queen of Heaven, Mistress of the World, Port of Salvation'. All this was echoed in influential and widely circulated Protestant texts later on – even in the official sermons published in the 1560s for Elizabeth I's Protestant Church of England.[69]

Erasmus has wrongly been credited with writing *Julius Exclusus*, a damaging satire on Pope Julius II, in fact by a senior English humanist churchman, Richard Pace; nevertheless it was not surprising that a man with so little time for the everyday life and public liturgy of the Church showed no deep affection for its institutions. Of course he said respectful things about both liturgy and Church, and on one occasion he even composed a rather moving liturgy of the Mass, but one should never place too much faith in individual writings of Erasmus, who wrote a great deal for effect, a great deal for money and a great deal to curry favour. The Church as a visible institution was chiefly important to him as one of his main sources of cash, as he sought a spectrum of patrons to sustain the writing and research which was his real concern; for that purpose, the court of a prince of the Church was as good as any other princely court. A piquant aspect of his career was that one of his regular sources of income was a grace-and-favour pension provided by an admiring Archbishop of Canterbury, William Warham, and diverted in typical medieval fashion from the parish revenues which ought to have sustained pastoral care in a Kentish village called Aldington. Aldington's main claim to fame was that, during the years of Erasmus's pension, it produced a massively popular but highly orthodox prophetess called Elizabeth Barton or 'the Maid of Kent', whose ecstatic Catholic visions would have caused the sage of Rotterdam some sarcastic amusement. Irony piled on irony after Henry VIII (who executed Barton for criticizing him) severed England's links with the Pope and appointed as successor to Warham the future architect of English Protestant liturgy, Thomas Cranmer. Erasmus's main concern at this news was that the Aldington pension would keep flowing – and because it did, Cranmer was in his eyes a most admirable man, despite his schism from the papacy.[70]

By contrast, Erasmus was enthusiastic for the role of the godly prince in the Commonwealth, as a substitute for what he saw as the failures of the official Church: 'the love of knowledge has decamped to secular princes and noblemen at court', he announced grandly to the English courtier Sir Henry Guildford in 1519.[71] With typical humanist optimism, he believed that he could improve the world with the help of the leaders of the Commonwealth (as long as they read and paid for his books), and that he could make his own agenda of universal education and social improvement into theirs. He believed that he could persuade them to abandon war, which threatened his programme for a sweetly reasonable and decently educated pan-European society. One of the most important sections of his *Adages*, a particularly sustained and impressive pioneering advocacy of pacifism, springs out of the proverb *Dulce bellum inexpertis* ('war is sweet to those who have not experienced it'). By his last years Erasmus realized that princes like Henry

VIII and François I had cruelly deceived him in their elaborate negotiations for universal peace, but his belief in the potential of princely power for good remained undimmed. Princes should even decide theological disputes: Erasmus was predictably horrified at the treatment of Johannes Reuchlin in the 1510s, and he was insistent that the Emperor Charles V should take on the responsibility of silencing Reuchlin's tormentor Pfefferkorn.

In a letter to his friend Abbot Paul Volz, antiquary and future Lutheran preacher, written to preface the 1518 edition of the *Enchiridion*, Erasmus asked the rhetorical question 'What is the state ('*civitas*') but a great monastery?'.[72] This had important implications. First, it was rejecting the idea that there was anything distinctive or useful about monasteries: if the city-state or commonwealth (that is, the whole of society) was to become a monastery, then the monastic vocation which Erasmus himself loathed and had escaped from was put firmly in its place, and perhaps his own personal guilt at his flight was exorcized. Second, in Erasmus's ideal society everyone was to be an active citizen of a '*civitas*' as in the city-states of ancient Greece, and everyone had a duty to behave as purely as monks were supposed to do under a monastic rule. Third, the person to make sure that they did so was the prince.

This message much appealed to secular rulers, and fitted in with the existing late medieval trend which we have already noted (chapter 1, pp. 47–52) towards princes and commonwealths acting as *Landesväter* and taking power in matters of religion and morality out of the hands of churchmen. Catholic and Protestant alike developed this theme of Erasmian humanism, so that the sixteenth and seventeenth centuries became an age that historians have termed 'the Reformation of Manners', when governments began to regulate public morality and tried to organize every individual in society in an unprecedented fashion – on both sides of the Reformation chasm. We will be meeting many examples of this as we discuss such matters as witchcraft and sexual regulation in chapters 13 and 16.[73] That was one of the most long-lasting consequences of Erasmus's writings, and in that respect, sixteenth-century Europe is his Europe.

Yet there was much more to his memory than that. Scholars used his scholarship; cultivated people showed their cultivation by enjoying his prose. The people of the Netherlands were proud of his birth there, and they did not forget his pleas for tolerance: well-educated radical Christians everywhere made their own creative use of his thought. Significantly, the Roman Inquisition at one stage tried to ban all his writings (chapter 6, p. 277). We will keep discovering his influence in all sorts of spheres and places, often unexpectedly, as we pursue the story of the Reformation.

Nevertheless Erasmus did not end his life feeling that his career was a success. The irony was that his project seemed at its most convincing and his reputation had reached its highest peak in a brief period after 1517, that same year which has sounded throughout this chapter like a passing-bell as the moment of Martin Luther's rebellion. One of Johann Froben's freelance employees in the publishing house wrote to Erasmus from Basel in December 1518: 'How blessed we are who happen to live in this present age, in which (with you to guide, lead and bring them to perfection) literature and true Christianity are born again!' The young man proved as inadequate a prophet as he was a proof-reader, but Erasmus himself was no better at prophecy. In May 1519, in the letter to Sir Henry Guildford already quoted, he spoke as one whose work was safely done: 'the world is coming to its senses as if waking from an ancient dream ... I see a golden age appearing, which perhaps I may not myself live to enjoy, since I will now be coming to the climax of my tale.'[74]

When Erasmus did die, on a visit to Basel in 1536, his chaste red marble monument was placed in the former cathedral, from where the bishop had already fled and where reformers had smashed the images of the saints, much to the elderly scholar's alarm and misery. For a decade and more before his death, Erasmus unhappily shifted his centre of operations (he never really looked for a home) around a circuit of western Europe, successively from Leuven to Basel to Freiburg-im-Breisgau. He was desperately trying to avoid taking sides in the storm that was surrounding him and tearing apart the world of elegantly phrased letters, high-minded reform projects and charming Latin-speaking friends that he had patiently extended across the face of Europe. As a result, increasing numbers on either side of the new divide regarded Erasmus as a time-serving coward who lacked the courage to take sides now that everyone was expected to do so. What had gone wrong? What had happened to the humanist project for changing the world through the power of a perfectly balanced Ciceronian sentence? To understand this, we will have to meet someone who had been dead for a thousand years before Erasmus was born, but whose writings had never ceased to cast a bleak shadow over the hopes and fears that we have surveyed.

3

New Heaven: New Earth 1517–24

THE SHADOW OF AUGUSTINE

The most distinctive feature of Renaissance humanism was its spirit of playful optimism; it bred an excitement about possibilities for the future. Humanists took for granted that human beings were created to do good: their outlook and conduct could be transformed by the persuasive power of poetry and rhetoric, or by regaining wisdom hidden in hermetic and cabbalistic literature, or by reading the Bible aright, so that humanity might equal or surpass the creativity of ancient Athens and Egypt. A classic expression of this mood was the Florentine Platonist Giovanni Pico della Mirandola's late fifteenth-century celebration of human free will and potential for improvement in his posthumously published *Oration on the Dignity of Man*: 'O great and wonderful happiness of man. It is given to him to have that which he desires and to be that which he wills.'[1]

As the sixteenth century wore on, realism and the disappointment of many political hopes took their toll. On the day of Pico's death in 1494, the troops of King Charles VIII of France marched into his own beloved city of Florence, disastrously for the whole Italian peninsula. Humanists increasingly now moved on a hundred years from Cicero's Latin oratory to focus on the historian Tacitus. Tacitus's various historical writings were clear-sighted and melancholy chronicles of Roman emperors subverting the institutions of Cicero's Republic and using them to create tyranny; he and his republican-minded contemporaries turned away in despair from the problems of their times and lost their faith in political action, even when circumstances forced them to become involved in it. Tacitus was now echoed for instance in the Italian historian Francesco Guicciardini, who chronicled the extinction of real independence and the general collapse of republican forms of government in Italy during the sixteenth century. This spirit was very different from the active engagement with the world to be found in his friend Niccolò Machiavelli's writings on politics, even though it is Machiavelli rather than Guicciardini who has come to be seen as the archetypal political cynic.

Yet Christian humanists had a far greater problem than the accidents of European politics. It is worth noticing that Pico's *Oration on the Dignity of Man* focused on the creation of humanity: it did not concern itself with that other foundation of Christian belief, the Genesis myth that in the Garden of Eden Adam and Eve had fallen from their paradise because of their disobedience to God. This tragedy of the Fall was at the centre of the Christian theology of Augustine of Hippo. Humanist optimism, and with it the whole project of calling on cultures older than Christianity to improve the Christian world, had from the earliest days of humanism clashed with this inheritance from Augustine, who has been as fundamental to western Christianity as he has been more or less ignored by the Greek eastern Churches. Educated in one of the major Latin universities of his day, he turned from a potentially distinguished career as a master of rhetoric in the imperial capital to become from 395 CE the bishop of an embattled Catholic community in the city of Hippo, at a time when the Catholic Church in north Africa was struggling for survival against a rival Christian Church. He lived through the sudden collapse of the western Roman imperial system in the first decade of the fifth century, a terrible disappointment after a decade in the 390s that had seemed to promise a brilliant Christian future for the ancient Empire, and he sought the meaning of this disaster for the civilization which he had loved so much. He found an explanation in the bleak picture of human worthlessness painted in the letter written by the Apostle Paul to the first Christian community in Rome. In the Epistle to the Romans, Paul finds only one solution to humanity's helpless slavery to sin: a gracious gift of salvation from God, 'through the redemption which is in Christ Jesus, whom God put forward as an expiation by his blood, to be received by faith' (Romans 3:24–25).

All Augustine's theology was shaped by various disputes in which he found himself embroiled, and the most significant dispute of all was over this question of sin and salvation. He was confronted by a group of enthusiastic, ultra-austere Christians, who had as one of their most prominent spokesmen a monk called Pelagius, probably from Britain. Pelagius (and associates who took his thinking further than he himself thought wise) tried to call Christians to the highest standards of behaviour by emphasizing that their future salvation depended on their own efforts to live with purity in this life. Augustine had no objection to austerity, but he found Pelagian advocacy of it grotesquely wrong-headed, because it was based on reasoning which conflicted with the picture of human corruption he found in Paul's writings. In the Epistle to the Romans, Paul gave an extended commentary on the

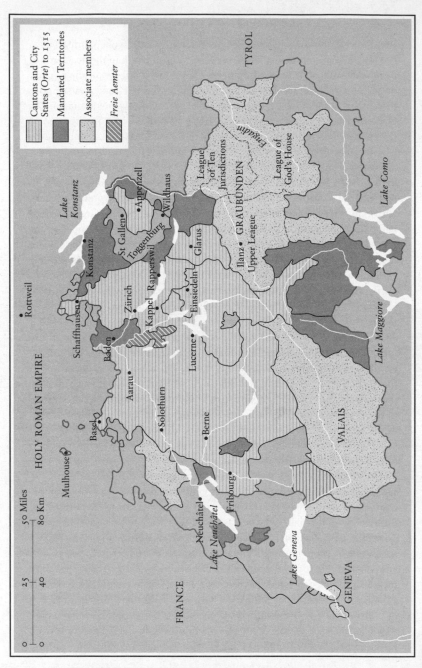

2. *The Swiss Confederation in the early sixteenth century*

biblical story of Adam and Eve as they committed the first act of disobedience to God in the Garden of Eden: the first sin. Augustine saw this corruption – original sin – as passed down from Adam to all humanity like a hereditary disease, and he linked sin to sex because like all heredity, sin was embodied in the act of procreation (even at the time, Pelagians criticized him for this view of procreative sex). All sin was thus Adam's first sin, and no human could escape it. How could beings so sunk in sin possibly do anything to earn themselves salvation, as the Pelagians claimed?

As Augustine argued with the Pelagians, his statement of his position grew ever more bleak and extreme. Everything depended on the grace of an all-powerful God, and God must show the completeness of his power by choosing which human beings he would save from the damnation they deserved. Since nothing about human beings after the Fall was worth saving, God's decision as to who should be saved was entirely arbitrary and mysterious, a reflection of his unchallengeable will. Augustine's intellectual formation had been in a late form of Plato's philosophy: Plato's deity was perfect, indivisible and incapable of suffering because suffering involves change, which implies imperfection. Since the perfect deity cannot change his mind, his decision about whom he chooses from humanity must be made only once. All the saved must be predestined to salvation (and though Augustine rarely said this explicitly, all the damned to damnation) before they have committed any deed of any sort: perhaps, in the words of one of the letters in the Pauline collection, 'before the foundation of the world' (Ephesians 1:4). Predestination became central to Augustine's beliefs about salvation – in theological jargon, his soteriology.

There is a terrible logic to Augustine's argument. The Christian message is full of polarities or opposed affirmations, and one of the most starkly drawn of these is the opposed affirmation of God's majesty as judge and of God's loving mercy as father. As Augustine contemplated this polarity, he was drawn to making majesty his starting-point in his account of God. He elaborated his theology against the background of a crisis in contemporary society more total than anything that the modern West has so far had to face, so it is understandable that he turned with relief from the chaos around him to contemplate in awe Plato's picture of a God immune from the changes and chances of this fleeting life. Yet Augustine's picture of a perfect deity gives no very good answer to the eternal Christian problem of where evil can have come from to turn Adam and Eve aside from paradise, if this all-creating, all-powerful God did not create it. One can also easily sympathize with the dry observation of the modern theologian Horton Davies that a God who cannot suffer is insufferable.[2]

It is essential to grasp these contours of Augustine's soteriology because otherwise it is impossible to understand why the Reformation happened or the profound nature of the issues at stake. Plenty of explanations have been offered for the cataclysm of the sixteenth century: the corruption of the old Church, the greed of monarchs for church wealth, the questing individualist spirit of humanism, vague forces of 'modernity'. None of these suggestions get to the heart of what happened, even if there might be some truth in all of them. We have seen enough of the medieval western Church now to know that it was not in terminal decay – obviously it suited Protestants afterwards to portray it in that light, but the myth was also convenient for later Catholics, who launched the Counter-Reformation as much to remedy the supposed faults of medieval Christianity as to combat Protestantism. The old Church was immensely strong, and that strength could only have been overcome by the explosive power of an idea. The idea proved to be a new statement of Augustine's ideas on salvation. That is why there is so much description of apparently abstract thought in my account of the Reformation, and why the discussion of this abstract thought sometimes has to get extremely intricate. Monarchs, priests, nuns, merchants, farmers, labourers were seized by ideas which tore through their experiences and memories and made them behave in new ways, sometimes admirable, sometimes monstrous. Social or political history cannot do without theology in understanding the sixteenth century.

Why did such a restatement of Augustine have such a particular impact at that moment? It was not as if he had ever been forgotten – far from it – and his views on salvation and predestination have repeatedly come to the fore in the Church's thinking. Before Luther's time, Anselm of Canterbury in the twelfth century and Thomas Aquinas in the thirteenth both called the Church back to what Augustine had said, just as the Swiss Protestant Karl Barth did again in the twentieth century. At other times there has been a counterpoint to this mood: theologies which emphasize God's fatherly mercy rather than his majesty as judge. Such was the case in late medieval Europe, when elaborations of the theology of Purgatory, God's merciful provision for humanity to do its best for its salvation, sat rather uneasily with what Augustine had said about human worthlessness. Late medieval nominalist theology, the so-called 'via moderna' or 'modern system', squared the circle by borrowing medieval economic theory and talking in terms of ascribed value and contract. Human virtues may be worthless but they can be treated like a token coinage issued in a time of emergency (after all, there could be no greater emergency for humanity than Adam and Eve's sin in Eden). Such temporary coins, unlike the normal silver coinage of medieval Europe, possess no value other than what the ruler decrees them to bear. The ruler has entered an agreement, a contract or covenant, with his people to sustain this fiction for the general good. So God in his infinite mercy ascribes value to human worth, and makes an agreement with humanity to abide by the consequences and let it do its best towards its salvation. In a famous phrase of the nominalist theologian Gabriel Biel, he allows a human being 'to do that which is in oneself' (facere quod in se est); even pagans may gain salvation through use of their reason. The system avoids troubled scrutiny of Augustine's soteriology, as long as one accepts its principles.

One reason why Augustine's influence has varied so much in the history of western Christianity is that there is much more to Augustine than his soteriology: he is at the heart of western thinking about the nature of the Church and its sacraments, and in some eras, it was this aspect of his thought that mattered more than what he said about salvation. When Martin Luther and other theologians in his generation recalled the Church to Augustine's soteriology, western Christians would have to decide for themselves which aspect of his thought mattered more: his emphasis on obedience to the Catholic Church or his discussion of salvation. In a well-known summary by the Princeton historian of theology B. B. Warfield, 'The Reformation, inwardly considered, was just the ultimate triumph of Augustine's doctrine of grace over Augustine's doctrine of the Church.'[3] So from one perspective, a century or more of turmoil in the Western Church from 1517 was a debate in the mind of long-dead Augustine.

A variety of scholars were stimulated to a new perception of Augustine by the first scholarly printed edition of all his known works, a formidable task which took the Basel printer Johann Amerbach sixteen years from 1490 to publish. The Reformation was not the necessary outcome of this renewed interest: other opinion-formers in the Church came to see the significance of what Augustine said about salvation, independently of Martin Luther but at exactly the same time. In France, when Bishop Briçonnet's protégé Jacques Lefèvre d'Etaples published his pioneering commentaries on Paul's Epistles in 1512, he stressed the total irrelevance of human works in God's salvation of humanity: this was five years before Luther began publishing the same views. In Italy, Luther's celebrated theological breakthrough has striking similarities with an earlier turning-point for a future Cardinal of the Church, Gasparo Contarini. He was a Venetian nobleman and diplomat whose reading in the Gospel of Matthew and the writings of Augustine brought him to a spiritual crisis, plunging him into despair about his worthlessness in God's sight. Close friends, Tommaso Giustiniani and

Vincento Querini, solved their similar crisis by joining the ultra-austere Order of the Camaldolese Hermits, and by subsequently devoting themselves to making its community life even more austere, but their efforts to persuade Contarini to join them only increased his misery. In 1511 he experienced a sense of mystical peace that released him from anxiety; suddenly he felt his worries foolish and unnecessary in the face of a gracious free gift of forgiveness from God.[4] When Lutherans began preaching Luther's message of free justification by faith, Contarini recognized what they were saying, and he devoted his distinguished later career in the Church to an effort (ultimately vain) to bring the opposing sides together (chapter 5, pp. 226–31).

Contarini was not the only leader of the old Church embracing Augustine's message. The new champion of Thomas Aquinas, Cardinal Cajetan, who was to play a fateful part in Luther's clash, was led back to emphasize predestination and the works of Augustine by his reverence for Aquinas. Dean Colet of St Paul's, London, repeatedly returned to Augustine in his commentaries on Paul's epistles, and he similarly emphasized God's decrees of predestination, not merely to salvation but damnation ('double predestination'), together with the worthlessness of human actions.[5] Bishop John Fisher of Rochester became one of Luther's chief literary opponents and died on the block in the Tower of London for opposing Henry VIII's break with the papacy. He was a humanist who also had an immense respect for medieval scholastic learning, and he was sensitive to the way in which Augustine rode roughshod over late medieval ideas about salvation and human good works. His answer was not to challenge the Church's teaching authority and legitimacy, as Luther found himself doing, but to construct his own intricate theology of grace and salvation. This insisted that the first element in being reconciled with God is an initiative from God: a gift technically called prevenient grace ('grace which goes before'). Prevenient grace opens the eyes of human beings to their sin and begins the process of making them reconciled with God – 'justifying' them. Either they then wait in penitent sorrow for further grace from God, which will inspire them to good works, or they hurry to receive the sacraments of the Church to find the grace of God that the sacraments offer. This includes performing the penances which they may receive in the confessional. So Fisher manages to hold in balance Augustine's thought, the authority of the Church and the importance of human works. Altogether, many influential people were taking their own profit from those newly published Basel volumes of Augustine's writings.[6]

As we gauge how humanism differed from the Augustinianism that now overwhelmed Europe, we must note that Desiderius Erasmus did not share in the general stampede to praise Augustine. He had too much respect for creativity and dignity in human beings to feel that the human mind had been utterly corrupted in the fall of Adam and Eve. Even before he turned towards theology as his main preoccupation, around 1489 he began drafting a work called the *Antibarbari*, eventually published in 1520. One of the aims of this was to defend humanist learning against scholastics, but there was a more general purpose underlying it: Erasmus was protesting against the whole perspective on knowledge that sees the only real truth as what is revealed by divine grace, rather than the knowledge which is available through the reasoning faculties of the human mind and through the acquisition of education. He was expressing his distrust of mysticism, such as that of the *Devotio Moderna* so strong in his native Netherlands, and he deplored the rejection of the created world which often accompanied it; his detestation of the monastic life was related to this feeling.[7] Augustinian pessimism was not for Erasmus. Instead he preferred the thinking of another giant of the early Church's theology, a brilliant Greek-speaking maverick who had lived in the eastern Mediterranean two centuries before Augustine, Origen. Origen had been a pioneer of meticulous commentary on the Bible, which was one reason why Erasmus admired him – but he had also been an audacious and speculative thinker, who aroused alarm and condemnation in the centuries after his death, as the Church had become more highly structured and regulated in its thinking. Origen had even suggested that, in the end, God envisaged that everyone, including the Devil himself, would be saved and return to paradise.

Origen's works first became readily available to Latin-speakers in a good scholarly edition in 1512, but Erasmus's esteem for Origen is evident well before that, in his first important devotional writing, the *Enchiridion*; during 1501 he was drawn to Origen by the enthusiasm of a new friend, Jean Vitrier, a famous French Franciscan preacher. One reason was Origen's distinctive view of humanity (in jargon terms, his 'anthropology'), which he had built on a passing reference in a letter of Paul to the Thessalonikan Church (1 Thess. 5:23): a human being was made up of three parts – flesh, spirit and soul. We have already seen (chapter 2, p. 102) that the concept of spirit became crucial in Erasmus's thought, and this was one major reason: of the three components of humanity, said Origen, only the flesh had been thoroughly corrupted, and the highest part, the spirit, was still intact. No wonder Erasmus made so much of the spirit in his theology: here was a splendid basis for humanist optimism in the face of Augustine.[8] Naturally, with his usual instinct for self-preservation, Erasmus made disapproving noises in his writings about the officially condemned side of Origen's thought, in other words the amount of Platonizing heresy which he had produced, and he also covered his tracks thoroughly against charges of Pelagianism, a word which Augustine had established as one of the ultimate put-downs in Christian vocabulary. However, when Erasmus wrote his interpretations of the crucial parts of the Bible on which Augustine had constructed his bleak view of humanity – Paul's Epistles to the Romans and Galatians – he frequently turned both to Origen and to Jerome's analysis of them, but he was notably silent on what Augustine had said. Likewise, Erasmus's fierce belief in pacifism, one of the consistent, strongly expressed and radical elements in his thinking, was opposed to the discussion of the legitimacy of war which Augustine had pioneered and which Aquinas had then developed into a theory of 'just war'.[9]

Erasmus's discreet fascination with Origen and his equally discreet cold-ness towards Augustine was a pointer to a possible new direction for western Christianity in the early sixteenth century. It was a direction rejected alike by mainstream Protestantism and those who remained loyal to the Pope, but it did inspire many of the more adventurous minds of the century, radicals who refused to be absorbed into the hardening theological cate-gories of the house divided – many of whom no doubt first encountered the unfamiliar name of Origen through the pages of Erasmus's *Enchiridion* – and we will be meeting them again many times, first in central Europe and Strassburg (chapter 4, p. 182). But as the future leaders of European religious thought took up their stance in the ghostly debate between Augustine and Origen, and sided decisively with Augustine, many of the qualities that had once distinguished humanism – its lively curiosity, its scepticism, its celebration of the possibilities for human creativity – were stripped from the humanist scholarship that took refuge either with Protestants or Catholics.

This is why one can never fully identify the humanist revolution with the 'New Learning' represented by Protestantism, which was the outcome of the Augustinian revolution sparked by Martin Luther in north-eastern Germany. It is significant that in the middle of the bitter literary clash between Erasmus and Martin Luther over free will (below, p. 151), Luther took the trouble to sneer at Origen's tripartite anthropology. Similarly, when Luther's colleague Philipp Melanchthon produced a first draft of the landmark statement of emerging Lutheranism, the 1530 Augsburg Con-fession (chapter 4, p. 174), he included a condemnation of Origen's views of salvation, and condemned Origen as a way of condemning Erasmus.[10] These were declarations of war by the Augustinian Reformation on the great humanist and his independent-minded exploration of Christianity's past, and to understand how such a clash developed we must meet Luther and follow his struggles to understand how he might be saved from eternal destruction.

LUTHER, A GOOD MONK: 1483–1517

Martin Luther was typical of the recruits to the monastic and clerical life on whom the smooth running and reputation of the Church depended: a bright boy from a hard-working middle-rank family with a shrewd respect for education. His father Hans, a younger son of prosperous small farmers, had done well for himself in the mining industry of Saxony, and married into a respectable urban family which included several distinguished graduates. Hans projected a career for his eldest son in secular law, the law of the Empire, paying for his education right up as far as university at Erfurt. But Martin branched out in his own direction to become a monk. The circumstances had the providential character which he would have recognized from reading the lives of the saints: caught in a fearsome thunderstorm in 1505, the twenty-one-year-old student was so terrified that he vowed to St Anne, the mother of Mary, that he would enter monastic life if he survived. When the storm was over he kept his vow, moving only a step down the road from his college to the Erfurt house of the Augustinian Eremites, a strict Order who had the austere reformer Egidio of Viterbo as their current Prior-General in Rome.

Hans Luther was annoyed at this sudden decision, but he could hardly gainsay St Anne, who happened to be the patron saint of miners as well as the grandmother of God. Much has been made of this rebellion of a son against his father, following a clever but misconceived psychological study of *Young Man Luther* by Erik H. Erikson, a Freudian psychoanalytical writer of the 1950s, who pointed to Martin's defiance as a way of explaining the grand rebellion which followed. There is no doubt that Luther was a passionate, impulsive man, who felt his theology rather than beginning with logical questions and answers about God, resulting in a theology full of paradoxes or downright contradictions. In any century in which he was born, Luther would have guaranteed a richly memorable night out, whether hilariously entertaining or infuriatingly quarrelsome. Yet Freud is of little help in understanding Luther, whereas, as I have already emphasized, Augustine of Hippo is of central importance. The Augustinian Eremites prided themselves in bearing the name of the acknowledged prince of western theologians. As Luther began his new theological studies at Erfurt, in an atmosphere of humanist learning, he met the writings of Plato and the Church Fathers, among whom Augustine stood as Luther's guide long after he had lost his interest in Plato and lesser Christian writers. Augustine would point him to a still greater authority: the Bible.

Luther was thus launched on a monastic career which was a complete contrast to Erasmus's years of frustration at Steyn: he did well, naturally took priestly orders (1507) and was soon marked out for senior responsibilities among the Augustinians. In 1510 he was chosen as one of the delegates to Rome on important business for a consortium of Saxon Augustinian monasteries, and although in later years he reminisced about the corruption he had seen in the papal capital, there is no evidence that at the time the effect on him was any more profound than the normal culture-shock suffered by northern Europeans in Italy. From 1511 he was sent by his Order to teach in a new university in Wittenberg, the little Saxon town which would become inextricably linked with the fortunes of his new movement. Wittenberg was ruled by Friedrich 'the Wise', Elector of Saxony, an enigmatic, highly cultured ruler, who was the most consistent long-term patron of Germany's greatest contemporary artists, Albrecht Dürer and Lukas Cranach the elder, as well as of the Augustinian monk who became the catalyst of the Protestant revolution.

There were many elements of luck which came together in Luther's position in Wittenberg, not least its location in what was known as 'Ernestine' Saxony. Since 1485, Saxony had been partitioned between two branches of its ruling Wettin dynasty; Duke Georg, the current ruler of the other part, Albertine or Ducal Saxony, proved to be one of Luther's most implacable enemies until Georg died in 1539. Friedrich the Wise's territorial section of the Wettin family inheritance was smaller than Albertine Saxony, but he did have one crucial advantage: the title of Elector, which gave him a pivotal role in the politics of the entire Holy Roman Empire. There were only seven Electors in the Empire, and they were the barrier preventing it becoming a hereditary monarchy. Every new Emperor had to be elected by them, and although the Electors' choice had fallen on a member of the Habsburg family since the early fifteenth century, they were always ready to make it clear that this was not an automatic outcome. The Emperor therefore had to be wary of Friedrich, and that became of great significance when in later years Europe's mightiest ruler was anxious to destroy Friedrich's protégé Martin Luther.

And for reasons best known to himself, Friedrich did obstinately defend Luther against his enemies. He remained a traditionalist in religion, who never saw the point of Luther's crisis of conscience, and who had virtually no personal relationship with him, but he was never prepared to betray his esteem for the turbulent university lecturer. Partly this may have been his commitment to his university foundation: Friedrich devoted much of his considerable energy to promoting the hitherto insignificant town of Wittenberg, and his pride and joy (apart from the large collection of relics which he accumulated in his family's Castle Church there) was the university, which he endowed in 1502. This was the first in Germany to be founded without the permission of the Church authorities, and it was a natural attraction for a printing-firm which set up in Wittenberg in the same year – another significant asset for Luther later on. The infant university's selling-point was its claim to offer an up-to-date humanist education, in contrast to the prevailing scholasticism of the rival older university in Albertine Saxony at Leipzig. Wittenberg's advertising handbook of 1508 referred equally disparagingly to the hundred-year-old 'pseudo-University' at Cologne.[11]

Because Luther was associated with this optimistic and rather brash little institution, and indeed quickly became the dominant figure in its Theology Faculty, it was not surprising that he was widely mistaken for a humanist scholar once his troubles became public knowledge in 1517. But despite Luther's use of humanist techniques in his teaching and writing, his increasingly dark view of human potential and his eventual insistence on the primacy of the revealed will of God in Scripture cannot be said to share much in the humanist spirit. As well as keeping his distance from humanism, he loathed the ethics of Aristotle, which were among his earliest teaching assignments, and he developed a lifelong hatred of this philosopher who was so important in scholastic learning.[12] His whole later career represented a rebellion against the scholastic nominalist theology and philosophy which remained standard components of a northern European education, and which were dominated by the softened view of humanity's role in its own salvation presented by the *via moderna*. There were indeed already nominalists who distrusted *via moderna* theology, and who were so insistent on the importance of Augustine that they were styled the 'modern Augustinian movement' (*schola Augustiniana moderna*.) It is not certain whether Luther had any contact with such writers in his crucial years, and as we will see, there is no particular reason why he should not have reached their conclusions for himself. From early on in the six quiet years at Wittenberg before the storm broke he was developing a certain individuality.

In 1513 and 1514 Luther lectured on the Psalter, a natural first choice for a monk for whom the chanting of the Psalms structured his daily life, and to help his students he had a batch of psalters printed for them with the text surrounded by wide margins, so that they could make their notes around the text as he spoke. As a humanist should, the lecturer was stripping the text of all the medieval commentary which provided a ready-made lens through which a student would have been expected to view the Bible. This forced them to look at it afresh and build up a new picture from scratch.[13] In 1515 Luther moved on in his lectures to Romans, that central text for Augustine's message about salvation: it is worth noting that all this fundamental groundwork for his interpretation of the Bible was done before Erasmus had published his edition of the New Testament, and so it owed nothing to that monument to humanist learning.

Already in the notes which survive from these two lecture courses (rivetingly, we can follow them in manuscripts from Luther's own hand) themes appear which later coalesced behind his proclamation of justification by faith: his presentation of the Psalms as a meditation on the message and significance of Jesus Christ, his affirmation that all righteousness comes from God, his pointers to a revelation of truth through the words of Scripture, a revelation that dwarfs any of the truths provided by human reason. When Luther turns to Romans, central to his presentation of the message of salvation is the doctrine of predestination: 'Whoever hates sin is already outside sin and belongs to the elect.' How could we get to this state without help from outside ourselves? There is a terrifying image in his notes that conjures the plight of a human being in the aftermath of the Fall in the Garden of Eden: so trapped in sin that both body and spirit are twisted up claustrophobically without any escape from their agony – *incurvatus in se* – 'turned in on themselves'.

Not everything of the later Luther is yet in focus in these commentaries: faith, the word that resounds through Luther's developed theology, has not yet assumed its crucial role.[14] The traditional picture of Luther's discovery of justification by faith makes it a story of agonized turmoil and release, a dramatic adventure of conversion that has been much imitated in the spiritual experience of evangelical Christians. Conversion has indeed subsequently become something of a required element in evangelical religion, with Luther's conversion standing in a succession of dramatic sudden turns first seen in the life of Paul of Tarsus, and then of Augustine of Hippo. Luther's turning-point has been linked to the picturesque tale of a 'tower experience' (*Turmerlebnis*), drawn from his own account long afterwards in 1545, and remarkably difficult to fit into a definite chronological point in his life.[15] The experience has been made all the more picturesque by a misunderstanding of the Latin in his story, which has sent him to sit on the monastic lavatory in the tower as he made a crucial breakthrough in a spiritual as well as a physical sense. Alas for admirers of Erikson's Luther and of the interesting stage interpretation which John Osborne drew from it, medical examination of the reformer's career reveals that his celebrated sufferings from constipation date from no earlier than his months in the Wartburg in 1521 (an understandable ailment at a time of huge tension, coupled with lack of exercise – see below, p. 132); thereafter they were not exceptional. The relief of constipation is thus not as compelling a metaphor for his discovery of justification by faith as is now often asserted.[16]

Whenever the *Turmerlebnis* occurred (and in fact it is almost certain to have been after 1517), Luther remembered or reinterpreted it as a turning-point which hammered home to him the key role of faith in salvation: his realization centred predictably on seeing in a new light a text from Romans 1:17, which itself contains a quotation from the Hebrew scripture Habbakuk 2:4: 'the righteousness of God is revealed through faith for faith, as it is written "he who through faith is righteous shall live" '. In this sentence, the words 'righteousness/righteous' could equally be rendered as they were in the Latin of the Vulgate, '*justitia/justus*'. Hence the word 'justification', which in Latin literally means the making of someone to be righteous. In Luther's understanding it rather meant the declaring of someone to be righteous: God 'imputes' the merits of the crucified and risen Christ through grace to a fallen human being, who remains without inherent merit and who, without this 'imputation', would remain unrighteous. Linked as the word *justitia* is in Romans 1:17 so closely with faith, we see how Luther constructed the notion of justification by faith from Paul's closely woven text. He had found the ultimate revealed truth in the Bible, and saw the Bible through new eyes: 'At this I felt myself straightway born afresh and to have entered through the open gates into paradise itself.'

There have been endless attempts to analyse the triangular relationship between the surviving texts of the early lectures, the Tower experience and Luther's state of mind in the six years before 1517, and there will probably never be a definitive solution. Later he represented his years as a monk in the Wittenberg Augustinian house as emotionally tortured and unprofitable; partly that was hindsight given all that had happened afterwards, and partly it can be accounted for by his constant efforts in later years to cheer up a long-term house-guest, Jerome Weller, who suffered repeated bouts of clinical depression, and who needed to hear about someone else who had successfully endured similar troubles.[17] Luther also freely admitted that he had been a good and conscientious monk, one of the best products of the healthiest parts of the monastic system – but indeed, that was the trouble. After all his frequent anxious visits to the confessional to seek forgiveness for his (in worldly terms, trivial) sins, he still felt a righteous God's fury against his sin. Reminiscing later, he said that he had come to hate this God who had given laws in the Old Testament which could not be kept.

The answer was to discover that God put aside his wrath as judge for human beings whom he chose as his elect. They received a gift of faith that had nothing to do with their own sinful actions. It was entirely in the will of God to grant this gift – to declare someone to be righteous: that was divine grace. Luther made this delighted discovery himself, but he freely acknowledged that he also found it proclaimed in Augustine, especially in one of his chief writings against the Pelagians, *On the Spirit and the Letter* (this is a work much referred to in the 1515–16 lectures on Romans).[18] His release from tension, when he sensed his sheer helplessness was known to a merciful God as well as an angry God, was now the centre of his experience and the guiding principle of the Protestant Reformation. 'My chains fell off, and I was free', sang the English hymn-writer Charles Wesley, whose Georgian verse has a rare ability to expose the heart of Luther's message, and still empowers evangelical Christianity worldwide. Luther clung on to this sense of release through all his later career, when the powers of Church and Commonwealth, and worse still, the contradictions of theology within his own mind, battled with the liberating simplicity of justification by faith.

As this theology gradually took shape in Luther's mind and brought him peace and spiritual security, a wholly unrelated event in southern Europe set up reverberations which reached Wittenberg and precipitated a crisis for him: the rebuilding of a church. Luther would not have considered church-building an unworthy cause – all Europe echoed to masons and carpenters building churches at the time – and this was something special, for it was the project for St Peter's Basilica in Rome, begun by Pope Nicholas V some seven decades earlier and still nowhere complete (see chapter 1, p. 42). Leo X was determined to move it along for the greater glory both of God and of his Vicar on earth, and conscious of the huge costs involved he turned to the usual late medieval method of raising funds, the issue of an indulgence, duly proclaimed as a solemn papal Bull *Sacrosanctis* in 1515. Every worthy institution sought money through indulgences at the time – England's hospitals could not have functioned without them – but this was an exceptionally ambitious scheme which needed pan-European co-operation. In Germany, the Pope had approached Jakob Fugger of Augsburg, current proprietor of the family banking business which financed the most powerful people in Europe. Fugger had done his best to stop Leo being elected Pope, but he was prepared now to broker a deal, linking it with the needs of another of his clients, Albrecht of Brandenburg, newly consecrated Archbishop of Mainz.

Albrecht, already Archbishop of Magdeburg and Administrator of the diocese of Halberstadt nearby, was an extreme example of the European noblemen who regarded the Church as an asset to be exploited for their family, in his case the great German dynasty of the Hohenzollern. He was determined to use his very considerable talents to continue the Hohenzollerns' steady accumulation of power. They already controlled one of the seven votes of the Imperial Electors, since a Hohenzollern (Albrecht's brother) was Elector as Margrave of Brandenburg, but now in 1514 an ecclesiastical Electorate, the Archbishopric of Mainz far away to the southwest, fell vacant. Albrecht acted decisively to secure his own election to this highly attractive see, which carried with it the office of Imperial Chancellor and also made him primate of Germany, but he was not prepared to give up his other bishoprics while taking on Mainz. Even by the acquisitive standards of Europe's clergy-cum-noblemen, this was an unusual ambition, which required big money to pay for dispensations from Rome, quite apart from the very large routine fees involved in becoming Archbishop of Mainz. Hence the deal, the public face of which was the bull *Sacrosanctis* (followed up in 1518 with a Cardinal's hat for the Archbishop). Albrecht would promote the Pope's indulgence in co-operation with a financial understanding worked out by the Fuggers. The faithful would benefit from the indulgences they bought: Albrecht would become an Elector as well as an Archbishop twice over, and St Peter's would be completed. Everyone would be a winner.

To understand why this did not prove to be the case requires an explanation of the indulgence system. It depends on linking together a number of assumptions about sin and the afterlife, each of which individually makes considerable sense. First is the assumption which works very effectively in ordinary society, that any wrong requires an act of restitution to the injured party. So God demands an action on the part of a sinner to prove repentance for a sin. Second is the idea that Christ's virtues or merits are infinite since he is part of the Godhead, and therefore they are more than adequate for the purpose of saving the finite world from Adam's sin. Additional to his spare merits are the merits of the saints, headed by Christ's mother Mary: clearly these are worthy merits in the sight of God, since the saints are known to be in heaven. This combined 'treasury of merit' is therefore available to assist in the work of a faithful Christian's repentance. Since the Pope is the Vicar of Christ on earth, it would be criminal meanness on his part not to dispense such a treasury to anxious Christians on earth. The treasury of merit can then be granted to the faithful to shorten the time spent doing penance in Purgatory: that grant is an indulgence.

All these ideas were drawn together in a bull of Pope Clement VI, *Unigenitus*, in 1343, by which time the Pope was seeking to rationalize a system of indulgence grants which was already well-established. It was only natural for pious Christians to show gratitude for such an act of charity on the Church's part. Eventually their thank-offerings became effectively a payment for the indulgence, even although all indulgences (including that sponsored by Albrecht) were very careful to lay down proper conditions for use, particularly instructions to the purchasers to go to confession, and also, in a specialized form of welfare relief, offered free indulgences for the destitute. In 1476, a very considerable extension of the system's potential occurred when the theologian Raimund Peraudi argued that indulgences were available to help the souls of people already dead and presumed to be in Purgatory, as well as living people who sought and received an indulgence; a papal Bull followed to implement this suggestion. With that the system was complete, and ready to have its disastrous effect on Martin Luther's volcanic temper.

Nevertheless, it is worth appreciating that indulgences were a minor outcrop of the doctrine of Purgatory, which could have stood as a system perfectly well without them. Indeed, Luther himself continued to accept the existence of Purgatory until around 1530, when he finally realized that his soteriological revolution had abolished it (a change of mind which then necessitated a certain amount of re-editing of some of his earlier writings).[19] What infuriated him about indulgences was that every assumption behind the indulgence system conflicted with justification by faith. To conflate Christ's merits with the merits of the saints was blasphemous. Human beings were worthless lumps of perdition, as Augustine had said, and could do nothing to gain their own salvation, least of all by buying a piece of parchment from Archbishop Albrecht's agents. In fact Luther found nothing distinctive about the *Sacrosanctis* campaign which was not equally objectionable in other indulgences: his first protests came in sermons of 1516 and were couched in general terms, disregarding (as idealistic academics tend to do) the fact that his own university was a financial beneficiary of the system which he was attacking.[20]

Luther was not the first theologian to express unease about what had happened to the original worthy aims of the indulgence system. Fifteenth-century Dutch leaders of the *Devotio Moderna*, John of Wesel and Wessel Gansfort, had condemned abuses of indulgences, as had highly respectable scholars in that bastion of orthodoxy, the Sorbonne in Paris; so did Thomas

Wittenbach, the teacher of the future reformer Huldrych Zwingli at Basel University.[21] Moreover, after 1515 there were many besides theologians who objected to the indulgence campaign launched by *Sacrosanctis*. The Elector Friedrich was furious and banned the campaign from his territories, not only because no Wettin could be pleased at seeing the Hohenzollern get their hands on a second Electorate, but also because *Sacrosanctis* suspended all other indulgences while it was being proclaimed, and that suspension drastically curtailed the revenue projections for his own beloved relic collection in Wittenberg. Humanist scholars and serious-minded folk generally were horrified at the exceptionally vulgar emotional blackmail of the campaign, which was run by Johann Tetzel, a Dominican friar, who turned a gift for preaching into a flair for a catchy commercial phrase. 'Won't you part with even a farthing to buy this letter? It won't bring you money but rather a divine and immortal soul, whole and secure in the Kingdom of Heaven.'[22] The Augustinians sneered at their traditional rivals the Dominicans for being caught up in such a debasement of true religion. There was therefore a ready audience for anyone who cared to speak out against what was happening.

AN ACCIDENTAL REVOLUTION: 1517–21

Reputedly Luther spoke out on 31 October 1517, celebrated in later years in German-speaking lands as Reformation Day. That day, he may or may not have publicly advertised his intention of setting up an academic disputation on the subject of indulgences by tacking to the Castle Church doors in Wittenberg a copy of ninety-five statements or theses to be disputed – much is uncertain in the anecdotes about these tumultuous years, and not even the doors themselves can bear witness, having been destroyed in a fire in 1760. Probably Luther did not see what he was doing as particularly important, since he had spoken on indulgences before, and he was currently much more pleased with his campaign against his bugbear Aristotle in faculty teaching, to be replaced (as he rather grandly told a friend in May 1517) by 'our theology and that of St Augustine'.[23] But he gathered together the conclusions of his lectures and his objections to the Tetzel scandal in crisp Latin, which attentive students in the Faculty must have heard often before. 'When our Lord and Master, Jesus Christ, said "Repent", he meant that the whole life of believers should be one of penitence.' Erasmus would have nodded approvingly at this opening shot, drawn from his own commentaries. 'Christians should be taught that, if the Pope knew the exactions of the preachers of indulgences, he would rather have the basilica of St Peter reduced to ashes than built with the skin, flesh and bones of his sheep.' That did not sound quite so academic or detached, though one might argue that it was intended to show a touching faith in Pope Leo X. The culminating two statements of the whole ninety-five summed up Luther's tormented inner experience, yet they might be taken as a simple and unexceptional statement of Christian struggles towards God: 'Christians should be exhorted to seek earnestly to follow Christ, their Head, through penalties, deaths, hells. And let them thus be more confident of entering heaven through many tribulations rather than through a false assurance of peace.'

Luther's low-key understanding of what he was doing was hardly surprising, because the ninety-five theses are hardly a call to revolution. They still assumed the existence of Purgatory, works of merit and the value of penance to a priest, even if they were couched in the sharp terms appropriate to points intended to provoke formal scholastic debate. However, Luther went to the extent of enclosing his acid little theses about the indulgence system in a protest letter, written in the most courtly terms on 31 October to the local Archbishop – none other than Albrecht of Brandenburg. By doing so, Luther made his challenge a public matter. Albrecht did his duty and forwarded the theses to the Holy Father in Rome. Meanwhile, printed copies of them circulated in Germany in both Latin and German and sparked a pamphlet war among German theologians; Dominicans naturally rushed to defend their colleague Tetzel against attack. It was not the first time that the new medium of print had provoked a general debate, way beyond those who could actually read the pamphlets and books involved: that had happened over the previous decade, when European authorities launched an ambitious publicity campaign to raise a new continent-wide crusade against the Turks. However, what the Luther furore now demonstrated was that there was an independent public opinion, and the printing presses which fuelled it could not be controlled by the existing hierarchies in Church and Commonwealth.[24]

It was difficult for Pope Leo to feel much interest in what appeared to be a familiar story of Dominicans and Augustinians squabbling. Italian politics had plenty to occupy him in 1517, after the murderous success of his campaign against his enemies among the Cardinals, and his capture of the rich little city of Urbino in a sordid dynastic war on behalf of his nephew Lorenzino de' Medici. If in more principled moments he took a broader view as the leader of Christendom, the appalling situation in the East would take precedence: Cyprus was under acute threat from the Turks after the fall of Egypt and Syria, yet Venice and France seemed more interested in settling scores with the Emperor and Spain than heeding strident papal calls for a new crusade. Accordingly, papal reaction was to instruct the German Augustinians to sort out this annoying matter themselves in their three-yearly meeting in Heidelberg in April 1518, while Rome got on with more pressing business.

Among brothers, Luther found a courteous audience, as well as meeting unexpected and gratifying public recognition and approval as he travelled to and from Heidelberg. Here he was able to talk less about the minor issue of indulgences and more about his general propositions on grace, and in consequence he produced less confrontation and more dignity. He talked movingly about the suffering of God which showed divine love for fallen humanity. He insisted specifically that one could not use Gabriel Biel's idea that humanity could be allowed 'do that which is in oneself' to attain salvation; all that we do ourselves amounts to the commission of mortal sin. In one of the many strong oppositions of ideas or paradoxes that were always to characterize his thought, he called his convictions a theology of the Cross: a loving God becomes weak and foolish to save his people. He set this against a theology of glory, which revels in wisdom and human achievement. In later years, he would more usually talk about gospel, which saves, against law, which condemns, but the paradox remained. 'A theology of glory calls evil good and good evil. A theology of the Cross calls the thing what it actually is.'[25] This was to move on subtly but decisively from Erasmus in the *Enchiridion*: he had said 'if your eye is not sound and you look elsewhere than towards Christ, even if you perform good actions, they will be unfruitful or even harmful' (see chapter 2, p. 102). For Luther, no eye was sound and no action was good. That was why God's love was so astonishing.

Luther's devout and learned audience and disputants would recognize here some of the more solemn and contemplative themes of later medieval theology, themes which they would have found in the writings of German mystics, or would sense for themselves as they knelt in silence before one of the many crucifixes in their churches and studies. We know that one Dominican observer present, Martin Bucer, who had a great future as a reformer, was entranced by what he heard Luther saying and went on to make God's love his watchword much more than did Luther himself (chapter 4, p. 180). It was a moment when Luther's rich paradoxes looked as if they were capable of producing a Christian theology for the weak and powerless without involving any attack on the existing Church, and without all the bids for power and politicking which followed. But that was not to be: Tetzel and his angry fellow Dominicans in Germany wanted a result, not more theology, and at the same time as the Heidelberg meeting, Tetzel issued another set of theses that highlighted the theme of obedience to the Pope's authority. Luther wanted to talk about grace; his opponents wanted to talk about authority. That chasm of purposes explains how an argument about a side-alley of medieval soteriology – indulgences – escalated into the division of Europe. Throughout 1518 Luther's opponents relentlessly called him to be obedient to Rome, and the incendiary idea of conciliarism constantly hovered around their diatribes. A veteran Dominican papal theologian and opponent of conciliarist thought, Silvestro Mazzolini of Prierio ('Prierias'), was commissioned to write against the ninety-five theses. He saw a familiar conciliarist enemy in Luther, and he discussed the infallibility of Church authority at such length that it made Luther much more inclined to wonder whether the Church might indeed be fallible.

At the end of October 1518 came a decisive meeting in Augsburg between Luther and the great Thomist scholar Cardinal Cajetan. This could have been a further opportunity for compromise, because the summons to meet the Cardinal modified Luther's previous summons to Rome in May on charges that he had shown himself heretical in questioning the authority of the Pope. Friedrich the Wise negotiated this concession on the strength of his crucial position in the imminent election of a Holy Roman Emperor, seizing on the useful coincidence that Cajetan happened to be present in Germany on a mission to the Imperial Diet to plead for Leo X's crusading project. Moreover, in less fraught circumstances, the little Italian friar would have been the ideal partner in a proper discussion of the indulgence question: immediately after the appearance of Luther's ninety-five theses, he had turned his formidable intelligence to an intensive study of indulgences, and his conclusions (published later at great length) were typical of his brusquely independent thinking. While defending the existence of indulgences, he took a realistic view of their historical origins, and he downplayed both the theology of merit and the proposition that the Church could be in control of measuring out lengths of penance in Purgatory.[26]

However, the Cardinal was also a Dominican and the Pope's representative, and he was not going to stand impertinence from an obscure German Augustinian lecturer. Impertinence was what he heard in response to his command for obedience to the Church. Luther was wise to leave Augsburg hastily after several unhappy meetings with Cajetan: he was in a state of deep disappointment, and now convinced that Thomists like the Cardinal had formed a powerful conspiracy with pagan Aristotle against the truth. The most likely dating of his *Turmerlebnis* is somewhere around this time. Its significance may therefore not be quite what his narrative presents (above,

p. 118): rather than the definitive breakthrough on justification by faith, it may have represented a moment when the balance between the claims of authority and the claims of faith seen through Scripture began to tilt in his mind. Passionate lover of the Church that he was, he had wanted to obey the Church, assuming that it would give him God's commands. Now he had seen that some of the most admirable members of the hierarchy were not prepared to argue Christian truth with him. What did that say about the Church hierarchy? Luther's answer to this question was to show a spectacularly disloyal form of loyalty to the Church; he appealed to a General Council to hear his case. This was precisely what Pope Pius II had forbidden in 1460, when the hopes of the conciliarists had lain in ruins. All over Europe, conciliarist sympathizers were astonished and excited at this long-silent fanfare against papal despotism. But those who saw Luther merely as a new champion for conciliarism found that the rapid momentum of events produced something alarmingly different.

In June 1519 Luther arrived in Wittenberg's rival university of Leipzig for a debate which he hoped would vindicate or at least clarify his position. Enlivened by partisan crowds of students and faculty, it took place in the atmosphere of festive adolescent aggression customary in large-scale encounters between universities committed to detesting each other. The guest speaker and Luther's chief opponent was central Europe's leading theologian, Johann Eck of the Bavarian university of Ingolstadt, who had turned from a courteous academic correspondent of Luther into one of his most effective enemies, remorselessly pursuing the theme of obedience to papal authority. This continued to be Eck's strategy at Leipzig, and in debating terms it was brilliantly successful. He pushed Luther on from uncompromising but perfectly safe affirmations of conciliarism, such as the statement that Christ, not the Pope, was head of the Church, into dangerous discussion of the rights and wrongs of the Hussite Church. Infuriated by his opponent, Luther made an honest but fatal comment: whatever opinions of the Hussites were heretical, 'I am sure on this, that many of Hus' beliefs were completely evangelical and Christian'.[27] This was to say that the Council of Konstanz, that golden moment in conciliarist development, had burned a man whom Luther was willing to commend. No attempt by Luther to move the argument in the debate from the Hussites to the equally anti-papal but far more respectable Greek Church could undo the damage. He had been defined as an enemy of the whole western Church. Less than two years earlier, nothing could have been further from his mind.

The year 1520 saw Luther condemned for heresy by a papal Bull, *Exsurge Domine*, and it climaxed in early December when he burned that bull at the gates of Wittenberg, along with works by Eck and volumes of canon law, which were the foundation of papal administration in the Church. This was enacted prophecy, as much as any ceremonial action of an Old Testament prophet: the symbolic culmination of a year in which he had sealed his break with the past in three key writings, none of them long enough to wear out the reader. At a time when he was pouring out a torrent of occasional pamphlets, preaching and debating, they represented an astonishing creative achievement, a harnessing of the fury which he now felt at the rejection of the good news and urgent advice he had offered the Holy Father. All three books showed how far the acute conflict of 1519–20 with the authorities in the Church had pushed him to think new thoughts. To be delivered so many hammer-blows by the institution which he had regarded as his mother was to liberate his imagination and give him the chance to look afresh at the Church which he saw in the New Testament.

First, the *Address to the Christian Nobility of the German Nation* was addressed in German to those in charge of decision-making in the Empire, and to the newly elected Emperor. It was the most popular of all three books, because it developed familiar anti-papal thoughts, often expressed over previous centuries, including the suggestion made at particularly heated moments in the conflicts between Pope and Emperor, that the Pope, far from being God's representative on earth, was an impostor put in place by the devil: Antichrist. Luther had first voiced this thought for himself in a private letter not long after his traumatic meeting with Cajetan.[28] At that stage, he may have been half-joking: now in the *Address*, he was not. The Pope was a threat to the good government of the Empire. If the Pope was Antichrist, imperial noblemen faced not merely a political task to discipline a papal jurisdiction that had become corrupted, but a God-given duty to overthrow a devilish confidence trick. But now not only the papacy was in Luther's sights; going way beyond medieval anti-papal rhetoric, he began saying that the whole organization of the clergy was a betrayal of the Church, which had been turned into a selfish interest-group for the benefit of its officials. Clergy had been made into separate beings, particularly by the command to compulsory celibacy; all marks of separation, especially the vows which sustained them, must be overthrown. 'If a little company of pious Christian laymen were taken prisoners and carried away to a desert, and had not among them a priest consecrated by a bishop, and were there to agree to elect one of them, born in wedlock or not, . . . this man would as truly be a priest, as if all the bishops and all the Popes had consecrated him.'[29] 'Born in wedlock or not'! Luther was emphasizing that even a bastard might represent God's people: this was a deliberate injection of Christian freedom into the Church, for the idea offended deeply against canon law – not to mention the Pope's power to earn money from dispensing bastards to enter the priesthood.

Frequently this is called a 'nationalistic' book, and so it was often interpreted when a nation-state of sorts called Germany was manufactured in the nineteenth and twentieth centuries. But one has to be careful to avoid misunderstanding the feeling to which Luther was appealing in his book: the 'nation' in his title was the sacred medieval institution of the Holy Roman Empire and its privileged nobility, not the totality of German-speakers in Europe, and he was calling for one universal set of representatives of God, the Emperor and his nobility, to punish the crimes of another universal claimant to universal representation, the Pope. Certainly German-speakers in northern Europe had long despised the supposedly debauched culture and decadent habits of people from south of the Alps, and resented the large sums of money which their rulers' previous deals with Rome allowed to travel south from the Empire to the papacy. Their feelings did not differ much from those of Poles, Scandinavians, Scots, English – the Alps were a major cultural barrier in western Christendom. Many saw familiar themes in what Luther was saying, and read the book accordingly, but he had a wider point to make about the whole Catholic Church, as it preached God's message throughout the world.

Luther developed this theme in *The Babylonian Captivity of the Church*, written in pungent Latin for the clergy; in this comparatively short work lie some of the most significant strands in shaping and also in disrupting the later Reformation. The title would of course have reminded the well-informed of its earlier use in relation to the papacy's fourteenth-century move to Avignon, but the implication was much more profound. Developing his theme of a clerical confidence trick, Luther directed the clergy's attention to the sacraments which they administered, and offered a redefinition of a truly scriptural sacrament which drastically reduced the seven major sacraments recognized in the medieval West. A true sacrament consisted of a divine promise marked by a divine sign, both of which were only to be found in scripture, and on this test only baptism, Eucharist and penance survived (Luther was already doubtful about penance, and later recognized his inconsistency in putting it on the same level as the other two). Naturally, like the Hussites, he said that the laity should drink wine as well as eat bread when they came to communion. Sensational was his attack on the theology of the Mass, fuelled by his loathing of Aristotle, who had provided the original terminology on which the Church had constructed its preferred explanation of the miracle of the mass: transubstantiation. Christ's sacrament should not be viewed through Aristotle's eyes, and treated as an object for rational analysis, but instead it should be accepted by faith through the plain words of Scripture, 'This is my body ... this is my blood.'[30] In these simple statements, quoting Christ's words recorded in the gospels of Matthew, Mark and Luke, lay a time-bomb which as we will see, soon blew apart any unity in Protestantism.

There was still more to Luther's analysis of the Eucharist. If he hated Aristotle, he also hated the idea that good works or human merit had value in God's eyes. So he insisted that the Mass could not be a work, therefore its performance could not be a sacrifice or be manipulated for any one human intention. It was a road of communication from the divine to the human, a channel of God's love: 'the word of divine promise in this sacrament sets forth the forgiveness of sins' – Christ on the cross had been the only sacrifice. A sacrifice is done by a priest, and so Christ had been the only priest, sacrificing himself. No sacrifice, no priest: so the clergy who administered communion were not set aside to be special priestly beings; that idea was part of the Roman cheat. Every faithful Christian was a priest, although only those called by the community or by a superior should exercise priesthood (much later hinged on this casual aside). Clergy were just servants (in Latin, 'ministers') of the Church: 'I cannot understand at all why one who has once been made a priest cannot again become a layman; for the sole difference between him and a layman is his ministry.'[31]

The third great work in this sequence, *The Freedom of a Christian*, took a different, less militant tone. It addressed the obvious question that has always perplexed those who take a grace-alone view of salvation: if human good works or merits are worthless in the sight of God and have no influence on a destiny to heaven or hell, what is the point of being good – or, perhaps more pressingly, what is the point of not being bad? Some might say that there was no point in morality at all – this was the problem of 'antinomianism' which continued to haunt the Protestant Reformation. Luther, however, refused to see it as a problem. His willingness to embrace opposites, to make a joyous art-form of paradox, was here seen at its most effective. The freedom of a Christian consists in the knowledge that no commandments can be kept properly, but that God does not condemn us for that – indeed he has come to die in anguish to save our anguish. Therefore 'A Christian is a perfectly free lord of all, subject to none. A Christian is a perfectly dutiful servant of all, subject to all.'[32] Good works come naturally to the saved Christian as an expression of love and gratitude for God's saving and loving nature, as naturally as it is to be good and loving to the person whom we love passionately. Luther was showing the idealism of a celibate here: the complex experience of marriage was yet to come for him. But he told a sound psychological truth: relationships of love are not played by rules. He did not say the last word on the Protestant problem of liberty versus license, but he gave some profound answers for others to wrestle with, and he had released the word freedom (*libertas*), to ring through Europe and excite a bewildering variety of reactions in its hearers.

What would the powers of this world make of his call to liberty? The authorities of the Church had already given their answer; now it was for the civil Commonwealth to pronounce, in the person of its most exalted representative, the Holy Roman Emperor. Charles V, elected in summer 1519 against all rival candidates to the huge relief of the Habsburg family, was then not out of his teens, but he was already king of Aragon and Castile and their overseas possessions: now, therefore, he ruled the largest empire that the Christian West had ever experienced. A serious-minded young man, whose sense of destiny as Christendom's leader was not diminished by his advisers, he was anxious not to jeopardize the unity of the dominion entrusted to him, but he was also anxious to do what God wanted. Eventually setting aside papal protests, he heeded Friedrich the Wise and decided to give Luther a formal hearing within the Empire at the first available meeting of its Diet, at Worms in April 1521. Luther arrived after a triumphal tour across Germany. Facing the Emperor, he acknowledged the long list of books assembled in the room as his own. Ordered to say 'yes' or 'no' to the question 'will you then recant?', he asked for a day's grace to make his answer. This was the turning-point on which his life depended: would he return to being the best monk in Germany, or go forward into an unformed future, guided only by what he had found in the Bible?

Luther's answer the following day was no single word but a careful and dignified speech. His books were of various sorts, some of which were indeed 'polemic against the papacy', which reflected 'the experience and the complaint of all men': 'If then, I revoke these books, all I shall achieve is to add strength to tyranny, and open not the windows but the doors to this monstrous godlessness, for a wider and freer range than it has ever dared before.' He spelled out to the Emperor that without a conviction from 'scripture or plain reason (for I believe neither in Pope nor councils alone)', he could recant nothing. It was such a momentous ending to his words that not long after his death, the first editor of his collected works, Georg Rörer, felt compelled to construct two tiny summary sentences in German, which have become the most memorable thing Luther never said: 'Here I stand; I can do no other.'[33] This can stand for the motto of all Protestants – ultimately, perhaps, of all western civilization.

Charles, likewise taking a night to gather his thoughts, behaved more honourably than had his forebear Sigismund and the Council of Konstanz to Jan Hus: he honoured Luther's safe-conduct, while issuing an edict condemning Luther as a heretic. After a few days the newly criminalized monk left for Wittenberg. Friedrich had made provision to keep him safe; once Luther was within Saxon territory, a staged kidnapping carried the marked man out of public view. Installed in the Wartburg, a Wettin stronghold on the wooded massif high above the city of Eisenach, familiar to him from his childhood, Luther vanished for ten months from an astonished world. When he reappeared in March 1522, it was in a desperate effort to put bounds on the revolution he had provoked.

WHOSE REVOLUTION? 1521-2

Before the traumatic experience of executing a king in the mid-seventeenth century British civil wars, most people who used the word 'revolution' understood the word as meaning what a modern engineer would mean by it: a turn around to the place where one should be, a return right back to the beginning. So the humanists' cry of '*ad fontes*' was a revolution in that sense.[34] Luther saw his task in the same way: returning the Church to where it should be. But did he have the right to be the leader of this return? His one qualification was as a Doctor of Theology, by grant of his university in 1512, at the unusually young age of twenty-eight, and in all his Reformation he never gained any other formal status as authority in either Church or Commonwealth, neither as bishop nor as prince. Rather than seeking to found a Church or a kingdom of God on earth, he simply claimed the right to pronounce on doctrine, like a one-man version of the Sorbonne, the theological faculty of the University of Paris, which for centuries had seen itself as having a peculiar privilege in this regard. But he felt also compelled to do so by an authority far higher than the Wittenberg university charter: he saw himself as God's prophet in the last days of the earth, spreading God's good news ('*euaggelion*' in Greek, '*evangelium*' in Latin). That is why his movement was straight away called 'evangelical', the description which predates the word 'Protestant' (above, p. xx).

While confined to the Wartburg, Luther devoted himself to a fever of writing: the most formidable task was the first part of his translation of the Bible into High German. It was an astonishing achievement at a time of great personal stress and amid the production of a welter of polemical writing. Although time only permitted him to complete the New Testament, and the complete Old Testament followed later, this was a extraordinary achievement, which has shaped the German language ever since. Luther was a connoisseur of language, just like his English contemporary Thomas Cranmer, whose speech has haunted formal English ever since, but his gift was different: Cranmer's meticulously calculated prose in his *Book of Common Prayer* was to present a public, ceremonial face of the Protestant Reformation in a restrained dignity, even sobriety, whereas Luther's gift was for seizing the emotion with sudden, urgent phrases. His hymns, first published in collections from Wittenberg and Strassburg in 1524, reveal his genius perhaps even more than his Bible, because they transcend the notorious and already then well-established tendency of the German language to pile syllable on syllable in conglomerations of compound-notions. Singers of Luther's verse can revel in strong words of one or two syllables, like his famous 'A safe stronghold our God is still' – '*Ein' feste Burg ist unser Gott, Ein gute Wehr und Waffen*'.

The Bible translation drew on Luther's scholarly training in a humanist fashion just as Erasmus would have wished, but nothing could be further from Erasmus's refined and cerebral spirituality than Luther's urgent purposes. Saturated as he was in Augustine's writings, he believed like Augustine that God exercised detailed control over all history and shaped it for his divine purposes; so he must look out to current events around him to read God's message. Like everyone in central Europe, he was desperately conscious of the coming of the Turks, who threatened the very existence of Christendom, and now bitter experience had also taught him that the Pope too was a manifestation on earth of Antichrist. This all indicated unmistakably that the evangelical message centred on the coming of the Last Days. Plenty of people agreed with Luther, and talked or wrote about him as the prophet of the Last Days, which were so keenly expected in early sixteenth-century Europe. He was commonly identified with Elijah: ironically the Swiss reformer Huldrych Zwingli, who was not destined to be numbered among his admirers, is the first person known to have done this.[35]

What message should the prophet preach? He had found some very specific central truths in the course of his spiritual turmoils. With his strong sense of paradox he drew a great gulf between law and gospel, between salvation by works and salvation by faith alone. Jesus Christ had come to fulfil the Old Testament law, freeing humanity from its demands (or at least, freeing elect humanity). Anything which stood in the way of this evangelical message must be thrust aside – even if it was to be found in scripture. His translation of the Bible in the Wartburg was an expression of a relationship of love with the word of God, which meant that he could be as familiar with or even as rude to the Bible as with the most intimate of old friends. He could treat the text in a startlingly proprietorial way. Wherever, for instance, Luther found the word equivalent to 'life' in Greek or Hebrew, he would extend it in his German to the phrase 'eternal life'. 'Mercy' became 'grace', and 'the deliverer of Israel' 'the saviour'. When he translated a crucial proof-text in Romans 3 'we hold that man is justified without works of the law, by faith', he made no bones about adding 'only' to 'faith'.

Luther also had no scruples about ranking different parts of the Bible as more or less valuable depending on whether they proclaimed the message which he had discovered. St John's Gospel, Romans, Galatians, Ephesians and 1 Peter were central; so were the Psalms, because they were prophecies of Christ. The Epistle to the Hebrews talks about faith in terms which did not suit him; he correctly recognized from its refined literary Greek that it could not have been written by his beloved Paul, despite the contrary opinion in majority Church tradition, but he also saw it as a confused work. Worse still was the Epistle of James, which seemed to maintain that good deeds under the law were necessary for salvation: 'a very strawy epistle', Luther snarled contemptuously, and he also loathed the book of Esther for its similar implications – let alone the book 2 Maccabees, which provided the traditional Church with one of the few good direct proof-texts for the existence of Purgatory. Fortunately for Luther, 2 Maccabees belonged to a set of books which had always raised doubts among commentators: were they part of the core of the Bible (its canon) or not? Luther answered emphatically in the negative, and in this he was followed by Protestantism generally. In his Bible edition of 1534, he separated out these books, and gave his grouping of them a title that has come into general use: 'Apocrypha'.[36]

Previously, if such breathtaking readjustments of perspective had succeeded in carrying along the mainstream of the Church, it had been because they had been initiated or approved by the Church authorities, Councils or Popes. The papal machine had now failed to give Luther a proper hearing; moreover, the bishops and abbots of Germany, notably Luther's own archbishop Albrecht of Brandenburg, had also failed to heed his prophetic words. So Luther had gone on to appeal from Church to Commonwealth. The supreme secular authority under God, the Emperor Charles V, had in his turn rejected him at Worms. Charles was in fact responsible for creating the first martyrs of the Reformation, when his government in the Low Countries reacted with extraordinary severity to the reforming preaching of Luther's fellow Augustinians at Antwerp: in 1523 the Augustinian monastery buildings there, which were only ten years old, were razed to the ground, and two monks, Hendrik Voes and Johannes van den Esschen, were burned at the stake.[37] Other European rulers like Henry VIII of England, the authorities in Venice and the Spanish governments in Naples and Castile all dutifully burned Luther's books just as the Pope wished in spring 1521, even before the Emperor issued his formal condemnation at Worms. Prompted by the most impressive of his bishops, John Fisher of Rochester, Henry VIII went further, commissioning a team of leading English theologians to help him write a defence of traditional theology, *The Assertion of the seven sacraments*, which he published in 1521. It was a remarkably effective critique of Luther which earned the King the Pope's gratitude and the title 'Defender of the Faith'.[38]

Two possible power-bases for the revolution did emerge outside the Empire and beyond German-speaking lands, but neither fulfilled their early promise. Bohemian Hussites, who happened to attend the Leipzig Disputation in 1519, were surprised and gratified to hear what Luther said about Hus, and provided him with fruitful contacts with the leading Hussite clergy in Prague. However, the Hussite Church proved to be divided between those who saw Luther as the external ally who had been missing for a century and conservative forces who were alarmed at his radicalism and sought a deal with Rome; the pro-Luther faction was roundly defeated in Czech political struggles during 1525.[39] In 1520 the cultured but cruel and power-hungry King Christian II of Denmark, Sweden and Norway, brother-in-law of the Emperor Charles V, invited various reformers to Denmark to advise on changes in the Church. They included Luther's university colleague Karlstadt, who quickly took fright at the unstable political situation and hurried back to Wittenberg – with some reason, because in 1523 the Danish nobility reached the end of their patience and expelled King Christian. Once his Scandinavian empire had fallen apart, the religious situation remained confused in Norway and Sweden, while the new king of Denmark, Frederik, was not as yet prepared to show his hand and reveal that he had genuine sympathy for evangelical reform. Meanwhile ex-King Christian moved to Wittenberg, where he lodged with the celebrated artist Lukas Cranach and loudly proclaimed his evangelical faith, but an exiled monarch who constantly tried to stir up rebellion in his former lands was hardly the greatest asset to the Lutheran cause.[40]

Where else might Luther look for support? He could persist in looking for God's chosen authorities on earth. In the Empire, God-given authority was multilayered, and it might be seen as just as much residing in its princes as in its Emperor. Perhaps they would take up his cause. And what of the imperial free cities, or the independent cities beyond the Empire's borders?

Or what, indeed, of every baptized Christian, who was 'a perfectly free lord of all'? Luther had after all said expansively when reacting against the Church hierarchy in *The Babylonian Captivity* that local communities ought to choose their own ministers. Here was a set of questions with the potential to throw society into confusion, particularly since no one provided particularly decisive answers straight away. The princes of the Empire proved a disappointment, breeding in Luther a lifelong suspicion of their good intentions. Some, like Duke Georg of Saxony, bitterly opposed him, Georg committing the ultimate sin of banning Luther's translation of the New Testament. Even the Elector Friedrich, who had conspicuously abstained along with the Elector Palatine from signing the Edict of Worms outlawing Luther, equally conspicuously abstained from giving any firm backing to Luther's reformation in his territories. Instead, individual towns in Electoral Saxony, and indeed over the next three years most of its towns, introduced measures of reformation as they saw fit. To the south, the wealthy imperial free city Nuremberg continued its medieval initiatives in shaping its own church by allowing evangelical preaching in 1521; this was a very big prize for the cause because the central legal and administrative institutions of the Empire were sited in Nuremberg.

Individual lesser German nobility also rallied to Luther's message. Far to the south-west, also in 1521, an imperial knight, Franz Sickingen, turned his estate in the Rhineland, the Ebernburg, into a refuge for Lutheran sympathizers and a centre of printed propaganda production. To the east of Saxony in Silesia, another knight and a member of the Teutonic Order, Kaspar Schwenckfeld, was an enthusiast for Luther's message as early as 1518. He used his considerable influence over Duke Friedrich II of Liegnitz to introduce reforms to the Duke's Silesian territories, although within a few years Schwenckfeld turned out to be too independent-minded to follow any model of the church which Luther would lay down.[41] Similarly in the German-speaking parts of Bohemia, noble families had many contacts with Saxony, particularly because they were using Saxon experts in developing a mining industry, and from at least 1521 they imported preachers and teachers who peddled the Lutheran message.[42] Overall, then, a confusion of at least three different models of secular authority first came hearkening to the Lutheran prophet – small urban communities with a dubious claim to have any sort of God-given power to make decisions, one major free imperial city and smaller fry among the nobility. None of them represented the elite audience which he had sought to persuade in his *Address to the Christian Nobility*. And now to complicate matters, in German lands far to the south in Switzerland, came stirrings of something different. An independent leader of revolution emerged, who found backing from a great city with virtually no allegiance to the Emperor, and who himself felt no allegiance to Luther: the leader was Huldrych Zwingli, and the city Zürich.

EVANGELICAL CHALLENGES: ZWINGLI AND RADICALISM 1521–2

Zwingli came from the same level of society as Luther. His family, prosperous farmers from eastern Switzerland, similarly sent their brightest child to Basel, Bern and Vienna for the best education available. Unlike Hans Luther, though, they managed to stop their boy from entering a cloister, in this case that of the Bern Dominicans. Instead, after a wide grounding in both humanist and scholastic learning, he returned to eastern Switzerland to become a parish priest at Glarus; he also accompanied Glarus men as an army chaplain on campaigns, when in the customary Swiss style they hired out their services as soldiers to the great powers of the day. In his abruptly truncated public career Zwingli was never to know the detachment from everyday pastoral concerns which was possible for the Wittenberg university lecturer – he managed to master Greek and some Hebrew, not at university but while carrying out his parish duties – and his vision of Christianity was enmeshed in a deliberate fashion in everyday concerns, as Luther's was not.

This was not just a matter of circumstances: Zwingli met Erasmus in Basel and became a thoroughgoing admirer, in contrast to Luther's growing coolness to the great scholar. He grew up in a Switzerland of independent-minded cantons and communities, who had pooled their energies enough to inflict a shattering defeat on Habsburg power in 1499; they felt a pride in their achievement, which bred optimism and combined with a widespread enthusiasm for humanism among the educated and prosperous. It was not surprising coming from such self-confident, self-reliant communities that Zwingli shared in Erasmus's belief that God intended Christianity to be an engine of change and improvement in human society; he also echoed Erasmus's passionate diatribes against war, having experienced its horrors at first hand alongside Swiss mercenary troops, and he warmed to Erasmus's distinctive theological emphasis on the Spirit as a key to understanding God's relationship to humanity. Above all, he was electrified when in 1516 he was able to read Erasmus's New Testament and began comparing the Church of his own day with the Church of Paul and the Apostles.

What, by comparison, did Zwingli owe to Luther? Nothing, he himself insisted, claiming that he turned to Christ and to Scripture in 1516, before there was any public hint of Luther's protest. Zwingli had naturally read Augustine for himself and, like the other humanists whom we have found encountering Augustine (Lefèvre, for example), he could have found the same radical pessimism about humanity's capacity for salvation without Luther pointing it out to him. However, the bad relations which developed between the two men may have coloured Zwingli's later recollections, and the historian Euan Cameron rightly observes that 'if Zwingli really did develop the distinctively "Reformation" message of salvation by free forgiveness, apprehended through faith, simultaneously but *entirely* independently of Luther, it was the most breathtaking coincidence of the sixteenth century'.[43] Certainly Zwingli's path to revolution was curiously roundabout. Like many ambitious medieval clergy, he became a pluralist in 1516, keeping his Glarus parish but spending his time ministering to pilgrims at a famous Swiss Marian shrine at Einsiedeln. In 1518, the year after Luther's indulgence protest, he added an honorary papal chaplaincy to a papal pension which he was already receiving, tokens of Rome's thanks for his efforts to stop Swiss soldiers serving the Pope's enemy the King of France.

At the end of 1518, a post became vacant in the wealthy collegiate church of the Grossmünster in Zürich. After the Grossmünster canons had decided that Zwingli's talents outweighed his shamefaced and penitent admission that he had broken his vows of celibacy with a young woman at Einsiedeln, he moved to this most powerful of Swiss cities, where he would spend the rest of his short life. Zwingli's post was once more pastoral: in theory he was a mere assistant, the people's priest or *Leutpriester* in subordination to the canons of the Grossmünster, but in fact his job was a crucial contact with the people of the city who had come to treat the great church as their own. Straight away on his arrival in 1519 he announced that he would begin systematically preaching through the Gospel of Matthew, brutally ignoring the complicated liturgical cycle of readings from the Bible which the Church laid down. The Book of Acts followed, taking him from the life of Christ to the subsequent founding of the first Christian congregations, and his preaching no doubt intensified for him the sense of how different the Church seemed to be in his own time.

Gradually through 1520 Zwingli's close relationship with his enthusiastic urban congregation began to fuse with his own convictions of the need for church reform, and with the news of disruption in Germany, although there is no evidence that he was reading any of Luther's major works published that year. Late in 1520 he quietly ceased to draw his papal pension; equally without fuss, he was beginning to make powerful friends in the city council, and in 1521, despite increasing worries from conservative canons of the church, he was appointed a canon, thus making him a citizen of Zürich. It was at a time when the Pope had infuriated much of Switzerland by making alliance with the Habsburgs, their traditional enemy: the battle of Bicocca which resulted in the following year caused the deaths of 3,000 Swiss mercenaries, and against the background of everything that was happening to the north in Germany, the old Church's reputation collapsed. Authorities in Switzerland were not going to kowtow to the Habsburgs by publishing Charles V's edict of Worms against Luther, yet neither did they wish to make any positive endorsement of a troublemaker far away in north Germany.[44] Tensions in Zürich must now find a breaking-point.

It was a sausage that proved to be the rallying-cry for the Swiss Reformation. Early in 1522, on the first Sunday in the penitential season of Lent, a Zürich printer, Christoph Froschauer, sat down with a suspiciously biblical tally of twelve friends or thereabouts, cut up two sausages, and distributed them to his guests.[45] Zwingli sat out the sausage, alone among the company, but when the row became public (as was surely intended), he first devoted one of his Sunday sermons to showing why it was unnecessary to obey the traditional Church's order not to eat meat in Lent, and then published what he had preached. For Zwingli, it was a matter of Christian freedom – but there was a crucial difference from the theology presented in Luther's *Freedom of a Christian*. Luther made a sharp contrast between Law and Gospel, so sharp that on occasion he was prepared to say that God had destroyed Jerusalem in ancient times as a divine judgement on the Jewish Law.[46] Zwingli's point in his sermon was that there was no Lenten commandment in the Gospel; it was a human command introduced by the Church, which might or might not be observed, but which obscured the real laws of God in the Gospel if it was made compulsory (see Plate 5). He called the Bible 'the Divine Law'; the Law represented the will of God. So right from this very first pronouncement, which openly identified Zwingli with the developing revolution, he was proclaiming the difference of Zürich's Reformation from the paradoxical message of the Wittenberg reformer.[47]

We must leave the Zürich Reformation, which was about to break, in order to rejoin Luther in the Wartburg at a moment of crisis. The tangled question of what authority had the right to further the Reformation had not been solved during 1521, and the situation in Wittenberg posed the question in ever more acute form; Luther's most important allies in the university in his absence had tried to steer events forward, without his guidance. One was a brilliant but very young man, Philipp Melanchthon, who in 1518 had been appointed professor of Greek in the university aged only twenty-one (and had taken the opportunity to turn his surname Schwartzerd,

'Black-earth', into Greek). He deeply admired his older colleague, and with a natural tidy-mindedness which Luther consistently failed to exhibit, he began reducing the chaos of theological insights which had poured from Luther's pen since 1517 into some sort of shape for people to appreciate as a whole. The result, the *Loci Communes* or 'Common Places' (that is, a topically arranged textbook), was published in 1521, and it was to have a long life in expanded and altered form as a central text of Lutheranism, once something called Lutheranism had begun to emerge.

Andreas von Bodenstein of Karlstadt, as he was commonly known, Melanchthon's senior in years and university office but not necessarily in maturity, was a minor nobleman and a man of impatient temperament and sudden enthusiasms. Karlstadt likewise saw himself as Luther's best interpreter, but in a very different way: instead of clarifying the message, he increased the disorder. During autumn 1521 he tried to put into effect ideas which were undoubtedly present in Luther's writings by preaching against compulsory clerical celibacy and the ritual of the Mass. He turned the priesthood of all believers into excited praise of the Christian wisdom of ordinary people; on Christmas Day he presided at a Eucharist in a common gown, rather than priest's vestments, and he gave both bread and wine to the people. The following day the middle-aged academic got engaged to a fifteen-year-old girl.

Over the next month this logical (or at least predictable) progress in Reformation attracted a number of other people to Wittenberg from elsewhere who were enthusiastic to push the various strands of Luther's revolutionary message still further. Some of them felt, just as Luther did, that they had the spirit of prophecy, yet they did not, like him, simply deliver a message which they thought to have found in the Bible, but they claimed to be receiving new revelations directly from God. Most were from the large Saxon town of Zwickau, which had not been far behind Wittenberg in officially adopting the Reformation, and they were soon known as the Zwickau Prophets. Semi-literate as they were, their charisma impressed thoughtful young Melanchthon: 'for various reasons it seemed as though the Spirit might be moving them', he wrote rather lamely to the Elector Friedrich, two days after Christmas.[48]

Some of the new arrivals wanted to be more radical than Luther about the Eucharist; while he had scorned the miracle of transubstantiation, they now scorned any miracle at all, and said that bread and wine were symbols, aids to memory in recalling the unique sacrifice of Christ, and could not in any sense become the body and blood of God. Karlstadt was struck favourably by this line of argument. Equally he listened seriously when the prophets

The Wittenberg Reformers in their early years.

AETHERNA IPSE SVAE MENTIS SIMVLACHRA LVTHERVS
EXPRIMIT·AT WLTVS CERA LVCAE OCCIDVOS

·M·D·X·X·

*Luther was still living as a monk when Lukas Cranach
the elder created this famous image in 1520.*

*Philip Melanchthon: Jean Jacques Boissard's version of an engraving
by Albrecht Dürer, c. 1526.*

fastened on Luther's insistence on the importance of faith; they consequently pointed out that while every example of baptism in the New Testament involved a confession of faith, it was impossible for small children to exhibit such faith; therefore they should not be allowed baptism. This was very difficult for Luther, for it was both logical and pointed up a real problem in his insistence on making Scripture the touchstone for the essential Christian message. Luther was determined to maintain infant baptism, yet it was clear that the New Testament contained not a single example of it. This was a problem which was not going to be solved simply by his later dispersal of the Zwickau Prophets.

The final straw came when Karlstadt pushed further an implication of one recommendation in Luther's *Address to the Christian Nobility*. Luther had been infuriated by the brand-new Marian cult of 1519 that had been as big an Empire-wide sensation as his own troubles that year – the miracles of the 'Beautiful Mary of Regensburg', whom we have already encountered healing an anti-Semitic demolition worker (chapter 1, p. 19). Accordingly Luther had urged the nobility to see all centres of pilgrimage 'levelled', making the shrine of the Regensburg Mary the climax of his list.[49] It was a small step from advocating destruction of the 'devilish deceit' of sacred places to Karlstadt saying publicly that all sacred images were examples of devilish deceit and should be destroyed. Accordingly, around the end of January 1522, the people of Wittenberg wrecked various specimens of religious art in their churches. The Elector Friedrich was furious: his beloved town and university were in turmoil, and his cousin Duke Georg was enjoying being proved right. Luther must return from the Wartburg to sort out the situation.

So he did, significantly wearing his monk's gown once more, preaching a series of Lenten sermons which were studiously moderate but firm expressions of the need for restraint and order, and summarily ejecting the Zwickau prophets from town – he contemptuously called them '*Schwärmer*' (fanatics). Karlstadt, increasingly at odds with his former hero, was gradually frozen out of the university and within a couple of years he had severed his links with Wittenberg, romantically casting aside his senior academic's gown and proclaiming his commitment to popular religion by dressing as a peasant. He began a life of wandering, ending in a 1541 outbreak of plague in Basel, after a torrid week which began with his complaints that a demon had been creeping around the pews in church while he was preaching – Luther, who was good at nursing grudges, was grimly satisfied by this sensational story.[50] By contrast, Luther would never again stir far from Wittenberg – his outlawed status throughout Charles's Empire in any case made that difficult. His return to the town in March 1522 represented a moment in his career almost as significant as 31 October 1517. He had now seen the effect of letting the idea of Gospel freedom have its head without careful direction. He must now concentrate on creating a shape for what – despite his intentions and his first expectation of ready reforming action from the Pope in Rome – looked more and more like the structure of a Church.

To begin with, this meant choosing which logical paths Luther would take from his earlier writings, and which he would eschew – for virtually everything that had happened in his absence had some good precedent in his own publications. There was not much he could do about the introduction of clerical marriage, which proved very popular with the clergy. In fact in summer 1525 he himself married Katharina von Bora, an aristocratic former Cistercian nun (Melanchthon was hurt and furious at not being invited to the wedding or even told about it).[51] Luther had at first somewhat unromantic intentions to give a good home to one of several destitute former nuns in return for being properly looked after, but Katharina turned out to be a high-spirited, long-suffering and extremely capable partner, who brought him much happiness and much-loved children (chapter 15, p. 650). She presided over a famously convivial atmosphere at the Luther family dinner table, usually with an admiring student or two ready to take down every passing thought or joke of Dr Luther, to contribute to a compilation which was eventually published as his 'Table Talk' (chapter 9, p. 347). The result of Katie's careful budgeting and generous catering can be seen in the marked contrast between the lean austere friar of Luther's first portraits and the married reformer who inspired the proverb 'as fat as Martin Luther' (see Figure 1, Plate 10).[52]

However, on other matters, Luther set up fences against change. On infant baptism, he was immovable. This was a matter of great importance, which straight away made a fundamental choice for the future of the Reformation. Back in the fourth century, the mainstream Christian Church had allied with the Roman imperial power after sudden and unprecedented favour from the Emperor Constantine I, and during the following century it had assumed a monopoly position among the religions of the Empire, establishing the union of religion, culture and society that we label Christendom. Fundamental to this was the principle that all members of society were also members of the Christian Church, and their membership was sealed by their baptism. The Zwickau Prophets threatened the notion of Christendom by rejecting infant baptism, and Luther was as determined to uphold Christendom as was his enemy the Pope. So infants must be baptized, whatever the price in terms of justifying the practice from scripture.

In this, as we will see, Luther was followed by all the mainstream reformers. The upholding of infant baptism became a main characteristic of what historians have termed the 'magisterial' Reformation, the movement of the 'masters' like Luther, Zwingli, Bucer, Calvin or Cranmer, who worked for the reconstruction of Christendom in alliance with the secular magistrates of Europe. But on other subjects, Luther struck a more conservative note than any other major reformer. His deep personal devotion to the Eucharist meant that he went on passionately defending the notion that the body and blood of Christ could be physically or corporeally present in the bread and wine on the eucharistic table: in his favourite simile, they were present as heat fills a piece of iron once fire has heated it up, and there is nothing more physical than the sensation of holding a red-hot poker. Above all, on the matter of images, the issue that had finally brought his recall to Wittenberg, he directly contradicted Karlstadt, and straight away he published those sections of his 1522 Lenten sermons that dealt with that question.

Having already given thought to the problem of sacred art, Luther decided that there was no problem. Once the most obviously absurd images had been removed in an orderly fashion, there was nothing wrong with sacred art in church; indeed, to destroy it meant that it had some power, and in fact it had none, other than to be a witness to the beauty of God's creation and a reminder of the biblical story. What could be wrong with pictures of God's mother or of Christ hanging on the cross? Luther used biblical arguments to justify his position: Moses, he pointed out, had made a brazen serpent, which had only been destroyed by a later king of Judah, Hezekiah, when it had been misused in Israel's worship. Paul the Apostle had gone to Athens and found many images, but rather than setting about them with violence, he had made a thoughtful speech to try to persuade the Athenians not to worship them. In later clashes with Karlstadt, he produced a lasting formula which conveyed the usefulness of images: 'zum Ansehen, zum Zeugnis, zum Gedächtnis, zum Zeichen' (for recognition, for witness, for commemoration, for a sign). After 1525, he rarely felt the need to enlarge on these points (see Plate 6).[53]

ZÜRICH AND WITTENBERG 1522–4

In the future, Luther's beliefs on the Eucharist and on sacred art became major distinguishing features of the Churches that followed his version of Reformation, because now on both Eucharist and images he immediately found himself at odds with the Reformation which was emerging in Zürich. Matters moved steadily forward there in the wake of the Lent 1522 sausage scandal. Very soon afterwards, and not long after Karlstadt in Wittenberg, Huldrych Zwingli got married. Although he kept it secret for the time being to avoid providing ammunition for conservatives, he was happy to be a signatory to a letter to the diocesan bishop at Konstanz saying that clerical marriage was a much better alternative to the notorious propensity of Swiss clergy to live with a woman without the Church's sanction. Published statements of his reforming views followed, and finally his supporters on the city council agreed to attend a public disputation in January 1523, at which he would defend a series of propositions to change the Church.

This was a remarkable occasion. Zürich had no university, nor was Zwingli a monk, so it did not follow the traditional format of the disputations which had figured so prominently in Luther's progress towards revolution. The proceedings were not in Latin but in German, so that the city councillors could understand what was going on. Suddenly the city community, the Commonwealth, was taking on itself to decide the future of its religious life and what it believed, without any reference to the Church dignitaries present – who, in angry awareness of this startling novelty, did not deign to give the occasion respectability by speaking in defence of traditional religion. Accordingly, Zwingli's views won by default, and because of the influential secular backing which he now enjoyed. The Bible was declared to be the only source of doctrine which the city council was prepared to accept.

Zwingli and a small group of colleagues were now only too willing to tell Zürich what the Bible said. It was actually his friend Leo Jud at St Peter's across the river from the Grossmünster who first set a pace which paralleled some of the radical steps already taken at Wittenberg in 1521-2. In a sermon of September 1523 Jud pointed out quite rightly that the Bible ordered the destruction of images, and did so in one of its most prominent and well-known texts, the Ten Commandments, which stated flatly 'you shall not make yourself a graven image, or any likeness of anything . . . you shall not bow down to them or serve them'. Jud was a distinguished Hebrew scholar: he noticed the significant oddity, forgotten by most of the western Church up till then, that there were two contrasting ways of numbering the Commandments. One system, used in the West and in particular given the authority of Augustine of Hippo, numbered the Commandments so as to make this command against graven images simply a subordinate part of Commandment 1 (the number ten was then made up by having two commandments about covetousness at the end). The other system, used by

Judaism (which has in most periods avoided creating religious art involving figures), was also still in use in the eastern Christian Church; this made a separate commandment, Commandment 2, out of the graven image command (see Appendix, p. 711, for the different arrangements).[54] It was obvious that the second system gave the condemnation of graven images extra importance; eastern Orthodoxy was, and remains, scrupulous and completely consistent in observing it by making all its numerous sacred images flat painted surfaces – icons – and maintaining a complete ban on carved statues.

Fairly defensible principles of biblical criticism lay behind Augustine's decision on numbering the Ten Commandments, but it was also easy for the reformers to seize on this as yet another example of the dishonesty of the Pope's Church. Jud gradually publicized his discovery in print, but there is no doubt that before that he was quick to spread the message in Zürich. What is remarkable is that Martin Luther, strenuously maintaining his insistence that images do not matter, refused to follow the Zürichers in renumbering the Ten Commandments. Quite the reverse: as early as 1520, when preparing teaching material on the Commandments, he showed his characteristic ability to play fast and loose with Scripture by omitting all reference to the prohibition on images.[55] The result, bizarrely, is that the churches of western Europe still number the Ten Commandments in two ways, and the split is not between Roman Catholics and Protestants, but between, on the one hand, Roman Catholics and Lutherans, and on the other all the rest – including the Anglican Communion. Great principles were at stake. Where Luther had opposed Law (bad) and Gospel (good), Zürich now opposed Law (good) and idolatry (bad). Zwingli, despite being a talented and enthusiastic musician, even banned music in church, because its ability to seduce the senses was likely to prove a form of idolatry and an obstacle to worshipping God. Turned into a point of principle by Zwingli's successor Heinrich Bullinger, this ban lasted until 1598, when Zürich congregations rose in rebellion against their ministers and successfully demanded the satisfaction of singing hymns in their services, since all the other Reformed Churches did. The printers of Zürich had in fact been happily printing hymnals for those other churches for the previous fifty years.[56]

A great division was being born in Zürich in the early 1520s, which would widen and come to distinguish the Reformed from the Lutheran branches of European Protestantism. For this was not just an abstract debate; the consequence of Leo Jud's preaching was that Zürichers started pulling down images from churches and from the roadside. This frequently involved disorder, and disorder has never appealed to the Swiss. The council had to do something. In October 1523 it arranged a second disputation, with as the main items on the agenda the image question and the allied question of the Mass: was that too an idolatrous image? The result within a month was the first official statement of doctrine produced anywhere in the Reformation, and then action: first images in June 1524 and then the Mass itself in April 1525 became the subject of banning orders by the council, much as a city council might today place parking restrictions on its streets. There could be no better symbol of the way that the Reformation ignored the decision-making structures of the traditional Church and was forwarded by the power of lay authority. Yet till that moment in April, astonishingly, Zürich still remained in communion with its traditional ally the Pope, who had let politics blind him to the seriousness of what was happening there, and who never made any official condemnation of the man who was steering events in the city.

But what form should the Eucharist now take in Zürich, and what theology would be recommended? Here Zwingli took a direction very different from Luther, and with basic principles bearing a marked resemblance to those of Karlstadt and the Zwickau Prophets. Like a good Erasmian, he emphasized the spirit against the flesh, taking one of Erasmus's favourite biblical proof-texts, John 6:63: 'The Spirit gives life, but the flesh is of no use' (see chapter 2, p. 102). Luther, he thought, was being crudely literal-minded to take Christ's statement at the Last Supper 'This is my body . . . this is my blood' – as being true as it stood, and meaning that bread and wine in some sense became the body and blood of Christ. After Luther had jettisoned the idea of the sacrifice of the Mass and the miracle of transubstantiation, why could the obstinate Wittenberger not see that it was illogical to maintain any sort of physical presence in the eucharistic bread and wine? Jesus Christ could hardly be on the communion table when Christians know that he is sitting at the right hand of God (this was an argument pioneered by Karlstadt, which may seem crass now, but which became a firm favourite with anti-Lutherans). In any case, what was a sacrament? Zwingli, as a good humanist should, considered the origins of the Latin word *sacramentum*, and discovered that the Latin Church had borrowed it from the everyday life of the Roman army, where it had meant a soldier's oath. That struck a strong chord in Switzerland, where the regular swearing of oaths was the very foundation of a society whose strength came from mutual interdependence and an overwhelming sense of local loyalty.

So the sacrament of the Eucharist was not some sort of magical talisman of Christ's body, which performed wonders: it was an equivalent of the symbolic and reverent daily saluting of the flag, an expression of the believer's faith (and after all, had not Luther said a great deal about faith?). The Eucharist could indeed be a sacrifice, but the sacrifice was one of faith and thankfulness by a Christian to God – a way of remembering what Jesus had done for humanity on the Cross and the promises which followed in scripture. And what was true for the Eucharist must be true for the other biblical sacrament, baptism. This was a way of welcoming children into the Lord's family, the Church; it did not involve some magical washing away of sin. For Zwingli, therefore, the meaning of the sacraments shifted from something which God did for humanity, to something which humanity did for God. Moreover, he saw the sacraments as inextricably linked with community; the intimate, shared life of a proud city profoundly affected his theology. The Eucharist was the community meeting in love: baptism was the community extending a welcome. And the community was Zürich; Zürich was the city, but it was also the Church, with no sense of separation between the two institutions. This was a nobly coherent vision of a united, godly, well-regulated society, living under God's laws set out in the Bible, a reformed version of Erasmus's vision of how the world might be changed. And it was utterly different from the raw paradoxes about the human condition, the searing, painful, often contradictory insights which constituted Martin Luther's Gospel message.

There were, however, serpents in Zwingli's garden: not angry supporters of the Pope or troublesome Lutherans, but his own most fervent admirers. In the city congregations there were plenty of people with a good humanist education who took up his message, read their Bibles as he told them to do, remembered Erasmus's picture of an informed, rational, active Christian life, and then drew their own conclusions. The cumulative result of these conclusions was to attack the principle which was so precious to Zwingli: the united community of Zürich. Zwingli had followed Erasmus in eloquently advocating pacifism; thoroughgoing or radical Zwinglians pointed out in addition that the Ten Commandments forbade people to kill, and so no one should join an army. Jesus Christ himself further told them not to swear oaths; so they should not take the oaths which the Swiss held so dear.

There was more. If the Eucharist was the spiritual matter which Zwingli made it, perhaps there was no need for a physical sign of bread and wine at all. If baptism was an expression of community faith, a soldier's expression of loyalty, it should not be administered to little children who could not show their faith like that. Many radicals noticed Erasmus's emphasis on Christ's command which is the climax of Matthew's gospel: a 'Great Commission' to all the disciples to go out baptizing all nations, 'teaching them to observe all that I have commanded you' (Matt. 28:18–20). So mission was a duty laid on every Christian; it was not to be left to authorities who might compromise the message and not teach all Christ's commands (like not swearing oaths or refraining from killing, for instance).[57] And if people did not observe all that Christ commanded when they heard it, it might be necessary to withdraw from the wider community, and form groups of true Christians, in order to show the purity which the Gospel as law demanded.

This assortment of views spread very rapidly through the canton of Zürich in the two years from 1523. The success of a radical version of Zwingli's own message was very serious indeed for him because of the great gulf opening up over the question of Christendom, the identification of Church and Commonwealth. The radical view of baptism in particular fatally risked splitting the community. Zwingli's reaction in this respect was just the same as Luther's to the radicals at Wittenberg. He was faced with the same problem about the authority of Scripture: why did the Bible not resolve such a fundamental question as infant baptism in his favour? Like Luther, he was in danger of being forced back unhappily towards saying that there were some things in the life of the Church that had been proved by their long usage in Christianity, even if they were not explicitly described in Scripture. The problem here was that traditionalists were increasingly using this argument to justify many developments in the life of the Church that the Reformers were now condemning; conservatives said that tradition, which was guarded by the institutional Church and ultimately by the Pope, was as important a source of authority as the text of the Bible. It would be safer for reformers to defend infant baptism against the radicals by finding some argument that was indeed based on Scripture.

In fact, Luther had done so, fairly casually, when he was trying to stiffen Philipp Melanchthon's nerve against the Zwickau Prophets back in January 1522. He wrote to his young colleague that baptism was like the ancient Israelite custom of circumcizing male infants, commanded in Scripture to be done on the eighth day. Just as circumcision had been done under the law as the symbol of entry to the old Israel, so baptism was done under grace for entry to the new Israel. Circumcision had been done to infant boys, so baptism could be done to infants on the same basis (the male-centred non-sequitur in the logic did not worry him, although some radicals did gleefully point it out in later years).[58] Luther himself did not go on to make much of this argument, but Zwingli and his colleagues seized on it with enthusiasm. It made much more sense for them than it did for Luther, because they took a much more positive interest in the Old Testament law than he did. Circumcision, as Genesis 17 spells out, was a symbol of God's agreement with his people – it was their covenant or *Bund*. This word meant a great deal to the Swiss cantons and cities, which had fought their way to success and kept their many divisions within bounds by their ability to make covenants with each other. So the place of law or covenant in the theology of the Zürich Church, so different from Luther's attitude, was much reinforced in these very first years by their urgent need to justify infant baptism; we will come to see how fruitfully it developed (in chapters 4, p. 178 and 8, pp. 389–91).

A political and social confrontation loomed in Zürich. The radicals were not anxious to avoid it, for they were becoming increasingly annoyed by what they saw as Zwingli's backsliding, and once more there was a precedent in the symbolic direct action which had been so important to Zwingli himself in 1522: Froschauer's sausage-eating party. Accordingly, in January 1525, a group of enthusiasts in the city baptized each other, some in public and some in private, and some laypeople among them demonstrated the priesthood of all believers by themselves breaking bread and drinking wine. The new reformed establishment, well past its days of making ostentatious gestures with sausages, had to respond: now a third disputation was held, and declared to be a victory for the forces of order. The dissident ultra-Zwinglians were given a hostile nickname which reflected the most threatening thing that they had done: they were called 'Anabaptists', meaning 'rebaptizers'. In a tragic aftermath, legislation of 1526 led to four of them being solemnly drowned in the River Limmat, and radical enthusiasm in the canton of Zürich subsided as quickly as it had begun. Even though only four martyrs ever died in Zürich, this Erasmian, Zwinglian and reformed community had thereby committed itself to a policy of coercing and punishing fellow reformers whose crime was to be too radical. Yet Zürich was not the first reforming community to do this; as we will see in chapter 4, terrible events of 1525 set the precedent. The Reformation throughout Europe was about to turn from popular carnival to something more structured, less dangerous, and more dour.

Perhaps this was inevitable, given the common allegiance of Luther and Zwingli to Augustine and to the theology of justification through grace. In Zwingli, an enthusiasm for Erasmus and a wish to build as perfect a community in Zürich as the great humanist might wish, jostled uneasily with a commitment to Augustine's pessimistic view of human beings' capacity for corrupting all their best intentions. For Luther, the struggle was much less complicated than for Zwingli: he began with a low view of human capacity, and he believed that very few would ever be chosen by God to be saved as true Christians out of the general slavery of sin. It was on this issue of human corruption that Desiderius Erasmus finally chose to confront him. Erasmus, much urged by traditionalist churchman to use his talents against Luther, held back from such a contest for as long as he could, but in the end he chose his issue carefully, to go to the heart of their difference: the question as to whether humanity has retained free will to respond to God's offer of grace. He set out his attack on Luther in a tract of September 1524, *A Diatribe on free will*. Fully aware that he must play by Augustinian rules, he emphasized that the initiative in grace was with God. After that, however, he sought to avoid dogmatism and an assertion of one single truth on grace; for him this was Luther's chief fault. His attack was as much on Luther's way of doing theology as the theology that resulted; it represented the same distrust of absolute claims to revealed truth that had inspired the writing of his *Antibarbari* (see above, p. 113). Luther was exposing controversial questions to public excitement when there was no need to do so. Erasmus preferred to compare opinions, look for consensus, put forward an opinion that seemed most probable – that process is actually the technical meaning of the word *Diatribe*.

Erasmus was a humanist pleading for people to be reasonable – and also saying bluntly that people who were not reasonable should not be brought into technical discussions of theology. Moreover, he believed that human beings could indeed be reasonable, because when Adam and Eve had fallen in the garden of Eden, their reason had not been fully corrupted, only damaged. Luther by contrast was a prophet proclaiming an inescapable message to all fallen humanity. In his response to Erasmus's *Diatribe*, uncompromisingly entitled *Of the slavery of the will* (*De servo arbitrio*; December 1525), Luther set out the full pitiless message that human beings could expect nothing but condemnation, and had nothing to offer God that would merit salvation. 'If we believe that Christ redeemed men by his blood, we are forced to confess that all of man was lost; otherwise, we make Christ either wholly superfluous, or else the redeemer of the least valuable part of man only; which is blasphemy, and sacrilege.'[59] This was the parting blow of his book, and it was the very heart of the Reformation's reassertion of the darkest side of Augustine: a proclamation that the humanist project of reasonable reform was redundant.

Erasmus could not accept this all-embracing view of the Fall. Luther was saying that the Fall made the use of human reason impossible in theology, and that offended Erasmus, who was sure that reason had come through the experience of the Fall wounded but not destroyed; he was highly suspicious of Luther's bold use of paradox in theology, which he felt was a deliberate assault on reasonable argument. It was not surprising that

Erasmus went on fighting, in two bulky and bitter volumes published in 1526 and 1527, in which he showed how Luther had forced him back to reaffirm his loyalty to the imperfect structures of the old Church. 'Therefore I will put up with this Church until I see a better one; and it will have to put up with me, until I become better.'[60] With this weary statement, he was confronting not only Luther, but also his own humanist sympathizers like Zwingli or Melanchthon, who had made the irrevocable decision to favour Augustine's doctrine of grace over Augustine's doctrine of the Church.

THE YEARS OF CARNIVAL 1521–4

Luther's stand against Rome aroused huge popular enthusiasm in the Empire and in German-speaking lands. A seemingly endless variety of individual acts of revolt against the old Church fed off his phenomenal volume of words rushing off the printing presses in both German and Latin. There were 390 editions of various of Luther's writings published in Germany in 1523 alone, and it has been calculated that beyond what he himself had written, around three million copies of related pamphlets (*Flugschriften*, or flysheets, mostly illustrated) were printed in German by 1525; Wittenberg's puny economy now boomed solely because of the sudden growth in its printing industry. Print could take the Reformation to anyone who was prepared to hear a pamphlet being read out or listen to someone explain the meaning of a printed picture. Even women had their thoughts printed to further the cause: a south German noblewoman called Argula von Grumbach briefly became a popular celebrity in 1524 when she published open letters to various representatives of authority, passionately calling them to the evangelical cause – Johann Eck and his colleagues in the theology faculty of Ingolstadt University were among those who came under the lash of her pen. It was a time of what the German historian Franz Lau has called *Wildwuchs*: wildfire-growth, as in a jungle or an abandoned garden.[61]

Why should the words of one German monk have such an impact? We need to remember the atmosphere of tense excitement mixed with extreme fear for the future that we have seen all over Europe around 1500 (see chapter 2). At all social levels, people were expecting something dramatic and decisive to happen. It was a mood which seized peasant women in Andalusia, cardinals in their Roman palaces and scholars in their studies. They were terrified of the Turks, and believed that God had sent the Sultan for a purpose, to show his wrath and proclaim the Last Days. They were also prepared to hear a Christian prophet for the Last Days; some expected it to be a Pope. Half a century ago Owen Chadwick opened a brilliant summary account of the Reformation with the sentence, 'At the beginning of the sixteenth century everyone that mattered in the Western Church was crying out for reformation.'[62] The statement is true but straight away needs modification in two ways: the cry went much further than the elites, and very few people who looked for reformation like this had any idea until Luther came along that the Pope was part of a conspiracy to stop the coming reform. Yet for much of Europe after 1517, the prophet of the Last Days turned out to be Luther; he thought so himself. Many decided to listen to his message that the Pope was the problem, not the solution.

How did Luther achieve this? Here one cannot ignore his individual genius and passion. He spoke at so many different levels: he debated with scholars, shouted from the pulpit, wrote vigorous German and sang his message in German hymns and songs. Perhaps the hymns were the most persuasive to the wavering because they were the least polemical. Luther's impact was naturally greatest on his fellow German speakers, but it was much wider than that in the 1520s. It was not just the impact of print, vital though it was: the Reformation was a matter of the spoken and sung (some might say, the ranted) word, as much as the word on paper. We have seen (chapter 1, pp. 21, 32-3) that the medieval Western Church was a religion full of sermons, that peculiar, intense form of dramatic mass communication that early Christianity seems to have invented: a struggle between the speaker, his God, the text of the Bible and an audience of believers. Now the pulpits stood as a ready-made communications resource, and they were hijacked by scores of renegade professionals, clergy who had been seized by what Luther said. They were furious because they felt that they had been cheated by a papal plot to pervert their own ministry, and that in their turn, their own blindness had led them to cheat their flocks. They wanted to convey their anger to ordinary people so that they might be saved from Hell, and the centre of their message was to expose the complicated mechanism of the confidence trick: the Mass and the industry of intercession for the dead. It is no coincidence that the mood was most intense and the effect most successful in northern Europe, north of the Alps, where the Purgatory industry was at its most developed.

Luther's theme was not just the negative exposure of a con-trick. His proclamation of Christian liberty was particularly fruitful, and it was easy to relate to his attacks on the institutional structure of the Church. The rich variety of the old system of devotion might be a burden both financially and emotionally, with its endless inducements to lavish money on sacred objects or pious practices, and its requirements of regular confession of sin to a priest. Laypeople were flattered at being told that they had been liberated from clerical deception to think for themselves; Zürich had shown the way with its disputations on theology authorized by the city council. Other great German cities like Hamburg followed Zürich's example and held disputations when they introduced Reformation; but it was not just the authorities who felt entitled to exercise this new privilege of making decisions about salvation.[63] Local communities seized what they wanted out of Luther's message, and they added their own grievances and enthusiasms to the turmoil, sometimes ending up with an officially sponsored change in religion, sometimes in a popular uproar. Very many decided that liberty meant that they were free not to pay exactions like tithes to church institutions, particularly abbeys or chantry colleges, from which they drew little direct benefit. That merged with heated rhetoric against clergy generally, which Luther would find difficult to repudiate since he had supplied most of it in and after 1520; clergy were accused of *Totenfresserei*, feeding on the dead, with their cultivation of chantries and endowments for soul-prayers, and of depriving living widows, children and the poor of the means of survival.[64]

Just as in past centuries, rebel clergy gave voice to much of this anticlericalism – especially friars. Social radicalism had always lurked within Franciscan ideology; it may be remembered what an incendiary role they had played in the social hatreds which made the 1514 Hungarian crusade such a grotesque disaster, and how from their earliest years they had nurtured unstable excitements around the prophecies of Abbot Joachim of Fiore (chapter 2 above, pp. 56, 96; and chapter 13, pp. 552–3). Many friars were the loudest in announcing the evidence of the Last Days: they noted with fascination the fifteenth-century Franciscan Johann Hilten's prophecy that a great reformer would arise in 1516, and they enthusiastically echoed Luther's identification of the Pope with Antichrist.[65] Conversely, we have seen that secular clergy had a tradition of envying and distrusting friars, so an attack on the tyranny of confession might really be an attack on the friars' boasts of special expertise in the confessional. At the same time, in countless monasteries and convents, the notion of Christian liberty fused with long evenings spent reading the refined sarcasm of Erasmus about monastic life to send monks and nuns joyfully out into the world to start a new Christian life, which for many meant exploring Christian liberty inside Christian marriage. Not only nuns and monks, freed from celibacy, rediscovered their sexual selves; laypeople trapped in unhappy relationships saw the godly revolution as a possible means of escape from an 'ungodly' partner and a chance for a new start (chapter 15, pp. 647–57).

All these varied and sometimes contradictory strands united to create a world turned upside down. It was wonderfully exciting. A natural way to celebrate liberation in a new world was to smash up symbols of the old oppression. The movement for destruction spread with startling speed during 1524: for the following three years the far north of Europe, all around the Baltic coast, was as full of violence against images as Switzerland, showing that there was nothing necessarily 'Lutheran' about the future of Baltic and north German religion. Just as with most developments in spiritualizing late medieval piety noted in chapter 2, the greatest destructive energy was in towns: peasants mostly preferred to refuse to pay tithes rather than to smash well-loved images. Characteristically also at this stage iconoclasm, like the early Reformation as a whole, was a movement of the young, naturally inclined to celebration and grand gestures. They could act out their sense of their personal liberation from a deception. In Riga (in Livonia, now Latvia) in March 1524, the younger members of a confraternity destroyed only the altar and reredos which their own organization had previously endowed, and left the other images in the church for the moment intact. Even for the older people who did join the destruction, the same demonstration of freedom was compelling. How interesting it is that in regions as widely separated as Germany and Scotland, images of St Francis became and continued to be a favourite target: this might be a mark of hostility to friars, but equally it might be a gesture by exultant former Franciscans, making a special point of humiliating the symbol of their former slavery.[66]

In the same year Riga also witnessed a pioneering but extreme example of the grim humour of iconoclasts as they humiliated objects formerly credited with power. A much-venerated statue of the Virgin Mary in the Cathedral was denounced as a witch, uprooted and ducked in the river Dvina: since the wooden object floated, the evangelical revellers pronounced it guilty and burned it at Kubsberg, the customary place to punish witches. Burning often seems to have been an important symbol: the old Church burned people, calling them heretics, so it was only right for the heretics to burn the trappings of the old Church. Satire merged with carnivalesque celebration and perhaps a fair amount of alcohol at festival-time; in Braunsberg (Braniewo), near Danzig, after a number of hilarious parodies of the Mass, the mayor celebrated Christmas Day 1525 by leading a crowd dressed in festival-season bearskins into the church in order to smash up the images. Significantly in this frontier area of Europe, the reformers did not spare Orthodox churches, beginning in 1525 when a German-speaking crowd destroyed icons in a small Russian Orthodox church in Dorpat (now

Tartu in Estonia). These painted icons were by definition not graven images but Leo Jud's careful elucidation of the Ten Commandments in St Peter's Zürich was a world away from Dorpat in more senses than one. The Orthodox did not forget such outrages: this was yet another layer of wrongs done them by western Christians. Throughout the Reformation they continued to associate their Lutheran neighbours with iconoclasm, long after Luther's revulsion had banished image-smashing from Protestant northern Europe and ensured that Lutheran churches there were full of decorous sacred art.[67]

Predictably, despite his own fiery temperament and dramatically brave personal stands against authority, Luther was horrified at the thought of *Wildwuchs*, spontaneous movements of the people which lacked the control of God's properly chosen representatives. In spring 1522 he had made emphatically clear that he was not going to accept rival prophetic voices when he had expelled the Zwickau Prophets from Wittenberg and snubbed Andreas Karlstadt's enthusiasm for the godly decisions of the people. Yet his own feelings remained confused, as became clear once more when his *bête noire*, Duke Georg of Saxony, sponsored a new saint in 1523, a five-centuries-dead bishop of Meissen called Benno. Luther wrote a vicious pamphlet against this aggressively traditionalist move by his arch-enemy, and had only himself to blame when in 1524 a cheerful crowd at Buchholz in Electoral Saxony enacted a parody of St Benno's new cult using the bones of horses and cattle.[68]

How could Luther stop the righteous indignation which saturated his own writings from moving to other people's direct action? He must turn for help to the lawfully constituted magistrates of the Commonwealth, whom he felt had been chosen by God, as the only powers to protect the Church. Increasingly one text from Romans came to assume a central role for him: it has often been seen, with some reason, as the most important text of the magisterial Reformation – 'Let every person be subject to the governing authorities. For there is no authority except from God, and those that exist have been instituted by God' (Rom. 13:1). And yet also resounding through the Reformation, as much for Luther as for others, was another text from Acts 5:29: 'We must obey God rather than man'. What would happen if the lawful authorities failed to assume the role which he wanted of them? Would Acts 5:29 trump Romans 13:1?

Still not a single prince had declared positively for the reform by 1525. Worse, the support which Luther had gained from knights of the Empire, led by Franz Sickingen, became a disastrous liability by the end of 1522 when their attempt at turning the renewal movement into an armed assault on churchmen with territorial jurisdictions was crushed by an alliance of alarmed princes, and Sickingen was killed. His most brilliant associate, the humanist poet turned reforming propagandist Ulrich von Hutten, was left a penniless fugitive and a few months later died in Zürich of syphilis, a widely known scandal which did nothing to promote the evangelical cause. Thereafter, two contradictory impulses ran through Luther's thinking on authority, and he never really resolved them. On the one hand, he wanted desperately to secure the support of the princes, and on the other, he was concerned to make sure that godly reformation was not threatened by unsympathetic princes. This contradiction was played out against the background of his continuing commitment to the idea of Christendom, which would mark out the future of the magisterial Reformation.

During 1522, before the failure of the knights' rebellion, Luther and Melanchthon had both set out a theory of 'two kingdoms', typical of the strong oppositions to be found within Luther's thought, and designed to preserve the freedom of the true Church against misguided rulers like Duke Georg of Saxony. So they said that it was not appropriate for the Church to exercise worldly government, but nor was it possible for temporal princes to rule in the Church and think that they could do anything to save souls. Then Luther went on in 1523 to publish *On secular authority: how far does the obedience owed to it extend?*[69] A significant feature of this new work was that in the wake of Sickingen's catastrophe it firmly proclaimed the authority of the princes, yet this was still maintained in tension with the two kingdoms theme: the realm of faith needs freedom, but the realm of temporal order needs coercion and rules. True Christians can know clearly where the boundaries lay, but there are very few true Christians, so they ought to submit to worldly powers.[70]

The 'two kingdoms' teaching would come to bear little relation to the future reality of Lutheran Church structures (chapter 4, p. 164), but that was a problem for the future. Immediately striking was that in the same year as he published *On secular authority*, 1523, Luther was still prepared to publish two different treatises affirming the right of congregations to elect their own pastors – in one case addressing himself to an exemplary local community, Leisnig in Saxony, and in the second to his friends in the Hussite Church of Bohemia.[71] This was an affirmation of the rights of ordinary Christians to make decisions affecting God's spiritual kingdom on earth. Luther had not yet seen the full implications of his capitulation to the prince. The traumatic events of 1524–5 now forced him to recognize what they were.

4

Wooing the Magistrate, 1524–40

The year 1524 opened inauspiciously for the scientifically-minded: a conjunction of planets in Pisces suggested a terrible deluge to come. This had been much anticipated all over Europe over the previous few years, and triggered some 160 gloomy new tracts and almanacs. Although the weather was indeed obligingly bad in 1524, including a disastrous hailstorm in July, affecting most of Germany, the actual weather conditions were probably less significant than the widespread panic and dread caused beforehand by the astrological predictions, which only added to the febrile mood of European society, already sent into turmoil by popular Reformation and more than half a century of expectation of the Last Days.[1] Encouraged by this unstable combination, social turbulence boiled over into the so-called 'Peasants' War', Europe's most massive and widespread popular uprising before the 1789 French Revolution.

Trouble started in summer 1524 in south-west Germany, which had known similar risings for more than two centuries, concerned with much the same unresolved issues: landlords' efforts to impose financial and legal burdens on their tenant farmers or *Bauern*. There were certain traditional understandings in such disturbances: the *Bauer* leaders of the disruption were generally the wealthy rural elite of their communities (the English translation of *Bauern* as 'peasants' misleadingly suggests something more humble), the sort of responsible, self-reliant families from whom Luther and Zwingli and so many other clergy had come. Equally, there were well-established ways of negotiating some sort of deal before matters went too far, ranging from mediation by the princes and cities of the Empire to legislation in its variety of courts, right up to the central *Reichskammergericht* which the Emperor had established in 1495.[2] The Reformation, however, injected an extra element of instability; all sides found it more difficult to play by the rules, particularly given the new excitement and bitterness against established authority generated in the years leading up to 1524. The tithe disputes, proliferating from the beginning of the 1520s, were infused with a new self-righteousness on the part of the protesters. Many landlords in renewed dispute in 1524–5 were rich monasteries, collegiate churches or cathedrals; this made the rhetoric of the Reformation a useful extra weapon for the protesters, but it was also a rhetoric much less in the control of village notables.

For this reason, the stakes were fatally raised. Landlords were more defensive and intransigent than before; village leaders lost face when they failed to produce results in negotiations, and consequently more extreme spirits rushed in to take their place.[3] Clashes flared all through the regions fringing the north of the Alps, and then in early 1525 trouble moved northwards in a broad band right across the Empire from Alsace to the borders of Bohemia. The Austrian lands to the east of the Alps, inspired by the exceptional leadership of Michael Gaismayr in the Tyrol, represented a new phase. Far to the east in Hungary, miners went on strike, furious at debasement of the kingdom's coinage, but also inspired (if the papal nuncio was to be believed) by preachers of religious reform. Hundreds of miles to the north, peasants in the Teutonic Knights' territories in the kingdom of Poland rose in rebellion.[4] Jews were among the victims of the uprisings, for they were traditionally seen as in league with the princes and the Church who protected them, part of the conspiracy to undermine peasant prosperity. Even where full-scale rebellion did not break out in northern Europe, crowds went on gleefully smashing religious images. The authorities in the reformed cities of Switzerland managed to contain violence within bounds much more effectively than elsewhere, but they watched their demonstrative radical inhabitants with increasing alarm, fearing greater trouble, and they became convinced that a coercive response was needed: hence Zürich's drownings of Anabaptists in the Limmat (see chapter 3, p. 150.)

Coercion in the Empire was delayed, but when it came, it was far more ruthless than in Switzerland. Most effective military force was initially tied up in the Habsburgs' Italian wars with the French, so it was only after the Emperor had won a shattering victory at Pavia in February 1525 that his soldiers could slowly be marched north across the Alps to begin the counter-offensive. No peasant army proved a long-term match for trained troops, and the repression which followed was as horrible as the affronted representatives of authority could devise: torture and death for thousands who had survived mass slaughter on the battlefield. Reactions to the catastrophe varied; many of the peasants' demands were discreetly conceded, once official vengeance had run its course. The Elector Friedrich the Wise brooded on his death-bed in May 1525 on whether the chaos around him was a punishment on the ruling classes for their years of ill-treatment of the 'common folk'.[5] A less reflective Elector, Cardinal Albrecht of Brandenburg, demonstrated a year later his genius for the inappropriate gesture when he commemorated the peasants' defeat by commissioning an elegant canopied public fountain for the city of Mainz: there it can still be seen standing in the square outside his cathedral.

Martin Luther's response to the two years of mayhem lacked the celebratory frivolity of the Archbishop of Mainz's fountain: he grimly and categorically endorsed the revenge meted out by God's magistrates on earth. In April 1525 he published *An admonition to peace*, directed at peasants and rulers alike, but only a month later, as the Habsburg armies advanced north amid the still spreading breakdown of law and order, he republished his tract with a furious appendix, entitled *Against the robbing and murdering hordes of peasants*. The text of Romans 13:1 sounded a tocsin throughout his biting prose, and it was given a murderous edge that did not appear in Paul's original text: 'Let everyone who can, smite, slay and stab, secretly or openly, remembering that nothing can be more poisonous, hurtful or devilish than a rebel.'[6] This poisonous stuff was made to look even worse because it happened to appear at exactly the moment that the princes of Saxony and Hesse cut to pieces rebel armies at Frankenhausen. Even at the time, respectable folk who were no rebels found Luther's words repellent. The Mayor of Zwickau, who had plenty of experience of popular tumult at first hand, wrote to one of his town colleagues that he could not regard the pamphlet as a theological work, calling as it did 'for the private and public murder of the peasants'. 'Is the devil, and those who do this, to be our Lord God?', he asked with despairing sarcasm.[7]

Luther the champion of the ordinary Christian had been transformed into an apologist for official savagery, for two reasons: his deep disappointment at the untrammelled course of evangelical Reformation, and his uneasy and unspoken knowledge that without his Reformation the events of 1524–5 would never have happened. His own ideas had fuelled the fire. It suited him at the time and has suited varied interest-groups since to portray the Peasants' War as the work of radical fanatics, alien to the true spirit of the Reformations of the mainstream leaders. It is true that very many leaders of radical groups in later years did first spring to prominence in 1524–5: one could point to Balthasar Hubmaier, Jakob Hutter, Melchior Rinck, Hans Hut, Hans Denck. Yet they were radicalized by the experience of the 1525 defeat rather than shaping the peasants' proceedings with their radicalism.

One person in particular has been given a prominence in the events which he does not deserve: Thomas Müntzer, a sometime protégé of Luther's, a sensitive musician and hymn-writer, charismatic preacher and inspired deviser of new liturgies for reformed communities. Newly arrived as vicar of St John's in the Saxon town of Allstedt in the heady year of 1524, Müntzer developed his own ideas about uniting Christian rulers and people in a 'Christian League' against ungodliness. He was happy then to recognize the power of secular rulers, given that the Last Days were at hand – an attitude to worldly power not that different to Luther's at the same time. Unlike Luther, however, he encouraged his flock to iconoclasm and non-payment of tithes in order to usher in paradise. After the Elector Friedrich's family forced Müntzer out of Allstedt, he took up a ministry in the nearby Thur-ingian city of Mühlhausen, jettisoned his interest in enlisting the authorities, and tried to turn the growing disturbances towards his own apocalyptic vision of world transformation.

It was very useful for Luther to draw attention to Müntzer in disassociat-ing himself from the Peasants' War: in his May 1525 tract he insisted 'in particular it is the work of the archdevil who rules at Mühlhausen, and does nothing else than stir up robbery, murder and bloodshed'.[8] Equally, the Communist regime of the German Democratic Republic, building on Marx-ist historical misuse of 1525 from Friedrich Engels onward, found it useful to elevate Müntzer into an earlier incarnation of Lenin. In reality Müntzer was an impractical mystic and dreamer (although his dreams were frequently vicious and bloodthirsty); far from his being a Marxist *avant la lettre*, his talk of the new elect church of the Holy Spirit echoed Abbot Joachim of Fiore, and he had no interest in the material betterment of the poor. His contribution to 1525 was marginal, apart from its result in leading himself and his scanty band of followers to a wretched death.[9]

The aims of most peasant leaders, especially as set out in the Twelve Articles published in the free imperial city of Memmingen in March 1525 and given very wide circulation in print, bore little relation to Müntzer's apocalyptic enthusiasms. Instead, this editing together of a diverse collection of demands from Swabian insurgents was an amalgam of legal, social and economic goals traditional among prosperous *Bauern*, mixed with ideas which sprang out of Luther's 1520 writings; notably, the first article echoed his call for communities to elect their pastors. Rather more ambitious was the programme of reform which Michael Gaismayr created further south in Tyrol beyond the Empire; this was codified after the 1525 defeat in a manifesto for the reordering of his native land, the *Tiroler Landesordnung*. Yet Gaismayr's emphasis was not the other worldly excitement of the radicals, but a coherent vision of a reformed political entity in Tyrol freed from Habsburg rule; it appealed to those such as miners, peasants and lesser townspeople with grievances against the nobility, but it was no more radical than much of the reforming rhetoric of Huldrych Zwingli. Zwingli in fact did have contacts with Gaismayr, and he was aware of the Tyrolean leader's political efforts to form an anti-Habsburg alliance with the neighbouring communities of the Graubünden, Venice and even with the Habsburgs' chief opponent among Europe's great dynasties, the King of France.[10]

PRINCELY CHURCHES OR CHRISTIAN SEPARATION: 1525–30

Luther would not have been surprised by this link between Zwingli and Gaismayr: he was, after all, inclined to dismiss Zwingli as a *Schwärmer*, no better than Thomas Müntzer or the Zwickau Prophets. He would not be able to let himself off the hook so easily: the popular movement of 1524–5 had regarded him as a major prophet and inspiration. It was particularly important that he should repudiate the association because ironically, just at this moment, in spring 1525, significant princes for the first time started unequivocally espousing his movement. Luther's consciousness of this new unfolding of God's purpose may go far to explaining the extreme language of his pamphlet against the peasants. Princes saw chaos surrounding them, and saw the need for action: as we have seen (chapter 1, p. 51), it had long been commonplace for them to regard themselves as the *Landesväter* of their people in all matters, and if that meant breaking with the Church hierarchy, some might well think that a price worth paying.

In a major coup, the first prince to come over was from a rather surprising quarter: he was the current Grand Master of the Teutonic Order, Albrecht of Brandenburg-Ansbach, a Hohenzollern who was a cousin of Cardinal Albrecht of Mainz. The Teutonic Order had met increasing reverses in its long struggle with Poland-Lithuania and, demoralized by major defeats in 1519–21, many of Albrecht's knights had turned to evangelical religion, quitting the Order. To save himself from ruin, Grand Master Albrecht begged another of his cousins, King Sigismond I of Poland, to remodel the Order's Polish territories in east (Royal) Prussia into a secular fief of the Polish kingdom, with himself as its first hereditary Duke; he did his first act of fealty to the gratified Sigismond in Cracow in April 1525. Naturally such a radical step as secularizing the territory of a religious Order needed a formal act of rebellion against the old Church, and the new Duke, who had already sounded out Luther in a face-to-face meeting in Wittenberg in late 1523, institutionalized this during summer 1525, creating the first evangelical state Church in Europe.[11]

Only a little while later than the newly minted Duke Albrecht, the Elector Friedrich's successor Duke Johann marked his accession in Electoral Saxony by abandoning the old Elector's studied caution towards Luther's Reformation and laying the foundations for an evangelical church system. Soon after that in 1526, Landgraf Philipp of Hesse, a young prince who had been prominent in suppressing the peasants, decided that he too would openly bring his territories to the Reformation. Luther never really trusted him, and with some justification in view of the catastrophe that Philipp's marital disorders brought to the Protestants (chapter 5, p. 229); yet over the next forty years the Landgraf was to prove the ablest, most politically competent and resolute princely defender of the evangelical cause in Germany. The university which he founded in his town of Marburg in 1527 (using confiscated monastic revenues and buildings) was the first consciously to be founded outside the papal obedience, ancestor of hundreds of Protestant universities in the future history of western Christianity. Many more princes across the continent might now follow. After Scandinavia's earlier false start in 1520 (chapter 3, p. 135), its extreme southern region, the Duchy of Schleswig-Holstein, began moving towards reformation; the Duchy's Diet declared in May 1525 for pure preaching of the Gospel. The Diet had the quiet backing of its Duke, King Frederik of Denmark, who was meditating on plans for his own newly acquired Danish kingdom – Frederik's son Christian, whom his father soon made Duke of Schleswig-Holstein, had been present at the 1521 Diet of Worms and had been much impressed by Luther's bravery there.[12]

There might be higher prizes still than Scandinavia or the principalities of the Empire. The Emperor Charles V's brother Ferdinand, who, having been born and raised in Spain, found the evangelical revolution profoundly distasteful, nevertheless faced challenges from the representative Estates (assemblies) of nobility and cities in his various central European territories; it was perfectly possible that these powerful political forces might end up successfully putting pressure on the Habsburg family to accept the Reformation. In 1525 the Estates in Upper Austria gave backing to Ferdinand's suppression of the peasant rebellions, but their price for further co-operation in the suppression of Anabaptists was to force him to tolerate evangelical activists and preachers in the mould of Luther. Ferdinand's Estates in the Bohemian crown lands of Moravia manoeuvred him into a similar position when he took the Bohemian throne in 1526 after King

Louis's tragic death in Hungary at the battle of Mohács. This allowed Moravia a century of extraordinary religious diversity.[13]

Given this significant turn in evangelical fortunes, it was not surprising that in that same year, Lutheran sympathizers in the Imperial Diet held at Speyer began setting out a position that became one of the major themes of the mainstream European Reformation, and turned Europe into a geographical kaleidoscope of opposing theologies: *cuius regio, eius religio*. Where you come from decides your religion, and within that region no other can be tolerated.[14] There was a natural corollary of this policy: most regions in Europe were ruled by a monarch, so he (or even she) should make the decision on which religion was to be adopted. Within thirty years there would be few parts of west and central Europe where *cuius regio, eius religio* was not the public position. Very few places came to enjoy the luxury of official co-existence of two religions achieved as early as 1526 in the remote Swiss Alpine valleys of the Graubünden – they could do this because they enjoyed the equal luxury of not having a prince. By agreements made at their chief town of Ilanz, the Graubünden allowed each village to choose to maintain either a Catholic or a Reformed church, without recourse to any external authority; despite much bickering, they kept this arrangement in operation for more than a century, by which time some imaginative thinkers elsewhere in Europe were just beginning to glimpse the sense in the idea.[15]

The spread of *cuius regio, eius religio* meant that monarchs would inevitably assume a much larger role in the running of the Church than Luther's 'two kingdoms' principle had suggested, but Luther now recognized and accepted the inevitability. After 1525 he ceased to talk about congregations electing their own pastors, and he agreed that matters which had in the past been the concern of the Church – administering its landed wealth and providing for the payment of its clergy – should now become the business of the secular prince. This change in direction left Luther's political thought as a tangle of intricate qualifications and balances that has confused observers ever since. Alert opponents like Duke Georg's viciously able Catholic polemicist Johannes Cochlaeus quickly noticed the changes in Luther's message and derided him accordingly, but the logic of events pushed him on further.[16] Matters were made worse because of the widespread popular disillusionment in the countryside about his message in the wake of the events of 1525; his reformation was disintegrating and without guidance from authority it might collapse.

By 1527 the Church in Electoral Saxony was descending into chaos. Luther, himself in the grip of serious and painful illness and increasingly depressed at the mass of unregenerate humanity around him, could see that the only person who could sort the mess out was the Elector Johann. Accordingly the Elector sent out commissions to visit the parishes of his territory and, in consultation with Luther and his colleagues in Wittenberg, issued orders to reform the Church. Luther himself was one of the inspectors, and the results of his investigations of ordinary people's understanding of his evangelical revolution further appalled him – 'Merciful God, what misery I have seen, the common people knowing nothing at all of Christian doctrine – especially in the villages!' He was still convinced that the Gospel would do its job, but he now felt that the Church would have to push the message more systematically: its chief task must be to teach. So he prepared a simple basis for instruction in the form of catechisms, which he constructed in 1529 in question and answer form: a Short Catechism which could be learned by ordinary people, and a larger catechism which was intended for the teachers and pastors who were attempting the task of instruction. They expanded on and explained the texts which everyone was expected to know by heart (and which will be found in the Appendix): Creeds, Ten Commandments and Lord's Prayer.[17] The Short Catechism was destined not only to be a cornerstone of evangelical doctrine – in fact the only universally accepted official Lutheran document written solely by Luther himself – but it was imitated on a huge scale both by Protestants and Catholics, turning its simple instruction into whatever doctrinal paths they regarded as fundamental to Christian faith (chapter 14, pp. 587–8).

Luther continued to regard the Elector Johann's intervention as in theory an irregular action: he later referred to a prince acting in this capacity as an 'emergency bishop', a *Notbischof*, doing his duty not as a ruler but as an ordinary Christian in the absence of competent Church authorities.[18] But in practice the Elector's action set the pattern for monarchical Protestant churches all over Europe in the future. Luther never really reconciled himself to it, still trying to balance Romans 13:1 with Acts 5:29, but Philipp Melanchthon, following Erasmus's enthusiastic humanist discussion of the role of the prince, was much more prepared than his colleague to consider it a natural responsibility of God's anointed in the Commonwealth to have a 'care of religion' (*cura religionis*), like an abbot or a schoolmaster.[19] So the alliance of magistrate and magisterial reformer rapidly hardened after 1525. There was no especial reason why more radical reformers should not have followed Luther in making their own accommodations with the secular power, in some version of his 'two kingdoms' principle, even as they tried to gather their own congregations of the godly out of the unconverted mass of the population; Luther shared their pessimism that more than a minority was capable of real conversion. We have already noted

Kaspar Schwenckfeld's early influence in the Silesian Duchy of Liegnitz; he was a spiritual elitist who nevertheless found it possible to work with a temporal ruler.

Similar possibilities opened up for the scholarly preacher turned Anabaptist leader, Dr Balthasar Hubmaier, who arrived in July 1526 in the Moravian town of Nikolsburg (now Mikulov) in the territory of the Counts of Liechtenstein, on the run from an unpleasant brush with Zwingli and the authorities in Zürich. He had long since repented his part in the anti-Semitic excitement of the 'Beautiful Mary' of Regensburg (chapter 1, p. 19, and chapter 3, p. 142), and was now anxious to promote a humanist evangelical Reformation, further than Zürich would allow. Already back in 1523 in his previous parish, the little German town of Waldshut on the Rhine far to the west, he had inspired the town council to implement Europe's first comprehensive civic reformation of religion, far outstripping anything that Wittenberg, Nuremberg or Zürich had done at that stage, and he had only left Waldshut for fear that his presence might cause Habsburg troops to intervene there. In Nikolsburg he quickly projected himself into a position of extraordinary influence with Count Leonhard von Liechtenstein, and set up congregations throughout the little territory, whose name he affectionately translated as 'Nicopolis', or its early Christian equivalent 'Emmaus', where the risen Christ revealed himself to his disciples. Learning from his own former intolerance, Hubmaier showed his patience with the less idealistic: he had already said after his experience of his previous pastorate in Waldshut that he would baptize infants if the parents 'are weak and still convinced of the need for baptism . . . I am weak for the sake of the weak for now until things improve.'[20]

As a result, Nikolsburg embarked on the road to creating an official Church which accepted the principle of believers' baptism. A more eschatologically minded Anabaptist leader, an Augsburg bookdealer called Hans Hut, then arrived, denouncing Hubmaier as a wicked compromiser with worldly powers. These were now irrelevant to God's purposes, said Hut, since it was clear to him that the world would end in 1528. In a public dispute in May 1527, Hubmaier vigorously defended his Church polity before the admiring Count with all the skill of a professional theologian: while deploring war and violence, he carefully set out a case for rejecting Hut's total pacifism in a manner which Erasmus would have recognized. He kept his nerve in the face of further popular uproar to defend in a second disputation a magistrate's right to use coercion in society. Here was a fascinating might-have-been in the future history of radical Christianity: an Anabaptist state church. Hubmaier was in fact much more positive than

Luther about the power of the prince, because like Zwingli or Melanchthon, he saw the magistrate as ordained by God. Christ's coming in flesh had not removed the God-given legitimacy of secular power, which was made explicit in the Old Testament. Even before Hubmaier had arrived in his favoured political position in Nikolsburg, while still pastor at Waldshut, he had defended the magistrate's right to use capital punishment.[21]

Yet only a few months after the first Nikolsburg disputation, a greater secular power than the Count of Liechtenstein intervened to destroy Hubmaier's Moravian Emmaus: the Habsburgs. King Ferdinand flexed his political muscles in his newly acquired Bohemian lands and forced Count Leonhard to surrender his pastor on heresy charges. After prolonged interrogation and torture, Hubmaier was burned at the stake in Vienna: 'Oh salt me, salt me well!' was his brave essay at donnish humour to the executioners as they rubbed gunpowder into his beard and hair, and at the last he shouted as so many victims did in the flames, 'Oh Jesus, Jesus!'[22] His wife, who had refused to abandon him, was weighted with a stone and thrown to her death into the Danube. It was the beginning of an exceptionally vicious period of persecution throughout the Habsburg lands, scattered from the Danube plains to the North Sea, and in the hereditary Austrian territories of the dynasty, the Lutheran nobility co-operated zestfully with their Catholic sovereign to root out all traces of religious radicalism. The historian of Anabaptism Claus-Peter Clasen has estimated that 80 per cent of a total of perhaps a thousand Anabaptists executed in central Europe between 1525 and 1618 died in the period 1527–33.[23]

The future of Anabaptism lay with the scattered survivors of these years, who now codified their deep disillusionment with all worldly powers, from treacherous backsliders like Zwingli or Lutheran Austrian noblemen to agents of the papal Antichrist like Ferdinand von Habsburg. Now radical spokesmen became steadily more radical in their hopes for the future. One aspect of this radicalism was something which terrified even some radical leaders: women began reconstructing Christianity for themselves. Thoughts previously confined to mystics and nuns were now heard in the streets. Medieval women religious had turned in their imaginations to intimate encounters with God, which were not fettered by the Church structures created by males, sometimes even ignoring the sacraments that the Church said Jesus Christ had entrusted to his male disciples. With no rules in a new situation, some of these explorations turned in strange directions, and they had a traumatic effect on those in the centre-ground of the Protestant revolution. Radical demonstrations of ecstatic religion in north-east Switzerland in 1524 were nearly as disturbing and confusing for male reformers as the violence of the Peasants' War in central Europe a few months later.

Women were not necessarily the only leaders in these incidents, but they seemed shockingly prominent simply because women were not normally in any sort of leadership role. St Gallen women decided to cut their hair short because they said it provoked lustful thoughts in men and so was responsible for sin: no amount of pleading from Johann Kessler, a chief local spokesman for moderate reformation in the town, could persuade them that they had misunderstood what St Paul had told the Corinthians about women and their hair. Magdalene Müller applied the words of Christ in St John's Gospel, 'the way, the truth and the life', to herself, while one of her companions Frena Bumenin, a servant girl from Appenzell, so identified herself with God that she proclaimed herself the New Messiah and gathered disciples. Bumenin's excitement turned to self-destructive delusion, and she became convinced that she was going to bear the Antichrist. The authorities were relieved that after this hysterical climax some women repented of their austerity and refashioned their desecrated jewellery, but a new horror emerged when the women ostentatiously began offering themselves sexually to the men in their devotional circle. 'Why do you judge?' they replied to the appalled townsfolks' rebukes. 'We have passed through death. What we now do is against our will in the spirit.'[24]

This was a new twist to Luther's talk of the 'bondage of the will': one can see how it shaded into some talk of radical male theologians like Andreas Karlstadt about how Christians should passively resign themselves to the will of God, and it had the ring of what some medieval female mystics had said in the privacy of their cells and hermitages about their experience of the divine. Yet it was not surprising that even Anabaptist leaders hastened to put careful boundaries on their movement. A statement or 'Confession' of a fully separatist Anabaptist grouping was agreed in 1527 at Schleitheim on the borders of Switzerland and the Empire. Those who compiled it, the 'Swiss Brethren', looked back to St Gallen and Appenzell and were aware that they were fencing themselves off on two sides: the Schleitheim articles began by bewailing that 'a very great offence has been introduced by certain false brethren among us, so that some have turned aside from their faith, in the way they intend to practise and observe the freedom of the Spirit and of Christ'.[25] Equally important now for the radicals was to regroup after their various sufferings at the hands of secular authorities, and to draw a firm line between themselves and the magisterial reformers, who in the eyes of the Schleitheim group, had committed the fatal error of confusing the Church with the world.

Accordingly the Schleitheim Confession was insistent on 'separation from the Abomination'. True Christians must not indulge in lawsuits in the world's courts, serve in the world's armies or swear the oaths which formed the sinews of everyday life in the outside world, especially in Switzerland. By making all these breaks with the way that fellow Europeans lived, the Swiss Brethren showed their allegiance to a concept which had begun to emerge in Switzerland as the 1524 stirs began gathering momentum: the Church is not truly the Church unless it is suffering, and that is unlikely to be the case with a Church which has identified itself with the interests of secular rulers. 'True believing Christians are sheep among wolves, sheep for the slaughter. They must be baptized in anguish and tribulation, persecution, suffering, and death, tried in fire, and must reach the fatherland of eternal rest not by slaying the physical but the spiritual': the young Zürich patrician Conrad Grebel wrote thus to Thomas Müntzer in 1524, before the tribulation had come.[26] This was a denial of the concept of Christendom, the alliance with worldly power that had sustained the medieval Church and that was now beginning to sustain the magisterial Reformations.

Hubmaier's surviving flock, asked to leave Nikolsburg after his arrest in 1528, added a last component in the spectrum of Anabaptist belief: communal living and community of goods. They sought to move further beyond the Habsburg grip, taking to the road alongside the more radical spirits who had recently shouted them down in the Nikolsburg disputations, and they ended up on the estate of sympathetic gentry not far to the north at Austerlitz (now the Moravian town of Slavkov). Wretchedly poor despite Count Leonhard von Liechtenstein's embarrassed farewell generosity to them, they shared what few goods they had, simply to avoid total destitution. Even if this started as a matter of expediency, once they established themselves as an organized community in their new home and joined with other refugees they agreed in 1529 to make this sharing of goods into a formal principle. Perhaps they remembered Hans Hut's excited command to sell all goods before the world's end (due the previous year), but they were able to look at the Bible and see a model of Christian community in the early chapters of the Book of Acts in which the first Christians held all goods in common. Maybe this arrangement had never existed, and certainly Christians had soon replaced it by more conventional family structures amid wider Roman society. Monasteries and friaries had represented one attempt to recreate it; now the monks and friars had gone, the radical experiment applied the Acts model to a whole society of men, women and children.

The new separated Church was initially under the guidance of an organizer of genius, Jakob Hutter (or Huter), who brought his own much-harried group of radicals from Tyrol to Austerlitz towards the end of 1529. Hutter was himself burned at the stake by the Habsburgs in 1536, but by then his wise direction had overcome the worst of the squabbles inevitable during this brave effort to remould a Christian life; he gave his name to the distinctive communalist separation from the 'Abomination' of worldly Europe, which established communities in defiance of the Vienna authorities. The territory of Moravia gave them the chance, because of the constitutional independence which its rulers had already negotiated from the Habsburgs (above, p. 163): Moravian noblemen and urban dignitaries collectively might not relish experiments in creating new societies, but they were well aware that the Habsburgs liked the idea even less, and that was a very good reason for toleration. In Moravia the Hutterites also found a degree of sympathy from the numerous communities of radical Hussites, the *Unitas Fratrum* or Bohemian Brethren (see chapter 1, p. 37), who had likewise taken advantage of Moravia's benevolent confusion. The Brethren's great fifteenth-century spokesman Petr Chelcický had anticipated some of the Hutterites' own passionate beliefs, such as pacifism and holding aloof from secular politics and administration; the Brethren had already taken an interest in the beliefs of the Swiss Anabaptists who had created the Schleitheim Articles.

More than any other group at the time, the Hutterites came to centre their community life on a group of elders under a principal whom they called a bishop: these elders were responsible for a programme of education, health and sanitation that would set a common standard for all. Under their careful hierarchical direction, the community (*Bruderhof*) pooled its skills in crafts and farming, in a structure anticipating the *kibbutz* movement of modern Israel. It paid much attention to communal upbringing and education for all children: this was the first society in Christian Europe to expect everyone to read and write. The children normally lived not with their families but from the age of two in a dormitory, first at 'small' and then at 'great' school, with regular visits from their parents. That took them up to their teenage years – there was no point in going further, for a university education would draw them back into the corrupt, individual-minded world beyond. Married couples, too, lived in dormitory houses rather than separate cottages. So these were disciplined, busy, self-contained people who belied any paranoid stereotypes of crazed anarchic fanatics – they liked to call their communities 'beehives'. As others started trusting them and they decided to use their industry to deal with the outside world, they made handsome profits from what they made and grew, and the wealth was put back into the community movement, invested in new settlements to accommodate their prolific birth rate. They flourished even beyond the bounds of Moravia: tens of thousands of people were members of Hutterite communities by the end of the sixteenth century.

THE BIRTH OF PROTESTANTISMS: 1529-33

We have noted (Introduction, p. xx) that the name 'Protestant' was the product of political manoeuvres in the Diet of Speyer in 1529: Landgraf Philipp of Hesse was able to unite evangelical-sympathizing free cities and princes of the Empire in a 'Protestation' against the decrees of the traditionalist majority. There could be no better symbol of the deep involvement of the existing powers of Commonwealth in the Reformation movements which followed. But if this 'Protestant' movement had simply been a political alliance, it would have soon found itself in the dustbin of history along with the Boeotian League, the Concert of Europe or the Dreikaiserbund. Instead, it produced enduring Christian identities within a world faith based on the assent of millions of ordinary people. Through the late 1520s and 1530s a real popular adherence to a mainstream evangelical faith emerged out of the widespread sense of disillusionment with Luther after the Peasants' War. Many rural areas took a long time to be coaxed or bullied back into an enthusiasm for the Protestants' message of repentance and free justification of sinners, but still very many thoughtful townspeople made a free decision that the religion of the book offered more to them than the religion of the Pope. Notably Germans, who could sing Luther's hymns and wrestle with the High German text of his Bible, responded quickly. All over the Empire, town councils with sufficient privileged autonomy continued their old tradition of deciding their own religious affairs, and in a great majority of cases that led them to align themselves with the Reformers. They rejected the alarming radicalism of the likes of Hutter, and they were pleased to hear the clerical leadership making the same rejection.

But the same message which had excited so many ordinary people of northern Europe in the early 1520s still exercised its fascination on the respectable burghers and citizens of the Empire. It was the message which Luther took from Augustine's thought and expressed so powerfully in his three great treatises of 1520, and in innumerable other pamphlets, that the laity had been the victim of a cheat. Citizens who believed that it was a God-given duty to spend their money wisely took that idea very seriously: those most affected were likely to be the people who had spent most money on traditional worship. White-hot Catholics, the most devout traditionalists, were likely to become white-hot evangelicals: the Reformation did not recruit the religiously indifferent. Angry and pious folk listened to evangelical preaching, then saw to the dissolution of chantries and indignantly took the jewels, silk and lace from Our Lady's statue. They also realized that once they had decided the Mass was blasphemous and chantries for the dead were a waste of money, they could redeploy a good deal of Church wealth for worthy civic purposes: schools, hospitals, rebuilding the city walls and gates. Inevitably there was much cynical and greedy robbing of the Church's wealth, and not everyone can have arrived at the Reformation through idealism, but we should respect the possibility that many did.

Yet the Protestants also found that they could not maintain a single identity. This was because of the continuing legacy of Augustine's theology on sacraments and grace which seethed through the preaching of reformers across Europe and made them passionate to defend their vision of truth not merely against the anti-Christian old Church, but also against each other's misunderstandings. The years around 1530 saw a process of definition and separation, capped by three momentous failures: unsuccessful doctrinal talks at Marburg in 1529, an abortive effort at Augsburg in 1530 to reunite the whole Church, and then in 1531 a disastrous defeat for the Swiss Reformation. The period also saw the emergence of ideas so radical that it would be a mistake to give them the new name of Protestantism at all.

First in the line of failures was Philipp of Hesse's effort to broker an agreement between Luther and Zwingli; this would have ended the damaging split among magisterial reformers and built on the new Protestant initiative at the 1529 Diet of Speyer. Accordingly, Philipp invited the leading theologians to a discussion (or 'colloquy') in his family's castle crowning the hill of Marburg; Zwingli himself and Johannes Oecolampadius of Basel travelled all the way from Switzerland to meet Luther and Melanchthon. The only real problem was going to be the nature of the Eucharist; whether or not bread and wine duly offered contained the body and blood of Christ: Luther and the Swiss remained silent on their other differences about images to concentrate on this matter. Martin Bucer, the theologically agile reforming leader of Strassburg, had already drawn up a formula about eucharistic presence for the Protestant allies at Speyer, but the Landgraf was now disappointed in his high hopes. Luther had already gone into print in 1527 bluntly describing Bucer, Oecolampadius and Zwingli as 'fanatics' (Schwärmer, like the Zwickau Prophets) because of their eucharistic beliefs; now he set the tone for his own contribution by chalking the words 'This is my body' on the table and then covering his inscription with a velvet cloth. He was not prepared to make any concessions as the Swiss carefully presented their logical humanist arguments, and he reduced Zwingli to near-tears in angry frustration at his crudely expressed intransigence. 'Pray that God will open your eyes!' was one of Luther's passing shots.[27]

This was a great missed opportunity. Even before Marburg, Zwingli had in 1527 summed up his reproachful feelings about the Wittenberg reformer's obstinacy: 'You were that one Hercules who dealt with any trouble that arose anywhere . . . You would have cleansed the Augean stable, if you had had the images removed, if you had not taught the body of Christ was supposed to be eaten in the bread.'[28] Yet having stood his ground at Marburg on the Eucharist to his own satisfaction, Luther was prepared to be sweetly reasonable in drawing up fourteen articles of doctrine on which all the reformers did agree, as well as a final fifteenth which bluntly left the eucharistic question unsolved. These fourteen articles naturally proclaimed the doctrine of justification by faith that all reformers saw as central to their understanding of Christianity, regardless of how they went on to apply the doctrine.

Now the Imperial Diet at Augsburg presented an even broader prospect than forming a common Protestant front: nothing less than ending the dozen years of western Christian schism. Faced with the most dire of Turkish invasion threats in the wake of Hungary's collapse, the Emperor Charles V was desperate to end the distracting quarrel within Christendom. In the course of the Augsburg discussions, Melanchthon used the fourteen articles of Marburg to create a studiously measured statement which he hoped would be acceptable to moderate Catholic opinion and form the basis for further negotiations (Luther was necessarily absent, as in all the major discussions of the next few years, since he was still officially an outlaw of the Empire after the 1521 confrontation at Worms). This new formulation of Melanchthon's was presented to the Emperor on 25 June 1530.

A settlement was not beyond possibility. There were plenty of Catholics in the Empire who were not at all certain that the Pope had been in the right in his quarrel with Luther, and the fact that most of the Emperor's senior advisers were Spanish was not as much of a drawback as it might at first sight seem. Among the most influential was Alfonso de Valdés, twin brother of the mystically minded theologian Juan (who was at that time forced out of Spain because of harassment by the Inquisition: see chapter 5, p. 214). The Valdés brothers, scholarly humanists from a gentry family with Jewish *converso* blood, were *alumbrado* sympathizers (see chapter 2, p. 64), keenly aware of the faults of the old church, and Alfonso, who had himself written Erasmian dialogues discussing Church reform, discovered that he had a great deal in common with Philipp Melanchthon.[29] Moreover, the Emperor's political quarrels with the Medici Pope Clement VII had led him to allow imperial troops in 1527 to sack the city of Rome itself, an extraordinary nightmare month marked by horrific atrocities; there was no guarantee that the multiple and intricate demands of his foreign policy would not lead him to contemplate a further humiliation of the papacy.

The moment passed. Charles V was caught between his longing for Christian reunification and his sense of divine destiny as defender of the Church. Fresh in his mind was his coronation by the Pope in Bologna in February; he was not to know that this was the last time that a Pope would crown a Holy Roman Emperor, and the symbolism of his reconciliation with Clement VII was potent. So Charles hesitated and listened not to Alfonso de Valdés but to the Pope's representative Cardinal Lorenzo Campeggio (whom Valdés detested): Campeggio set a tone of bitter rejection towards the Protestants. Now, far from being a compromise document to reunite Catholic Christendom, Melanchthon's draft found a new career as the 'Augsburg Confession', theological cornerstone for a new branch of Christendom that would soon take on the abusive nickname already applied to it by its enemies – 'Lutheranism'. Moreover, over the next four decades the Confession became the starting-point for drafting many other Protestant statements of faith that did not subscribe to a strictly Lutheran line. At the end of 1530 the evangelical princes and cities of the Empire decided that they must create a defensive league against possible attack by Catholics now that the Emperor had rejected Protestant overtures: they agreed their alliance in the Hessian town of Schmalkalden. Until its destruction in the late 1540s (see chapter 6, p. 271), this Schmalkaldic League was the most powerful Protestant political force in Europe, and what is particularly significant about all its political and military activities is that they were inspired by religious zeal. The League was only in existence to do God's work: it was not merely a diplomatic association of convenience. This did not bode well for the future peace of Europe.

The results of Marburg and the Diet of Augsburg, then, were twofold: they shaped a distinctive Protestantism which could be described as Lutheran, and established its difference from another form of Protestantism that regarded Luther as part of the problem, not the solution. As yet this second alignment was characterized mainly by its lack of deference to Luther and by its general alignment with Zürich and Zwingli, but readers may find it useful to apply the name which emerged for it as boundaries and beliefs became clarified: 'Reformed Protestantism', in which the word 'Reformed' is not a vague adjective but a technical description. In these crucial years, the Reformed had also tried to create a political and military alliance; in 1531 their enterprise crashed in ruin, albeit after an interesting beginning which had lasting consequences. The late 1520s had seen increasing divisions between Swiss cantons and communities accepting the evangelical message and those loyal to the old church. In general, the division mirrored existing social and political cleavages. Evangelicals, following the model of the Reformation in Zürich, appealed to widely based communal forces such as urban gilds, and where they were strong they often combined proclaiming the Reformation with breaking the power of narrow patrician and traditionalist oligarchies, expelling their leading members.[30]

Zwingli encouraged the new evangelical communities to come together in a political alliance, the Christian Civic Union, formed in 1529. It even brought in the powerful city of Strassburg some way down the Rhine beyond the Swiss Confederation's borders, so the Union was an evangelical force with the potential to spread a more communally-based or 'civic' Reformation than was likely to be encouraged by the German princes who later created the Schmalkaldic League. The Union took its cue from Zwingli's vision of his beloved city of Zürich as a united community of Christian believers working to build a godly society; it was also unmistakably aggressive in intention. There is disagreement about the extent of Zwingli's ambitions for the Union, but there is no doubt that his immediate aim was to pull over into evangelical faith the so-called 'Mandated Territories' scattered through Switzerland, which were mandated to be jointly ruled by all the Swiss cantons; with cantons now dividing between reform and traditionalism, these might be manoeuvred towards religious reform.[31] Accordingly, Zürich brushed aside the worries of its evangelical allies and fought a brief war against the Catholic communities in summer 1529. The Peace of Kappel-am-Albis which followed this war was something of a compromise, but Zwingli gained his aim for the Mandated Territories. Following the precedent in the Graubünden, where individual communities had already decided to make choices about their religious future (above, p. 164), he secured the right of each parish or village to choose by a majority of the male inhabitants which religion to adopt; he personally led a vigorous and charismatic campaign with his carefully trained Zürich preachers, which resulted in most communities choosing the evangelical option.

Majority voting was a new idea in communities which had previously made decisions by reaching consensus; it was also an obviously useful device for overcoming traditionalist minority obstruction. Zwingli extended the principle by organizing territorial assemblies, including both clergy and lay delegates who would make common decisions on worship for the parishes of each territory. He thus created the first evangelical church synods, which in many later more fully developed Reformed systems formed part of a tiered structure of such decision-making bodies, some alternatively called presbyteries. This was a precedent of huge significance, not just for Reformed Churches throughout the world but for the shape of western political life generally. Often the English point complacently at their 'mother of Parliaments' as the source of western democratic ideals. They forget that by modern standards there was nothing especially democratic about their parliamentary system for most of its history, whereas the synodical, representative form of Church government in Reformed Christianity was much less inclined than English parliamentarians to show deference to the established hierarchy in society. The synodical model was of particular importance when after 1776 the leadership in the fledgling United States of America drew on its own experience of Reformed Churches in creating its new forms of government. Within western Christianity, synodical systems have come to dominate all western Christian churches over the last century – even Roman Catholicism has begun to be affected.[32]

Zwingli and the Zürich leadership then fatally overreached themselves. Dissatisfied with what they had got out of the first Peace of Kappel, considering it a betrayal of their holy community's war for the Gospel, they imposed economic blockade on the Catholic Inner States of Switzerland. They were then surprised to find an angry and desperate Catholic army advancing towards Zürich territory. Their attempts to stop it were ill-organized and confused: a pitched battle on the mountain slope above the former Cistercian abbey at Kappel turned into a rout. Zwingli, in full armour, was cut down and butchered as his detachment of troops tried to make a stand. Luther's reaction to the news was heartless and also heartlessly repeated, but it was not unjust as a comment on the incongruously military end of the Erasmian pacifist: 'All who take the sword die by the sword'.[33] Poor Johannes Oecolampadius, already gravely ill in Basel, was broken-hearted when he heard about the defeat, and died soon afterwards. It was the end of the Christian Civic Union, the end of fruitful political alliance with the German evangelical cities to the north, and the end of any attempt to impose the Reformation by force in Switzerland.

It was little thanks to Zwingli that his work in Zürich did in fact recover. The city's Reformation was steered back to stability by Heinrich Bullinger, a wise and patient man and a great preacher. He was one of that numerous though officially non-existent tribe, the son of a Swiss parish priest. He had once had ambitions to quit the world altogether and become a Carthusian monk, but now when only twenty-seven he was appointed as *Antistes* (religious leader) in one of central Europe's greatest cities, less than a month after the Kappel disaster, to sort out the mess left in Zürich. Bullinger was notably loyal to Zwingli's memory in his long career as *Antistes*, which only ended with his death in 1575, but he also tactfully and tacitly modified aspects of Zwingli's legacy which might prove troublesome. He soon decided to avoid open involvement in politics either in Zürich or in the Swiss Confederation, although he did insist that his new masters in the city council should be prepared to accept 'Relations', formal private memoranda from their clergy whenever the ministers felt it important discreetly but firmly to make their opinions known to the government.[34] Bullinger's vision of the Church, however, was continent-wide. He made it his life's work to reach out across the divide created at Marburg in 1529 and he did his best to reunite the fractured Protestant world; he became a letter-writer on a scale to rival Erasmus's European-wide correspondence, busily forming friendships by post that might lead to reconciliation or greater understanding. So while he very rarely left Zürich in person, 12,000 of his letters survive, testifying to his spider's web of contacts across the Continent.

Bullinger sensed that in the course of controversy Zwingli had been led into statements about the Eucharist that were too uncompromising or insufficiently nuanced; indeed, before his untimely death, Zwingli had been beginning to explore what might be said about this mystery using the language of presence. Accordingly, Bullinger began trying to find ways of speaking about the Eucharist that might not alienate admirers of Luther. There was no possibility that he would abandon Zwingli's insistence that the value of the Eucharist was as a symbol, but he wanted to say more than Zwingli had done. If we are to do his thought justice in this vital topic, we must not flinch from some discussion which may seem dauntingly technical: the reward will be to glimpse some of the distinctions which were among the most important matters in the world to people in Europe five centuries ago. Accordingly I make no apology for introducing an analysis of how Protestants viewed the Eucharist, developed by a modern American historian of theology, Brian Gerrish.

Gerrish is first concerned to explain how Zwingli and Bullinger differed when they talked about eucharistic bread and wine as symbols. He describes Zwingli as a 'symbolic memorialist'. For Zwingli, the importance of the symbolic bread and wine was that they recalled people to what Christ had done at the Last Supper and on the Cross and so drew them through the drama of the Eucharist towards God's grace; like a memorial statue to a hero, or an *aide-memoire* like the proverbial knot in the handkerchief, they jogged the believer's memory of spiritual truth. By contrast, Gerrish sees Bullinger as a 'symbolic parallelist': he did indeed regard the taking of bread and wine as a memorial drama, but affirmed that in parallel to these physical actions with physical objects, God reaches out to meet his people spiritually and anew. We will see later that John Calvin in Geneva staked out further ground in what Gerrish calls a 'symbolic instrumentalist' understanding of the eucharist, but Bullinger proved sufficiently generous-spirited to find a good-enough agreement with his fellow reformer over their difference (see chapter 6, p. 251).[35]

Bullinger also developed one aspect of Zwingli's theology in a way which set up long-term echoes throughout Reformed Protestantism: his discussion of the idea of Covenant – a treaty or agreement between God and humanity.[36] Here, as with the Eucharist, we must be prepared to find our way through the thickets of the Old Testament as nimbly as any Reformation student of the Covenant motif. We have already noted that God's Law set out in Scripture was very important to Zwingli, not least because it gave him a good reason to justify infant baptism against Anabaptists by analogy with Israelite circumcision, the seal of the covenant (chapter 3, p. 150). The Old Testament speaks a great deal about the Covenant between God and Israel as the agreement to keep his law, but it also develops this simple idea in various ways; it talks about Covenants in different contexts, and with different implications.

Some forms of the Covenant between God and Israel come with divine conditions laid down: so God tells Adam not to eat from one particular tree in the Garden of Eden (Genesis 2:15–17), gives Moses Ten Commandments for Israel to keep (Exodus 34:27) or orders Abraham to institute circumcision (Genesis 17). Others appear to be free gifts from God with no strings attached: Abraham (confusingly) seems to receive one of these in Genesis 15:18; Noah hears that God will never flood the world again in Genesis 9:8–17, and King David proclaims in 2 Samuel 23:5 that God has given him a Covenant. So God's Covenants can be conditional or unconditional.

This rich variety of usages for a fertile concept which is full of hope and reassurance means that the idea can take off in various directions. Where Zwingli had used the theme of Covenant only in relation to infant Baptism, Bullinger organized his whole discussion of Christianity around it, though he still took as his main starting-point the conditional Covenant with Abraham in Genesis 17. God's people must continue to keep his law. In his plan for history, God had fulfilled the Covenant with Abraham by the coming of Christ. So far from seeing God's promise as restricted to the Jews, because it was associated there with circumcision, Bullinger saw the proclamation as being for 'a multitude of nations', as that same Genesis passage also proclaimed – for all people. Now the culminating glory of the Reformation in Bullinger's own day was that it was a renewal of the Covenant, after centuries in which God's people had broken faith with him.

The sacraments of Baptism and Eucharist were the Covenant's marks or 'seals' – a word which went on resonating through Reformed eucharistic discussion thereafter.

Covenant was nevertheless still a divine promise to a single 'nation': so it embraced the people's social, economic and political as well as their religious life (for the Swiss it also reminded them of their own treasured political Covenants). So even if Bullinger personally avoided politics, his theology was full of political and social implications, and that was to be a leading characteristic of Reformed theology thereafter. The Covenant idea went on growing and diversifying, partly because it helped Reformed Protestants find an answer to a great problem posed by Luther's proclamation of justification by faith: how to persuade people to be moral beings if God had saved them without any effort on their part. Luther had provided his majestically paradoxical answer in *The Freedom of a Christian* (Chapter 3, p. 130); not everyone found this adequate, and the idea that God made demands of his chosen people in a Covenant was an attractive one. Later Reformed 'Covenant theologians' built on Bullinger's use of Covenant, especially in England and the Rhineland, and added their own opinions as to how it could be used, with consequences which still resonate throughout the world (chapter 8, pp. 389–91; chapter 12, p. 536).

STRASSBURG: NEW ROME OR NEW JERUSALEM?

All this was, of course, in the future, as Bullinger painfully began his job of rebuilding Zürich's shattered confidence. In 1531–2, a well-informed observer of the developing Protestant phenomenon asked to predict the future centre of gravity in the new movement would look not to the shattered Swiss Protestants, nor even to university lecturers in far-away Wittenberg, but to one of Europe's greatest cities, Strassburg. The leading city in the imperial territory of Alsace, placed both on the Rhine (one of Europe's main water thoroughfares) and on the chief European land route east and west, as well as being on the cultural frontier between German and French-speakers, Strassburg was a bustling commercial and industrial centre of around 20,000 people, an Imperial Free City with a proud tradition of independence; so it was ideally placed to become the capital of the Protestant world. The beginnings were rather like those in Zürich: in 1523 Strassburg's most popular preacher, Matthis Zell, used his influential pulpit in the cathedral to proclaim the evangelical message, provoked widespread enthusiasm, and drew more and more leading clergy to his side. The select patrician elite who dominated the city's affairs carefully and gradually steered it towards the evangelical camp during the upheavals of the 1520s, moving further as the majority among them listened to the preaching in the city churches and themselves became convinced evangelicals; they finally prohibited the celebration of Mass in Strassburg in 1529, the year that it joined the short-lived Christian Civic Union. They took Strassburg into the Schmalkaldic League when it was formed, but for several decades they kept aloof from fully identifying with Wittenberg's Reformation. In these years there was a real chance that Strassburg would gather the diverse strands of reform and become the new Rome for western Christendom – or at least take on the role which Geneva later played for much of Protestantism.

The Strassburg councillors were encouraged to keep their theological options open by the most prominent churchman among the team of talented Protestants whom they employed to channel the city's reformation into disciplined paths: he was a former Dominican from nearby Sélestat in Alsace, Martin Bucer. Bucer has suffered in the story of the Reformation because he left no worldwide 'Bucerian' Church behind him; even Strassburg went in a different theological direction after he left it in 1549, becoming more and more conventionally Lutheran. Moreover, Bucer was a nuanced and subtle thinker whose theology is not made easier to understand by his inability to say anything concisely: Martin Luther (who was irritated by his independence of mind) unkindly but accurately called him a *'Klappermaul'* – chatterbox – and a modern historian has equally acidly remarked of his writings that 'his fairy godmother . . . withheld from him a pleasant and acceptable style'.[37] Nevertheless, even Bucer's enemies and detractors recognized his importance: like Bullinger he devoted himself to Christian unity, but unlike Bullinger, he was not burdened with defending an existing theological legacy. He also cast his net wider, even towards papal loyalists. For that reason European rulers repeatedly brought Bucer into a variety of situations to act as a go-between or a facilitator for advancing particular Reformations.

In negotiations, and in his theological writings generally, Bucer talked a good deal more about the love of God than did many of his fellow Reformers. Moreover, he was capable of seeing the good in people who were deeply at odds; he preserved fond memories of how impressive he had found Luther amid the fast-moving events of 1518, but he was also deeply moved (at least in the mid-1520s) by what Karlstadt and Zwingli said about the Eucharist, and he regained his humanist delight in the wisdom of the early fathers of the Christian Church, more quickly than did most early Protestants. By the late 1520s he was convinced that he held the same beliefs about the Eucharist as both Luther and Zwingli, and that therefore fundamentally they both agreed with each other – a discovery which won him no thanks from either side, particularly when he tried to spin his improbable insight into formulae for agreement. Bucer even saw good in the views of the radical Christians who inspired anger and fear in most magisterial theologians, and he tried to organize the Church in Strassburg in ways which would meet some of their objections to the direction that the mainstream Reformation was taking.

In particular, Bucer stressed the importance of proper discipline in the Church, something that mattered a great deal to radicals who were forming separate communities to preserve their holiness of life. He loved the Epistle to the Ephesians, a detailed blueprint by the Apostle Paul or one of his followers for how a church community should work; uniquely among his large volume of writings Bucer produced not one but two commentaries on Ephesians, at the beginning and the end of his reforming career. Protestants were beginning to discuss how one could distinguish a true Church from the false claims of Rome. Luther expressed various opinions about this, but in general he thought that it had two characteristics or marks: right administration of the sacraments and true preaching of the Gospel. Being a firm believer that the world was about to end, Luther was not much interested in how the Church should be structured, but Bucer insisted that discipline was a third mark of the true Church. He noted with interest what Johannes Oecolampadius had said when promoting the Reformation in Basel in the 1520s: the Church should exercise its own discipline of love over its members, independent of the secular discipline which the authorities of the Commonwealth should impose on their citizens or subjects. Oecolampadius insisted that the new Church, like the old unreformed Church, should have the power to exclude erring members from Communion (excommunicate them), and that this was a sacred duty which was no concern of a secular magistrate. He made sure that this belief was reflected in the way that the Basel Church was officially restructured in 1529.[38]

Oecolampadius's views clashed with the strongly unitary model of church and commonwealth that Zwingli and Bullinger sponsored in Zürich, so he was not much listened to on this matter elsewhere in Switzerland. Instead his discussion of excommunication and church government gained their future through Bucer and some sympathetic reformers in south German cities. Bucer did not always carry the suspicious Strassburg civic authorities with him when he tried to put such ideas on discipline into practice and establish independent structures for the life of the Church, but he impressed many subsequent Protestant thinkers (particularly, as we will see, John

Calvin). So the stress on discipline that was already becoming a feature of radical communities became central to the Reformed tradition as well. Radicals appreciated Bucer's seriousness on this matter. Hundreds of Anabaptists in Hesse rejoined the official Protestant Church in 1538, after Landgraf Philipp had imported Bucer to stage a series of sympathetic and reasonable debates with them: this conversion was a unique event in the sixteenth century, when rulers usually dealt with Anabaptists not by persuasion but by expulsion, persecution and execution, and therefore rarely scored up any success in claiming them from radicalism.[39]

Bucer's open-mindedness and search for peace were shared by his leading colleagues in the city ministry, Wolfgang Capito and Matthis Zell – not to mention Zell's wife Katharina Schütz, a talented hymn-writer of wide sympathies, who had a kindly attitude towards radical spirits and a brusque contempt for male intolerance. She welcomed a wide variety of guests to the Zells' home without enquiring closely into their opinions, saying 'it is our duty to show love, service, and mercy to everyone; Christ our teacher taught us that'. Towards the end of Katharina's life, the ministers of Strassburg (by now stiff Lutherans) refused to officiate at funerals of two sisters from a patrician Strassburg family that had become enthusiastic for the spiritualist teaching of the radical Kaspar Schwenckfeld, himself a former house-guest of the Zells. Indignant at this bigotry, Katharina took it on herself to preach sermons and officiate at the burials of these well-deserving women. She was old and ill herself: on both occasions she had to be carried to the graveside from her sickbed.[40] Such attitudes encouraged a wide variety of highly individual versions of Reformation to develop in the crowded streets of Strassburg.

The city councillors were certainly intolerant of any excitable rhetoric which reminded them of the dark days of social disturbance in 1525: in 1527 they went so far as to execute Thomas Saltzmann for denying that Jesus Christ was God, and in 1533 they drowned Claus Frey, a radically minded furrier, whose radicalism had taken the unusual form of leaving his wife to live with an aristocratic widow whom he proclaimed to be the second Eve and the Virgin Mary. However, in general the Strassburg authorities were prepared to tolerate religious diversity if it did not disturb the peace. Tolerance was good for trade, and it emphasized that they were not going to be pushed around by outside forces demanding religious uniformity. Anabaptists were told to leave the city's territory if they got too tactlessly noisy, but there were ways of surviving.[41]

As a result an extraordinary number of prominent radicals appeared in Strassburg in the late 1520s, and were briefly enabled to discuss and develop

*The leading Reformers of Strassburg: two images from
Jacques Boissard's Icones (1597).*

Martin Bucer.

Matthias Zell.

their ideas and gather disciples. Naturally, there was no room in a tightly regulated urban community for the sort of experiments in communal living that the Hutterites were pioneering in Moravia, but instead a number of creative people proposed new answers to ancient Christian problems, and they also brooded on the future of the Christian Church in God's plan for history. Martin Luther and magisterial reformers of the 1520s like Bucer himself had been radical in their own strictly limited way. They posed a radical challenge to the authority claimed by the western Church's hierarchy, but they did so in order to claim for themselves the first five centuries of Christianity: indeed, the essence of their case was that the official Church had unjustifiably added doctrine to this hard-fought original package. The old Church denied that its medieval additions of doctrine were anything more than developments of the truths which the early Church (culminating with Augustine of Hippo) had discovered; hence B. B. Warfield's insight that the sixteenth-century Reformation was a struggle within the mind of Augustine (chapter 3, p. 111). What happened now, however, was that a great variety of challenges arose beyond the contested area of authority, taking up matters on which Luther, Zwingli and the Pope agreed. More radical spirits denied that the outcome of the early Church's history was the right one, the outcome that God wanted.

We have already seen that Anabaptists in Switzerland and central Europe in the 1520s challenged one basic assumption of Augustine's Church: that Christianity should embrace all society, baptize all society's members, and accept many of society's institutional structures, such as war and private property. Ungrateful for the Emperor Constantine I's alliance with the Church back in the fourth century, they insisted that Christians should return to being a minority community, selected by God to do him glory by suffering in the fallen and evil world. Now some of the radicals who found a precarious haven in early 1530s Strassburg posed even more profound questions about the Church after Constantine: they said that it had radically misunderstood the nature of God. To understand how, we will need to return to that debatable ground which is always lurking behind the Reformation story – the early history of the Church.

The problem lay at the heart of Christianity. It centred on the paradox that the Church in its earliest days identified the crucified man Jesus not merely as the Messiah or Christ expected by the Jews, but as God himself, even though born in human flesh (incarnate) of a woman, Mary. Moreover, Christianity affirmed that this incarnation had taken place through the power of God, the Holy Spirit, which was an active force in the world, and this Spirit could also be called God. So a religion which inherited a strong conviction that God was one, also talked about him in three aspects: Father, Son and Holy Spirit. The Church spent its first four centuries arguing about how this could be. It needed to reconcile its story of a triune God made human both with its Jewish heritage of monotheism and with its Greek heritage from Plato, who said that the ultimate reality of a perfect God could have nothing to do with the confused, messy imperfection of the human world. These theological arguments, which were bitter, intricate and increasingly mixed up in power politics, culminated in decisions made during the fourth and fifth centuries at a series of councils of the Church, from Nicaea (325 CE) to Chalcedon (451 CE).

These decisions envisaged a unity of God that comprehended three persons, Father, Son and Holy Spirit, equal and sharing in substance. The Son was both fully God and fully human, Jesus the Christ. Assertions about this were summed up in two different but similar easy-to-learn statements or creeds, created at much the same time in the late fourth century CE: the Apostles' Creed and 'Nicene' Creed (see Appendix). They are regularly recited at various points in Christian liturgies; they were supplemented at the Council of Chalcedon by a carefully balanced formula about the divine and human natures in Jesus Christ, the Chalcedonian Definition. This completed the Church's official christology (that is, its doctrine of the natures of Christ). We viewed the completed story in dramatic form in the Doom painting of the little Suffolk church of Wenhaston (chapter 1, p. 6), and it lay behind the preaching of eastern Orthodox, western papal loyalist and western Protestant alike. The Protestants acknowledged the value of the first four great Councils of the Church (Nicaea, Constantinople in 381, Ephesus in 431 and Chalcedon), even although they saw later Councils of the Church as having increasingly fallen into error.

Now radicals who believed that Constantine's alliance with the Church had represented a wrong turn for the Church also noted that the following century was the era of those first Councils. No wonder that the more historically aware of them felt that theology decided in this era was tainted: they preferred the pre-conciliar theological genius Origen to Augustine, who had lived in the post-Constantinian era of Ephesus and Chalcedon. Erasmus had discreetly provided them with the pointers to Origen (chapter 3, p. 113): now they began rethinking the problem of the Trinity and in particular the place of Jesus Christ within it. From that starting-point, their radicalism could go in two precisely opposite directions, but both options brutally dispensed with the balancing act of the Chalcedonian Definition, and returned to older alternative christologies, which in different ways were unitarian rather than trinitarian. Some unitarian radicals affirmed that

Christ was fully divine, and that it was blasphemous to suppose that he had any genuine element of humanity. If he had the appearance of coming in flesh, or of undergoing suffering on the Cross, it could not be more than an appearance – a doctrine known as docetism, from the Greek *dokein*, 'to seem'. On the other hand, other unitarian radicals said that the idea of the Trinity was a Nicene (and therefore tainted) doctrine, not seen in the Bible. The unity of God demanded that Jesus Christ the Son could not be considered as fully God in the same sense that the Father was God. Both christological propositions were heard in Strassburg around 1530, but it was the first option which was most loudly proclaimed and which found its home in regions of Europe west of the Rhine.

Several trains of thought, both recent and ancient, converged to deny Christ's humanity and stress his divinity. For many radicals, as for humanist theologians like Zwingli, the place to begin was the hated focus of late medieval western devotion, the Mass. As we have seen, Desiderius Erasmus had habitually stressed the spiritual against the physical; one of his favourite texts was John 6:63. Zwingli followed him in warming to John's affirmation that the spirit gives life and the flesh profits nothing, and on it he had built his eucharistic doctrine of remembrance, denying the physical or corporal presence of Christ in the Eucharist (chapter 3, p. 147, and chapter 4, p. 177). It was not surprising that when such respected authorities distanced themselves from physicality, more adventurous spirits developed the thought. If Christ's body in the Eucharist was a spiritual and not an earth-bound flesh, that had implications for his incarnation on earth. It was logical to suppose that his flesh in his earthly life was created not of the Virgin Mary, but in heaven: it was celestial. That was a good argument to condemn another focus of devotion in late medieval religion which infuriated evangelicals: what they saw as excessive reverence paid to Christ's earthly mother. Moreover, many radicals saw the Church (which was the Body of Christ) as a spiritual community whose corruption came from turning towards the physical world. To be pure, Christ's body must be exempt from such taint.

Besides this rooting in contemporary humanist scholarship, various older theologies made Christ exclusively divine. One strain within mainstream medieval mystical piety had affirmed and meditated on Christ's celestial flesh. A different medieval inheritance came from radicals like the English Lollards or the Taborites of Bohemia, who were angered by the Marian cult and sought to downgrade Mary; they often rationalized their anger by drawing on the ancient male fantasies about reproduction made respectable in Aristotelian biology, where a woman was considered merely as a vessel for the receptacle of male seed. If no male seed was involved in Christ's incarnation, it was logical that he did not partake of human flesh. The eighth-century Byzantine Emperor Constantine V, who was a supporter of the iconoclastic movement seeking a more spiritual Christianity free of images, had expressed the 'vessel' theory of Mary in a vivid metaphor: 'When she bore Christ within her womb, she was like a purse filled with gold. But after giving birth, she was no more than an empty purse.'[42] The Emperor's aphorism had a long history, although the many generations who repeated it over some eight centuries no doubt had little idea of its origin. The common variant motif among English radicals in the sixteenth century was that Mary was like an empty saffron bag, in which the smell of the precious former contents lingered. In the Netherlands of Charles V, Pieter Floriszoon, a tailor in Gouda, said that Our Lady was like 'a sack that had once held cinnamon, but now only retains the sweet savour'; in a rather less flavoursome version, Willem die Cuper said that she was like a flourbag from which the flour had been emptied.[43]

The first known celestial flesh christology of the Reformation came from Strassburg. In 1524 a lay preacher, Clement Ziegler, developed a theory that the celestial body of Christ had existed before he took on visible human flesh at the Incarnation.[44] On this foundation two radical spokesmen from northern Europe, who both took refuge in Strassburg in 1529, built more thoroughgoing but also differing doctrines of celestial flesh: the gentle ex-Teutonic Knight Caspar Schwenckfeld, now in voluntary exile from the official church he had helped to found in Silesia (chapter 3, p. 136), and a leather-seller from the Baltic lands turned wandering preacher, Melchior Hoffmann. Hoffmann produced an alternative metaphor for Mary to that of the bag, unconciously echoing the second-century Gnostic thinker Valentinus when he described Christ as passing through Mary 'as water through a pipe'; he may actually have derived this metaphor from a well-known sermon by a pillar of twelfth-century orthodoxy, the Cistercian Bernard of Clairvaux.[45]

But almost as soon as this series of celestial flesh solutions to the Incarnation problem developed, it was confronted by the opposite form of unitarian radicalism, taking up in more extreme form the same line of argument promoted by Arius in the fourth-century Church: Jesus was not God at all, but a human prophet of God, and the whole doctrine of the Trinity was an unbiblical sham, thought up in the years of the Church's decay. This belief was first picked up by scandalized mainstream evangelicals at trials of radicals in Augsburg in 1527, and paradoxically it was given wider currency among radicals when official publication of statements from the trials deliberately or inadvertently ascribed the doctrine to the widely respected radical leader Balthasar Hubmaier – entirely without foundation.[46] It was developed by a restless and extremely talented physician and scholar from Navarre called Miguel Serveto (Michael Servetus). His views may be accounted for by a sensitivity to the culture wars of his native Spain: he knew how offensive the doctrine of the Trinity was to Jews and Muslims, and wanted to present Christianity more sympathetically to show that it really was a universal religion. He had courteous conversations with Bucer and Capito while he was in staying in Strassburg in 1530, and gained their personal protection, but the following year he profoundly upset his various Protestant acquaintances when he published his first attack on the conventional concept of the Trinity at Hagenau (ten miles to the north of the city). This was only the beginning of Servetus's career of omnivorous intellectual curiosity, much of it spent on the run, which we will find ending in Geneva in one of the most famous of the many martyrdoms of radical thinkers in the sixteenth century (chapter 5, p. 244).

Melchior Hoffmann not only developed a new celestial flesh christology, he also fuelled the excitement about the Last Days so common in the 1520s and 1530s, drawing once more on the literature inspired by Joachim of Fiore, which sought to find God's threefold pattern in the history of the world. Strassburg so impressed Hoffmann that he decided God had chosen the city to be the New Jerusalem, the scene of Christ's return in judgement. He predicted this would take place in 1533, and would be followed by the thousand-year rule of the saints predicted in the Bible. Between 1530 and 1533 he preached this 'millenarian' message not merely in Strassburg but northernwards throughout the Low Countries as far as East Friesland, and he combined his preaching with a programme of adult baptism like that which had spread through central Europe in the 1520s. Unlike rationalist radicals like Servetus, Hoffmann was vitally concerned with mass evangelism, in order to gather the saints in Strassburg. Yet the Strassburg authorities were not grateful for his accolade. Their alarm increased as they were flooded with destitute 'Melchiorite' radicals, who were escaping persecution or simply economic hardship elsewhere, and who took Strassburg's generous and efficient charity provision to be a sign that Hoffmann was right about the New Jerusalem. When Hoffmann returned to the city in 1533 to await Christ's Second Coming, he was arrested.

Baffled by Hoffmann's eloquence, and reluctant to go the way of the rest of Europe by instituting heresy trials against honourable dissidents, the city council refused to put him on trial. They resorted to imprisoning him in vile conditions, hoping that it would make him see sense. Alas for both them and him, Hoffmann remained true to his expectation of the end of the world; he died so obscurely that we have no exact idea how long he survived. It is likely that he spent a decade or so in his wretched cage; thus he outlived the nightmare consequences of his prophetic message in the city of Münster in 1535 (see below, pp. 204–8). The shock of this episode paradoxically sealed the alliance of magisterial Protestantism with the traditional powers of the Commonwealth in Europe, and began to convince some secular rulers that there were worse threats to mainstream Christianity than the Protestant reformers.

KINGS AND REFORMERS, 1530-40

It is worth noting that in 1531 the future of the Reformation seemed to be in the hands of a city council. Various princes of the Empire had now openly declared for the reforming cause, but still not a single sovereign monarch had done so. Moreover, the accidents of heredity meant that evangelical leaders seeking to convert the kings of Europe faced an exceptional generation of talented and long-lived monarchs, all well-established on their thrones by 1530 and mostly destined to reign until mid-century, throughout the two decades of religious realignment that followed. These leaders of the major European dynasties would need a good deal of persuading that Luther, Bullinger or Bucer were any safer investments than Caspar Schwenckfeld or Melchior Hoffmann. Prime among them was the Habsburg world-monarch Charles V, first King of Spain, then also Holy Roman Emperor (1516–55), together with his brother and later successor Ferdinand. Ferdinand was Archduke of the Austrian lands, and from 1526 to 1564 King of Bohemia and (rather more shakily) Hungary. Standing alongside the Habsburgs in the first rank of military, dynastic and political power were the Jagiellon King Sigismond I Stary ('the elder') of Poland–Lithuania (1506–48) and the Valois King François I of France (1515–47).

Lesser kings included the cousins Henry Tudor (VIII) of England and Ireland (1509–47) and James Stewart (V) of Scotland (1512–42). They were both shrewd and touchily proud extroverts who were keenly and jealously aware of King François's easy showmanship and artistic patronage; since their resources did not match their political or cultural ambitions, they were prompted to cast an interested eye on the wealth of the old Church, which opened up possibilities for evangelicals. In the far north, the two newly separated Scandinavian monarchies of Denmark and Sweden remained weak and contested in the 1530s after the 1523 collapse of the Scandinavian Union of Kalmar; only at the very end of the decade did either king made an unequivocal jurisdictional break with Rome, and much remained to be done before Scandinavia experienced fully evangelical reformations in the classic German Lutheran mould (chapter 7, pp. 335–6; chapter 8, pp. 365–7).[47] Progress for Protestantism was at best halting and equivocal in the second-rank kingdoms, while among the 'big three', Jagiellon and Valois proved to be as personally hostile as the Habsburgs.

The Emperor Charles had set his face against religious revolution at Worms in 1521 and Augsburg in 1530, and from the early 1520s he had unleashed a harsh persecution against evangelicals in his Low Countries dominions; yet Protestants could note that he was still intent on reunifying the western Church. Ferdinand was equally savage against Anabaptists where he had a free hand, but everywhere in his fragmented and decentralized dominions he faced obstruction from noblemen prepared to favour the Lutherans or even more radical spirits – often precisely because this annoyed and inconvenienced the Habsburgs. In his Bohemian dominions Ferdinand was further constrained by inherited traditional understandings with the Hussite Utraquists (chapter 1, p. 37). In any case, the Habsburg brothers were rarely prepared to make defence of the traditional Church authorities a priority over the urgent need to defend Europe against further Ottoman advance. The Reformers were naturally aware of these cross-currents, and remained anxious to do business with the Habsburg monarchs.

The Kingdom of Poland and Grand Duchy of Lithuania, ruled as a joint monarchy by the Jagiellon dynasty, comprised the largest single area of territories in sixteenth-century Europe. Even in the early seventeenth century after the loss of some of its lands, it was still twice the size of France, and at its zenith in the fifteenth century it had stretched from the Black Sea to the Baltic, from the Carpathian mountains in the south to Danzig in the north, from the Ukraine in the east to Silesia in the west – a bewilderingly multilingual and multicultural area. In 1500 the Jagiellons also ruled in the kingdoms of Bohemia and Hungary. It was only their disaster at Mohács in 1526 (chapter 2, p. 54) that gave the Habsburg family a territorial advantage over them and moved the centre of power in Europe westwards – another accidental spin-off of Ottoman Turkish expansion. Uniquely among major European kingdoms, Poland-Lithuania straddled the boundary between western Latin and eastern Orthodox Christianity; besides the Commonwealth's twenty-one dioceses of western Latin obedience (all but two of which were in Poland), the vast majority of the Ruthenian population in the Grand Duchy of Lithuania ignored the fairly vestigial Latin Church organization in the Ukraine and looked to the Orthodox Metropolitan (Archbishop) of Kiev.

Another dimension of Jagiellonian Poland was unique in sixteenth-century Europe: the privileged position of the Jews. After 1549, they formed an officially recognized fifth estate of the realm, alongside clergy, nobility, burghers and peasantry. They were no more exotic than the German-speaking governing classes of the towns, and indeed they spoke their own dialect of German richly mixed with Slavic, Hebrew and Romance elements, the language now known as Yiddish (itself a German adjective simply meaning 'Jewish'). King Sigismond himself strengthened their already entrenched legal position in the kingdom, encouraging Jewish immigration from elsewhere and allowing Jews to arrange their royal taxation as they thought best. Like all privileged groups, they attracted jealousy from the less fortunate, who could draw on medieval anti-Semitic clichés, particularly the 'blood-libel', to rationalize riotous violence against them. Nevertheless, the sixteenth century was a golden age for the Jews of Poland-Lithuania: their scholarship flourished amid peaceful conditions, and they began to spread out of the towns and cities into the countryside. There they could enjoy the protection of the nobility, just as Protestant groups did in the same era; landowners found very useful their commercial and administrative skills and their frequent occupation as bankers. However none of these professions were calculated to win the Jews friends among the peasant population of the eastern plains: a long-rooted antagonism waxed and waned, but culminated monstrously in the twentieth century.[48]

Even before the Reformation, therefore, the Jagiellon monarchs could never ignore the fact that their subjects were from two different religions, and the Christians were from two different confessions. From the beginning of the 1520s, the break-up of the Western Church complicated matters still further. Luther's teaching had great impact in the culturally German cities and towns which clustered around the Baltic coast, dominated trade on the rivers inland and were crucial for the Commonwealth's economic life. Lutheran teaching also initially had much success in attracting the Lithu-anian-speaking population away from the old Western Church: they had been excluded from becoming clergy in the Teutonic Order's territories, and even in the Grand Duchy of Lithuania they were largely kept out of impor-tant or wealthy office in the Church in favour of Polish-speakers among the Polonized Lithuanian nobility. Lithuanians thus had an incentive to favour the Reformation if they did not wish to choose the cultural option of identifying with the Polish elite.[49] The first book printed in Lithuanian was an edition of Luther's Short Catechism, published in (Polish) Ducal Prussia at Königsberg in 1547; the Luther Catechism was the second published work in the related language of Lettic, at Königsberg in 1586.

Altogether the monarchy faced a potentially explosive religious mixture, all the more because of the distinctively self-assertive role of the nobility throughout the Commonwealth. Their self-description as *Szlachta* derived from a cluster of Old Low German words relating both to family or race, and the notion of a blow or a strike: so they saw themselves as an exclusive military caste, even prepared to claim a unique racial or biological status. Within this noble caste there was little notion of a separate elite of wealthy aristocracy distinct from lower gentry, and in fact a fierce sense of equality. Forming around a tenth of the population, the *Szlachta* owned perhaps 60 per cent of the Commonwealth's land by the mid-sixteenth century. Their legal and financial privileges grew even in the face of their economic decline, and they were not slow to take action either to defend those privileges or to right any injustices which they perceived in the Commonwealth, relying on a legal institution of constitutional armed force known as 'confederation'. The Polish monarchy could never ignore this formal right of noble resistance: the *Szlachta* came to elect Polish kings, and also enjoyed very considerable constitutional powers of obstruction in the Polish Diet (the *Sejm*). Throughout the Reformation, if a nobleman of the Commonwealth chose to defend a particular religious grouping, there was not much that any external force could do about it.[50]

On this basis, Poland-Lithuania went on to exhibit one of the most richly varied and interesting of all the local religious developments in Reformation Europe. Throughout the century, the Jagiellon kings were never convinced to join any of the many Protestantisms in their territories, but neither were they prepared to do much more than passively support the old Church amid its delicate balancing act of interests within the Commonwealth. Sigismond I and his formidable Milanese wife Bona Sforza were personally opposed to the new doctrines, but were also enthusiastic patrons of humanist learning and literature, which often allied with reformist teaching. On one occasion Sigismond said sarcastically to Johann Eck, 'Please permit me, Sir, to be King of both the sheep and the goats'. Sigismond's son Sigismond II Augustus was a reflective, subtle man, elected king in his father's lifetime and from 1529 ruling as Grand Duke in Lithuania. He took a more favourable attitude than his father to the Protestant activists of his territory, seeing their power-base among the townsmen and the Lithuanians as a useful counterweight to the pretensions of some of his magnates and of the Catholic bishops of Wilno (Vilnius): he announced that he would be 'King of the people, not of their consciences'.[51] Throughout his long reign (he succeeded his father in 1548 and died as late as 1573), Protestants continued to hope that he might incline openly to their cause.

In France it was much more important for evangelicals to win the monarchy's sympathy because a series of French kings had done much to rebuild Valois power and central administrative effectiveness at the end of the ruinous English aggression and civil wars of the fifteenth century, and they continued to consolidate that power. However, as part of this royal agenda, King François I secured a useful deal limiting papal interference within his kingdom through the Concordat of Bologna of 1516 (chapter 1, p. 46). This powerfully inclined him not to disturb a satisfactory working arrangement with Rome, and François was also influenced to be hostile towards the reformers by his mother Louise of Savoy. Louise flexed her political muscles during a brief ascendancy as Regent in 1525, when François was a prisoner of the Emperor Charles V after his defeat and capture at the battle of Pavia: conservative theologians and lawyers in Paris now secured a blanket ban on the publication of vernacular Bibles in France, a drastic end to a pious commercial activity which had previously been a well-developed aspect of the printing industry in the service of the official Church. In an ironical consequence, French Bible-printing was delivered into the hands of clandestine or exiled evangelical publishers for the next four decades.[52]

However, François himself was not especially well disposed towards conservative French theologians: they were often conciliarists opposed to the growth of royal power, and in particular had shown their ill-will towards the 1516 deal with the Pope. Moreover, through his deeply affectionate relationship with his sister Marguerite d'Angoulême the King was in touch at one remove with French humanist circles. Duchess Marguerite, herself an articulate and nuanced writer both on religion and romantic love, was patron to the grouping that included Guillaume Briçonnet and Jacques Lefèvre d'Etaples (chapter 2, p. 93); from 1517 many of them took great interest in Martin Luther, because they initially mistook Luther's doctrine to be the reformist message of their hero Erasmus. Marguerite's part in securing her royal brother's release from his imprisonment in Spain in 1526 consolidated her influence, but his goodwill was undermined by his alarm at growing popular disruption. By the late 1520s, evangelicalism was spreading beyond the beleaguered group of courtly Erasmian writers and senior clerics whom Marguerite continued to protect as much as she could: people were beginning to call the province of Normandy 'little Germany' because of stirrings of activism among its urban merchants and artisans.[53]

A series of violent evangelical outrages were powerful factors persuading François that warnings from conservative clergy were justified, beginning with the smashing of an image of Our Lady on a prominent street corner in Paris in 1528. Immediately, with royal support, this triggered public displays of repentance for the polluting presence of evangelicals in France, a theme which became characteristic of the bitter inter-confessional struggles in the kingdom later in the century: the battered statue became the focus of a traditionalist anti-iconoclastic cult which was strengthened only when evangelicals targetted it for further attack.[54] Even more infuriating for the King, because it touched directly the royal honour and security, was the Affair of the Placards in October 1534. Printed posters ('placards') attacking the Mass were nailed up in prominent places throughout the kingdom, including, many said, the door to François's own bedchamber in his favourite château at Amboise on the river Loire.[55]

This proved to be the turning-point for the King. Two dozen executions followed, and a number of academics and writers who till then had hung on hoping for better times now hastily fled the country. Typically, François soon moderated his position and sought an alliance with the Schmalkaldic League against his enemy Emperor Charles V; he even tried to get Philipp Melanchthon to visit Paris, and in 1536 pardoned French opponents of the Mass ('sacramentarians'). But it was now no longer possible to preserve the polite atmosphere of public non-alignment among Marguerite d'Angoulême's protégés: humanist sympathizers with reform were now being forced to make decisions, and most of the evangelical intellectuals who went into exile in 1534–5 did not come back.

Most significant for the future, not merely for France but for all western Protestantism, was the flight of a young humanist lawyer-academic, Jean (John) Calvin. Calvin's road to evangelical conviction from around 1530 had been as slow and hesitant as for most French humanists of his generation, but by 1533 he was sufficiently openly identified with reformism to make a hasty withdrawal from Paris when his associate, the Rector of the University of Paris, Nicolas Cop, provoked traditionalist fury with a public oration provocatively incorporating evangelical themes and phrases. The Affair of the Placards, and increasing hostile official attention, now convinced Calvin that he must leave France altogether. During 1535–6 he was in the safety and congenially academic atmosphere of Basel, devoting his time to writing a Latin textbook of evangelical faith, *An instruction in Christian faith (Christianae Religionis Institutio)*. It was the first version of the work which all Europe came to know simply as the '*Institutes*'. Applying his formidable powers of organization and presentation to his task, he wrote quickly and effectively, publishing the work (anonymously) in March 1536 even though the preface was only dated in the previous August.

This first version of his work was admittedly comparatively brief, arranged in six divisions deriving straightforwardly from Martin Luther's

Short Catechism, but the remarkable feature of it is that Calvin, an adherent of evangelical theology for only three or four years, had already worked out the main themes that continued to characterize his theology. In the greatly expanded later editions and the complete rearrangement he made in 1559 not long before his death, virtually all the original text is still there. The opening sentence was never displaced, though Calvin enlarged its scope from a reference simply to 'sacred [i.e. Christian] doctrine' to all human knowledge; so in the 1559 version it reads 'Nearly all the wisdom we possess, that is to say, true and sound wisdom, consists of two parts: the knowledge of God and of ourselves.'[56] From this premise, Calvin leaps immediately to another assumption of his book, that was fundamental from 1536 onwards: the result of scrutinizing ourselves honestly after we have contemplated God is bound to be shame. None of our talents or capacities can lift us from this abyss in our fallen state, only an act of free grace from God. This is Augustine restated, the Luther of the *Bondage of the Will* restated. For Calvin the theme of the 'double knowledge' (*duplex cognitio*) lay at the heart of Catholic Christianity, and it was to become his life's work to recall his beloved France to a real version of the Catholic Church.

Symbolic of this agenda, Calvin kept his first preface of August 1535 in all subsequent editions of the *Institutes*. It was a passionate plea to King François to distinguish his loyal evangelical subjects, the true Catholics, from the radical vandals of 1528 and 1534; the King had identified them with the Anabaptists who were being rounded up in the city of Münster as Calvin wrote. Much of Calvin's subsequent development of his theology was designed to show how different he was from an Anabaptist; significantly, his *Institutes* was the first statement of Protestant belief to include a lengthy discussion of civil government (although in later editions he changed his emphasis significantly in this discussion, away from his first enthusiastic endorsement of monarchy). Calvin's preface was nevertheless a piece of self-deception. His own evangelical circles were closely linked with the aggressive demonstrations in France; his assertions that discipline and suffering were characteristic of the true Church were also Anabaptist themes. When preaching in Geneva on that crucial text (Acts 5:29) about obeying God rather than man, he performed an unhappy balancing act when he told his listeners that this was a demand for resistance to the deceitful Church of Rome, but that Anabaptists 'and other fantasists' used it even though they 'only wished to govern themselves in accordance with their foolish brains, under the pretence of wishing to obey God'.[57] Many of Calvin's followers proved indeed over the next century that they could be as destructive and politically revolutionary as any Anabaptist.

Even without that hindsight, the King was unmoved by Calvin's plea, and the lawyer from Picardy was condemned for the rest of his life to look longingly at his homeland from a city which never became home: Geneva. His arrival there in 1536 was an accident: when he left Basel in order to settle in the evangelical Mecca of Strassburg, war forced him to divert from the normal route to make a temporary halt in this city-state on the edge of the Swiss Confederation. Like Augustine long before him in Hippo, the traveller immediately found himself assaulted by passionate demands to stay and do God's work, in this case to consolidate the frail Reformation struggling to take shape in Geneva, which had thrown off its overlord the Duke of Savoy only in the 1520s. The assailant was another French exile, Bishop Briçonnet's former protégé Guillaume Farel, a fiery, headstrong individual whose talents were more for inspiring a crowd to enthusiastic action than organization. Farel now knew that he had found the man who could make up for his own deficiencies.[58]

Calvin could see the potential significance of this city for evangelical revolution. It was even more of a natural continent-wide meeting-place than Strassburg, lying between the French, German and Italian cultural zones and at one of the cross-routes between northern and southern Europe – ideal for infiltrating France. A man with acute political antennae, he may quickly have appreciated the significance of Geneva's political make-up after its recent struggle for independence: the city's small patrician elite had won the victory and there was no strong rival gild system to build exclusive privileges for native artisans and traders to inhibit outside arrivals. It was possible for immigrants, including numerous evangelical-minded refugees from France and Italy, to prosper here, and the city's population was becoming swollen with incomers until it grew larger than its rivals over the Swiss border – Bern or Zürich.[59] So Calvin obeyed Farel's call, but he never forgot thereafter that God had sent him for inscrutable reasons to a city that over the next quarter-century at best admired rather than loved him, and at worst, regarded him as a pest to be eliminated. It is not surprising that as Calvin wrote and preached, his thoughts turned on occasion to the image of Jonah, the prophet whom likewise God sent kicking and screaming on a mission to save the detestable city of Nineveh from its sins: not surprising, moreover, that predestination and an awareness of God's all-watchful providence came to play a central part in the system which his theological successors constructed out of his writings and sermons.[60]

Calvin's first interventions in Geneva were not a success. He and Farel clashed bitterly with the city leadership about the future government of the Church, and in 1538 they found themselves pointed firmly down the road to Strassburg. This humiliation in fact proved an admirable education: installed as pastor to the French exiles in Strassburg, Calvin had the chance to observe how another Reformer, the great Martin Bucer, had to a large extent succeeded in organizing a city-state Church (Calvin also married in Strassburg, the widow of an Anabaptist). He began rewriting and enlarging the *Institutes*, including the production of a French translation which demonstrated his unrivalled mastery of a cool, clear French style. In his new edition of 1539, he paid much more attention to the theology which might underpin a visible, working Church. He did not forget his Strassburg experiences when in 1541 he had the remarkable satisfaction of finding himself invited back to Geneva by a chastened set of city governors. The religious chaos in their city had deepened, and the only remedy they could see was to re-employ their austere former guest. The circumstances of Calvin's return subsequently became his greatest asset: whenever the confrontations which he continued to face in Geneva looked as if they might turn against him, his ultimate weapon was to threaten to leave again – a second withdrawal would have been intolerably embarrassing to the city authorities. So from 1541 he and Farel could settle down not merely to build a version of the true Catholic Church in Geneva, but to use the city as a base for their all-important mission to the France of François I.

Calvin now emerged as the leader among the exiles who from retreats over the French borders discreetly encouraged the small groups of evangelicals who were emerging in towns scattered throughout the kingdom. One of his strategies for basing international religious revolution in Geneva was to develop a printing industry in the city, with a particular eye on the French market. Many exiled Paris printers helped him in this enterprise, which rapidly became a major employer in Geneva, significantly boosted its economy and was yet another attraction for immigrants to the city. Genevan publishers imported to France a fleet of unobtrusive and easily hidden popular evangelical books, of which the bulky 1542 French translation of the *Institutes* was the flagship: an official campaign to burn the books of Calvin and others inaugurated in 1544 made little difference to their distribution.[61]

The evangelical message was encouraged within France by a movement to establish colleges (town schools) independent of church control; inevitably what might start as an assertion of municipal independence against overbearing clergy linked up with ideas of which those clergy might disapprove. Notorious, for instance, was the Collège de Guyenne in Bordeaux, a port whose near access to the Atlantic seaboard gave this Latin school an interesting cosmopolitanism. The Collège's principal teachers were distinguished

Portuguese crypto-Jewish scholars of dangerously individual views, whom the French monarchy nevertheless cultivated because they provided useful contacts with Portugal. Further exoticism among the staff appeared in the 1540s in the form of the brilliant Scots evangelical humanist scholar and poet George Buchanan (later a much-hated tutor to James VI of Scotland). Around thirty such municipal colleges were set up in the three decades after 1530 – a symptom of a situation utterly different from that in German cities and principalities. Without any central organization or open official backing, the towns of France were developing an informal evangelical network.[62] The fact that certain of the kingdom's great noblemen were also moving from the discreetly humanist evangelical sympathies of Marguerite of Navarre towards more open backing for evangelicalism made a new confrontation with the French monarchy only a matter of time. In his last years from 1544 to 1547, King François now set his face against evangelicals: he backed the civil legal authorities in savagely intensifying executions for heresy to numbers never exceeded under his successors.[63]

In the Atlantic Isles, with their two royal dynasties of Tudor and Stewart, Martin Luther attracted an immediate reader in King Henry VIII of England, and his reaction was wholly negative: he threw himself whole heartedly behind the Church's campaign against Luther (chapter 3, p. 135). The subsequent rather convoluted course of the Reformations in the Atlantic Isles revolved around this initial and very public clash: Luther and Henry never laid aside their mutual loathing, and that could never be ignored in Henry's relationship with the academic or popular evangelical activists who emerged in England and Scotland, let alone in his often disastrous relationship with his proud royal cousin James V. It also significantly affected Henry's treatment of the very traditionalist religious practice in his second territory, the Lordship of Ireland, for the King's quarrel was only ambiguously with traditional religion, and much more straightforwardly with the Pope. For this loyal son of the papacy notoriously began having problems with his loyalty in the late 1520s when Pope Clement VII disagreed with the King that God was angry because he had married his deceased brother's widow Catherine of Aragon.

Henry became convinced that his lack of a male heir proved that a previous Pope should never and could never have given him dispensation to let this marriage go ahead; now it must be declared null. This undoubtedly genuine conviction quickly coincided with his discovery of a fascinatingly intelligent and high-spirited new potential bride, Anne Boleyn. The Roman bureaucracy, already infuriated with the English for their reluctance to help the effort to defend Europe against the Turks after the disaster of Mohács, obstructed the annulment of the Aragon marriage, and from the moment when this obstruction became open, at the end of a hearing of Henry's case at Blackfriars, London, in summer 1529, Henry began looking around for an alternative strategy to secure what he and God wanted; he suddenly became alerted to the supposedly ancient truth that he was Supreme Head of the Church within his dominions.

The King now set a new task for his team of theological experts. Previous teams had ghost-written his *Assertion* against Luther and argued for his annulment: now they must show that England was, in contemporary political jargon, an Empire, without any superior on earth. They duly found what he wanted in (among other places) the stories of King Arthur, which appeared to them to be perfectly respectable history.[64] This programme became a series of legislative Acts, steered through the English Parliament between 1533 and 1536 by a new chief minister, the obscurely born Thomas Cromwell, a layman of protean talents, who had risen in the service of the previous humble boy turned all-powerful royal minister, Cardinal Thomas Wolsey. Henry probably did not fully realize that Cromwell was a discreet but highly motivated evangelical. The centrepiece of the new legislation was an Act of Supremacy of 1534, which spelled out without qualification the royal Supreme Headship over the Church of England. Henry had now broken with the Pope, the first king in Europe fully to do so. Now he must decide what this break had to do with the Reformations in progress across the North Sea.

Among Henry's theological researchers was a taciturn diplomat and Cambridge don, Thomas Cranmer, on whom the discovery of the royal supremacy seems to have had a traumatic effect: it propelled him out of his previous conventional piety and distaste for Martin Luther into hating the papacy and taking an interest in the Reformation's message. This crystallized during one of his diplomatic missions abroad, when in Nuremberg in 1532 he expressed his newfound convictions by marrying the niece of Andreas Osiander, the city's leading Lutheran theologian. Cranmer's marriage (see below, chapter 16, p. 650) was only one sign of a cosmopolitan outlook which was destined to bind the developing English Reformation closely into other Reformations on the European mainland. But immediately there was an alarming surprise: Cranmer found that Henry VIII, valuing an efficient and trustworthy royal servant, had chosen him to succeed the late William Warham as Archbishop of Canterbury. Cranmer decided to keep quiet about his wife, returned to England, and went through all necessary formal motions to secure papal co-operation with his consecration in 1533, while secretly repudiating papal obedience. He felt this dubious procedure justified by his genuine reverence for Henry, coupled with his new passion for reforming the Church.[65]

As Archbishop, Cranmer quickly declared Henry's Aragon marriage annulled. Now the new royal marriage to Anne Boleyn could openly be acknowledged. Anne was already Cranmer's patron, and a vigorous and well-informed patron of the evangelical cause: she was a major promoter and importer of evangelical printed literature, especially from France, and had introduced her husband to some important elements of it. She had the perfect opportunity to promote other evangelical activists after an extraordinary crop of deaths of distinguished elderly bishops who might have proved awkward obstacles for the evangelical cause. Between 1532 and 1536 nine died (eight apparently coincidentally of natural causes, one – John Fisher – at the executioner's block), plus a further two resignations, and many of their replacements were effectively Anne's nominees from among her evangelical clients.[66] Cranmer was not only encouraged by Anne, he now worked closely with Cromwell, his old acquaintance. Cromwell did more than encourage church reform amid other royal business: he took it over. The King used his Royal Supremacy to set up the royal minister with a new title as Vice-Gerent in Spirituals (now often carelessly misspelt as Vice-Regent!).

What Henry had done was to delegate his new royal supremacy over English religion to Cromwell: he thus gave him powers in the Church equivalent to those previously enjoyed as the Pope's local representative (legate) by Cromwell's former employer, Cardinal Wolsey. Cromwell seemed unstoppable. When he quarrelled with Queen Anne and helped engineer her downfall and execution in 1536 on absurd charges of incest and adultery, he was able to preserve the quiet progress of infiltrating evangelical Church reforms into the King's dominions (and he took the less steely Archbishop Cranmer with him, leaving Cranmer's former Boleyn patrons a spent force in politics). Their plans were nearly derailed by serious rebellions during 1536 and 1537: first in Lincolnshire and soon afterwards a much larger rising involving most of northern England, which took the intimidating title of 'Pilgrimage of Grace for the commonwealth'. The risings expressed popular fury at the evangelical leadership and their policies, and most northern notables allowed themselves to be drafted in as figurehead leaders for the rebels: the whole 'commonwealth' of the north was making known its hatred of religious change. Henry was outraged by this insult to his majesty: deceiving the rebels with false promises in what seemed their hour of triumph, he engineered their defeat. After cruel reprisals, Cromwell was left more powerful than ever.[67]

Cromwell administered the dissolution of all monasteries over which the

Tudor monarchy had control with remarkable speed and efficiency between 1532 and 1540, thus destroying monastic life throughout England and Wales and in about half of Ireland. The Pilgrimage had been in large measure a cry of anguish at this process: the Pilgrimage's defeat only speeded it up, and may have decided King and minister on making it total. The King no doubt regarded the dissolutions chiefly as a welcome source of cash, but they had the incidental effect of eliminating much traditional religion. Similarly the friaries were dissolved in a single campaign in 1538, accompanied by much negative government propaganda to neutralize public worries: the friars included some of the most effective preachers of traditional faith and thus posed a real danger to Cromwell's plans. The Vice-Gerent also mounted a determined attack on shrines, and with Cranmer's enthusiastic support he began moving against the church furniture and imagery which sustained the old devotion. All the time, however, Cromwell's position was fragile and dependent on the King's favour in the face of a host of aristocratic enemies who resented either his reformist policies or low birth or both. One horrific political mistake proved fatal: he recklessly furthered a fourth marriage for Henry to a German princess, Anne of Cleves, who was convenient for Cromwell's religious diplomacy but who proved sexually repulsive to the King.

In his embarrassment and frustration, Henry started listening to Cromwell's enemies as they pointed out and exaggerated his undoubted evangelical sympathies – not to mention pointing the King back to a pretty young lady at Court, Catherine Howard, who had previously attracted royal attention. In July 1540 the Vice-Gerent was executed on charges of treason and heresy; two days later Henry cruelly emphasized his commitment to his personally devised religious 'middle way' by executing three papal loyalists and burning three evangelicals. One of the latter, Robert Barnes, was a prominent English Lutheran academic, one of very few magisterial Protestant leaders to be burned at the stake in the whole Reformation – and by the Pope's great enemy, the King of England! Richard Hilles, an exiled English evangelical, later sarcastically commented to Heinrich Bullinger that Henry made a habit of celebrating a new wedding by burning someone at the stake.[68] The King soon regretted his rashness in destroying Cromwell, but Cranmer was left for a time without a strong ally to represent the evangelical cause in high politics, and with no asset other than the King's personal affection and trust. The Archbishop narrowly missed suffering the same fate as Cromwell in 1543, and only gradually in the old King's last seven unpredictable years did Henry's complex religious views begin moving crabwise in an evangelical direction.[69]

Ireland's puppet Parliament dutifully shadowed English Reformation legislation, but it could only be enforced in areas of effective English rule in eastern Ireland (the 'Pale of Dublin'). Equally, evangelical religious policies exported to Ireland on the back of the break with Rome produced meagre results. George Browne, an Englishman and a former friar made Archbishop of Dublin to enforce the Cromwellian religious changes, found that his clergy adamantly refused to take part in the preaching campaign which he ordered; he found little support from the Dublin royal administration, and after 1540 he lapsed into intimidated passivity. Royal government in Ireland was conscious of its fragility, and without Cromwell's prodding it was not prepared to confront conservatives. Dublin governors were traumatized by a major rebellion staged in 1534 by the King's Vice-Deputy of Ireland, Lord Thomas Fitzgerald, son of the ninth Earl of Kildare and so heir of the island's greatest magnate family. Fitzgerald demanded that the Irish take an oath to the Pope, Charles V and himself, and a substantial part of the community even in the Pale was willing to make this complete transfer of allegiance away from the Tudor Crown.

Such an ideological component had no precedent in medieval Ireland's frequent rebellions, and this was perhaps the first incident in Europe to reveal how the Reformation or those who hated it might unseat a dynasty. Fitzgerald was defeated only with difficulty; thereafter Henry's administration was very cautious about alterations to Irish religion. Until the King's death, the island enjoyed Catholic religious practice without the Pope – there was none of the continued innovation which England and Wales experienced.[70] Typically, Henry did emphasize the exclusive nature of his royal relationship with God by changing the political status of Ireland. Previously it was a lordship of the English Crown; in 1541 the Dublin Parliament obediently followed Henry VIII's wishes and proclaimed Ireland a kingdom of itself, separate from the English Crown. Far from an Irish declaration of independence, this enabled Henry to begin tidily binding the chief powers in Ireland more closely to English forms of government, and the move had a second important dimension. It was widely believed that back in the twelfth century the English-born Pope Adrian IV had granted Henry II of England the Lordship of Ireland by a papal Bull. Henry's Tudor namesake could not abide that thought, and so he proclaimed his own sovereign independence just to emphasize that the papacy had no power to hand out territory to secular rulers.

Even before Thomas Cromwell steered Henry VIII towards involvement with the Reformation, evangelical ideas found a popular response in some parts of England and Scotland. In both kingdoms, academics and merchants with Continental links were prominent in bringing ideas over, but penetration was small-scale until a sudden burst of enthusiastic activity inspired by the arrival of the first English printed New Testaments. This translation was the work of an Oxford scholar in exile, William Tyndale, and published abroad in 1525-6. Tyndale came from the remote west-country Forest of Dean on the borders of Wales, and it is not fanciful to see his fascination with translation as springing out of market-days in his childhood, listening to the mixed babble of Welsh and English around him.[71] He was a gourmet of language: he was delighted that he could use two good Anglo-Saxon words, 'gospel' and 'worship', when biblical translators into other languages were stuck with versions of Greek '*euaggelion*' and Latin '*cultus*', and it also pleased him to discover – as he moved into translating the Old Testament – that Hebrew and English were so much more compatible than Hebrew and Greek.

Tyndale's Bible translation, together with the completions of it made by his assistants, formed the basis of all subsequent English Bibles up to the twentieth century: it has had a huge impact on the future of the English-speaking world. Surreptitiously read and discussed during the 1520s and 1530s, it worked on the imaginations of those who had no access to public preaching because of official repression or lack of provision. It may be significant that there was a perceptible nationwide decline in ordinations in England during the 1520s: perhaps the traditional Church was losing its grip on those thinking of a clerical career. Tyndale was the first biblical translator of the Reformation to die – arrested and strangled in his Low Countries exile by the Holy Roman Emperor's officials with the connivance of the Bishop of London and Henry VIII. Yet even before the time of Tyndale's martyrdom in 1536, perhaps 16,000 copies of his translation had passed into England, a country of no more than two and a half million people, with at that stage a very poorly developed market for books.[72]

Cromwell and Cranmer began the slow work of supplementing this Bible-reading by recruiting and financing preachers. In 1537 Cromwell also persuaded Henry VIII to order general provision of English Bibles for parish churches, and further promoted an official translation in 1539. Even after Cromwell's fall, Henry himself gave the parishes an effective extra spur to provide Bibles in 1541 by the threat of fines if they did not. The resulting popular enthusiasm for the Bible was sufficiently noticeable for the King to take fright. In 1543 he pushed Parliament into ordering that only upper status groups in society, presumably deemed less excitable, should be allowed to read it at all. Interestingly, in the same year the Scottish Parliament, dominated after James V's death by a regency regime toying with church reform, passed an Act which for the first time allowed lieges, that is landowners, to possess the Bible; the Scots were thus newly allowed access to the Bible approximately equivalent to its newly restricted access in England. It was a brief moment of concession: for the most part, successive Scottish governments in the 1530s and 1540s remained hostile to the Reformation and did their best to curb its growth.

In both England and Scotland between the 1520s and 1550s, enthusiastic evangelical communities took shape in ports all along the east coast, despite hostility to begin with from both Henry VIII and James V. In south-east England, evangelical activists merged inland into pre-existing Lollard groups. Probably ordinary people were more affected than clergy and the landed elite, who had more emotional and financial investment in the old system. For Scottish evangelicals, traditional trading links with the Baltic and north Germany were initially as important as those with England; they therefore had a direct relationship with the rapidly institutional-izing Lutheran churches that was not so easy for the English, faced with Henry VIII's studied hostility to Martin Luther. However, Scottish reform-ers did not gain even a limited foothold in James V's government, unlike Thomas Cromwell and Thomas Cranmer in 1530s England, and Scotland failed to follow the example of the similar northern kingdoms, Denmark and Sweden, which in the 1530s were beginning to make tentative moves to embrace an official Lutheran Reformation. Scotland tended to follow the model of French government, and King James aped King François in defending the traditional Church in order to exploit it for the financial and political benefit of his dynasty.

A NEW KING DAVID? MÜNSTER AND ITS AFTERMATH

The last monarch of the 1530s to need consideration is a rather different figure; his journey to his terrible end in the city of Münster in 1536 will require tracing from the arrest in 1533 of Melchior Hoffmann, whom we then left in his fetid Strassburg prison cell (see above, p. 189). As Hoffmann's 1533 deadline for the coming of Christ began ticking away, a charismatic Dutchman, a baker from Haarlem called Jan Matthijszoon, came to promin-ence among Hoffmann's frustrated and increasingly excited followers in the northern Netherlands. He prevailed upon the Melchiorite congregation in Amsterdam to recognize him as one of the two witnesses whom Revelation 11 described as having the duty to prophesy and punish the wicked cities of the world; thus empowered, he determined to improve on Hoffmann's message. Hoffmann, he decided, had made a mistake in paying attention to existing worldly powers. Not only had he foolishly placed trust in the treacherous city council of Strassburg, but in his horror at the suffering when Charles V's officials had begun executing those who had received adult baptism, Hoffmann had ordered that such baptism must be suspended until the Second Coming.

Now Matthijszoon decreed defiance of the civil authority and the resumption of baptism. He identified the New Jerusalem not as Strassburg but as the north German city of Münster.[73] Münster was not only much more geographically convenient for the northern Netherlands, but was also in the throes of a Reformation showing interesting signs of veering drastically from its Lutheran origins under the direction of its principal preacher, Bernd Rothmann. Change began in 1531 in a fashion typical of urban German Reformations: a majority on the city council, encouraged or intimidated by popular trade-gilds, chose to side with Rothmann and the Reformers against the newly installed aristocratic Prince-Bishop of Münster, Franz von Waldeck. Rothmann was a young man of humble origins, who had become a scholarly theologian acquainted with Bucer, Capito and Melanchthon. There were aspects of his thought that projected him far beyond the common magisterial mould of evangelicalism, rather as Zwingli might have travelled if he had possessed less self-restraint. Rothmann showed a willingness to see the Reformation promoted by violence (as of course Zwingli had in his final months), and he insisted on the role of active faith in the sacraments, which encouraged him to reject infant baptism.

Now, because of Matthijszoon's excitement at his work, Rothmann found exhilaratingly numerous supporters. Notably, in complete contrast to most Reformations so far, the movement of Dutch enthusiasts that coagulated in Münster was led apart from Rothmann himself by laymen and not clergy – partly because the Habsburgs had destroyed the existing Dutch clerical evangelical leadership. Multitudes heard Matthijszoon's proclamation of the Last Days in Münster. All over northern Europe humble people had been excited by Luther's cry of liberty, then bitterly disappointed when in 1525 this had turned out not to involve a radical transformation of society and a righting of injustice: then they had been further traumatized by the Habsburg persecutions in the Netherlands. What more natural than to turn to the Bible made newly available by the evangelical reformers, to read its accounts of the tribulations which awaited the faithful before their triumphant victory, and the coming of a thousand-year rule of the saints on earth? So the new version of Hoffmann's millenarian message, preached by envoys sent across the flatlands of north Germany and the Low Countries, sent thousands to seek adult baptism to qualify for their place in the millennial kingdom, and to travel exultantly towards Münster.

In February 1534 the growing crowds of Anabaptists seized the city with the help of Rothmann and his supporters on the council. Anabaptist congregations in north-west Europe mushroomed in response to this sign that the Last Days were indeed arriving. Bishop von Waldeck now besieged the city; soon he gained support from Lutheran princes and towns, in a stark admission that the new situation was too serious for Catholics and magisterial Protestants to waste time quarrelling. Matthijszoon was killed in a sortie from the city, mistaken in his belief that God would protect him, and leadership passed to another Dutchman, Jan Beukels, a charismatic young former tailor, soon to be known to the world as 'John of Leiden'. Jan developed a regime with two aims: to usher in the Last Days (all the more urgent when the predicted Second Coming failed to materialize in April 1534), and also to sustain the urgent needs of a crowded city in military crisis. Property was forcibly redistributed for communal use; the remaining city notables were exempted from this measure, but expected to use their wealth for the common good. Jan gathered an apocalyptic council of Twelve Elders, and instituted polygamy – again a measure both biblical (a measure to make God's chosen Israel 'increase and multiply') and practical: to provide security for the women who formed a large majority among the Anabaptist volunteers. When the Bishop and his allies decided in the summer to close all exits and try to starve Münster into submission, Beukels reacted by proclaiming himself messianic king of the world, with all the royal trappings of a new David in Israel. He minted a symbolic gold and silver coinage and had it distributed throughout northern Europe.

As the besiegers tightened their grip, Jan's kingdom became an increasingly desperate permanent carnival amid growing hunger and misery in the city. Finally, in June 1535, the Bishop's forces, now belatedly reinforced by imperial troops, were led through the defences by two turncoats from the city and ended nearly seventeen months of extraordinary social experiment. The public executions of Jan and his two main surviving supporters in front of Münster's principal parish church were unsurprisingly exercises in exemplary sadism. The giant pincers which were heated red-hot and used to tear their tortured bodies still survive, as do three iron cages in which the corpses were once displayed, having endured war and rebuilding still to hang on St Lambert's church tower. A vigilant visitor to Münster today finds other reminders: the city churches reveal plenty of evidence of the city's medieval wealth, but a marked lack of pre-1534 furnishings – no stained glass, no tombs. Evidently the Anabaptists, trapped in the besieged city, had ample time to eliminate everything that they hated. A poignant discovery in the 1890s was a series of fragments of a beautiful fourteenth-century font, recovered from inside the rubble of one of the city wall towers; it can be identified as having come from the Benedictine abbey church known as the Überwasserkirche, and it was evidently smashed up and contemptuously redeployed by the defenders in a symbolic humiliation of infant baptism. Likewise, one of the distinctive features of Münster churches is the amount of mid-sixteenth-century art: the product of a frantic effort of refurnishing. The priority of the triumphant besiegers was to edit the immediate past and remember only what they needed to.

Münster's fall brought despair and anger in the Dutch heartland of Anabaptist recruitment, which in parallel to the Münster siege saw local uprisings of militants and proclamations of the New Jerusalem during 1535. Some kept up the fight; even after the capture of their leader Jan van Batenburg, son of a Dutch nobleman, in 1537, terrorist raids on churches and monasteries took some time to peter out. However, most radicals were sickened by continuing violence and were deeply disillusioned by the horrific events in Münster. Some turned towards a variety of undemonstrative (even clandestine) mystical beliefs. The Dutch stained-glass artist and poet David Joris carefully sought out former Münsterites to persuade them that he and not the butchered King of Münster was in fact the Third David. Joris had learned his lesson about enthusiastic openness in proclaiming a message: back in 1528, as an enthusiastic radical convert to the Reformation, he had led attacks on a procession of Mary in Delft and suffered a flogging and the boring-through of his tongue, while subsequently his followers were a particular target of official savagery. Now for his own sake and theirs he spread his message more discreetly. He ended his days in prosperous respectability, living in Basel under a false name, a valued member of the humanist academic establishment there, but still the subject of widespread unobtrusive devotion, which persisted long after his death.[74]

Such traditions of discreetly thoughtful dissent attracted well-educated people with leisure to make religious choices. They remained strong in the prosperous urban society of the Netherlands, but throughout Europe, people quietly listened to what the likes of Joris had to say. This was an extreme form of that tendency within literate late medieval religion to retreat into private contemplation of printed wisdom or one's own thoughts (chapter 2, p. 75). Collectively such believers have come to be labelled 'spirituals', because one thing which united them was a conviction that religion or contact with the divine was something from within the individual: God's spirit made direct contact with the human spirit. Like many of the first patrician radicals in Zürich in the early 1520s, the spirituals were often admirers of the writings of Erasmus, and took his side in his disputes with Martin Luther: they could not stomach Luther's radical pessimism about the human condition, but neither could they stay with what they saw as an authoritarian and corrupt traditional Church as Erasmus had done. Hence the attraction for these humanist intellectuals of concentrating on the inner spirit – yet another adaptation of Erasmus's favourite text 'The Spirit gives life, but the flesh is of no use' (chapter 2, p. 100). If that was so, Scripture might even be seen as a fleshly irrelevance: a 'paper pope'. As for the sacraments, as early as 1526 Kaspar Schwenckfeld and his spiritualist-minded colleagues in Liegnitz (chapter 3, p. 136) made a solemn decision never to receive the Eucharist again until everyone could agree on what it meant.[75] So any help from Scripture, sacrament or pulpit was at best of secondary importance: hence it might also be of secondary importance loudly to proclaim one's dissent from Scripture, sacrament or pulpit.

The most extraordinary sect of this sort to develop in western Europe was the Family of Love, founded by a prosperous merchant, Hendrik Niclaes, whose origins are obscure and can only be placed through the dialect of his writings in the great triangle of German and Dutch lands between Utrecht, Emden and Cologne. In 1532–3 he was in trouble with the authorities at Amsterdam for heresy, but unlike so many others from that recruiting-ground for the Münster adventure, he was not swept up into the crowds seeking the new Jerusalem. Instead he interested himself in the quieter message of spiritualist thinkers. By the early 1540s he was in that busy little northern entrepôt of religious dissent, Emden, proclaiming his own message of inner enlightenment: he habitually signed himself in his writings by his initials H. N., which by a happy or divinely inspired coincidence also stood for *homo novus*, 'New Man'. He took up a radical version of a traditional mystic Christian idea derived from writings of the Apostle Paul, that God unites himself with saved humanity: he told his followers that they were so full of God's Spirit that they were part of the Godhead. He personally undertook unobtrusive missionary journeys as far as England in the time of Edward VI and perhaps even in the unpromising reign of Mary.[76]

Niclaes's intoxicating message appealed particularly to creative people with a good education, who knew the power of their own minds. The Family became distinctive in combining an urgent desire to spread their good news with disinclination to risk their semi-divine skins by proclaiming themselves as religious dissenters. They were happy to fade into the background of whatever established Church they found, quietly confident in their cosmic elite status. Familists were often artists, musicians or scholars: the great painter of landscape and townscape, Pieter Brueghel the Younger, was one of them. They also had a penchant for the powerful. In Antwerp, chief commercial city of the Spanish Netherlands, King Philip II of Spain's printer Christophe Plantin was a Familist: by day he printed the King's Catholic breviaries for the Counter-Reformation Netherlands, and by night, Familist literature. One of the King's Spanish councillors, Benito Arias Montano, a close collaborator with Plantin in the production of the prodigious officially sponsored Antwerp Polyglot version of the Bible, also became a Familist sympathizer (as a man of Jewish *converso* descent, he knew all about concealment).[77] Both men died in their beds, much-honoured. At the Court of Philip's great rival and nemesis Elizabeth I of England, great was the consternation in the 1580s when some of the Yeomen of the Guard, her personal security force, turned out to be Familists. Puritans raged: Elizabeth, most enigmatic of monarchs, did nothing, which may raise some questions about her own beliefs. There were still Familists among her successor James I's Court officials, including the keeper of the lions in the Tower of London.[78]

Equally enjoyable Familist speculations can be built around a journey to Balsham, a little English village in Cambridgeshire, to meet its Rector, one Dr Andrew Perne. Perne was a very senior academic, Master of Peterhouse Cambridge, who has remained famous as one of the most shameless floor-crossers in the English Reformation. When he donated a weather-vane to his college, bearing his initials, it was said that 'AP' swung to 'A Papist, a Protestant, a Puritan' depending on the way the wind blew. As Vice-Chancellor of Cambridge University in Catholic Queen Mary's reign, he presided over the exhumation and solemn burning of the bones of the lately deceased Martin Bucer; as Vice-Chancellor in Queen Elizabeth's reign, he presided over an equally solemn university ceremony in the same church amounting to an apology to Bucer's missing ashes. One way or another, he too knew a lot about self-concealment: scurrilous Puritans said he had once been the homosexual lover of John Whitgift, later Archbishop of Canterbury, with whom he went to live in old age at Lambeth Palace.[79]

In Balsham, this mysterious intellectual quietly allowed the Familists to set up one of their most blatant colonies in all Europe. Familists served as churchwardens in Balsham. To the fury of those villagers not in the clique, one of the leading Familists was afforded an especially honourable burial in 1609, reusing the graveslab of a medieval priest, which implied that he was the local Mr H. N. Another member helped in that stormy and significant year of 1609 to pay for three new bells in Balsham church tower, which can still be seen and heard: one of them bears the unusual Latin inscription, 'I do not sound for the souls of the dead but for the ears of the living.' How the Family must have smiled as they heard Balsham's church bells ringing. During the seventeenth century the whole movement faded away; some have wondered whether its English members then joined a new group which also believed in Inner Light, the Society of Friends, or Quakers (chapter 12, p. 526).

The bizarre story of the Family of Love is one very unexpected pathway from the ruin of Münster. Other radicals in north-west Europe, usually more humble in social status and education, persevered in organizing separate congregations which scorned any concealment while specifically rejecting all forms of physical force. The principal spokesman and inspirer of these quietist separatist communities was a former country priest from West Friesland, Menno Simons, who was horrified by the terrible fate of the crowds who had travelled to Münster. He was determined to minister to the traumatized people who remained. In the face of vicious Habsburg persecution he persevered, nurturing congregations which continued patiently (at least until disillusionment set in at the end of the sixteenth century) to await an imminent Second Coming. They also affirmed Melchior Hoffmann's views on the celestial flesh of Christ; they made common cause with the Swiss radicals who had created the 1527 Schleitheim Confession (see above, p. 168), although memories of Münster discouraged Dutch Mennonites from following the Hutterites in establishing a community of goods. So they eventually grew and prospered in the independent northern Netherlands. The resulting Mennonite tradition (interestingly, it never refers to itself as Melchiorite) survives in different church organizations on both sides of the Atlantic to the present day.

The radicals got little credit for their general renunciation of violence. The image of John of Leiden continued to provide the rationale for rulers to persecute and marginalize radicals, and added to their sense that order in society was something very fragile and in need of constant repressive vigilance. Most magisterial Protestant reformers lost whatever inhibitions they had possessed about persecuting heretics, even though Catholic rulers were simultaneously persecuting magisterial Protestants for heresy. Luther's separation of sacred and secular in the 'two kingdoms theory' might have been taken as an argument for tolerating honest religious dissent, but the persistence and diversification of radicalism after the Peasants' War already led him by 1530 to approve of the death penalty for blasphemy and idolatry (the actual word 'heresy' remained difficult for evangelicals). In 1531 Luther tried to hang on to the separation of the 'two kingdoms' by endorsing

Melanchthon's view that Anabaptists should be put to the sword only because they were politically seditious. By 1536 he was prepared to join with Melanchthon and their Wittenberg colleagues Johann Bugenhagen and Caspar Cruciger in signing a document affirming that the civil power had a religious duty to suppress blasphemy. This hopelessly blurred the boundaries between ecclesiastical and civil power, but the times seemed to demand it.[80]

Still for some there remained the uneasy memory that in the beginning there had been a common rising-up against the Roman Antichrist. One Anabaptist woman of Augsburg, when arrested and questioned by the city authorities, did her best to make Urbanus Rhegius, the suavely scholarly Lutheran Reformer, feel thoroughly uncomfortable: Rhegius's son records her shouting sarcastically at him: 'you dispute elegantly, Brother Urbanus, sitting there beside the councillors in your soft cloak, while I am cast on the ground in chains, which in itself could take away my courage. And you speak as from the Delphian tripod.'[81] In England, the fiery reformer John Bale looked back in 1545 on the time seven years before when King Henry VIII had burned a number of Anabaptists, including a German called Peter Franke in Colchester: Franke's brave death, he noted, converted several Colchester people from papistry to evangelical faith, and 'I dare boldly say that his life was good'. Bale's own pamphlet which made this candid admission was itself printed secretly, away from King Henry's wrath in Antwerp, a city where the Catholic authorities were continuing to burn heretics both evangelical and radical without any discrimination between them.[82]

Despite such qualms, the shock of Münster further stimulated the strong impulse among magisterial Protestant reformers to codify their teaching and practice: to accept that they had created separate church bodies, which in order to avoid the theological disintegration typified by Bernd Rothmann in Münster must now take on all the trappings of authority from the old Church and become a new establishment. It is significant that Luther (for whom church structures were never a matter of great concern) did not trouble to draft a liturgical rite for ordaining clergy until 1535, the year of the Münster siege.[83] It is further significant that a requirement for parish registers of baptisms, funerals and marriages became widespread in Europe in the mid-sixteenth century, for instance in England by a Vice-Gerential order of Thomas Cromwell in 1538; one powerful incentive was to keep an eye on those who were not bringing their children to the font because they did not believe in infant baptism. Münster also probably disturbed a good many people enough to make them newly appreciate traditional religion, thus paving the way for the Roman Church's revival in the Counter-

Reformation. So the 1540s continued the battle for the hearts and minds of rulers between Catholic and Protestant; it also saw a variety of efforts to see how the Catholic Church of the Latin West could be rebuilt after twenty years of chaos. What was the best road to reunion? Negotiation? Confrontation? Spiritual renewal? Religious war? By the early 1550s, clear answers (although not necessarily the best answers) were beginning to emerge.

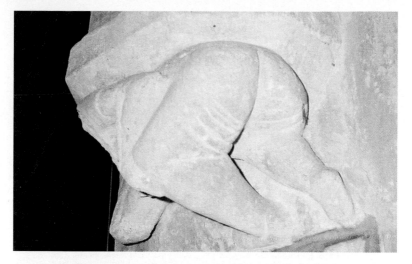

Supporting figure for chancel arch, *c.* 1320, Preston Bissett (Buckinghamshire, England). This figure, its rear facing the high altar, formed part of the ensemble screening the priest's chancel from the people's nave.

1b. Holy Roman Emperor Maximilian I commissioned Hans Burgkmair to engrave an imaginary triumphal procession (1517–18, unintentionally coinciding with Luther's first protests). Here (at the tail end), in one of the earliest European representations of native Americans, are so-called 'Indians' or inhabitants of 'Calicut', Maximilian's new subjects in America, ripe for conversion to Christianity.

bus expofito digno fide fomnio: per
q̅d vniuerfos leuificauit. Erat aūt bu
iufcemodi vifus omiaq̅ fuerat fum/
mus facerdos virū bonū z benignum
verecundū vifu:modeftū mozib̅z elo
quio decoz:z qui a puero in virtutib̅z
exercitatus fit manus ptendentē:oza
re pzo omni pp̅lo iudeoz. Poft b̅ ap/
paruiffe z aliū virū etatez g̅ra mirabi
lem:z magni decozis babitudine cir/
ca illū. R̅ ñdente vero oniam dixiffe.
Hic eft fratrū amatoz z pp̅li ifr̅l. Hic
eft q̅ multū ozat pzo pp̅lo z vniuerfa
fcra ciuitate bieremias ppha dei. Et
reddiffe aūt bieremiā dexterā z dediffe
iude gladiū aureū dicente. Accipe fan
ctū gladiū munus a deo:in q̅ deijcies
aduerfarios pp̅li mei ifrael. Exbozta
ti itaq̅ iude fmonib̅z bonis valde de/
dbus extolli poffet imped z animi in
nenū pfoztari: ftatuꝭt dimicare z cō/
fligere foztiter vt p̅tus d̅ negocijs in
dicaret:eo q̅ ciuitas fancta z templū
periclitarent. Erat eñi pzo vxozibus
z filijs:iteꝗz pzo fratribus z cognatis
minoz follicitudo: maximus v̅ oz pm̅z
pzo fanctitate timoz erat tepli. Sed
z eos q̅ in ciuitate erant non minima
follicitudo bebat pzo bis q̅ cōgreffu
ri erāt. Et cū iam oes fperarent iudici
um futurū boftefq̅ adeffent atq̅ exer
citus erat ozdiatus:beftie eq̅refq̅ op
poztuno in loco cōpofiti pfideräs ma
chabeus aduentū multitudinis z ap
paratū variū armoz ac ferocitate be/
ftiaz extendēs manus in celū: pdigia
faciente d̅ñm innocauit: q̅ non fm ar
moz potentiā fed p̅ut ipfi placet dat
dignis victoziaz. Dixit autē innocans
boc modo. Tu dñe qui mififti angelū
tuū fub ezechia rege iuda:z interfeci/
fti de caftris fennacherib centū octo/
gintaquinꝗz milia:z nūc dfiator celo
rūz mitte angelū tuū bonum añ nos
i timoze z tremoze magnitudinis bra
chij tui:vt metuant q̅ cū blafphemia
veniunt aduerfus fanctū pp̅m tuum
Et bic q̅dem ita pozauit. Nicanoz āt
z q̅ cum ipo erant cū tubis z canticis
admouebāt. Judas v̅o z q̅ cū eo erāt
inuocato deo:per ozoes pgreffi funt
manu q̅de pugnátes:fed z dñm cozdi
bus ozátes pftrauerunt no̅ minus tri
gintaꝗz milia pñcta dei magnifice
delectati. Cunꝗz ceffaffent z cū gau
dio redirent:cognouerunt nicanozem
ruiffe cū armis fuis. Facto itaꝗz cla/
moze z pturbatiōe excitata pfia voce

oïpotenté d̅ñz b̅ñdicebant. Pzecepit
autē iudas qui per oïa cozpozet aïo
moti pzo ciuibus paratus erat caput
nicanozis z manū cum bumero abfcif
fam bierofolymā pferri. Q̅uo cū̅ ꝑue
niffet ꝗuocatis ptribulibus z facerdo
tib̅z ad altare acceffit ad eos q̅ in ar
cerant. Et oftéfo capite nicanozis z
manu nefaria quā extenderat d̅ domū
fancta omnipotétis dei magnifice glo
riatus eft. Linguaz etiā impij nicano
ris pciffam iuffit pticulatim auibus
dari:manum aūt dementis d̅ templū
fufpendi. Oēs igitur celi b̅ñdixerunt
d̅ñm dicentes:b̅ñdictus qui locū fuū
incontaminatum feruauit. Sufpendit
aūt nicanozis caput in fumma arcevt
euidés eét maïfeftū fignū auxilij dei
Itaꝗz oés cōmuni pfilio decreuerunt
nullo modo dié iftum abfꝗz celebzita
te pterfire:babere autem celebzitatem
tertiadecima die menfis adar: que d̅
voce fyziaca p̅die mardochei die Jgit
bis erga nicanozé geftis:z ex illis tp̅i
bus ab bebzeis ciuitate poffeffa: ego
ꝗz in bis faciam finē fermonis. Et fi
quidé bene z vt biftozie cōpetit boc:z
ipfe velim:fi aūt minus digne conce/
dendūz eft mibi. Sicut eñi vinūz fem
per bibere:aut femp aquam cōtrariū
eft alternis aūt vti delectabile:ita le
gentib̅z fi femp exactus fit f̅mo: non
erit gratus;b ergo erit cōfummatus.

¶Scd̅s liber Machabeoz explicit.
¶Epiftola beati bieronimi ad dama
fum papā in q̅ttuoz euāgeliftas fcipit

Beatiffimo papa damafo. Hiero
nimus. Nouū op̅ me facere co
gis ex veteri: vt poft exemplaria fcri
pturarū toto ozbe difperfa quafi qui
dam arbiter fedeam:z qz inter fe vari
ant que fint illa que cum greca cōfen
tiant veritate decernam. Pius labor
fed periculofa pfumptio iudicare de
ceteris ipfm ab olbus iudicandum: fe
nis mutare linguā z canefcentem iam
mundū ad initia retrabere paruuloz
Quis eñi doctus pariter vel indoct̅z:
cum in manus volumen affumpferit
z a faliua quam femel imbibit viderit
difcrepare q̅d lectitat:non ftatim erū
pat in voces:me falfarium me clamās
effe facrilegum :qui audea m aliq̅d in
veteribus libzis addere:mutare coz
rigere. Aduerfus quam inuidiam du
plex caufa me cōfolatur:quod et tu q̅

2. A Vulgate Bible, a small reading edition of 1511 printed in Lyon: the end of 2 Maccabees, in what Protestants would later call the Apocrypha, but here forming the end of the Old Testament. The biblical text at this date was divided into chapters but not yet numbered verses. This copy reached England early and may have belonged to Archbishop Thomas Cranmer: one Tudor owner here dutifully follows Henry VIII's orders, twice erasing the word 'papa' ('pope') in a letter of Jerome to Pope Damasus about the Gospels, which immediately follows the Maccabees text

3. This painting (from *c.* 1500) of the Last Judgement or Doom, at Wenhaston (Suffolk, England) was a backdrop to carved figures of the Rood, Our Lady and St John (now represented only in outline): it shows saved and damned in judgement. It was painted over at the Reformation – hence the black-letter biblical text at its foot – then in 1894 saved from destruction when overnight rain washed whitewash off the boards, which were stacked in the churchyard for firewood.

4. The massive statue of Charlemagne on the south face of Zürich's Grossmünster symbolized the medieval city's gradual acquisition of power from the nuns of the Fraumünster. Zwingli and the city authorities let the statue stand through the Reformation despite Zürich's general destruction of imagery, reasoning that no one would worship Charlemagne; it also well symbolized their own theology of close union of Church and civil Commonwealth. This statue replaces the original, now protected in the church crypt.

HVLDRYCHVS ZVINGLIVS,
DVM PATRIÆ QVÆRO PER DOGMATA SANCTA SALVTEM,
INGRATO PATRIÆ CÆSVS AB ENSE CADO,

OBIIT AÑO DÑI, M,D,XXXI, OCDOB,X
ÆTATIS SVÆ XLVIII,

5. This picture in the Swiss National Museum is the best of the few authentic likenesses of Huldrych Zwingli. Zwingli holds the New Testament, interestingly in the Erasmus Latin version, open at a passage from Matthew 11–12, 'Come to me all that are heavily laden ...', emphasizing the dangers of religious legalism – a dig at medieval Catholicism, and perhaps a reference to the famous incident with the sausage. The inscription at the top celebrates his death in battle for his country and his faith.

6. Nuremberg had an exceptionally conservative Lutheran Reformation, and the two chief parish churches kept their magnificent medieval saint's shrines. The bronze/latten shrine of St Sebaldus in the church of that dedication, begun *c.* 1488, was only finished in 1519.

7. St Janskerk in Gouda has a remarkable range of sixteenth-century stained glass, which with Dutch tolerance includes windows commemorating both Philip of Spain and William the Silent who rebelled against him. This window shows King Philip and his wife Queen Mary of England at the Last Supper with Christ and the Apostles.

8.The Emperor Charles V commissioned this magnificent portrait from Titian (now in the Prado Museum, Madrid) to commemorate one of his most satisfying victories, at Mühlberg in Electoral Saxony on 23 April 1547, during the Schmalkaldic Wars against his Protestant princes. His triumph was short-lived and he was forced to the compromise Peace of Augsburg in 1555. The armour in the portrait still survives in Madrid.

5

Reunion Deferred: Catholic and Protestant, 1530–60

A SOUTHERN REVIVAL

Religious renewal was not confined to the evangelical revolutions of the north in the 1530s. In southern Europe, cross-currents of official initiatives, fresh enterprises in the regular religious life, and intense personal explorations of spirituality offered a range of possibilities for the future. Some of these impulses might well have led to the reunification of the western Church, but the outcome was a strengthened Church of Rome, much less inclined to strike deals with the increasingly divided Protestants, and having made choices as to which of various spiritual energies it would legitimize and nurture. Protestants, too, made decisions that crystallized their division into Lutheran and Reformed, and a new generation of leaders emerged, the most prominent of whom proved to be the French exile John Calvin.

In chapter 2 (pp. 58–65) we saw how the confrontation with native Islam and Judaism released movements of spiritual excitement and unrest in Spain, and how in Italy decades of military misery and political confusion triggered in the 1490s had much the same effect. The horrors of the 1527 sack of Rome by Charles V's troops were a rude shock to those who were expecting a new Golden Age to emerge from these years of tribulation. The Pope's humiliation also suggested that God was reinforcing the message already proclaimed through the chaos in northern Europe that the Church must reform itself. Some Italians turned to read the writings of Luther or of other northern evangelicals, clandestinely repackaged or translated. Nevertheless, although many Italian readers would not have suspected the origins of works which had been given false names to avoid official censorship, there would always be limits on how much people south of the Alps were prepared to place faith in barbarous northern authors.[1] Less alien voices would stand more chance of a wide hearing. One important catalyst for the concerns and diverse spiritual longings in Italy was a scholarly refugee theologian from Spain, Juan de Valdés.

Valdés, the twin brother of the Emperor's adviser Alfonso (chapter 4, p. 173) came to Italy in 1530 to escape the interest of the Spanish Inquisition. He felt secure enough in Italy to settle in the Spanish-governed dominions in Naples, and there, from his arrival in 1535, he developed a circle of friends and admirers, wealthy or talented or both, who shared his passion for humanist learning and his deep commitment to promoting a vital, engaged Christian faith. Among these were two powerful preachers, leading figures in their respective religious Orders, Bernardino Ochino from the newly founded Franciscan reformed Order, the Capuchins, and Piermartire Vermigli ('Peter Martyr' in his later north European career), an Augustinian who became Abbot of S. Pietro ad Aram in Naples. Brooding on the message of his Order's patron Augustine of Hippo, Vermigli developed a predestinarian theology of salvation as thoroughgoing as anything in the Protestant north.[2]

Also among Valdés's admirers were talented members of some of Italy's premier noble families, such as the two poets, artistic patrons and lay theologians Vittoria Colonna, close friend of Michelangelo, and Vittoria's cousin by marriage Giulia Gonzaga, a celebrated beauty who in her widow-hood had retired to a Neapolitan convent. With such influential support (the Colonna had produced two popes and claimed others as ancient family members) there was a ready entry to the courts and noble palaces of northern Italy; Valdesian ideas in turn filtered into the lively world of humanist discussion in Italian cities, hospitable to a variety of opinions on the inad-equacies of official religion. Valdés was soon in touch with Gasparo Contar-ini, the Venetian nobleman who had fought his own lonely way to discovering justification by grace alone (chapter 3, p. 111), and through Contarini he also gained the attention of a cultured emigré cousin of King Henry VIII of England, Reginald Pole. Pole was born with a rather better hereditary claim to the English throne than King Henry; after some hesita-tion (a feature of his whole career), he bit the royal hand that was feeding him in an expensive Italian education and sided with the King's wronged wife Catherine of Aragon. This led to Pole's permanent exile in Italy from the early 1530s. His enforced leisure, exalted birth and reasonably comfortable income combined with a strong sense of duty and a thoughtful, introspective piety to make him a major player in the ferment of Italian theological exploration. Like Contarini, he emphasized the central role of grace by faith in the Christian life, and he was aware that Martin Luther had proclaimed the same message.

Divergent themes naturally emerged from such a creative and articulate group, yet central was a renewed emphasis on the grace which God sent through faith, together with a consistent urge to reveal the Holy Spirit as the force conveying this grace – so that associates of the movement were soon characterized as *Spirituali*. Within these broad limits there were different emphases as to how the Spirit showed its power. Valdés was an assiduous commentator on and translator of the Bible, and there is evidence that he read Luther with interest. However, he parted company with north European evangelicals in his belief that the Spirit progressively offered its light to Christians: he believed that some favoured children of God would be led to ever deeper union with Christ, and the Scriptures might not be the only or the chief illumination on the way. He was notably reticent in what he said about the Trinity, perhaps because he regarded it as one of the deeper mysteries of the faith for initiates, but perhaps for more dangerous reasons which led some later unitarians to claim him as one of their intellectual ancestors. He also had little to say about the sacraments or the institutional Church – an Erasmian indifference, perhaps, but one has to remember Valdés's *converso* ancestry via his Jewish mother: his uncle had been burned by the Spanish Inquisition. Among Valdés's circle, Vittoria Colonna became the subject of discreet pressure from Reginald Pole in order that she might more fully acknowledge that the visible structures of the Church were of vital importance in the Christian life.

Pole's insistence that the institutional Church should not be ignored seemed more plausible because in the mid-1530s the papal machine seemed at last to be taking notice of its potential resources. Poor Pope Clement VII, overwhelmed by multiple catastrophes, died in 1534. Cardinal Alessandro Farnese, who succeeded him with little opposition as Paul III, came from the same northern Italian aristocratic circle, and devoted much of his fifteen years as Pope to scandalous promotion of the interests of his unattractively omnivorous children and family, just like his notorious predecessor and former patron Alexander VI. However, Paul was also a perceptive and intelligent Renaissance prince anxious to capitalize on all his assets. While making two of his teenage grandsons Cardinals in 1535, he additionally bestowed Cardinals' hats on men who were symbols of reform in the Church: Reginald Pole, Gasparo Contarini, Jacopo Sadoleto, Giovanni Pietro Carafa (of whom we will hear much more) and the imprisoned English bishop John Fisher. Fisher may or may not have been grateful for this honour, the news of which immediately led to an infuriated Henry VIII ordering him from his cell in the Tower of London to the executioner's block. The Pope even appointed Contarini, Pole, Carafa and like-minded men to a commission to consider reforms in the Church, and although this commission, *De emendanda ecclesia*, confined itself in its report of 1537 to recommending an administrative shake-up in the system, its frankly expressed picture of corruption and misused resources immediately proved a godsend to Protestant polemicists. Paul also began making plans for a General Council of the Church, much to the alarm of northern European rulers who had broken with papal obedience: the Emperor Charles V was also extremely suspicious of the papal initiative, and his obstruction was one of the main forces that postponed the Council's meeting for nearly a decade.

Pope Paul's mixture of reforming zeal and cheerfully stereotypical Renaissance worldliness was typical of many senior Italian churchmen's reaction to the Reformation. Cardinal Ercole Gonzaga provides another good example. Cousin of the deeply devout *Spirituale* Giulia Gonzaga, he was effectively ruler of the family Duchy of Mantua for two decades, and he was its bishop for much longer than that; he sired five children and did not bother to proceed to full priestly ordination until 1556, or to receive consecration as bishop until 1561, two years before his death. Nevertheless, he was a close friend of Pole and Contarini, and he much admired the reforming work of the neighbouring bishop Gian Matteo Giberti of Verona, whose intensive energy in visitations of his dioceses and promoting the laity's education and personal devotion became a model for the reforms of bishops in the Counter-Reformation. Gonzaga imitated these reforming activities in his own diocese and he also showed increasing sensitivity to his own complex involvement in absentee sources of church income. He was evidently guided by a sense of family honour; God had given the Gonzaga their wealth and power, so it was his duty not to diminish these family resources, but it was also a matter of honour to make his diocese as devout, well-instructed and well-regulated as God or a Gonzaga would wish.[3]

So far, then, we have noted two different impulses in Italy: the open-ended, mystically inclined piety of the *Spirituali*, and the *noblesse oblige* reformism of some aristocratic senior churchmen and their relatives. Both these impulses interacted with the optimistic spirit of enquiry in humanist scholarship. There were reformers among the evangelicals of northern Europe who would recognize familiar agendas amid these preoccupations, yet the widely distributed reformists in aristocratic, mercantile and artisan circles did not develop an open Italian Reformation. Militant mass support and a charismatic leadership prepared to make a break with the old structures were both lacking. As already noted, the anti-clerical rhetoric, which in northern Europe gave an inflammatory edge to interest in reform, seems largely missing from late medieval Italy, with its distinctive form of gilds, out of which developed the various Oratories (chapter 1, pp. 16–17, 33).

By the time that dissenting activism and leaders were openly emerging and acknowledging a debt to northern evangelicalism in the 1540s, the moment had passed when such a militant stand could have enough political plausibility to appeal to Italian princes – as it was doing in Germany, Scandinavia and England. Moreover, Italian religious revival contained other elements which pulled powerfully in a different direction.

The Oratories fostered an intense, activist and eucharistically centred piety which might well merge with *Spirituale* concerns: so Contarini was associated with the Oratory of the Divine Love in Rome (founded in 1517) and was one of the movers in setting up a similar group in Venice. However, other prominent churchmen who were inspired by the Oratory moved in a different direction: notably the Neapolitan nobleman Giovanni (Gian) Pietro Carafa. A papal official, he turned away in disgust from his comfortably pluralist career in the Church. In 1524 he joined with Gaetano da Thiene, a nobly born priest from Vicenza and a fellow member of the Roman Oratory, to found a congregation of clergy under special vows ('clerks regular') to lead an austere life which would provide a shaming example of vocation to less conscientious priests. Carafa was at that time Bishop of Chieti or 'Theate', hence the new Order was called the Theatines. In northern Europe such a level of commitment for serious-minded articulate clergy was rapidly being diverted into new forms of Protestant clerical ministry: the vital difference in this contemporary Mediterranean initiative by a former papal diplomat was its complete loyalty to Rome.

Thereafter Carafa's career, which after his work in founding the Roman Inquisition (below, p. 231) saw him become Pope Paul IV in 1555, was marked by a concern for obedience to the traditional discipline of the Church. This was no less obsessive for being combined with a complete inability to discipline his own violent temper. His perspective on church reform was further distorted because he loathed Spaniards, deeply resenting Spanish rule in his ancestral Naples (his years as papal nuncio in Spain had apparently only made matters worse). As Cardinal-Archbishop of Naples from 1537 Carafa would have proved to be an uncomfortable father-in-God for Juan de Valdés if the Emperor Charles V had not thoroughly obstructed his efforts to administer his diocese. Carafa was happy to co-operate with Pole and Contarini in the work of the Commission *De emendanda ecclesia*, but his friendly personal relations with them were increasingly strained by his suspicion of their religious agenda and by his own conviction that any concession to the Protestants was a blasphemous betrayal of the Church. Those senior clerics sympathetic to Carafa's bleakly rigorist and authoritarian agenda have often been seen as a party contrasting with the *Spirituali* and described as the *Zelanti* ('the zealous ones'). In the confused and developing situation of the 1540s, relationships never amounted so crudely to two team line-ups, but the descriptions still have some value in identifying two polarities while clergy and theologians argued about the best way to save the Church. As we observe the answers emerging, some of these untidy cross-currents will become apparent, notably in the development of one of the greatest forces for revival in the Roman Church, the Society of Jesus.

IGNATIUS LOYOLA AND THE EARLY JESUITS

The founding of the Jesuits unites two themes: the western Church's constant renewal and remodelling of forms of religious life under vows, and the creative (if often fraught) relationship between Spanish and Italian culture, which had already brought Juan de Valdés to Italy. All through the decades around 1517, we have noted the steady continued emergence of new religious orders and similar groupings, just as in the centuries before: various new forms of the Augustinian and Franciscan lifestyle, up to and including the Capuchins, regional reforms in Benedictine Congregations, the *Devotio Moderna* communities, the Oratories and the Theatines. Further new movements appeared during the 1530s. Noticeable in these fresh movements is a common emphasis on large-scale teaching of basic Christian doctrine, not primarily in the form of preaching, but of catechizing. This systematic instruction, based on patient repetition of lessons, and often in the sixteenth century phrased in question and answer form, was a long-established practice in medieval Spain, where it was a symptom of the militant Christian culture accustomed to dealing with often reluctant converts from Islam or Judaism. Now the Church found itself waging a civil war against evangelical subversion, and since evangelicals from Luther onwards had quickly seen the need for catechetical instruction (chapter 3, pp. 164–5), traditional religion needed to seize the minds of congregations before it was too late.

Such instructional work was undertaken by laywomen and laymen as well as by clergy, and it is no coincidence that three important initiatives all came from northern Italy – Brescia and Milan – much fought over by armies of north European mercenaries and geographically nearest to the evangelical contagion. Angela Merici, companion to a widowed noblewoman in Brescia and herself very limited in formal education, drew on her experience of activism as a Third Order Franciscan and a member of the local Oratory of the Divine Love when she conceived the plan of setting up a society of unmarried women and widows; they would live a life of charitable works and teaching the poor while still living in their own homes, in a fashion reminiscent of the early female Beguine communities which had been set up in northern Europe three centuries before. Her community, named Ursulines from the then popular cult of the supposed fourth-century martyr St Ursula, was formally organized in 1535. After her death Pope Paul III granted it an approved Rule, pulling it more closely into the institutional forms of earlier religious Orders for women, but still the model of the Ursuline Rule was the flexible organization of the medieval Augustinians. Not everyone in the Church approved of this potential for female self-assertion, and we will discover different efforts to influence the future of the society from Archbishop Carlo Borromeo of Milan and from the Society of Jesus (Chapters 9, p. 412, and 16, pp. 642–6). In fruitful dialogue with these external pressures, within a century the Ursulines had become one of the largest and most varied of female Orders.

Not long after Spanish armies seized Milan in 1535, an elderly Milanese priest Abbate Castellino da Castello began catechetical work in the city, bringing boys to church with a gift of an apple, and more to follow if they turned up again; girls (usually less in need of such bribes) were taught in separate classes. Castello repeated his work in nearby Pavia, and his initiative spread elsewhere; a quarter-century later it was formalized in Rome as the Confraternity of Christian Doctrine. This is the first instance of a 'Sunday school', that separate institution for teaching children, which over the next three centuries spread to become the mainstay of western Christianity both Catholic and Protestant. The 'confraternity' label is significant as showing that this was yet another development out of Italy's medieval gild culture, and laypeople remained important in its teaching work. It is not surprising that Gian Pietro Carafa should also have become involved in the movement for basic instruction of the laity. He took a sympathetic interest in an organization for clergy modelled on the Theatines, also pioneered in Milan. In the early 1530s the young priest Antonio Zaccaria secured permission for an order of priests with a particular mission to foster lay enthusiasm for worship. Nicknamed the 'Barnabites' from the dedication of the base church in Milan, which they took over after Zaccaria's early death, they were never numerous, but their extrovert open-air devotional processions and preaching missions provided one influential model for future Counter-Reformation popular instruction (chapter 8, pp. 415–17).

Amid these various witnesses to the continuing creativity of traditional religion in southern Europe, the Society of Jesus might not at first have seemed the most promising initiative. Its founder was a gentleman from the Basque country in the far north-east of Castile, Iñigo López de Loyola, who would be known to history as Ignatius after a scribal error over his Christian name when he matriculated in the University of Paris.[4] He is often described as a soldier, but his first ambition was for advancement at the Castilian Court, and his training in courtly self-assurance and in knowing how to behave in the presence of the powerful proved to be a useful asset in his later years in the Church. Military service and adopting the posturing of medieval chivalry were nevertheless necessary elements in the career of a successful Iberian courtier, and it was in the course of a heroic but unsuccessful mission in 1521 to defend the citadel at Pamplona from capture by the French that Iñigo received serious injuries, leading him to return home to convalesce. In the course of a long recovery from excruciating operations on his legs, he sought diversion in reading, but instead of the courtly romances which he would have preferred, there were only the old-fashioned devotional classics of a dull country house: a popular meditational fourteenth-century *Life of Christ*, and that thirteenth-century Dominican work so much despised by sophisticated humanists, the *Golden Legend* (chapter 2, p. 82).[5]

Using his powerful imagination to extract every ounce of meaning from these familiar materials in his long months of recovery, Iñigo transformed his inner life. He was increasingly empowered to comprehend his own reactions to the books, his shifting enthusiasms, the motivations behind them. He was developing an extraordinary ability to analyse the workings of the mind and the emotions, an ability which he described as the 'discernment of spirits', a traditional term used by a confessor or spiritual director. He found himself drawn to refashion his thirst for knightly glory into a service still greater than that of his Habsburg monarch: Our Lady and her Son. He would reject the life of the Court which he had enjoyed to the full, and his chivalric quest would now be redirected to Jerusalem. The Holy City was not just the ultimate goal of the medieval pilgrim, it was a natural preoccupation for a man who had aspired to be a Spanish grandee, and who was therefore inevitably obsessed with the Iberian heritage of crusading against Islam.

The transformation was symbolized by the night's vigil Loyola spent before the pilgrimage statue of the Black Madonna at Montserrat on her feast of the Annunciation (25 March 1522); it was meant to be the eve of his proposed (though in fact subsequently much-delayed) departure for Jerusalem, and he was dedicating himself as a knight on the eve of his knighting, while throwing off the outward splendours of a Castilian courtier. Luther's parallel solitary struggles with God led him ultimately to a sense that his salvation was an unconditional gift of God, making him free of all his natural bonds; this freedom empowered him to defy what he saw as worldly powers of bondage in the medieval Western Church. Iñigo found that his encounter with God was best expressed in forms drawn from the Iberian society which had created the most triumphant form of that same Church: chivalric expressions of duty and service. The contrasting conversion experiences thus led respectively to rebellion and to obedience. It was a momentous symbol of what came to separate Protestant Reformation and Catholic Counter-Reformation.

Soon, amid many false starts, disappointments and changes of direction, in a painful and poverty-stricken search to understand his new call to divine service, Loyola was beginning to note down his changing spiritual experiences. This was the raw material for a systematically organized guide to prayer, self-examination and surrender to the divine power; he soon began using the system with other people, and it reached a papally approved final form in print in 1548 as the *Spiritual Exercises*. This has become one of the most influential books in the history of the Western Church, even though Ignatius did not design it for reading any more than one would a technical manual of engineering or computing. It is there to be used by clerical spiritual directors guiding others as Ignatius did himself, to be adapted at whatever level might be appropriate for the situation of those who sought to benefit from it, in what came to be known as 'making the *Exercises*'.

Inevitably such an independent spiritual initiative alerted the Spanish Inquisition. As with their suspicious scrutiny of Juan de Valdés in the same years, they saw in Loyola a suggestion of the deplorable mysticism of the *alumbrados* and, like Valdés, Loyola judged it prudent to leave Spain. He had already undertaken a great deal of study in Spanish universities and now in 1528 he continued this in the Mecca of traditionalist western theology, the University of Paris. Here he formed a circle of like-minded student friends, including one of the most outstanding future personalities of the Catholic revival, a tough and extrovert Navarrese nobleman's son named Francisco de Javier (Francis Xavier). Initial personal tensions among this abrasive group were resolved after a particularly rigorous experience of the *Exercises*, and in 1534 they resolved to pursue Ignatius's first preoccupation in his conversion and repeat his earlier journey to Jerusalem. However, when after many trials an augmented party of enthusiasts eventually liaised in Venice in 1537, they faced a major disappointment. A rare triumph of pan-European diplomacy had constructed a coalition of the Emperor, the Pope and the Venetian Republic to wage war on the Ottoman Turks, and all commercial sailings to the Holy Land were cancelled.

The bedraggled and deflated group bravely made the best of this fiasco. They agreed that if no ship became available (and it did not), they would offer their talents for whatever service the Pope required. They also decided that they would call themselves the Company of Jesus; this Italian word *compagnia* was yet another name for a confraternity or gild, and its Latin equivalent was *societas*. So the Society of Jesus was born, soon to be known informally as the Jesuits: a gratuitous weapon to be placed in the Pope's hand. The initial reception in Rome was mixed, and its casting around for a suitable ministry was not without set-backs: Ignatius had hastily to abandon his efforts to turn the city's large population of prostitutes to penitence when his motives were widely questioned.[6] He had powerful enemies, not merely Spanish Inquisition officials and Spanish senior clergy still suspicious of his orthodoxy, but also Gian Pietro Carafa, who paradoxically detested him because he was a Spaniard (though there may also have been personal clashes). Carafa's hostility was all the more bitter because *Spirituale* sympathizers gave the members of the new Society a warm welcome, finding their evident devotion to the interior life of the soul a familiar and congenial theme. Vittoria Colonna gave them much-needed hospitality in a difficult period in Ferrara in 1539, while in the same year Cardinal Contarini made the *Exercises* under Loyola's direction; in 1540 Contarini proved one of the influences in getting Pope Paul III's personal approval with a Bull of Foundation for the new Society.[7]

An additional irony of Carafa's hatred was that the closest model for the Jesuits' developing constitution was his own non-monastic association of 'clerks regular', the Theatines – to the extent that the early Jesuits were often called 'Theatines' by outsiders, rather to their discomfort. They in fact turned down the Theatines' offer of a merger in 1545. 'We are not monks!' insisted Jerónimo Nadal, the Majorcan who became one of the principal shapers of the Society as it mushroomed in numbers in the 1550s: 'the world is our house'.[8] That phrase was only slightly adapted two centuries later in a Protestant context by the English founder of Methodism, John Wesley – 'the world is my parish' – and Wesley's tightly organized body of travelling Methodist preachers, committed both to exploring the depth of personal spirituality and to meeting ordinary folk in their own situation, had much in common with Ignatius's new Society. The Jesuits took their precedents not merely from the Theatines but from the older Orders of friars, Dominicans and Franciscans. Jesuit core tasks, preaching and hearing confessions, were the same as the friars', and it was not surprising that the Society soon attracted their resentment.

The Jesuits also made crucial and controversial innovations in their work,

Two early champions of Catholic renewal.

Gasparo Contarini.

Ignatius Loyola, holding his constitutions for the Society and flanked by leading Jesuit scholars of the next generation, including Luis de Molina. They are dressed simply as academics, since the Society has no regular habit.

again thereby not endearing themselves to monks and friars (whom, it must be said, they treated in an infuriatingly patronizing manner on occasion). They eliminated two normal features of religious community life: regular decision-making gatherings of the community in chapter and a daily structure of communal worship 'in choir' in the community church – moreover they refused to develop a distinct uniform dress or habit for members to wear. The Society was nevertheless far from unstructured or directionless: the Superior-General made policy and conveyed it to Superiors of provinces which generally corresponded to major political or regional units like Spain or Italy. During the 1540s, Ignatius delicately finessed the Society's principle of papal obedience so that it was clearly understood that the Superior-General and not His Holiness was responsible for directing mission policy.[9] Within this discipline, and with an increasingly rigorous and structured training for Society members based on the psychological insights of the *Exercises*, Jesuits had scope for extraordinary feats of personal initiative and adventuring.

Ignatius needed all his formidable political skill (and that of certain devoted female supporters) to protect such idiosyncratic provisions, but they were soon to be vindicated by the spectacular numerical growth and achievements of the Society – 3,000 members only a quarter-century after 1540, working in three continents.[10] Moreover, the Jesuit style addressed the problem of excessive clericalism which had been one of the rallying-cries of the Protestant revolution; thus the Jesuits provided an effective riposte to Protestantism. They did not seek to become an enclosed monastic Order because Ignatius passionately wanted to affirm the value of the world and say that it was possible to lead a fully spiritual life within it – he was, after all, a cultured ex-courtier who had seen more of the world than most Europeans, in wanderings which had taken him from the Basque lands as far as London and Jerusalem. The medieval western Church harboured a tendency, never exclusive or all-embracing, but real enough, to assume that the spirituality of monks and priests was superior to that of the laity, and that clergy had a better chance of getting to heaven. Resentment against such clericalism had been one reason why so many read with such relish Luther's *Address to the Christian Nobility of the German Nation* and the genre of anti-clerical evangelical literature that it spawned.

There had already been a strong reaction in perfectly orthodox medieval traditional devotion against clericalism, most notably, of course, in the *Devotio Moderna*, which vigorously affirmed that the clergy had no especial privileges in the eyes of God (chapter 1, p. 23). It is no coincidence that the book with the most influence on the developing spirituality of Iñigo López de Loyola, discovered soon after his 'knightly' vigil before Our Lady of Montserrat, was that *Devotio* classic, *The Imitation of Christ* by Thomas á Kempis. Ignatius remained an extremely unclerical cleric – it was not surprising that the Spanish Inquisition and the likes of Gian Pietro Carafa remembered the *alumbrados* when they scrutinized his devotional style. Ignatius thought of his Jesuits as 'apostles' rather than priests: a call to the Society was not a call to priesthood, and in any case, Jesuit clergy confined their spiritual ministry to two of the Church's seven sacraments, Communion and Confession. Notably, Loyola waged an irritable battle to stop Jesuit churches staging elaborately sung high masses, although when the Society realized that festive music and splendid ritual were effective evangelistic devices in the mission field, it relented on this puritanism.[11]

In its first decade, the Society lacked two features which later seemed an essential part of its mission: aggressive confrontation with northern European Protestantism, and involvement with education. The Counter-Reformation was still in the future. So when the Genevan Pierre Favre, one of Ignatius's closest associates from his Paris student days, instructed fellow Jesuits in how they should treat Lutherans, he stressed that it should be a matter of simple Christian witness, 'speaking with them familiarly on those topics which we have in common and avoiding all contentious arguments in which one party might seem to beat the other'.[12] The confrontational stance only emerged in the 1550s (Chapters 6, p. 309 and 7, p. 323). As for education, the Society more or less blundered by accident into this work that proved so vital over the next two centuries. While it quickly set up 'colleges' in certain university towns, they were simply intended as lodging-places for students who were members of the Society. However, potential lay benefactors were not excited by the inward-looking reference of such projects, and that was an incentive to think about expanding the colleges' role.

The significant pioneering move here came in Spain in 1546: with endowments secured by the Valencian nobleman Francisco Borja Duke of Gandía (later Superior-General of the Society), a small college was set up at Gandía, which for the first time was not part of an existing university, and yet which rapidly secured university status from the Pope. Two years later, at Messina in Sicily, a more elaborate development of the Gandía initiative was promoted by the Spanish viceroy and his wife Leonora Osorio (one of the most energetic of Ignatius's circle of aristocratic female admirers): the locally endowed school was staffed by a cosmopolitan cross-section of some of the Society's leading members. Ignatius may have thought of this primarily as a way of securing endowed education for Jesuits, but within half a decade city authorities right across Europe were scrabbling to secure such de luxe school facilities for their own children. Moreover, although education in these schools was proudly proclaimed as free of charge (and the Society put a huge and increasingly professional effort into fund-raising to make sure that it was), the Jesuits concentrated their limited manpower on secondary education. The consequence was that it was very difficult for children of the poor to get the necessary primary grounding to enter the system. Thus there came about a Jesuit educational mission to secure the minds of the next generation of merchants, gentry and nobility – in other words, the people who mattered in converting Europe back to the faith. This mission evolved without any single policy decision, and not until the end of the 1540s.[13]

HOPES FOR A DEAL: THE 1541–2 CRISIS

At the beginning of the 1540s, therefore, many within the Roman Church did not associate their enthusiasm for the burgeoning religious renewal with an unbending attitude to northern Protestants. The Jesuits were linked to the circle of Contarini and Pole, and in turn Contarini and Pole were friends and patrons of theologians like Valdés, Ochino and Vermigli, who were quietly exploring what northern evangelicals might contribute to their own religious synthesis. Such forces in Italy had the chance to steer the Church into the sort of reasonable reassessment of its faults and a restructuring of its theology that Erasmus had sought before the Luther crisis had broken: to take a peace-seeking ('eirenical') approach. If they could do this, they would win the warm gratitude of Charles V. The Emperor's military prestige was high after recent successes against the Ottomans and in Muslim north Africa, but he was also only too conscious of the fragmentation which the religious quarrels had brought to the central European territories of the Empire and the kingdoms of his brother Ferdinand. He may also have been aware that his own sister Mary (widow of the unfortunate King Louis of Hungary, and now Charles's Regent in the wealthy and restless Low Countries) was a discreet patron of learned evangelical clergy at her Court in Brussels.[14]

Particularly given what had happened at Münster, there was much support among the leading figures of the Empire for some sort of general deal to restore an ordered peace. Several important princes had not yet made a definite decision in the Reformation. The Elector Joachim II of Brandenburg, for instance, had a Lutheran brother-in-law but also, in the King of Poland, a Catholic father-in-law for his notoriously unhappy marriage. Since additionally Cardinal Albrecht of Mainz was Joachim's uncle, it is perhaps not surprising that the Elector was not overfull of reverence for the old Church hierarchy, and he took it upon himself in traditional *Landesvater* style to enact his own religious settlement for Brandenburg, specifically declaring it to be temporary until there could be a general settlement throughout the Empire. He made no break with Rome, but confiscated much of the Church's lands and dissolved monasteries, just as Henry VIII was doing at the same time in England, and with almost as much lack of concern to reinvest his winnings.[15]

Philipp Melanchthon in 1538 contemptuously called such people the '*Mittelhauf*', the mob in the middle, but only a year later he was prepared to co-operate with Joachim in further moves on Church reform, and he had shown himself capable of some remarkable gestures across the divide: in 1531 he suggested to Henry VIII that he should solve the Aragon marriage *impasse* by getting the Pope to provide a dispensation for bigamy.[16] In 1532, Melanchthon had dedicated his commentary on Romans to Cardinal Albrecht no less, pleading with him to use his position as Primate of Germany to act as a mediator, and equally his dedication of his 1535 *Loci Communes* to King Henry of England was a rather optimistic casting of bread upon the waters. No wonder that Martin Luther remarked acidly that his colleague wrote his best dedicatory prefaces to 'the naughtiest boys'.[17] Moreover, for all his harsh words about temporizers in the late 1530s Melanchthon was himself taking an interest in new moves in the archdiocese of Cologne.

The current Archbishop of Cologne was a powerful nobleman, Hermann von Wied. He was no great scholar, and his acquisition of the Archbishopric while still only a sub-deacon in 1515 did not suggest that he would break the mould of aristocratic German church leadership any more than his fellow-Elector in Mainz, Cardinal Albrecht: in fact, von Wied became an energetic reformer in his wealthy and powerful Rhineland prince-bishopric (which was another of the seven Electorates of the Empire). He called on the services of a distinguished theologian, Johann Gropper, to write an *Enchiridion* to be a positive and constructive statement of the Church's belief as well as a response to Melanchthon's *Loci;* Gropper included a nuanced discussion of justification that much interested the Italian circle of Contarini and Pole. In 1536 the Archbishop summoned a provincial church synod to Cologne, and its reforming provisions were published in 1538 along with Gropper's *Enchiridion*; they were in the tradition of humanist efforts to tidy the faults of the existing structures by recalling clergy to the strictest moral standards, and making sure that these clergy went on to give the laity proper and regular instruction in basic Christian doctrine. Copies circulated throughout Europe, and as far away as Scotland they were seen as the best programme available for a local church reform.[18]

Here was an Archbishop of the Western Church who openly regretted the failure of repeated efforts to reform the Church, while still proclaiming his loyalty to the Holy See; Archbishop Cranmer in England's separated but still very theologically hybrid Church watched with interest. More remarkable still, in 1539 von Wied invited Melanchthon and Martin Bucer to help him in preparing a more thoroughgoing scheme of reform for his diocese, and although Melanchthon eventually refused to compromise himself in this way, Bucer accepted. Similarly, in the same year, Bucer joined with Georg Witzel, a married priest whose early enthusiasm for Luther had cooled and who had returned to Roman obedience, in drafting a Church structure for Ducal Saxony in the wake of the death of Luther's instransigent enemy Duke Georg. Was this the way forward for a reconciliation across the 1520s divide?

The Protestants, particularly the indefatigable Bucer, had likewise not given up hope of healing their own wounds inflicted in the Marburg discussions about the Eucharist. Philipp Melanchthon was now a experienced and self-confident negotiator, who had long ago modified his uncritical youthful idolization of Luther. Although he remained publicly as loyal as possible to Luther when he was acting officially on behalf of Wittenberg, in the early 1530s he had privately come to the conclusion that Luther was misguided in much of what he said about the Eucharist, an opinion which led to some fruitful discussions with Bucer, much to the pleasure of Philipp of Hesse. Melanchthon generally kept a discreet silence about his differences from Luther in the matter, writing no more than a page or two about the Eucharist over a ten-year period, but he was quite prepared to modify the 1530 Augsburg Confession (after all, he had written it himself). In 1540 he produced a modified ('Variata') version, one of the main variations of which consisted of a form of words about eucharistic presence designed to accommodate the main worries of non-Lutheran evangelicals: the body and blood were not now described as 'truly and substantially present', and they were said to be 'shown forth' ('exhibeantur'), rather than 'distributed' ('distribuantur') to communicants. Luther was furious, and would not accept these changes as representing his beliefs, but the Variata form of the Augsburg Confession did have an effect on future formulations of Reformed eucharistic doctrine.

Against this background of attempted accommodations and adjustments, a moment of opportunity arose in 1540–1 that Charles V was determined to seize. He had a bizarre stroke of luck – a severe dent to the prestige of his most truculent Protestant opponent within the Empire, Philipp of Hesse, which also damaged the reputation of the leading German reformers. It was revealed that Philipp had recently committed bigamy, with the express if reluctant written agreement of Luther, Bucer and Melanchthon. Their action was the ultimate in Protestant wooing of the magistrate. The signatories' logic (apart from the unspoken acknowledgement of how much they owed to Philipp) was that bigamy was better than the adultery which had characterized Philipp's chaotic private life over the previous decade; Melanchthon and Bucer in particular were only being consistent with the advice about bigamy that they had offered Henry VIII a few years before (chapter 13, p. 227). Nevertheless the evangelical theologians' belief that both their action and the bigamous marriage could be kept secret was a colossally naive political misjudgement, bringing predictable and gleeful expressions of moral outrage from their Catholic opponents. Charles graciously granted an imperial pardon to his prince, who could in theory have suffered the death penalty for bigamy as newly laid down in the 1532 imperial law code (*Lex Carolina*). Melanchthon was so shattered by the self-inflicted catastrophe that he became gravely ill.

Apart from this demoralizing moment for the evangelicals, an extra incentive to come to agreement was a sudden renewal of Ottoman military activity, which reached a terrifying stage in 1541 with the beginning of their long-term occupation of the former royal Hungarian capital of Buda. With all sides therefore showing welcome signs of vulnerability, preparations for discussions cautiously went ahead. Much hung on the outcome of these events. The great nineteenth-century German historian Leopold von Ranke saw them as 'a period of vital importance for Germany and even for the world': perhaps the definitive moment at which the Holy Roman Empire failed to go the way of France or England into becoming a unified state, and when the middle ground failed to carry with it the old Church of Rome.[19]

After a number of false starts, useful discussions began in January 1541. Johann Eck and Melanchthon achieved the remarkable feat of agreeing in four days a statement on original sin, and Bucer and Gropper followed up their previous discussions in Cologne. Gropper's work offered the chance of reaching agreement in the theological minefield of justification. Deeply learned in the writings of the early Fathers of the Church, he returned to Augustine of Hippo and rediscovered (as had Lefevre, Luther and Contarini) Augustine's deep pessimism about the human condition. This seemed to counter what late medieval theology had said about the possibility that human righteousness might be able to match up to God's requirements: 'to do that which is in oneself', in Gabriel Biel's phrase (chapter 3, p. 111).

Gropper argued that when a human being met God on judgement day, even the combination of the grace which the Church's sacraments conveyed and what remained of merit in human beings would not stand up to divine scrutiny. This combination was not negligible, he said, but it would necessarily have to be supplemented by the righteousness of Christ. God in his mercy would allow this 'alien righteousness' to be imputed to the unworthy sinful human through grace. What Gropper had done was to find a way of squaring the circle of the medieval theology of merit and Luther's theology of imputed merit by grace through faith (chapter 3, p. 119). Bucer was impressed by Gropper's statement of what is often called 'double justification' (perhaps it should really be triple justification: sacraments, human merit, the grace of Christ). He did little to modify what Gropper had drafted. Their agreement on justification and other matters became known as the 'Regensburg Book'.[20]

This was preliminary to the opening in March 1541 of the Imperial Diet at Regensburg (Ratisbon), in parallel to the theologians' conference (or colloquy). Even the schismatic English were keen to cash in on the atmosphere of reconciliation: King Henry sent over his most prominent conservative Bishop, Stephen Gardiner of Winchester, to make Catholic noises to the Emperor. Rome signalled its commitment to doing real business at Regensburg by sending the eirenical Cardinal Contarini, who had impressive experience as a diplomat in the service of the Venetian Republic. When introduced to Bucer, he observed 'How great will be the fruit of unity, and how profound the gratitude of all mankind'. Bucer replied equally graciously: 'Both sides have failed. Some of us have overemphasized unimportant points, and others have not adequately reformed obvious abuses. With God's will we shall ultimately find the truth.'[21] Such optimism soon faded. Powerful forces were still very suspicious of any deal at Regensburg: some of the Emperor's own princes were not anxious to see the Habsburg family's problems solved, even less so the King of France, who would have been a necessary party to any final agreement. But in any case, the theologians proceeded over the next two months to ruin the deal before the politicians had any opportunity to do so. Contarini could not give ground on the eucharistic doctrine of transubstantiation; the Protestants were not prepared to say that confession to a priest was necessary. Their measure of agreement on justification in the Regensburg Book was therefore irrelevant. Then messages from both Rome and Luther in Wittenberg made it quite clear that even that would not be accepted.

The failure of the Regensburg Colloquy was not merely a disaster for the Empire, it precipitated a crisis in Italy that had profound consequences for the future of western Christianity. Contarini had aroused many fears in Rome by his willingness to compromise and he died under house arrest, a broken man, in August 1542. By then, the more confrontational *Spirituali* were alert to the danger of their position. Valdés avoided the testing time by his death in 1541, but Bernardino Ochino was summoned to Rome when his sermons became ever more outspoken. Sensibly disregarding the order, he had time to say goodbye to the dying Contarini before he left on horseback for Switzerland and Calvin's Geneva, and he was closely followed in his flight by Peter Martyr Vermigli, whose wanderings eventually took him to a warm welcome from Bucer in Strassburg. The sensation was huge at the flight of these preachers whom all Italy knew, and theirs were only the first in a series of defections of Italian scholars and theologians to the Reformed world across the Alps.

Gian Pietro Carafa's hour had come. The conciliators had not merely produced nothing out of the Regensburg Colloquy (an enterprise which he had denounced from the beginning), but many of their brightest stars now shamelessly revealed themselves as traitors to the Church, at the same time tainting all their friends and associates who stayed, particularly those whom they had contacted in the course of their flights northward. Peter Martyr, it emerged, had used his most recent base in Lucca in Tuscany during 1541–2 to encourage a popular movement which looked like the classic tumultuous first stages of a northern European urban Reformation: evangelical preaching, denunciations of the papacy, even Swiss-style Eucharists. Now Carafa had a cast-iron case to persuade Pope Paul III to set up a Roman Inquisition, modelled on the Spanish Inquisition, and with the Cardinal-Archbishop of Naples himself as one of the Inquisitors-General. The papal Bull was promulgated on 21 July 1542. 'Even if my own father were a heretic, I would gather the wood to burn him,' Carafa vowed.[22]

There was much less incentive now for remaining Italian *Spirituali*, evangelical humanists or humble bible-readers to feel any commitment to the traditional Church. Cardinal Pole, who always tried to avoid closing options or drawing clear boundaries, did what he could to protect his own dependents, who included some of Valdés's former admirers, and to keep them faithful to the Church. Pole's friend, Cardinal Giovanni Morone, kept the Inquisition at bay in his religiously turbulent diocese of Modena by an extensive campaign of swearing leading citizens to a Formulary of Faith, designed by Contarini to persuade truculent evangelicals back into the fold. Yet because the secular and religious leaders of Italy so rapidly fell into line after 1542, there was every reason for adventurous individuals clandestinely to pursue their own lines of spirituality without the disciplining which

Two Italian refugees from the downfall of the Spirituali.

Peter Martyr Vermigli.

Bernardino Ochino.

evangelical opinion was experiencing in the institutional churches of northern Europe. Wealthy citizens in Lucca in particular went on fomenting underground religious radicalism for two decades after Peter Martyr's flight.

In what seemed the relative safety of Venice, a community of radicals gathered, who were from time to time able to meet with Anabaptists from the Alpine regions to work out some common basis for their Christian belief. In 1550, during the course of a marathon forty days of discussion, prayer and Eucharist, they agreed that the Bible gave no basis for believing that Jesus was God. In the new atmosphere of repression, the strain of being different eventually broke the nerve of one of their leading members, a former priest and admirer of Ochino, Pietro Manelfi. In the following year he handed himself over to the Inquisition, who were delighted now to have the chance to wipe out nearly the whole of the Italian radical movement. Those who could followed the example of Peter Martyr and Ochino and fled northwards; the rest (and we will never know how many they were) faded silently back into the mainstream church in Italy. A variety of very independent thought, ending up in both unitarianism and Swiss-style Protestantism, remained untidily connected to Pole's papal palace in Viterbo, Colonna's salons or Michelangelo's artist's studio.[23]

The most influential work of Italian spirituality in these years, the *Beneficio di Cristo* (published 1543, and apparently selling in tens of thousands before translation into other European languages), illustrates this continuing shapelessness – it was itself a somewhat shapeless work. It was written by a Cassinese Benedictine monk Don Benedetto da Mantova, through whom it gained a characteristically Cassinese colouring of the great Fathers of the fourth- and fifth-century Greek Church like John Chrysostom (Chapter 2, p. 91). It was then revised by Benedetto's friend Marcantonio Flaminio, a protégé of Valdés and Pole, to heighten its presentation of the spiritual and mystical themes of Valdesian theology, and it also silently incorporated substantial quotations from the 1539 edition of Calvin's *Institutes*! The text emphasized justification by faith alone, and celebrated the benefits of suffering for the faith; yet Cardinal Morone loved it for its eloquence on the benefits of the Eucharist. The Inquisition's opinion of it can be gauged by the fact that of all the thousands of copies printed in Italian, none was seen again from the sixteenth century down to a chance find in the University Library in Cambridge, England, in 1843. That disappearance, dismal proof of the Inquisition's energy when it felt the need, is an eloquent symbol of the exclusion of the *Spirituali* from the future of the Catholic Church.[24]

A COUNCIL AT TRENT: THE FIRST SESSION
1545-9

The dramatic shift in the balance of influence in the Roman Church that sprang from the crisis of 1541-2 was of great significance, because it was now that the long delays in convening a General Council of the Western Church finally ended – at a moment when there was no chance of even moderate evangelical representation from northern Europe, and when the conciliatory or *Spirituale* voices in high ecclesiastical circles were in disarray. There had been a series of false starts ever since the Pope had unsuccessfully called Europe's bishops to Mantua in 1537, although after that the Pope and Emperor at least settled on a venue which did not discountenance either of them: the prince-bishopric of Trent in the Tyrol was in imperial territory, but it was also south of the Alps. The opening ceremony finally took place there on 13 December 1545, still with only about three dozen official representatives besides the advisory theologians in attendance. Although numbers did roughly double for later sessions, around 600 European bishops were at that stage still more or less loyal to the traditional Church, and the number of important absentees was always large, especially from France, the Atlantic Isles (no royally appointed representative ever attended Trent from the Atlantic kingdoms of England, Scotland or Ireland) and the remaining Catholic parts of northern Europe. The Franconian Prince-Bishop of Würzburg, for instance, found better things to occupy him in Germany, and he consistently ignored all papal pleadings to attend the Council in person, as did his successor throughout its third session in the 1560s.[25]

Most bishops who did appear at Trent were Italians, as one would expect. That did not necessarily mean that they were unthinking tools of papal policy (which was in any case a shifting commodity), nor were hardliners in the mould of Carafa the only voices to be heard. The host and chairman of the Council as Bishop of Trent, Cristoforo Madruzzo, was a *Spirituale* sympathizer and a former student and patron of one of Italy's leading conciliarist scholars; he was also an old friend of Reginald Pole.[26] Pole was himself one of the three legates sent by the Pope, and he prepared the opening sermon, which had a sternly penitential tone and drew attention to the hierarchy's faults, urging them to imitation of Christ.[27] Among the insultingly small number of French bishops who made the long journey to Trent was a rare crypto-evangelical, Gérard Roussel, the Bishop of Navarrese Oloron: he was a survivor of the Lefèvre-Briçonnet circle and still chaplain to that steadfast champion of French reformists, Marguerite d'Angoulême. However, Roussel would soon despair of the tone of Trent's proceedings. A series of decrees began spelling out the detail of doctrines which had previously been surrounded with a certain latitude; it became virtually impossible to sustain the nuanced spectrum of belief which had helped many reformers stay in the Church through the storms of the previous three decades.[28]

The first significant decree came on 8 April 1546, and concerned the basic question of authority, out of which Martin Luther's confrontation with the Church hierarchy had been manufactured in 1518–20. There was no question of a 'scripture alone' view of the authority question. The truth of the divine revelation was declared to be presented to humanity through two channels, both of which were in the custody of the Church: 'this truth and this discipline are contained in written books and in unwritten traditions, which were received by the Apostles from the lips of Christ himself, or by the . . . Apostles, at the dictation of the Holy Spirit, and were handed on and have come down to us . . . preserved by unbroken succession in the Catholic Church.' The case for a status for a communal tradition of 'unwritten verities' alongside scriptural authority was, after all, plausible in the face of radical reinterpretations of Christianity; as evangelicals quickly and uncomfortably discovered it was otherwise difficult to defend infant baptism effectively, to say nothing of lesser matters like the observance of Sunday as the weekly day of worship or the proposition that the Virgin Mary had remained perpetually a virgin (see Chapter 15, pp. 613–14). However, Protestants might (and did) observe that the principle of 'unwritten verities' was as capable of almost as infinite extension as the doctrinal explorations of the radicals.

Equally momentous and a direct confrontation with the core issues of the 1520s was the decree on the nature of justification. The debates over this Somme-like battleground were painful and long drawn-out. The result was a firm rejection of the possibilities offered by Gropper's discussion of double justification, and an attempt to continue to hold in perpetual tension the theological polarities which had been so unstable in the medieval Western Church: Trent decreed that God necessarily takes the initiative in salvation through grace, 'through the redemption that is in Christ Jesus', as Augustine had insisted, but also that humanity retains free will after the Fall in Eden. The Council rejected Luther's assertion that sinful humanity cannot fulfil the Law – 'God does not command impossibilities'. God's grace is available through the good works which humans can perform, including participation in the Church's sacraments of baptism and penance (in March 1547 all seven sacraments of the medieval Western Church were reaffirmed as 'instituted by

Jesus Christ'). Several months before the long and intricately balanced text of the Decree on Justification was finally passed in January 1547, Cardinal Pole had left the Council, never to return. An acute modern commentator on the Council considers that the strain of trying to hold his line on justification had driven him to virtual nervous breakdown. To remain loyal to the Church, all he could do was to plead illness and leave; only thus could he find the strength to submit to the Council's unwelcome decisions.[29]

Pole was not the only one to feel that the decree on justification was a turning-point. As much as the 1542 crisis, this marked a moment when many Italian evangelicals ceased to regard themselves as part of the same church as the Bishop of Rome; they now gathered in their own secret conventicles. Equally, Charles V was increasingly displeased with the Council's proceedings, which closed any remaining possibility of a deal with the Lutherans. There might have been a new chance to bring in chastened German evangelicals after the Emperor's crushing military victory over the Schmalkaldic League at Mühlberg in April 1547 (chapter 6, p. 271), but just at this juncture Paul III chose to move the Council from Trent south to the papal city of Bologna, officially to avoid an outbreak of the plague in Trent. Charles was enraged by this move to the second most important city of the Papal States, and several bishops who wished to assert episcopal rights against the papacy were equally suspicious of the Pope's motives. The Council which convened at Bologna was a shadow of its previous self, although its proceedings drifted on for a few more months into 1548 before the Pope suspended it under pressure from the Emperor.[30] Nothing more could happen while Paul III lived; the old man was increasingly distracted by the dire results of his dabbling in Italian politics on behalf of his grasping and often sensationally scandalous family. His eventual death on 10 November 1549 offered a last chance to turn the tide of authoritarianism in the Roman Church, for one of the favourite candidates to succeed Paul as Pope was Reginald Pole himself.

The fact that Pole could be considered a plausible Pope is a tribute to the continuing respect in which he was held, despite all that had happened, and despite the inconvenience that as yet he was still only in deacon's orders. There were many diverse hopes invested in him – too many and too diverse for his own good. Even the dying Paul III had recommended him. The Emperor approved of him because he had (belatedly) championed Charles's aunt Catherine of Aragon against Henry VIII, because he was of royal blood, and because he was not Italian. Pole's upbringing linked him to the high-minded, tidy-minded clergy and their royal admirers who had made early Tudor England one of the best-run parts of Christendom: Dean Colet,

Bishop Fisher, Lady Margaret Beaufort, Queen Catherine. His cosmopolitan education made him a humanist scholar at the centre of a cultured international circle worthy of Erasmus. His patronage and friendship had attracted some of the most creative minds of southern Europe, from Valdés to Contarini and Colonna, and despite his pathological inability to write any readable work of devotion, he was generally recognized as one of the most thoughtful churchmen of his day. Perhaps only Marguerite d'Angoulême could rival him as a magnet for reformers who wished to remain true to the old Church, and it is debatable whether the fact that she was a woman or the fact that she was French was more of a bar to her ever becoming Pope.

Yet Pole failed. On the first ballot in the conclave of Cardinals, he came within four votes of a majority. On the second, Carafa dramatically intervened, waving a file of papers that he claimed proved that the Englishman was a heretic; nevertheless, Pole's vote rose, and this time there was only one vote short. But now the proceedings became drawn out (it was one of the longest conclaves in papal history) and Pole did not have the stomach for a face-to-face fight in such atmospheres of bitterness. Once more he drew back from the brink instead of seizing the hour. The new Pope, Julius III, was an Italian papal civil servant who was no especial friend to Carafa, but who had no great vision of reform either. In the Cardinals' vote which elected Julius on 8 February 1550, the last chance passed away for a Reformation such as Erasmus had sought.[31]

CALVIN IN GENEVA: THE REFORMED
ANSWER TO MÜNSTER

In the years during which the Council of Trent first began to give legislative shape to the structures of belief and practice that would become the Counter-Reformation Catholic Church, John Calvin was also beginning to create a working model of what a Reformed Catholic Church might look like. It will be recalled that from 1541 he was back in Geneva after nearly three years of exile in Strassburg. His task was not simply to expand his ordered presentation of a Reformed theology from the 1536 *Institutes*. In striking contrast to Luther, he took a precise and detailed interest in how the Church should be structured, and now in Geneva he had the sort of opportunity to try out his ideas that the Anabaptists had enjoyed in Münster in 1534. Calvin's interest was equalled by the Genevan city elite's concern to make sure that such a structure would be under their control; neither side fully achieved its goal, but the creative tension embodied in the *Ecclesiastical Ordinances* which the city authorities ordered Calvin to draft in 1541 had resonances throughout the continent. Calvin drew his models from Bucer's Strassburg, fortified by his observations during his exile: Bucer had experienced his own tensions and frustrations with the civil authorities there, but Calvin was able to go much further than Bucer in creating decision-making and disciplinary bodies for the Genevan Church that formed a hierarchy of authorities alongside those of the city. It was a consistent application of the 'two kingdoms' theory of the Church that Luther and Melanchthon had taken in a radically different, and confusing, direction (chapters 3, p. 157, and 4, p. 164).

To structure the Genevan Church in the *Ordinances*, Calvin borrowed Bucer's assertion that the New Testament indicated four functions of ministry: pastors, doctors, elders and deacons. Calvin was not particularly worried about the forms that this fourfold system might take, as long as all its functions were properly carried out: his successors were more doctrinaire about forms than he was, and tried to copy exactly what had been done in Geneva. Pastors carried out the general ministry of care of the laity exercised by medieval parish priests and bishops; doctors were responsible for teaching at all levels, up to the most searching scholarly investigation of the Bible (Calvin, who was himself never ordained as priest or minister in any Church, primarily identified himself as a doctor). Together the pastors and the senior doctors, who were obviously close to them in ministry, notably Calvin himself, formed a Company of Pastors. Elders bore the disciplinary work of the Church, that function which Bucer considered so important that he had proclaimed it to be the third mark of a true Church (chapter 4, p. 181): Bucer had advocated the establishment of just such an eldership in his *Von der wahren Seelsorge* (*On the true care of souls*, 1538).

So Calvin managed to do what Strassburg council opposition had prevented Bucer from achieving: he set up an eldership functioning citywide, together with a committee in which the pastors and elders could combine to exercise discipline. Calvin named this committee as the 'Consistory' rather casually in passing in the *Ordinances*: this was meant to wield a different sort of authority from the dry legalities of the secular courts, advising and guiding people in broken relationships of neighbourliness or marriage. Similarly exercising Christian love alongside the Consistory's discipline were the deacons, the fourth order of biblical ministry, who took the function described for them in the book of Acts, looking after charitable giving, either administratively or practically. This diaconal function was very necessary when the medieval structure of charity run by religious orders or confraternities had been so comprehensively dismantled in the Reformation, and Calvin also saw their role as demonstrating love in action: so their often very practical and down-to-earth activities were intimately connected with the acts of Christian worship. After his death, this connection was expressed in the liturgy of the Genevan Church, when a solemn act of alms-giving was instituted.

The balance of power thus created in the *Ordinances* was interestingly subtle. It reflected the fact that Geneva was being swamped by immigrant religious enthusiasts in a manner strikingly reminiscent of Münster in its Anabaptist days. Apart from the hundreds of ordinary laypeople who arrived, all the ministers in the city were immigrants, mostly French; in fact, astonishingly between the 1540s and 1594, the Genevan ministry did not include a single native Genevan. Yet Calvin's evangelical message was much more firmly tied into existing political structures than had been that of Bernd Rothmann and Jan Matthijszoon. The patrician city authorities in Geneva, in contrast to those of Münster, were determined to keep the immigrants from challenging their authority. Already when they had evolved civil institutions for the city in the wake of their independence struggle from Savoy, they had made their own innovations in constitutional practice. They created a hierarchy of decision-making councils, the real power being kept in the smallest and most exclusive, the 'Council of 24'. They laid down for the first time that citizenship of Geneva was restricted entirely to the native-born, and only citizens could become members of the Council of 24 or its associated major offices. However, to neutralize discontent from outsiders and to give appropriate immigrants a stake in Genevan society, the councillors also created a category of 'bourgeois', who joined with citizens in being eligible for membership and election of the larger, less powerful city councils, of 60 and 200. It is noticeable that Calvin only achieved this 'bourgeois' status in 1559, when he was put in charge of the city's proud new institution of higher education, the Academy: until then he was merely a member of the third and numerous category of strangers living in Geneva, immigrant 'habitants' without political rights. That did not stop him building up a unique power-base within the city.

From 1541, the pyramid of councils in the civil government stood alongside the system which Calvin had created for the Church: the Company of Pastors, the Consistory of pastors and elders and the diaconate. The *Ordinances* carefully ensured that all the civil councils had some say in choosing the elders of the Church, but by contrast and crucially, they left the main initiative in choosing pastors in the hands of the pastors themselves, although they allowed for due provisions for scrutiny by senior councilmen and even by congregations. Thereafter the Genevan pastoral ministry formed a self-perpetuating body, with a strong sense that God had chosen it to choose itself. Calvin and Bucer, after all, had demonstrated that God himself had provided for the Church's government in the fourfold form of ministry. What better reason than God's authorization to develop a sturdy self-confidence in the forms of the ministry, and to maintain an independent attitude to civil commonwealth? It was a far cry from the clerical ministry simultaneously evolving in Luther's Germany, effectively a wing of the bureaucracy of princes or city councils, and chosen by them as they would choose their other officers. It was in fact much more like the high clericalism of the old Western Church.

It should be obvious why the 'two kingdoms' theory was thus so graphically expressed in the Genevan situation in the 1540s. At the head of the civil government was a small elite of the native-born Genevan patriciate, while at the head of the Church's government was a small exiled elite of some of the best minds in France, supported by that large element of the immigrant population who were in Geneva as godly refugees for religion's sake. Nevertheless, the Church structure which arose from this peculiarity of the Genevan political situation was copied all over Europe wherever Calvin's independent form of the Church was admired, even though the original reason for the structure was not present. A Church that stood alongside the civil authority and felt a God-given right to criticize it if necessary, while still aspiring to minister to the entire population which the civil authority administered, was a powerful expression of militant Catholic Christianity. It might be particularly militant if it was formed independently of the civil power – but such consequences lay in the future.

Though the *Ordinances* represented an agreed deal between Calvin and the Council of 24, including some last-minute alterations on which the Council insisted in order to improve its position in relation to the Church authorities, tensions persisted. One constitutional issue, first raised two decades before by Johannes Oecolampadius in Basel (chapter 4, p. 181) remained a crucial litmus test in Reformed Churches of where power lay: who possessed the right to excommunicate Church members – the Church's own disciplinary authorities such as the Consistory, or the civil authorities? Calvin obstinately refused to acknowledge that the *Ordinances* delivered the power of excommunication into civic hands, and there were many other features of his ministry that increasingly irritated some of the citizens who had done most to secure his recall. Proud of Geneva's heritage, they were infuriated that Calvin's hatred of idolatry led him to ban the name of Claude, the city's own saint, for babies baptized in the city; in fact, there were a number of ugly scenes at the font when ministers refused to confer this and other 'superstitious' names on the children presented to them.[32]

City opposition did not come so much from Catholics, whose power had long been broken, as from evangelicals who did not feel that the Reformation should have turned out like this; the city elite had staged their revolution to rid Geneva of a tyrannous bishop and a foreign overlord, and now they found themselves being lorded over by a set of foreign clergy who in some spectacular cases succeeded in subjecting them publicly to humiliating church discipline. Calvin had a talent for inventing abusive nicknames and he styled this amorphous opposition 'Libertines', which had a conveniently scandalous resonance, while also reflecting the undoubted fact that his opponents sought a freedom for which he saw no need. Ultimately it is fairly safe to add the conclusion that many people opposed Calvin because they detested him. If one would have been justified in anticipating a good night out in the company of Martin Luther, the same cannot be said for the buttoned-up French exile who wanted to stop the citizens of Geneva dancing. Calvin was in delicate health from his youth, and he was not inclined to conviviality; his only recorded frivolous indulgence, apart from an occasional round of quoits, was the game known to schoolboys in twentieth-century England as shove ha'penny.[33] He did, however, relish getting his own way, which he identified with doing the will of God.

Apart from an increasingly formidable political opposition from some of the most influential native Genevans, Calvin was also challenged by individuals within the immigrant community, who naturally included independent-minded and articulate people with strong opinions. One of the earliest was the Savoyard Sébastien Châteillon (now more usually called Sebastian Castellio), a considerable biblical scholar whom Calvin brought from Strassburg in 1541 to become the Rector of Geneva's municipal college (a school like those in French towns and cities: see chapter 4, p. 197). Castellio chose his own stance on a number of biblical and theological problems, the most irksome of which for Calvin was his refusal to accept that the Old Testament's erotic poem, the Song of Songs, should really be a 'canonical' part of the Bible. Calvin was determined to defend the canonicity of the Song of Songs; his theology was based on the principle that God's revelation of his Word was definitively contained within the Bible, and unlike Luther, he was not prepared to pick and choose where the Word was best expressed within the Bible's covers. The Bible was God's to define, however unpromising the sensuous lyrics of the Song of Songs might seem.

However, this raised the uncomfortable question of how the canonical boundaries of the Bible had been set in the early Church, as Calvin, a humanist scholar with a sense of historical perspective, readily appreciated. At some point the Church had made decisions about what should be in the Bible and what should not. In securing a condemnation of Castellio's views, Calvin was forced to talk afresh about the tradition of the Church: 'our first plea and entreaty was that he should not rashly reject the age-long interpretation of the whole of the Church' – this was only a couple of years before the Council of Trent was to make such age-long interpretation an equal source of divine revelation with the biblical text.[34] Nevertheless, for all his talk of pleas and entreaties, once Calvin had won his point with the civil authorities, he forced Castellio to leave Geneva. The infuriated Savoyard eventually took up residence in Basel, where the city and Church authorities were rapidly developing the principle that no one who hated Calvin could be all bad.

Challenge on a different front came from a French refugee theologian, an ex-Carmelite friar, Jérôme Bolsec. He tackled the question of predestination in a lecture audaciously delivered to the Company of Pastors in 1551, declaring that the formulation which Calvin had made of double predestination to salvation and reprobation (damnation) effectively made out God to be a tyrant and the author of sin. Here Calvin was on uncertain ground. From Luther's first proclamation of justification by faith through God's grace, it should have been obvious that a logical conclusion of the doctrine was divine predestination of humanity to salvation or damnation, but many Protestants were not prepared to follow that logic all the way. Among Lutherans, Philipp Melanchthon had begun his career as a reformer by enthusiastically echoing Luther's affirmation of predestination and the bondage of the will, but just as on the Eucharist, he had second thoughts. From the late 1520s he grew increasingly concerned that an unqualified doctrine of predestination not only suggested that God was the author of evil but also pulled Christianity too close to pagan philosophies of determinism and human helplessness like Stoicism or Manichaeism.

So, in various writings from around 1527, particularly in successive revisions from 1535 of his highly influential theological textbook, the *Loci Communes*, Melanchthon began to draw back from and then openly to modify the notion of predestination. He preferred to say that God 'called' those who were saved and went to heaven, the divine mercy allowing a movement of the human will to receive grace, while not treating this movement as meritorious or as a cause of justification. Already in 1530 Melanchthon had virtually excluded all mention of predestination from the Augsburg Confession when he drafted it.[35] Similarly, the Protestant theologians of Zürich and Bern were not happy with the increasingly rigorous statements of predestination that appeared during the 1540s in Calvin's published work. It was not possible therefore for Calvin to act as severely against Bolsec as he would have liked, but he did make sure that Bolsec was banished from Geneva by the city authorities. Bolsec did not forgive and forget, and he devoted the rest of his career to attacking both predestination and Calvin. In old age once more a member of the Roman Catholic Church, he got his revenge by producing a viciously vituperative anti-biography of Calvin and his successor Theodore Beza; there, among other choice morsels, he accused them both of sodomy.

Bolsec's challenge was only one of a number of critiques of Calvin's views on predestination that drove the Reformer to spell out what he believed on the subject (Castellio also published a critique of Calvin's approach). Consideration of predestination had hardly appeared in the first 1536 version of the *Institutes*, but Calvin's Augustinian theology of the majesty of God predisposed him to explore the idea in the expanded editions from 1539. Once more he was much influenced by Bucer, who devoted much discussion in his biblical commentaries to the predestination both of the saved and of the damned. It is a mistake to see predestination as the dominant idea in Calvin's theology, although for some of his Reformed successors, it seems often to become so. Rather it was part of Calvin's growing conviction that he must proclaim the all-embracing providence of God in every aspect of human life and experience, so just as affirmation of a double predestination grew in Calvin's successive remoulding of the *Institutes*, so did his positive and comforting discussion of providence. Yet predestination made more than one connection for him; it was also intimately linked to his theology of the Church, to his worries about Anabaptists, and to his puzzlement that after two decades, the Reformation had not through the providence of God carried all before it. His discussion of predestination in the final version of the *Institutes* begins with that puzzlement: 'In actual fact, the covenant of life is not preached equally among all men, and among those to whom it is preached, it does not gain the same acceptance either constantly or in equal degree.'[36]

God must surely have predestined such a superficially disappointing result, and in fact God had given a model for how he chose his people in the Old Testament, in his relationship with the people of Israel. The theme of Israel became very important for Calvin, because it helped him develop his view of the Church, and answer the charge of radicals, particularly Anabaptists, that a state-sponsored Church like that of Geneva, gathering all the city's motley population, could not possibly be the true Church. An Anabaptist might say (like Calvin) that it was not surprising that few listened to God's message, because God had planned it that way. However, the Anabaptist inference from this was that a true Church should be the gathering of the minority who did listen to the word. Calvin looked at Israel in the Old Testament and drew a different conclusion. Israel was the Old Testament equivalent of the true Church; it had been a covenanted, chosen nation. Everyone in Israel was elect: they enjoyed a 'general election'. But not all Israelites followed God's commandments, and so 'we must now add a second, more limited degree of election, . . . when from the same race of Abraham God rejected some but showed that he kept others among his sons by cherishing them in the Church'.[37] So because Israel had been a mixed Church, so was the New Testament Church of Christ. The Anabaptists were mistaken.

Calvin was perfectly aware that the determinism of divine predestination was 'dreadful indeed' to humanity. Moreover, like most believers in predestination (Luther and Augustine included), he felt that only a minority would be saved – it was not Calvin but Augustine in one of his savage late anti-Pelagian works who observed that God had arranged this in order to give the elect all the more reason to be grateful for their elect status.[38] Calvin was not prepared to put a figure on the proportion of the saved, varying his estimates for artistic effect from his habitual estimate of one in a hundred to one in twenty, or even one in five in more generous moods. He was also very wary of saying that people could be certain of their own election, let alone identify others among the elect.[39] He relentlessly criticized leaders of the magisterial Reformation who disagreed with him on predestination; he usually avoided naming names in print, but many would recognize his assaults in the *Institutes* on the wayward theologians of Zürich or on Melanchthon. Calvin must particularly have enjoyed penning a swingeing attack on the alternative determinism of astrology, since it was notorious that Melanchthon was an enthusiast for astrology as a heavenly show-case in nature for God's purposes. The Wittenberg humanist even set great personal store by the horoscope which warned him against taking a ship across the Baltic Sea.[40]

The most dramatic challenge which Calvin faced was from a maverick thinker from Navarre whom we have already met, Michael Servetus (chapter 4, p. 188). Servetus began corresponding with Calvin from southern France in 1546, sending him early manuscript versions of his culminating work on theology, the *Restoration of Christianity* (this title, *Christianismi Restitutio*, was clearly an audacious reversal of Calvin's own *Christianae Religionis Institutio*). As was repeatedly the case with radicals in the sixteenth century, Servetus's medical expertise had protected him for a long time: as personal physician to the Archbishop of Vienne and enjoying this senior churchman's favour, he was able to get his *Restitutio* secretly printed in neighbouring Lyon in 1553. Now began an extraordinary saga of ecumenical viciousness. The Inquisition in Lyon arrested Servetus, but the main documentary proof of his guilt was out of its reach in Calvin's filing-system in Geneva. Soon (though Calvin always denied direct involvement) the proof ended up on the Lyon Inquisitor's desk, and Servetus was condemned. He then cheated the Inquisition out of a tidy resolution of the case at the stake by escaping; he travelled over the French border to Geneva, where he committed the extraordinary folly of turning up in the church where Calvin was preaching. Perhaps he thought that he would act as a rallying-point for the increasingly militant opposition to Calvin in the city, but instead his charmed life was at an end.

Calvin was as clear as the Roman Catholic inquisitors in Lyon or the papal Antichrist in Rome that Servetus must die. The Genevan city authorities determined that the heretic's fate should be the traditional one of burning at the stake, and although Calvin would have preferred a more mercifully summary method of execution, he did not oppose the burning on 27 October 1553. Quite apart from his own feeling that Christendom was under threat, there was a political consideration: to show mercy would be to show weakness, and that would encourage his enemies in Geneva just at a moment when they hoped to triumph. He had ensured that there had been careful international soundings among Protestants about the sentence; after all, the legality of Geneva burning someone who had merely been passing through the city was not immediately obvious.

On the whole, Calvin gained a solid endorsement: Bullinger in Zürich and Lutherans like Melanchthon and the Württemberg religious leader Johann Brenz were among the most prominent voices in favour. The most discordant noises came from Basel, where one anonymous pamphlet with bitter sarcasm described the Genevan Church as proclaiming 'its good news with flames'.[41] Sebastian Castellio was outraged at the cruelty and intolerance of what had been done, and with the discreet connivance of the Basel city authorities he wrote trenchantly on the subject of toleration; his work became the flagship of the Basel attacks on the principle of persecuting heretics. Calvin continued to feel that Castellio was one of his most dangerous enemies in all Europe – Castellio's ideas might undo all that had been done to make Geneva a beacon of Reformed practice – and Geneva devoted much energy to unsuccessful efforts to silence him and destroy his reputation.[42]

However, even Basel did not officially condemn Calvin. The burning of

Servetus strengthened his position not only in Geneva itself but throughout Europe; it was from this moment that he began widely to be perceived as not one reformer among many, but the major voice in Reformation Protestantism. He had shown his seriousness as the defender of Catholic Christianity. His victory was symbolized by the fact that the suppression of Servetus's *Restitutio* was almost as thorough as the Roman Inquisition's efforts with the *Beneficio di Cristo*: only three known copies of the original printed edition remain in the world today, one of them formerly owned by one of Calvin's fellow pastors.[43] Domestically, the serious crisis in which Calvin had found himself by 1553 came to a head over the next two years, when his very success at widening his support in the civic elite drove the infuriated opposition to open confrontation. Calvin gleefully seized on this as an attempted *coup d'état*. Four of his chief opponents who did not flee the city were beheaded, and their defeat, Calvin's triumph, was represented as God's triumph. Over the severed head of one of the victims was coldly inscribed

> For having fallen into the misfortune
> Of loving a man more than God
> Claude de Genève has his head
> Nailed up in this place.[44]

Calvin won his victory against very considerable, sustained and principled opposition, partly because he was skilled at judging the political situation, partly because of his ultimate weapon of deterrence, a threat to leave the city a second time (chapter 4, p. 197) – but above all because of his extraordinary abilities as a preacher. It is easy to concentrate on the political crises which beset Calvin. His perspective would have been different. He was, after all, primarily a doctor (teacher) of the Church rather than a pastor, and in the pulpit he became a towering force, bitterly lambasting the faults of his city and fearlessly defending his version of the faith. Between the year 1549 and his death, 2,000 or so of his sermons (more or less two a week) were noted in shorthand by two successive scribes – itself a formidable achievement – and were then written up in forty shorthand volumes. Bizarrely, the Genevan city authorities sold off all but one of these volumes in 1805, and so far less than half the sermons have been recovered. But these represent the heart of Calvin's activities: they were either based on or formed the basis of the weighty series of biblical commentaries which he published after 1551, and the *Institutes* represented for him the topically arranged twin of his pulpit examination of the biblical text. (See Plate 14a).[45]

Calvin's preaching represented an intensive examination of the details of God's Word that few other expositors would equal, sucking the last drops of meaning from every last syllable and turn of phrase: 189 sermons on Acts between 1549 and 1554, 174 on Ezekiel from 1552 to 1554, 200 on Deuteronomy in 1555–6.[46] This could be liberating to an audience precisely because it was so demanding: Calvin and the preachers who followed him asked a lot of their audience and were thus taking them seriously, as adults in the faith. Reformed congregations were expected to absorb and understand complex and abstract material and therefore were encouraged to see the value of education. They were, of course, expected to know their Bibles, and it was no coincidence that a Reformed printer invented a system of referencing the text by individual fragments defined as verses, in addition to the traditional chapter numbering. This made it much easier to locate biblical quotations; the godly loved to swap texts in argument or in devotion. The printer was Robert Estienne (Stephanus), former official printer to the King of France and a biblical scholar in his own right. He fled the kingdom in 1551 and followed Calvin to Geneva: his first enterprise there was his pioneering verse-divided edition of the Greek New Testament. Within a decade, English admirers of Calvin produced a similar verse-divided English 'Geneva' Bible, which proved a bestseller in the English-speaking world; soon even Roman Catholics were getting used to reading Bibles with the new device (see Plate 20).

Calvin won in Geneva where Jan of Leiden had lost in Münster. From the 1555 *coup* his position in the city was secured, and in the next few years he was at last given a recognition of his status as the doyen of Geneva's 'Doctors' when in 1559 the city council appointed him to head a newly founded civic institution of higher education, the Academy: a project which had first been announced in the 1541 Ecclesiastical Ordinances. Now there would be a proper training-school for ministers to preach with all Calvin's intensity. It was not a college under Church control, as Calvin would have preferred, and it could not claim to be a university, since it did not teach the whole range of subjects that university status demanded (the principal omission was medicine). Nevertheless, the Academy was his to staff and the curriculum his to mould as he wished, and the institution soon recruited students from all over Europe. Those dutiful young men from Scotland, England, the Netherlands, Hungary, France and Poland, toiling towards Geneva for their education, make an interestingly symbolic contrast with the excited crowds that had congested the roads to Münster back in 1533 and 1534.

CALVIN AND THE EUCHARIST: PROTESTANT
DIVISIONS CONFIRMED

While Calvin was thus finally consolidating his position in Geneva in the 1550s, his relations with Lutheran and non-Lutheran Protestants took a decisive turn, over the vexed question of the nature of the Eucharist. The outcome of what turned into a bitter row placed him as the champion of a non-Lutheran Reformed axis. We have already seen what a divisive issue the Eucharist became in the 1520s and 30s, with Martin Luther and Huldrych Zwingli radically disagreeing whether bread and wine could objectively and corporeally become the body and blood of Christ in a eucharistic service. The division, expressed with distressing clarity at Marburg in 1529, was a source of great concern to Protestants who were not blind partisans of either man, and many had tried to do something towards healing the breach, including Zwingli's successor Heinrich Bullinger, Martin Bucer and Luther's colleague Philipp Melanchthon (above, p. 228, and chapter 4, p. 172).

It was inevitable that Calvin, obsessed with his project to define the boundaries of a Reformed Catholicism, devoted much energy to finding a formulation about the Eucharist to give it due reverence but avoid saying either too little or too much about it. His first instinct had been to disapprove of Zwingli's ideas; in the midst of fierce debate with Lutherans in the mid-1550s, he admitted that he had been impressed a quarter of a century before when he read Luther saying that Zwingli and Oecolampadius 'left nothing of the sacraments but the bare figure' and that for a long time he therefore avoided reading their books. He continued to feel that Zwingli's presentation of the Eucharist lacked an appreciation of the mystery which it embodied, 'which plainly neither the mind is able to conceive nor the tongue to express'.[47] In his attempt to take a middle way in the controversy in a short treatise in that year of failed ecumenism 1541, he said that Zwingli and Johannes Oecolampadius of Basel 'laboured more to destroy the evil than to build up the good'.[48]

However, although Calvin found Zwingli's discussion of the Eucharist inadequate, he also strongly criticized Luther in his 1541 pamphlet. He deeply disapproved of Luther's insistence on finding the body and blood of Christ physically present in the eucharistic elements. To understand why, we need to consider some of his other deeply held beliefs, for more than one consideration drove him to reject Luther's eucharistic theology. First was Calvin's preoccupation with the dangers of idolatry. Paying undue attention to physical, visible objects obscured the worship of God 'in spirit and in truth' – this is a phrase from a passage in the fourth chapter of John's Gospel that scores frequent references in Calvin's *Institutes*. Zwingli, of course, had been one of the pioneers of the evangelical war on idols, but where Zürich had restricted its purifying efforts to the interiors of churches, Calvin was suspicious of the visual arts generally. Like the mainstream tradition of Judaism, he felt that imagery in relation to the divine was best restricted to words, where it could be as extravagant or as startling as he pleased: in one sermon on Deuteronomy preached in 1555–6, for instance, he radically adapted some words of Jesus in order to compare God's coming in flesh in the birth of Jesus Christ to a hen stooping down to the ground.[49]

Calvin's determination to avoid distraction from the worship of God was so thoroughgoing that he was even suspicious of any attempt to give honour to Mary the mother of God. This was very relevant to the eucharistic question, because Mary was the symbol and the means of Christ's Incarnation, the miracle of Christ's coming in flesh and blood in his earthly life in Palestine. Both Zwingli and Luther had written movingly about Mary because they felt real love and reverence for her, and they saw her as a guarantee of the Incarnation. Calvin showed nothing of the same spirit of reverence for Mary. In the whole of the text of the *Institutes*, so soaked in biblical citations, there is only one passing reference to the *Magnificat*, Mary's biblical song when she learned from the angel Gabriel that she would bear the Christ-child. Luther had cheerfully remarked in 1523 that Gabriel's greeting 'Hail Mary' was no danger to those of firm faith, and the churches of Zürich continued to recite this biblical salutation in their liturgy until as late as 1563 – but already in 1542 Calvin bitterly denounced any use of it as 'execrable blasphemy', together with the traditional titles of honour for Mary which Luther was happy to commend.[50] Calvin could not ignore Mary's part in the story of the Incarnation, for Christ was 'born of the Virgin Mary' and 'was incarnate by the Holy Spirit of the virgin Mary', but he and his successors felt that when Christians had recited these statements in the Creeds, they should not dwell further on them in case idolatry loomed. It was not surprising, therefore, that Calvin should not warm to Luther's emphasis that Christ's coming in flesh by the Virgin could be experienced in every eucharistic service.

So although Calvin naturally wanted to proclaim a Catholic doctrine of the Incarnation, he found Mary a problem rather than a reliable ally in this. Instead, in accordance with his humanist fascination with history, he turned to the successive Councils of the early Church. The climax of these statements was the work of the Council of Chalcedon in 451, with its careful crafting of the 'Chalcedonian Definition'. Christ was one person in two natures inextricably linked: he was God the Son and so fully part of the Divine Trinity, while at the same time he was Jesus the human being, born in Palestine. Chalcedon had a particular significance for Protestants, who saw it as the last General Council of the Church to make reliable decisions about doctrine in accordance with the core doctrines proclaimed in scripture – magisterial Protestants were all the more inclined to respect the early Councils because radicals rejected their legacy (chapter 4, p. 185). The balance of statements within the Chalcedonian Definition, with its emphasis on the indivisibility of the two natures of Christ, gave Calvin a model for a general principle which became very important to him: distinction, but not separation (*distinctio sed non separatio*). It was the perfect model to be used by this theologian so consciously striving for a Catholic balance: it can be seen, for instance, in Calvin's discussion of the Church, both visible and invisible, or of election, both general and particular – and above all, in what he says about the Eucharist.

With the 'distinction but not separation' principle in mind, Calvin made a firm distinction between 'reality' and 'sign' that nevertheless would not separate them. The old Church betrayed this principle by confusing reality and sign, attributing to the signs of bread and wine worship which was only due to the reality behind them. Luther, he felt, had also wrongly attributed to the signs that which was only true of the reality: in particular when he asserted that the physical body and blood of Christ were capable of being everywhere (*ubique*) wherever the Eucharist was being celebrated in the world: a Lutheran doctrine called ubiquity, which Calvin devoted a substantial section in the final version of the *Institutes* to ridiculing. He thought on the other hand that Zwingli had separated sign and reality too much. Calvin was firm against Zwingli by stating his conviction that 'in the sacraments the reality is given to us along with the sign'.[51] Typically, he returned to Augustine of Hippo, and like so many Reformers, was grateful for the crisp Augustinian definitions of the sacraments as 'a visible sign of a sacred thing' or 'a visible form of an invisible grace'.[52]

For Calvin, then, the signs of bread and wine become an instrument of God's grace in uniting the believer to Christ: hence Brian Gerrish's characterization of Calvin's views on the symbolism of bread and wine as 'symbolic instrumentalism' in contrast to Zwingli's 'symbolic memorialism' or Heinrich Bullinger's tactful move away from Zwingli to 'symbolic parallelism' (chapter 4, p. 177). Calvin distinguished himself from Luther by emphasizing that God's grace, which unites eucharistic sign and reality, and which makes that sign an instrument of Christ's presence, is offered not to the whole congregation at a Eucharist, but only to God's elect. The Body of

Christ is not ubiquitous on earth in the Eucharist, as Luther said, but in heaven at the right hand of the Father. God's grace, brought by the Holy Spirit, lifts elect believers to Christ's presence in heaven.[53] The ancient words of the Mass, 'Lift up your hearts' (*Sursum corda*) beautifully express this idea: already in the 1520s Johannes Oecolampadius had found this a poetic and inspiring way of making clear that the elements of bread and wine were not too closely associated with the body and blood of Christ.

So here was a consciously Chalcedonian and Augustinian construction of eucharistic theology, which carefully avoided approaching the Incarnation through an emphasis on the role of Mary, and which vigorously rejected Luther's view of bread and wine as objectively Christ's body and blood. After prolonged and often acid-toned correspondence during the 1540s, Heinrich Bullinger and Calvin gradually recognized that more united them on the Eucharist than divided them. The military triumph of the Emperor Charles in central Europe in 1547-8 galvanized them into trying harder to find agreement – particularly when a large imperial army placed itself alarmingly close to Zürich in autumn 1548 and abruptly and permanently ended the Reformation in the city of Konstanz. A further accidental and unfortunate spur came from Calvin's personal tragedy when his deeply loved wife Idelette died in April 1549: the gentle pastoral sensitivity which Bullinger showed for Calvin's profound grief was not insignificant in producing a remarkably quick result when the two men met face to face in May. By the autumn they were able to consult with other Swiss cities, principally Bern, to produce a joint statement on the sacraments of Eucharist and (far less contentiously) Baptism. Since the nineteenth century this has been given the shorthand name of the 'Zürich Agreement' or *Consensus Tigurinus*.

The *Consensus* is a remarkable piece of theological statesmanship and a tribute to both Calvin's and Bullinger's common sense and ability to be gracious when circumstances cried out for it. All too rarely in the sixteenth century did theologians acknowledge that they had substantial differences, but then go on to produce a joint statement that both sides could find acceptable. Calvin wanted to embody his insistence that the sacraments were instruments instituted by God for conferring grace; although this word 'instrument' – so important to Calvin – was actually excluded from the text, its work was done by the assertion that Christ 'makes us participants of himself in the Supper'. Bullinger wanted to emphasize that (as the *Consensus* expressed it) 'God alone ... acts by his Spirit, and although he uses the ministry of the sacraments, in this he neither infuses his own power into them, nor detracts anything from the efficacy of his Spirit.'[54] So partisans of both sides could find their favourite expressions or insights carefully laid side by side in the text – the great precedent for such balance was of course the Chalcedonian Definition itself. It was an inspired decision to bring in other Protestant cities like Bern (which had long had a peculiarly fraught relationship with Geneva) to lend endorsement. Various of Calvin's colleagues in Geneva, including his long-term survivor Thedore Beza, were not altogether happy about the emphasis in his theology on receiving the substance of Christ's body through the mystery of the Eucharist, and so it suited them to adhere closely to the careful language of the *Consensus*. Its achievement was to create a broad enough area of agreement on the sacraments for the non-Lutheran Protestant Churches of Europe to regard themselves as a single family; the statement lay behind four major 'Confessions' or statements of Reformed belief that were formulated in quick succession between 1559 and 1563. This had profound implications for the future direction of the Reformation from the Atlantic Isles to the Carpathian mountains.

Luther had died in 1546 and so was no longer around to express righteous indignation at this outbreak of eucharistic agreement at Zürich. However, there were plenty of ministers and theologians in Germany determined to champion his views, the chief among them being the principal pastor of Hamburg, Joachim Westphal. Westphal's first pamphlet salvo against the *Consensus* in 1552 was full of personal abuse in German well down to the standards of Luther at his most truculent; Calvin became the 'cow' (*das Kalb*) and Bullinger inevitably the 'bull' (*der Bulle*). The 'Supper-strife' which followed, centring on increasingly substantial replies to Westphal from an enraged Calvin, made only too distressingly clear the gulf between the two sides. Major figures of the older generation who might have bridged the gap could now have little moderating influence: Bucer died far away in Cambridge in 1551. Melanchthon was actually offered the succession to Bucer's academic job in Cambridge by the government of Edward VI of England (see below, p. 258), but he remained caught unhappily in Wittenberg because of King Edward's sudden death in 1553; for years before his own death in 1560 he was himself the object of grave suspicion from self-appointed guardians of Luther's legacy, who denounced aspects of his teaching, which they regarded as treacherous and labelled 'Philippism' (chapter 8, pp. 347–51).

The division signalled so long ago at Marburg therefore hardened. German and Scandinavian Lutherans behaved inhospitably in the 1550s to Protestant refugees from Roman Catholic persecution (for instance, people fleeing from Mary Tudor's England to Lutheran Denmark) whom they regarded as belonging to the party of the *Consensus*.[55] It was particularly unfortunate that when a settlement of the wars in central Europe was hammered out in Augsburg in 1555, the Lutheran negotiators had no interest in bringing Reformed Protestants into the framework of the resulting settlement. The hopes of the early 1540s for a real reunion were dashed. It was not merely that Catholics and Protestants now turned from bringing together the house divided: Protestants too were increasingly accepting that their divisions were not going to be healed. The 1560s only made matters worse.

REFORMED PROTESTANTISM: ALTERNATIVES TO CALVIN 1540–60

John Calvin's reputation has so mushroomed in the centuries after his death that it is easy to equate with his name the whole of Reformed Protestant theology and practice, and then rather crudely award it the label which started life as a term of Catholic or Lutheran abuse: 'Calvinism'. Calvin himself, a reticent and private man despite his steely abilities in politics, would not have approved of this.[36] He was in any case a second-generation Reformer, and even as the reputation of his work in Geneva grew, there were plenty of currents within the Reformed Protestant world that did not automatically look to him for leadership. The 1549 *Consensus Tigurinus* was not (and not intended to be) a victory for Geneva over the older centres of Zwinglian Reformation in Zürich and Bern, and they continued to influence Reformed Protestantism as it expanded in the 1540s; likewise the models of Strassburg and Cologne were remembered even after their misfortunes at the end of the decade (chapter 6, pp. 271–3). These varied sources of the Reformed tradition provide one reason why Reformed Protestantism turned out to be so much more cosmopolitan than Lutheranism with its single ideological base in the German heartland.

One significant early accession to the Reformed Protestant family was far away from Switzerland, in the extreme north-west corner of Germany on the shores of the North Sea: the little imperial territory of East Friesland, where the great north German plain meets the marshes and waterways which become the Netherlands. In 1540 its ruler Count Enno II died, leaving his widow Anna von Oldenburg with three young sons. A resourceful and cultured woman, Countess Anna brushed aside opposition to her assumption of regency power on behalf of her children, planning to build them a secure and well-governed inheritance in East Friesland that might form the basis of greater things for the dynasty. In politics she sought out alliances with rulers who, like herself, wanted to keep out of religious or diplomatic entanglements. In her own religious policy, in pursuit of what might today be termed a 'third way', she likewise sought to avoid alignment with either Lutherans or Catholics.[57]

Accordingly Countess Anna chose as principal pastor in her little port-capital at Emden an exotic and cosmopolitan figure from the Polish noble caste, Jan Łaski (usually known in his international travels as Johannes à Lasco by non-Polish Latin-speakers trying to get their tongues around Polish pronunciation). Łaski's uncle, also Jan Łaski, had been Primate of Poland and a great statesman in the Polish-Lithuanian Commonwealth. The younger Jan, while a generously financed student in Basel, became a great favourite with Desiderius Erasmus: as always, Erasmus was susceptible to youthful male charm and scholarly talent but more particularly he appreci-ated Łaski's lavish kindness in buying the elderly scholar's library in rever-sion – the equivalent of providing him with a pension fund. Jan's predictably smooth scaling of the Polish ecclesiastical career ladder – he became a titular bishop and was Archdeacon of Warsaw from 1538 – came to an abrupt end in 1540 when he got married; two years later he was putting his talents as church leader to a new use in Emden. Yet he never lost his pride in his ancestry, continuing uncompromisingly to wear the distinctive shaven scalp, quiff and long beard of a Sarmatian nobleman. His air of being born to command (as well as his reputation as Erasmus's friend) was a considerable asset in wanderings which took him far from Poland before his last years back home.[58] The remarkable career of Łaski is a symbol of how effortlessly the non-Lutheran Reformation crossed cultural and linguistic boundaries, and it is arguable that by the end of his life in 1560 he had become more influential in the geographical spread of Reformed Protestantism than John Calvin.

Łaski's contacts with the distinctive Reformations of Strassburg and of Cologne marked him out as the perfect exponent of the Countess's third way. He developed fruitful links with Martin Bucer, he was a close friend of von Wied's assistant Albert Hardenberg, and he much admired what the Archbishop was attempting in Cologne. Like Bucer, he was a sensitive and even sympathetic opponent for Anabaptists, instrumental in persuading many among the large number of radicals active in Countess Anna's terri-tories to join her new official Church. As Superintendent in East Friesland – in effect its bishop – he impressed Anabaptists because like Bucer he was insistent on firm discipline for the Church and created structures which would enforce it. The Cologne *Pia Consultatio* of Bucer and Albert Hardenberg (chapter 6, p. 270) was an important influence on him as he developed his plans for the Church and its worship; his eucharistic theology nevertheless developed beyond Bucer's towards the symbolic understandings of Switzerland (he had after all known Oecolampadius's city of Basel back in the 1520s). He followed Bucer and the Swiss in declaring war on imagery in churches. But, as with von Wied and Bucer, Charles V's victory and the coming of the *Interim* interrupted his church-formation: under external pressure, Countess Anna reluctantly asked her guest in 1549 to find another setting for his talent. Łaski explored various options and in the end decided on England, which he had already visited in 1539 and 1548.

This was by no means the end of Emden's importance in the story of Europe's Reformations, as we will see. Although Countess Anna's plans for her dynasty were later ruined by her sons' quarrels, and East Friesland never expanded into an absolutist state in the manner of Brandenburg or Bavaria, its port-town capital was particularly crucial in the second blossoming of Dutch Protestantism (chapters 6, pp. 310–13 and 7, pp. 336–7). For the moment in 1549, however, Łaski made a significant choice. He had recognized that England was emerging as another new potential centre of leadership for the Reformation under its boy-king Edward VI. A few years earlier, in the reign of Henry VIII, England would have seemed an unlikely candidate to supplant Zürich or Geneva, even after Henry's 1533 break with Rome. However, despite Henry's masterful if confusing 'middle way', keeping the balance between evangelicals and religious traditionalists (chapter 4, p. 201), the old king, amid the ill-health of his last years, had appointed evangelical-minded tutors for his much-cherished only son Prince Edward, and he had generally allowed evangelical politicians to gain political advantage against their conservative opponents.[59] So Edward VI's accession (1547) brought a regime based on a close association of politicians headed by Edward's uncle Edward Seymour, Duke of Somerset as Lord Protector of the young king, and with the now veteran evangelical Archbishop Cranmer as a prominent member. It immediately began accelerating religious changes, despite the constraints of Charles V's suspicion, combined with hostility to change from most English bishops and noblemen. Yet even in Edward's first regnal year, a royal visitation promoted renewed destruction of religious imagery, an official collection of homilies (sermons) set forth evangelical theology, the old heresy laws were abolished and the final dissolution of chantries was enacted.

All this was against the background of a subtle shift in theological stance among the English evangelical leadership. In general in Henry VIII's time they had been broadly Lutheran in sympathy, mostly for instance continuing to accept the real presence in the Eucharist (which one has to point out, made their relations with the King a good deal less dangerous than otherwise might have been the case). But Henry's occasional bursts of traditionalist intransigence in his last years – his brief attempt, for instance, to restrict the reading of the Bible to respectable people (chapter 4, p. 203) or a last campaign in 1546 to burn evangelicals who proclaimed disbelief in the real presence – gave greater credibility to more radical evangelical voices urging less compromise with Henry's eccentric agenda (advice, naturally, for the most part given from the safety of exile).[60] Around the time of the old King's death, Archbishop Cranmer became convinced that Luther was wrong in affirming eucharistic real presence. One might cynically call this a convenient moment to change his convictions, but we should never underestimate the psychological effect of suddenly being released from the hypnotic power of Henry's extraordinary personality. The immediate practical result when King Henry died in January 1547, clinging in his last moments to his faithful Archbishop's hand, was that England was suddenly poised to act as a refuge for prominent European Protestants caught up in the Schmalkaldic Wars and Charles V's imposition of the Augsburg *Interim* (chapter 6, pp. 271–3).

Accordingly, from late 1547 Cranmer welcomed to England many prominent overseas reformers who had been displaced by Catholic victories in central Europe; his vision of the Church was resolutely international and the refugees whom he found most congenial were now non-Lutherans like Peter Martyr Vermigli, Jan Łaski and Martin Bucer (with whom he had been discreetly corresponding for the previous sixteen years). Vermigli and Bucer were given the leading professorial chairs in Oxford and Cambridge: it was in Oxford that Vermigli first made an international reputation as a major evangelical spokesman through his disputes with conservative theologians, as well as his regular and wide-ranging courses of lectures. In their wake came hundreds of lesser refugees, among them a significant number of printers who were also enthusiastic Protestants. In 1546 Charles V had suddenly intensified his persecution of Protestantism in the Low Countries, and the flourishing Antwerp printing industry was a prime victim, to England's benefit. The influx of foreign experts in a previously underdeveloped English publishing market brought higher standards and triggered a sudden outpouring of cheap evangelical literature in English. For many in England this was an exciting time when any change seemed possible – even union with the old national enemy, Scotland. When Protector Somerset pursued a dynastic war against the Scots in 1547 to try to enforce the marriage of the young Mary Queen of Scots to King Edward, his military march north was incongruously accompanied by propaganda addressed to the Scots, talking warmly of religious change and offering the prospect of a new united kingdom, 'Great Britain' – an unprecedented use of this phrase. Remarkably, some Scots evangelicals listened and were enthusiastic for the idea: once more, a significant indication of the way in which Protestantism might foster the breakdown of ancient political and cultural boundaries.[61]

Over the next few years Cranmer masterminded two successive versions of a Prayer Book in English, the first in 1549, and he drew extensively on the liturgical changes in Lutheran Germany and those proposed by Archbishop von Wied in Cologne. Official campaigns also began to curb and even eliminate the elaborate choral and organ music of traditional worship. Cranmer was generally cautious in orchestrating the pace of change, to the annoyance of many less politically minded evangelical English clergy, and his caution was justified when a major uprising in western England in summer 1549 specifically targeted religious innovation, notably his first Prayer Book. Yet simultaneous popular commotions in southern and eastern England, far from showing unhappiness with the government's religious agenda, displayed positive support for it, and indeed their demonstrations seemed fuelled by enthusiasm for the reformation in Church and Commonwealth that the Duke of Somerset's official pronouncements ostentatiously proclaimed.[62]

The result of this sudden eruption of trouble was Somerset's summary removal in October 1549 by his colleagues, to be replaced by the reassuringly less colourful John Dudley, Earl of Warwick (from 1551 Duke of Northumberland). Yet the Reformation continued and accelerated its pace, encouraged by Cranmer and the King's own adolescent evangelical enthusiasm: evangelical bishops supplanted several conservatives, which in turn made it easier to impose the religious revolution. In 1550 Jan Łaski was given an extraordinary position as Superintendent in charge of a London 'Stranger Church' intended to embrace all the various refugees who had descended in their hundreds on the city from mainland Europe: the English government, anxious to use his firm leadership to curb religious radicalism among the refugees, gave him a handsome salary and one of the largest churches in the city. Łaski administered his kaleidoscopic congregation to show how England might set up as pure a reformed Church as he had been building in Emden (this was clearly the aim of several leading English politicians). In the careful plans he made for the Stranger Church's everyday life he allowed the laity to have a real voice in decision-making, even to the extent of choosing ministers. John Calvin, who was not a great admirer of the independent-minded Pole, would deplore this degree of democracy, yet the model had a great influence throughout Reformed Protestantism after

Łaski published the *Forma ac Ratio*, in 1555 retrospectively describing both the Church government and the liturgy of the Stranger Church, by then dispersed.

Cranmer, in fruitful dialogue with Peter Martyr Vermigli and Martin Bucer, produced a second Prayer Book in 1552 far more radical than the stopgap version of 1549; the theology of the Eucharist that its liturgy expressed was clearly within the range of symbolist views expressed by Martyr or Heinrich Bullinger, and so it was close to the nuanced statements of the *Consensus Tigurinus*. Cranmer also presided over the formulation of a statement of doctrine (the forty-two Articles) and the drafting of a complete revision of canon law. A remarkable feature of this work, testimony to Cranmer's vision of England as leader of Reformation throughout Europe, was that Peter Martyr and Łaski were both active members of the working-party that drafted the law reform – even though Łaski had often vocally disapproved of the slow pace at which England was implementing religious change. Cranmer even tried wooing Philipp Melanchthon over to England to succeed Bucer at Cambridge, accurately sensing that the Wittenberg reformer was increasingly unhappy in the role forced on him of guardian of Luther's theological legacy. Plans went far enough for the financially hard-pressed English government to send Melanchthon lavish travel expenses for his new appointment in spring 1553.[63]

In the event everything was left unfinished, and Melanchthon never came to England. In early 1553 King Edward, on whose life the whole programme depended, sank into a fatal illness (probably pneumonia). He and Northumberland desperately tried to divert the succession from the next designated heir, Henry VIII's traditionalist daughter Mary, to a Protestant member of the royal family, Jane Grey, but although England's local and central governing elites complied, the scheme met unexpectedly fierce popular resistance. Even many Protestants supported Mary's claim to the throne, drawn by her relentless reminders that she was the old King's daughter and designated successor (she carefully avoided talking about religion throughout her *coup d'état*). Mary rode to London in triumph; the Protestant establishment was thrown into complete disarray, and it looked as if England's Reformation was over. Łaski (accompanied by his newly-wed young English second wife), Peter Martyr and many other refugees set out wearily once more back to mainland Europe; this time they were followed by hundreds of English Protestants. Even though Mary's reign proved, equally unpredictably, to be no more than a five-year restoration of Roman obedience to England, never again did the kingdom play the captaining role which Cranmer had planned for it among the Reformed Churches.

It will be noted that Calvin has played no part in these stories of northern Europe's Reformed Protestantism. In Edward VI's England, his few efforts at intervention by letter from far-away Geneva were usually ill-informed and ill-timed, and the works of Heinrich Bullinger were at first circulated and translated in print among the English far more than those of Calvin.[64] The Genevan reformer's role on the international stage only changed as a result of the 1553 Servetus affair (see above, p. 244), and the Reform had begun spreading out of its Swiss and south German base well before that. This expansion of Reformed Protestantism without much help from Calvin was not merely to East Friesland or England, but also with spectacular success into eastern Europe, from Poland in the north down through the Hungarian plain and Transylvania, as far south as the Adriatic coast.

The vast expanse of the former kingdom of Hungary provided a ready audience for the evangelical faith among the nobility because the old hierarchy in Church and State was both dismantled and discredited by the disaster inflicted by the Turks. It looked as if God was angry with the old Church, and the uncompromising message of the Reformed in particular was a congenial call to purification and repentance. After the 1520s, the Habsburgs only succeeded in clinging to the north and western rim of the old kingdom, the area which was now known as 'Royal Hungary'. Here the institutions of the kingdom maintained a rump existence and the Hungarian Diet exhibited much the same contrariness on constitutional and religious matters that the Habsburgs found so awkward in their hereditary lands to the west. The bulk of the great Danube plain and the mountainous 'Danube bend' which contained the former royal capital of Buda were from the 1540s firmly in the hands of the Turks, who tolerated the practice of all varieties of Latin Christianity, for the moment on rather easier terms than they did the churches of Orthodox Christianity further east. But east of these Turkish dominions lay further regions of the kingdom that had been rescued from Ottoman attack by local rulers, beginning with a former royal governor of Transylvania, János Zápolyai. Challenging the Habsburgs for the title of King of Hungary through a decade and more after the disaster of 1526, János left his territories in a state of such military strength that eventually the Habsburgs had to accept that they could not assert their authority over his successors. These princes instead judiciously recognized the overlordship of the Ottoman Sultan in order to keep their independence, and they ruled over the mountainous principality of Transylvania, together with certain easternmost provinces of the Hungarian plain known as the Partium.

Political fragmentation in Hungary encouraged free choice among the surviving local Christian magnates. The plains and mountains of Hungary and Transylvania also contained plenty of German-speaking settlements several centuries old that could absorb various evangelical messages coming out of western Europe and then retransmit them to other surrounding cultural communities, principally the Magyars (Hungarian-speakers). In 1557 the legislative Diet of Transylvania granted the three-century-old Saxon settlements in Transylvania known as Siebenbürgen, the right to practise Lutheran religion – but German doctrine could travel from Switzerland as well as Wittenberg. Heinrich Bullinger, busily surveying the whole European scene from his study in Zürich, took a great interest in the eastern lands, and he was naturally unenthusiastic at the prospect of Luther's heirs setting the tone for the Reformation there. In 1551 he wrote a book addressed to the people of Hungary to encourage them in their resistance to the Turks, the *Brevis et pia institutio* (published in 1559), and his theological outlook came greatly to influence Hungarian-speaking as well as German-speaking theologians in the Danube basin and beyond. Several local leaders had spent time in Wittenberg between the 1520s and 1540s, but even there they could listen to Melanchthon's nuanced message as much as to Luther himself, and then they could choose to assimilate whatever else seemed appropriate to their situation.

The humanist scholar Valentin Wagner provides an example of this. He was among the pioneers of German-speaking evangelical Reformation as schoolmaster and pastor in Kronstadt, one of the Siebenbürgen towns. Now Braşov in Romania, lying in a dramatic narrow valley in the Carpathian mountains in remotest eastern Transylvania, the city was home to the region's first printing press. In 1550 Wagner used this press to publish a catechism in Greek to use with his cosmopolitan mixture of school pupils in Kronstadt. Varied influences around him shaped the text: his experiences in Wittenberg, his contacts with non-Lutheran evangelicals and his ambiguous feelings about the Orthodox Christians around him. Uneasy about the Orthodox description of the Virgin Mary as 'God-bearer' (*Theotokos*) he tried an individual effort of theological engineering by restricting her role to that of 'Son-bearer'. His Lutheran convictions did not prevent him adopting Leo Jud's numbering of the Ten Commandments to emphasize God's prohibition of graven images (chapter 3, p. 145): that was probably because he had Orthodox icons in mind, and so he was as wary of religious pictures as any Zürich preacher.[65]

For several decades many local developments of eastern European Protestantism drew, as they chose, on both Lutheran and non-Lutheran evangelical sources, in the fashion of Valentin Wagner. In the small north-western section of Hungary controlled by the Habsburgs, many Protestant communities adopted the 1530 Lutheran Augsburg Confession, not out of any special enthusiasm for Luther, but because from the mid-1550s it was clear that King Ferdinand and his family were prepared to tolerate Lutheranism, whereas they would not put up with anything which savoured of Switzerland or Geneva. Many must therefore have regarded the Augsburg Confession as not much more than a convenient theological figleaf for their own convictions. To the east, beyond the Habsburgs' influence, in the Partium and in Transylvania, a series of evangelical synods met from the mid-1540s to organize their fledgling communities: they too gave general assent to the 1530 Augsburg Confession, but they could not agree on the details of what it meant.[66] The existence of Melanchthon's 1540 *Variata* version of the Confession gave more scope both for argument and for untidy compromise. Such communities only gradually decided whether or not they would sign up to a Lutheran confessional package – hardly surprisingly, for not until the 1570s did such a package take definitive shape in the Lutheran heartland in the Holy Roman Empire (chapter 8, pp. 352–3).

The official churches of Zürich, Bern or Basel were not the only influences in eastern Europe more radical than Lutheran evangelicalism. One distinctive feature of the region was the spread of extremely varied and sometimes startlingly unconventional views, all in effect rebellions against the Christianity of the late Roman Empire, which both Catholic and mainstream Protestant alike accepted as normative. Most of these arose from the fall-out of the religious crisis in Italy which exploded in 1542, and which within two decades had made it virtually impossible for evangelicals to survive in the Italian peninsula (see above pp. 230–36, and Chapter 9, p. 406). At first sight a surprising link between eastern Europe and Italy, it relied on the flourishing and long-established Italian merchant communities in such major cities of central Europe as Bratislava and Cracow to serve as conduits taking Italian evangelical refugees as far north as Poland. Here, a distinguished Italian community included artists and humanist scholars, encouraged by King Sigismond I's formidable Italian consort Bona Sforza.

The initial stage in many of these evangelical migrations from Italy was directly northwards to the benevolent religious anarchy in eastern Switzerland, Valtellina and the Graubünden (chapter 4, p. 164). Displaced from the restraints of their home settings, some Italian religious refugees drew on the more adventurous strains of the *Spirituale* movement, perhaps taking their cue from Juan de Valdés himself (chapter 5, p. 215), and they began questioning such assumptions of conventional Christianity as the divinity of Jesus Christ and the doctrine of the Trinity. It was one more ecumenical task for Heinrich Bullinger during 1549, besides his negotiations for the *Consensus Tigurinus*, to encourage more conventional Italian-speaking Church leaders in the Graubünden to curb this emerging radicalism. As a result, many of the Italian dissidents then moved on further east, along the well-trodden paths of Italian commerce.[67] The non-Trinitarian Christianity which they took with them to Hungary, Transylvania and Poland was to have a richly complex future, of great importance for all western Christianity, as we will see (chapter 17, pp. 692–3).

The first success for the radicals was in the principality of Transylvania and the Partium. In their complex confrontation with both Ottomans and Habsburgs, the Transylvanian princes were understandably anxious to conciliate as many Hungarian nobility as possible, and that meant taking a benevolent attitude to the varieties of religion that the nobility sponsored. Most of this variety was now some form of evangelical belief rather than the remnants of the old Church, but it proved impossible to find some common agreement among the quarrelsome clergy of the Principality, despite repeated demands from the Transylvanian Diet. Matters were complicated still further when no less a figure than the superintendent of the Reformed Church, Ferenc Dávid (who had already moved on from leadership of the Hungarian Lutherans), announced in 1565 that he had grave doubts about the doctrine of the Trinity. He gained sympathy from many clergy and nobility and even from the Prince, János Zsigmond Zápolyai, whose court physician had influenced him in favour of Dávid's doctrine – here was another case like that of Servetus, where a well-placed doctor used his position to cultivate radical religion (see above, p. 244). The result was extraordinary by the standards of the time. The Diet, meeting in the town of Torda in 1568, decided to recognize the legal status not only of Catholics, Lutherans and Reformed, but by implication also gave recognition to Dávid's newly-emerging anti-Trinitarian community, with this trenchant declaration:

ministers should everywhere preach and proclaim [the Gospel] according to their understanding of it, and if their community is willing to accept this, good; if not, however, no one should be compelled by force if their spirit is not at peace, but a minister retained whose teaching is pleasing to the community . . . no one is permitted to threaten to imprison or banish anyone because of their teaching, because faith is a gift from God.[68]

This was the first time that radical Christian communities had been officially recognized in sixteenth-century Europe, with the brief and ill-fated exception of Balthasar Hubmaier's experiment in little Nikolsburg back in 1526–7 (chapter 4, pp. 166–9). The Torda agreement trumped even the open religious policy of the Swiss Graubünden. The anti-Trinitarian communities of Transylvania never again succeeded in attracting official princely support; they became split by internal dissension, and from 1600 they faced hostile Reformed pressure which further sapped their strength. Nevertheless, this toleration endured into the seventeenth century and it also provided an example for the much larger Polish-Lithuanian Commonwealth in its 1573 Confederation of Warsaw (chapter 7, pp. 343–4). The model provided by Transylvania and Poland is instructive. It can be no coincidence that these were the frontier regions of medieval Europe where Orthodoxy met Latin Christianity: Christians here, unlike the rest of Latin Christian Europe, had centuries of experience in making compromises with other Christians, however grudgingly, and however often mixed with acts of spite and bigotry.[69]

It is also worth noting, amid the Italian radicals who had such an effect on eastern Europe, a last startling echo in Hungary of Cardinal Reginald Pole. One of Pole's close associates, and in fact his first biographer, was a Hungarian humanist called András Dudic. After accompanying the Cardinal in his ill-fated papal legateship to the England of Mary I (chapter 6, pp. 280–86), Dudic became sickened by the association of Roman Catholicism with persecution and returned to his native Hungary to play a prominent role in the Reformed Protestant Church. He never ceased to treasure the memory of Pole and he never became an anti-Trinitarian, but he did talk as radically as a sixteenth-century European could on the subject of religious toleration. By the 1570s Dudic was prepared to say openly that 'each religion has its own rationale, as do all arts and sciences', and he seemed to be looking for a new synthesis of divine truth. The message of the *Spirituali* had travelled a long way. Might there have been room for the views of Pole's biographer in a Catholic Church with Reginald Pole as Pope?[70]

Poland-Lithuania's open political situation was ideal for piecemeal Reformations of choice sponsored by local magnates, as we have seen (chapter 4, p. 192), and just as in Hungary, much of this Reformation energy was openly radical. Here, the unitarianism which had travelled from Italy met and mixed with dissident views coming from the other direction: Russian Orthodox Christianity. During the 1540s there were stirrings of dissent in Muscovy (Russia) that involved both proclamations of radical social views and denials of the Trinity. In 1552 one of the leading dissident Muscovite spokesmen, Feodosii Kosoi, escaped with a group of supporters to Lithuania, allegedly signalling his arrival in the city of Vitebsk by a campaign among the Orthodox population to eject icons from their churches and houses. In due course, one of Kosoi's prominent supporters, Foma, conformed to more mainstream Protestantism and became a Reformed pastor in Polotsk (now in Belarus, to the west of Vitebsk). He was butchered there, along with the rest of the Jewish and Protestant population, by invading Russian armies of Ivan IV 'the Terrible' in 1563: the Russians regarded the Jews and the Protestants as equally detestable because of their shared objection to sacred images.[71]

Besides this growing and diverse anti-Trinitarian grouping, the surviving radical wing of the Hussites, the *Unitas Fratrum* or Bohemian Brethren, established a presence in Poland. After King Ferdinand had routed the 1547 Bohemian rebellion (Chapter 6, p. 273), Brethren were forced to scatter from Bohemia, some to the Moravian lands of the Bohemian kingdom where Ferdinand had no legal right to harass them, but many more northwards into the Polish-Lithuanian Commonwealth. The radicals added further diversity to an already proliferating evangelical movement in the Commonwealth. By the 1540s well-established Lutheran organizations were officially recognized in the primarily German-speaking towns and cities of Poland-Lithuania, having emerged locally and piecemeal as in the free cities of the Empire. Then, from around 1546, Reformed organizations also began developing, backed by members of the noble caste. At a first synod of Reformed evangelicals in Słomniki, not far to the north of Cracow, noblemen claimed the right to divert revenues from the old Church to their own purposes, and Polish provincial diets prevented the Catholic hierarchy from harassing noblemen who had declared for the Reformed cause.[72]

A significant moment came with the death in April 1548 of King Sigismond I, after a reign so long that no one could accurately remember what ceremonial would be appropriate at his funeral.[73] Protestants expected great things from his tolerant and politically experienced son Sigismond II Augustus, and although it was disappointing that the King issued a royal edict against heresy in December 1550, the edict remained unenforced. Moreover, at the 1555 meeting of the Polish Diet (the *Sejm*) at Piotrków, there was a proposal that the King should lead a national Church. Leading figures within the Polish Church treasured the memory of Erasmus's close personal links with Polish scholars, and wanted to hold out for a united and tolerant Church against the blunt certainties being expressed on both sides of the Reformation divide, notably the royal secretary Andrzej Frycz Modrzewski and Jakub Uchánski, who was to become Primate of Poland in 1562. Sigismond himself forwarded to Pope Paul IV (a predictably unsympathetic recipient) a series of demands made by the *Sejm*: vernacular services, communion in both kinds, an end to compulsory clerical celibacy. Interestingly, the resolutions embodying these proposals pointed out that all these practices were commonplace for Orthodox Christians, normally so much the object of contempt among Western Catholics, and yet also so numerous within the lands of the Jagiellon monarchs.[74]

In the wake of these proposals at Piotrków, which might have changed the future of the Polish Church, all the non-Lutheran evangelical groups met at Secemin in January 1556. This 'Synod' sought a Protestant unity, but in fact began crystallizing the later divisions within their ranks. Most importantly, Secemin witnessed the first open statements of radical Christianity in any major public council of the Reformation. The speaker was from the border country of Lithuania and Poland, Peter Gonesius from Goniądz near Białystok: his cosmopolitan studies had taken him to Italy, Switzerland and Germany, and he was much influenced by the great Italian legal scholar Matteo Gribaldi, who had recently gained European-wide fame for his attacks on Geneva's execution of Servetus (see above, p. 245n). Gonesius appeared in the assembly wearing a wooden sword as a symbol of his pacifist convictions, but it was not so much his pacifism that shocked those present: he shared this with the more radical elements among the Bohemian Brethren. He attacked the developed doctrine of the Trinity expressed in the Creed of Nicaea and the so-called Athanasian Creed. Soon he was also making clear his opposition to infant baptism. He found support, and from then on such powerful advocacy from one born and bred in the Commonwealth began inspiring many followers among the evangelical groupings.[75]

Jan Łaski naturally took a keen interest in developments in his native Poland after the old King's death, and he kept in touch with Sigismond Augustus, hoping to repeat his achievements in Emden and London on a much greater scale. In that significant year of 1555 Łaski dedicated to Sigismond the *Forma ac Ratio*, his published description of his former London Stranger Church, as a prospectus for a future Polish Church. At the specific invitation of the King he returned to Poland in 1556 after a contentious time in Germany. He was even able to secure a royal grant of official refuge to one of his former English patrons, Catherine, Duchess of Suffolk, a vigorously Protestant member of the English royal family, who could not stomach the Catholic regime of Queen Mary. The Duchess took up honoured quasi-regal residence in Lithuania, protected by the King's fervently Reformed Protestant cousin Prince Mikołaj Krzysztof Radziwiłł, the Lithuanian Chancellor, until the accession of Elizabeth of England allowed her and her family a triumphant return home in 1559.[76] Up to his death in 1560, Łaski continued in efforts to pull together the various factions among the Polish evangelicals, using Melanchthon's 1540 *Variata* form of the Augsburg Confession as possible common ground. However, time was too short, and no similar statesmanlike figure replaced him in what turned out to be an impossible task. A meeting of non-Lutheran Churches held at Piotrków in 1565 witnessed a serious schism, in the same year that Ferenc Dávid dropped his anti-Trinitarian bombshell in the Hungarian Reformed Church. At Piotrków the Trinitarian majority among the Reformed finally rejected the anti-Trinitarians, who defiantly formed their own synods in a 'Minor Reformed Church' and were henceforward frequently known as Arians. So the 1550s proved the high-water mark of the Polish monarchy's flirtation with reform, and Polish Protestantism began fragmenting at the moment of its greatest chance of success.

For a brief moment in the 1560s it indeed looked as if Polish Protestantism would trigger eastern Europe's first official alliance between Protestantism and the civil power. However this was not in Poland-Lithuania itself but to the south-east and right outside the frontiers of Latin Christianity, in the overwhelmingly Orthodox Christian principality of Moldavia, stretching between the Carpathian mountains and the Black Sea. Unsurprisingly, given the setting, this pioneering Reformed Balkan experiment was short-lived and bizarre, for it depended on the genius or opportunism of one man. Jakob Heraklides was a Greek soldier of fortune from the Aegean island of Samos, who made a career in western armies and became fascinated by Latin Europe and western Christianity. Clearly charming and charismatic, he won the good opinion of Philipp Melanchthon during time in Wittenberg, and he successively served in Charles V's armies and in Poland-Lithuania. His contact there with the Reformed magnate family of Radziwiłł encouraged him away from his enthusiasm for Lutheranism, and it was also Prince Mikołaj Krzysztof Radziwiłł who recommended him to service of the Voivode (Prince) of Moldavia. Having arrived there, Heraklides scented an opportunity to harness discontent against a ruler who was widely hated for collaborating with the Turks. Creatively drawing on his varied acquaintance in the West, he led an army backed both by the Habsburgs and by Lithuanian magnates, and in 1561 he succeeded in his bid to take over in Moldavia, taking the Greek title of Despot. Like the Princes of Transylvania, he prudently paid tribute to the Turkish Sultan, but he also saw himself as a champion of Christianity, and most remarkably it was Protestant Christianity with a bias to the Reform of Poland; he regarded the religion of his birth with contempt.

Heraklides ordered Protestant worship at his Moldavian Court, appointed a Polish Reformer as a bishop, and called scholars from all over the Protestant world, including sympathizers of Melanchthon. Some were optimistic enough to accept the invitation, which was a mistake, because Heraklides' rule was rapidly undermined by his genuine and urgent commitment to Reformed Protestantism, in a land which knew only small communities of non-Moldavians not owing loyalty to the Orthodox hierarchy of bishops. If anything destroyed his carpet-bagger regime it was the issue which marked out the Reformed from everybody else – their hatred of sacred images. In the Despot's need for cash to support his shaky government and army he plundered the treasure of Orthodox monasteries, not exempting various precious metal crosses which were regarded with particular veneration, or worse still, the precious metal frames of icons; out of this bullion he minted a coinage which as was customary, bore his portrait.

Nothing was more calculated to enrage the Orthodox population, because it recalled for them the iconoclastic disputes which had torn apart the Byzantine Empire nearly a millennium before – the Orthodox have long memories. Those ancient destroyers of icons had denounced images, but showed no problems with the portraits of monarchs on coins: this inconsistency had been seen as a symptom of their wickedness by the victorious champions of icons. Now the same rhetoric was turned on Heraklides by the furious leaders of the Orthodox Church, even though he had actually spared the wooden icon-pictures themselves. When Heraklides married the daughter of a great Polish aristocrat, rather than a Moldavian, his fate was sealed. His army melted away and he was butchered without mercy, as was the hapless widow of his late Polish bishop and anyone else whom the infuriated Moldavians decided was a Protestant. Heraklides' extraordinary adventure into monarchy lasted just two years, and the first major encounter of the Reformation with the Orthodox had proved extremely bloody.[77]

Amid all this Europe-wide expansion of the Reformed during the 1540s and 1550s, if one is going to find the influence of John Calvin beyond Geneva, it is where one would expect, and where he passionately desired it: in France. Already Calvin was one of the most frequently read contemporary authors in French: there were seventy-seven editions of forty-six titles of his works before 1551, easily outstripping his nearest rival Pierre Doré, then a popular but now long-forgotten Dominican devotional and polemical Catholic writer.[78] The French evangelical movement at first consisted of small groups where the simple framework of Reformed worship (prayers, singing and Bible-reading) was not difficult to maintain even in the absence of a minister. The gradual incremental growth of these private groups accelerated when King François I died in 1547, bringing a halt to the savage persecution of his last years; this gave Protestants more confidence. More of them were now prepared to listen to Calvin's furious diatribes against hiding one's faith: in a bitter tract of 1544, *Excuse á Messieurs les Nicodemites*, he sarcastically compared secret Protestants to Nicodemus the Pharisee, who would only come to Christ by night, out of cowardice (John 3:1–21; 7:50; 19:39). This was a high-profile intervention in a debate that was already lively wherever evangelicals faced official Catholic persecution. In both France and Italy, those whom Calvin was dismissing as 'Nicodemites' could point out that it was much easier to take such a purist line if one was sitting safely in Geneva. Soon the same debate divided English Protestants, facing Catholic Queen Mary after July 1553.[79]

Protestant activity achieved critical mass in France through two events in 1555. In that year there was the first formal meeting of a consistory constituted in Genevan style in Paris: the most prominent of a growing number of such French creations of a structured church congregation which was definitively separated from official Roman Catholicism. Equally important for the future was a decision by the titular Queen of Navarre in the northern flank of the Pyrenees, Jeanne d'Albret (daughter of Marguerite of Angoulême), to convert to the Protestant faith, even though she postponed making a public declaration of her conversion until 1560. There was no way of predicting at the time that Queen Jeanne's son would go on eventually to be King Henri IV of France (chapter 10, pp. 465–72), but the conversion of a member of the French royal family who was also a territorial princess was a symptom of a new phenomenon: the active involvement of the higher nobility in the attempted Reformation of France, pulling the hitherto dispersed Protestants into the cockpit of national power politics.

King Henri II's accession in 1547 offered as much hope to Protestants in France as Sigismond Augustus's in Poland. At first he favoured some measures of Church reform, particularly during his intense quarrel with the Pope in 1551; in that same year he ordered all the French bishops to tour their dioceses, following the best practice of reform-minded French prelates like Charles de Guise, Cardinal of Lorraine, who were in turn belatedly imitating what Guillaume de Briçonnet had attempted in Meaux thirty years before (chapter 2, p. 93).[80] However, the growing visibility of Protestantism began to alarm the King. He abandoned his confrontation with Rome and under the influence of his mistress, Diane de Poitiers, he became more active in persecuting heretics; increasingly he invested his formal title as 'Most Christian King' with a new significance as his calling from God.

So in two of Europe's leading monarchies, France and Poland, an activist Reformed Protestantism now confronted the powers of the supreme civil magistrate, and the Reformation in France was on the verge of turning from reticence to political and even military activity. In these circumstances, it was perhaps not surprising that Calvin, the figure so central to developments among French Protestants, should increasingly outstrip Bullinger, Łaski or Peter Martyr Vermigli as the dominant Reformed voice. Once the Lutherans, battered and demoralized by the equivocal results of the wars after 1547, had reached an understanding with the Catholic Habsburgs in the 1555 Peace of Augsburg, the chief confrontation in Europe's divided house proved now to be between the Pope and the Reformed cause.

6

Reunion Scorned, 1547–70

CRISIS FOR THE HABSBURGS, 1547–55

The 1555 Peace of Augsburg was a compromise after a near-decade of war from 1547, in which the fortunes of those opposing and supporting the Reformation changed with bewildering rapidity. It was remarkable that general warfare had been postponed for so long in the wake of Luther's 1517 protest and the gradual separation of various monarchs, cities and princes from Roman obedience. But now the military crisis further narrowed the options for the future of western Christianity and dealt more blows to the hopes of reunion or reconstruction that seemed to have substance at the beginning of the 1540s. The gulf went on widening through the 1550s and 1560s.

We have already seen that the 1541 fiasco at Regensburg and the 1542 religious crisis in Italy closed down various avenues to alternative futures; a parallel historical dead end came with the collapse in the late 1540s of the programme which Archbishop Hermann von Wied was developing in Cologne in co-operation with Martin Bucer. Von Wied had been deeply disappointed with the failure at Regensburg and his sympathies increasingly turned towards the Protestants: in 1543–4 he published a summary of his proposals for a thorough reformation in his diocese. Effectively ghost-written by Bucer, it was directed both to local laity and an international audience, since it appeared both in German and Latin; the Latin version (translated by the Archbishop's newly acquired assistant, Albert Hardenberg, a recent convert to Protestantism) was entitled the *Pia Consultatio*. The Archbishop showed how far he had moved away from traditional religion in his book's condemnation of prayer to saints and the misuse of images; his adoption of the 'Zürich' numbering of the Ten Commandments (chapter 3, p. 145) emphasized that point. Naturally the instructions for preaching that he laid down proclaimed the doctrine of justification by faith, while the liturgical section of the work included a strongly worded attack on the traditional theology of the Mass. We have seen von Wied's liturgical proposals in the *Pia Consultatio* were important to Archbishop Thomas Cranmer as he prepared a vernacular prayer book for the Church in England (chapter 5, p. 257), and already by 1547 two different versions of the work had been translated for the English market.

The conservative canons of Cologne Cathedral did not share Cranmer's enthusiasm. They rallied protests against their Archbishop's plans and enlisted his former ally Johann Gropper to write a stinging attack on the *Pia Consultatio*, the *Antididagma*, which also sold briskly throughout Europe from its publication in 1544. It was increasingly obvious that von Wied could not remain in the papal obedience, and as a prince-bishop, he was not merely a harmless clergyman, but a major player in the increasingly tense situation in the Empire. He allied with the zealous Lutheran princes of the Schmalkaldic League. Unfortunately for him, Charles V, free at last from years of warfare with the King of France, now decided that it was time to deal with the increasingly aggressive and assertive activities of the League's leadership: their protestations that they were loyal both to him and to true religion were wearing thin. Steadily building up his military resources and treasure, the Emperor made no effort to meet Protestant demands at the Imperial Diet at Regensburg in spring 1546. Instead he determined to strike at the heart of the League by destroying the power of its military leader, Johann Friedrich the Elector of Saxony.

The old Wettin family rivalry between Electoral and Ducal Saxony was a useful tool for Charles's plans: the ruthlessly ambitious young Duke Moritz of Saxony, although himself a Lutheran, agreed to assume the leadership of the armies invading his cousin Johann Friedrich's territories on the Emperor's behalf. Archbishop von Wied was now an obvious target. Charles V had long respected his personal piety, but ridiculed his lack of education and saw him as a political menace. So while the Emperor's bizarre alliance with Moritz was in preparation, the Pope declared von Wied deposed. Menaced by the Emperor's troops and facing fierce opposition in Cologne, the Archbishop resigned in February 1547 and retired to his family estates, dying as a declared evangelical in 1552. So the 'Schmalkaldic Wars' which now broke out eliminated the last major player who tried to bridge the divide between Rome and the Protestants, and Cranmer was left in England as the only leading Archbishop in Europe to declare for the Reformation.

By spring 1547 the Protestant cause in the Empire was in a desperate state, after the Emperor's stunning victory over Johann Friedrich at Mühlberg in Electoral Saxony, on 23 April 1547. Charles profited both from commanding a much larger army than the Elector's and from a surprise attack: it was one of the high-points of his life and he commemorated it with a portrait by Titian which has become one of the most famous images of the Emperor, in full armour on his horse, a chivalric knight resplendent in the cause of God and the Empire (see Plate 8). The Elector was a prisoner, the Schmalkaldic League's other leading figure Philipp of Hesse soon surrendered as well, and at last a triumphant Charles seemed in a strong position to order the affairs of the Empire as he wished. He continued to seek a settlement which would include as many moderates as possible; among his advisers was Johann Gropper, still advocating Catholic reformation as long as it did not end up in the von Wied mould. Finding it impossible to secure a voluntary agreement from his Protestant subjects, by an edict of May 1548 at Augsburg the Emperor imposed a temporary religious solution (the *Interim*) on the Protestants: this recognized the existence of married clergy and allowed the laity to receive communion in both kinds, but otherwise rode roughshod over Lutheran theological and devotional sensibilities. Duke Moritz (now declared Elector of Saxony) proclaimed a slightly more accommodating *Interim* document from his capital of Leipzig, but that was met with scarcely less fury than the Emperor's action. It is interesting evidence of the way in which the German Reformation had already attracted solid popular support, particularly in the towns and cities, that the victorious Emperor found so much opposition to his plans.

Nevertheless, the *Interim* had a significant short-term effect on Protestantism. It provoked bitter quarrels between those who decided to accept it and those who would not, prompting many of the more hardline evangelicals to leave the Empire. This actually encouraged the development of Reformed Protestantism in new areas, and yet it also struck a permanent blow to the prospect of Strassburg becoming the centre of European Protestantism, as seemed very likely in the 1530s. The city authorities made an uncharacteristic diplomatic blunder when they committed themselves to their allies in the Schmalkaldic League. Normally they kept firmly aloof from the tangle of warfare raging around their little territory, and their involvement in the Schmalkaldic Wars was one of only two occasions on which they were formally at war during the whole sixteenth century. The city paid dearly for its mistake, for it was now at Charles V's mercy and forced to compromise with the long-exiled Catholic bishop of Strassburg, even returning some of the city parishes to Catholic worship.

Despite bitter popular opposition in Strassburg to accepting the *Interim* and attendant Catholic humiliations, the prominent theologians who most obviously stood out against its imposition found it increasingly difficult to remain. From late 1547, several of the distinguished refugees who had enjoyed Strassburg's hospitality went elsewhere, notably Peter Martyr Vermigli, who was given a warm official welcome in England by Edward VI's new government, and although Bucer tried to stay on as long as he could, by spring 1549 he too took up a royal invitation to England, abandoning a quarter-century of ministry in the city. Bucer died in Cambridge before he could return, and when Martyr left England on Queen Mary's accession in 1553, he found a much changed atmosphere in Strassburg which made him move on to Zürich in 1556. The Strassburg authorities now increasingly inclined to Lutheranism, abandoning the independent theological stance which had made the city so attractive to a wide range of evangelicals earlier in the century. Despite the widely diffused influence that Bucer's thought and pastoral practice had throughout Europe, he did not leave a Church or a confession to treasure his name and memory as did Luther, Zwingli or Calvin.

Charles V could not enjoy his German victory for long: too many people were alarmed at his new power, including his own Catholic princes within the Empire. Charles's brother King Ferdinand failed to raise an army to support the Emperor in his kingdom of Bohemia: he faced a formidable opposition not only from Hussites and adherents of the *Unitas Fratrum* (chapter 1, p. 37), but also from Lutherans, plus numerous noblemen and city governors who simply resented the Habsburgs' efforts to curb Bohemia's privileges and freedom of action. Their anger escalated into full-scale rebellion. Much of Ireland had risen in 1534 against Henry VIII in the name of papal loyalty (chapter 4, p. 202), but this was the first time in Reformation Europe that a ruler faced an uprising from his subjects that drew on slogans of mainstream Protestantism. Not only did it anticipate the much more widespread rebellions in Europe in the 1560s, it also prefigured the Bohemian rising of 1618 against the Habsburgs, which led to the Thirty Years War (chapters 6, pp. 306-13, 11, pp. 492-5).

Although King Ferdinand eventually succeeded in asserting his authority in Bohemia through military action and harsh reprisals against his rebellious subjects, he had faced a setback that made him and his successor-monarchs extremely wary of Bohemian religious dissidents, and loth to do too much to upset them. In Moravia the King had even less room for manoeuvre than in Bohemia, for the paradoxical reason that the Moravian Estates had refused to join the Bohemian revolt and thus gave him no excuse for military intervention. Quite the reverse: the price the Moravian Estates demanded for their loyalty was confirmation of Moravia's long-standing religious plurality, which Ferdinand was forced to concede in 1550 – this degree of toleration was unparalleled in the Habsburg dominions and it remained intact down to 1618. Furthermore, when the Ottoman Turks once more began military pressure on his eastern frontiers in 1551, Ferdinand was even less well placed to help his brother. All this made him determined to get some sort of general deal in central Europe as quickly as possible.[1]

The situation in Germany likewise turned against the Habsburgs. By 1551 the Elector Moritz of Saxony had decided that his alliance with Charles was a wasting asset, and that he needed to get in his treachery before the Emperor did. His characteristic pragmatism this time led him to ally not only with other German Protestant princes but with the Catholic King Henri II of France: within a year this alliance routed the imperial forces, sending Charles fleeing out of Germany and Austria. Protestant lands in the Empire gleefully began abandoning the *Interim*. King Ferdinand negotiated a peace with Moritz at Passau on the Danube in August 1552, with his imperial brother's grudging agreement; it was an important moment in the German Reformation. Although Charles continued grimly to fight the French in the west until 1555, and Moritz died of wounds in 1553 after a battle with one of his own former Protestant allies, Passau at last created the basis of a settled understanding between Catholic emperor and Protestant imperial territories. Many of its terms would now be incorporated in a comprehensive settlement which shaped the future of central Europe for more than half a century, and its ghost would reappear to haunt Europe in the course of the Thirty Years War.[2]

In 1555, with Charles deeply depressed and exhausted and determined to abdicate the imperial throne, King Ferdinand took the leading part in negotiations at the Imperial Diet. These led to a general settlement recognizing the inevitable – a religious division of the Empire. As had already been accepted at Passau, church lands which were in Lutheran hands in 1552 were to be accepted as definitively lost to the old Church. There was no more talk of the *Interim*. Princes and lords could make a decision to make their territories Catholic or Lutheran: even the free cities could make the choice, provided that if they were Lutheran they left some provision for Catholic worship inside their walls. This was the principle of *cuius regio eius religio* first proposed back in 1526 at the Diet of Speyer: it gave the final signal that leadership of the Reformation in the Empire was in the hands of its rulers. There would be no more years of *Wildwuchs* for Germany (chapter 3, p. 152), no more Anabaptist kingdoms in Münster or anywhere else.

There was of course one vital difference between the religious situation in 1526 and 1555, but the Augsburg settlement chose to ignore it: the division between Lutherans and the Reformed, now so bitter because of the

'Supper-strife'. The Lutherans hated and feared the Reformed almost as much as they did the papalist Catholics: so with Lutheran princes as the negotiators with the Catholics at Augsburg, the official choice of Protestantism was to be limited to Lutheranism as defined by the 1530 Augsburg Confession, and the Reformed had no legal existence. The shortsightedness of this was shown when only four years after 1555, one of the key evangelical princes of the Empire, the Elector Palatine Friedrich III, abandoned Lutheranism for Reformed Protestantism (chapter 8, p. 354). Although one of his successors temporarily returned to Lutheranism, Friedrich's conversion made his Palatinate territories one of the most important centres of Reformed theology. Since the Elector agreed to recognize the *Variata* version of the Augsburg Confession, he escaped outright confrontation with the terms of the 1555 Settlement; yet the Palatinate's official shift from Lutheranism marked the beginning of a 'Second Reformation' in the Empire in which many rulers and cities converted to the Reformed cause. The 1560s saw the beginnings of a Reformed power-bloc right across Europe (see chapters 8, 10). Reformed Protestantism was not going to go away, and in the end the fundamental structural contradiction in the Peace of Augsburg was one of the factors fuelling the crisis of 1618. Even so, one has to acknowledge the achievement that the Peace of 1555 embodied: central Europe experienced more than sixty almost unbroken years of peace under its provisions.

Against the background of political confusion and shifting confessional fortunes during the Schmalkaldic Wars, it was not surprising that the traditional Church's Council of Trent did not achieve much when it reconvened in a second session during 1551–2. Pope Julius III (with little enthusiasm) summoned the bishops back to Trent for spring 1551. The Emperor was determined to make this a more inclusive occasion than the first session, and worked hard to get Protestants invited from the Empire: there were even overtures to the Protestant English government, which only resulted in abortive English efforts to convene a rival Protestant General Council in London.[3] Some German Protestants did turn up in Trent from late 1551, but given the turn of warfare against the Emperor they were in truculent mood and particularly angered by the Council's one new achievement: a decree of October 1551, which for the first time in the history of Christianity laid down a single official method of understanding the miracle of the Eucharist, through the medieval scholastic terminology 'by the Holy Catholic Church conveniently and properly called transubstantiation'.

Even within the Council, disagreements verged on the catastrophic. The bishops attending from Spain certainly hated Protestants, but just as in the first session of the Council, they were also deeply suspicious of the papacy: their private correspondence with the sympathetic imperial diplomat Granvelle, furiously critical of the conduct of the Council's proceedings by the papal legate Cardinal Crescenzi, was so inflammatory that in the late seventeenth century a Protestant editor in England published it in translation as anti-papal propaganda.[4] King Henri II of France, now in alliance with the Elector Moritz against the Emperor, was so much at odds with Rome that he threatened to hold his own Gallican assembly in France and make a break with papal obedience as Henry VIII of England had done. In the end the Council broke up in April 1552 because French armies were menacing Trent in the course of France's war with the Emperor. Since, as we will see (below, p. 278), the next Pope, Paul IV (Gian Pietro Carafa), was bitterly hostile to any thought of bishops making decisions in a Council, the next session at Trent was delayed for another seven years until the old man was dead.

1555: AN EMPEROR'S EXHAUSTION, A POPE'S OBSESSION

As important as the Peace of Augsburg in 1555 was the prospect of new accessions to western Christendom's premier titles, the thrones of the Holy Roman Empire and the Papacy. The Emperor Charles V was profoundly weary of more than three decades of defence of his family inheritance and of the shattered Catholic Church. He left the distasteful task of signing the Peace of Augsburg to his brother Ferdinand, but it still represented the failure of his family's programme of maintaining a united Western Church and reasserting Habsburg authority over the princes and cities of the Empire. His mother Juana 'the Mad' died in April 1555 in the seclusion of her castle at Tordesillas in northern Spain, after nearly half a century of listless withdrawal from the world which had followed her husband's early death; Charles, though himself only approaching fifty-five years old, now decided that it was time for his own retirement. In October he began partitioning his vast dominions by dispensing with his sovereignty in the Netherlands: symbolically he first resigned his headship of his Burgundian ancestors' Order of the Golden Fleece, and then handed over rule in the Netherlands to his son Philip. In January 1556, he completed his resignation, making over his Spanish dominions to his son as King Philip II, and the Holy Roman Empire to King Ferdinand (although it took two years to bring the Electors of the Empire together to ratify this unilateral decision).

Habsburg genealogical accidents and marital scheming had united under Charles's anxious care a world-embracing array of territories from Mexico to Munich, from Sicily to the Zuyder Zee. No single ruler ever again enjoyed that inheritance, even though Spanish and Austrian Habsburgs continued to do their best to act together to defend the interests of the Catholic faith. The possibility of universal monarchy was within Charles's grasp in the 1530s; now, to the relief of much of Europe, particularly Protestant Europe, it would never happen. For his last years, Charles von Habsburg returned to Spain, the land of his first monarchies, to tranquillity in a little villa beside a monastery of the Jeronimites at Yuste. He died in 1558. His son the King of Spain later saw to it that he was reburied in a much more magnificent newly built Jeronimite monastery, the Escorial, symbolic centre of Philip's own attempt to found a world empire to carry on his father's work.

Considerably less serene than the retirement of the Emperor Charles V in Yuste were the last years of that veteran opponent of religious compromise, Gian Pietro Carafa. His election as Pope Paul IV in May 1555 at the age of seventy-nine was a surprise decision caused by a wholly unpredictable misfortune: the death of his predecessor Marcellus II after only twenty days on the throne of Peter. Many felt deep and justified apprehension at Carafa's election: it added to the misery of Charles V as he made his decision to abandon his imperial crown, and Ignatius Loyola feared the worst for his Society of Jesus. Carafa knew that his time was short, but his energy was undiminished and he worked fast. At last he had the power to put into effect the rigorous agenda that might be expected from the founder of the Roman Inquisition; he could treat the world with the same austere Puritanism which governed his own life (with the exception of his own relatives, to whom he was almost as indulgent as any of his aristocratic Italian predecessors).[5] It was during Paul IV's pontificate, in 1557, that the Roman Inquisition first issued a general Index of forbidden books for the whole Church, following precedents set not only by the Sorbonne in the University of Paris in the 1540s and the Spanish Inquisition in 1551, but also – curiously – in Henry VIII's schismatic England. Within a year, even the independent Inquisition in Venice, always careful to keep papal power at bay, had followed suit, and on its own initiative it burned 10,000 books in March 1558. In the Pope's new Index, the Roman Inquisition included all the works of Desiderius Erasmus, whose reputation as fomenter of the whole Reformation catastrophe had thus come a long way since his years of serene celebrity on the eve of Luther's 1517 protest.

Erasmus was not the only *bête noire* for Paul IV. He was a good hater, and his hatreds ranged from the trivial to the profoundly politically important. He hated nudity in art, and famously commissioned a forest of figleaves for the sensuous religious painting and sculpture of Renaissance Rome, including Michelangelo's forty-year-old frescos on the Sistine Chapel ceiling. He hated Jews, and confined the Jewish communities of the Papal States for the first time in ghettos and made them wear distinctive yellow hats. He hated the independent spirit of the Jesuits, and once they had lost the temporizing skills of their founder Ignatius on his death in 1556, Pope Paul forced them to surrender much of their freedom of decision-making and began remodelling them into a more conventional religious Order. He also hated the senior clergy who had fostered the *Spirituali* and who, after their 1540s débâcle, had tried to preserve something from the wreck.

For Pope Paul, Reginald Pole and Giovanni Morone were no better than Lutheran heretics. The Inquisition did good business during his pontificate, becoming the main agent of policy in the Vatican and sponsoring a wave of arrests and interrogations. Morone was thrown into gaol, and the remnants of Italian evangelicalism were ferociously assaulted wherever the Inquisition could exercise power. The Pope met angry defiance from devout Catholic monarchs when he tried to recall prominent eirenical churchmen to Rome for trial for heresy by the Inquisition. Queen Mary of England refused to allow the return of Cardinal Pole (see below, p. 284), and similarly Sigismond Augustus of Poland-Lithuania blocked a papal summons to the open-minded Bishop Jakub Uchánski: he had recently promoted Uchánski to a diocese without the Pope's consent, and a few years later he pointedly made him Primate of Poland.[6]

Above all, Paul's old loathing of Spaniards was undiminished: they had stolen Italy, and he would do his best to see them expelled. It was not merely the Society of Jesus which suffered for its Spanish associations: Paul detested the Habsburgs who ruled Spain. So amid the crisis of the Catholic Church, a Pope regarded the devoutly Catholic Holy Roman Emperor and King Philip of Spain not as the Church's best defences but among its chief enemies, and he behaved accordingly; he would not even recognize Ferdinand I as successor-Emperor to Charles V. Paul's obsession with the Habsburgs naturally propelled him towards their chief enemy, King Henri of France, reversing Henri's previous anti-papal stance in a Franco-Papal alliance against Philip of Spain that became open war in 1557. In Italy, the outcome of this warfare was precisely the opposite of Carafa's hopes: when Spain and France eventually made peace at Cateau-Cambrésis in the old man's dying months in 1559, the Spaniards were more deeply entrenched in his beloved Italy than ever – an ignominious end to the last Italian challenge to Habsburg power until the upheavals after 1789.

Overall, it is no exaggeration to see Pope Paul's behaviour as a lunatic and disastrous extension of his lifelong preoccupations. He not only made enemies of some of the most passionately committed Catholic rulers in Europe, but he was deeply hated by his subjects in the Papal States. The news of his death in August 1559 sparked riotous celebrations; in Rome the crowd sacked the offices of the Inquisition to destroy their files, and to the north in Perugia there was a similar mob attack on the church of S. Domenico which housed the local headquarters of the Inquisition.[7] The new Pope was Cardinal Giovanni Angelo Medici, a Milanese namesake of the Florentine Medici family and an old enemy of the Neapolitan Carafa; he took the title Pius IV. He was chosen by the Cardinals as a deliberate contrast to Paul: Medici had gone so far as to withdraw from Pope Paul's Curia in 1558 to demonstrate his displeasure at the policies being implemented.[8] He systematically cleared out Pope Paul's relatives from positions of power, even executing two of them, one a Cardinal. The senior clergy whom Paul had arrested were now all released without charge, although some had already died in gaol; Cardinal Morone was once more free to contribute to the work of reforming the Church, which included a new session of the Council of Trent and beginning the gigantic enterprise of implementing the conciliar decrees (see below, pp. 303–6, and chapter 7). The Jesuits quietly secured the undoing of the changes that Paul IV had imposed on them, and they continued expanding their work in their own style.

Nevertheless, Carafa's shadow did not entirely lift from Rome on his death. He had created several cardinals during his pontificate who were determined to promote his rigorist agenda and who were frustrated by the comparatively relaxed regime of Pius IV – Benedetto Ascolti, one of their more unbalanced admirers, even tried to assassinate Pius because he was not doing enough to persecute heresy. The rigorists' last chance came after Pius IV's death in 1565, when Cardinal Michele Ghislieri was elected as Pius V. Ghislieri, a Dominican friar, had been Carafa's Inquisitor-General and his preferred successor as Pope before the triumph of Giovanni Medici. Pius V's canonization in 1712 shows that a sanitized version of the Carafa agenda has never lost its attraction to certain elements in the Church of Rome.

As personally austere and grimly focused as Carafa, Ghislieri did not suffer his mentor's tragic loss of self-control as he energetically promoted change in the Church, but his pontificate was marked by political misjudgements born of misplaced zeal, notably his condemnation of Queen Elizabeth I of England (chapter 7, p. 334); moreover, he had not forgotten Carafa's ancient battles with the *Spirituali* and the admirers of Juan de Valdés. During his pontificate the Inquisition spent much time drawing up schedules of evidence to blacken the name of two leading symbols of that lost enterprise, Cardinal Pole and Vittoria Colonna – both by then long in their graves.[9] Moreover, by the 1570s the Inquisition finally harried evangelicalism out of Italian-speaking lands except in the most remote valleys on the Italian side of the Alps. It was not surprising that in the three decades from the mid-1550s, much of Europe found entirely plausible the common assertion in Reformed Protestant circles that the Pope was Antichrist. Such hammers of heresy as Paul IV and Pius V would only increase the militancy of the heretics they opposed. Subsequent Popes from the 1570s made increasingly less convincing Antichrists, and in time the rhetoric of confrontation had a chance to soften once more.

A CATHOLIC RECOVERY: ENGLAND 1553–8

Pope Paul IV's loathing of all things Habsburg or Spanish proved to be a wretched complication in what appeared in the 1550s to be the most promising gain for Catholic revival in all Europe: the joint reign of Queen Mary Tudor and Philip of Spain in the kingdom of England. While Habsburg hopes for a restored uniformity were crumbling in central Europe, and just as assertive Protestantism was beginning to emerge in France and the Netherlands, the sudden death of young King Edward VI in 1553 opened up the prospect of a recovered Catholic kingdom in the Atlantic Isles. Mary won her half-brother's crown with every advantage: she defeated and humiliated Queen Jane Grey's Protestant regime in a virtually bloodless *coup* with massive popular support (chapter 5, p. 258), and now had the chance to exploit widespread conservative frustration and fury at Edwardian religious changes. To begin with, she got her way. Mary was not an imaginative woman (her Court rapidly gained the reputation among foreign diplomats of being one of the dullest in Europe), but she had a generous share of the Tudor family traits of courage and stubbornness. She forced the kingdom's political leadership to accept two decidedly unpopular personal initiatives, one a marriage alliance with her Habsburg cousins, the other a return to Roman obedience.

Mary needed to find a husband if she was to preserve England for the Catholic faith. The next designated Tudor heir, the Lady Elizabeth, was widely known to be a Protestant, and although Mary was thirty-seven at her accession, she felt acutely a biological destiny to provide an heir who would block Elizabeth gaining the throne. She insisted on the bridegroom being a Habsburg: Charles V, Mary's cousin and faithful supporter through her twenty years of political eclipse, felt that he was too old a widower to offer himself as a husband, so his son Philip, soon to be King of Spain, was brought to the task. The idea was not popular with Mary's subjects, who were well aware of how the Habsburgs had created an empire out of such marriage alliances; additionally, marriage to a King of Spain raised popular fears which reflected new tensions between Spaniards and the English, already born out of England's Reformation (chapter 7, p. 338). However, there was also a lot to be said for seeking a Habsburg husband. Not only were the Habsburgs Mary's own close relatives, but they ruled England's chief overseas trading partner, the Netherlands, and so for two centuries English monarchs had seen them and their predecessor dynasties as the normal mainland European ally for England.

Mary successfully outfaced all domestic opposition to this marriage, even defeating a dangerous rebellion in Kent by former supporters of Lady Jane Grey in January 1554: the rebel leader Sir Thomas Wyatt tried unsuccessfully to emulate Mary's own bipartisan appeal in her *coup* six months before, and concealed his Protestant purposes under the secular cause of stopping England being overwhelmed by Spaniards. In summer 1554 the Queen met her new husband in a wedding ceremony in Winchester Cathedral, one of her few days of pure fulfilment in a life of unmerited marginalization and disappointment (see Plate 7). Philip brought his lifelong sense of duty to what was not a personally exciting match with a woman eleven years his senior. He bore with remarkable good nature the distinctly ungenerous bargain that English politicians struck with him – he was not to inherit the kingdom if there was no heir by the marriage, he was not given the honour of a coronation (particularly galling for a ceremonialist Habsburg) and he was not even granted the customary personal landed estates of an English royal consort.

It was the end of the same year 1554 before Mary could achieve her other dearest goal, reunion with Rome. Prolonged negotiations were necessary with the English nobility and gentry, who showed less enthusiasm for the Bishop of Rome than they had for a restored Latin Mass, and who were determined not to surrender their recently acquired former church lands in any deal. Only when English landowners had secured their claims did Julius III's representative arrive in November 1554 to reconcile the realm: this legate was Cardinal Reginald Pole, at last given a chance of real power to exploit his years of brooding on the reform of the Church. Pole addressed an emotional English Parliament with his customary gracefulness: 'I come to reconcile, not to condemn. I come not to compel but to call again. I am not come to call anything in question already done, but my commission is of grace and clemency to such as will receive it.'[10] He could not as yet take the power of the Archbishopric of Canterbury because the hiatus of jurisdiction between England and Rome had prevented the legal removal of the former Archbishop Thomas Cranmer. Mary could have executed Cranmer for treason for supporting Queen Jane, but she saw him as the author of both England's misfortunes and her own over two decades, and she was determined to see him tried for heresy.

This proved to be a mistake, but only by a hair's breadth, on a confused day of high drama on a rainy Saturday in March 1556. After more than two years of imprisonment, Cranmer was weakened by increasing isolation, by his own turbulence of guilt and confusion about betraying Henry VIII's daughter, and by the pressure of argument with skilled exponents of contemporary Catholicism. He broke down and signed six recantations of his whole Protestant career, each one more abject than the last, even after he knew that Mary would not allow him to escape the stake. The Marian regime seemed to have won the biggest prize of reconversion in the whole European Reformation, but at the last moment Cranmer, given a pulpit in the crowded University Church in Oxford to expound his penitence, dramatically and unexpectedly withdrew all his recantations. He died in the flames in Oxford extending his writing hand into the fire, and screaming out while he still could, 'his unworthy right hand'. He had ruined the government's propaganda victory.[11]

Nevertheless Pole was now at last ready to begin his work of reconstructing a version of the Catholic Church that would be worthy of the noble vision of reform nurtured in his long years of exile. He had enthusiastic backing from his cousin the Queen and allies provided by King Philip, who was passionately committed to the restoration of the Catholic faith. Philip brought to England some of the best minds of contemporary Habsburg Catholicism, Spanish members of the Dominican Order: his father's confessor Pedro de Soto, Juan de Villagarcia, Bartolomé Carranza. Symbolically, de Soto and Villagarcia were given the university chairs previously occupied by Martin Bucer in Cambridge and Peter Martyr Vermigli in Oxford, and they nearly broke Cranmer's spirit in the months before his death. This was to turn England from a beacon for Reformed Protestantism towards the rival enterprise of international religious reconstruction, this time centred on Spain and on the work already done in the opening sessions of the Council of Trent. Often the Marian regime has been criticized for not calling on the other bright hope of Catholic evangelism, the Society of Jesus, but what could the Jesuits have done at the time in England which those elite Dominicans could not? There was no English member of the Society until 1555, so their preaching, like that of the Spanish Dominicans, would have had to be in Latin to a university or court audience. In a mission already taking on a world dimension, it is not surprising that the Jesuits did not press themselves on a kingdom which had other promising Catholic resources, and so a Jesuit envoy's arrival was delayed until the month that Mary died.[12]

Cardinal Pole took many promising initiatives in establishing a renewed Catholicism. Like Cardinal Wolsey before him, he had the advantage of his special legatine powers giving him control over both archbishoprics of England, not merely his own province of Canterbury. Some of his actions were basic reversals of the developing Protestant church infrastructure, particularly in re-equipping churches with images for devotion and providing a minimum kit of vestments and eucharistic plate for traditional liturgy. Some 2,000 married clergy were separated from their wives, and those priests not considered incorrigibly Protestant (the vast majority) were redeployed in new pastoral cures in the Church. These major administrative operations were carried out with prompt efficiency, reminiscent of Henry VIII's great minister Thomas Cromwell. Pole also called together a legatine synod (assembly) for the entire kingdom: among the legislation it enacted were measures which anticipated what would later be done throughout the entire Roman Catholic world after the Council of Trent. Marian England became the first country to introduce a new piece of church furniture to reserve consecrated eucharistic bread: a container or tabernacle placed at the centre of a church's main altar. Such altar tabernacles were destined in Counter-Reformation Europe to be treated with increasing splendour as the focus for devotional contemplation and liturgical adoration. The synod ordered bishops to be resident, and it also made provision for clergy training schools, seminaries, which would be based in cathedral closes and which would serve each diocese: the first time that the Catholic Church had seriously addressed the problem of equipping a parish clergy to equal the developing articulacy of Protestant ministers.[13] For the first time in more than a decade, recruitment to the English clergy began rising.

The developing profile of Marian Catholicism interestingly revealed how a thoroughgoing Protestant Reformation affected a restored traditional Church. The regime took lectern Bibles out of the churches, but the medieval total prohibition on the Bible in English was not restored, and Pole made plans in his own provincial assembly, the Convocation of Canterbury, to commission a new reliable English translation of at least the New Testament.[14] Some things from the past seemed difficult to bring back. It was perhaps not surprising in what turned out to be a short reign that few monasteries were re-established or new chantries founded; such action demanded a large commitment of money and landed endowment as well as faith. However, some devotional activities which needed little financial commitment did not seem to return: few shrines were retrieved from their destruction under Henry VIII and Edward VI, and the gilds which had previously been so important in parish life were not much revived. Preachers found it difficult to talk about purgatory, which had been firmly marginalized even in King Henry's portmanteau statements of doctrine, and the Pope's name was still not a winning theme in published literature – no doubt this reflected twenty years of concentrated propaganda venom against Rome.

Nevertheless, all this might be undone with proper teaching, and the regime did not neglect preaching and popular instruction. Bishop Edmund Bonner of London imitated his Protestant former colleague Archbishop Cranmer by producing a catechism and a collection of homilies (see above, p. 255). Two of his homilies were actually borrowed from the hated Cranmer's 1547 set: an astonishing piece of pragmatism, even if they were on uncontroversial subjects. Bonner's homilies were widely used in England, and even translated into the minority Celtic language of Cornwall.[15] Pole put Bartolomé Carranza to work to write a new catechism for the kingdom; the translation from his native Spanish was not completed before Mary died and so became redundant in the English situation, but it was destined for a long life internationally as it became the basis for the official catechism published in the aftermath of the Council of Trent. Even if the Jesuits did not arrive in person, their spirituality was available in all good English bookshops in the form of an adaptation of Ignatius's *Spiritual Exercises* made by a Dutch mystical theologian, Nicolaus van Esch, and published in English translation by the newly appointed Provincial of the English Dominicans, William Perin.[16]

Mary had to live with the bitter irony that one of the chief enemies of Rome's most loyal daughter turned out to be the Pope himself, when Gian Pietro Carafa became Pope Paul IV only six months after England's reconciliation with Rome. Not only did he declare war on her husband King Philip, but he also pursued his old vendetta with Cardinal Pole, revoking Julius III's grant to Pole of legateship *a latere* for England, and summoning him back to Rome to put him on trial as a heretic. Mary sensibly refused to let Pole go, and the unfortunate Archbishop had to rely on her defiance of the Pope to continue in his conscientious efforts at restructuring the English Church. Yet all was left unfinished at Mary's death in 1558. The greatest unfairness of a life filled with disappointments came when her hopes for a pregnancy turned out to be the beginnings of stomach cancer. In her last year of life, her regime died around her. King Philip's war with France and the Papacy, successful enough for Spain, brought disaster and humiliation to the Queen when the French walked into the ill-defended enclave of Calais, last remnant of England's medieval empire in mainland Europe and a town so integrated into the kingdom that it sent MPs to Parliament in Westminster. Calais was lost for ever to the English Crown, although the English could not bring themselves officially to acknowledge this until 1801.

At home, even while the Queen's health broke down, her campaign of burning Protestants rolled grimly on, with stubborn support from Mary herself and from a number of zealous supporters, including a few of her bishops and traditionalist activists among the local justices of the peace. It had begun in 1555 after Parliament rather reluctantly restored medieval heresy laws: the note of reconciliation that Pole had struck in his November 1554 speech was soon forgotten. Pole himself kept notably at arms' length from the continuing programme of bonfires, though he was harsh enough in the case of Cranmer. It was another irony that this champion of Christendom's renewal and reconciliation in the 1530s and 1540s ended his days as ecclesiastical figurehead in the Church of 'Bloody Mary', whose reputation has been shaped by its persecuting intolerance – while the Pope still believed him a heretic. In under four years nearly 300 people died, numbers unprecedented in England, though alarmingly reminiscent of what the Habsburgs had done in the Netherlands and central Europe from the 1520s, or Francis I had done in France in the 1540s.

Faced with death, most victims behaved with defiant dignity, the perfect material for restoring the credibility of English Protestantism after its 1553 débâcle. Popular lack of enthusiasm for the government's programme of burnings was a fertile seedbed for Protestant propagandists, chief of whom was an exiled Protestant clergyman, John Foxe. From his various refuges in the exile communities abroad Foxe began gathering material which placed England Protestant sufferings against the background of the international fight with Antichrist. As *Acts and Monuments*, its English version first published in 1563 in the safety of Elizabeth's reign and quickly nicknamed 'Foxe's Book of Martyrs', this massive and repeatedly expanded compilation became one of the cornerstones of English Protestant identity, a potent reminder of the militant character of the English Reformation.

Meanwhile, in a final insult of fate, the Queen and Cardinal Pole died on the same day in November 1558, Pole the victim of an exceptionally vicious influenza epidemic. With no opposition, the Lady Elizabeth took the throne, with a ready-made team of advisers who had been senior administrators in the Protestant government of Edward VI, principally William Cecil and Nicholas Bacon. Elizabeth was the daughter of Anne Boleyn, whose marriage to Henry VIII had caused the original break with Rome (chapter 4, p. 198); everyone knew that she represented the Protestant Reformation. The new Queen could thank influenza for removing many powerful elderly figures in Church and Commonwealth who might have proved an obstacle in her way, and she could also thank the late Cardinal Pole for his efforts at sorting out twenty years' chaos in the finance of the English Church. Yet now this woman of twenty-five, long isolated from the power struggles of the English Court, and with no personal experience of government, found herself presiding over one of the most bitterly polarized kingdoms in Europe. She was plunged into a series of crises, engulfing not only her own dominions, but the neighbouring realms of Scotland, France and Spain.

1558-9: TURNING-POINTS FOR DYNASTIES

Elizabeth's accession in 1558 was only one element in a watershed series of events for several of Europe's ruling dynasties: Tudor, Stewart, Valois, Habsburg. The year 1559 was dominated by the peace treaty between the kings of France and Spain signed at Cateau-Cambrésis on the French border of the Low Countries. This proved an enduring settlement to the wars between the Valois and the Habsburgs that had disrupted Europe since the 1490s: not till the early seventeenth century did the French monarchy once more confront the Habsburgs in war, and meanwhile the prospect seemed to open up of Catholic monarchs forgetting their differences and combining against the Protestants in Europe. In reality, matters did not work out like that, because of a catastrophic accident that was a direct result of the Treaty; jousting in a tournament to celebrate dynastic marriages cementing the new world order, King Henri II of France was horribly injured by an unlucky lance-thrust to the face, and died after lingering nearly a fortnight in agony. A convinced Catholic monarch in the prime of life and political effectiveness left government in the hands of his Italian widow Catherine de' Medici, anxiously defending the interests of her young sons. Her sickly eldest boy King François died in 1560 after only a year on the French throne: his death had its own subsidiary effect in sending his young widow Mary Queen of

Scots to deal as best she could with a newly established Protestant Reformation in her own kingdom of Scotland.

Mary, as we will see, eventually proved unequal to the Scottish situation (see below, p. 295), but even Catherine de' Medici, with her far greater capabilities, found it in the end impossible to impose a female regent's authority over the increasingly unstable political atmosphere in France. New divisions between Catholic and Protestant were adding dangerously to the already considerable assertiveness of the nobility. In these years the French Protestant acquired the nickname 'Huguenot', a mysterious word which may be derived from the 'Eidgenossen' or associates who had started Geneva's revolt from Savoy in the 1520s and who had thus provided the conditions for Calvin's organization of the Genevan Reformation.[17] Thanks to the sporting accident of 1559, France now faced a future in which, for four decades, religion tore the kingdom apart.

In the face of the formidable array of Catholic power apparently building up in 1559, the new Tudor Queen Elizabeth had to make choices about how to structure the religion of her traumatized and rudderless kingdoms of England and Ireland. Her regime was guaranteed to be a break with that of her half-sister Mary, and indeed the daughters of Henry VIII could hardly be more different: they were their mothers' daughters, both physically and in terms of their characters. Mary was straightforward, pious, impressively brave and decisive in a crisis, but not especially bright, and she spent her adult life trying to undo the wrong done to Catherine of Aragon and her mother's Catholic world (chapter 4, pp. 198–200). Elizabeth's mother Anne Boleyn was the equal of Catherine in stubbornness and her definite superior in intelligence – the only one of Henry's six wives whose marriage to the King had regularly been called her 'reign' by contemporaries. Mary's teenage experience of her mother's downfall after 1530 had been one of total loss and humiliation, after a childhood of privilege and honour. Elizabeth's was the other way around: too young to remember her three years as heir to the throne before Anne was executed in 1536, then seven years until the age of ten in a highly ambiguous and probably uncomfortable role as a bastard daughter of the King.

Just at an age when Mary's world had begun collapsing, things began getting better for Elizabeth: after 1543 Henry's last wife Catherine Parr rebuilt the King's family. Catherine was part of a Court circle of evangelical humanists who felt that a good classical education was the best way to change the world and destroy Catholicism. This education was not wasted on Elizabeth: she read the New Testament in Greek every day – which may be something of a corrective to a common cliché about the coolly secular

Elizabeth, contrasting with lushly pious Mary. Parr was entangled in Elizabeth's teenage years in another way: after Henry VIII's death in 1547, the girl was lodged with the Dowager Queen, whose fourth husband Lord Thomas Seymour, an unscrupulous and ambitious man, then made sexual overtures to her. The Seymour experience clearly left a permanent scar on Elizabeth: the memory may have been one component in the problems she seems to have had with marriage and close emotional relationships for the rest of her life, despite her gift for friendship. Through her youth, in fact until she came to the throne, she took significant care to dress very simply: she was not going to risk getting a racy reputation.[18]

The young woman who became Queen in 1558 had thus suffered an unrivalled education in the dangers and complexities of power politics, and had learned the hard way about the subtleties of dealing with other people. Keeping a judicious obscurity under Edward VI, she was disinherited as much as Mary by Queen Jane Grey's accession, but once Mary was on the throne, Elizabeth in her turn became a symbol of Protestant hopes. That might have destroyed her if she had made just one wrong decision. Characteristic of her long reign became a political caution and deliberation which frequently infuriated her male councillors. Given this instinct, the decisive action that she and her advisers took when she came to the throne is all the more striking. In much traditional historical writing about English religion, the emphasis has been on the religious compromises Elizabeth made in her 1559 religious settlement, which has formed the basis of the Church of England (and therefore of worldwide Anglicanism) to the present day. It would be more sensible to note how little compromise Elizabeth made in swiftly and decisively setting up an unmistakably Protestant regime in Westminster. The new Queen proved a past master at making soothing noises to ambassadors from dangerous Catholic foreign powers, but few people could be deceived about the nature of her programme.

Among several other significant symbolic gestures, in Elizabeth's formal entry to her capital London in January 1559 (always a major propaganda opportunity for a new monarch), Elizabeth allowed two ardent Protestant publicists Richard Hilles and Richard Grafton to script the lavish Protestant pageantry, which could not have been a more aggressive statement that she was breaking with the past. This public drama was received with massive popular enthusiasm in the city.[19] At the same time, the elections to the House of Commons in her first Parliament produced a remarkably large majority of MPs prepared to back Protestant changes. These are significant results: London crowds were not easily overawed by government pressure, and no English regime could orchestrate parliamentary elections as it wished.

Elizabeth's acute political antennae had convinced her that there was a large enough body of convinced Protestants at least in the politically vital south-east of England to make her religious gamble worthwhile – indeed, from the beginning of her reign she showed herself highly skilled at appealing to the broadest possible constituency of her subjects, and openly emphasized that she had been preserved through the dangers of her sister's reign by the support of the 'common' people rather than the nobility.[20]

Elizabeth's religious Settlement, planned meticulously by her chief ministers William Cecil and Nicholas Bacon and already drafted in the first weeks of her reign, made no significant concessions to Catholic opinion represented by the church hierarchy and much of the nobility. There was no question of offering it for inspection by the overwhelmingly Catholic clerical assemblies, the Convocations of Canterbury and York, and its parliamentary legislation faced stiff opposition from the Catholic majority in the House of Lords. This meant a delay until April 1559, when two Catholic bishops were arrested on trumped-up charges and the loss of their parliamentary votes resulted in a tiny majority for the government's bills in the Lords.[21] The resulting Settlement was a snapshot of doctrine and liturgy in Edward VI's Church in autumn 1552: a moment perhaps chosen because the boy-king's later months had been unacceptably dominated by the effort to put Jane Grey on the throne – thus thrusting aside Elizabeth as well as the Lady Mary.[22]

The revival of Edwardian forms was completed in 1563, when Archbishop Cranmer's forty-two doctrinal Articles of autumn 1552 were reissued as thirty-nine Articles, with only minor alterations. The 1559 legislation made a number of small modifications in Cranmer's 1552 Book of Common Prayer and its associated liturgical provisions: some traditional vestments were allowed (noticeably, however, not those associated with the Eucharist), and those who wished to might see the liturgy affirming a real presence of Christ in the eucharistic elements of bread and wine. It is nevertheless absurd to suppose that these concessions were intended to mollify Catholic-minded clergy and laity, whom the Settlement simultaneously deprived of the Latin Mass, monasteries, chantries, shrines, gilds and a compulsorily celibate priesthood. They were probably aimed at conciliating Lutheran Protestants either at home – Elizabeth had no way of knowing the theological temperature of her Protestant subjects in 1559 – or abroad: the Lutheran princes of northern Europe were watching anxiously to see whether the new English regime would be as offensively Reformed as the government of Edward VI had been, and it was worthwhile for Elizabeth's government to throw the Lutherans a few theological scraps.

The new Church of England was still different in tone and style from the Edwardian Church. Edward's regime was characterized by its commitment to (and even its bid to lead) militant international Protestantism in a forward-moving revolution. Many Edwardian leaders had gone into exile under Mary to parts of Europe where they saw such militant change in action, and they expected to carry on the good work now that God had given them the chance to come home. Elizabeth begged to differ, taking particular exception to returning exiles associated with Geneva. She excluded them from high office in the new church, because she was furious with the Scots Edwardian activist and Genevan enthusiast John Knox for challenging the right of women to rule (his disastrously timed pamphlet, *The First Blast of the Trumpet against the monstrous regiment of women*, had been aimed from Geneva in 1558 against the 'monstrous regiment' or unnatural rule of the previous English queen, Mary). Moreover, Elizabeth did not appreciate condescension from overseas Reformed leaders like John Calvin and Jan Łaski, who thought that they could mix their diplomatic congratulations on her accession with patronizing advice to a young female. Her own brand of Protestantism was peculiarly conservative, including a liking for some church imagery and elaborate choral music in worship, a lack of appreciation for frequent preaching and a suspicion of married clergy – perhaps she had remained with the cautious Henrician evangelicalism of her stepmother Catherine Parr, who was such an important figure in her life in her crucial adolescent years in the 1540s. Her package of beliefs recalls the idiosyncratic 'third way' religious policies of various rulers of the 1540s such as Anna von Oldenburg, Wilhelm of Cleves and Philipp of Hesse. Few other Protestants shared her outlook by 1559, either at home or overseas.[23]

In one respect, the new Queen did gather like-minded people as she planned the religious future. She and all her leading advisers (including her new Archbishop, Matthew Parker) had conformed outwardly to the traditional Catholic Church under Queen Mary, in other words, they were what John Calvin sneeringly called 'Nicodemites' (chapter 5, p. 268). They knew the specialized heroism of making choices about concealing opinions and compromising in dangerous times, rather than the luxury of proclaiming their convictions in unsullied purity. No other Protestant Church in Europe had such a beginning. It meant that the Queen sympathized with traditionalist Catholics who kept similarly quiet in her own Church – towards the end of her reign, Sir Nicholas Bacon's philosopher-son Francis said admiringly that she did not seek to make windows into men's souls. Elizabeth, a subtle and reflective woman, who learned about politics the hard way, showed no enthusiasm for high-temperature religion, despite the private depth and quiet intensity of her own devotional life.

Many of her Protestant subjects found this extremely frustrating, particularly when it became clear in the 1560s that she would permit no change in the 1559 Settlement. Her senior clergy had not at first appreciated this. In a watershed meeting in 1563 of the Convocation of the Province of Canterbury, England's most important clerical assembly, the bishops (notably even including Archbishop Parker) proposed a series of further Protestant reforms, only to find them blocked. When they tried again in the 1566 Parliament, it was obvious that the main obstacle was the Queen, who refused to allow them to proceed with such initiatives.[24] Idiosyncratic features of the Settlement, randomly preserved in her fossilization of the Edwardian Church, came over time to exercise a pull away from the world of Reformed Protestantism, making the Church of England unique in the European Reformation: the traditionally shaped threefold ministry of bishop, priest and deacon, together with the preservation of the devotional life and endowments of cathedrals (chapter 12).

England's renewed Reformation coincided in 1559 with an independent religious revolution in Scotland, the first time that European Protestants carried out a successful armed rebellion against their Catholic rulers in both Church and Commonwealth. What is particularly noteworthy about the Scottish experience, proving prophetic for events throughout Europe over the next few decades, is that this Protestant uprising was Reformed Protestant and not Lutheran in character. In the 1550s the Lutherans were in disarray in the aftermath of the Schmalkaldic Wars, despite their accommodation with the Holy Roman Emperor. In Scotland, as in England, the Lutheran character of the early Reformation evaporated during the 1550s; Scottish evangelical contacts with English Reformers had a lot to do with this change of atmosphere. In 1546 the pro-French Cardinal David Beaton, ruler of Scotland during the minority of the infant Mary Queen of Scots, was murdered by a group of Protestant conspirators, but they were eventually forced to surrender Beaton's castle at St Andrews, and they had not displaced the pro-French and conservative character of the Scots government, which was taken over by young Queen Mary's French mother, the widowed Queen Mary of Guise. The Protestant failure resulted in the exile to France of a minor associate of the conspirators, a notary and priest recently converted to evangelical faith – John Knox.

After release from a harsh sentence of slavery in the galley-ships of the King of France, which permanently wrecked his health, Knox joined the work of

Reformation in Edward VI's English Church. Throughout his later tangled history, he never lost his admiration for the forward Protestants of England. Knox has done his best to conceal these wider dimensions of himself by his own relentless self-fashioning: after focusing his activities on the Reformation in his native land, he wrote an autobiographical history of the Scottish Reformation that contrives to be indispensable in its first-hand observation, and tantalizing in what it conceals. Most of what we know about Knox's part in the English Reformation comes from sources other than himself, and it is remarkable that he has covered his tracks so thoroughly that no important new information about him has emerged over the last century of Reformation research. Particularly striking is the veil which he managed to draw over his years before 1546 as a faithful son of the undivided Western Church.[25]

The tensions of international politics in the 1550s meant that Mary of Guise's devoutly Catholic but reformist regime had little contact with the work of Mary of England in restoring and redeveloping Catholicism there: the leading reformist Catholic clergy in Scotland were linked rather with Germany and Paris, for instance John Hamilton, Archbishop of St Andrews, who soon after his arrival in office in 1549 instituted two successive councils to consider reform. Hamilton's Scottish catechism of 1552 (admittedly drafted, it seems, by an English Catholic exile) shows a concern to be conciliatory to evangelical critics of the Church, in a manner reminiscent of Hermann von Wied's major efforts at reform in the archdiocese of Cologne in the 1530s and 1540s (chapters 5, pp. 227–30, 6, pp. 270–71). Yet little was achieved. The Regent Mary, exhausted, fatally ill and desperate to maintain disintegrating national unity, forced the calling of another Church council in 1559. Once more it had few concrete outcomes, and its failure represented one of the last international attempts at ecumenical reconciliation. In despair, several leading humanist Catholic clergy went straight over to the campaign for a Protestant Reformation in Scotland.

The Scottish nobility's parallel frustration with French political influence in 1559 further discredited Mary of Guise's Catholic policies and led to a Protestant insurrection. The rising was led by prominent noblemen (including the Earl of Arran, heir presumptive to the throne and half-brother to Archbishop Hamilton), but it also relied on mob violence. This led to the comprehensive sacking of certain monasteries and friaries, mostly urban, but also including the remote and ancient royal enthronement abbey church of Scone. This was a popular Protestant aggression without parallel in any other stage of the Reformations in the Atlantic Isles, and it anticipated what was going to happen in France and the Netherlands over the next decade. The source of this sudden outburst of energy in Scotland remains mysterious;

certainly in the crisis of 1559 it was much encouraged by fiery preaching from the returned John Knox, but during Knox's absence in the 1550s, popular fervour had built up in certain parts of the kingdom in a manner that frankly astonished him. On a brief visit back to Scotland in 1555–6, he wrote to his English mother-in-law and intimate confidante Elizabeth Bowes: 'If I had not seen it with my eyes in my own country, I could not have believed it . . . Yea, Mother, their fervency doth so ravish me, that I cannot but accuse and condemn my slothful coldness.'[26]

During the 1550s Knox's eyes nevertheless remained fixed on England and a prospect of his return there if his second exile from Mary Tudor's Catholic regime should come to an end: it was the combination of Queen Elizabeth's hostility to him and the sudden new possibilities in Scotland that turned his life in a new direction in 1559. This was not mere opportunism on Knox's part: like so many in his Protestant generation, he was a fervent internationalist, and he was prepared to be led where God took him. If the accidents of politics had not allowed him back into the Atlantic Isles, he might have been content to become a distinguished peripatetic exile in the manner of Peter Martyr Vermigli or Jan Łaski. His flight from Mary's England in 1553 took him to Geneva and Europe's most celebrated European exile John Calvin; Knox's plans for the Kirk were now shaped by his fervent admiration for Geneva rather than by the model of Archbishop Cranmer's Edwardian church reforms. Knox had clashed with Cranmer in England during 1552–3. Although later he was prepared graciously, but perhaps a little condescendingly, to remember the English martyr as 'the mild man of God', he had been temperamentally closer in Edwardian England to Jan Łaski, who looked back witheringly from the 1560s on King Edward's Church as being tainted with 'Parliamentary theology' – a Reformation hamstrung by political manoeuvring.[27]

Accordingly, during 1560 the Scottish Protestant leadership, backed enthusiastically by lesser Scottish lairds and barons, legislated into existence in the Scottish Parliament a radically new Protestant Church: the 'Kirk'. Knox and his clerical colleagues, several of whom were very recent converts from reformist Catholic views, carefully planned to take the Kirk towards the models provided by Geneva and other 'best Reformed Churches'. Some of the bishops of the old Church joined the new to take up leading roles in its administration, but the new Church gave them and other prominent Protestant ministers a new role as regional 'superintendents' in a rationalized version of the old diocesan system; these superintendents had a similar position to that which Jan Łaski had assumed in the Stranger Church of Edwardian London.

Two Reformed leaders of northern Europe.

*John Knox: he steered Scotland's national revolution of 1560
and led opposition to Mary Queen of Scots.*

*Jan Łaski (Johannes a Lasco): his Sarmatian nobleman's
hairstyle is hidden by his Reformer's cap.*

There was no question of the new Kirk retaining as many traditional features as Queen Elizabeth had allowed the year before in England. The Scottish revolution was admittedly aided by Queen Elizabeth's English government: England's vigorous military intervention avoided the mistakes of English military adventures in Scotland under Edward VI, while still drawing on the Scottish Protestant anglophilia which had been a curious accompaniment to those earlier campaigns. That anglophilia continued to be exhibited in the new Kirk: its handbook of liturgical guidelines, the Book of Common Order, was originally compiled for the English exile congregation in Geneva in 1556, and the Bible it used, the Geneva translation of 1557-60, was written in the English of London, not that of lowland Scotland. Yet the success of this English investment in Scottish Protestantism was balanced by a fact uncomfortable for Elizabeth: the Scottish Reformation was based on a rebellion against God's anointed monarch. The contrast with the English Reformation, directed at every turn by the Crown, was significant, and it constantly recurred up to the end of the seventeenth century.

The Scottish situation was complicated by the arrival from France in 1560 of Queen Mary on the death of her young husband François II. Mary, beautiful and charming yet without any political skill, moved from inexperience through attempts at religious inclusiveness and conciliation to exceptional political incompetence, alienating Protestant politicians who had done their best to remain loyal to her. Her errors of judgement included tolerating the murder of her second husband Henry Stewart Lord Darnley and marrying his murderer as a third husband – James Hepburn, Earl of Bothwell. The ensuing civil war resulted in a series of Protestant and mostly pro-English regimes. From 1567 they ruled in the name of James VI, Mary's infant son by Darnley, after she fled to the reluctant and embarrassed hospitality of Queen Elizabeth in England. Mary remained alive as an English prisoner for the next twenty years, heir presumptive to the English throne, and so a destabilizing element in the politics of both England and Scotland.

The partition of the Habsburg dominions was completed in 1558 when the Emperor Charles V's successor finally achieved recognition by the Electors of the Holy Roman Empire. The new Holy Roman Emperor Ferdinand I had a formidable record in central Europe of persecuting mainstream and radical evangelicals alike, but three decades of maintaining a tangled territorial inheritance had taught him realism. Lutheran princes in the Empire, Lutheran noblemen in his own lands beyond the Empire and the still-powerful Hussites of Bohemia were all too capable of damaging his family's interests, particularly if they managed to combine against the Habsburgs: they could not be eliminated, and they might be conciliated. The Emperor therefore continued to seek some settlement which would go some way to meeting the symbolic issues of public worship that concerned Lutherans and Utraquist Hussites. As early as 1537 he had unsuccessfully tried to get a decision out of the clergy of the traditional Church's province of Salzburg that would make clerical marriage possible.[28] Now he was prepared to press for changes within the Catholic Church that included Masses where both kinds (bread and wine) were offered to the whole congregation, in the context of worship in vernacular languages, and with married clergy offici-ating. If such an external settlement could be created, then theologians might be left to debate issues of theology that did not need airing in public, such as justification by faith alone. It was the programme which had lain behind the 1548 Augsburg *Interim*, combined with the recognition in the 1555 Peace of Augsburg that Lutheranism, was here to stay.

The Austrian Habsburgs were not united behind the Emperor's pragmatic strategy, which was in any case carefully modulated to suit the specific circumstances of his various territories and which would always have a bias in favour of the old Church. His long-lived (and favourite) younger son the Archduke Ferdinand worked for a newly aggressive Roman Catholicism once appointed governor in Bohemia in 1549. He introduced the Society of Jesus to Prague in 1556, and he was also instrumental in securing the appointment of a Roman Catholic Archbishop in Prague in 1561, after a lapse in succession since the early fifteenth century because of the Hussite schism. His father ensconced the Archduke as ruler of the southernmost Habsburg dominion in the Tyrol in 1563, and the younger Ferdinand was soon busy implementing an aggressive Catholic agenda there, with the Emperor's covert blessing. Yet back in Bohemia, when the new Archbishop of Prague, Antonin Brus z Mohelnice, finally took up his office in 1564, the Emperor insisted that he should ordain Hussite clergy, much to the fury of the Jesuits, who harassed the unfortunate prelate and his successors on this issue. Ferdinand also successfully wheedled Pope Pius IV into recognizing the practice of administering communion in both kinds (a concession with-drawn by Pope Gregory XIII in 1584). Politics dictated this selective imperial moderation.[29]

In the same year 1564, the Emperor set up a commission to draft a settlement for his dominions that might even be based on the Augsburg Confession. Those involved were Catholic theologians who shared his agenda, the Netherlandish scholar Georg Cassander, veteran of Archbishop von Wied's reforming programme and a consultant for the 1561 Colloquy of Poissy (see below, p. 302), together with the notoriously floor-crossing clergyman, Georg Witzel.[30] The Emperor Ferdinand's death in 1564 meant that Cassander's commission reported to his eldest son and successor as Emperor, Maximilian, but still they found a sympathetic audience. Maximilian II, unlike his younger brother the Archduke Ferdinand, was passionately committed to his father's policy of a middle way – more sincerely, indeed, than the old Emperor. At his court in Vienna, he gathered a remarkable multicultural array of scholars and diplomatic and political advisers (notably few theologians). By their very diversity they were to contribute to a harmonious culture worthy of Christendom's Emperor: prominent among them were a Silesian Protestant physician Johannes Crato (formerly one of Martin Luther's lodgers), a Reformed Protestant scholar Hugo Blotius from Leiden, who presided over the imperial library, an historian from Mantua Jacopo Strada, and a Swabian soldier and diplomat Lazarus von Schwendi, who saw the toleration of religious diversity as essential to consolidating Habsburg power in central Europe.

Nevertheless, all the while the Emperor had to face opposition from more resolute Catholic forces in his dominions, principally the Jesuits; he also endured open criticism from his brother the Archduke Ferdinand, who managed to outlive him by nearly two decades. With Maximilian's death in 1576, and the accession of his highly cultured but increasingly eccentric son Rudolf II, the Habsburg pursuit of a middle way in religion began to falter after half a century of conscientious effort, although shifting alliances in family squabbles prolonged it into the early seventeenth century (chapter 11, pp. 486–93). Because the Habsburgs maintained a policy of partible inheritance within their family, moderates like the Emperor Maximilian could never impose their policies consistently throughout their dominions, and the uncompromising Catholicism of the Archduke Ferdinand became the dominant family policy. The eventual outcome was the religious confrontation which sparked the Thirty Years War, rather than the search for consensus which was the main emphasis in the 1560s.[31]

For Habsburg Spain, 1559 had the same significance as in Tudor England: it would be remembered as marking the beginning of a long and stabilizing reign, when a resident king returned for the first time in sixteen years. Philip II, so recently King-Consort of England, was no longer burdened by his conscientious pretence of affection for Mary Tudor. He wasted little effort on his proposal of a further marriage to the new English Queen, although the desultory negotiations were valuable to Elizabeth as a way of muffling Spanish hostility to her religious changes and avoiding immediate confrontation. Instead, Philip turned his attention southwards, travelling south from the old imperial capital at Brussels to sort out a rising tide of turbulence and financial chaos in his Iberian kingdoms; he immediately based himself not in his paternal ancestors' kingdom of Aragon, but at the centre of the Iberian peninsula, in the kingdom of Castile.

Philip built as his home and also as his tomb the Jeronimite monastery-palace of the Escorial outside Madrid: it was dedicated to St Laurence, on whose feast-day Philip had won his crushing military victory over the French at St Quentin in 1557. From 1559 until his death in 1598 he based himself in Spain, ruling his worldwide empire with a bleak sense of mission as God's chief champion of the Catholic faith. The cold splendours of the Escorial, enshrining the memory of his divinely granted victory, symbolized Philip's resigned sense that not simply his father Charles V but God himself had singled him out for a rocky road of dedication to be universal monarch: that mood was only increased when he inherited the throne of Portugal and all its empire in 1580. Very early on, visitors noticed that the huge palace's grid-plan was reminiscent of the gridiron on which St Laurence had been roasted alive, and the King's driven personality did nothing to dispel this unique association of a palace-home with an instrument of torture. It is more certain that the Escorial's architect had been instructed to draw on the biblical description of the temple of King Solomon in his design – so that Philip lived in a re-creation of the Holy City, Jerusalem.[32] The King's portraits, generally showing him dressed in black, reveal a man convinced that true magnificence lay in self-restraint. One can contrast his great rival and one-time putative marriage partner, Queen Elizabeth of England, who was determined to have a good time as well as to govern her realms, and who to prove it happily rummaged through her extrovert wardrobe whenever she commissioned an artist to capture her likeness (see Plates 7, 9).

The return of Philip to Spain focused the issue of how Spanish Catholicism should be shaped for the future. There was even less chance than in Italy that Protestantism would make any headway in Spain, but by mid-century the Spanish Inquisition had still not succeeded in disciplining all the multi-form energies of early sixteenth-century Spain. A number of groups in the underworld of Spanish religion retained the *alumbrado* fascination with pushing the boundaries of religious exploration, which included reading what northern European Protestants were saying. One of the largest of such conventicles was in the far south in Seville, where from the mid-1530s the cathedral preacher Juan Gil (Dr Egidio) had been privately encouraging dissent and making contact with like-minded people elsewhere.

Juan Gil was forced to retract before the Inquisition in 1552, but the major Inquisition crack-down came in 1557–8, uncovering interconnected groups as far apart as Seville, Valladolid and in the kingdom of Aragon, after a chance discovery of a courier's bundle of subversive literature. Many victims were rounded up for prolonged investigation and many burned at the stake in *autos da fé*, but some of the monks and laypeople involved were lucky enough to escape to permanent exile in Protestant northern Europe. One of them, safe in Reformed Heidelberg, published anonymously in 1567 an account of the 'arts' of the Spanish Inquisition, *Sanctae Inquisitionis hispanicae artes detectae ac palam traductae*, which became a bestseller in many translations. The book was one of the key elements in the formation of the 'Black Legend' of the terrifying work of the Spanish Inquisitors, which was to be so prominent first in the consciousness of European Protestants and later of southern European anticlericals. It also contained a good deal that was alarmingly accurate.[33]

King Philip thus arrived back in his Spanish kingdoms in autumn 1559 amid an atmosphere of official paranoia and repression. Might he have avoided being sucked into this unyielding drive for conformity? There were Erasmian or *alumbrado* voices raised against what was happening, hoping to benefit from the new start offered by the King's succession to Charles V. Among those Spanish scholars who wrote advice on the practice of kingship at that time was Felipe de la Torre, an associate of *Spirituali* such as Reginald Pole and Marcantonio Flaminio, the author of the final version of the *Beneficio di Christo*. He published his *Institución de un rey christiano* in the rather more relaxed atmosphere of Antwerp in 1556, making a plea for toleration in Spain and expressing cautious criticism of the Inquisition.[34] De la Torre survived the trouble which might have arisen from his views by drawing on the support of King Philip's confessor, and in the end he even became a royal chaplain, but otherwise the King remained unmoved by calls for a change of official direction. Almost as soon as Philip had reached his Castilian capital at Valladolid, he attended one of the Inquisition's *autos da fé* of their 'Lutheran' suspects; his message of support for the Inquisition's work was clear.[35]

In 1559 the Spanish Inquisition produced its own Index of prohibited books for Spain, which to begin with even banned Ignatius Loyola's *Spiritual Exercises* – most of the Inquisitors were Dominicans and kept all their old suspicions that the founder of the Jesuits was the worst sort of *alumbrado* in a thin disguise. All Spanish books printed outside Spain were banned from the peninsula; moreover a blanket ban was imposed on Spaniards studying abroad (so much for Loyola's fruitful years in Paris), and all teachers or students currently abroad were ordered to return home. Such bans were, in the manner of all early modern bureaucratic measures, difficult to police and were surmountable with discretion; yet still Philip's government had committed itself to the proposition that there was only one way to be a Spaniard, and that this was to be a traditionalist Catholic untainted by unsupervised contact with alien thought. Protestantism was added to the list of unSpanish traits that already included Islam and Judaism.

The Inquisition's paranoia swept up some unlikely victims. The later troubles of those great and totally orthodox mystics, John of the Cross and Teresa of Ávila, are well-known (chapter 9, pp. 423–7), but their harassment was anticipated at the end of the 1550s by the suspicion which fell on one of their most admired predecessors, Luis de Granada, a veteran Spanish Dominican who had become Provincial of the Portuguese Dominicans in 1556: Granada was unhealthily interested in the writings of Savonarola and Erasmus, and his own works of devotion were put on the Spanish Index in 1559. Granada's connections at the courts of both Portugal and Spain saved him from serious trouble, but even a much more socially eminent figure, Francisco de Borja, former duke of Gandía and Viceroy of Catalonia, now a star recruit to the Society of Jesus, was subject to the unwelcome attentions of the Spanish Inquisition. They placed some of Borja's writings on their Index and ruined his work for the Society in Spain; in 1561 he left his native land for Rome in a state of fury, depression and physical collapse. Borja and his fellow Jesuits with characteristic creativity turned this humiliation to good use, since from 1565 he became one of the most outstanding Superiors-General in the Society's history.[36]

Most bizarre of all was the fate of the great Dominican Bartolomé Carranza, whom we met helping Cardinal Pole in the reconversion of England, particularly through his draft for a national catechism (see above, pp. 282, 284). He was a widely respected churchman, who had not only played a prominent part in both the first and second sessions of the Council of Trent but when in Spain had also been energetic in helping the Inquisition. He was an obvious choice for Philip to make Archbishop of Toledo, the primatial see of Spain, and once he was able to begin his work there in 1558 he began implementing a comprehensive programme of reform, until suddenly in summer 1559 the Spanish Inquisition arrested him on suspicion of heresy. Carranza's misfortune was to be the victim of two separate but related paranoias, supplemented by the usual individual grudges which any powerful cleric would attract from lesser clergy. One paranoia was that of Pope Paul IV: for Paul and his circle, the fact that Carranza was a friend of Reginald Pole linked him to all the other unfortunates whom the Carafa papacy was pursuing. In parallel to that obsession, the Spanish Inquisition in its increasingly fevered investigations into Spanish theological deviance noted that the Archbishop's decade and more of vigorous involvement in combating Protestantism in northern Europe involved the reading of a great deal of Protestant literature. They eagerly scanned his private files and found detailed notes on heretics in whom no decent Spaniard should take even a critical interest.

The luckless Archbishop Carranza spent nearly seventeen years in prison, the second half spent in Rome to get him away from the worst that the Spanish Inquisition might do to him, and he died there a few months after his eventual release. A consequence of particular black comedy arose when the last session of the Council of Trent appointed a commission to create a single official catechism for the Church. The resulting work of 1566 was based on the catechism that Carranza had drafted for Reginald Pole in England, and which was clearly worth recycling. Because this Tridentine Catechism, the ultimate expression of the Counter-Reformation, was thus associated with Carranza, the Spanish Inquisition persistently refused to allow it to be used in Spain! Carranza was remembered in his native land with puzzlement and regret. His first biographer Pedro Salazar de Mendoza recalled travelling several years after the Archbishop's death through the olive-groves of Andalusia with a distinguished Franciscan friar: the Franciscan observed drily that he was looking forward to the Day of Judgement because he would find out what the truth was in the Carranza affair. Some have seen Carranza's arrest as depriving Spain of its Carlo Borromeo, the model Counter-Reformation diocesan bishop.[37]

The religious uniformity imposed by the Spanish Inquisition was out of the question in France after the death of Henri II. It was impossible for the Regent Catherine even to maintain the unchallenged authority of the Crown in the face of the increasingly partisan behaviour of leading noble families, who were adding religious polarization to their personal rivalries at the same time as clandestine Protestant congregations were spreading with alarming and baffling speed through the kingdom. Most prominent and dangerous to national unity were the Guise and the Bourbons. François duke of Guise, his brother Charles de Guise, Cardinal of Lorraine, and their sister the Queen Dowager of Scots Mary of Guise, mother-in-law to the young François II, represented traditional Catholic loyalty. The house of Bourbon was headed by Antoine de Bourbon, titular King of Navarre, an unimpressive individual who was a good deal less important in his family than his formidable Protestant convert wife Jeanne d'Albret and his younger brother Louis the Prince of Condé, who publicly announced his conversion to evangelical faith in 1558. A third great noble family, the Montmorency, were more divided in religious affiliation: the traditionalist Constable of

France Anne de Montmorency was counterbalanced by his nephew by marriage Gaspard de Coligny, Admiral of France, who soon emerged as one of the most important Protestant leaders. The poisonous atmosphere generated by the Guise–Bourbon rivalries reached its height in the Conspiracy of Amboise in March 1560, an attempt by Huguenot supporters of Navarre to take control of King François and thus seize the initiative from the Guise. Their failure was marked by savage torture and executions of the conspirators – just at the moment when Queen Catherine had issued a decree of amnesty to Protestants.

In this desperate situation, both the Queen and the Cardinal of Lorraine sought to draw back from the brink. Both of them were committed to the traditional church – the Queen, after all, was niece to the late Pope Clement VII – but the Huguenots now seemed too powerful to destroy: their formally constituted Genevan-style church organizations (*Eglises dressées*) were being set up in towns and cities throughout the kingdom. 'This plague has spread into every layer of society,' the alarmed Venetian ambassador wrote home from France in 1561, and he noted the especially disturbing feature that Protestant support came especially from the nobility and people under forty.[38] Even some French bishops were showing an interest in the Reformed cause; Lorraine was not among them, but he understood the power of the new movement. He has often been misrepresented as a unbending Catholic fanatic, not least by his Huguenot opponents at the time, but his outlook was that of the French reformists of previous decades, even that of Archbishop Hermann von Wied in his glory days: he sought a middle way that might bring in moderate Protestants. The growing atmosphere of repression in Spain was a factor in his calculations: Lorraine and his family had been among those in the French leadership most hostile to Spain throughout the 1550s.[39] If the Cardinal could find a basis for compromise then the French Church might be saved, and typically in mid-century, he looked to the 1530 Augsburg Confession as the possible way forward, just as so many did in central Europe.

Accordingly the Regent Catherine summoned Catholic and Protestant theologians to a discussion or colloquy at Poissy, a little town north of Paris on the Seine, whose chateau as the birthplace of the royal saint King Louis strongly symbolized the French monarchy's sacred trust for its people. The colloquy opened in September 1561, nominally presided over by Catherine's young son, King Charles IX. She had invited not only Calvin's colleague in Geneva (soon to be his successor), the exiled French gentleman Theodore de Bèze or Beza, but also her own countryman, Peter Martyr Vermigli; Martyr was now based in Zürich and came to represent the Zürich Church, his last major service to international Protestantism before his death in 1562. Beza and Martyr were an impressive duo to lead the Reformed Protestant delegation. The fatal flaw was the fact that the Cardinal tried to rally moderate opinion behind the Augsburg Confession. Open French evangelicalism had long ago parted with Luther; there was never going to be much chance of agreement with Reformed Protestants, who found Lutheranism almost as wrong-headed as papalist Catholics on the subject of the Eucharist. 'Look at the Augsburg Confession on that and you will stand condemned by the Churches which accept it,' Lorraine hectored his opponents.[40] His middle way could easily be seen as a mischievous attempt to divide and rule, and it only strengthened the resolve of the Reformed party; even Martyr seemed too moderate for them. Poissy decisively associated the French Reformed movement with Geneva. With the failure of the Poissy discussions within a month, intransigent Catholics and Protestants began arming themselves for open confrontation. This was the last conference to attempt general reunion in the sixteenth century.

THE LAST SESSION OF THE COUNCIL OF TRENT, 1561-3

Pope Pius IV's alarm at the French monarchy's independent initiatives at religious conciliation was one powerful motive for his summoning yet another session of the Council of Trent. This infuriated Catherine de' Medici and the Cardinal of Lorraine, who wanted a newly convened Council into which Protestants might be drawn; they saw that a revived session of Trent would enrage Protestants and further damage the prospects for reconciliation. Naturally the Emperor Ferdinand felt the same way but equally predictably his nephew Philip II took the contrary view and backed the Pope's desire to continue the previous Council. Accordingly, the opening of the Council met with Protestant rebuffs; the Protestant princes of the Empire, assembled at Naumburg, refused the invitation, and the young Queen of England and her chief adviser William Cecil were more ostentatious in their snub. They arrested one of the late Queen Mary's chief officers, Sir Edward Waldegrave, together with two other members of Mary's Privy Council, for being too open in patronizing and attending traditional Masses; Waldegrave died in prison in the Tower of London.[41]

The Council opened in January 1562. Since the commanding heights of traditional doctrine had already been reaffirmed in previous sessions, most of its work concerned the life and structuring of the Church. There were decrees on the reform and structural centralization of religious orders. Provisions for the training of parish clergy in seminaries took up the beginnings made by Cardinal Pole in Marian England (his old friend Cardinal Morone, now safe from the dead Paul IV's vindictiveness, took a major part in steering the Council's proceedings). Clandestine marriages (marriage vows exchanged by the parties alone, without the presence of a priest) were forbidden, constituting a major declaration of policy in the official Church's long campaign to gain control over this vital decision in the lives of human beings (chapter 16, p. 636). The Council tried to tidy up devotional practices associated with the cult of saints and the doctrine of purgatory, and in a major case of shutting the stable door after the Lutheran horse had bolted, it forbade the sale of indulgences.

One matter which might be regarded as administrative but in fact had much more profound implications for the Church came near to wrecking this last session of Trent: the question of the role and authority of the bishops of the Church. There was clearly a great deal of work to do to turn the Catholic episcopate, a job-lot of noblemen, semi-detached monks and friars and career-minded scholars, into an effective leadership for the Church, capable of providing an impressive alternative to the highly motivated leadership of Protestant churchmen. However, any move to produce such zealous leaders straight away raised a question: how did the bishops relate to the bishop of Rome, whose claims as Pope had accumulated piecemeal and without any single general act of affirmation or consent over the previous centuries? The attendance at the last session of Trent was larger than in either of the previous sessions: around 200 bishops were involved in proceedings, and many, especially the substantial delegations from Spain (around half its total of bishops), France and the dominions of Venice as far away as Cyprus, were not inclined to allow the Pope much room for manoeuvre. There was a controversial aspect even to something as apparently uncontentious and obviously commendable as the order that bishops should be resident in their dioceses: was residence demanded by God's law, as Spanish bishops maintained?

The point at issue here in what proved to be some very angry exchanges concerned papal authority. A divine command for episcopal residence was a strong indication that the Pope should not exercise a right to dispense bishops for non-residence – this was in fact the same argument which Henry VIII of England had deployed to say that a Pope had had no right to dispense his marriage to Catherine of Aragon because the marriage contravened a divine command. There was a wider question of divine right. This arose when (after dealing with other business in a cooling-off period of several months) the Council tried to tackle a major unresolved issue of doctrine, the nature of ordination in the Church. There was no question of denying that ordination was a sacrament, as Protestants did, but what was the relation of episcopal office to the sacrament of orders? Had bishops emerged in the very early days of the Church as a necessary but historically contingent development, or had Jesus Christ himself instituted the office? If he had not done so, that indicated that the Church's divine authority rested in the Pope, the successor of Peter, chosen by Christ to be the rock on which he built his Church (Matthew 16:18). That would indicate in turn that the authority of bishops came from the Pope, rather than that every bishop was a direct representative of the authority of Christ.

The debates on this issue nearly wrecked the Council. Two of the Pope's delegates died within a few days of each other in March 1563, and the stress of the debate may well have been a factor in their deaths.[42] In the end it proved impossible to formulate an answer that would satisfy everyone present, and it took some masterly drafting to create a formula that would not definitively locate exclusive divine authority in either the papacy or the general body of the episcopate. In practice, many of the centralizing reforms of institutions in the later part of the century put the advantage in the hands of the papacy, particularly because these reforms gave the Pope and his officials the prime responsibility for interpreting what the decrees and canons of Trent actually meant. In the very different situation of the nineteenth century, the first Vatican Council of 1870 formally made the resolution in favour of papal primacy that had been impossible in the conditions of the 1560s.

The mere fact that the Council had not broken down and that there was now a coherent body of decrees and canons for the Church was a source of general relief to those present: as the Council climaxed in ceremonies of thanksgiving in December 1563 there were emotional scenes of bishops in tears, and rounds of applause amid the solemn liturgy. Two hundred and twenty-six bishops signed the Council's documents, and Pope Pius IV swiftly ratified them, putting in train a process of enactment throughout the Catholic world that proceeded piecemeal over the next century, dependent on the willingness of Catholic rulers to accept the decrees. In any case, regardless of the immediate reaction from secular powers, many former clerical sceptics like the Cardinal of Lorraine now decided that there was no point in seeking conciliation with Protestant opponents. Lorraine had gone to Trent in 1562 still hoping to secure worship in the vernacular and communion in both kinds in the French Church; in 1563, he took the opposite ideological route to so many of the Scots reformist Catholic clergy in 1558–9 (see above,

p. 292), and became one of the foremost senior churchmen in France pressing for the implementation of Trent's decisions.[43] The Council decisively
shaped the future of papal Catholicism, which is thus usefully described as
Tridentine (*Tridentum* being the Latin name for the city of Trent).

PROTESTANTS IN ARMS: FRANCE AND THE LOW COUNTRIES, 1562–70

Even before the Council of Trent had drawn to its close, there was good
reason for the Cardinal of Lorraine to despair of conciliation. In March
1562 open warfare broke out in France after François Duke of Guise and
his retinue found a 500-strong Protestant congregation illegally gathered at
prayer at Vassy in the Champagne country, and killed scores of them (rather
unconvincingly claiming that they had acted in self-defence).[44] While the
Guise went on to rally their forces in Paris, Louis de Bourbon, the Prince of
Condé, led similar moves for the Huguenots. Protestants took the opportunity to make a series of armed seizures of power in French cities, taking
advantage of divisions between moderates and hardliners on the Catholic
side: briefly, major centres from one end of the kingdom to the other – Lyon,
Orléans, Le Mans, Rouen, Caen – fell into the hands of the Huguenots.
They were rarely able to sustain their early success, and their failure to win
Toulouse, the capital of southern France (the Midi), was a significant reverse
which indicated the fragility of their military gains. Yet Huguenot strength
among the nobility meant that Protestantism could sustain resistance over
long periods: from 1562 until a final exhausted recognition of compromise
in 1598 there were eight phases of warfare in France, and little more
than ten years that could be considered times of peace. Even during these
comparative lulls, relations between French Protestant and Catholic militants were marked by an extraordinary degree of bitterness and savagery.

Yet this was not a straightforward ideological clash between two sides: it
soon became clear that the struggles in France were three-cornered. Caught
between the extremists on both sides was the French Crown, desperate to
maintain national unity and also determined to suppress the self-assertion
of great noble families that characterized both Catholic and Huguenot
militancy. That might mean pragmatic alliances for the Crown with either
side at various different stages in the conflict. The Regent Catherine de'
Medici was a shrewd woman, who derived entertainment from reading the
biliously partisan Protestant pamphlets abusing her.[45] It was easy for her to
deplore the sort of murderous vendetta that developed between Guise and

Montmorency when the Duke of Guise was assassinated in 1563, and the Guise family were convinced that Admiral Gaspard de Coligny was involved. However, when in September 1567 the Huguenot party, including Coligny and the Bourbon Prince of Condé, nearly succeeded in an effort to capture the young King Charles IX and seize the capital in the 'surprise of Meaux', Catherine was enraged and her attitude to the Huguenots was permanently transformed. In 1568 she put a price on Coligny's head, and it is very likely that she was implicated in the poisoning of his brother François Sieur d'Andelot that same year. All this was preparatory to the great disaster of St Bartholomew in 1572 (chapter 7, p. 337).[46]

The outbreak of war in 1562 was the culmination of a decade of extraordinary growth in French Protestantism. There may have been two million adherents in around a thousand congregations by 1562, while in the early 1550s there had been only a handful of secret groups; the phenomenon is even more spectacular in scale than the sudden emergence of popular Protestantism in Scotland in the same years that had so astonished John Knox. How had such rapid expansion taken place? Public preaching had not been possible on a significant scale to spread the message in France; there had not been enough ministers, and limited opportunities to gather to listen to sermons. Books played a major part, but the two central texts, the Bible and Calvin's *Institutes*, were bulky and expensive and could not have had a major circulation in the years of persecution before 1560, while a massive increase in Bible publication came only after 1562. Lesser, more easily concealed pamphlets could be more easily distributed and read, but in one respect the Protestant crowds who emerged to fight their Catholic neighbours ignored what Calvin and the ministers of Geneva wrote. Until open war began, Calvin was relentless in conveying a message of moderation and avoidance of conflict. Very few seem to have listened: the clerical leadership was then swept along against its will by popular militancy marked especially by gleeful smashing of images.

The explanation for this mass lay activism may lie in the one text which the Reformed found perfectly conveyed their message across all barriers of social status and literacy. This was the Psalter, the book of the 150 Psalms, translated into French verse, set to music and published in unobtrusive pocket-size editions which invariably included the musical notation for the tunes (see Plate 21b). In the old Latin liturgy the psalms were largely used in monastic services and in private devotional recitation. Now they were redeployed in Reformed Protestantism in this metrical form to articulate the hope, fear, joy and fury of the new movement. They became the secret weapon of the Reformation not merely in France but wherever the Reformed brought new vitality to the Protestant cause. Like so many important components of John Calvin's message, he borrowed the idea from the practice of Strassburg in the 1530s. When he arrived to minister to the French congregation there after his expulsion from Geneva in 1538, he found the French singing these metrical psalms, which had been pioneered by a cheerfully unruly convert to evangelical belief, the poet Clément Marot. Calvin took the practice back to Geneva when he returned there to reconstitute its Reformation. Theodore Beza finally produced a complete French metrical psalter in 1562, and during the crisis of 1562–3, he set up a publishing syndicate of thirty printers throughout France and Geneva to capitalize on the psalm-singing phenomenon: the resulting mass-production and distribution was a remarkable feat of technology and organization.[47]

The metrical psalm was the perfect vehicle for turning the Protestant message into a mass movement capable of embracing the illiterate alongside the literate. What better than the very words of the Bible as sung by the hero-King David? The psalms were easily memorized, so that an incriminating printed text could rapidly be dispensed with. They were customarily sung in unison to a large range of dedicated tunes (newly composed, to emphasize the break with the religious past, in contrast to Martin Luther's practice of reusing old church melodies which he loved). The words of a particular psalm could be associated with a particular melody; even to hum the tune spoke of the words of the psalm behind it, and was an act of Protestant subversion. A mood could be summoned up in an instant: Psalm 68 led a crowd into battle, Psalm 124 led to victory, Psalm 115 scorned dumb and blind idols and made the perfect accompaniment for smashing up church interiors. The psalms could be sung in worship or in the market-place; instantly they marked out the singer as a Protestant, and equally instantly united a Protestant crowd in ecstatic companionship just as the football chant does today on the stadium terraces. They were the common property of all, both men and women: women could not preach or rarely even lead prayer, but they could sing alongside their menfolk. To sing a psalm was a liberation – to break away from the mediation of priest or minister and to become a king alongside King David, talking directly to his God. It was perhaps significant that one of the distinctive features of French Catholic persecution in the 1540s had been that those who were about to be burned had their tongues cut out first.

If French Protestant crowds were militant, so were Catholic crowds, and they were generally more murderous: where Protestants smashed images, Catholics butchered people. There were some rational explanations for their hatred: the loathing that the vast majority of people in Paris showed for

Huguenots over several decades was connected to the campaigns of Protestant forces around the city in the second civil war in 1567, which left permanent memories of the starvation and general misery which they caused. However, the hatred ran much deeper: the counter-attacks that swept many of the temporary Protestant regimes in towns from power in 1562-3 were followed by triumphant massacres of hundreds of Protestants. The massacres after the unsuccessful Huguenot attempt to seize Toulouse in May 1562 were notable for a feature that frequently recurred thereafter: many of those killed were drowned in the local river. Protestant corpses were in a similar manner deliberately humiliated, either similarly by being flung into water or kicked into mud or sewage or obscenely mutilated with knives, often merely because they had been given a Protestant funeral.

All this seems to be an attempt to purify the community from the pollution caused by Protestantism. Protestants had tainted the sacredness of French society, and they deserved the most extreme exclusion from it. Protestant iconoclasm had a similar purifying purpose, to stop divine worship being tainted by idols.[48] If the violence from Catholic crowds was spontaneous in the 1560s, the mood was reinforced by the rapid official reinforcement of Catholic institutions of popular devotion in the years after the Council of Trent. The Jesuits, full of their newfound enthusiasm for confronting Protestantism, established a presence in major French towns immediately after the 1562-3 crisis, and they encouraged the refoundation of religious confraternities or gilds, often with a very specific anti-Protestant commitment. Such popular associations became the backbone of an increasingly militant Catholic response to the growth of popular French Protestantism, and they sustained the bitterness of the next thirty years, which found its chief expression in the Catholic Ligue (chapter 10, pp. 446-71).

The crisis which broke in the Habsburg territories in the Low Countries in the same years as the outbreak of war in France revealed a similar combination of political and religious motives. Once more, as in Scotland and France, one major component was an initially clandestine growth of Reformed Protestantism, a revival of Protestant activism in the 1550s reversing a trend of evangelical decline in the region. Since the 1520s, the Habsburg authorities had put more consistent effort into persecuting religious dissent than anywhere else in Europe, and their campaigns had borne fruit: both radical and magisterial Protestant activity showed every sign of contraction and demoralization in the 1540s.[49] The revival of the 1550s was made possible and was sustained to a significant degree because there were bases beyond the Habsburgs' reach that could welcome exiles, and that could also offer support to those still at home through clandestine publication of evangelical literature and returning missionaries. The first important help came from the England of Edward VI, where Dutch exile communities were established not merely in Jan Łaski's London Stranger Church, but also with the encouragement of Archbishop Cranmer in Kent – an easy sail across the North Sea.

When the Edwardian Protestant regime collapsed in 1553, rescue was at hand immediately north of the Netherlands beyond the Habsburg border, in Countess Anna's territory of East Friesland, where once Łaski had fostered the local Reformation. Both English and Dutch Protestant exiles moved from England to the East Frisian capital of Emden in large numbers, and virtually overnight they turned the little port into a major centre of evangelical printing: between 1554 and 1569 230 separate titles came off the Emden presses. It assisted infiltration into the Low Countries that Groningen and west Friesland, the Habsburg provinces closest to Emden, were the least subject to the control of the central administration in Brussels.[50] Once Elizabeth was on the throne after 1558, England also opened up as a refuge again. The chief Inquisitor in the Netherlands Pieter Titelmans wrote in frustration to the Habsburg Regent Margaret of Parma as order broke down in 1562 that 'in the countryside and villages . . . the poor simple people have been misled by these people who can go back and forth to England and other places'.[51]

By itself, this growth in Protestant activism might not have been enough to confront the might of the Spanish Habsburg regime. The persecuted Protestants within the Low Countries held anxious debates about how open they dared to be, particularly after the disastrous consequences which followed public Protestant demonstrations in Antwerp in June 1558; these quarrels over Nicodemism, so characteristic of the mid-century, did not help Protestantism's morale.[52] It took the heavy-handedness of the regime in Brussels to combine the zeal of the Protestant minority with the fierce pride of the Dutch nobility in their traditional local privileges. Trouble began with quarrels over heavy taxation which King Philip II had attempted to extract from the Low Countries at the beginning of his reign: they were, after all, the richest part of his dominions, and he was in dire financial difficulties which led to a declaration of bankruptcy in Spain in 1557. Equally reasonable was the plan of church reorganization that he left for his half-sister Margaret of Parma to implement as Regent when he left for Spain in 1559. A plan first devised by Charles V, it addressed the absurdly small number of four dioceses that covered the densely populated Low Countries, seeking to establish fourteen bishoprics and three archbishoprics to offer Catholic pastoral care and the suppression of heresy in a more effective way.

This plan was opposed by all interested parties except the Habsburg administration in Brussels. The current bishops and the neighbouring church hierarchies in France and the archdiocese of Cologne were joined by Low Countries nobility, horrified that all the new bishops would gain voting rights in the local Estates alongside them. The nobles also resented the administrative power which Philip had allowed to concentrate in the hands of the bishop of Arras, Antoine de Perronet, sieur de Granvelle; in 1561 Granvelle was made a Cardinal and designated Archbishop of Mechelen (Malines) in the new scheme. However, anxieties spread more widely through Low Countries society. There was a deep popular fear that the already active local Inquisitions would be supplemented by an introduction of the Spanish Inquisition; there was a lively awareness among the Dutch of the recent sudden increase in Inquisition activity in Spain (see above, p. 298). Their fears seemed justified when in 1561 Philip sent a Spanish army administrator Alonso del Canto to reinforce the work of the over-stretched local inquisitors in seeking out Spanish heretics fleeing the intensi-fied persecution back home. Local notables who had backed the work of the Inquisitions for decades now pointedly withdrew their active support.[53]

The King's plans for rationalization in Church and Commonwealth now clearly threatened the complex liberties of the lands which the Habsburgs had inherited from the Dukes of Burgundy seventy years before. Whereas the French nobility in their manoeuvrings in the 1560s were seeking new and greater power in relation to their monarchy, the Dutch nobility, who now resisted the royal plans, sought to keep the local power that was theirs by right. Alongside these localist grievances, Protestant activism came into the open. The first public services were held in 1562, and already in 1561 the churches now taking on formal structures in the manner of the French *Eglises dressées* had formulated a Reformed confession of faith, the Belgic Confession. It was closely modelled on a confession of faith that the French Reformed Churches had created in 1559, but it was modified to meet the challenge of the strong body of radical opinion in the Netherlands: there was much more detailed discussion of the Trinity, and of how the newly constituted Church differed from Anabaptist groups.

When discontent became general during 1563 the government response was fatally incoherent. Philip reluctantly ordered Granvelle to leave the country, but then in 1565 insisted that the local authorities should continue to enforce the heresy laws, further infuriating those notables charged with carrying out the King's will. Issues of local autonomy were now being associated with religious protest. In 1566 a group of several hundred lesser noblemen petitioned the Regent Margaret against the heresy laws, and she yielded to their demands: this wavering in authority encouraged Protestant enthusiasts to abandon their caution, and control of the situation slipped from the nobility in what Protestants later remembered as 'the wonder-year'. Exiles returned enthusiastically from England and Emden: preaching fanned popular demonstrations which turned into celebratory attacks on the symbols of the old religion; mobs sacked churches in an iconoclastic 'fury' which outstripped the similar previous attacks in Scotland and France. Philip could hardly avoid drastic action against this defiance of his government. In 1567 he sent a large army commanded by the Duke of Alva, a Spanish veteran of Charles V's campaigns in the Schmalkaldic Wars, to restore order, which he did, with ruthless cruelty. The Regent Margaret, appalled by Alva's actions, resigned from government, and the Duke ruled the Netherlands through a 'Council of Troubles', known to his terrified subjects as the 'Council of Blood'.

Alva's punishment of the region lived up to the worst fears inspired in the previous few years: he executed two leading noblemen in 1568, together with about 1,000 others, and the Spanish army behaved like an occupying force in enemy territory. Thousands fled from the Netherlands: it was a highly significant moment for the Reformed as their community in Antwerp, northern Europe's leading centre of culture and intellectual enquiry, dispersed across northern Europe to sympathetic refuges in London, Emden and the German territories of the champion of Reformed Protestantism, the Elector Palatine. The senior surviving political notable in the Netherlands was Willem of Orange (nicknamed 'William the Silent'), whom in 1559 Philip had appointed to the traditional governor's office of *stadhouder* in three Low Countries provinces.[54] Willem was now forced into the leadership of the opposition by the power vacuum which the executions created and by the wrongs personally afforded him by Alva's administration. He concluded an alliance with the French Huguenot leaders Coligny and the Prince of Condé; his own religious outlook was Protestant, but not strictly Reformed. He went so far as to propose that the Protestants of the Netherlands should unite around the Augsburg Confession, but it was too late for such gestures of unity, given the strong links of most Protestant preachers with the Reformed Churches in Geneva, France and London. Theodore Beza was particularly influential in blocking the suggestion.[55]

Orange's efforts at military action against Alva were a failure. At the end of the 1560s, the Protestant cause seemed again lost, and a fresh wave of refugees flooded out of the Netherlands: perhaps 100,000 people left, many of them once more northwards over the border into Emden or across the North Sea to England.[56] This was one of the greatest dispersals so far of the many movements of people caused by the Reformation, and it might have been permanent. Religion alone might not have been enough to reverse the situation, but the arrogance of the new Spanish administration, now openly despising assertions of traditional privilege and arbitrarily imposing heavy taxes, kept alive a spirit of resistance that turned once more to rebellion in 1572. In the Netherlands, as in France and Scotland, the hopes of conciliation and the reconstruction of a single Catholic Church were at an end. After this second wave of militant popular Reformation in the 1560s, Europe's house was destined to remain divided.

PART II

EUROPE DIVIDED:
1570–1619

7

The New Europe Defined, 1569–72

NORTHERN AND SOUTHERN RELIGION

The end of the 1560s marked a watershed in the Reformation. Most of the leaders of the early struggles, when the shape of the Reformation had still been uncertain, were now dead. A generation had passed since Zwingli's corpse lay on the battlefield at Kappel; Luther died on the eve of the Schmalkaldic Wars in 1546. Calvin, racked by tuberculosis and mourning in his dying months the descent of chaos on France, went in 1564 to an unmarked grave in Geneva, as he had insisted. Most of the great Reformed pioneers had predeceased him, although Heinrich Bullinger survived to steer the Church of Zürich as late as 1575. The Protestants had divided into two camps, Lutheran and Reformed, which could not agree on such vital matters of doctrine as the Eucharist, the right use of images and ceremony or the role of predestination to salvation. They buttressed their differing positions with an increasing array of confessional statements, saying exactly what they did and did not believe: for Lutherans, the 1530 Augsburg Confession; for the Reformed, the 1563 Heidelberg Catechism or the statements of various national Reformed Church groupings like the French Confession of 1559 and the Belgic (Netherlands) Confession of 1561.

Historians have named this transformation of western Christianity in the century or so from the 1560s the era of 'confessionalization'. Churches tried to make their confessional statements essential parts of the consciousness and sense of identity of their followers, and most civil powers now backed their efforts. Another symbolic death heralding this new age was that of Philipp of Hesse in 1567, that same Landgraf Philipp who had sponsored the Colloquy of Marburg as a young man. Until his dying day Philipp refused to allow the Protestant Church in his dominions to be identified with any one variety of Protestantism. Similarly Albert Hardenberg, that old friend of Archbishop von Wied, Martin Bucer and Jan Łaski, loyally maintained Countess Anna's 'third way' in East Friesland up to his death in

317

1574; yet Hardenberg had only taken over the leadership of the Church in East Friesland because he had been expelled from the free city of Bremen in the course of struggles for power between Lutherans and Reformed. Only Queen Elizabeth of England maintained her own personal third way in religion to the end of the century, to the bafflement and disapproval of most of her subjects who expressed opinions about such matters.

The differentiation which the Landgraf Philipp, Hardenberg and Elizabeth resisted was not merely a matter of the details of belief laid down by governments; most people made choices and internalized the new identities of Protestant and Catholic remarkably quickly, often even in the absence of major pressure from a state authority. The Reformed were showing a talent for creating mass movements across cultural and linguistic boundaries, witnessed by the extraordinary diffusion of John Calvin's writings: between 1565 and 1600, nearly half of all Calvin publications were English, German or Dutch translations from the original Latin and French.[1] By contrast, the Lutherans consolidated within the cultural frontiers of *Deutschtum* (wherever German-speakers might be found in Europe) and in Scandinavia. Indeed, in the wide scattering of German settlement beyond the boundaries of the Habsburg lands and the Empire, German identity was increasingly understood to involve a confessionally Lutheran relationship with Wittenberg. As far away as Transylvania, the stately medieval German churches of Siebenbürgen now resounded to Lutheran hymnody and services conducted with the sober liturgical splendour being devised by the Lutheran clergy (one French visitor to a Siebenbürgen Lutheran parish commented that the main clue that he was not at a Roman Catholic service was the abuse of the Pope afterwards).[2] The rival Reformed and Lutheran identities were both confronted with a Roman Catholic Church which after the Council of Trent was now equipped with more precise formulations on doctrine and worship than ever before, and which was filled with a determination to win back ground lost over the previous forty years.

This divergence was at its greatest and the future clearest at the southern and northern extremes of Europe. In the Baltic region, the Atlantic Isles and the mainland bordering the North Sea centring on the German heartland of the early Reformation, the advantage swung decisively towards Protestantism (see below, chapter 8). By contrast in Iberia and Italy, the lands of Philip of Spain and the seat of papal power, Tridentine Catholicism routed its rivals (see chapter 9): a symbol of the contrast was that after the death in 1523 of Adrian VI (a Dutch former tutor of the Emperor Charles V), up to 1978, every Pope was an Italian. However, in a swathe of central Europe, the outcome of events remained uncertain and the political situation was dangerously unstable (see chapter 10). In the Netherlands, sixty years of warfare eventually led to partition between Catholic and Protestant, and so radically different destinies developed for the northern and southern lands which before the Reformation had the shared identity of the Low Countries. In the prolonged civil wars of France, Protestantism found its centre of gravity not in the north but in the west and south, where the kingdom bordered on the Atlantic and the Mediterranean. Switzerland was equally divided in religion, though in much more complex territorial fashion and without the mayhem that followed events in France and the Netherlands in the 1560s. In much of the Empire and other Habsburg lands, the religious balance of power remained precariously even between the Catholic Habsburgs and their Protestant subjects, and in the great plain of Hungary, along the eastern Adriatic coast and in the Balkans, the balance tipped for the moment towards Protestantism. Although the religious situation remained as chaotic as the politics of the area under the constant threat of aggressively expansionist Islam, the princes of Transylvania emerged as the champions of a militant Reformed Protestantism, which might prove an ally to hard-pressed Protestants elsewhere.

All generalizations in history cry out for qualification. On the western fringe of Europe, Queen Elizabeth outfaced Roman Catholic opposition in England, but in her other kingdom of Ireland, her official Protestant Church began losing momentum by the end of the 1560s (chapter 8, pp. 394–9). In the midst of the mostly Lutheran cities, kingdoms and principalities of the Baltic, northern Germany and Scandinavia, the future of the greatest civil Commonwealth of them all, Poland-Lithuania, remained deliberately and proudly open (see below, pp. 340–44). History indeed is good at confounding and confusing labellers. Reformed Protestants were often called 'Calvinists' at the time and since, but our lengthy mid-century foray in chapter 5 into East Friesland, the England of Edward VI and the Churches of eastern Europe shows that there were alternative Reformed voices to John Calvin – Bucer, Cranmer, Peter Martyr, Melanchthon, Łaski, Bullinger. For the most part, they had done their work before Calvin, and although they generally honoured and admired what they knew of his achievements, they did not look to him as an authority, and frequently disagreed with him. Geneva was never Protestantism's Vatican – in fact, as we will see in chapter 8, its dominance was a matter of a couple of decades at most from the mid-1550s.

Did Calvin ever become a Reformed Pope? The effect of his example and his writings was greatest in those Churches created during the popular upheavals of the 1560s – Scotland, France, the Netherlands – also in the attempted Reformations 'from above' in Germany's 'Second Reformation' (chapter 8, pp. 353–8). Even in such settings, the other great Reformers were read and their thought was influential – in Calvin's own beloved France, many Protestants followed Jan Łaski in believing that local congregations ought to have more power than Calvin's system of Church government offered them, and that was a continuing source of quarrels among the Huguenots.[3] Generally those Reformed Protestant Churches founded in the militant 1560s and after were more likely to fall into a Calvinist mould than those that had taken shape before the 1560s. That resulted in a long-term divide: there were more varied, flexible patterns of life in the Churches of Switzerland (for Geneva was not Swiss in the sixteenth century), England, Hungary/Transylvania, Poland-Lithuania, than in Calvinist Scotland, Huguenot France or the official Church of the United Provinces of the Netherlands. We shall be seeing some consequences of this divergence within Reformed Protestantism, particularly in the way that different Churches exercised church discipline (chapters 10, 12–14).

Catholicism, even in its areas of strength, also continued to face impulses and obstacles pointing away from the uniformity of 'confessionalization' and the central control implicit in the Pope's view of what had happened at the Council of Trent. Like Poland-Lithuania to the north, the central European Habsburg lands beyond the Holy Roman Empire witnessed a delicate balance of power between Catholic Habsburgs and Lutheran, Reformed, religiously radical or undecided local magnates. That produced parishes where clergy indifferently played the role of Protestant minister or Catholic massing priest, depending on consumer demand, as late as 1600.[4] Yet even the most devoutly Catholic secular rulers continued to see themselves as fathers of their territories (*Landesväter*); their grandfathers before the Reformation had often been inclined to create out of the universal Western Church *Landeskirchen* or locally run churches (chapter 1, p. 51). Not all these rulers had broken with the old Church in the Reformation, but neither did they necessarily change their proprietorial attitudes. The most fiercely devout of traditionalist Catholic monarchs, Philip II of Spain, was not going to yield any of his ancestors' independence from direct papal interference in his dominions. He was one of the first monarchs to implement the decrees of the Council of Trent; in fact he was so quick off the mark that he did so without waiting for the Pope to ratify them. From the 1560s the decrees were enacted through Spanish provincial Church councils convened by the King, with Philip's royal 'observers' in reality presiding over the proceedings, and whatever the King found difficult in the decrees he altered to suit himself. In the same spirit, when Philip wished to introduce into the Spanish dominions the 'Tridentine' breviary newly authorized for the whole Catholic Church, he commissioned a local edition from Plantin, his official printer in Brussels, which made some deliberate minor alterations to get around the monopoly privilege granted to an Italian printer by the Pope.[5]

Similarly, the ideology of Gallicanism did not disappear from France with the Reformation. A high proportion of French lawyers and scholars viewed the history of their country through traditional Gallican eyes: they saw no necessary clash between loyalty to the old Church and loyalty to the French monarchy, but if a clash should indeed occur, their first loyalty was to the King. A whole series of late sixteenth-century French historians drew their view of the relations between Church and Commonwealth from early fourth-century Rome, when the Emperor Constantine was converted to Christianity and immediately took it upon himself to summon Councils to decide questions of Church doctrine and discipline: they pointed out that after the baptism of King Clovis of the Franks, the same thing had happened in France. This was not merely antiquarianism, as a representative splutter about the Council of Trent from the celebrated Gallican Catholic lawyer Charles du Moulin makes clear: 'This new pretended Council has sought to deprive the King of France of his ancient honour by subjugating him and preferring another [the Pope] to him. This other was elevated to his position long after the institution of the Crown of France, which delivered him from the pagans and the Saracens and installed the Catholic faith by means of the succours and victories of Charlemagne and the Franks.'[6] But Gallicanism was more than just an attitude of mind among politicians. It was allied with the French monarchy's desperate efforts to unite the kingdom in the face of the split between Huguenots and papalist Catholics, and reflected a widespread horror at the extremism which papal loyalty might produce, extending as far as the assassination of two Catholic Kings of France. It was a mood that spread well beyond France, and the consequence was that Roman Catholicism in northern and western Europe never marched entirely in step with the southern Counter-Reformation (chapter 10, pp. 479-84).

Before pursuing these various loose ends, however, we will take stock of the polarized extremes of Catholicism and Protestantism, and also examine an extraordinary sequence of major crises and decisions across the Continent which, within no more than half a decade around 1570, set the courses of northern and southern Europe in opposite directions. The dynamic of these events made it possible for the partition of Europe to become permanent in the mid-seventeenth century. They culminated in 1572 in a catastrophe in France, the Massacre of St Bartholomew, which not only showed how unstable and divided that once-powerful kingdom had become, but also reinforced the feeling in the minds of both Catholic and Protestant that their enemies were bent on eliminating them altogether. From then on, the fates of southern and northern Europe clearly began to diverge, and subsequent chapters in this section of this book recognize that reality by telling separate and localized stories of the struggles for the soul of the Continent.

TRIDENTINE SUCCESSES

By the end of the 1560s there was an obvious recovery of self-confidence and effectiveness in the life and organization of the surviving Roman Catholic Church. After the Council of Trent closed, the Council's work was completed by various major documents intended for the whole Church throughout the world: the catechism issued in 1566, developed as we have seen from the work of the imprisoned Archbishop Carranza (chapter 6, p. 301), a Breviary (1568) to regulate the non-eucharistic services of the Church, and then a single rite for the Mass itself, the Missal of 1570. This Tridentine Mass became the symbol of the new dispensation, to be used everywhere except in carefully specified circumstances. In general, a Roman Catholic could now walk into a church of papal obedience anywhere in the world and know that he or she would hear exactly the same Latin drama being performed. The medieval western Church had been a house of many mansions: now they were all to be tidied up and given a uniform Tridentine colour-scheme in a Roman Catholic Church.

The Pope was obviously placed to be the symbol of unity in Tridentine Catholicism. The rebuilding of St Peter's Basilica in Rome beside his principal palace the Vatican – that rebuilding which had been the unwitting cause of Luther's first protest back in 1517 (chapter 3, p. 120) – continued serenely on into the 1620s, the steadily grander scale of the project providing a fitting setting for the new splendour and renewed self-confidence of the Bishops of Rome. Their ambitious building projects in the city were paired with a reconstruction of papal government which enabled the papacy to seize the initiative in the Roman Catholic Church: papal nuncios (ambassadors) to Catholic rulers in Europe were given more to do, and some were issued permanent commissions with instructions to promote local reforms in the Church.

Transforming the central organization of the Church in a brief reign from 1585 to 1590, Pope Sixtus V expanded the departments of state or Congregations to administer both his own Italian territories and the wider Church; one of them ran the Vatican's first printing press, a remarkably late recognition in Rome of the role that publishing now played in ideological battles. An even later addition to these Congregations in 1622, the Congregation for the Propagation of the Faith, had the task of co-ordinating the worldwide mission which was an increasingly important aspect of the Roman Catholic Church's work, although in fact its first priority was severely European: the new opportunity for recatholicizing central Europe provided by the military catastrophe of Protestantism in the early stages of the Thirty Years War (chapter 11). A symptom of this new papal centralization was that it now became automatic to look to Rome to decide doctrinal matters. In the medieval Western Church it had been the universities, especially Paris, that had done this, but their role was now eclipsed; no doubt their dismal failure to produce a unified or convincing judgement on King Henry VIII's marital difficulty over Catherine of Aragon (chapter 4, pp. 198-200) was one factor in discrediting them as theological referees.

The papacy's new power was backed up by the recently founded religious organizations which also had a central focus. The Capuchin friars were a pioneering example actually before the Reformation had begun, but above all there was the Society of Jesus. From the 1560s the Society was ready to take on a leading role not merely in promoting the programme of the Council of Trent, but also in actively combating Protestantism. In the Jesuits' revised statement of their purpose in 1550, they added the idea of 'defence' to 'propagation of the faith'. The programme this implied was accelerated after Ignatius Loyola's assistant Jerónimo Nadal visited Germany in 1555: the degree to which Protestantism had taken over the German Church profoundly shocked Nadal, and convinced him that the Society must devote its talents to reversing the situation there. This represented a major change in direction for the Society, for confrontation with Protestants had not been part of its agenda in its earliest years. Nadal, who did much to remould the image of the Society after Ignatius's death, now came deliberately to promote the inaccurate idea that the Jesuits had been founded to combat the Reformation.[7] The Jesuits thus moved from 'Catholic Reformation' to 'Counter-Reformation'. They were not always popular with the Popes whom they were pledged to defend, and with remarkable skill they defended themselves from the Council of Trent's efforts to subject regular clergy to the control of local bishops. In their eyes, the new era of Tridentine regulation applied to everyone but themselves, as it would restrict their freedom and flexibility in promoting the new era of Roman Catholicism that was now beginning.

An essential feature of the tidy new Tridentine world was the Church's determined effort to regulate society – part of its recovery of nerve and affirmation of its authority against the assertive secular rulers of Europe. Erasmus had encouraged kings, princes and city councils to become 'abbots' in the 'great monastery' of their territories (chapter 2, p. 104); it was time for the Church to recapture the moral high ground from the princes, and also to show that in the competition to create a 'Reformation of Manners', it could create a society even better-run and better-disciplined than that of Protestant heretics. Accordingly, the Church made more concentrated scrutiny of the sexual lives of the faithful, both inside and outside marriage (chapter 15). Rather less commendably in modern eyes, in most parts of Europe, Catholic and Protestant churchmen alike took a new interest in the pursuit and punishment of witches, an activity with little precedent in medieval Europe, even though medieval people had been just as serious in their belief in witches as people in the sixteenth century (chapter 13, pp. 563–75). Naturally the laity would stomach such regulation much more willingly if they experienced the Church's compassion as well as its discipline. Churchmen in Catholic Europe renewed their commitment to relieving the distress of the poor: much medieval provision for poor relief was in the hands of gilds which had been widely disrupted by Protestant hostility to their religious functions, or in Italy by the half-century of Valois–Habsburg warfare. Religious Orders and the Jesuits were now prominent in taking over gild activities in order to restore them; with greater clerical leadership came a greater emphasis on examining the spiritual as well as the physical condition of the unfortunates who were being helped, to save their souls alongside their bodies.[8]

In reasserting itself, the old Church had advantages over Protestants. It could draw as Protestants could not and would not on its obvious continuity with the medieval Church, laying claim to those centuries of history and devotional practice, presented in the best light possible. This did require some reassessment. Protestants had targeted the wealth, magnificence and ritual splendour of the old Church, and for several decades reformers in the traditional Church felt their vulnerability on this point: the immediate reaction was to simplify and combine grandeur with austerity and restraint in the Church's visual, liturgical and music presentation. Since a church building had sparked Luther's anger, it was worth considering whether a renewed Church needed a renewed architecture, making a break with the compromised medieval past. Queen Mary of England, for instance, gave generously to the restoration of Worcester Cathedral (burial-place of her mother Queen Catherine's first husband Prince Arthur): the Cathedral's eastern parts had been comprehensively trashed by the Protestant Bishop John Hooper under Edward VI in order to purify the building for evangelical worship. The Queen probably intended to set a good example to her subjects in a showcase cathedral of how they might do something about England's shattered churches: interestingly, her money was used in the years after 1556 not only on a new organ and choir-stalls, but on removing the remaining medieval stained glass from the choir windows to lighten the church, and the modish classical style of the new Cathedral furnishings broke with the building's Gothic architecture.[9]

In a similar break with the past, the Jesuits sought to make an impression by a style of almost Puritan grandeur when they began acquiring enough funds to put up major church buildings. One of their prototypes was the massive but deliberately undemonstrative western façade and simple hall-plan of their Portuguese headquarters church in Lisbon, St Roch (begun in 1555), and its ideas were followed on an even grander scale from 1568 by the Jesuits' chief church in Rome, the Gesù. However, it is significant that simplicity is not the impression made today by either St Roch or the Gesù: their interiors are a riot of colour and sculpture, which began accumulating within half a century of the foundation. The deliberate plainness (we might even call it Puritanism) of the early Counter-Reformation quickly dissipated into the emotional turbulence of Baroque architecture and design, as the Catholic Church realized that dramatic artistic statements were one of its best weapons against the restrained Protestant aesthetic.

This progression from elaboration to restraint and back again was equally true of music for the liturgy. Liturgical music in the late medieval Church reached a pitch of professional sophistication and gorgeous complexity of instruments and voices rarely equalled since: during the fifteenth century, even the last refuges of musical austerity, the funeral service and the solemnities of Holy Week, were taken over by the professional singers.[10] The reaction of the early sixteenth century reforming bishop Gian Matteo Giberti of Verona to such musical excess was as extreme as that of many Reformed Protestants: he banned the lot, leaving only unison plainsong. Few of Giberti's fellow Catholic Reformers went that far, although we have already noted Ignatius Loyola's disapproval of sung high masses (chapter 5, p. 225). The short-lived Pope Marcellus II (1555) was one of those encouraging simpler forms of unaccompanied polyphonic choral music, and one Roman composer of genius under his patronage, Giovanni Palestrina, showed just how moving such aesthetic restraint could be in a Mass dedicated to his memory, the *Missa Papae Marcelli*, which has become the archetype of such composition. The Council of Trent laid down guidelines following the moderate course that Palestrina's music indicated, rather than wholly depriving the Church of the liturgical treasure-chest which was soon recognized to be as potent as the contemporary effect of Reformed metrical psalms. However, within a few decades, any restraint evaporated, encouraged by the extrovert liturgical practice of the Republic of Venice, which had never shown particular enthusiasm for Tridentine Puritanism. Giovanni Gabrieli and Claudio Monteverdi, from the late sixteenth century successively given free rein in the Venetian Doge's church of St Mark, have rarely been surpassed in liturgical music in their audacious manipulation of the peculiar acoustic in that great building, stunning the listening worshipper through their divided groupings of choirs exuberantly battling with bands of stringed and wind instruments.

While the traditional Church had the capacity to draw on devotional resources which Protestants rejected, it could equally well exploit the weapon of communication that Protestants now regarded as paramount: the sermon. As we have seen (chapter 1, pp. 31–3), there was no shortage of preaching in the late medieval Church, but it tended to be the province of specialists, either friars or a small elite of highly educated secular clergy. The friars went on with their work, and they were now joined by the Jesuits, who may have borrowed their ideas for church planning from the open-hall designs of the preaching-spaces in medieval friars' churches. Pulpits took on a new prominence in these unified liturgical rooms, though not the total dominance that they assumed in Reformed Protestant church interiors. The ideal was now to make all the clergy effective preachers, even if not of their own sermons.

The one thing that the Council of Trent could agree on amid its near-fatal quarrels about the role of the bishops (chapter 6, pp. 304–5) was that the prime duty of the episcopate was to preach. That directed bishops towards considering how the clergy under their care might also convey the message. New textbooks on preaching proliferated, and both old and new collections of ready-made sermons became staples of Catholic publishing – the equivalent of Luther's *Postils*, Bullinger's *Decades* or the English official Homilies of Edward VI and Elizabeth I. In a Catholic liturgical setting, the drama of sermons was not in competition with the drama of music, liturgy and imagery, but each could reinforce the other. One preaching manual published in Perugia in 1579 includes a picture that is a broad hint to clerical readers to use their imaginations when trying to communicate their message: a Franciscan preacher standing in the pulpit is using a impressively long teacher's pointer to draw his congregation's attention to the pictures of sacred art all around them in their church building.[11]

Such schoolmasterly panache was only one example of how much more was now demanded of the parish clergy than before 1517. To be more

*Ad sensus aptat coelestia dona magister,
Aridaᵹ eloquij pectora fonte rigat.*

In his study of pulpit rhetoric and technique, the Franciscan Diego
Valadés illustrated how Franciscan preachers in Mexico used visual aids
in preaching to illiterate Indio congregations, complete with pointers:
the same technique could be used in rural Europe. Significantly, the
paintings he is using are a series of martyrdoms, flanking Christ's
crucifixion. The pulpit has an acoustic sounding-board, a sixteenth-
century innovation, though here it may also be keeping off the sun.

precise, much had been required of them before by reforming Councils of the medieval Church, but now there was a settled determination for reform not to lapse as it had so often done before. Trent insisted that parish priests should teach the catechism to their congregations; since this was principally taught to children, it implied an increased degree of clerical involvement in bringing up children beyond the expectations of medieval parishes. Counter-Reformation bishops ordered parish clergy to hear confessions regularly, rather than accepting that friars were the experts in such matters. That hyper-energetic paragon of a reforming Archbishop, Carlo Borromeo of Milan, popularized a new item of furniture for churches, the confessional: a wooden double sentry-box divided by a latticed partition, in which a kneeling penitent could be distanced from the invisible confessor yet still experience an intense one-to-one relationship during the course of confession. By the early seventeenth century it was possible to consider that a parish clergyman might act as a spiritual director to his people: a rare phenomenon indeed to medieval Europeans, whose instinct would have been to look first to the friars, second to the older religious Orders.

Bearing in mind Protestant denigration of the medieval clergy and the early Reformation's devastating attacks on monastic life, these Counter-Reformation measures thus amounted to a resounding vote of confidence in the parish system. They confidently looked to the formation of an activist, well-instructed laity, steered by an activist and well-trained clergy. Trent not only planned an unprecedented European-wide system of diocesan clergy training – the seminaries – but also required that parish clergy show evidence that they had a private income to sustain them apart from any parish revenues.[12] It proved a slow task to enforce this clerical means test, but reforming the clergy had to proceed on many fronts. The laity were co-opted into improving clerical standards by the general raising of moral expectations: the enforcement of clerical celibacy was an obviously central symbolic issue. In northern France, for instance, one local study has highlighted the way in which from the 1580s, leading laypeople in villages were denouncing clergy who kept concubines, something that previously had provoked little comment, and this shift in social mores could be given many parallels elsewhere.[13]

The task of reconstruction in the parishes was huge, and it was naturally easier to reform the religious Orders, who had community rules to act as a benchmark for improvement, and an ethos of expecting such action. So the most immediate changes were in fact among monks and friars; here too the recovery begun in the 1560s was cumulative but in the end spectacular.

The Franciscan Conventual friars, who had suffered catastrophic losses through defection and dissolution in the early Reformation, increased their numbers from around 20,000 in 1517 to 25,000 by 1775: by 1700 the Dominicans had more than doubled their early sixteenth-century strength to around 30,000.[14] With the return of self-confidence to the regular clergy, it was possible to launch missionary efforts, with the agenda that much of Europe was as much a mission field as any of the colonial or trading ventures of the Spanish and Portuguese empires (chapter 9, pp. 414-17).

Beyond renewal in parishes and religious orders lay a revival of that traditional sphere of lay activism: pilgrimage to holy places and the shrines of saints, which when suitably regulated and sanitized, could stir the imaginations and devotions of the faithful once more (chapter 10, p. 454). The Virgin Mary, whose cult was a principal target of Reformation anger even among the Lutherans, could be considered an especially powerful ally in defending the old ways. The Hail Mary was the centrepiece of a form of devotional recitation known as the rosary. This became popular in northern Europe during the fifteenth century and confraternities were then set up to promote its use, much encouraged by the Dominicans. What happened next was one example of the Counter-Reformation fixing on the practice of serious-minded northern Europeans and making it general throughout Catholic Europe. From the 1560s the Jesuits took up the rosary as a useful way of stimulating lay devotional activity; it was included in the new Roman Breviary, and in a bull of 1569 Pius V for the first time gave a detailed official description for the practice.

Confraternities of the rosary now proliferated, encouraging their members to frequent communion, something controversial in the medieval West (chapter 1, p. 22). Their great attraction was that in the rosary and the confraternity Masses they offered laypeople a vehicle of prayer that was as structured, corporate and intense as anything enjoyed within a religious community under a rule – a riposte to the stereotype assiduously peddled among Protestants that traditional faith relegated the laity to second-class status. Moreover, the rosary was a physical object as well as a form of prayer: the set of beads helped the user keep a tally of the number of prayers made, and one Redemptorist preacher called it 'the ladder to paradise'. As such, it was a satisfying and comforting holy possession, which for many became the equivalent of a personally owned relic – something that the poorest people might keep with them.[15]

THE CATHOLIC DEFENCE OF CHRISTENDOM, 1565–71

In the years around 1570 the champions of Tridentine Catholicism, principally King Philip of Spain, were responsible for beating off one of the most serious threats from Islam to Latin Christendom in more than a century. A favourite project of the ageing Ottoman Sultan Süleyman 'the Magnificent' was to finish the business he had begun forty years before in expelling the Knights of St John from the island of Rhodes, amid his spectacular victories through the eastern Mediterranean (chapter 2, p. 54). In the 1550s he had encouraging success: the Knights, now in what they regarded as unwelcome and uncomfortable exile in Malta, suffered a series of appalling reverses, and the Ottoman fleets effectively dominated the central Mediterranean. In May 1565 Süleyman determined to crown his efforts by sending his generals to capture Malta: for an anxious Europe, Christendom's future might seem now to be in the hands of two warriors in their seventies, the Sultan and the Knights' Grand Master Jean Parisot de La Valette.

No more than 9,000 Christian fighting men, scattered through the Knights' Maltese island strongholds, faced the Ottoman generals' 35,000 soldiers and nearly 200 ships through a vicious series of sieges and battles during four nightmarishly hot summer months of 1565. La Valette's fierce determination kept the Christian defence going: even though he was left with only 600 men capable of fighting, his Ottoman opponents lost thousands, and eventually the (scandalously delayed) arrival of a relieving fleet from the Spanish Viceroy in Naples at last prompted an ignominious Ottoman withdrawal. In an appropriate tribute to the Grand Master, the Knights' monumental new city headquarters on the site of the most crucial battle of the siege was named Valletta, and the older town across the Grand Harbour was renamed Vittoriosa.

Even this epic defeat of one of the most powerful Ottoman forces ever assembled did not decide the outcome of the struggle. Süleyman died the next year on another frontier of Ottoman warfare in western Hungary, but his successor Selim II was determined on revenge. He began by inflicting a catastrophe on the Latins on their most vulnerable front, far to the east: the long-dreaded Ottoman attack on Latin Christian Cyprus came in 1570–1. The Venetian government had spent frantically on upgrading the defences of the chief cities, but in vain. Famagusta, the last major stronghold to fall, was defended with heroism and at length. After the surrender in 1571, the Turkish treatment of its small garrison was unusually sadistic. The ruined city centre there is still an eloquent witness of an especially dark moment in the struggle between Islam and the Latin West, the desolation of Famagusta long predating its repetition in the bitter late twentieth century replay of Christian/Islamic conflict in Cyprus. Yet at the time, the Cypriot Orthodox Church, which now emerged from four centuries of suppression, was not sorry to see the Latin Christians humiliated by the Ottomans. It lost nothing when the greatest medieval Gothic churches of the island were converted into the chief mosques for the new regime, their stained glass smashed and their spires replaced with minarets.

The attack on Cyprus galvanized the western Mediterranean powers to unite, after a frantic effort of lobbying by Pope Pius V. The Venetians were desperate to gain allies, and the Pope importuned the General of the Jesuits Francisco de Borja, despite his age and illness (Borja died soon afterwards), to embark on missions to Spain, Portugal and the independent states of Italy. The resulting emergency alliance was styled a Holy League for the defence of Christendom. Don John of Austria, illegitimate brother to King Philip, led eastwards a remarkable muster of the noble and princely families of southern Europe, with a formidable fleet largely composed of Venetian galleys. They met the Turks in the mouth of the Greek Gulf of Corinth or Nafpaktos, then known to westerners as the Gulf of Lepanto. The two fleets were fairly evenly matched, and the loss of life was immense on both sides, yet what proved to be Europe's last major encounter between two fleets of galley-rowed ships left the Holy League's forces more or less intact, while it crippled the Ottoman fleet and killed the Turkish commander-in-chief. Sultan Selim was soon distracted by warfare on his Persian frontier, and he was in any case a pale shadow of his father in capacity and energy. There would be a last great Ottoman effort to the north in the 1680s, which brought the Turks to the gates of Vienna in 1683 – but to the south, the victory of the Catholic empires in 1571 had stopped the Sultan's war machine in its tracks, and never again did the Ottomans try to dominate the Mediterranean beyond the bounds of their existing empire.

All Christian Europe could celebrate this triumph. The Pope put his own Tridentine Catholic interpretation on it, attributing the Christian success to Mary's intercession with God, invoked by the faithful praying the rosary. He declared the battle day of 7 October as the Feast of Our Lady of Victory, and his enthusiasm was a major boost to the already-proliferating rosary devotion.[16] The city of Rome witnessed a triumphal entry of a military commander to equal anything of its ancient Emperors when the papal general Marc' Antonio Colonna came home from the fleet; later Colonna threw off his splendour, and bareheaded and barefoot, set out on a pilgrimage of thanksgiving to Our Lady of Loreto. There had even been a sprinkling of Protestant volunteers on the galleys which sailed to Lepanto. It was one of the few moments in the Reformation when Protestants could feel real pleasure at a Catholic success, or could at least envy Catholic noblemen because they were doing what Christian noblemen were tradition-ally supposed to do – defend the faith in battle against infidels. Far away in Scotland, the young Protestant king James VI wrote an epic poem celebrating Don John's achievement in the battle.

MILITANT NORTHERN PROTESTANTS, 1569–72

Nevertheless, if one reads James's celebration of the defence of Christendom at Lepanto, his confusion of feelings is obvious. When the King had his epic published in Edinburgh in the 1590s (he was a reckless self-publicist), he felt constrained to explain rather uncomfortably in a preface why 'contrary to my degree and religion, like a mercenary poet', a Protestant monarch had written 'in praise of a foreign Papist bastard', Don John. He also tacked on to the end of his work the poetic health warning 'God doth love his name so well, / That so he did them aid / That serv'd not right the same.'[17] The Scottish King, an acute observer of the European scene, naturally remembered that his own reign had started amid the crises which set most of northern Europe on a decisively Protestant course, and that in the years around 1570 the military skills of Protestant noblemen were normally displayed not against the foes of Christendom but against the perverters of western Christianity – papalist Catholics.

James himself had not been a player in these events, since he was a baby of a few months old when a consortium of Scots Protestant nobility had declared him King in place of his mother Mary Queen of Scots in 1567 (chapter 6, p. 295). Mary was soon afterwards a refugee and then a prisoner in England, but for the time being she did keep significant support in the Scottish political nation. Although that support was by no means all Catholic in religious allegiance, the gradual defeat of the Marian party in the six years that followed signalled the end of Catholic hopes in the northern kingdom of the Atlantic Isles. Steadily Marian politicians defected to James's regime, and in 1573 her last significant stronghold, Edinburgh Castle, was starved and battered into surrender, finally placing the King's capital in his own hands. Lending aid to James's forces in the siege was a contingent of English troops – indeed, it was on this occasion that Queen Elizabeth of England's carefulness with money reached its most celebrated height, when she ordered that her troops should economize by crawling around under the castle ramparts to retrieve spent cannon-balls for reuse in the bombardment.[18]

Elizabeth's precocious contribution to recycling should not obscure the importance of what was happening. Protestant religion had now brought together the ancient enemies Scotland and England in what proved to be a permanent alliance, cemented when James VI succeeded the childless Queen Elizabeth in 1603 by hereditary right as James I of England. The flight of his mother to England in 1568 was as significant for the future of England as for Scotland, because her presence as a Catholic heir to the English throne jolted the delicate political balance which Elizabeth had maintained since creating her Protestant religious settlement in 1559 (chapter 6, pp. 288–91). Elizabeth was determined to avoid forcing conservative gentlemen into open opposition while her new Church consolidated itself. Receiving little leadership from Catholic clergy, English conservatives did not cause large-scale trouble through the 1560s: the Queen's Protestant councillors tried to remove Catholic gentry from the county commissions of the peace and other positions of local authority, but they met with only partial success since the government was not anxious to offend traditionalist noblemen with particular local spheres of influence. If one political issue did cause tension, however, it was royal marriage. At first, efforts were made to persuade Elizabeth to marry, preferably a foreign prince who would be a diplomatic advantage to England, but from 1568 a search was also underway for a suitable fourth husband for Mary Queen of Scots; her marriage would be an exercise in damage limitation for the English government to control this unpredictable heir presumptive.

Quarrels at the English court over Mary's marriage joined with a major diplomatic crisis in 1568, which finally ended the long-hallowed English alliance with the Holy Roman Empire and Spain; Elizabeth, desperate for cash, seized an Italian treasure fleet contracted to deliver bullion to the Spanish government in the Netherlands. These tensions persuaded conservative English gentry that enough was enough in conformity to a schismatic Church. Prominent Catholic sympathizers openly ceased to attend regular worship in their parish churches and became 'recusants' (from the Latin *recusare*, to refuse). In 1569 bitter quarrels at Court forced the flight and arrest of Thomas Howard, Duke of Norfolk, irresolute patron of conservative interests, and there followed an abortive rising in the north led by his kinsmen the Catholic Earls of Westmorland and Northumberland. From his cell in the Tower of London, Norfolk half-heartedly involved himself in further Catholic plots with an Italian banker, Roberto Ridolfi, to depose the Queen. For the first time these involved the possibility of a Spanish invasion: so in 1572 Norfolk, England's premier peer, was finally led to the executioner's block. The conservatives had exposed their hand, but had failed disastrously. With Catholic sympathizers eclipsed, Elizabeth's Court and Privy Council were a good deal more united and Protestant in complexion than before; Elizabeth's chief adviser William Cecil was never again in serious danger of disgrace or worse, as he had been at intervals in the previous decade. No avowed Roman Catholics were returned to the House of Commons after 1571, and the 1570s witnessed local conservative elites in towns and counties nationwide struggling usually without success to retain local power.

It was doubly unfortunate for English Catholics that in 1570 Pope Pius V issued a Bull, *Regnans in Excelsis*, condemning Queen Elizabeth as a heretic and absolving her subjects from their allegiance to her. The Bull had been intended to help the northern rebels, but it was not issued and advertised in England until after they had been defeated (with reckless bravery, a Catholic gentleman called John Felton tacked a copy of it to the gate of the Bishop of London's palace, and suffered the usual hideous execution of a traitor when he was caught). It provided a new embarrassment for Catholics instead of helping them. How could they dodge the question of whether their loyalty was to the Queen or to the Pope? The Pope's successor Gregory XIII issued an 'explanation' of the bull in 1580, saying that things being as they were, Catholics were not bound by the bull until it could be publicly executed. This did not alter the fact that the practice of Catholicism offered a public challenge to the Elizabethan government. Pius's action was so generally recognized as a political blunder that it was even remembered in the 1930s when the papacy considered how to react to Adolf Hitler's regime: discreet voices in the Vatican privately recalled the bad precedent, and behind the scenes it was a factor in preventing a public papal condemnation of Nazism.[19]

The English government now had much less inhibition in proceeding against Catholics; it pushed drastic legislation against Catholic practice and recusancy through the 1571 Parliament, including a major assault on the remaining conservative-minded clergy in the Church, requiring all those not ordained under the Protestant Ordinal to subscribe to the Church's Protestant Thirty-Nine Articles. Simultaneously efforts were made to remedy the Protestant Church's defects: the Convocation of Canterbury indulged in a flurry of activity during 1571, which produced modest but useful reforms in church administration. A round of promotions among the bishops between 1570 and 1572 favoured those most active in promoting religious change. It was a hopeful time for Protestants looking for further reformation in the Church of England.

The year 1570 also saw a shift in balance towards a Protestant future in the Scandinavian kingdoms, although less decisively. The Reformation was most secure in Denmark, where the long reign of King Christian III, secured by military victories over his rivals in 1536 and his firm commitment to Lutheranism, provided decades of stability for the new Church to take roots. His other kingdom of Norway was a much more difficult proposition; there was little indigenous early support for the Reformation before the King himself began trying to extend the Danish Church Order to Norway in 1537. Most of the native senior clergy were strong opponents of the Reformation, and their firm stand may be responsible for the disproportionate number of Norwegians among the Scandinavians who trained as Jesuits at the Society's Polish college in Braunsberg after its foundation in 1564 (see below, p. 342). Only gradually did Christian feel confident enough to introduce into the Norwegian Church hierarchy reliable outsiders from Denmark who would implement his policies as Lutheran superintendent-bishops. The most important appointment was that of Jørgen Erikssøn to the diocese of Stavanger in 1571: in the course of a long and energetic episcopate up to his death in 1604, he earned the tribute of being called 'the Norwegian Luther', and three years after he died the Norwegian Church finally received its own Lutheran Church Order.[20]

Like Norway, the kingdom of Sweden experienced a hesitant version of Reformation before 1570. King Gustav Vasa and his successors suffered from the shaky origins of their regime back in 1523 in the overthrow of the Scandinavian King Christian II (chapter 3, p. 135); all the time they had to take into account the opinions of their subjects, their leading churchmen and their Parliament (the *Riksdag*). Gustav was not a man of strong religious feelings, and he did not sense any widespread support for the Reformation; he was also aware that his deposed predecessor Christian ostentatiously proclaimed evangelical beliefs and reminisced fondly about the time that he had spent in Wittenberg. Gustav's own relations with the leading evangelical clergy, the brothers Olaus and Laurentius Petri (Olaf and Lars Petersson), remained tense. So from the 1520s the King gave only intermittent backing to the Petris or other evangelical activists: he confiscated church lands and allowed Olaus Petri to introduce Swedish vernacular services, but use of the Latin Mass remained widespread. When Gustav introduced his own church settlement in 1539, it was mainly designed to rein in the independent initiatives of the clergy. By 1540 his relationship with Olaus had deteriorated to the point where he threatened the pastor with death.

During his long reign (he died in 1560) he curbed any further moves to identify the Swedish Church with changes elsewhere in northern Europe. In his last years, the old King inclined to the 'third way' of East Friesland, marrying his eldest daughter to the Countess Anna's son Count Edzard II, and encouraging Dutch exiles in the Frisian capital of Emden to move on once more and settle in Sweden, but really his interest was in acquiring some economically energetic foreigners rather than in their religious views: he even invited Bohemian Brethren to come to his kingdom, with the same aim in mind.

Gustav's son Crown Prince Erik had a principal tutor who was a Reformed Protestant, Dionysius Beurreus. When he succeeded as Erik XIV in 1560, the new king went on encouraging Reformed immigrants, considering them a useful balance against the increasingly confessional Lutheranism of Swedish Church leaders. However Erik also faced the problem of uniting the powerful figures of the kingdom in the face of an outbreak of war with Denmark in 1563 and a continuing menace from Ivan IV of Muscovy: Laurentius Petri, since 1531 the first avowedly Protestant Archbishop of Uppsala, determinedly exploited this weakness in order to promote Lutheranism, and this halted any drift towards the Reformed cause.[21] In any case Erik was increasingly mentally unstable to the point of dangerous insanity, and he was deposed in 1568; his brother the Duke of Finland was then elected as Johan III. An able theologian and scholar, Johan proved to have sympathies for Tridentine Catholicism. His views were an incentive for his Protestant nobility and clergy in Sweden to defend their position and to push forward from the shapeless Church-Commonwealth of the previous three decades. After a decade of argument, in 1571 a Church Order drafted by Archbishop Petri was agreed for the kingdom and for the first time committed the Swedish Church to an evangelical confession of faith. It was a major step forward for Scandinavian Protestantism, although not as yet explicitly Lutheran. Sweden experienced four more decades of political and religious turbulence before successive monarchs, noblemen and churchmen settled their differences and agreed permanently to align the kingdom with the Lutheran cause (chapter 8, p. 366).

The fate of the Netherlands was equally uncertain in 1571, but in that year Dutch Protestants met to decide their future in a synod which proved a turning-point for the Reformation in the Low Countries. Because of the disasters they had suffered after the arrival of the Duke of Alva's army (chapter 6, p. 312), their meeting had to take place over the border in the safety of Emden. Here the exiled church leaders determined on a settlement that would unmistakably ally itself with Geneva: all ministers must be prepared to subscribe to the 1561 Belgic Confession, and Church order would be presbyterian, in which all ministers and elders would have an equal voice. The Emden Synod planned an ascending structure of presbyterian committees, from consistory to provincial synod to national church synod, like the Reformed Church in France – all this for a Church which currently had no territory at all in which to set up such a structure.

Yet the Emden Synod's quixotic faith in a better future was vindicated. Alva's arrogance and arbitrary government created a mood of increasing fury in the Low Countries, and while Willem of Orange cautiously laid plans to exploit this potential defiance with an invasion, he was forestalled by a motley band of Reformed activists and refugee noblemen only tenuously connected to his command, who styled themselves the 'Sea Beggars' (*Gueux de mer* or *Watergeuzen*). In April 1572 they seized the small island fortified town of Brielle (Brill): they rounded up and later executed nineteen Catholic priests, an act of brutality that was ideologically fuelled. William hastened now to intervene in order to appeal to a wider constituency, and much of the northern Netherlands rose in rebellion against Alva; the Duke's continued cruelty only recruited more rebels. The Spanish government recognized the failure of his policy by recalling him in 1573, but the Spaniards now found themselves in a prolonged confrontation with the Protestant powers of northern Europe, which by the 1590s became a war on a global scale. At the end of this war, the Habsburgs acknowledged that they had permanently lost the northern half of the Low Countries, which before the Reformation had been the birthright of the Dukes of Burgundy and their Habsburg successors.

THE MASSACRE OF ST BARTHOLOMEW, 1572

Protestantism thus newly in the ascendant in Scotland and England, and newly on the offensive in Norway, Sweden and the Netherlands, met its most horrifying check in France with nationwide massacres of Huguenots by Catholics in August 1572. It was a mark of the murderous tensions and deep hatreds that had developed during France's decade of unrest and warfare that these tragic events were sparked by a wedding in Paris designed to heal the kingdom's wounds: Queen Catherine de' Medici had negotiated the marriage of her daughter Marguerite to Henri King of Navarre, now the head of the Huguenot party in France. Among those attending was the Protestant leader Admiral Gaspard de Coligny, only the most prominent of an array of Huguenot noblemen of significance. Coligny's arrival was straining Queen Catherine's tolerance, considering the outrage she had felt at his effort five years before to kidnap her son, the King; it was rash in the extreme of Coligny to insist on being a wedding guest, considering that there was still a reward of 50,000 écus on his head (chapter 6, p. 307). Four days after the wedding an assassin tried to shoot him dead in a Paris street, and succeeded in badly wounding him.

At this stage, with the atmosphere explosive, any wrong move spelled disaster, and everyone made the wrong move. The Huguenot leaders reluctantly agreed to stay in Paris, accepting royal assurances of protection: however the royal Council was so unnerved by Huguenots' fury at the attempt on Coligny that it decided that a pre-emptive strike against them was the only safe thing to do. The young King Charles IX and Queen Catherine backed the Council's scheme, and on Sunday 24 August, St Bartholomew's Day, royal troops, following the King's orders, murdered the Huguenot leaders still in the capital. When news spread, Catholic extremists in the city, who loathed everything that the Protestants stood for, gleefully took up this example of their social superiors: three days of the most savage killings and mutilations of known Protestants followed, and over the next few weeks they were repeated in major cities throughout the kingdom. Overall, it has been calculated that around 5,000 victims were slaughtered.[22] The bridegroom Henri of Navarre, trapped at Court, escaped only by converting to Catholicism, and he was under house arrest for the next few years.

This bloodbath took place only a month after the Sea Beggars had butchered the priests in Brielle. The two widely separated atrocities were a grim demonstration of a new phase in the European Reformation. Since the early 1520s the largescale slaughter inflicted on thousands of unfortunate Europeans had mainly been the consequence of official violence: persecution of heretics, repression of rebellions (such as the savage reprisals against conservative uprisings in England in 1536 and 1549, or the destruction of the Münster Anabaptists in 1535), or wars like the Schmalkaldic Wars of 1547–51, which resulted from power politics and the ambitions of princes. Gradually, however, ordinary people were beginning to own the religious labels that the officially agreed confessions and the decisions of Councils were creating: they found that they were Protestant, Catholic, Lutheran, Reformed. They were proud of these identities, and they often grew to hate people of different religious opinions. Often these hardening outlooks became associated with popular stereotypes of whole kingdoms. Already in the 1530s, Spanish ports were becoming unsafe places for English sailors, because the local population had heard of Henry VIII's dissolution of English monasteries and were appalled at such blasphemy: an English visitor to Corunna and Cadiz in 1538 noted how 'the King's subjects hath here in all parts little or no favour . . . they be all taken in derision and hated as Turks, and called heretics and *Lutarios*'.[23]

Perhaps the most bitter of all such popular hatreds were between neighbours rather than between nations. Twentieth-century Belfast, Mostar or the towns or villages of Rwanda echo such hatreds witnessed in the streets of Rouen or Antwerp in the era of St Bartholomew. These furies were brought to a new level by the mass eruptions of Reformed Protestant excitement that took place in the 1560s. Spontaneous violence between rival mobs became familiar: ordinary people were now capable of being seized with a frenzy for eliminating their fellow human beings simply because they represented an idea. In Paris, a woman variously described as a nun or a lay sister stirred up hatred even while the Navarre wedding was being prepared, proclaiming that God had entrusted her with the duty of telling Parisians that their city would be destroyed if they did not kill every Huguenot.[24] In the end the city militia could not control the fury of the Catholic crowds, and even the Guise family, long-standing Catholic enemies of Coligny, were galvanized into dragging Protestants away from the mobs for safety.[25]

The shock-waves reverberated around Europe: governments trying to conduct normal diplomacy across the religious divide realized that suddenly the rules of international relations had been changed as decisively and negatively as the Peace of Augsburg had brought some positive stability and mutual acceptance. Of course, governments could also use such mass emotions; we will see in chapter 14 (p. 601) how Elizabethan England constructed a usefully unifying loyalty to kingdom and dynasty, with the aid of a growing popular hatred of Catholic Spaniards who had once been the allies of the English. In France, the effect on the Protestant population of the Massacre of St Bartholomew was devastating well beyond the numbers of killed and bereaved. Never again did the Reformed communities feel the excitement and self-confidence which had led to such dramatic expansion over the previous decade, even at times when the military situation had turned against them. Many adherents simply gave up and faded back into the mainstream Catholic Church, particularly in the north of the kingdom, where the Guises took a lead in eliminating the local footholds which Huguenots had established in the 1560s, using all their resources of local patronage and family connections.[26]

The remaining strength of Protestantism (indeed into modern times) came to be in the south, away from Paris. Among those who remained there was a defensiveness which sprang from a justified fear that many Catholics were prepared to repeat the savagery of 1572. It has been noticed, for instance, from studies of the baptismal register of the beleaguered Reformed congregation in Rouen (Normandy) that after the massacre, far fewer babies were given names which were demonstratively taken from the Bible, especially from the Old Testament: such names would mark the children out as Protestants as they grew up and make them vulnerable. In the parts of France where Huguenots became weak, particularly in the north, they came to respect the rhythm of the Catholic liturgical year, so that communities that had once firmly ignored the Catholic taboo on weddings in the penitential seasons of Advent and Lent, in the course of time quietly refrained from such celebrations and even noted the seasons in their registers.[27]

Inevitably also the Huguenots fought back in the 1570s. They still had formidable support among the French nobility, and their military strength meant that once alerted to their danger, they could not be eliminated. The story of the warfare that continued over the next quarter-century is one of repeated efforts by the French monarchy to find the authority to impose a solution that would accommodate this embattled community and yet command the assent of militant Catholics. The effort cost the lives of two successive Kings of France, Henri III and IV, both murdered by Catholic fanatics (chapter 10, pp. 469–71).

POLAND 1569–76: AN ALTERNATIVE FUTURE?

To turn to Poland from the Massacre of St Bartholomew amid perhaps the most wretched few decades in French history is to find a cluster of events around 1570 that hearteningly defied the contemporary trend to confessional definition and confrontation: an affirmation that religious diversity should be accepted and indeed must form an essential part of the Polish-Lithuanian political system. At the beginning of the 1560s it would have been impossible to say whether the religious future of Poland-Lithuania lay with Roman Catholicism, Lutheranism or the Reformed. Even in 1600, the identification of Catholicism with Polish identity, which in the twentieth century was capable of surviving Hitler and Stalin, producing a Polish Pope and crippling the power of Soviet Communism, still remained remote. Like the Graubünden far away in Switzerland, the Poles defied the inevitability that Europe's divided house would seek to recreate the unity of Latin Christianity by violence and systematic persecution; they yoked creative political change to religious toleration.

No religion was capable of asserting a monopoly in 1560s Poland.

Lutherans, mostly German-speakers in the towns and cities, were vital to its economic life, and from 1544 they had the advantage of a newly founded confessional university at Königsberg, created by the Polish king's vassal Albrecht of Brandenburg Duke of Ducal Prussia, and led by Abraham Kulwieć (Culvensis), a Lithuanian former student of Melanchthon, and other Lithuanian and German Lutheran scholars. The Reformed not only boasted one of the most statesmanlike of European Protestant leaders, Jan Łaski, but they also commanded the allegiance of some of the greatest families in Poland-Lithuania, in particular the Radziwiłłs, who lived like kings and controlled the main armed forces of the Grand Duchy of Lithuania. Perhaps a fifth of the nobility became Reformed in allegiance, and in the Polish Senate in the 1560s and 1570s an absolute majority of the members who were not clergy were Reformed sympathizers or adherents.[28]

After the Protestant schism of the 1565 meeting at Piotrków (chapter 5, p. 266) the anti-Trinitarian radicals in their own 'Minor' or Arian Church enjoyed a more open life and institutional structure than any similar group of believers in Europe except for their near allies in Transylvania (chapter 5, p. 262). Remarkably swiftly, in 1569 they were even able to open their own institution of higher education, the Academy of Raków, complete with printing press to spread their message, and by the early seventeenth century it was teaching more than a thousand school pupils and students: the catechism of Raków produced in 1609 became in its Latin version a internationally known statement of non-Trinitarian belief. The Academy was at the heart of another bold effort to provide an alternative to the normal organization of society: like the Hutterites of Moravia (chapter 4, p. 170) the community held property in common, held to strict pacifist principles and observed no distinctions of rank, but unlike the Hutterites it was not suspicious of independent thinking or advanced learning. It represented the most thoroughgoing challenge so far to the hierarchical assumptions of sixteenth-century Europe.

Against this rich variety of Protestant activity, Roman Catholicism had some advantages. It never lost control of the Church hierarchy or the landed endowments of the old church, which were in any case rather more modest than further west in Europe, and therefore perhaps less vulnerable to secular greed. Crucially, the Polish monarchy never finally broke with the old Church, and that, combined with the unbroken adherence of the bulk of the lower orders in the countryside, proved decisive over a century and a half in securing one of very few successes for Catholic recovery in northern Europe. After the vigorous expansion of Protestant activity in the 1550s that had aroused the cautious interest of King Sigismond II Augustus (chapter 6, pp. 264-6), Counter-Reformation Catholic activists were quick to mount a counter-attack. At a meeting of the Polish *Sejm* in Parczew in 1564, the Senate and Sigismond Augustus solemnly received the decrees of the newly completed Council of Trent, and in the same year the most resolute among the Catholic bishops, Stanislaw-Hozjusz (Hosius), saw to it that the Society of Jesus established its first base in Poland-Lithuania, at Braunsberg, an estuary port associated with the powerful trading-group the Hanseatic League and strategically sited on the Baltic coast between Lutheran-dominated Danzig and Königsberg. This was of high significance for the future of Poland, and potentially it might be the bridgehead for a general Catholic recovery throughout the Baltic region.[29]

Amid this competitive religious market, the political leaders of Poland-Lithuania launched vital political changes with profound implications for Polish religion. In response to increasing military pressures from Muscovy on the eastern border in the 1560s, the nobility reached an agreement with King Sigismond II·Augustus to create a new set of political arrangements: a closer association between the kingdom of Poland and the Grand Duchy of Lithuania in the Union of Lublin (1569). The resulting Commonwealth (*Rzeczpospolita* in Polish) was the greatest power in the east of Latin Christendom, but it was not a monarchy in the mould of the monarchs consolidating their power in Spain, France, Scotland or England. Significantly, European diplomats came to refer to it by the title enjoyed by the aristocratic republic of Venice far to the south, 'Serenissima Respublica'.[30] This title was a mark that the Polish monarchy's powers were carefully and explicitly balanced with those of the thousands of nobility within the Union, including the vital fact that the nobility now elected the king.

Given the Polish-Lithuanian nobility's proud insistence on deciding their own individual responses to the Reformation, this meant that Europe's growing divisions were challenged by another European model of how western Christians should be governed. Even before the Union of Lublin, and only a year after the *Sejm* had received the decrees of the Council of Trent, the King was prevailed upon to order royal administrators not to enforce any decrees of the old ecclesiastical courts against members of the nobility.[31] It is easy to be misled by the misfortunes of Poland in a later age, when in a very different political situation from the 1770s, the descendants of the centralizing monarchs of Europe dismembered the Polish-Lithuanian Commonwealth and wiped Poland from the European map for a century and a half. In the sixteenth and early seventeenth centuries, there was no reason to suppose that the pluralist religious and political situation created by the Union of Lublin in a vigorous and self-confident Commonwealth might not represent the future in much of Europe.

An opportunity to enshrine this pluralism in the constitution of the Commonwealth came with Sigismond Augustus's death in 1572: after a tragically tumultuous marital history, he was the last of the Jagiellon male line. Now the provisions of the constitutional settlement of the Union of Lublin came into operation: the election of a new monarch was in the hands of the noblemen of the Commonwealth. A majority among them was determined to keep the Habsburgs from adding to their collection of European thrones, and the obvious alternative candidate would come from the Habsburgs' chief dynastic rivals in Europe, the Valois dynasty of France. Accordingly, negotiations began with the younger brother of King Charles IX, Henri Duke of Anjou. A major complicating factor, however, was the arrival in Poland in early autumn 1572 of the shocking news of the St Bartholomew's Day massacre and the resulting atrocities against Protestants across France. It was not surprising that the Reformed nobility were determined that Henri would not take the Polish throne without a guarantee that nothing similar would ever happen in the Commonwealth.

The result was a meeting of the *Sejm* in Warsaw on 28 January 1573, in which the assembly unanimously approved a clause on religious freedom in the agreement ('Confederation') proposed with the new King. True to the principles of the Commonwealth, it was couched as a declaration of the nobility's intent, which Henri would have to recognize if he were to gain his throne. The crucial resolution ran thus:

Since there is in our Commonwealth (*Respublica*) no little disagreement on the subject of religion, in order to prevent any such hurtful strife from beginning among our people on this account as we plainly see in other realms, we mutually promise for ourselves and our successors forever . . . that we who differ with regard to religion will keep the peace with one another, and will not for a different faith or a change of churches shed blood nor punish one another by confiscation of property, infamy, imprisonment or banishment, and will not in any way assist any magistrate or officer in such an act.[32]

The young King Henri duly agreed to this among the other conditions of the Confederation of Warsaw, despite misgivings from his French advisers and furious protests from the Polish episcopal hierarchy (only one member of which was prepared to sign the Confederation). Henri's stay in his new realm was not prolonged, however. He was dismayed by the unfamiliarity of his vast realm, by the alarming enthusiasm of his middle-aged prospective bride (the last of the Jagiellons), and by the discovery that the Polish nobility were even more lacking in deference than the nobility of France. Then, only a few months after his coronation in Cracow, he received astonishing news: his brother Charles was dead and he was by hereditary right King Henri III of France. He wasted little time in reacting to this unexpected deliverance. His secret flight from Cracow across Europe back to Paris in June 1574 was a bitter blow to his subjects in the Commonwealth, and they swiftly disabused him of any illusion that he could keep his Polish throne in addition to France. After a two-year interval of extreme political chaos, a replacement candidate emerged who could block the Habsburgs' further efforts to impose themselves on the *Sejm*: the Prince of Transylvania, Stefan Bathory (István Báthori in his own country). Bathory, who proved to be an excellent choice as a monarch of exceptional wisdom and military capacity, was a devout Catholic, but he was not going to jeopardize his chances of the Polish throne by objecting to the toleration clause of the Confederation of Warsaw, which in any case had already been anticipated eight years earlier in the legislative diet of his native Transylvania at Torda (chapter 5, p. 262). Neither did his successors. Into the mid-seventeenth century, the Confederation remained a cornerstone of Polish political and religious life.[33]

PROTESTANTISM AND PROVIDENCE

The Polish-Lithuanian Commonwealth thus remained set on a path of religious coexistence unique among the great European powers of the time, and only paralleled in other states on the eastern frontiers of Latin Europe. Amid the various events of the early 1570s deciding the fortunes of Protestant north and Catholic south, the sequence of events that took Poland from the 1569 Union of Lublin through the Confederation of Warsaw to the accession of King Stefan Bathory kept the future situation in the Commonwealth open to either side. In western Europe, the 1569–72 crises left three cockpits of conflict with an ideological dimension: France, the Netherlands and England. These wars could not be separated from each other: the Huguenots of France looked to their fellow Reformed in the Netherlands and England for military support. The presence of Mary Queen of Scots as a Catholic heir to the throne imprisoned in an English castle was a spur to European Catholics to consider how they might follow up Queen Elizabeth's condemnation by the Pope, and try as she might over the next decade, Elizabeth could not avoid eventually being drawn into the battles across the North Sea on the side of the Protestants. That meant that she found herself the enemy of the former ally Spain and her brother-in-law King Philip. Many of her Protestant subjects were now only too happy to fight Spaniards wherever they should encounter them. As a result Reformed Protestants, especially in England and the Netherlands, began taking seriously the possibility of winning overseas territories that would challenge the worldwide empire built up by Spain over seven decades. The quarrels of Europe were now to be extended across the oceans, with effects that have shaped the politics and power structures of our present-day world.

It would be easy as a Protestant in the 1570s to ignore the achievements and successes of the Reformation, and feel that God in his unfathomable wisdom was allowing the enemies of truth to overwhelm his little flock. In fact, the spectacular expansion of Reformed Protestantism in the 1550s and 1560s had saved the Reformation cause from comparative stagnation and compensated for the military defeats suffered by the Lutherans, but it was still easy to read the story as a disappointment of great hopes. The first reformers in the 1520s had believed that all that was necessary to right the faults of the old Church was to preach the true Word and to provide it for all to read in a freely available Bible. Astonishingly, however, many listened and did not act on what they had heard, and there was confusion and division even among those who acknowledged the message. Now the miseries inflicted on the Netherlands, the horror of St Bartholomew and the constant threat of assassination that hung over Queen Elizabeth, together with the continuing menace to Christendom from Islam, promised affliction rather than deliverance.

Of course the faithful could never believe that God would abandon them completely, but the Book of Revelation alarmingly laid out the suffering which his people would have to face before the end of time. Apocalyptic thinking, and detailed anxious reading of the details of visions of the future in the Bible, seemed both realistic and practical, and it was easy to identify contemporary appearances of the Antichrist described in the Bible with particular human figures who had been particularly active in thwarting the Reformation: the English conservative bishop of Winchester Stephen Gardiner, for instance, or the Scottish Cardinal David Beaton – above all, the Pope. Moreover, John Calvin's stress on the providence of God, and of God's plan for his elect minority in predestination, convinced so many in Europe and made his version of Reformed Protestantism so attractive, precisely because his religious system gave good answers to Reformation problems and worries. The Last Days seemed at hand (chapter 13).

John Foxe, creator of the hugely influential English 'Book of Martyrs' which introduced so many Catholic villains like Gardiner and Beaton to an eager Protestant readership (chapter 6, p. 285), expressed this mood of fear and excitement in an extended prayer-meditation delivered to the crowd at the open-air pulpit outside St Paul's Cathedral, London, on Good Friday 1570. The solemn commemoration of Christ's death on the Cross was an appropriate time for Foxe to remind both God and his audience of the sufferings of Christ's Church, even to the latest invasions by the Turks in Hungary and Austria: 'Only a little angle of the West parts yet remaineth in some profession of thy name.'

But here (alack) cometh another mischief, as great, or greater than the other. For the Turk with his sword is not so cruel, but the bishop of Rome on the other side is more fierce and bitter against us; stirring up his bishops to burn us, his confederates to conspire our destruction, setting kings against their subjects, and subjects disloyally to rebel against their princes, and all for thy name. Such dissension and hostility Satan hath sent among us, that Turks be not more enemies to Christians, than Christians to Christians, papists to protestants; yea, protestants with protestants do not agree, but fall out for trifles.[34]

Foxe was now an old man who had experienced the whole sweep of the early Reformation. Born a year before Luther's first public protest, then a choirboy amid traditional liturgical splendours in one of England's most lavish collegiate churches, he had lived through England's break with Rome, the urgent atmosphere of religious revolution in Edward VI's reign, the fears and frustrations of being a refugee in mainland Europe under Catholic Queen Mary, the growing division among Protestant Churches – and now he looked down with doubt and compassion from his pulpit on a London crowd who should be better Protestants than they were. In the turmoil of Europe's Reformation, he could see only one possible escape from looming catastrophe: 'forasmuch as thy poor little flock can scarce have any place or rest in this world, come, Lord, we beseech thee . . . and make an end, that this world may have no more time nor place here, and that thy Church may have rest for ever'. But that was indeed the best prospect of all. Once Queen Elizabeth, who for all her faults and hesitations had brought back godliness to her nation, had run her allotted span, then it would be time for God to intervene.

Foxe was one of the many in his century who confidently expected an imminent end of the world to be a reward for all their labours. Instead, they and their Catholic opponents between them inadvertently created a very different Europe which bred a worldwide 'western' culture. That culture has still not quite succeeded through its quarrels in bringing about a secular version of the end-time which Foxe sought from his God.

8

The North: Protestant Heartlands

DEFINING LUTHERANISM: TOWARDS THE FORMULA OF CONCORD

As Martin Luther receded further into the past after his death in 1546, he became an increasingly mythical figure for Lutherans, and finally he looked suspiciously like a medieval saint. His Saxon birthplace at Eisleben soon became a centre of pilgrimage, called by its devotees a 'New Jerusalem', and legends grew celebrating the continuing power of the dead reformer; it was said that pictures of him would miraculously survive house-fires, and they were therefore useful forms of elementary home insurance if pinned to a cottage wall.[1] At a more sophisticated level, Luther's academic and clerical colleagues hastened to gather all his wisdom for the benefit of posterity. The first effort was a collected thematic reprint of those writings that Luther himself had published in his lifetime, in an edition which took twenty years to complete from 1539. A second attempt from 1555 tried to ingest every possible fragment of the great man's words – even eventually his jokes and conversation at the dinner table, the basis of the famous and fascinating *Table Talk*.[2]

These two editions of Luther's works were in fact rivals produced in an atmosphere of mutual bitterness, the first from the presses of the University of Wittenberg, the second sponsored by a new college at Jena, founded by the former Elector Johann Friedrich in the much-truncated fragment of Saxony left to him after his 1547 humiliation in the Schmalkaldic Wars (chapter 6, p. 271). The editions were not just commercial competitors: the two sets of weighty volumes glaring at each other across the floor of the Frankfurt Book Fair symbolized the contested legacy of Luther's theology, and the uncertain future of Lutheranism as a body of doctrine. The complicating factor in this rivalry was the independent mind of Luther's former colleague and collaborator Philipp Melanchthon, whose thought, as we have already noted (chapter 5, pp. 228, 242), clashed with Luther's unruly

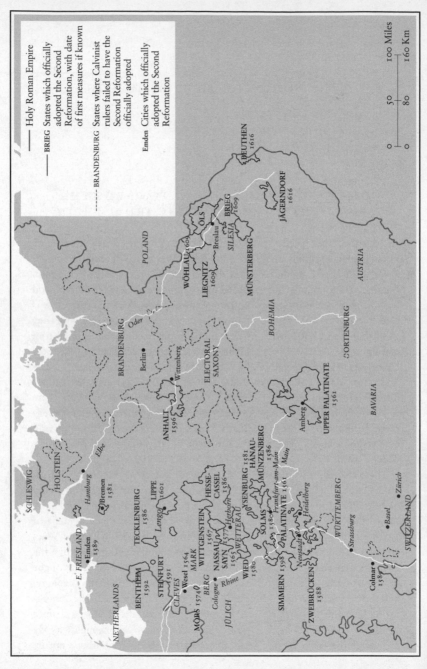

3. *The Holy Roman Empire, c. 1600, showing Second Reformation territories*

assertions of basic principle in two main respects. The first was humanity's means of salvation: Melanchthon had withdrawn from the logic of double predestination implied by Luther's doctrine of justification by faith in order to accommodate his own insistence that God wished human beings to exert a measure of free will in receiving divine grace. Second, Melanchthon had placed a large question mark over Luther's assertion that bread and wine in the Eucharist could objectively become the body and blood of Christ; he went public with his self-assertion in the 1540 *Variata* form of the Augsburg Confession.

Disagreement on such basic matters of the faith were bound to be hard-fought, but circumstances conspired to make them worse. The Lutheran misfortunes in the Schmalkaldic Wars suggested that God was sending tribulations to his faithful in preparation for the Last Days. It was a matter of urgency to please him by seeking right belief – particularly when he set such grievous aptitude tests as the 1548 Interims of Augsburg and Leipzig, which posed inescapable questions about what it meant to be true to Luther's legacy. So the ongoing Wittenberg edition of Luther's works during the 1550s became the property of Melanchthon sympathizers, Georg Major and Caspar Cruciger, while the Jena edition was associated with intransigent clients of Johann Friedrich, who shared the ex-Elector's fury at his defeat and regarded themselves as defenders of the authentic Luther against backsliders like Melanchthon. The Jena edition also picked up one of the editors from the 'other side', Georg Rörer, who had come to disapprove of his Wittenberg colleagues' views.

Posterity has christened these Lutheran ultras and those who thought like them as 'gnesio-Lutherans' – 'gnesio-' being Greek for 'the real thing' – while those who, like Melanchthon, were more concerned with uniting Protestantism than remaining faithful to Luther, have been labelled 'Philippists'. It was a gnesio-Lutheran, the well-known pastor in Luther's birthplace of Eisleben Cyriakus Spangenberg, who was prepared to make the astonishing claim that 'Luther was the greatest and best prophet the world had since the time of the apostles, and he was superior to all other teachers since that time, made comparable to the Old Testament prophets by God'.[3] Chief among these watchful, angry souls was a scholar of Hebrew and historian commonly known by his academic Latinization of his Croatian birthname (Matija Vlačić-Ilirik) as Matthias Flacius Illyricus. Born in 1520, the year of Luther's breach with Rome after excommunication, Flacius spent his adult life in Germany. As a young academic in Wittenberg, he suffered a deep spiritual crisis, and he was fired by his memories of the elderly Luther's kindness during this time of misery to become a noisy opponent of the 1548 Interims, with which Melanchthon tried to find some accommodation. Flacius quit his academic post at Wittenberg University to express his views freely in the city of Magdeburg, which had become a stronghold of those resisting compliance with the victorious Emperor. This marked him out for the rest of his life as an outspoken critic of compromisers like Melanchthon.

Like Luther, Melanchthon had been good to Flacius in his Wittenberg years, but it had been Luther's proclamation of justification by faith that had comforted Flacius in his wretchedness. So Flacius's gratitude to Luther led him to set out the starkest possible presentation of the 'bondage of the will' from which humanity was rescued by external ('forensic') justification. For Flacius, Adam's fall had been so catastrophic and complete that human nature had actually changed in substance, and humanity had become kins-folk of the Devil. Humanity was actually becoming more wicked as time rushed to its conclusion: some of Flacius's gnesio-Lutheran admirers pointed with gloomy relish at well-publicized contemporary examples of deformed births to show how humanity's spiritual corruption was being manifested in physical monstrosity.[4] It was not surprising that Flacius was appalled and abusive when Melanchthon said that justification by faith alone did not stop God mercifully allowing human beings free will to open their souls to this external gift of faith. Similarly the Wittenberg Luther-edition editor Georg Major became a particular target of Flacius's polemic because he taught that human good works were a sign of God's gift of faith externally bestowed on the justified.

This argument over faith and works may sound abstruse, but it arose from a fundamental problem in the Reformation's proclamation of justifica-tion by faith. A logical conclusion of the doctrine might be antinomianism, the idea that all restrictions on human conduct by laws and regulations have become irrelevant to those saved by the gift of faith (chapter 3, p. 130). An antinomian might therefore feel entitled to ignore all the agreed rules and restraints of everyday society, confident in ultimate salvation. As early as the 1521–2 Wittenberg disturbances (chapter 3, p. 142), Melanchthon had been unnerved by seeing the anarchic results of this doctrine apparently put into practice, and the eventual outcome was his careful restoration of a free will doctrine to Luther's message of salvation. The problem was just as acute for the Reformed as for Lutherans, and we will find them developing their own varied answers in the thought of Jacobus Arminius and William Perkins (below, pp. 373–8, 389–91).

Lutheranism's internal arguments about salvation and the Eucharist became all the more bitter because after the 1555 Peace of Augsburg they represented not only a contest for God's favour but a political competition to possess the newly acquired legal status of Lutheran Protestantism within the Empire. Worse still, they were played out against the background of the disputes between Lutheran and Reformed Protestants: these reached a defining moment in the decade after the 1549 *Consensus Tigurinus*, when the emerging champion of Reformed theology John Calvin exchanged insults with the Hamburg gnesio-Lutheran Joachim Westphal about eucharistic doctrine (chapter 5, p. 252). To complicate matters further, Calvin emphatically agreed with the 'original' Luther (and therefore with the gnesio-Lutherans) against Melanchthon on predestination, but he disapproved of Luther's assertions about eucharistic presence and sympathized with Melanchthon in his efforts to modify them. In the end, in the intricate and convoluted disputes leading to a resolution of the doctrinal impasse within Lutheranism, it was what Calvin or the Reformed believed that decided what mainstream Lutheranism would pronounce as orthodoxy. If Calvin had affirmed it, then they were against it (although naturally this was not how they argued in public or in print).

The Lutheran quarrel with the Reformed over the Eucharist proved particularly bitter. The Reformed objected that the physical body and blood of Christ were in heaven and that it was against nature for them to be everywhere in the world in the forms of bread and wine. Hardline Lutherans therefore defensively revived an idea of Luther: in his quarrels with Zwingli he had creatively redeployed an important doctrine of the early Church, forged in the intricate fourth- and fifth-century disputes over Jesus Christ's humanity and divinity. This doctrine, known technically as the *communicatio idiomatum*, asserted that properties of the divine Christ could be attributed to the human Christ because of the union of Christ's two natures. Applying this doctrinal principle, it could be argued that it was a property of divinity to be everywhere, so that could also be true for Christ's physical body and blood in the Eucharist. Luther's resulting doctrine of 'ubiquity', or the eucharistic potential of Christ's body to be everywhere (already attacked by Zwingli and sneered at in Calvin's *Institutes*), now became a central plank of developed Lutheran eucharistic doctrine.[5] In battles around the theology of eucharistic presence in the late sixteenth century onwards, partisan German universities both Reformed and Lutheran returned to the study of metaphysics – that medieval university specialism which Luther had so despised – because otherwise they could not construct the fine distinctions that were necessary to set out their respective arguments.[6]

Lutherans also stoutly affirmed aspects of worship that the Reformed regarded as popish survivals: certain traditional ceremonies in baptism and marriage, a renewed elaboration in funerals to proclaim the Christian victory over death, the use of church music beyond metrical psalms, and a tolerance of much surviving medieval sacred art – even a performance of the Eucharist that retained a great deal of the traditional Latin. The Eucharist was naturally full of opportunities to emphasize difference, all the more because its symbolism spoke of communal unity. The Reformed made a point of using ordinary bread for it, the Lutherans insisted on specially baked wafers, rather like those used in the pre-Reformation western Church. The Reformed laid great stress on a small moment of liturgical action that had safe biblical precedent in the narratives of Christ's institution of his Supper: the 'Fraction', when the minister solemnly broke the bread. They regarded this as a symbol of Christ's benefits shared throughout his community. Lutherans found this offensive, because of their conviction that Christ was corporeally present in the bread by the doctrine of ubiquity: they regarded a minister making the Fraction as carrying out a renewed human assault on Christ's body. Accordingly, Lutheranism revived a different moment of medieval eucharistic theatre, which in the early Reformation had generally been considered a dangerous symbol of priestly power: the elevation of the host – the presiding pastor lifted up the eucharistic bread as he pronounced the prayer of consecration over it.[7] Altogether, it is not surprising that many Reformed found the whole attitude of Lutherans to the Reformation scandalous and even wondered whether they ought to be regarded as Protestants.

Lutheran Germany's bundle of distinctive beliefs and practices became the theological equivalent of a litmus test which could confirm Lutheranism and exclude Reformed deviation, and it was inevitable that efforts should be made to set the Lutheran boundaries and overcome internal arguments. During the 1570s Lutheran belief was successively refined in a series of agreements between the various Lutheran interest-groups, encouraged by the Lutheran rulers of Saxony, Brandenburg, Württemberg and Brunswick-Wolfenbüttel. These culminated in a 'Formula of Concord', chiefly brokered by a leading scholar in Württemberg's university of Tübingen, Jacob Andreae, together with the Brunswick theologian Martin Chemnitz; this was first given official status in Saxony and Brandenburg in 1577. The fiftieth anniversary in 1580 of the creation of the Augsburg Confession provided the perfect emotional lever to secure very widespread adherence to this Formula among Lutheran cities and principalities, although for decades afterwards hardline supporters of Flacius Illyricus persisted in regarding it with contempt.

The 1580 Book of Concord which embodied the Formula recognized certain key texts that defined Lutheran belief. It was remarkable that only three of these texts were actually from Luther's pen: his Small and Large Catechisms of 1529 (chapter 4, p. 165), and an aggressively anti-Roman statement of belief which he had created for the Schmalkaldic League to present to a General Council of the Church if it had in fact met in 1537. It is noticeable that Luther's three great treatises of 1520 and his *Bondage of the Will*, which mean so much to Protestants today, were not included; they might prove too disruptive of the actual end-result of Luther's Reformation. Otherwise it was the works of the gnesio-Lutherans' *bête noire* Melanchthon that were given hallowed and official status in the agreement: the 'unvaried' 1530 Augsburg Confession and his commentary on it, and a further anti-papal work from his pen. Lutheran orthodoxy therefore emerged as playing down the doctrine of predestination (with Melanchthon) and affirming the real presence in the Eucharist (against Melanchthon).

The newly self-identified Lutherans took over the once-general Protestant label 'Evangelical' to describe their Churches, just as the non-Lutherans were monopolizing the name 'Reformed'. The Lutheran achievement was to become the prime religious identification for the majority of Germans by 1600: we will note the proof of this in the resistance put up to many Calvinist-style 'Second Reformations' (below, pp. 357–8). In what John Bossy has described as 'an invigorated traditionalism', once the time of destruction and purging was over Lutheranism took on much of the shape of the late medieval Western Church in the north.[8] It now represented a successful effort by much of the ruling caste in central Europe to graft a religious revolution on to traditional forms of life, to ensure the stability of their rule. The *Landesvater* tradition of government in the Empire meant that on the whole such rulers were much more conscientious than the monarchs and nobility of the Atlantic Isles in redeploying the confiscated wealth of monasteries, chantries and gilds not for private gain but for public purposes, from paying clergy stipends to supporting hospitals and schools. Indeed, some Lutheran rulers were even prepared to allow some communities of male and female religious to continue their communal life under Evangelical auspices, and some of these Lutheran lineal descendants of medieval monasteries have survived into modern times.[9]

THE 'SECOND REFORMATION' IN GERMANY

Statesmanlike in recognizing Melanchthon's vital contribution to the shaping (indeed reshaping) of Luther's Church, the 1580 Formula of Concord nevertheless guaranteed that any immediate prospect of union between

Evangelical and Reformed was out of the question. This slamming of the door was all the more unfortunate because a significant number of Protestant temporal rulers in Germany were dismayed at the closer definition of Lutheranism. Anyone who in the 1540s and 1550s might have been inclined to seek a 'third way', in the manner of Countess Anna of East Friesland or Philipp of Hesse, was now forced to identify with the Reformed if he or she were not to capitulate to the strict Lutheran package of doctrine. The first such ruler of significance was the Elector Palatine Friedrich III. A festively inclined minor Wittelsbach prince, in 1559 he found that the quirks of his family tree had left him with the succession to the scattering of territories in the Rhineland and further east that made up this important Electorate. Friedrich was sobered (fairly literally) by his new responsibilities and power, and while earnestly reading the Bible and trying to work out for himself what he believed as a Protestant, he made a great effort to forge a church settlement which would satisfy Melanchthon's sympathizers as well as prove compatible with the Reformed theology of central Europe.[10] To help him achieve his aim, he collected a talented set of Protestant academics in the university of his Rhineland capital at Heidelberg: notably Zacharias Ursinus, Kaspar Olevianus, Thomas Erastus and the Italian exile Girolamo Zanchi. Ursinus led the team which produced a new 'Heidelberg Catechism' as a confessional statement for the Elector's Church Order.

When the drafters of the Catechism dealt with the sacraments, the most contentious issue to be discussed, they had an eye on all those contemporary Protestants who were not hardline Lutherans. The text of the Catechism therefore included that which would unite Zürich, Geneva and the Philippist supporters of the late Melanchthon, and it tried to avoid saying anything which would annoy any of them (and there was certainly material to annoy if the drafters had put their minds to it). This was a deliberate act of compromise in the fashion of the 1549 *Consensus Tigurinus*, and as such it predictably earned the rage of Matthias Flacius Illyricus. Perhaps helped by the seal of gnesio-Lutheran disapproval, the Heidelberg Catechism went on to have an astonishing success as a confessional statement in non-Lutheran countries: it was translated into around forty different languages, more than any other such statement produced in the era of reform.[11]

Nor was this Heidelberg's only contribution to international Protestant dialogue. Ursinus developed Heinrich Bullinger's discussion of the idea of 'covenant' in the Christian life, an idea which had a major effect on Reformed Protestantism (see below, pp. 389-91). Heidelberg also co-operated with Bullinger in his continuing efforts to unite Switzerland with sympathetic churches from the Atlantic Isles to eastern Europe. When in 1566 Bullinger drew up a new statement of belief for the Reformed Churches, the Palatinate was particularly active in promoting his 'Second Helvetic Confession'. The Palatinate territories and Heidelberg were now emerging as a centre of Reformed theology to rival and indeed to become a northern replacement for Geneva. Geneva's real leadership in the Reformed world began to diminish as soon as Calvin died in 1564, and from the 1580s the city was severely harassed by the Catholic Dukes of Savoy: its population went into steep decline, and despite the continued presence of Theodore Beza into the 1590s, the Genevan Academy attracted fewer students and internationally renowned staff. Instead, students flocked to Heidelberg University from the furthest bounds of Protestant Europe, so that by the 1610s a third of the non-German student body had travelled to the Rhineland from Slavic eastern Europe, from Lithuania in the north to Transylvania in the south.[12] Heidelberg saw itself as a second and better Wittenberg, a German university which would complete the half-finished Reformation of the Lutherans. Picking up this thought, modern historians have referred to the emergence in northern Europe of a self-consciously Reformed impulse to remodel existing Protestantism as 'the Second Reformation'.

Such a showcase role for Heidelberg and the Palatinate brought problems. Even although the Heidelberg Catechism successfully strengthened the 1549 compromises on sacramental doctrine between Zürich and Geneva, strains remained within Reformed theology on the question of Church and Commonwealth. The integrated model of church and city government that Zwingli and Bullinger had developed in Zürich (chapter 3, p. 148, and 4, p. 178) clashed with the ideal of a careful separation of powers and functions for which Calvin had fought in Geneva (chapter 5, pp. 238–46). The presence in Heidelberg of Thomas Erastus, a lifelong friend of Heinrich Bullinger, raised this issue in acute form: he proclaimed in line with Zürich practice that the final right to excommunicate sinners lay with the secular magistrates, not the church authorities in a Genevan-type consistory. This originating statement of 'erastianism' (a word often now misused in a loose sense to describe any belief in a state-dominated Church) provoked fury in 1568 from George Wither, an English enthusiast for the Genevan Church, then at Heidelberg University.

The ensuing bitter row was highly embarrassing to Ursinus; as the most prominent theologian of the Palatinate, he was naturally anxious to keep open lines of communication to both Zürich and Geneva. There was the additional factor that the Reformed cause in the Palatinate and else-where in Germany was patently much more dependent on the initiative of the secular ruler than it had been in Calvin's Geneva, and the power of consistories needed to be carefully balanced with that of princes like the Elector Friedrich: this was a problem which would afflict any princely version of the Second Reformation. Only gradually did Ursinus work out a compromise which brought a modified version of Geneva's presbyterian system to the Rhineland, although it was an advantage to him when Erastus's party was badly compromised after 1570: some of their clerical supporters were convicted and one beheaded for promoting an Arian view of Christ's relationship to the Godhead.[13] The 1570s saw attempts by Ursinus and Zanchi to produce a single confession of faith for all Reformed Churches in Europe, since at that time the Lutherans were drawing together in the negotiations which produced the Formula of Concord. In the end all that was done was the publication in Geneva of a *Harmony of Confessions*, but this compendium of existing confessional statements was significant in showing the breadth of Churches that could now be considered Reformed: not only those of Germany, Switzerland, the Netherlands and France, but also those of the Atlantic Isles, so that among the texts set out in the *Harmony* were the Thirty-Nine Articles of the Church of England.

A further trial for the Reformed cause in the Palatinate was a rapid shift in official opinion when one ruler was succeeded by another. Friedrich III died in 1576; his eldest son and successor as Elector Palatine Ludwig VI was by contrast a Lutheran sympathizer who took much satisfaction in withdrawing favour from the Reformed clergy and academics. Prominent figures like Ursinus were forced to take refuge in the small enclave of Neustadt, ruled by Ludwig's younger brother Count Johann Casimir, an enthusiastic Reformed Protestant. The Reformed clergy were given the chance to reassert themselves in 1583, when the accession in turn of Ludwig's young son Friedrich IV as Elector enabled Johann Casimir as principal regent to extend his influence through the entire Palatinate. The returning ministers celebrated their triumph with a sustained campaign of destroying surviving medieval art in the churches of the Elector's territories, much to the anger of the bulk of the population.[14]

This tangled story in the Palatinate illustrates the stark reality of the *cuius regio eius religio* principle in central Europe. It is also a further reminder that the 'Second Reformation' in Germany consisted largely of second thoughts about Protestantism among princes, dukes and the leaders of a few imperial cities, rather than a socially broad-based alliance against Roman Catholicism, as was the case in Scotland, France or the Netherlands. These German secular elites and their Reformed preachers felt deep contempt for Lutheran practice: when the Elector of Brandenburg Johann Sigismund converted to the Reformed cause from Lutheranism, the great

Palatinate divine and celebrated Heidelberg Court preacher Abraham Scultetus said with relish that 'the leftover papal dung is to be swept completely out of Christ's stable'.[15] As the Reformed tried to change local religious practice, simplifying liturgical custom and purging church interiors, very frequently they encountered traditionalist opposition and localist pride, which Lutheran church leaders were quick to turn to their own purposes and mould into an affirmation of emerging Lutheran practice. As early as 1566, at much the same time that enthusiastic crowds in France and the Netherlands were giving violent support to the Reformed religion, there were riots when the Palatinate authorities tried to assert their religious beliefs and remove images from the churches in Amberg, principal city of the Upper Palatinate and significantly just to the east of ostentatiously conservative Lutheran Nuremberg (see Plate 6). For decades afterwards, Amberg remained a thorn in the flesh of its Reformed Electors.

Such expressions of popular outrage became a consistent pattern in later decades wherever Calvinizing rulers decreed changes in Protestant Germany. A turning-point was a violent protest provoked in 1605 by Landgraf Moritz V of Hesse-Kassel when he tried to introduce a full-scale Reformed Church throughout his territories (the bulk of the former Hessian lands of his famous grandfather Landgraf Philipp). Popular fury in Hesse-Kassel was so great that although Moritz eventually succeeded in setting up a Reformed Church organization including a Consistory, his difficulties were a deterrent to other Reformed rulers contemplating similar measures. In the next decade, the Calvinist convert Elector Johann Sigismund of Brandenburg took heed of the Hessian experience. On the advice of Abraham Scultetus, he abandoned plans for wholesale change in Brandenburg: Scultetus advised that he should leave the parish churches untouched in their Lutheran state, but only reform his own Court chapel and the Cathedral in Berlin, to act as an example to his subjects. Even this was an explosive move in one of the most conservative Lutheran states in the Empire, where the liturgy had long retained much of its medieval extravagance after the piecemeal Reformation of the old Elector Joachim (chapter 5, p. 226). The Elector faced riots from infuriated Berliners, and his Calvinist pastors had their houses sacked.[16] Scultetus promoted the same policy in Prague under the Elector Palatine Friedrich in 1620, with even more disastrous results (chapter 11, p. 495). Indeed, after the difficult outcome of Landgraf Moritz's initiative in Hesse-Kassel in 1605, no seventeenth-century European ruler again tried to change the official religion of his territory without using reliable military force. Not just in Germany, but across the Continent, popular religious habits were now becoming entrenched in the various moulds produced by Reformation and Counter-Reformation, and it would take more than the decisions of a prince to change them.

The division of Protestant northern Europe thus hardened into opposed habits and patterns of life. Lutherans often looked more favourably on Roman Catholics than on their supposed brethren of the Reformation. The stand-off and ill-will between the two Protestantisms was nowhere better symbolized than by the bizarre fortunes of the Cathedral in the wealthy trading-port of Bremen which, with its crucial position in the north-west of the German lands, had once been the very heart of early medieval Christianity's first mission to the peoples of north Germany and Scandinavia. Bremen went over in the 1530s to the Lutheran cause against the opposition of its Catholic archbishop, but by 1561 the growth of Reformed belief among the merchant elite delivered control of the city into Reformed hands, after fierce intra-Protestant disputes inevitably centring on the Eucharist. The aristocratic canons of the Cathedral, however, remained staunch Lutherans: the resulting clash between city and Cathedral authorities closed the doors of the building to worshippers. For an astonishing seventy-seven years after 1561, the vast church, locked and silent, cast its shadow over the busy life of the two principal city markets, the medieval treasures of its interior preserved unused though undefaced. Only in 1638 did the intervention of Danish Lutheran troops force the Reformed city authorities very grudgingly to allow the large number of convinced Lutherans in the city to use the Cathedral once more for Evangelical worship.

BALTIC RELIGIOUS CONTESTS:
POLAND-LITHUANIA AND SCANDINAVIA

In Chapter 7, pp. 340–44, we followed the sequence of events around 1570 that made the Polish-Lithuanian Commonwealth defy the European trend towards confessionalization and enshrine toleration in its constitution. The great modern Polish historian Janusz Tazbir coined a description of the Commonwealth in the sixteenth and seventeenth centuries that has now become celebrated: 'A state without stakes'. As with most striking generalizations it is easy to find exceptions: from time to time, people did die for their religion in the Commonwealth, although in rather unusual circumstances. For instance, 1611 saw a young Italian Reformed Protestant Franco de Franco die in punishment for his suicidal aggression in making a public protest during a Catholic procession in Wilno; in the same year a Ruthenian Arian, Ivan Tyschkovitch, was dismembered and burned in Warsaw, after

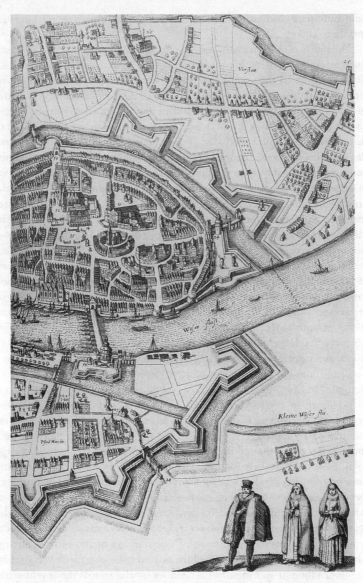

A bird's-eye plan of Bremen of 1653 shows how the Cathedral (the large church with prominent single spire, no. 21) dominated the eastern half of the city and its market-places. One of the Cathedral's twin west towers had collapsed during its long closure and was not rebuilt till the nineteenth century.

an exceptionally bitter factional feud had drawn attention to his religious beliefs.[17]

Yet although such stories are reminiscent of contemporary western Europe, where in 1612 that philosopher-king James I of England was still ready to order the burning at the stake of two anti-Trinitarian believers, western Europeans were less prepared for the situation that confronted and plainly deeply disconcerted a Spanish Dominican, Damian Fonseca. In the course of an official visitation of the Commonwealth's Dominican friaries, he had occasion to visit the Court of a great magnate of the Grand Duchy, Prince Mikolaj Jerzy Czartoryski. The Czartoryski family were fairly recent converts from Orthodoxy to Catholicism, and Fray Damian was there in order to baptize one of their children, but still he found Catholic, Orthodox and Arian noblemen enjoying relaxed and friendly relations during the extended and presumably bibulous celebrations. The friar was called on to dispute the divinity of Christ with another guest who held Arian beliefs – not an experience which would be familiar to him in Spain.[18] In Poland it was necessary for radical anti-Trinitarians to argue in their church gatherings as to whether or not believers were justified in possessing serfs, for the very practical reason that anti-Trinitarian patrons were normally serf-owning noblemen. This was a very different version of radical Christianity from that of the unassuming Hutterite craftsmen in their communalistic *Bruderhof* in Moravia.[19]

It was in Poland, the land where the Minor Church and the Raków Academy flourished, that the most central figure of moderate Unitarianism, the exiled Italian Fausto Paolo Sozzini, found a permanent home from 1579 to his death in 1604. Sozzini built on the teachings of his uncle Lelio Francesco Maria Sozini (the spelling difference of their surnames was habitual), who represented that generation of radicals who had matured their doubts about the full divinity of Christ during the last harassed years of the *Spirituali* in Italy in the 1540s (chapter 5, p. 233). The days were long gone when such radical views could survive in their native land, but although the younger Sozzini found himself rabbled out of Cracow in 1598, he had influential friends in Poland who protected him thereafter. It is after him that unitarians were often (abusively) labelled 'Socinians', a label which would come to cover a multitude of questionings of the early Church's formulation of Christianity, and which proved to be of great importance in the unravelling of Reformation certainties by the end of the seventeenth century (chapter 17, p. 693).

King Stefan Bathory was not in a position politically or militarily to discourage such religious diversity, even if he had wanted to. He wanted to encourage the revival of the Roman Catholic Church, 'not by violence, fire and the sword, but by instruction and good example', which meant actively encouraging the Society of Jesus in the Polish work which it had begun in 1564 and which was already greatly expanding before his accession.[20] He was responsible for founding three major colleges in the far north-east of the Commonwealth at Polotsk, Riga and Dorpat, deliberately chosen as the towns where the Reformed Churches were at their strongest, and by the early seventeenth century every important town (more than two dozen scattered throughout the Commonwealth) had a Jesuit school. From the late 1570s there was a Jesuit-run Academy (university college) in Wilno, the chief city of the Grand Duchy: Lutheran and Reformed schools could not compete with such large-scale educational enterprise.

If anything turned back the tide of noble and popular Protestant advance it was this Jesuit offer of high-quality education, employing a curriculum decided at international level and so guaranteeing an international standard of excellence. Small wonder that the elites began sending their children to such schools, their ambitions for their children often outweighing their suspicion of Catholic indoctrination, and small wonder that the children so educated increasingly turned to Roman Catholic belief. During the seventeenth century the educational effort became two-pronged, when the Order known as the Piarists arrived from Rome first in central Europe and then in Poland, dedicating itself to the schooling of the poor with a curriculum consciously different from and more practically oriented than that of the Jesuits. In Poland, they particularly directed their efforts to the large proportion of the nobility who possessed a title and ancient noble ancestry, but not much else.[21] The effect of education was aided by charitable work and preaching from a wide variety of revived religious Orders, particularly friars, while there was a vigorous restoration of female contemplative communities, restoring the battered prestige of enclosed monasticism. All the European-wide literary and devotional resources of the Counter-Reformation could strengthen traditional practice in Poland; so pilgrimage to shrines underwent a great revival in the early seventeenth century just as in southern Europe, and by the end of the century open-air reconstructions of Calvary and shrines of Our Lady were numbered in their hundreds throughout the Commonwealth; mass pilgrimage remains characteristic of Polish and Lithuanian Catholicism.[22]

Stefan Bathory's tactful benevolence towards Catholic revival was replaced by a far more partisan Catholic monarchy when in 1587 the *Sejm*'s customary efforts to keep the Habsburgs at bay resulted in the election of a son of King Johan III of Sweden. He became King Sigismond III of Poland, the first of the Vasa dynasty on the Polish throne and following his Jagiellon mother, an ardent supporter of Roman Catholicism. During Sigismond's four decades and more as King of Poland, the monarchy began (as far as the constitution permitted) to discriminate against Protestants, habitually preferring to choose Catholics as members of the Senate, and allowing the newly established Crown Tribunal to make legal decisions detrimental to Protestants.[23] The Jesuit Piotr Skarga, former Rector of the Wilno Academy, now royal chaplain and a fearsome preacher, encouraged Sigismond in a 'Regalist' outlook that deplored the constitution of the Commonwealth both because it limited royal power and because it belittled the Catholic faith.

It was not surprising that Sigismond met armed resistance from a nobility outraged at his obvious hankering to set up a Catholic hereditary monarchy and to accumulate military and financial resources in the manner of some major western European monarchies – his acquisition of a Habsburg bride did not help matters. The resulting internal warfare from 1606–9 curbed royal ambitions, but it also began to weaken the delicate balance of the constitution in the Commonwealth, beginning its later fatal divisions.[24] Nor did the conflict between the nobility and the Crown stop the steady advance of Catholicism. As everywhere in Europe, the splendours of the royal Court exercised a powerful fascination over noblemen, however much they might have tried to stand up to royal power. If the entrée to Court life in Warsaw was a profession of Roman Catholic faith, then that was a powerful temptation to embrace Catholicism; and there were plenty of opportunities provided by the Jesuits for favourite sons to get a good Catholic education.

The greatest single triumph of Catholicism in the Commonwealth came in the 1590s, with a large-scale union of Orthodox believers under Roman Catholic obedience. The Orthodox Church in the Ukraine, with its Metropolitan at Kiev, had formerly been under the jurisdiction of the Patriarch of Constantinople, but it suffered from the fifteenth-century collapse of the Byzantine Empire; contacts with Greece dwindled and it became hard for the Metropolitans to maintain their independence, caught in conflicts between the Jagiellon monarchs and the last independent Orthodox ruler in Muscovy. Church discipline suffered and many Orthodox noblemen of the Grand Duchy converted to Catholicism – some even to Protestantism. When the Muscovite Tsar Feodor persuaded Patriarch Jeremiah of Constantinople to recognize a Patriarchate in Moscow in 1589, the situation of Orthodoxy in the Commonwealth became particularly awkward. Patriarch Jeremiah's journey to Moscow through the Commonwealth's Ruthenian lands during 1588 was itself a cause of contention, because his well-intentioned attempts to discipline the Ruthenian clergy suggested a future of renewed external interference in the Church, both from Moscow and Constantinople.[25]

Accordingly, several Ruthenian bishops began looking with more favour on proposals for some form of union with Rome, a possibility which Jesuits had been canvassing since the 1570s. The precedent was there in the abortive union between eastern and western Churches declared after negotiations in Florence in 1439, but the furious popular reaction in Orthodox lands that had defeated that union in the fifteenth century was an indication of the problems to come. In 1595 a group of bishops was able to conclude articles of union with a Roman delegation at Brest, while another group, supported by the majority of Orthodox monks, furiously denounced the deal; on 8 October 1596 the Union of Brest was finalized. Those who adhered to the Union in a 'Greek-Catholic' Church (often also known as the Uniate Church) agreed to accept the Tridentine doctrine of the Eucharist, acknowledge papal supremacy and submit to the discipline of the Curia in Rome; in return, they retained their Slavonic liturgy and a separate episcopal hierarchy and the parish clergy continued to have the right to marry, in contrast to Western clergy of the Roman obedience.

This was one of the greatest achievements of the Counter-Reformation, the result of long and careful preparation much encouraged by King Sigismond and the secular powers of the Commonwealth (papal diplomats went on to engineer a similar agreement with a section of the Coptic Church in Egypt in 1597). The Greek-Catholics did not get all that they were promised; their bishops were never granted a place in the Senate of the Commonwealth, so it was all the more easy for those who had not accepted the Union to denounce them as dupes of Rome, particularly as insensitive proselytizing by Western-Rite Roman Catholics gained momentum throughout the Commonwealth. Bitterness continued, often erupting into violence, even the murder of a particularly energetic (not to say aggressive) Uniate Archbishop of Polotsk, Josaphat Kuncevyc, in 1623. The Uniate Church did persist, and many of its bishops were of high calibre, but it remained vulnerable either to its faithful deciding to adopt the Western Rite in the Roman Catholic Church, or to conversions back to the independent Orthodox Church.

Those Orthodox who stayed out of the Union galvanized their shattered Church organization back into new life, particularly under the energetic leadership of a cosmopolitan Moldavian nobleman, Piotr Mohyla, who was born in the very year of the Union, educated in Paris, served in the Polish army and then entered an Orthodox monastery. There were still prominent Catholics who remained proud of the Commonwealth's commitment to tolerance, and after the death of the intransigently Catholic Sigismond III in 1632, they combined with Orthodox nobles to encourage his son Wladyslaw IV officially to recognize the independent hierarchy of Orthodox bishops. With the new King's assent in royal 'Articles of Pacification' (fiercely opposed by intransigent Catholics, notably the Jesuits), Mohyla became the Metropolitan in Kiev. Conspicuously loyal to the Polish monarchy and so prepared to keep the Moscow Patriarchate at bay, he could see what might be useful to Orthodoxy in western culture. So he founded a college in Kiev that would teach along Jesuit lines in order to equip the Orthodox with an education to match their opponents in the western Church: it was the first institution operating at university level in the modern Orthodox world. Later, graduates of this 'Mohyla Academy' would be very useful to Tsar Peter the Great when he sought to westernize Russia.[26]

In the face of this three-pronged renewal of Roman Catholicism, Greek-Catholicism and Orthodoxy, there were distinct signs of contraction among the various Protestant communities of the Commonwealth after 1600. In 1598 King Sigismond failed in his efforts to secure his other throne of Sweden, and his defeat came at the hands of the Protestant ascendancy in Sweden (see below, p. 366). The continuing claim of the Polish Vasas to the Swedish throne became entangled with territorial rivalries between the Commonwealth and Sweden in the Baltic, and in the resulting seventeenth-century wars against the aggressively Protestant power of Sweden, the patriotic cause of Poland became increasingly identified with that of Catholicism. Poland may have been 'a state without stakes', but its activist Catholic population increasingly challenged the Commonwealth's toleration. In towns and cities where Catholics felt confident, and were often inflamed by Jesuit or Capuchin preaching, Protestant church buildings or funeral processions were attacked, and in some places, churches permanently closed down as a result. As the Catholic cults of pilgrimage to sacred places revived, there were instances of crucifixes or wayside shrines being provocatively erected near to communities of Protestants; if these offensive images were then attacked, that gave an excuse to take official reprisals. It was after an incident of this sort that the famous anti-Trinitarian Academy at Raków was closed down in 1638. In the far north, too, Protestant communities were especially badly harassed by Muscovite or Cossack raiders during the various frontier wars with the Commonwealth, for the same reason: the Orthodox were outraged by Protestant traditions of scorning or destroying religious imagery.[27]

All this made the Commonwealth's Protestants very insecure, especially as the protection of their Protestant magnates began to lapse or fall away through piecemeal conversions to Rome. The number of Reformed Protestant communities more or less halved between the late sixteenth and the mid-seventeenth century, at a time when the Jewish population of the Commonwealth continued to expand in wealth, self-confidence and numbers.[28] Spurred on by the shock of the Union of Brest, Reformed Protestants made overtures to the Orthodox to see if some sort of agreement could be made among the non-Catholics of the Commonwealth; a synod of representatives from both sides met at Wilno in 1599. There was little result. Everyone present could agree in loathing Counter-Reformation Catholicism, but theological differences were too deep, particularly on the question of images. When the synod drew up a set of eighteen points of agreement, discussion of images was notably omitted; the Wilno synod was a dead end which only emphasized the growing ineffectiveness of Polish Protantism, which had only four decades before seemed poised to become the dominant religious force in the Commonwealth.[29] A Protestant elite united might have prevailed, but with an estimated thirty-four different sects in Lithuania alone at the height of the Reformation, the hierarchical structure of the Catholic Church and the huge reservoir of traditional religious practice in the countryside proved too formidable to overcome.[30]

Roman Catholicism's success in Poland contrasted with its failure to make a comeback in Scandinavia. In both cases the Vasa royal family of Sweden were the leading actors. The Roman cause was given a chance to reassert itself because of the accession of Johan III to the Swedish throne in 1568: his wife Catherine, sister of Sigismond Augustus of Poland, was a fervent Catholic, and in 1578 he himself was openly received into the Roman Church by the Italian Jesuit Antonio Possevino. Even before this potentially momentous shift in the balance of power in northern Europe, Johan, with his wife's encouragement, introduced a new liturgy for the Swedish Church that included elements borrowed from the Tridentine rite, and he allied with the more ceremonially minded members of the Protestant clergy. He even restored the famous royal foundation for Bridgettine nuns, the mother house of the Order at Vadstena, lavishing gifts on it, and drawing on the advice of Fr Possevino in the restoration. Perhaps more significantly for the future, he gave his blessing to the scheme of a Norwegian who was covertly a Jesuit, Laurentius Nicolai, to open a theological college in Stockholm in 1576. Since there was no competitor in higher education in Sweden, this might well prove the beginning of the sort of educational initiative that was already bearing such fruit for Catholicism in Poland.

Johan's imitation of the Polish model seemed to be much boosted when in 1587 his son Sigismond was elected to the Polish throne (after Johan's previous unsuccessful efforts to get himself elected). Now, however, his Catholicizing project in Sweden was running into difficulties. The programme Johan was trying to put into place had been inspired by the proposals for compromise made back in the 1560s by the eirenical Catholic theologian George Cassander, protégé of the Habsburg Emperors Ferdinand and Maximilian II (chapter 6, p. 296). These moderate Habsburg policies had already faltered in the 1570s, and after the hostility which Rome and the Jesuits had shown to compromise in the Habsburg lands, there was no likelihood of the Pope showing greater approval in Sweden's case. When Johan tried to get papal blessing for a Habsburg-style 'middle way', Possevino proved less than helpful in Rome, and by 1580 it was obvious that no deal could be struck.[31] Worse still, the Swedish royal family was not united in religion. Johan's brother Karl Duke of Södermanland was a Protestant of convinced Reformed sympathies, and he could ally with the growing opposition to the King's schemes among clergy and laity of Lutheran convictions. For the time being, the Catholic threat overrode internal Protestant divisions, and in the early 1580s demonstrations of popular anti-Catholicism increasingly hamstrung the King's efforts. A fresh crisis erupted on Johan's death in 1593: now the openly Catholic King Sigismond of Poland returned to claim his rightful second throne, provocatively accompanied by Jesuits and by a papal nuncio. He was met by a Church which in its assembly in Uppsala had decided finally to commit itself to the Augsburg Confession and Luther's Catechism, and which was now determined to make the King accept this religious *fait accompli*.

Sigismond's few months in Sweden were exceedingly uncomfortable, and he did not return again to his northern kingdom until 1598. By that time, his uncle Duke Karl was firmly established in power – already in 1594 the Duke ostentatiously sent the Bridgettine nuns packing from Vadstena – and King Sigismond's efforts to assert his position by armed force in a military expedition proved futile. He left Sweden for ever, and Duke Karl was elected King Karl IX. The Catholic cause in Scandinavia was finally lost. With this possibility at an end, Swedish religious politics reverted to a more normal northern European pattern: a struggle between a monarch trying to carry out a Calvinist-style 'Second Reformation' and an entrenched and increasingly self-confident Lutheran Church establishment backed by popular attachment to Lutheran ceremonial. It was not surprising that the Swedish nobility were eager to unite with the clergy against the schemes of a king who obviously identified the Reformed religion with the advancement of his own power, so Karl never achieved his religious goals. By his death in 1611, the triumph of a virtually monolithic confessional Lutheranism around the Baltic coast was complete.[32]

THE NORTHERN NETHERLANDS: PROTESTANT VICTORY

The 1570s and 1580s saw the partition of the Low Countries that eventually led to the permanent establishment of a Roman Catholic southern state, now the kingdom of Belgium, and a Protestant north, which in its modern form as a kingdom has annexed the old name of the Netherlands. The ideological division became so deep that when in 1815 the victors of Waterloo tried to impose reunion on the seventeen provinces of the old Low Countries under a Protestant monarch of the House of Orange, the marriage proved impossible to sustain. There is irony in this: in the early stages of the Dutch revolt in the 1560s and 1570s, the backbone of Protestant militancy had been the south, and in particular the great commercial city of Antwerp. Nor had there been at first any intention of repudiating Habsburg sovereignty: it was extremely difficult in the sixteenth century for subjects collectively to make the leap of imagination which was required before repudiating allegiance to a long-established ruling dynasty. It was the Reformation that provided the impetus in the Netherlands, just as in the early 1530s resistance to the Reformation had made some Irish noblemen prepared to envisage the same drastic action against the Tudors (chapter 4, p. 202).

The road to ideological and territorial partition was complex after the renewal of revolt in 1572 (chapter 7, pp. 336–7). In July that year there was a meeting of rebels in Dordrecht (the river-port whose name is customarily abbreviated by the Dutch as Dordt): this assembly declared itself to be the States-General of the provinces of the Netherlands, and took Willem of Orange as *Stadhouder* of the provinces to lead defence against foreign invasion. Already Catholics were finding themselves in an awkward position, identified with the excesses of Spanish rule; the province of Holland quickly took the initiative in dismissing Catholic magistrates in favour of Protestants. The Reformed Church theoretically mapped out in 1571 at the exiled Synod of Emden was now taking shape, and Willem somewhat reluctantly declared his allegiance to it in April 1573; he was never particularly at ease with the Church leadership's insistence on their tidy package of confessional beliefs summed up in the Belgic Confession and the Heidelberg Catechism. The fiction of allegiance to the Habsburg monarchy became steadily more transparent; while the military fortunes of both sides fluctuated, the ill-paid Spanish armies alienated more and more of the population by their brutalities. By 1576 the States-General loyal to the Habsburgs were prepared to negotiate with the rebel provinces, ending up with a compromise deal, the Pacification of Ghent of 1576. This looked as if it might restore the old autonomy of the Netherlands while retaining Habsburg overlordship, and it gained reluctant assent from Philip II; Orange triumphantly entered the royal capital at Brussels, and took his oath to the King and the States-General in 1578.

The Pacification proved a dead end. The Habsburg authorities were divided over policy, Don John of Austria (the victor of Lepanto and now Spanish military commander) consistently seizing opportunities to undermine the agreement. On the other side, militant Calvinists infuriated Orange and greatly alarmed Catholics by extending their control by force where they could, and they began attracting international support: Count Johann Casimir, champion of Reformed religion in the Palatinate (see above, p. 356), intervened with troops in 1578, encouraged by Elizabeth of England at least until she grew alarmed at his Calvinist partisanship. Now a division between north and south emerged among the nobility and political leaders. A strong Catholic party in the southern provinces was prepared to try for a new deal with the Spaniards: this was a fatal step in deepening the schism, making it much more plausible for Protestants to say that the cause of freedom from Spanish rule was also the Protestant cause. The northern provinces led by Holland retaliated in January 1579 by agreeing at Utrecht on a Union: this was the basis of the grouping which was to survive up to the French Revolution as the Protestant state known as the United Provinces of the Netherlands. Large-scale military victories by the new Spanish commander the Duke of Parma undermined Orange's efforts to stop this Union splitting the country: he had no choice, if he were to survive politically, except to identify with the Union of Utrecht. In retaliation, King Philip declared Orange outlawed in 1580, and in turn in July 1581, the States-General of the United Provinces took the drastic step of solemnly deposing their hereditary ruler, the King of Spain.

To devise a replacement form of government proved very difficult in the middle of continuing bitter warfare now becoming international in scale. The expedient of offering the crown to the younger brother of Henri III of France, François, Duke of Anjou, was not a success: his Catholicism and self-assertiveness outweighed his usefulness as a French counterweight to Spain and possible marriage partner for Elizabeth of England. A catastrophic loss was Willem of Orange, whose diplomacy and experience had done so much to bring coherence to the revolt – shot dead by a French Catholic terrorist in 1584. The impeccably Reformed Protestant English nobleman Robert Earl of Leicester was appointed Governor-General after he arrived with an English expeditionary force in 1585, but this proved no more happy than the Anjou experiment. Not only did Leicester infuriate his own Queen Elizabeth by taking such power, but he increasingly identified with the hardline Calvinist grouping in the United Provinces, who in turn drew their strength from provinces dissatisfied with the lead taken by the wealthy and populous province of Holland. One of the triggers of war, after all, had been the outrage felt by provincial elites at Spanish threats to their autonomy: having ejected the Spaniards, they were not going to fall for what might be seen as a new tyranny, and their refusal to surrender their freedom for the sake of the war effort proved a major handicap in confronting the Spanish armies. Haplessly caught in the labyrinth of Dutch politics, Leicester finally resigned in 1588 and died back home in England in a state of exhaustion.

Nevertheless, gradually the war turned in the Protestant provinces' favour. One advantage for them was that as a world leader Philip of Spain had much else on his mind. Any one of the challenges facing him would have been daunting for a capable ruler: masterminding the peaceful takeover by Spain of the entire Portuguese Empire, facing the continuing threat of Islam in the near East, devising a strategy to contain or even destroy the growing Protestant power of Queen Elizabeth's England. In 1588 the King launched a long-delayed and staggeringly ambitious scheme to invade England, which came within hours of achieving its strategic aim of linking a fleet from Spain and an army in the Netherlands – but instead the plan failed and Philip's Armada fleet was scattered and mostly lost in the Atlantic. His last attempt to make the Netherlands strategically useful rather than a rebellious liability swallowing up military resources had thus proved a disaster, and he knew it: during the 1590s, the Spanish Netherlands armies were used mainly in containment of the increasingly effective and self-confident United Provinces. In 1590 the United Provinces decided definitively to cease looking for a monarch and declared their own States-General sovereign, to form a new republic still highly decentralized and proud of the Protestantism which had fuelled its success. They found a general of dogged competence in Willem of Orange's son Maurits of Nassau, together with a politician, Johan van Oldenbarnevelt, who had the skills to overcome the worst of the provinces' mutual suspicions, and who played a great part in securing the title of *Stadhouder* for Maurits in all but one of the United Provinces.

In the south, the Spaniards consolidated their rule in their remaining ten provinces and devoted their efforts to building up a territory which would be a showcase for the Counter-Reformation, all the more urgent a task since once it had been the heartland of the Protestant revolt. The Spanish Netherlands would also have to do its best to keep up with the economic achievements of the Protestant north: one of the remarkable features of the Dutch Revolt. C. P. Hooft, a distinguished contemporary burgomaster of Amsterdam, expressed it with a mixture of wonder and complacency: 'It is known to all the world that whereas it is generally the nature of war to ruin land and people, these countries on the contrary have been noticeably improved thereby.'[33] The economic miracle in the United Provinces, based on Dutch energy and expertise in worldwide seaborne trade, and ingenious development of varied manufactures at home, became one of the wonders of seventeenth-century Europe, not least because of the wide distribution of the resulting prosperity among its people: the northern Netherlands were one of the first territories in Europe (along with England) to escape the constant danger of mass starvation following harvest failure.[34]

But there was more for a visitor to wonder at in this busy, crowded little land of waterways and wide skylines, bristling with the church steeples of villages, towns and cities. It had an established Protestant Church, for sure, but that Church found much to its chagrin that it could not create a monopoly of recognized religion on the normal western European model. Just as in Poland, the reason for this lay in variety of opinions and constitutional pernicketiness among the secular governing elites. Since Netherlands society was far more urbanized than the vast and sparsely-peopled plains of the Commonwealth, the most powerful voices were not necessarily territorial magnates in the mould of the Radziwiłłs or the Czartoryskis, but oligarchies of merchants (known as 'Regents') in Dutch towns and cities, whose riches placed them in the seven provinces alongside the rural nobility. Calvinism emerged mainly as an urban religion when it made its comeback in the 1570s, organizing its congregations and disciplinary structures in town churches as it found opportunity. Willem of Orange, no enthusiast for strict doctrinal definitions, had exercised considerable tact in gathering a variety of urban oligarchies into his anti-Spanish alliance, and his efforts meant that more towns were persuaded to adhere to the Protestant cause than doctrinaire Calvinist clerics might have won over by their own efforts. As a result, the critical mass of the Protestant party was extended beyond strict Calvinist circles. The crucial adherence to the cause by the great and wealthy city of Amsterdam in 1578 was hesitant and late, and Catholics continued to sit on its corporation: this was no overwhelming vote in favour of ideological purity (see Plate 14b).[35]

Around 1600, one estimate suggests that only about 10 per cent of the Dutch population had become full members of the Reformed Church and thus willingly subjected themselves to consistory discipline. This may be too pessimistic, but even the most generous figure, including non-member attendants at the parish churches (*Liefhebbers*), would give the Reformed Church the allegiance of only just over half the people.[36] Beyond this was a great diversity of evangelical belief in the Netherlands, reflecting the complex and troubled early history of the Reformation there: the fierce repression of Protestantism by the Habsburgs (chapter 4, p. 207) had encouraged Dutch evangelicals to turn to quiet forms of rebellion against Rome, rebellions which had no Church structure to restrain them, and often therefore became very radical. In a wealthy society, literacy and general education levels were high, the memory of Erasmus's open and tolerant spirituality was treasured, and there was a ready audience for some of the writings or personal proselytizing of the most independent-minded thinkers of the period: this was the land which produced the Mennonites, David Joris and the Family of Love (chapter 4, pp. 207–12), and it is not an exaggeration to say that such people kept Protestantism in the Netherlands in existence through the dark years of Habsburg persecution in the 1540s. They represented the type which John Calvin had in Geneva abusively termed 'Libertine'; they would more neutrally be called Spirituals. A large section of the Dutch people simply did not believe in rigid Church structures, and in a Nicodemite fashion (another of Calvin's pet hates) they were willing to put up with whatever pattern was imposed on them, while keeping their own counsel as to what they did believe. Moreover, the stubborn localism of the provinces made it impossible to impose a uniform church settlement across the United Provinces.

A pattern therefore quickly emerged where Dutch civil authorities, even though committed to the Protestant cause, were not prepared to sign up themselves or their citizens to churchmen's demands for strict observance of Calvinist norms. The standoff between secular oligarchies and the presbyterian Church hierarchy reached a crisis during the Earl of Leicester's time in the Netherlands, and the ignominious collapse of his rule between 1586 and 1588 represented a decisive and permanent snub for the ambitions of the hardline Calvinist ministers whom he had supported.[37] Pragmatic secular politicians were well aware of the continuing religious diversity of their territories: quite apart from differing opinions among Protestants, there were still plenty of Catholics in the United Provinces, especially in the far north, and many of them had fought against Spanish rule – it would be folly to prolong ideological conflict once a political settlement had been reached.

But more than that, many Libertines felt a principled commitment to toleration: like Erasmus, they loved Holy Scripture, but they believed that God had given people brains to think out for themselves what it meant, and they distrusted clergy who tried to usurp this function.

Some ministers agreed. The celebrated pastor Hubert Duifhuis of the Jakobskerk in Utrecht (himself a Nicodemite spiritualist radical in younger years) stressed that personal discipline should come from within rather than be imposed by a Church court. He gave full Church membership to anyone who applied without enquiring into their doctrines, and communion was open to all who chose to come to his church.[38] Yet even Duifhuis's Jakobskerk was eventually shoehorned into the Calvinist Church disciplinary structure after his death, a lesson not lost on broad-minded civic authorities. In the middle of a row between the Calvinist Church authorities and the town council in Leiden, some town councillors were reported as recalling the people of Leiden's heroic survival of a Spanish siege, and saying menacingly that they might prefer the Spanish Inquisition to Genevan discipline.[39]

Amsterdam provides a prime example of a deliberately tolerant civic elite, facing a notoriously hardline Calvinist parish clergy and determined to keep them in their place. When the Amsterdam Regents rebuilt their city hall in the 1640s and 50s, the most prominent artistic theme in the Chamber of Magistrates was the story of Moses descending from Mount Sinai with the Ten Commandments, ready to rebuke the Israelites for the idolatrous worship of the golden calf set up in his absence by Aaron. To the highly biblically literate Dutch, the message would be clear: Moses the secular magistrate knew better than Aaron the priest, who had been foolish enough to indulge the religious passions of the Children of Israel, with disastrous consequences.[40]

The result was Europe's first established Church where in normal times it was possible to opt in or opt out without any great penalty, even though the Reformed had a monopoly on the parish church buildings and on public worship. The States of Holland, with predictable grudging efficiency, set a lead for other provinces by paying for their pastors from consolidated public funds, mostly confiscated from the pre-Reformation Church. This gave the pastors of the province a certain independence from their parishioners, but it also made them beholden to their secular masters in a way which would not have pleased Calvin. Parish ministers right across the northern Netherlands discovered to their dismay the problem which would later become the common lot of established Churches in the modern western world: they had to provide convenient spiritual amenities like baptisms, weddings and funerals for a religiously amorphous public, while simultaneously looking after the minority of pious souls. In remote rural areas they might achieve something like a monopoly of ministry, but they were consistently hampered from doing so in the numerous towns and cities in the United Provinces.

The Church's problem was especially revealed in its relation to that key Reformed preoccupation, discipline (chapter 14, pp. 591–600). In the Netherlands, consistory discipline became much more a matter of persuasion than in Calvinist societies like Scotland where the whole weight of community opinion could be brought to bear on an offender. Some Dutch people who initially admired the Reformed faith for its strict discipline found this lack of comprehensive authority intolerably worldly, and left their parish churches for radical sects where a more stringent community discipline could be exercised, in particular among the Mennonites.[41] The Mennonites were at their strongest in the far north, especially in the Province of West Friesland: here their roots in the preaching of the local boy Menno Simons and their readiness to communicate like him in Frisian rather than Dutch meant that they penetrated a largely rural society more quickly than the urban-based ministry of the Calvinist ministers. It is significant that in those parts of Europe – Poland, Transylvania and the Netherlands – where it was possible to make free choices in religion, a substantial minority of the population chose radical groups: perhaps 12–14 per cent in West Friesland.[42] And such people also cherished their intellectual independence: the Mennonites were among the most disciplined of radical groups – they took pride in that – but that did not stop many of them finding spiritual profit in the writings of David Joris, that ecstatic wayward genius who had abhorred any form of communal discipline.

THE NORTHERN NETHERLANDS: THE ARMINIAN CRISIS

One should not become too carried away with a picture of benevolent Dutch pluralism. Indeed, the French historian Dominique Colas has gone so far as to call the religious patchwork of the United Provinces a 'multiplication of intolerances and fanaticisms within the different religious groups', and a wry Dutch proverb runs 'One Dutchman, a theologian; two Dutchmen, a Church; three Dutchmen, a schism'.[43] The story of Jacobus Arminius will show how murderously high religious passions could rise even inside Dutch Protestantism: Arminianism was to prove not only disruptive in the United Provinces of the Netherlands but later also in the Atlantic Isles (chapter 12). It became a solvent for the certainties of the whole Reformation. So the condemnation of Arminianism at the Synod of Dordt in 1618-19 represented a defining moment.

Arminius (as the boy Jakob Hermanszoon became as a clergyman and academic) was an unlikely traitor against Dutch Calvinism, because his career initially suggested a textbook model for a godly minister in a country newly brought to a hard-won Gospel purity. When only fifteen he experienced the full horror of the struggle for independence when most of his family were massacred by Spanish troops in the sacking of the town of Oudewater. In 1576 he began studying in the brand-new University of Leiden, which symbolized both the Protestant quest for excellence in scholarship and the heroism of the Low Countries struggle: it had been founded only a year before Arminius's arrival, and popular mythology soon saw it as the town's reward for beating off the Spanish armies in an epic siege. Arminius went on from Leiden to study at Geneva with Theodore Beza, High Priest of Calvinist orthodoxy, and while there he received a call to become a minister of the Gospel in Amsterdam. He was ordained in 1588 and distinguished himself in his pastoral and administrative work in Amsterdam; a call back to Leiden University to teach theology followed, and from 1603 to his death six years later, he remained on the academic payroll there, much esteemed as a teacher by his students.

A worthy record of service, then, to a church struggling to shape a newly independent country in its own Calvinist mould; however, Arminius had too acute a mind to rest content with the synthesis of thought produced by the second generation of Reformed scholars like Theodore Beza at Geneva or Ursinus and Zanchi at Heidelberg. In his thinking, the Reformed tradition reached the dilemma of any fertile intellectual system which aspires to completeness: new circumstances and existing internal contradictions in its logic will send it off in new directions, transforming it beyond recognition. The issue was the foundation of the Reformation from Luther onwards: how humanity relates to God. In the rows between developed Lutheranism and the Reformed, Calvin's successors became ever more dogmatic in their assertions, ruthlessly spelling out questions about salvation that Calvin had generally left understated. Beza emphasized double predestination, and maintained that even before Adam and Eve had committed sin by disobeying God in the garden of Eden, God had drawn up his complete scheme of the damned and the saved in the human race (a view known as supralapsarianism or antelapsarianism). Calvin reconciled his wish to maintain Jesus Christ's universal concern for humanity with his belief in God's pre-ordained choice of an elect, by asserting that although Christ had died for all humanity on the Cross, he did not go on to pray for all when he interceded for human salvation at the right hand of the Father. This was not good enough for Beza; for him, Christ died for the elect only.[44] To many non-Calvinist Christians, Beza's interpretation of the whole human story after the Fall in Eden savoured suspiciously of a divine put-up job; one could accuse God of being the author of Adam and Eve's fault and hence of all human sin, which was indeed the doctrine which Jerome Bolsec claimed to find in Calvin's teaching back in 1551 (chapter 5, pp. 242–3).

This was the developed Calvinism that gave Arminius his education. He was not the first thinker to agitate the fledgling Protestant church in the Low Countries with doubts about the Calvinist approach; the great Dutch humanist Dirck Volckertszoon Coornhert – patriot, vernacular writer, playwright, fastidiously independent in his critical adherence to a non-sectarian Christianity – had raised these questions at disputes at Leiden in 1578.[45] For Coornhert, like so many other Libertines, the Dutch revolt was about freedom of conscience, and now the Calvinist Church had become the biggest threat to it: he well knew and consciously echoed what in earlier years Sebastian Castellio had said about Calvin's intolerance (chapter 5, p. 245). Two Calvinist ministers were deputed to oppose Coornhert, but they ended up agreeing with him, and in turn Arminius was asked to defend the doctrine of his old master Beza against the turncoats. The problems which Arminius experienced led him down the road of doubt as he brooded on the text of the Apostle Paul's epistle to the Romans – the very text at the heart of the Augustinian tradition's pessimism about the human condition. By 1591 he was voicing his doubts publicly in his teaching ministry in Amsterdam, and causing a great furore in the process. In his pastoral work in the city, he faithfully visited the sick during a severe outbreak of plague in 1602, and he was particularly alarmed by the despair of a pious couple facing death who could not feel proper Calvinist certainty of divine remission of their sins. Going through relevant passages of the Bible in order to comfort them, he was convinced of the necessity of speaking very carefully and with fine distinctions on such a grave matter as salvation.[46]

The greatest scandal and danger for the Reformed Church of the Netherlands was that Arminius was no outsider like the Libertine Coornhert or some benighted Lutheran, but a clergyman with impeccable Calvinist credentials. Throughout his career, in many ways Arminius remained loyal to his Calvinist roots. He never denied the doctrine of predestination; indeed, on occasion, he was even prepared to defend the thesis that God both decreed salvation for some and damnation for others, but with the significant modification that those damned suffered by 'their own fault' as well as by the judgement of God.[47] Always cautious in his assertions, he went no further than saying that 'I never taught that a true believer can either totally or finally fall away from the faith and perish, yet I will not conceal that there are passages of Scripture that seem to me to wear that aspect.'[48] His great act of rebellion was to move from these very guarded statements to deny the irresistibility of God's grace: in other words, to say that alongside those whom God has eternally decreed to be elect to salvation there are those who choose to reject the offer of God's grace, and fall away into damnation. In their case, God foresees their act of will leading to their own damnation rather than himself decreeing it. Moreover, Arminius had the audacity to suggest that the doctrinal statements treasured by the Dutch Reformed Church since its struggles for survival in the 1560s – the Belgic Confession and the Heidelberg Catechism – might not represent the last word in theological perfection; they might even have to be revised.

Why should these debates within Calvinism be so bitter? One has to remember that when Arminius began questioning developed Calvinist doctrine in the 1590s, the Reformed Church still felt very fragile. It had enjoyed some sort of existence in the Low Countries for only four decades, and its doctrinal statements were no older, while its grasp on the adherence of the Dutch people was, to say the least, incomplete; if the Calvinist ministers had failed to impose a godly discipline on the nation then they were certainly not inclined to give up any further ground in doctrinal matters. Nor was the dispute about Calvinism merely theological; Calvinism had become inextricably linked with the Low Countries' fight for independence from Spain, a fight which realistic observers by 1600 could see had achieved only partial success. Even after the Protestant military gains against the Spanish armies in the 1590s, the independent United Provinces controlled less than half the area of the old Low Countries, and they were losing all hope of recovering the southern provinces, which was the original home of Calvinist protest in the 1560s. The Reformed Church in the north had a large number of clergy and laypeople who were exiles from the south for the sake of their faith, and their Calvinism was reinforced by their fierce longing for a lost home. For them, any attack on the doctrine for which so many had fought and died was an act of political treachery as well as a blasphemy against God's plan of salvation; and it would remind them of the many indisputably treacherous acts which the cause of independence had suffered during the long years of struggle. Many must have regarded Arminius as no better than the assassin of William the Silent.

Arminius thus stirred up potent enmity and his health was undermined by constant theological rows, particularly with his ultra-Calvinist colleague at Leiden University, Franciscus Gomarus. Yet he died in his bed unscathed;

despite repeated efforts to have him condemned by a variety of church and university disputations, his enemies could never win a successful verdict against him. Clearly he could count on a good deal of support. Part of this was intellectual: the Libertine conviction that religion should not be forced into an ideological straitjacket by Reformed churchmen any more than by Catholic prelates. Part was political: leaders and laypeople suspicious of the pretensions of the Calvinist clergy saw in the efforts to silence Arminius an unacceptable assertion of clerical power. Regents in the free Netherlands were not going to have church synods encroaching on their jurisdiction, and time and again, attempts to bring Arminius to book for his views petered out in a wrangle over jurisdiction between Church courts and civil authority.

Freed of Arminius's restraining influence, his supporters rapidly adopted confrontational tactics against the Calvinist clerical establishment. During 1610 they published the results of a meeting at Gouda that had agreed on a statement or Remonstrance addressed to the States-General of the United Provinces; henceforward those championing Arminius's affirmation of the resistibility of divine grace would be known as Remonstrants. Increasingly the doctrinal dispute was absorbed by the question of where the balance of control lay between Church and civil power; clergy and congregations lined up on both sides, and by the middle of the decade a state bordering on civil war was paralysing the United Provinces. The Church showed itself incapable of resolving the dispute unaided; naturally the politicians stepped in. The two chief contenders were the veteran statesman Johan van Olden-barnevelt – consistent in his suspicion of the Calvinist clergy and his wish for a less divisive faith to unite the infant state – and Prince Maurits of Nassau, *Stadhouder* of all but one of the Provinces in the independent Low Countries and lifelong military leader in the struggle against the Spanish. Oldenbarnevelt had won Maurits his political position, but the two men found their interests and policies increasingly diverging, particularly after 1609 when Maurits bitterly opposed a twelve years' truce which Oldenbar-nevelt negotiated with the Spaniards. In practical terms the truce represented a recognition that the Spanish-controlled southern provinces were perma-nently separated from the independent North, so Maurits's opposition to this end to the war coincided with a bitter sense of betrayal felt by many Calvinists of southern origins.

Almost inevitably, therefore, Maurits and the Calvinists became allies, and the struggle between Remonstrants and their opponents resolved itself into a trial of strength between the most powerful political leader Oldenbar-nevelt and the most powerful military leader Maurits. In 1618 Maurits staged a successful military coup against Oldenbarnevelt's supporters, and within a few months a national synod of the Reformed Church had been called to Dordt to destroy the Remonstrants theologically as well as politically. Swiss, German and English Reformed divines were among those invited, making this the most representative gathering ever seen in the Protestant Reformation; the Remonstrants were treated as under accusation and condemned with a ferocity that dismayed some of the foreign delegates. The Synod formulated conclusions under five headings which would remain the reference points of developed Calvinism: the unconditional decree by God of election, the limiting of Christ's atoning death for humanity to those elect to salvation, the total corruption of humankind, the irresistibility of God's grace, and the unchallengeable perseverance in saving grace of God's elect.

The defeat of the Remonstrants was sealed by the judicial murder of Oldenbarnevelt as the Synod ended: bitter persecution followed of Remonstrant clergy and lay supporters. Although after Maurits's death in 1625 the situation eased, the Remonstrants were permanently alienated from the established Dutch Reformed Church, and the boundaries of Reformed Protestantism had been drawn more tightly than ever. By its uncompromising defence of ultra-Calvinism at Dordt, the official Dutch Reformed Church established itself as the chief point of reference for the Reformed tradition worldwide, the chief fighter against twin menaces: not only Arminianism but also the anti-Trinitarian Socinian movement, which the orthodox Reformed (with some justice) regarded as linked to it. This theological ascendancy was helped by two external factors: the first was the disaster for the Reformed cause brought by the Palatinate's defeat and the destruction of Heidelberg University in 1622 (chapter 11, p. 495); the second was the gradual withdrawal of the established Church of England from the Reformed world after 1660 (chapter 12). The Netherlands was thus left with no great rival for primacy this side of the Atlantic, although during the eighteenth century the Reformed religion was to find a new and very significant flowering in the universities and churches of north America (chapters 12, pp. 544–5 and 17, p. 700).

A REFORMED SUCCESS: SCOTLAND

The kingdoms of Scotland, England and Ireland all experienced Reformations in the Reformed Protestant mould, yet they were very different in nature, and had very different outcomes. The Scottish Reformation proved the most thoroughgoing and the most internationally minded, and although there were tensions between the Calvinist churchmen and the monarchy, in parallel fashion to the disputes between Church and Commonwealth in the Netherlands, a workable solution emerged during the long reign of James VI (1567–1625). This Scottish Reformation began in a national revolution in 1559, and it was therefore not the Crown but Protestant churchmen and their lay supporters who took the lead in shaping the future: as King James grew to adulthood, he reacted as best he could to a series of *faits accomplis* worked out when he was a boy, but he showed himself extremely skilful in bending the situation to his own purposes. He inherited a remarkable ecclesiastical deal patiently worked out for the Scottish Kirk amid the political turmoil of the 1560s. A Reformed Church polity was founded to cover the whole country (chapter 6, pp. 293–5), but this Kirk was to coexist with the ghost of the old Catholic Church system, preserved for the lives of its old office-holders; they continued to draw two-thirds of their former revenues even if they did not play an active part in the new Church.

This shrewd and realistic expedient shows that the supposed English genius for compromise was rather more effectively displayed during the Reformation in Scotland (it should also be pointed out that the Scottish Reformation was a good deal less bloody than that in England, with no more than twenty-five Protestant and two Catholic martyrdoms against Tudor England's 500 or more deaths both Catholic and Protestant). The many absentee and pluralist clergy in the pre-Reformation parish system made the compromise about parish revenues easier: after all, hardly any of those resources had benefited medieval parishes, and providing a third of them to the active parish minister normally represented an improvement in the real finance available to working clergy. Half the old clergy did in any case choose to work actively in the new Kirk. Most Scottish monasteries were not suppressed (although the potentially more dangerous Orders of friars were): they were allowed to fade gradually away, a significant measure of their irrelevance to Catholic survival. Several were legally remodelled into secular lordships: a logical step, since most Scottish monasteries had been headed by a lay commendator in the century before the Reformation (chapter 2, p. 90).

The Scottish Kirk was capable of being more hardline than the Reformations of Switzerland and Geneva that it so admired and imitated. From 1561 it officially disapproved of the non-scriptural feast of Christmas, and so although it adopted the Helvetic Confession of Faith in 1566, it explicitly excluded the observation of Christmas that the Zürichers had allowed (it took another three decades to get the Scottish Parliament to agree with the Kirk on this abolition). However, after the death of the anglicized and comparatively moderate Calvinist John Knox (1572) two tendencies emerged. One was a broadly-based Protestantism which accepted the institution of bishops or superintendents and a strong role for the secular government in church affairs, rather on the English model; the other, led by the leading scholar Andrew Melville after his return from Geneva in 1574, was a more doctrinaire presbyterianism, determined to assert equality among ministers in the Kirk and also the Kirk's independence of Crown interference, just as Calvin or Beza would wish.

Three-way political struggles between these two groups and Catholic noblemen in the 1580s resulted in further compromise. As King James VI reached political maturity, he struggled with considerable success to increase the power of the bishops and of the Crown within the system, but he also allowed the growth of a nationwide structure of presbyteries. That gave the General Assembly of the Kirk a major place in Scottish life alongside the Scottish Parliament. The Calvinist self-assertion of the General Assembly contrasted markedly with the marginalized role of the English Church's provincial Convocations of Canterbury and York in English politics. Nevertheless, after several failed negotiations, aimed at giving the Kirk a say in Parliament itself, bishops anomalously also continued to hold their seats in Parliament among the peers, generally providing a useful bloc of tame support for the King's purposes.[49]

Sixteenth-century Scotland was a kingdom of two languages and cultures: lowland English and highland Gaelic. The latter (the *Gaidhealtachd*) was a society of clans in which all those of the same surname looked to a chief for leadership and hospitality in return for loyalty and service. Scottish Protestantism was fortunate that among the most powerful of these chiefs were early and enthusiastic converts: principally the fourth and fifth Earls of Argyll (both called Archibald Campbell) who were both leading actors in the national revolution of 1559. The Clan Campbell had a presence in many areas of the highlands and on the fringes of the lowlands, and was thus well-placed to mediate the new Protestant culture of English-speaking Scotland to the very different world of the north and west. The Earls and their principal relatives could do this partly by their own efforts: they customarily spent their time touring their territories from castle to castle, and now in addition to the feasting and celebrations which accompanied their visits they could add Protestant services and preaching. However, preaching needed preachers, and preachers who could perform convincingly in Gaelic. That must be done by winning over the learned orders of Gaelic society: the lawyers, doctors and poets, much of whose tradition was transmitted orally and so potentially might have little contact with the print culture which characterized the Reformation.

The Campbells discovered in their retinue the ideal representative of this learned tradition to proclaim the Protestant message: a notary named John Carswell. Thanks to the Earl of Argyll, during the 1560s Carswell was set up as Superintendent of Argyll and Bishop of the Isles, with wide grants of land and two impressive castles to emphasize his position, just at the time when the Scottish Church's wealth was otherwise draining away into the pockets of the Scots secular nobility. In 1567 Carswell published a free translation of the Kirk's *Book of Common Order* (*Foirm na n-Urrnuidheadh*), combined with a version of Calvin's small catechism: this was the first book printed in Gaelic, in a literary form of the language common to Ireland and Scotland, and there is evidence that it was used in Gaelic Ireland too, to the alarm of the English government. However, most of the transmission of Reformed Protestantism was oral, and it is clear from the names of ministers in the Highlands through the Reformation that the old learned families continued to serve the Kirk. With the Kirk's dominance of a primarily oral Gaelic culture, Highland Scotland quickly became Protestant, despite a feature very unusual among developed European Reformed cultures: it had no complete Bible in the vernacular language until 1801. Instead, ministers translated spontaneously from the English Bible into whatever local Gaelic dialect they encountered; they also preached and used Carswell's catechism in Gaelic. It was a remarkably effective combination: Franciscan friars coming from Ireland in the 1620s to try and win the *Gaidhealtachd* back to Catholicism were so alarmed by the success of Protestant Gaelic sermons that they got permission from their superiors to attend parish church services incognito, so that they could learn what arguments they needed to counter in their own preaching. The achievement did not usually get much credit from the English-speakers who dominated the Kirk in the south, and whose culture steadily encroached on this Gaelic world from the seventeenth century onwards.[50]

In what amounted to an optional Reformation, there was little opportunity for the Scots to form a distinctive and self-conscious Catholic recusant grouping, in contrast to England and Ireland; it took the early seventeenth-century Franciscan missionary work to win a paltry few of the Gaelic-speaking western isles back to Catholicism. A Scots College in Rome came rather late, in 1600; additionally, a small exile community of activist Scottish clergy established itself abroad, successfully laying claim to three ancient but redundant Benedictine monasteries in the Holy Roman Empire by creatively misunderstanding the fact that long ago they had been founded by 'Scoti' (a word which in fact had originally meant Irish).[51] Scottish members of the Society of Jesus tended to be socially well-connected and rather looked down on their more humbly born English counterparts; they scored some successes among their aristocratic relations back home in stiffening loyalty to the Catholic cause, but never enough to shift the majority of the nobility from the mid-century conversions to Protestantism.

The prime Jesuit aim in Scotland was to repeat their achievement in Sweden and secure the monarch himself. James (whose own Danish Lutheran wife Anne did indeed convert to Catholicism in the mid 1590s) toyed with Catholic overtures for his own purposes, mainly in his interminable schemes to make sure that he became King of England after the childless Queen Elizabeth, but he never genuinely shifted from his ecumenically minded Reformed Protestantism.[52] He was anxious to be as inclusive as possible to Scottish Catholic magnates willing to be loyal, so it was possible for them to gain high positions in royal favour: the Jesuit-educated crypto-Catholic Alexander Seton, Earl of Dunfermline, took a leading place in Scottish government for nearly three decades from the 1590s, despite snarls of disapproval from the more austere ministers of the Kirk.

ELIZABETHAN ENGLAND: A REFORMED CHURCH?

When James finally inherited the English throne with remarkably little trouble in 1603, he also inherited a Church of England which had similarly undergone a contest for its identity. After the political crisis of 1569–72 (chapter 7, pp. 333–5), the Protestant future of the Church of England seemed secure, but for many it also seemed unexpectedly and alarmingly static: Queen Elizabeth was determined to defend her idiosyncratic religious settlement of 1559 without any further progress towards the best Reformed Churches, the movement that had been proceeding so rapidly during the reign of Edward VI. The English bishops who in the 1560s had seen themselves as the natural leaders of such change (chapter 6, p. 291) now found themselves defending a status quo in which many of them did not believe; however they were prepared to do their best in making the structure work for godly reformation, and new recruits to the bishops' Bench were inevitably more inclined to defend the existing structure with positive enthusiasm. Among the younger generation of Protestant clergy and gentry now emerging from the universities, many were frustrated by the bishops' unwillingness to stand for change. Such people were styled by those who did not like them 'precise', or less frequently but in the end more lastingly, 'Puritans' – they were inclined to call themselves 'the godly'.[53] For many Puritans, episcopacy was now revealing itself as part of the problem, not the solution: the obvious goal was to replace it with a presbyterian system like Geneva.

It is important not to fall into the trap of thinking that every Puritan was a presbyterian (although there is no problem in identifying all presbyterians as Puritans). A much wider range of issues persuaded many in the Church of England between the 1560s and the 1640s that it was hindered from doing the work of a Reformed Church. Cranmer's Book of Common Prayer was too elaborate and fixed; it preserved the ghost of the ordered liturgical world of saints' days and prescribed recitations. Lurking behind it might even be 'that popish dunghill, the Mass', which one widely read Puritan propaganda work co-authored by John Field unhesitatingly named as the source of the Prayer Book, even though Cranmer had died at the stake for his hatred of the Mass.[54] Observation of the way in which the Prayer Book was used had increasingly disenchanted Puritans with liturgical approaches to God. They became convinced that preaching was the only way in which Christians should in normal circumstances receive God's truth: Calvin said similar things, but had never been so categorical in asserting that a sermon was 'the ordinary means of salvation'. Now they felt it a matter of scandal that there were not enough sermons in England – a major proof of the Church's corruption. Not all bishops would disagree, and they might consider it most unjust when they found themselves under attack from Puritans.

The first person to publicize presbyterian views was Thomas Cartwright, Lady Margaret Professor of Divinity at Cambridge. In a course of lectures in spring 1570 he compared the Church of England with the New Testament Church as portrayed in the Acts of the Apostles; in such a contest the Church of England was bound to come off worst. Cartwright's advocacy of parity in the ministry brought him the loss of his Cambridge professorial Chair and a pointedly warm welcome to Geneva when he left England. However, getting rid of Cartwright was not going to end controversy; he had only said out loud what many had been thinking. During the 1570s a good deal of public agitation and efforts to make progress in Parliament showed the level of discontent among the Protestant political nation, while the Queen forced her bishops into disciplining clergy who would not conform to the details of her 1559 Settlement, for instance in liturgy or specialized clerical dress. It would be up to the bishops to win back the trust of such people by proving that they could carry out reform.

The chance occurred when the kindly and scholarly but much-harassed

Archbishop Parker died in 1575; the Queen chose Edmund Grindal as his successor. As a former Marian exile, Grindal's Protestant credentials were impeccable: he had been an energetic Bishop of London and Archbishop of York, a good friend to the returned immigrant communities of foreign Protestants in their presbyterian Stranger Churches, and an assiduous opponent of the powerful body of Catholic gentry in the north. His tragedy was that his very determination to make progress cost him his freedom of action: he refused to give way to the Queen by suppressing 'prophesyings'. Considerably less dramatic than their name might imply (it came from the institution for clergy training in Zürich, the *Prophezei*), these were gatherings or 'exercises' for clergy to practise their preaching skills and ability to use scripture, with interested laypeople gathered for the public part of the proceedings. Regular exercises had become widely established, and the bishops generally welcomed them: not so the Queen. The reasons for her dislike are not clear: perhaps the name suggested lurid connotations of disorder, and in any case the Queen's respect for preaching was not sufficiently great to prevent her on more than one occasion from rudely interrupting sermons which annoyed her.[55]

Grindal's response was defiance of the Queen culminating in a 6,000-word defence of the exercises and of the vital place of preaching in the Church: he pursued this document to a fatal sentence, 'Bear with me, I beseech you, Madam, if I choose rather to offend your earthly Majesty than to offend the heavenly majesty of God.' The 'Puritan' Archbishop had brooded on the history of the Church Catholic, and had remembered that great fourth-century prince of the Church Ambrose, Bishop of Milan, who likewise dared to lecture a Roman Emperor on his duty. Ambrose had succeeded in his bids to overawe Theodosius, but Elizabeth was not to be treated thus. In spring 1577 Grindal was placed under house arrest in his own palace at Lambeth. The Queen, for once forced to abandon her habitual use of the bishops to do her disciplinary work, summarily forbade all prophesyings by circular royal letter (they later quietly resumed under the more neutral name 'exercises' apparently without her noticing). Grindal, still enjoying the esteem of less forthright episcopal colleagues and of many Protestant courtiers, was saved from formal deprival, but his active career in directing the Church was over – cut short like that of the Protestant archbishops von Wied and Cranmer. Blind and in increasingly bad health, he died in 1583, and with him, any possibility of moving the English Church beyond the beginnings made under Edward VI.[56]

Grindal's disgrace brought to prominence a generation of bishops whom we might call 'conformist' because they could see nothing in the existing settlement of the Church that was an obstacle to godly reformation. Led by John Whitgift, made Bishop of Worcester in 1577 and Archbishop of Canterbury in 1583, they reflected the Queen's determination to discipline those who deviated from her settlement, and they were backed by her newly risen favourite, Sir Christopher Hatton (a politician only just emerging from crypto-Catholicism into tepid Protestantism), against the Puritan sympathies and patronage of Elizabeth's more long-established favourite the Earl of Leicester.[57] Accordingly, one feature of English religion over the next decade and a half was an internal Church battle between conformists and a spectrum of the discontented, the most extreme of whom were presbyterians. Whitgift sought to impose a degree of tight conformity on the clergy that often alarmed the Queen's senior politicians like William Cecil, Lord Burghley (one of the architects of the 1559 Settlement), but the Archbishop was aware that he faced a movement designed to provide an alternative presbyterian church, with a leader, John Field, who had the assets of energy, efficiency, discretion and a wide acquaintance. At a local level, many Puritan clergy met in embryo presbyteries: Victorian historians called these *classes*, and christened their activities the 'Classical Movement'. Perhaps many members of such groups were not doctrinaire presbyterians but joined for clerical fellowship and support, but amid the fierce passions aroused by Whitgift's campaign, moderation was becoming almost impossible.[58]

When a Parliament was called for November 1584, the Puritans viewed this as a perfect opportunity to demonstrate their strength. This was probably the most fiercely contested English general election of the century; significantly, it returned an unusually large number of people who were MPs for the first time. Yet the election result did not represent a Puritan landslide. Whitgift may have angered many gentry and clergy, but the Puritans had themselves aroused powerful antagonisms. Perhaps some of the opposition to the Puritans was Catholic-sympathizing traditionalism; perhaps some was the beginning of a familiarity with and acceptance of the ways of the 1559 Church Settlement which resented Puritan criticism of it. Puritans certainly tried to array their forces in the Commons, but most were elected for boroughs with small electorates, often dominated by fellow-Puritan nobility or gentry: where they faced electorates numbering thousands in the shire (county) elections, they had much less success, even in East Anglia, the puritan heartland.[59] This may well have encouraged the Queen in her blanket defiance of all parliamentary agitation about religion and proposals for reform, the result of which over the next two Parliaments was precisely nil.

The 1580s were ambiguous for Puritans. As England drifted into war with Spain over the Netherlands in 1584-5, the Dutch hero Willem 'the Silent' was murdered and Catholic plots uncovered to murder the Queen, the forward Protestant policy which Leicester championed still made sense. In rapid succession came official sponsorship of a fund to support Geneva under Catholic siege from Savoy in 1582-3, a nationwide Bond of Association in 1584 in which peers and gentlemen swore to pursue to the death anyone who attempted to harm the Queen, and in 1585 Leicester's royal commission for the Netherlands military expedition. The greatest success was the Parliamentary agitation combined with steady Court pressure on the Queen that led to beheading the imprisoned Mary Queen of Scots in 1587. Politicians took advantage of a momentary lapse in Elizabeth's studied reluctance to take the life of an anointed monarch; this was a judicial decision to execute a woman who was associated both in her own kingdom and in England with political murder, designed to promote the Catholic faith. The funeral of the great Protestant warrior-poet, the Earl of Leicester's nephew Sir Philip Sidney, who died heroically on 5 November 1586 in the Netherlands fighting the Spaniards, may have been deliberately delayed until February 1587 in order to provide a ceremonial counterpoint to Mary's death and show what a true and godly martyr was like – the Sidney funeral was held eight days after her execution, and made a great popular impression.[60]

Mary's execution was an ideological assertion of Reformation against dynastic legitimacy, echoing the Netherlands' landmark decision in 1581 to repudiate the King of Spain, and it was deeply repugnant to Queen Elizabeth's conservative instincts. But like King Johan III in Sweden at the same time, she had to face the fact that there was now a noisy public opinion which was emphatically Protestant and which was not prepared to show unquestioning deference to monarchs. The 1584 Bond of Association might even be seen as the assertion of a 'monarchical republic' in England, an example of a feeling increasingly common among sixteenth-century Europeans that 'monarchy was too important a matter to be left to monarchs'.[61] Between 1570 and 1584 Elizabeth faced increasingly vocal public alarm at her marriage negotiations with a succession of Catholic princes. In the end this forced her to abandon the idea of a dynastic marriage, although then with characteristic ingenuity she made the best of a bad job by adopting the rhetorical role of the 'Virgin Queen' that the opposition had forced on her.[62] With the political nation in such a mood, Puritans might justly claim that they were the true loyalists in the Elizabethan state, providing the logical corollary to growing national anti-Catholicism by advocating thoroughgoing reformation. Yet they were always in danger of isolation, particularly those pressing for a presbyterian system; they could count on widespread goodwill from those who cared about the advancement of the Protestant faith, as long as they did not seem to be subverting the life of the Protestant nation.

A combination of factors eventually served to isolate and weaken the Puritan group, culminating in troubles in 1588: not least was a series of outrageously humorous attacks on leading conformist clergy published on secret fugitive presses by the pseudonymous 'Martin Marprelate'. It was Marprelate who accused Archbishop Whitgift ('John Cant') of sodomitical relations with the Master of Peterhouse (chapter 4, p. 209). Here is Martin ranting against one of his *bêtes noires*, John Bridges the Dean of Salisbury, who had written at length defending the Church of England's polity – it is typical in its dense and allusive mixture of racy personal cheek, often with a scandalous edge, veering unpredictably into high seriousness on religion:

Sir Bridges, do you not know before whom you speak? You think now that you play my Lord of Winchester's fool, do you? Or that you are in the monastery of Sarum [Salisbury Cathedral] among your roaring choristers. I would advise you, learn this of me: that the Church government is a substantial point of religion, and therefore of the substance of the building . . . his Grace [Whitgift] shall one day answer me this point or very narrowly escape me a scouring, and you, Dean John, go forward: I am content to let you pass my fingers at this time.[63]

The Marprelate Tracts were widely enjoyed, but horrified senior Puritan clergy, who were not used to their cause being promoted in this way. The government never succeeded in bringing the author to justice, despite imprisoning and torturing those associated with the project, but at the same time as the Marprelate scandal broke, death deprived the Puritans of level heads and powerful friends. The Earl of Leicester and John Field both died in 1588, followed by a series of other key figures. The spectacular disintegration of the 1588 Spanish invasion Armada was also a paradoxical piece of ill-luck for Puritanism (see Plate 9). A medal commemorating the defeat expressed a common opinion in echoing the words of Exodus 15:10, 'he blew with his wind and they were scattered'. It would be difficult to resist the conclusion that if God felt that strongly about England, there could not be too much wrong with its established Church. Conditions were therefore ripe for a further conformist assault on the Puritans.

Now Archbishop Whitgift's chaplain Richard Bancroft, a good hater of Puritans and a notable precursor of Sherlock Holmes, scored a coup: he was investigating the Marprelate Tracts, but stumbled across evidence of the presbyterian organization created over the previous decade. The ringleaders, including the veteran Puritan spokesman Thomas Cartwright, found themselves in 1591 facing first the ecclesiastical High Commission, and then, even more intimidatingly, the Court of Star Chamber. It was an extraordinary piece of bad luck for them when in the middle of London's Cheapside Edmund Copinger and Henry Arthington, two extremist Puritans who hero-worshipped the ministers under examination, proclaimed a disturbed individual called William Hacket as the new Messiah and supplemented it with an announcement that Queen Elizabeth was deposed. Naturally Hacket was swiftly executed. What better for the conformists than this demonstration of the depths to which Puritanism could sink? Although the Puritan presbyterian leaders were all eventually released, their spirit was broken, and the 'Classical Movement' collapsed.[64]

The conformists sealed their triumph by a crack-down on the small group of Protestants who had separated from the national Church: separatism could be represented as the ultimate fruit of espousing Puritan opinions. In 1593 three separatist leaders, Henry Barrow, John Greenwood and John Penry, were executed for sedition; this martyrdom of sincere godly Protestants, in no way heretical in theology, was a remarkable contrast to the fierce anti-Catholicism of the 1580s that had inspired penal legislation and executions of Catholic clergy and laity (see below, p. 392). Equally symbolic was the government's manipulation of further measures against Catholics proposed in the 1593 Parliament, creating the first legislation to apply similar legal ferocity against Protestant separatists.

What is striking after that is the lack of theological controversy. Conformists had received backing from on high because of the quarrel over church polity; in other respects it was difficult to portray Puritans as a danger to the English way of life, and the issues which conformists tried to take up were simply not significant enough. Differences in outlook between conformist and Puritan did not represent the gulf between Reformed and Arminian theologies that proved so explosive in the 1620s and 1630s (see chapter 12).[65] In the conformists' year of triumph 1593, Whitgift encouraged a clergyman called Richard Hooker to begin publishing a sustained if highly nuanced conformist attack on the Reformed approach to theology, the *Laws of Ecclesiastical Polity*. This work was highly important in the future of the English Church (chapter 12, pp. 506-8), but at the time it was a damp squib, and only one Puritan writer belatedly bothered to attack it six years later.

Whitgift's Puritan opponents were not disposed to cause further trouble in public. Puritans were terrified by the government's attempts to associate their activities with the apparently subversive intentions of separatism, particularly since they would be conscious of the sharp increase in popular unrest and disturbance that characterized the economically disrupted, hungry and anxious years of the 1590s. Useful Puritan contacts at Court had dwindled. The Puritan gentry who were so important in many counties both for local government and for the sustaining of Puritan ministers in the church's system were becoming isolated from Court politics, an unhealthy development for English political life. Instead of pursuing the national agitation for change that had gained such meagre results during the 1580s, they devoted their religious energies to unobtrusive protection of Puritan ministers and of lay activity at a local level.[66]

So Puritan literature changed from the presbyterian polemic of Field and Cartwright or the knockabout abuse of Marprelate, to weighty and intricate moral analysis, complete with printed diagrams of the path to salvation, from the Cambridge theologian William Perkins. This was bestselling Puritan divinity: Perkins's publications were rapidly outstripping the number of English editions of his hero Calvin when the Cambridge don died in 1602.[67] Significantly, Perkins hardly ever mentioned questions of church government: he was the latest and perhaps the most important exponent of 'Covenant theology' (also known as 'federal theology', since Covenant is '*foedus*' in Latin). This became one of the most characteristic features of the Puritan outlook, and we need to plunge into the intricacies of Perkins's thought-world to see what it meant and why Puritans came to think as they did.

From the early days of Reformed Protestantism in Bullinger's Zürich, the theme of Covenant was an attractive metaphor in societies which were trying to live up to the divine plan for Israel. A further reason for its attractiveness was that it provided an answer to that familiar problem of 'antinomianism': free grace might seem to destroy the importance of moral law in human affairs if God's plan of salvation had nothing to do with morality (see p. 350, and chapter 3, p. 130). The scheme of a divine Covenant usefully restored the notion that God cared about his law and wanted it kept. The Heidelberg theologians Ursinus, Olevianus and Zanchi explored the Covenant motif, but it was developed more systematically in *Sacra Theologia*, a book published in 1585 by a young English theologian Dudley Fenner. Fenner, like all interested in the Covenant motif, observed that the Bible talked of covenants with different characteristics: some were unconditional, others had strings attached. So Fenner constructed a theology of the Christian life that contrasts two different Covenants.

On this scheme, there is a *conditional* Covenant of works, which is part of God's creation of the world, so it remains binding on all human beings and is still dependent on observance of God's moral code. There is then an *unconditional* Covenant of grace, which God makes only with true Christian believers. The theological advantage of this scheme of things is that it emphasizes the importance of God's saving work, precisely because humanity is caught in a tragic dilemma. We are still compelled to try to keep God's law under the Covenant of works, while finding it impossible. Only grace can release humanity from the trap, and then those under the Covenant of grace will do good works out of gratitude and love of God. Either way, human beings whether saved or damned are directed away from antinomianism.

Fenner died young, and it was left to Perkins to develop Covenant theology further. Perkins's starting-point was an idea of Calvin's which he took up and made peculiarly his own: some of those whom God has chosen to reprobate (irrevocably condemn) to damnation are given *temporary* faith. This may stay with them for some time, perhaps even for a lifetime, but is completely different from the saving faith of the elect, and it leads to the fires of hell; they are still under the Covenant of works, not the Covenant of grace. Belief in temporary faith makes for an unattractive doctrine (and it must be pointed out that Perkins died in what appears to have been a state of clinical depression): nevertheless, one can see how pastoral experience might drive a minister to embrace the idea if he became exasperated at unctuousness or self-righteousness among his flock, and wanted to shock them into a more gritty piety. Besides, temporary faith had a necessary corollary in a doctrine of assurance: a claim that individuals are capable of discerning that their own faith is of the saving rather than of the temporary variety. This discernment comes from an experience of true belief, or is, in Perkins's phrase, 'experimental'.

It is understandable that Perkins concentrated on moral issues and personal piety, given the idea of temporary faith at the heart of his thought, and it is also apparent that it must make questions of election and predestination central to one's religious life. Each individual believer is forced to come to a conclusion about his or her experience of belief. It is no coincidence that the modern type of confessional diary emerged as a literary genre among English Puritans around 1600: these were journals intended to examine oneself for proofs of genuine election by God. There was also another feature of experimental Calvinist piety: it might encourage separation either to find groups of the likeminded within the established Church or to withdraw completely from the community which seemed to contain so many with no consciousness of election. Among English Puritans who sailed across the Atlantic to found a new, purer version of Protestant Europe, the

Covenant became a central, comforting and strengthening ideal in the midst of their dangers and struggles, and it remains a bedrock idea in the Protestant ideology that is deeply embedded in American consciousness (chapter 12, pp. 533–45).

Perkins's style of moral theology spread east as well as west across the Atlantic. One of his most attentive students at Christ's College Cambridge was William Ames, an outstandingly talented theologian not prepared to make the compromises with the Church establishment that had given Perkins his honoured place in English ecclesiastical life. As a result he left England for the Netherlands in 1611, and eventually settled in 1622 in the little West Frisian university of Franeker, which prided itself on its Calvinist orthodoxy and had a surprisingly international student body which had travelled to the remote Frisian coast because of this. Given this cosmopolitan audience, Ames became very important in European Reformed Christianity; his influence was felt as far away as Transylvania, where the writings of Perkins and Ames were enthusiastically studied, and where Ames's theology of the Christian life and of Church organization became a major point of contention (chapter 10, pp. 459–63).

Ames and like-minded Dutch theologians were a major force in developing a new intensity of devotion in small groups in the Dutch Reformed Church. Like the self-selected local circles of enthusiasts within English Puritanism, they took up the message of covenant theology to emphasize the great gulf between the spiritually reborn and the unregenerate mass of the population, and they did their best to live up to the highest moral standards. The movement has been styled by Dutch historians a 'further Reformation' (*nadere Reformatie*), in parallel with the 'Second Reformations' of Germany, and it anticipated by half a century a similar movement of 'Pietism' that was to develop in the established Churches of Lutheran Germany.[68]

Back home in England, by 1600, Puritanism seemed to have abandoned its vision of transforming the institutional structures of the English Church. As in the Netherlands, it gave priority in the manner of William Perkins to cultivating the individual soul in pilgrimage to the blessings promised to the elect of God. Generally English Puritans did not now link this to the more confrontational stance on Church government taken up by Perkins's student Ames, which had led Ames to abandon Cambridge in favour of Franeker and Utrecht. By doing so, English Puritans were both contained and influential within the Elizabethan and early Stuart Church; they remained an integral part of its Protestant life.

By contrast, the programme of activist Catholics to win back England to Roman obedience was a failure. From the late 1560s, when a 'recusant' group emerged refusing to attend services of the established Church, there were problems. The 1569–72 crisis (chapter 7, pp. 333–5) left committed Roman Catholics with the poisoned chalice of the papal Bull *Regnans in Excelsis* condemning Elizabeth as a heretic. How could they dodge the question of loyalty: to the Queen or the Pope? Moreover, as old priests ordained before the final break with Rome in 1558 died off, English Catholicism might wither away. To prevent this, in 1568 William Allen, a former Oxford academic now in exile, founded a college at Douai in Flanders that began training priests; other seminaries in the mode envisaged by Cardinal Pole and created by the Council of Trent were set up in mainland Europe. The first missionary priest arrived in 1574, ending the government's hope of a slow death for English Catholicism: missionary priests were automatically considered traitors, and their hosts were liable to punishment. Savage 1570s and 1580s parliamentary legislation ordered death, banishment, life imprisonment, forfeiture of property or fines. Priests had to be hidden, often in specially constructed 'priest holes' within Catholic houses; secret printing presses produced devotional and propaganda works. The Jesuit Edmund Campion made a point of announcing his mission to England in 1580, and when betrayed in an English hiding-place, was horribly tortured before his execution after a show trial. In a decade between 1581 and 1590, seventy-eight priests and twenty-five laypeople were executed, with executions still numerous between 1590 and 1603: fifty-three priests and thirty-five laypeople. Seventy more priests were executed between 1601 and 1680. In fact England judicially murdered more Roman Catholics than any other country in Europe, which puts English pride in national tolerance in an interesting perspective (see Plate 13).[69]

However, amid this heroism, tensions developed among English Catholics, partly because Rome gave them no overriding authority like a local bishop. Allen fulfilled this function in part, since he was much respected and in 1587 was made a Cardinal, but he died in 1594. It was also undeniable that he was powerfully influenced by the Society of Jesus, like many students of Douai and other colleges founded later. Secular priests were often jealous of Jesuits, and some contested the Jesuit insistence that every Catholic should first obey the Pope, and keep separate from the English Church. Some seculars blamed the Jesuits for government persecution, and hoped that if they left England, seculars could gain toleration. On the other side, the Jesuits were inclined to emphasize that England was as much an empty mission field ripe for conversion as any jungle in south America, and they took the absence of settled jurisdiction as an opportunity to operate as they thought fit without outside interference. Very similar tensions could be found in the Protestant northern Netherlands, where Catholics, although much more numerous than in England and not so bitterly persecuted, found themselves facing the same issues; we will also find Catholic hostility to Jesuits as a major force in France as the French Church reconstructed itself in the early seventeenth century (chapter 10, p. 479). Indeed, lurking behind such disputes was a wider question about the identity of Catholicism that still haunted the old Church throughout Europe: had the Council of Trent provided all the answers about how the Church should be governed, and how it made doctrinal and practical decisions?

The English government was naturally delighted at what it saw of the Catholic troubles: a 1602 proclamation offered personal protection against the treason laws for priests willing to deny that papal power could depose an English monarch. This first cautious step towards toleration of more than one religious group within England only served to intensify Catholic quarrels. If divisions undermined the potential effectiveness of the mission to England, there were also plenty of incentives to avoid confrontation with the Protestant regime. English government was very untidy; astute Catholics could benefit from this and escape persecution. To the fury of Puritans and Jesuits, who both deplored such duplicity, many gentry became 'church papists': the family head attended Protestant services, which satisfied the anti-recusancy laws, while his wife (a non-person in English law) remained a Catholic recusant. He turned a blind eye to what went on at home, as she saw to the education of his children and organized clergy to lead Catholic worship.[70] The gentry did not encourage the priests (who were largely dependent on their protection) to conduct large-scale missionary work; few people apart from the recusant or 'church papist' gentry and the tenantry whom they could protect were able to sustain their faith in the face of the official pressure to become Protestant. Immense sacrifices preserved Catholicism, and they were vital, because the government wanted to destroy the practice of Catholicism even if not necessarily to destroy Catholics. Nevertheless, English Catholicism fossilized as a largely upper-class and faintly exotic sect, before a new spectacular expansion in the nineteenth century.

IRELAND: THE COMING OF THE COUNTER-REFORMATION

The contrast in religious outcome between England and the other Tudor kingdom of Ireland could hardly be greater: in Ireland, official Protestantism became the elite sect and Roman Catholicism the popular religion, in a result unique in the whole Reformation. In no other polity where a major monarchy made a long-term commitment to the establishment of Protestantism was there such failure. This was not merely the result of a culture clash: Ireland was a land of two languages, Gaelic and English, but so was Scotland, and there the Protestant Reformation was an outstanding success. The chief problem was the ambivalent attitude of the Tudor dynasty to Ireland after Henry VIII had unilaterally erected the medieval Lordship into a Kingdom in 1541 (chapter 4, p. 202): were the Tudors to make a reality of this status, negotiating and co-operating with the existing Irish chiefs, nobles and notables as they did with the nobility and gentry of England, or were they going to remodel Ireland into another England through land confiscation and colonization imposed by brute force, as the Spaniards were doing in the New World? Rarely did the Tudors have the resources or the concentration of purpose to be consistent in their policies to Ireland, but their urge to exploit usually won out over their urge to understand or accommodate. In the process, the Reformation which the Tudors sought to introduce lost allegiance from the bulk of the native Irish population, both Gaelic and English speaking (the so-called 'Old English'): both communities experienced its enforcement (however hesitant and untidy) as an aspect of an alien attack on their identity and their way of life.

The early years of the Reformation in the 1540s and early 1550s were indeed marked by negotiation rather than exploitation. Under the long-term guidance of the experienced and tactful Lord Deputy Sir Anthony St Leger, himself no enthusiast for Protestantism, a cautious beginning was made in introducing English-style religious changes. Nearly all Irish bishops accepted the oath of supremacy under Henry VIII, although many of them hedged their bets and also kept open channels of communication with Rome; under Edward VI, the government secured widespread use of the first (1549) English Book of Common Prayer, and there was even a Latin version of it, which could meet the problem for the Gaelic lordships that government plans for a Gaelic translation were not implemented. Only in the far north was innovation entirely ignored, in the remote and predominantly Gaelic portions of the Archdiocese of Armagh, from where Archbishop

Dowdall fled abroad rather than co-operate with the Edwardian government.[71]

Queen Mary's restoration of traditional religion to Ireland (enthusiastically welcomed) was modified in one crucial respect: the Pope was persuaded to modify his twelfth-century predecessor's grant by recognizing Henry VIII's *fait accompli* in proclaiming an Irish kingdom. Mary was not going to lose that title, and her determination was significantly coupled with the beginnings of a new policy towards her second kingdom: the implementation of plans to plant immigrant 'New English' settlers in the midland areas of Leix and Offaly that had been mooted in her brother's reign. It was no coincidence that her husband was the King of Spain, the great colonial power of the New World, but it is also a curious irony of history that a Catholic monarch began the colonization spawning the resentment out of which Irish Catholic nationalism was eventually born. Queen Elizabeth promoted further plantation schemes, and as the flagship of English policy in Ireland into the seventeenth century, plantation eventually proved fatal to 'Old English' religious loyalty to England, as well as an obstacle to any similar loyalty taking root among Gaelic lords.

It is instructive to make the contrast between Elizabethan governmental incompetence and the Reformation's failure in Ireland, with the Tudor success in Wales. In 1559 there was little native Protestantism in either of these predominantly non-English-speaking territories, and many more historic reasons in Wales than in Ireland to remember English oppression; yet the Tudor government now treated Welsh identity and cultural distinctiveness as allies not obstacles. It helped that the Tudors were by origin Welsh princes, even if they did not choose to emphasize this to their English subjects: they were more sensitive to Welsh interests than to Irish, and the Welsh remained proud of the Welsh blood in the ruling dynasty. In a new departure, most bishops appointed by the Crown to Wales after 1559 were native Welshmen, and several gave patronage to the bards who played an important part in Welsh society. This was like the integration of the learned classes into Protestantism in Gaelic Scotland (see above, pp. 380–81), and completely unlike the English attitude to the Gaelic bardic class in Ireland. A significant factor in binding the Welsh cultural and social elite into the agenda of a Protestant government was the foundation in 1571 of a new college in Oxford University, Jesus College, which immediately augmented an already significant Welsh presence in the university and proved to be a seedbed for Protestant Welsh clergy and gentry.

The Elizabethan authorities also worked creatively alongside a handful of Welsh Protestant enthusiasts to encourage publication of Welsh translations of the English Prayer Book and Bible. The Bible, completed in 1588 by a Cambridge-educated Welsh parish clergyman, William Morgan, was decisive not only in winning the Welsh to Protestantism but in preserving Welsh as a viable language into modern times. Its historical introduction emphasized inaccurately but inspiringly that the Reformation was a restoration of ancient Celtic religion that had been subverted by Roman corruption: so to be Protestant was to be truly Welsh. As a result, Roman Catholicism in Wales atrophied, despite much traditionalism in religious practice and continuing problems in financing the official Church. A survey of 1603 indicates no more than about 3,500 practising Catholics amid a churchgoing population of 212,450: a smaller proportion than in the most conservative parts of England.[72]

In Ireland, there was a completely different atmosphere: the new English plantation strategy made it easy to see all incoming Englishmen as enemies, and the English authorities and their settlers saw Gaelic culture as an obstacle to their schemes. Plantation provoked major warfare in Ireland in the 1570s and 1590s: the Gaelic aristocracy now allied with agents of the Counter-Reformation and with England's Catholic enemies in mainland Europe, principally Spain, which made repeated if unsuccessful efforts to aid Irish Catholics with expeditionary forces. The Tudor regime banned celebrations of the Roman Mass in Ireland in 1568, but this proved to be a futile gesture.[73] Religious energy was all on the Catholic side: having formed its political alliance with the Irish nobility, the Counter-Reformation also began to remould Irish traditionalist religion in its own image, helped by growing prosperity in Ireland that was only partially disrupted by the colonial wars. By the 1580s the older Irish clergy, many of whom had continued to lead worship in traditional forms while officially conforming, were either dying off, or losing heart and quitting the established Church in favour of the Roman obedience. Their replacements had to choose between allegiance to Elizabeth or allegiance to the Pope, and increasing numbers chose the Pope.

As a result, the Irish aristocracy, gentry and town rulers established their own contacts with the rest of Europe independently of Tudor England. Gaelic Ireland, with its long coastline providing abundant sea access to Europe that could bypass England, was a cosmopolitan culture with the ultimate badge of cosmopolitanism in the period – widespread knowledge and use of Latin. A Spaniard from the Armada shipwrecked in north-west Ireland in 1588 was astonished to find peasants who could communicate with him in Latin.[74] Thousands of Irish left for Catholic Spain or France, either permanently or to get an education in a non-Protestant setting. Spain and Portugal proved particularly hospitable to the founding of colleges: between 1590 and 1649, no fewer than six colleges were set up in Iberia, with the prime but not exclusive role of training clergy. Such clergy returned home to build on the existing popularity of the mendicant Orders, whose communal life was unbroken through the Reformation in many parts of western Ireland beyond effective English control, often still in their pre-Reformation buildings. Franciscan Observants led the mission in the field, and after some initial blunders in launching initiatives in Ireland, the Jesuits established a permanent presence from 1597.[75]

In parallel to these developments, by around 1600 life was trickling out of the medieval parish system of the Protestant established Church. Extraordinary anomalies remained in it: unlike in England, Irish chantries had never formally been dissolved, and sometimes their revenues were used to support Catholic clergy. Even in the royal capital Dublin, a covert arrangement of this sort at St Audoen, one of the major parish churches, survived undetected as late as 1611, and still continued thereafter. Given that most of the urban elites were Old English of Catholic sympathies, only a handful of major Irish towns established anything like the life of a well-regulated English Protestant parish, and even in such settings there were further odd survivals which would not have been tolerated in England: for instance, a Corpus Christi play officially sponsored by the city Corporation survived at Kilkenny until at least 1637.[76]

Was there any future for Protestantism in Ireland? The foundation of Trinity College, Dublin, in 1594 very belatedly provided potential for educating a new Protestant governing class, and Trinity came into its own with the eclipse of the Catholic nobility in later years. This was at a time of a major new initiative in establishing a Protestant ascendancy that has cast a long shadow in Irish history: the greatest plantation scheme of all, implemented in Ulster from 1609. The plantation was a reaction to the fact that this far northern region was the most Gaelic and recalcitrant part of the island, and the heartland of military campaigns in the late 1590s by Hugh O'Neill, Earl of Tyrone, which had nearly destroyed English rule in Ireland. Tyrone's eventual failure was followed in 1607 by his flight to exile in mainland Europe along with some of the most important noblemen of the north. In order to fill the power vacuum, and to further the integration of his three Atlantic kingdoms, James VI and I backed schemes to import settlers to Ulster, mostly from the traditionally lawless areas of Scotland on the border with England, where the government felt that they would not be missed.[77]

These new arrivals may not have been particularly convinced Protestants to begin with, but they had every incentive for them to discover and then emphasize their Protestantism in a land-grabbing scheme backed by Protestant money from the city of London. The plantation even reserved estates for the Church of Ireland. One of the chief symbols of the new regime was a newly built cathedral for the diocese of Derry in the renamed city of Londonderry, which was designed to look like the ideal English Protestant urban parish church, and which still dominates the city (see Plate 23b). Not just in Ulster, but throughout the country, New English settlers, characteristically holding a Calvinist theology predisposing them to think of themselves as God's elect set down among benighted and barbarous papists, now came to dominate the established Church of Ireland.[78] Some despised what they regarded as the half-heartedness of the Irish Church's discipline and looked to Scotland, where the established Protestant Church had developed proper presbyteries on the Genevan model.

It was not surprising that in contrast with the vernacular success of the Protestant Church in Wales, attempts to promote Protestantism in Gaelic were late and half-hearted. This was certainly not the fault of Queen Elizabeth: she took a personal interest in efforts to translate the Bible into Irish Gaelic, and since she had paid for the special typeface required, she was particularly angry at the delays which killed the project (a complete Bible did not come until 1685).[79] John Kearny, a Cambridge-educated clergyman and treasurer of St Patrick's Cathedral, Dublin, published a Protestant catechism and alphabet in Gaelic in 1571 in parallel with the Welsh initiatives, but otherwise only after 1600 was a considerable amount of Protestant literature put into Irish Gaelic. By then, the chance that it might have a widespread effect had already been lost. Significantly, the customary Irish Gaelic words for a Protestant became 'Albanac̓' or 'Sasanac̓' – 'Scotsman' or 'Englishman'.[80] By 1600, some Catholic missionary clergy were indeed making that equation between Catholicism and Gaelic culture that later became a powerful myth in much Irish nationalist history. That was an equation that the Catholic Old English (including the Jesuits) deeply resented, and which they were still resisting in the seventeenth century; nevertheless, nearly all the Old English scorned official attempts to bring them over to the Protestant Reformation as much as did the Gaelic regions.

In 1621 the Dublin secular administration officially suspended enforcement of the monetary fine for Catholic recusancy, to the fury of the Protestant bishops. This was one of the chief indications that the established Church of Ireland was grudgingly admitting defeat and handing over pastoral responsibility for most of the population to Roman Catholics, who by now had roughly the same number of clergy working within the island as the Protestants. By 1635 there was a newly-built Jesuit Church in Dublin, where Protestants could go to gawp tourist-fashion at the extraordinary sight of the Counter-Reformation resplendently operating in the King's dominions, complete with glittering high altar and confession boxes straight out of a Mediterranean landscape.[81] Thus in Ireland, the Counter-Reformation achieved one of its greatest victories, although the misguided actions of a Protestant government were probably an indispensable pre-requisite for this Catholic success. In moving now to southern Europe, we will see what Counter-Reformation Catholicism could achieve when the secular power enthusiastically co-operated with the authorities of the Roman Church, and also began to take its version of western Christianity into worldwide empires.

9

The South: Catholic Heartlands

By the 1570s southern Europe was secured for the old Western Church, from the Atlantic coasts of Spain and Portugal to the Venetian towns and territories on the Dalmatian coast of the Adriatic Sea. The great majority of European dioceses not lost to the Protestants were in the south: from a total of around 620 surviving Roman Catholic bishoprics around 1600, no fewer than 315 were Italian, and 67 were in Spain (where dioceses had always been larger and wealthier); that compared with rather fewer than 60 in total surviving in northern Europe, eastwards from the Spanish Netherlands through the Holy Roman Empire to Poland-Lithuania.[1] In the absence of Protestantism, the task of Catholic churchmen was to remould the multifarious patterns of medieval devotion and religious practice that might be considered vaguely Christian into a form compatible with the strategies laid down at the Council of Trent.

This was no small task. One sixteenth-century Portuguese Archbishop was dumbfounded when in the course of his visitation a well-meaning procession of peasants welcomed him to their community, chanting 'Blessed be the Holy Trinity and His sister the Virgin Mary'.[2] To some extent the creation of Tridentine Europe was a matter of using the apparatus of coercion possessed by both Church and civil power. However, Tridentine Catholicism would have been a barren and empty creed if it had not also genuinely sought to make people do more than understand their faith – love it and claim it for their own. The story of southern Europe is partly about monarchs, bishops and inquisitors, but it is also a tale of intense personal searches for God and his saints, pursued in settings as various as the bleak cork-lined cells of a Portuguese Capuchin hilltop convent battered by Atlantic gales, the newly-gilded splendours of Baroque basilicas, or the crowded market-places and street-corners of the Mediterranean world. Since the missionary effort of Tridentine Catholicism stretched out into the Americas, Asia and Africa, there is good reason to see it as the largest such enterprise since the Church's expansion in the first five centuries after the life of Christ.

ITALY: THE COUNTER-REFORMATION'S HEART

To appreciate the dual face of the Counter-Reformation it is logical to begin at its heart: the papacy newly consolidating its position in Rome in the wake of the Council of Trent. Any visiting traveller in the late sixteenth century would be impressed by Rome's outward symbols of rebuilding and growth beyond its medieval urban core. Within the vast walled circuit of the ancient imperial capital spanning the Tiber, streets, houses and shops were springing up in areas where for centuries there had been little but fields, lonely churches, ruins and waste ground; the sound of building and rebuilding was everywhere. This was the setting for some of the greatest achievements of the new triumphalist architecture of the Church, culminating in the sensationally monumental (as well as sensationally expensive) rebuilding of St Peter's, repeatedly extended in conception and grandeur by its succession of architects (see Plate 11). Around the base of Michelangelo's dome, shining in giant gold letters far above the great seated statue of the apostle and the crypt which housed his tomb, was the Latin proclamation 'Thou art Peter; and on this Rock will I build my Church' – this was the biblical basis of the Pope's new power, founded on the earliest days of Christianity, and a fitting motto for what was taking place in Rome. For the rebuilding of the city had an unexpected and sensational by-product: the rediscovery of a lost aspect of its Christian past. The early Christians had tunnelled into the soft Roman tufa stone to create underground labyrinths of tombs: some of these catacomb complexes were very large indeed, and millions of bodies had been interred in them. Many tombs became the object of early pilgrimage, but in Rome's eighth- and ninth-century troubles, devotions concentrated in more secure locations and the catacombs were abandoned and nearly all forgotten.

The first major rediscovery was in 1578, and was quickly followed by others: for many scholars, it was the frescos and sculpture which aroused humanist and antiquarian interest, but from the beginning the myriad bones and skulls also stirred the imagination of the excavators. They were much encouraged by the popular and charismatic priest Filippo Neri, who in the 1570s was securing the foundation of a new company of secular priests known as the Congregation of the Oratory. As early as the 1540s Neri was fascinated by the only catacomb then known, and he gave the catacombs a special place in his intense vision of Catholic vocation; the Oratorians continued to be at the heart of the catacomb explorations. It was obvious from dating these tombs that they contained a cloud of witnesses to the early

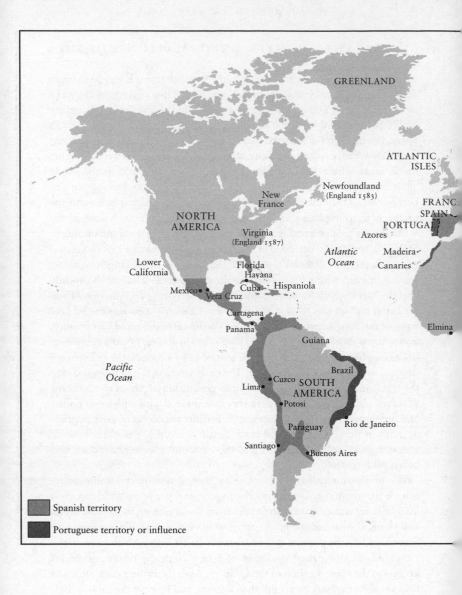

GREENLAND

ATLANTIC
ISLES

Newfoundland
(England 1583)

FRANCE
SPAIN
PORTUGAL

New
France

NORTH
AMERICA

Virginia
(England 1587)

Azores

*Atlantic
Ocean*

Madeira

Lower
California

Florida

Canaries

Havana

Mexico

Cuba

Hispaniola

Vera Cruz

Cartagena

Panama

Elmina

Guiana

*Pacific
Ocean*

Brazil

Cuzco

Lima

SOUTH
AMERICA

Potosi

Paraguay

Rio de Janeiro

Santiago

Buenos Aires

Spanish territory

Portuguese territory or influence

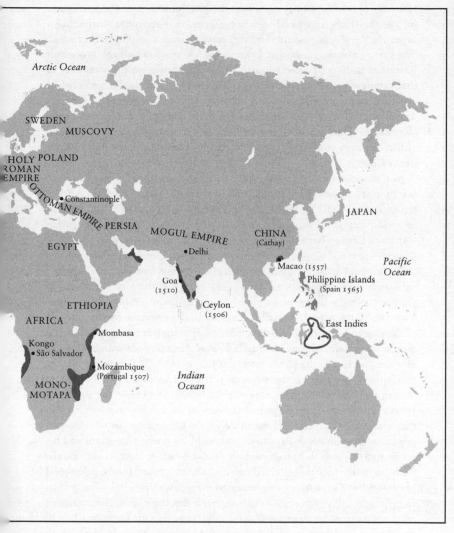

Arctic Ocean

SWEDEN
MUSCOVY

HOLY POLAND
ROMAN
EMPIRE

OTTOMAN EMPIRE
• Constantinople

PERSIA

EGYPT

MOGUL EMPIRE
• Delhi

CHINA
(Cathay)

JAPAN

Pacific
Ocean

Macao (1557)

Philippine Islands
(Spain 1565)

Goa
(1510)

Ceylon
(1506)

ETHIOPIA

AFRICA

Kongo
• São Salvador

Mombasa

East Indies

Mozambique
(Portugal 1507)

Indian
Ocean

MONO-
MOTAPA

4. *The Iberian world empires, c. 1600*

Church's heroic days of persecution: the general absence of identification for the skeletons, combined with some genuine martyrdom stories and a generous helping of wishful thinking, now proved a helpful combination. The catacombs were a potent weapon for a Church which the Protestant Reformation had attacked because it had departed from the standards of that same early Church, but whose trump card against the Protestants had always been the sneering question, 'Where was your Church before Luther?' The Church of Rome had reaffirmed old certainties in the decrees of the Council of Trent: now God was favouring it by revealing a new supply of authentic saints who mocked the Protestants' claims to be the new martyrs of the Church.[3]

Just as these ancient martyrs were revealed once more, Catholics were beginning to be martyred afresh, both in mission fields overseas and in the struggle to win back Protestant northern Europe: the catacombs proved to be an inspiration for many to action and to heroism. In 1597 the Oratorian Cardinal Cesare Baronio, the greatest contemporary historian of the Church's past and assistant of Filippo Neri, decided to restore the neglected little church of SS Nereus and Achilleus from which he took his Cardinal's title, in a quiet marshy area of the city near the ruins of the Baths of Caracalla. To dominate the interior, he commissioned a sequence of frescos from the Mannerist artist Niccolò Circignani, depicting the martyrs' deaths of the twelve Apostles. Most of them manage to look reasonably composed during their awful deaths, but Bartholomew cannot restrain an expression of agony amid the ghastliness of being flayed alive. This fresco cycle has rarely been surpassed in the sado-masochism of its detail, but Circignani was already something of an expert in this genre. In 1582–3 the Society of Jesus commissioned him to provide frescos of ancient and modern English martyrs for the chapel in the English College at Rome, together with martyrdom sequences in other Roman churches. In all these, Circignani and his Jesuit patrons had the programmatic intent of inspiring heroism for the faith, just at the time that emigré English students training for the priesthood in the English College were beginning to return to Elizabeth I's England to face torture and death (see Plates 12, 13). From the 1620s, the catacomb excavations were further turned to benefit the worldwide Catholic Church: bones were extracted, provided with a name where necessary, declared to be those of martyrs, bureaucratically processed and sent out from Rome to strengthen and excite the faithful wherever there was need.[4]

The great rebuilding of Rome and the civil service which fostered it had to be paid for, and most of the money came from the papacy's inheritance of territories in central Italy that formed the Papal States. Indeed, with the

9a. The Armada Portrait of Queen Elizabeth I attributed to George Gower, *c.* 1588–9. In this most triumphant of images of Elizabeth, at 55 looking implausibly youthful as usual, the Queen casually rests her hand on a globe showing the Americas, while in the background, 'before and after' pictures reveal the destruction of the Spanish Armada around the English coast.

9b. The gable of the south porch at Priston parish church, Somerset, contains the memorial of 1589 to the parson Thomas Wats, including a fierce exhortation to repentance. The inscription probably replaced a statue of a saint in a niche.

S·Vrſula Deonoti Cornubiæ in Anglia reguli filia cum undecim
millibus uirginum prope Coloniam Agrippinam ab Hunnis pro
Chriſti fide et uirginitate ſeruanda, partim in Rheno merſæ, partim
ſagittis confixæ duplices palmas adeptæ ſunt·

12 One of Niccoló Circignani's English martyrs depicted in the chapel of the
English College in Rome (now only surviving in engraved form) was St Ursula,
with her improbable eleven thousand virgins: she was included since she was
said to have come from Cornwall. Against the background of Cologne, the
Huns are methodically setting about Ursula and her virgins with arrows or
drowning the rest in the Rhine. Her name was borrowed for the vastly
successful sixteenth-century foundation of the Ursulines.

Viri plurimi in Anglia pro fide Catholica retinenda hoc qui expressus
est modo eousq; cruciantur donec uniuersi corporis artus singulatim
luxentur. Sic Edmundus Campianus Societatis Iesu religiosus,
Rodulphus Sheruinus, Alexander Briantus, alijq; Sacerdotes summ.
Pontificis Alumni acerbissimè torti fuere. Anno Dñi 1581.1582.et 158

13. A Roman Catholic priest is tortured on the rack in the presence of an
English Protestant bishop and Privy Councillors of Elizabeth I, with two
further captive priests observing. The caption names the former students of the
English College martyred between 1581 and 1583 (the date of Circignani's
frescos in the chapel), beginning with the exceptionally brutal torture and
execution of the Jesuit Edmund Campion as a traitor at Tyburn, London.

14a. An ingenious transformation by the late seventeenth-century German writing-master Johann Michael Püchler of Henrikus Hondius's sixteenth-century portrait of John Calvin: the elderly Reformer with his thin beard is clothed in the words which were his stock-in-trade – a biographical description and texts from scripture and the Reformed metrical psalter. In the more relaxed decades after the Thirty Years' War, Püchler was ecumenical in his artistry, creating similar images alike of Luther, Protestant and Catholic monarchs and Catholic saints.

14b. Amsterdam seen from the ships in harbour in its glory days in the late seventeenth century. Chief city of the Reformed Protestant Netherlands, it was also a haven for Jews and the unorthodox of all descriptions.

15a. The soaring magnificence which is the familiar modern image of Cologne Cathedral was woefully incomplete after work stopped in the 1560s: this is the south view of the Cathedral in 1824. The giant crane on the west towers had been in place since the sixteenth century.

15b. The pilgrimage church of Our Lady of Victory by the Czech architect Jan Blazej Santini-Aichel (1677–1723) commemorates the battle of the White Mountain (Bila Hora), outside Prague, which shattered the Bohemian Protestant cause. It is a superb miniature example of Czech baroque.

Actus fidei prout in Hispania celebratur

16. This seventeenth-century Dutch engraving claims to be a picture of Spain, but the background scene is Dutch: a reminder that the Spanish Inquisition would have come to the Netherlands if the war for independence had failed. Note the procession of accused and convicted in their sanbenitos, the prominent altar complete with reredos flanked by royal and episcopal 'boxes', and the generally theatrical design of the scaffold and spectators' seats.

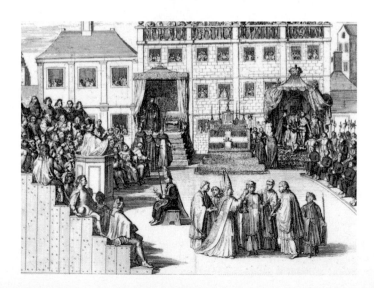

loss of revenues from northern Europe, the Pope came to rely for around three-quarters of his income on the Papal States: from being one of the most lightly taxed political units in Italy, they became one of the most burdened, particularly after a ruthlessly thorough reorganization by the energetic Pope Sixtus V (1585–90). The government of the Papal States was also unique: like all other European monarchs, the Pope was intensifying his bureaucratic control over his subjects, but this did not produce a secular administrative class, since all the posts of any importance remained in the hands of clerics. Papal governors were indeed now given the chance to appropriate power which had previously been exercised by the old civic authorities: in his own fashion the Pope was embarking on state-building, like many contemporary secular monarchs of Europe.[5]

At the head of the remodelled clerical bureaucracy were the cardinals. In the early seventeenth century, the College of Cardinals was at the height of its power and influence; the cardinals' extensive households provided opportunities for advancement then unparalleled in Europe, although from mid-century the French monarchy's recovery of stability and power sent alert careerists northwards to Paris rather than to Rome. Many cardinals were from the leading ancient noble families of central Italy, but in the decades after the 1520s, the upheavals in the Church's central administration triggered by the shock of the early Reformation resulted in a considerable influx of new talent in Roman administration which eventually affected the College of Cardinals.[6] Once established, they were able with luck or perseverance to promote their family into the ranks of the highest secular nobility: the benchmark for such ambition was provided by the new arrivals from Siena, the Borghese, who owed their huge wealth and exalted status to the election of Cardinal Camillo Borghese as Pope Paul V in 1605.

Such good fortune needed much nourishment with money and land: a host of privileges, lucrative administrative licences and permissions to acquire church lands trickled outwards from the papal desk to grateful relatives of deserving clerics. The wealthy layfolk of Italy thus became 'the silent share holders in the church' – a solid foundation of support for Tridentine Catholicism. Catholic rhetoric of reforming the Church significantly shifted before and after the Council of Trent: earlier, the demands were for a thoroughgoing reform of the system of providing to church office, an end to pluralism, simony (the buying of clerical positions) and nepotism (promotion of relatives). Later, the emphasis was on personal devotion, the reform of theology, the creation of new or reformed religious orders. Some structural change had occurred in the meantime – there were many fewer pluralist bishops, for instance – but otherwise there were still plenty of unreformed opportunities for benefiting from the Church's wealth, and a good deal less attention to doing something about it.[7]

If an alert visitor from northern Europe tried to get to grips with the religious scene in Italy, one absence would be immediately obvious: there were no vernacular Bibles in the houses of the laity. Pope Paul V was perfectly serious when in 1606 he furiously confronted the Venetian ambassador with the rhetorical question 'Do you not know that so much reading of Scripture ruins the Catholic religion?'[8] One of the tasks of the 1564 Tridentine Index had been to keep vernacular Bibles away from the faithful; anyone wanting to read the Bible in a modern language required permission from the local bishop, and in the 1596 Roman Index the ban became complete and without exception. In Italy, the Index's ban was enforced. Bibles were publicly and ceremonially burned, like heretics; even literary versions of scriptural stories in drama or poetry were frowned on. As a result, between 1567 and 1773, not a single edition of an Italian-language Bible was printed anywhere in the Italian peninsula.[9] Even a visitor from the Catholic parts of Germany would find this astonishing: there a ban on Bibles would have been highly dangerous to a Church constantly confronting biblically literate Protestants. By 1600, however, Italy had no Protestants to worry about. Thanks to the vigilance of the Roman Inquisition, the last remnants of Italian evangelicalism were dispersed into exile in the 1560s, and by the 1580s heresy had more or less disappeared.

With no Bibles to sustain evangelical belief, this was hardly surprising. Thereafter, Italian dissent where it appeared tended to be the result of an individual's independent imagination, and it was likely to end up as free thought or atheism rather than Protestantism. The only exceptions were Protestant communities which managed to survive in the north, in remote Alpine valleys on the borders with Switzerland. Up to the mid-seventeenth century, the ancient dissenting communities of Waldensians in the western Alps beat off military efforts by the Dukes of Savoy to destroy them, and their troubles drew them closer to their one immediate source of Protestant support, the city of Geneva, which supplied them with pastors and gradually remoulded their distinctive beliefs into more conventional Reformed paths. In the high country to the south of the Savoyard capital of Turin, the small Marchesate of Saluzzo was for decades a haven for religious dissent because the French captured it in 1548. Saluzzo was therefore protected against the aggressive Catholicism of the Dukes of Savoy until Henri IV handed it over to Savoy by a peace treaty in 1601, bringing an end to the Marchesate's *de facto* toleration for Protestantism. Similarly, the valley of Valtellina and its outrunners in the mountains north-east of Milan benefited from the jurisdiction which the Swiss Graubünden held over them; they imitated the religious openness to be found in the Graubünden until the Spanish garrisons in Milan brutally dispersed Valtellina's Protestants in the early seventeenth century.[10] Thanks to the effect of the Index and of the ecclesiastical cultural repression that accompanied it, much was marginalized which was not Protestant and represented the best of Italy's past culture: among the works that the Church ordered Italians not to read were Boccaccio's *Decameron*, the poetry of Petrarch and Ariosto, the writings of Castiglione on conduct and Machiavelli on politics. It is arguable that what the Franco-Italian wars of the half-century after 1494 had begun in curtailing the achievements of the Italian Renaissance and the vibrant civic life on which it was based, the Tridentine version of the Counter-Reformation completed in the next half-century.[11]

It would nevertheless be highly misleading to portray the Catholic Church's power in Italy as monolithic. The Roman Index of forbidden books and the work of the Roman Inquisition got off to a shaky start, associated as they were with the discredited regime of Pope Paul IV (chapter 6, pp. 277–80). To begin with, the officials running the Index were not professional scholars equipped with skills in languages or theology, and they were overwhelmed by a task for which no coherent strategy had been devised. The muddle and infighting were reduced when Robert Bellarmine, a Jesuit who was a very considerable scholar, joined the team trying to censor all the books of Europe. Bellarmine had the breadth of vision to see what was dangerous to the Counter-Reformation project and what was not, and he established his own priorities: Latin mattered more than vernacular languages, since it was the tongue that anyone of any importance could read. However, even Bellarmine found himself in trouble when his own *Controversies*, a massive and authoritative refutation of Protestant heresy, infuriated the masterful Pope Sixtus V because it placed limits on papal claims to jurisdiction over secular monarchs: Sixtus (who thoroughly distrusted the entire Jesuit enterprise) actually wanted this work placed on the Index. Even though Bellarmine survived this clash and spent three decades in charge of censorship, the work of the Index was never as effective as he might have wished. As is so often the way with such efforts, a listing of a book on the Index was a positive incentive for the irreverent to acquire the banned item: it could provide the best international publicity that a publisher could desire, and all free of charge. It was probably at least as good for sales as an entry in the *Bibliotheca selecta* of 1593–1603, the Jesuit Antonio Possevino's attempt to provide a positive reading-list for good Catholics.[12]

The Pope also had to face the fact that outside his own central Italian dominions, other civil rulers had their own agendas. Amid the Italian peninsula's political confusion, the great external power of Spain directly occupied Sicily and the south, and also the Duchy of Milan in the far north: the Spanish authorities were not going to let the Roman authorities usurp power belonging to the King of Spain. In the north-west was the Duchy of Savoy, Catholic Italy's line of defence against the heretics of Geneva, the city which had once acknowledged Savoyard allegiance. Carlo Emanuele I, Duke for fifty years from 1580, was an outstanding ruler: physically slight, he was cultured, quick-witted and a ruthless military campaigner. He was a devout son of the Church, and the papacy was grateful to him for his repeated attacks on and long-term economic blockade of Geneva, which did much to isolate and weaken the city. Nevertheless, what came first for Carlo Emanuele was the promotion of his Duchy and the strengthening of the power of his ducal house of Savoy, which in the end in the nineteenth-century reunification of Italy proved the nemesis of Habsburg power in the peninsula, and which after 1870 humiliatingly corralled successive Popes inside the walls of the Vatican.

Equally self-conscious in defence of its interests and much more openly confrontational in its attitude to the papacy was the Republic of Venice. Venice emerged from the traumas of the early sixteenth-century Italian wars battered but unbowed, as the only truly independent state in the peninsula outside Spain's control, still holding its Mediterranean empire maintained by a powerful fleet. The city itself was proudly Catholic in its own fashion – of its population of around 135,000 in the 1580s, more than 4,000 were priests, monks or nuns, and Venice's rich devotional life was sustained by powerful lay-run confraternities, whose broadly based membership embracing rich merchant and poor artisan alike contributed much to the city's famous social and political stability.[13]

Yet the Republic's authorities had spent centuries on the religious frontier between eastern and western Christianity, and their cosmopolitan and commercial history left Venetians with a reputation for religious cynicism, to which they added in the Reformation era a profound distrust of Spanish intentions, not excluding Spanish Catholicism. They generally kept the local Inquisition on a short leash, and with European-wide commercial interests, they were not inclined to persecute visiting foreign Protestants who might be important for trade. The famous University of Padua in the Venetian Terraferma continued to attract Protestants from as far away as England, long after the Council of Trent had sought to exclude such heretics. With pleasing irony, after Henry VIII permanently suspended the study of canon law in English universities, the high-flying ecclesiastical lawyers of England's

Protestant Reformation kept up to date by legal studies in Padua. Here, northern Europeans from troubled and contested Reformations might meet in a more relaxed world, as when in 1574 the young Philip Sidney, white hope of militant internationalist-minded English Protestantism, was among those witnessing the doctoral examination in law of the self-exiled English Catholic John Hart.[14]

In Venice, more than anywhere else, voices were openly raised against the package of doctrinal and administrative reform that emerged from the Council of Trent, providing expression for the anger of many southern European bishops and conciliarists at Rome's efforts to centralize authority. The governors of the Republic listened sympathetically to local spokesmen of such clergy, particularly when quarrels between Rome and Venice over jurisdiction and the administration of church property culminated in 1606 in a tense stand-off between the Republic and Pope Paul V: the Pope laid Venice under an interdict. The Venetian government retaliated by choosing as its official theological consultant a friar prominent in the small Servite Order, Paolo Sarpi. He openly talked of Rome usurping episcopal power and showed alarming interest in Protestant theology (not surprisingly, Rome blocked repeated Venetian nominations of him to bishoprics). With Sarpi's encouragement, the Venetian authorities ignored the interdict, which the Pope was forced to withdraw after a year. The affair was of huge interest to northern European Protestants, particularly to the open-minded King in the Atlantic Isles, James VI and I, who saw what was happening in Venice as offering great possibilities for his own vision of a rapprochement across the Reformation divide (chapter 12, pp. 513–17). His ambassador in Venice, Sir Henry Wotton, optimistically commissioned a translation of the English Book of Common Prayer into Italian, and used it to show off English worship for Venetians in his embassy residence.[15]

Even after the Pope's reconciliation with Venice, Paolo Sarpi retained his office in the city up to his death in 1623 (even though he may well have privately abandoned dogmatic Christianity in his last years), protected despite his papal excommunication and at least one assassination attempt. He wrote an acerbic but well-informed history of the Council of Trent, portraying it as a lost opportunity for genuine all-embracing European church reform. His book was so controversial that he had it first published anonymously in Protestant London, an enterprise overseen by an exiled clerical colleague of his from the Venetian dominions, Marcantonio de Dominis, the Archbishop of Spalato (now Split, in Croatia). De Dominis, a scholarly Dalmatian nobleman, accomplished astronomer and former Jesuit, was so furious at papal interference in his Dalmatian archbishopric that in 1616 he left his native land to join the Church of England, causing a great sensation. An exotic trophy for northern Europe, he was welcomed as a celebrity and made Dean of Windsor, but he was disappointed at not finding the ecumenical spirit that King James I had led him to expect in English Protestantism. After six years he was back to Roman Catholicism and Italy, though his naturally combative nature led to further rows, and he died in a prison of the Roman Inquisition.[16]

By contrast, an Archbishop in another great northern Italian city has come to be seen as the archetype of the Italian Counter-Reformation: Carlo Borromeo, Archbishop of Milan. Borromeo was propelled into the service of the Church through archetypal unreformed nepotism: while still in minor orders and without a theological training, he became Cardinal-nephew and secretary to his uncle Pope Pius IV. His administrative gifts were much in evidence in saving the last sessions of the Council of Trent from breakdown, and in 1560 he was also appointed Administrator of the Pope's native archdiocese of Milan. Even then, he might have emulated his aristocratic cousin Markus Sittich, who the following year through the same papal uncle's favour became Bishop of the equally strategic diocese of Konstanz, and outlived Carlo by a decade, but after only eight years had virtually abandoned his unruly charge for the comforts of Rome.[17] Instead, Carlo discovered a steely priestly vocation out of a family tragedy which burst on him without warning and triggered a conversion experience: his elder brother, head of the Borromeo line, died suddenly in 1562, and Carlo found himself expected (even by his uncle the Pope) to do his family duty and marry. Like Luther he rebelled against the Pope, but in a rebellion that adroitly made condemnation impossible, he rebelled into sacred obedience and contrived to be clandestinely ordained priest.

This creatively independent view of what constituted submission to papal authority is reminiscent of Borromeo's hero Ignatius Loyola, and it characterized his subsequent hyperactive career as Archbishop, the first to be resident in Milan for eighty years. After some heart-searchings about whether to become a monk, and following some decorous haggling with the Pope, Borromeo was eventually consecrated Archbishop in 1565. He pointedly made his triumphal entry into the city in his archbishop's robes, not dressed as a cardinal, the emissary and servant of Rome.[18] The Roman Catholic Church has nevertheless subsequently made sure that in the iconography of this prelate who has become a model of a saintly church leader, he is always portrayed in the robes of a cardinal rather than those of an archbishop.

In practice, Borromeo proved very ready to take his own initiatives in imposing his own vision of what the Council of Trent represented. He took a high view of his episcopal authority as successor to Ambrose, the great Milanese Bishop of the fourth century, and his self-assertion had a double aspect: like Borromeo himself, Ambrose had been an aristocrat who could (and did) outface both Pope and Emperor. Just as Protestant Edmund Grindal, far to the north in England, was inspired by the memory of Ambrose to defiance of the civil power (chapter 8, p. 384), Borromeo was ready to confront the civil authority, the Spanish Governors of Milan, if he felt the need. However, he got away with more than Grindal found possible under Queen Elizabeth, because he could draw on his reservoir of support in Rome as a Cardinal of the Church. He successfully excluded the Spanish Inquisition from his archdiocese, even though it was operating in the southern Spanish territories of Naples and Sicily, and in one particularly bitter row with the government over jurisdiction in 1573, he went so far as to excommunicate Governor Requesens.[19]

Such struggles were the background to two decades of energetic reform and reorganization, in a city of particular strategic importance both to Spain and to the Roman Church: it was on the frontier with Swiss Protestantism and so something of a showcase for what the Tridentine reforms might mean. Borromeo led by example, showing notable heroism in personal action during city crises like outbreaks of plague. He had the advantage of being able to harness the various existing corporate initiatives of reform in clerical and monastic life pioneered in Milan and northern Italy in the 1530s (chapter 5, pp. 218–19), but he was also an obsessive administrator, believing in the virtues of centralization, standardization and filing systems. He was determined to regulate the elite activism of such clerical associations as the Theatines and the Barnabites and extend it throughout his entire parish clergy: he was one of the first founders of a diocesan seminary as decreed by the Council of Trent, to the extent that he has become the patron saint of seminarians – an historical injustice to the English Cardinal-Archbishop Reginald Pole, the true pioneer of this work. Borromeo ordered all priests with pastoral charges to preach every Sunday and feast day, and he even organized monthly congregations of these clergy in which (after discussion of reports on the parishes) designated victims practised their preaching in front of him; afterwards they had to deposit their text with the Archbishop for inspection. Once more there is a striking comparison with his Protestant contemporary Archbishop Grindal, determinedly defending the clerical 'prophesyings' to Elizabeth I – but Borromeo possessed the effective coercive power which Grindal lacked.[20]

Borromeo was convinced that confession had a crucial role in regulating the lives of the faithful, and he was determined that the practice should be under his close control. He introduced the confessional box to churches (chapter 7, p. 328). Naturally, he paid close attention to the quality of clergy hearing confessions: they were forbidden to operate without his licence and were given frequent and detailed instructions, to the extent of having to attend weekly classes in confessional technique. This was a notable innovation, and just like the Archbishop's promotion of the parish clergy's preaching ministry, it struck a blow against the specialist roles of the Orders of friars as preachers and confessors, which was one of the most notable features of the late medieval church – the friars, of course, had largely been free of the authority of diocesan bishops. Other bishops copied Borromeo's move, and for the same reasons.[21] More easily brought under episcopal discipline than the friars were the newly established female communities of the Ursulines, who were already committed to the instruction and education of girls: seeing the value of this resource, Borromeo devoted much energy to restructuring and disciplining the Ursulines' communal life, making them a more conventional order of enclosed nuns. Having achieved this, he ordered that all the dioceses of his province should support their work (chapter 16, p. 644). In the parallel task of educating boys, he vigorously supported and systematized the work pioneered by Castellino da Castello in the Confraternity of Christian Doctrine (chapter 5, p. 219), with astonishing results: by the time of his death, the diocese of Milan had 740 schools, around 3,000 teachers and 40,000 pupils under instruction.[22]

Borromeo's personal emblem was taken from an element of his family heraldry, the word HUMILITAS ('humility') crowned. It was a useful reminder that his own autocratic nature did not incline to humility, and needed constant self-discipline, producing in him what one modern historian has called an 'emaciated joylessness', a Puritanism which one might have more readily associated with the likes of Archbishop Grindal.[23] The demands he made on himself made him harsh and demanding to others. Harassed, overworked clergy must have sighed when some fresh order came down from the archiepiscopal palace, for instance regulating the exact size of linen cloths for the Eucharist, or requiring the replacement of sponges with bristle-brushes for the sprinkling of holy water, so that the faithful could more effectively be reminded of the biblical cry that they should be purged with hyssop.[24]

There were more damaging excesses. Borromeo's pressure on both confessors and the confessional was pushed to unwise limits: one-to-one confession in total confidentiality is potentially one of the most intimate and individual relationships constructed by humanity, and Borromeo tried to turn it towards social engineering. From 1576, in a well-intentioned effort to reduce infant mortality, he ordered confessors to check whether women were obeying an ecclesiastical order to keep their babies in a separate cradle rather than sleeping with them in their own beds. Women laughed at these earnest interfering celibate men, or worse still, they stopped coming to confession during the twelve first months of their child's life to which the decree applied. Borromeo ordered that dancing should cease on Sundays and feast-days, on penalty of the offending dancers being unable to marry for two years afterwards – that was very serious, because the main point of such dancing was as a courtship ritual. When he tried to suppress the Milanese carnival, the fury of people and civic authorities alike was so great that both Rome and the King of Spain had to intervene to calm things down. Small wonder, then, that many of Borromeo's conscientious contemporaries among the Italian episcopate felt that he had gone too far in his enthusiasm.[25]

Tridentine regulation in the style of Carlo Borromeo would always be a paradise for the authoritarian or the small-minded, but there were also clergy with the common sense and compassionate concern for their flocks to make it work in a more humane fashion – indeed, Carlo's rather more tactful cousin Federigo Borromeo did much in his own years as Archbishop of Milan to implement a modified version of his predecessor's schemes, making them a model of how to run a Counter-Reformation diocese. Given sensitivity, the Italian Tridentine project could benefit from a huge resource of entrenched popular devotion. In the large towns and cities in particular, the well-developed medieval network of confraternities could be revived and extended (preferably under firmer clerical supervision). By 1600 it is likely that one in every three or four adult males in these urban settings belonged to a confraternity, with substantial numbers of women and teenagers as well.[26]

Besides confraternities, shrines took a new lease of life, aided by the sudden accession of the Roman catacombs. Symptomatic of the revival of confidence and the renewed interest in saints is that a new canonization of a saint by a Pope took place in 1588, after an interval of sixty-three years, and it was followed by the creation of one of the new centralized agencies of the Church, the Sacred Congregation of Rites and Ceremonies, which to this day has as part of its brief the examination of claims for sainthood. This was an attempt to bring scholarly and bureaucratic exactitude to a process which had long been a matter of group intuition and popular acclamation, and its work remained in creative tension with the enthusiasm of the ordinary faithful.[27] Laypeople's appetite for holy places and hagiography still often stayed beyond the control of senior clergy, many of whom had university training which made them uneasily aware of the standards in historical evidence set by some humanist scholars over the previous century. Other clergy encouraged their flocks in their appetite for marvels. Orazio Torsellino, a Jesuit enthusiast for the Holy House of Loreto, published a bestselling guidebook to its wonders in 1594: his work was worthy of a modern popular novelist, and with about as much historical content, and it hugely boosted the shrine. The supposed Carmelite friar-saint Simon Stock furnishes another instructive example.

The Carmelite friars had long enjoyed an imaginative relationship with their history, which they prolonged back from the twelfth century to the time of the prophet Elijah, and which they used as a weapon in battles for prestige against their fraternal rivals the Dominicans. The Dominicans claimed particular favour from the Virgin Mary, whom they asserted had provided them with their distinctive dress, together with privileges for laypeople who died wearing that part of it known as the scapular. The Carmelites duly discovered that Our Lady had duplicated her scapular promise to Simon Stock, an early English Carmelite (himself remarkably elusive in ordinary historical documents). By 1609, an unsympathetic official of the Portuguese Inquisition smelled a rat in Simon Stock's vision and banned all mention of it. Rome backed up the inquisitor, until it became evident that the faithful throughout southern Europe were furious at the prospect of losing the benefits of Carmelite scapulars, whereupon the Roman Inquisition hastily climbed down. By 1613 Carmelite supporters among the laity were once more in legal possession of their scapulars. Boosted by this consumer confidence, the Carmelites remained little abashed by the Inquisition's strong recommendation to play down their more extravagant claims for the scapular.[28]

When neither Carlo Borromeo nor the Roman Inquisition could guarantee to get their own way, it is not surprising that the restructuring of Italian religion was slow and difficult, particularly in the remote south. It was a slow process even to renew leadership there: in the great Archdiocese of Naples, the first archbishop to exemplify the new Tridentine style was a Theatine, Paolo Burali d'Arezzo, who was not consecrated until 1576.[29] Trent had emphasized the role of the parish clergy, properly trained in a seminary provided in each diocese, but these colleges cost money to set up properly and needed sustained expertise to staff efficiently: as late as 1630, fewer than half the dioceses of Italy had established some form of seminary, and some had failed, so probably most parish priests had not so far received seminary training. In the south, most dioceses did not acquire a seminary until the mid-eighteenth century.[30] It was not easy to reform secular clergy who did not wish to be reformed, particularly when they were members of some well-entrenched collegiate church with plenty of friends among the nobility.

Some other strategies must be devised to capture the people's devotion not so dependent on the inadequate clerical resources locally available. The answer was for professional missionaries to treat much of Italy as a mission field, just like the expanding Iberian conquests in the New World or the Portuguese territorial toeholds and commercial contacts in Africa and Asia. Leading this work as part of their worldwide task were the Jesuits, who began experimenting with this approach in the Terra d'Otranto in the far south-eastern peninsula of Italy in 1573; they pointedly referred to such areas (and similar remote parts of Catholic Europe) as the 'Indies'. In the same way that they were prepared to adapt the non-essentials of Christianity to suit local conditions in Asia (see below, pp. 433–4), they set out to accommodate their message to the setting, and what rapidly became clear to them was that they must leave behind the austere devotional style preferred by Ignatius Loyola: they must use every device of dramatic sensation to capture the imaginations of a people who had a fixed idea of what the Church represented, and apparently thought little about it. The Jesuits became actors and showmen: their visit must be a heart-stopping special occasion, bringing God's circus to town.

The show the Jesuits staged was the setpiece devotional mission, the elements of which, with their usual ability to borrow a good idea from others, they adapted from the earlier revivalist processions and eucharistic devotions of Antonio Zaccaria's Barnabites in Milan (Chapter 5, p. 219). The classic exponent was the Modenese Jesuit Paolo Segneri the elder, who was reckoned to have travelled barefoot through more than 540 missions in north and central Italy during the mid and late seventeenth century; his extraordinary dedication and persistence built on a tradition well established in previous decades.[31] The pattern for the mission was to identify some central market town with a hinterland of villages: the main rallies would be in town, but during the eight or ten days of the event, representatives of the mission toured the outlying areas in what they called 'raids' – *missioni scorriere*. Besides dramatic preaching, the focus of the mission was the Blessed Sacrament in the form of the consecrated eucharistic wafer: it was borne in triumphal procession through the streets, but also exposed or exhibited for devotional contemplation in one or more churches, surrounded by glowing banks of candles, customarily for forty hours as the Barnabites had first done in Milan. The Jesuits quickly saw the potential of this devotion. In 1556 they staged the 'forty-hours' during a mission in the central Italian city of Macerata, and for the first time they deliberately fixed the date to clash with the local carnival: the two shows were in competition, and it was the Jesuits' aim to upstage their rivals.[32]

Carnival was a time when normal social values were deliberately turned upside-down. The mission sought to do the same in order to shock the audience into repentance and true love of God. Preachers could flourish the Church's ultimate trump card in the game of toppling human pretensions: death. Onofrio Saraco SJ used a particularly demoralizing version of this gambit: he would preface his sermon by calling out to ask whether various local notables were present, drawing on a list of the recently dead which he had discreetly obtained beforehand. When the response came that the people named were all dead, he had the perfect opening for reminding his audience of their human frailty and parading before them the terrors of hellfire. When addressing an elite audience, preachers might adroitly play up this deconstruction of the social order to emphasize the shockingly claustrophobic and undeferential atmosphere of Hell: respectable folk would be herded together with their social inferiors in an eternal prison, 'pressed together, distilled in decaying and contagious humours, and touching mouth to mouth'.[33] As the impact of the missions grew, living local dignitaries willingly co-operated with such carnivalesque inversion: they were increasingly ready to humiliate themselves in the missionary carnival, for instance forming groups known as 'the slaves of the Virgin', loaded with chains and headed by a crucifix, or leading the *strascino* devotion in which the penitent licked the ground in token of worthlessness.[34]

Such carnivalesque missions had an extraordinary impact across the social divides. The missioners were given adulation as fervent as that offered a modern pop star: they were regarded as living saints, and their converts lovingly preserved small relics of their visits, personal possessions or clothes. The missionary clergy sought to leave an infrastructure in their wake, founding confraternities which would carry on their work in devotion to the Eucharist or the Blessed Virgin, but they returned repeatedly to stage missions in the same territory, anticipating the mechanism of religious revival that became such an integral part of British and American evangelical Protestantism during the eighteenth century, and which seems a recurrent feature of western Christianity. The religious behaviour of southern Italy was permanently moulded in this pattern of processional drama and devotional exhibitionism.

Further north, the pattern was more mixed. Jesuits and Capuchins carried the same aggressive missionary strategies to the frontiers of Protestantism, in Savoy, southern Germany and France. Borromeo took a particular interest in promoting Catholicism in Switzerland on which his archdiocese bordered, and he himself travelled widely through the mountains; he vigorously promoted the efforts of the Capuchins in the Swiss cantons, and there they rather than the Jesuits proved the main agents for promoting the Counter-Reformation in remote rural settings. In such circumstances, where there were Protestants to convince, not all Catholics engaged in mission felt that it was wise to flourish eucharistic and Marian devotion as a badge of difference, or to hector religious opponents: the outstanding French missionaries François de Sales and Vincent de Paul exemplified a quieter style, eschewing drama and seeking to persuade in less confrontational ways. The difference in style within the Catholicism of the contested areas of central Europe had wider implications, as we will discover (Chapter 10, pp. 478–84).

SPAIN AND PORTUGAL: KING PHILIP'S CHURCH

In his time, through half a century of power up to 1598, King Philip II of Spain rivalled the Emperor of China as the most powerful human being alive. He ended his days ruling wider dominions than his father Charles V had bequeathed him: the first truly global empire, and one that proclaimed its Tridentine Catholic faith. Philip could claim the credit for saving Christendom at Lepanto in 1571, and in 1580 he won Portugal and its overseas empire by a decent hereditary claim and with a minimum of opposition. Yet he is difficult to envy. Modern rulers with his degree of power generally have the satisfaction of fulfilled ambitions; whether through violent revolution or democratic mandate, they have clawed their own way into supreme position, driven by their own compulsions. Philip had no choice: he was born into his unique inheritance – indeed he was the ultimate hereditary monarch, for his Habsburg, Trastamara and Burgundian ancestors had built up their dominions largely by judicious marriage (with reckless disregard for the baleful longterm effects of an over-restricted gene pool). He was both beneficiary and prisoner of this genetic accumulation.

Once installed in Spain after 1559, Philip was never allowed to rest. As late as 1591 he faced a major revolt in his kingdom of Aragon, led by a former senior servant, which proved hideously expensive to put down and which he decided necessitated cruel reprisals. In Portugal, he did his best to please his newly acquired subjects, punctiliously housing the bodies of the last members of the royal House of Avis in reverent magnificence in the royal mausoleum-monastery at Belém, lavishing money on the Jesuit head-quarters in Lisbon, and making a present to the Portuguese capital of a grandiose rebuilding for its central Augustinian abbey church of St Vincent, as a showcase of the most up-to-date Spanish architecture. But the Portuguese failed to love their new king, even if they also failed to show much support for the rival pretenders to the Portuguese throne. In 1640 they finally threw off the rule of his grandson Philip IV in favour of a native nobleman. In northern Europe, Philip's sense of divine destiny met a force which he could not understand, let alone suppress – the Protestantism of England and the United Provinces of the Netherlands. He had been convinced that his 1588 Armada was on a holy mission for the Catholic Church, and he was shocked that God had sent such storms to scatter his ships.

Philip realized his need for information in order to grapple with such huge problems, and he had remarkable success in mobilizing his resources to accumulate it. He commissioned not simply words but pictures: townscapes, landscapes and maps, so that he could imagine himself in his various dominions. However, once all this had piled up in his study in the Escorial, what could he do next? Frequently despair. 'I do not understand a word of this. I do not know what I should do. Should I send it to someone else for comment, and if so, to whom?' A truly competent ruler would have had the answer, but Philip rarely delegated his decision-making. Worse still, he even spent precious time writing in the margins of his pile of documents about how weary he was and how little time he had. His austere piety taught him that all worldly splendour comes to nothing, and the saddest portrait we possess of him is a sketch from the 1590s of the aged monarch slumped in the sixteenth-century equivalent of an orthopaedic chair, clad from head-to-foot in a sort of romper-suit specially designed to ease pressure on his arthritis. Unable to stand upright, for his last two years of life Europe's most powerful man was confined to this chair, struggling to stop his empire from falling to ruin. Cynics whispered that his own physical decay was mirrored in the decline of his vast dominions, many so recently accumulated; imperial maintenance cried out for an expenditure often outstripping even his unparalleled resources.[35]

Philip's Spanish reign began in the wake of the Inquisition's clampdown on heresy in 1557–8. Despite the false start and continuing jurisdictional complications caused by Archbishop Carranza's downfall, he gave consistent backing to the campaign to reconstruct a Catholic Spain in the mould of the decrees of the Council of Trent – suitably controlled, modified and indeed sometimes obstructed by royal priorities.[36] Since the militant edge of Counter-Reformation reform derived in great part from the characteristic

Philip II of Spain in his last years in the 1590s, so crippled and in pain that he had to have a surgical chair and padded suit.

frontier militance of medieval Spanish Christianity, much of what needed to be done was simply to pick up initiatives from the Spanish past. For instance, the monarchy continued to intensify Cardinal Ximénes's not always successful efforts to reform existing Spanish religious houses; like Ximénes, royal officers often employed armed force to crush fierce opposition from monks, friars and even nuns.[37] While continuing the reform of the regular clergy, the Counter-Reformation added its effort to raise the quality of ministry in the parishes. Seminaries were set up (an impressive twenty-three in Castile between 1564 and 1610), and there were soon perceptible effects on the education of the lower clergy.[38]

Improving the clergy must be allied with education for their flocks. Catechizing the laity was an old Spanish custom, and it was practised with a new intensity in the 1540s, at the same time as the new initiatives in the Spanish-dominated parts of northern Italy (chapter 5, pp. 218–19). Church authorities were now assiduous in using the printing press to produce simple, vividly illustrated tracts and primers which would spread the basic content of the faith or publicize the burgeoning number of holy places, and there was much commercial competition to supply this booming market. Naturally all this instruction was in the vernacular, particularly in Spain's literary languages Castilian, Catalan and Galego: such activity had its effect. By the 1580s it was noticeable that 80 per cent of those appearing before the tribunal of the Inquisition in the central Castilian diocese of Cuenca could recite the basic Christian texts (see Appendix), and the figure increased thereafter: this was a remarkable achievement, and probably in advance of the results of catechizing in Protestant northern Europe.[39]

There were other ways in which Catholicism in the peninsula built on its traditional life. Church authorities had their worries about the boisterous activities which made up local carnivals, which were as much a feature of Iberian community life as in Italy. They did not adopt the unrealistic blanket hostility shown by Archbishop Carlo Borromeo (whom his Spanish contemporaries regarded with annoyance rather than reverence). Rather than shutting down the celebrations, they simply ordered that the carnival figures dressed as dwarves, giants, dragons or saints should move out of the church building and perform their mock fights in the square outside. The combats were, after all, about the victory of good over evil, and therefore not to be discouraged.[40] Yet popular culture was not excluded from church: the clergy were anxious to help those who knew no Latin to participate in the Church's formal liturgy. A charming and distinctively Spanish tradition of ecclesiastical music grew up during the seventeenth century, the *villancico*: this developed as a vernacular carol sung in parish churches on great festivals of the Christian year as an affectionate parody of parts of the monastic liturgy. These carols were full of humour, and featured characters on the picturesque margins of society such as gypsies, negresses or confidence tricksters, temporarily made unthreatening and comic in the service of God.[41]

Naturally, the Church's use of Spain's past was selective. The royal tribunals of the Spanish Inquisition continued their project of creating a culturally homogeneous Spain, preoccupied with the dangers from Spaniards of Jewish or Moorish descent. The Inquisition went on warning people against the menace of the vanished 'luteranismo' – in the deservedly sarcastic phrase of Jaime Contreras, 'a permanent spectre . . . which was made to "collaborate" in the task of stabilizing a feudal, aristocratic, and authoritarian social order. Never was an enemy made use of so profitably.'[42] The Inquisition even told artists within the Iberian empire how they should treat the subjects of religious art: in the early seventeenth century the artist Francisco Pacheco acted as the Holy Office's painting censor, and his guidelines were posthumously published as *The art of painting* (*El arte de la pintura*), inspiring others to imitate his work.[43]

The power of the Inquisition was seen at its most public in its *autos-da-fé*, great dramas often with thousands of spectators (see Plate 16). Frequently but not invariably including the burning of convicted offenders, they paralleled the secular violence in the bullfighting spectacles of Iberian culture, but also reached out to the eternal world as did the Mass itself. The *auto-da-fé* has been described as a 'mimesis of the Last Judgement', like the doom painting in Wenhaston church brought to life as a play: all human society was represented standing before God, from the King (often physically present in a royal box) to the humblest of his subjects.[44] Repentant prisoners represented to spectators repentance in that part of sinful humanity reconciled to God, while the fate of unrepentant blasphemers, sexual deviants or Judaizers represented that of the damned in the fires of hell. All were dressed up in costumes called *sambenitos*, painted with symbols of their offences and indicating their fates – pardon or flames. These *sambenitos* spread the power of the Inquisition still further because they were hanging on the walls of nearly every parish church in the kingdoms of the peninsula. Once they had been worn in the *auto-da-fé*, they were taken for display in the offender's parish church, to symbolize his or her shame before the whole community.

One should nevertheless not fall into the old stereotype of an organization that kept its place in Spanish society by sheer terror. Certainly the Inquisition used torture and executed some of its victims, but so did nearly all legal systems in Europe at the time, and it is possible to argue that the Spanish Inquisition was less bloodthirsty than most – as we will see, it showed a healthy scepticism about witches and put a stop to witch-persecution where it could (chapter 13, p. 574). After a period of undoubted severity in the crisis decades around 1500, soon after its foundation, the Inquisition's execution rate between 1540 and 1700 was around 2 or 3 per cent per year for those brought before its various tribunals. That was lower than virtually any contemporary secular court of justice in Iberia or elsewhere (admittedly, that might not have been much consolation to those burned at the stake).[45] 'Old Christians' usually welcomed and supported the work of the Inquisition, and it could not have so successfully fostered attitudes of exclusive Catholic Spanish identity had not the bulk of the population thoroughly approved of the idea. Catalonia provides interesting evidence: it was on the frontiers of heterodox France and it was also a province in which the Inquisition was notably weak as an institution (chapter 2, p. 63), but Catalonia was as firm against heresy as any other part of the peninsula. This was not because it was kept in ignorance or isolation: its literacy rate was much higher than in Luther's Germany, and its capital Barcelona was one of the world's great seaports. It may actually have been the area's consciousness of the world beyond – its suspicion of the alien ways of the many French immigrants in Catalan communities, or of the Jew-loving Italians – that kept it aloof from heresy.[46]

In other respects, Counter-Reformation Spain needed to model itself anew. This included inventing a past for Christian Spain in areas where the course of actual history meant that it was lacking: repeating in Spain the impact of the discovery of the catacombs in Rome. An enterprising Jesuit, Jerónimo Román de la Higuera, created ancient chronicles for authors whom he named as Flavio Destro, Maximo and Luitprando, and these imaginary worthies provided a useful flood of ecclesiastical history otherwise unknown. The city of Granada, so gloriously provided with architectural reminders of its Islamic heritage, was particularly anxious to show that it was a more ancient and distinguished Christian centre than Toledo or Santiago de Compostela, and it also wanted to outface the upstart royal capital Madrid. These aims were much assisted by the 'discovery' from 1588 onwards of a series of forged early Christian relics (*plomos*, or lead books) hidden in the minaret of the former main Granadan mosque and in various nearby caves. The *plomos* conveniently illuminated Granada's lost Christian history, to the point where the first Mass in Spain could be said to have been celebrated in the city by no less a figure than Santiago de Compostela's St James the Apostle (Santiago), the patron saint of Spain. The site of these discoveries became the foremost place of pilgrimage in southern Spain: external scepticism, and even an official condemnation from Pope Innocent XI in 1682, had as little effect on local enthusiasm as Rome's similar health warnings imposed on St Simon Stock's scapular vision.[47]

Other restructuring concerned patterns of worship. One of the notable features of the Counter-Reformation in southern Europe was the way in which it highlighted aspects of Catholic devotional practice previously more characteristic of northern Europe. We have already observed this in the rise of rosary devotion (chapter 7, p. 329), but another major import from the north was the emphasis on the funeral Mass with the aim of benefiting souls in purgatory: the purgatory industry had been a distinctive strength (and ultimately also a weakness) in the countries that listened to Luther's message, but it was not previously so prominent in the south. All over the Iberian peninsula from the later sixteenth century there are examples of the inflation in the number of masses expected by the dying – an eight-fold average increase in Madrid, for example – and a much greater elaboration of the ritual that accompanied them. It is even possible that so much investment in the cult of the dead had a seriously distorting effect on Iberia's already fragile economy and contributed to the decline of the Spanish empire in the seventeenth century. Whether or not that could be substantiated, there is no doubt that Iberian Catholicism became more dominated in its practice by the concerns of the clergy: in the historian Henry Kamen's phrase, it turned from 'a formal but basically non-clerical and non-sacramental Catholicism ... rooted in community norms and agrarian ritual' to 'a religion rigorously defined in terms of clerical privilege, sacramental duty and performance of social obligations'.[48]

It would be an injustice to see the reshaping of Spanish religion merely as a project of self-aggrandizing clergy, tidy-minded Inquisition officials or the devout busyness of Philip II. These forces could not have produced, neither could they eliminate, the spiritual energies released by centuries of Iberian conversations between the three monotheistic religions of the Middle East: Judaism, Christianity and Islam. That interaction, in all its complexity and frequent cruelty, had not merely left a population with a very mixed past, but fostered currents of mystical spirituality that sat uneasily within the official structures of the victorious Christian Church. It can be no coincidence that one of the most distinctive forms of Iberian monasticism was that of the Jeronimites, who unlike most medieval monastic Orders did not spread beyond their origins to establish a presence in all parts of Europe; they emphasized the solitariness of encounter with God, and consistently they attracted *converso* recruits – later also in the era of the Reformation, sympathizers with Protestantism. We have already noted the spiritual turmoil in Spain after the final Christian triumph of the 1490s: the wild prophecies, millenarian expectations and spiritual wonders of unofficial religion, and then the diffusion of spiritual religion through the *alumbrados* and on through Juan de Valdés into the *Spirituali* of Italy (chapters 2, pp. 63–5, and 5, pp. 213–15). The Inquisition did much to tame this maelstrom and bring the remnants within the Church. Out of that repressed yet still multitextured world grew an extraordinary flowering of mysticism, of which the outstanding but by no means the only representatives were Teresa of Ávila and John of the Cross.

Teresa was herself from a *converso* family of Ávila in central Castile. She entered a convent of Carmelite nuns in Ávila in 1535 at the age of nineteen without her father's consent, and her feelings about leaving her family always remained tangled. To her emotional turmoil was added prolonged and severe illness, out of which came visions of both reproach and consolation. She soon began writing down what she experienced, casting the intensity of her meetings with the divine in terms of the most passionate and intimate of human relationships: she spoke of the piercing of her heart, of her mystical marriage with the divine. There were orthodox precedents for this in female mystical expression from various parts of medieval Europe, for instance in the work of Bridget of Sweden or Catherine of Siena, but it was not surprising given the tense religious atmosphere of contemporary Spain that her brand of ecstatic and personal mystical piety attracted a good deal of suspicion. Her imagination had been fired by a rich heritage of devotional literature in the vernacular, virtually all of which the Spanish Inquisition regarded with downright hostility and placed on its Index in 1559.[49]

Luckily for Teresa, she also earned sympathy and respect from influential early Jesuits (who experienced their own troubles with the Spanish Inquisition), and even from Dominicans, many of whose members were active in the Inquisition. Crucially, she met King Philip II himself and came to win his firm support. Those who encountered her could hardly fail to be impressed by her horror at what she had heard of Protestantism and its destruction of churches in northern Europe, or by her determination to undertake something distinctive to strengthen the Church in holiness and spiritual power. She would pray the Church into new life, and she would create an army of women to do so.[50] Her plans began taking shape in the early 1560s, when she was already well into middle age. She drew on the spirituality of her Carmelite Order, who in the course of its complex medieval evolution from cave-dwelling hermits in Crusader Palestine had come to combine an intense experience of solitary piety with a vocation to the travelling active life in the world maintained by friars. Teresa was determined to bring the Carmelites back to their radically austere origins and to reject, as they had once done, all compromises with the lifestyles of the secular world.

Accordingly she founded her first new convent for women in Ávila in 1562, and more followed, together with a campaign to reform friaries for men and to found new houses. Her fellow Carmelites of the Reform would go barefoot ('discalced') as Carmelites had first done, and there would be no distinctions of social rank within her convents, contrary to the custom at the time. Teresa was never afraid of paradox: she was 'an enclosed nun constantly on the roads, nagging and manoeuvring her new communities into existence'.[51] She struggled to persuade the Church authorities to make a leap of imagination: to allow the Carmelite balance of contemplation and activism for the women who joined her, and through many troubles and setbacks at the hands of the ecclesiastical authorities she developed what one of her admirers has called 'the gift of making men give her the orders she wanted to obey'.[52] She did not get everything that she sought, for like all the activist female religious of her day she found herself up against a male establishment which would not countenance women taking up the mendicant and preaching role of male friars (chapter 16, pp. 642–6). Nevertheless in 1580, only two years before her death, her Order of Discalced Carmelites won official recognition.

Teresa had extended her mission of reforming conventual life from women to men after meeting Juan de Yepes, a much younger Carmelite. He also witnesses to the extraordinary power of Spanish mysticism, and has come to be known by the name which he took in religion, John of the Cross. Like Teresa, Juan was from a *converso* background, although unlike her he knew grinding poverty in his youth. A hospital administrator in Medina del Campo saw something exceptional in the diminutive boy and recruited him to work as a nurse in his institution. There Juan was presented with some of the most dire human misery of the age, because the hospital (nicknamed las Bubas) specialized in ulcers and contagious diseases – primarily that traumatically shaming and physically appalling scourge of the period, syphilis.[53] He was only a little older than Teresa had been when he felt in his turn a call to the Carmelite life, and he entered a newly founded Carmelite house in his town in 1563. He practised the rule of the Order as strictly as his community would let him, and sought out solitude and silence to a degree that often seemed dangerous and threatening to others. It was not surprising that his mission came to combine with Teresa's.

Teresa and Juan met in 1567, when Teresa came to Medina del Campo to found one of her convents. She was already turning her attention to how the male houses of the Carmelites might take up her reform, and she begged Juan to abandon his plan of leaving the Order to pursue his solitary vocation in the more congenially austere setting of the Carthusian Rule. Juan accepted, and in 1568 he headed the first attempt to found a male house to follow her principles. Their relationship was always a complex one. Teresa found that Juan was one of the few men who was not always prepared to defer to the force of her personality. Yet beyond their particular arguments, there was a commonality of purpose sealed by the bitterness of the struggle which they had to face to secure their goals. In 1571 Teresa was appointed Prioress of the convent in Ávila where she had begun her religious life. She exercised the prerogative which she regarded as one of the cornerstones of her reform by personally appointing a priest-confessor to her community – naturally it was Fray Juan.

This was the spark of great troubles for both of them. Many of Teresa's nuns were apprehensive at what the austerity of the two combined might mean for them: Juan's fellow friars harboured grave suspicions about the relationship, and several among the Carmelite authorities were appalled at the potential of these two to reshape the life of the Order to suit themselves. Through the 1570s and 1580s, Teresa and Juan were drawn into bitter internal battles within the Order, which brought out the worst in their powerful opponents. At one point in 1577–8, Juan suffered nine months' close and degrading imprisonment from which he had to effect a dramatic escape, but which also renewed in him his consciousness of how a human might look on the depths of despair and isolation and out of it construct a sense of serenity and purpose. He expressed his experiences in poetry and prose that rank among some of the most profound Christian explorations of suffering and redemption. The title of one of his writings after his prison experiences, *The Dark Night*, has become familiar, even beyond the bounds of Christian spirituality, to those who feel that they too are passing through the dark night of the soul.

Yet John of the Cross's writings are full of joy and delight – and like Teresa's they are expressed in terms of an intensely personal and even physical relationship with God. For both Teresa and Juan the erotic biblical poem the Song of Songs becomes a key text for the divine revelation. Juan is not afraid of picturing himself again and again as the lover, and frequently the bride, of Christ, appropriating for himself the image which is more conventionally given to the institution of the Church, and often expressing himself in ways which sound startlingly homoerotic. This is possible for Juan because he sees the self as not an exclusive, bounded individual: the relationship of the bride is the relationship of all the creation of a good and loving God to its creator. Within that, the human soul fearfully and joyfully finds its place. And Juan finds that even the ancient technical language of theology, the Chalcedonian Definition, can be fired with his own vision of the meaning in the Song of Songs:

After the soul has been for some time the betrothed of the Son of God in gentle and complete love, God calls her and places her in his flowering garden to consummate this most joyful state of marriage with Him. The union wrought between the two natures and the communication of the divine to the human in this state is such that even though neither change their being, both appear to be God.[54]

It is a tribute both to the creative power and persistence of Teresa and Juan, as well as to the continuing richness and complexity of Iberian Christianity amid authoritarianism and bureaucratic pettiness, that the lives of these rebellious Carmelites came to be seen as one of the great spiritual glories of their age. The Discalced Carmelites faced fresh battles after Teresa's death. A new (and of course, male) Provincial of the Order curtailed the degree of independence and freedom of action which Teresa had won for prioresses of her Reform. When John of the Cross supported the nuns against these manoeuvres, the Provincial also saw to his removal from authority within the General Chapter of the Order.[55] Still the Discalced Carmelites were left flourishing, an influential and vibrant spiritual force at the highest levels of Spanish society. They were determined not merely to see Rome recognize their foundress as a saint (which they achieved in 1622, only forty years after her death) but in a much more ambitious project, to see her replace Santiago himself as the patron saint of Spain. This was both a devotional act and a political self-assertion against all the forces of the Church that had made life so difficult for Teresa and Juan: luckily for the Carmelites it had the backing of the Spanish monarchy.[56] In 1618 King Philip III persuaded the Pope to designate Teresa co-patron of Spain. Pope Urban VIII, alarmed by some fierce Spanish opposition, but also mindful of continuing support from powerful figures like Philip IV's minister the Count-Duke Olivares, negotiated a compromise in 1630 whereby recognition of this co-patronage could become a local option. The canonization of John of the Cross remained more controversial; it was not until 1726 that he was finally officially declared to be a saint of the Church.

THE COUNTER-REFORMATION AS WORLD MISSION

Reformation Protestants did very little missionary work outside the boundaries of Europe; during the sixteenth century they were still too busy fighting for their existence against Catholics, and also fighting among themselves to establish their identity. Even in the seventeenth century their continuing troubles limited their efforts to imitate Roman missions – the main energy of Protestant missionary work would not appear until the eighteenth century (chapter 17, p. 699). Meanwhile, Counter-Reformation Catholicism performed spectacular if not always well-rewarded feats of missionary exploration in America and Asia, using the Spanish and Portuguese empires as its vehicle. The Council of Trent said nothing in its official statements about the world mission of the renewed Catholic Church, but this mission became one of the most distinctive features of southern European Catholicism: a project of taking Christianity to every continent, which has made Roman Catholicism the largest grouping within western Christianity, and made the Spanish and Portuguese languages the chief modern rivals to English as the mode of western communication.

Trent's silence seems all the more surprising since the Catholic world mission had been in operation for more than half a century when it met – this was not like the Council's silence on the menace of militant Calvinism, which had hardly begun to emerge as a real problem in the years that the Tridentine fathers were in session. Committees are even more prone than individual human beings to miss the point in the business in front of them, but it is worth observing that there was little that Rome could do about the mission – at the beginning of the century, the papacy had signed away control of Catholic activity in the overseas empires by the King of Spain's *Patronato* and the King of Portugal's *Padroado*. It was no coincidence that Portugal was one of the first kingdoms on which Ignatius Loyola concentrated the efforts of his infant Society, founding as early as 1540 a headquarters in Lisbon and only two years later a Jesuit college for missionary training, set up with royal encouragement in the university town of Coimbra. A new world mission based on Portugal would more than compensate for Ignatius's abortive plans for the Holy Land.

While the Jesuits rapidly began following up their initial advantage in the Portuguese territories in Africa, Asia and Brazil, their difficulties with the Spanish Inquisition in mid-century (chapter 5, p. 225, and 6, p. 300) meant that they were comparatively late on the scene in the vast Spanish empire in central and south America. The Society began arriving only in the 1560s and 1570s, by which time patterns had already been well established by Franciscan and Dominican missions (see Fig. 6, p. 327). It was the friars who were first forced to think out a new theology of mission. For centuries this had not been a feature of any part of western Christian activity outside Iberia, with the specialized exception of Lithuania's capitulation to Catholic Christianity in the fourteenth century. They were doing so in conditions where they had overwhelming military force on their side: it has been calculated that as a result, by 1550 around ten million people had been baptized as Christians in the Americas.[57] In central America, this was accompanied by the obliteration of the structures of pre-Christian government and society, in which the friars vigorously co-operated. As the Church had done in late Roman and early medieval Europe, they took various important pre-Christian sacred sites and neutralized or converted them by building major churches, but they also took a lead in pioneering an entirely new pattern of settlements of villages and towns laid out on a grid plan and centring on a church: this redrew the map of central America. Spaniards got much of the cultivable land thus made available, but since European-imported diseases cruelly reduced the size of the Indio population, there was a good deal left to distribute to the natives.[58]

We have already seen how the friars also quickly provoked very considerable discussion about the manner of these rapid Spanish military conquests in the 'New World': it has been well said that the Spanish empire is unequalled in history among similar great territorial enterprises for its insistent questioning of its own rights to conquer and colonize.[59] Yet as

Christianity took shape in the new colonies it was hardly surprising that even those most concerned to protect the welfare of the native 'Indio' populations brought with them from Iberia the exclusive attitudes of Christian monopoly culture: there was going to be no more room for the survival of rival religions in the 'New World' than there was back in Spain. In fact, since Dominicans like the theologian Francisco de Vitoria denied that the Pope had the right to grant temporal rights of conquest in the New World in 1493, they were driven to stress the rationale of what he had done in terms of bringing the good news of Christianity and banishing Satan. Franciscans coming from Iberia were particularly prone to be affected by the millenarian enthusiasm which gripped southern Europe around 1500, and which the Franciscan Order had long fostered: they believed that they were living in the last times, and so their task of bringing good news to new peoples was desperately urgent. Nothing could be further from their minds than any thought that there was a need for Christianity to develop a long-term strategy of coexistence with other world faiths.[60]

The arriving clergy noticed curious analogies with Christian practice in central American Aztec religion – an apparent sign of the cross, or belief in the virgin birth of a God for instance. This did not inspire them with a pleasurable fellow feeling for indigenous religion: these were devices of Satan to mock and deceive God's Church as he struggled against God's imminent Second Coming.[61] Their attitude hardened from the 1530s. In 1541 and 1546, major uprisings of the Maya population of Yucatan were directed against all things Spanish, including Catholicism; they involved savage revenge attacks on the Spanish settler population and were naturally suppressed with equal cruelty. In 1562, Franciscan missionaries in Yucatan discovered to their horror that some of their converts were continuing secretly to practise pre-Conquest religious rites: it was bad enough to find that people had been burying figures of the old gods next to crosses so that they could go on publicly worshipping them undetected, but those whom the Franciscans questioned even reported cases of human sacrifice, some including crucifixions, staged with satirical blasphemy during the Christian solemnities of Holy Week. The Franciscan provincial Diego de Landa set up a local Inquisition which unleashed a major campaign of brutal interrogation and torture on the Indio population. A newly appointed bishop, horrified at zeal gone wild, abruptly removed de Landa from all his positions of authority and put a stop to the atrocities, but the Indios had already paid a terrible price for their defiance.[62]

In the long term, the effect of such disappointments was radically to limit the trust which the Spanish clergy were prepared to place in the Indios.

Indios might become assistants in the liturgy, but never the principals – catechists, sacristans, cantors and instrumentalists, but not priests. When the Church in New Spain (central America) held its first provincial council in 1555, it made explicit the ban on ordaining Indios, half-castes (mestizos) or the slaves who were beginning to arrive from Africa; to begin with, Indio men were also not allowed to enter religious Orders. A provincial council for the west coast of South America at Lima in 1568 introduced similar bans. It was only in the eighteenth century that significant numbers of Indios became priests, at a time when consciously non-Christian religious practice in peoples under Spanish control had long ceased.[63] There were even serious debates throughout the sixteenth century as to whether Indios should be banned from receiving the eucharistic elements when they came to Mass – after all, European laity only did so once a year, and these people were barely fit to be considered full Christians.[64] In south America, first under Portuguese rule in Brazil and then in the south-eastern Spanish territories, Jesuits treated their hunter-gatherer Indio converts almost as children, organizing them into large settlements to protect them against the greed and exploitation of the other colonists, but always in a benevolent European-led dictatorship of estates, the 'Reductions'. When the Jesuits were forcibly expelled from the Americas after 1767, they left their Indios without any experience of leadership, and the carefully structured Indio communities in the Reductions quickly collapsed.

Within this framework of cultural imperialism, the Church did achieve a remarkable degree of synthesis between Christianity and those elements of native culture that it allowed to survive. Naturally the friars and the Jesuits worked with the languages they found, particularly since they were reluctant to open the Indios up to unhealthy influences from colonists by teaching them Spanish. Their concern to speak local languages sprang from utterly different priorities from the Protestant Reformation's insistence on the vernacular. Protestants would demand vernacular Bibles, but for Tridentine Catholics, not even vernacular preaching mattered as much as the need to safeguard the confidentiality of sacramental confession: if a priest heard a penitent's confession through an interpreter, many felt that it made a mockery of the sacrament. As missionaries developed their vernacular work, they tended to privilege certain languages in order to simplify and unify their task, choosing for instance in central America the former official lingua franca of Nahuatl. Into these native languages, they imported Latin theological terms, to avoid further conscious or unconscious local syncretism with pre-Christian concepts.[65]

Above all, the missionaries realized that after the traumas and frequent horrors of the conquest they must show that there was joy and celebration in the new religion. Frequently they turned their catechisms into song, just as Francis Xavier in his missions in India turned the creed into poetry to be recited, and out of these initiatives sprang a vibrant indigenous tradition of music in church; many clergy also encouraged the Indios to dance, even inside the church buildings.[66] A forest of new churches coated the map of the Iberian colonies, and the extrovert art and architecture of the developed Counter-Reformation gleefully fused with native Indio artistic traditions to create some of the most sumptuous monuments of the Catholic world. The festival days of the Catholic Church began as symbols of the new conquerors' dispensation, but as community celebrations they were soon also assimilated into the joys and fears of the whole population and appropriated to local purposes. In Peru, where the pre-conquest aristocracy survived the trauma of Pizarro's conquests, Inka nobles might send their daughters to convent school to receive a good Spanish education from nuns who were creole (people of supposedly pure Spanish blood), but then on Corpus Christi day or the like the nobles joined the eucharistic procession proudly wearing Andean costume and insignia, to emphasize their continuing privileged position within indigenous Andean society.[67]

The long-term success of Spanish evangelism in the Americas was to make the Catholic Church an essential part of Indio culture as well as a tie binding it to the cultures of southern Europe. In Mexico this is symbolized by the central role in national identity played by the Virgin of Guadalupe. This apparition of Our Lady is supposed to have been experienced by an Aztec convert with the Spanish name Juan Diego. As Diego was affirming the truth of her appearance in front of his bishop, her image became miraculously apparent in the cloak he was wearing; the cloak and its painted image remain to this day an object of prodigious veneration at the shrine of Guadalupe Hidalgo. These events are said to have taken place in 1531, but the tradition in written form cannot be traced earlier than the work of Fr. Miguel Sánchez in 1648; that hardly matters in terms of the impact of the Guadalupe cult. It perfectly united old and new central American cultures in a common affirmation of divine motherhood – the very name Guadalupe comes from Arabic Spain and a Marian shrine there, yet it was to an Indio that this sign of special divine favour had appeared. The most recent study of the 'miracle' also draws attention to the achievement of Sánchez: he drew on the biblical commentary of Augustine of Hippo and the eighth-century Greek theologian John Damascene in meditating on the Guadalupe miracle, in order to illuminate the discovery of sacredness and glory in the landscape of a people whom he passionately loved. It is an extraordinary tribute to the many-sided legacy of Augustine, who was the source of the Reformation of Luther and Calvin, that he should also fire the imagination of this Mexican priest. Such a synthesis might itself be considered a miraculous triumph of human imagination and creative making of connections.[68]

Whereas in southern and central America Christianity could rely on official backing from the colonial governments of Spain and Portugal (subject to the hundred and one other concerns of colonial administrators), this was not so in Asia or Africa. Here the Portuguese were the main European Catholic power, and even after Philip II of Spain gained the Portuguese throne in 1580, the weakness of the Portuguese colonial enclaves (chapter 2, pp. 65–7) meant that there was little or no military backing for Christianity, particularly against the far stronger native empires that ruled in India and China. Moreover, in the small enclaves where the Portuguese authorities were able to exercise real control, especially in their Indian fortress-headquarters of Goa, they often made matters worse by insisting on the paramountcy of Portuguese culture and Portuguese ecclesiastical jurisdiction as granted by the Pope in the *Padroado* (the Archbishop of Goa became primate of all Catholic churches around the Pacific Ocean). They were frequently jealous of and obstructive to missionaries from areas of Europe beyond Portugal.

Once outside these uncomfortable Portuguese bases, Christianity in Asia had to make its own way on its merits, often in situations where missions by eastern Christians in earlier centuries had already known success followed by gradual decline and contraction. Only in the Philippine Islands, a Spanish colony named after King Philip II, did Christianity eventually secure a substantial foothold among a large population in Asia – but the reason for this exception proved the rule. Here, as in America, the Augustinian friars who led the Church's mission could rely on backing from colonial authorities with substantial military force. In fact, in a link-up which at first sight seems bizarre, but illustrates the Philippine analogy with Spanish American experience, the bishopric of Manila in the Philippines was first ranked as a part of the archdiocese in New Spain (Mexico), thousands of miles across the Pacific, since most links with the home government in Madrid were via America.

Presenting the Christian message without backing from strong military force posed considerable problems for a missionary priest. Nearly always a member of the Society of Jesus or one of the various Orders of friars, he faced Asian peoples with age-old and subtle cultures, full of self-confidence and likely to be profoundly sceptical that these westerners could teach them anything of value. The Muslim rulers and the Hindu elites of the Indian sub-continent could contemplate with sarcastic interest the normally dire relations between the Christian newcomers and the small and ancient Christian Church in India deriving from Nestorian Syrian roots: Portuguese contempt for Christians they regarded as schismatics or heretics, and the schisms and disputes which Portuguese interference provoked in these Churches, were not impressive demonstrations of Christian brotherly love. Unlike the Syrian Christians, Catholic clergy did not at first appreciate a perennial problem in India: Hindu converts to Christianity automatically lost caste. It was not surprising that the missionaries' main early success was with the peoples lowest in the caste system. João de Cruz was a former Hindu merchant who converted to Christianity in Lisbon in 1513. His efforts to restore his shaky finances led him to trade on the Fisher Coast of south India, where he was touched by the misfortunes of the poverty-stricken pearl-fishers (Paravas), who were facing extermination by local rulers and their Arab merchant allies after an act of desperate rebellion. He advised the Paravas that their one hope of deliverance was to seek Portuguese protection – that would necessarily mean adopting Christianity. Twenty thousand Paravas are said to have been baptized as a result.[69]

This initiative by someone who knew the sub-continent as an insider was an exception, however. The Jesuits began building up their strength after the beginning of Francis Xavier's prodigious decade of Asian mission in 1542, and after that European missionaries did begin to make an effort to understand Indian culture, language and literature (although it must be said that Xavier was also responsible for recommending the introduction of the Portuguese royal Inquisition to the capital at Goa).[70] Now a new attitude emerged among the Jesuits, very different from that of Iberian mission in the Americas that the friars had pioneered: there might be something in the other world faiths that could be of value and reflect God's purpose. The most interesting and bold experiment was made in southern India by an Italian Jesuit, Robert de Nobili. He took the logical but unprecedented step of working in the same way as a high-caste Indian and adopting the dress appropriate to an Indian holy man; fluent in the appropriate languages, he also took particular care to point out to those to whom he preached that he was not a *Parangi* (a Portuguese). The Portuguese authorities fiercely opposed de Nobili's work, but finally lost their case against him in Rome in 1623; his reports back to Europe in the course of these disputes are among the earliest careful western European accounts of Hinduism and Buddhism. Whatever success the Church had in the Tamil country of South India was entirely thanks to Nobili and his Italian successors, but their work went on to suffer during the eighteenth century both from severe Muslim persecution and from the 1773 official suppression of the Society of Jesus as a result of high politics back in Europe.[71]

The case of China shared features with the Indian experience, but Portugal had even less leverage there. The Chinese were not especially interested in large-scale contacts with foreign countries, not even for trade, and with their military might they were certainly not prepared to let the Portuguese in the small trading enclave of Macau adopt the ruthless proselytizing methods put into practice in Goa. The Jesuits, with their usual flexibility and imagination, quickly took the decision that missionaries must adapt themselves to Chinese customs, but such was their ignorance of the country to begin with that their first great missionary, the Italian Matteo Ricci, began on his arrival in 1582 by wearing the dress of a Buddhist monk (bonze), without realizing that the bonzes were little esteemed by the people who mattered in China. When the Jesuits realized their mistake, they began dressing as Confucian scholars, and they determined to show that their learning was worthy of respect in a culture which had a deep reverence for scholarship. In this they had the advantage of the network of colleges and educational experience that they had built up back in Europe in the previous decades. The Chinese upper class was indeed impressed by the Jesuits' knowledge of mathematics, astronomy and geography, and the Society gained an honoured place at the Emperor's court through its specialist use of these skills, even taking charge of reforming the imperial calendar.[72]

However, as in India, the sheer scale of the task before the missionaries, with inadequate resources of money and men, meant that their impact through China was tiny. At the peak of the Chinese mission's success at the end of the seventeenth century there were perhaps around a quarter of a million adherents, but even at that time only seventy-five priests to serve them.[73] To make matters worse, the Portuguese authorities in Macau and Goa remained suspicious of the majority of the Jesuits working in China who were not Portuguese. When the Dominicans and Franciscans arrived in China from the Philippines in the 1630s, the friars launched their own bitter attacks on their religious rivals, and raised major matters of missionary policy. The friars, coming from the background of America and a total confrontation with previous religions, violently disagreed with the Jesuits in their attitude to the Chinese way of life, particularly traditional rites in honour of Confucius and the family: they even publicly asserted that deceased Emperors were burning in Hell. They took their complaints against the Jesuits as far as Rome itself, and after a long struggle they won condemnations of the Chinese rites from successive Popes in 1704 and 1715. It was not surprising that after this western Christianity's first major effort to understand and accommodate itself to another culture ended in relative failure.

Christian work in Japan was the most extreme story, in which the most spectacular success of any mission launched from Portuguese bases in Asia or Africa was followed by almost total defeat.[74] Loyola's companion Francis Xavier and his fellow Jesuits arrived as early as 1549, only seven years after the first Portuguese visit to Japan, and Jesuits continued to dominate the Japanese mission. They quickly achieved results: by the end of the century there were perhaps as many as 300,000 Christian converts in Japan, aided by a determined and imaginative effort to meet Japan on its own terms. From the beginning, the Jesuits took Japanese culture seriously: 'these Japanese are more ready to be implanted with our holy faith than all the nations of the world', Xavier affirmed, and he recommended using members of the Society from the Low Countries and Germany on the mission since they were used to a cold climate and would work more efficiently in it.[75] The Italian Jesuit Alessandro Valignano envisaged the formation of a new native clergy, and a Portuguese Jesuit, Gaspar Coelho, was active in recruiting some seventy novices for the Society by 1590, with a particular concentration on the sons of noblemen and samurai who would command respect in Japanese society – however, his colleagues felt more cautious and restrained his initiative.[76]

The background to this remarkable success was a fatal entanglement with politics, both that of Portuguese trading policy and of the internal concerns of Japan. The Portuguese trade was led by their so-called 'Great Ship' trading in bullion and luxury goods annually: the Jesuits not only invested in this to support what proved to be an extremely expensive mission, but also encouraged the Ship to travel to as many Japanese ports as possible to excite interest in Christianity. The arrival of the missionaries and merchants occurred opportunely at a time when Japan was split between rival feudal lords. Many of these saw Christianity as a useful way of attracting Portuguese trade and also of furthering their own political aims: particularly the powerful Tokugawa family, who initially encouraged the missionaries. By 1600 the Tokugawa had eliminated all their rivals in politics, and they now saw Christianity not as a convenience but a nuisance, even a threat. They had some reason: the Philippines fell under Spanish royal control with such comparative ease because missionary activity of Augustinian Friars had preceded the arrival of King Philip's ships and soldiers.

Matters were made worse for the mission when Franciscan friars arrived in Japan to establish a missionary presence in 1593: they were used to the missionary conditions of the Spanish Empire, and in parallel to the controversies that developed between Jesuits and friars in the Chinese Empire, they adopted an aggressively negative attitude to Japanese culture, which led to a number of them suffering death by crucifixion. In the early seventeenth century the Tokugawa expelled Europeans from Japan except for one rigorously policed trading-post. They launched one of the most savage persecutions in the history of Christianity, and their repression of Japanese Christians was not without some military assistance from the Protestant Dutch, who were doing a good job of wrecking Portuguese power in eastern Asia, and had few regrets about campaigns against Jesuits and friars. The Church in Japan, despite the heroism of its native faithful, was reduced to a tiny and half-instructed remnant. It struggled to maintain any sort of secret existence for more than two centuries until Europeans used military force to secure free access to the country after the 1850s, and rediscovered it with astonishment. The Japanese persecution is a standing argument against the old idea that the blood of the martyrs is the seed of the Church.[77]

In Africa the Christian mission was likewise based on Portuguese trading-posts and contacts with local powers, and as in Japan it achieved some success among local elites, although without any single traumatic turning-point like that which crippled the Japanese mission. There were even efforts to create an indigenous clergy, spurred on by a chronic shortage of clerical manpower: the climate and disease ecology proved lethal to most European missionary clergy. However, there was a different fatal flaw to the mission in Africa: its association with the Portuguese slave trade, which produced an unholy synthesis across the Atlantic between the colonial empires of America and the seaborne outposts of Portuguese power on the African coast. Millions of men, women and children were rounded up in the African interior through the agency of local rulers and shipped out through the Portuguese forts across the Atlantic to sustain the economy of American plantations; they introduced a third element to the racial kaleidoscope of the Iberian American empires. The Portuguese possessions in Brazil accounted for the largest number – perhaps 3.5 million people over three centuries – but from the late sixteenth century the Portuguese were (unwillingly) sharing this trade with the English and Dutch, and hundreds of thousands of slaves were taken to new plantations in Protestant colonies in north America.[78] The Spaniards were not actively involved in the shipping trade, but their colonies could not have survived without it. Depressingly, as we have noted in discussing the passionate polemic of Bartolomé de las Casas (chapter 2, pp. 67–8), the expedient of importing African slaves was in part meant to protect the Indio population from exploitation by the colonists.

Not many clergy saw into what a moral disaster their enterprise had led them. One Franciscan based in the university of Mexico city, Bartolomé de Albornoz, in the course of a book on contract law published in 1571, had the clear-sightedness to condemn the common argument that Africans were being saved from pagan darkness by their removal to America, remarking sarcastically 'I do not believe that it can be demonstrated that according to the law of Christ the liberty of the soul can be purchased by the servitude of the body'.[79] His words found few echoes. There were only two entry points for slaves in the whole of the Spanish dominians, the Mexican port of Vera Cruz – a place where a True Cross might indeed be found on the quaysides – and Cartagena in what is now Colombia. In Cartagena two maverick Jesuits, Alonso de Sandoval and Pedro Claver, spent years amid terrible conditions doing their best to minister to and baptize those West African slaves who had managed to survive the Atlantic crossing and newly arrived in the docks. A telling detail of the Jesuits' ministry was that they made sure that their baptismal ceremony included plenty of cool drinkable water; the desperate and grateful slave would be more receptive to the Christian message. In its context, their pastoral work was bravely counter-cultural, arousing some real disapproval among the settler population, but their efforts to instil first a sense of sin (particularly sexual sin) and then repentance in their wretched penitents now seem oddly placed amid one of the greatest acts of communal sin perpetrated by western Christian culture.[80]

This was a predictable failure of imagination. Missionary clergy were frequently slave-traders themselves, and the great historian of the Iberian overseas empires Charles Boxer was able to observe that the Catholic Church in West Africa was almost entirely maintained on the profits of the slave trade. It was hardly surprising that popular mission was hampered or that the native population despised Christianity. Canon Manuel Severim de Faria, an enthusiastic seventeenth-century Portuguese historian of his country's empire, noted sadly that in a century and a half of existence, the Portuguese West African slaving fortress-post of Elmina had not succeeded in spreading Christianity beyond three or four nearby villages, despite the theoretically wide territorial jurisdiction at its disposal.[81] The story was little different in West Africa where a local elite did decide to convert: the rulers of the little West African coastal state of Warri (in what is now Nigeria) took up Christianity for a period of nearly two centuries, but their subjects generally did not; the slave trade remorsely eroded the popular impact of a message which proclaimed love and freedom.[82]

The most promising initiative for Catholic Christianity under powerful

This was the first view which African slaves had of Cartagena, the largest town on south America's northern coast: a symbol of high Iberian civilization with its Spanish-style two- and three-storey houses and rich convents. Once past the defensive chain at the harbour entrance, all that Africans could look forward to there was Jesuit baptism, with plenty of cool water.

local patronage rather than at the command of Portuguese guns was in the central African Atlantic kingdom of Kongo. Here the ruler Mvemba Nzinga became a fervent Christian and adopted the Portuguese title of Afonso I. Afonso welcomed Iberian priests to his extensive lands, saw to it that one of his sons was consecrated in Portugal in 1518 as a bishop, opened schools to teach the Portuguese language, and created a stately inland cathedral city, São Salvador, as his capital; he has been called 'one of the greatest lay Christians in African Church history'.[83] His successors continued officially Catholic into the eighteenth century, and together with their nobility they created a genuinely indigenous Church. Yet even this remarkable success story anticipates the experience of Christianity amid nineteenth-century European colonialism in Africa. The Kings of Kongo were constantly at odds with the Portuguese monarchs who tried to impose their *Padroado* rights in the appointment of bishops: that inhibited the arrival of European clergy, severely limited the creation of a native clergy, and drew attention to official Christianity's entanglement with the slave trade. When the kingdom descended into political chaos in the seventeenth century, the disruption also crippled the organization of the Catholic Church. What remained was a variety of creative popular syntheses of Christian belief with previous religions: this was the first major burgeoning of independent Churches, which are such a feature of African Christianity today.[84]

In Ethiopia there was already an ancient (Monophysite or Coptic) Christian culture, which had been the ultimate source of western Europe's vain hopes to meet a great ally against Islam, Prester John. In fact events turned out the other way, and in the 1540s a Portuguese expeditionary force at very great cost in lives helped the Ethiopian kingdom defeat an Islamic holy war that had nearly annihilated it. Western Europeans could therefore count on great goodwill. Yet the Jesuits thereafter dissipated the advantage, despite zestful and heroic wanderings, which for instance may have led them to be the first Europeans to see the source of the Blue Nile, a century and a half before the Scotsman James Bruce.[85] The contemporary European battles with Protestants created a blind spot in the missionaries: just as with the Nestorian Christians of India, the Society was much less prepared to make allowances for local custom in fellow Christians than it was for other world faiths such as Hinduism, Shinto or Confucianism. There was also a fatal reminiscence of Iberia's cultural wars. Jesuits violently criticized the Ethiopian Orthodox Church for what they saw as Judaizing deviations – celebration of the Sabbath, male circumcision and avoidance of pork. Eventually the Ethiopians were infuriated enough to retaliate: a brutal expulsion of the Jesuits, and some executions, followed in the 1630s.[86]

Again and again missionary Jesuits and friars proved their heroic commitment to spreading their Christian message in such situations. The prolonged sufferings and ghastly deaths of Jesuit missionaries at the hands of hostile first nations in Canada in the early seventeenth century are legendary. Even the hazards of travel were a martyrdom in themselves: of 376 Jesuits who set out for China between 1581 and 1712, 127 died at sea on the way.[87] The perpetual trouble in all these mission-fields was the European reluctance to accept on equal terms the peoples whom they encountered, even when Europeans distinguished between what they saw as varied levels of culture. The Jesuit José de Acosta expressed the diverse policy of his Society to different groupings of 'barbarians' in his *On securing the salvation of the Indies* (1588). His first category embraced the great civilizations of India and east Asia, whose culture ought to be respected and who could be persuaded into Christianity by rational argument. A second category were those cultures like the Inkas or Aztecs, which had developed complex political organization but had no worthwhile literature and whose religion showed bestial features such as human sacrifice: they needed proper firm Christian government, but might be helped to manage their own affairs. Last of all were the peoples without proper government or settled life, who should be treated like children before they could even be educated into behaving like proper humans: such were the Indios who formed the population of the south American 'Reductions'.[88]

Such attitudes meant that the missionaries were always loth to create native priests on a large scale or with equal authority to themselves. Even the Jesuits would not recruit for membership of the Society from Acosta's first privileged category of culture apart from the Japanese, with a few later admissions of Chinese and Koreans in the seventeenth century. Where initiatives were taken in other areas, as in the Portuguese settlements in west and central Africa, the native clergy were treated as inferiors and very rarely became bishops. In Kongo, many of them (generally from elite backgrounds) were so infuriated at being patronized or marginalized by European colleagues that they became a major force in articulating local hatred of the Portuguese. An additional problem in Africa was the Church's insistence on the rule of compulsory clerical celibacy, restated with renewed vigour in the Counter-Reformation: this was profoundly alien to the mores of most indigenous cultures. It was not surprising that when a Church infrastructure which remained European fell into decay in any area of the world, the Church as a whole soon began to fade away.

Such became the case in many parts of the Catholic mission field of Asia and Africa in the later seventeenth and eighteenth centuries, and it was directly connected to the increasing weakness of the Spanish and Portuguese empires. It had been a marvellous achievement in the first place for these comparatively ill-endowed Iberian kingdoms to put together world empires, but they faced mounting problems and increasing interference from other European powers, first the Protestant United Provinces of the Netherlands, and later Britain and France. With their decline, the Catholic missionary impulse suffered a great setback, as power shifted from the Catholic south to central Europe and the Atlantic Isles. Our next three chapters deal with the fortunes of this fiercely contested part of the divided house.

IO

Central Europe: Religion Contested

By the early seventeenth century, the destinies of far south and far north in Europe were clearly marked respectively for Roman Catholicism and Protestantism: not so in a broad central band of territories across the continent, stretching from France to the Black Sea. A telling difference between Catholicism in central and in southern Europe was that in this central band, virtually nowhere was it possible to introduce or sustain the work of an inquisition. Bishop Georg Stobaeus, adviser to Ferdinand, the devoutly Catholic Archduke of Inner Austria, sarcastically dismissed a papal nuncio's proposal to introduce an inquisition to the duchy. He pointed out that an inquisition's job was to seek out and investigate heresy: in the lands with which he was familiar there was nothing to investigate, since all the important officials were Protestants and the heretics cheerfully practised their religion in public.[1] It was in the unstable religious and political situation of central Europe that the fatal breakdown of peace was to come in 1618: thirty years of destructive war followed, with the aim on both sides of radically tipping the religious balance one way or the other. This chapter deals with the conditions leading to the 1618 crisis, beginning with the territories of central and eastern Europe in which the Thirty Years War was incubated.

THE EMPIRE AND HABSBURG LANDS: A SHATTERED CHURCH

From the southern provinces of the Low Countries under Spanish rule eastwards to the Carpathian mountains and the Balkans, very few parts of central Europe could ignore claims to power by various branches of the Habsburg family. The most straightforward outcome was on that far west coast: the survival of Roman Catholicism and Spanish Habsburg power in the southern Netherlands, which was the result of hard-fought military campaigns against the Protestant north, over three decades from the first rising of 1566. As the long military emergency gradually dissipated in the 1590s, the Spanish monarchy was able to experiment with renewed autonomy in Brussels. This led from 1598–9 to King Philip II granting joint sovereignty to his favourite daughter Isabel and her newly acquired husband Albrecht (Albert), son of the Austrian Habsburg Holy Roman Emperor Maximilian II. Over three decades of their careful guidance as Archdukes, and with a treaty at last concluded with the United Provinces in 1610, the south began to stabilize and to prosper once more; alas, the Archdukes had no children to inherit their efforts, and the return to Spanish rule in 1633 proved a less happy experience.

Isabel and Albert still hankered after the reunion of the Low Countries under Roman obedience, and they were determined to make their realm a showcase of well-instructed, lavishly funded Roman Catholic practice to impress the northern heretics. They encouraged the restoration of ravaged churches and the building of new ones, and they fostered the usual Counter-Reformation array of revived monasteries, nunneries, friaries, Jesuit communities and confraternities. The famous university at Leuven was still a powerhouse of Catholic scholarship, with the advantage over its more southerly Catholic competitors that it was a long way from Rome and less under the eye of tidy-minded Roman officials. The old humanist scholarly traditions of the Netherlands continued to be respected there, much to the unease of government representatives of Church and State visiting from Spain, and the university authorities discreetly managed to exclude any Jesuit foundation, well knowing the Society's tendency to take over any educational establishment in which it established an interest. We will see the consequences of this relative freedom when we come to examine the disruptive Catholic theology known as Jansenism (see below, pp. 480–84).

Elsewhere it was the Austrian branch of the Habsburg family, centring on the imperial residence in Vienna, who faced the conundrum of how to deal with Protestantism. There was an additional problem of geographical priority in the vast and complex inheritance of Habsburg family jurisdictions and rights. Should a Habsburg look north-west, or south-east? To open a westerly-facing window in Vienna's Hofburg was to be reminded of two centuries during which the Habsburgs had worn the crown of the Holy Roman Empire. To look south or east was to survey the conglomeration of duchies making up the hereditary family lands beyond the Empire, or the two great kingdoms of Bohemia and Hungary, all constantly menaced by the power of the Ottoman armies on a shifting border. Outside the Austrian hereditary lands, the chief subjects of the Habsburgs in both Empire and

North
Sea

Finland

S W E D E N

Stockholm

Estonia

R U S S I A

Baltic Sea

Riga

Moscow

DENMARK AND NORWAY

Copenhagen

Hamburg

Danzig

Ducal
Prussia

L i t h u a n i a

United
Provinces

Amsterdam

Brandenburg

Magdeburg

P O L A N D

Cleves

Cologne

Warsaw

Spanish
Netherlands

Silesia

Dresden

Vistula

Kiev

Frankfurt am Main

Prague

Cracow

Dnieper

Rhine

Bohemia

Carpathian Mountains

FRANCE

Danube

Bavaria

Austria

Munich

Vienna

Buda

Debrecen

Partium

Kolozsvár

Transylvania

Savoy

Hungary

Gyulaferhérvár

Kronstadt

Milan

Venice

O T T O M A N

Florence

Papal States

Dalmatia

Adriatic Sea

E M P I R E

Rome

Naples

Mediterranean
Sea

5. *East and central Europe, 1648*

kingdoms rarely let them forget that their crowns were elective and not hereditary, and everywhere – in Empire, kingdoms and duchies alike – there were representative Estates and Diets where landed nobility and chief towns were alert to defend their financial and political interests. Virtually everywhere during the first five decades of the Reformation, the local rulers had decided that this ought to be coupled with a declaration for Protestantism, which would be a useful weapon against any aspirations by the Catholic Habsburgs to increase their power. In Bohemia and Moravia, Lutherans (and in Bohemia also the Hussites) had long enjoyed concessions from their monarchs (chapter 4, p. 163). The Habsburgs were usually desperately short of money with which to sustain their government, particularly their armies, and they were uncomfortably aware that the Estates might withhold grants of money if the dynasty ignored their wishes.

The head of the family, the Holy Roman Emperor, naturally tended to be preoccupied with the situation in the Empire, circumscribed as it was after 1555 with the compromise of the Peace of Augsburg. The Emperor faced a set of secular imperial princes who had almost all ended up backing the Reformation, with the important exception of the Wittelsbach ducal house in Bavaria (to whom we will return); likewise, by the end of the sixteenth century, fifty out of sixty-five free cities of the Empire had accepted the Reformation.[2] It was this fact of entrenched Protestant strength that shaped the mediating and inclusive strategy of the Emperor Ferdinand I, despite his personal loathing of Protestantism: Ferdinand's policy was continued as a matter of conscientious and enthusiastic conviction by his son the Emperor Maximilian II, as we have noted (chapter 6, pp. 296–7), and central Europe owed several decades of peace largely to their moderation. However, it was much less obvious to other members of the Habsburg family, particularly to Archdukes who ruled in the hereditary lands, that action to help the old Church regain its ascendancy was unrealistic. Successive Archdukes from Maximilian's younger brother Ferdinand onwards began co-operating with Rome in order to introduce the Counter-Reformation. They were particularly helped in a crucial decade from 1572 by the close interest which Pope Gregory XIII took in the affairs of central Europe: he showed warm support for the Society of Jesus, the chief agents in the campaign of reconversion. Pope Gregory saw the Archdukes as a useful counterbalance against the policies of the Emperor Maximilian, whom he profoundly mistrusted.

Even though the Habsburgs were able to exercise much more control over their hereditary lands than in the Empire, the cause of Roman Catholicism still faced daunting obstacles, for the nobility and German-speaking population beyond the Empire were overwhelmingly Lutheran by the 1570s. The nobility of Tyrol in the extreme south were a notable exception, remaining staunchly Catholic all through the Reformation, but Tyrol's peculiarity is significant. It related to a specially advantageous deal on tax and local revenue that local magnates struck early in the sixteenth century with the old Emperor Maximilian I – he had a special affection for Tyrol and intended to make it the centre of his dominions. There was thus much less incentive here than elsewhere for nobles to make a stand against imperial power, and so less incentive for them to become Lutheran when the Reformation arrived. Already in the 1560s, the Archduke Ferdinand began exploiting the religious possibilities which this opened up. German-speaking towns, free peasantries and mining communities in the hereditary lands responded to evangelical preaching from the 1520s onwards and joined the Lutherans, although their own contentions with Protestant territorial nobility over jurisdiction and taxes meant that Protestantism was not always capable of presenting a united religious front against Catholic aggression.[3]

Indeed, aristocratic exploitation of feudal rights such as compulsory labour created fury among the rural peasantry that was a serious potential weakness for the Reformation since Protestantism became closely identified with aristocratic support. This was especially true where there was a substantial non-German-speaking element in the peasantry: in the provinces of Lower Styria and Carniola, Slovene peasants were repeatedly involved in savagely fought risings against their German feudal lords, and it was no coincidence that mid-century missionary efforts by a native Slovenian Lutheran, Primus Truber, were a failure, despite his pastoral work and his labours in translating the Bible into south Slav languages. Instead, alienated from Lutheranism, Slovenes uniquely expressed their radical longings for a renewed religion in a 'Leaper' (*Springer*) sect which represented an intensification of their traditional piety. They listened eagerly to visionary prophets who proclaimed messages from the Virgin and the saints, significantly prompting them to build new churches. Leaper enthusiasm proved a useful ally in the eventual coming of the Counter-Reformation, although the Catholic authorities were themselves quick to repress Leaper activities once official Catholicism was firmly established. By then the Leapers had served their purpose.[4]

By contrast with the secular powers of the Empire and beyond, all the important imperial bishops and archbishops who enjoyed independent territorial power resisted pressure to convert to Protestantism, as far north as the lonely outpost of Catholicism in the Westphalian Prince-Bishopric of Münster, little more than thirty miles from the border with the Protestant Dutch. This general faithfulness (only betrayed, and then unsuccessfully, by

Hermann von Wied of Cologne) certainly preserved the husk of the old Church in Germany and Austria through its most dangerous years in mid-century, but it was less clear that the imperial prelates were going to be much better disposed to the Counter-Reformation than they were to the Reformation. The election of these bishops and their conduct in office still remained governed by the deal that Rome had struck with the Holy Roman Emperor in the Concordat of Vienna back in 1448 (chapter 1, p. 46). Few imperial bishops were likely to be sympathetic to the sort of centralizing interference in dioceses envisaged by the Council of Trent (a gathering at which few of them had deigned to appear) – more importantly, there was little that Rome could do to compel them to show any deference to papal wishes. They still mostly came from the ancient noble families of the Empire and were elected by cathedral chapters with the same social profile, which meant that many of them had close contacts and sometimes some sympathy with aristocratic supporters of the Lutheran Church.

The consequences could be seen in the German and Austrian Catholicism of the 1560s and 1570s. Like various senior Austrian Habsburgs, many prelates were well-disposed to the project (which Rome detested) of offering the chalice of wine to the laity in the Mass, and they did not discourage the practice in their dioceses. The bishops could not understand the southern preoccupation with the dangers of the vernacular Bible, and often in their synods, in an effort to counter Protestant emphasis on Bible-reading, they encouraged their parish clergy to own Bibles and use them in a way which was unthinkable in Italy.[5] The German bishops were annoyed at interference with centuries of varied local liturgical custom when the papacy tried to enforce use of the Tridentine Mass, and they were particularly lukewarm about Rome's efforts to impose universal clerical celibacy. It was extremely difficult for either them or their subordinate clergy to see the point of this, when all around them the Lutheran clergy offered examples of happy and decorous marriages. When the papal nuncio Germanico Malaspina gloomily surveyed the archdiocese of Salzburg in 1581, he found that in the Styrian territories of its jurisdiction, fewer than ten out of 220 parish clergy did not have a concubine or claim to be married, and clergy defiantly cited the example of Lutheran pastors, whom they regarded 'as good as the priests of other provinces'. As late as 1612 the aristocratic Archbishop of Salzburg, Wolf Dietrich von Raittenau, who in other respects was well disposed to Catholic reform, set his clergy a notable example by living with a concubine who bore him fifteen children, and it was not this misdemeanour but political misadventuring that brought his eventual deposition and imprisonment.[6]

How could the Counter-Reformation vision be implemented when most of the German diocesan clergy and episcopal hierarchy were so manifestly out of sympathy with it? Sometimes the combination of an outstanding local clergyman and a single-minded civic elite produced the required result. Rottweil was an Imperial Free City in the far south-west of Germany, which was conveniently remote from its nominal and ineffective episcopal superior, the Bishop of Konstanz; it could therefore direct its own religious life with little outside interference. The city council, unusually, took the decision to stay Catholic, but Rottweil than behaved very like the Protestant free cities of the Empire by seeking a prominent clergyman to lead the city's preaching and teaching. Johannes Uhl, a local boy from the city elite, was their chosen candidate, and over half a century from 1559 he did a remarkable and imaginative job there – acting rather like Martin Bucer in Strassburg or Heinrich Bullinger in Zürich, but here in the interests of reviving Catholic devotion.[7]

Rottweil was an exception, particularly since its well-ordered Catholic life was led by a secular clergyman: since 1517, such local initiatives in the tradition of late medieval civic religious activism had rarely led to the Counter-Reformation, and nearly always to Protestantism. It would be tempting for outside observers like Germanico Malaspina to see a powerful symbolism in the embarrassing state of Germany's most ambitious church building, Cologne Cathedral. Money finally ran out there in 1560 after more than three centuries of construction, leaving the staggeringly tall choir rearing its torso over the city and the river Rhine, with everything else no more than a monstrous stump; work on the building only began again (under the sponsorship of a Protestant monarch) in the nineteenth century (see Plate 15a). Catholic Germany desperately needed some external initiative. It was the pro-German Pope, Gregory XIII, who began tackling the clerical problem when in 1573 he saw to the foundation in Rome of a College for Germany. The ingenious idea of this 'Collegium Germanicum' was to circumvent the problems posed by the Concordat of Vienna by training up a properly motivated aristocratic clerical elite who were highly likely to become canons of German cathedrals, and who should eventually therefore make a respectable job of electing well-disposed bishops. Gradually the strategy produced results, although the experience of life in Rome was not always calculated to make a German nobleman enthusiastic for papal obedience.[8]

Inevitably, as with most new educational initiatives in the Counter-Reformation world, the Jesuits were closely associated with the Germanicum, which was actually a remodelling of an earlier unsuccessful foundation of their own. After all, it had been the dire state of Catholic

Germany in the 1550s which first refocused the Jesuit mission on combating Protestantism (chapter 7, pp. 323–4). Just as in the unsatisfactorily staffed dioceses of southern Italy, the Jesuits viewed the German lands as a specialized form of virgin mission field, in which the existing hierarchy needed to be bypassed if an effective and distinctive Catholicism was to be re-established (chapter 9, pp. 415–17). It was easy for others to construe this attitude as arrogance and condescension, and in some circumstances it won the Jesuits a good deal of ill-will. In Münster, where the Society did actually arrive with the sponsorship of the local bishop, many of the faithful still found the Jesuits almost as alien as Reformed Protestants: the incomers annoyed leading citizens by speaking High rather than Low German, they offended the local sensibilities of north Germans by drinking wine instead of beer, and as usual in their missions, they tried to abolish the local carnival customs, in this case with a rare lack of success. In the diocese of Speyer in the central Rhineland, the discreet hostility of the local bishop prevented the Jesuits founding a college until 1575; thereafter, continuing opposition from the city much hampered their work, and at the end of the Thirty Years War they faced such obstructions from the cathedral Chapter that they virtually ceased operations in the diocese.[9]

HABSBURGS, WITTELSBACHS AND A CATHOLIC RECOVERY

The situation in Speyer highlighted a general difficulty for the Jesuits. For their work to begin, they relied on a local invitation, and they also tried as far as possible to make the institutions that they then founded financially viable with a proper endowment. If they were going to overcome the general indifference or even hostility of the local Catholic clergy or the even more dangerous opposition of Protestant nobility and town councils, they must find backing from well-motivated (and rich) members of the German lay elite. This began to emerge from some members of the Habsburg family, but also from another great family of the Empire, the Wittelsbachs. One Protestant branch of the Wittelsbachs provided the Electors of the Palatinate, who from the 1550s came to play such a crucial role in Germany's 'Second Reformation' (see above, chapter 8, pp. 354–7; below, chapter 11), but in the duchy of Bavaria a succession of Wittelsbach dukes (who as a result of the Thirty Years War would become imperial Electors) embraced the renewal of Catholicism with extraordinary fervour and effectiveness. Bavaria was one of the largest political units within the Empire, and its

Wittelsbach rulers therefore experienced in miniature the same sort of political problem facing the Habsburgs in their various dominions: self-assertive noblemen and civic elites, most of whom found adopting Protestantism to be a useful asset in their frequently combative relations with the Dukes of Bavaria. Both for Habsburg and Wittelsbach then, genuine devotion to the Catholic faith conveniently coincided with their wish to strengthen their own power. Catholicism was an ally in these dynasties' efforts to build an institution that is a recognizable ancestor of the modern centralized bureaucratic state.

A remarkable dynastic and confessional alliance now developed between the two families, who had by no means always appreciated each other's virtues (chapter 1, p. 49). The first fruit was marriage in 1571 between Duke Albrecht V of Bavaria's daughter Maria and Archduke Karl of Inner Austria. Karl joined his elder brother Archduke Ferdinand of Tyrol as one of the chief instigators among the Habsburgs of an aggressive policy towards Protestantism in their dominions, in conscious opposition to their eldest brother the Emperor Maximilian. Soon afterwards, Karl completed long drawn-out negotiations to bring the Society of Jesus to his Inner Austrian capital of Graz, which was at that time also a prominent centre of the Lutheran church and had a flourishing Lutheran school. The Jesuits now set to work to provide a college and school designed to supplant the efforts of Protestant education, and they did well enough to expand their institution into a university in 1586; already by then it was recruiting significant numbers of students from neighbouring Hungary and Croatia. Simultaneously Duke Albrecht was financing a Bavarian Jesuit college to strengthen his cherished university of Ingolstadt, already famous as a bastion of Catholic orthodoxy through the worst crises of Catholicism in the Empire, after the long years that Luther's dangerous opponent Dr Johann Eck had spent there.[10]

These highly motivated Catholic rulers continued to work closely together, and kept in touch with Pope Gregory XIII. In 1579 a crucial face-to-face conference took place in Munich between Duke Albrecht's son and successor Wilhelm V and the two Archdukes Ferdinand and Karl. They were prompted by alarming proof of how successful the Estates in Inner Austria could be in furthering their Lutheran religious interests. Between 1572 and 1578 the Estates used their financial leverage on Archduke Karl to extract from him (and also to publish) a 'Pacification' granting sweeping concessions for Lutheran Protestantism. This Protestant success in one part of central Europe spelled disaster for the nascent Counter-Reformation in a much wider field, and the three rulers debated how to regain the advantage for Karl in Inner Austria in the face of the Graz Pacification. They agreed that military action was impractical and undesirable, and instead they recommended a gradual policy of legal and political attrition of Protestant privileges, coupled with a steady promotion of the Catholic cause, using every incentive of promotion or Court favour that was at the Archduke's disposal. If necessary, reliable Bavarian or Tyrolean Catholics could be imported to take up influential offices. Change, they decided, would come 'not with sound and fury, but surreptitiously and slowly; . . . not with words but with deeds'.[11]

This was indeed the programme which Karl adopted, carefully liaising with his fellow rulers while he implemented it, for instance through another threeway summit meeting in Innsbruck in 1584. He was followed by his son Ferdinand (the future Emperor Ferdinand II): the new Archduke's intense Catholic piety had been reinforced by a Jesuit education at Ingolstadt, and his advisers were likewise Jesuit-trained or themselves members of the Society, mostly from the Spanish Netherlands. The successive Archdukes whittled away at the position of Protestant churches until in 1598 the younger Ferdinand finally abolished the Protestant ministry in Graz and closed the school. They first favoured Catholics in appointments to lesser Court offices, gradually working up the scale of importance until only their War Council still contained a significant number of Protestants (it would not do to enrage Protestant magnates in this crucial strategic body). Ferdinand also packed Catholics into local judicial appointments to intimidate local councils, and it became clear to anyone with ambition that imperial service meant a profession of Catholicism.[12]

In 1599 the Archduke, who had just paid a secret visit to see the Holy Father in Rome face to face, introduced a new aggression into his campaign and widened it from town to country by a new use of 'reformation commissions'. These were extensions of the traditional episcopal visitation, but apart from being led by a senior cleric whom Ferdinand could trust, they were reinforced by senior Habsburg officials and an intimidatingly large body of troops. They hurled thousands of Protestant books on to bonfires. They not only expelled Lutheran clergy if they found them exercising their ministry, but even desecrated Protestant graveyards or tore down Protestant churches, seeing them as too polluted to be reused by Catholics even if they were handsome buildings – some of them they blew up with gunpowder. It was significant that Slovenian peasants, smarting from the destruction of their own 'Leaper' cult churches by Lutherans and delighting in the discomfiture of their German landlords, gleefully joined the commissioners in the desecration.[13]

The Bavarian Wittelsbachs also followed the Munich agreement in carrying out a programme of careful attrition against local Protestantism in their own territories, but additionally they were drawn into direct military intervention within the Empire. Here their successful action proved equally decisive in halting further Protestant advance. The issue was the possibility of wholesale defection of the imperial bishoprics into the Protestant camp if their incumbents converted from Catholic obedience. This was, after all, how Protestantism gained its first significant territorial Church, back in 1525 when Grand Master Albrecht of the Teutonic Order had renounced Catholicism and celibacy to establish a secular dynasty in Ducal Prussia (chapter 4, p. 162). Over the next decades a whole series of abbots, abbesses and collegiate deans had followed suit. By contrast, virtually no major bishop did so without external pressure, and a clause of Reservation in the 1555 Peace of Augsburg sought to make sure that this could not happen: any bishop or prelate of the imperial Estates who converted to the new faith would automatically lose office and imperial territory.

The issue was forced when in 1582 the Lutheran Hohenzollern administrator of the Archdiocese of Magdeburg, Prince Joachim Friedrich, sought to attend the imperial Diet under the title of Archbishop of Magdeburg. After Catholic protests, the Emperor Rudolf decided to order him to withdraw. This was a useful precedent in a crisis which developed in the same year: after prolonged disputes in the Archdiocese of Cologne between Archbishop Gebhard Truchsess von Waldburg and his cathedral chapter, the Archbishop decided to defy the Augsburg Reservation by declaring both his Protestantism and the fact that he had married, while refusing to renounce his title. It was a replay of the Hermann von Wied episode in the 1540s: the prospect of the rich Rhineland archbishopric moving to the Protestant camp, and the capture for a Protestant of one more vote in imperial elections. The emergency galvanized Duke Wilhelm of Bavaria; just as Charles V had made effective the papal deposition of von Wied by force, troops were now needed to resolve the issue. Acting in concert with Spanish Habsburg forces from the southern Netherlands, the Duke's armies removed the would-be Protestant Archbishop, with little Protestant intervention except from Duke Wilhelm's indefatigable Calvinist cousin, Count Johann Casimir of the Palatinate.

The reward for the Bavarian Wittelsbachs was the acquisition of the archdiocese of Cologne; from 1583 to 1761 every Archbishop was a member of the Bavarian ruling house. The first nominee was manifestly unfit for office and epitomized the worst scandals which had afflicted the medieval German Church: Prince Ernst had been Bishop of Freising since the age of twelve, and besides holding the important sees of Liège and Hildesheim, he went on to enjoy alongside Cologne the prince-bishopric of Münster, where two of his successors up to 1688 were also members of the Wittelsbach family. Brusquely ignoring the ideals of the Council of Trent for resident and competent bishops, Pope Gregory XIII was happy in this case to exploit the possibilities of imperial episcopal corruption, and he encouraged Ernst's inappropriate candidacy for Cologne, confident that the house of Bavaria was a useful investment. In a concordat also agreed with Duke Wilhelm in the decisive year of 1583, the Pope conceded the Duke a great measure of control over his clergy, including taxation rights. Both parties gained as these provisions were designed to rein in the inconvenient independence of one section of the German Church.[14]

The 'Bishops' War' over Cologne dragged on for five years from 1583, but it was remarkable that otherwise the strategies agreed at Munich in 1579 did not lead to much more widespread warfare before the great 1618 crisis in central Europe. It was a measure of the ideological commitment of Archduke Ferdinand that he implemented his highly confrontational policy of 'reformation commissions' at the height of a war which he was waging against the Ottomans, yet his gamble paid off: despite a good deal of local fury and violent clashes with the commissions, the war effort was not seriously disrupted. Indeed, the constant state of threat from Islam was a useful asset to the Habsburgs as they implemented their deeply unpopular Catholic religious policies. However angry the Lutheran nobility might be with the ruling dynasty, they were at one with them in the absolute necessity of fighting the Turks. An additional neurosis which bound the nobility to the Habsburgs was the memory of the events of the Peasants' War of 1525–6, when the charismatic Michael Gaismayr in Tyrol had been one of the most successful leaders of popular armies enthused by evangelical slogans, threatening the end of noble and Habsburg power alike (chapter 4, p. 161). The Estates were therefore terrified of any suggestion of militancy or disruption of the social order in their Protestantism, and as Lutherans they were generally hostile even to conventional Reformed Protestantism. Consequently they chose to draw on Luther's theories of non-resistance rather than his theories of resistance, despite the more militant urgings of some of their clergy. They failed to make a stand even to save their effective and cherished schools and colleges.[15]

Amid this adroit Catholic combination of military force and partisan restructuring of power, the Counter-Reformation in central Europe began taking shape. Wherever the Jesuits were able to establish themselves they led the work of re-education, followed later by the Capuchins and the Piarists as the mission began to widen its social base and tackle the instruction of the rural masses. The Jesuits benefited particularly from the patronage of the Dukes of Bavaria: their huge new headquarters church of St Michael, dominating a main street in Munich, was the first major new Catholic church-building project north of the Alps when it was begun in the Catholic 'wonder-year' of 1583, and the work absorbed alarmingly large quantities of Wittelsbach revenues. Far to the north in Münster, it was the uninspiring and pluralist Wittelsbach Bishop Ernst who was prompted to invite the Society to its contentious mission there. Rarely in Germany did the Jesuits risk the sort of dramatic travelling preaching missions or histrionics that made such an impact in southern Europe. It was as late as 1594, for instance, before they introduced the practice of the Forty Hours Devotion to Graz as a penitential exercise at a particularly threatening moment of the Turkish Wars. Sometimes the low-key nature of the work in central Europe, teaching assignments in parishes or pastoral ministry to condemned prisoners, bored some of the adventurous spirits in the Society: they had to be reined in or told firmly that they had to persist, rather than transfer to some more glamorously dangerous sector of the Jesuit mission.[16]

One essential task was to win back from the Lutherans the sense that the Catholic Church represented the traditional norm in German religion. Accordingly, when the Society built its local headquarters in the centre of Cologne in the early seventeenth century, its stately church paid tribute to the ancient churches of the city by being deliberately designed in an old-fashioned Gothic style, with high turrets in Rhineland Romanesque, architecturally obsolete for four centuries. The Jesuit church further up the Rhine in Bonn boasts similar archaizing Romanesque towers. But these architectural references were only symbols of a greater project to reclaim and revalue the sacred places and sacred history of Catholic Germany. Cologne was well placed in this respect as the last resting place of St Ursula and her 11,000 virgins (see Plate 12). Although this multitude of ladies appears to have been the result of a medieval scribal error, they had generated an obligingly large number of bones: the Jesuits used their international organization to spread specimens as objects of devotion throughout the Habsburg dominions both Austrian and Spanish, and even beyond into the Iberian seaborne empires.[17]

Everywhere in central Europe, relics of the saints were brought out of hiding, and shrines desecrated by Protestants were lovingly restored. The unfortunate St Benno of Meissen, whose cult Duke Georg of Saxony had tried to launch in 1523, now found himself rescued in the more sympathetic atmosphere of Catholic Munich when his remains were acquired for Duke Albrecht of Bavaria in 1576, and he became much celebrated in the city, giving his name to one of its favourite beers. After the Thirty Years War, the Lutherans of Bremen Cathedral preferred Catholic hard cash to their golden medieval shrine of Sts Cosmas and Damian, which similarly went to Munich, further to adorn the Jesuits' church of St Michael.[18] Thousands of bones were also imported from the Roman catacombs to reinforce the depleted local larders of sanctity in churches all over the region: a great help in this process was the newly developed glass technology which made it possible to build clear display-cases for whole skeletons. Some saintly arrivals pandered to the same instinct that today leads to the acquisition of personalized car number-plates: they bore the same name as the pious purchaser. Others were testimony to a more scrupulous but still optimistic faith, as I observed in a relic cabinet in St Peter's, Augsburg, where one catacomb bone is labelled *Sancti martyris ignoti* – 'of an unknown holy martyr'.

Unsurprisingly the Bavarian Wittelsbach family were chief patrons in the campaign, especially in importing catacomb saints to their territories. To enter the private oratory of the Wittelsbachs off the Long Gallery of their palace in Munich is to be overwhelmed by a glittering little room which substitutes human bones and their jewelled cases for wallpaper. This collection was designed as an arsenal of holiness, the living heart of the Wittelsbach project to restore the Roman obedience and also to build the dynasty a confessional and absolutist state. To give the saints their due honour was to symbolize the defeat of Protestantism and to encourage an attitude of militant anger among Catholics that God's holy people should thus have been dishonoured. On the eve of the Thirty Years War the leading specialist in the restoration of shrines in Bavaria, Fr. Matthäus Rader SJ, urged on good Catholics to get ready to fight 'those who have declared eternal war on the saints, dug up their relics like dogs and destroyed them with fire and water'.[19]

As a centrepiece of this campaign to rehabilitate the saints and through them the Catholic Church, the Jesuits stressed devotion to Mary, the Mother of God, which Martin Luther's own Marian enthusiasm had not saved even in Lutheran Protestantism. They promoted use of the rosary (which after all had its origins in fifteenth-century Cologne) and directed confraternities specifically dedicated to Mary; echoing the political militancy of Jesuit confraternities in France (chapter 6, p. 309), significant popular resistance to Archbishop Gebhard's Protestantizing project in Cologne was mobilized by these 'Marian congregations'.[20] As soon as they could, the Jesuits sought to revive Marian shrines, a particular target of the reformers, by reminding the population of their spiritual power. As early as 1570, the Jesuit Provincial of Upper Germany Peter Canisius contributed to the revival of the Bavarian shrine of the Black Madonna of Altötting by exorcizing the Devil from a noblewoman there. This caused a great sensation, and the following year the miracle was well publicized in a new guidebook by the shrine church's Provost, Martin Eisengrein: his often-reprinted *Our Lady of Altötting* was one of the first examples of a newly hagiographical tourist literature that burgeoned in central Europe over the next century.[21]

Once the revival of shrines gained momentum, it made the cult of Mary the chief symbol and agency of Counter-Reformation renewal. The Austrian churchman Melchior Khlesl owed the Jesuits his childhood conversion from Protestantism, before becoming a prominent Austrian church administrator and Chancellor of Vienna University (subsequently also Cardinal and Bishop of Vienna). He seized every opportunity far beyond his administrative responsibilities to promote the Counter-Reformation, and was a chief agent in restoring Marian pilgrimage in central Europe. In 1599 he personally led a crowd of 23,000 pilgrims to the Upper Styrian shrine of Mariazell; with the enthusiastic backing (and cash) of senior Habsburgs including the Emperor Ferdinand III, this became one of the most well-patronized and loved of the region's shrines, not merely in Austria, but far beyond in Moravia and Hungary, contributing much to undermining the dominance of Protestantism in these areas. Mariazell was a highly important means of binding together disparate Habsburg territories through Catholic devotional practice. In the Spanish Netherlands, the same function was filled by the restored Marian shrine of Scherpenheuvel ('Sharp Hill'), which was usefully on the borderland with the United Provinces; once the holy place was securely under the military control of the Catholic government in the south from around 1580 and rescued from Protestant desecration, it started once more producing miracles to strengthen the faith of Catholics and impress Protestant doubters.[22]

The results of all this concentrated effort were apparent by 1600. Those who have systematically studied the preoccupations of Roman Catholic bishops in visitations of south and west Germany have noticed a shift in their interest around this date: previously the questions and reports of misdemeanours focused on the conduct of the parish clergy, particularly the fundamental problems of non-residence and concubinage or clerical marriage. From 1600, the reports concerned lesser quirks of the clergy's personal behaviour such as drunkenness, and in any case such deficiencies apparently become less numerous; attention was shifting to the associates of the pastor, such as the sacristan or the schoolteacher, or whether the church roof was in good shape. No Church system ever matches up to its own ideal standards, but these changes indicated that there was now at least a functioning system which could respond to the probing of the episcopal authorities.[23] Between them, Rome, Jesuits, Habsburg and Wittelsbach had turned the tide of Lutheran Protestantism in much of the German lands. Not merely Lutherans but the Hussite and Reformed subjects of the monarchs in Bohemia, Moravia and Hungary were entitled to feel very apprehensive about the future.

TRANSYLVANIA: A REFORMED ISRAEL

East of the Habsburg hereditary lands, Latin Christianity struggled to recover from the collapse of the Kingdom of Hungary in the 1520s, with Habsburgs, Ottomans and local rulers contending for political advantage. The result, as we have seen (chapter 5, pp. 259–60) was a three-way split between western and northern Habsburg Royal Hungary, the great expanse of Turkish-occupied plains in the centre of the old kingdom, and in the east the autonomous 'Partium' plains and the mountainous principality of Transylvania. The numerous German communities and elites stretching far into the Balkans generally identified with the developing Lutheran Church, but other cultural groupings did not. Very few stayed with the old Catholic Church, so thoroughly discredited by the catastrophe at Mohács in 1526, and so the critical mass of the non-German-speaking Latin Church coalesced around Reformed Protestantism, often in variants so radical as to alarm mainstream Reformed leaders (chapter 5, pp. 260–63). By 1600 more than three-quarters of over 5,000 parishes in Hungary and Transylvania were Protestant, and over 2,000 of these 4,000 or so Protestant communities were Reformed.[24] To appreciate the remarkable story of Hungarian Protestantism will take us well into the seventeenth century, for this was a late as well as an intense flowering of the international Reformed Protestant movement.

In 1570 Transylvania and the Partium gained formal recognition as an independent principality, acknowledging not Habsburg but Ottoman overlordship, after bitter warfare ended in a three-way agreement, leaving the bulk of Hungary in Ottoman hands. The principality of Transylvania was thus the only Latin Christian territory to find itself to the east of Muslim power, as well as on the frontier of Orthodox Christianity, and it took its responsibilities to western Christendom very seriously. Successive princes came to see themselves as protectors of Christians in Ottoman Hungary, and also defenders of Protestants in Royal Hungary whenever the Habsburgs tried to move against them. It was not surprising that Hungary's and

Transylvania's Reformed ministers were drawn to see the heroism and suffering of the Hungarian people as a modern parallel to the epic of God's ancient chosen people, Israel: like the 'Scythians' who had migrated to Hungary, the Israelites had wandered until they conquered a Promised Land, and then they suffered many misfortunes and the destruction of their kingdom at the hands of the ungodly. Nevertheless, the sixteenth-century Princes of Transylvania were not yet adherents of Reformed Protestantism, and one of the most capable, István Báthori (who was also elected King of Poland, chapter 7, p. 344), was actually an enthusiastic Catholic. In 1579 Báthori tried to extend his benevolent encouragement of Catholicism from Poland to Transylvania by inviting the Jesuits to operate in the principality. It was significant how little support this popular and respected prince received for his action: the Society found its work severely constrained, and the Transylvanian Diet saw to its expulsion in 1588 – two subsequent returns and expulsions took place before 1606. Bereft of support from the magnates, with no determined backing from the monarchy after Báthori's death and with no resident bishop, the Catholic Church for the time being remained a shadow of its former self in the principality.[25]

The Reformed gained their ascendancy in Hungary not least because Reformed Protestantism was an emphatic rejection of Habsburg allegiance. This became apparent in 1604–5, when István Bocskai seized power, and a new era for the Reformed Church opened up. He was a wealthy Reformed Protestant landowner from the Partium who became increasingly impatient with the close links built up between the Báthori princes and the Habsburgs; that alliance was supposed to be directed against the Turks, but the Emperor Rudolf II clearly intended it to promote Habsburg rule and the Catholic faith in Hungary. Habsburg armies won few successes against the Turks, and instead in 1603–4 they began occupying Transylvania and maltreating Protestants in Royal Hungary. Leading a revolt against Habsburg and Báthori rule, Bocskai was first recognized as Prince by the Transylvanian Diet in 1604 and was then proclaimed by the rebellious diet of Royal Hungary as prince-protector and 'Moses of the Hungarians'. His bid for power thus couched in Old Testament terms was inseparable from his claim to be the champion of religious liberties. Although this new Moses was prepared to do a deal with the Emperor in 1606, relinquishing claims to Habsburg western Hungary, he still secured from the Habsburgs a grudging promise of freedom of worship there for both Reformed and Lutherans.

Bocskai died suddenly in 1606, and it could never thereafter be said that Transylvania was a model of political tranquillity, but successive princes were masterful and competent military leaders, and they achieved a degree of support from their nobility that the Habsburgs might envy. This was based on a shared commitment of the Prince and the great majority of noblemen to Reformed Protestant faith. The Reformed Church now emerged as the religion of the Court and virtually an established Church, with its ministers receiving generous financial backing and even privileges of nobility. A mark of the Church's new status was that it placed increasing restrictions on the anti-Trinitarian Church, despite the uniquely magnanimous provisions made for all Christians in 1568 by the Declaration of Torda (chapter 5, p. 262). In other respects, there are parallels to be drawn between this easternmost of Reformed Churches and Europe's westernmost Calvinism in the western coasts and isles of Scotland (chapter 8, pp. 380–81). Both were firmly based on the dominance of secular territorial magnates, and both managed to identify strongly with a traditional cultural identity. Both, interestingly for a religion of the book, were remarkably late in acquiring a complete Bible in the native language – the nineteenth century in the case of Scotland, and here not until 1590.[26]

The Transylvanian Church was keenly aware of its geographical isolation and its lack of educational resources. The great upheavals of the 1560s and 1570s, which sent thousands of refugees from France and the Netherlands travelling to other lands, did not spill them this far east to bring cosmopolitan communities of foreign Protestants. There were few schools, and no university until Prince Gábor Bethlen established an academy at the princely capital of Gyulaférvár (now Alba Iulia in Romania) in 1622. As the Church grew more hostile to the anti-Trinitarian congregations, it wanted its ministry to get a sound training in the latest arguments to counter the poison of radicalism. The Transylvanian authorities therefore placed a great emphasis on sending promising young hopefuls for the ministry to study abroad. Students travelled of course to Europe's leading Reformed academy at Heidelberg, but many were brave enough to seek out reliably Calvinist universities as far away as Franeker in West Friesland or over the Channel to Cambridge in England: in Franeker and Cambridge they might sit at the feet of theological stars like William Perkins and William Ames (chapter 8, pp. 389–91). All this was possible because the international language of scholarship was still Latin, although the system was not infallible: one hapless young Hungarian found himself staring in bewilderment at a large cathedral in a city called Canterbury, when he had asked directions to the English university town of *Cantabrigia*.[27]

Transylvanian Protestants thus triumphantly overcame their remoteness. Once the Thirty Years War broke out, the horrors of life in central Europe produced a good supply of distinguished refugee foreign academics ready

459

to come to the Gyulaférvár Academy and other Transylvanian schools, especially because Gábor Bethlen had set a benchmark for offering lavish salaries – some of the greatest names of the Reformed diaspora like Johann Heinrich Alsted or the Bohemian Brethren pastor Jan Amos Komenský (Comenius) arrived. Yet exposure to the wider world brought its own problems. A Hungarian student enthused by the Puritanism of Franeker or Cambridge would notice contrasts on coming home. It was not merely that to step into a Transylvanian Reformed church building was often to find a riot of newly painted colour and even figure decoration that would alarm censorious western European Calvinists (see Plate 19a).[28] A striking feature of the Reformed Churches in both Hungary and Transylvania was their hierarchical organization. Perhaps predictably for Churches so dependent on feudal magnates, they did not model themselves on the principle of equality of ministers as in the presbyterianism of Geneva, the Netherlands and Scotland. The Transylvanian Church had seven superintendents, who were often referred to without any sense of incongruity as *episcopi* or bishops, assisted by archdeacons in local church districts. There were local decision-making councils which might seem like presbyteries, but they contained only clergy and appointed no lay elders.[29] This is a reminder that Reformed Protestantism can never be simply identified with Calvinism: the idea of strong superintendency derived from Heinrich Bullinger's Zürich, or from the provisions for church organization in Jan Łaski's *Forma ac ratio*, dating back to the days of his Stranger Church in London in the 1550s (chapter 5, p. 257).

Many students who studied abroad came home to criticize their Church's leadership and to demand the introduction of a proper presbyterian system with lay elders. Some went further and followed William Ames in stressing the right of each congregation to make decisions and run internal discipline – what in England would come to be called 'Independency' (chapter 12, p. 523). They also brought back an intense concern with personal morality in the style of Perkins and Ames, and they were extremely censorious of the Church's continued coexistence with blasphemous anti-Trinitarians. They even ostentatiously sang Hungarian metrical psalms to foreign tunes ultimately deriving from the Geneva psalter, and many of them wished to abolish superstitious festivals like Christmas and Easter that were still part of local church life. Soon the writings of Ames and Perkins found a ready market in Hungarian translations and became theological bestsellers. A significant commercial success was *The Practice of Piety*, a standard English work setting out an intense personal morality, first published in the 1610s by a Calvinist-minded Welsh bishop, Lewis Bayly, and translated into

Hungarian in 1636 by one of the most energetic, charismatic and eloquent of the returned scholars, Pál Medgyesi. These young zealots were in fact Puritans, and those who found their religious style infuriating used this English word abusively for them; ultimately the enthusiasts themselves adopted the label in defiant pride.[30]

Thus in Transylvania developed western European Calvinism met another and older style of Reformed Protestantism, with more varied and cosmopolitan origins: it is worth remembering that one of the important formative figures in the Hungarian Reformed Church had been Cardinal Pole's former servant and consistent admirer, the humanist András Dudic (chapter 5, p. 263). It was not that the Transylvanian Church authorities had anything against social discipline or ordered Christian life, for moral enforcement and discipline formed the major business of the archdeacons in the Church. Hungary and Transylvania had also willingly adopted the Heidelberg Catechism of 1563. At root, what worried the clerical establishment about the new Puritanism was that these young enthusiasts would make religion an elitist matter, despising the bulk of Christians; one Transylvanian superintendent also said that the Puritans were privileging 'heart knowledge' or emotion over 'head knowledge', reflective understanding of religion. Others thought that Puritans' intensely personal and experiential piety devalued the role of the sacraments of Baptism and Eucharist in Christian life. Such debates are still potent in modern Protestant Christianity, where very similar criticisms are frequently levelled at charismatics or fundamentalist evangelicals.[31]

So from the 1620s the Transylvanian Church experienced Puritan-conformist convulsions with strong echoes of those which fifty years before had begun disrupting the Reformed Church of England (chapter 8, pp. 382–91). Those earlier English disputes were the ultimate source of the new Transylvanian stirs, more than 1,500 miles to the east of Dover. The link between these far-separated situations was underlined in the 1650s when a remarkable clergyman of the Church of England turned up in Transylvania. Isaac Basire was born into a minor French noble family of Huguenot belief, but after ordination in England he became a high-flying Royalist Anglican, serving as a chaplain to King Charles I in besieged Oxford during the first English Civil War (chapter 12, pp. 522–4). When Charles's war effort collapsed, Basire fled the country and travelled to the Middle East with the ambitious (some might think quixotic) project of drawing eastern Orthodoxy to a version of High Church Anglicanism. His flamboyant bravery and energy preserved him through journeys as far as modern-day Iraq, and although he had no discernible success in exporting Anglicanism, he won the admiration of the Transylvanian Prince György II Rákóczi, who in 1656 appointed him director of the Gyulaférvár Academy. Rákóczi had already become annoyed by the hectoring tone of Transylvanian Puritan clergy, and he was very willing to listen to Basire's often first-hand accounts of what Puritans had done in England, up to and including the beheading of King Charles I. The thought had already occurred to the Transylvanian Prince that there might be a connection between presbyterianism and the overthrow of monarchies.

Basire wrote exultantly back to Charles II in the exiled English Court in Paris, telling the tale of his Transylvanian campaign against 'Independency and presbytery (flown over here from England)'. His fulminations against presbyterians were better received in Transylvania than his efforts to convince the Transylvanians that their Church superintendents were really bishops in a proper Catholic succession (as he naturally believed Anglican bishops were). In fact the rival Puritan party had a formidable asset in the shape of Prince György's mother, the Dowager Princess Zsuzsanna Lórantffy, the Transylvanian equivalent of those intimidating aristocratic or gentry matriarchs who were the mainstays of English Puritanism. Lórantffy was an intense admirer of Puritan clergy and a constant agitator for Presbyterian church government. In her frequent letters, and no doubt more frequently face to face, the unfortunate Prince György heard the words of mothers down the centuries: 'I have already written many times of this to you, and I do not see any point in it . . . I only see from you harsh deeds against me.' Her championing of presbyterianism also won support from an increasing number of noblemen, less impressed by Basire's threat of King Charles's Head than by the thought that lay elders might prove useful in curbing the pretensions of the Reformed clergy.[32]

Predictably given this balance of forces, the furious debates on Church polity in Transylvania eventually produced an untidy compromise, which would have disappointed Basire had he not already returned home after Charles II's Restoration to a comfortable retirement in the cathedral close at Durham. Basire's eloquence and influence on the prince had not succeeded in overturning an agreement hammered out in a national synod of 1646, by which local churches could form presbyteries with lay elders if they wished to. Nevertheless Hungarian Reformed Protestantism has always maintained its clerical hierarchy, and the part played in it by lay elders long ago diminished. Its current honorary President, Laszlo Tokés, is an elected bishop who in 1989 staked a claim to history and demonstrated the continuing militant tradition of Hungarian Calvinism, when his outspokenness and quarrel with local Communist party bosses as pastor in Timişoara

(Temesvár) proved to be the catalyst for the revolution against Romania's last Communist dictator Nicolae Ceausescu.

Perhaps the Hungarian Puritan movement might have won its case on church government outright if its energies had not been sapped by a series of severe military reverses which hit Transylvania from the 1650s. These were largely self-inflicted wounds, because they centred on a disastrous invasion of Poland on which Prince György II Rákóczi embarked in 1656. To begin with his military adventure relied on an alliance with Sweden, the Protestant great power of the day, and the aim was no less than for Rákóczi to seize the throne of Poland-Lithuania to promote the cause of Protestantism, as István Báthori had once done for Catholicism. Rákóczi went against all precedent for a vassal of the Turkish Sultan in pursuing his crazy campaigns in Poland without any authorization from Constantinople, and he persisted in the face first of strong warnings from the Ottomans and then of catastrophic defeats at the hands of Polish, Tartar and Turkish armies. He died of battle-wounds in 1660, his death preventing him from witnessing the complete humiliation of the principality by the Ottomans. Historians have been puzzled by the apparently suicidal foreign and military policies of a prince who was clearly intelligent and effective, but Rákóczi was motivated by religious zeal. The princely Court resounded as it had done for half a century with sermons proclaiming that Transylvania was the Israel of its day, destined to lead God's Protestant people all over Europe to victory against false religion whether Catholic, Orthodox or Muslim. In this story Rákóczi was cast as King David, who might usher in a golden age for humanity. The preacher at his funeral called him 'Israel's illuminating candle'.[33]

This was no narrow Transylvanian nationalism: one of the reasons that exiled intellectuals such as Johann Heinrich Alsted and Jan Comenius were attracted there, apart from their urgent need to make a living, was that they saw the principality as an essential component in God's plan for the end of history (Alsted saw this coming in 1694): they made their calculations explicit to their hosts. One of the loudest voices urging on Prince György in his schemes was Comenius, who during the 1650s held a lecturer's post in the principality as an honoured guest of Zsuzsanna Lórantffy and the Rákóczi family. In Comenius's sermons and writings he confidently looked for a new future for Europe hurried on by victorious Transylvanian armies. It was not the first time that Comenius had placed such hopes in a Calvinist prince: he was among those who had expected great things from the unfortunate Elector Palatine Friedrich V, whose election as King of Bohemia sparked the Thirty Years War (chapter 11). Comenius actually presided at the wedding of a daughter of ex-King Friedrich to Prince György II Rákóczi's younger brother in 1651, and in the years of Transylvania's disasters he put frenzied energy into unsuccessful efforts to chivvy help for the principality out of godly European rulers as far away as Lord Protector Oliver Cromwell in England.[34]

The wreck which overtook Transylvania in the late 1650s was thus one more episode in the internationalist militancy of Reformed Protestantism starting in Scotland in 1559, exploding in France and the Netherlands in the 1560s, and then one of the major destabilizing factors in early seventeenth-century Europe. The very fact of Transylvania's eventual failure after so much Reformed excitement was a severe blow to the morale of eastern European Calvinism. The principality of Transylvania was not destroyed by its mid-century misfortunes, but it never regained its early seventeenth-century strength, and Protestant fortunes suffered accordingly. The Habsburgs did not now need to take into account the opinions and the military muscle of the Transylvanian princes; they pushed forward Catholic fortunes in Hungary against the Protestants in step with their new victories against the Ottomans, and they did their best to promote both Roman Catholicism and Uniate Orthodoxy in Transylvania itself, with considerable success. It was a telling symbol of changed times when in the late seventeenth century the Rákóczi family, now no longer the princely dynasty, converted to Catholicism.

FRANCE: COLLAPSE OF A KINGDOM, 1572–98

While the Habsburgs successfully avoided major religious war in central Europe for more than sixty years and yet steadily promoted Catholic fortunes, France had to emerge out of some of the most wretched decades of civil war in the kingdom's history before finding a settlement of religion. When King Henri III returned from his ill-fated adventure as monarch of Poland-Lithuania to succeed his brother Charles IX in 1574, he found an even worse situation than that from which he had just escaped: a kingdom still traumatized and divided in the aftermath of the Massacre of St Bartholomew (chapter 7, pp. 337–8, and pp. 343–4). It is arguable that the traumas and divisions of later French history, often attributed to the Revolution of 1789, in fact take their roots from this period and the murderous bitternesses which it encouraged.

The new king has usually been seen through the eyes of his religious enemies, who plumbed the depths of personal abuse in attributing vices to him, topping the mixture with accusations of what they regarded as the ultimate devilish vice, homosexuality. Certainly the King enjoyed intense relationships with male favourites (*mignons*): they were charming young men who were drawn from outside the world of French power politics, and who showed him an affection which he did not find elsewhere in the poisonous political atmosphere. He was a passionate, intelligent and sensitive man, prone to extravagant gestures which ranged from theatrically self-abasing Catholic penitential devotion under the influence of Jesuit confessors, through to ruinously expensive and desperately frivolous presents for his favourites.[35] Like his much-insulted mother Catherine de' Medici, he could be engagingly good-humoured when criticized: after a particularly savage attack from a Parisian preacher in 1583, the King sent the Catholic zealot 400 crowns in money, with instructions 'to buy sugar and honey to get him through the Lenten fast and to be used to sweeten his bitter mouth'. Such pointed wit failed to charm the humourless or the bigoted.[36] In tranquil times Henri might have left a golden reputation as an imaginatively reforming ruler or as patron of the arts. Instead, as he did his best to hack his way out of his impasse during the 1570s and 1580s, he left matters worse, and lost his life in the effort.

To begin with, an optimist might have considered it possible to control the great magnates of the realm – Guise, Bourbon, Montmorency – whose self-assertion had wrecked the realm since 1559 (chapter 6). Two of the most troublesome were at least curbed by being confined to the Court. One was the bridegroom at the centre of the Massacre of 1572, Henri of Navarre, present head of the house of Bourbon, now maintaining a show of Catholic allegiance to save his life. The other was the King's own younger brother, the talentless but boundlessly ambitious François Duke of Alençon – he was later to trouble the affections of a middle-aged Queen Elizabeth of England, before failing to charm the Dutch as a potential monarch (chapter 8, p. 368; by then he had gained the ducal title of Anjou). The leading survivor of the Protestant leadership, Navarre's cousin Henri Prince of Condé, was in exile, while the Guises, uncertain whether to ally with Navarre or Alençon, were for the moment biding their time. All this soon changed; first Alençon, then Navarre escaped from Court, each bidding for support from the nobility. Condé returned to lead the Huguenots of southern France, now regrouping and far less inclined than before 1572 to make allowances for a Catholic King. Some French Protestants were even now talking about a republic, or at the very least a radically decentralized kingdom, and an autonomous government was becoming a reality in the south, in a loose alliance of Protestants and opportunist Catholics.

No less than the Habsburg Emperor Ferdinand in the 1560s, King Henri went against his Catholic convictions to adopt a policy of inclusion and compromise that might buy time for the monarchy. Not only was the French Crown politically crippled, but its finances had collapsed: in 1574, more or less a year of civil peace, net royal revenue was 4.5 million livres against expenditure of 20 million, even after savage economies.[37] Accordingly in 1576 Henri sponsored a deal which somewhat unfairly came to be known after his brother Alençon's courtesy title as 'the peace of Monsieur', and which was embodied in a royal edict promulgated at Beaulieu. It conceded an autonomous government to southern France that had already existed in practice over the previous year, and revived a scheme for fortified places of safety for Protestants under royal guarantee. By now the chances of getting any such deal to last were remote. From the moment of the monarchy's first efforts at conciliating Protestants in the 1560s, every such proposal had sparked a political league (*Ligue*) of Catholic intransigents in opposition. Now the largest-scale yet of such Ligues was put together, with the head of the ultra-Catholic Guise family, Henri Duke of Guise, as a figurehead leader. The King unwittingly gave the Ligue a platform by summoning a meeting of the Estates General to Blois for December 1576, in order to raise money and pursue a national settlement: he found the Estates packed with supporters of the Ligue, who even defied precedent by refusing the Crown a money grant. The King was trapped; he wept in public as he accepted the Ligue's terms for a campaign against the Huguenots. It would not be the last time that he chose ostentatiously to shed public tears at such vengeful Ligueur policies.[38]

Between the dismantling of the Peace of Monsieur and King Henri's death in 1589 there were three periods of declared civil war, and the last extended beyond the King's death through most of the 1590s; the intervals of peace were no more than armed truces. The pattern of negotiated peaces instantly betrayed by ultras on both sides, of local deals, local atrocities, continued in a desperate cycle of violence; by the late 1580s, France had ceased to be a functioning commonwealth. Philip II of Spain took advantage of the chaos afflicting his family's traditional enemy to dabble in the politics of French Catholic extremism: the reward might be double, in the shape of Spanish hegemony and the furthering of the interests of Holy Church. Philip's interest became urgent when François, Duke of Anjou died in 1584. In a remarkable coincidence of biology or malign accident, all four sons of King Henri II, including three successive kings, had now failed to produce an heir to the throne and the Valois male line was on the point of extinction. Monsieur had failed to convince either as prospective king-consort in England or as monarch in the Netherlands, and now even his death brought fresh disaster, because he had at least represented the prospect of a Catholic succession on the death of the childless Henri III.

The quirks of genealogy and French royal succession law meant that Henri, King of Navarre, once more openly a Protestant, would succeed as king on Henri's death. King Philip, with an eye on his war in the Netherlands as well as on the French succession, was determined to stop that happening. Accordingly in December 1584, the King of Spain made arrangements with the Guises and Navarre's Catholic uncle, Charles, Cardinal de Bourbon: on King Henri's death, the Cardinal would succeed to the French throne backed by Spanish troops. This aged nonentity would be a useful figurehead to make France safe for Catholicism. A renewed and augmented Ligue would make an open statement of the altered succession, and rally Catholics to the cause. When the Ligue declared its hand in 1585, Pope Sixtus V was called in to excommunicate the Protestant leaders Navarre and Condé. Naturally the vicious Catholic abuse of King Henri as a self-indulgent sodomite redoubled, even though he was now helplessly co-operating in Navarre's disinheritance; this was because the whole strategy of the Ligue and the rationale for its taking up arms on Bourbon's behalf depended on portraying Henri as incapable of fathering an heir to the throne.

Navarre for his part was not going to give up his rightful claim to the throne. In his campaigns he proved an inspired and innovative military leader, and he could also draw on Huguenot naval power, which far out-classed the royal navy.[39] He had leadership qualities which Henri III lacked: charismatic populist energy, zest in riding out a crisis, and a cheerfully extrovert heterosexual hedonism which effortlessly matched the conventional stereotype of male monarchy. His support came not only from Protestants. Plenty of Catholics were sickened by Catholic extremism and violence and were furious that the Pope should take it upon himself to set aside the kingdom's customs and decide who should become king. Looking back over the nightmare years of the Ligue's activities from the new peace brought by Henri IV, the aged lawyer and historian Etienne Pasquier, a judicious traditionalist 'Gallican' Catholic (chapter 1, p. 46), drew a distinction which was in effect a rejection of the Counter-Reformation: 'I love, respect and honour the Catholic, Apostolic and Roman religion, just as our predecessors have done in this France of ours ... I hate the sect of the Jesuits, who, feigning obedience to the Holy See, have introduced their novelties there.'[40] The Catholic ultras gave a single sneering name to the various moderate forces: they called them '*politiques*', with all the overtones of amorality and lack of principle that the word implied.

In reality, *politiques* never constructed a coherent party like the Catholic Ligue, and they had principles in plenty: Gallican distrust of Rome, love of peace and the rule of law, horror at a Catholic king's humiliation, and often a genuine conviction that people with different religious principles had no right to force their beliefs on each other. There was a Puritan intensity about Ligueur piety, much encouraged by Jesuit preaching, which many found as distasteful as Calvinist attacks on traditional culture. The great Norman city of Rouen, for instance, boasted a carnival society called the Abbaye des Conards: on the eve of Lent, in innocent days before the world turned bad, generations of high-spirited young men from the prosperous sectors of the city had staged shows satirizing local society, including the Church, whose institutions their mock-hierarchy mimicked. When Huguenots became numerous in the city in 1562, they stoned the Conards' processions because of their frivolous impiety. Once the Huguenots had been put down, the Conards returned with local government support, albeit taking more care in their satire. Then the Ligue in its turn closed down the Conards altogether when it dominated the city in the years after 1589. Religion was no longer a laughing matter: the Conards prudently kept away from the topic even once royal authority was restored and the Ligue dispersed. All through the Conards' troubles there were many who would see them as less of a menace to the city than the clear-eyed ideological tidiness of Huguenots or Ligueurs.[41]

King Henri's trials reached a new low in spring 1588. Throughout his reign, in an effort to ride the tiger, he had been normally resident in Paris: since the 1560s the city had been the rallying-point for hatred of Protestantism, and it was natural that its government slid into the hands of Ligueur Catholics, who loathed and despised him. The Ligueurs of Paris invited their hero Henri, Duke of Guise to meet the King, who forbade him to enter the city. Guise ignored his order, and in a bid to assert royal authority after the city's rapturous welcome for Guise, the King tried to deploy Swiss mercenary troops in the streets. The people of Paris threw up barricades which pinned down the troops. The memory of the popular victory on this occasion has resonated through the centuries, prompting similar actions through various French crises after 1789, and even in tragi-comic mode in the student protests of 1968. The King fled his own capital, all pretence of authority gone. He was forced to call a meeting of the Estates-General to his palace-town at Blois, which promised to recapitulate the Ligueur triumph of 1576.

At this point the King's frustration turned murderous. He summoned the Duke of Guise out of an early morning meeting of the royal council to a private conference: Guise, who did not believe that Henri had the nerve for really desperate action, was cut down in the royal ante-chamber, dead before he could say a word, while the Cardinal de Bourbon was seized and arrested. According to the English ambassador, King Henri reported to his mother in person: 'Madame, I am now come to tell you that I am King without companion and that the Duke of Guise, the enemy of all my proceedings, is dispatched.' Catherine de' Medici, who had witnessed so much butchery in her long widowhood, coolly replied 'that he had given a great blow, so all the rest might succeed accordingly'.[42] What succeeded was naturally not what the King had planned. The Ligue now had every reason to cast off all restraint. All over France, funeral sermons for Guise became rallying-cries for revenge, and the preacher Jean Guincestre's rhetorical discovery that Henri de Valois was an anagram for 'vilain Herodes' was only one small shaft of witty malice amid an agenda of destruction.[43] The Ligueurs in Paris set up a provisional government for the realm, and the theological experts of the Sorbonne declared that King Henri had forfeited the allegiance of his subjects.

The cycle of death continued into 1589. Royal supporters were murdered, and although Pope Sixtus had previously refused to have anything to do with the proposal of one Jesuit, lately King Henri's confessor, to kill his former penitent, plenty of volunteers were prepared to do God's will without papal permission.[44] The honour fell to a Dominican lay brother, Jacques Clément, who in July 1589 took a knife to King Henri. Clinging to life through a day of agony, Henri called on his followers to support Navarre, whom he prayed would convert once more to Catholicism. Now Ligueur preachers mounted their pulpits to preach first exultant anti-funeral sermons for the dead king and then eulogies on his assassin Clément. Ligueur instructions were for sermons to include comparisons of the executed assassin with the ancient Jewish heroine Judith, who (according to a biblical book which Protestants would consider as Apocrypha) had sawn off the head of an enemy of God.[45] This Catholic enthusiasm for destroying a monarch outstripped anything that had been said among Huguenots in the previous decade, and it had few equals in the rhetoric of rebellious Protestants in Scotland, England or the Netherlands over the previous thirty years.

In the eyes of those who respected the kingdom's traditional law, the King of Navarre was now King Henri IV of France. Over the next nine years, he battled to make that a reality. His siege of Paris in 1590 was particularly bitterly fought and full of more horrors than the Prussian siege of 1870: thousands (some said 30,000) died of starvation rather than surrender to a heretic. There were desperate expedients to survive: the Spanish ambassador, trapped in the city, successfully suggested grinding up dry bones in the cemeteries to make a paste for bread for the poor. In the end Henri had to withdraw and lift the siege.[46] By 1593 the King was weighing up his chances of uniting the kingdom: the Cardinal of Bourbon was now dead, and Henri therefore had no convincing rival for the throne within the kingdom. As a Protestant he would always remain divisive: as a Catholic he might shift more of his potential Catholic subjects out of Ligueur enthusiasm into the ranks of the politiques, and make matters a good deal easier for convinced Gallicans. When negotiating with moderate Ligueurs in 1593, he is often said to have mused that 'Paris is worth a Mass'. Although this famous quotation is even more insecurely founded than Martin Luther's precisely contradictory sentiment, 'Here I stand, I can do no other', it is worth remembering in the same way as conveying an essential reality of the moment: in its weary rejection of ideological principle, it shows what many of Europe's politicians and rulers felt about the Reformation and Counter-Reformation after seventy years of fighting.[47] The King took Catholic instruction and attended Mass in the royal abbey church of St Denis: in 1594 he achieved the apparently impossible when he was received with great enthusiasm in Paris itself, at Mass in Notre Dame Cathedral.

Theodore Beza, who all through his long years in Geneva had corresponded with Navarre, regularly received cash from him and was devoted to him as a new King David in Israel, was devastated at Henri's betrayal of the godly cause. Beza nevertheless remained loyal, and sadly consoled himself with a different Old Testament image: God's champion in Israel, Samson, sacrificed his life to slay his enemies, and now perhaps King Henri was making an even greater sacrifice of his soul in God's cause. He also continued to regard himself as on King Henri's payroll.[48] It took Pope Clement VIII two years to bring himself to place an equivalent faith in the royal convert, but in 1595, to the horror of Philip of Spain, the Pope reluctantly granted Henri absolution for his earlier lapse from Catholicism. The Pope's action was evidence that by now, with the carnage in France continuing, he had lost confidence in the Ligue's ability to deliver a Catholic kingdom; in any case he was no admirer of King Philip. The war was veering in King Henri's favour: the Ligue was badly split over who if anyone should replace Henri, and more and more local governors were beginning to feel that the Ligue's fervent activism was a threat to traditional authority. Extremist partisans of the Ligue reinforced this insight with repeated freelance bids to kill the King. At around one major assassination attempt a year, the murderous persistence of their religious zeal would have won admiration in the 1990s from devotees of the Ayatollah Khomeini's fatwa against Salman Rushdie. Eventually in 1610 one of their number, an embittered schoolmaster and failed aspirant to the Society of Jesus, François Ravaillac, achieved their goal, and struck down the heretical hypocrite in the name of pure religion.

Quite apart from increasing public revulsion against the worst extremes of Ligueur activity, it became evident to patriotic French Catholics in the late 1590s that the main impulse behind the continuing fighting was external military support from the King of Spain. They must weigh up a Ligueur internationalist militancy for the Catholic faith against their loyalty to the French Crown and their suspicions of Spanish intentions. The numbers opting for Catholic internationalism dwindled. In May 1598 the Spaniards, exhausted and demoralized, signed a treaty with Henri at Vervins. Their ambitions in France had been brought to nothing; within a few months King Philip was dead, and Europe had learned that its greatest empire was not invincible. At last the French Crown was in a position to craft the religious compromise which successive monarchs had been seeking for more than thirty years. It was embodied in Henri IV's Edict signed in the Breton city of Nantes at the submission of the last major Ligueur governor, the Duke of Mercoeur. The peace negotiations with Spain had left the Catholic Ultras without any external support, and so although there was still bitter Catholic opposition to accepting the Edict, this time a French monarch won his aim; not enough people believed in fighting on. The faithful Beza felt that his patience had been rewarded.

The Edict provided for a general amnesty for the crimes committed on all sides over the previous decades, in return for loyalty to the Crown. It allowed freedom of worship for both Catholic and Reformed Protestant in what was proclaimed to be perpetuity. Specified Ligueur strongholds, including Paris, were allowed to exclude Protestant worship, while the Huguenots were once more granted officially guaranteed towns which (over a renewable period of years) they could garrison for their security; special law-courts were set up to hear law cases for Protestants, half of whose legal officers had to be drawn from Protestants to ensure an impartial trial. Significantly, some of the settlement's provisions were embodied in royal warrants because Henri knew that Catholic-dominated legal institutions would not register them. It was a symptom of an increasing tendency of the French Crown to get its own way without reference to constitutional bodies: this centralizing impulse of the monarchy and its increasing reluctance to meet representative legislative bodies would not finally be curbed until the financial and political crash of 1788–9.

There was little in the provisions of the Edict of Nantes that had not been proposed before, particularly in Henri III's sequence of abortive attempts at peace settlements from the Peace of Monsieur in 1576 through to the Treaty of Nérac (1579).[49] Huguenots might have seen the deal as not exactly a liberation, more a containment, and after the death of Henri IV they experienced a series of moves of attrition against their privileges, up to the sudden and arbitrary revocation of the whole Edict by Louis XIV in 1685. The worst period before the 1680s was the series of Huguenot revolts which broke out after 1620 when Louis XIII had decided to restore Catholicism in the small principality of Béarn in the extreme south-west, newly annexed to the French Crown and previously boasting an established Protestant Church under its Huguenot princely rulers. These risings brought disaster to the Protestant cause, culminating in the destruction in 1628 of the greatest guaranteed Huguenot stronghold, the Atlantic port of La Rochelle, after an epic siege. After that, Huguenots lost the military refuges and the privileges in politics granted in 1598, but still the King's chief minister Cardinal Richelieu did not seek their destruction and saw to it that the toleration of Nantes was reaffirmed. Many Catholic zealots deplored his comparative openness, but Richelieu never forgot what zealotry had done to France in the second half of the previous century.

The Huguenots therefore had nearly a century after 1598 in which to maintain their everyday devotional life and the scholarship of their academies. They were a literate, highly organized and highly motivated national community: when around 200,000 of them were scattered across Europe in 1685, their industriousness and professional, technical and commercial abilities benefited every community in which they settled (I speak with bias, since my mother's family fled from France to England in the 1680s to bring their skills as weavers to a new life in Staffordshire). Their Calvinism was distinctively shaped by their environment. Huguenot reading habits reveal an interesting contrast with the increasing moralism of English Puritan covenant theology (which, as we have seen, was elsewhere so influential in settings as widely separate as the Netherlands and Hungary). Huguenots did not read so much of this literature of moral self-examination, and they did not keep diaries like many English Puritans. They did not need to agonize about seeking out everyday proofs of their elect status: their past struggles and their present watchfulness against Catholic encroachment and proselytizing were quite enough to prove their status as God's suffering chosen people.[50]

Overall Huguenot numbers contracted remarkably little through the seventeenth century. This was despite the phenomenon perceptible all over seventeenth-century Europe when a Catholic monarchy put pressure on

Protestant nobility; the greater magnates tended to give way and convert, loth to forgo pleasures and honours at the royal Court (cf. chapter 8, p. 362). Even under the influence of these important losses, the Huguenot community lost no more than around a quarter-million by 1685 from its peak of about a million in 1598, with the main losses in the wars of the 1620s: the faint-hearted had already been whittled away during the sixteenth-century civil wars.[51] On the whole, the smaller towns without a substantial Roman Catholic presence suffered least from attrition. In the Catholic diocese of Nîmes on the Mediterranean coast (where there was not even a proper seminary for the Catholic clergy until 1667), Protestants actually formed the majority of the population and could defy the efforts of the local Catholic bishop to win over converts; even after the official elimination of the Huguenots in 1685, the local population there remained steadfast in the faith, and there were as many Protestants around Nîmes in the nineteenth century as there had been in the seventeenth.[52]

If French Huguenots were harassed and eventually in the 1680s found themselves betrayed, that was hardly the fault of Henri IV. In one of Henri III's earliest attempts to heal the kingdom's wounds, in his Ordinances of Agen in April 1576, the King had proclaimed the principle that 'we are all friends and citizens of the same country'.[53] 'Citizens' – such a secular word has more resonance of the French Revolution than of the Most Catholic Kings of the Valois house. The dire emergency of the kingdom had forced Henri III to use his imagination and think in terms which set aside the dividing wall of religion created in the Reformation. Henri IV did all he could to turn his predecessor's aspiration into a reality against the opposition of religious exclusivists on both sides of the divide. He bequeathed France a carefully crafted recognition of the legal existence in the same realm of two contending forms of western Christianity, something unique in western Europe, and a statesmanlike reversal of their previous vicious conflict. It was especially remarkable that adherents of the minority religion were not excluded from public office. For most of the seventeenth century, despite many imperfections, France stood alongside Poland-Lithuania and Transylvania as a symbol of toleration, in contrast to Protestant monopoly states like England or Catholic monopoly states like Spain, and at a time when the Habsburgs had done their best to dismantle similar provisions in central Europe during their victories in the Thirty Years War.

The end of toleration in 1685 left a legacy of bitterness and instability in France, for it failed to destroy the Huguenots, while encouraging an arrogance and exclusiveness within the established Catholic Church. In the great French Revolution after 1789 this divide was one of the forces encouraging the extraordinary degree of revulsion against Catholic Church institutions, clergy and religious that produced the atrocities of the 1790s; beyond that it created the anticlericalism which has been so characteristic of the left in the politics of modern southern Europe. In the history of modern France, it is striking how the areas in the south that after 1572 formed the Protestant heartlands continued to form the backbone of anti-clerical, anti-monarchical voters for successive Republics, and even in the late twentieth century they were still delivering a reliable vote for French Socialism.

FRANCE: A LATE COUNTER-REFORMATION

So much Catholic energy had been poured into civil war for two generations by 1598; only now could something positive be done to revive the shattered French Catholic Church and begin reconstructing it along Tridentine lines. Peculiarities remained in the French situation, quite apart from the carefully fenced position of the Huguenots. The greatest oddity was the delay in giving official status to the decrees of the Council of Trent; Henri III had nearly been forced to do so back in the 1580s, but that initiative had been overtaken by the ruin of all his policies. Henri IV steadily resisted receiving the Tridentine decrees, secure in the strength of Gallican sentiment among influential Catholics, especially secular lawyers. Even when they were partially received in 1615 after Henri IV's death, the monarchy would only recognize the doctrinal sections, leaving the Church's own institutions to implement disciplinary measures under its own authority. The Jesuits remained on the defensive in France because of their links with extremism during the civil wars: quite apart from Ravaillac's murder of Henri IV in 1610, a former student of the society had been responsible in 1594 for one more in the sequence of unsuccessful assassination attempts on the King, and that led to the expulsion of the entire Society for the following nine years. There was a continuing strain of anti-Jesuit feeling in French Catholicism, paralleled in other parts of western Europe. A Counter-Reformation here would have a character different from that in other areas of Catholic Europe.

Remarkably, given the contemporary situation in the German-speaking lands (see above, pp. 446–7), the French bishops were among those taking the lead in promoting change. Up to the end of the civil wars, the French episcopate was on the whole as unreformed and ineffectual as any other set of mitred aristocrats in Europe. The general tendency for bishops to be younger sons of noblemen continued, but after 1600 there was a sudden and marked improvement in qualifications: bishops were now almost automatically university graduates, and increasing numbers of them took the trouble to be ordained priest before being nominated to the episcopate. That might seem a ludicrously basic expectation, but it had been uncommon among sixteenth-century French bishops, and the change was significant. Forty-nine per cent of bishops nominated by Henri IV came to the episcopate as priests, and that percentage rose to 63 per cent under his son Louis XIII – the figure became 91 per cent among those nominated in the twenty years from 1642 when Cardinal Jules Mazarin was chief minister of the kingdom.[54] The bishops' model now became Carlo Borromeo, that serious-minded nobleman who had transformed his episcopal charge in Milan. As we have already noted, Borromeo was a usefully ambiguous figure in his interpretation of the Counter-Reformation, for he had asserted the rights of bishops in their dioceses with as much tough-mindedness as any Gallican cleric might wish (chapter 9, p. 410).

Structural renewal in the French Church also needed to include the older monastic Orders. They had not merely to undo physical damage to their monasteries done by Huguenots, but also to restore standards which well before the Reformation had already fallen foul of royal and aristocratic exploitation (chapter 2, p. 90). It was not always easy to extract wealthy monasteries from the hands of Catholic magnates: between 1528 and 1621, for instance, a continuous succession of members of the Guise family headed the once-illustrious abbey of Cluny, and these Guise abbots did little for the welfare of their enormously rich house.[55] The Cistercians more than the Benedictines were troubled by the obvious contrast between their austere founding ideals and the ease that they had come to enjoy: even during the civil wars, a substantial number of Cistercian houses began adhering to patterns of reform set by certain leading abbeys, for instance abstaining from meat in their diet. Such changes in lifestyle, entirely justified under the earliest rules for the Order, caused furious arguments, but they carried with them around a third of Cistercian houses.[56]

After Henri IV's death, such reform movements received much support from his devoutly Catholic widow Marie de' Medici and from Louis XIII. Although hindered by demarcation disputes between the Crown and the papacy, many monasteries were remodelled under the energetic supervision of a royal and papal commissioner, Grand Almoner Cardinal La Rochefoucauld, a nobleman who achieved the delicate balancing-act of being simultaneously a commendatory abbot, a diocesan bishop and a conscientious reformer. Symptomatic of the changes were signs of the laity's renewed respect for traditional monasticism. In Paris, the heart of French Catholic devotional activity, increasing numbers of laypeople now sought to provide for their burial in monastic churches, and among the impressive total of forty new religious houses founded in the city in only forty years after 1600, a significant number were foundations for the pre-Reformation religious Orders.[57]

François de Sales, one of the most outstanding contributors to restoring the reputation of French Catholicism, came from a noble family beyond the eastern borders of France in the Duchy of Savoy; although he had much contact with activist Catholic circles in Paris, he spent most of his career in Savoy. His title as bishop could not be more resonant of the struggle with Protestantism: in 1602 he was appointed Bishop of Geneva, having previously already headed the impoverished former cathedral chapter exiled from Calvin's city, now deprived of most of its old endowments and based just south of Geneva in the Savoyard town of Annecy. He visited Geneva itself on three occasions, and had courteous meetings there with the venerable Theodore Beza. Not all Catholic dignitaries could have carried off such an encounter, but de Sales was remarkable for his mildness and lack of ostentation or pomposity. As bishop he was assiduous in promoting Catholic instruction and preaching, and his devotion to the poor was exemplary. He was capable of winning over the peasantry of his Savoyard diocese by the reality of his pastoral concern for them, rather than by the intimidation (let alone the Duke of Savoy's troops) which another bishop might have used: 'We must hold it a sure truth that men do more for love and charity than under severity and rigour.'[58] This was a very different style of episcopal reform from that of Borromeo and it sprang from an urge to open up everyone to an intense personal experience of divine love. When de Sales spoke of this love, one of his favourite images was the Sacred Heart of Jesus: French Catholicism took this up as a major metaphor for the divine, and hence it became a widely popular object of devotion.

On the basis of the universality of divine love, de Sales proclaimed his conviction that every section of society, cleric or lay, male or female, was capable of finding an appropriate road to God. One can well believe that his generous vision of divine grace was fruitfully stimulated by the narrower forms of the Calvinism with which he came into contact, and indeed in his younger days he had been badly frightened by the prospect of divine predestination. Like the fiery Scottish Calvinist John Knox, despite their very different religious styles, the majority of his most deeply articulated relationships were with women rather than men. Two of these women, Barbe Acarie and de Sales' cousin by marriage Jane Frances de Chantal, devoted their years of widowhood to promoting religious Orders; de Chantal chose Annecy to be the centre of a new Order of the Visitation in which

476

young women or widows could lead a disciplined contemplative life without facing the extreme physical austerities of other reformed Orders. De Sales's correspondence with de Chantal and the works that he wrote with her in mind are among the most important expressions of his spirituality. Acarie represented a different style of the religious life from that of de Chantal: she was active in bringing to France the strenuously ascetic contemplative Rule of St Teresa of Ávila's Discalced Carmelites, taking the name Marie de l'Incarnation when she joined the Carmelites herself. Through the circle of Acarie, the ecstatic Carmelite mysticism pioneered by Teresa and John of the Cross was opened up for the potential benefit of the ordinary Catholic faithful of Europe.

Rather different from de Sales's optimistic vision of a divine grace for everyman was the mystical spirituality of his friend Pierre de Bérulle, who had nevertheless also much encouraged Acarie in her introduction of the Carmelites to France. Bérulle was in a politically exposed position as chaplain to Henry IV, and he was eventually made a Cardinal in recognition of his practical contribution to the renewal of the French Church, so his mysticism was no withdrawal from the world. It was only natural that, like de Sales, he had a lively awareness of the power of Reformed Protestant theology, which had sustained the Huguenots through so much suffering and which still sustained the community against the Catholic Church. The Reformed drew their strength from their sense of God's providence underpinning their communal life through all their troubles as a chosen people, like the children of Israel: Bérulle turned to a different vision of community, the ancient writings of the so-called 'Dionysius the Areopagite', whom we have encountered already, bringing inspiration to Jean Gerson and John Colet a century and more before (chapter 1, pp. 33–4, 40–41). This pseudonymous mystic had a special attraction for French divines, having long been arbitrarily conflated with an early French bishop to become St Denis, patron saint of the kingdom and of the royal mausoleum abbey near Paris.

Like Gerson and Colet, Bérulle was fired by Dionysius's picture of God's creation as a hierarchy of order and orders of being: the divine grace descended from heaven to the Church's priests on earth, then, through their mediating ministry, out to the whole of the human race. 'The Church is divided into two parts ... One is the people, and the other is the clergy. One receives holiness, and the other brings it about.'[59] Priests were entrusted with the awesome power of the divine light of grace: like Colet before him, Bérulle called on the priests of the Church to be no less than the angels in heaven as they ministered to the laity, for their priesthood was a reflection of Christ's priesthood, and the Eucharist that they celebrated was the chief means by which humanity made its encounter with the divine. Every priest must find the strength and the wisdom to become a director of souls. This was a revolution from the general medieval view of the clergy as performers of the Mass, among whom only a well-trained minority would be capable of going further and offering spiritual counsel to the laity. It reflected the challenge that the training of the Protestant ministry offered the Church of Rome.

Bérulle followed Dionysius in meditating on the union of the created order with God (luckily for his contemplations, the Cardinal did not realize that the mystic had evolved this view with a heretical agenda, in conscious opposition to the carefully balanced theological definitions of the Council of Chalcedon of 451). Like Dionysius, he saw the human Christ as lost in the immensity of the Christ who was the divine Word in heaven; in the same way, Christians should become lost in the divine, surrendering the self to the power of God. 'This humanity has been lifted out of the sterile soil of the common and ordinary existence of its specific nature and happily transplanted into the very soil of divine and personal existence.' He talked of the need for humans to enter spiritual servitude to Jesus and to his mother Mary, who was the 'first to share in Jesus, [and] the first as well to share the cross and the humiliation of Jesus'.[60] Bérulle saw a practical consequence of his mystical vision for himself: his particular servitude was to improve priestly vocations. He was responsible for founding a version of St Philip Neri's Congregation of the Oratory, with a significant modification: each congregation of the Italian Oratory had an independent life, but in keeping with Bérulle's instinct to see the world in hierarchical terms, he subordinated all his French congregations of priests to his control as superior-general.

Alongside Bérulle's Oratorians came a second French foundation for the clergy: the Congregation of the Mission created by Vincent de Paul (often known as Lazarists from their Paris headquarters of St Lazare). Vincent had already devoted his energies to serving the poor and encouraging laymen and laywomen to form confraternities for charity work among the desperate (chapter 15, p. 646); he directed this priestly Congregation to the task of holding travelling missions in remote countryside and to training other clergy. He esteemed equally de Sales and Bérulle, and his work reflected aspects of their contrasting outlooks. Like de Sales, Vincent was optimistic about human potential: even the most wretched and debased galley slave could be rescued to lead a life full of God's love. Bérulle's mysticism had stressed the importance of the inner spiritual life rather than outward shows or external expressions of piety, and likewise Vincent's missionary style was a deliberate contrast to that of the Jesuits: there were no theatricals, no dramatic preaching, no more than the most low-key of devotional processions. Such fireworks might anger and repel French, Genevan or Savoyard Calvinists, rather than showing them what Catholic holiness was about.

Amid these richly varied French approaches to spirituality – mystical, contemplative, practical, emotional – there is one common feature: an emphasis on the ordinary work of the parish priest and his father-in-God, the bishop. In fact both de Sales and his chief admirer and collaborator among the French bishops, Jean Pierre Camus, Bishop of Belley, insisted that the role of the parish clergy (and therefore of the bishop) was primary in the Church. Borromeo's strategy for his diocese of Milan was based on the same assumption. The parish clergy of France were being called to exalted standards of concentrated commitment, and many of them were being trained to exceptional levels. One long-term consequence was that the parish priest in France was to become a somewhat more remote figure to his parishioners than elsewhere in Europe: the parishes of France came to be dominated by the *curé* in the black soutane and cap, who in the French cultural wars of the nineteenth century was confronted by the equally symbolic figure of the secular-minded village schoolmaster.

There was a further implication in the work of Bérulle, Vincent de Paul and de Sales. They placed a large question-mark against the notion that only the religious Orders and those under special vows were capable of producing people with a powerful enough spirituality to guide the laity. Significantly, the Oratorians and the Lazarists were not committed to any vows beyond those made by all priests of the Church. If parish clergy were doing their job properly, why would there be any need for organizations like the Society of Jesus? It would be wrong to suggest that this led automatically to hostility to the Jesuits or other religious. Like Borromeo, both Bérulle and de Sales had close personal links with the Jesuits and esteemed their work, and they rejoiced in the expansion of contemplative religious Orders which their friends Acarie and de Chantal did so much to assist. Nevertheless, there were clergy and devout laity who combined their commitment to renewing parochial and diocesan ministry with Gallican attitudes and memories of the negative part played by some friars and Jesuits in the Catholic activism of the Ligue. Moreover, as we have already noted (chapter 8, p. 392), the French phenomenon of anti-Jesuit feeling among Catholics was echoed elsewhere in those parts of western Europe where Catholicism and Protestantism faced each other, and where the Catholic episcopal hierarchy was trying to regain its old authority – particularly in England, Ireland and the Netherlands.

A symptom of this was that Bishop Camus's book stressing the superiority of secular priests was translated into English in 1635 as *A spirituall director disinteressed*. The translation was associated with a group of English secular clergy who in the previous decade had founded an English-speaking seminary in Lisbon: its specific purpose was to train secular clergy for the English mission, outside the control of the Jesuits which was so universal in the other overseas English seminaries. Richard Smith, the Pope's appointed Catholic bishop in England, who had experienced his own bruising encounters with the English Jesuits, was given complete authority over the Lisbon College, and he appointed a Principal, Thomas White alias Blacklo, who loathed the Society. It was common for such English clergy to have a conciliarist attitude to Church government, downgrading the authority of the Pope, just as the Gallicans did.[61]

These rifts were not just a matter of quarrels over status (though that is always a prime temptation among clergy), or of resonances from France's wretched recent history. A more profound theological division began to arise, a return to the shadow of Augustine that has so haunted the whole story of the Reformation. Just like de Sales or Vincent de Paul, many serious-minded western European Catholics meditated on the reasons for the successes of Protestantism since 1517. Much could be written off as the product of human sin and the greed of unscrupulous rulers and nobility, but just as Cardinal Contarini had uneasily felt that Luther had got much right about the means of salvation, so some theologians who read Protestant theology concluded that they found some accurate perceptions of the great Augustine amid the lamentable heresy. They must construct a theology for the Catholic Church which would take this into account, and describe more accurately the means of grace as Augustine had done.

Chief among these thinkers was a Dutch theologian, Cornelius Jansen, who spent most of his career in the Universities of Leuven and Paris before being made Bishop of Ypres at the end of his life.[62] Born in the province of Holland in what became the Protestant United Provinces, and so an exile in adulthood, Jansen had reason to be particularly conscious that his native land had been torn apart by the claims of rival religions. Jansen studied the writings of Augustine at Leuven under the influence of academics who followed the teachings of the Leuven theologian Michael Baius: Baius had been condemned by Rome in 1567 and 1579 for expounding the savage pessimism about the human condition that he had found in Augustine, and he was a particular target of Jesuit attacks. Jansen saw Augustine in the same light as Baius did, and he was driven to contrast what he read of Augustine writing on grace and salvation with aspects of what the Society of Jesus taught. Even in basic principles, he perceived a fundamental chasm between his own outlook and that of prominent Jesuit theologians, who mostly followed the thought of a Spaniard from the previous generation, Luis de Molina (see Figure 4, p. 223).

Molina shared the concern of late medieval scholastic theologians and of Desiderius Erasmus to safeguard human free will. Just as in their case, this meant a good measure of finessing of the thought of Augustine (who could not be ignored or avoided) to deal with his emphasis on God's absolute power and human helplessness. Molina did this by an ingenious presentation of God's powers of creation and his will to save humanity, which shaped Jesuit thought on the matter until modern times. God, as an all-powerful creator, was able to create an infinity of possible world orders, but he had made the decision to create the one we know. God not only knew everything that might happen (what are called in the jargon of philosophy hypothetical future contingents), but out of all those possible choices he foresaw the things which actually did happen. So our world and its history was a result of God's sovereign decision (as Augustine maintained), and the world and its history contained within themselves God's foreknowledge of all human acts, which was part of that decision. Yet God chose in his mercy to regard this foreknowledge as foreknowledge of free human choices, as much as any human decision out of the myriad hypothetical future contingents would be. Molina saw this as ensuring that the choices which human beings made in seeking salvation were indeed real human choices.

If the reader has survived this brutally swift summary of an intricate system, the consequence of Molinism may become apparent. Just like the late medieval nominalist theological school of Gabriel Biel (chapter 3, pp. 110–11), and despite a very different starting-point in Biel's thought, Molina and later Jesuits stressed the importance for salvation of the particular actions of human beings as sinners struggled through life's dilemmas to gain the vision of God. Even though Molinism was careful to keep on the right side of Augustine, this was a thoroughgoing theology of works. Luther had rejected Biel's ideas because he saw them as violating the biblical view of God's power and divine grace as expounded by Augustine: now Cornelius Jansen rejected Molinism for the same reason. He deplored Jesuit casuistry, the detailed discussion of particular moral cases that had become a speciality of Jesuit spiritual advice: he regarded casuistry as a recipe for avoiding the great moral choices and for cloaking dishonest or even criminal acts with a gloss of morality.

Jansen was thus seeking to remodel the Counter-Reformation through a rigorous stripped-down Augustinian reform – a new Reformation, but now pursued within the bounds of the Catholic Church. General moral principles mattered more than flexibility – Jansen was bitterly critical of what he regarded as Cardinal Richelieu's unprincipled softness towards the Huguenots, and it is also consistent with his presuppositions that Jansenists were prominent in opposing Jesuit proposals for being theologically adaptable in the mission field in China and India (chapter 9, pp. 432–5).[63] Jansenists predictably disliked the exuberant missionary work sponsored in Europe by Jesuits and Capuchins, regarding such emotional theatricals as examples of what the twentieth-century Protestant theologian Dietrich Bonhoeffer would call 'cheap grace'. They were the first movement in the Counter-Reformation actively to recommend that all Christians, not just clergy, should read the Bible.[64] The relevance of Jansen's critique of Jesuit casuistry to the Catholic dilemmas of France in the civil wars should also be obvious. In the hands of its madder exponents, and occasionally with the tacit compliance of the higher reaches of the Society, casuistry had justified the killing of kings. It was not surprising that Jansen's dark analysis of Augustine struck a chord among French Gallicans and all those who had reasons for hostility to the Jesuits: it was likely to attract formidable support within the French Catholic Church.

Jansen avoided much direct confrontation with the Jesuits in his lifetime, and personally he was fervently and genuinely loyal to the Holy See, but at his death in 1638 he left a timebomb in the shape of a treatise on grace baldly titled *Augustinus*, ordering his executor to publish it. The Jesuits got wind of the publication and invoked a papal decree forbidding published discussion of the topic of grace: by 1641 they had secured the Pope's condemnation of the book, but by then it was a *succès de scandale* among theologians and its edition came with the endorsement of several leading scholars of the Sorbonne. The content of the work, which Jansen said had taken him twenty years to write, was a pitilessly detailed survey of Augustine's controversy with Pelagius (chapter 3, p. 107), which led on to an equally detailed and pitilessly hostile dissection of Molinism. Humanity was seen as radically corrupt and the human will to good therefore non-existent: Luther and Calvin, though not Melanchthon, would have applauded.

There were plenty of graduates of Leuven University among the senior clergy of France and the Low Countries who had heard this message in their student days and found it congenial. Many contrived to misunderstand the Holy Father's opinion of Jansen's work in order to continue a benevolent interest in it, and his thought and general approach to theology became especially influential in France. In Paris it was championed by an austere and much-respected community of nuns who originated among the newly reformed Cistercian houses, and who then secured their own autonomy, exporting the name of their original rural monastery of Port-Royal when they opened two new establishments in Paris. All through the seventeenth century French Catholicism was convulsed by the struggle between Jansenist supporters of Port-Royal and the Jesuits, and the struggles became entangled with the politics of the French Court.

Among the several strands of conflict in this situation was a contrasting vision of the future of the Roman Catholic Church. Was it to be directed by the wisdom of the Pope in Rome, or was its theology to be constructed from the creative arguments of the wider Church? Where did authority lie to make decisions in such controversies, with a papal monarch or with a collegiate decision by the bishops of the Church? In the Netherlands, such arguments led at the end of the seventeenth century to the Roman Catholic Church's first major schism since the Reformation, when Jansenist Catholic clergy in the United Provinces refused to accept Rome's decisions on the appointment of a bishop, secured the consecration of their own candidate by a dissident bishop, and created an 'Old Catholic' Church. In France, the debates did not end with the persecution of the Port-Royal community, which culminated in an official order for the destruction and deliberate profanation of its chief house in 1710. Around the memory of Jansenism, all sorts of dissident strains in both Church and State gathered. When the Society of Jesus was dissolved in the eighteenth century it was not unbelievers of the Enlightenment but a surviving network of Jansenists who contrived its destruction in France, and the degree of viciousness inflicted on the dispersed Jesuits was extraordinary, considering that both sides professed loyalty to the Catholic Church.[65]

The issues of authority which Jansenism raised are still those that threaten to blow apart the modern Roman Catholic Church. That is reflected in the call back to a vision of papal monarchy, away from the conciliarism of the Second Vatican Council, sounded by Pope John Paul II from 1978. It is curious that history has made it seem natural for a Polish Pope to enunciate such doctrines, which in the seventeenth century would have sounded better on the lips of Jesuits in southern or central Europe, and which were generally remote from the style of Catholicism in northern European Catholic lands like Poland-Lithuania. It was that era that coined a name for the centralizing impulse in Catholicism that minimizes local autonomy and the need for consultation with the whole Church: significantly the name derived from the geography of Europe. The Alps became the symbolic barrier, and the perspective was that of northern Europeans. The centralizers were known as 'ultramontanes' – those from beyond the mountains. Less frequently heard now is the symmetrically opposite name 'cisalpine' ('this side of the Alps') to denote a decentralizing Catholicism, such as was evolved by Gallicans or Jansenists, and which might be more inclined to feel that Protestants and even Protestantism were not all bad.

We have surveyed southern Europe as the heartland of the Counter-Reformation, and now when dealing with Europe's central lands from France to the Habsburg territories we have witnessed two rival styles of Catholicism. The outbreak of the Thirty Years War gave a great advantage to the Catholic intransigents in central Europe and swept aside much of the Protestantism which had endured there for nearly a century. The outcome was to fossilize the religious divisions of Europe that endured through the French Revolution and the Napoleonic upheavals and that still shape the life of the continent today. To this landmark confrontation between the forces of Reformation and Counter-Reformation we must now turn.

11

1618–48: Decision and Destruction

The word 'crisis' started life in Greek, and then meant a decision. We have already encountered one of the great decisions of the crisis years 1618–19: the Synod of Dordt committed the Dutch Reformed Church to an extreme version of Calvinist predestination and set it as a standard for Reformed Protestant Churches generally (chapter 8, pp. 377–8). The Synod did not carry all the Reformed with it: quite apart from dissident (and for the moment persecuted) Dutch Arminians, who now began thinking new thoughts, the ultra-Calvinist triumph of Dordt paradoxically marked a moment of loss for Calvinism, after which the Church of England began to drift out of the Reformed family towards a different future (chapter 12).

In the same year 1618, much of Europe was faced with another crisis: the beginning of a climactic battle for possession of the continent, which threatened for a couple of years to sweep back all Catholicism's gains in the Counter-Reformation. The Catholic struggle to hold the line against Protestantism brought thirty years of misery to millions of Europeans: opinions vary, but within the German lands one modern estimate is that 40 per cent of the population met an early death through the fighting or the accompanying famine and disease, and even the most cautious reassessment of the evidence comes up with a figure of 15–20 per cent.[1] Such was the bitterness that when the combatants had fought themselves to a standstill, they could not bring themselves to negotiate together: Catholics and Protestants had to meet imperial representatives in two different Westphalian cities some thirty miles apart to create the Peace of Westphalia, which finally brought an official end to the carnage on 24 October 1648. The great Gothic chambers in the city halls of Münster and Osnabrück, where the formal work was completed, are each proudly celebrated in their cities as the 'Peace Hall' (*Friedenssaal*), a mark of the impact which these years have had on European memory.

At the centre of the conflict were two great German dynasties whose names have resounded through the events of the Reformation: Habsburg

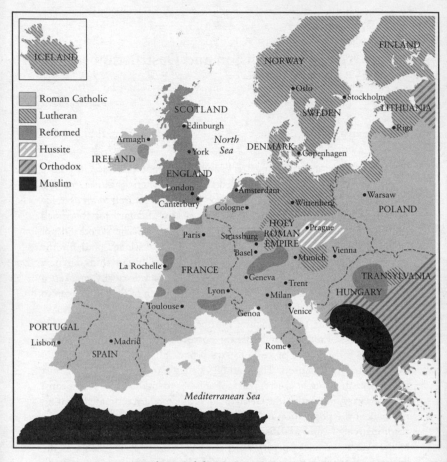

6. *Confessional divisions in Europe, c. 1600*

and Wittelsbach. One cynical and secular view of what happened after 1618 would be to see it as yet another episode in centuries of dynastic rivalry between the two families, a struggle for power through mastery of the intricate mechanisms of the Holy Roman Empire, into which others in the clique of ruling European dynasties plunged for their own purposes, whatever the cost to their wretched subjects. This would be a truth that missed the point: religion, religious zeal and religious hatred were at the heart of the outbreak of war in 1618, and both sides believed that they could effectively eliminate those who took a different view of the Christian message. Both dynasties were split over religion. The Wittelsbach Elector Palatine Friedrich V, a Reformed Protestant, confronted his Bavarian Catholic Wittelsbach cousins, whose ideologically inspired marriage alliance with a Habsburg Archduke had been such a crucial moment in the turning of the Protestant tide in central Europe in 1571 (chapter 10, p. 450). For the Habsburgs, a family debate was now being resolved: the time of religious moderation and straining to keep the balance in central Europe was over. The fervent Counter-Reformation Catholics in the family were determined to end the policy of successive Emperors from Ferdinand I to Matthias, who had to one degree or another accepted that different Christian confessions should co-exist.

During the 1610s, the most likely heir to the ageing and childless Emperor Matthias was the Archduke Ferdinand of Inner Austria, who succeeded him as the Emperor Ferdinand II in 1619, when the war had already begun. Ferdinand was the fruit of that dynastic alliance of 1571. We have met him systematically dismantling Protestantism in his duchy during the 1590s (chapter 10, pp. 450–51); he never forgot his political apprenticeship in that turbulent time, and he took a good deal of trouble to build a stately burial-place for himself in his first capital Graz, the Inner Austrian town which he and his father had struggled with such success to wrest out of the hands of the Lutherans.[2] His considerable personal charm masked an austere and intense piety: no mistresses enlivened or disfigured his Court, and his life between his steady commitment to his duties of government was a constant daily round of hearing Mass and the Offices of the Church, with pilgrimages to the newly rebuilt shrines of the saints as his main self-indulgence.

Ferdinand's advisers were kindred spirits, chiefly successive Jesuits, the most formidable of whom was a former lecturer at the College in Graz, a farmer's son from Luxemburg, Guillaume Lamormaini. One might liken Lamormaini's closeness to Ferdinand to Theodore Beza's constant watching over the policies of Henri IV in France, anxiously judging whether the monarch was living up to God's expectations of his chosen servant, and always ready to express his feelings if the servant seemed to be falling short (chapter 10, p. 470). Not all members of the Society were happy that Jesuits should immerse themselves with such obvious relish in the high political struggles and atrocious warfare of central Europe, but that was of little concern either to the implacable Lamormaini or to Adam Contzen, his likeminded Jesuit colleague at the Court of the devout Bavarian Duke Maximilian.[3]

While the Archduke Ferdinand was the son of a Bavarian Wittelsbach princess, his adversary in the 1618 crisis was a distant Wittelsbach cousin, the Elector Palatine Friedrich V, current head of the ruling family of the Palatinate. From the end of the 1550s the Electors Palatine had been among the chief champions of Protestantism in the Holy Roman Empire, and after some flirtation with Lutheranism had returned to a firm commitment to the Reformed cause (chapter 8, pp. 354–6). One should never underestimate the power of genealogy in early modern politics: Friedrich was projected by his family tree into the role of a Protestant warrior for all Europe. His grandfather was the lost hero of a previous generation, Willem 'the Silent', whose campaigns for a Protestant Netherlands had been halted by a Catholic assassin's bullet. It is not easy to get an impression of Friedrich through the fog of adulation and abuse that he inspired, but the man under the myth seems to have been inclined to let mythology overwhelm him: handsome, sincere, amiable, imaginative, but not a strong personality.

Friedrich's equivalent of Lamormaini or Contzen was a lay political adviser, Prince Christian, himself the ruler of a small territory, Anhalt-Bernburg. Christian of Anhalt was a fervent Calvinist who managed to combine his Reformed faith with a lively interest in the contemporary frontiers of knowledge, a combination of mystical philosophy, magic and practical investigation that looked back to the mysterious ancient *Corpus Hermeticum,* the ebullient sixteenth-century eccentric Paracelsus and the English magus John Dee (chapter 17, pp. 679–84). It was to prove a dangerous mixture. By the time that Friedrich succeeded to the Electorate in 1610, Prince Christian was a veteran in the government of the Palatinate, and he believed that this was a providential chance to campaign in God's service on a rather larger stage than his own Anhalt inheritance afforded: his goal was to break the anti-Christian alliance of Pope, Jesuits and Habsburgs. Most people blamed him for the events that followed.[4]

This Protestant and Catholic posturing was played out in acute consciousness of the fragile balance within the Empire. Of the seven Electoral dignities, three (the Palatinate, Brandenburg and Saxony) were in the hands of Protestants. Among the permanent holders of the three chief imperial titles of dignity, two, the Elector Palatine and the *Reichsverweser*, who governed the Empire while the throne was vacant, were Protestants, and only the Imperial Chancellor, the Archbishop-Elector of Mainz, was a Catholic. The Peace of Augsburg had made no allowance for Reformed Protestants, yet in the course of the 'Second Reformation' many Protestant princes and some cities had abandoned Lutheranism for Calvinism; they had no legal right to do so, nor any legal protection. There were genuine efforts at avoiding the obvious dangers, and in 1601 even an essay at dialogue between Roman Catholics and Protestants at Regensburg, sponsored by the leading Catholic Duke Maximilian of Bavaria and the major Lutheran activist in imperial politics, Count Palatine Philipp Ludwig of Pfalz-Neuburg. Symbolically it took its rules for debate from those operated in the 1519 Leipzig confrontation between Martin Luther and Johann Eck (chapter 3, pp. 127–8); the princes acted as monitors and clergy on both sides were invited to lead communal prayers during debates. But this promising initiative led nowhere.[5]

It proved little easier to get a union of Protestants against the Catholic menace. A whole series of attempts sought some sort of ecumenical theological understanding, mostly led by conciliatory Reformed divines, who were aware of the legal vulnerability of their faith; yet Lutherans and Calvinist clergy remained constantly at each others' throats, the Lutherans feeling secure in their legal privileges of 1555 and disinclined to give any ground. Several Protestant rulers felt compelled to ignore these difficulties after two military emergencies: the Bavarians occupied the fractiously Lutheran imperial city of Donauwörth, claiming a need to protect its Catholic minority, then the ducal succession in the Duchy of Cleves-Jülich was disputed between Catholics and Protestants. The result was the formation of a defensive alliance, the Protestant Union, in 1608: the Catholics led by Maximilian of Bavaria set up a Catholic League the following year. The battle-lines of the future were being established, but so were hesitations among various Lutheran princes who disliked their fellow Protestants almost as much as they hated the papal Antichrist. The confusion and disarray on the Protestant side, despite the efforts to reach across the confessional divide, convinced many godly folk that a major turning-point in God's plans for the world was about to reveal itself. Who would be his agent? Some thought that it might be Henri IV of France, who in 1610 intervened in the Cleves–Jülich affair with a substantial army – but then suddenly that same year, Ravaillac's knife abruptly halted French interest in foreign military adventures.

Christian of Anhalt had no doubts after Henri's murder that his young master in the Palatinate fitted the divinely appointed role. In 1613 the Elector Palatine Friedrich married Elizabeth, daughter of Europe's most powerful Reformed Protestant monarch, James VI and I of Scotland, England and Ireland. The couple proved to be devoted to each other, Princess Elizabeth proving a rock of strength in her family's troubles in later years (indeed the characters of the opponents Archduke Ferdinand and Elector Friedrich might persuade one that a strong commitment to marital fidelity is a dangerous quality in international statesmen). Everyone saw the splendid wedding ceremony in the Chapel Royal at Whitehall as forging a pan-European Protestant alliance against popery: the presiding minister, George Abbot, the Archbishop of Canterbury, was himself a fervent Calvinist who was eager to see the Atlantic kingdoms play an Elizabethan role as the defender of Europe's beleaguered Protestants. The only dissenting opinion, but a crucial one, was from the father of the bride. King James was one of the few European rulers who regarded peace as always better than war, and his vision of the marriage was that it should form part of a dynastic lowering of the international temperature, to be balanced by a wedding of his son Charles to a Spanish Catholic princess. Amid the excitement of the wedding, no one seems to have taken any notice of James's agenda, perception of which might have dampened the fervour of anticipation that built up in central Europe over the next few years.[6]

The young couple returned from London to Heidelberg, to transform the Palatine castle high above the river Neckar into one of the most magnificent Courts in the continent: a place where the England of Inigo Jones, William Shakespeare and Orlando Gibbons met the Renaissance culture and scholarship of all Europe.[7] It was not surprising that the Elector Palatine was inclined to believe Christian of Anhalt's enthusiastic vision for his future, or that many others saw him in the same light. Protestant Germany was no less ready for a divinely ordered climax to world history than it had been in the carnival days of the 1520s (chapter 3). The very disappointments of the Reformation, as it settled down into institutional forms and fell short of initial hopes, made people look all the more anxiously for signs and wonders sent from heaven, urged on by their clergy.[8] The centenary of Martin Luther's first declaration of rebellion in Wittenberg approached in 1617. Lutheran historians much encouraged the idea that such patterns of years were important: indeed, the scholars nicknamed the 'Centuriators of Magdeburg', led by that ultimate gnesio-Lutheran Flacius Illyricus, had more or less invented the century as a significant unit of historical measurement. The celebrations of the anniversary mounted as the outlook for Protestantism

Lutherans were pioneers in the concept of commemorating historical centenaries. This medal, issued in the later stages of the Thirty Years War in 1630, commemorates the Augsburg Confession of 1530. It shows Martin Luther (who did not actually attend the Augsburg Diet) and on the reverse, the Pope sits on Antichrist's throne; inscriptions celebrate the defeat of papal tyranny.

seemed ever more uncertain. Poetry, plays and pamphlets all took the celebration of Luther as Germany's Moses to new heights.[9] Even Halley's Comet contributed to the sense of a coming moment of decision by putting in its appearance in 1618. If Luther had been Moses, then King David could not be far behind.

Symptomatic of all this was a bizarre additional excitement: the publication by one 'Christian Rosenkreuz' between 1614 and 1616 of a series of manifestos describing a centuries-old society of wise and benevolent philosophers, the Rosicrucians, who had previously kept their existence secret from the world. The Rosicrucian tracts were eagerly and widely read; their principal author is now known to have been an imaginative Lutheran pastor of Württemberg, Johann Valentin Andreae, whose distinguished clerical grandfather Jacob Andreae had been one of the chief architects of the Lutheran Formula of Concord (chapter 8, p. 352). Later historians have not known what to make of this literature, and have generally ignored it, particularly since in later years it has become a happy hunting-ground for the naive and muddle-headed, despite the obvious fact that the Rosicrucians never existed. It was a brilliant work of interpretation published by Frances Yates in 1972 that revealed the original significance of the Rosicrucian publications. She saw that they were a symptom of the febrile atmosphere which led to the Thirty Years War, and that they were full of indirect references to the coming role of the Elector Palatine Friedrich. The promise made by these creations of a learned Lutheran pastor and his collaborators was a new world of enlightened culture, harmony and human achievement, a measure of the way in which Protestant Europe's expectation now transcended a narrow Reformed Protestant militancy. The Rosicrucian manifestos sprang from the same intellectual world as the hermetic, Paracelsian, magic and mystical enthusiasms of Christian of Anhalt. If the Elector Friedrich acted, then a new phase of human history might begin, and the fiction of the Rosicrucians would become reality.[10]

With one of the principals thus being groomed for a Protestant messianic role, the preoccupation of the other was to secure the future of the Habsburg dominions both for himself and for the Catholic cause. Matters might not go smoothly for the Archduke Ferdinand: genealogy and politics still gave the Habsburgs and their imperial throne many possible futures. Several members of Ferdinand's family, including his uncle the Emperor Matthias, were alarmed by his closeness to the Jesuits, while his Spanish cousin King Philip III had a good enough prospective title to use it as a bargaining counter for a share of the Austrian Habsburg empire. Ferdinand decided to capitalize on his assets and deal with the King of Spain. He was aware that the Spaniards needed allies: the twelve years' truce which they had signed with the Protestant Dutch in 1609 (chapter 8, p. 377) would expire in 1621, and the steadily escalating but undeclared war that the two powers had been fighting overseas was likely then to become official once more and return to Europe. It was worth ceding territory to the Spaniards in Alsace and Italy to secure recognition of his title to the imperial throne, plus a large cash sum. It was also worth Ferdinand overcoming his studied contempt for his uncle Matthias in order to take further joint action for the future. Archduke and Emperor travelled together to Dresden to enlist the backing of Elector Johann Georg of Saxony – the Elector was chief among the princes whose hardline Lutheranism and traditionalist loyalty to the Holy Roman Empire made them hold back from joining the Protestant Union. By now it was the summer of the Reformation Jubilee year 1617.[11]

Secure in his various sources of support, Ferdinand escorted the increasingly frail Emperor to meetings of his royal Diets, first in Bohemia and then in Royal Hungary. Both Diets agreed to Ferdinand's election as King designate, and he did not waste time waiting for Matthias to die before acting in his new Bohemian inheritance. He was now determined to end the privileged existence of Churches which repudiated Roman obedience: an affront which in Bohemia predated Luther's Reformation and went right back to the Hussite risings of the early fifteenth century. Among the nobles and towns of the Bohemian kingdom, the King-designate was faced with an extraordinary variety of religion to outrage him: Utraquist Hussites, radical Hussite Bohemian Brethren, Lutherans, Reformed Protestants. The offence of Bohemia to Ferdinand was all the greater because of the very recent concessions which the Bohemian Protestant nobility had secured. Matthias, while still only an Archduke, had clashed with his brother the Emperor Rudolf II in a conflict which Ferdinand regarded as treasonable. Matthias had joined with the Protestants in order to strengthen his own position: he connived with the Bohemian Estates in 1609 to force the wretched and by now half-crazed Rudolf into granting a Letter of Majesty, much extending the rights of non-Catholics. Having then supplanted Rudolf as King of Bohemia, he had confirmed the Letter himself. As a result, all over Bohemia Protestant communities showed signs of exultant revival. Now was the time for Ferdinand as King-designate to roll back this Protestant advance: he revoked the Letter of Majesty. His handpicked officers (regents) began to harass Protestant congregations where they could, to censor printed publications and to exclude Protestants or Hussites from office-holding.

Such provocation was bound to lead to an explosion. First was a famous violent demonstration which arose from the breakdown of Bohemian negotiations with the Habsburg authorities. When imperial officials ordered the Bohemian Estates to end their meeting in Prague, held under the terms of the Letter of Majesty, the delegates seized the Palace, rounded up two of Ferdinand's regents and a secretary, and as their Hussite ancestors had done two hundred years before, threw them out of a window – the 'defenestration of Prague' (23 May 1618). As the humiliated officers climbed painfully out of a providentially placed compost heap, the eyes of Protestant Europe were on events in Prague. In an age when people believed that God guided events in patterns as surely as in the pages of the Old Testament, Protestants throughout the Continent were well aware that the armed proclamation of the Reformation had started with the Hussites in Bohemia long before Luther; it was only symmetrical that God should orchestrate his finale in the same place. Indeed, the Bible could be seen as saying so. Far away on the East Anglian shores of the Wash, the scholarly Puritan preacher John Arrowsmith later comforted his troubled King's Lynn congregation, in the middle of England's own civil wars, with a reminder of Bohemia's apocalyptic significance in God's plan: 'That this should be the course of the Sword to come where the Gospel hath first been, and then opposed, is not obscurely prophesied of, Revelation 6.'[12]

The Bohemian Protestants firmly believed that such biblically based enthusiasm would be translated into concrete support. There was some reason for their faith in international Protestant solidarity: when the Emperor Rudolf's Letter of Majesty allowed the erection of Protestant churches in the Catholic Old Town of Prague in 1610, the subscribers to a provocatively grand and expensive new church building there had been an ecumenical roll-call of Europe's Protestant elite, headed by King James I of England, but also including Lutherans like the Elector of Saxony.[13] Now once more the Bohemian Estates saw their best chance as coming from the Reformed, the more outspokenly militant element of the Protestant scene, and they were not alone: Archbishop Abbot of Canterbury eagerly looked in 1618 for an alliance which would stretch from Scotland to Transylvania, so 'by piece and piece, the kings of the earth that gave their power unto the Beast shall now tear the whore and make her desolate'.[14]

The loudest voice which the Bohemians heard was that of Prince Christian of Anhalt. Through him they made their fatal invitation in August 1619 to the Elector Palatine to fulfil his destiny and accept the throne of Bohemia in place of the Habsburg King-designate Ferdinand. Events moved very quickly now. The Emperor Matthias had finally died in March 1619, and by August the imperial Electors decided on the Archduke Ferdinand as his successor: the intransigent Catholic had triumphed. But if Friedrich became King of Bohemia, he would have two votes of the seven in future imperial elections, and the Protestant vote would shift to a majority. 'It is a divine calling which I must not disobey,' Friedrich declared: 'my only end is to serve God and his Church'. The ever-bellicose Archbishop Abbot wrote from England likewise that it was a religious duty for the Elector to accept the Bohemian throne.[15] As the Bohemian electors were making their decision for Friedrich as King, the militantly Calvinist Prince Gábor Bethlen of Transylvania made his own bid to attack the enemies of Israel (as well as to acquire the Hungarian throne) by routing the Habsburg armies in Hungary and taking over the Habsburg territories there; the Ottoman Sultan then offered his support to the Transylvanians. All the provincial Estates of the Habsburg hereditary lands now rose in rebellion. In this intoxicating moment it would have seemed folly to turn aside. The new King of Bohemia travelled in triumph from Heidelberg to Prague, and he was crowned by Utraquist clergy in St Vitus's Cathedral. It was to prove the last public act of the Utraquist Church after two centuries of existence.

Almost immediately the atmosphere in Prague began to sour. The new Reformed regime looked askance at the liturgical conservatism of the Utraquist Church, which seemed to Friedrich and his Reformed advisers to be stuck in a weird timewarp of pre-Tridentine Catholicism. Consequently during the winter of 1619–20 they committed an ideological folly by tearing down and publicly destroying statues and sculptures in the very cathedral in which King Friedrich had been crowned. This self-inflicted injury was immediately associated in the minds of outraged Utraquists with the veteran Calvinist Court preacher of the Palatine dynasty Abraham Scultetus, who seemed to have learned nothing from the failure of his similar plan for graduated change in Lutheran Berlin only five years before (chapter 8, p. 357): Scultetus was singled out for bitter abuse in pamphlets from the Prague presses.[16] Other cultural differences between the Bohemians and their new Court, such as the Queen's extravagantly English taste in fashion, increased the atmosphere of disunity, and now the Bohemian forces faced an invading Catholic army commanded by the Emperor Ferdinand's fellow zealot Duke Maximilian of Bavaria.

There was no help for them. Already the Habsburgs had bought off the Transylvanians, for Prince Gábor Bethlen's greed for new Hungarian territories outweighed his wish to play King David. Most Lutheran princes were in any case contemptuous of the new Calvinist monarch, and no Protestant ruler followed up the earlier expressions of support: the Dutch were only just emerging from the political and religious crisis of Arminianism (chapter 8, pp. 376–8), the Protestant Union of the Empire had shown little enthusiasm for the Bohemian candidature, and as ever, King Friedrich's father-in-law James I adamantly sought a mediated peace in what he had always regarded as a crazy venture. At the Battle of the White Mountain on 8 November 1620, Maximilian's army annihilated the isolated Protestant Bohemians. Today a stately church of Our Lady of Victory stands on the site, a centre of pilgrimage for Czech Catholics (see Plate 15b). The dream of a continent-wide Protestant paradise was over: it was no coincidence that the production of Rosicrucian literature ceased abruptly in 1621.[17] Soon Bavarian armies were overrunning the Upper Palatinate, and from being a monarch twice over, Friedrich found himself a landless refugee, who had to wander Europe until the Dutch allowed him to create the shadow of a royal Court in the safety of the Hague. His Electoral dignity was transferred to his Bavarian cousin Maximilian. In 1622 the troops of the Catholic League sacked Heidelberg and took great delight in seizing the world-renowned library of the Electors Palatine (see Plate 17). Maximilian wanted it for himself, but after some broad hints from the Holy Father he dutifully sent it off as a trophy of a religious victory to Rome, where it still remains separately shelved: a Calvinist prisoner in the Vatican.[18]

The battle of the White Mountain proved an irredeemable catastrophe for Protestantism in central Europe. Immediately Maximilian set about dismantling Protestant Church structures and promoting Catholicism: the Emperor Ferdinand, after some initial hesitation, even overturned the 200-year-old agreement with the Hussites and destroyed the Utraquist Church. The recatholicization of Bohemia was frequently brutal, to the dismay of Catholics who were prepared to try the same policies of persuasion that François de Sales had implemented in his Savoyard diocese. One campaigning Jesuit, Father Firmus, later in the century took to wearing heavy clogs with sharp metal spikes so that he could stamp on the feet of peasants until they revealed where they had hidden Protestant books; if that did not work, he pulled their hair and boxed their ears. There were many similar tales.[19]

Thus the Utraquist Hussites disappeared altogether from the European scene, the only major Church ever to do so in western Christianity: most either became Catholics or left for exile, where they found Lutheranism their most natural home.[20] The radical Hussites, the *Unitas Fratrum*, nearly followed the Utraquists into oblivion; they were sustained by the heroic efforts of their internationally respected bishop Jan Amos Comenius (chapter 10, pp. 460, 463). Later a fervently Pietist Lutheran nobleman, Count Zinzendorf, gave a remnant of them refuge on his estates in Saxony and started them on a remarkable new career: generally known as the Moravian Brethren, they aroused much enthusiasm in Georgian England, and at one stage became a great influence on that most eclectically creative of Protestant Church leaders, John Wesley. It was indeed a curious symmetry that the Hussite movement, which had taken much inspiration from the Lollards of fourteenth-century England, should thus through Wesley and the Methodists have such an effect on the religious renewal of eighteenth-century England. The Hutterite Anabaptists likewise left their century-old settlements in Moravia. They began wanderings through Europe that eventually led them across the Atlantic Ocean: here they found greater expanses of land than they had ever previously enjoyed, and could start their separate life afresh. They survive to the present day, many of their communities (like later 'Amish' Anabaptist emigrants from Switzerland to north America) preserving a German dialect and a way of life that does its best to reflect the era in which they left behind the persecutors of central Europe.

Through the rest of the 1620s, the Habsburgs won further victories in Germany, and having first targeted the Protestant Bohemian nobility, they turned their attention to the Lutheran nobility of the Habsburg hereditary lands. In 1628 the Emperor completed the process when he decreed the expulsion of all Protestant landowners in Inner Austria, ignoring the Pacification of Graz which his father Archduke Karl had so resentfully granted to the Protestants in the 1570s (chapter 10, p. 450). Most nobles did their best to avoid leaving their estates; they outwardly converted to Catholicism and became 'Nicodemite' crypto-Protestants, waiting for better times which never came. Habsburg reverses in the next decade raised their hopes, but effectively this was the end for Austria's once-flourishing Lutheranism.[21] Ferdinand and his hardline advisers were not content: as their military victories in northern Europe mounted up, they wanted to extend their triumph to the Holy Roman Empire. Urged on by leading Catholic clergy within the Empire, in March 1629 the Emperor promulgated an Edict of Restitution. Among other provisions which strengthened the position of clergy who were also territorial rulers, he decreed the return to the Catholic Church of all lands and bishoprics seized from it since the Treaty of Passau, back in 1552 (chapter 6, p. 274). The Edict also reinforced in newly explicit terms a ban on Reformed Protestantism throughout the Empire except in the free cities.

The Edict proved to be a disastrous move which undermined the Habsburg gains of the previous decade. Even moderate Catholics were uneasy at its intransigent terms, but the Emperor's Lutheran allies among the imperial princes were furious, seeing it as a travesty of the 1555 Augsburg settlement. Lutherans began serious talks with Calvinist theologians on resolving or at least ignoring their theological differences; these culminated in a protocol agreed at Leipzig in 1630, which for the first time used the significant word 'toleration' in proposing a new relationship between the two Protestant confessions.[22] More seriously still, the manifest aggression which the Edict promised, and its prospect of further accretions of power for the Habsburgs, alarmed two major European powers which had previously been occupied elsewhere and had avoided major engagement in the Empire's troubles: Catholic France and Lutheran Sweden. The Swedish king Gustav Adolf brought his armies south in 1630 to fight against the Habsburgs.

Gustav Adolf was a brilliant general, whose victories (much aided by French subsidies) for a moment raised the sort of wild Protestant hopes that the Elector Palatine had inspired a decade earlier. His intervention in Germany and central Europe did indeed save the Protestant cause, although together with the actions of France against both Spanish and Austrian

Habsburgs, it also gave the war a truly continent-wide scale. The King of Sweden treated the ex-King of Bohemia with great respect, and briefly Friedrich was once more able to walk in his lost lands of the Palatinate. Yet within a year of the Swedish intervention, and only a few days apart in November 1632, both men were dead, Friedrich of the plague, Gustav Adolf of the wounds which he sustained in defeating an imperial army at Lützen.[23] In later years, only Prince György II Rákóczi of Transylvania became a contender for the role of universal military saviour for the godly cause (chapter 10, p. 463); he failed to impress his fellow rulers, and the fiascos of his campaigns in the 1650s finally persuaded Protestants in Europe not to look for a general deliverance from one of God's anointed. It was a significant moment in robbing European monarchies of their sacred aura.

Europe had to endure sixteen years more of misery after Lützen. It took five years from 1643 to finalize the peace of Westphalia at Münster and Osnabrück, because it involved resolving internal squabbles on both sides as well as finding a deal that would give some sense of finality to the religious issues. In the negotiations, eventually Protestant unity proved greater than on the Catholic side, where many parties in the Empire, quite apart from France, were still determined to stop the Habsburgs gaining excessive advantage. The eventual deal did much to deliver Protestantism from its most extreme disasters of the previous decades. All parties agreed on an arbitrary decision to freeze the map of Europe at a particular moment in the fighting that represented some rough parity of misfortune, by restoring the territorial position as it had been in 1624. This meant that the Habsburg lands in central Europe were lost to Protestantism, but it also meant that the Edict of Restitution of 1629 was past history. Religious minorities saw their rights to worship in private restored wherever such rights had existed in 1624, and the Catholic Church was prevented from reclaiming any land or goods that it had not held in that year.

This account of the Thirty Years War has highlighted its character as a conflict of two religious confessions. That is how it began, and much of its atrocious course had a bitterly confessional character. The episode which lodged itself most deeply in the Protestant imagination was the sack and virtually complete destruction of the Imperial Free City of Magdeburg by an imperial army in 1631. The majority of Magdeburg's 20,000 inhabitants, overwhelmingly Protestants, are said to have died, either killed outright or burned alive in the fires which raged through the city and left it a wasteland. It was fairly normal for captured towns to be sacked after a long siege, particularly since armies were rarely well-paid or provisioned and felt entitled to a reward for effort and revenge for losses. However, the scale and brutality of what happened in Magdeburg were exceptional, and they had an extra symbolism. In the whole Reformation, through a century of vicious confrontation and mutual barbarism, never had one of the Empire's free cities suffered such a fate – moreover, Magdeburg was one of the greatest Imperial Free Cities, and since the days of the Schmalkaldic Wars it had been a symbol of Protestant pride and independence. The Babylonian destruction of Jerusalem was the comparison which straightaway rose to mind, and it was frequently repeated in the scores or even hundreds of pamphlets published across Europe that analysed, exaggerated and moralized the horrors at Magdeburg. To cast Magdeburg's disaster in biblical terms was an additional reason to see what was happening as part of the events of the last days: an incentive to all sides to cast off all restraint in what might be God's intended Armageddon. The atrocities which Ireland experienced as the most ideologically charged arena of the wars of the 1640s and 1650s in the Atlantic Isles (chapter 12, p. 524) owed much to the memory of Magdeburg and the apocalyptic mood which the sack of 1631 reinforced.

Yet even at the time it was possible to see alternative, less mythically dramatic forces in the conflict. We have noted how virtually no Protestant prince, let alone the incorrigibly pacific James I, came to the aid of the King of Bohemia in 1620–1 – a belated English effort at intervention in 1625 was half-hearted, short-lived and characterized by utter logistical ineptitude. Even Gábor Bethlen of Transylvania was prepared to cut a deal with the Emperor over gaining territories in Hungary, despite being a zealous Reformed Protestant monarch who was reputed to carry a Latin Bible in his pocket wherever he went.[24] Practicality and considerations of statecraft thus very frequently won over religious commitment. Most striking was the role played by France throughout the war, particularly in its interventions on the Swedish and anti-imperialist side after 1629: the prime concern was to limit Habsburg power rather than promote the universal cause of Catholicism. French foreign policy through most of the war was in the hands of Cardinal Richelieu, whom we have already seen taking a pragmatic attitude to the toleration of French Protestants (chapter 10, p. 472). As early as 1616, before his years of supreme power, Richelieu commented that 'the interests of a state and the interests of religion are two entirely different things'.[25] If the Cardinal had a religious idealism, it was different from that of *dévots* like Ferdinand II: he wanted to restore peace to Christendom and he saw an alliance with Protestants against the Habsburgs as the best way of doing it. It is also worth noting that Richelieu's contemporary Pope Urban VIII agreed with him: the Pope was no lover of either Spain or the

Spanish Habsburgs, and he regarded their forward policies as directed to their own interests more than those of the Church. He was even prepared to give thanks for the victories of Protestant heretics.[26]

At the end of it all, western Christianity would have to face some new realities. On the outbreak of war, many believed strongly in the sacred reality and God-given destiny of the Holy Roman Empire: it was still a principle which in the case of a serious-minded prince like the Lutheran Elector Johann Georg of Saxony might well outweigh his suspicion of the intentions of the Catholic Emperor Ferdinand. After 1648, there was no prospect that this foundation institution of the medieval western Christendom was ever going to become a coherent, bureaucratic and centralized state, not even on the open model of the Polish-Lithuanian Commonwealth. Its institutions continued to operate, and it provided a framework for German life, but Christian rulers would have to devise other ways of understanding how and why they ruled. Having seen the results of religious war through the years of the Reformation up to 1648, fewer of these rulers would be inclined to embark on crusades for the faith, especially against fellow Christians; crusades simply had not worked. Catholics and Protestants might mutually despise each other, and rulers might still persecute religious minorities for religious reasons, yet there was now a willingness to do business in government and diplomacy that there had not been before. In 1676–9, another prolonged peace conference sought to end a war between Catholic France and the Protestant United Provinces. This time, unlike the Westphalia negotiations, Catholic and Protestant diplomats sat down with each other face to face as they hammered out an agreement. Europe was beginning to follow Richelieu's principle: religion and politics need not be identical.

René Descartes was a soldier in the French armies who fought in the Thirty Years War. Jesuits educated him in the France of the first decade of the seventeenth century as it embarked on its late Counter-Reformation, and Cardinal de Bérulle had taken a friendly interest in his studies. Descartes chose to spend much of his later career in Amsterdam, the greatest city of the Protestant United Provinces, one of the most pluralist communities in western Europe, where the established Church had never achieved the monopoly position or the coercive power that it sought. He had witnessed at first hand the horrors of wars in which armies had been urged on to their business of death by clergy proclaiming religious certainties, certainties that in many instances contradicted each other and sought to destroy the rival system of belief. His reaction was to peel back the layers of certainty that he could find in his consciousness of the world around him. At the end he was left only with himself. 'I think, therefore I am'. From that he could begin to reconstruct certainties. Still a devout Catholic, he found that a sense of God was the first fundamental conviction that he could identify after his consciousness of himself. Not all those who followed him would be so sure of that.[27]

12

Coda: a British Legacy, 1600–1700

There are several reasons why the story of the Reformation in the Atlantic Isles after 1600 deserves special treatment. The three kingdoms ruled by the Stuart dynasty from 1603 managed to avoid any substantial direct involvement in the Thirty Years War, whose convulsions drew in the rest of Europe, but they endured twenty years of their own internal wars from 1642. These wars, which the peculiar insularity of English history is inclined to reduce to a single conflict called 'the Civil War', did as much as the horrors in mainland Europe to challenge the idea of divinely sanctioned monarchy, which was one of the most characteristic institutions of western Christendom. Nowhere else in Europe had a reigning monarch ever been put on formal trial by his people and then executed: this fate overtook Charles I of England, Scotland and Ireland in 1649. During the same period, and partly in response to the tensions which led to these wars, the Atlantic Isles launched a colonial enterprise which has shaped the modern world – the settlements on the east coast of the 'New World' which later joined to form the United States of America. Out of this turmoil also emerged a Church of England which began to take a different course from the other Reformed Protestant Churches of Europe, and eventually gave a name to this different identity: Anglicanism. This is now a worldwide communion, and including the Episcopal Church of the United States it forms a distinctive form of western Christianity.

NEW ENGLISH BEGINNINGS: RICHARD HOOKER AND LANCELOT ANDREWES

What is this Anglicanism, and how did the Church of England come to differ so much from the Churches with which it started out in partnership in the Reformation, such as Zürich, Geneva, the Netherlands, Transylvania? A journey to a little English parish church, Priston in the quiet Somerset hills to the south of Bath, provides a way of contemplating the mystery. Priston church now looks archetypally Anglican: soberly ceremonial inside, undemonstrative, yet proudly exhibiting layers of history from medieval times to the present day, a symbol of the unruffled continuity of English history. One small feature then pulls us back to Reformation tumult. The church's entrance porch was put up before the Reformation happened, but its stone gable is a slightly later rebuilding. In this gable, where previously a saint's statue would have stood in a niche over the porch entrance, there is placed instead a memorial tablet to Thomas Wats, 'preacher of the word of God', who died here in 1589 (see Plate 9b). But the stone is no mere pious reminder of Mr Wats: it has a wider purpose – the inscription in stern capitals begins 'PRISTON, REPENT AND BELIEVE THE GOSPEL'! Now that Mr Wats could no longer glare down from his pulpit in person at his little Somerset congregation, his message of justification by grace through faith was designed to confront the villagers every time they entered their church, brusquely supplanting their old popish devotion to the saints. So Priston affords us a little taste of the shock of the Protestant Reformation as it could be found all over northern Europe. Wats's memorial is a symbol of the international revolution that overtook England in the sixteenth century.

If we start finding out a little more about Mr Thomas Wats, the picture becomes more complicated. The parson of Priston was a learned man, as a godly preacher should be, and he had been to Oxford University, to Corpus Christi College, where he was made a scholar in 1568 and took his bachelor's degree four years later.[1] In the same year that Corpus granted Thomas Wats his scholarship, one Richard Hooker came up from Devon to study at the college, aged only fourteen: Wats would have known him well over the next four years, and a year after Wats, Hooker likewise took his BA. Wats might have envied Hooker's international Protestant credentials, for the shy but precociously intelligent boy was nephew to John Hooker alias Vowell, a cosmopolitan historian and scholar from Exeter who had lodged with the famous Peter Martyr Vermigli while studying in Strassburg. Student gossip would also reveal that young Richard was only at Corpus because one of England's greatest Protestant names, Bishop John Jewel of Salisbury – exile for the faith under Queen Mary, personal friend of Heinrich Bullinger and writer of Elizabeth I's official defence of her Church Settlement – paid for him to come to the Bishop's old college.[2]

From this exemplary Reformed Protestant background, Richard Hooker took a surprising turn; in the end he could not have been more different from his Corpus contemporary Thomas Wats, and the great book that he wrote, *The Laws of Ecclesiastical Polity*, was one of the chief starting-points

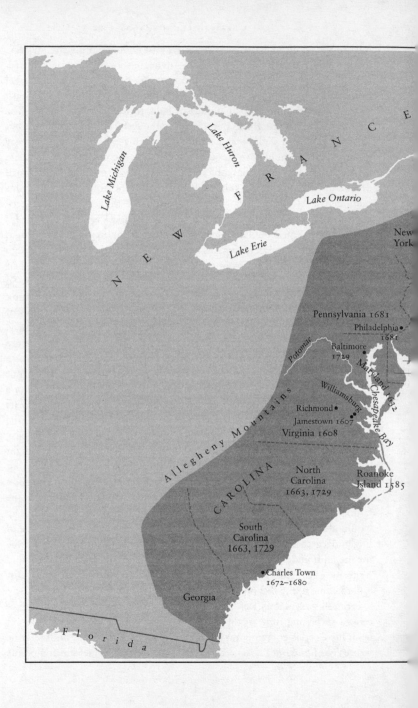

Lake Michigan

Lake Huron

Lake Ontario

Lake Erie

NEW FRANCE

New York

Pennsylvania 1681
Philadelphia •
1681

Baltimore
1729

Potomac

Maryland 1632

Chesapeake Bay

Williamsburg

Richmond •
Jamestown 1607
Virginia 1608

Allegheny Mountains

CAROLINA

North
Carolina
1663, 1729

Roanoke
Island 1585

South
Carolina
1663, 1729

Charles Town
1672–1680

Georgia

Florida

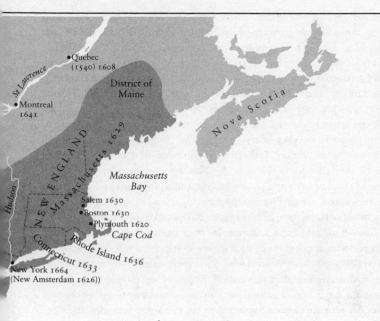

St. Lawrence

• Quebec
(1540) 1608

District of
Maine

• Montreal
1641

Nova Scotia

NEW ENGLAND

Massachusetts 1629

Hudson

Massachusetts
Bay

• Salem 1630
• Boston 1630
• Plymouth 1620

Cape Cod

Connecticut

Rhode Island 1636

• New York 1664
(New Amsterdam 1626))

Connecticut 1633

Delaware Bay
Delaware 1638
(England 1664)

Atlantic Ocean

| 0 | 125 | 250 Miles |
| 0 | 200 | 400 Km |

Extent of British territory about 1748

7. North American seaboard, c. 1700

for England's move away from mainstream European Protestantism. The two men symbolize a great divide which opened up in the Church of England: its long-term future was more with Hooker than with Wats. Much of Hooker's career, after some years as an Oxford don, was likewise spent in rural parishes, but he was the reverse of a country Puritan: he became fascinated by the life of London, then at the height of its Elizabethan cultural brilliance, was intimate with the printers' workshops in the city, and kept up with the latest plays of Shakespeare. In his one London appointment, ministering to the lawyers of the Temple, he clashed with a prominent Puritan spokesman Walter Travers, and this won him esteem from the scourge of Puritans, John Whitgift, Archbishop of Canterbury. Whitgift encouraged Hooker to write a book which would contribute to his campaign against Puritanism; the first part of the *Laws* appeared off the press in 1593, at the moment of the fiercest action against Puritans (chapter 8, pp. 387–9).

The *Laws* had little impact at first. Its poor success and Hooker's early death in 1600 meant that much of it then still remained to be put in print, and its publishing history proved long and complicated. Nor did the book make any wider impression in Europe: it was never published in Latin, which would have been essential to win an international audience, and western Christendom outside Anglicanism has remained resolutely indifferent to Hooker. Yet the scale of Hooker's work was grander than its occasion, and only gradually did readers realize that its arguments combated the whole mindset behind the sermon-based 'bible alone' style of English Reformed Protestantism, let alone the arguments for a presbyterian future for the English Church. Hooker placed the specific debates in a framework of a philosophy of human action, motivation and discipline, analysed as expressing God's laws for his creation. Central to his argument was a careful sifting of the ways in which scripture should be used as an authority for Christian life and practice, and the ways in which it should not. The purpose was to widen the areas which could be regarded as matters indifferent, *adiaphora*. These might then be considered using a variety of norms, and so they were open to the authorities of Church and Commonwealth to regulate in the wider public interest.

By meticulous definition and argument, Hooker extended such areas way beyond those which scripturally-minded Protestants would consider appropriate: notably in the field of Church government. In such matters which did not affect salvation, Hooker's criteria for making decisions became as much the weight of collective past experience and the exercise of God-given reason as the commands of scripture itself. History mattered, and there was no great break in the Church's history in the Reformation:

perhaps there might even be good in the Church of Rome, and it was not appropriate to call the Pope Antichrist, as most English Protestants were inclined to do. Hooker went on to the practical outworkings of his principles, starting in Book V of his work with a massive defence of aspects of English Church worship attacked by Puritans: a remarkably relentless defence of the exact shape of Queen Elizabeth's 1559 Settlement of Religion (chapter 6, pp. 288–90). After reading it, one feels that if the parliamentary legislation of 1559 had laid down that English clergy were to preach standing on their heads, then Hooker would have found a theological reason for justifying it.

Hooker knew that he was on dangerous ground in terms of the intellectual orthodoxy of his day, and when he went on to say unconventional things about salvation and predestination he was extremely careful in works intended for publication not to challenge Reformed propositions too directly.[3] His views on the sacraments were not exceptional for a Reformed commentator: nearer to Calvin than to Zwingli in his sacramental outlook, he was also typical of English theologians of his time in briskly dismissing Lutheran real presence views of the Eucharist, as much as the Romish doctrine of Transubstantiation. A celebrated section of Book V is a sensuous expression of our participation in Christ through the Eucharist, yet it has an impeccably Reformed climax – a rhapsodic quotation which Hooker borrowed from a twelfth-century text edited by a Huguenot pastor.[4] What was individual, however, was what Hooker did with this discussion.

Deliberately and at some length Hooker re-emphasized the role of the sacraments and liturgical prayer at the expense of preaching; he felt that the sermon had been over-emphasized in the English Church. His reassessment of preaching might have had something to do with the fact that he was notoriously dull in the pulpit: it is however more charitable to note that Hooker had been considered one of the best lecturers in logic in his generation, at a time when the nature of Oxford University's curriculum encouraged students to make a choice between considering logic or rhetoric a priority. It would not therefore be surprising if the master of logic looked down on the claims of pulpit rhetoric. Whatever the motivation, Hooker's attitude to preaching was not at all a popular stance to take at the time. He made choices in his avant-garde views: he chose not to echo fellow conformist English polemicists who in the 1590s were beginning to emphasize divine right claims for episcopacy (see below, p. 509). Even if Hooker thought that the Church was best governed by bishops, he did not go so far as denying that presbyterian Churches were true Churches, any more than he approved of calling the Pope Antichrist. In a similar independent fashion, when it came to secular government, unlike many contemporary ecclesiastical lawyers who might otherwise be congenial to him, Hooker did not let his anti-Puritanism take him down the road that produced arguments for divine right secular monarchy.

It was this sheer individuality, the stubborn independence of mind, the number of hares started by Hooker's indefatigable quest in his subject, that made him such a protean source for commentators in the future. Yet one person would have been pleased if she had read the *Laws*: Queen Elizabeth I. Hooker had few recorded encounters with the Queen, but the accumulated vision of his work is uncannily close to the idiosyncratic private religious opinions of this very private woman. She too defied contemporary wisdom in her reluctance to characterize Rome as Antichrist; she too was sceptical about excessive claims for episcopacy; she too had an ambiguous attitude to preaching and valued prayer more than sermons; she too loved dignified church ceremonial. Even her views on the Eucharist veered towards Reformed formulations because of her growing irritation with German Lutheran dogmatism, and so she would have sympathized with Hooker's Calvin-like talk of mystical participation.[5] In this sense, Hooker's theology is truly Elizabethan.

Hooker provided many clues to the future thought of 'Anglicanism', yet he was a loner who died comparatively young and in a country parsonage. Among his close friends and admirers was Lancelot Andrewes, a clergyman who chose a much more glittering career, and who was destined to foster a startlingly new style of devotion in the Church of England. Son of a London merchant, he went up to Cambridge University, and like Hooker his early connections were in the vanguard of Reformed Protestantism: Andrewes's first patron was Queen Elizabeth's austerely Puritan adviser Sir Francis Walsingham. Walsingham, a near neighbour to the Andrewes family in London, was loyal to a boy whose brilliance had clearly impressed him, and he was helpful even up to the time when Andrewes was made Master of his Cambridge college, Pembroke. Yet in the 1580s, Andrewes had already begun to diverge from the Elizabethan norm: he also proved to be in a strong position to protect himself and encourage others, being a noted controversialist against Roman Catholicism and an increasingly popular Court preacher.[6]

The whole style of Andrewes's preaching and theological writing marked him off from the Reformation mainstream, largely ignoring the work of the sixteenth-century Reformers to concentrate on writings from the early Church. He found the Reformed doctrine of predestination cruel and unhelpful. He expressed a sensual delight in the beauty of God's creation, emphasizing the Eucharist as the ultimate fruit of creation, and stressing the role of human reason in appropriating the truths of Christianity. Take one of his Christmas sermons, in which (in typically intense and layered style) he reminded his congregation that 'Bethlehem' meant 'the house of bread':

The town itself never had the name rightly all the while there was but bread made there, . . . 'the bread of men'. Not till this Bread was born there, which is *Panis Angelorum*, as the Psalm calleth it, 'and man did eat Angels' food.' Then, and never till then, was it Bethlehem, and that is in the Church, as truly as ever in it. And accordingly the Church takes order we shall never fail of it. There shall ever be this day a Bethlehem to go to – a house wherein there is bread, and this bread . . . Shall we forsake our Guide leading us to a place so much for our benefit?[7]

Such a message would have sounded very startling in the Elizabethan Church, yet Andrewes was already boldly preaching it to the large congregation of his London parish church in the 1590s, and in 1601 he was made Dean of Westminster Abbey. He had survived and prospered when other similar voices in the Church had been suppressed – some had indeed converted to Roman Catholicism in despair.

One of the most remarkable new developments in the late Elizabethan Church was the proposition that God had intended bishops to be a necessary part of Church structure: no other Church of the Reformation developed such a theology. Andrewes clearly held such views, but the idea was first promoted by contemporaries who did not share his sacramental rhetoric or his distaste for predestination, when they wrote against Puritanism in the late 1580s and 1590s. Such conformist polemicists were in fact going further than Archbishop Whitgift; when defending the episcopal structure of the English Church earlier, he had simply argued that it was appropriate and convenient for the English situation. Whitgift did not try to justify the Elizabethan Church polity by detailed reference to the New Testament Church, declaring 'I find no one certain and perfect kind of government prescribed or commanded in the scriptures to the church of Christ; which no doubt should have been done, if it had been a matter necessary unto the salvation of the church.'[8] This, of course, was the heart of the presbyterians' disagreement with him. The essence of their case was that there was indeed one certain and perfect kind of church government to be discerned in the New Testament, and it was presbyterian in character; anything else represented disobedience to God's word and was a fatal hindrance to the salvation of the Church. Presbyterianism was commanded by divine law: *jure divino*. Now by contrast, the conformists (who included Whitgift's sharp-eyed chaplain Richard Bancroft, chapter 8, p. 387) took up this *jure divino* claim and reapplied it to the institution of episcopacy. This adroit reversal of the argument went beyond the aggression of Whitgift's drive for subscription in 1583 to attack the presbyterians on their own theological ground.[9]

The final new element to note in the new mood emerging in the 1590s was an emphasis on the difference and special character of the Church of England: a mood at its clearest in Andrewes, but also implicit in Hooker, that the Reformation was something which happened not here, but somewhere over the English Channel. On this reading of recent history, if there were disturbingly Protestant features in the English Reformation, such as iconoclasm, or unacceptably minimalist views about the nature of the Eucharist in Cranmer's Prayer Book, then they were the result of foreign interference from the likes of Peter Martyr, Bucer or Calvin. Curiously, such arguments had first been heard not from members of the Church of England but from Roman Catholic polemicists attacking it; now they were borrowed in order to reshape the Church from inside.[10] Anglicanism in later centuries has continued steadily to distance itself from the rest of international Protestantism – indeed, from the nineteenth century, very many Anglicans would be embarrassed to be called Protestants, and would insist on being thought of as Catholics, even inventing the label 'Anglo-Catholic' to distinguish themselves (but not too much) from 'Roman' Catholics.

These modern Anglicans are echoing a distinctive synthesis of all the ideas which we have surveyed that emerged into a coherent body of thought around 1600. It was voiced by a group of English clergy and a few laypeople (generally those who had been to university with the clergy), who began uniting all these strands of thought together into a distinctive outlook on the English Church. They saw themselves as offering a more authentic Catholicism than that offered by the Church of Rome. It is difficult to find a satisfactory name for them: one common label, 'High Churchmanship', is vague and begs many questions, and the label 'Anglo-Catholicism' is best left applied to the heirs of the Oxford Movement in the nineteenth century. Another name which we will encounter and use, 'Arminianism', also has problems; 'avant-garde conformism', a term very recently coined by the historian of theology Peter Lake, sounds clumsy but accurately conveys the flavour of what was happening. The 'avant-garde conformists' sought to impose conformity on the Church, but they actually wanted to alter what conformity represented.[11]

Where had all these individual voices behind 'avant-garde conformism' come from, or what had inspired them? A vital factor must be a feature of the 1559 Settlement unique among European Protestant Churches: the

survival of cathedrals and a handful of similar surviving collegiate foundations as corporations without substantial alteration. Elsewhere in Europe
the buildings might be preserved, and in some European Lutheran state
Churches the shadow of the organization, but there was nothing like the
English cathedral close, with its round of regular liturgy involving a large
staff of clergy and elaborate music sung by paid professionals, nothing of
which seemed at the time to have much relevance to a Protestant Church.
The English survival is a puzzle: a cynical view is that cathedral estates and
offices could act as a reservoir of patronage for the powerful to dispense to
the deserving or the greedy. But perhaps more important was the stubborn
love of church choral music shown by that midwife of the Church of
England, Elizabeth I. Since her choir in the Chapel Royal went on singing
and her composers went on producing music of superlative quality, then the
cathedrals were emboldened to follow suit, despite considerable strains of
finance. Strangely, this exquisite sacred music, with a continuity broken
only by the seventeenth-century civil wars, had virtually no effect on musical
and devotional life in English parish churches from Elizabeth's reign to the
time of the 'Oxford Movement' in the nineteenth century: the parishes sang
metrical psalms in the manner of Geneva, at least until the major evangelical
'revival' in the eighteenth century popularized a new sort of hymn which
was not exclusively based on the text of the psalter. Nevertheless the survival
of the cathedral tradition had huge significance for the future of Anglicanism.
It struggled through what might have seemed unpromising Elizabethan
years to reveal the potential for liturgical splendour in Cranmer's Book of
Common Prayer (a development which, almost certainly, he would not have
welcomed).

Naturally those involved in such a devotional life did not regard the
pre-Reformation past with the same loathing as many Reformers. They did
not regard beauty as an obstacle to worshipping God. They would certainly
be inclined to put preaching in its place alongside prayer, and give a special
value to the highest form of prayer, the sacrament of holy communion. They
might come to re-evaluate bishops, seeing them not so much as Reformed
superintendents but as endowed by God with a special authority as guardians of the Christian tradition. If we seek one place that most fostered such
a complex of attitudes, it was Westminster Abbey, the royal mausoleum
which was only briefly the centre of a diocese from 1540 to 1550, but
thereafter continued to behave more like a cathedral than most cathedrals.
Here the English choral and ceremonial tradition was at its most spectacular
and well-funded outside the Chapel Royal, a permanent reminder that the
Reformed character of the Church of England never quite achieved total

dominance. Standing immediately beside the Houses of Parliament, the chief law-courts and the principal royal palace of Whitehall, the Abbey provided a liturgical showcase for inspection (either puzzled, admiring or suspicious) by Parliament men, litigants and foreign ambassadors. Gabriel Goodman, Dean for forty years from 1561, was marked out as the very opposite of a Puritan in his churchmanship: a most unusual figure among senior English Protestant clergy, as was his successor as Dean Lancelot Andrewes.[12]

A further piece in the jigsaw is the powerful political backing that the Abbey enjoyed from the royal ministers William Cecil Lord Burghley and his son Robert, the dominant figures in the 'vill' (town) of Westminster. The Cecil connection was crucial in promoting avant-garde conformism among the English clergy, because the Cecils themselves began sympathizing with such theology. In his last years, old Lord Burghley, that veteran of Edward VI's Reformation, came to deplore rigid predestinarian Calvinism. Robert Cecil was an enthusiast for art and beauty, and was not prepared to exclude them from his devotional life like most Reformed Protestant grandees of the time; he came to have an intense reverence for the Eucharist.[13] One Cecil protégé is a crucial link in a story which is all about political and personal connections: an avant-garde conformist clergyman who determinedly promoted like-minded clergy, Richard Neile. Neile had been brought up in the shadow of Westminster Abbey, in an Elizabethan parish, St Margaret, which like the Abbey was peculiarly old-fashioned and ceremonial in its devotional style. The memory never left him. He owed his education to Dean Goodman and to the Cecils, whose chaplain he became, and he succeeded Lancelot Andrewes as Dean of Westminster in 1605. Before that, Neile's Cecil connection had brought him a vital piece of preferment. When King James VI came south in 1603 to take up the throne of England on the death of Queen Elizabeth, he sought to appoint a new English private chaplain (the quaintly named Clerk of the Closet). The choice was Richard Neile, and there can be little doubt that the new King's chief minister Robert Cecil made the recommendation. Now Neile was in a uniquely influential position. In 1608 he became a bishop, and the chaplain he appointed in turn was a promising Oxford academic called William Laud.

EARLY STUART ENGLAND: THE CHURCH'S
GOLDEN AGE?

The Scottish ruling dynasty of Stewart (generally spelled Stuart in an English context) had a tortuous path to the English throne. The Scots and the English had considered themselves hereditary enemies until the Reformation had drawn the two Protestant kingdoms together: worse still, the new King James's mother Mary had not only been involved in plots to murder the previous English Queen but had eventually been beheaded on her orders (chapter 8, p. 386). King James was well aware of this tangled heritage and spent many anxious years before finally being reassured (thanks to judicious liaison with Robert Cecil) that old Queen Elizabeth would not stand in the way of his hereditary claim from Henry VIII's sister. He was delighted at his good fortune in inheriting a far more wealthy kingdom than Scotland, and he was determined to have a good time in his remaining two decades of life; he frequently drove Cecil to despair by disappearing from government for prolonged deer-hunting expeditions. But James was not simply an idler, let alone the 'wisest fool in Christendom' of traditional cliché. He was a highly intelligent man who enjoyed a good joke, and he had been a remarkably successful king of Scotland in frequently very difficult circumstances.

James could be personally disconcerting. It has been plausibly suggested that some of his personal characteristics, such as his speech impediment and regular incontinence, are indications that he was born with mild cerebral palsy.[14] His English subjects found difficult his breezy informality and his thick Scottish accent under the speech impediment, and in any case they were uneasy at having a foreigner as king. English noblemen resented the consequences of the King's homosexual affections, which as in the case of Henri III of France (chapter 10, p. 465) threatened to divert the normal sources of advancement and wealth at Court into the hands of male favourites who were not generally from the established political elite. People were also baffled that the King did not seem to hate Roman Catholics, even when a Catholic terrorist group tried to blow him up with all Parliament and the royal family – he talked regardless of reuniting the entire Christian world, and even proposed that eventually a reformed papacy might resume primacy in the Western Church.[15] James's obstinate search for universal peace seemed very odd behaviour in a monarch. His Danish wife Anne was not only a Roman Catholic convert from Lutheranism but hugely extravagant, and James himself was inclined to spend more money than was available either in the Treasury or from Parliament, which gave rise to some very serious political rows. Given all these disadvantages, James performed a remarkably accomplished balancing-act in his English reign, not least in religion. After his death and in the light of the events which followed it, people felt nostalgic for him.

The new King surprised many people in 1603 by being greatly enthusiastic for the Church of England. Roman Catholics were disappointed, because in the course of his struggles for the English succession, he had privately promised them much. Puritans were disappointed, because he came from an emphatically Reformed Church of Scotland which they considered could teach England a great deal. However, they had not sufficiently noticed that James had often been at odds with presbyterians in Scotland, and he had done much to restore the position of bishops in the Scottish Church alongside the presbyteries. It was true that James considered himself a Reformed Protestant, and was a glutton for listening to sermons. He did call a conference to his Palace at Hampton Court in 1604 to hear Puritan grievances, but he granted them no Church reforms of consequence except the establishment of a project to create a new version of the English Bible: this was the 'Authorized Version' completed in 1611, which as the 'King James Bible' is still a major symbol of English-speaking Protestant culture. At the time, this would seem less significant than the fact that at the Hampton Court Conference, avant-garde conformists for the first time boldly put forward their point of view in a public context, rather than in the protected atmosphere of university lecture-rooms. Richard Neile was already Clerk of the Closet. What did that mean for the future of the Church?

English Puritans were not the only ones worried by the rise of Andrewes, Neile and the like. Scottish churchmen were alarmed by what they heard of such opinions. When there was need for a new Archbishop of Canterbury on the death of Richard Bancroft in 1610, King James passed over Andrewes (even though he was in many ways well qualified and had already been promoted through two bishoprics) largely because the Scots would not have approved; instead the King chose the strongly Calvinist-minded former Oxford don George Abbot. Many clergy and laity in England would have been horrified to think of themselves as Puritans, but they still regarded their Church as part of the international Reformed consensus; they were highly distrustful of the new tendency in divinity, and the new Archbishop Abbot shared their distrust. During the 1610s they gave avant-garde conformists a foreign name in allusion to the disputes about predestination that were currently tearing apart the Dutch Reformed Church – 'Arminians'.

This was not so much because the English 'Arminians' were interested in the issues about salvation and predestination that preoccupied the Dutch.

Although many of them did reject what they saw as a Calvinist doctrine of predestination, and there were friendly contacts between Dutch and English Arminians, the English party was more concerned with promoting ceremonial worship, use of the sacraments and a high view of clerical vocation (shockingly to many they had no hesitation in regularly calling ministers of the Church of England 'priests'). None of these issues had any parallel in Dutch Arminianism. The Arminian label was a symbol that England was witnessing a rebellion against European Reformed orthodoxy as serious as that of the Arminians in the Netherlands. Some also nicknamed the developing Arminian clique 'the Durham House set', since from 1617 Richard Neile was Bishop of Durham, and Durham House, his London residence in the Strand, became an unofficial headquarters for the group, the shadow equivalent of Archbishop Abbot's Lambeth Palace across the river Thames.

King James had decades of experience in dealing with squabbling clergy, and he kept a characteristically careful balance among all these tendencies in his fractious Church, promoting some, enjoying the sermons of others, as he saw fit. He was not impressed by the higher-flying Arminian claims of some English bishops, and was prepared to give (slightly gingerly) royal approval to an ostentatiously non-episcopal synod of English and Scottish clergy who ministered to English-speaking congregations in the Netherlands.[16] James also quietly made appointments of senior clergy across the boundaries of his three national Churches as a way of bringing them closer together, and he manoeuvred the Scottish Church by a mixture of bullying and genial persuasion into accepting modifications that would bring it more into line with the English set-up – observing Christmas and Easter as festivals, for example. He kept carefully in touch with other Reformed Churches, and took a firm dislike to the Dutch Arminians, making sure that there was a heavyweight delegation of reliable Reformed English and Scottish divines to the Synod of Dordt in 1618 (chapter 8, pp. 377–8). It was notable that the Synod was particularly considerate to the British delegates: despite the Dutch Church's presbyterian convictions, a special seat was provided with a canopy for the one bishop among the British, George Carleton of Llandaff, to mark his episcopal status (admittedly the canopy annoyed some of the Dutch present).

In King James's time, the Church of England might be seen as enjoying a golden age, fulfilling many of the hopes both of anxious Elizabethan bishops and pernickety Elizabethan Puritans. The King brought in legislation to stop Church estates being further exploited either by the Crown or other laypeople; he encouraged a proper codification of English Church law, something which the earlier Reformation had left unfinished. Decades of efforts at improving clerical education reached the point where virtually all the clergy had been to university and had a degree, which meant that the Puritan ideal of a preaching minister in every parish was at last a reality. Yet the rise of the Arminians soon destabilized the English Church and brought it crashing down in ruin. The beginnings of this were in King James's last years: he was ageing and ill, losing his sureness of touch and relying too much on his latest favourite, George Villiers, Duke of Buckingham. Buckingham chose to ally himself with the Arminians, William Laud in particular, but equally the King began favouring Arminians, in pursuit of his wider diplomatic goals.

We have seen James marrying his daughter Elizabeth to the Elector Palatine Friedrich V, and also the disastrous aftermath with the young couple's Bohemian venture in 1619–20 (chapter 11, pp. 488–96). King James's reaction to this crisis of godly religion was not to help the Elector with military might or money (he had little of either); instead, to the bewilderment and fury of many of his Protestant subjects, he redoubled his efforts in the cause of peace, trying to marry his son Charles to a Spanish princess. James knew how much this project angered the Dutch United Provinces, and he also knew that Archbishop Abbot was a cheerleader for militant Protestantism (chapter 11, pp. 490, 494). Accordingly the King began favouring the Arminians, who he knew did not share the popular mood. In 1623, he even issued a proclamation banning discussion of predestination, because (he said) sermons on the subject were getting contentious and causing trouble. The real reason was that he wanted to stop members of the Church's Reformed establishment such as Archbishop Abbot defending the accepted theology of predestination against Arminian attack. There was then such a huge national outcry that the old King remembered his native pragmatism and withdrew the proclamation.

However, this was only a temporary setback for the Arminians. They had the ear not only of the Duke of Buckingham but of the heir to the throne, Prince Charles. Lancelot Andrewes, who combined his gentle Catholic spirituality with a feline surefootedness in politics, had seen to this. From 1619 the Bishop was Dean of the Chapel Royal, a position which gave him the opportunity to choose the chaplains and preachers to whom the impressionable young prince listened in his own private chapel: naturally their tone now turned solidly Arminian.[17] From then on Charles was a devout High Churchman, and when he came to the throne in 1625 he promoted Arminianism in every sense. A wry joke went the rounds, a question about belief: 'What do the Arminians hold?', to which the answer

was 'all the best deaneries and bishoprics'.[18] The most highly promoted of
all was William Laud, who directed Church affairs as Bishop of London
from 1628, although he had to wait for Canterbury until Archbishop Abbot
had the good taste to die, in 1633. Laud was prominent in a royal regime
which after 1629 ceased to trouble itself with meeting Parliament and
instead tried to sort out England's problems with royal proclamations, Privy
Council orders and the decisions of law courts. Its enemies sarcastically
named the period 'Thorough', and looked back on it as the 'Eleven Years'
Tyranny'.

Laud had a reputation for being kind-hearted to the poor, and he showed
engaging affection for his pet cats and his giant tortoise (a beast that survived
all the subsequent upheavals at Lambeth Palace until it was accidentally
killed by a gardener in the mid-eighteenth century). He was also a lonely
little man, confiding his erotic dreams about the Duke of Buckingham and
others to his private diary.[19] Laud's homosexual leanings showed none of the
extrovert cheerfulness of King James. His tidy-mindedness and humourless
dedication appealed to King Charles, another self-contained little man;
between them they showed no awareness that they might need to inspire
popular enthusiasm for the innovations in religion that they now foisted on
a horrified Church of England. This was an attempt at Counter-Reformation
without the Jesuits. A new royal proclamation in 1626 once more gagged
the pulpits on predestination, and this time it was not withdrawn but
repeated later on. The well-informed might have wryly noted that the
previous year, the Pope had issued a similar prohibition about discussion of
grace, in order to curb the parallel Roman Catholic row over Jansenism
(chapter 10, pp. 480–83).[20]

This was only one symptom of a new regime in the Church that redefined
some of the most senior figures in the ecclesiastical establishment as Puritans,
simply because they disagreed with Arminianism. Bishop John Williams of
Lincoln, a quick-witted and politically minded Welshman who showed
sympathy to protests and challenged Arminian theology effectively, found
himself imprisoned in the Tower of London in 1637 and crushingly fined.
Unmistakable Puritans were treated worse: there were savage Star Chamber
punishments which went beyond ruinous fines to the cropping of ears for
some of the noisiest opposition voices, including one clergyman, Henry
Burton, who had been private chaplain to King Charles's deceased elder
brother Prince Henry. Astonishingly for anyone who had a perspective on
the Reformation, in 1630 the Arminian Archbishop Harsnet of York banned
the sale in northern England of any works by the great William Perkins
or by the doyen of Heidelberg theologians Zacharias Ursinus. Laud also

launched a single-minded campaign to discipline the eighty-year-old Stranger Congregations for foreign refugees, saying that these symbols of England's international Protestant friendships were 'nurseries of ill-minded persons to the Church of England'.[21]

All this was taking place in the decade that Heidelberg's Palatine castle stood a blackened ruin after its sack by Habsburg armies (see Plate 17), when Magdeburg burned and Protestant and Catholic armies fought for the soul of Europe, with the English government not lifting a finger to help the Protestant cause. Meanwhile Charles's Queen Henrietta Maria was a French Roman Catholic, there was an official papal representative in London for the first time since the death of Queen Mary in 1558, while Capuchin friars semi-publicly sang their services in a purpose-built chapel in Somerset House on the Strand. It was not surprising that many should see Laud as the agent of a papist plot to take over the English Church. What was worse, it was clearly also a clerical plot, in which country gentry and noblemen saw clergy taking positions in local government as justices of the peace which they had not enjoyed since the Reformation, and asserting the dignity of the clergy with a new self-confidence. Laud's close associate Matthew Wren, Bishop of Norwich (a London merchant's son), once provocatively remarked that he 'hoped to live to see the day when a minister should be as good a man as any Jack Gentleman in England'.[22] In Ireland, the King's Lord Deputy, Thomas Wentworth, Lord Strafford, launched a ruthless campaign to recover for the Church of Ireland estates and property which had been appropriated by gentry and English settlers over the previous eighty years: in Scotland, the Crown made moves to restore titular abbacies so that in a similar way church lands could be recalled from secular hands. The Habsburgs were doing similar things to Lutheran nobility in central Europe. What could be more alarming than an attack on the laity's property rights?

Angry gentlemen therefore forgot that Laud had participated in a major debate against Roman Catholicism, which had kept the Duke of Buckingham from converting to Rome and had been published as *A conference with Fisher the Jesuit*; neither did they know that the little Archbishop had indignantly turned down the Pope's offer of a Cardinal's hat.[23] Laud deplored the Church of Rome's errors: the problem was that he and his sympathizers clearly thought that the Reformation had been the wrong way to tackle the errors. In a myriad of ways the Arminians showed their contempt for the Reformation: some borrowed a Roman Catholic piece of abuse and anticipated Dr Johnson by calling it a 'Deformation'.[24] They built new churches in a style which deliberately imitated pre-Reformation architecture, and which was the first 'Gothic revival' rather than Gothic

The architects of Arminian policies in England.

Charles I, King of England, Scotland and Ireland.

William Laud, Archbishop of Canterbury.

survival – some might have known that the Counter-Reformation was doing the same thing in the Empire and central Europe as it rolled back the frontiers of Protestantism (chapter 10, p. 454). One of the most offensive English examples was the new chapel of Peterhouse, Cambridge, built by Bishop Matthew Wren as Master of the College: it mocked the University's Puritans with its stained glass and prominent façade aggressively thrust towards the main street, artfully combining Gothic with what looked distinctly like Counter-Reformation Baroque trimmings.

Newly crafted Arminian silver church plate carefully copied the shape of pre-Reformation chalices and patens, of which few survived from the thousands which on the orders of the early Elizabethan bishops had been melted down nationwide and replaced with robust congregational drinking-cups for the Lord's Supper (see Plate 18).[25] This was literally to thrust Arminian eucharistic thought in the faces of communicants; moreover, the faithful were told to treat their church's communion table as an altar, and they were now forced whether they liked it or not to kneel to receive the bread and wine at the communion rail (an innocent piece of church furniture which Laud thus turned into a political issue). In the Laudians' zeal to make worship and church interiors more holy, they offended against long-standing silent understandings of religious behaviour: they even tried to stop people bringing their dogs to church. The English were already a nation of dog-enthusiasts if not dog-lovers, and they tolerated dogs in church on the same basis as children, as long as both groups behaved themselves: there was much fury among churchgoers at the cat-loving Archbishop's intolerance. All over the country, churchwardens were ordered to spend large sums of money on reordering the interiors of their churches on Arminian principles, often not long after the parish had spent large sums on rearranging the same churches for godly preaching.[26] The result was that in the commotions after 1642, Peterhouse Chapel was gleefully wrecked, and all over the kingdom the collapse of Laud's plans was marked by bonfires of communion rails. How had the golden age of the Church of England come to this?

WAR IN THREE KINGDOMS, 1638–60

In the 1630s King Charles embarked on a revolution in the Churches of England and Ireland against the Protestant landowning and clerical establishment which had been in control since the 1559 Settlement. If he had had any imagination, he might have found food for thought in the fate of royal attempts to turn back the Reformation in Sweden under Kings Johan III and Sigismond, or in the trouble which various German princes experienced in imposing a Calvinist 'Second Reformation' on predominantly Lutheran populations (chapter 8). He coupled his religious changes with assaults on the accepted conventions of English politics: he clearly did not intend to meet Parliament again after he dissolved a particularly acrimonious session in 1629, and he encouraged a recklessly unqualified rhetoric of the divine right of kings. There was little in this which had not been said by Queen Elizabeth or King James (or indeed by most medieval monarchs), but it sounded different when it was not balanced by any respect for the country's representative institutions, and when Charles's clerical allies were also loudly proclaiming the divine right of bishops, a radically new doctrine in England. All this was coupled with busy, pernickety attempts to streamline the country's administration and raise royal finance without Parliament, often by recourse to precedents which were so archaic that they sounded dangerously novel.

What was remarkable, and a tribute to English habits of obedience to the monarchy, was that for most of the decade the King seemed to have got his way in imposing his new religious policies, his political innovations and his move to raise revenues without calling Parliament. A mark of his apparent success was that several leading gentry and nobility who opposed Arminianism made despairing plans to leave the country and begin afresh in the north Atlantic or Caribbean colonies (see below, p. 535). However, what ruined Charles's plans was his mishandling of his third kingdom, Scotland. Although he had been born in Scotland, he had spent his life south of the border, and he showed a suicidal disregard for Scottish public opinion. He did not deign to revisit the land of his birth and receive a Scottish coronation until 1633, and on this visit he should have been alerted to possible trouble by the astonishment and anger which the sight of an English clergyman in a surplice aroused in the spectators at Holyrood Palace. Instead, the King went ahead with plans to bring the Scottish Church into line with the English; he left behind his father's cannily gradualist policies towards the Kirk and listened only to a few Arminian sympathizers among the Scottish bishops. In 1637 he imposed on Scotland a version of the English Prayer Book, modified in a fashion which Arminians would secretly have liked to achieve in England: a move back to the first English Prayer Book of 1549, which had many more 'Catholic' features than the post-1552 English liturgies, in particular making it easier to proclaim a theory of the real presence in the Eucharist.

There had been no consultation with the people who mattered in Scotland,

and the kingdom exploded in indignation. There were riots. In the cathedral church of Brechin, Bishop Whitford led the service from the new book glowering at the cathedral congregation over a pair of loaded pistols, just in case they tried to rush him in his desk – a remarkable case of episcopal tough love.[27] In two successive 'Bishops' Wars' in 1639 and 1640, the Scottish leadership showed its rejection not only of the new Prayer Book but also of the bishops who had collaborated with its introduction. In the process they totally defeated two royal armies sent from England, whose hearts were not in the job of defending their royal master and his popish ceremonies against fellow Protestants. Charles's critics in England, who in their fury had begun a secret and unprecedented collaboration with the Scots, were now able to unite the whole kingdom in rage against him. After tumultuous general elections in 1640, they dominated the first meeting of Parliament for eleven years. When Charles, not liking the message he heard from the assembled peers and members of the Commons, rapidly dismissed this 'Short Parliament', a second round of elections produced the same result, and the 'Long Parliament' was launched on its turbulent career at Westminster. Laud was arrested and sent to the Tower, and Strafford executed.

For a few months in 1640–1, England experienced a version of the exuberant hopes for a better future that Protestant central Europe had felt when the Palatine Elector rode towards his coronation in Bohemia in 1618. Yet as the leadership in the newly convened Westminster Parliament imposed a drastic settlement of their religious and political grievances on their King, many within the political establishment began to be worried by their radicalism. Mobs wrecked the houses of Roman Catholic gentry, seized by the firm belief that a popish plot was in preparation, and parish churches suffered vandalistic attacks on anything which excited Protestants might decide was a symbol of Arminian corruption. It was all very well to get rid of Charles's Arminian bishops and ministers, but now many of his parliamentary opponents seemed to be intent on the destruction of all bishops and the Church of England as well. Accordingly amid intense political activity in 1641, thousands of worried people were now prepared to sign petitions in favour of the Church of England, but they couched their petitions in very revealing terms: this was a Protestantism prepared to defend the apostolic origins of bishops, but carefully silent about their *jure divino* claims, glorying (John Foxe-like) in the Marian martyrs' blood which consecrated the Prayer Book text; applauding Elizabeth I and James I but stony-faced on the subject of the reigning monarch, and happy to denounce the imprisoned Laud.[28] Many were reluctantly coming to the conclusion that there might be a need to rally to the defence of their obnoxious monarch in order to stave off worse evils.

The fatal split of 1641 came when a major national rebellion broke out in Ireland. The Catholic population – both Gaelic and English – had finally decided to take their revenge on Protestantism and its settler culture. There were terrible atrocities, and worse reports as news sped across St George's Channel: a sober modern estimate is that a maximum of 12,000 Protestants died in the province of Ulster alone, but this already ghastly figure was soon magnified to 154,000, four times the actual settler population of the province.[29] Once more the fires of Magdeburg raged in the imaginations of English Protestants, with the extra horror that their own kith and kin were involved. They knew that they must defeat the Irish, but the country was split down the middle as to whether the King could be trusted with an army to invade Ireland. A majority in Parliament thought not. Charles's own slippery conduct towards the opposition in England did not inspire confidence, and very many firmly believed that he was secretly co-operating with the Earl of Antrim and other Irish Catholics.[30] So it was around this issue of raising troops that the first English Civil War broke out in 1642, as Charles withdrew from his capital in order to rally provincial support for his army. Given the powerful mystique of monarchy at the time, the growing backing for the King was not so remarkable as the great body of his subjects who were prepared to fight against him in the name of liberty and true religion. A series of civil wars followed in the three kingdoms right up to 1660.

One of the major issues to be fought between Charles's supporters and the opposition leadership who ruled in Parliament at Westminster was what should happen to the Church of England. Increasingly the whole 1559 Settlement was identified with the King's cause, particularly since Charles did his best to pose as defender rather than subverter of the Church of England in order to rally people to the royalist armies. On the Parliamentarian side, a split developed between 'Presbyterians', who were prepared to follow the Scottish line and set up an English Church with a presbyterian structure, and 'Independents' who were suspicious of Parliament's Scottish allies and wanted a much more loose church system, with a minimum of central organization for England's religious life. The Presbyterians had their strength in the Westminster Parliament, and it was Parliament which set up a synod in 1643 to reform the Church in England. Predictably, this 'Westminster Assembly', which came to include Scottish representatives, produced a Confession of Faith which was Calvinist and presbyterian in form.

This Westminster Confession of 1646 still has an honoured place in the doctrinal standards of the Church of Scotland, but it has had a much lesser role in English religious life. The reason was that the Independents had their power-base in the army which Parliament had built up to fight the King, and as the army became ever more successful against Charles, its leaders started making up their own minds on England's future. The total defeat of the King in 1646 made matters worse, because Parliament and the army now quarrelled about what to do with him as well as about how to reshape national religion. A military *coup d'état* (Pride's Purge, 1648) ousted the parliamentary Presbyterian leadership and led the way open to a state trial and a verdict of execution on the King for waging war on his own people. He died with serene dignity in January 1649, doing much more for the Church of England in his death than in his life: his (ghost-written) spiritual reflections in prison, *Eikon Basilike*, became an instant clandestine best-seller, and promoted the image of a saintly royal martyr. This book can claim to be one of the most influential published in England during the seventeenth century, even though it is now virtually forgotten. It helped to prolong the idea of sacred monarchy in England for at least another century.

What could replace the King? The next eleven years are often neutrally known as the Interregnum ('the time between the reigns'), which disguises the fact that England became a republic, translating the Latin *Respublica* in the new regime's ostentatiously vernacular public documents as 'Common-wealth', on the analogy of Poland-Lithuania. The army's leading general, Oliver Cromwell, was a brilliant and often ruthless soldier, who around the time that King Charles's 'Thorough' policies had begun had come to a deeply held and intense Protestant faith, in a recovery from what appears to have been a serious nervous breakdown.[31] Now this dourly high-principled, blunt-spoken minor gentleman's son from Huntingdon was becoming master of the entire Atlantic Isles. In Ireland, as he steam-rollered the destruction of the Roman Catholic Confederacy and allied royalist forces, he had no compunction first in perpetrating massacres of Roman Catholic garrisons and then confiscating the lands of Roman Catholic gentry. Cath-olic landowners were exiled to the bleakest part of the island, with all the concentrated confessional spite which Habsburg government was showing simultaneously against Protestants in central Europe.

Cromwell was less adroit as a politician than as a soldier, and he now faced the task of working out a new structure of government for the Commonwealth, which after his conquests embraced the whole of the Atlantic Isles. It proved a hopeless task. The root problem was that Scotland

and Ireland did not wish to be ruled from England, so the army was needed in all its power to overawe them. This was not merely very expensive, it was deeply offensive to those English people who longed to return to pre-war normality. The nation which in the 1630s had been one of the least militarized in all Europe had become one of the most militarized by the 1650s. The English increasingly hated the army, while the army developed political and religious agendas of its own. Any English parliament elected on a reasonably representative basis clashed with the army, while everywhere else in the archipelago could only be ruled using the army. Cromwell unhappily experimented with a variety of new national assemblies, but he could not square this political circle and he was eventually forced to set up a military-backed dictatorship. It looked more and more like the old monarchy, though he would not take any more monarchical title than Lord Protector on the (not exactly encouraging) precedents of the murderous fifteenth-century Richard Duke of Gloucester and the inept sixteenth-century Duke of Somerset (chapter 5, pp. 255–7). Poland-Lithuania kept its Commonwealth going for three centuries: the English Commonwealth managed eleven years.

When Cromwell died in September 1658, on the night of one of the worst storms to hit Europe in the whole century, there was no one of similar standing to take his place as Protector, and in desperation, after two years of mounting confusion, one of the army leaders led a successful move to restore the old monarchy with the exiled Charles II, son of the executed King. This seemed to be a 'revolution' in the old sense: a turn right back to the political and ecclesiastical conditions of 1641. Matters were not that simple, because much had changed in the intervening twenty years. One important religious change was that during the 1650s organized groups of Protestants took permanent shape outside the established national Church: in the course of time these would come to form denominations, Congregationalists or Independents and Baptists. During Elizabeth I's reign there had been small separatist congregations which approximated to these later groups: some were significantly strong in areas affected by pre-Reformation Lollardy, some were former Puritans who had come to despise the official Church, while others had been influenced by the radical Reformation in mainland Europe. They remained few in number before the war: Puritans in the established Protestant Church thought ill of such people, who offended against the assumption of mainstream Protestants that Church and Commonwealth should be closely linked.

Then the war altered everything. The whole structure of the pre-war Church was dismantled, and with the end of government control people could begin to make religious decisions for themselves. Parliament's army was particularly affected by religious radicalism, for in it men were risking their lives for a godly cause and were free of any control from the traditional parish system. In all branches of religious life there was a feeling that the Last Days were about to come, especially after the King had been executed, and this apocalyptic excitement spawned many sects who wished to play the part of the faithful remnant before God's throne. Some tried to overthrow all previous society. The Diggers tried to dig up common land to establish and maintain self-sufficient communes (they were broken up by furious consortia of those with legal rights on the commons). Groups whom scandalized respectable folk called 'Ranters' believed that God had sent them a particular revelation, which surpassed that in the printed pages of the Bible: it amounted to an 'inner light' – a belief that takes us back to some of the more radical thoughts of the 1530s (chapter 4, p. 207; chapter 5, p. 215). Such 'Ranters' sometimes expressed their God-given antinomian freedom from all worldly and spiritual laws by such gestures as ecstatic blasphemy, joyous tobacco-smoking and running naked down the street. Such tales lost nothing in the telling among the rest of the population, especially in the burgeoning sensationalist journalism of those years.[32]

Among the movements of enthusiasts, some gathered around the powerful figure of George Fox, who was determined to harness such energies to a godly purpose and end the excesses. Those who (more or less) accepted his centralizing direction came to call themselves 'Friends of the Truth', while others sneeringly nicknamed them Quakers, after an incident in which Fox told a judge in a law court to tremble at the name of the Lord. At the time the Friends horrified and infuriated everyone else by their deliberate flouting of social convention to show that they acknowledged no power but God's: they refused to doff their hats respectfully to social superiors, and they used the familiar forms 'thee' and 'thou' to everybody (a gesture slightly undercut by the fact that this linguistic idiom was then going out of fashion). Almost alone among the more exotic groups of the Interregnum, they survived and transformed their character into a peaceable, self-restrained people who, even though they still rejected all sacramental forms in their worship, seemed almost like a contemplative religious Order in the universal Church. Their present-day association with peace, disarmament and ecological movements is a quiet return to their original commitment to questioning all established authority.

Such groups as these terrified the mainstream supporters of the Common-wealth and Protectorate, most of whom had fought Charles I to preserve the old England as they understood it, not to usher in a new Zion. In 1656 a Quaker called James Nayler re-enacted Christ's triumphal entry into

Jerusalem in Bristol, escorted by a crowd of adoring women waving leafy branches: Parliament voted him a vicious punishment, including branding and bodily mutilation. Cromwell was much more torn in his reaction, disapproving of such institutional violence even though Nayler's blasphemous theatricals profoundly shocked him. Leaders like Cromwell were caught between their longing to establish a truly godly state in England, which would indeed be a new Jerusalem, and their wish as English gentlemen to restore the stability of the past. Usually conservatism won out, and radicals found themselves forced out of positions of power in Cromwell's army and government. Nevertheless Cromwell was committed, against the Presbyterians whom he had defeated in Parliament, to establishing a broad and truly comprehensive Protestantism in the religion of England.

Under Cromwell's guidance, the English Church became more widely based than it would ever be again. Equally, while he proved himself a brutally thorough enemy to Irish Roman Catholicism, in England he encouraged an unprecedented toleration. The Roman Catholic minority found itself less persecuted in the Interregnum than under the monarchy, despite its general support for the King during the wars of the three kingdoms. The Anglican gentry minority who wanted the episcopal system of the pre-war Church were left alone as long as they caused no trouble, and they settled down unwillingly to being an upper-class sect like the Roman Catholics, nursing and honing their grievances against the new Church establishment, and burnishing the memory of the late King Charles as a martyr. Cromwell even allowed the Jews back into England after an official expulsion which had lasted since 1290 – but in this he showed himself not an enlightened modern liberal but a devotee of the Protestant enthusiasm that eagerly awaited the Last Days.

All well-informed Bible-readers knew that the Last Days would never happen until the Jews were converted, but in England there were no Jews to convert. Menasseh ben Israel, a celebrated rabbi in the Jewish community of Amsterdam, was well aware of such apocalyptic longings: he paid visits to England in which he spent much time raising excitement among apocalyptic-minded Christians, and Cromwell showed his practical commitment to the Last Days by granting the Dutch rabbi an annual pension of £100. In a fashion which (rather typically for the Interregnum) disguised the drama of what was happening, the eventual resolution of the situation was less apocalyptic. After the outbreak of Anglo-Spanish war in 1656, a Jewish merchant resident in London had his property confiscated as a Spaniard: he took his courage in his hands and complained to Cromwell that he was not Spanish but Jewish. The Admiralty lawyers duly handed the property back without fuss: their action implied without any big ideological fanfare that there was no problem with Jews either being resident in England or holding property. Charles II, on his Restoration four years later, seemed anxious to conciliate the Amsterdam Jews, perhaps in return for cash, and England has been home to an openly Jewish community ever since.[33]

In the new situation, the Church in England became a vast federation of parishes, with virtually no central structure apart from a London committee known as the Triers, set up to examine candidates for the ministry, and drawn from all shades of mainstream Protestant opinion. As a result, parishes could go their own way, which usually meant a personal adaptation of the supposedly illegal Book of Common Prayer in a Protestant direction (exactly what Puritans had been seeking for a hundred years), or an equally selective use of the Prayer Book's lawful Parliamentary replacement of 1645, the Directory of Public Worship.[34] In some areas, ministers of presbyterian convictions managed to set up a local presbytery on a voluntary basis, but groups also emerged alongside the parish system, wishing to worship as a 'gathered congregation' of those who were moved to join together. These were linked to the separatist groupings which had begun to take shape in Elizabeth's reign. There was a broad division between those who accepted infant baptism (Independents) and those who rejected it (Baptists). It was an untidy divide, because many congregations were prepared to tolerate individual opinions on this important subject among their members in the interest of Christian love, freedom and common worship. There were even divisions within the division, especially between 'Particular' Baptists who still held to a Calvinist belief in predestination, and a growing number of 'General' Baptists who rejected that doctrine. Each main grouping developed structures so that they could associate with like-minded Christians: regional organizations for the Particular Baptists, and national meetings which drew up policy guidelines for the General Baptists and Independents.

A SPECTRUM OF PROTESTANTISMS, 1660–1700

The restoration of Charles II in 1660 abruptly cut across all the Interregnum religious experiments. Much to its astonishment, the Presbyterian leadership, prominent in inviting back the new King, found its mass support swept away in a wave of nostalgic (and perhaps shame-faced) enthusiasm for the executed Charles I, the old ways of Cranmer's Prayer Book and the episcopal structure of the Church. The leading episcopal clergy waiting in the wings made full use of this mood, completely outmanoeuvring the Presbyterians

Lambeth Palace from the Thames after 1660: Archbishop Juxon's lavish rebuilding of his ruined palace, particularly the reconstructed great dining hall in the centre where archbishops entertained the English nobility and gentry, symbolised the remarkable return of a self-consciously Anglican and episcopal established Church with Charles II.

in setting up a new Church and an only lightly revised Book of Common Prayer by 1662: episcopal clergy who had been driven out of their livings over the previous two decades now in turn triumphantly ejected their successors with grim satisfaction.

It is one of the most astonishing and least remarked-upon phenomena in English history that bishops and even the cathedrals with their deans and chapters were given back all their lands in 1660–2 without the landowners of England rising in indignant revolution. Apart from a good measure of guilt or sheepishness among the English landed elite, it suggests a slow build-up of emotional reaction against the governments of the Interregnum, a reaction of revulsion which made the old Church seem like a good investment. Oliver Cromwell's government had closed theatres, taken down maypoles and ordered shopkeepers to stay open on the superstitious feast of Christmas Day. Fatally in the late 1650s, a small number of enthusiastic army officers had been created 'Major-Generals' with charge of designated areas of the country to enforce such measures as well as to raise taxes for the army, and they were cordially loathed by most of the population. Christmas Day and *Eikon Basilike* between them defeated Oliver Cromwell's heirs, and revenge after 1660 was sweet.[35]

The now re-established Church of England proved to be much more exclusive in its doctrine than it had been before 1642. For the first time since the reign of Mary it had acquired martyrs, indeed a martyred king. Equally importantly, it was steered by a large number of ousted clergy who had been victimized over two decades for their loyalty to episcopacy and Cranmer's liturgy, and who were therefore now all the more attached to them as a matter of principle. Most of these clergy also turned their backs on the Calvinist or Reformed Protestant theology which had been so overwhelmingly dominant in England until the 1620s, now associating it with Puritan revolution. That meant that the Church of England no longer emphasized that it was part of the international Reformed Protestant world, despite indignant protests from some old-fashioned churchmen, especially in that inveterate home of lost causes, Oxford University.[36] Laud was rehabilitated as a martyr alongside Charles I, and although the restored Church leadership discreetly sidelined the more extreme elements of Laud's programme, his insistence on the *jure divino* character of both bishops and monarchy became an essential part of the Church's doctrinal stance. The team of liturgical experts who undertook the task of revising the old Prayer Book were supposed to be conciliating Presbyterians in an inclusive spirit, but virtually all their changes were designed to accommodate long-standing 'avant-garde conformist' worries as to whether Archbishop Cranmer had been sufficiently 'on-message' in 1552 on matters such as divine presence in the eucharistic bread and wine.

The new boundaries of what was possible in the established Church were symbolized by the departure of nearly 3,000 clergy who could not fit into the new system, together with lay people who supported their stand. With an inadvertent symbolism long remembered by those affected and their followers and successors, the deadline for their departure coincided with the ninetieth anniversary of the St Bartholomew's Day massacres of Protestants in France (chapter 7, p. 338). This was a posthumous triumph for Lancelot Andrewes and Richard Hooker, although the triumph also involved a certain amount of rewriting the life and thought of both these divines to suit the new situation.[37] Now there was a Church of England which could accurately be described as 'Anglican'. It could never be completely the Church that Laud had wanted, because Reformation memories were too deeply ingrained in England. The nation went on lighting bonfires and setting off fireworks to commemorate the defeat of the Armada and the foiling of Guy Fawkes's conspiracy to blow up King James; the good folk of Lewes in Sussex (a Protestant stronghold since the 1530s) still burn the Pope in effigy on 5 November. England remained the land of Foxe's Book of Martyrs, and its established Anglican Church has oscillated between the poles of Protestantism and Catholicism ever since, producing an interestingly subtle and reflective version of Christianity in the process.

Sublety or reflectiveness were nevertheless in short supply in 1662. By their hard-line stance, the Anglicans created 'Dissent' out of those who had been part of the united pre-war Church of England: Presbyterians now found themselves alongside the Independents and the Baptists (together with the Quakers whom they all despised) outside the new establishment. English Protestantism was fractured in a way that has yet to be healed, and the reign of Charles II saw Dissenters putting up a desperate struggle to survive against often severe persecution from the Anglican authorities in Church and state. Legislation made the holding of public office dependent on taking Holy Communion in the Anglican form, and this perverse use of the sacrament of unity as a political 'Test' was not abolished in England until the nineteenth century. This was a persecution of Protestants by Protestants unique in Europe in its intensity and bitterness: another major question-mark against the complacent English boast of a national history of tolerance.

The persecution was also paradoxical, because although it was promoted by a vengeful Anglican establishment, King Charles himself, Supreme Governor of the Church, gave it only the most reluctant and coerced support. He had seen too much earnestly held religion in his childhood and turbulent exile to take it very seriously. If his Maker had cross-questioned him on the subject, he would have opted for Roman Catholicism, rejecting the Church of England which so fiercely proclaimed its loyalty to him – in the end, the cheerfully cynical monarch converted to Roman Catholicism on his deathbed. Before that last-minute decision, he spent the last years of his reign concentrating his intermittently formidable political skills on securing the rights of his openly Roman Catholic brother James, Duke of York, to succeed to the throne, crippling the ultra-Protestant opposition as far as he could. It was not his fault that when James succeeded as James II and VII in 1685 the new King took only three years to throw away this golden political legacy.

The Reformation now contrived to remove yet another king from the three thrones of the isles, although this time his head was not severed from his shoulders: James achieved the remarkable feat of uniting all British Protestants against their old religious enemy, the Church of Rome, after a quarter-century of internal Protestant quarrels. James's problem was that unlike his brother he was serious (as well as not very bright). A convert to Roman Catholicism during the 1660s, he now earnestly tried to improve the position of his fellow Catholics in such an inept way that he aroused the fears of both the Anglican establishment and the Dissenters. His replacement on the throne in 1688 by his Dutch son-in-law Willem of Orange was virtually bloodless because the whole English political establishment stood by and let it happen, earning the event the name of the 'Glorious Revolution'. This happy title is a disguise for the fact that Willem was (so far) the last foreign ruler to lead a successful military invasion of England, and the English did nothing to stop it. James's efforts to regain his thrones by rebellions in Scotland and Ireland were a good deal more bloody: the final defeat of his Catholic Irish forces at the battles of the Boyne and Aughrim in 1690 and 1691 remains one of the most explosive memories in the unhappy history of Catholic and Protestant relations in Ireland.

In England, James's defeat brought an untidy and long-contested deal between Anglicanism and Dissent. The new King William III (who, to provide a figleaf of constitutional respectability, ruled as joint monarch with his devoutly Anglican Stuart wife Mary) was a Dutch Calvinist, from the family of Willem 'the Silent': he devoted much of his life to fighting the Catholic menace offered to Protestant Europe by Louis XIV of France, and his conquest of England had been part of his grand Protestant design against Louis (chapter 17, p. 671). Neither William nor the Anglican establishment could ignore the memory or the potential of the united Protestant front against James, and some leading churchmen tried to find ways of bringing Dissent back into the Church of England through some sort of 'Comprehension'. In the event, political circumstances meant that there was a much more illogical compromise: Dissenting bodies were given the chance to worship legally alongside the Anglican parochial system on certain restrictive conditions, laid down in a Toleration Act in 1689. During the early eighteenth century, hardline Anglicans repeatedly tried to put the clock back to the 1660s, but the Act proved the beginning in a long process of granting full civil rights to those outside the established British Churches. A few anomalies still remain, such as the restriction of the British throne to Protestants, but emancipation was virtually completed during the nineteenth century.

The Act of Toleration was thus an event of great significance, for like the outcome of the Thirty Years War, it was a faltering step in allowing Christians of opposing views to live side by side. Whatever its official claims, the Church of England had now surrendered in its attempt to represent the only Christianity which could have a true existence in the kingdom, as the Dutch Reformed Church had done in the United Provinces decades before, in a rather muted aftermath to the Arminian defeat at the Synod of Dordt. This produced a very different texture in the Protestantism of the English-speaking world to that of overwhelmingly Lutheran or Calvinist states in mainland Europe. A fractured Protestant ascendancy produced a more open politics, even while the three kingdoms were increasingly drawing together into a single state of Great Britain: the British monarchy found it increasingly difficult to maintain its real power against the self-assertion of a Protestant Parliament in Westminster and politically active Protestant Dissenters. After 1690, besides England's episcopalian Anglicanism and Protestant Dissent, the Church of Scotland finally lost its bishops and became exclusively presbyterian in polity, and the majority of Scottish settlers in Ireland also reaffirmed their presbyterian loyalty. So several different faces of British Protestantism were each destined to give rise to worldwide families of Churches. Moreover, the centre of gravity in these bodies other than Anglicanism was destined to move from the Atlantic Isles to the western seaboard of the ocean, to the new English-speaking colonies of America.

AMERICAN BEGINNINGS

One result of Charles I's religious policies in the 1630s was to further English colonization in north America, but the beginnings were eight decades earlier. As soon as northern European Protestants began establishing themselves against Rome, they became envious of the Iberian Atlantic conquests: from the earliest days, religious and economic motives were inextricably mingled. The English had long fished in north Atlantic waters and visited north American shores, but they were to some extent distracted from America by their own rather more accessible Atlantic New World in Ireland: here they could plant true religion and steal land from people whom they were often inclined to regard in much the same light as the Spaniards did the native peoples of America. While the English were making their first Irish plantation attempts in the reigns of Edward and Mary (chapter 8, p. 395), French Protestants took the lead in challenging the Iberian powers across the ocean, making efforts to set up colonies in Brazil and Florida in the 1550s and 1560s. The aristocratic Protestant leadership was encouraged by the French monarchy, which was happy to see the Habsburgs harassed in another world sphere, but both Brazilian and Floridan ventures ended in disaster, and during the long decades of civil war in France there was no incentive to follow them up. It was therefore the Protestant English who took up the task from the French. They turned their attention first to the lands well to the north of New Spain: southern Europeans had found these less enticing, particularly since the latitudes turned progressively colder as the coastline stretched further north.

From the 1580s the English made a series of efforts to rival the Spanish success by founding their own colonies on the seaboard to the north of the Spanish empire. The first efforts were as abortive as the earlier French ventures, but England had enough political stability and enough will to try again. After much loss of life and capital, a settlement established a precarious but continuous existence from 1607: it borrowed the name Virginia (after the lately deceased 'Virgin Queen' Elizabeth) from the earlier unsuccessful Elizabethan efforts to colonize the north American coastline. The settlers of Virginia brought with them a conformist clergyman of the Church of England and quickly provided for financial support for a parish ministry. Virginia established a Church which certainly identified itself as Anglican, but which also remained more like the undemonstratively Protestant Church of James I than the Arminianism of William Laud. Even after the execution of Charles I the colony stayed fiercely loyal to the Prayer Book and episcopally ordained clergy, which made its relations with Cromwell's Interregnum regimes strained and difficult – together with the rather similar regime on the Caribbean island of Barbados, it was one of two places in the world where Anglicanism survived as an established Church through the 1650s.[38] Yet after 1660, the Virginian colonists' theoretical love of bishops was not ardent enough to lend much support to proposals to establish a bishop on their side of the Atlantic, let alone a system of English-style church courts. They also made sure that their parishes were run by powerful 'vestries' of laypeople rather than giving control to clergymen. Virginian Anglicanism was thus made safe for gentry who appreciated a decent and edifying but not over-dramatic performance of the Prayer Book.

Virginia remained more like the hierarchical countryside of Old England than any of the other English ventures, particularly those which followed on the coasts northward. These expeditions represented those who saw the early Stuart Church of England as too flawed to be truly God's Church. America was not their automatic first choice when they looked for a place to build a purer community in which to worship God. Some migrated to the Protestant United Provinces of the Netherlands, as discontented English godly folk had done since the middle of Elizabeth's reign, but however godly the atmosphere in this properly reformed Church setting, there was little land to spare and rather too many Dutch people. Ireland offered better possibilities, but the drawback by the late 1620s was that Arminianism was pursuing settlers from England and making godliness impossible in Ireland as well; after Strafford had arrived to lead the government in Dublin in 1632, he even made major concessions to Irish Roman Catholics (chapter 8, p. 398). So the best alternative was to be found in the new lands of America.

The godly made their venture far to the north up the Atlantic coast from Virginia, in an area of forests and deep sea inlets which was soon named New England. The first colony in this northern region, Plymouth, in what later became a part of Massachusetts, was founded in 1620 by self-conscious separatists who made no bones about their wish to separate completely from corrupt English religion. These 'Pilgrim Fathers' had first migrated as a single congregation to the Netherlands, but now sought a more challenging and less restricting place to become a 'civil body politic, for our better ordering and preservation'.[39] For all its subsequent fame in American mythology, their settlement remained small and poor, for not many wished to join them; they made their brave voyage in the years before the group around William Laud had achieved power in England. Notably, for all their intense practice of piety, there was no clergyman among them for the first nine years of Plymouth's existence.

The impulse during the 1630s was different: the radical religious changes brought about by Charles I's regime encouraged many gentry, clergy and ordinary people who had no inclination to separatism to uproot themselves and try the hazards of a long Atlantic voyage. Up to the 1630s there were fewer English migrants to north America than to north Africa, where there were thousands of English slaves, Muslim converts, traders and adventurers: now that quickly changed. In that decade perhaps as many as 20,000 emigrated to the New World – rather more than the entire contemporary population of Norwich, the largest city in early Stuart England after London.[40] Some colonists established themselves far to the south in islands in the Caribbean, financed by Puritan grandees who saw these as useful bases for harassing the Spanish colonies in the manner of the great Elizabethan Protestant captains like Francis Drake. Most did not. They followed the earlier separatists to New England and in 1630 founded a new colony of Massachusetts, taking under their wing an ailing earlier venture in that region sponsored by the prominent Dorchester minister John White (chapter 13, p. 557). A significant difference from the Virginian and Caribbean enterprises was that the New England leadership was generally less socially prominent – ministers and minor gentry – and those in charge now proposed to migrate to the colony themselves rather than stay back home in England. This was a measure of their commitment to starting England afresh overseas.

The first governor of Massachusetts was John Winthrop: like Oliver Cromwell, he was an East Anglian gentleman of no great local standing who had come through a similar (though less traumatic) experience of financial and family crisis in the late 1620s (see Plate 23a). His family had a tradition of cosmopolitan Protestantism stretching back to the 1540s; mindful of his troubles in England, and rejected in his attempt to secure election to Parliament to promote the godly cause, he now devoted his talent for leadership, previously confined in the roles of justice of the peace and minor royal official, to a grander enterprise.[41] Winthrop's associates included a number of university-trained ministers ejected from or not prepared to serve in Laud's Church, and as early as 1636 they founded a university college in Massachusetts to train up new clergy. Significantly, they placed the new college (soon named Harvard after an early benefactor) in a town named Cambridge, and equally significantly, they took care to furnish Cambridge with a printing press; the third book to be printed was a new version of the Genevan-style metrical psalter so familiar back home in the parish churches of England. They ignored the other component of English worship, the Prayer Book: Laud had tainted that irredeemably. With great satisfaction John Winthrop recorded in his journal for 15 October 1640 the miracle of the Puritan mice. One volume in his son's library was a Greek New Testament, a book of psalms and the Book of Common Prayer all bound up together. Mice gnawed at every leaf of the prayer book, but left the New Testament and the psalter intact. Thus Mr Winthrop's library, like Massachusetts itself, put its mark of scorn on the popish Church of England liturgy.[42]

The rhetoric of this emigration sprang out of the Puritan rhetoric which had sounded from pulpits throughout England since the 1560s. Naturally the idea of covenant, first resounding in Bullinger's Zürich in the 1530s, was prominent. A highly influential book, *Seven Treatises called the practice of Christianity*, was written by one of the principal Puritan ministers of East Anglia, Richard Rogers; published in 1603, it had gone through eight editions by the time of the Massachusetts venture in 1630. One of its highlights was a description of how twenty years before, Rogers had covenanted with those people in his Essex parish of Wethersfield who were prepared to separate themselves from the delights and temptations of the world: their covenant had endured ever since, said Rogers. This was a potent image which many in Puritan circles noted, and the communities that set themselves up in New England were prompt to covenant for their future.[43] They were a chosen people, who had made an agreement with God and with each other. Other words beside covenant might inspire people as they leafed through their Bibles and meditated on what they had done, confined in the cramped and stinking ships of the Atlantic voyage or amid the deep snow of a New England winter. They found themselves in a wilderness, as the Children of Israel had done, but was this any worse a wilderness than the Church of England under the leadership of the Arminians? Might they rather be re-entering an Edenic garden, which they might tend and bring to order and peace such as their communities had known before the time of Laud? So they named their new communities Boston, Dedham, Ipswich, Braintree, to begin the task of cultivating and replicating these gardens of godly England that they had lost to the weeds and pollution of Laud's religion.

Although the New England settlers made their colony much less like Old England than Virginia was intended to be, it is important to remember that the vast majority were not separatists but Puritans. They wanted a truer form of established Church, which somehow (perhaps uncomfortably) would also have the characteristics of a Church of the elect. It was the same impulse which lay behind the covenanting back in Wethersfield, or the pietist-style 'further reformation' in the Dutch Reformed Church (chapter 8, p. 391), or the disruptive movements of exclusive piety in the Reformed Church of Transylvania (chapter 10, p. 460). The venture in New England was more than wilderness or garden: it was (in the words of Governor Winthrop as his party prepared to sail out from Southampton) 'a city upon a hill'. This quotation from Matthew 5:14 has become a famous phrase in American self-identity, but Winthrop did not intend to convey any sense of a particular special destiny for the new colony: he meant that like every other venture of the godly, and as in the quotation's context in Matthew's Gospel, Massachusetts was to be visible for all the world to learn from it. At such a moment of crisis, with England's Protestant Church in disarray, those who left Southampton would have been conscious that the eyes of many in England and perhaps as far away as Transylvania were upon them.[44]

The form assumed by the Church of Massachusetts was therefore the paradoxical one of an established Reformed Church run by local assemblies of the self-selected godly – a congregationalist form of Church government. The early foundation of Harvard College meant that Massachusetts was unique among the north American colonies in never being short of ministers to serve its parishes, and that made the task of a establishing a single dominant Church all the easier. The clergy ministered to a federation of parishes made up of laity who were devotees of the religion of the book: possibly the most literate society then existing in the world. They felt as keenly as any godly congregations in the worldwide Reformed Protestant family that they must fulfil the hopes of a century of Reformation in the universal Church; they kept in close touch with like-minded congregations in England all through the century and beyond, and were very conscious of their international heritage. John Cotton, for forty years minister first of Boston (England) and then of Boston (Massachusetts), and the man who gave currency to the word 'Congregationalism', was remembered as declaring (with rather alarming relish) 'I love to sweeten my mouth with a piece of Calvin before I sleep.'[45] The great reformer of Geneva might have been surprised, but perhaps gratified, to hear himself likened to a toothbrush.

Technically this was not a theocracy, a State run by the Church, but the Church's government ran side by side with secular government. The elect, the 'Saints', were in charge of the Commonwealth; they were nevertheless still a minority of the population, particularly as children were born and grew up without having experienced the excitement of committing themselves to emigration and a new life. Winthrop and his fellows were in any case conscious that not all who had crowded the Atlantic migration boats were pure in heart or sought godliness, and that some might have other and more murky reasons for fleeing England than objections to Laud's sacramental theology. Such people should not be allowed to pollute the purified Church, and should be excluded from government. In 1631 the franchise for the colony's assembly was limited to Church members. Still it was compulsory for everyone to go to their parish church (known in New England simply as a 'meeting-house'), and the Massachusetts government tried to stop people settling beyond a certain distance from the meeting-houses so that they could be properly supervised.

Government back home in England came to look pleasingly more like the Massachusetts model in the years of Cromwell's Protectorate, but then the return of Charles II in 1660 threatened to bring everything to ruin. As the leadership argued about how to preserve the delicate balance of their polity, they evolved a compromise which ingeniously built on their favourite notion of covenant. In 1662, after every congregation had voted on the issue, they agreed on establishing a 'Half-Way Covenant': some could remain members of the Church by virtue of their baptism only, but the fully committed would have to offer proof of repentance and lively faith to gain the full Church membership which allowed them to receive communion at the Lord's Table. Thus godliness, a wide franchise in the Massachusetts Assembly, and an established Church could all be preserved. New England's Congregationalism faced many challenges: the arguments around the 'Half-Way Covenant' proved very disruptive of the ministers' authority as rival clergy lobbied the congregations against their opponents, and after royal intervention in the 1680s there was the extra annoyance of a governor appointed by the Crown who was rarely sympathetic to the Congregationalist ministry. Nevertheless the Congregational establishment continued to rally its support in the legislature in the name of independence from outside interference. It retained its dominant position until challenged by the disruptive religious enthusiasms released in the North American colonies' eighteenth-century 'Great Awakening'.

The new Commonwealth of Massachusetts, self-consciously a protest against King Charles's Church, itself in turn produced dissent. As early as 1635 an independent-minded Boston woman called Anne Hutchinson horrified the leadership by challenging the whole framework of Puritan piety established by the covenant theology of William Perkins. She criticized the constant search for proofs that the elect were growing in holiness, and worse still, she asserted her authority for these 'antinomian' views by holding her own devotional meetings and claiming special revelations of the Holy Spirit. The ministers of Massachusetts were split as to whether her charisma was from God or from the Devil, and all sorts of personal clashes became mixed up in the dispute.[46] After two years of tense confrontation, Hutchinson was banished from the Commonwealth and travelled south to join a scattered set of coastal communities called Rhode Island. This had been set up by Roger Williams, a strict separatist minister, who had himself fled Massachusetts to escape arrest for his religious views in 1636; it soon became a haven for an intimidating variety of the discontented, and the fastidious godly of Boston looked on it as the 'latrina of New England'. As Williams struggled to create order out of chaos, any thoughts of a single Church of God quickly disappeared. He came to embrace complete religious toleration, even including Jews and 'Turks' in his envisaged freedom (in practice Turks were probably thin on the ground in Rhode Island, but it was a striking rhetorical gesture). Calvinist that he still was, Williams believed that all the non-elect would go to Hell, but it was not his responsibility to make matters worse for them in this life. In 1647, his Rhode Island towns proclaimed that 'all men may walk as their consciences persuade them, every one in the name of his God'.[47]

Another challenge to the Massachusetts system was the arrival of the Quakers in 1657, determined to spread their ecstatic message of freedom and inner light, apparently spoiling for martyrdom, and raising bitter memories of Anne Hutchinson as they encouraged women to preach. Their wilful separation from secular life aroused fears for the stability of the colony, still no more than a quarter-century old and bound together socially as well as in religion by its covenants. The Congregationalist government of New England publicly flogged the Quakers and cropped their ears. Then between 1659 and 1661 it even hanged four of them for missionary activities – one of the victims was a woman, Mary Dyer, who had deliberately returned from banishment to see her previous sentence fulfilled. This caused a sharp reaction of protest both in New England and in the home country. Charles II ordered the executions to stop, even though his government had little time for Quakers and was imprisoning them back home: it was ironical that a royal regime so like the one from which the Puritan settlers had fled should now restrain their zeal for persecution. The executions now placed a question-mark for many New Englanders as to whether even the religiously obnoxious ought to be treated in such a fashion.

Roger Williams was one of the few early colonists who thought of making an effort to spread Christianity among the native American population, taking the trouble to learn and analyse their languages and publish a guide to them. However, he too came to let this part of his ministry lapse, and the New England Churches waited for a personal initiative by one minister, John Eliot, who began his work in 1646: by 1663 he had produced the first Bible of any language to be printed in America, in a dialect of Algonquin now extinct. The early English Protestant neglect of evangelizing among indigenous peoples makes a curious contrast with the early Spanish attention to converting Indios in south and central America, or French efforts to the north in Quebec. It cannot simply be accounted for by the early difficulties of the colonies in surviving at all, or the tensions and cultural incomprehensions between the two societies that sometimes boiled over into open warfare. Elizabethan writers who published propaganda for the founding of colonies, principally George Peckham, Thomas Harriot and Richard Hakluyt the younger, had made a good deal of the importance of bringing Christianity to the peoples of America: that makes the seventeenth-century slowness in taking up the work all the more surprising.[48]

The explanations are probably theological rather than the result of inertia or straightforward racism (both of which the Iberian colonists had also exhibited in generous measure). We should consider the nature of Puritan covenant theology, which may have inhibited the idea of mission: believers in covenant theology might well feel that the natives should prove their status as part of God's elect by spontaneously showing an interest in and making an effort to imitate the Christian beliefs of their neighbours, without any artificial effort on the colonists' part. Roger Williams and John Cotton were also affected by their longing for the imminent arrival of the Last Days, because they both shared Oliver Cromwell's biblically based belief that this event must be heralded by the conversion of the Jews. Logically, therefore, that should happen first, and any conversion of new Gentile peoples would form a later stage of God's plan.[49] It took Eliot's generous imagination to overcome such theological or psychological barriers in order to translate the whole of the Bible and produce a catechism in the main local language. His thirty years of intensive work produced thousands of Indian converts, organized in 'prayer towns' next to English-cultivated territory, governed by the natives themselves, but imitating as far as possible English models of life. Few settlers displayed Eliot's spirit of openness. As the colonies expanded in numbers and territorial ambitions through the century, the future of such settlements was generally destroyed by warfare and colonial betrayal: a beginning to a long-drawn-out and wretched story of suffering for the indigenous people of north America.

Slavery formed another problem for and a blot on English-speaking Christian mission. As the southern colonies developed a plantation economy, particularly for tobacco and sugar (cotton came much later), they became deeply enmeshed in the system of importing African slaves to America that had sustained the Iberian colonies since the sixteenth century. The numbers rocketed at the end of the seventeenth century: blacks outnumbered whites in South Carolina by the 1710s and in Virginia the proportion of blacks to whites shot up from less than 10 per cent in 1680 to about a third in 1740. Anglican clergy in the south did make efforts to convert slaves to Christianity, but they met a good deal of resistance from masters, which was a major obstacle in a Church so dominated by the laity. The further south, the larger the number of slaves, and the less likelihood that white laypeople would be sympathetic; so as late as 1762 one Anglican missionary sadly calculated that of around 46,000 slaves in South Carolina, only 500 were Christians.[50] It is admittedly possible that he really meant that only 500 were Anglicans: he was writing in the midst of the major evangelical religious revivals which swept through the colonies in the eighteenth-century 'Great Awakening'. These eventually made spectacular breaches in the earlier barriers to evangelization, and fostered an Afro-American Christian culture which expresses itself in the fervency of extrovert evangelical Protestantism rather than in the cooler tones of Anglicanism.

Virginia in the south and New England in the north thus created two models of English-speaking colony by mid century. Both northern and southern colonies were firmly committed to their different patterns of established Churches, just as back in Europe, though Rhode Island remained as a thorn in the side of the New England establishments and was a model for their gradual loosening of official restrictions on other Protestant congregations. In the long coastal wetlands, plains and inland hills between the two regions, a variety of 'Middle Colonies' were set up, not all of them English. Swedish Lutherans settled on the Delaware River, and the Protestant Dutch seized a spectacular natural harbour in the Hudson estuary

that they named New Netherland: annexation by an English flotilla commanded by James, Duke of York, in 1664 made it English, and its capital
New Amsterdam on the Manhattan peninsula became New York. Once
more the aim of the Swedes and Dutch had been to reproduce the national
Churches back home, but English rule fatally complicated this. Moreover
the religious cosmopolitanism of the Netherlands was already reproduced
in New Amsterdam whether the Dutch Reformed Church liked it or not,
including pragmatic Dutch toleration of a wealthy Jewish community. It
was New York that first experienced the bewildering diversity of settlers
that during the eighteenth century swelled into a flood, and made any effort
to reproduce old Europe's compartmentalized and discrete confessional
Churches seem a lunatic enterprise.

Further religious experiments continued to link with civil war and Interregnum England's burst of assorted religious energies. In 1632 Roman
Catholic aristocrats friendly with Charles I sponsored a colony in the region
known as the Chesapeake to the north of Virginia, which they named
Maryland after the King's Catholic wife Henrietta Maria. In fact the royal-
ists' defeat in the English civil wars meant that Catholics did not take the
leading role in Maryland. Feeling their already tenuous position under
threat, in 1649 the Catholics seized a brief opportunity of local strength to
create a unique freedom to practise their religion by making a huge concession which outmanoeuvred their Protestant opponents: they guaranteed
complete toleration for all those who believed in Jesus Christ. They ordered
fines and whipping for anyone who used an elaborately specified list of the
normal religious insults of seventeenth-century England: 'heretic, schismatic, idolator, Puritan, Independent, Presbyterian, Popish priest, Jesuit,
Jesuited Papist, Lutheran, Calvinist, Anabaptist, Brownist, Antinomian,
Barrowist, Roundhead, Separatist'.[51] This was an extraordinary effort to
blot out all the bitter history of the Reformation century; it was approaching
a similar result to Rhode Island's universal toleration by a very different
route. Maryland showed the limits of its vision by still ordering property
confiscation and execution for anyone denying the Trinity, and tidy-minded
Anglicans seized control of the colony in the 1690s, doing their best to
restrict Roman Catholic rights. Nevertheless, amid the steadily encroaching
diversity of the whole colonial seaboard, the Maryland example was not
forgotten.

A new chance for the hard-pressed New World Quakers came when
William Penn became interested in founding a refuge for them. A Quaker
himself, he was also the son of an English Admiral and friendly with the
Catholic but nautically minded heir to the throne, the future James II; with

these useful connections, in 1682 he got a royal charter for a colony to be called Pennsylvania, in territories lying between Maryland and New England. His plan was bold and imaginative: going further than the Catholic elite of Maryland, he renounced the use of coercion in religion, granted free exercise of religion and political participation to all monotheists of whatever views who wished to seek refuge in his colony, and he also tried to maintain friendly relations with the native Americans. Soon Pennsylvania came to have a rich mix not simply of English Protestant expression, but also Scottish Presbyterians, Lutherans and the descendants of radical Reformation groups of mainland Europe like Anabaptists and Moravian Brethren, fleeing from the intolerance of Roman Catholicism in central Europe. All this diversity proved destructive for Penn's original vision of a community run according to Quaker ideals – under pressure from the English government, Pennsylvania's assembly even disenfranchised Catholics, Jews and non-believers in 1705.[52] Good relations with the native population were also soon badly compromised.

Pennsylvania still set a notable example. No one religious group could automatically claim exclusive status, unlike nearly all the other colonies where a particular Church continued to claim official advantages even if it was a minority. This was the first colony to evolve the characteristic pattern of religion of the modern United States of America: a pattern of religious denominations, none claiming the exclusive status of Church, but rather making up the slices of a Protestant 'cake' which together adds up to a Church. Established Churches might have been able to resist this process better if they had more effectively set up their structures of government, but virtually everywhere except Massachusetts the colonies suffered a shortage of clergy in the first formative century, and lay leaders of local religion were generally less inclined to take an exclusive view of what true religion might be than professionally trained clerics. In this they were aided by a strong consideration swaying many promoters of colonies that religious coercion discouraged settlement, and was therefore economically bad for struggling colonial ventures.

This was the creation of a different ideal from the development of religious toleration as we have seen it in most of Reformation Europe: now religious liberty was developing. Toleration is a grudging concession granted by one body from a position of strength; liberty provides a situation in which all religious groups are competing on an equal basis. We have already seen the precedents in central and eastern Europe. First in the 1520s the Graubünden in Switzerland had settled their local problems by a pragmatic version of this solution, then the Hungarians and Transylvanians in the Declaration of Torda, then the Polish-Lithuanian Commonwealth's Confederation of Warsaw. Just as old Europe was abandoning these sixteenth-century ideals in its increasing confessional rigidity of the seventeenth century, a new European enterprise took up the challenge once more.

Anglicanism did manage to strengthen its position in the southern English American colonies after Charles II's restoration, gaining established status in other places besides Virginia. However, the origins of so many colonies in religious protest against a 'proto-Anglican' system guaranteed that Anglicanism would never be as dominant as it was in England, and the circumstances of the thirteen colonies' successful rebellion against the mother country in 1776–83 ended any chance Anglicanism had of general establishment. So the eighteenth-century federal Republic established a principle of the formal institutional separation of Church and State. Curiously this has consistently been yoked in America with a more general observance of religious practice than remains in the formally established Protestant Churches of northern Europe. Anglicanism remains as the Episcopal Church of the United States; though still influential, it is a relatively small body, and its rather restrained and European ethos of devotion is not characteristic of American Protestantism.

There is irony here, for the first lasting American English-speaking colony was Anglican Virginia. The rhetoric of covenant, chosenness, of wilderness triumphantly converted to garden, has come down into American political and religious consciousness from elsewhere: the immigration of Governor Winthrop to New England. Since Winthrop's Congregational Church establishment has long faded, the varied spectrum of American Protestantism has grafted on to its memories of Massachusetts the appearance of the obstinate individualism and separatism of the Plymouth Pilgrim Fathers (an ethos which Winthrop and his covenanting congregations deplored). All of this is served up with a powerful dose of extrovert revivalist fervour which ultimately derives from Scottish Presbyterianism (chapter 14, pp. 603–4).

The consequences of the civil wars in the Atlantic Isles between 1640 and 1660 were therefore wholly out of scale with what could have been expected in the seventeenth century from a marginal, second-rank European power. Because the USA has so far retained its Protestant and English-speaking ethos, the American varieties of English Protestantism, complete with the rhetoric of the English Reformation, form the most characteristic forms of Protestant Christianity today, and indeed they are probably the most dynamic form of Christianity worldwide. American Roman Catholicism too has largely left the Counter-Reformation behind, and in much of its behaviour and attitudes it has been enrolled as a subset of the American

Protestant religious scene. This is a Christianity which has been shaped by a very different historical experience from that of western Europe, and the similarities in language and confessional background may mislead us into missing the deep contrasts. If Britain has a role to play in modern world politics, it may be to interpret the pervasive and exuberantly assertive (some might say strident) culture of Protestant religion in the United States to a Europe that has begun to forget what the Reformation meant.

PART III

PATTERNS OF LIFE

13

Changing Times

The last section of this book explores how it felt to live during Europe's Reformations and Counter-Reformations. First, the experience of changing times: time changed in a literal fashion during the Reformation and the change turned into chaos because of it. For 1,500 years, Europe used the calculation of the calendar year made in the Roman Republic by the order of Julius Caesar. It had been a great improvement on its predecessors, but it still made the year 11 minutes 4 seconds too long, and that built into a considerable error over centuries. Drawing on the scientific expertise of the Jesuits in the newly established Roman College, principally their distinguished mathematician Christopher Clavius, Pope Gregory XIII decided with characteristic energy to sort out the Julian Calendar's error. In 1582 he decreed that ten days should be suppressed in the year: 4 October should be considered 15 October. He also ordered that a new year should be reckoned from 1 January rather than 25 March, thus rather surprisingly restoring the practice of the pagan Julius Caesar rather than doing honour to the Virgin Mary on her feast of the Annunciation.

Naturally, both Protestants and Orthodox Christians regarded such decisions by the Papal Antichrist with acute suspicion, even though the experts knew that Gregory and his Jesuits were right. At first, implementing the change of time was an index of attitudes to the Roman Catholic Church: France, Spain, Portugal and Italy showed their loyalty by changing straight away. Poland-Lithuania's famed tolerance did not extend to allowing Orthodox subjects of the Catholic monarchy to observe the old calendar: that became yet another grievance of the Orthodox against Rome, and in Russia it took the Bolsheviks to catch up with Pope Gregory in 1918. Many Lutherans recalled the calendar changes made to the calculation of Easter by the first Council of Nicaea in 325, which Lutheran historians linked to the time when Antichrist first troubled the Church, so they scorned the new arrangements.[1] The resulting patchwork of local decisions makes dating documents written in the Holy Roman Empire between 1583 and 1700 a nightmare for historians, only surpassed by the confusion in the cantons of Switzerland. Dates of the month could change overnight with a military victory or show of force, especially as the Habsburgs rolled back the power of Lutherans in their various central European territories before and during the Thirty Years War. Reformed Protestants in the Habsburg-ruled parts of Hungary also fiercely resisted the Emperor Rudolf's decree of 1584 imposing the Gregorian calendar, and it was sixteen years before pressure from the Hungarian Diet brought an end to the resulting confusion.[2] In the same year of 1600, Reformed Scotland decided to snub the Virgin Mary and start reckoning the year from 1 January, while still resisting the popish subtraction of the ten days. That meant that for a century and a half there were two different dating-systems in the Atlantic Isles, because the kingdoms of the Tudors resisted all change until 1752 (the famous story that rioting English crowds then demanded the return of their missing eleven days is, disappointingly, only an eighteenth-century joke).

TIME ENDING

There could hardly be a better symbol of the way in which the Reformation tore apart the fabric of European society than this disagreement about dating. An issue which could hardly seem more practical or a matter of rational calculations was caught up in passions which left rationality at a discount. To those living in the age of European Reformation, the changing of time had far more resonances and urgent meaning than the redating of a day. Human beings are inveterate pattern-makers, as a way of trying to remain sane in the face of the bewildering arbitrariness of their lives. When history was moving fast, it was only natural to look for the patterns put there by a benevolent creator God. The Reformation would not have happened if ordinary people had not convinced themselves that they were actors in a cosmic drama plotted by God: that in the Bible he had left them a record of his plans and directions as to how to carry them out. Their revolution was not simply a search for personal salvation. They changed the way that their world worked because they were convinced that this visible world was the least important part of the divine plan.

Above all, large numbers of Europeans were convinced in varying ways and with varying degrees of fervour that the momentous events through which they were living signified that the visible world was about to end. If so, it was vitally important for the world's condition at its end to correspond as closely as possible to what God wanted. The perpetual threat from the

Turks was proof enough, even before the Reformation (and some will have known that their Islamic enemies were also widely convinced that the world would end in the Hijra year of 1000, the equivalent of the Christian 1592). Repeatedly we have seen the practical outcome of this belief in the Last Days. Without that pervasive expectation of an imminent, dramatic change, few might have listened to Luther's challenge to the Church. Without it, Savonarola could not have seized Florence, thousands would not have trekked to Münster to set up a new Jerusalem, Franciscans might not have toiled to convert the Indios in the Americas, Friedrich V might not have travelled to Prague, Transylvanian princes would not have found a sense of crusading mission, Oliver Cromwell might not have readmitted the Jews to England.

Without appreciating this background of thought, much of the Reformation will only be understood as a vandalistic, mean-minded or money-grabbing assault on a settled round of devotion and a world of beauty and celebration. Such, for instance, has often been the reputation of the English Reformation in the time of the boy-king Edward VI. Rather, we should view the enthusiastic Edwardian wrecking of church interiors, the banishing of ancient ceremonial and obscenely vicious propaganda against the old Church in the light of words from one of the England's star preachers, Bishop Hugh Latimer, when he proclaimed the imminent end before the King's cousin the Duchess of Suffolk in Advent 1552: 'we know by scripture and all learned men affirm the same, that the world was meant to endure six thousand years. Now of the six thousand be passed already five thousand five hundred and fifty-two, and yet this time which is left shall be shortened for the elect's sake, as Christ himself witnesseth.'[3] So the time would be all the shorter if God was pleased with the elect.

As Latimer pointed out, there was every reason for Christians to believe this because their Bible told them so. In fact different parts of the Bible said so much about these events that it was possible to construct any number of accounts of when and how the Last Days would happen. Christ himself had left a short but detailed and terrifying picture in Matthew 24; the prophet Daniel had described the rise and fall of successive empires; John the Divine had in the Book of Revelation (the Apocalypse) set out his vision of a cosmic clash ending in God's triumph and glorification. On the margins of the Bible, a composite Hebrew work known as II Esdras added further visions of the end, and although it had failed to enter the Christian biblical canon, Christians had never forgotten it. Such literature had been the product of peoples in crisis seeking comfort and meaning in their disasters, and while in settled times the Church tended to discourage excitement about it, new crises repeatedly brought the message to life once more. Repeated disappointed expectations only indicated that God's script had not been properly interpreted.

Besides the data contained in the Bible, there were the opinions of Latimer's 'learned men', who were ironically very often leading figures of the old Church against which Protestants fought. In the twelfth century the Italian Cistercian monk Joachim of Fiore expressed the excitement of many monks in his age at western Christianity's new flowering of the monastic life. He pictured history as patterned after the Trinity itself: the days of the Old Testament had been an Age of the Father, up to the coming of Christ, who had initiated an Age of the Son, and that was to be replaced soon after Joachim's own time by the Age of the Spirit, in which the world would be run by monks like himself. The failure of this to happen as Joachim predicted did not dampen the enthusiasm with which his message was heard. It became the particular property of the Franciscans, who reapplied Joachim's vision of a renewed Age of the Spirit to their own activities. Some of them on the radical or 'Spiritual' wing of the movement were so carried away with Joachimite enthusiasm in the thirteenth and fourteenth centuries that they denounced the corruption of the institutional Church and sought a literal renewal of society; many Spirituals were thereafter burned as heretics. The readers of Umberto Eco's great and mischievously learned novel *The Name of the Rose* will be familiar with their anguished debates.[4]

The Franciscans, who survived their early troubles to become a recognized religious Order, did not forget Joachim, and others continued to expect apocalyptic talk from them. We have repeatedly seen Franciscan radicalism in action, and noted the wide impact of the *Apocalypsis Nova* of the 'Amadeist' writer, who gave his publication of 1502 a Franciscan pedigree to enhance its impact (chapter 2, p. 96; chapter 3, pp. 154–5). Joachim might have been a monk, but in the explosion of the Reformation, Protestants were prepared to overlook this in their eagerness to believe that history had a shape if only one could discern it. Many turned Joachim's prediction of a third age into an expectation of a thousand-year rule of the saints on earth before the Last Judgement – the strict definition of the word 'millenarianism', a belief with acute political implications, which can also be derived from passages in Daniel, Revelation and II Esdras. Radicals especially loved Joachim's literary legacy: it was Joachimite literature that inspired Thomas Müntzer and Melchior Hoffmann in their dreams of world revolution. Those trying to control the Reformation were not slow to see the dangers in this emotional exaltation, and they were troubled by the book at the centre of it all, the Book of Revelation. Predictably, Revelation had not appealed to Erasmus's coolly detached spirituality: he doubted whether it should be considered canonical, and it was the one New Testament book on which he failed to comment in his influential biblical *Paraphrase*.

In this respect, the first generation of leading Reformers imitated Erasmus. Even Martin Luther, torn between his self-image as a prophet of renewal and his duty to maintain the God-given order of society, felt ambiguous about Revelation. He distrusted its message, but unexpectedly he insisted on employing the great artist Lukas Cranach to fill this book of his German Bible with majestically exciting engravings of its story, the only part of his biblical text that he treated in this pictorial fashion. The justification seems to have been that Cranach and Luther decided that the pictures should be vividly anti-papal, and anti-papal readings of Revelation provided one respectable reason for taking the book seriously. Most mainstream leaders of the early Reformation, hurt and surprised by the outbursts of radical religion around their own efforts to bring a controlled godly revolution, kept an uncomfortable silence about Revelation, and there were few early commentaries on it – yet significantly, the earliest biblical commentaries on the Book of Revelation to be written by declared adherents of the Reformation were by two ex-Franciscan friars, François Lambert in 1528 and Sebastian Meyer in 1539.[5] Melanchthon and Bucer normally did their best to ignore the book of Revelation, and Calvin rarely quotes from it in his writings (one significant exception being his bitter pamphlet against those whom he considered cowardly traitors to God, the Nicodemites).[6] Archbishop Cranmer virtually omitted it from the cycle of daily Bible-readings that he constructed for the services of the English Church in 1549.

Heinrich Bullinger was the first Protestant star-name to take up the challenge of writing a commentary on the Apocalypse, and he was spurred to do this by a grave crisis for the Reformation: the accession of Queen Mary of England in 1553, which forced a distinguished group of English Protestants to flee their country (chapter 5, p. 258). Many of them ended up in Zürich, and their arrival inspired Bullinger to preach a series of sermons on the Apocalypse that formed the basis of his commentary: he dedicated his work to the English exiles, comforting them in their affliction by reminding them of the glorious outcome of persecution, the sign of a true Church. He was prepared to speak well in his text of both Joachim of Fiore and Savonarola. These were themes previously more characteristic of Anabaptists or radicals, but amid the bitterness of the new struggles of Reformed Protestantism against Counter-Reformation Catholicism from the 1560s, such ideas found greater respectability, and the Book of Revelation's stock rose accordingly among mainstream Protestants.[7] The English martyrologist John Foxe borrowed the scheme of history in Bullinger's work in his own highly influential *Acts and Monuments*: like Bullinger he spoke of a 'golden age' of the Church's first thousand years, the period when it had only marginally been affected by Antichrist's corruption, and then a half-millennium which was a 'brazen age' when 'began corruption to enter and increase'. All would soon be well, Foxe believed. In the course of his voluminous writings he toyed with other versions of Joachim's schemes, and his work was eagerly devoured (not merely by English-speaking readers), producing many new variants on the Last Days theme.[8]

Thus, if anything, expectation of the Last Days strengthened rather than died away in the course of the Reformation; it was a particular mark of Reformed Protestantism to conceive itself as a crusade against the Papal Antichrist, but in this respect the Lutherans were not far behind. Lutheran schoolchildren, for instance, were often educated through Johann Sleidan's short textbook introducing the shape of world history, which was structured by reference to the Book of Daniel and emphasized that the last Empire was approaching.[9] The appalling weather conditions of the 1590s, triggering the worst harvests in living memory and probably for some centuries, were an extra incentive to belief, and when the memory of these was beginning to diminish, politics provided a new set of catastrophes with the outbreak of the Thirty Years War: so, of the Four Horsemen of the Apocalypse, famine and war had both entered and taken their bow on the stage. The fear of the Last Days only began to fade in the last years of the seventeenth century (for the time being – the French Revolution would bring it back), but for decades after 1660 it was possible for respectable Anglican bishops to defend their episcopal Church of England by such arguments as asserting that 666, the Number of the Beast in the Book of Revelation, coincided in alphabetical significance with the name of Oliver Cromwell's Commonwealth of England.[10] Sir Isaac Newton, so often taken as a symbol of the scientific changes which brought the dominance of a despiritualized, mechanical world-view in Europe, devoted as much energy to his writings on theology, including much speculation on the meaning of the Book of Revelation, as to his work on motion and gravity (chapter 17, p. 683).

Both Protestants and Catholics experienced God constantly intervening in the world and ready to make direct announcements to it, either through natural phenomena or through the voice of his elect messengers. Calvin's view of God's relationship to his created world particularly stressed all-encompassing divine providence, but the underlying assumption was as characteristic of Catholic and Lutheran as of Reformed Europe. Protestants were in fact particularly prone to take notice of natural signs and wonders such as monstrous births or abnormal weather conditions, because they had discounted the powers of the saints to work miracles and wanted to stress the immediacy of divine power.[11] One result was that while Spain and Italy had been full of prophets and prophetesses around 1500, so were Lutheran Germany and Scandinavia later: perhaps 300 can be traced there between 1550 and 1700, many of them bearing messages conveyed via angels.[12] In Elizabethan England, the Queen's chief minister Lord Burghley kept a file of letters from such people, who included a John the Baptist, a variety of Old Testament prophets, and a son of God the Father and Queen Elizabeth, who had been snatched away at his birth by the Archangel Gabriel.[13]

Such people were not just isolated lunatics but represented the outer margin of beliefs which were at the centre of the Reformation. Burghley kept their letters because he thought they were politically dangerous. Preachers denounced them as deluded, but that is because there was a certain professional rivalry involved: the work of preaching was itself a form of prophecy, in a form authorized by Church institutions. Reformed Protestantism, following Calvin's stress that Jesus Christ was prophet as well as priest and king, made a particular point of this idea. One Scottish minister was not untypical of Reformed preachers when in 1597 he brought to a climax the solemnities of his reception into his new parish of Gullane by demanding his congregation's 'obedience to the voice of God in his mouth'. Scottish ministers were indeed prima donnas of the pulpit, dramatic performers who might themselves claim or be awarded powers and popular reverence previously associated with the saints. The Revd John Welch, minister of Ayr around 1600 (and John Knox's son-in-law), was reputed to be a frequent miracle worker, up to and including causing a sarcastic papist fellow guest at dinner to be struck dead, and on another occasion bringing a more godly young man back to life.[14]

HEARING GOD'S VOICE

Once northern European worshippers were outside their church doors, the sermon still ringing in their ears, they became a large and socially varied reading public who fuelled a boom in cheaply produced tracts and pamphlets, giving ready publicity to God's interventions in nature, politics and personal affairs. Readers avidly devoured these marvellous tales, some medieval Catholic in origin, though suitably retold for Protestant use; the stories often derived from preaching and were equally often later recycled once more in the pulpit. The market for wonders crossed frontiers: when in

1597 Norwegian fishermen landed a freak herring apparently covered in mysterious writings and signs, within months English readers were marvelling at the printed story of *A most strange and wonderful herring*, complete with illustrations. Herring seem to have been particularly inclined to be ominous, because a decade before, King Frederik II of Denmark had been much upset by sinister hieroglyphs in Scandinavian herring catches, and notoriously, only a year after that, he was dead. Every disaster could provoke speculation: what particular sin was God out to criticize? In the great 1580 earthquake which shook England, northern France and the Netherlands, had God used geology to topple a pinnacle of Westminster Abbey and make the sea foam in Sandwich Bay, or was it blasphemy to consider such natural secondary causes?[15]

There was of course much room to argue amid the Reformation's conflicts on what clues disasters provided to God's opinions on current religious controversies. When fire caused by lightning severely damaged London's St Paul's Cathedral in 1561, was God shocked at Protestant worship in the sacred fabric, as Catholics confidently bragged, or was he annoyed with the loiterers who used the Cathedral as an amusement arcade, as the Protestant Bishop of Durham argued when he was drafted in to refute the Catholic canard? (It would not be the last time that a Bishop of Durham was troubled by lightning in a cathedral.) When a floor collapsed under a clandestine London Catholic congregation in 1623, killing ninety, including the Jesuit preacher, God's outrage at popery seemed obvious – particularly to gleeful London bystanders, who aided God's wrath by attacking the wounded and dying as they were removed from the ruins. Roman Catholics either riposted that God afflicts most those whom he loves most, or they became more rationalist than Protestants and blamed Jacobean cowboy builders.[16]

Often the psychological effects of such spectacular events were long-lasting. The historian of English providentialism Alexandra Walsham speculates that the 1580 earthquake turned many prominent English people against commercial theatre and produced a century of skirmishing over the legitimacy of public drama. It certainly provided an excuse for the city authorities of Coventry to suppress the traditional Corpus Christi play, to avoid further displays of God's anger, and the replacement was a Protestant play on the appropriate subject of the destruction of Jerusalem. It is thus possible that the general public readiness to accept the 'Reformation of Manners', that regulative spirit so noticeable in early modern European society, was attributable to fear of divine retribution triggered by a sixteenth-century concentration of catastrophes. After the English town of Dorchester was destroyed by fire in 1613, rigorous Puritan government led by a charismatic local minister John White turned the town into a mini-Geneva: the bastardy rate slumped, and the town became strikingly generous to good causes (as well as one of the earliest recruiting-grounds for the efforts to found colonies in New England – chapter 12, p. 535). The townsfolk even founded a public library where they could turn the globes to learn their geography, or contemplate the world beyond in the pages of John Calvin.[17] This was an extreme example of a common reaction: discipline and self-denial would please God and avert further disaster.

By this reasoning, fasting was a key course of action in times of trouble. Bucer and Calvin, with their strongly communal vision of the Church's disciplinary life, were the first Reformers to advocate reviving fasting as a solemn public act of the Church. In Scotland, the official Protestant Church was inclined to out-Calvin Calvin, and consequently provided a model to which envious English Puritans could only aspire. The Scottish Kirk became the only branch of Christianity to create a liturgical service as a setting for communal fasting, and did so as early in its career as 1565, during its years of bitter conflict with the Catholic Mary Queen of Scots. How better to rally militant Protestantism to the fight? What was important about this rite was that it was not to be used at ritualized set times (unlike the old popish Church's Lent or dietary abstinence on Fridays), but instead whenever it seemed good to the Kirk. Fasting was a weapon against disaster always at the ready, to be ordered by the authorities in such emergencies as visitations of plague or war with the English. It must be said that there were many more days of official fast than official feast in post-Reformation Scotland.[18]

Such communal acts, which in Scotland could last from one day up to several weeks in acute crises, provided a satisfying sense that an entire community could do something positive to relieve its own misery: public fasts had all the collective drama of repentance which the Jesuits were creating in their parochial missions in southern Europe (chapter 9, pp. 414–17). From the 1560s, English Puritans likewise imitated the Genevan practice as far as they could wherever they had local strength in their half-Reformed Church. Protestants were proud of such fasts, contrasting them with superstitious Catholic penitential processions and intercessions to saints that were only 'Popish toys to pacify God': the fast was thus an immobile equivalent of (or replacement for) the pious energy expended by Catholics in pilgrimage. When the government of Charles I became particularly obnoxious to many in England and Scotland, such local declarations of solemn fasts became powerful communal acts of defiance against Laudian religion and arbitrary royal rule, and they provoked government fury and repression.[19]

FIGHTING ANTICHRIST: IDOLS

For Reformed Protestants, a prime cause of God's wrath was idolatry (misplaced worship), which in Calvin's eyes as in the Apostle Paul's is the primary sin of humankind. If God was an imminent visitor because the Last Days were approaching, He would be particularly angry to see His people still tolerating idols in His holy places. Everything must be dealt with if God's will was to be done, hence the emphasis in Reformed Europe on the duty of smashing images. This was as much a measure of community protection as the fast; it was not generally an act of individual or adolescent self-expression, although the young no doubt derived plenty of fun from the various bouts of communal iconoclastic fervour that affected Europe. The use of images was of course one of the major areas of theology where the emphatic and individual opinions of Martin Luther made a major difference to Lutheran Europe, and separated it very obviously from the Reformed. Thanks to Luther's resolute indifference to images, once Lutherans had removed some of the more offensive religious art of the medieval West, they started bringing back into their churches pictures of suitably Christ-centred devotional subjects such as the Crucifixion. It has been plausibly asserted that in later sixteenth-century Germany, more new painted altarpieces were put in place in the churches of the Lutheran north than in the traditionalist south – hence the bitterness caused by the various Reformed Protestant attempts at 'Second Reformation' (chapter 8, pp. 353–8).[20]

At times the destruction of images did indeed consist of spontaneous and furious acts of mob violence, as generally throughout the regions affected by the *Wildwuchs* of the 1520s (chapter 3, pp. 152–6), or in the turbulent birth of mass Protestant movements in Scotland, France and the Netherlands in the 1560s (chapter 6, pp. 291–313). Otherwise images were the victims of considered reflection and bureaucratic meticulousness, particularly in areas where Reformations were led by noblemen. For instance, when all the non-Lutheran evangelical groups of Poland-Lithuania held their first major meeting in Secemin in 1556 (chapter 5, p. 265), the Reformed noblemen present had a chance to draw on the century of experience of reform represented by the delegates of the Hussite Brethren. One of those taking part advised noblemen who were the patrons of local churches to make their reforming changes cautiously, to avoid infuriating their peasants: altars should be closed off and images should be covered with sheets, and then taken out of the main body of the church to less public places. Some places in Poland did indeed adopt the old Hussite practice of turning around church images to the walls, thus depriving them of their power, and generally in eastern Europe the removal of images was an orderly affair, carried out by the patrons of churches and their parish clergy. The example of the disastrously precipitate enthusiasm of Jakob Heraklides in Moldavia (chapter 5, p. 266) should have been enough to convince local governors of the wisdom of this.[21]

There are many examples of such careful and selective action in the cathedrals and the thousands of medieval parish churches of England. Here mob iconoclasm was a rather marginal phenomenon at certain brief moments in the Tudor Reformations, before an equally brief revival in the first English Civil War. Most English images were taken down by lawfully constituted authority: bishops, churchwardens, JPs – who knew like Polish noblemen that the main issue was one of sacred power. An image need not be totally destroyed in order to remove its power: indeed, damaged images or the ruins of an entire monastery speak very precisely of the defeat of superstition, and so the purging of the holy place. Hence the large amount of medieval art that has survived in England in a fragmentary state (although Victorian antiquaries and High Churchmen have often fooled us by lovingly restoring what they found). Look closely at the figures of saints painted on English medieval rood screens, and sometimes you will see that their faces have been carefully scraped out – such action made no sense unless the rest of the image remained visible (see Plate 21a). Look at the inscriptions on medieval tombs: the prayer for the soul may have been meticulously chiselled off, leaving the rest to give details of the deceased. Look at the figures in stained glass, and there often only the heads have been removed (glass is after all very expensive to replace on a large scale). We know of many cases where stained glass was actually whitewashed rather than taken out of windows ('washing out images', the churchwardens of Great St Mary's, Cambridge, vividly termed it), which rather undermines the idea that church buildings were filled with more light after the Reformation than before, and which also explains how so much medieval glass has been preserved.[22]

In the place of images came words. The church interiors of Reformed Protestant Europe, England included, were covered in painted and often exuberantly floridly framed biblical texts, plus big boards bearing the three texts which all Protestants should know by heart: Nicene or Apostles' Creed, Ten Commandments and Lord's Prayer (see Appendix). A church became a giant scrapbook of the Bible, and of course it also resounded to the Word of God from the pulpit. Naturally all this played a part in teaching congregations (see below, pp. 584–91), but we also need to bear in mind the talismanic power of all those words. Protestantism is often said to have brought an end to the notion of sacred space when it destroyed so much beauty and wrecked shrines and religious houses. That is a mistake. Admittedly, some early mainstream Reformers did at first despise the old church buildings, and so did the continuing radical tradition: the Quakers, late arrivals at the Reformation Ball, contemptuously called them 'steeple-houses'. At much the same time in the 1640s and 1650s, Bristol Baptists emphasized their separation by calling the city's stately medieval parish churches (some of which they nevertheless regarded as being served by godly ministers) 'Redcliffe public place' or 'Nicholas, the public place' – clearly different from and inferior to their own properly gathered congregation in an upper room.[23]

This was not the usual reaction of established Protestant Churches. Leading Reformers from Luther and Zwingli onwards rapidly overcame any sense of revulsion that they might have had for the architectural setting of the hated Mass. Once they had purged church buildings and brutally dispensed with the buildings which were not necessary, such as monasteries and friaries, then they went about creating their own sort of sacred space – so 'the temple well purged' was one of the satisfied captions of the panoramic engraving in the 1563 version of John Foxe's *Acts and Monuments* that summed up the Reformation of Edward VI.[24] When a parish congregation came to sit in their newly stripped, whitewashed and lavishly betexted church building, they could know that the Word of God was literally all around them, protecting them from the assaults of the Ancient Enemy, some of whose broken symbols they could also see surviving in their church, as tokens of his defeat. In Transylvania, preachers brought further comfort to their congregations when they pointed to the white walls and reminded their flocks that the whitewash symbolized the cleansing power of the blood of Christ and of the Holy Spirit available to wash away the sins of those who were repentant.[25] This was a transformed sacredness, not the end of the sacred place. Protestants were not afraid of sacred pictures in their proper place, not in church but either to add a little seriousness to the home or safely between the covers of a book. Calvinists were more miserly with their book illustrations than Lutherans, but they scored a notable commercial success in their English Geneva Bible by introducing an unprecedented sort of sacred picture with a contemporary appeal to an age of exploration: a map of the Holy Land (see Plate 20).

The war on the idols was paralleled by another war which has remained a lasting memory from the story of the Reformation and Counter-Reformation, and which is perhaps the aspect of that period most remote from the experience of modern western Europe: the war on the Devil's

A panoramic allegorical engraving in the 1563 version of John Foxe's
Acts and Monuments *constructed by John Day from earlier engravings
summed up the Reformation of Edward VI: at the top image-smashing
and burning proceeds, and Roman Catholics ship sacred objects abroad.
Below, the King distributes the Protestant catechism book of 1548 to his
bishops and councillors, and in a purged church building, Reformed
baptism and eucharist are administered, while a godly preacher addresses
a large congregation.*

agents known as witches. The connection can be seen at its most intimate in the careers of three East Anglian Puritans of the English Civil War period, who lived only a mile or two apart on either side of the river Stour. English tourist cliché now characterizes this tranquil valley (which contains Flatford Mill and Willy Lott's Cottage) as 'Constable Country', but then it was what Americans would later call 'burned-over country', a hotbed of evangelical fervour and fiery godly preaching since the 1530s. One of the three Puritans was a self-educated yeoman enthusiast for destroying images called William Dowsing, who devoured godly literature in his painstakingly acquired library and convinced himself that God had chosen him to purge church buildings of remaining idolatry. During the very course of the war, in 1643, he lobbied the local parliamentary military commander and obtained an official commission to remove all 'monuments of superstition'.[26]

This Dowsing did with extraordinary thoroughness, making a chilling inventory in a journal (which mostly still survives): stained glass smashed, altar steps levelled, tomb inscriptions scraped out or ripped up. One of his assistants even clambered up the stairs and ladders of church towers to chip medieval prayers to saints off the bells: the inscriptions in their belfries might be invisible to everyone else, but they were still causing the bells to ring out a message of superstition. Such was Dowsing's war on Satan. Just across the river Stour from Dowsing's Suffolk home at Stratford St Mary lies the Essex town of Manningtree, from whence came two minor gentlemen even more odious in modern eyes, Matthew Hopkins, self-styled 'Witchfinder-General', and his close collaborator John Stearne. In a period of three years immediately after Dowsing had made his vandalistic East Anglian church-crawls, Hopkins and Stearne were touring the same area with their own agenda: they examined and tortured around 240 women and men, including one parish minister, and were responsible for around a hundred hangings and at least one burning at the stake. Hopkins was regarded by simple country folk as having 'infallible and wonderful power', although his excesses did arouse unease both in Parliament and among some local ministers, one of whom courageously wrote against him. It is significant that the bubble of credibility that sustained the campaign of Hopkins and Stearne did not burst until 1647, when the first English Civil War was over. Like Dowsing, Hopkins and Stearne could plausibly portray their activities as part of the Westminster Parliament's war effort against Antichrist, which also included the victories over Charles I at Marston Moor and Naseby.[27]

FIGHTING ANTICHRIST: WITCHES

Despite such a clear association with religious warfare in the crisis of the Atlantic Isles, much remains puzzling about the 'witch-craze' of Reformation and Counter-Reformation Europe. Europeans believed in witches long before the Reformation, and went on believing in them long after, yet only in the period after 1500 did they turn this cultural assumption into major episodes of assault on fellow human beings, and then their newly murderous feelings were exhibited in both Catholic and Protestant lands. The witch-craze was a major killer in the Reformation, although not as virulent as the combined totals caused by heresy trials plus the confessional wars from Münster in 1535 to the Peace of Westphalia in 1648. There is now general agreement among historians that between 1400 and 1800, between forty and fifty thousand people died in Europe and colonial north America on charges of witchcraft (which is about double the population of the city of Magdeburg when the majority of the city's inhabitants died in its destruction in 1631 – chapter 11, p. 498). The executions took off in substantial numbers around 1560, intriguingly just about the time when large-scale executions of Protestant or radical heretics by monarchs and Church authorities (which had probably numbered about 3,000 over forty years) were coming to an end.[28]

To appreciate the problems involved in understanding this new departure in European history, we must get a sense of when and where supposed witches were persecuted and killed. The chronology and geography are as episodic and developmental as the gradual spread of a slowly incubating disease. After initial symptoms in early fifteenth-century Switzerland, there was a break-out of active persecution in central Europe in the mid-sixteenth century, then occasional outbreaks in Protestant England, sometimes severe but always marginal to the mainland pathology; Ireland and the Catholic Iberian peninsula remained islands of virtual immunity, and Dutch Protestants made an early recovery. The pathology intensified in central Europe, especially among Catholics: it also spread outwards to produce some intense late persecutions in Protestant Scotland from the 1590s, and the famous but shortlived and wholly isolated repetition of Protestant English paranoia in Salem, Massachusetts, in 1692, which led to nineteen deaths. There was an even later start in Lutheran Sweden and its subsidiary territory Finland, resulting in a sudden leap in executions in the 1660s and 1670s, brought to an equally sudden end (with a few late strays) after some spectacular volte-faces by witnesses who admitted that their evidence was fantasy.[29]

In areas on the boundaries of Reformation Europe and beyond to the east, the paranoia started later, lasted longer and in fact climaxed in the eighteenth century: by then half of those charged with witchcraft in Poland ended up being burned, whereas the proportion had been around 4 per cent in the sixteenth century: the 'state without stakes' was increasingly belying its reputation, in step with the decline in its tolerance of religious diversity. The executions there ended only with a Polish royal decree in 1776, by which time perhaps around 1,000 people had died, a similar figure to that in Hungary and Transylvania through the same period. The eastern persecutions had thus escaped any direct connection with the Reformation and were being fuelled by new and different crises and social tensions in the steadily disintegrating polities of the east. Like Scandinavian, Finnish and Balkan persecutions, Poland and Russia reversed the usual gender balance found in western Europe, where the majority of victims were female: in the east, the imported western stereotype of the witch seems to have interacted with the widely distributed eastern institution of male shamans, who had pivotal community roles in providing magical help for their communities, or with Balkan cultures which were familiar with other predominantly male participants in 'night-battles' with spirits.[30] Even in the West, the victims were not necessarily marginal or eccentric figures who provoked accusations because of the fears or guilty feelings of their neighbours, let alone fulfilling the traditional image of the gnarled, hook-nosed female: one survey of witchcraft accusations in England has shown that the accused were characteristically prosperous or significant figures in their community, though commonly not the most peaceable.[31] Accused witches were young, old, male, female, child, adult, poor, rich.

How do we construct any explanation for all this? We can start with the shared assumption at all levels of society that powers existed beyond everyday physical powers and were available for manipulation by humans. The medieval Church's power over the Body and Blood of Christ in the Mass was after all only one example of this. There was a continual contest over who should have a stake in administering this power, and the Church's battle with magic has always had something of the air of a trades union closed shop about it. In 1499 an energetic Archbishop of Canterbury, John Morton, decided to stage a major visitation of the diocese of Norwich before the new Bishop was installed there. His visiting officials fastidiously recorded the confession of Etheldreda Nyxon that she ran a business recovering stolen property using her extraterrestrial contacts. Marion Clerk more ambitiously claimed that she could visit heaven, prophesy and find hidden treasure, through powers granted her by God, Our Lady 'and the gracious fairies', and in the wake of her mother's long-standing contacts with elves – this Suffolk family represented the outer edge of the prophetic excitement sweeping much of Europe in those years. The Clerks at that date suffered nothing more serious than a repeated performance of public penance; the consequences might have been worse for them later.[32]

One reason for the new atmosphere was a newly confrontational attitude to witchcraft on the part of the intellectual elite, which had an association with the flowering of humanist scholarship and with late medieval religious reform. Humanism did not necessarily represent what we might consider as rationality, particularly when it explored the esoteric and magical resources of ancient hermetic literature (chapter 2, p. 80). We have already met a representative of this face of humanism, Abbot Trithemius of Sponheim, historical faker, code-breaker and would-be angelic postmaster (chapter 2, p. 91). Scenting professional rivals in his magical activities (particularly galling if they were female), Trithemius was insistent that witchcraft demanded harsh penalties. Such a learned man was taken seriously.[33] Besides humanism, and often of course overlapping with it as with Trithemius, there was the anxiety to renew the Church that, as we have seen, was so important around 1500 (chapter 2, pp. 83–97). Around the time that Archbishop Morton's officers were conscientiously exercising due traditional discipline on Nyxon and the Clerks, other reform-minded clerics in central Europe began turning their attention to witches, with a new and more systematic agenda in mind.

Two Dominican Inquisitors in the Holy Roman Empire, Heinrich Krämer (or 'Institoris') and Jakob Sprenger, produced what became a classic text on witchcraft, the *Malleus Maleficarum* ('Hammer of Witches'), first published in Strassburg in 1487. Three years earlier Krämer had launched one of the first systematic witch persecutions in the Tyrol, and it was not a success – he was ignominiously thrown out of the territory, and the local bishop woundingly dismissed him as a senile old man. The writing of the *Malleus* was Krämer's act of self-justification and revenge. His co-author Sprenger was a notable and much respected innovator in popular piety: he organized in Cologne the first confraternity to be devoted to the Rosary and secured papal recognition of the Rosary devotional movement that had such a spectacular future in the Counter-Reformation (chapter 7, p. 329). With such impressive credentials and powerful contacts in Rome, the two Dominicans got the best ally they could in the form of a papal Bull of 1484 (*Summis desiderantes affectibus*) endorsing their activities against witches.[34]

This was a winning combination for the future. The *Malleus* was not treated with universal respect: there were no editions of it between 1520 and

1585. Humanists and Counter-Reformation scholars frequently regarded it with contempt as a degenerate piece of medieval scholasticism, leading to a bulky replacement textbook on witchcraft and magic by a brilliant and cosmopolitan young Spanish Jesuit, Martin Del Rio, whose publication in 1595 made it the most frequently reprinted authority on the subject for a century.[35] However, in conjunction with the papal backing for its authors, the *Malleus* had for all its faults still given credibility to the urgent need for a war on witches. The very fact that Del Rio a century later turned his exceptional intellectual energies to the task of replacing it was a measure of its success: the *Malleus* had proved to be a catalyst to give shape to already existing worries in the minds of those prepared to deal with their worries by turning to the literature of experts.

Like Trithemius's discussion of witchcraft, the *Malleus* was marked by the explicit and scholastically precise misogyny of its clerical authors (the Virgin Mary, subject of Sprenger's Rosary cult, being the obvious exception to prove the rule). Krämer and Sprenger confidently asserted that women were more likely to be witches than men, 'a fact that it were idle to contradict, since it is accredited by actual experience, apart from the verbal testimony of credible witnesses'.[36] This misogyny was hardly exceptional: most of contemporary European public culture had a misogynist flavour. The *Malleus*'s tired clichés about women being less rational, more subject to passions and less able to discern spiritual matters – thus more open to perversion by the Devil – could fit into a vague mush of male preconceptions. They were a major contributing factor to the general rule through most of western Europe outside Scandinavia that a majority of the victims of witchcraft persecution were indeed women. Nevertheless it would be an exaggeration to follow some feminist scholars as seeing the witch-craze as a male campaign against female power – not simply because of the number of men and boys who were also accused. It is true that a disproportionate number of those ending up in courts were post-menopausal women, mostly widows, and that does require explanation. Some have launched on elaborate theories about societal fears of pollution or of the perceived redundancy of women beyond their fertile years. A simpler structural explanation comes from the fact that many of these indicted widows can be proved to have been the subject of accusations over many decades before being formally prosecuted. It is likely that the death of their husbands (who statistically generally predeceased them) now left them without a man who could defend them against such assaults, and so made them much more vulnerable to accumulated ill-will.[37]

The resource of learning provided by the *Malleus* combined with the deep anxieties of ordinary people to launch the attack on witches. The final piece in the unattractive jigsaw came when Europe's leading secular authority, the Holy Roman Emperor, added his endorsement to that of the Pope. In 1532 Charles V's new codification of imperial law, the *Lex Carolina*, prescribed the death penalty both for heretics and witches, and brought the secular law authorities into the process of trying witches; given the unusual seriousness of the crime, the code overrode the usual procedures of investigation and authorized the use of torture. That provision had a wide effect on legal systems even beyond the Empire, such as that of Sweden, where existing legal practice specifically forbade torture in interrogation, but where torture was frequently used in witchcraft cases.[38] The question remains as to why witch-persecution became an ecumenical matter.

It is easy to understand why so many Catholics remained enthusiastic for a godly activity commended by a Pope, inquisitors and the Holy Roman Emperor. Del Rio, in the introduction to his textbook (first published at Leuven, in acute consciousness of the religious division of the Low Countries), reminded his readers in salty language of the connection between heresy and witchcraft – 'demons were accustomed to deceive people through heretics, like beautiful whores . . . just as brothel-keepers make a procuress out of a whore when the whore loses her looks, so demons make witches out of heretics when the first appearance of heresy so decays that it is less enticing to people . . . We formerly saw Calvinism, Lutheranism and Anabaptism eating everything like caterpillars in the Netherlands . . . and now that they are wasting away, and at last almost expiring, we see swarms of sorcerers laying waste the whole North [i.e. the Protestant United Provinces], like locusts . . . To those heretics, many of our Society [of Jesus] strongly opposed themselves' – so now Del Rio was complementing that earlier Jesuit work to meet the new threat.[39] It was Del Rio, with his authoritative and careful synthesis (and even a certain moderation in the penalties which he recommended for witchcraft), who systematized the belief which remained vague and marginal in the *Malleus* that witchcraft involved sabbats, that is ritual devotional meetings with Satan himself. As a result, ideas of witches' sabbats and aerial rendezvous and sexual encounters with the Devil became more common, long-lasting and widely disseminated in Catholic Europe than in Protestant areas.[40]

Why had early Protestants nevertheless not already rejected outright the work of fanatical and crafty Dominican Inquisitors in the same way that Martin Luther came to dismiss so many of the clerical institutions of the late medieval Church? Why did witch-persecution not go the way of Transubstantiation, the five unbiblical sacraments or compulsory clerical celibacy? One part of the explanation must be the competition for moral legitimacy in the age of the 'Reformation of Manners': when both sides were striving to show that their version of western Christianity was better calculated to instil morality, it might be embarrassing to show hesitancy in the struggle against obvious agents of the Devil. A further reason must be the increasing expectation of the Last Days among Protestants. The fight with Satan was hotting up: everyone should look for further proof of his activities, and the *Malleus* and associated literature showed how one could find it – the fact that it had been written by Dominican friars could be pardoned, just as Protestants implicitly pardoned Joachim of Fiore for being a Cistercian monk. It is noticeable that Lutheran states, where the official level of expectations of the Last Days was generally rather lower than that of Reformed Protestants, were the least active in witchcraft persecutions in the Holy Roman Empire.[41] Secular rulers particularly enmeshed in Reformed Protestant apocalyptic enthusiasm might be especially prepared to view the fight with witchcraft as part of their divinely commissioned vocation: it bolstered their authority and might be a useful weapon against rivals.

This was the case in the turbulent political life of Transylvania. Its turn-of-the-century struggles between the deeply pious Reformed Protestant political adventurer Gábor Bethlen and the Catholic ruling Báthori family (chapter 10, p. 458) resulted in Bethlen supplanting Prince Gábor Báthori in 1613. Bethlen's wife Zsuzsanna Károlyi fell desperately ill in 1618, and Bethlen accused Anna Báthori, sister to Gábor Báthori, of causing her illness by witchcraft. The charge was lent some colour by association with the undoubted and spectacularly criminal activities of Anna's relative, the famous lesbian mass murderess Erzsébet Báthori, imprisoned by her own family ten years before: reportedly Anna survived her witchcraft conviction only because Bethlen believed that she might have the power to reverse her spells on his wife. Whatever the level of Bethlen's real feelings about the case, the diabolic contest was a considerable political benefit to him in consolidating his power in the Principality.[42] We should also not forget the simple fact that plenty of people believed themselves to be witches and to be possessed of extraordinary powers. They might not be too pleased to be tortured, burned or hanged, but paradoxically to a great extent they were active collaborators in the witch-craze and gave it credibility. Their activities, if malicious (as they often were), merged into other forms of malice that nowadays would be considered secular terrorism or criminality.

An example of how witchcraft might be constructed is provided by the bizarre phenomenon of 'greasing' that periodically emerged during the century after the 1530s, in Switzerland, south-west France and northern

Italy. This was the supposed spreading of plague by special ointments smeared on buildings or animals. Insofar as this was a real activity, it must have reflected acute social hatreds or personal desperation in a region which frequently fell helpless before epidemics, and which was riven by much acute poverty as well as by religious confrontation between Catholicism and Reformed Protestantism. Calvin's Geneva was at the epicentre of the greasing phenomenon, but only gradually in his time did the authorities associate a number of cases of it with witchcraft, at a crisis point amid an epidemic of plague in 1545. Calvin was nevertheless already prepared in the 1540s to think of the greasers' activities as involving some form of sorcery, and he gave his full approval to the execution of the convicted. There was after all good scriptural basis: Exodus 22:18 says 'Thou shalt not suffer a witch to live' – in fact Calvin amalgamated that punitive message with a list of sinners in Deuteronomy 18:10–11 that extended the possibility of the death penalty even to benevolent witchcraft. After Calvin's death, with his opinions of sorcery as warrant, and with official witch-hunting now becoming common in central Europe, the Genevan authorities began from 1571 routinely classifying greasing as a form of witchcraft, in which those accused were defined as consciously in league with the Devil, and were made under torture to confess to contacts with him.[43]

No doubt many similar if perhaps less exotic examples of societal misbehaviour could already have been found in medieval Europe, forming part of a spectrum of malice with the performance of witchcraft. What made the situation different in the Reformation years was the frequent coincidence of new anxieties and excitements among powerful and articulate people in Church and Commonwealth with common and traditional anxieties and excitements of the general population. The relationship was never a simple one: it was affected by a whole set of local accidents and interactions in particular political settings. Two situations in Reformed Protestant commonwealths make an interesting mirror-image: the Protestant Netherlands and Scotland. The northern Netherlands witnessed hardly any judicial executions of witches after 1578, and the last was in 1610, even though the majority of Dutch people long continued to be deeply concerned about witches.[44] These were extraordinarily early dates, contrasting not only with the steady rise of the witch-craze in the neighbouring Catholic Spanish Netherlands, but also with the Protestant Scots, who started systematic witch investigations in 1590 and turned them into a fine art.

One factor in the Dutch situation was an opportunely published statement of scepticism, *De Praestigiis Daemonum*, by Johann Weyer, a Dutch-born physician to Wilhelm, Duke of the nearby duchy of Cleves-Jülich (and brother to Henry VIII's most fortunate of spurned wives, Anne of Cleves). Until the Duke was completely overcome by his chronic ill-health in the 1560s, he was a thoughtful, humanist-educated ruler who, like Countess Anna of East Friesland or Landgraf Philipp of Hesse, sought a moderate reformed 'third way' in religion (chapter 5, p. 253, chapter 7, p. 317); Weyer shared his outlook. His was the first book to make serious criticisms of witch-beliefs and persecutions, while retaining credibility in contemporary terms by accepting that witches existed. Weyer's message had a limited impact in Germany, because the 1560s saw the last gasp of the 'third way' amid increasing confessional polarization – 1563, the year in which *De Praestigiis Daemonum* was first published, was also the year of the publication of the Heidelberg Catechism and of the Church of England's Thirty-Nine Articles and marked the end of the Council of Trent, not to mention the promulgation of hard-line new witchcraft legislation in England and Scotland. Nevertheless an edition of Weyer's book, that he dedicated to the Reformed German city of Bremen (so long the home of that steadfast 'third way' theologian Albert Hardenberg), actually persuaded the city authorities to abandon witch trials.[45] In the Netherlands, likewise, politics were in Weyer's favour: officials of the King of Spain pressed hard the case for witchcraft prosecutions as part of their general efforts in the 1560s to impose a tidy Catholic uniformity on the Low Countries. Consequently when the Dutch rebelled against Spain and its efforts to discipline them, scepticism about witchcraft became a plausible point of view to many of the humanist-educated nobility and merchants leading the rebellion.

Thus when the northern Netherlands won its independence, a voice like Weyer's, that could be respected as that of an expert professional, could have a real effect, just like the expert professional voices of the *Malleus* or of Del Rio, but with precisely the reverse result. Having escaped Catholic clerical tyranny, the Dutch might well have taken up Reformed enthusiasm for witch persecution, but the fraught relationship between town councils and the developing Reformed Church (chapter 8, pp. 370–73) soon predisposed the secular Regents to moderation precisely because the Reformed Church became so excited about witchcraft. When a later Dutch minister, the aggressively sceptical Balthazar Bekker, wrote his influential *Bewitched World* (1691), which finally shamed many Protestant authorities in Germany into giving up witch-trials, the Dutch Reformed Church was furious with him. The city of Amsterdam did not specifically comment on Bekker's outrageous views, but it went on paying his salary right up to his death and resolutely ignored the Church's call to appoint a substitute minister.[46]

One might have expected the situation in the Scotland of James VI to go the same way as the Netherlands, given the fact that King James was a thoughtful scholar-monarch frequently at loggerheads with the self-assertive leaders of the Reformed Kirk, and given the previous comparative blood-lessness of the Scottish Reformation. In fact it was the reverse: the King became the instigator and also the publicist of a sudden, intense and atrocious persecution, which subsequently escaped his control and became a major preoccupation of the Kirk. Curiously, the Scottish and English Parliaments had passed legislation against witchcraft in the same year, 1563, with the Scots prescribing death for witches, but in neither kingdom did this lead to a rush of prosecutions, with no more than a handful of executions in Scotland.[47] The Scots' persecution awaited James's marriage to the Danish princess Anna, who in 1590 found herself prevented by spectacular storms from sailing to Scotland to meet her royal bridegroom. With uncharacteristic heterosexual bravado, James himself then set out, voyaging through the terrible weather to meet her in Denmark. On the King's return to Scotland, James plunged himself into one of the most lurid and extraordinary affairs in Scottish history.

Personally leading an investigation to discover the causes of the storms, James uncovered a story of a gathering at North Berwick parish kirk the previous Hallowe'en (31 October 1589) over which the Devil himself had presided, with the agenda of planning the King's destruction, principally through manipulation of the weather. The details were abundant, or at least became so after the suspects had been subjected to prolonged torture. Careful modern analysis of the North Berwick affair has revealed a number of political motives for James's actions: he drew into the accusations one of Scotland's most troublesome magnates, Francis Stewart, Earl of Bothwell, a raffish Renaissance intellectual, notorious for his interest in the occult and in hermetic literature. The King may also have been attacking Catholics: the North Berwick gathering may in fact have been a clandestine but perfectly orthodox celebration of the Mass.[48] What is striking when all this has been explained is that after his stay in Denmark, and possibly as a result of his exposure to that different culture, James was genuinely convinced of the diabolic element in the North Berwick assembly and of the diabolic attack on his kingdom: from now on, official Scottish views on witchcraft emphasized its satanic side with all the conviction of Martin Del Rio. In 1597 James (who regarded himself as schoolmaster both to his kingdom and to all Europe) published one of the classic affirmations of witchcraft, *Demonologie*, one of whose features was a bitter attack on Johann Weyer's *De Praestigiis Daemonum*.[49]

Although the proud royal author published an edition of *Demonologie* in southern English idiom when he came to the English throne as James I, the book now became something of an embarrassment to him. This was not only because he was already becoming uneasy about the Kirk's enthusiastic pursual of his witchcraft campaign in Scotland, but because in the England of 1603 he found a different combination of forces interested in witches and the fight against the supernatural. Over the previous two decades, both English Roman Catholic clergy and several English Puritan ministers had made rival bids for charismatic authority by performing spectacular exorcisms. Both sides represented a challenge to the episcopal hierarchy of the Church of England led by Richard Bancroft, Archbishop of Canterbury, whose moderate Protestant style the new King found very congenial (chapter 12, pp. 513–15). The changed situation was crystallized by a new English *cause célèbre*, the supposedly diabolic possession of a young woman called Anne Gunter, that developed from a local Oxfordshire feud through Puritan clergy publicizing her possession, to a trial for fraud in Star Chamber in Westminster in 1606–7. The King once more sprang into action, but with very different results from those in the North Berwick case. After Gunter's father contrived to introduce her to the King, James interviewed her several times and exposed her as an impostor.[50]

By the time of the Gunter case, Archbishop Bancroft and like-minded conformist English clerics, furious at Puritan and papist pretensions to special spiritual powers, had moved to a position of resolute scepticism on resorts to exorcism (of course, the ceremonialist 'Arminian' clerics like William Laud in the next generation also hated Puritans, and so they followed Bancroft in becoming rather unexpected exponents of a rational view of supernatural phenomena). In his major revamping of the English Church's canon law in 1604, Bancroft forbade clergy to conduct exorcisms without their diocesan bishop's permission, which was a sore affliction to zealous Puritan ministers. James now agreed with Bancroft and the sceptics. In the English Parliament of 1604 he backed new legislation about witchcraft that laid down harsher penalties for the crime, but also had the effect of taking the prosecution of witchcraft and magic out of the hands of the Church and passing it more completely to secular courts, thus further undermining the activities of Puritan clerical exorcists.[51] In fact, through his reign, witchcraft prosecutions noticeably declined in England.

In Scotland, by contrast, there was not much that James could do to influence the Kirk. At intervals over eight decades after 1590 it instigated one of the most intense persecutions in all Europe: in this relatively small and underpopulated kingdom, it is likely that there were more than a thousand executions during the period, much greater in absolute let alone relative numbers than in its southern neighbour England (which had more than three times its population). The varying intensity of Scottish prosecutions was also suspiciously coincident with periods when the Kirk's leaders wished to assert their authority against the secular power. Nor did the Kirk shrink from torture, despite contemporary doubts. The modern Church of Scotland exhibits no readiness to trumpet its innovative discovery around 1600 of the usefulness of sleep deprivation, both as an effective form of interrogation and as a legally less dubious alternative to the torturing techniques more usual in the period.[52]

There is thus a general correlation between those European Churches both Protestant and Catholic that evolved an effective and largely unchallenged disciplinary system, and a high incidence of witchcraft prosecutions. The Catholic Counter-Reformation was as atrocious in its persecution as that of the Reformed Protestants. Some of the worst in Europe took place in the Archbishopric of Cologne during the time of Ferdinand of Bavaria, who from 1594 was the second in the long series of Bavarian Wittelsbach Archbishops installed there after the Catholic victory in 1583 (chapter 10, pp. 452–3). Ferdinand (whose uncle Ernst, the previous Archbishop of Cologne, had been the dedicatee of Del Rio's book) was a typical specimen of the radical self-discipline and austere crusading spirit which characterized both his own dynasty and the contemporary champion of the Counter-Reformation, Habsburg Archduke Ferdinand of Inner Austria – that spirit which was such an important trigger of the Thirty Years War (chapters 10, pp. 449–57, and 11, p. 487). It has been plausibly suggested that these devoutly Catholic rulers were struggling with more than the Protestantism that certainly obsessed them. Their Jesuit mentors had instilled in them a preoccupation with sin and judgement that was strengthened by the new disciplinary demands of clerical celibacy, now for the first time properly enforced on senior clergy in central Europe. These were major motives for them to look for the Devil's agents in the world. They were struggling with their own temptations, and witches were very visible symbols of the general temptations with which Satan tormented their society.[53]

The Cologne situation is also a reminder that forms of customary justice and the structures of power which controlled them were likely to make one local situation very different from another. In small political units such as the Catholic German Prince-Bishoprics, pressures from popular fears or the opinions of one significant personality in the ruling elite were liable to produce some of the worst panics (although conversely, in such situations one strong-minded personality could also withstand popular panics).[54] Larger political units were more likely to have a legal system whose slow processes and greater detachment from local emotions brought restraint. England had a precociously strong system of central justice that stoutly ignored influence from exotic foreign law codes like the *Lex Carolina*: it had a noticeably patchy distribution of prosecutions (some of the most concentrated being in the 'burned-over' Puritan territory of Essex). Interrogation under torture remained abnormal in the English legal system, and this undoubtedly made confessions of English witches less sensational and less likely to conform to the stereotypes of active diabolic contact that were developing in the expert literature of Europe. The contrast with Scotland's interrogatory techniques and its development of the diabolic stereotypes is significant. The Essex Puritan Matthew Hopkins in the national crisis of the 1640s was the first (and last) in England habitually to use torture like the Scots, and predictably he came up with confessions more like the common diabolic European norm.

Finally it is worth considering the two areas of Catholic Europe which did not opt in to the witch-craze. In the case of Ireland, one explanation for the near-absence of witch-trials must be the strong gulf in religious and political sympathy which opened up between the royal government and the Gaelic and 'Old English' populations during the later sixteenth century (chapter 8, pp. 394–9). This meant that the common combination of popular demand and elite preoccupations was disrupted; nevertheless it is still odd that such an increasingly polarized society did not exorcize some of its tensions in witchcraft accusations. It is possible that on the Catholic side, the Catholic Irish clergy's strong links with Iberia were significant, because Counter-Reformation Spain and Portugal stand out as the second region where witchcraft persecutions were positively discouraged by the Church authorities. This was all the more remarkable when one considers that in the northern territory of the Spanish Habsburgs, the Spanish Netherlands, witch-trials burgeoned at exactly the same time as they were being suppressed in Spain, and with the backing of repeated royal decrees.

In the Iberian case, the unlikely heroes of this self-denial were the Spanish and Portuguese Inquisitions. In the Spanish Netherlands the royal authority and secular courts led the attack on witches, without an Inquisition to comment on their activities, and some of their colleagues in the secular administration in northern Spain enthusiastically followed suit. Inquisitors scrutinized various outbreaks of persecution that did occur in the peninsula, particularly on the fringes of Iberia in the Basque country. They decided that evidence required for a satisfactory verdict of guilty was extremely difficult to obtain, and that in fact there was very little evidence for the widespread existence of witches, let alone active pacts with the Devil. They regarded even most confessions of witchcraft as delusions, to be treated with pastoral discipline not death, and they generally disciplined colleagues who took extreme measures, much to the fury of various secular officials who wanted to forward persecution. The chief personality holding the line against punitive viciousness was the Navarrese Inquisitor Alonso de Salazar Frias, a careful and scrupulous lawyer who wrote up his findings after a particularly atrocious convulsion of executions in Navarre on the French frontier in 1609–10. Salazar roundly declared in the wake of examining thousands of cases: 'I have not found the slightest evidence from which to infer that a single act of witchcraft has really occurred.'[55] Before one gets too carried away in saluting the Inquisitions' common sense, one should remember that they were already in hot pursuit of two ready-made scapegoats for the cultural fears of the Iberian population, secret Judaism and Islam, and witches were superfluous to the paranoias either of the elite or the people. It was indeed the Inquisitions' long experience in persecuting these two minority groups that gave them a particularly sensitive ear for the nuances of evidence. Such was the devious route which led the Inquisitors of Iberia for a moment to sound more like the contemporaries of modern secular westerners than might John Calvin or Philipp Melanchthon.

14

Death, Life and Discipline

NEGOTIATIONS WITH DEATH AND MAGIC

One reason why the issue of witchcraft did not become controversial between Catholics and Protestants was that it did not affect the great Catholic–Protestant fault-line – the late medieval Church's claim to be able to offer living humanity an active part in directing the fate of the dead to damnation, Purgatory or heaven. This was something that from the beginning of the Reformation, Luther's affirmation of justification by faith alone absolutely denied. Hence Protestant Europe's attack on the soul-prayer industry and destruction of chantries; hence also the wholesale attack on the position of the saints, because the old devotion saw them as humans whose heavenly credentials made them still powerful and available as agents in the apparatus of negotiation with God.

In England, both pre-Reformation and post-Reformation wills customarily made their first bequest that of the testator's soul, and optimistically expressed the hope that it should end up in heaven. However, there was a great difference either side of the religious divide: the medieval will usually left the soul to a committee consisting of God, Our Lady and 'the holy company of heaven' (all the saints). After the Reformation, the beneficiary was God alone, and the more well-informed Protestants or their scribes would emphasize the point by saying specifically that they hoped to be saved only by the merits of Jesus Christ. The changes in these formulae have often been used to chart the spread and development of the English Reformation in the mid-sixteenth century, and despite much scholarly argument and many problems of method, the effort does produce some worthwhile results.[1]

Naturally Protestants did their best to remodel and tame the liturgical expression of the moment of death, the funeral, since they rightly saw the requiem Mass as one of the strongest cards that the traditional Church could play. If one reads the funeral service in England's Book of Common

Prayer, it quickly becomes apparent that Archbishop Cranmer took great care in his much simplified final version prepared in 1552 to remove any sense that those present can do anything for the dead. His previous compromise version of 1549 had kept from the old funeral rite a direct address by the officiating priest to the dead corpse and its departing soul, but now his liturgy contained no sense of any continuing relationship to the corpse (or even much sense of its presence at the service): the ritual addresses the living audience only.[2] In the first days of the Reformation, evangelicals had gone much further. They had emphasized living humanity's helplessness in the face of death by holding burials without ceremony or clergy and often by night, much to the horror of their Catholic neighbours, and soon also to the unease of the emerging Lutheran establishment. Nocturnal burial was one of the practices which the first Electoral visitation commission of Saxony in 1527–8 (chapter 4, p. 165) moved to suppress. Several German Lutheran cities nevertheless moved cemeteries to new sites outside the city walls to keep a firm separation between the living and the dead. The Reformed were punctilious in following suit: hence John Calvin's insistence on an unmarked grave in Geneva. Scotland prohibited ministers from going to the grave or from doing anything more than give an address on death and resurrection afterwards, and likewise New England, in its enthusiasm for building a society which Calvin would have admired, at first excluded clergy altogether from funerals.[3]

The dismissal of superstitious ceremony around death was fine in theory, but cross-currents both from above and below opposed these minimal rites of passage. Luther himself, with his strong sense of the teaching importance of ceremony, decided when drawing up the instructions for the 1528 Saxon visitation that the Church ought to help people mock their fears of death through a satisfying liturgical drama, so he reinstated an elaborate ritual with procession and hymns.[4] Equally, in the Reformed world, many both lay and clerical felt a desperate wish for suitable remembrance of the dead in this world even if nothing could be done for them in the next. Statements of social hierarchy quickly reasserted themselves: after all, the magisterial Reformers had committed themselves to the proposition that social hierarchy was part of God's purpose. The defeat of simple funerals became a general rout because it was led by the secular paymasters of the new Churches, the nobility and gentry. Both in Lutheran Germany and in England, one odd result was that during the seventeenth century night funerals came back into fashion for the upper strata of society: having started as statements of the irrelevance of ceremonial in the early Reformation, now they provided an opportunity for sombre magnificence under the lights of many nocturnal torches – and more opportunities to exclude the lower orders.[5]

There were all sorts of good reasons to reinstate funerals as memorable occasions. The secular leaders of Protestant societies adroitly annexed Protestantism's insistence on the Word of God, and made sure that the first commemoration which they would receive in their communities on their deaths would be a sermon. Some Swiss reforming theologians did their best to oppose this idea, but even Reformed clergy were torn: Archbishop Cranmer's sometime chaplain Thomas Becon, bestselling devotional writer of mid-Tudor England, already assumed in 1561 in his *Sick Man's Salve* (a do-it-yourself guide to a good death) that a decent Protestant funeral would include a sermon. Quite apart from the duty to reaffirm the God-given hierarchy of society by giving due respect to noble birth, the pastoral opportunity of a funeral sermon was obvious, and it would not have escaped the notice of Reformed preachers in France that from the 1560s French Roman Catholic preachers were making the sermon at funerals a major opportunity for partisan propaganda as well as pious reflection. In England the funeral sermon enjoyed equal popularity indifferently among Arminians, conformists and Puritans. Soon printed versions of such sermons became a major commercial enterprise for the publishing industry. They remained so well into the eighteenth century, when early versions of the modern newspaper or journal began featuring obituary notices in their pages instead – sometimes with a pious framework, but increasingly often with little religious rhetoric.[6]

The sermon was not the only way to offer a moral lesson at a funeral. Hungarian and Transylvanian ministers were customarily prepared to heap shame on notorious dead sinners by giving them what were known as 'ass's funerals' – burying the corpse with insulting perfunctoriness outside the churchyard, with no attendant processions or passing bell. Such deliberately liturgical lack of liturgy only made sense against the assumption that good Christians deserved honourable and ceremonial burial: Calvin, of course, would have thought that no Christian deserved such ceremonial frivolities, but that is a reminder that Transylvania was not Geneva.[7] Funerals were also a chance to reaffirm the positive links which bound communities. Anyone who died blessed with surplus wealth was likely to feel constrained to leave something for the poor, and possibly also provide food and drink ('doles') on as large a scale as possible, despite Protestant worries that this was a return to the charity which had sped people through Purgatory. In England there did tend to be an association between doles and the more conservative northern and western parts of the kingdom, and the English gentry and nobility began giving them up during the seventeenth century as they made their funerals more private affairs. Nevertheless, doles at death kept a powerful community symbolism: for instance, decades after Queen Elizabeth's accession, they actually emerged as a new custom in one of England's first industrial communities, the County Durham coal-mining village of Whickham, where people were closely knit in a specialized and dangerous trade. Many English parish officials also laid on food and drink at pauper funerals in a kindly effort to do something to cheer this most wretched moment in the lives of the wretched.[8]

No more than Catholics did Protestants wish their funeral service to be the last remembrance of themselves. Far from tombs disappearing from church buildings, in most European settings the Protestant dead made their presence felt ever more stridently and in greater numbers. Some of England's greatest Puritan magnates have some of England's largest and most splendid tombs keeping their memory alive, and in the English church floors which Victorians have not tidied up with their tiling, the leger-slabs of the lesser dead vie with each other for the interest and respect of the living. Sometimes these monuments emphasize the gulf which divides them from old superstition by being aggressively placed where medieval altars had stood: even in some cases (to the huge offence later of Victorian High Churchmen) in the place of the high altar in the chancel.[9] The cool, white spaces of Dutch churches likewise are paved with monuments of the wealthy dead. Even the Church of Scotland lost the battle against the monuments. It started out in 1581 confidently forbidding the building of tombs inside churches, through which papists had turned God's house of prayer into a 'cairn of dead men's skulls', but its proclamations grew ever more shrill and are patently contradicted by the majestic monuments which survive in many of Scotland's old church buildings. Eventually canny Scottish church officials saw that principle could be combined with profit by levying supposedly punitive fines on offending tomb-builders, which were effectively a tax on burial in church.[10] And outside, all around in Scottish kirkyards, four centuries of monuments both humble and grand now afford the serious-minded tourist much varied visual delight.

It might be thought that such adjustments of Protestant theory are explicable simply as the cynical pressure of the powerful, bending theology to suit their own interests, pretensions and preoccupations. However, there were other adjustments in allied spheres that are evidence that the sensitivities of Protestant Churches extended towards all their flocks, and that their religious life was full of negotiations with the preoccupations, joys and worries of the population at large. Christianity as a religious system is at least two-fold: it is religion as prescribed by the professionals (which on both sides in the Reformation was reformist in intent and agenda), and it is religion as actually practised, which even among Reformation Protestants tended inevitably to conservatism. The whole area of death and the super-natural was full of such compromises, part of a continuing 'black economy' of spirituality that was as old as institutional Christianity itself.

The medieval Church officially insisted that at the moment of death God made a decision about the fate of a soul: either heaven, Purgatory or hell. Even at an official level there was a complication to this: regardless of its various disagreements over Purgatory, Christianity has always been uncomfortable about relating the idea of an immediate individual decision to the contradictory notion of God's Last Judgement which it has also inherited from the New Testament. The everyday experience of death intro-duced a degree of popular scepticism. There was a widespread and under-standable conviction that many souls, particularly those who experienced a 'bad death', continued to wander the earth for some time either as ghosts or as forces which could possess living human beings. Theologians were not unanimous in what to think about this, but most followed the lead provided by the great Augustine of Hippo and insisted that demons and not human souls were responsible for such possessions. Ordinary folk were not neces-sarily overawed by Augustine's authority, and they were sometimes quite prepared to stand their ground and argue with know-all clergy on the subject. It was probably this popular belief about the danger of souls hanging around without proper assignment that led to the laity buying so enthusiastically into the medieval institutional Church's provision of a month's-worth of Masses (a 'trental') to pray for the soul of the deceased.[11] Not surprisingly, at the Reformation this semi-detached popular theology was perfectly able to slip its moorings to the medieval Church system and seek an attachment to the official Protestant replacement.

Magisterial Protestant Reformers therefore found themselves with a prob-lem, particularly since they had just abolished Purgatory, a middle state which had given the official medieval Church some leeway in negotiating with popular beliefs about ghosts and indeterminacy after death. Protestants were also initially riven with disputes arising from the old ambiguity in Christian belief between immediate and Last Judgement. Many were attracted to a radical solution affirming the sleep of individual souls until God's final round-up, which would decisively dispense with any dangerous notions of Purgatory. Luther (after he had ditched his belief in Purgatory around 1530) openly affirmed soul-sleep: that was one of the reasons that he encouraged the siting of new cemeteries outside the noisy bustle of towns, so that the sleep of the dead could be properly and decorously symbolized.[12] The English Bible-translator William Tyndale shared Luther's belief, but Calvin devoted the first theological tract he wrote (probably in 1534, published in 1542) to rubbishing the idea, possibly with Luther in mind – the name he gave his tract, *Psychopannychia*, has come to be used to describe the doctrine of soul-sleep, despite meaning precisely the opposite in Greek ('the all-night vigil of the soul'). Subsequent Protestantism in general quietly signed up to Calvin's point of view. Partly this was because the despised radicals and Anabaptists were often proponents of soul-sleep, but probably pastors also instinctively felt that the prospect of remote universal judgement was less of an incentive to moral behaviour than an immediate and one-to-one interview with the Almighty after death.

The decision against soul-sleep still left Protestantism with a division between the dead and the living much more radical and impermeable than in Catholicism. Moreover, Protestants had to minister to a population which would not be shifted out of its ghost-beliefs – in any case, leading Reformers themselves believed in ghosts, even the great humanist Melanchthon confidently affirming that he had seen them. Mainstream Reformers now found Augustine of Hippo a useful ally. They affirmed with him that ghosts were demonic in character, and having held the line on that point of principle, they set about helping ordinary people cope with the ghosts which they experienced. So one of Heinrich Bullinger's ministerial colleagues in Zürich, Ludwig Lavater, published a widely translated guide to ghosts in 1569 (the *Gespensterbuch*), which undertook that dual task of remaining faithful to Augustine and being practically useful. With symmetry and logic the Reformers also sought to bring comfort to people by emphasizing that they should believe not just in demons but in angels and their powers to help. There was a double usefulness in angels: they were abundantly biblically attested, and they could step into the shoes of the evicted Catholic saints as ideologically appropriate friends of humanity. Even the austerity of post-Reformation Scottish kirks could on occasion be relieved by newly painted pictures of angels without threatening the prohibition on idolatry (see Plate 19b).[13] In fact Protestant Europe was restoring to western Christianity a view of angels as powerful and effective servants of God, which had lapsed in the medieval western Church during the centuries that the cult of the saints had become so all-consuming.[14]

It is remarkable what a large degree of popular belief in the supernatural and in magic Protestantism in practice allowed to remain in place. In Lutheran regions, one extra factor was the Church's official theology: the strongly realist sacramentalism which Luther had bequeathed the Church.

After all, Luther still believed that bread and wine became corporally the body and blood of Christ, and he also persisted in his conviction that water used in baptism had a peculiarly sacred quality. The results were not always what the Lutheran Church authorities wanted, but were predictable nonetheless: in Saxony in the 1580s orders had to be issued that people should not approach church vergers to buy water from the font after baptisms or left-over bread from communion, with magical purposes in mind.[15] The English Church had a similar problem, because the 'arrested development' of its Reformation after Elizabeth I's 1559 settlement of religion left it with a Prayer Book prescribing more ceremonial than any other Reformed Church. The official Church, for instance, kept the custom of signing a cross in water on the baby's forehead in baptism. Puritans thought this was superstitious and popish, and Elizabethan bishops had an uneasy feeling that they were right, despite Good Queen Bess's command. So the Church leadership was in an awkward position: it simultaneously tried forcing Puritans to allow their babies to be signed with the cross, while it tried to stop other people thinking that this was a magical rite which was the centre of the whole christening.[16]

Superstitious use of liturgical practices obviously could not be countenanced, and all forms of non-official magic ought equally to have been condemned. In Reformed territories there was the precedent of Calvin's exceptionally hard line against benevolent as well as malevolent magic (chapter 13, p. 569). Nevertheless the Reformed disciplinary authorities, even in Scotland with its dark record on witch-hunting, generally took a soft line on folk-healing, and often without further penalty simply warned healers to cease their activities – effectively leaving them to their own devices. Similarly, Scottish Kirk Sessions were in most circumstances significantly lenient on those who went a-maying to ancient holy wells, or drank and danced on Midsummer Day. They might grumble at the idolatry of 'putting the well in God's room' in seeking healing there, but in 1649 one set of Highland elders gloomily concluded that proper godly correction of well-visits was impossible because 'there were few in the parish that could purge themselves from going thereto', especially since 'this abuse had not been punished this long time bygone'. Often Church elders seem to have regarded such occasions as the basis for parish revenue-raising through fines, just as they treated those who broke the Kirk's prohibition on burial in church buildings. Much folk custom should have been viewed as potentially just as bad as magic, because it reflected the contours of the hated Catholic Church's liturgical year, but wherever one looks in the Protestant world one repeatedly finds this sour-faced and ungracious tolerance of popular magic and ceremony – in Lutheran Württemberg as much as Calvinist Scotland or Reformed England.[17]

This lukewarm Protestant reaction to such survival may seem puzzling, given everything that we have noted about the witch-craze and high-temperature expectations of the Last Days. It should nevertheless be seen as reflecting a judicious sense of priorities among the clergy of Protestant Europe. Once the outlines of settled Churches began emerging in the mid-sixteenth century, they found themselves with a huge task on their hands. They might destroy the commanding heights of the old system through the campaign against idolatry and the introduction of radically simplified liturgy, but a daunting job of education remained, with the aim of transforming patterns of life and thinking in the entire population. Faced by the enormity of this agenda, ministers might well regard as harmless enough the survival of a custom such as baking a special flat loaf on Good Friday, marking it with a cross and keeping it all year – as long as those who did it had more or less forgotten that the 'hot-cross bun' had started life as the consecrated Mass-wafer, housed in churches through Good Friday and Holy Saturday in a special Easter Sepulchre. It did not matter too much in traditional-minded Lancashire when families marched out on All Souls' Night led by a forkful of burning straw, and prayed on a hillside for the souls of relatives until the straw burned down; they no longer tried to do that sort of thing in church.

Such communal customs pleased people, did not do any systematic harm to the Protestant message, and crucially had been detached from the round of worship in the parish church, so they could not pervert people's official or public devotional life. Ronald Hutton has magisterially surveyed an astonishing variety of survival of such custom in England and Wales – in many cases they have lasted up to the present day, when Anglican parish clergy have often come to see many folk-observances as useful allies in the task of defending local communities against disintegration. He suggests that many Reformation clergy may have taken the pragmatic attitude of an eighteenth-century English parson who collected evidence of such survivals: the Revd Henry Bourne conceded that 'vulgar antiquities' might be 'the produce of heathenism' or 'the inventions of indolent monks', but said that the main question was whether they were 'sinful and wicked' in practice. Many weary ministers must have decided to forget what Calvin had said, and judged that they were not.[18]

TELLING OUT THE WORD

Protestant clergy would only have had the confidence to do this if they felt that they were winning the main battle for their evangelical message – and they were indeed. In the century and a half after Luther's first rebellion they scored an extraordinary success in religious instruction within the territories of confessional Protestantism. Only in Poland-Lithuania and Ireland did the Reformation in either Lutheran or Reformed shape fail to take over the framework for popular culture to the north of the Counter-Reformation's central European frontier. This was all the more remarkable because of the shocks and setbacks that Protestants faced in their first two decades. Luther and his early admirers amid the spontaneous *Wildwuchs* of the 'years of carnival' in the early 1520s had believed that the Bible alone would convince people by its power. Then came the traumas of the mid-1520s, and the continuing radicalism centring on Münster in 1534–5. Their suppression left much of rural northern Europe sullenly resentful of mainstream evangelical efforts to discipline it. These confrontations revealed the dangers of leaving the Bible in people's hands unsupervised and without proper explanation, and Lutheran state Churches increasingly restricted access of children in schools to the Bible, preferring to present them with instruction in catechisms, and to leave Bible-reading to the fully educated. It was a strange reversal of Luther's initial hopes.[19]

The Reformed, who had so benefited from the new popular movements of the 1560s in France, Hungary, the Netherlands and Scotland, were much more inclined than Lutherans to encourage their flocks to read the Bible for themselves, but even they were anxious that it should be read in the right way. Reformed editions of Bibles throughout Europe are characterized by a mass of tiny print in the margins: detailed commentaries which act like a minister looking over the reader's shoulder and directing how the reading should go. Brooding on his defeat in the English Civil War of the 1640s by the parliamentarian armies who had read their Geneva Bibles only too thoroughly, Charles I's northern general William Cavendish, Duke of Newcastle, commented sourly: 'The Bible in English under every weaver's and chambermaid's arm hath done much harm . . . for controversy is a civil war with the pen which pulls out the sword soon afterwards.'[20] This Protestant but ultra-Royalist aristocrat was (no doubt unconsciously) echoing the sentiment of Pope Paul V four decades before (chapter 9, p. 406). Unsurprisingly Roman Catholics remained highly suspicious of lay use of the vernacular Bible. Even if they could not ban it outright in northern Europe as became the case in Italy (chapter 9, p. 406), they saw reading the Bible primarily as a professional necessity in arguing with Protestantism. So the most prominent cleric among the English Catholic exiles William Allen, when writing to a colleague in 1578, saw it as a regrettable necessity that his students at the Douai college were having to discuss the biblical text in English:

... it would perhaps be desirable that the sacred writings should never be translated into the vernacular, nevertheless since in these days, either because of the spread of heretical opinions or for some other reason, even men of good will are apt to be inquisitive ... it is more satisfactory to have a faithful catholic translation than that they should endanger their souls by using a corrupt one.[21]

The result was that when English Roman Catholics created their first English biblical translation in exile at Douai and Reims, it was not for ordinary folk to read, but for priests to use as a polemical weapon – the explicit purpose which the 1582 title-page and preface of the Reims New Testament proclaimed. Only the Jansenists of early seventeenth-century France came to have a more positive and generous attitude to promoting Bible-reading among Catholics (chapter 10, p. 482).

The long-term task for Protestants was to show people how to use the Bible in a disciplined way and still love it: to build on the officially provided resources so that everyone could make Reformation their own, rather than merely passively accepting what their betters decided for them. Central to this task was preaching: disciplined presentation of the word by a duly authorized minister. In the pre-Reformation ordination service used in Scotland, the priest was given as symbols of his office keys to the kirk and the font cover, a missal, a chalice and vestments: after the Scottish Reformation, he got a Bible, plus a key to unlock the pulpit.[22] Besides his pulpit key, an essential asset for a minister now became a loud or clear voice. The problem of audibility was a real one in the very large town churches of Scotland and the Netherlands, but it was at its most acute in Huguenot congregations in France, where the restrictions imposed by the Catholic royal government meant that each town or city would have only one very large venue for often over-excited worshipers who might number a thousand or even more.

The size and grandeur of newly built Protestant pulpits were permanent reminders of the paramountcy of the sermon, and led to the drastic restructuring of Reformed church interiors from Ireland to Lithuania. This dramatically canopied wooden preaching-turret now became the chief focus of the congregation's eyes rather than the altar or communion table. Commonly in the existing long, narrow medieval church buildings, the furnishings were turned around through ninety degrees, pulling the congregation away from the old climax of the altar at the east end and facing them either on to the long northern wall, where sunlight could fall on the preacher's face as he brought his people to struggle with God's word, or on the south, where in dramatic silhouette he could scan the eyes of his flock as he spoke. Pulpits were furnished with hourglasses to give a measure to the preacher's performance, although it was the expectation in most Protestant societies (particularly among their civil magistrates) that only star preachers should risk the patience of God and humanity with a second hour.[23]

The sermon at its best was popular theatre on a far greater scale than its rival, the playhouse. In Shakespeare's London there were a hundred sermons each week in a period when there were only thirteen playhouses, which were not all open at the same time. The Transylvanian Reformed Church in the years of its greatness in the mid-seventeenth century set as its ideal four sermons a week in its parish churches, on Wednesdays and Fridays and twice on a Sunday.[24] Everywhere sermons were the great occasions of the week. Once Dutch churches had become well supplied with preaching ministers, they customarily made a point of not announcing the name of the preacher in advance, in order to avoid personality cults or connoisseurs of sermons moving from church to church or service to service to hear their favourites. The Dutch clergy were conscientiously trying to counter the fact that the official Dutch Reformed Church was effectively a voluntary organization, which made competitive self-advertisement a great temptation for ministers in order to swell their congregations.[25]

Scotland, where there was no latitude for attendance as in the Reformed Netherlands, developed the community drama of the sermon to its height. It was preceded by the prolonged ringing of the church bells which had once rung the faithful to Mass; during the half-hour allowed for the congregation to troop in and arrange itself, the Kirk official known as the reader would be solemnly reading a whole book of the Bible. Once everyone was in, the doors would be locked (in the western Highlands, this led to ghastly incidents of murderous inter-community malice, when on at least two occasions clans set fire to parish kirks filled with their clan enemies at sermon-time). Scottish congregations might then be encouraged to participate in the sermon-drama, being urged to shout out responses, cries of praise or 'Amen', in the manner that has been inherited by American evangelical Protestantism. After everyone had dispersed, the sermon would go on resonating through the community, because the Kirk required parents and masters at home to listen to their children and servants repeating what the minister had said that day.[26] This was a highly effective way to promote mental agility throughout the population, and it gave at least the option of mulling over some abstract ideas during the toil of the week ahead. The Scots became as a result a formidably theologically minded people, and they also came to value a good education for all, in a fashion which has never quite seized their English neighbours.

Some people revelled in the culture of the sermon. The Lutheran funeral sermon of one woman from the civic elite of Leipzig recorded at length her husband's account of her death-bed discourses in 1579, and included her exclamation 'Oh, in what a blessed time I have lived, in which I have heard many splendid and lovely sermons, which my parents under the Pope did not hear!' This rather charming cry is admittedly the sort of remark that preachers were only too pleased to relay, but listeners would not have accepted it if it had been too far from reality.[27] However, many also fell asleep during the sermon, misbehaved or failed to get the message. What should be done then? The main answer was the alternative hard slog of class teaching for both children and adults, on the model pioneered by Luther at the end of the 1520s: catechizing. It was slow, labour-intensive work and lacked the glamour of the pulpit, and it also needed the right printed materials to back up the teaching. A host of individual ministers and laypeople as well as official Church consortia constantly sought to make these little textbooks more user-friendly and effective, with or without official patronage or finance.

This was a massive enterprise on a European-wide scale, which for more than a century was the most common form of education throughout the continent. It became a very competitive commercial market: Lutheran Germany produced around thirty or forty different new editions of printed catechisms every decade after 1550, and more than a thousand different catechisms produced in England between 1530 and 1740 have been identified (many further examples of this very disposable genre will have left no trace at all). As usual, the Scots outdid most other Protestants, even demanding catechizing before baptisms and weddings. The elders and ministers of Glasgow and lesser burghs such as Perth or Leith had organized themselves enough by 1600 to conduct weekly catechisms, which on a rota basis would cover their entire population over a few weeks – in the case of Glasgow, that involved between four and six thousand people.[28] In the long term all this effort worked: the pious of the parish came to value catechizing and backed up the clergy's work. Already in the 1570s, German Lutheran congregations might complain bitterly if their church officials or pastors neglected catechizing. The English historian Christopher Haigh, who would be the last to admit enthusiasm for the achievements of the Reformation, has nevertheless observed a threefold progress in England over seventy years: first, early Elizabethan bishops struggled to get their clergy to catechize, later, Elizabethan clergy struggled to get their people to learn, and by the reign of James I both had largely succeeded in the task.[29]

Roman Catholics followed suit. Naturally they carefully modelled their essays on the Tridentine Catechism of 1566, although the 1587 edition of Luther's Small Catechism produced by the Jesuits in Graz was a specialist exercise in negative education, gleefully pointing out Luther's doctrinal inconsistencies in the margins of his text, in order to annoy Graz Lutherans. French bishops, trying to steer France's early seventeenth-century revival of Roman Catholicism against the Huguenots, were especially assiduous, more or less every diocese making the effort to produce its own authorized catechism.[30] An element beyond catechism in Roman Catholic publication was devotional literature that helped its readers in private meditation on divine mystery and glory. Sixteenth-century Protestantism was remarkably slow to produce similar material, possibly because Protestant clergy were so busy preaching and catechizing that they had little time for quiet and reflection. Indeed, Protestants – even English Puritans – actually read specially sanitized versions of Catholic devotional tracts for lack of their own literature in this genre, the most notorious case being the *Christian Directory* or *Exercise*, a devotional work of the famous (and much-hated) English Jesuit Robert Parsons: there were twenty-four bowdlerized Protestant editions of Parsons's tract, minus references to Purgatory, the Virgin Mary and the like, in contrast to only four Catholic editions.[31]

There can be no doubt that the effort of catechizing and the task of listening to a weekly diet of abstract ideas from the pulpit made Protestant Europe a society generally more book-conscious, and perhaps also more literate, than Catholic Europe. One scholar, Kari Konkola, has made some heroic calculations for total book production in Protestant England. On a conservative estimate he suggests that 1,342,500 whole Bibles and New Testaments were printed for the English market between 1520 and 1649, enough for every English household in that period to have one. Among these were half a million copies of the Geneva Bible, which significantly when one looks at surviving copies have usually been read to bits – my own copy of 1606, typically bound up with a metrical Psalter, is particularly fragile and fingered around Paul's epistles. Perhaps 7.5 million copies of what Konkola defines as 'major religious works' were published in England between 1500 and 1639, in contrast to 1.6 million secular poems, plays and sonnets, for a population which hovered around three million. Between 1580 and 1639 William Perkins, the doyen of Puritans, scored 188 editions, putting in the shade William Shakespeare's 97. The printing presses of Venice supplied half the Italian religious book market by the 1590s, and yet they produced only a twentieth as many as the major religious books produced for the English market.[32] Study of the book-owning habits of French Huguenots produces a similar contrast with their French Catholic neighbours: on the evidence of people's possessions recorded in probate inventories from the city of Metz, the proportion of French Catholic households owning books was roughly half the proportion in Protestant households in the same city, and also roughly half the figure in Lutheran Germany.[33]

Crucially for the Reformation, the Word could be sung as well as spoken or read. Even more than the text of a book, sacred music is flexible in its use and effect: it can be a matter of individual appreciation and meditation, passive enjoyment, or the occasion for active communal performance. Faced with these choices, the Lutherans and the Reformed sent up different devotional noises to God. The English Church, as we have seen (chapter 12, pp. 510–12) was uniquely schizophrenic between its cathedral choral music and the Reformed character of its parish churches with their metrical psalms. Lutherans did not exhibit such a sharp divide, but they did also operate with two musical genres. First, Luther loved much of the music of the old Church, and encouraged his followers to preserve it. Like the English cathedrals, therefore, but in urban parish churches where there was a well-educated and wealthy leadership, Lutherans went on developing choral polyphonic music and even used the old plainsong, with detailed seasonal reference to a trimmed-down version of the medieval liturgical year (later to find triumphant expression in the cantatas of J. S. Bach, written largely for urban congregational appreciation). Alongside that, and appropriate to the humblest devotional settings, Lutherans also had an increasingly rich new repertoire of congregational hymns stemming from Luther's lively appreciation of singing.

Luther's own hymn-writing set the highest of standards: the early seventeenth-century Jesuit Adam Contzen ruefully said that the Reformer's hymns 'killed more souls than his works and sermons'.[34] Lutheran worship thus offered a double richness to its congregations: the performance of choirs in the great churches and the opportunity for congregations to sing vernacular hymns. It was a musical choice which did not attract anything like the ideological freight that divided the English devotional public between Arminian ceremonialist and Reformed Protestant on the subject of music. Nevertheless, in the late seventeenth century, the coming of the intensely personal devotional German movement known as Pietism (chapter 17, p. 699) did place a question-mark against the traditionalist side of Lutheran music and ceremonial, and in the end it killed off the Lutheran retention of Latin in much of the Eucharist. The Lutheran love of hymns spilled over into a distinctive genre of sermon based on the words of a hymn (a *Liedpredigt*): these sermons began as meditations on Christmas hymns or carols for congregations to enjoy as a Christmas treat, but they spread to cover other seasons of the Church's year as well, and even became a common means of preaching at funerals.[35]

Reformed Churches frowned on the Catholic or Lutheran frivolity of singing non-biblical texts in church, and their singing was confined to the psalms of David in metrical form. In most Reformed territories they also insisted that this singing should be done without the benefit of the pipe-organ, which they regarded as part of past superstition and generally destroyed: this was just as much the case in English parish churches, where nationwide from around 1570 organs were nearly all removed or terminally neglected, as they were in Zürich or Scotland. Only in the Netherlands did the Reformed parish churches continue to boast increasingly elaborate and splendid organs, and that is an illustration of the peculiar balance between church and civil authority there. Ministers might disapprove, but the urban Regents liked the splendid sound, and insisted on maintaining organs for recitals for public enjoyment even if the festively decorated instruments were not used in the worship of the Church. They were deliberately overriding the clergy's objections to show who was boss.

We have already noted the power and dynamism of the metrical Psalter – that secret weapon of the Reformation – in the years of struggle in the 1560s and 1570s (see above, chapter 5, pp. 307–8). In more peaceful days, the psalms were a joyous unaccompanied roar in church that might capture the interest even of those bored by the sermon, but they could also be sung at home, or at work in the fields. The English Puritan minister Richard Greenham, who by example and friendship in his Cambridgeshire country parsonage shaped the ministerial careers of a multitude of Elizabethan Cambridge graduates, saw singing as important as prayer and meditation 'to whet up affection' in constructing a personal relationship with God – and he meant metrical psalms.[36] The metrical psalter was a very significant unifying factor across the boundaries of culture and language. Having started with Clement Marot's French metrical psalmody in the specialized and refined French setting of John Calvin's Geneva, it reached out to all Reformed Europe and beyond into north America.

A fine example of this multiculturalism is provided by the German and

Hungarian versions of the metrical psalter. As always, the starting-point was Marot: Ambrosius Lobwasser, a distinguished lawyer from Saxony, was travelling in France and was struck by the beauty of Huguenot French psalm-lyrics, even though he himself showed no Reformed sympathies and spent his life in the service of Lutheran princes. His German translation was published in 1573, and became an extraordinary success in the German-speaking world. Around a hundred separate editions appeared in the next 200 years; in fact there were only five years between 1573 and 1800 when some version was not coming off the press. Even Lutherans borrowed from it, and it was probably as influential as Luther's Bible in standardizing the linguistic forms used in High German.[37] In turn, Lobwasser's work spawned a very effective Hungarian translation by Albert Szenczi Molnár, published in 1607: knowing German but no French, Molnár worked closely with the French Reformed Pastor in Frankfurt to make sure that he reproduced the power of the French verse in the very different rhythms of Hungarian.

Once Molnár's translation had become established, the singing of his version, complete with French tunes, became symbolic for those 'Puritans' in the Transylvanian Church wanting to bring their country further into the mainstream of international Reformed Protestantism (chapter 10, pp. 460–61). They sought to replace the melange of traditional hymns that the Hungarian Church authorities had allowed to survive in bowdlerized form in church services, and they sparked bitter debates with the partisans of the native musical tradition.[38] If anything can justify the application of the originally abusive label 'Calvinist' to the Reformed Protestant tradition, it is the international use of the metrical psalter which started life in Calvin's Geneva and was more all-embracing in its impact than the theology of the *Institutes*.

GODLY DISCIPLINE

Discipline was a very positive word in the Reformation: for those in the Reformed Protestant tradition, it became almost a sales slogan, conveying the promise of the right ordering of the world and the pleasure of Almighty God, not merely some pettifogging interference by humourless self-appointed tyrants with individual personal freedom. We must realize the gap between our society and theirs in this respect. Those who have been shaped by the modern West think of discipline as primarily a matter of personal choice or of legislative regulation by a secular state. It is therefore particularly difficult for us to understand or sympathize with a world in which one of the main tasks of the Church, and one of its most useful functions in the eyes of contemporaries, was to be the active agent of discipline.

When looking at the Reformation, it is therefore easy for us to sneer at the repressors and take the side of the repressed, even when they are indulging in what in our own everyday life we would condemn as casual brutality. We may feel a sneaking sympathy for the Genevans who called their dogs 'Calvin' so that they could give the great Reformer a good kicking at one remove.[39] Modern liberal academic historians have been particularly prone to this tendency as in recent years they have started (very commendably) taking an interest in the history of the weak and the powerless, and have tried to write 'history from below'. One of their number, the distinguished social historian of the Reformation, Gerald Strauss, came to realize what he called 'the dilemma of popular history': 'how can I, in my scholarly work, applaud the ways of ordinary people in former times when, as an inhabitant of my own historical moment and milieu, I feel so little sympathy for, and virtually no sense of kinship with, the popular culture of my contemporaries?'[40] No one would dispute that to most scholars, the all-night party and the revolutionary echo of smashing glass sound sweeter at a distance of five centuries.

That delicate intellectual Desiderius Erasmus was the prototype of Strauss's dilemma: his enthusiasm for the theory of popular religion combined uneasily with his distaste for the reality of how ordinary people expressed their religion, or indeed expressed themselves generally. Erasmus was at the heart of the drive for social discipline in the Reformation: he made fashionable the idea that every human life could be lived in as holy a manner as monks claimed to do. Roman Catholics and Protestants alike followed him in this, and rulers both Catholic and Protestant hastened to fulfil the role of abbot in which he had cast them (chapter 2, pp. 104–5). We will find both sides seizing the chance to regulate the sex lives of the people of Europe (chapter 16). The disasters of the Reformation decades, the brooding threat of the Last Days, all instilled a mood of sombre penitence, which has been described as the symbolic triumph of Lent over Carnival. That triumph was as much the work of Archbishop Carlo Borromeo of Milan and the Jesuit mission preachers as of John Calvin.[41]

The disciplinary mood was not necessarily solely for staid magistrates: it was the stance of revolutionary puritans on both sides who wanted everyone to be as pure as themselves. We have already noted that during the French Civil Wars, both Huguenots and Catholic Ligue enthusiasts successively ruined the fun of the boisterous young carnival-players of Rouen, the

Abbaye des Conards (chapter 10, p. 468). Once the revolution was over, the revolutionaries might also turn on former allies to promote the Reformation of Manners. While the early English Reformation was still a revolution, evangelicals were commonly excluded from pulpits, so they spread their message outside churches – in alehouses, in ballads, and on the stage. By the 1580s, Puritans started disapproving of alehouses, ballads and the stage: because the Protestant Church was now firmly established and they had a chance of using the Church's structure to forward the godly society which they sought, they did not need these alternative forms of communication.[42] In taking this stance, Puritans were still at odds with the Elizabethan establishment, because conformist Protestant magistrates disagreed with them, and considered their hostility disruptive of good fellowship and due hierarchy. The ultimate symbol of changed times was the growing custom in London after 1600 that on Shrove Tuesdays (the eve of Lent) thousands of city apprentices and their friends burst into the city brothels and theatres and wrecked them. One might term that an action by the Provisional Wing of the Reformation of Manners.[43]

The ideal of Christian discipline is set by words attributed to Jesus Christ in Matthew 18:15–22: hardly surprisingly in an organization which was in its first generation both small and self-consciously separate from ordinary society, the method described is personal and private. 'If your brother sins against you, go and tell him his fault, between you and him alone. If he listens to you, you have gained your brother.' So two people should sort out their own dispute; if they cannot, then other Christians should be involved, and if remedy still fails, the whole Church should intervene. Discipline should thus come from within, both individually and within the Church's community, and should as far as possible avoid any secular system of law – 'if [the offender] refuses to listen even to the Church, let him be to you as a Gentile and a tax collector', Jesus commanded only as a last resort.

With this principle in mind, the medieval Western Church's practice of confession started as a public community act of reconciliation for sinners, but it had gradually become a one-to-one transaction, with the added overlay of the idea of sacramental penance: the priest hearing such an individualized 'auricular' confession was not only the candid friend but the bringer of divine absolution. Alongside confession was the system of church courts operating canon law, that system which Martin Luther had seen as the corner-stone of papal corruption, symbolically burning the books of papal decretals that embodied it. The Counter-Reformation Church naturally still kept private confession as the centerpiece of its discipline along with all its other surviving disciplinary structures. We have seen Archbishop Borromeo characteristically doing his best to intensify the system (chapter 9, pp. 412–13), but he was only one agent of the new Catholic drive for proper penance under clerical guidance. The Jesuits used their network of schools to recruit for after-hours devotional associations: after the Pope had given these associations institutional status in 1584, they could offer the benefits of plenary indulgence in return for daily Mass attendance and regular confession. Jesuits particularly promoted a favourite device pioneered by Ignatius after Spanish precedents, the general confession. This was a solemn systematic review of the sins of one's life, a carefully guided form of self-examination that recalled the growing contemporary Reformed Protestant interest in 'experimental' proofs of election to salvation.[44]

Some parts of Protestantism were stranded between the old disciplinary system and the much more systematic Reformed reassessment and restructuring inspired by Martin Bucer in Strassburg and then given its classic expression in Calvin's Geneva. The English Church began towards the end of Edward VI's reign tackling the problem of replacing medieval canon law, proposing a new structure of disciplinary courts with an elaborate liturgy of public penance, but politics intervened to kill this reform and after that nothing radical was done.[45] From 1559 the English had to do the best they could with the medieval ecclesiastical court system, to the disgust of many forward Protestants, including some bishops: gradually and painfully they restored the credibility which these popish church courts had lost in mid-century, and they did indeed achieve some considerable success, particularly in the regulation of sexuality (chapter 16, p. 635). Nevertheless, lack of proper Reformed discipline was as significant as the survival of cathedrals in differentiating the English Church from the other Reformed Churches of Europe.

In part-compensation for these deficiencies, the English Prayer Book continued to allow for the possibility of private confession to a clergyman, though on nothing like the systematic scale of Counter-Reformation Catholicism, and detached from the medieval confessional context of Purgatory and compulsion. Lutheran clergy, like the English, were unable to exercise church discipline through consistories and elderships in the Reformed manner. Much more systematically than in England, they revived the practice of private confession to a pastor, and it remained prominent in German Lutheran practice down to the eighteenth century. In Norway, as Lutheran orthodoxy established itself after 1600, pastors insisted on one-to-one confession as a prerequisite for receiving communion, and an enclosed desk was provided for the purpose on the north side of a church altar – by the eighteenth century these had become full-scale confessional-boxes which would have been instantly recognizable to a Counter-Reformation Catholic.[46]

England was not the only Reformed Church to face difficulties in securing discipline. Both in France and the Netherlands the court system of the consistory, run by ministers and elders on the Genevan model, was hampered by its lack of coercive powers: in France, because it was only the internal disciplinary apparatus of a tolerated minority, and in the Netherlands because its powers only extended to those who had taken the decision to sign up to full membership of the Dutch Reformed Church. In such circumstances, the option of excommunication – exclusion from the self-selected community – might be a powerful weapon, but it was something of a nuclear option that might do as much damage to the whole community as to the individual. As a result, consistories were much more reluctant to exclude people than in the monopoly culture of Geneva or Scotland: excommunication was much rarer in France than in Geneva, and even rarer in the Netherlands than in France.[47] Paradoxically the consistory's problems were in some ways greater in the Protestant Netherlands than in Catholic France, because many Dutch civil magistrates were unconvinced that there was any need for church courts now that the war of independence had produced Protestantism. As the Amsterdam burgomaster C. P. Hooft put it, the ministers were making the mistake of confusing 'a church which is under the protection of a Christian magistracy and one which is under the cross' – in other words, consistories were only suitable for times of emergency and suffering.[48]

Nevertheless, even in such contested circumstances, the consistory could exercise powerful social sanctions. Calvin had valued discipline so highly because it was the means of protecting the Eucharist from pollution, and that aspect of the consistory's work was a matter of community as well as of theological significance. When the consistory made a decision to readmit an offender to communion after a period of suspension, that was a major statement of the worth and probity of the person so favoured, in a society in which public reputation was a matter of great importance. In Scotland, the distribution of metal tokens provided an admission ticket to communion: for the same reason, these little objects were much prized and often worn prominently for a day or two during the public preparations for communion as visible signs of the community's affirmation of an individual's godliness and worth (some cared enough to forge the tokens, so designs had regularly to be changed).[49]

The strength of Reformed church discipline as it developed in France, the

Netherlands or Scotland was that it genuinely represented its community. It helped to reconcile people in their quarrels, in this respect doing what the gilds had done for much of medieval Europe before the Reformation abolished them. It delivered justice free of charge, unlike most civil courts, and since it was based on individual congregations, it was remarkably reactive and local, unlike the continuing archdeaconry or diocesan courts of the Roman Catholic or English Church, or the new disciplinary courts of Lutheran state Churches administered by princely or civic authority. Reformed discipline was constructed from below, not imposed by a prince: the congregation made decisions as to who would be an elder in the consistory along with the minister. Although they would naturally tend to choose people who were socially prominent, every church member had the opportunity to make judgements on the capacity and moral fitness of their betters, while the authority of the consistory would also benefit from the existing social prestige of its members.

The laity were thus given back power in the Church that the abolition of the gilds had removed: in a consistory which might number between one and two dozen elders, the minister's voice was never guaranteed to carry the day. One of the reasons for the undoubtedly rapid success of the Scottish Reformation was its immediate establishment of a consistory system in the parishes, the 'Kirk Session' – in the 1560s and 70s in the Lowlands, and throughout the Highlands by 1600. In a society dominated by lairds and noblemen, where personal violence and anti-social behaviour were common and which had nothing like the secular system of royal justices of the peace well-developed in contemporary England, this was an authentically local means of community regulation – for ill as well as good, as the coming of the witch-craze in the 1590s was to reveal. We may well recoil from the pettiness, the tyranny and the repression of difference and nonconformist behaviour that were all too likely products of such a system. But there would be no part of Europe in the Reformation or Counter-Reformation that did not experience such disciplinary pressures. Virtually no one enjoyed our luxury of freedom of personal choice, and few would have taken the imaginative leap into envisaging such a luxury or even considering it desirable. At least Reformed discipline set itself the goal of representing its community rather than representing the opinions and preoccupations of inquisitors or princes.

In all circumstances of Reformed disciplinary systems, the responsibility of eldership was heavy and time-consuming for people who usually needed to earn an everyday living as a lawyer, merchant or a farmer, and this unpaid work was generally undertaken with a seriousness and commitment that

17. Heidelberg was the greatest centre of Reformed Protestantism in the early seventeenth century. Its siege and capture by the great Habsburg general Tilly in 1622 was symbolic of the catastrophe that central European Protestants suffered in the Thirty Years' War. The Elector Friedrich V's castle, with its library and magnificent gardens, is shown intact at this stage of the siege; soon it was in ruins.

18a. Even a small English parish (Charsfield, Suffolk) could acquire a fine assembly of Elizabethan communion plate, thanks to the local wealthy Protestant knightly family of Wingfield. Note the communion cup, like an ordinary secular drinking-goblet.

18b. This chalice, presented to Staunton Harold church (Leicestershire) in 1640 at the height of Charles I's confrontation with Scotland and the English Parliament, returns aggressively to medieval forms of eucharistic plate, including sexfoil foot and stem knop: the cross on the cover would also be thought popish. The donor was Sir Robert Shirley, a convinced Laudian who later rebuilt his church in careful and ideologically charged imitation of medieval Gothic.

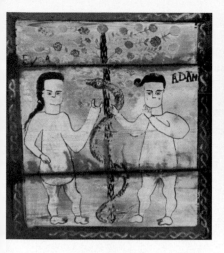

19a. Two panels from the ceiling of Tancs (Tonciu) parish church, Transylvania, near Cluj Napoca: Adam and Eve with the Tree of Knowledge and serpent, and Noah in his ark: probably late seventeenth century. Such figure painting would have been frowned on in western European Reformed church interiors, but notably most images at Tancs are from the Old Testament, a pictorial source less tainted by Catholic 'idolatry'.

19b. The cheerful decoration on the early seventeenth-century Mariners' Gallery at Burntisland parish church, Fife (Scotland), show that even the Reformed Scots were not afraid of depicting angels.

¶ The defcription of the holy Land, conteining the places mentioned in the foure Euangelifts, with other places about the Sea coafts, wherein may

be feene the wayes and iourneys of Chrift and his Apoftles in Iudea, Samaria, and Galile: for into thefe three parts this Land is diuided.

The places fpecified in the Mappe, with their fitua-
tion by the obferuation of the degrees concerning their length and breadth.

Afcalon	65, 24: 31, 32	Corafim	66, 53: 32, 29.	Ior, the other fountaine whence	
Azor	65, 35 : 32.	Dan, one of the Fountaines		Iorden fpringeth 67, 31.33.7	
Bethlehem	65, 55 : 31, 51.	whence Iordane fprin-		Magdalon, called alfo Dalma-	
Bethphage	68, 31, 58.	geth	67,25: 33,18.	nutha	66, 48 : 32, 28.
Bethfaida	66, 51 : 32, 29.	Ennon	66, 40 : 32, 18.	Naim	66, 35: 32,33.
Bethabara	66, 34: 32. 1.	Emmaus	65, 34: 31,59.	Nazareth	66, 56 : 32, 42.
Bethania	66, 31,59.	Ephen	66. 8, 31.	Ptolemais	66, 50 : 32, 58.
Cana of Galile	66, 52: 32,48.	Gadara or Garaza	66,48: 32,29	Samaria the city	66, 22 : 32, 19.
Capernaum	66, 53 : 32,39.	Gaza	65, 10: 31,40.	Sidon	67,15: 33, 30.
Carmel mount	66,31 : 32,50.	Iericho	66, 10 : 32, 1.	Silo	66,27: 32, 19.
Cefarea Straton	66,16:32,25.	Ierufalem	66, 31,55.	Tyrus	67, 33, 20.
Cefarea Philippi	67, 39: 33, 5.	Ioppe	65,40:32,5.	Tiberias	66,44: 32, 26.

THE

20. This 1606 edition of the Geneva Bible's New Testament is prefaced by a map of Palestine (one of the work's innovative features), with the ships conveying a lively sense that the Bible story is contemporary with the seaborne explorations of the Reformation age.

21a. This rood screen of *c.* 1500 at Roxton (Bedfordshire, England) has been cut down to waist-height, losing its upper parts and gallery, and the faces of the saints have been scratched out. These are St Sebastian and St Dorothy.

21b. This tiny bilingual psalter of *c.* 1640, little bigger than this picture, could have fitted unobtrusively in a housewife's purse or a soldier's pack. Its paired Dutch and French text made it saleable to the many French-speaking Protestant refugees from the southern Netherlands in the Protestant United Provinces: the French psalm shown here is in Theodore Beza's translation.

22. In this fresco by Domenichino (Domenico Zampieri, 1581–1641) in the Treasury of S. Gennaro, Naples Cathedral, the local and the universal Church combine against heresy. The Virgin Mary intercedes with her son for the Church: below, Naples's own Saint Gennaro (Januarius) holds up a reliquary containing his famously liquefying blood. Right at the foot are heretics and the books of Luther and Calvin trampled underfoot – and note that heresy has a German moustache.

23a. John Winthrop, the Suffolk gentleman who became first governor of Massachusetts, was at the centre of the New England colonial enterprise: he has been described as America's 'lost founding father'. This portrait of 1834 by Charles Osgood closely follows an original miniature now much damaged.

23b. Derry Cathedral, seen here before Victorian extensions. Built in the 1620s as part of the London colonial city of Londonderry in the Protestant plantation of Ulster, it was modelled on contemporary English urban parish churches, just as the parish churches of colonial Virginia later in the seventeenth and eighteenth centuries imitated the English churches designed by Wren and Gibbs.

24. Anna Maria van Schurman, 'the Learned Maid of Utrecht'. In the background is the tower of Utrecht's former cathedral, and she is surrounded by the curtain which protected her in university lectures.

were not always mere pomposity or self-promotion. Elders had a weighty role to play in reconciling the wounds of their community, and on the principle of Matthew 18, they would succeed if they could end a case without involving their colleagues. A lucky find of the private notebook of one such elder in early seventeenth-century Utrecht, the prominent lawyer Arnoldus Buchelius, reveals that the official records of the Utrecht consistory recorded only about 30 per cent of the disciplinary business in which he was involved: formal minutes would concentrate on matters such as marriage disputes which self-evidently needed some official note to be made, while Buchelius did his best privately to sort out quarrels or secure signs of contrition for bouts of drunkenness or inappropriate dancing. Investigations of the preoccupations of consistories show that in France, the Netherlands or Scotland, the elder was concerned much more than the medieval confessor with sins that could be defined as public rather than private: matters which affected the community as a whole, rather than the inner thoughts of the heart.[50]

One important aspect of Reformation discipline was that it revived the communal aspect of penance that the growth of auricular confession had to a large extent obscured, so that church authorities could involve everybody in the process of making a wrongdoer repentant. Public ceremonies of repentance had never died out in the medieval West: the *auto-da-fé*, after all, was very precisely a communal penitential act (chapter 9, p. 420). The practice of penitents standing in humiliatingly skimpy clothes, bare-legged, in white or sackcloth sheets, during service time, remained common through the medieval centuries, and the principle of public penance was reaffirmed at the Council of Trent. Many bishops and archdeacons in the Elizabethan Church of England, still operating the old court system, made efforts to revive the largely lapsed custom of penitents standing in the town market-place to show their repentance before they processed to their parish church, and it is significant that many of the first instances of this in an English context are connected to clergy who had contacts with the developing Church of Scotland. For if any one part of Protestantism exemplified and systematized the recovery of communal repentance and reconciliation, it was the Scottish Church.[51]

In the matter of penance, the Kirk showed no worries that extrovert traditional outward ceremonial might foster superstition. It actually elaborated on the medieval apparatus of humiliation, the white sheet and bare legs, eliminating only the popish lighted taper held by the penitent, but often replacing that with a symbol of the crime to be repented, such as the sword or knife of a violent quarrel. It introduced a new piece of liturgical church furniture, the stool of repentance, which is otherwise only to be found far away in the Reformed Church of Hungary and Transylvania, from much the same time in the 1560s (see Illustration 14).[52] Evidence of the stool's unfamiliarity in other cultures was provided by the English traveller who in 1598 turned up for worship at St Giles High Kirk in Edinburgh and made for what he thought looked an honourable and conveniently empty seat: the unfortunate gentleman thus provided sustained innocent merriment for the assembled congregation before he eventually fled. The stool of repentance was not like the private setting for repentance represented by the confessionals of the Counter-Reformation or of Lutheran Norway: it was a dramatic public siting of the penitent in the context of public worship. The stool often belied its simple description by having separate sections at different heights for different offences, the worst at the top for extra humiliation – in Elgin, the slanderers were placed lower than the adulterers.[53]

The ritual around this was designed to provide a theatre of forgiveness that would bring an offender back into the fold of the community from outside, a drama which often assumed the form of a cliffhanger serial in several episodes spread over successive Sundays. At its most elaborate this was literally an exercise in what anthropologists would call reducing liminality, for the penitent might move in a series of stages from the kirk prison to the burgh market-place to the kirk door to the stool in the centre of the kirk before finally hearing forgiveness pronounced. As far as possible, the culmination of a series of appearances for the sinner was timed to coincide with one of the occasional communion services, to emphasize the message of forgiveness and reconciliation. Some church buildings had separate entrance-doors for communicants and non-communicants: at communion-time the penitent was customarily situated at the communicant door, so that he or she (dressed in humiliating white or sackcloth) would meet the gaze of the certified godly clutching their communion tokens as they filed into the building.

Once at the stool, and having endured the hour of the sermon under the gaze of the assembled parish, the penitent must make a speech of repentance, and it should be sincere: the congregation was the judge as to whether the tears were real, and there would be more penances to come if the general opinion was that the offender was scorning the system. If the verdict was positive, then the repentant sinner was customarily welcomed back to proper fellowship with a symbolic gesture: a handshake or a kiss. The congregation's participation was not mere voyeurism: sin of whatever variety hurt the whole community, damaging its relationship with God, so

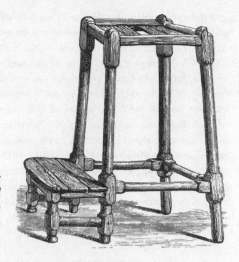

The Stool of Repentance formerly in Greyfriars Old Kirk, Edinburgh: now in the National Museum of Scotland.

it was only right that the whole community should judge and express its forgiveness. This was an ultimate expression of what the Reformation meant: no longer was the act of absolution in the control of a clergyman, but was in the gift of all God's people. Even the clergy were subject to it.

This intensely interventionist society is likely to seem uncongenial to modern westerners (although the modern western tabloid press provides its own not dissimilar and less regulated rituals of public humiliation for specialized classes of sinner). It worked then because people wanted it to work. Rates of reoffending were low. For many, it provided a structure for controlling a frighteningly violent and arbitrary world, and for others a release of personal guilt and conflict. There are instances of people taking the initiative to confess crimes at the stool that could have easily remained secret: the married couple of Aberdeen, for instance, who felt tormented because they had indulged in sex at home during a proclaimed fast of the Kirk, or the visiting Dutch sea-captain, who could easily have sailed away from Leith without coming forward to make repentance at the Leith kirk stool for his spree of drunkenness and fornication in the waterfront red-light district.[54]

From Scotland to Transylvania the Reformed Church derived its disciplinary system explicitly from the Word of God. That gave it an extraordinary self-confidence which made it a good deal less respectful of social rank or convention than was to be expected in early modern Europe. The wealthy and powerful rarely stood at the Scottish stool of repentance, but they were not exempt from the Kirk Session's withering comment, and they paid heavily for their exemption in fines for the Kirk's welfare funds. In 1589 the Kirk of Edinburgh publicly disciplined and witnessed the repentance of Francis, Earl of Bothwell (see above, p. 571) for the crimes of murder and treason. It followed the ceremony with a spirited sermon on the sins of the nobility from Robert Bruce, one of Edinburgh's chief ministers, in front of both Bothwell and the rest of the Scottish noblemen present. Bothwell did rather take the shine off the day's proceedings by raping the daughter of the late Earl of Gowrie after he had left St Giles Kirk, but the very fact that one of Europe's most wayward and dangerous noblemen, one of Scotland's most powerful magnates, had submitted himself to such a public shaming was a remarkable tribute to the range and ambitions of Reformed discipline.[55]

A SPIRIT OF PROTESTANTISM?

Even if we do our best to understand and empathize with the world of iconoclasm, fasting and the Kirk Session, it is not easy to avoid the suspicion that thoroughgoing Protestants were out to create a society corresponding to the definition of Puritanism by that great American newspaper editor H. L. Mencken: 'the haunting fear that someone, somewhere, may be happy'. Certainly Protestants massacred the number of holy days (holidays) which were available for public festivity and private rest, even in England where a suitably purged band of the saints retained a toehold in the Book of Common Prayer. Yet this world would not have worked on repentance and purging alone: it had its own forms of celebration. We have already noted some of them: the special activities which marked out Sunday, now that it had exclusively drawn to it the sacredness of the week away from the old saints' days of the old Church's Kalendar – the sermon, the hymns, the drama of disciplinary reconciliation.

For the first generations, the abolition or simplification of the old Kalendar did not only mean the loss of holidays, but gave a sense of release from ecclesiastical tyranny, symbolized by the deliberate breakdown of the old fasting regulations for Lent. In frontier areas like the Rhineland, Catholic butchers often complained about the advantage that this gave Protestant butchers during the Lenten season.[56] Protestant England rather illogically kept the old rules about eating fish without the religious justification, repeatedly reminding the population that the fishing industry needed support: everyone could agree that this was a good cause, but it did not suggest that hellfire followed the consumption of a Lenten sausage.[57]

There were also new Protestant festivals to compensate for the loss of the saints, usually to do with commemorating Protestant successes. The England of Elizabeth I developed a clutch in the month of November. It was an adroitly morale-boosting choice, since the spirits of northern Europeans are prone to sag as the dark nights lengthen and the cold intensifies, but its origins were in the accident that Queen Elizabeth had come to the throne on the death of her half-sister Mary on 17 November 1558. During the Queen's first decade, without any apparent government initiative, some parishes seem to have begun ringing their church bells and building bonfires on Accession Day: this spread through the nation. In 1588 the English government finally staged its thanksgiving for the destruction of the Spanish Armada in November (perhaps leaving it that late to make sure that the threat was indeed over), so this new festival was appended to rejoicings for the Queen. Even the Scots, who had not been directly involved in the Armada's defeat, were soon celebrating this major deliverance for the faith. Then Catholic conspirators in 1605 again coincidentally chose 5 November for their effort to blow up the opening of the Westminster Parliament with gunpowder.

By now, ordinary English people had made Protestant November very much their own. They consciously used their November celebrations against the government of Charles I when he seemed to be betraying Protestant England in the 1620s and 30s. They pointedly made much of the memory of Queen Elizabeth and King James, while (to government fury) they did not do much at all to celebrate the birthday of Catholic Queen Henrietta Maria, which unfortunately also fell in November. In 1688 Prince Willem of Orange intensified the sense of November destiny still more when he chose that month for the invasion which sent Catholic James II and VII packing from his Atlantic thrones. November was the month when bells, bonfires and fireworks made the English and the Scots pleased to be Protestant. Under James VI, the Scots added August celebrations for King James's deliverance from the Gowrie Plot: this was a conspiracy of 1600 which almost no one but the King believed had actually taken place, but which was still a good excuse for a party.[58]

We should not look only to the secular calendar to find Protestant celebration, but remember that Christianity is based around a celebratory taking of bread and wine: the Eucharist. Many people have the mistaken impression that Reformation Protestants downgraded the Eucharist in their theology and devotional practice: that was not so, though it is much more often the case in modern evangelical Protestantism. By now readers should have realized that it is obviously not the case for Luther. Zwingli, whose eucharistic thought is commonly described as making the Eucharist a 'mere' symbol, would have been horrified at such a caricature, since he saw its celebration as the highest expression of a Christian community, the outward sacred sign of God's loving purpose for the world – in his case, the community of Zürich. Calvin did feel that Zwingli had not got his eucharistic theology quite right, but that is because Calvin wanted to say even stronger things about the presence of God in the service. As we have observed (see above, p. 250) his view of discipline was so strict because he wanted to save the Eucharist from pollution. For Reformation Protestants, reception of the eucharistic elements was one of the most solemn moments of their lives, but it was also a moment of joy and fulfilment. Because it was so special, it was not a moment to be repeated too often: in fact it became much less frequent than Calvin and the early Reformers had planned. Protestants regarded the repetition of Masses in the Roman Catholic tradition as a blasphemous cheapening of the sacrament.

Once more the Scottish Church provides the most striking post-Reformation example of this recasting of the Eucharist as a high festival of community life. Most parishes in Scotland celebrated Communions once or at most twice a year, and they turned them into a major event, usually held in the spring about the time of the old festival of Easter, and culminating in a weekend of high excitement. There would be preparation and catechism running over several days, weeks or even months, then examination and a preparation sermon on Saturday. At the Communion service itself on the Sunday, everyone in the congregation sat at specially erected long tables and passed each other the bread and the cup. As we have seen, there were also likely to be penitents ready to leave the stool of repentance to take up their full place among the people once more. The Communion sermon was one of special solemnity and would often be recorded by both preacher and listener in distinctive notebooks: on the Monday there would be a further gathering, with a sermon of thanksgiving, to allow emotions to cool. This eucharistic festival was a chance for the whole community to gather – thousands, in the case of the towns – for people to straggle in from the hills, to row over from island to island to the kirk (often the Kirk authorities paid for the ferries). It united everyone who had given their allegiance to the national Church. Very frequently, the crowds were so huge that the kirk building could not contain them, and a veritable open-air fairground of events, communal meals and huddles of catechizing sprang up. These great occasions became known as 'holy fairs'.[59]

The Scottish parish festivals of Eucharist became peculiarly entwined with the great national outburst of fervour, anger and excitement that swelled up during the 1620s and 1630s as the royal governments of James VI and Charles I lost touch with the religious feelings of their Scottish subjects. One prime mover was a young clergyman called John Livingston, who never held his own parish because he opposed the growing power of bishops in the Scottish Kirk: instead he travelled extensively in south-west Scotland, and particularly targeted the parish communions, where his preaching galvanized the population. Reportedly the people of Shotts in Clydesdale stood for two and a half hours in pouring rain while he preached in 1630, some swooning not because of the weather but because of the 'strange unusual motion' of his words. This was no dangerous Anabaptist event: it was still firmly in the parochial framework and Calvinist tradition of the Kirk, as was symbolized by the venerable presence during the events at Shotts of that same Revd Robert Bruce who had harangued the thuggish Earl of Bothwell thirty years before (see above, p. 600).[60]

On the other side of the Irish Sea, the Scottish settlers of Ulster, anxious, rootless, looking for identity in a strange land and beset by fears of the Catholic menace around them, also flocked with enthusiasm to the combination of Eucharist and spiritual renewal. They anticipated Scotland's extraordinary events at Shotts in the County Antrim Six-Mile-Water Revival which began in 1625, a 'bright and hot sun-blink of the Gospel': a festival of evangelical fervour in which the beleaguered community felt itself empowered and renewed.[61] One young witness who later became a minister vividly recalled the same patterns of behaviour as were emerging in the Scottish Kirk: 'I have seen them myself stricken, and swoon with the Word – yea, a dozen in one day carried out of doors as dead, so marvellous was the power of God smiting their hearts for sin.'[62] The revival galvanized the Ulster Scots communities over eight years from 1625; the same population, surviving the murderous traumas of the 1641 Rebellion (chapter 12, p. 523), was to go through the same fiery rededication repeatedly in the future, and for better or worse Ulster Protestantism has never lost the tradition to the present day. The revivalist communion gathering was remarkably reminiscent of the great festivals of a Catholic shrine: at much the same time, the Catholic Irish were flocking to St Patrick's Purgatory or the ancient monastic complex of Glendalough. It was also the first example of a phenomenon which has become a key mechanism of evangelical Protestantism worldwide: the revivalist meeting.

It would be difficult to overestimate the importance of these beginnings amid the political and cultural turbulence of an impoverished outer corner of the European Reformation. Emigrants moved on from Scotland and from the Protestant settler culture of Ulster to the north American colonies, taking with them a Presbyterian and evangelical Protestantism which had vigorously rejected bishops over half a century of Scottish struggles from 1638 to 1688. In America, they enshrined the rhetoric of revival because they brought with them the custom of the 'holy fair'. Large-scale seasonal communions, gathering hundreds or even thousands of widely scattered people to them in sudden outpourings of good fellowship and extrovert expressions of religious fervour, were as suited to the American frontier as they had been to the glens, moors and islands of Scotland and Ulster. Revivalism spoke to the excitements and anxieties of the new American settlers as it had done in colonial Ulster after 1625. To Presbyterian ardour was added in the eighteenth century the fervour of English evangelical leaders who felt confined by the newly developed conventions of Anglicanism, and had discovered for themselves the intoxicating religious possibilities of open-air preaching: John Wesley, the early Methodists and George Whitefield. In the American colonies this produced 'the Great Awakening' from the 1730s to the 1760s, one of the most important formative moments in the creation of American culture. Against the mobile, adaptive fervour of the Scots-Irish Presbyterians and English Methodists, rapidly following the moving frontier of colonial north America, southern Anglicans or New England Congregationalists found that their measured piety and cautious investment in ecclesiastical structures put them at a considerable disadvantage. Revivalist enthusiasm still fires the rhetoric of American religion. It has reached the White House and the Pentagon. In the charismatic if unlikely persona of Bill Clinton, descendant of Ulster Protestants, it spoke to its mother-culture in Protestant northern Ireland, with more success in moving towards peace than anyone else had yet achieved in that land overburdened by religious history.

Max Weber, a nineteenth-century German sociologist of genius, constructed out of his understanding of Protestantism a theory which still remains influential, particularly among those who are not historians. In a classic work first published in 1904, *The Protestant Ethic and the Spirit of Capitalism*, he suggested that there was a causal link between these two phenomena, more particularly between Calvinist Protestantism and modern capitalism – thus adroitly standing on its head the contention of Karl Marx and Friedrich Engels that Protestant ideology was the superstructure of change in economy and society. His work formed the basis of the English Christian Socialist R. H. Tawney's equally influential book *Religion and the Rise of Capitalism* (1926). Tawney, who had more refined historical instincts than Weber, both widened and restricted the phenomenon. He pointed out that an urge to accumulate capital and monopolize the means of production can be found in very many cultures and civilizations, but he also contended that this instinct found a particular partner in 'certain aspects of later Puritanism' – individual self-discipline, frugality, self-denial.[63] From vague memories of the combination of these two authorities comes that still frequently heard cliché, the 'Protestant work ethic'.

The Weber-Tawney thesis still has its defenders, and there is much in the picture of the Reformed Protestant ethos which we have explored in this chapter and elsewhere that might make it seem plausible. We have met disciplined, self-reliant people, with a powerful sense of their elect status and ready to defend their right to make decisions for themselves. We have also noted their frequent suspicion of religious art, and in England the growing Puritan suspicion of particular forms of cultural expression such as the theatre: Elizabeth Eisenstein perceptively observes that artists have a vested interest in idleness, and in an audience that loves to stand and stare.[64] Nevertheless it is missing the larger picture simply to find the Weber-Tawney thesis vindicated in particular historical situations, like the late nineteenth-century southern Germany and Switzerland which was the setting for Weber's own observations of contrasting Catholic and Protestant economic and social behaviour. Tawney was of course right in seeing a wider canvas, and he would have been further vindicated had he seen the explosion of emphatically non-Christian Indian, Pakistani and east Asian entrepreneurial energy in the late twentieth century. Above all, there are major questions of cause and effect. Protestant England and the Protestant Netherlands undoubtedly both became major economic powers in the seventeenth and eighteenth centuries – pioneers in economic production and virtuosi in commerce and the creation of capital and finance systems, while formerly entrepreneurial Catholic Italy stagnated. Why?

Any simple link between religion and capitalism founders on both objections and counter-examples. One could point out that rather than taking its roots from religion, this new wealth and power represents a shift from Mediterranean to North Sea which has political roots: particularly the disruption caused by the Italian wars from the 1490s, and the long-term rise of the Ottoman Empire, bringing a terrible social and economic blight to Mediterranean Christian coastal regions (chapter 2, p. 57). Striking counter-examples would be the economic backwardness of Reformed Protestant Scotland or Transylvania. That suggests that the prosperity of England and the Netherlands arose precisely because they were not well-regulated Calvinist societies, but from the mid-seventeenth century had reluctantly entrenched religious pluralism alongside a privileged Church. Just as in the case of Judaism in medieval Europe, tolerated but disadvantaged minorities such as the Protestant Dissenters of Stuart England found the best way to social advancement that was available to them: excluded from political power, ecclesiastical office or the law, they turned to commerce and manufacture. French Huguenots and eighteenth-century English Methodists followed their example.

One powerful objection to the whole notion of a structural or causal link between Reformed Protestantism and capitalism comes from the very dubious further linkage which is often made between Protestantism generally and individualism. Individualism, the denial or betrayal of community, is after all seen as one of the basic components of the capitalist ethos. It is very frequently suggested that medieval Catholicism was somehow more communitarian and collective-minded than the Protestantism which replaced it, which was a dissolvent of community and promoted the sort of individualism which is embodied by that apocryphal cry of Luther, 'Here I stand; I can do no other'.[65] Yet the evidence which I have drawn together here goes against such assertions. Calvinism is a Eucharist-centred and therefore community-minded faith. Its discipline at its most developed was designed to protect the Eucharist from devilish corruption, and the resulting societies formed one of the most powerful and integrated expressions of community ever seen in Europe. Certainly Protestants disrupted some forms of community, the structures created by medieval Catholicism, but they did so precisely because they considered them harmful to the community, just like witches or images. They then rebuilt those communities, and did so most successfully where Reformed Protestantism was at its most effective and thoroughgoing: Scotland, Hungary and New England. Such places were not at the forefront of the birth either of modern individualism or of modern capitalism. In the United States, it is not Congregationalist Salem or Boston that are the best symbols of modern capitalist enterprise, despite their once-flourishing ocean-going trading fleets; it is the determined and foundational pluralism of New York or Pennsylvania's Pittsburgh.

The 'spirit of capitalism' debate shows how sensitive we should be in placing theology in its context before making our efforts to put together cause and effect. Equally we should never forget that theology is an independent variable, capable in the Reformation of generating huge transformations in society, modes of behaviour and the very shape of the year. Reformations and Counter-Reformations always interacted with and were modified by other aspects of the peoples and the societies in which they operated. That will become just as apparent when we turn to consider the most intimate aspect of peoples' lives: their sexuality, their perception of themselves as men and women, and their ways of expressing their most intimate relationships not merely with other human beings but with the world beyond.

15

Love and Sex: Staying the Same

A COMMON LEGACY

Archaeologists investigating human prehistory find that for around 150,000 years there has been no appreciable change in the physiological make-up of male and female human beings: our bodies have remained the same.[1] It is reasonable to suppose that over that timespan we have changed little in our package of emotions and feelings about ourselves and each other, our own bodies and other people's bodies. Certainly for those millennia during which humans have left us written information about themselves, there is abundant evidence that they could feel love, lust, self-assertion: that they could show tenderness and altruism, or play power-games of varying degrees of ruthlessness and sadism with each other. What has changed over time has been the range of ways in which we have been taught to express these feelings and interactions and understand what they are about – how we have seized on available ideologies to give meaning to what we think and do. For 2,000 years – a very short period in this long and mostly lost history of self-understanding – Christianity has become a voice in the long conversation about sexuality. Out of a precarious amalgam of its sacred writings and a good many unexamined presuppositions, it has constructed a series of propositions that it claims encapsulates God's opinions on the subject.

Naturally, like Christianity's pronouncements on many subjects (for instance, on the justification or condemnation of slavery) these propositions have varied greatly over time, often to the point of outright contradiction. The greatest fault-line in Christian attitudes to sex lies in the status of virginity and celibacy relative to heterosexual marriage. Christianity looks to both a Jewish and a Greek inheritance of thought. Judaism exalted marriage and the family because it affirmed the goodness of God's physical creation, but within Greek thought there was a powerful strain of opinion downgrading fleshly pleasures, which runs through the thought of Plato, the most influential voice in Greek philosophy. Early Christianity was much affected by this contrasting attitude, which seeped in through those parts of early Christianity following the Greeks more than the Jews, the 'gnostics' (chapter 2, p. 80). One independent variable were various comments on marriage to be found in the epistles of the Apostle Paul: his personal attitudes to marriage were remarkably cool for a Jew, and some of his remarks provided some fuel for those later commentators who were also less than enthusiastic about marriage.

From the first appearance of hermits and monks on the fringes of the institutional Church in the late third century CE, the status of virginity grew and marriage was relegated to a secondary good, whose virtues were praised by most commentators (nearly all unmarried clerics even if they were not monks) with a certain condescension, or worse. The influential fourth/ fifth-century theologian and biblical Latin commentator Jerome went further than most in exalting virginity at marriage's expense, and he was much echoed later. One of the most widely copied medieval commentators on morality, the thirteenth-century French Dominican Vincent of Beauvais, said bluntly that 'a man who loves his wife very much is an adulterer. Any love for someone else's wife or too much love for one's own is shameful.'[2] The outcome of such attitudes in the medieval Western Church was the long battle waged from the twelfth century to impose compulsory celibacy on all clergy, not just monks as had been the case in earlier centuries.

The Counter-Reformation Church, under strong Protestant attack on this point, completed its affirmation of old certainties in the very last stages of the Council of Trent in 1563. The Council then made it a point of faith to affirm the inviolability of vows for nuns and male clergy, and pronounced anathema (the most solemn curse possible) on anyone claiming (like Desiderius Erasmus and mainstream Protestantism) that 'the married state excels the state of virginity or celibacy, and that it is better and happier to be united in matrimony than to remain in virginity or celibacy'.[3] This theology was starkly expressed in Cardinal Bellarmine's 'larger' catechism of 1598, by definition a document intended for public lay education, when Bellarmine set out a common ancient cliché from the advocates of celibacy: 'Marriage is a thing human, virginity is angelical. Marriage is according to nature, virginity is a thing above nature.'[4] The Protestant Reformation, therefore, brought a momentous change in direction in the Christian history of sexuality. It denied this theology: it reaffirmed marriage and proclaimed that compulsory celibacy, like compulsory seasonal fasting, was part of the papal confidence trick which they had uncovered.

Nevertheless sixteenth-century Protestants and Catholics alike took over most medieval commonplaces about sex, because they listened to what the experts said about it. From its beginnings in the Greek-speaking culture of the Mediterranean seaports, Gentile Christianity borrowed heavily from the pronouncements of pre-Christian Greek and Latin science, fitting a bundle of beliefs derived from Scripture around a pre-Christian cosmology and view of the human body. The medical world's accepted gender scheme assumed the existence of four humours: in combination these dominated the body's content. They had their special characteristics, expressed in the fluids of the body: hot and moist (blood – so a 'sanguine' temperament), hot and dry (choler), cold and dry (black bile, which translates as 'melancholy') and cold and moist (phlegm). Different individuals had different mixtures – producing sanguine, choleric, melancholy or phlegmatic temperaments. Although cold humours were associated with women and hot with men (and Aristotle considered that hotter meant superior), the combination might be distinctive in one particular person. This happily explained why some women broke all the rules by being masterful (note the word): why, for instance, Queen Elizabeth I of England was such a good monarch despite being a woman.[5]

The Christian understanding of the roles of women and men in reproduction were also much influenced by the pre-Christian Aristotle, who presented the act of procreation as depending entirely on male seed. A man's semen contained the entire foetus in embryo: so anything which stopped male seed doing its job was an act of murder – anything, from masturbation to contraception to same-sex sexual relations. The idea was taken up by the second-century Christian teacher Clement of Alexandria, and it has become deeply embedded in the Christian moral tradition, lying behind many of the pronouncements of the modern Roman Catholic church on sexuality. There were further confident pronouncements on the sexual organs in human bodies. The ancient medical expert Galen had said back in the second century CE that males and females were the same human being reversed: ovaries were testicles, the penis a cervix and vagina, and so on. For reasons owing little to logic and everything to the fact that males had thought up this scheme, a witness to men's superiority was that their versions of the various organs hung on the outside, because the natural heat of men required it, rather than hiding away inside the body as did women's (in both sexes, breasts rather complicated the theory).

These assumptions in non-Christian authorities such as Galen were given further resonances by early Christian writers, particularly that towering authority Augustine of Hippo, who during his career as theologian and bishop steadily developed a morbid horror of disorder, which was the product of fallen human self-will. He saw orgasm as the ultimate disorder, and tied it to the Christian myth about the disobedience of Adam and Eve in the Garden of Eden. 'And the eyes of them both were opened, and they knew that they were naked': for Augustine, this crucial moment of the Fall described in Genesis 3:7 was the moment when sexual shame entered the world (this exegesis of the text was unusual, separating Augustine from most biblical commentators in the early Church, especially from those in the Greek and Eastern Churches). Who had started the disobedience, Augustine asked, and thus ushered in disorder and shame to history? A woman, Eve, when she had badgered Adam into eating the apple off the tree. And so all women were a threat to order (though as we will see when discussing sodomy, there were worse disorders of nature than being female). Augustine speculated wistfully about the time before the Fall in Eden, when Adam and Eve's private parts had behaved in an orderly fashion. The Church has been trying to tell private parts what to do ever since.[6]

What Christian theologians asserted about men, women and sexuality was nonsense, but it was ancient nonsense, and humanity has always been inclined to respect the assertion of ancient wisdom. The classical and Christian package of ideas also had a lunatic coherence: it seemed to make sense, explained a baffling aspect of human experience, and contained a good deal of room for flexibility of interpretation. No doubt our own medical theories will seem equally lunatic to generations to come. Eventually in the seventeenth century, medical discoveries showed up the ancient physiological theories for the nonsense they were, but old cliché and new discovery jostled uneasily side by side in discussions of gender, until a new framework of discussion, based on the new idea of the human nervous system, drove out older ideas. And even then, both ancient and revised theories worked towards one agenda: men were superior and women inferior. This consistent agenda can be termed patriarchy, the organization of society for the benefit of males at the expense of females. Even now it fights a rearguard action. It adapted in order to survive, so that its rationale was very different in 1800 from 1500: the notions of maleness and femaleness had been redefined in the intervening years. Society, once integrated by the cosmology of humours and by Galen's theories, with gender a continuum, was from around 1700 conceived in terms of rigidly divided opposites – especially gender. By 1800, men were told that they must exercise rigid self-control and never shed tears; women that, after all, they were not uncontrollable and lustful like Eve, just passive and gentle crybabies, to be shielded from life's brutality.[7]

One might have expected that in the sixteenth century, the more generous or pluralist impulses of humanist scholarship would have an effect in widening the possibilities open to human beings: there was, after all, a strain of opinion among humanists, including Erasmus, that exceptional women should be given access to all-round education. Humanists might also have recommended an end to the double standard in morality that victimized female sexual transgressions more than male. There was nevertheless a double problem: humanist scholars were mostly men, and the powerful lay and ecclesiastical rulers who picked and chose what they wanted to hear from their humanist clients were also mostly men. A good example is Queen Mary I of England's former tutor Juan Luis Vives. He wrote a popular treatise, *The Education of a Christian Woman*, which did indeed recommend education for all women, but that thought was rather overwhelmed by a good deal of traditional talk about women's need to control their passions, battle against their weak nature and obey their husbands. Vives also made explicit a double standard in chastity, based on all the important tasks which fell to the male sex: 'human laws do not require the same chastity of the man as the woman', he said reassuringly: 'men have to look after many things; women are responsible only for their chastity'.[8]

With such texts in mind, one female scholar of the 1970s posed the question 'Did women have a Renaissance?' and having surveyed Renaissance humanism across Europe, came up with a resounding negative.[9] If anything, the formal legal position of women grew worse in the sixteenth century, especially in the Holy Roman Empire, where free cities that had allowed citizenship to women withdrew the privilege: a major factor was the growing adoption of Roman law, which had assumed the inferiority and mental incapacity of women.[10] Crucially, women normally remained barred from that key to power, a classical education. Exceptions were found among those women whom accidents of genealogy destined to hold positions of power, like the two daughters of Henry VIII; likewise in the early years of the Reformation, some Protestants of humanist sympathies (for instance, Sir Anthony Cooke, one of the tutors of Henry's son Edward VI) made sure that their daughters were as well educated as any boy. That mood largely passed in the later part of the century. In the early seventeenth century there was a famous example, 'the learned Maid of Utrecht' Anna Maria van Schurman, who thanks to the enthusiasm of her independent-minded father had a de luxe classical and theological education; with the blessing of the great scholar (and rigid Calvinist) Gijsbert Voetius she even attended university lectures in Utrecht, decorously hidden behind a curtain (see Plate 24). She wrote much about the necessity of educating women as well as she had been, but she was regarded by the male world of scholarship merely as a phenomenon and a wonder, a living demonstration that some women could transcend the limitations of their sex.[11]

When Protestants struggled against what the old Church said about sex, they were therefore still burdened by the fact that most of what was said (or at least recorded in print and manuscript) had been said by men. That led to some surprising modifications of the revolutionary spirit of the Reformers. Medieval Christianity had installed one powerful female who modified Christianity's inbuilt tendency to talk about three male archetypes, Father, Son and (less certainly or consistently) Holy Spirit. She was Mary, the mother of God, who became so all-pervasive in the devotion of the Church both in the West and the East by the fourth century CE. The excesses of Mary's cult amid the busy energy of the pilgrimage industry repelled Protestants right from Luther's first condemnations, and that was a major incentive in destroying both pilgrimages and the imagery which was associ- ated with them (chapter 3, pp. 155-6). Yet both Luther, who decided that images were not important, and Zwingli, who decided that they were, and therefore must be destroyed, alike treated the Mother of God with genuinely deep reverence and affection. They did so because she was a guarantee of the Incarnation of Christ – an idea which some more radical and adventurous spirits in the Reformation were exploring anew and sometimes denying (chapter 4, pp. 182-8).[12]

There were other reasons for leading Reformers to treat Mary with kid gloves. Even when Calvin took a much harder line on her cult than Luther, Zwingli or Bullinger, he shared the insistence of all Protestant Reformers on one very surprising reaffirmation of traditional Catholic doctrine, that Mary had remained a virgin not only in the birth of Jesus Christ but throughout her life: she was 'ever-virgin'. This was surprising because the doctrine of Mary's perpetual virginity defies all the criteria of Protestant views of Scripture, as Erasmus had already made clear before the Reformation started. It is based on allegory and a discrepant Greek or Latin translation of a verse in the Hebrew original of Isaiah's prophecies (chap- ter 2, p. 101), plus a good deal of special pleading around references in the New Testament to Jesus's brothers and sisters – who have to become his cousins or older step-siblings in order to preserve Mary's perpetual virginity. Normally Protestants would gleefully have followed Erasmus in ignoring such arguments; logically they should have said like him that the doctrine could not be found in Scripture. They had a particular incentive to do so, because to disagree with Erasmus on this matter was to confirm the old Church's privilege of making doctrine through its control of tradition, rather than simply looking to Holy Scripture for answers. It was a dangerous line to take, which threatened any Protestant defiance of traditional doctrine.

Despite this, Protestants ignored Erasmus on the perpetual virginity: they rediscovered a taste for medieval allegorical interpretation, which in other circumstances they would have regarded as distinctly suspect, and they pointed confidently to the Catholic proof-texts Ezekiel 44:2 and Isaiah 7:14.[13] At one level, one can ascribe this neurotic attachment to the perpetual virginity among the magisterial Reformers to the general worries about sexuality that thanks to Augustine have been especially pervasive within western Christianity. Jesus Christ and his mother needed to be distanced from the more messy realities of human reproduction, if one was to show true love and reverence for him, however much the Church continued to stress the doctrine of his true humanity in solidarity with the first Council of Nicaea and the Council of Chalcedon. At a more conscious theological level, a vital real impetus was once more the challenge from voices more radical than mainstream Protestants. Many radicals had indeed looked at the Bible and noted that the New Testament said that Jesus had brothers – so they were more perceptive and logical advocates of 'scripture alone' on this matter than the likes of Luther, Zwingli or Calvin.

The trouble for the mainstream Reformers was a different issue, which was one of the other major concerns of radicals: the affirmation of adult against infant baptism. In both cases the question of scriptural authority was the same. Two beliefs which the magisterial reformers felt passionately were valid and important for Christianity, the perpetual virginity of Mary and the necessity of infant baptism, had distinctly shaky justification in scripture. Any admission of that meant toying unhappily with some notion of Church authority in addition to the authority of scripture, and that meant vulnerability to radicals and conservatives alike. One Lutheran spokesman, Hermann Busche, innocently let the cat out of the bag when debating with Anabaptists at Münster in 1533, while debate was still possible in that ill-fated city. After admitting that infant baptism was not explicitly found in the Bible, he said that there were many things 'not mentioned in the Bible which are still perfectly acceptable. For example the perpetual virginity of Mary or that the Bible nowhere mentions the baptism of the apostles.'[14] It was with such debates in mind that Mary's perpetual virginity assumed the importance that it did. When Andreas Osiander of Nuremberg wrote to Huldrych Zwingli in 1527 that the sum total of religion consisted in the satisfactory proof of the Virginity of Mary, or when in the same year Johannes Oecolampadius of Basel told Zwingli in strikingly similar terms that the whole of Christendom stood or fell on the acknowledgement of Mary's perpetual virginity, it was because they wrote in the aftermath of the first radical assertions that Jesus Christ was no more than a prophet.[15]

So as we explore how Reformation and Counter-Reformation affected

European sexuality, we will certainly find change, but just as in the case of witchcraft we must also be alert for shared beliefs and presuppositions which the Reformation did not disturb, or at least pretended not to disturb, for a variety of reasons which were not always made explicit. People do not always do what they are told, even when they indignantly insist that they do; nowhere in human behaviour is this more apparent than in sexual behaviour. The story of both Reformation and Counter-Reformation is full of successful subversions of patriarchy by women, and full of other discreet adaptations of public ideals to reality. It is also a fascinating dialogue between theology and circumstance: sometimes Christian theory was capable of transforming situations, while sometimes theologians discreetly found ways of dealing with and explaining situations in danger of escaping their control. To examine the Reformation and Counter-Reformation in relation to marriage, gender, sexuality and the family is to weigh up that balance of massive practical continuity against equally significant change and transformation.

THE FAMILY IN SOCIETY

What did early modern Christians say about the family, and what was the reality behind the theology? Several decades of effort by modern scholars at reconstructing how people actually lived together and brought up their children in previous centuries makes it possible to sketch some generalizations about family structure in the age of the Reformation, and what is striking is that the basic structures did not change. From at least the late medieval period to the Industrial Revolution there were two forms to be found in Europe: the 'extended' and the 'nuclear' family. Geographical distribution was not absolute or rigid, but there were clear and significant dominances in the two types. In eastern and in Mediterranean Europe, together with the Celtic far west of the Atlantic Isles (Ireland and western Scotland), the dominant type was that of multi-generational households, which included extended patterns of kinship.

By contrast, north-western European society – Scandinavia, the Holy Roman Empire and the Netherlands, northern France, England and English-speaking Scotland – was dominated by the nuclear family model. This is our basic pattern of continuity, which seems to have been unaffected by religious change. The divide in Europe was not a match between the religious divisions brought by the Reformation: the dates of its establishment well predate the Reformation, and the north-west area includes both northern

France (whereas the Huguenots found their stronghold in the south) and southern Germany, which as we have seen was eventually won back for the Counter-Reformation. Contrariwise, the eastern area of extended family patterns includes Hungary, Transylvania and Poland-Lithuania, so it both straddles the Catholic/Orthodox divide and includes the richly mixed religious environment that saw Reformed Protestantism and varieties of radical anti-Trinitarian Christianity flourish.[16]

The continuity and stability of the nuclear family in north-western Europe is remarkable. Certainly in England there is good evidence for its presence in the fourteenth century, and one cannot say that any social function which the nuclear family was playing in 1400 was any less well-developed then than in 1700.[17] Moreover, the institution has largely survived the Industrial Revolution into the twenty-first century (with one significant difference, as we will see). What were its characteristics? They can be well seen in the intensive research done on the English situation. Most obviously, a typical nuclear family household consisted only of two generations, parents and children: few other members of the family lived there. The very elderly tended to continue living in their own home, or perhaps with an unmarried child – again, therefore, in two-generation units. This is not to say that such families did not value kin ties; they did, at all social levels. But wider kin did not live in the household, and there was an individuality and flexibility about how people kept in touch with and drew on the resources of their kin. This was summed up in England in the fact that the word 'cousin' was used in a highly adaptable way to describe all sorts of relationship, forming a 'selective and voluntary basis' to kindred.[18]

Within this two-generational structure, people married relatively late, in their middle and late twenties. For seventeenth-century Englishmen, the age hovered at around twenty-eight, for women just over twenty-six – a rapid fall in these ages began only after 1700.[19] This was not because marriage was difficult to achieve: technically it was very easy to accomplish, needing only the consent of the couple, and attempts at reform in the Reformation generally did not make much practical difference to that. The late marriage age had importance consequences: it affected family size. In a society which was normally efficient in curtailing extra-marital pregnancy, the first pregnancy was late; that was a very effective way of limiting population growth. However, there was a further dimension of the very small average gap between the age of husband and wife: it made the all-pervasive theory of patriarchy rather less convincing in practice. It might not be that easy for a twenty-eight-year-old to convince an adult wife around eighteen months younger (who, as we will see, commonly had lived away from the parental home for ten years or so previously) that he had a God-given right to rule. Marriage in the nuclear family was therefore open to constant negotiation between patriarch and supposedly deferential wife.

The one feature of the early modern nuclear family alien to modern versions of the same institution was the presence of servants: instead of kin, unmarried servants lived in the household, except in the humblest and poorest units. In a society which mostly lived in rural communities and supported itself by its own farming, servants were essential in making a household and a farm function, in a way which is now almost inconceivable in our largely urban society, supported by readily available food, the convenience of supermarkets, and the household gadgets of the electric and digital age. Servants were in plentiful supply because early modern Europe was a much more mobile society than is often now realized. There were plenty of people who expected to travel to look for work and security in their early twenties before the customary age of marriage; they would become either farm or household servants or enter the system of apprenticeships and journeymen that provided the training programme for most crafts and trades.[20] So servants were mostly at a particular stage in their lifecycle, before they in turn could marry and found similar nuclear units: they were teenagers or twenty-somethings. This phenomenon of 'lifecycle servants', the one difference from the twenty-first-century family, was highly significant for the nature of social relationships generally, and it meant that nuclear families were paradoxically less fixated on blood-relatives than now. Children grew up in the presence of outsiders: household servants were usually lively young adults, but like the family's children they had no appointed part in making decisions which affected the family, and so they were in a sense on the same level as the children themselves.

Why has the nuclear family proved so long-lasting? It was economically efficient, and adaptable to new circumstances. In time of sudden crisis it could rapidly expand its focus and reactivate contact with kin as appropriate, while its formation consciously related to economic opportunity.[21] Such households were usually only established when it was economically possible to do so: hence the late age of marriage. For instance, both the percentage of the population marrying and the actual age at which they did so can be shown to relate to the level of wages in the wage-earning part of the population.[22] The nuclear family also experienced a different sort of flexibility: a high turnover within marriage because of the death of one partner. Up to one-third of marriages in Stuart England were second or later marriages – in the much-studied village of Clayworth in Nottinghamshire, for instance, 39 per cent in the late seventeenth century. Between a quarter and a fifth of all seventeenth-century children had lost one birth-parent: a much higher proportion than in the 1980s, when the proportion of children experiencing a step-parent in a marriage was one in six.[23] As a result, the Church's insistence on lifelong marriage meant something very different then than now: one partner or other would have the experience of serial monogamy at much the same rate as is now created by the secular deaths of marriages through divorce or legal separation.

The European age structure also had significant influences on the thinking of society. The population was young, although not as young as in many modern developing countries, where the proportion of under-fourteens may be more than half. In England between 1541 and 1751, the highest proportion in the population of those who were fourteen and under occurred in 1556 (37 per cent), the lowest in 1671 (29 per cent) – those who were sixty and over hit a low point after years of disease in 1566 (7 per cent) and a high in 1716 of 10 per cent.[24] The large proportion of the young was a great incentive for society on either side of the Protestant and Catholic divide to emphasize and enforce hierarchy and obedience, both in rhetorical terms and with the rod: otherwise the hordes of boisterous and inexperienced youth might bring chaos. At the same time, the aged had a certain rarity value, and there was a predisposition in society to treat their opinions with respect – a further reinforcement for the hierarchical values of the age. Since women then as now were liable to live longer than men, this gave elderly women a useful chance to be key fifth columnists against patriarchy. Aged nuns and widows had a lifetime's experience of manipulating the rhetoric of the patriarchal system to their own advantage, while widows could also exercise the primeval skills of mothers and grandmothers in intimidating their offspring with a cold stare or sustained barrages of good advice. With time on their hands and a lively consciousness of the approaching afterlife, elderly women often became key players either in enforcing religious norms or promoting religious change.

One should not underestimate another continuity in the nuclear family: it could be the centre of intense emotion. That might well turn bad (the intensity of human relationships being what it is), but many people may actually have enjoyed being mothers, fathers and children, just as they still can even amid the most dire economic and social stress. There was a fashion among late twentieth-century historians (particularly those influenced by French social history) to assert that medieval or early modern families were radically different from those of today, and that affection was largely missing from family relationships. The evidence for these assertions was always selective, and it has crumbled whenever subjected to sustained investigation.

Much of it was based on the particularly abundant evidence from elite families in England, where the peculiarities of English inheritance law distorted norms and were likely to exaggerate the constant temptation among landed elites to turn marriage into a commercial transaction.[25] There is plenty of testimony from both medieval and Reformation Europe that it was as possible to associate love and marriage then as now. Parents could love each other and their children. Whether they were rich or poor, it is to exercise the condescension of posterity to suppose that they were incapable of mourning the deaths of spouse or child as deeply as at any time in human history.

We will see (chapter 16, p. 648) that the Reformation did make a new contribution to this, as clergy began to experience marriage for themselves and comment on it. One might not expect the Reformed Protestant Church of Scotland to be a witness for romantic love, but in its first official provision for marriage in 1560, when the infant Kirk was organizing itself through its *First Book of Discipline*, it already emphatically declared that the attraction between young people was 'a work of God'. So seriously did the Scottish ministers take this principle that they were prepared to override the commonplace assumption of both Catholic and Protestant that marriages should have parental consent. The *First Book* said that if parents stood in the way of their children's desire for 'no other cause than the common sort of men have, to wit lack of goods and because they are not so high-born as they require', then the minister should try and win the parents round – but if that did not work, he should overrule them and go ahead with a marriage. 'For the work of God ought not to be hindered by the corrupt affections of worldly men': a principle worthy of any romantic novelist.[26] One can find echoes of this conviction in Reformed Protestantism all over Europe.

North-west Europe's distinctive patterns of nuclear family life in the Reformation years carry with them one great question-mark: given the late age of marriage, how should we account for the missing sexual years for the teenagers and twenty-somethings, the household servants, the apprentices and journeymen waiting to take their place in the system and establish their own family units? Children may have physically matured into puberty rather later than they do now, but the evidence for that is shaky; in any case, that still leaves a gap of around a decade of sexual maturity unfilled. On this question, there is a great silence in the sources, except for the noise of authority calling incessantly for chastity. Not everyone can have listened to these calls. Certainly the missing years did not give rise to high rates of bastardy. There were fluctuations, but for the period 1580–1660 the overall bastardy rate in the English part of the nuclear family system was as low as about 3 per cent of all births. Could there have been much use of contraceptive practice? Certainly there was knowledge of various contraceptive methods, but the more research has been done on them, the less overall effect they seem to have had on the birthrate before the eighteenth century.[27]

Might there have been courtship customs which acted as a safety valve? In many parts of north-west Europe there is evidence that among the poor there was a custom which formed no part of the Church's official moral system: the formal sharing of a bed by courting couples, subject to widely recognized constraints about what sort of sexual contact was permissible. When the custom arrived in north America, where it lasted into the nineteenth century, it was known as 'bundling', but curiously there is an almost total silence about the practice from the obvious possible source for its American manifestation, England.[28] What does that leave? Apart from the chastity recommended by the authorities, the alternatives would include masturbation, heavy petting, heterosexual anal intercourse, and resort to prostitutes – there is plenty of evidence for that last activity, though as we will see, official attitudes to prostitution hardened in the sixteenth century (chapter 16, p. 632). There have been some attempts to assess this most private of areas in human experience: the tentative conclusion is that before the eighteenth century, much more heterosexual sexual activity was non-penetrative, and therefore non-procreative, than it was later.[29] And in a world of small crowded houses where it was routine for people of the same sex to share beds, there was another alternative: the discreet practice of homosexuality.

THE FEAR OF SODOMY

In any period of history, attitudes to same-sex emotional and genital activity are a useful litmus test of the nature of attitudes to sexuality generally. Thus the history of homosexuality in the medieval and Reformation epochs instantly provides confirmation of the dominance of patriarchal assumptions, because that history, in relation to Roman Catholicism and Protestantism alike, is largely about the fears of homosexual activity among males. This was the central phenomenon in a range of sexual activities then normally given the collective label sodomy. Male homosexuality involves a group which has generally been seen as marginalized in the Judaeo-Christian tradition – yet this group by definition overlaps with the group which has undoubtedly been dominant in the Judaeo-Christian tradition: that is, men. So a man in Reformation Europe who found his emotional or sexual preferences were primarily for the same sex could step in and out of roles of power. Contemporary expression of same-sex sexual preference, just as in repressive sexual cultures today, involved strategies for concealment and disclosure: sometimes for appearing visible, distinctive and available in some culturally recognizable way, sometimes being able to melt into the background of the dominant gender identity – for saying things obliquely or keeping significant silences. John Calvin would have recognized the character of the Nicodemite in the closet gay man.

In the late nineteenth century, optimistic pioneers of gay self-assertion made much of the Renaissance as an age when humanists rediscovered the more generous attitudes revealed in much literature from the classical past to same-sex love, both male and female. It is true that the Renaissance did inspire a genre of poetry and prose imitating classical homosexual models. As a young man Theodore Beza left a hostage to fortune in a published collection of his French poetry by including a set of verses addressed to a male and a female intimate friend. He playfully said that they both wanted to have him ('*tenere Bezam*'), but if forced to make the choice, he would prefer dear Audebert to dear Candida, while quieting with a little kiss any protests the spurned girl might make. Catholics led by the embittered Jérôme Bolsec exploited this sexual *bonne-bouche* mercilessly when Beza had become a great Reformer in Geneva (chapter 5, p. 243) but probably the apprentice humanist was only trying out his skills as a writer of fashionable classical verse.[30]

For others who had no doubts about their same-sex preference, classical literature could provide a framework for understanding and expressing their feelings, as well as the possibility of making them respectable in the eyes of other people. In Venice, that most cosmopolitan of cities, a remarkable example is provided by a raunchy study of *Alcibiades the schoolboy* by a Conventual Franciscan friar called Antonio Rocco, which he published there in the mid-seventeenth century. Fr Rocco graphically used the theme of this notoriously ambiguous Athenian playboy charmer to trumpet the superiority of same-sex relations over heterosexual: 'if there are other Paradises, I willingly trade them for this one'. There was nothing theoretical about Rocco's advocacy, to judge by the details in worried investigations by the Venetian and Roman Inquisitions into his private life, some time before his book was published, and also considering the outspoken praise of sodomy that was attributed to one of his clergy associates. Yet Rocco's book was widely read, and he died in his bed uncondemned.[31]

Rocco was exceptionally lucky as well as exceptionally candid. Humanist antiquarianism remained a minor strain in comparison with the majority voice in the writing of the period: the predominant tone is deep panic, which parallels the great reluctance in most humanist texts to challenge the existing stereotypes of women. In fact little had changed in attitudes to sodomy since that landmark 'formation of a persecuting society' in western Europe back in the eleventh and twelfth centuries (chapter 1, p. 26). Previously, Christianity had shown an ambiguity about homosexual behaviour, not surprisingly considering the contrast between the total silence of Jesus Christ on the subject and the obvious hostility from the Apostle Paul. The Church indeed showed some surprising forms of acceptance of same-sex sexual behaviour in a Christian context: some eastern Orthodox liturgical books even provided ceremonies which gave formal blessing to same-sex friendship. The twelfth-century Western Church, in its widening efforts to bring a new discipline to European society, enrolled sodomites in a demonic pantheon of social and theological deviants, the enemies of good Christians: other occupants of this category were heretics, Jews and even eventually malevolent lepers.[32] Thereafter, homosexual behaviour was seen as so bad that it even shocked the devil: 'a sin so odious that the fame of it will fright the damned in the darksome Pit' was the description by the French Huguenot poet Guillaume du Bartas in his internationally bestselling poem 'The week.' It is interesting that all through the most lurid testimony produced (usually by judicial torture) in the European witch-craze of the sixteenth and seventeenth centuries, virtually no witches were recorded as being involved in homosexual activities – their orgies were heterosexual. Some poets and playwrights developed a literary motif that although the offspring of sexual unions between witches and Satan customarily turned out to be sodomites, Satan himself was not pleased by this outcome – 'the Devil if he saw it sure would fear it' was the Elizabethan writer Michael Drayton's opinion of the monstrous sodomitical moon-calf twins resulting from such a union, in his poem 'The Moon-calf.'[33]

This horror was made all the worse by the sensational vagueness of the language involved. Sodomy was a general word, wider than just homosexual behaviour as understood today; it was part of a notion of extreme debauchery that involved a whole variety of unregulated sexual acts. Moreover, because sodomitical acts were reckoned to be an aspect of general debauchery, it was very difficult to imagine on the basis of the official tirades that these acts denoted or defined a particular group of people. There was no descriptive term at all in the prescriptive literature for the notion of a homosexual identity; sodomy was a matter of corrupted individuals making choices to carry out certain acts. All people could fall, and the consequences were dire, not just for the individual but for all society. So in 1509, a bad year for Venice, the patriotic journal-keeper Girolamo Priuli blamed the Serene Republic's humiliating military defeat at Agnadello on God's displeasure at the combined (and equally shocking) misdeeds of Venetian sodomites and randy nuns – both groups were perverting nature by their activities.[34]

While Augustine had seen all sexual activity as associated with disorder, sodomitical sexual activity was such an intense form of this disorder that it resulted in total chaos in God's natural creation. This was exemplified in the Bible by the fire, earthquakes and salt-storms which had brought the fall of Sodom and Gomorrah, and by the Apostle Paul's link between disobedience to God's commands and same-sex activity, spelled out in his epistle to the Romans (Romans 1:26–7). Therefore sodomy was linked to any group which could be represented as threatening the structure of society. The medieval Catholic Church used the fear of sodomy in this way in relation to heretics such as the southern French dualist Albigensians (famously, the word 'bugger' is supposed to be derived from dualist Bulgar or Bogomil heretics from the Balkans). In a similar fashion, we have already seen the Jesuit expert on witchcraft Martin Del Rio see witchcraft as Satan's next ploy after heresy (chapter 13, p. 567). In Spain, where witches were comparatively safe, the Inquisition's punishment was the same for sodomites and unrepentant heretics – burning without benefit of strangulation: between 1570 and 1630 around 150 'sodomites' suffered this terrible fate.[35]

With a similar agenda, during and after the Reformation, Protestants linked sodomy to popery, helped by the old Church's commitment to a celibate Roman clergy, who were seen as active and proselytizing practitioners of sodomy. The polemicist of the early English Reformation John Bale became quite obsessional on the subject: perhaps this was fuelled by some traumatic personal experience of abuse during his years as a Carmelite friar, but his denunciations of Catholic clergy's 'changing of the natural use unto a use against nature' also carried the theological resonance (using the Apostle Paul's arguments in Romans 1:26–7) that all people were tempted to fall back into the unnatural vice of popery, in the same manner as contemporary theory saw all people as liable to fall into sodomitical activity. Both vices were forms of idolatry, perverting humankind's true purpose of worshipping God.[36] Not only Catholics or Protestant heretics faced the sodomy stereotype. Everyone saw the Turks and Muslims generally as habitual practitioners of sodomy. It was an aspect of the real threat they posed to the very existence of Christian Europe, an attitude interestingly mirrored in modern fundamentalist Islam's view of the evil materialist West. When Europeans created overseas empires by grabbing land from indigenous populations, they frequently associated the practice of sodomy with the native peoples they were encountering, which was a convenient way of making them less than human and so justifying their maltreatment and exploitation (an equally useful ploy was to describe them as habitual cannibals).[37]

There was a dilemma in adopting this official blanket hostility. Commentators were uncertain as to whether they should be instructively revealing or prudently concealing the awfulness of sodomy: it was a sin, in the phrase of English law, 'not to be named among Christians', and since sodomy was seen in ecclesiastical theory as a universal temptation, to undertake that naming might put ideas in people's heads. This was the problem faced by the star preacher of fifteenth-century Italy, Bernardino of Siena, who was strikingly fond of frank discussion of sexual matters in his sermons: a favourite theme of his was denunciation of sodomitical acts, both heterosexual and homosexual. A number of mothers in the audience at his open-air performances in Siena became so furious when he named shocking sexual activities in front of their daughters that on one occasion in 1427 they marched out of the piazza, leaving the preacher lamely shouting after them 'Don't go, don't leave; wait, so that you perhaps hear things that you haven't ever heard!' That was, of course, precisely what the ladies were determined to avoid.[38] Similarly in Beza's Geneva, when in 1568 the city authorities took the very rare step of prosecuting a woman repeatedly involved in lesbian sexual activities, the leading Genevan lawyer Germain Colladon privately advised that 'it is such a case in which one is well advised not to publish the details of this case, only that it is about a detestable and unnatural crime'.[39]

In the privacy of lawyers' offices, by contrast, there was frequently a remarkably precise assessment of deviant sexual behaviour. The city courts of Geneva might use the catch-all label of sodomy in their prosecutions, but in the voluminous records that they have left us concerning these prosecutions, they show an ability to discriminate between cases that indicates a surprising degree of convergence with modern western definitions of sexual activity beyond married heterosexual sex (combined, of course, with a completely different punitive attitude in dealing with such cases). In cases of rape, Geneva's lawyers were able to see that trauma caused by rape might lead to the victim making a false accusation in later life. In their investigations they could define cases of child sexual abuse by adults, and separate those out from cases of childish sexual experimentation or consensual sex between adults of the same sex. They might also investigate the motives of a child-abuser, and they demonstrated on occasion that they were aware that abusers had often themselves been abused, although the courts' bewilderment that children and even parents would not immediately report cases of child abuse is revealed in the intensity of their questioning on this problem. In the case of sodomy between adults, to a surprising degree, Geneva's judges saw same-sex sexual activity as an unlikely lapse for those who could be shown through cross-questioning also to have engaged in heterosexual acts, and they treated differently men who had engaged only in same-sex sexual activities. In this respect lawyers were ignoring the opinions of theologians about the universal temptation of sodomy and approaching something like the modern conception of a separate homosexual identity.[40]

In fact the idea of sodomy publicly promulgated by legal and clerical authorities became so horrific and alien that it was difficult for ordinary people to associate it with behaviour in which they were involved, or which in their crowded everyday lives they witnessed going on between others. Same-sex sexual behaviour actually recorded in the archives is far from disordered; it is in fact a parasite on the overwhelmingly family-based structure of early modern society, and a predictable consequence of people of the same sex regularly sharing beds. Homosexual activity undoubtedly acted as one important outlet for the 'missing years' of sexuality before the late age of marriage, and so it formed a common part of the family lifecycle. Evidence for this becomes apparent from some Italian cities like Florence and Venice where records are abundant, and although Italians were seen by contemptuous northern Europeans as particularly prone to perversion, it is likely that this simply meant that southerners had a different public etiquette about revealing what they were doing. Bernardino of Siena clearly recognized this 'lifecycle homosexuality' in the culture of his native Tuscany, although naturally he regarded it as the entrance to the pit of hell. It is not surprising that even in northern Europe, when ordinary people were brought before the courts on sodomy charges, they often seemed bewildered that what they had done could be associated with the crime not to be named among Christians.[41]

Above all, homosexual activity throughout most of Reformation and Counter-Reformation Europe mimicked the ordered authority structure of the family by being characteristically a hierarchical activity between superior and inferior: adult and adolescent, master and servant, schoolmaster and pupil, college tutor and undergraduate. Thus it was far from disordered or the gateway to anarchy.[42] The humanist inheritance of comment in classical literature provided a model for this, since such asymmetry was the usual way in which classical authors described same-sex relationships – as in the case of Alcibiades, on which the Venetian priest Antonio Rocco had seized.

Hierarchically asymmetrical homosexual relationships fulfilled social and educational functions within the same-sex institutions of society – especially in churches and convents, schools and universities. In such controlled settings, the authorities who made such loud noises about the appalling evil of sodomy might show a surprising degree of toleration, or at least lethargy.

Two cases from Tudor England where schoolmasters abused their positions provide examples. In 1594 the Archdeaconry Court of Colchester summoned an Essex schoolmaster for 'beastly behaviour among his scholars', but it seems to have taken no further action when he failed to appear to answer the charge. Much more high-profile was the scandal at Eton College in 1541 when investigations into a theft of some school plate accidentally revealed that the headmaster Nicholas Udall was sexually involved with one of his boys. Udall was examined by the Privy Council and suffered a brief imprisonment, but his high-flying career in schoolmastering (featuring much enthusiastic beating) was not for long interrupted, quite apart from his output of pious evangelical writings and bawdy drama – he was one of the period's great survivors.[43] If officialdom could be so inconsistent in its reaction to flagrant cases, it is predictable that in everyday life there are also indications of practical long-term toleration of persistent same-sex behaviour, often until it became tangled up in some other dispute, such as rivalry between tradesmen – much the same pattern of long delay and sudden external provocation, indeed, as can be found in some witchcraft accusations.[44]

Caught between the reality of hierarchical inequality in same-sex activity and the concentration on acts rather than identities in the condemnatory literature, an individual of the period needed a good deal of imagination and self-confidence to imagine lifelong adult homosexual relationships based on equality: it was almost as difficult as imagining thoroughgoing atheism. There was indeed one well-known visible social model of such same-sex relationships, the position of male favourites in the courts of some male monarchs (such as Henri III of France, James VI and I of Scotland and England, or in the historical literature of the time, the fourteenth-century Edward II of England). The role of the favourite was nevertheless not an encouraging one, for more than one reason: first because it was the creation of those strange exalted beings, monarchs, and thus remote and exotic behaviour to common folk, but second because it aroused strong social disapproval precisely through offending against hierarchy. Favourites rarely possessed the independent social standing giving them the right to be so intimate with one of God's anointed, let alone the right to exercise the power and patronage that stemmed from such a position. Given patriarchal assumptions, the favourite's male status was far more threatening to hier-archy than that of low-born royal mistresses, who as women were regarded as of no consequence in the structures of power. Literary hangers-on of royal male favourites (such as the philosopher-politician Francis Bacon to James I's Duke of Buckingham) made unhappy efforts to conceptualize their patrons' position in terms of another classical model, the friendship of equals: the frequent awkwardness of what they said on the subject testifies to the problems of categorization that the role brought.[45]

The model of intimate and equal same-sex friendship was more safely and unselfconsciously applied to situations of great adversity such as that of Protestants under persecution. John Foxe, in his account of the letters passing between the imprisoned and soon-to-be martyred John Careless and John Philpot in the reign of Mary I of England, depicts some surprisingly emotional and even erotic exchanges of letters between them. Careless, the subject of playful puns from Philpot on his surname, came up with his own affectionate set of biblically generated plays on words: 'O pot thrice happy, in whom Christ hath wrought a great miracle, altering thy nature, and turning water into wine, and that of the best, where out the Master of the feast hath filled my cup so full, that I am become drunken in joy of the Spirit through the same.'[46] One parallel is the practice of some English and Scottish Puritan ministers in publishing rhapsodic devotional writings which portrayed their relationship with Christ in terms of the biblical Song of Songs: Christ was the bridegroom and they were the very willing bride (reminiscences from eighteenth-century Scotland suggest that the writings of one of these ministers, Samuel Rutherford, were sometimes read as pornography in default of anything else available). Probably unconsciously, these Puritans were echoing the Spanish mystic John of the Cross, but rather than sharing John's mystical concerns they may have had a pastoral motive arising from a Protestant context. Married clergy in every age have needed to reconcile their strongly asserted personal masculinity with the feminine role of nurture and care that is such an important part of the clerical pastoral task. Puritan devotional writers may have found that a reassuringly biblical feminine role helped to square the circle.[47]

Yet the evidence of court depositions occasionally enables us to glimpse people who were prepared to go further than such rhetoric, contradicting both hierarchical models and the official separation of sexual act and sexual identity: they linked up their same-sex instincts and actions to the language of love between equals. Such was the (married) baker of Frankfurt-am-Main Ludwig Boudin, who at the end of some passionate embraces with an acquaintance urged him to come home to sleep with him or 'he would get crazy' – this was by no means his only declaration of love for male friends in the last two decades of the sixteenth century, before his rather exceptional prosecution by the normally indifferent secular courts of Frankfurt. From Catholic Europe, the vigilance and archival meticulousness of the Portuguese Inquisition have preserved for us a number of love letters, some of which reveal long-standing same-sex relationships.[48]

Such instances do seem isolated in the sixteenth and seventeenth centuries, and what might be termed a recognizably gay subculture emerged only right at the end of our Reformation era, in the 1690s. From then on, some individuals began making choices of a continuous and unambiguous homosexual identity and lifestyle, and interestingly they did so in late seventeenth-century Europe's two most pluralist cities, Amsterdam and London. In both settings a gay sub-culture emerged and has never since been suppressed: clubs and pubs, a distinctive language and shared jokes which shaped a semi-public lifestyle shot through with parody and irony. In turn this provoked periodic purges and moral panics targeted specifically on homosexuals, which had not been possible previously in early modern London or Amsterdam when there was no such social phenomenon to panic about.[49]

Why did this remarkable revolution in western culture happen, and why did it happen when it did? I suggest that this new phenomenon was a reflection of a decline of the integrated divine view of society, the desacralization of the world, in which ecclesiastical prescriptions and proscriptions were no longer able to provide a coherent framework and hold the imagination of everyone in society. The Netherlands and England were the places in western Europe where this fragmentation first emerged, thanks to the peculiar outcomes of their Protestant Reformations, which by 1700 had hamstrung the coherent exercise of ecclesiastical discipline and instruction through much of their territories. (We will see many other examples of their pluralism later.) These were also the two European societies which by their economic development had banished famine from their experience. Their increasingly general distribution of surplus wealth brought a new emphasis on leisure and hence personal choice to a wider cross-section of society than anywhere in medieval or Reformation Europe, where leisure and personal choice had only been the experience of a tiny privileged elite.

Such a choice might well include a decision to adopt a long-term personal identity other than that imposed by society. It must nevertheless be noted that the boundaries and possibilities of that decision were still generally determined by evolving ideas about gender in society at large. The decline of the humours theory and of Galenic ideas about the continuity of gender meant that male and female identities drew increasingly further apart.

Accordingly, the homosexual man in such environments as the gay bars of London and Amsterdam evolved what amounted to a third sexual identity: a man who was wholly attracted to other men but who represented this 'unmasculine' preference by acting in a highly feminized way. Symmetrically in this scheme, a fourth sex was the mannish 'lesbian', a word actually invented during the eighteenth century and so predating the word 'homosexual' by about a century.[50]

This was a transformation in understanding. Characteristically in the Reformation era, the older gender presuppositions had associated 'effeminacy' with men who were excessively and unnaturally interested in sex with women. So when a Catholic propagandist of the reign of Queen Mary of England, Miles Huggarde, sneered in the 1550s at the likes of Cranmer, Ridley and Latimer as 'bishops effeminate', he was mocking their unprecedented enthusiasm for getting married.[51] The same mockery was applied to Charles II, that most ebulliently heterosexual of monarchs, so the switch in meanings thereafter was very sudden. The new eighteenth-century stereotype of the theatrically effeminate homosexual has had a long life after Georgian London; it still has its adherents, and remains both a source of mockery and of self-reassurance in masculinized heterosexual cultures. This radical change in the perception and self-perception of homosexuality after 1700 has its own significance in the story of the Reformation. It might indeed be said to mark the end of the Reformation, and we may find other evidence for that end as we now consider the changes in attitudes to love and sex that are traceable between 1400 and 1700.

16

Love and Sex: Moving On

THE 'REFORMATION OF MANNERS'

We have reviewed some continuities in attitudes from the medieval to the Reformation worlds – now we can explore what changed. Underlying much of the change was a new departure which began in the fifteenth century before the Reformation broke out: an increasing atmosphere of official regulation and strictness. This 'Reformation of Manners' naturally took as its centrepiece the regulation of sexual behaviour. Once more, attitudes to sodomy provide an indicator through the index of rising numbers of court cases. Convictions for sodomy rose tenfold in Venice between a mid-fourteenth-century sample of cases and a mid-fifteenth-century sample (110 between 1448 and 1469), though here there was a decline in prosecutions from the mid-sixteenth century and an actual cessation of executions after 1600. Between 1459 and 1502 convictions for sodomy in Florence quadrupled to an average of 48 a year.[1] England, rather later on the scene, passed a parliamentary statute against buggery in 1533: this was the first time that the English Parliament had concerned itself with regulating personal sexual morality, and significantly it came amid Henry VIII's general assault on the jurisdiction of the Church and his assertion of royal power. For what is interesting in these examples (and others) is that the secular rather than the ecclesiastical courts in Venice, Florence and England were now showing a concern for a moral issue which had hardly concerned secular lawyers previously. This was part of the phenomenon we surveyed in chapter 1: the reassertion of 'Commonwealth' against 'Church' and the emergence of the secular ruler as *Landesvater*, the father of his territory. Naturally fathers had a duty to look after the moral welfare of their families. Besides that general principle, two further encouragements for this new mood of regulation predated the Reformation: first, the arrival of a new disease, the second the arrival of Desiderius Erasmus.

We have seen (chapter 2, p. 94) that Italy had a bad year in 1494: not only the French military invasions which wracked the peninsula for half a century, but the coming of the 'French pox', the disease christened syphilis by the doctor Girolamo Fracastoro in his poem of 1531. What modern doctor would analyse an unknown disease by writing Latin verse about it addressed to the muse of astronomy? Yet no one in the sixteenth century made fun of Fracastoro when he did just that, and indeed what he said about the French disease was marginally more sensible than most other contemporary medical opinion (in fact the most practical contemporary medical advice, from Pope Alexander VI's Valencian doctor Pere Pintor, was to run away very fast on hearing of an outbreak of syphilis). Like AIDS in the twentieth century, the French pox developed its own literature, because it became the uninvited guest of the powerful and the articulate – which then meant noblemen and clergymen rather than people in Wall Street, the media and the arts. In Italy, Renaissance scholars tried to use all their cultural resources to make sense of a baffling and terrifying disease: they seriously debated whether the French pox could exist at all, since it apparently lacked a proper Latin or Greek name. A killer plague which had nothing more than an Italian nickname lacked respectability. If it could not be described by a word recognizable in the ancient world, then there was no basis for starting to work out a treatment. For humanists besotted with classical wisdom it took a leap of the imagination, beyond even most clever people at the time, to suppose that reality could extend beyond the knowledge of a dead philosopher.

While the scholars thus argued, urgent practical action against syphilis was needed, if Italy was not to become a chaos of stinking, panic-stricken and contagious beggars. Syphilis, like the religious renewal movements of the period, was at its most intense in urban settings: the crisis was one major stimulus for the emergence in various Italian cities of the activist devotional Oratories and Confraternities of the Divine Love, such an important part of the prehistory of the Italian Counter-Reformation (chapter 1, p. 17). A fleet of new purpose-built hospitals was set up, often dedicated to that boil-stricken hero of an Old Testament tale, Job, now turned into an honorary Christian saint and patron of syphilis cures. The flagship among these institutions was an impressive foundation in Rome (which predictably was one of the cities worst-affected). The hospitals were called *Incurabili*, a happily inaccurate name, since the death rate in them was surprisingly low. One treatment seems to have worked, or at least made patients feel that something positive and relatively painless was being done for them: the use of a wood called *guaiacum*, both for drinking in infusions and for bathing skin problems. The wood had been discovered by chance in the jungles of the new Spanish colonies in America, so it had to be imported, and it was reassuringly expensive. Charitable ladies held fund-raising drives ('World Pox Day'?) to pay for it and for the work of the *Incurabili* generally.[2]

Many doctors resented *guaiacum*: it was indecorous and inconsiderate of an unprecedented disease to have an unprecedented cure. Protestants were also suspicious of the wonder-drug. They took their cue from the great intellectual maverick and scientific innovator Paracelsus, who in a work published as early as 1529 drew attention to the fact that the Fugger banking dynasty of Augsburg was making a huge profit from its monopoly of *guaiacum* (in fact the Fuggers showed their gratitude for their profits appropriately by founding in Augsburg the largest dedicated pox hospital in the Empire, which as part of the great hospital complex known as the *Fuggerei* still exists). This was the same banking firm that in 1517 had financed the scandalous indulgence of Cardinal Albrecht of Brandenburg, the very trigger of the Reformation. The *guaiacum* treatment, sneered Paracelsus, was thus not only useless but part of a renewed plot between the Fuggers and Rome: was it not another German Cardinal, the imperial Chancellor Matthäus Lang, who was promoting this form of cure for the disease?[3] The first effective drug treatment for malaria suffered similar confessional prejudice in the seventeenth century because the Jesuits developed it in the course of their pastoral work in south America: it took a long time to persuade Protestants that anything good could come out of the Society of Jesus.[4]

As a disease quickly identified with sexual transmission, syphilis undoubtedly played a major role in the increased sexual regulation of the sixteenth century. Fear of catching syphilis affected people's sexual behaviour, for instance keeping Francis Xavier a virgin at university. It was also a major motive behind one of the more remarkable ecumenical phenomena of the sixteenth century: the large-scale closure of the licensed brothels that were such a feature of medieval city life. Luther had already called for this in his *Address to the German Nobility* of 1520, and such closures became an invariable feature of urban Protestant Reformations – Nuremberg, always more conservative than most Lutheran cities, was unusually late in waiting until 1562 to take action. Henry VIII of England also rather belatedly imitated mainland European Protestants by closing the Bishop of Winchester's long-established licensed brothels in Southwark in 1546, but Roman Catholics also joined the stampede: the Most Christian King of France did so in Paris in 1561, while successive Popes had to make two attempts in Rome, in 1555 and 1566, before getting their way.[5]

Admittedly, few of the public statements about closure conceded the connection with a disease: for instance, Henry VIII gave moral rather than medical reasons in his proclamation closing down the Southwark brothels. But at the same time throughout Europe, outside Finland and the areas dominated by the Ottoman Turks, public bath-houses also disappeared: there was no plausible religious justification for this, and fear of promiscuous contact must have been paramount, although ironically the disappearance of public baths must also have resulted in generally lower standards of personal hygiene. There is evidence that personal codes of manners and gestures, encouraged by prescriptive literature on the subject, changed so as to avoid too much physical contact with other people. Panic about syphilis has even been linked with the sudden emergence of the witch-craze after 1500, with a certain amount of plausibility: after all, the mythology surrounding witches included a good deal of sexual misbehaviour, while the new disease was associated with both sexual sin and shame: perhaps God would spare his people if there was a new urgency in combating witchcraft.[6]

To syphilis one has to add the effect of the primly asexual Desiderius Erasmus and his extensive writings on moral and social questions. With his temperamental aversion from the physical, he intensified the tendency of humanism and the book culture of printing to privilege the abstract over the concrete in all aspects of life (chapter 2, pp. 74–5), and that was calculated to throw a more intense spotlight on the Church's ancient worries about the physical body. Erasmus bequeathed his spiritualist and interiorized vision of Christian faith to Catholic and Protestant alike, though he was not alone in this: we have seen the Thomist Cardinal Cajetan step in in 1506 to quash what he saw as the alarming implications of uncontrolled emotion in the growing cult of the sufferings of Mary (chapter 2, p. 87). Equally significant was Erasmus's remark of 1518 that the state was 'a great monastery': everybody, laity just as much as clergy, should aspire to the same self-restraint as was demanded in the ideal of monasticism. Music to the ears of princes was the additional implication that they should play the role of abbot in their great monastery (chapter 2, p. 104).

Catholic clergy did not resist this notion, as long as such regulation was undertaken by loyal sons of the Church: in fact, the Jesuits encouraged rulers to become moral regulators, and so avoid falling into the mould of the amoral ruler portrayed with a shocking degree of approval in the writing of Niccolò Machiavelli. So one of the first acts of that enthusiast for Jesuit advice, Duke Maximilian I of Bavaria, on succeeding to power was to draw up a Law for Morality and Religion (1598), equally severe on sin and on Protestantism.[7] Catholic writers on public morality were conscious of being in a competitive market in advice on statecraft, not just from the notorious and much-condemned Italian, but also from Protestant moral commentators like Philipp Melanchthon. Just as in the promotion of the witch-craze, rulers on both sides of the religious divide battled for the honour of being the most ready and able to impose strict morality on their subjects, and did so in the humanist clichés conveniently provided by Erasmus. So the brothels were closed and secular courts renewed their efforts to discipline European society. Protestant and Catholic Church authorities vied eagerly with secular princes in this Reformation of Manners; many senior Catholic churchmen conscientiously struggled with the consequences for their own lives of Tridentine Catholicism's emphatic reassertion of clerical celibacy, and they may well have projected their own personal struggles on to their efforts at regulating the sex lives of others (cf. chapter 13, p. 573). It has been suggested that a significant rise in the rate of recorded suicides during the seventeenth century may have been one cost of this official interference in people's lives.[8]

A prime example of such interference is provided by the Europe-wide campaign to change the laity's attitude to espousal custom in the process of getting married. The medieval Western Church had relabelled marriage as one of seven sacraments, and then battled to convince the laity to accept a central implication of this: a sacrament necessarily needed to be administered within the framework of the Church's liturgy, so marriages ought to take place in church and cohabitation should not begin before that had happened. In this the medieval Western Church failed. The laity clung to the conviction (accepted officially in earlier centuries of the Church's life) that although marriage might be a gift of God, an act of marriage consisted of an act of consent between the man and the woman concerned. Sexual relations started from that point, and a wedding in church, if it happened at all, was an optional extra. All that changed in the sixteenth century. Protestants and Catholics, regardless of their different attitudes to the sacramental status of marriage, both relabelled as fornication sexual activities which had been popularly seen as the first stage of marriage, and they re-educated populations to see this activity as sinful.

Not surprisingly, the tightly regulated city-state of Geneva from the time of John Calvin's ascendancy in the 1540s furnishes an emphatically efficient example of this campaign. So does Basel, which set up a new marriage court in 1533 as part of its Reformation, and which likewise by the end of the sixteenth century made increasingly active interventions against engaged couples indulging in what was now defined as premarital sex. In this the Protestant authorities in Basel were in tune with new and similar disciplinary preoccupations in the Catholic diocesan Church courts of the Kingdom of Aragon in Catalonia.[9] It might seem less predictable that the Protestant

Church of England established in the wake of Elizabeth I's settlement would score a major success. This was among the most significant victories of the English Church courts in reasserting and perhaps even strengthening their pre-Reformation authority, despite the great volume of Puritan criticism that they were hardly reformed from popish days. Hesitantly and at different times in different places, depending on the strength of residual regional conservatism, the late sixteenth-century Church of England succeeded in destroying the ancient custom of espousal before church wedding. From about 1580 the courts were taking notice of ante-nuptial sexual activity that would previously have been considered as justified within espousal custom, prosecuting it as fornication, and correspondingly there was a rise in the proportion and number of church weddings.[10]

The English achievement, in a court system which had suffered a good deal of disruption and loss of authority in the early years of the Reformation, shows that the new discipline was not imposed on an unwilling population, but went hand in hand with increasingly widespread strictness in sexual morality. Perhaps in England the shift to church weddings was encouraged by growing popular fear of popery: English Catholics naturally preserved older traditions to avoid weddings in the Protestant parish churches.[11] There were other more general factors: the serious economic stress of the 1590s across Europe disrupted many wedding plans and led to a rise in the bastardy rate (and the need to support bastard children) that probably particularly frightened the tax- and poor rate-paying population. But the natural way of dealing with this fear was to turn to the accepted institutions for social control – the church courts. They wielded a powerful weapon, the system of public penance: even if in England this was not exercised with all the liturgical relish of contemporary Scotland (chapter 14, pp. 597–600), public shame was still a major incentive to conformity. The effects of the combination of public opinion and the work of the church courts can be seen in the falling English bastardy rates of the early seventeenth century. Although the English Church courts were brought back after Charles II's Restoration, they never regained their full effectiveness, and significantly the number of irregular weddings began to rise once more in the years of their relative decline.[12]

The ultimate effort at regulation in the Reformation was the attempt to introduce into secular law the Old Testament penalty for adultery (sex with a partner other than one's spouse) – death. Pope Sixtus V, a zealous reformer, tried to introduce this in Rome in 1586, but more commonly Reformed Protestantism, with its emphasis on the positive value of Old Testament law, was the setting for such efforts. Calvin's Geneva led the way and

Scotland was not far behind – in both cases, the admittedly small number of those who were executed were persistent offenders. In all such legislation there was a patriarchal double standard which demanded harsher penalties for an adulterous married woman: she had offended against the obedience due her husband, and thus she had approached the crime of a sodomite in transgressing on the natural order, so death was appropriate. Men (except those committing adultery with another man's wife) were generally punished on the same level as fornicators – gaoling and fining.[13] The English Puritans, in their years of precarious triumph after their military victories in the 1640s, tried to bring into England proper Reformed discipline at last: the flagship of their policy was the introduction in Parliament in 1650 of legislation permitting the death penalty for incest and adultery, but virtually no cases were even tried. It is true that in the 1650s the recorded percentage of bastard births fell to its lowest level since reliable records began, but this is probably more a statistical illusion because of the Interregnum breakdown in church record-keeping than a reflection of reality. The Puritan attempt to impose biblical discipline was a resounding failure, and it seems to have left a permanent memory of the resentment that it caused.[14]

CATHOLICISM, THE FAMILY AND CELIBACY

The Reformation of Manners therefore was a strange combination of the efforts of fifteenth-century revivalists, widespread anxieties triggered by syphilis, Erasmus's personal preoccupations, Protestant stringency and the determination of Catholic bishops not to be left behind in being rigorous. From this starting-point one might expect to find Protestants changing attitudes to sexual matters, but it is worth first considering Roman Catholicism to demonstrate that behind the façade of continuity there was a good deal of movement here too. As the remainder of the old Western Church recovered its nerve in the later part of the sixteenth century, it had a double task: both to demonstrate that it was as serious about marriage and the family as the Protestants, and to reinvigorate the discipline of compulsory celibacy, which had proved such a weakness and an opportunity for hostile propaganda in the early Reformation. Naturally the Council of Trent devoted its attention to both matters. On marriage, the central act was one of the Council's last decisions in 1563, the decree *Tametsi*. Like other conciliar decisions, this was not put into operation immediately everywhere, but it set a new standard, and its aim of securing uniformity and simplicity in practice found sympathy among secular authorities in Catholic lands. *Tametsi* sought to impose the Church's control over the process of marriage like the Protestants. It did so by laying down as strict conditions as possible about what constituted a marriage: now it had to be shown to have involved a declaration of consent in front of a clergyman, together with two witnesses, thus drastically simplifying a complicated set of possibilities of couples privately exchanging vows either with immediate or future intentions.

The creation of new clear rules inevitably strengthened the hand of the ecclesiastical courts which administered them – that was part of the general tightening-up of control by the Church authorities. Husbands and wives unsatisfied with their marriages would readily turn to the courts in the hope of finding an aspect of the rules that showed that their marriage had never been a reality. This became a major business: in the century after *Tametsi*, the people of Venice were bringing to the court of the Patriarch (the Venetian Church's highest official) around one request for separation every month, and around four petitions for outright annulment every year. Some laypeople developed their own expertise in exploring these rules. An extreme case was the aggrieved Venetian husband who in 1645 discovered (or claimed to have discovered) that his second wife had used the courts to argue her way out of no fewer than three previous marriages, before deciding that he should become her latest wealthy spouse. Such ingenuity in playing the system made the secular authorities in Venice increasingly convinced that the Church courts were too soft on obstreperous and ingenious wives, out of a misguided desire to defend them from male exploitation: this being Venice, the secular authorities set up their own rival court which came to monopolize trials of breach of promise cases.[15]

Nevertheless Catholic Church and Commonwealth were in general agreement about promoting the family by emphasizing its sacred quality. The Spanish secular authorities in particular were acutely conscious that they needed people both in the home kingdoms and in the vastly extended empire overseas: as a result both of natural disasters and the manmade and self-inflicted disaster of racial expulsion, Spain's peninsular population fell drastically between 1596 and 1650 from 8.5 to 6.5 million, and the average size of families went down from five to four.[16] The new emphasis on the family already perceptible in the fifteenth century provided the necessary rhetoric, with the Holy Family (Jesus, Mary and Joseph) being cited as the model for other families. This resulted in a remarkable boost for the position of Joseph. Before the fifteenth century he had been little regarded in western Christian iconography, and in fact he was usually a figure of fun in medieval sacred drama, an elderly little Jew too stupid to give ready acceptance to the miraculous nature of his betrothed's pregnancy. Suddenly he became a major cult figure, now said to be of noble birth, and celebrated by such leading fifteenth-century churchmen as Jean Gerson and Bernardino of Siena; his feast-days multiplied in number and importance. Later, François de Sales sang his praises and Teresa of Ávila made him her spiritual father. In the Spanish Empire, he became the single most important cult figure after the Virgin Mary herself – he became Mexico's patron saint, and from 1679 Spain's official protector.

Why did St Joseph's stock rise so dramatically? He was important because the Holy Family was important: it provided a (significantly nuclear) image of the monogamous family in settings where there were often alternative native models of family organization. Yet Joseph's status in the Holy Family also presented some problems which required careful negotiation, and which revealed the tensions within the official Catholic view of family life. Joseph was not a good advertisement for the primary place of procreation in marriage, for on the assumption of the perpetual virginity of Mary it was likely that his marriage was unconsummated (although one common explanation of the Bible's mention of Jesus's brothers and sisters was that they were Joseph's children by a previous marriage). One late sixteenth-century Japanese convert, Fabian Fucan, made this a reason for renouncing the Christian faith which the Jesuits had taught him: 'Jesus was born from a couple who had sworn chastity. What kind of a virtuous ideal is that? . . . The universal norm is that every man and every woman should marry. To go against that natural law is evil.'[17] The Spanish Inquisition, aware of the difficulty, told painters to keep a judicious balance in depicting Joseph: he should not look too young, in case he seemed to lack experience, and if he was too old he would be like everyone's image of the comic cuckolded husband.

Yet the dimension of apparent cuckoldry was an essential part of Joseph's importance in religious instruction. He contradicted the common lay assumption that sexual prowess was an important aspect of being a man, and that gave clergy the chance to emphasize to men that chastity was an important male virtue. Clergy could also point out that Joseph began by thinking that his wife had committed adultery, and yet he had not repudiated her: an admirable lesson in forgiveness within the tensions of married life. Joseph's doubts and fears even gave him the status of a suffering martyr, and might be an inspiration to men in their own private worries about themselves as family men. More than that, he offered indigenous peoples in the Spanish Empire a model of conversion, by his eventual realization of the glorious truth in Mary's pregnancy – he was the second person to hear about the Incarnation. In a different context, St Joseph might be a comfort to the many English Catholic gentlemen after the Reformation who were 'church papists', going to their Protestant parish church while their wives kept up Catholic practice at home, to spare the family punitive government fines or confiscation of estates. These Church papist heads of families were suffering like Joseph for the sake of their family, by sacrificing their ordinary moral assumptions and their uncomplicated leadership role, while their wives enjoyed the morally superior role of uncontaminated Catholic devotion, just like Mary with her sacred burden of maternity.

The Virgin Mary remained of course a constant presence in the churches and the lives of ordinary Catholics. Yet there are changes perceptible with her as well. As Joseph became ever more prominent as the model husband, Mary became a quieter figure. We have already seen (chapter 1, p. 87) that medieval preachers paid a great deal of attention to the bodily aspect of Mary's role, revelling in her active and demonstrative part in the mysteries of Incarnation and Atonement; late medieval art was very ready to picture her physically swooning away with grief. In the wake of Cardinal Cajetan's criticism of this theme, and the general tightening-up of attitudes to emotion and the body, Counter-Reformation preachers played down the physicality, meditated more on the spiritual dimension of the Mary-Jesus relationship and looked to Mary's passivity, silence and humility. When extravagantly swooning females re-emerged in the Church's art of the Baroque period, they tended not to be the Mother of God but visionaries like the fifteenth-century Catherine of Siena, who had seen herself as mystically married to Christ, or the sixteenth-century Teresa of Ávila (though it is unlikely that Teresa would have been at all pleased to see herself portrayed so orgasmically ecstatic as in Bernini's famous mid-seventeenth-century statue in Our Lady of Victory in Rome). Likewise the common medieval portrayal of the Virgin suckling her infant son was phased out of the art of the Counter-Reformation Church: it was too physical and indecorous.

This change was not universal, and it was more marked in northern Europe where Catholics had to face Protestant criticism of extravagant Marian devotion. In these contexts Catholic preachers had to emphasize God's grace working in the Incarnation, or proclaim Mary as a more effective example of quiet faith than the Protestants' favourite archetype, the Old Testament patriarch Abraham. Significantly François de Sales, lifelong contestant with Calvinism as Bishop of Geneva, was among the most revisionist of preachers on Mary, and the passive neo-Platonic mysticism of Cardinal de Bérulle's circle was a further incentive for his French Catholic contemporaries to picture the passivity of Mary (chapter 10, pp. 476–9). In the Mediterranean far south, safely beyond Protestant reach, preachers might be as hyperbolic as before. They would be more inclined to remember that Mary had crushed the Ottoman Empire at Lepanto in 1571: she was Our Lady of Victory (chapter 7, p. 331). So in that same church bearing this dedication in Rome where Bernini's St Teresa lies stricken in ecstasy, the main ceiling fresco shows Mary presiding imperiously from a cloud while angels beat back four heretics and their books. In Naples Cathedral, Mary transmits the prayers of the faithful to her son, and He causes the Archangel Michael to trample underfoot a very miserable-looking Luther and Calvin (see Plate 22). In such settings, Mary is far from humble, spiritual or passive.[18]

The complications of the Counter-Reformation's promotion of the Holy Family revealed the pull between its earnest commendation of family life and its simultaneous privileging of celibacy. One dramatic symptom of this was the determined Tridentine campaign against clerical partnerships: this campaign was a major component of the Catholic Church's effort to distance itself from Protestantism in central Europe and France (chapter 7, p. 328; chapter 10, p. 447; chapter 13, p. 573). However, a further tension arose from a growing competition for financial resources between the family and the celibate community. The boom in foundations of religious institutions and monastic communities as the Catholic Church found a new energy in the religious life was a constant source of potential conflict with families who might well feel resentful at tying-up family wealth in these institutions. The story of the consolidation and expansion of the Society of Jesus illuminates several strands within this competition, and the complex set of relationships that it could involve.

Ignatius Loyola, a courtier by aspiration and training, was notably successful in his intense (and chaste) relationships with women: in this he shows an unexpected similarity to that other austere Church reformer, John Knox (see below, p. 655). In the early years of his efforts to establish his mission, his motley group of brilliant mavericks had few friends among the male clerical establishment: instead, a set of noblewomen (mostly married) in the chief courts of Europe helped to bring his infant Society in from the cold. Centrally important was Loyola's pastoral care for Margaret of Austria, illegitimate daughter of the Emperor Charles V, who had the misfortune to be married to one of the loutish grandsons of Pope Paul III. Loyola's concern for Margaret in her misery saved her marriage, which had important diplomatic as well as personal significance, and this success was the main reason for the surprising papal readiness to grant an untried Society its generous Bull of Foundation in 1540. A strong-minded, cultured and celibate

Portuguese noblewoman Leonor de Mascarenhas was the much-loved governess of the two legitimate daughters of Charles V: she served as a counterweight to the Emperor's considerable suspicion of the early Jesuits, and she did much to promote the Society's early moves into Spain at the beginning of the 1540s. Leonor's kinswoman by marriage Elena de Mascarenhas, wife of the celebrated Portuguese diplomat and statesman Pedro de Mascarenhas, at the same time helped her husband to complete the Jesuits' pincer movement on Iberia by her own influence in Portugal. When the corporation of Lisbon put up a strong fight against furnishing the Jesuits with an enviably centrally placed headquarters at St Roch's church in the city, she bullied the city councillors into falling into line, so that she could have convenient access to Jesuit ministry near her own house.[19]

In a pattern very common in both Reformation and Counter-Reformation, once the emergency years were over, the Jesuits turned their public attention from unconventional – that is, female – patrons to conventional male magnates and churchmen. A Roman noblewoman, the Marchesa della Tolfa, provided the lion's share of the funding for the Jesuits' college in Rome, but in the course of time it became named after Pope Gregory XIII as the 'Gregorian'. The danger of sexual scandal, which had from the beginning been a worry to the Society, was a major factor in this change: some Jesuits refused to hear the confessions of women for that reason. As extrovert processions became a key feature of Jesuit missionary exploits around the Mediterranean (chapter 9, pp. 414–17), the Society also tried to exclude women from the extravagant displays of penitence, fearing inappropriate popular reactions if women indulged in such activities as mass penitential flagellation. These exclusions were not always successfully imposed, thanks to what one half-admiring cleric described as female 'holy obstinacy'. Likewise, when one of Leonor de Mascarenhas's two charges, the Archduchess Juana, demanded to be made a full member of the Society, the Jesuits could not gainsay a sister of King Philip of Spain and a strategically vital enthusiast for their work, but they swore her to silence on her membership and made sure that no woman ever again became a Jesuit.[20]

Nevertheless the Jesuits continued to take an interest in exploring new ways in which women might play an active part in their renewal movement. They targeted wealthy women, especially widows, to seek proper endowments for their mission and their ambitiously conceived free educational system, in a sustained and massive effort which made them the pioneers of professional charitable fund-raising. They perfected techniques of orchestrating begging letters, arousing enthusiasm with detailed reports of their work, and then pouncing with solicitations for specific projects. They sought legacies and donations and in return judiciously developed what Ignatius's early Jesuit biographer Ribadaneira delicately described as one of his chief characteristics, 'the virtue of gratitude'. A set of prominent women in Bologna raised the money for founding and equipping the Society's Bolognese headquarters, and they were all anxious in return to enjoy the title of 'Mother of the Church': the Jesuits courteously explained that that honour was reserved for the one who could raise the largest sum. It was not surprising that many wealthy families were furious at this asset-stripping of their corporate resources, and were particularly worried about what might go on in the confessional. Sexual solicitation was bad enough – and growing numbers of accusations of solicitation by priest-confessors are one of the spin-offs of the Counter-Reformation's new stress on regular confession – but the thought of a large dowry ending up in the Church's hands as the result of one particularly penitent occasion was equally alarming.[21]

The Jesuits were well aware that they were only one component in the revival of celibate life in the Catholic Church. One of the most remarkable changes of the period, and one that has persisted to the present day, was the spectacular growth of female Orders; previously nunneries had been in a distinct minority over against male institutions, but this was set to reverse over the next few centuries. The number of nuns in Florence well outstripped population growth over two hundred years: 933 in a population of 43,000 in 1427, 3,400 in 1552 and 4,200 by 1622 in a total population of 76,000. Valladolid in Spain, through a period of steady political and economic decline, managed in the century after 1545 to found five new male monastic institutions, but no fewer than twelve nunneries, and in France women religious overtook men in numbers during the early seventeenth century, encouraged by what has been styled the 'mystical invasion' of the Discalced Carmelites (chapter 10, p. 477).[22] The most extreme case was in Venice, where in the period 1580–1642 around half the women in the city's wealthy ruling class became nuns, thus saving their families a fortune in marriage dowries as well as performing a useful task of prayer for their loved ones. The Patriarch of Venice Giovanni Tiepolo rather gave the game away when he described these nuns as 'locked up in convents as if in a public tomb . . . making of their own liberty . . . a gift not only to God, but to the fatherland, the world, and their closest relatives'.[23]

The mushrooming of female participation in the regular life was far more than just a cynical development in the economy of wealthy families. Much of its impetus came from women who wanted to play their full part in the movements of renewal that the Church was fostering. It was thus a powerful reaffirmation of an independent role for women in the Church, but just because of that the male Church authorities had mixed feelings about the growth: all those nuns needed controlling. The men were especially determined that women should not exercise an active ministry in the Church; their ministry must be an enclosed life of prayer and contemplation, with minimal contact with the outside world. Even before the Council of Trent, the battle-lines were being drawn up. As with so many Counter-Reformation policies, it was Fernando and Isabel's 'Reformation before the Reformation' in fifteenth-century Spain that began the campaign to confine women to the cloister, but Trent formalized the move, followed up by a papal Bull from Pius V in 1566. Often this 'enclaustration' would mean literally the building of a cloister: archaeology has indicated that medieval nunnery buildings had not tended to follow the classic cloister-centred architectural layout of the male monastery, but now they would be forced to do so. If the Tridentine Blessed Virgin Mary was generally quieter and more passive than she had been in the medieval Church, so, in the same way, the ideal Tridentine convent was 'wealthy, silent, and invisible.'[24]

The new move to enclosure faced formidable opposition. Many well-born nuns had only regarded life in the convent as a bearable option because there would be plenty of possibilities for a social life involving the wider world, and they were appalled when new grilles were installed at the convent entrance. Another in Ignatius Loyola's circle of great ladies was Doña Leonora Osorio, wife of the Spanish Viceroy of Naples (the same Viceroy who sponsored the Jesuits' first municipal school in Messina: chapter 5, p. 225). She made it a particular personal ministry to tour Italian nunneries to persuade such mutinous nuns to accept enclosure. She was in a better position than most men to make them listen, being equal if not superior in rank to these often very socially elevated ladies, with the added prestige of her husband's viceregal status – and of course as a laywoman she was able to move from place to place as the nuns could not.[25]

Yet by no means all the opposition to strict enclosure was from outraged social butterflies. Many women desperately sought to play an active part in the revivalist work of the Church in the world at large, particularly as they watched the achievements of the friars and the Jesuits. The problem was that there was very little precedent in western Christianity for such a role for women, and there was the alarming contemporary parallel of female prophets among the radical sects of the Reformation. The Society of Jesus was not at all opposed to the new possibility, particularly because of its worries about being vulnerable to scandal if it entered directly into pastoral work with women: women might undertake this without such a danger. Yet the Jesuits realized that such initiatives had to be carefully negotiated.

One spectacular defeat was that of the English gentlewoman Mary Ward, who was determined to found an organization very similar to that of the Jesuits, with the same combination of freedom of action and central direction responsible to no one but the Pope; her eye was on the missionary opportunity provided by her native land, where the Jesuits had already laboured with such heroic self-sacrifice. Her Institute of the Blessed Virgin Mary was founded in 1609, but then it aroused such acute fears among the Church hierarchy that after twenty years it was suppressed by papal command, and Ward herself even suffered a period of imprisonment in a convent of the Poor Clares. Ward's mistake was to create a society threatening male assumptions about the Church by being too similar to male authority structures. Still her institute quietly persisted: in 2004 it gained the name she sought, the Congregation of Jesus.

The Ursulines, with Jesuit assistance, did much to sidestep such fears, partly because of the sheer scale of their activities. Before the male clerical establishment could do much about it, they had spread very widely through Catholic Europe from their beginnings in the Brescia of the 1530s (chapter 5, p. 218). We have seen Archbishop Borromeo's reaction to the phenomenon in Milan: he turned the Ursulines in his archdiocese into a conventional and conventual religious Order, so that he could more easily direct their work (chapter 9, p. 412). The Jesuits were less doctrinaire: they could see the potential of such an energetic movement to be a partner in their own very varied enterprises. In the late sixteenth century, they took on the spiritual direction of the Ursulines; they both fostered Ursuline expansion and took a major voice in how that expansion could operate. They encouraged choices among the originally varied aims of the Ursulines, steering them away from their work among the sick and the poor and promoting their interest in education, which did not require the sisters to move around so much in the ordinary world. They also steered the Ursulines into a more elevated social milieu. Ursulines had in the early decades normally been humble women and girls with little education: that began to change, as the Jesuits encouraged the daughters of their aristocratic patronesses to take up the work, and in turn to provide education for daughters of the wealthy and powerful, just as the Society did for their sons. Usually that indeed meant building convents to house the ladies (again, predictably, paid for by a wealthy woman), but that chimed with the intentions of the Council of Trent and the Society was as ready to adapt to circumstances in this as in everything else.[27]

Despite these general trends in one particular direction, it was important that the Ursulines never developed a single central organization – something symbolized by the fact that, like the Jesuits, they never adopted a single recognizable dress-code. The lack of one single voice at the top made it much more difficult for a male leadership to enforce strict enclosure on them, and in any case many local bishops and even some Popes did not sympathize with Borromeo's strict line on this matter of policy. The decentralized structure also gave an opportunity for strong-minded and creative individual Ursulines to make their own experiments and undertake new initiatives despite the general activities of the Order. There was for instance the work of the French Ursuline Anne de Xainctonge, a great admirer of the Jesuits, who created education for poor girls in day-schools and who with Jesuit help wrote a distinctive rule for her communities that made them remarkably like the open uncloistered houses of the Society. She could do this because she chose to operate in areas where the control of Catholic bishops was weak: the independent frontier territories between the Empire and France, and the Catholic cantons of Switzerland.[28]

Equally distinctive was the joint enterprise in the French settlements of Canada, spearheaded from 1639 by two aristocratic French widows, Marie Martin (who took the name in religion Marie de l'Incarnation) and Marie-Madeleine de la Peltrie. Their husbands' deaths brought them early release from unwelcome arranged marriages: their families had fresh plans for them, but with a good deal of covert Jesuit help, they escaped. Strengthened by Mme de la Peltrie's defiant removal of her considerable fortune from France (to the rage of her relatives), the two ladies were free to begin an educational mission to the first-nation population of Quebec: Mère Marie learned the languages of the Algonquin and Iroquois peoples and wrote dictionaries and devotional works for them, at a time when the Protestants in the English colonies to the south were doing little to bring Christianity to their native neighbours (chapter 12, p. 540). They shared at one remove the early struggles of the Jesuits and acted as a reservoir of strength and encouragement for them in the Society's frequently harrowing sufferings at the hands of hostile native peoples. Their frontier monastery in Quebec was a long way from the carefully bolted doors of the Milan Ursuline convents.[29]

The history of the Ursulines illustrates a pattern in the Counter-Reformation that is recurrent, although it has rarely been made explicit in the official story. Energetic and talented women, often those freed from demands of family life by the opportune death of a more-or-less lamented husband, started an organization which would maximize and perhaps enlarge the skills customarily regarded as a mother's responsibility and therefore allowable for women: nurture, nursing, the passing-on of domestic skills, elementary education for little children and even advanced education

for girls. The form of such an organization might be that of the confraternities which had been a vehicle for lay activism in the late medieval
Church. Such enterprises flourished: if so, men stepped in with the aim of
turning them into a monastic Order on medieval lines. The more ingenious
women then used the language of deference and subservience in order to
subvert this assault, either finding allies among sympathetic men, playing
off rival male authorities against each other to postpone irrevocable
decisions, or gravitating towards emergency situations such as that in the
Canadian mission, in which the Church had to waive the normal rules in
order to preserve the mission. If one female initiative became frozen within
the religious Orders, another took its place, and the best chance of with-
standing being herded into the cloister was to shelter under the authority of
a charismatic male sponsor.

One of the best examples of this began in seventeenth-century France.
Here that cheerful and modest priest Vincent de Paul collaborated with yet
another aristocratic widow, Louise de Mérillac (Le Gras in marriage), in
order to set up a female Confraternity of Charity, which gained the significant nickname *Filles Séculières*. With political good sense, Fr Vincent habitually commented that neither he nor Mademoiselle were the founders of the
work, since neither of them had envisaged founding a community. Based
on this tactful vagueness, the work of the community managed to achieve
recognition by the Archbishop of Paris in 1646 while navigating its way
past the possibility of enclosure: 'For your grille, the fear of God, for
your veil, holy modesty' were the ingeniously phrased recommendations of
Vincent in the informal rule which he devised for his sisterhood. The Sisters
of Charity of St Vincent followed the Ursulines to the open conditions of
the frontier society of Quebec, while back home in France they managed
over two centuries to retain much of their freedom: operating from communal homes, they organized education alike for rich and poor girls, ran
soup-kitchens for the desperate, nursed in hospitals and even undertook
work in parishes under the direction of parish clergy, who might appreciate
that there were areas of life to which a celibate male priest did not have
access. In their schools, they were actually giving catechetical instruction to
their charges, though naturally they were careful not to offend against male
proprieties by calling catechesis by its name – that was man's work, after
all. So might Catholic women find their own way around the patriarchal
assumptions of Mother Church.[30]

PROTESTANTISM AND THE FAMILY

The Reformation era saw a barrage of rhetoric about the importance of the family, and the role of the father as its head. There was very little new in this, but what was new was its assertion among Protestants at the expense of the role of virginity and celibacy. In fact just as with the emergence of a 'Reformation of Manners', the tendency can be seen gathering strength in the fifteenth century. This was the time when the *Devotio Moderna* was re-establishing the idea in northern Europe that married couples could experience as close and loving a relationship with God as any monk (chapter 1, pp. 22–3), and when cults of the 'Holy House' – the childhood home of the boy Jesus at Nazareth with Joseph and Mary – achieved a spectacular new success through pilgrimage to Holy Houses at Walsingham in England and Loreto in Italy. After that, one commonplace genre of moral comment within existing medieval attitudes, praise of the family, was given greater official currency by being put into print in conduct books that were intended to show families how to live their lives.

In this respect Desiderius Erasmus echoed themes from the *Devotio Moderna* piety which he had experienced in his youth. In 1518 he published the first version of what proved a very popular and influential essay in praise of marriage (*Encomium matrimonii*). As so often with Erasmus, one cannot easily tell how sincere he was in what he was writing, and in fact in the introduction to the work he claimed that he had written it twenty years earlier as a rhetorical exercise for the benefit of Lord Mountjoy, the young Englishman who was first in his series of glamorous aristocratic patrons. That dating would take the work's composition back to the years immediately after Erasmus had escaped from his miserable time in the monastery at Steyn. It is likely that much of his enthusiasm for marriage (which was always at second hand) was motivated by his consistent desire to belittle monasticism, for the essay is as much a diatribe against celibacy as a commendation of marriage.[31]

Whatever his motivation, in his essay Erasmus tackled medieval clerical assumptions head-on. Bluntly he stated in the *Encomium* that the single state is 'a barren way of life hardly becoming to a man ... let us leave celibacy for bishops ... the holiest kind of life is wedlock, purely and chastely observed'.[32] In 1518 it might still have been possible to have presented such statements as theologically uncontroversial, but in the helter-skelter pace of events over the next two or three years, Erasmus's assertions about marriage proved as much of a hand-grenade lobbed into Europe's controversies as were his biblical commentaries. He soon came under fire from that bastion of traditional theological orthodoxy, the University of Paris, where the leading theologian Josse Clichthove went into print in 1522 to reproach him for undermining chastity by his praise of marriage. Erasmus's reply to Clichthove was pugnacious, and he felt strongly enough to invite further clashes with the conservative establishment of the Church, repeating what he had said about marriage and celibacy in a second work of 1526, the *Institutio christiani matrimonii*.[33]

Erasmus's rhetorical praise of marriage was then given an enormous boost through the Reformation: it was given precedence over the rival rhetoric in praise of virginity, discredited in Protestant eyes through its association with compulsory clerical celibacy and monasticism. One fact explains the particular upsurge in interest in the family in Protestant Europe: the clergy were allowed to marry. The overwhelming majority did, with great enthusiasm, not uncommonly in the early days to ex-nuns: Martin Luther's marriage to the former nun Katharina von Bora (chapter 3, p. 143) was the most famous example and among the most successful (see Plate 10). Clerical enthusiasm for marriage counteracted the fact that Protestants, in their reduction of seven sacraments to two, had ceased to number marriage among the sacraments. They still found ample biblical basis for exalting marriage over celibacy: ordination had also been demoted from the seven sacraments, but that did not stop Protestants valuing the ordained ministry. Hence the new insistence on weddings in church, which was as strong among Protestants as Catholics: it reflected a conviction that marriage might not be a sacrament, but it was still sacred.[34]

The first major exponent of such discussion was not so much Luther as Martin Bucer of Strassburg, never inclined to stint himself in writing on any subject which interested him. A former Dominican friar, he was one of the first clergy to take the imaginative leap of getting married, as early as 1522 – three years before Luther, and also to an ex-nun. His second wife of 1542, Wibrandis Rosenblatt, was actually recommended to him by his first wife Elisabeth as she lay dying from the plague; with this encouragement, Bucer remained a widower for only a few months. Wibrandis was herself virtually a one-woman Reformation. She had previously married and buried a humanist artist of Basel, Ludwig Keller (Cellarius), then two successive prominent clerical Reformers, Johannes Oecolampadius of Basel and Wolfgang Capito of Strassburg: she accompanied Bucer to England when he became Regius Professor in Cambridge, and outlived him too.[35]

Anxious to justify his serial married bliss, Bucer turned to the story of Creation and the account in Genesis 2 of Eve being made out of Adam's rib.

For the misogynistic authors of the anti-witchcraft classic, the *Malleus Maleficarum*, the main point of this story was that Eve had been created out of a perversely bent rib, and had thus (they asserted) been imperfect from the outset (which did not say much for God's abilities as a creator).[36] Bucer, by contrast, pointed to God's justification for creating Eve: 'it is not good that the man should be alone'. If a man was alone, all the sexual corruption of the celibate clergy followed. This emphasized that marriage was there for companionship, to stave off human loneliness. Significantly, Bucer saw this as God's intended primary purpose for marriage, rather than procreation: his other key biblical text apart from Genesis 2 was from the epistle to the Ephesians (5:23–4), which likewise described marriage in terms of relationship (the husband's relationship to his wife being like that of Christ to the Church). Bucer also reminded readers of Genesis 2 that the story showed that the first marriage happened before the Fall of Adam and Eve, not after: there was no necessity to see it as part of the story of sin. Clergy should lead the way for their people by showing how good and godly marriage could be, in their own lives. In this, as in many other aspects of his theology, Bucer was prepared to make love, both human and divine, the centrepiece of what he had to say: human love gave a glimpse of the divine.[37]

Bucer's two key biblical texts share another feature: they firmly commend patriarchy. It had been for the man's benefit that Eve had been created, and Christ is the head of his Church, not the other way around. So Protestants not only exalted marriage, but male headship within it. In the practice of developed Protestant Churches, that was further emphasized by the new stress on family communal prayer: no longer was it a matter of a mother teaching her child such formulae of the Church as the Hail Mary or Lord's Prayer. Now the ideal Protestant father would be expected to lead his family in prayer, and bring to that task the spontaneity or sense of particular occasion that characterized the minister's sermon in his pulpit. It is perhaps significant that the model of faithfulness in the Christian life in the literature and discourse of Protestant churches swapped gender, shifting from the Blessed Virgin Mary to the literally patriarchal Abraham.[38]

The reality may have been somewhat different. It was not without consequence that many of the early clergy marriages were to nuns: ex-nuns tended to come from rather more exalted social backgrounds than their menfolk, and they may well therefore have been able to put their clerical husbands in their place from time to time. One can equally well imagine that Wibrandis Rosenblatt had developed her own ways of managing her four successive husbands – although interestingly Bucer complained that she did not correct him for his own good as his first wife had done.[39] Her close friend in

Protestant Strassburg's small clerical world, the redoubtable Mrs Katharina Zell (chapter 4, p. 182), certainly stood no nonsense from men. Female self-assertion would not necessarily in turn provoke stereotyped male out-rage. The early clerical partnerships in particular were between people who shared memories of the epic religious struggle which had made their marriages possible: such heroic equals could reach beyond the rhetoric to which they were expected to subscribe. Many historians have solemnly quoted various apparently misogynistic and male-centred remarks of Martin Luther without realizing that he liked to tease his Katie.

Among fathers, the newly married minister nevertheless did his best to provide an example in patriarchal masculinity. Protestant clergy emphasized that their male sexuality was no different from that of laymen, in order to make a theological point that clergy were not a caste separate from the laity. How might ministers symbolize their newly recovered maleness? Commonly they grew beards (it also helped their central task of preaching that a full beard would make them look like everyone's picture of an Old Testament prophet). Luther led the way in 1521 during his stay in the Wartburg while he was pretending to be a secular gentleman, 'Junker Jörg'; he made a personal decision thereafter to restore his shaven chin even when he got married, but others ignored his change of heart and most Reformers were bearded by the 1540s, led by the majestically bushy Heinrich Bullinger in Zürich, who also wrote Protestant Europe's standard textbook on marriage (see Illustration 15a). In England in 1547, Archbishop Cranmer celebrated the death of Henry VIII, which gave him the opportunity to come out as a married evangelical, likewise by growing a full-length beard, and so he contributed his authority to the fashion. When John Hooper, Worcester's first aggressively Protestant bishop, arrived in the diocese in 1552, complete with wife and daughter, one of the few things which a disgusted local chronicler was prepared to note about his repulsive innovations was that he had 'a long beard' – presumably previously unknown among the senior clergy there.[40]

Where the great Marian martyrs like Cranmer and Hooper led (and as their pictures in Foxe's *Book of Martyrs* portrayed them), many English clerical chins followed. The most prominent Puritan clergyman in the city of Norwich in Elizabeth I's time, John More, was said by his awestruck contemporaries to have the longest beard in the Church of England.[41] All this was no mere symbol. Cranmer was a clear enthusiast for marriage: he had twice knowingly endangered his academic and clerical career by getting married. The first time was before he was ordained, but he still lost his Cambridge College fellowship as a consequence, and the second time in

1532 he was officially a priest of the old Western Church committed to celibacy, breaking cultural as well as theological boundaries to marry the niece of a German Lutheran theologian in Nuremberg. Cranmer's brother Edmund, also a priest, followed his example in marrying with equal illegality and secrecy in the early 1530s, promptly starting a family. These were principled decisions to rebel against the old world: a very different choice from that of clergy in the old Church who chose to take concubines.

Archbishop Cranmer created a fully vernacular wedding service for the Church of England in the Book of Common Prayer of 1549 (the same year that the English Parliament at last reluctantly and ungraciously legalized clerical marriage). It was logical but also revolutionary that right from its 1549 version the service affirmed that marriage could be enjoyable for human beings – that one of its purposes was 'for the mutual society, help, and comfort, that the one ought to have of the other'. Cranmer's was the first marriage liturgy in Christian history officially to say this, and thus to turn Martin Bucer's insight from Genesis 2 into an observation heard by all English newly-weds on their special day. Additionally, Cranmer was following Lutheran precedent (as he habitually did in his liturgical work) in making sure that clergy presided over all marriages and affirmed their sacred character. Reformed Protestants were divided on this matter, just as they were with funerals (chapter 14, p. 577): most Protestants eventually decided that the public character of a church wedding would reinforce their efforts to eliminate clandestine or perfunctory wedding contracts. Seventeenth-century New England kept clergy out of weddings as much as burials, to avoid superstitious notions of marriage as a sacrament, but by that time the Scottish Church had already long concurred with the English in letting the clergy in, to the point of making sure that weddings took place in the midst of Sunday worship. Characteristically, Scottish ministers saw a marriage as an opportunity for theological education: intending newly-weds were expected to attend special catechism sessions before a church wedding, and so were parents bringing their children for baptism.[42]

With Cranmer's sonorous liturgical encouragement, England's Protestant clergy cheerfully celebrated their family lives. By the mid-seventeenth century Jeremy Taylor, an Anglican bishop of Laudian outlook and therefore sympathetic in many respects to traditional Catholic spirituality, nevertheless spoke from enjoyable experience of marriage when he spoke of children in one of his marriage sermons: 'no man can tell', he said, 'but he that loves children, how many delicious accents make a man's heart dance in the pretty conversation of those dear pledges; their childishness, their stammering, their little angers, their innocence, their imperfections, their necessities, are

Two important Reformation beards.

Heinrich Bullinger, Antistes of Zürich.

Thomas Cranmer, Archbishop of Canterbury, after 1547:
his standard Reformation image. Only in the more decorous
Anglicanism of the later seventeenth century did his earlier
clean-shaven portrait of 1545 become the normative picture.

so many little emanations of joy and comfort to him that delights in their persons and society'. In what was surely a conscious refutation of Cardinal Bellarmine's catechism (chapter 15, p. 609), Bishop Taylor commented in another of his sermons that 'Single life makes men *in one instance* to be like angels, but marriage *in very many things* makes the chaste pair to be like Christ.'[43] Taylor was also an enthusiastic advocate of mothers breast-feeding their children rather than handing them over to wetnurses. As a young country parson he must have disconcerted as well as entertained his congregation in a sermon which vigorously recommended this practice, both as an imitation of the Blessed Virgin Mary herself, and as a proof that those 'exuberant fontinels', a mother's breasts, are not 'needless excrescencies'. One cannot imagine a bishop of the Counter-Reformation entertaining his flock with such rhapsodies.[44]

Clerical families were precarious in their status at first. The English Parliament's reluctance to recognize the *fait accompli* of clerical marriage until 1549 was common among Europe's leading laity, so it was not until 1555 that one of the Habsburgs' unenthusiastic concessions in the Peace of Augsburg was to give a secure legal status to Lutheran clergy unions and offspring within the Holy Roman Empire. Many called the new clergy wives whores – and indeed to begin with, these women had often been the unofficial partners of their clerical menfolk under the old regime. Such a shaky start meant that clerical families looked to each other for comfort: in all Archbishop Cranmer's voluminous surviving correspondence the only reference to the family which had so endangered his career and meant so much to him is one Latin greeting, passed on to them in a letter from that pioneer of clerical family life, Martin Bucer.[45] The inward-looking atmosphere of a clerical trades union persisted into more settled times: many of the clergy's sons in turn followed their fathers into the ordained ministry and founded long-lasting clerical dynasties. Daughters were no less important. William Barlow (successively Bishop of St David's, Bath and Wells and Chichester) was another English clerical high-flyer who, like Thomas and Edmund Cranmer, secretly married in the 1530s while Henry VIII still forbade the practice: he fathered five daughters, all of whom married clergy who became bishops (and in one case an Archbishop of York) in the Elizabethan and Jacobean Church. Barlow was thus in a fairly literal sense the father of the Church of England.

The clergy wife, from being abused and despised by conservatives in the parish, came to provide a new model for all the wives of Protestant Europe: she was now without any female rival for iconic status since nuns and anchoresses had been banished from Protestant society. Following the

Bucerian ideal, she was of course obedient to her husband, but she was also a calm and experienced companion, ready to give advice and help to parishioners – also to sustain the cheerfulness of her spouse and her children in a publicly enacted life which made them all potentially rather lonely objects of the curiosity and envy as well as the emulation of others. And so the parsonage or the manse, not so well-supplied with spare cash as with books, high ideals and high thinking, negotiated its way through a social position which was continually poised self-consciously and uncertainly between gentry and people. It took its place as one of the great cultural forces in Protestant societies, both in the Old World and the New. In the upheavals of the Enlightenment and after, it produced some of the most eloquent and troubled voices to face up to doubt and unflinching reassessment of the family business: Søren Kierkegaard, Friedrich Nietzsche and Karl Barth were all the sons of pastors.

The newly positive view of marriage that the clergy of Protestant Europe borrowed from Erasmus was perhaps surprisingly at first sight paired with a new acceptance that on occasions marriages can end and ought to be pronounced dead through the mechanism of divorce. This was in fact a logical corollary of Protestants' theological revolution: since they declared that marriage was not a sacrament, they brought it back to its original character as a contract between two persons. Even if the contract had been blessed by God and the Church, by its nature such a contract could be abrogated. While the medieval western sacramental view of marriage had made divorce an impossibility, Martin Bucer pioneered discussion of divorce, in terms characteristically much more generous than with some later commentators: he believed that both parties in a divorce should have the right to remarry, and he also emphasized that badly treated women should be treated as fairly as possible. This fair-mindedness made Bucer sympathize with poor Queen Catherine of Aragon, and just as much as the Pope, he infuriated Henry VIII by refusing to give him a good theological excuse for annulling his unwanted marriage: in this case there was no justification for either divorce or annulment. Furthermore, both Bucer and Philipp Melanchthon shocked that most pious of monarchs by suggesting that he solve his marital dilemmas by an act of bigamy, which was after all perfectly normal practice among the Jewish patriarchs of the Book of Genesis. Notoriously, in 1539–40 they also convinced another European monarch, Philipp of Hesse, to rush into bigamy where King Henry had feared to tread, with disastrous results for their own public reputations (chapter 5, p. 228).[46]

Bucer and Melanchthon's adventurous thinking on marriage should alert us to the unstable state of Protestant thought on the subject in the early decades of the Reformation. Protestants were liberated to be radical by the destruction of traditional sacramental theology, just as Luther experimented with the radical idea of soul-sleep in relation to the afterlife because he had rejected the old Church's doctrine of purgatory (chapter 14, p. 580). One exciting and thoroughly destabilizing notion in an era of acute religious conflict was a perfectly valid biblical possibility raised by that most respectable of all Christian pioneers, Paul of Tarsus, who left a time-bomb in his first epistle to the Corinthians (7:12). Although he suggested that Christians who found themselves married to an unbeliever should not seek to leave their spouse, he did so in a remarkably tentative fashion, offering merely a personal opinion ('I say, not the Lord'), and he further ruled that an unbeliever might well feel entitled to leave a Christian spouse. Martin Bucer discussed this 'Pauline privilege' more than once: he said that it was a sin knowingly to marry an unbeliever, but taking advantage of Paul's hesitations he set out some circumstances in which he was prepared to go beyond the Apostle and allow a believer to take the initiative in dissolving such a marriage. If Bucer could be that cavalier with Paul, it was not surprising that many early evangelicals decided to take the initiative and rid themselves of obnoxious papist spouses.[47]

Anabaptists and other groups who separated from mainstream Protestantism for conscience's sake long continued to argue whether or not marriages outside the gathered Church were valid, but equally this was a common theme in early mainstream Protestantism. Prominent in the martyrology of the English Reformation, for instance, was a brave and eloquent gentlewoman whom her male chroniclers John Bale and John Foxe referred to as Anne Askew. She was tortured and burned at the stake by Henry VIII's ministers in 1546 for denying the real presence in the Eucharist, and she left a vivid diary of her sufferings and defiance of her tormentors that Bale and Foxe published with edifying commentary. The surname they gave her was a misspelling of her family name Ayscough, one of Lincolnshire's most prominent knightly families, and in any case it concealed the fact that history ought to have known her as Anne Kyme, the surname of her husband, who was a traditionalist gentleman also from Lincolnshire (as well as being a brute). The plain fact was that Anne had left him and would not go back – and yet she was treated in the fashion of a saint by her evangelical contemporaries. Similarly John Knox (most of whose significant close relationships appear to have been with women) inspired another enthusiastic gentlewoman, Elizabeth Bowes, to leave her unsympathetic husband and most of her children in England so that she and her daughter Marjorie could follow her spiritual mentor into his Genevan exile. She never returned to the family. Knox soon married Marjorie, and after her death Elizabeth moved in to take care of her son-in-law and her grandchildren. Knox was thus very much 'effeminate' by the standards of the sixteenth century.[48]

Mrs Bowes was by no means unique, especially in that turbulent period of the English exile under Mary I. Plenty of other women chose to follow God rather than their man. An unfortunate Catholic nobleman from the south of France, while travelling home after army service in Italy, decided on a whim to be a tourist and see what wicked Calvinist Geneva was like. He went to hear John Calvin preach, and to his horror and astonishment he saw his wife and daughter sitting enraptured at the front of the church, when they should have been far away in France. Naturally he made a huge protest. Calvin and the Consistory gave him the choice either of conversion or losing his family: he stuck to the Catholic Church and went home, his family life in ruins.[49] We do not need to follow the prurient comment of contemporary Catholics to realize that these high-minded spiritual relationships and unilateral decisions were a radical rewriting of the conventions of marriage in the interests of godly Reformation. One Catholic propagandist for Mary I's English Catholic revival knew that he would be believed when he portrayed evangelical preachers as explaining 'that there were two sorts of fornication, for which men or women might be divorced, one carnal, and another spiritual. Carnal, as when the wife had committed adultery with another man, or the husband with another woman. Spiritual, when the woman or man was a papist, and an enemy to God's word, as they called it.'[50]

Thus many people now felt that they had the best of reasons to bring unhappy relationships to an end: far from their divorce or separation being a source of shame, they would be reassured that they were doing God's will, while gaining release from spiritual as well as emotional bonds. This was one element in the sudden welling-up of revolutionary popular Protestant excitement, first in the 1520s and then again in the 1560s: a spreading conviction that some of the most intimate human relationships were now ready for radical reconstruction. In the wake of those two great periods of excitement, clergy in the newly established Protestant Churches were naturally intent on calming things down and re-establishing social boundaries. That was the agenda of the new marriage courts in Zürich and Basel, established on the ruins of the old church courts in the 1520s and early 1530s, at the same time as these cities excluded the Reformation's first waves of religious radicalism.

The role of women was a particularly delicate issue to negotiate. As we have seen from the extraordinary events around St Gallen and Appenzell (chapter 4, pp. 167–8), women might discover that God intended previously unheard-of possibilities for them in the early years when Protestantism was still not even a name, and when the main traditional outlets for women's independent religious life had been destroyed with the suppression of nunneries. The general pattern in Protestantism was very similar to the experience of women religious in the Counter-Reformation Catholic Church: self-assertion, followed by male reassertion and renewed traditional discipline. Female self-assertion was possible in periods of uncertainty and crisis. It was accepted for the time being by men, partly because any help in the fight against Antichrist was welcome, and also because the male-centred conventions of the time had a paradoxical side-effect: women were less likely than men to be punished for breaking rules, especially in matters of conscience, because their opinions did not matter as much as those of men. So women might defy repressive religious authorities and sustain the godly with rather more chance of avoiding death than if they were male.

The English Marian exiles were sustained largely by a group of devoted and wealthy women, some of whom were able to move quite freely between England and the places of exile abroad, but until recent years they were virtually written out of the story of the Marian exile, even by the twentieth-century woman scholar who made it her life's work to study it. In her biographical dictionary of the Marian exiles, Christina Garrett provided no separate entries at all for females.[51] This pattern was not confined to Protestants. In the next reign, Roman Catholic women were to have the same experience in Elizabethan England, exploiting legal anomalies and social attitudes to create that fundamental means of Roman Catholic survival – 'church papistry' (chapter 8, p. 393). The resulting society of Catholic gentry households in the heroic years of persecution by Elizabethan and Jacobean government has even been described as the community's 'matriarchal era'.[52]

When times quietened, there was a gradual reining-in of possibilities for women, together with a rewriting of history (here there are distinct echoes of the early history of patronage among the Jesuits). We have seen the stance for toleration taken by that remarkable woman Katharina Schutz, the hymn-writing wife of one of Bucer's most prominent ministerial colleagues at Strassburg, Matthias Zell (chapter 4, p. 182). Male attitudes hardened towards Katharina over time. Johann Kessler, who had faced at first hand the alarming female enthusiasts of St Gallen, said condescendingly but also admiringly of Mrs Zell in the 1520s that 'it is amazing to see such high gifts in such a weak vessel of a woman'. By contrast, her husband's successor as minister at St Laurence Church in Strassburg, Ludwig Rabus, a pugnacious gnesio-Lutheran, described her variously as a heretic, prostitute, drunkard and foolish, ignorant old gossip, and said that her writings were 'heathen, unchristian, stinking and lying'.[53] The treatment of Lutheranism's pioneer female hymn-writer and contemporary of Mrs Zell was equally telling: Elizabeth, wife of Luther's colleague Caspar Cruciger, was author of one of the best-loved Lutheran hymns '*Herr Christ der einig Gottes Sohn*' ('Lord Christ, the only Son of God'), which Miles Coverdale translated into English as early as 1535 – but within a generation the hymn was usually attributed to a male pastor of faraway Riga, Andreas Knoepken.[54]

The second wave of popular Protestant activism in the 1560s encouraged the Reformed to pay fresh attention to the idea of women's equality before God, and sometimes even to their active part in the life of the Church. Yet such calls from the Reformed were always ambiguous. One of the pioneers of Reformation in Geneva was Marie Dentière, a former Augustinian Abbess from Tournai, whose presence in Geneva with her second husband Antoine Froment (a pastor) predated the arrival of her fellow Picard John Calvin; her writings included a lively account of Geneva's deliverance from Roman Catholicism, the latter part being testimony from her own experience, and she played a major part in closing the last convent of nuns in the city. Yet when Dentière began in her writings to encourage other women to write and speak out, the Genevan authorities were not pleased. No further writings by women were published in the city during the sixteenth century.[55] A striking and very unusual contrary affirmation of the possibilities for women came from a landmark gathering of Dutch ministers and laypeople meeting in exile in the German town of Wesel in 1571: among other proposals for the future of a Reformed Church in the Low Countries, they decided that where it seemed appropriate, women of exceptional quality and advanced years should be ordained to the diaconate to take care of prisoners and the sick. It should nevertheless be noted that this proposal was made during the heroic days of struggle against Spanish Catholic rule, and any idea that ordination might be involved was soon played down in the Dutch Reformed Church when it was properly established.[56]

Even radical groups were in practice little more adventurous. Women did continue to have a somewhat less confined role in radical groups than in mainstream Protestantism, one good reason being that emergency conditions of persecution persisted much longer for radicals. Spiritual groups like that of the charismatic Dutch artist David Joris (chapter 4, p. 207) stressed the religion of inner light and inward contemplation: these were themes which had been the particular prerogative of women in the medieval

Western Church, and it was neither surprising that mystically inclined women were drawn to such sects nor that they were accorded respect and equality within groups which rejected most trappings of hierarchy. Yet still the radical groupings were generally very wary of betraying the assumption that men ought to be leaders in the Church, particularly those sects like the Hutterite Anabaptists who sought to recreate their own society within and separate from the society around them. One influential sixteenth-century formalizer of Hutterite identity, Peter Riedemann, when drawing up one of the most prominent Hutterite confessional statements in 1540, set the tone of his discussion of the role of women by sounding an utterly traditional note: 'We say, first, that since woman was taken from man, and not man from woman, man hath lordship but woman weakness, humility and submission, therefore she should be under the yoke of man and obedient to him.'[57]

There was little breach in such conventional attitudes of male superiority among the Hutterites until the later seventeenth century. No women are recorded as writing Hutterite hymns, and yet hymns were one of the fundamental bonds of these communities: neither in all the varied Anabaptist communities is there any record of any Anabaptist woman performing that other essential community function, baptism.[58] A Hutterite community was, after all, called the Court of Brothers (*Bruderhof*). The one area in which the Hutterites did allow their social radicalism to enter the sphere of human relationships was in their bureaucratic remodelling of courtship in marriage: responsibility was taken out of the hands of a prospective couple and given to the community elders (men, naturally). The elders would decide on a small group of eligible young people from among the whole group and bring together those selected, so that these few might choose a partner suitably monitored, and thus avoid 'the inclinations of the flesh'. The Hutterite marriage ceremony proved to be one of the greatest points of internal contention in this determinedly peaceable society. A century after the Hutterites' foundation, one of their most distinguished bishops had to put a stop to widespread blatant fraud, as young lovers attempted to 'jerrymander' the choice of those chosen for particular wedding occasions, and the dispute rumbled on until in the mid-nineteenth century the Church authorities finally admitted defeat and gave up their prerogatives.[59]

If there was such hesitation about changing the relationship of the sexes even among the most radical reformers, it was not surprising that careful management of change soon characterized mainstream Protestantism. In the process of taking firm control of marriage after the years of excitement, and in the wake of the Philipp of Hesse débâcle, magisterial Protestants firmly suppressed all favourable commentary on bigamy. They said primly that that sort of mistaken use of the Bible was exactly what one would expect from the Anabaptists, and they pointed to the polygamous excesses of John of Leiden back in Münster in 1535, as a welcome diversion from the Hesse affair which had occurred five years later. Great was the scandal in 1563 when Bernardino Ochino, the outspoken Italian theologian and former star preacher of the *Spirituali*, published a dialogue in which one of his imaginary speakers argued a rhetorical case for polygamy: in fact Ochino had plagiarized much of it from a semi-official attempt to justify the Philipp of Hesse case.

In his own character, Ochino spoke for monogamy in his tract, but the very mention of polygamy was too much for his host city Zürich. After all, its leading minister Heinrich Bullinger had written Protestant Europe's bestselling guide to marriage, which secured much of its popularity in many languages by its sensible and low-key advocacy of divorce along Bucerian lines: the authority of Zürich to pronounce on matters matrimonial could not be polluted by the speculations of an Italian, however brilliant. Faced with an order for his expulsion and even with threats from infuriated citizens, Ochino sadly quit Zürich to seek a more open atmosphere, first in Poland and then (moved on by diplomatic pressure on the Poles from an implacable Archbishop Borromeo) to a last refuge in the benevolent anarchy of Moravia, sheltered by a community of Hutterites. So like so many Italian exiles, in his old age the former prebendary of Canterbury Cathedral and star of both Catholic and Reformed theologians found the radicals more hospitable and more congenial than the new Protestant establishments, let alone his old Catholic colleagues.[60]

Divorce by contrast became established as part of normal marriage law in virtually all Protestant countries, although just as Bucer had suggested in his pioneering discussion on the subject, it was an absolute last resort and generally rare, rather like the death penalty for persistent adultery. John Calvin's own brother Antoine divorced his wife in Geneva in 1557, after her second lapse into adultery.[61] Alone among Reformed Protestant polities, England did not introduce a divorce law, and that stemmed from a sheer sequence of accidents. The comprehensive reform of canon law planned by Edwardian parliamentary legislation and carefully chaired by Archbishop Cranmer made full provision for divorce; the reform was ready in 1553, but as the political crisis of Edward VI's last year gathered momentum, the plan was derailed by entirely irrelevant political antagonisms within the regime itself. Catholic Queen Mary's accession followed, and when Queen Elizabeth revived her brother's Protestant Church structure, the proposed canon law reform was the one major aspect that she did not activate. So the Church of England remained without divorce law, and in fact, through this accident rather than any basic theological conviction, right up to the end of the twentieth century, it kept the strictest laws on marriage in all western Christendom, scarcely mitigated by the numerous ingenious reasons for annulment with which Roman Catholic Church lawyers relieve Catholic canon law on marriage.[62]

Despite the anomaly in England, the Protestant view of marriage crystallized: no longer a sacrament but regarded with the utmost solemnity, and an icon of the social order where the role of a father was a microcosm of the role of a prince as father of his people. The family was almost a church of itself, for as one Scottish commentator described it, it was 'a Bethel, or the house of God'.[63] Strict Calvinism even provided for parents' worries about how God's sovereign decisions in predestination might discriminate against their beloved children: when the Synod of Dordt of 1618–19 refined the Reformed doctrine of salvation, it stressed (slightly uncomfortably) that children were included in the benefit of the covenant of grace with their parents, and so predestination to election might be hereditary (the same presumably also applied to predestination to damnation). The Protestant family now had no serious competitor in social organization: Protestants had eliminated most gilds and confraternities and (with some unimportant Lutheran exceptions) wiped out the alternative societies of monasteries and nunneries.

Symptomatic of the break with the past was the gradual disappearance in Protestant Europe of a liturgical closed season for marriages in the penitential seasons of Lent and Advent. The Church of England tried half-heartedly to preserve the closed season, but Puritans attacked it as super-stitious, and the Church leadership was not convinced that they were wrong; Church courts were certainly not going to fight to preserve it in the way that the Church fought to abolish traditional espousal custom. In the more conservative north of England, the taboo was still entrenched in 1600 but it had virtually gone by 1650. Even English Roman Catholics followed suit, about fifty years later: that was a real triumph for the Reformation in changing habits, and an interesting mirror-image of the way in which the minority community of Huguenots eventually conformed to the closed season in Catholic France.[64]

The new image of the family was a redefinition of the sacred just as much as that other radical redefinition, the destruction of devotional imagery in churches. It was therefore logical that it should have a similarly radical effect on parish church interiors: the family now commonly became the dominant unit in parish church seating. The sexes had usually been segre-gated in church before the Reformation: the custom was favoured by some

Reformers, lingered on in some traditionalist Protestant rural areas, and remained common in Catholic Europe. Later on, seating segregation was often enforced anew by enthusiastic dissenting Protestant groups when they had the chance to put up their own church buildings, but during the later sixteenth century, as parishes undertook extensive schemes of seating to meet the new emphasis on the sermon, many Protestant territories witnessed an innovation in the church building which represented the whole community. Generally the new pews seated people in their family households without any gender divide, so the interiors of churches could become a map of the social structure of a village. In Catholic days, the hierarchical procession on a great feast-day of the Church might have symbolized the unity of the parish: now the seating-plan in the church building was like a frozen procession, fulfilling the same purpose since in theory it should seat everyone within the parish boundaries. One late seventeenth-century English country parson, Richard Gough, wrote a marvellously detailed and gossipy history of his Shropshire parish entirely in terms of the seating layout of households in his church. One of the many ways in which the bachelor Archbishop Laud misjudged the mood of the English nation was in launching his bishops on a campaign to dismantle what he regarded as offensively obtrusive family pews.[65]

It was a widespread belief prominently affirmed among Protestants that such family arrangements would not be confined to the church pews, but would persist in the afterlife, where the blessed would meet their loved ones again. Did not the Apostles' Creed talk about the resurrection of the body? Surely that implied that bodily relationships would be part of the afterlife. Not all clergy approved of this logic. Many of them felt that celestial enjoyment of family relationships might prove a distraction from what Christianity affirmed to be the main occupation of heaven, eternal contemplation of the Almighty – but as we have already seen (chapter 14, p. 579), the laity were often capable of deciding that they themselves knew best about the afterlife. Consumer demand swept aside official reservations about family reunions. Clergy resistance was weakened by their disagreements about when the body might be resurrected, at the moment of death or at the Last Judgement (chapter 14, p. 580), and now in any case clergy were family men as well as being theologians. So the memorial brass of the Sussex widow Elizabeth Alfraye (who died in 1590) confidently looked forward to her soul seeking out her husband's soul 'among the saints above / And there in endless bliss enjoy her long desired love'. No one seems to have suggested by contrast that meeting one's relatives anew might be among the punishments of hell.[66]

CHOICES IN RELIGION

In surveying attitudes to love and sex during the three centuries from 1400, we have found women both Catholic and Protestant finding opportunities to worship their God in their own way, amid what might seem an over-whelming phalanx of male clichés about male superiority. Often that meant making such clichés their own and exploiting them to the full. Take the words of another one-woman Reformation, Anne Vaughan (usually known from one of her three marriages as Anne Locke). She sounded meek enough when she wrote in 1590 that there were 'great things by reason of my sex I may not do', but then she added the significant rider 'that which I may I ought to do'.[67] In Anne's case, one meaning of this was that she had endured a long life spent at the storm-centre of the entire English Reformation – she was the daughter of one of Thomas Cromwell's chief business agents Stephen Vaughan, who (more than half a century before she wrote those words) had tried to save William Tyndale from Habsburg judicial murder in the Netherlands; later she was yet another devoted female friend and correspon-dent of John Knox. Her second husband Edward Dering was a famously outspoken young Puritan minister, who had infuriated Queen Elizabeth I by criticizing her Church settlement in the royal presence.

But 'that which I may do' meant much more for Mrs Locke than being a Zelig-like witness to history. She was an active supporter and encourager of men who were waging a struggle for godliness against a backsliding English Church establishment; she was an accomplished translator of foreign devotional works, including Calvin's sermons (many clever women in her period felt it more decorous to translate other people's prose than compose their own original texts), and also one of the best creators of English biblical poetry in her generation. Her sonnet sequence on Psalm 51 was the first in the English language, predating Shakespeare's sonnet sequence by thirty years.[68] Anne Vaughan seized to the full the opportunities given her to do what she ought to do: she realized what the boundaries were and strained them to the uttermost, as did Mère Marie de L'Incarnation and Mme de la Peltrie, Katharina Schutz or Teresa of Ávila.

From the beginning of the Reformation there were patterns of devotion that were predominantly female: one commentator who knows intimately the Germany of the *Wildwuchs* years in the 1520s has suggested that already in that excitable decade one can see different religious texts lighting up for men and women, with men preferring to collect published books of sermons and favouring hymns which spelled out doctrine, while women read general works of piety and showed especial affection for more personally expressed hymns.[69] What was less predictable was the beginning in the seventeenth century of a great change which has become one of the distinctive features of modern western religion. The devotional practice of Christianity was becoming an activity in which more women than men participated. The spectacular growth of female religious communities in Counter-Reformation Catholicism was one symptom, but in Protestantism there was a different phenomenon: in various settings, church attendance was becoming skewed, and congregations were beginning to contain more women than men.

The first signs of this so far detected are in those parts of western Europe where voluntary religion was possible: the Netherlands and England. In many parts of the Netherlands, as we have seen, even the officially established Dutch Reformed Church had the character of a voluntary organization: people chose whether or not to go to their parish churches. Studies of the far north of the United Provinces in the early seventeenth century, the province of West Friesland, where so many people opted to join groups like the Mennonites, already show an imbalance in membership between men and women, even for the official Church.[70] The same was true in England in the 1640s when the coercive structures of the established Church collapsed on the eve of the Civil Wars: in membership lists of the growing number of voluntary churches, Independents, Baptists, Quakers and the like, women often outnumbered men by two to one.[71] At much the same time on the other side of the Atlantic, the authorities in the established Congregational Church in Massachusetts also began to notice the phenomenon of gender-skewed church attendance.

Why was this happening? One of the most perceptive modern commentators on religion in the early English colonies of north America has noted that the mismatch between male and female church attendance does not appear in the Anglican-dominated colonies from Virginia southwards in the seventeenth or eighteenth centuries. She suggests that this is related to the resolutely non-clerical character of Anglican leadership in these colonies: consequently, as we have already observed (chapter 12, p. 534), laymen ran the parish system in their parish vestries, and the Anglican clergy had little power. Massachusetts, by contrast, was dominated by a strong and well-trained ministry emerging out of the most effective seminary in America, Harvard College: lay male leadership was atrophying, leaving the Congregational Church in the hands of devout women and male ministers.[72] This idea would be worth testing out in other circumstances, but probably no single explanation will do. It would hardly apply in the Reformed Church of West Friesland, with its strong Calvinist structure of consistories and elders, and it also seems less convincing amid the sects of Civil War England.

Amid the major disruption of English religious life in the 1640s and 1650s, it is certainly likely that a disproportionate number of women joined the independent congregations because they had more room to assert themselves than in the established Church. This assertion was at its greatest among the extreme radicals such as the early Quakers. In the 1650s, Quaker women could enjoy prophetic roles reminiscent of those in the early days of some radical groups in the mainland Europe of the 1520s and 1530s, and we have seen the fatal consequences when outspoken women of the Friends came up against the outraged male establishment of the Church in Massachusetts (chapter 12, p. 539). Just as in the sixteenth-century radical groups, the male leadership of the Quakers over subsequent decades steadily moved to restrict women's activism. By the early eighteenth century the appeal of the Quakers to women may have been different: its resonance with that more traditional distinctively female form of spirituality, the quiet waiting on the Lord, which now characterized the worship of the Friends. In late seventeenth-century Germany, there developed among the official Lutheran Churches the intimately devotional renewal movement known as Pietism: small private groups developed a spirituality which likewise emphasized the inner encounter with the divine, although in this case the devotional group took its place alongside the public worship of the Lutheran Church. It is interesting that these Pietists were among the few people to take an interest in the writings of women activists from the earliest days of the Lutheran Reformation, like the outspoken noblewoman Argula von Grumbach.[73]

A welter of different circumstances seem to be converging to produce a single phenomenon. One contemporary explanation of the high proportion of women in Massachusetts churches provided by the leading late seventeenth-century Massachusetts minister Cotton Mather is particularly worth noting: he felt that women had a greater moral seriousness than men because of their constant consciousness of death in childbirth.[74] Whether he was right or not, his notion was a very important turnaround from traditional medical talk of humours and the continuous spectrum of gender, or of Augustine's disparaging theological comments on women's nature. As women appeared to be showing themselves more devout than their menfolk (and gratifyingly to ministers, perhaps more appreciative of the clergy's toil), the ancient Christian stereotype of women as naturally more disordered than men and more open to Satan's temptations began to look less and less convincing. So we have arrived at a phenomenon which we have already noted in a different context: the radical reconstruction of the relationship of the sexes, which now opened up a great divide between male and female identity (chapter 15, pp. 611, 628).

There is another common factor in all this that we have also met before. In the Netherlands, Civil War and Interregnum England and the increasing religious variety of Anglophone north America, there was a precocious ability to make choices that has gradually spread to other regions of western culture. Amsterdam and London were among the first places where the scale, pace and resources of metropolitan life offered the chance to form one's identity and way of life primarily through choosing voluntary associations, clubs, theatres, dissenting churches, or parish churches with particular styles of worship. These consumer cities were a conman's paradise, because now very many people, not just a privileged few, had a chance amid the complexity of urban life to reconstruct who they were, and that is a task not that much different from a confidence trick. I have argued (chapter 15, p. 628) that one demonstration of this new situation was the increasing ability to make a choice of sexual identity, which emerged in exactly the same European settings in late seventeenth century: Amsterdam and London witnessed the first widespread male same-sex subcultures in western Europe. Furthermore, it was no coincidence that these were the cities in which the coercive discipline of the 'Reformation of Manners', so carefully built up since 1500, first began to disintegrate. Many people showed no sign of mourning its demise.

One of the most instructive pieces of evidence for this was the ignominious failure in England of the 'Societies for the Reformation of Manners': the very organizations that have provided historians with that useful label. The Societies were voluntary English organizations set up from the 1690s in London and other provincial towns to enforce public morality: they took on the task for the very good reason that amid the precarious but ultimately irreversible religious pluralism of England after the Glorious Revolution of 1688, the Anglican Church's ecclesiastical courts were now incapable of acting effectively for social discipline. The Societies represented a not altogether stable rainbow coalition of all those who mourned the collapse of discipline: frustrated Puritans, worried bishops and High Church Anglicans who wanted to reassert the power of the Church. They sought to secure a large network of informers to tell them about the sexual and social misdemeanours of others – blasphemy, sabbath-breaking, 'lewdness', brothel-keeping – so that these offenders could be prosecuted in the courts.

This plan for a Protestant subscribers' version of the Spanish Inquisition found few recruits to do the informing. England was the country that had been heartily sickened half a century before by Interregnum Puritans trying to improve on the old discipline of the Church of England. By the 1730s the work of the Societies for the Reformation of Manners had collapsed, aided by their internal doctrinal squabbles. The majority within England's new urban culture had made its choice against moral snoopers, and despite a century-long but superficial detour into Victorian seriousness, the English public has since shown little sign of changing its mind. Snooping is now left to tabloid journalists out to entertain for profit.[75]

At the end of three centuries of Catholic and Protestant Reformation trying to mould and restructure Europe's outlook on love and sex, there were some surprising continuities. The family remained a stable centre, despite the excitements of the 1520s and the further upheavals of the mid-sixteenth and mid-seventeenth century. Patriarchy seemed still in place in 1700, though now it was expressed through new stereotypes, while in church it faced the peculiar desertion of males from the pews in more and more Protestant and later also some Roman Catholic settings. Moreover, around 1700, patriarchy was ceasing to be a microcosm of God's purpose in creation and more an expression of what was considered the natural make-up of a mechanical universe. Mrs Anne Locke, the Puritan translator and friend of John Knox, had a great-great-great-nephew, the late seventeenth-century philosopher John Locke. Locke and the even more iconoclastic English philosopher Thomas Hobbes between them removed the idea of God's regular and intimate intervention in the physical world that had been so important to the thinking of the Reformation.

Neither Hobbes nor Locke nor their mainland European contemporaries in philosophy abolished God in their portraits of the nature of society, but they did abolish a close theological analogy which had given a sacred character to the family. When discussing politics they weakened the possibility of comparing three different levels of relationship: God to his creation, ruler to his subjects and father to his household. Locke still clung to the idea of patriarchy, but now in his system the only secure basis of religious belief, as of everything else, was reason. His primary justification of patriarchy was no longer higher divine authority; he felt that rule within marriage 'naturally falls to the man's share', on the pragmatic and reasonable grounds that men are 'abler and stronger'.[76] It was only a matter of time before this practical patriarchy was undermined in its turn; the present generation of Americans and Europeans may be witnessing its death-throes. With that disintegration of patriarchy, a large question mark appears against many of the religious assumptions which had been the shared property of Bernardino of Siena, Martin Luther, John Calvin and Ignatius Loyola.

17

Outcomes

Here is a hymn about the Reformation:

> Faith of our fathers! Living still
> in spite of dungeon, fire, and sword;
> O how our hearts beat high with joy,
> whene'er we hear that glorious word:
> *Faith of our fathers, holy faith!*
> *We will be true to thee till death.*

These stirring words were written in the nineteenth century for Roman Catholics to sing, when the Catholic Church was beginning to realize the power of popular hymnody. Their author, Frederick W. Faber, a former High Church Anglican clergyman and a talented hymn-writer who had converted to Rome, was thinking of the 'dungeon, fire and sword' which the Protestant English Reformation had inflicted on his new co-religionists. But Methodists, who are always greedy for a good hymn, soon heard Faber's work and fell in love with it. They hastened to incorporate it in their own hymn-books, but they were given some pause when they arrived at Faber's confident prediction that Victorian England would return to the Roman obedience:

> Faith of our fathers, Mary's prayers
> Shall win our country back to Thee;
> And through the truth that comes from God,
> England shall then indeed be free.

The Methodists were not going to let go of their prey; so with a little judicious tweaking, that verse began 'Faith of our fathers, God's great power / Shall soon all nations win for thee', and the reference to England was painted out. Thus suitably doctored, the hymn has enjoyed a huge worldwide success among evangelical Protestants, and can now be down-loaded from scores of evangelical websites, most of whose creators are probably innocent of its origins.

Several morals might be drawn from this curious tale. One might optimis-tically take it as a theme for the Christian ecumenical movement, whose growth has been a feature of Christianity over the last century, a sign that even amid Reformation conflict, so much united the two sides that they might easily end up singing each other's hymns. More negatively, it might remind us of an ecumenism of purpose rather less attractive to modern eyes: repression of religious radicals as early as the 1530s by Protestant and Catholic alike, increasing common strictness or censoriousness in matters of personal morality and discipline, shared persecution of people labelled witches. More harshly still, in view of the contraction of Christian practice in modern Europe, it might seem to symbolize a Reformation which was a story of two bald men fighting over a comb: an ultimately futile struggle over issues which now seem trivial or irrelevant.

Much of what I have presented in previous chapters has pointed to an end to the Reformation around 1700, a convergence of various strands of contrary thought which in the course of time transformed the way in which the descendants of Reformation and Counter-Reformation Europeans viewed themselves, their society and their place in the world around them. We have not yet finished gathering together these contrary impulses: so our final task is to see what western Christendom looked like at the end of the seventeenth century, and then to assess what now remains from those three centuries of upheaval in western religion.

WARS OF REFORMATION

At first sight, the Reformation struggle seemed far from over in 1700. Averagely aware Europeans at the turn of the seventeenth and eighteenth centuries were only too conscious that the boundaries of Protestant Europe had hugely contracted over the previous hundred years: Counter-Reformation Catholicism seemed triumphantly unstoppable. In 1590, around half the European land-mass was under the control of Protestant governments and/or Protestant culture: in 1690 the figure was only around a fifth. The greatest losses were in central and south-eastern Europe in the wake of the early Habsburg victories in the Thirty Years War: Bohemia, cradle of successful religious dissent long before Luther, and the once-kaleidoscopic religious landscape in Moravia were now utterly transformed, together with the Austrian lands where Lutheranism had once seized the advantage. The Reformed (yet equally kaleidoscopic) principality of Transylvania was a shadow of its former self and could do little to stem the onward eastern march of Catholic Habsburg power, newly self-confident after overcoming the last great Ottoman threat in the siege of Vienna in 1683.

The frontier of Protestantism had thus retreated hundreds of miles north by 1700, from the borders of Italy to the Germanic middle territories of the Holy Roman Empire. Geneva in the south now seemed a lonely outpost. In the western Alpine regions, ruled by the Duchy of Savoy, from the 1650s to the end of the 1680s ancient Waldensian communities of Italian Protestants faced massacres from ducal armies that shocked all Protestant Europe and sent even the far-away English scrabbling in their purses to help the terrified and brutalized refugees. In the Polish-Lithuanian Commonwealth, inexorable pressure from Catholic education, missionary work and royal interference was undermining the variety of Protestantisms and radical Christianities that had once been the life-blood of the Commonwealth, now itself politically enfeebled and increasingly at the mercy of its political neighbours. Arian and Reformed noblemen were abandoning their faith for Catholicism, leaving their Protestant protégés to fend for themselves: Lutheran-led towns and cities in the Commonwealth seemed increasingly isolated in their religion as well as in their German speech and culture.

It is true that by the end of the Thirty Years War many Europeans, including many European rulers, felt sickened by wars of religion, yet the most powerful people in Europe kept the idea alive with a vengeance. Along with the newly minted Bavarian Elector, the Habsburgs had made sure that their hereditary territories were exempted in the Peace of Westphalia from the general provisions for toleration of religious minorities; throughout the first half of the eighteenth century they grimly pressed on with their programme of restoring the Catholic faith and dispersing Protestant populations from their dominions. Late seventeenth-century Europe was dominated by the king at the centre of Roman Catholic advance in western Europe, Louis XIV of France: a devout Catholic, determined to extend the boundaries of his faith as well as his dominions right up to his death as an exhausted and defeated old man in 1715. In his prime, he directed an army of 400,000, supported by a taxable population of twenty million. Louis spurred on the Duke of Savoy in his murderous campaigns against his Protestant subjects: Louis overturned his grandfather's religious settlement for France by revoking the Edict of Nantes in 1685: Louis conquered largely Protestant lands of the Empire in Alsace, finally making a Catholic

Strasbourg out of Martin Bucer's proud Strassburg, which long before had been the prime candidate to lead the Protestant world. Louis stood behind the plans of the former King James and his son to regain their island kingdoms in the Atlantic and permanently re-establish a Catholic Stuart dynasty there.[1]

In his military campaigns of 1672, King Louis nearly succeeded where the Catholic Spanish monarchy had failed in overwhelming the Protestant United Provinces of the Netherlands – and in that ambitious venture lay the seeds of his own failure. For the outrage of French invasion provoked Prince Willem of Orange to take up arms against the Catholic Leviathan just as his murdered ancestor Willem 'the Silent' had done a century before. Willem eventually humbled French Catholic power, taking revenge for the disaster suffered by the Elector Palatine Friedrich (his great-uncle by marriage) through the Habsburgs back in 1620. As a by-blow in the course of his relentless campaigns against Louis, Willem gained the throne of England in the Glorious Revolution of 1688. After his death, English-led armies continued to fight the French under his British successor Queen Anne, and they decisively blocked what had seemed an inexorable advance. John Churchill gained his title of Duke of Marlborough, and the money to build Oxfordshire's Blenheim Palace, one of Europe's most splendid houses, because of British public gratitude for his brilliance in commanding the armies which permanently halted the Catholic tide from washing away all surviving Protestant power. It was not surprising that the people of northern Europe were still virulently anti-Catholic in 1700. They still read their sixteenth-century martyrologies – John Foxe for the English, Adriaan van Haemstede for the Dutch, Ludwig Rabus for Lutherans, the *Martyrs' Mirror* for many Anabaptists – but Protestants had no need merely to recycle passions from the days of the Reformation martyrs. The Catholic menace was a living reality.

The Reformation might indeed be viewed simply as two centuries of warfare: the sixteenth century witnessed fewer than ten years of complete peace, and there were less than a couple of years during the first half of the seventeenth.[2] The starting-point was earlier, in the Franco-Habsburg wars in Italy in the 1490s, but the Reformation took only six years from its outbreak in 1517 to become a major trigger of violence in the Peasants' Wars of the German lands. Very soon it was the single greatest motive for the killing, as the Lutheran-inspired Schmalkaldic Wars unfolding from 1547 were succeeded by the Reformed-inspired wars of religion between the 1560s and 1590s, and then by the horrors of the Thirty Years War. Wretched columns of refugees were repeatedly sent straggling along the roads of Europe for the sake of their faith, or even moved voluntarily to find a more welcoming religous atmosphere. These Reformation wars involved the biggest population movements in Europe between the 'barbarian' upheavals which dismantled the western Roman Empire and the twentieth century's First and Second World Wars. Hundreds of thousands of people decided to follow the example of the English, quit Europe and brave the terrors of the Atlantic to find a new life in north America. As early as 1662 some of the Duke of Savoy's Waldensian victims in the Alpine valleys took ship for a sympathetic Dutch Reformed colony; they found a new safe home on Staten Island, amid the great natural haven which would become New York.[3]

European wars spiralled in cost as armies grew ever larger and evolved ever more sophisticated weapons and defences. In order to finance the monster as efficiently as possible, government grew in complexity and sophistication, to the point that it became possible to envisage it as an autonomous force, the 'state' – a significant new translation of that Latin word 'respublica' which had previously commonly been rendered 'commonwealth' (chapter 1, p. 44). The growth of governments generally increased their power and the desire of monarchs to have as few obstacles to obedience as possible. The Reformation thus inadvertently promoted the already growing power of state machines, both Protestant and Catholic. Indeed it helped to transform many of them from loose dynastic territories, dependent on consent from noblemen and representative assemblies, to much more tightly organized monarchies: the Protestant states in Sweden or Brandenburg-Prussia, for instance, or the Catholic states in France, Spain or the Habsburg lands. The great exception was Poland-Lithuania, where conflicting religious loyalties served to hobble the constitutional power of the monarchy in the religious Confederation of Warsaw (chapter 7, p. 343): the consequent struggles of Polish monarchs to seize back the initiative were one major factor in eventually bringing down this greatest of European aristocratic Commonwealths.

The newly strengthened monarchies in turn sought to build up their subjects' potential enthusiasm for fighting the subjects of other monarchs, by stressing a common cultural and religious identity. Usually they privileged one language among others, for administrative simplicity's sake, or even one version of a language among others: Castilian Spanish, northern French, High German and the English of London were among the prime beneficiaries. Latin, the esperanto of educated Protestants as much as of Catholics, fought a rearguard action among scholars: during the seventeenth century, the Catholic philosopher René Descartes, the Dutch Arminian legal theorist

Hugo Grotius, the English Socinian Protestant theologian-scientist Isaac Newton all still addressed an international audience in Latin. Yet within a generation after 1700, the transition to certain favoured vernacular languages was complete, alike for philosophy, theology and the newly expanding 'natural philosophy' of the physical sciences. Now the 'state-nation' was developing. Soon such 'state-nations' turned into 'nation-states': this change came through the consolidation of one majority culture within a state, the overthrow of many monarchies after the French Revolution of 1789, and the furious reaction of many cultures to Napoleon Bonaparte's imperial ambitions. National consciousness and not a royal dynasty now became the prime point of loyalty.

In 1700, that was still in the future. During the growth of dynastic states in the Reformation wars, some Catholic and Protestant theologians justified the increase in royal power as they felt fit, elaborating theories of divine right or royal absolutism blessed by God. Other theologians, caught up in struggles against monarchs of contrary religious views, developed increasingly elaborate theories of resistance which put power in the hands of the people (or at least godly people), and even laid down circumstances in which monarchs might be eliminated. In the long civil and religious wars which eviscerated late sixteenth-century France, Reformed Protestants, ideologically charged Ligueur Catholics and some of the more ruthless Jesuits alike all put their minds to such theories. Catholics in those years specialized in terrorist assassinations – Willem of Orange, Henri III and Henri IV of France were among their victims, and they did their best to eliminate Elizabeth I and James I of England. Reformed Protestants achieved the same end differently. Concerned to express the mind of God's people through decisions publicly agreed, they appealed to judicial process involving public consent from representative bodies: for instance, the English Bond of Association agreed by Protestant English gentry and nobility against Mary Queen of Scots, or her later trial and execution (chapter 8, p. 386), then the trial and execution of Charles I in 1649 (chapter 12, p. 524).

Reformation and Counter-Reformation thus shed much blood and shortened or ruined countless lives in the course of their warfare. By the early years of the eighteenth century, with political boundaries more or less stabilized after Marlborough's victories against Louis XIV at Blenheim, Ramillies, Oudenarde and Malplaquet, the wars also produced a great divide between the everyday life of Catholic Europe and the surviving fragment of Protestant Europe. This was far greater than the ancient divide between the chilly north and the more relaxed atmosphere of the Mediterranean. Much more now united the cultural consciousness of sun-scorched

Seville and the windswept plains and pine-forests of Catholic Poland than united the Poles to their Lutheran and Reformed neighbours, thanks to the common focus of Catholics in Rome. In 1622 the Pope canonized a twelfth-century Spanish farm labourer St Isidore the Farmer, after strong advocacy from King Philip of Spain. Far away in Poland Isidore's cult soon began to flourish, much encouraged by Catholic nobles of the Common-wealth who calculated that a hardworking labourer-saint would be a good example to their serfs and estate workers.[4]

TOLERATING DIFFERENCE

The difference between Catholic and Protestant Europe would be instantly obvious to any traveller bundled up, blindfolded, set down at random in a street on a Sunday morning, and told to listen to the church bells. During the Reformation, Protestants had culled countless unwanted bells to be melted down for armaments and for sale, adroitly combining profit with iconoclastic destruction of popish superstition. Nevertheless, Protestants had not dispensed with bells altogether, because before the invention of the electric telegraph, bells were only rivalled by fire-beacons as the most effective means of communication over a long distance. Even Protestant Scotland, which has been more ruthlessly practical in disposing of its incon-venient medieval churches than any other country in Europe, to this day retains a surprising number of pre-Reformation church bells. But after the Reformation, the sound on the Catholic and on the Protestant street would be very different. A Sunday morning in Catholic Europe would be full of the competing clangour of a bewildering variety of encounters with God. Just as before Martin Luther's agonized rebellion, the parish churches, the cathedral, the collegiate chapters, the monasteries, the nunneries, the hospitals would all still be sending up their cacophony of noise, not only to summon people to myriad celebrations of the Mass, but also repeatedly to tell the faithful out in the streets or in the fields that God had been seen once more in bread and wine in the priest's act of consecration. The triumphal din would be incessant, perhaps all the stronger if the ringers were conscious that there were Protestants within earshot.

In Protestant Europe, the parish church eliminated all its competitors. The monasteries were ruinated, demolished, or turned to useful purposes such as warehouses, workhouses, schools, libraries – the cathedral buildings (except in England) demoted, if they were kept at all, into large parish churches. So a single bell might austerely be summoning the parish to hear the Word of God. Lutherans might be more inclined than the Reformed to keep a whole belfry-full of bells, but now these would be sounding only from the parish church tower. Our blindfolded victim on the street might have one distinctive experience which would instantly tell him that he was in that strange and self-satisfied kingdom, England: the church bells here were doing something very odd. They were ringing out in regular melodic patterns, changing in a complicated pre-ordained scheme from sequence to sequence. Towards the end of Elizabeth I's reign, as most of the English came to accept the Queen's official Reformation in various fashions to suit themselves, they invented a game with their church bells not found anywhere else in Europe. They called it change-ringing, and developed a huge enthusiasm for it, frequently indulging in great competitive bouts to see how long a team could last without repetition, even without the excuse of a church service to announce. Change-ringing became part of the fun of being an English Protestant.[5] It was one curious symbol that the Reformed Church of England had begun taking a distinctive path from the other Reformed Churches of Europe, thinking of itself in a different way, and puzzling all other European Protestants.

By definition the sound of bells was the sound of established Churches, those which had been given the privilege of announcing their presence in the landscape by assaulting the ears of the entire population. Many people in Europe decided against joining official Churches. In most Catholic lands, official pressure and harassment meant that Protestants had small chance of hanging on to open profession of their deviant beliefs, but in Protestant Europe, south of Scandinavia, with its development of a remarkably uniform Lutheranism, there was a significant spread of alternative religious bodies. Some were pockets of Roman Catholics, Lutherans or Reformed who found themselves under the wrong regime. In Scotland after 1690 there was even an aggrieved body of Protestant adherents of Church government by bishops. On the other side of the border in England these 'Episcopalians' would have been part of the Church establishment, but now they were excluded from Scotland's established Church by a deal between the new King William III and the presbyterian party in Scotland, and they were treated as dangerous subversives because most of them supported the exiled Stuart pretender to the throne.

Besides such fragments of Churches that would have liked to enjoy established status, there were some groups who rejected association with the civil power on principle, for instance the Independents and Baptists in England. There were also followers of the many radical forms of Christianity for whom Protestants (with some justice) begrudged the name of Protestant:

Anabaptist Mennonites or Hutterites, Schwenckfelders, Quakers – a host of small sects following the insights of some particular charismatic leader of the previous two centuries. In eastern Europe there were Orthodox, in Poland-Lithuania even some Muslims. Such diversity presented the official Churches of Europe with problems. How far should religious dissent be tolerated? It was surely offensive to God, as well as offensive in its disloyalty to the wishes of God's anointed, the rulers in Church and Commonwealth. Here it is possible to argue that the most significant contribution of the two Reformation centuries to Christianity was the theory and practice of toleration, although it would also be possible to argue that the contribution was inadvertent and reluctant.

Christianity's previous record on toleration, either of Christian deviance or of other religions, might kindly be termed unimpressive. The eastern Churches (the Orthodox, the Copts and other Churches of Monophysite or Nestorian belief) generally have a better record than the Latin West, but that has been forced on them by circumstance: power was taken out of their hands by the Muslim invasions, and they have had much less chance than the steadily more centralized Latin Church of being successfully intolerant. Some of them have had plenty of experience of being persecuted by Latin Christians (chapter 2, p. 55, and 8, p. 363). Indeed western Christianity before 1500 must rank as one of the most intolerant religions in world history: its record in comparison with medieval Islamic civilization is embarrassingly poor. It put up with Jews (more or less) only because they played a part in the Church's view of its own future (chapter 1, p. 8), it hated and feared Islam and did its best to destroy it whenever possible.[6] Its attitude to Greek Christianity was at best condescending and at worst contemptuous, resulting in consistent failure for medieval negotiations on Christian reunion.

It was not that medieval western Christians did not have the mental resources to envisage religious toleration. As modern scholarship has rediscovered, they frequently talked about it as a theoretical possibility, but they did precious little about it unless forced to, as the Hussites forced the Pope in fifteenth-century Bohemia, or as circumstances forced the atrophied Catholicism of late medieval Lithuania and Ukraine to tolerate Orthodoxy.[7] At the beginning of its 'formation of a persecuting society' (chapter 1, p. 26), the western Church started burning people whom it defined as heretics (the first recorded example being in 1022 in France), and in the course of its wars against Christian deviance in southern France in the thirteenth century it introduced inquisitions as a method of examining unusual Christian theology. It is probably significant that in the whole history of Muslim–

Christian relations, the volume of voluntary conversion from Islam to Christianity has been minimal, but the traffic in the other direction has been very much larger.

This dismal record began to change in the Reformation, though once more in the first instance through force of circumstances, as the rival bidders for a monopoly on the expression of Christianity found that they could not impose that monopoly. So the first implementations of toleration in western Europe were mostly concessions by the powerful whose power was not complete: a grudging recognition of something which ideally would have remained forbidden. Concessions were made from a society which had not fundamentally adjusted its structures or the ideologies that legitimized them, even though it put up for the time being with an alternative set of ideas. This was the assumption allowing French Catholics to accept the Edict of Nantes after 1598; the Dutch Reformed Church to put up with its infuriating variety of competitors from the 1580s; the vengeful ultra-royalist gentry of Charles II's England to leave some marginal existence to dissenting Protestants as well as to the traditional hate-figures of Roman Catholics, when they passed punitive legislation for uniformity in 1662.[8] Few in such societies openly said that it was a bad principle to persecute or kill people for religion, although Protestants were rather more hesitant than Catholics about executions, given their own sufferings at Catholic hands. Notable among the minority who did condemn all executions for heresy were two chief chroniclers of Protestant martyrdoms, John Foxe and Adriaan van Haemstede. Haemstede was in fact dismissed by his outraged congregation of Low Countries refugees in Elizabethan London because he obstinately persisted in affirming that Anabaptists were among his brethren.[9]

There was a more generous atmosphere in eastern Europe, where people were more familiar before the Reformation with having to live and let live. We have heard the sentiments of Transylvania's pioneering Declaration of Torda from 1568 ('faith is a gift from God') and of the Confederation of Warsaw of 1572 – 'we will not for a different faith or a change of churches shed blood' (chapters 5, p. 262, 7, p. 343). It is one of history's saddest ironies that Transylvania is now celebrated for the imaginary grotesqueries of Count Dracula rather than for its clarion call for sanity amid sixteenth-century Europe's distractions. It is also sad that the more intolerant attitudes of southern and western Europe gradually contaminated the open-mindedness of the east: during the seventeenth century, for instance, western Reformed Churches much encouraged the Transylvanian Reformed establishment to crack down on the Unitarian Church. In 1638, the Transylvanian Reformed Church went so far as an execution for heresy, when it had the

Unitarian János Toroczkai stoned to death for saying 'if Jesus would come to earth, I would send him to work in a vineyard'.[10] The memory of an eastern Europe of diversity and hospitality to independent thought is worth placing against the more recent images of the region: the malign later history of Poland which (with the unsought assistance of Nazi Germany's crimes against the Jews) has now left the nation's religious character virtually monochrome, and the break-up of Yugoslavia in the 1990s, achieved with the aid of slogans of religious bigotry.

It took a great leap of imagination, beyond most sixteenth-century people who enjoyed power, to think that toleration might be not only a useful or necessary expedient, but that the ultimate aspiration might be to seek religious freedom for all – 'indifference to certain kinds of difference'.[11] To begin with, the idea was the product of outsiders, like John Calvin's *bête noire* Sebastian Castellio in mid-century Basel, reacting among other provocations to Geneva's burning of Servetus (chapter 5, pp. 241, 245), but gradually other voices joined in. Particularly significant was the addition of those who had experienced first power and then persecution: misfortune gave them a chance to rethink their earlier attitudes. The Arminians of the Netherlands, faced in the 1620s with vicious repression by hard-line Calvinists after the Synod of Dordt (chapter 8, p. 378), produced a number of impressive statements of the new case, especially from the leading Arminian clergy Johannes Uyttenbogaert and Simon Bischop (Episcopius). What was the point in persecution, asked Episcopius, when there were so many different possible interpretations of Scripture and opinions that could be derived from it? This being so, it was a positive advantage and a way of clarifying the real truths of Christianity to allow as many views as possible to be heard.[12]

Gradually during the seventeenth century, such statements ceased to be shocking; the flourishing economy and growing power of the Netherlands, where such things were being said, was one good reason for taking seriously the idea of toleration. Governing authorities began to lose their faith in crusading. They became more hesitant and more shamefaced about persecution for religious opinions, let alone adding to the 5,000 or so executions for religion that the Reformation and Counter-Reformation between them had produced in western Europe.[13] A consortium of secular magistrates and Jesuits in the Catholic Spanish Netherlands went so far in 1597 as to bury alive an Anabaptist servant-girl, Anneke van den Hove, but that was almost the end of the killings for heresy in this northern Catholic setting. The English burned two anti-Trinitarian radicals in 1612 for the last time, and indeed, considering England's generally dismal record on toleration during the Reformation, there was a noticeable absence of any further burning of heretics during and after the mid-seventeenth century Civil Wars in the Atlantic Isles, which in other respects were often atrociously bitter. On the contrary, the Interregnum in England was a very important moment when amid lively debates about the future of English religion, advocates of toleration began raising their voices. Some of these voices were lucky in having the ear of Lord Protector Oliver Cromwell.

Progress was crabwise. Cromwell's readmission of the Jews to the Atlantic Isles (chapter 12, p. 527) was a permanent achievement, but the Restoration regime of Charles II was exceptional in its renewed repression of Protestants by Protestants, and when John Locke published his celebrated *Letters concerning toleration* in the aftermath of England's Glorious Revolution, he still excluded Roman Catholics and atheists from his proposals, on the grounds that they were enemies to the English state. England had recently witnessed its final judicial murder of a Roman Catholic with the execution of Archbishop Oliver Plunkett, at the height of politically inspired anti-Catholic hysteria in 1681; the Presbyterian Church of Scotland had a last convulsion of punitive violence in 1697 when it secured the hanging in Edinburgh of a wild young medical student, Thomas Aikenhead, for blasphemy, including denial of the Trinity. By then, even some Scottish ministers pleaded that Aikenhead be spared; and in 1736, the British Parliament pulled back a further frontier of official repression when it repealed the savage provisions of the English and Scottish legislation against witchcraft. Once more that turning-point around 1700 emerges as significant.

CROSS-CURRENTS: HUMANISM AND NATURAL PHILOSOPHY

There are yet more convergences to explore. All through the story of the sixteenth and seventeenth centuries, we have occasionally glimpsed other currents of thinking, which did not form part of the Reformation and Counter-Reformation's set-piece battle within the mind of Augustine (chapter 2, p. 111). Humanist scholarship had sheltered such alternative views because it had opened up so much of the non-Christian literature surviving from the ancient world, innocent of Christian theological preoccupations. Both Renaissance humanists and the Reformers embraced new ways of thinking, yet their aims were not identical, and the Reformers transformed humanism as much as humanism created the Reformers. Luther and Zwingli saw many humanist preoccupations as irrelevant as any excess of scholasticism to humanity's absolute need for salvation by external grace. Accordingly the archetypal humanist scholar and activist Zwingli ended up supporting the primarily scholastically trained lecturer Luther rather than his former humanist hero Erasmus, when in 1524 the classic conflict over human free will emerged between them. Humanists found themselves forced to make choices, as confessional divides became pronounced. Humanist scholarship was then commandeered for the purposes of rival Churches.

Both Reformers and Romanists exploited humanist scholarly techniques, but then harnessed them to theological warfare. They deployed the skills of philology and historical criticism, but rarely valued objectivity; they drew on creative humanist discussion of schooling, the more efficiently to drum uniformity into young minds (the Lutheran Johann Bugenhagen, one of the great remodellers of education in north Germany and Scandinavia, described his ideal curricular focus as 'the catechism and languages'). They drew on humanist aspirations to make society better by legislation, but now their aim was to tidy everyone into confessional moulds. What they usually forgot was the cement that originally bound all this together: a delight in exploring truth even when it produced uncomfortable results, a hermeneutic and rhetoric of doubt. Neither revolutionaries nor counter-revolutionaries had any use for such preoccupations, and they despised and often persecuted those who tried desperately to assert their continuing importance. So already in 1524, Luther accused Erasmus during their clash on free will of wanting 'to compare everything, affirm nothing'. Equally, the Council of Trent has recently been described as 'a veritable Counter-Renaissance'.[14] The suppression of humanist doubt proved temporary, yet the scholarly but confessionally engaged kept on trying.

Faced with the change of atmosphere in the 1520s, some humanist scholars withdrew into an interior exile, ceasing to publish or moving to fields of enquiry such as secular classical history that could not be so easily drawn into theological controversy.[15] By doing this they were reminding the literary public that there were matters other than the Reformation that might be important, and other perspectives on religion. The humanists had rediscovered or taken a new interest in various forms of esoteric literature: the hermetic books, neo-Platonic writings from the Roman Empire and Jewish Cabbala (chapter 2, pp. 80–81). Some of them combined this fascination with a commitment to church reform well before Martin Luther: we have already met Egidio of Viterbo, who believed that Hebrew was the only real sacred language, and the alchemist and magician Abbot Trithemius of Sponheim (chapter 2, pp. 91–2). Some Protestant theologians continued this enthusiasm. Reformed Protestants after all drew many central theological themes from the Old Testament, and it was natural that they welcomed other apparent shafts of light on Hebrew wisdom: these might have bearing on that common Reformation preoccupation, the timing of the Last Days, or provide new answers to some of the many theological problems which caused so many murderous arguments in the Reformation.

Perhaps the most surprising outcrop of Reformed Protestant interest in the esoteric was the phenomenon of Freemasonry. This now very varied worldwide movement, despite much mythology tracing its origins to the ancient world, actually began in late sixteenth-century Scotland. This was an age when in the new conditions of comparative peace brought by that shrewd monarch James VI, there was a sudden surge of energy in building, as the Scottish nobility and gentry rehoused themselves in greater comfort and amid spectacular outward display. Those who commissioned buildings naturally took a great interest in the work done for them, especially the theory behind the new classical architectural styles involved: they were educated men who were seized with enthusiasm for Renaissance redis-coveries of classical wisdom, and they linked this with the craft traditions of those whom they employed in their building. A key figure was the royal Mason of Works, William Schaw, a crypto-Catholic. From the 1590s, various Scottish notables in contact with Schaw joined trade 'lodges' of the masons and builders, which clearly replaced in their esteem the devotional gilds that the Scottish Reformers had destroyed only a few decades before. Soon they were adding dignity to their socializing by drawing on the rich resource of esoteric literature which was so prized in the Renaissance: medieval masons had already sought to express their craft pride by con-structing histories for themselves out of such material. The Church of Scotland, in interesting contrast to its growing hostile preoccupation with witchcraft (chapter 13, pp. 570–73), showed no signs of alarm at the new departure. From all this the Scottish Freemasons constructed their impressively ancient history, which was gradually transmitted throughout Europe and eventually beyond as their organizations spread.[16]

One of the most original figures to weave his own (often far from sober) path through the Reformation was the multi-talented Theophrastus Paracelsus. His mysterious-sounding surname is simply an imaginative classicization of his ancestral home in Württemberg: he was the son of a doctor who had settled in the little Swiss shrine-town of Einsiedeln (he would have known Huldrych Zwingli there). Paracelsus ranged in his curi-osity over a bewildering variety of areas of knowledge, usually with a breezy disrespect for any received wisdom: 'Shit on your Pliny, Aristotle, your Albertus, Thomas, Scotus', he advised the world of scholarship.[17] The tone is remarkably like Martin Luther at his most outrageous, and Paracelsus has been called 'the Luther of medicine': scoring some real achievements such as an analysis of diseases associated with mining, he despised classical medical authorities like Galen. When he embarked on his massive and multiform speculations in theology, he was equally disinclined to listen to either Catholics or Protestants, to their puzzlement and fury. At one stage in the 1520s, when he was moving around some of the most disrupted and revolutionary parts of central Europe, he even speculated at length as to whether the Virgin Mary should be considered part of the Godhead, a direction which took him on precisely the opposite road to the rest of the Reformation.[18]

There was a practical reason for Paracelsus to leave aside the canonical texts of philosophy and theology: he was temperamentally restless and frequently on the move (often to avoid the wrath of conventional authorities), so he could carry few books with him apart from the Bible. That, however, did not stop him greatly respecting those ancient authorities whom he thought had been deliberately sidelined: the Cabbalistic and hermetic writers or the early Christian gnostics. Abbot Trithemius was among those who influenced him in his enthusiasms. Paracelsus was fascinated by the theme of the Magi, the astrologer-magicians who had visited the Christ-child, and this incessant traveller saw the Magis' journey to see Jesus as the model for his own efforts to fuse natural observation with sacred knowledge to create a 'magical' system of universal wisdom.[19] He wrote at obsessive length, but sensibly put very little into print in his lifetime, so the European-wide fame of his achievements was often combined with considerable confusion as to what they actually were. Many would-be disciples with their own axes to grind forged writings in his name to gain authority for their views, and these became part of the 'Paracelsian' corpus of literature; other more respectable admirers eventually published some of his works with the alarming sections censored out.

Hence Paracelsus became an all-purpose symbol for wide-ranging investigation which riskily combined irreverence with a sense of magical possibilities. He particularly excited less conventional Protestants (especially Protestant doctors) who saw the Reformation as a liberation from centuries of falsehood. So a heady mixture of Paracelsianism, hermeticism and Cabbala bred optimism: the ancient books became more rather than less important as time went on, particularly in the universities of central Europe, where in the early seventeenth century ecumenically minded scholars were trying to find ways of bridging the gulf between Lutheran and Reformed theology. Hermetic wisdom and Paracelsianism lay behind the febrile excitement of the Rosicrucian literature, inspired by a Lutheran, Johann Valentin Andreae, but intimately entwined with the attempted Reformed Protestant crusade of the Elector Palatine against the Habsburgs that sparked the Thirty Years War (chapter 11, pp. 491–2). The renowned Reformed Protestant scholar Johann Heinrich Alsted proclaimed calculations of the divinely ordained end-time, which in the course of a European-wide impact, helped inflame the political ambitions of Reformed Transylvania: much of his theorizing (eventually choosing 1694 as the crucial date) was drawn not from the Bible but from hermetic literature.[20]

The grave political disappointments which followed these predictions did not dampen scholarly enthusiasm for ancient esoteric wisdom: it was still current at the end of the seventeenth century. Sir Isaac Newton provides one of the greatest examples of that blend of fascination with a mysterious past, innovative observation and abstract thinking, which despite the intentions of most of its practitioners began to give precedence to a new area of human enquiry over theology. We define this exploration as 'science'. Commonly in the modern West it has been seen as a rational mode of enquiry, waging an ideological battle with a irrational foe, Christianity, but 'science' is a very imprecise word, and in the era of the Reformation and Renaissance it simply meant knowledge. The discipline which is the ancestor of modern specializations like astronomy, biology, physics or chemistry was then called natural philosophy: it demarcated itself from theology's concentration on the world beyond by concentrating on evidence from nature, the visible created world. That did not make it any less an examination of God's creation, since evidence from the world might have its own mysterious or magical dimension if seen through the eyes of a Paracelsian or neo-Platonist. Rarely did such investigation contain any sense of clash of purpose or intention with religion – that was why Newton wrote as much about the Book of Revelation as about the theory of gravity.[21] Newton, Alsted and other international and ecumenically minded contemporary scholars like John Dury or Jan Comenius were intent on forwarding all knowledge, which is why they saw classical esoteric literature as an ally in enquiry and not a series of ancient dead ends, as their scientific successors now tend to do.

By no means all theologians or philosophers were enraptured by esoteric wisdom even then: some took their cue from Erasmus, who had despised it. Some Reformed Protestants were keenly aware of a basic contradiction that esoteric enthusiasts chose to ignore: an Augustinian Christianity stresses the helplessness of humanity before God's purposes, while magic or hermetic wisdom emphasizes the empowerment of those with the right knowledge.

James I of England, in this matter an orthodox Reformed Protestant, disapproved of the omnivorous enquiries and magical experiments of the internationally renowned English Platonist and admirer of Paracelsus, John Dee: the King was not inclined to help the old man in his declining years. James was also pleased to be the dedicatee of a book by the former Genevan professor turned English clergyman Isaac Casaubon, which pitilessly analysed the hermetic writings to show that far from being age-old wisdom, they sailed under false colours, and in fact post-dated the coming of Christ.[22]

Neither did the Rosicrucians fool everyone. The English politician-philosopher Francis Bacon showed some interest in the Rosicrucian manifestos but then brusquely rejected them, seeing them as a symbol of the folly of paying too much respect to ancient authority and mystical secrets. He turned his attention to practical investigations and condemned preconceived theories, even though he was still fascinated by natural magic and valued the symbolic role of the Magi as much as Paracelsus before him.[23] Bacon's emphasis on the practical produced something of a blind spot in him: for instance, he regarded mathematics as too close to the number-symbolism that fascinated many esotericists (and in any case he was privately not sure that he understood how it worked). Not only was he unimpressed by the work of astronomers following up Copernicus's theories (see below, p. 685), he did not appreciate William Gilbert's discoveries in magnetism, because he rightly saw Gilbert as a neo-Platonist admirer of John Dee.[24] Conversely, Bacon's English contemporary William Harvey, who shaped his remarkable discoveries about the circulation of the blood with the aid of ancient Aristotelian method used in a new context, was cool towards Bacon's work because Bacon despised Aristotle. Harvey famously declared with no friendly intent that Bacon wrote philosophy like a Lord Chancellor – that is, like an unimaginative lawyer.[25] This gulf between Bacon – often seen as 'the father of modern science' – and some of his most creative contemporaries in the exploration of natural knowledge is a useful reminder that there was no clear war between 'science and religion' in the Reformation centuries.

One or two areas of natural philosophy did reveal tensions with theology. One was medicine, where for centuries doctors had been inclined to see practical observation as more important than what the textbooks told them: this shocked theologians, who were inclined to take very seriously what Aristotle or Galen said about the human body (chapter 2, p. 86; chapter 15). Ironically, humanist doctors were generally more conservative in medicine than doctors with a medieval scholastic training, simply because they placed a new value on ancient texts: there was a problem for humanists, for instance, when they tried to understand the new disease syphilis, which was unknown to the ancient writers (chapter 16, p. 631). An even more difficult frontier between natural philosophy and theology was astrology and astronomy. Natural philosophers concerning themselves with the planets and the stars had things to say about the heavens that might seem to be the business of theological faculties, particularly since the Bible makes certain confident pronouncements on the make-up of the visible heavens. Once more the divisions were unpredictable: we have seen Melanchthon and Calvin flatly disagreeing about the value of astrology (chapter 5, p. 244), and Lutheran ministers lined up behind Melanchthon against Calvin in seeing astrology as a respectable and valuable guide to God's purposes.[26]

At least astrology was a scholarly pursuit with a long history. Much more problematic was a growing body of opinion that the Bible contained a mistake about the physical universe: its assumption (on the few occasions that it addressed the question) that the sun revolved around the earth. The 'heliocentric' proposition that the truth was the other way around predated Luther's rebellion and was the product of quiet reflection and calculation by a mathematically minded canon of the cathedral of Warmia at Frauenburg (Frombork) in Poland, Nicolaus Copernicus. Copernicus circulated his findings in manuscript in 1514 and soon they were much discussed throughout Europe, even though not put into print until the very end of his life in 1543. By then theologians on both sides of the new religious divides saw heliocentric theory as presenting difficulties, contradicting as it did not only the Bible but Aristotle and the standard ancient authority on astronomy, Ptolemy. Worse still for the Reformers, Luther's theological revolution followed Augustine of Hippo in emphasizing the catastrophic effect of the Fall on creation. The earth's central position in traditional cosmology might be seen as a perfect symbol of this catastrophe: it was in the lowest and therefore the most humble position in the cosmos, a corruptible place, whereas the sun, the moon and the stars were part of a better incorruptible world. Copernicus's ideas challenged both these theological assumptions, so they were in danger of prompting a new arrogance in humanity: they implied that the corruptible universe below the heavenly sphere was much greater in extent than anyone had previously thought, and certainly included the sun, the moon and the stars.

Accordingly the printed version of Copernicus's De Revolutionibus of 1543 followed advice from the Lutheran pastor of Nuremberg Andreas Osiander, who knew of Wittenberg's disapproval: to conciliate Luther and Melanchthon just as much as to avoid any Catholic condemnation, the work's prologue (dedicated to Pope Paul III) emphasized that its contents were merely theoretical proposals. After Copernicus's death, John Calvin preached just as bitterly against Copernican theorists ('frantic people who would like to change the order of nature') as he denounced astrology.[27] There was indeed much to think about and refine before Copernicus's preliminary sketch made more sense than traditional cosmology: one essential requirement was practical observation which was not possible in Copernicus's time, in order to confirm his calculations. That came with the invention of an effective telescope in the early seventeenth century. In the next few years, while the Jesuits were still marshalling their formidable research capacity to explore the potential of this new tool of enquiry, there occurred a damaging clash between the Catholic Church and one representative of the new natural philosophy: the condemnation of Galileo.

October 31 has two particular resonances for the papacy. On that date in 1517 Martin Luther made his protest about indulgences, while on that date in 1992, Pope John Paul II made the nearest thing the Roman Church has achieved to an apology for its treatment of Galileo Galilei. Galileo was condemned by the Roman Inquisition in 1633 for advocating Copernican astronomy, after the Church in 1616 had declared Copernicus to be in error. This coincidence of dates has a piquant symbolism. Without the papacy's defensiveness after Luther's rebellion, it is unlikely that the Catholic Church would have made such a major miscalculation as it did in the Galileo affair. Galileo's trial happened during the Thirty Years War: a destructive battle for the soul of Central Europe between Catholic and Protestant, and a time when the Pope was feeling unusually vulnerable.

Worse still for any calm consideration of Galileo's contentions, the case of Giordano Bruno four decades before provided an alarming precedent for adventurous discussion of cosmology. This Neapolitan hermeticist, mystic and astronomer-priest, one of the most fascinating and independent intelligences of sixteenth-century Europe, had fled his Dominican friary and embarked on continent-wide travels which made him the client of such arch-enemies of the Church as Robert Dudley, Earl of Leicester and Sir Philip Sidney. The establishment of Oxford University loathed Bruno during his English visit in 1583–5, but they did not possess the powers enjoyed by the Roman Inquisition, which ended up burning him at the stake in Rome in 1600. Among the many charges against him, including his deep contempt for Jesus Christ and a blasphemous flippancy about the Mass, he had said that the universe had an infinite number of earths revolving around an infinite number of suns. After Bruno, it was easy to see all new astronomy as a danger to Christianity.[28]

The main issue, and a legitimate one for the Church's concern, was biblical interpretation. Galileo's astronomical observations could only be squared with certain biblical texts if scientists like himself were allowed to explain those texts in new ways: that would amount to the Church surrendering the power to expound the Bible's meaning to men who looked through telescopes. If the Church did that, how could it justify any of its power? Galileo suffered from a fatal inability to suffer fools gladly, a gift entertaining to the detached observer, but rarely appreciated by fools: that helped to bring his downfall out of the many coincidences, misunderstandings and failures of communication in his long drawn-out case. Yet impressively he turned his humiliation by the Roman authorities to positive use: after they forced him in 1633 to abject recantation for the boisterous boldness of his astronomical discussions in the *Discorsi*, he set to work under house arrest to produce a new version in secret, calmly discussing the physics of motion. This last work before his death was perhaps his greatest contribution to western science: an enterprise of truly rational investigation of empirical evidence, ignoring the pressure from powerful traditional authority. It was beginning to transcend the old category of natural philosophy.[29]

Around Galileo, the battle-lines were never simple. Francis Bacon characteristically distrusted Copernicanism because it seemed too based on abstract ideas, like the mystical neo-Platonism which he had come to detest. Gisbertus Voetius, the great ultra-Calvinist scholar of Utrecht, might have been open-minded enough to welcome Anna Maria van Schurman to his university lectures (chapter 15, p. 612), but he loathed all Copernicans, just as much as he loathed Arminians and hermeticists: Voetius felt they were all talking perversely, twisting the words of the Holy Spirit in the Bible. Conversely, over the border in the Spanish Netherlands, Geoffroi Wendelin, a learned and Jesuit-educated priest, went on publishing works which all through the Galileo affair openly discussed Copernican cosmology in favourable terms. As far as Wendelin was concerned, it was only common sense to say that the moon like the earth was simply a corruptible planet, and he said as much in formal debate before the papal nuncio to Brussels. He died in his bed at the age of eighty seven, a respected canon of Tournai Cathedral.[30]

The long term embarrassment for the Catholic Church in the Galileo affair was that although many Protestants might rage against Copernicans, they did not take action against Copernicans as the Inquisition had done in the Galileo case; moreover the Roman Inquisition's action did seem all of a piece with its action in trying to ban so much of the creative literature of the previous century and earlier. There was no doubt that amid the complexities and divisions of the Protestant world, natural philosophy had more room to manoeuvre, and that it was gaining new strength and confidence in northern Europe by the end of the seventeenth century.

Increasingly, natural philosophy emphasized its rationality, and if its practitioners had a close interest in Christianity, they often cherished an agenda
to make Christianity as reasonable a creed as natural philosophy was
becoming. But there were still other sources for that project.

CROSS-CURRENTS: JUDAISM AND DOUBTS

Running through the story of the Reformation has been the presence of a
separate and much disadvantaged religion within the bounds of western
Christendom–Judaism. Throughout medieval Europe, the position of Jews
was always difficult and uncertain, dependent on changeable opinions of
monarchs who might or might not honour agreements which they or their
predecessors had set out, and the equally changeable opinions of ordinary
people (chapter 1, p. 8). The late fifteenth century had brought the greatest
single disaster for the Jewish people since the Roman Empire's destruction
of Jerusalem back in 70 CE, their official expulsion from the Iberian peninsula and the creation of a 'Sephardic' diaspora (chapter 2, pp. 59–63). The
Portuguese were never as single-minded as the Spaniards either in expulsions
from their territories or in efforts to achieve proper conversions, although
after a serious 'converso' rebellion the Portuguese monarchy did set up
its own imitation of the Spanish Inquisition in 1536. In consequence, a
cosmopolitan crypto-Jewish community developed, adopting Portuguese
customs and language while travelling, and settling wherever it seemed
safe in western Europe. The Portuguese Sephardic Jews prospered, usually
through trade, but also through practising that usefully marginal profession,
medicine, and sometimes teaching in the less rigidly exclusive or more
unwary universities. The Portuguese monarchy, always on the lookout for
ways of stretching its strained resources, could see the usefulness of this
talented and mobile community, and it was inclined to look the other
way if some community members seemed less than whole-hearted in their
Christianity – much to the displeasure of the Inquisition.[31]

One might think that the humanist Renaissance, with its sense of new
possibilities and criticism of old stereotypes, would have acted as a counterweight to the Iberian declaration of war on Judaism. The reality was that
Jews benefited from the Renaissance even less than women. We have met
Cardinal Ximénes, that ambiguous patron of Spanish humanism, who was
also one of the major architects of Spain's ethnic cleansing (chapter 2,
pp. 61–4). Even those humanists fascinated by cabbalistic writings seldom
felt much warmth towards the people who had created them; rather, indeed,

they considered, like Johannes Reuchlin (chapter 2, p. 85), that this literature needed to be rescued from the Jews, particularly since one of the reasons to regard it as precious was that it provided clues to prophecies of Jesus Christ in the Hebrew scripture. The same was true of the Hebrew language. Humanist biblical scholars realized that they would have to study it if they were to make any progress in refining the text of the Old Testament, but Hebrew never attained the academic status or commanded the general respect apparent in the study of Greek in humanist higher education. The exiled English Catholic humanist scholars who created the first Catholic English translation of the Bible defended their decision to stick close to the Latin Vulgate's faulty readings of the Old Testament rather than paying attention to the original Hebrew: they confidently affirmed that Christian scholars had always known that the Jews had deliberately corrupted their text. It was predictable that the Spanish Inquisition regarded with acute suspicion any biblical scholars who showed excessive interest in Hebrew studies.[32]

Desiderius Erasmus set the tone for those who considered themselves in Europe's intellectual vanguard by being a notable hater of Jews. He loaded onto them all his prejudices about ceremonial religion, plus his deep distrust of cabbala and other mystical literature. When he savagely attacked Reuchlin's opponent Johannes Pfefferkorn he made much of the fact that Pfefferkorn was a converted Jew, implying that this was why he was standing in the way of truth.[33] Criticizing the scholar Wolfgang Capito, the kindly future reformer of Strassburg who showed a rare positive enthusiasm for Hebrew studies, Erasmus sneered in 1518: 'I see [the Jews] as a nation full of most tedious fabrications who spread a kind of fog over everything: Talmud, Cabala, Tetragrammaton, Gates of Light – words, words, words. I would rather have Christ mixed up with Scotus than with that rubbish of theirs.' One of the reasons that the great humanist gave for not taking up his repeated warm invitations to Spain was that the place was full of Jews.[34]

In this respect Erasmus was at one with Luther, whose theological stress on Law's replacement by Gospel was not calculated to make him love the Jews. Characteristically, Luther can be found saying precisely opposite things on the subject, and equally true to form, his more generous thoughts came earlier in his career, in a widely read tract of 1523 that pointed out the obvious, *That Jesus Christ was born a Jew*. Luther's two main motives in writing this pamphlet had little to do with positive feelings for Jews and much to do with his wish both to defend himself and attack Catholics: he wanted first to explain that he was not denying the virgin birth when he had said that Jesus was born of the seed of Abraham, and then to berate the

Catholics who made this accusation against him for their irrational cruelty to the Jews. He went on to make a further polemical point that his new proclamation of the Gospel was more likely to convert the Jews than was Catholic malice towards them. The conversionist theme reappeared in negative form in his infamous book of 1543, *On the Jews and their lies*: together with an even nastier tract of later the same year, this expressed Luther's furious disappointment that despite the obvious signs that the Last Days were approaching, Jews were refusing to fulfil their appointed destiny in the end-time by converting to Christianity.[35]

Luther's writing of 1543 is a blueprint for the Nazis' *Kristallnacht* of 1938. It recommends that in retaliation for Jewish obstinacy, synagogues should be burned, Jewish literature confiscated, Jewish teaching forbidden and vengeance taken for the killing of Christ. The fact that the aged and ailing Reformer was saying equally unpleasant things about Turks, Catholics and Christian radicals does little to exonerate him. Among Lutherans, only Andreas Osiander of Nuremberg, whose independent theological thinking eventually ruined his career in the city and sent him to a refuge in far-away Königsberg, stood out strongly against such sentiments; he deplored Luther's later outbursts. Osiander was not always an easy man to live with, but it took considerable intellectual courage for him to write a devastating attack on the 'blood-libel' myth about Jewish slaughter of Christian children. Rather to his embarrassment, it was then published by two grateful Jews in 1540. Among other arguments, Osiander pointed out how little real evidence there was for this ancient tale: even Jewish converts to Christianity, always ready to blacken the character of Judaism, had never made a single accusation of child-murder against their former faith. Predictably, his enemies said (wrongly) that he was a Jew himself, which as far as they were concerned annulled any force in his arguments.[36]

The creators of the Protestant Reformed tradition were at first little better than Luther, with certain honourable exceptions such as Wolfgang Capito (above, p. 689). Martin Bucer was surprisingly much less tolerant of Jews than of Anabaptists. In a 'Memorandum on the Jews' (*Judenratschlag*), written just at the time in 1538 when he was using sweet reason to persuade the Hessian Anabaptists into the mainstream Protestant Church (chapter 4, p. 182), he protested against his patron Philipp of Hesse allowing Jews to stay in his territories. Bucer suggested conditions of life for the Jewish community that amounted to an expulsion order, marshalling arguments from history that were feeble even by the low standards of the time. He sounded the same note as Luther in calling the Jews the enemies of Christ, and in a cliché characteristic of anti-Semitic Protestants, he flatly said 'Papist and Jewish belief and religion are thus simply identical.' Landgraf Philipp to his credit ignored Bucer's advice, even though it was backed up by the leading pastors of his territories.[37]

Matters improved after the 1550s, when many Reformed Protestant leaders experienced for themselves the miseries and anxieties of being refugees: that gave them something of a fellow feeling for the Jewish diaspora and for the rhetoric of exile and longing for home that is such an important theme in the Hebrew Scripture. Moreover, the fact that Luther said such negative things about Jews was an incentive for the Reformed to take a different attitude when the two groups moved apart. Of the major Reformers, Calvin was least interested in the idea of the Last Days, so the conversion of the Jews was not such an urgent priority for him as it was for others. There was an extra factor in the Reformed interest in Old Testament law, especially when the Reformed deployed the analogy of infant circumcision against radicals to justify the custom of infant baptism (chapter 3, p. 149). This was admittedly something of a theological tightrope to walk, since the Reformed also wanted to say, like Luther, that justified Christians were free of the Law, but as we have seen (chapters 13, p. 569, and 16, p. 635) they were much attracted to reviving Old Testament penalties such as death for blasphemy, adultery and sorcery.[38]

The practical consequences of all this were that throughout the sixteenth century Jewish fortunes continued to be as varied in Protestant as in Catholic lands. It helped that Christians now had alternative scapegoat groups for their fears and murderous hatreds: Europeans had now discovered the dangers of witches (chapter 13), not to mention each other's profession of Christianity. Generally, new examples of the 'blood-libel' were fewer, although there was no way of telling where it might appear again: while Oliver Cromwell was preparing for the readmission of the Jews to England, opponents such as William Prynne and Matthew Newcomen, who in any case disapproved of the Lord Protector for not instituting a properly disciplined presbyterian Church, duly revived the ancient myth as part of their campaign against the measure.[39] Despite such bigotry the Jews generally stood a better chance in territories dominated by the Reformed. The Transylvanian prince Gábor Bethlen, eager to improve the economic well-being of his territories, encouraged a colony of Jews to move from the Ottoman lands in 1623, even allowing them to wear Christian clothes so that they could blend in and avoid insults from the Christian population (he also welcomed Anabaptists, with the same economic motive).[40]

The Jews' long experience of surviving amid Christian prejudice soon alerted them to the places which were least dangerous. In eastern Europe there was a great flourishing of Yiddish-speaking Jewish culture (chapter 4, p. 191). In central Europe, Prague proved a meeting-place and cultural melting-pot for various strands of European Jewry of Iberian, eastern and Ottoman origins – Prague was the first city north of the Alps in which Jewish books were printed, in 1512, and it remained a great centre of Jewish scholarship. This was despite the best efforts of the Bohemian Estates, who while casting around for scapegoats for the threat from the Turks, sought to remove all Jews from Bohemia. In this respect, the Habsburgs proved more tolerant than their subjects, and in 1567 the Emperor Maximilian II permanently annulled an expulsion order which the Estates had extorted from King Ferdinand in the military crisis year of 1541 (chapter 5, p. 229).[41] But above all there was Amsterdam in the Reformed Protestant United Provinces (see Plate 14b). As it rose to commercial greatness in the wake of the War of Independence from the Spaniards, Amsterdam became a major haven for Judaism, especially the Sephardic community which was looking for a new secure home to replace the lost glories of Iberia. The tolerance which the 'regents' of the Netherlands and of Amsterdam in particular maintained (against the wishes of most of their Reformed clergy) allowed some remarkable cross-fertilization. In this most cosmopolitan of urban settings, where by the late seventeenth century the stately synagogues were a tourist attraction and an object of astonishment all over Europe, there developed a Jewish culture which acted as a solvent on the certainties that the Reformation and Counter-Reformation sought to establish.

The Iberian débâcle of the 1490s had already left its mark on the Christian upheavals of the sixteenth century. In Spain it created a peculiarly intolerant form of official Christianity obsessed with conformity to a Catholic norm, but Spain also fostered a different form of religious expression, which was destined to have a rich and varied future. We have traced the way in which the traumas, excitements and uncertainties released by the destruction of Muslim and Jewish civilization in Spain fed into Spanish Christian mysticism: not only elements like the Carmelite spirituality of Teresa of Ávila and John of the Cross, which managed to hang on inside the official Church, but also the amorphous movement which was labelled *alumbrado* (chapter 2, pp. 64–5.) From there, via the mystical theologian Juan de Valdés and other refugees from Spain, some of whom were more straightforwardly crypto-Jews, the *alumbrado* style of Christianity influenced the *Spirituali* movement in Italy.

In turn, when the *Spirituali* were dispersed in the 1540s, the Italian evangelicals spread all over Protestant Europe in their own *diaspora* (chapter 5, pp. 231–3; pp. 261–3). Many of these Italians proved remarkably independent-minded once they were released to think for themselves – again, Spanish crypto-Judaism was an influence here. They made a great contribution to the anti-Trinitarianism or Unitarianism which flourished in eastern Europe, notably the Polish movement which took its name from the Italian Sozzini to become known as 'Socinianism' (chapter 8, p. 360). Catholic Spain in combination with John Calvin also produced the classic martyr for radical religion, Miguel Servetus, whose project for reconstructing Christianity was inspired by his consciousness of what had happened to religion in his Iberian homeland. All these stirrings were question-marks against Christian orthodoxy, and now they met new forces of doubt among the Sephardic Jews of Amsterdam.[42]

Doubt of course was nothing new. At the time, it was generally given the blanket label atheism, just as a whole variety of sexual practices of which society pretended to disapprove were given the blanket label sodomy. Specific examples of doubt are generally hidden from us throughout the Reformation and Counter-Reformation, since it was suicidal for anyone knowingly to proclaim doubt or unbelief, and the kindly instinct of priests and pastors was no doubt normally to still doubts in their flock rather than risk their parishioners' lives by exposing and recording cases of 'atheism'. The exceptions were unsurprisingly the various Inquisitions, who in their anxiety to purify the world have preserved some precious fragments of unbelief or wild belief that no one else would have felt it appropriate to record. The Roman Inquisition (now famously for modern readers) discovered the miller of Friuli in northern Italy, Domenico Menocchio, who used his little stock of reading and a heritage of dualist heresy to re-envision the Christian message: for instance, he saw a good analogy for the process of God's creation of the cosmos in the curdling of cream into cheese, complete with the eventual appearance of worms within it as symbols of angelic life. He also felt that a tree might as well hear a penitent's confession as a priest.[43]

Similarly, rare survivals from the books of accusations compiled by the Spanish Inquisition in the late fifteenth century reveal a world of casual unbelief and jokes about religion, much of which does not sound like the anger and frustration of recently Jewish *conversos*, but the small-talk of the bored and frivolous. 'Peace be with you' intoned the parish priest of one Spanish village in his Latin chanting of the Gospel one day in the 1490s – 'as the ass said to the cabbages' came back the response in Spanish from the acolyte serving the Mass. He was quoting a popular song of the time.[44] This was not profound doubt which was going to bring down the fabric of Christendom. Jokes like that rarely expressed any coherent religious viewpoint: equally this category of flippancy or independence of mind could never

693

win the public approval of people in positions of power and responsibility, however much an excess of alcohol might on occasion make them fall from grace in similar ways.

Educated and powerful people in the sixteenth century of course did speak seriously of doubt, but rather like medieval discussion of toleration, or of same-sex sexual activity at all times since the fall of the Roman Empire, such talk had to be understood as theory only if it was to be considered respectable. The best way (as with sodomy) was to shelter behind interest in classical literature. The scrupulously dispassionate Latin poet Lucretius and the Greek satirist of philosophy and religion Lucian were widely read in educated circles, while the sceptic Sextus Empiricus was rediscovered in the sixteenth century (giving his name to 'empiricism'). Although Christian leaders regularly expressed their deep disapproval of these 'atheistic' writings, it was difficult to burn someone simply for reading a classical author. What was different about the movement of the seventeenth century was that gradually doubts melded into a systematic and self-confident confrontation with religious tradition, a confrontation which has become part of western culture and has deeply affected the practice of Christianity itself. At least one impulse provoking this seismic shift in religious outlook came – with something like poetic justice – from the Iberian Inquisitions. They demanded a profound and complete conversion from people, many of whom held a profound and well-organized faith already. Among many possible outcomes of this shattering experience, one effect for some was to breed scepticism about all religious patterns.[45]

The same was true in another region subject to an intense Catholic effort to eliminate one set of religious beliefs in favour of another: the Netherlands. Plenty of Dutch people, those whom the Reformed contemptuously called 'Libertines', were very wary of all strident forms of religion by the end of the sixteenth century.[46] They were joined in the 1620s by some of the most conscientious of Dutch Reformed clergy and people, the defeated Arminians. When Sephardic Jews gravitated to this interesting land and regrouped in the bracingly pluralistic atmosphere of Amsterdam, they had many possible identities to adopt. Many who had been almost completely cut off from their old religion by Iberian repression and later wanderings through Europe now painstakingly reconstructed their ancient belief with a new depth of devotion and orthodoxy. Others emerged from their experience of comparing one religion with another, still conscious of their heritage, but prepared to take very new directions. In the Netherlands they met Christians – Libertines, Arminians, Socinians quitting an increasingly inhospitable Poland – who were prepared to do the same thing.[47]

At the centre of this fusion of ideas was Baruch or Benedict Spinoza. Son of a Portuguese-Jewish merchant in Amsterdam, and so more or less ineligible for a normal university education, he quietly taught himself amid all the intellectual opportunities that the city had to offer – and in his teenage years, those included contact with the great mathematician and natural philosopher René Descartes, who had stripped down human certainty to individual consciousness alone. In 1656, at the age of twenty-three, Spinoza was sensationally expelled with the utmost solemnity from the Amsterdam synagogue. Not only had he ceased to identify with his family's religion, but to incur such an extreme penalty he must already have questioned some of the basic principles of all the great Semitic religions: that there was no immortality for human beings, and no God who intervened in human affairs.[48] In Spinoza's remaining two decades of life, he produced two revolutionary treatises. The *Tractatus Theologico-Politicus* (1670) among other things demanded that the Bible be treated as critically as any other text – particularly the so-called miracles within it; the *Ethics* (1677) saw God as undifferentiated from the force of nature or the state of the universe. Naturally such a God is neither good nor evil. Soon Spinoza was regarded as the standard-bearer for unbelief, even though pervading his carefully worded writings there is a clear notion of a divine spirit inhabiting the world and a profound sense of wonder and reverence for mystery. It was too much for the authorities in the Dutch Republic: they banned the *Tractatus* in 1674, and more predictably the Roman Inquisition followed suit in 1679, after the work had been widely circulated in French translation.

Around Spinoza, and generally in interested awareness of what he was writing, other voices began to be raised that also challenged the ancient wisdom of religion. Few of them had the dour talent of the Englishman Thomas Hobbes, who denied that it was possible for a God to exist without material substance, who delicately ridiculed the Trinity out of existence and who gave broad hints to his readers that they should take no Christian doctrine on trust.[49] Spinoza and Hobbes were followed around 1680 by another work from the Netherlands: the anonymous *Treatise of the three impostors* was too shocking to put in print until 1719, but from the beginning of the eighteenth century it was widely circulated throughout Europe in manuscript, often with a false attribution to Spinoza to give it authority. Written in French, probably by refugee and renegade French Protestants, it was a crude attempt to popularize an anti-religious version of the message of Spinoza's *Tractatus*, married with freely-adapted ideas of Hobbes and other sceptical writers. Its 'three impostors' were Moses, Jesus Christ and Mohammed, and in its condemnation of all three Semitic faiths it proclaimed that 'there are no such things in Nature as either God or Devil or Soul or Heaven or Hell ... theologians ... are all of them except for some few ignorant dunces ... people of villainous principles, who maliciously abuse and impose on the credulous populace'.[50]

A community of ideas and personal connections unites these pioneer doubters and gleeful iconoclasts. There is the recurrent Sephardic connection: one more voice of doubt in the years when Spinoza was reaching his moment of crisis with the Amsterdam synagogue was a French Huguenot Isaac La Peyrère, whose name reveals him underneath its French guise as yet another product of the Portuguese diaspora. His publication in Amsterdam and elsewhere of *Prae-Adamitae* ('Men before Adam') was one of the publishing sensations of 1655, followed by an English edition only a year later and then one in Dutch: reputedly it even became light reading for the Pope and his Cardinals. A product of the feverish apocalypticism of the time, it urged Jews and Christians to reunite to bring on the Last Days, but, as its title implied, it threw the Creation story into the melting-pot by arguing that there had been races of humans earlier than Adam and Eve.[51] La Peyrère also introduces us to another imperilled and highly articulate community which produced radical spirits contributing to the reassessment of religion, the Huguenots of France. They were part of that Reformed Protestant international which raised its hopes of apocalypse and divine consummation so high, only to have them dashed in the Thirty Years War and the other political disappointments of mid-century ranging from England to Transylvania. After the Revocation of the Edict of Nantes in 1685, the Huguenots had their own catastrophe to ponder as they followed the Jews into continent-wide exile.

The other main connection is the now familiar pair of twins, the Netherlands and England: the places where people first made choices on a large scale in religious, personal, social and sexual identities. These were the chief settings in which the millenarian or apocalyptic excitement of Reformed Protestantism, the conviction that God was preparing infinite possibilities for his people in the end-time, met the unpredictable energies of Judaism, now also in a mood of messianic excitement. The meeting of the two cultures was perfectly symbolized in the negotiations of Menasseh ben Israel, the great rabbi of Amsterdam, with Oliver Cromwell and the English enthusiasts for the Last Days (chapter 12, p. 527). The schemes of Interregnum apocalypticists not only encompassed the specific goal of readmitting the Jews to England: they gathered strength around two of Europe's most creative and restless Protestants scholars, Jan Comenius and John Dury, and envisaged a new flowering of scholarship and new discoveries in the many different fields of natural philosophy amid the new possibilities opened up by England's Republic.[52]

The efforts of the Interregnum optimists did not have quite the result that they expected. There was no second coming of Christ, but there were significant and practical consequences, not only the readmission of the Jews but after Charles II's restoration, the foundation of England's premier forum for gentlemanly discussion of natural philosophy, the Royal Society. Then the England of the Glorious Revolution, with a Dutch monarch on the throne, experienced that significant watershed of many choices around 1700. The English Parliament did pass in 1697–8 an 'Act for the effectual suppressing of blasphemy and profaneness', by which it principally meant systematic anti-Trinitarian belief: an admission by the legislators that it was now possible to see 'Socinianism' as a serious threat to the Church, and that the Church was not capable of taking its own action against the threat. Yet it was the Scots and not the English who executed poor Thomas Aikenhead earlier that year, and the Act proved as futile an effort to stem the tide of change as the activities of the Societies for the Reformation of Manners (chapter 16, p. 666).[53]

In the Netherlands there was a further element. The aftershocks of the Synod of Dordt (chapter 8, pp. 377–8) produced not only a separated 'Remonstrant' Arminian Church, but a movement of former Remonstrant laypeople who were left with no clerical leadership: they solved the problem by continuing to meet without a preacher, in gatherings which they called 'Colleges'. The 'Collegiants' deplored fanaticism about religion, which they saw had produced first Spanish Catholic tyranny in the Netherlands and now the schism in the Dutch Reformed Church and the persecuting mania of the victorious Calvinists after Dordt. The Collegiant movement attracted many new recruits, drawn by its firm rejection of dogmatism: not merely the traditional Dutch radicalism of Mennonites, Libertines and Schwenckfelders, but also the new arrivals, the Socinians. Collegiant Christianity that emerged from this marriage of traditions stressed, as so many past radicals had done, an inner light, but increasingly it was the light of reason rather than a direct inspiration from the Holy Spirit. So the Collegiant writer Jan Bredenburg of Rotterdam proclaimed in 1684, 'Reason, which takes its origin from the eternal being, offers men eternal truth and is the light . . . and the guiding star of all human practice.'[54]

THE ENLIGHTENMENT AND BEYOND

There is in all these connections a prehistory of the Enlightenment. What were the intentions of those who were proud to give themselves the 'Enlightenment' label? In one form, the eighteenth-century Enlightenment did indeed set itself against Christianity, proclaiming itself the enemy of mystery and the emancipator of humankind from the chains of revealed religion. Much of this started as being anti-Catholic rather than anti-Christian: a powerful consideration was the memory of the arch-Catholic Louis XIV of France's great betrayal of trust in revoking the Edict of Nantes. Often doubt, scepticism or hatred of the Church then moved on to become what we would define as atheism. So an anti-Christian Enlightenment encompassed the anger of Voltaire against clerical stupidity, David Hume's serene indifference to any hope of life after death that so shocked the diarist James Boswell, Maximilien Robespierre's cold hatred of Catholicism and the French Revolution's replacement of the Catholic Church with the goddess of reason. The authors of *The treatise of the three impostors* would have been delighted by all that, and they should also have been humbled by the quality of some of the minds which they had recruited by their clumsy diatribe.

Yet so much of the story so far has not been about unbelief at all, but sincere and troubled belief. When children of the Reformation and Counter-Reformation, and children of the Jewish Diaspora, turned on the religions which had bred them, they mostly sought not to abolish God but to see him in a clearer light. That was the project of the many groups in the Netherlands, England and beyond who coalesced around the Socinians and made it their goal to produce a more rational Christianity: so far as Spinoza has allowed us into his thoughts, this seems to have been the intention of his writings too. It was the agenda of those who had seen the esoteric literature of the hermeticists and the cabbalists as keys to understanding divine purposes both in the physical world and beyond. Such interests coalesced with a renewed Protestant mysticism and personal religion which to begin with, the 'magisterial' Reformation had held at bay. All that too found its way into the Enlightenment, and it meant that much of the Enlightenment was not anti-Christian at all: it was able to alter Christianity and open it to ways of reformulating the questions and answers which made up Christian belief. That is why to look at the eighteenth-century Enlightenment in England, Scotland or Germany is to see a movement which was as much an ally of Protestant Christianity as its supplanter.

Mainstream Protestantism in the sixteenth century had been very good at replacing the all-embracing medieval Western Church as the public expression of a particular society: Scotland and Scandinavia were especially effective examples, but England, northern Germany, the Baltic and Transylvania were also success stories. We have also already noted that Protestantism was less effective in becoming an expression of devotional reflection or meditation. Protestants had rejected monasteries, solitary religious life and devotional confraternities, and it took a long time for them to find replacements: they even had to borrow devotional literature from the Jesuits (chapter 14, p. 588). One reason for this was that some of the early Protestant leaders most sympathetic to exploration of inner encounters with God – Andreas Karlstadt, Kaspar Schwenckfeld, Andreas Osiander – were quickly marginalized by their colleagues and labelled as deviant. When mysticism returned after 1600, it was through figures who were unhappy that Protestantism had settled down into dogmatic patterns dependent on public community worship. Many of them now listened to radicals and alternative voices: outstanding was the mystically minded Lutheran farmer's son Jakob Boehme, who loved the writings of Paracelsus and sought to rediscover what he thought of as the feminine aspect of the Godhead alongside the male.

A craving for a more personal, private religion emerged in many different contexts in Protestant Europe: the community became less important than a search for God in small intimate groups or even alone. In England this quest for a personal spirituality was associated with two mutually antagonistic groups: on the one hand the radical sects like the Family of Love or the Quakers, on the other the 'avant-garde conformists' or 'High Churchmen' around Lancelot Andrewes and Archbishop Laud, who unusually in Protestant Europe were led straight back to Catholic precedents through the survival of the English cathedral ethos (chapter 12, p. 511). In the early seventeenth-century Reformed Netherlands there appeared the 'further Reformation' (chapter 8, p. 391); rather later in Lutheran Germany came the movement of Pietism, which managed the balancing-act of both drawing on adventurous mystical sources like Boehme and capturing the centres of power within many Lutheran state Churches, while also reaching out to similar-minded Reformed Protestant Germans. In the eighteenth century, very many of these groups began linking with each other in an unprecedented fashion, across Europe and out into the northern European colonies in north America.

Involved in much of this new and generous-minded release of Protestant energy was one Englishman who exemplifies the extraordinary eclecticism of the period: John Wesley, the founder of a 'Methodist' movement which (against his will) became a series of separate Churches in the Atlantic Isles and America. Wesley was a High Church Anglican priest who had a Puritan grandfather ejected from the ministry in Charles II's Restoration. He was inspired not only by contact with the Moravian Brethren (chapter 11, p. 496) but with Lutheran Pietists. Wesley was a reluctant convert to revivalist preaching which derived from Scottish-Irish Presbyterianism (chapter 14, p. 604) and an avid reader and editor of Catholic and even eastern Orthodox mystical devotion. He was also engrossed in the Enlightenment's exploration of knowledge, and in his own voluminous writings he sought to introduce it to his English and American flocks: he was a religious and intellectual omnivore.[55] Equally a man both of the Enlightenment and of evangelical revival was Jonathan Edwards, the New England Congregationalist Calvinist and champion of the American religious 'Great Awakening': he saw the Enlightenment's use of reason as an essential ally in reaffirming the message of the bondage of the human will, in as stark terms as Augustine of Hippo, Martin Luther and John Calvin before him.

Between them Wesley and Edwards represent two faces of a new movement of revival, which has borrowed a label from the Lutheranism of the Reformation and calls itself Evangelical. It is not a paradox, then, that the century of the Enlightenment also witnessed a new flowering of Protestantism. From the low-point that Protestantism had reached by 1700, with much of Europe lost to Catholic dynastic state machines, it witnessed a huge expansion in a new area, north America, fuelled by the remarkable European-wide coming-together of Protestant forces across the divisions of the Reformation. Leading European Protestants, including religious leaders in Britain, were fully aware of and involved in the explosion of religious energy across the Atlantic.[56] The expansion continued into the nineteenth century, as thirteen British colonies became the United States of America and embarked on their expansion across the north American continent, while Protestant Britain compensated itself for the loss of the thirteen colonies by acquiring the largest and most widely flung territorial empire the world has yet seen.

The result was a worldwide Protestantism increasingly expressing itself in the forms which have become predominant in the United States, speaking in the language of revival first heard in early seventeenth-century Ulster, and making a judicious selection from some of the central themes of the Reformations of Luther, Zwingli and Calvin. The principal carrier of all this is now Pentecostalism, a late offshoot of Methodism, with origins in both America and northern Europe. It is always unpredictable as to which beliefs from the Reformation past will suddenly re-emerge. So in the 1980s the United States experienced the presidency of Ronald Reagan, who believed in the Bible's predictions of an imminent arrival of the apocalyptic time as firmly as any of the Protestant savants of Interregnum England or the seventeenth-century princes of Transylvania. In western and southern Africa, the large-scale killing of witches has emerged in certain societies, and this is a direct borrowing from the western Christian inheritance, with little precedent in indigenous African cultures.

The founding fathers of the Reformation would find such beliefs familiar, but they would also be surprised by what is missing from modern Protestantism. During the twentieth century Protestant Christianity quietly ceased to talk about one of the forces which had given its original urgency: the fear of Hell. The evangelicalism which has swept the world has accordingly largely abandoned the Reformed preoccupation with predestination, even in those Churches still calling themselves Reformed: a posthumous victory for Arminius, and for the Methodist ethos of John Wesley (who ostentatiously managed a house-journal for Methodism called *The Arminian Magazine*), against the Calvinism of Jonathan Edwards. Also baffling to the first leaders of Wittenberg, Zürich and Geneva would be modern western Christian acceptance of religious pluralism or choice: Protestant Church establishments finally acquiesced in this when they abandoned repressive religious measures during the eighteenth century. The founding fathers might be slightly mollified in their indignation if it was pointed out to them that this religious pluralism has prevented Anglo-American culture being affected by the vicious anti-clericalism which still haunts the countries of southern Europe and Latin America, which are the heirs of the Counter-Reformation.

In reaction to the shock of the French Revolution, the Catholic Church also achieved a remarkable recovery of nerve. After 1815 it reasserted itself as a more tidy form of Tridentine Catholicism. This took to new heights the power of the papacy at the centre of a worldwide organization, and the first Vatican Council of 1870 completed the agenda of papal monarchy tactfully left incomplete in 1563 (chapter 6, p. 305) by declaring the doctrine of papal infallibility. Catholicism also began a new worldwide expansion, even though the Spanish and Portuguese colonial empires were in decline, because it could piggy-back on to Protestant religious toleration and undertake missionary work in the new Protestant empires. It could also take advantage of the ambiguous attitude of French colonial authorities as France built up a new overseas empire: despite the anti-clericalism of many French governments, they often grudgingly saw Catholic missionaries as agents of French civilization and therefore worth allowing their head in the colonies.

The new presentation of Roman Catholicism still entailed a rejection of much that the Enlightenment had proposed, and only in the twentieth century, with the deliberations of the Second Vatican Council from 1962 to 1965, did the bishops of the Catholic Church make any serious effort to enter dialogue with that legacy. Then from 1978 came the three-decade pontificate of John Paul II, one of the most powerful personalities to occupy the throne of Peter in its long history. His aim was a confident reaffirmation of a version of the Counter-Reformation, replaying many themes of obedience and dogmatic certainty that would have been familiar to Carlo Borromeo or the early seventeenth-century Jesuit advisers of the Habsburgs and Wittelsbachs. The weakness of this variety of Catholicism has been that it has continued to take the Enlightenment to be its enemy, and has sought to exclude or silence those Catholics who take a different view.

The Reformation and the Counter-Reformation are far from dead, therefore. Nevertheless, the versions of Christianity that they created have had to face a new reality, a phenomenon which began in the sixteenth century even as the Reformation was taking shape: Christianity's direct encounter with the whole range of other world faiths, not simply the old Christian entanglement with Judaism and Islam, but Hinduism, Buddhism and the religious of China and Japan – let alone the variety of local religions that world faiths have in the past ignored or casually swept aside. Such varied meetings have made any claim to exclusive religious truth look very strange, although that has not stopped very many western Christians announcing such claims with ever more stridency. There are now choices far wider than even that extraordinary range which emerged in London and Amsterdam around 1700.

Developments in western Christianity that have accompanied this consciousness of choice, and that at least in part result from it, have taken puzzlingly different forms either side of the Atlantic. In Europe, most people whose ancestors and even parents were practising Catholics and Protestants have ceased to practise public religion in any systematic way, and religious practice has the increasing air of a series of sectarian sub-cultures. In the United States, and in other areas of the world to which western Christianity has been exported, religious practice remains the norm. So, between 1990 and 1995, Church membership remained stable in the USA at around 46–47 per cent of the entire population, and of the declared Christian population 67 per cent were formal Church members. In the United Kingdom, the same period saw the proportion of formally declared Church members decline from 17 per cent to 16 per cent even of the declared Christian population, and according to the figures compiled by British Churches themselves, the decline has continued since. The minority status of Christian practice is at its most pronounced in northern Europe, especially Scandinavia, but the Catholic south and Catholic Ireland have also experienced steep decline around the millennium years.[57] In Europe, religion is only a major issue in the politics of certain enclaves trapped in particular understandings of their local history, such as Northern Ireland. In the United States, the rhetoric of religion, generally in the modified form of the Protestant Reformation already described, appears to be strengthening. No one has yet satisfactorily explained the contrast, but it remains one of the most likely causes of misunderstanding and failure of communication between Europe and the USA over the next century.

Even to chronicle and highlight such differences is to reveal oneself as a child of the Enlightenment. The urge to compare, to assess, rather than to contemplate and acquiesce, is one of the distinctive features of that movement which swelled out of the religious pluralism of the seventeenth-century Netherlands and England. The most important symptom of this has not been the 'scientific revolution' of recent centuries but the virtually unprecedented western effort to understand history. Westerners have sought to investigate the past with as few preconceptions as possible, or at least with as wide an understanding as possible of what preconceptions they bring to their study, and they have developed a new allied discipline, archaeology. The results have been remarkable in establishing the shapes of world history way beyond the story of the Christian West. In the early nineteenth century, for instance, it was a series of British scholars resident in India who, through archaeological exploration and careful thought about the results, made the unexpected discovery that there had once been a flourishing and indeed dominant Buddhist civilization in the Indian sub-continent: a major historical fact which Hindu and Muslim India had chosen to forget.[58]

Uniquely among world religions, western Christianity has applied this comparative, analytical impulse to the history of its sacred book, the Bible; only Jewish scholarship has made a serious effort to follow suit. Like religious toleration, this might be said to be an unintended outcome of the Reformation, whose struggles if anything at first hindered progress in biblical study on the foundations of humanist scholarship. Desiderius Erasmus was the first major scholar to borrow the techniques of humanism in philology and historical criticism from the students of Greek and Roman literature and apply them to the Bible. In the next two generations, Protestants and Catholics imitated his scholarship (mostly on the Protestant side) either to score points off each other or to do their best to illustrate great dogmatic truths laid out by the likes of Luther, Zwingli, Bullinger, Bucer, Calvin. Any intelligent critic in such a thought-world might see anomalies in the biblical text, but just like intelligent critics both Jewish and Christian in previous centuries, they would generally look for devotional meanings or hidden clues to God's purposes in such anomalies. So when in the mid-sixteenth century the great Spanish biblical exegete (and sympathizer with radical Christians) Benito Arias Montano was masterminding the ambitious project of the Antwerp Polyglot Bible sponsored by Philip II, he considered the problem that the Bible did not mention the American continent now revealed to Europeans thanks to Philip's royal predecessors. Montano was convinced that everything that should be known must somehow be mentioned in the Bible, and so in an appendix to the great work he added a list of ancient Hebrew versions of American place-names.

Only in the seventeenth century, in the period generating so much other reassessment, did sincere and devout Christians make a consistent return to the humanist project of historical criticism in considering the biblical text. Some of the earliest work in this was done among French Huguenot scholars, particularly at Saumur's Royal Academy for Protestant theology, before it was closed by Louis XIV (Louis retained the pioneering Academy for cavalry instruction, which formed part of the same foundation at Saumur). The earliest stage, undertaken by the Saumur scholar Louis Cappel in the early seventeenth century, was to show that the elaborate system of vowel pointing and accenting in the Hebrew text of the Old Testament was not as ancient as it claimed to be. Many regarded this comparatively minor philological correction as a dangerous attack on the integrity and divine inspiration of Scripture, implying error within it: but Cappel was clearly right in his conclusions, and by the end of the century his discovery had become part of accepted wisdom among Protestants. That was the basis for much more searching scholarly investigation of both Old and New Testaments, which has continued ever since. It has revealed the many-layered historical character of these complicated texts, and has done much to suggest historical contexts and historical motives for this literature, which is a library of books more than a single book.

The result has been a remarkable exercise in honest thinking. In the words of the great Roman Catholic theologian Hans Küng: 'modern biblical criticism . . . belongs among the greatest intellectual achievements of the human race. Has any of the great world religions outside the Jewish-Christian tradition investigated its own foundations and its own history so thoroughly and so impartially?'[59] The results of historical work on the Bible have triggered a revolution in the way that western religion constructs the authority for what it thinks, believes and does. That entails a painful reassessment of sources of authority, which is still convulsing both Protestantism and Catholicism. Although for Protestantism the primary problem has been the authority of the Bible, and for Catholicism the authority of the Church, in both cases the issue at the centre of the conflict has become the same: the Christian attitude to various aspects of sexual behaviour, that most intimate of human activities, which we have already seen as a major aspect of the transformations in western society that took place around 1700.

The sexual challenge to the authority of Tridentine Catholicism has been twofold. The first was the fiasco of Pope Paul VI's encyclical *Humanae Vitae* (1968), promulgated in the face of much anxious expert advice to the contrary, which sought to ban the use of artificial contraception among Roman Catholics. The Catholic faithful of Europe and north America have overwhelmingly, although largely without fanfare, rejected the papal pronouncement: the first such instance in the history of the post-Reformation papacy, and a source of bewilderment and pain to the Pope. The second challenge, still unfolding in its consequences, is the revelation of child abuse by certain clergy and religious of the Church. Already this has had a catastrophic effect on the perception of the Church hierarchy in the English-speaking Catholic world, and if Catholics in other cultural settings react in the same way when they begin to take notice of what has happened, the effects on Roman Catholicism are likely to be profound. The crisis places a question-mark against the imposition of compulsory celibacy on the Church's ministry as formidable as any posed by Protestants in the first decades of the Reformation.

Protestantism is faced with an equally momentous challenge to its assumptions of authority: the increasing acceptance in western societies of homosexual practice and identity as one valid and unremarkable choice among the many open to human beings. This is an issue of biblical authority. Despite much well-intentioned theological fancy footwork to the contrary, it is difficult to see the Bible as expressing anything else but disapproval of homosexual activity, let alone having any conception of a homosexual identity. The only alternatives are either to try to cleave to patterns of life and assumptions set out in the Bible, or to say that in this, as in much else, the Bible is simply wrong. There are other issues which might have been chosen as the basis of this stark choice: after the horrors of the Nazis' efforts to destroy world Jewry in the 1940s, some Christians have begun to face up to the plain anti-Semitism which runs through so many sections of the text of the New Testament. On another front, most have chosen to forget the

New Testament's clear acceptance of slavery as a normal part of social structure, though once upon a time western Christians used it to justify the transport of countless Africans to slavery in the Americas.

Instead, homosexuality has become the chosen battle-ground. The issue is now the front-line between those modelling their view of biblical authority on the general assumptions of western society as expressed before or after 1700: a deeply symbolic matter which threatens to split many Churches in the western tradition. The divisions are not tidy even among those Protestants who call themselves Evangelical, in the sense of the eighteenth-century revivals and the Great Awakening. Conservative Roman Catholics and conservative Evangelicals have more to say to each other about this than to other members of their own Churches who think differently. There is certainly still a house divided among the heirs of the Reformation and Counter-Reformation, but now the partitions have been replaced and put up in different places. The outcome of that debate remains one of the defining open questions of western culture for the coming century.

Eastern Christianity also has new experiences to face. It may benefit from contemplating the Reformation story, because it is now encountering the same Enlightenment culture as Protestantism and Roman Catholicism without ever having had the experience of Reformation. Orthodoxy has been, in an irony of history, protected from modernity by its enemies, first through its marginalization by the Ottoman Empire and then through its cruel persecution by Russian Communism. Now it has no excuses in confronting the pluralism and primacy of choice which characterize the modern West, and the experience is likely to be traumatic.

Modern Westerners – including modern Christians – are likely to deplore much in the struggles of the Reformation. Both late medieval Christianity and the mainstream Protestantism which sought to destroy it were religions of fear, anxiety and guilt, although they also both claimed remedy and comfort for anxiety and guilt through the love exhibited by God to humanity in Jesus Christ. The Reformation arguments were in large part about how human beings best approached this love of God, and whether anything in human behaviour and actions could influence God into saving them from eternal despair. Protestant Churches have naturally been concerned to emphasize the coherence of their founding doctrines that sought to answer such questions, so the haphazard and sometimes contradictory construction of thought within the surviving religious systems has not always been apparent. Radical thinkers and preachers in the early stages of the Reformation in particular represented possible future identities for Latin Christianity. Yet they have been marginalized and rejected by Catholics and

Protestants alike, because they radically questioned the grim certainties which both sides shared, and suggested new, more constructive approaches to divine power and its interplay with humanity. Very often mainstream Christianity is only now re-examining these alternative views of the future and recognizing how much value there is in them. A modern Anglican – or even a modern Roman Catholic – is likely to be more like a sixteenth-century Anabaptist in belief than he or she resembles a sixteenth-century member of the Church of England.

Few people in modern Europe now understand how urgent these arguments were in the sixteenth century. That urgency gave rise to what has been called 'theological road-rage', and we have viewed many of the dire consequences.[60] Europeans were prepared to burn and torture each other because they disagreed on whether, or how, bread and wine were transformed into God, or about the sense in which Jesus Christ could be both divine and human. We have no right to adopt an attitude of intellectual or emotional superiority, especially in the light of the atrocities that twentieth-century Europe produced because of its faith in newer, secular ideologies. Anxiety and a sense of imperfection seem to be basic components of being human, for those of no religion as well as the religious. Some continue to call the answer to these miseries by the name of God. The wise and much-lamented Dominican theologian Herbert McCabe echoed his Dominican predecessor Aquinas when he suggested that God may be the question.[61]

The answers of the past to human agonies may not seem like sensible answers now, but they deserve our respect and our attempt at comprehension. We have witnessed across continents and oceans a flux of angers, joys, destructive violence, search for silence and search for the infinite. It is worth remembering that the people of the Reformation and Counter-Reformation were as capable of ruefulness and humility as, at our best, we can be. Arthur Golding, an Elizabethan gentleman of wide Protestant sympathies, encountered a French translation of that mysterious spiritual meditation the *Beneficio di Cristo* – doomed product of Benedictine devotion, Italian Catholicism, John Calvin and the agonies and exaltations of *Reconquista* Spain (chapter 5, p. 233). He was driven to translate the *Beneficio* into English, and then to meditate on the folly of his times:

This may be counted among the greatest evils with which this age is infected, that they which are called Christians are miserably divided about Christ; and yet in truth as the Apostle saith unto us, there is but one God, which is the Father, of whom are all things, and we in him, and our Lord Jesus Christ, by whom are all things, and we by him. To discourse on this division, and the cause thereof would be to some pleasing, to some it would be displeasing. For what one truth can please minds so diversely divided? Would God it could please all to become one in that one Christ, whose name we all do carry.[62]

Appendix of Texts: Creeds, Lord's Prayer, Ten Commandments, and Hail Mary

The following texts are provided to illuminate the assumptions behind the conflicts portrayed in this book. The Creeds and Lord's Prayer are translated as close as possible to the Latin versions of the original Greek, the Commandments to the original Hebrew. Together they represent the minimum doctrinal kit that both Catholics and Protestants of around 1600 expected the population of Europe to possess. The Angelic Salutation (the Hail Mary) would additionally be expected of Roman Catholics. It is composed of two parts: the first, a conflation of Luke 1:28 and 1:42, was in general use in the medieval West. The second, a more specific prayer to Mary, did not come into general use until after the Reformation began.

THE 'NICENE' CREED (AN EASTERN CREED OF THE LATE 4TH CENTURY)

I believe in one God, the Father Almighty, Maker of heaven and earth, and of all things visible and invisible.

And in one Lord Jesus Christ, the only-begotten Son of God, begotten of the Father before all worlds; God of God, Light of Light, very God of very God; begotten, not made, being of one substance with the Father, by whom all things were made.

Who, for us for our salvation, came down from heaven, and was incarnate by the Holy Spirit of the virgin Mary, and was made human; and was crucified also for us under Pontius Pilate; He suffered and was buried; and the third day He rose again, according to the Scriptures; and ascended into heaven, and sits on the right hand of the Father; and He shall come again, with glory, to judge the quick and the dead; whose kingdom shall have no end.

And I believe in the Holy Ghost, the Lord and Giver of Life; who proceeds from the Father and the Son; who with the Father and the Son together is worshipped and glorified; who spoke by the prophets.

And I believe one holy catholic and apostolic Church. I acknowledge one baptism for the remission of sins; and I look for the resurrection of the dead, and the life of the world to come. Amen.

THE APOSTLES' CREED (A WESTERN CREED OF THE LATE 4TH CENTURY)

I believe in God, the Father almighty, creator of heaven and earth. I believe in Jesus Christ, his only Son, our Lord. He was conceived by the power of the Holy Spirit and born of the Virgin Mary. He suffered under Pontius Pilate, was crucified, died, and was buried. He descended to the dead. On the third day he rose again. He ascended into heaven, and is seated at the right hand of the Father. He will come again to judge the living and the dead. I believe in the Holy Spirit, the holy catholic Church, the communion of saints, the forgiveness of sins, the resurrection of the body, and the life everlasting. Amen.

THE LORD'S PRAYER

Our Father in heaven, hallowed be your Name, your kingdom come, your will be done, on earth as in heaven. Give us today our bread for the morrow. Forgive us our sins as we forgive those who sin against us. Save us from the time of trial and deliver us from evil. For the kingdom, the power and the glory are yours, now and for ever. Amen.

THE TEN COMMANDMENTS

In the Old Testament there are two versions of the Ten Commandments, whose texts contain some minor differences. The version here is found in Exodus 20, presented in the Revised Standard Version of the Christian Bible; it may be compared with Deuteronomy 5. The text is annotated with the numbering as generally used on the one hand by Augustine of Hippo, the Western Latin Church, then the Roman Catholic and Lutheran Churches [A], on the other by Judaism, the Orthodox Churches, the Reformed Protestant Churches and the Anglican Communion [B]. The tabulation is taken from M. Aston, *England's Iconoclasts I. Laws against images* (Oxford, 1988), p. 373.

And God spoke all these words, saying,

[A1] 'I am the LORD your God, who brought you out of the land of Egypt, out of the house of bondage. You shall have no other gods before me.
[B2] 'You shall not make for yourself a graven image, or any likeness of anything that is in heaven above, or that is in the earth beneath, or that is in the water under the earth; you shall not bow down to them or serve them; for I the LORD your God am a jealous God, visiting the iniquity of the fathers upon the children to the third and the fourth generation of those who hate me, but showing steadfast love to thousands of those who love me and keep my commandments.
[A2] [B3] 'You shall not take the name of the LORD your God in vain; for the LORD will not hold him guiltless who takes his name in vain.
[A3] [B4] 'Remember the sabbath day, to keep it holy. Six days you shall labour, and do all your work; but the seventh day is a sabbath to the LORD your God; in it you shall not do any work, you, or your son, or your daughter, your manservant, or your maidservant, or your cattle, or the sojourner who is within your gates; for in six days the LORD made heaven and earth, the sea, and all that is in them, and rested the seventh day; therefore the LORD blessed the sabbath day and hallowed it.
[A4] [B5] 'Honour your father and your mother, that your days may be long in the land which the LORD your God gives you.
[A5] [B6] 'You shall not kill.
[A6] [B7] 'You shall not commit adultery.
[A7] [B8] 'You shall not steal.
[A8] [B9] 'You shall not bear false witness against your neighbour.
[A9] [B10] 'You shall not covet your neighbour's house;
[A10] 'You shall not covet your neighbour's wife, or his manservant, or his maidservant, or his ox, or his ass, or anything that is your neighbour's.'

THE ANGELIC SALUTATION (THE HAIL MARY)

(1) Hail Mary, full of grace, the Lord is with thee; blessed art thou among women, and blessed is the fruit of thy womb Jesus. (2) Holy Mary, Mother of God, pray for us sinners now and in the hour of our death.

Notes

ABBREVIATIONS USED IN THE NOTES

ARG: *Archiv für Reformationsgeschichte*

Bireley, *Refashioning*: R. Bireley, *The Refashioning of Catholicism, 1450–1700* (Houndmills, 1999)

Bonomi, *Under the Cope of Heaven*: P. Bonomi, *Under the Cope of Heaven: religion, society and politics in Colonial America* (New York and Oxford, 1986)

Calvin, ed. McNeill and Battles, *Institutes*: J. Calvin, ed. J. T. McNeill and F. L. Battles, *Institutes of the Christian religion* (2 vols, Philadelphia: Library of Christian Classics xx, xxi, 1960). Citation in square brackets to the conventional divisions of the 1559 *Institutes* text.

Chadwick, *Early Reformation*: O. Chadwick, *The Early Reformation on the Continent* (Oxford, 2001)

CH: *Church History*

Cottret, *Calvin*: B. Cottret, *Calvin: a Biography* (Grand Rapids and Edinburgh, 2000)

Cunningham and Grell, *Four Horsemen*: A. Cunningham and O. P. Grell, *The Four Horsemen of the Apocalypse: religion, war, famine and death in Reformation Europe* (Cambridge, 2000)

CWE: *Collected Works of Erasmus*, various editors: Toronto edn.

Davies, *God's Playground*: N. Davies, *God's Playground: a History of Poland. 1: the origins to 1795* (Oxford, 1981)

Eisenstein, *Printing Revolution*: E. Eisenstein, *The Printing Revolution in early modern Europe* (Cambridge, 1983)

Ellington, *Mary*: D. S. Ellington, *From Sacred Body to Angelic Soul. Understanding Mary in late medieval and early modern Europe* (Washington DC, 2001)

EHR: *English Historical Review*

Gordon and Marshall (eds), *Place of the Dead*: B. Gordon and P. Marshall (eds), *The Place of the Dead: Death and Remembrance in Late Medieval and Early Modern Europe* (Cambridge, 2000)

Grell and Scribner (eds), *Tolerance in the Reformation*: O. Grell and B. Scribner (eds), *Tolerance and Intolerance in the European Reformation* (Cambridge, 1996)

HJ: *Historical Journal*

HT: *History Today*

JEH: *Journal of Ecclesiastical History*

JHI: *Journal of the History of Ideas*

Kłoczowski, *Polish Christianity*: J. Kłoczowski, *A History of Polish Christianity* (Cambridge, 2000)

Lualdi and Thayer (eds), *Penitence*: K. J. Lualdi and A. T. Thayer (eds), *Penitence in the Age of Reformations* (Aldershot, 2000)

Luther's Works: J. Pelikan and H. T. Lehmann (eds), *Luther's Works* (55 vols and 1 companion vol., Philadelphia and St Louis, 1958–86)

MacCulloch, *Cranmer*: D. MacCulloch, *Thomas Cranmer: a life* (London and New Haven, 1996)

MacCulloch, *Later Reformation*: D. MacCulloch, *The Later Reformation in England, 1547–1603* (revised edn, Basingstoke, 2001)

MacCulloch, *Tudor Church Militant*: D. MacCulloch, *Tudor Church Militant: Edward VI and the Protestant Reformation* (London, 1999)

Marshall and Ryrie (eds), *Beginnings of English Protestantism*: P. Marshall and A. Ryrie (eds), *The Beginnings of English Protestantism* (Manchester, 2002)

Matheson, *Imaginative World*: P. Matheson, *The Imaginative World of the Reformation* (Edinburgh, 2000)

Michalski, *Reformation and Visual Arts*: S. Michalski, *The Reformation and the Visual Arts: the Protestant image question in western and eastern Europe* (London, 1993)

MQR: *Mennonite Quarterly Review*

Murdock, *Calvinism on the Frontier*: G. Murdock, *Calvinism on the Frontier 1600–1660: international Calvinism and the Reformed Church in Hungary and Transylvania* (Oxford, 2000)

Naphy (ed.), *Documents*: W. R. Naphy (ed.), *Documents on the Continental Reformation* (Basingstoke, 1996)

O'Malley, *First Jesuits*: J. W. O'Malley, *The First Jesuits* (Cambridge MA, 1993)

Pettegree (ed.), *Early Reformation*: A. Pettegree (ed.), *The Early Reformation in Europe* (Cambridge, 1992)

Pettegree (ed.), *Reformation World*: A. Pettegree (ed.), *The Reformation World* (London, 2000)

Pörtner, *Styria*: R. Pörtner, *The Counter-Reformation in central Europe: Styria 1580–1630* (Oxford, 2001)

PP: *Past and Present*

PS: Parker Society publications

RSTC: A. W. Pollard and G. R. Redgrave, revised by W. A. Jackson and F. S. Ferguson and completed by K. F. Pantzer, *A Short Title Catalogue of Books printed in England, Scotland, and Ireland and of English Books Printed Abroad before the year 1640* (3 vols, London, 1976–91)

Rummel, *Humanism*: E. Rummel, *The Confessionalization of Humanism in Reformation Germany* (Oxford University Press, 2000)

SCH: *Studies in Church History*

SCES: *Sixteenth Century Essays and Studies*

SCJ: *Sixteenth Century Journal*

Todd, *Protestantism in Scotland*: M. Todd, *The Culture of Protestantism in Early Modern Scotland* (New Haven and London, 2002)

TRHS: *Transactions of the Royal Historical Society*

WA: *D. Martin Luthers Werke* (Weimar, 1883–)

Williams, *Radical Reformation*: G. W. Williams, *The Radical Reformation* (London, 1962)

Yates, *Rosicrucian Enlightenment*: F. Yates, *The Rosicrucian Enlightenment* (1st published 1972; new edn. London, 2002)

Introduction

1. For 'Picard' in the 1570s applied to the Unitas Fratrum in Bohemia, see Naphy (ed.), *Documents*, p. 110.

2. D. MacCulloch in P. Collinson (ed.), *The Short Oxford History of the British Isles: the sixteenth century* (Oxford, 2002), pp. 110–11.

3. MacCulloch, *Tudor Church Militant*, p. 2.

4. Matheson, *Imaginative World*, pp. 3–4.

1 The Old Church 1490–1517

1. The same subject is found in a wall-painting at Corby Glen, Lincolnshire, and in a stained glass window formerly at Heydon, Norfolk: see M. R. James, *Suffolk and Norfolk* (London, 1930), p. 165.

2. A useful summary of these arguments can be found in J. Edwards, *The Spanish Inquisition* (Stroud, 1999), pp. 33–5.

3. A useful summary discussion can be found in E. Kerridge, *Usury, Interest and the English Reformation* (Aldershot, 2002), Ch. 1.

4. S. Yarrow, *Saints' Cults and Miracle Narratives in Twelfth Century England: Negotiating Communities* (Oxford, 2003), Ch. 4. On the blood-libel generally, see R. Po-chia Hsia, *The Myth of Ritual Murder: Jews and magic in Reformation Germany* (New Haven and London, 1988).

5. J. Cohen, *The Friars and the Jews: the evolution of medieval anti-Judaism* (Ithaca, NY, 1982), especially pp. 42–4, 239–40, 244.

6. H. Christmas (ed.), *The Works of Nicholas Ridley* (PS, 1843), p. 366.

7. Useful discussion is C. S. Watkins, 'Sin, penance and purgatory in the Anglo-Norman realm: the evidence of visions and ghost stories', *PP* 175 (May 2002), 3–33.

8. G. Duby, *The Early Growth of the European Economy: Warriors and Peasants from the Seventh to the Twelfth Century* (London, 1974), pp. 48–56, 125.

9. W. D. J. Cargill Thompson, 'Seeing the Reformation in medieval perspective', *JEH* 25 (1974), 297–307, at 301.

10. S. K. Cohn Jr., 'The place of the dead in Flanders and Tuscany: towards a comparative history of the Black Death', in Gordon and Marshall (eds), *Place of the Dead*, 14; Pettegree (ed.), *Reformation World*, pp. 17–43, at 23; J. D. Tracy, *Europe's Reformations 1450–1650* (Lanham, 2000), p. 42; H. Kamen, *The Phoenix and the Flame: Catalonia and the Counter-Reformation* (New Haven and London, 1993), pp. 11–12, 19–21, 82–3, 127–9, 168–9, 194–5. See below, chapter 9, 422–3, and for another example of this transfer process, the rosary devotion, chapter 7, 329.

11. A. T. Thayer, 'Judge and doctor: images of the confessor in printed model sermon collections, 1450–1520', in Lualdi and Thayer (eds), *Penitence*, pp. 10–29, at pp. 11–18; I have drawn my own conclusions from this data.

12. K. Farnhill, *Guilds and the Parish Community in Late Medieval East Anglia, c. 1470–1550* (Cambridge, 2001), esp. pp. 154–5, 160–2; cf. MacCulloch, *Later Reformation*, pp. 107–8. R. A. Houlbrooke, *Death, Religion and the Family in England 1480–1750* (Oxford, 1998), pp. 110–16.

13. R. Hutton, *The Stations of the Sun: a History of the Ritual Year in Britain* (Oxford, 1996), esp. Chs 22, 40.

14. N. Terpstra, *Lay Confraternities and Civic Religion in Renaissance Bologna* (Cambridge, 1995).

15. W. Childs, 'The perils, or otherwise, of maritime pilgrimage to Santiago de Compostela in the 15th century', in J. Stopford (ed.), *Pilgrimage Explored*

(York, 1999), pp. 123–44; C. Burgess, ' "Longing to be prayed for": death and commemoration in an English parish in the later Middle Ages', in Gordon and Marshall (eds), *Place of the Dead*, pp. 44–65, at p. 52n.

16. Pettegree (ed.), *Early Reformation*, p. 74.

17. R. Gillespie, 'Going to hell in early modern Ireland, or why the Irish Reformation failed', unpublished paper, and cf. R. Gillespie, *Devoted People: Belief and Religion in Early Modern Ireland* (Manchester, 1997), pp. 159–60; G. Williams, *Recovery, Reorientation and Reformation in Wales c. 1415–1642* (Oxford, 1987), p. 80.

18. N. Vincent, *The Holy Blood: King Henry III and the Westminster Blood Relic* (Cambridge, 2001); on Wilsnack, C. Zika, 'Hosts, processions and pilgrimages in fifteenth century Germany', *PP* 118 (Feb. 1988), 25–64, at 48–59; on Hailes, E. Shagan, *Popular Politics and the English Reformation* (Cambridge, 2002), pp. 166–8.

19. P. Heath, 'Between Reform and Reformation: the English Church in the 14th and 15th centuries', *JEH* 41 (1990), 647–78, at 673–4.

20. On chapels of St Anne, see N. Orme, 'Church and chapel in medieval England', *TRHS* 6th series 6 (1996), 75–102, at 89–90.

21. M. Huggarde, *The displaying of the Protestantes* ... (London, 1556, RSTC 13558), 105; J. Stow (ed.), *Survey of London* (London, Everyman edn., 1956), p. 384.

22. S. Wabuda, *Preaching during the English Reformation* (Cambridge, 2002), Ch. 4.

23. Ellington, *Mary*, pp. 48, 63, 121–2; translation from p. 63 slightly adapted.

24. Ibid., pp. 98, 129.

25. R. W. Pfaff, *New Liturgical Feasts in Later Medieval England* (Oxford, 1970), p. 129.

26. M. Rubin, 'Europe remade: purity and danger in late medieval Europe', *TRHS* 6th ser. 11 (2001), 101–24, at 106.

27. J.T. Rhodes, 'Syon Abbey and its religious publications in the 16th century', *JEH* 44 (1993), 11 25, at 12–14.

28. R.W. Scribner, 'Ritual and popular religion in Catholic Germany at the time of the Reformation', *JEH* 35 (1984), 47–77, at 57–8.

29. G. Macy, 'The doctrine of transubstantiation in the Middle Ages', *JEH* 45 (1994), pp. 11–41.

30. D. MacCulloch, *Groundwork of Christian History* (London, 1987), Ch. 9; R. I. Moore, *The First European Revolution* (Oxford, 2000); R. I. Moore, *The Formation of a Persecuting Society: Power and Deviance in Western Europe 950–1250* (Oxford, 1987).

31. A. Bellenger and S. Fletcher, *Princes of the Church. A History of the English Cardinals* (Stroud, 2001), pp. v–vi, comment on the more usual pious explanation for the word 'cardinal' as being a 'hinge' of the Church.

32. H. Martin, *Le métier de prédicateur en France septentrionale à la fin du Moyen Age, 1350–1520* (Paris, 1988), pp. 618–19.

33. W. D. J. Cargill Thompson, 'Seeing the Reformation in medieval perspective', *JEH* 25 (1974), 253–66, at 305.

34. On Protestantism and printing, see chapter 2, p. 72, and chapter 6, *passim*. R. Rex, 'Friars in the English Reformation', in Marshall and Ryrie (eds), *Beginnings of English Protestantism*, pp. 38–59, at pp. 58–9; A. Hudson, *The Premature Reformation: Wycliffite Texts and Lollard History* (Oxford, 1988), p. 512.

35. Pettegree (ed.), *Early Reformation*, p. 121.

36. Cf. for example the preaching of the south-west German Franciscan Johannes Pauli around 1500: J. Atkinson, 'Luther Studies', *JEH* 23 (1972), 69–78, at 77.

37. H. Bettenson, *Documents of the Christian Church* (London, 1963), p. 135; translation slightly adapted.

38. G. H. M. Posthumus Meyjes, *Jean Gerson, Apostle of Unity: his church politics and ecclesiology* (Leiden, 1999); M. Rubin, 'Europe remade: purity and danger in late medieval Europe', *TRHS* 6th ser. 11 (2001), 101–24, at 107, 111.

39. C. Shaw, *Julius II: The Warrior Pope* (Oxford, 1993), p. 315.

40. A. Pettegree (ed.), *The Reformation of the Parishes: the Ministry and the Reformation in Town and Country* (Manchester, 1993), p. 2.

41. P. Blet, *Histoire de la représentation diplomatique du Saint Siège: des origines à l'aube du XIXe siècle* (Vatican City, 1982), pp. 221–2.

42. Davies, *God's Playground*, p. 125.

43. Pettegree (ed.), *Early Reformation*, p. 107. Geographically, Malmø is in what is now Sweden.

44. K. Trüdinger, *Stadt und Kirche im spätmittelalterlichen Würzburg* (Stuttgart, 1978).

45. J. Eltis, 'Tensions between clergy and laity in some western German cities in the later Middle Ages', *JEH* 43 (1992), 231–48, at 244–6.

46. M. C. McClendon, *The Quiet Reformation: Magistrates and the Emergence of Protestantism in Tudor Norwich* (Stanford, 1999), pp. 71, 100–5.

47. C. Dolan, *Entre tours et clochers: les gens d'Eglise à Aix-en-Provence au XVIe siècle* (Quebec, 1981), esp. Ch. 3 and pp. 196–206, 225–39. See also L. J. R. Milis, 'Monks, Canons, and the City: A Barren Relationship?' *Journal of Interdisciplinary History* 32 (2002), 667–88.

48. Davies, *God's Playground*, p. 127.

49. H. A. Braun, *Das Domkapitel zu Eichstätt. Von der Reformationszeit bis zur Säkularisation (1535–1806)* (Stuttgart, 1991), pp. 63–69; on Magdeburg, Eltis, 'Tensions', op. cit., 243.

50. Eltis, 'Tensions', op. cit., 243.

51. Pettegree (ed.), *Early Reformation*, p. 44.

52. M. Schulze, *Fürsten und Reformation: Geistliche Reformpolitik weltlicher Fürsten vor der Reformation* (Tübingen, 1991), pp. 39–40; my translation adapted from that of Tom Scott in *JEH* 44 (1993), 126–7.

53. R. K. Rittgers, 'Private confession and religious authority in Reformation Nürnberg', in Lualdi and Thayer (eds), *Penitence*, pp. 49–70, at p. 58.

54. J. J. Tyler, *Lord of the Sacred City: the episcopus exclusus in late medieval and early modern Germany* (Leiden, 1999), esp. Ch. 3.

55. Schulze, *Fürsten und Reformation*, op. cit., pp. 67–111.

56. I. Saulle Hippenmeyer, *Nachbarschaft, Pfarrei und Gemeinde in Graubünden 1400–1600* (2 vols, Chur, 1997), esp. p. i, Chs 1, 2–4.

57. This idea is developed, perhaps to excess, in R. J. Bast, *Honor your fathers: catechisms and the emergence of a patriarchal ideology in Germany 1400–1600* (Leiden, 1997).

58. Schulze, *Fürsten und Reformation*, op. cit., pp. 125–7, 136.

2 Hopes and Fears 1490–1517

1. The angel supporters of an early sixteenth-century canopy from the Franciscan Church are now in the Paphos Archaeological Museum.

2. N. Housley, 'Crusading as social revolt: the Hungarian peasant uprising of 1514', *JEH* 49 (1998), 1–28.

3. P. Ayris, 'Preaching the last Crusade: Thomas Cranmer and the "Devotion" Money of 1543', *JEH* 49 (1998), 683–701.

4. R. C. Davis, 'Counting European slaves on the Barbary coast', *PP* 172 (Aug. 2001), 87–124, esp. 90, 94, 110, 117–18, 123–4.

5. M. H. Harris, *Aztecs, Moors and Christians: Festivals of Reconquest in Mexico and Spain* (Austin, Texas, 2000).

6. D. Nirenbert, 'Mass conversion and genealogical mentalities: Jews and Christians in 15th century Spain', *PP* 174 (Feb. 2002), 3–41, esp. 21–5.

7. J. Edwards, *The Spanish Inquisition* (Stroud, 1999), Ch. 4, well summarizes these events.

8. The cautiously revised but still massive figure for expellees is from Edwards, *Spanish Inquisition*, p. 88.

9. M. D. Meyerson, *The Muslims of Valencia in the age of Fernando and Isabel: Between Coexistence and Crusade* (Berkeley, 1991); J. Edwards, 'Portugal and the expulsion of the Jews from Spain', in *Medievo hispano: estudios in memoriam del Prof. Derek W. Lomax* (Madrid, 1995), pp. 121–39.

10. H. E. Rawlings, 'The secularisation of Castilian episcopal office under the Habsburgs, c. 1516–1700', *JEH* 38 (1987), 53–79, at 55.

11. Edwards, *Spanish Inquisition*, p. 85.

12. J. R. L. Highfield, 'The Jeronimites in Spain, their patrons and success, 1373–1516', *JEH* 34 (1983), 513–33, at 531–2.

13. R. C. Davis, 'Counting European slaves on the Barbary coast', *PP* 172 (Aug. 2001), 87–124, 90. For European insults to Spaniards, see Nirenbert, 'Mass conversion and genealogical mentalities', op. cit., 35–6.

14. R. L. Melammed, *Heretics or Daughters of Israel? The crypto-Jewish women of Castile* (New York, 1999), ch. 8, and p. 164.

15. W. A. Christian, *Local Religion in sixteenth-century Spain* (Princeton, 1981); W. A. Christian, *Apparitions in late Medieval and Renaissance Spain* (Princeton, 1981).

16. J. Edwards, 'Trial of an inquisitor: the dismissal of Diego Rodríguez Lucero, inquisitor of Córdoba, in 1508', *JEH* 37 (1986), 240–57. On confiscations, Edwards, *Spanish Inquisition*, p. 93.

17. H. Kamen, *The Phoenix and the Flame: Catalonia and the Counter-Reformation* (New Haven and London, 1993), ch. 5.

18. Bireley, *Refashioning*, p. 160.

19. S. A. Bedini, *The Pope's Elephant* (New York, 2000). J. W. O'Malley, 'Fulfillment of the Christian Golden Age under Pope Julius II: Text of a Discourse of Giles of Viterbo, 1507', *Traditio* 25 (1969), 265–338.

20. Quoted in S. G. Payne, *A History of Spain and Portugal* (Madison, 1973), p. 239.

21. See comment on the Canaries by P. E. Russell in *JEH* 31 (1980), 115.

22. Kłoczowski, *Polish Christianity*, p. 76.

23. G. Schurhammer, *Francis Xavier: his life, his times* (4 vols, Rome, 1973–82), pp. ii. 1.

24. J. Trithemius, *In Praise of Scribes*, ch. vii, quoted in T. J. Brown, *JEH* 27 (1976), 82. I am grateful to Elizabeth Eisenstein for pointing out the echo of Jerome.

25. A. Pettegree, 'Printing and the Reformation: the English exception', in Marshall and Ryrie (eds), *Beginnings of English Protestantism*, pp. 157–79, at pp. 158–9.

26. J. E. Cox (ed.), *Works of Archbishop Cranmer* (2 vols, PS, 1844, 1846),

ii. p. 395; J. Strype (ed.), P. E. Barnes, *Memorials . . . of . . . Thomas Cranmer . . .* (2 vols, London, 1853), vol. ii p. 286, quoted London British Library Cottonian MS Cleopatra E V 325.

27. 'R. V.', *The olde faythe of Greate Brittayne and the newe learnynge of Inglande, wherunto is added a symple instruction, concernynge the Kinges Maiesties procedinges in the comunyon* (London, 1548), sig. C iiiv. *RSTC* 24566 wrongly guesses the date of publication to be 1549; it is clearly a year earlier. This predates the well-known remarks of John Foxe in the *Book of Martyrs* on the same subject: see G. Townshend and S. R. Cattley (eds), *The Acts and Monuments of John Foxe* (8 vols, 1837-41) vol. iii, pp. 718-22.

28. London, Public Record Office, E.135/6/56 (1476); *RSTC* 14077c.106.

29. Cottret, *Calvin*, pp. 93-4.

30. Eisenstein, *Printing Revolution*, p. 84.

31. Ibid., pp. 54-7, 80, 141.

32. A fine discussion of the primer is E. Duffy, *The Stripping of the Altars* (New Haven and London, 1992), chs. 6-7. See also V. Reinburg, 'Liturgy and the laity in late medieval and Reformation France', *SCJ* 23 (1992), 526-64; C. Richmond, 'Religion and the fifteenth-century English gentleman', in R. B. Dobson (ed.), *The Church, Politics and Patronage* (Gloucester, 1984), pp. 193-208: a comment of 1559 from England echoes Richmond's argument, PRO, STAC 5 U3/34, Answer of William Siday.

33. B. Stock, *The Implications of Literacy: written language and models of interpretation in the eleventh and twelfth centuries* (Princeton, 1983), pp. 246-50.

34. Rummel, *Humanism*, p. 10.

35. R. Rex, 'The New Learning', *JEH* 44 (1993), 26-44.

36. H. Baron, *The Crisis of the Early Italian Renaissance* (2 vols, Princeton, 1955).

37. The phrase, applied specifically to the city of Rome, is Stephen Wolohojian's: see *SCJ* 31 (2000), 1117.

38. II. Jones, *Master Tully. Cicero in Tudor England* (Nieuwkoop, 1998), esp. p. 77, and chs 1-4.

39. The foundation study here is F. Yates, *Giordano Bruno and the Hermetic Tradition* (London, 1964).

40. *De causis corruptarum artium*, II, quoted in S. Ditchfield, 'Sanctity in early modern Italy', *JEH* 47 (1996), 98-112, at 106n.

41. G. W. H. Lampe (ed.), *The Cambridge History of the Bible: 2. The West from the Fathers to the Reformation* (Cambridge, 1969), p. 301.

42. Rummel, *Humanism*, p. 11.

43. M. R. Ackermann, *Der Jurist Johannes Reuchlin* (Berlin, 1999).

44. Rummel, *Humanism*, p. 28.

45. H. O. Oberman, 'Discovery of Hebrew and Discrimination against the Jews: the *Veritas Hebraica* as Double-Edged Sword in Renaissance and Reformation', in A. C. Fix and S. Karant-Nunn (eds), *Germania Illustrata: essays on early modern Germany presented to Gerald Strauss (SCES 18, 1992)*, 19–34, at 32–4.

46. H. Wansborough and A. Marett-Crosby (eds), *Benedictines in Oxford* (London, 1997), p. 150; for other examples, see D. MacCulloch, 'Two dons in politics: Thomas Cranmer and Stephen Gardiner, 1503–1533', *HJ* 37 (1994), 1–22, at 3, 6.

47. S. Perfetti, 'Il commento di Pomponazzi al *De partibus animalium*', *Documenti e studi sulla tradizione filosofica medievale*, 10 (1999), 439–66, at 458; Perfetti, 'Three ways of interpreting Aristotle's *De Partibus animalium*', in C. Steel et al. (eds), *Aristotle's animals in the Middle Ages and Renaissance* (Leuven, 1999), pp. 297–316, at pp. 308–10. I am indebted to Prof. Ian Maclean for pointing me to these references.

48. Ellington, *Mary*, p. 193. See also below, chapter 16, 639.

49. C. D'Alton, 'The Suppression of heresy in early Henrician England', unpublished Melbourne Ph.D. thesis, 1999, pp. 22, 28, 31, 36, 50.

50. N. H. Minnich, *The Fifth Lateran Council (1512–17): Studies on its membership, diplomacy and proposals for reform* (Aldershot, 1993).

51. J. A. Bergin, 'The Crown, the papacy and the reform of the old Orders in early 17th century France', *JEH* 33 (1982), 234–55, at 236, 238.

52. For a convincing statement of this 'revisionist' view, see J. G. Clark, 'The Religious Orders in Pre-Reformation England', in Clark (ed.), *The Religious Orders in Pre-Reformation England* (Woodbridge, 2002), pp. 1–33.

53. J. W. O'Malley, *Giles of Viterbo on Church and Reform: a study in Renaissance thought* (Leiden, 1968).

54. K. Arnold, *Johannes Trithemius* (Würzburg, 1971).

55. H. O. Old, *The Patristic Roots of Reformed Worship* (Zürich, 1975), ch. 1; J. K. Nye, 'Johannes Uhl on penitence: sermons and prayers of the dean of Rottweil, 1579–1602', in Lualdi and Thayer (eds), *Penitence*, pp. 152–68, at p. 135.

56. M. Veissière, *L'évêque Guillaume Briçonnet (1470–1534)* (Provins, 1986).

57. J. Arrizabalaga, J. Henderson and R. French, *The Great Pox: the French Disease in Renaissance Europe* (New Haven and London, 1997), chs 1, 2.

58. Q. Skinner and R. Price (eds), *Machiavelli: 'The Prince'* (Cambridge, 1988), p. 21.

59. On England, E. Clarke in G. Rowell (ed.), *The English Religious Tradition and the Genius of Anglicanism* (Wantage, 1992), p. 139. O'Malley, *First Jesuits*, p. 262.

60. L. Polizzotto, *The Elect Nation: the Savonarolan movement in Florence, 1494–1545* (Oxford, 1994).

61. J. Jungić, 'Prophecies of the Angelic Pastor in Sebastiano del Piombo's portrait of Cardinal Bandinello Sauli and three companions', in M. Reeves (ed.), *Prophetic Rome in the High Renaissance period* (Oxford, 1992), pp. 345–70.

62. P. S. Allen, H. M. Allen and H. W. Garrod (eds), *Opus Epistolarum Des. Erasmi Roterodami . . .*, (12 vols, Oxford 1906–58), iii, no. 879, and see refs. at ibid; iii, p. 417; see also the comment by Geoffrey Nuttall, *JEH* 35 (1984), 311, n. 1.

63. There has been much modern embarrassment and obfuscation on Erasmus and Rogerus, but see the sensible comment in J. Huizinga, *Erasmus of Rotterdam* (London, 1952), pp. 11–12, and from Geoffrey Nuttall, *JEH* 26 (1975), 403.

64. L.-E. Halkin, *Erasmus: A Critical Biography* (Oxford, 1993), p. 229. Halkin points out that Erasmus's close friend Bishop John Fisher continued in his preaching to make use of the Song of Songs in relation to Mary.

65. *Opera Omnia Desiderii Erasmi Roterodami* (Amsterdam, 1969–), vi, 5, pp. 490–2.

66. Halkin, *Erasmus*, p. 225: cf. *Opera Erasmi*, i, p. 146–7. On Protestant problems about Mary, see chapter 15, 613–14.

67. On the precedent in Agricola, see A. Levi in *JEH* 34 (1983), 134.

68. *CWE, XXXLX–XL: Colloquies*, ed. C. R. Thompson (1997), vol. ii, pp. 630–3, 636; *An admonition showing the advantages which Christendom might derive from an Inventory of Relics*, printed in *Calvin's Theological Treatises*, ed. H. Beveridge (3 vols, Edinburgh, 1844–51), i, pp. 287–341, esp. pp. 316–18.

69. *CWE: Colloquies*, vol. i, p. 355; *Opera Erasmi*, i, pp. 155–6, 172. M. Aston, *England's Iconoclasts: 1. Laws against Images* (Oxford, 1988), pp. 320–5, esp. n. 96.

70. MacCulloch, *Cranmer*, pp. 98–9.

71. Allen et al (eds), *Opus Erasmi Epistolarum*, iii no. 966, p. 585, ll. 16–18.

72. Allen et al (eds), *Opus Erasmi Epistolarum*, iii no. 858, 1. 561, p. 376. Cf. a similar more extended passage in a letter to Servatius Rogerus in 1514, ibid., i, no. 296, ll. 70–88, 567–8.

73. A good discussion is to be found in J. Estes, '*Officium principis christiani*:

Erasmus and the origins of the Protestant State Church', *ARG* 83 (1992), 49–72.

74. Allen et al (eds), *Opus Erasmi Epistolarum* vol. iii, no. 904, p. 446, ll. 23–5; no. 966, pp. 585–6.

3 New Heaven: New Earth, 1517–24

1. Quoted in C. Trinkaus, 'Free will in Renaissance and Reformation', *JHI* 10 (1949), reprinted in P. O. Kristeller and P. P. Wiener (eds), *Renaissance Essays* (Rochester, NY, 1962), pp. 187–98, at p. 193.

2. H. Davies, *The Vigilant God: Providence in the thought of Augustine, Aquinas, Calvin and Barth* (New York, 1992), p. 115.

3. B. B. Warfield, *Calvin and Augustine* (Philadelphia, 1956), p. 332.

4. H. Jedin, 'Contarini und Camaldoli', *Archivio Italiano per la Storia della Pietà* 2 (1959), 51–118.

5. J. B. Gleason, *John Colet* (Berkeley, CA, 1989), p. 70; W. J. Hankey, 'Augustinian Immediacy and Dionysian Mediation in John Colet, Edmund Spenser, Richard Hooker and the Cardinal de Bérulle', in D. de Courcelles (ed.), *Augustinus in der Neuzeit, Colloque de la Herzog August Bibliothek de Wolfenbüttel, 14–17 octobre, 1996* (Turnhout, 1998), pp. 125–160, at pp. 136–41.

6. A. Null, *Thomas Cranmer's Doctrine of Repentance* (Oxford, 2001), pp. 76–81.

7. B. Bradshaw, 'Interpreting Erasmus', *JEH* 33 (1982), 596–610, at 597–601.

8. CWE, lxvi: *Spiritualia: Enchiridion; De Contemptu Mundi; De Vidua Christiana*, ed. J. W. O'Malley (1988), pp. 3, 34, 51, 69, 108, 127.

9. A. Godin, *Erasme lecteur d'Origène* (Geneva, 1982).

10. J. I. Packer and O. R. Johnston (eds), *Martin Luther: the Bondage of the Will* (London, 1957), p. 300; *WA*, xviii, pp. 774–5. G. B. Graybill, 'The evolution of Philipp Melanchthon's thought on free will', Oxford Univ. D.Phil. thesis, 2002, p. 159.

11. Rummel, *Humanism*, p. 19.

12. R. Marius, *Martin Luther: the Christian between God and Death* (Cambridge, MA and London, 1999), pp. 72–3.

13. G. L. Bruns, *Hermeneutics ancient and modern* (New Haven, 1992), pp. 139–40, quoted in J. Pelikan with V. R. Hotchkiss and D. Price, *The Reformation of the Bible: The Bible of the Reformation* (New Haven, 1996), pp. 28–9.

14. Marius, *Luther*, Chs 6, 7, esp. at p. 108. For the text, see W. Pauck (ed.), *Luther: lectures on Romans* (Philadelphia and London: Library of Christian Classics 15, 1956).

15. Abridged version in G. Rupp and B. Drewery (eds), *Martin Luther* (London, 1970), pp. 5-7.

16. J. Wilkinson, *The Medical History of the Reformers* (Edinburgh, 2001), pp. 25-6.

17. M. Brecht, *Martin Luther: Shaping and Defining the Reformation 1521-1532* (Minneapolis, 1990), pp. 378-9; cf. pp. 395-6.

18. Marius, *Luther*, Ch. 12.

19. C. M. Koslofsky, *The Reformation of the dead: Death and Ritual in Early Modern Germany 1450-1700* (Basingstoke, 2000), pp. 34-9.

20. Pettegree (ed.), *Reformation World*, p. 78.

21. W. D. J. Cargill Thompson, 'Seeing the Reformation in medieval perspective', *JEH* 25 (1974), 297-307, at 299.

22. See other examples in Naphy (ed.), *Documents*, pp. 11-12.

23. Rupp and Drewery (eds), *Luther*, op. cit., p. 15; see the crucial documents of 1517 set out ibid., pp. 17-25.

24. Eisenstein, *Printing Revolution*, p. 145.

25. Rupp and Drewery (eds), *Luther*, op. cit., pp. 27-9.

26. B. A. Felmberg, *Die Ablasstheologie Kardijnal Cajetans (1469-1534)* (Leiden, 1998).

27. Naphy (ed.), *Documents*, p. 18.

28. Marius, *Luther*, p. 188.

29. Rupp and Drewery (eds), *Luther*, op. cit., p. 43. 'Born in wedlock' translates '*ehelich*', which has often been bowdlerized in English translation to its less likely meaning of 'married': cf. *Address to the Nobility* (*Luther's Works*, vol. xliv), p. 128 and n.

30. *The Babylonian Captivity of the Church* (*Luther's Works*, vol. xxxvi), pp. 33-4.

31. Ibid., pp. 57, 116, 117.

32. *The Freedom of a Christian* (*Luther's Works*, vol. xxxi), p. 344.

33. E. Wolgast, *Die Wittenberger Luther-Ausgabe: zur überlieferungsgeschichte der Werke Luthers im 16.Jahrhundert* (Nieuwkoop, 1971), col. 122. For the speech, Rupp and Drewery (eds), *Luther*, op. cit., pp. 58-60.

34. On the shift, see C. Hill, 'The word "revolution" in seventeenth-century England', in R. Ollard and P. Tudor-Craig (eds), *For Veronica Wedgwood: These Studies in Seventeenth-Century History* (London, 1986), pp. 134-51.

35. Cunningham and Grell, *Four Horsemen*, pp. 23-4.

36. S. L. Greenslade (ed.), *The Cambridge History of the Bible: the West*

from the Reformation to the Present Day (Cambridge, 1963), pp. 7, 20-1, 25, 100; Rupp and Drewery (eds), *Luther*, op. cit., pp. 87-91.

37. A. Duke, 'The face of popular religious dissent in the Low Countries, 1520-1530', *JEH* 26 (1975), 41-67, at 42.

38. C. D'Alton, 'The Suppression of heresy in early Henrician England', unpubl. Melbourne Ph.D. thesis, 1999, pp. 106, 122; Pettegree (ed.), *Early Reformation*, p. 221.

39. Pettegree (ed.), *Early Reformation*, pp. 28-30.

40. Ibid., p. 96.

41. Williams, *Radical Reformation*, pp. 106-17.

42. Pettegree (ed.), *Early Reformation*, pp. 32-3.

43. E. Cameron, *The European Reformation* (Oxford, 1991), p. 182.

44. Pettegree (ed.), *Early Reformation*, p. 75; G. Ehrstine, 'Of peasants, women and bears: political agency and the demise of carnival transgression in Bernese Reformation drama', *SCJ* 31 (2000), 675-98, at 678-9.

45. Naphy, *Documents*, p. 38.

46. P. L. Avis, 'Moses and the Magistrate: a study in the rise of Protestant legalism', *JEH* 26 (1975), 149-72, at 153.

47. U. Gäbler, *Huldrych Zwingli: his Life and Work* (Edinburgh, 1986), pp. 52-4.

48. Naphy, *Documents*, p. 30.

49. *WA*, vi, p. 447, 1. 18, and n.

50. B. Gordon, 'Malevolent ghosts and ministering angels: apparitions and pastoral care in the Swiss Reformation', in Gordon and Marshall (eds), *Place of the Dead*, pp. 87-109, at p. 88.

51. E. Cameron, 'Philipp Melanchthon: image and substance', *JEH* 48 (1997), 705-22, at 721-2.

52. J. C. Smith, 'Katharina von Bora through five centuries: a historiography', *SCJ* 30 (1999), 745-73. Cf. Wilkinson, *Medical History of the Reformers*, op.cit., p. 15.

53. M. Aston, *England's Iconoclasts: 1. Laws against Images* (Oxford, 1988), pp. 39-43; Michalski, *Reformation and Visual Arts*, pp. 19, 29, 176.

54. Aston, *England's Iconoclasts*, op. cit., pp. 373, 379-81.

55. Ibid., pp. 378-9.

56. K. H. Marcus, 'Hymnody and hymnals in Basel, 1526-1606', *SCJ* 32 (2001), 723-42, 731-2.

57. Useful material in A. Friesen, *Erasmus, Anabaptists, and the Great Commission* (Grand Rapids, 1998), although Friesen is too ready to make this theme the sole source for Anabaptist thinking.

58. Rupp and Drewery (eds), *Luther*, op. cit., p. 78.

59. Packer and Johnston (eds), *Luther: the Bondage of the Will*, op. cit., p. 318; *WA* xviii, p. 786.

60. *Hyperaspistes*, in *CWE*, LXVI: *Controversies*, ed. C. Trinkaus (1999), p. 117.

61. Pettegree (ed.), *Early Reformation*, pp. 10, 16; P. Matheson (ed.), *Argula von Grumbach: a woman's voice in the Reformation* (Edinburgh, 1995).

62. O. Chadwick, *The Reformation* (London, 1964), p. 1.

63. On flattery, see effective discussion by Cameron, *European Reformation*, op. cit., pp. 311–13. On Hamburg, O. Scheib, *Die Reformationsdiskussionen in der Hansestadt Hamburg, 1522–1528: zur Struktur und Problematik der Religionsgespräche* (Münster Westfalen, 1976).

64. Gordon and Marshall (eds), *Place of the Dead*, p. 8.

65. On Hilten, Cunningham and Grell. *Four Horsemen*, p. 21.

66. Michalski, *Reformation and Visual Arts*, pp. 83, 90–1.

67. Ibid., pp. 86, 92–3, 95, 132.

68. T. Johnson, 'Holy fabrications: the catacomb saints and the Counter-Reformation in Bavaria', *JEH* 47 (1996), 274–97, at 276.

69. *WA*, xi, pp. 245–81; H. Höpfl (ed.), *Luther and Calvin on Secular Authority* (Cambridge, 1991).

70. J. Estes, 'Erasmus, Melanchthon and the office of Christian magistrate', *Erasmus of Rotterdam Society Yearbook* 18 (1998), 21–39, at 30; J. Estes, 'The role of godly magistrates in the Church: Melanchthon as Luther's interpreter and collaborator', *CH* 67 (1998), 463–83, at 471.

71. H. Bornkamm, *Luther in mid-career 1521–1530* (London, 1983), pp. 122–7.

4 Wooing the Magistrate, 1524–40

1. Cunningham and Grell, *Four Horsemen*, pp. 77, 320.

2. T. F. Sea, 'The Swabian League and peasant disobedience before the German Peasants' War of 1525', *SCJ* 30 (1999), 89–112.

3. G. P. Sreenivasan, 'The social origins of the Peasants' War of 1525 in Upper Swabia', *PP* 171 (May 2001), 30–65.

4. Pettegree (ed.), *Early Reformation*, p. 59; Kłoczowski, *Polish Christianity*, p. 98.

5. Matheson, *Imaginative World*, p. 67.

6. G. Rupp and B. Drewery (eds), *Martin Luther* (London, 1970), p. 122.

7. T. Scott and B. Scribner (eds), *The German Peasants' War: a history in documents* (Atlantic Highlands, 1991), pp. 322–4.

8. Rupp and Drewery (eds), *Luther*, p. 121.

9. T. Scott, 'The "Volksreformation" of Thomas Müntzer in Allstedt and Mühlhausen', *JEH* 34 (1983), 194–213; E. G. Rupp, *Patterns of Reformation* (London, 1969), Pt. III.

10. A. Stella, *Il 'Bauernführer' Michael Gaismair e l'utopia di un repubblicanesimo popolare* (Bologna, 1999).

11. Davies, *God's Playground*, p. 143; H. Bornkamm, *Luther in mid-career 1521–1530* (London, 1983), Ch. 12.

12. Pettegree (ed.), *Early Reformation*, pp. 98–9.

13. Ibid., pp. 45–7.

14. Bornkamm, *Luther*, pp. 635–6.

15. I. Saulle Hippenmeyer, *Nachbarschaft, Pfarrei und Gemeinde in Graubünden 1400–1600* (2 vols, Chur, 1997), especially i, pp. 171–82.

16. M. U. Edwards, 'The Luther Quincentennial', *JEH* 35 (1984), 597–613, at 601.

17. Useful extracts of the Short Catechism text, including the above exclamation from its introduction, in B. J. Kidd (ed.), *Documents illustrative of the Continental Reformation* (Oxford, 1911), no. 97.

18. Luther did not use this term until 1539: J. Estes, 'Luther's first appeal to secular authorities for help with church reform, 1520', in R. J. Bast and A. C. Gow (eds), *Continuity and Change: the harvest of late medieval and Reformation history* (Leiden, 2000), pp. 48–76, 67n.

19. J. Estes, 'The role of godly magistrates in the Church: Melanchthon as Luther's interpreter and collaborator', *CH* 67 (1998), 463–83, esp. at 472.

20. Naphy (ed.), *Documents*, p. 92.

21. Williams, *Radical Reformation*, pp. 60, 136, 205, 218–27.

22. Ibid., p. 229.

23. C.-P. Clasen, 'Executions of Anabaptists 1527–1618: a research report', *MQR* 47 (1973), 115–52, esp. 118–19. Pörtner, *Styria*, p. 16.

24. A. Jelsma, 'A "Messiah for women": religious commotion in the northeast of Switzerland, 1525–1526', in W. J. Sheils and D. Wood (eds), *Women in the Church* (*SCH* 27, 1990), pp. 295–306.

25. Jelsma, ' "Messiah for women" ', p. 296. For the text of the Confession, see J. C. Wenger, 'The Schleitheim Confession of Faith', *MQR* 19 (1945), 247–51.

26. L. Harder, *The Sources of Swiss Anabaptism: the Grebel letters and Related Documents* (Scottdale, PA, 1985), [no. 63], p. 290.

27. Useful extracts from the discussion in Naphy (ed.), *Documents*, pp. 94–100.

28. G. R. Potter (ed.), *Huldrych Zwingli* (London, 1978), p. 100. It was this 'tribute' that provoked Luther's 1527 pamphlet, calling Zwingli a fanatic.

29. J. Edwards, 'Kindred spirit? Alfonso de Valdés and Philip Melanchthon at the Diet of Augsburg', unpublished paper.

30. T. A. Brady Jr., *Ruling Class, Regime and Reformation in Strasburg 1520–1555* (Leiden, 1978), p. 238.

31. G. W. Locher, *Zwingli's Thought: New Perspectives* (Leiden, 1981), pp. 270–4.

32. G. R. Potter, 'Zwinglian synods in east Switzerland, 1529–31', *JEH* 26 (1975), 261–6.

33. G. R. Potter, *Zwingli* (Cambridge, 1976), p. 414.

34. See extensive discussion of the clergy's Relations or *Fürträge* in H. U. Bächtold, *Heinrich Bullinger vor dem Rat* (Bern, 1982).

35. B. A. Gerrish, *Grace and Gratitude: the eucharistic theology of John Calvin* (Minneapolis and Edinburgh, 1993), esp. pp. 166–7; and cf. also Gerrish, 'Sign and reality: the Lord's Supper in the Reformed Confessions', in Gerrish, *The Old Protestantism and the New* (Chicago and Edinburgh, 1982), pp. 118–30, esp. p. 128; on Zwingli, Gerrish, *Continuing the Reformation: Essays on Modern Religious Thought* (Chicago 1993), pp. 64–75.

36. J. W. Baker, 'Heinrich Bullinger, the Covenant, and the Reformed Tradition in retrospect', *SCJ* 29 (1998), 359–76.

37. D. F. Wright (ed.), *Common Places of Martin Bucer* (Appleford, 1972), p. 18; T. H. L. Parker writing in *JEH* 35 (1984), 668.

38. Rupp, *Patterns* pp. 37–42.

39. D. Mayes, 'Heretics or nonconformists? State policies toward Anabaptists in 16th century Hesse', *SCJ* 32 (2001), 1003–25, at 1007–8.

40. Williams, *Radical Reformation*, pp. 248–9; E. A. McKee, *Katharina Schütz Zell* (2 vols, Leiden, 1999), pp. i, 222–4, 418.

41. L. J. Abray, 'Confession, conscience and honour: the limits of magisterial tolerance in 16th century Strassburg', in Grell and Scribner (eds), *Tolerance in the Reformation*, pp. 94–107, esp. p. 104; Williams, *Radical Reformation*, pp. 286–8, 292.

42. E. Mâle, *Religious Art* (London, 1949), p. 167. On the medieval background to celestial flesh doctrine, see Williams, *Radical Reformation*, pp. 325–35.

43. A. Duke, 'The face of popular religious dissent in the Low Countries, 1520–1530', *JEH* 26 (1975), 41–67, at 52.

44. Williams, *Radical Reformation*, p. 245.

45. Ibid., pp. 329, 330–2. On Bernard, see Ellington, *Mary*, p. 128.

46. Williams, *Radical Reformation*, pp. 176–8.

47. The best summary account of these Scandinavian events is by O. Grell, in Pettegree (ed.), *Early Reformation*, Ch. 5.

48. Davies, *God's Playground*, pp. 126, 103–1, 190–1, 440–4.

49. A. Hermann and W. Kahle (eds), *Die reformatorischen Kirchen Litauens. Ein historischer Abriss* (Erlangen, 1998).

50. Davies, *God's Playground*, pp. 202–12, 238, 281.

51. Ibid., p. 145.

52. Pettegree (ed.), *Reformation World*, p. 117.

53. Ibid., p. 218.

54. Cottret, *Calvin*, p. 49.

55. For samples of the text of the Placards, lost until 1943, see Naphy (ed.), *Documents*, p. 54.

56. Cf. Calvin, ed. McNeill and Battles, *Institutes*, p. 15 and Calvin, ed. McNeill and Battles, *Institutes*, p. 35 [*Institutes* I.i.1.]

57. J. W. Balke and W. H. T. Moehn (eds), J. Calvin, *Sermons on the Acts of the Apostles* (Neukirchen, 1994), pp. 160–1.

58. A similar incident brought the great fifteenth-century preacher Johann Geiler von Kaysersburg permanently to Strassburg: cf. D. Steinmetz, *Reformers in the Wings* (2nd edn., Oxford, 2001), pp. 9–10.

59. W. G. Naphy, *Calvin and the Consolidation of the Genevan Reformation* (Manchester, 1994), Chs 1, 4.

60. Cottret, *Calvin* pp. 134, 136.

61. D. Potter, *A History of France, 1460–1560: the emergence of a nation state* (Basingstoke, 1995), p. 248.

62. Pettegree (ed.), *Reformation World*, p. 218; P. J. McGinnis and A. H. Williamson (eds), *George Buchanan: the political poetry* (Edinburgh, 1995) pp. 6–7, 16–18, 313.

63. W. Monter, *Judging the French Reformation: heresy trials by 16th century Parlements* (Cambridge MA, 1999) is an important revision of earlier uncritical use of the martyrologist Jean Crespin, who laid emphasis on martyrdoms a decade later.

64. V. Murphy, 'The literature and propaganda of Henry's divorce', in D. MacCulloch (ed.), *The Reign of Henry VIII: Politics, Policy and Piety* (Basingstoke, 1995), Ch. 6; G. Nicholson, 'The Act of Appeals and the English Reformation', in C. Cross, D. Loades and J. J. Scarisbrick (eds), *Law and Government under the Tudors* (Cambridge, 1988), pp. 19–30.

65. On Cranmer in what follows, see MacCulloch, *Cranmer*.

66. K. Carleton, *Bishops and Reform in the English Church, 1520-1559* (Woodbridge, 2001), pp. 63-5. On Anne and books, J. P. Carley (ed.), *The Libraries of King Henry VIII* (London, 2000), pp. lvii-lviii.

67. R. W. Hoyle, *The Pilgrimage of Grace and the Politics of the 1530s* (Oxford, 2001).

68. H. Robinson (ed.), *Original Letters relative to the English Reformation* (2 vols, PS, 1846-7), pp. 241-2.

69. MacCulloch, *Cranmer*, Chs 7-9, and see below, chapter 5, p. 255.

70. H. A. Jefferies, 'The early Tudor Reformations in the Irish Pale', *JEH* 52 (2001), 34-62, esp. 44-7.

71. On locating Tyndale's origins, see A. J. Brown, *William Tyndale on Priests and Preachers with new light on his early career* (London, 1996), Chs 1, 2.

72. O. O'Sullivan (ed.), *The Bible as Book: the Reformation* (London, 2000), p. 47.

73. A good summary account of the following events, albeit unsympathetic to the Anabaptists, remains N. Cohn, *The Pursuit of the Millennium* (London, 1957), Ch. 13.

74. G. Waite, *David Joris and Dutch Anabaptism 1524-1543* (Waterloo, Ont., 1990).

75. Williams, *Radical Reformation*, p. 114.

76. A. Hamilton, *The Family of Love* (Cambridge, 1981); C. Marsh, *The Family of Love in English Society 1550-1630* (Cambridge, 1993); Marsh's superb study is the basis of much of what follows, though some of the conjecture is my own.

77. Eisenstein, *Printing Revolution*, pp. 82, 175-6; on Plantin, see also Hamilton, *Family of Love*, pp. 43-48 and Ch. 4.

78. C. Marsh, *The Family of Love in English Society 1550-1630* (Cambridge, 1993), pp. 282-3.

79. P. Collinson, 'Andrew Perne and his times', in P. Collinson et al., *Andrew Perne: Quatercentenary Studies*, Cambridge Bibliographical Society 11 (1991), pp. 1-34, at pp. 1, 24, 34; on the insinuation, see also below, chapter 8, p. 387.

80. P. L. Avis, 'Moses and the Magistrate: a study in the rise of Protestant legalism', *JEH* 26 (1975), 149-72, at 155.

81. Rummel, *Humanism*, p. 110.

82. J. Bale, *A mysterye of iniquitye contayned within the heretycall Genealogye of Ponce Pantolabus* (Antwerp, 1545, RSTC 1303), fo. 54v.

83. R. F. Smith, *Luther, Ministry and Ordination Rites in the Early Reformation Church* (New York, 1996), Ch. 3.

5 Reunion Deferred: Catholic and Protestant, 1530–60

1. Pettegree (ed.), *Early Reformation*, p. 195. Luther's works were similarly translated with no mention of the author in Henry VIII's England: A. Pettegree, 'Printing and the Reformation: the English exception', in Marshall and Ryrie (eds), *Beginnings of English Protestantism*, pp. 157–79, at p. 166.

2. F. A. James III, *Peter Martyr Vermigli and Predestination: the Augustinian Inheritance of an Italian Reformer* (Oxford, 1998), Part II.

3. P. V. Murphy, 'A worldly reform: honor and pastoral practice in the career of Cardinal Ercole Gonzaga', *SCJ* 31 (2000), 399–417.

4. P. Caraman, *Ignatius Loyola* (San Francisco, 1990), p. 80.

5. Philip Caraman points out that the López family copy of the *Golden Legend* was at least in a recent edition, of 1511: Caraman, *Loyola*, p. 28n.

6. O. Hufton, 'Altruism and reciprocity: the early Jesuits and their female patrons', *Renaissance Studies* 15 (2001), 328–53, at 333.

7. O'Malley, *First Jesuits*, pp. 34–5; but on female influence in securing the Bull, see chapter 15, p. 640 below.

8. O'Malley, *First Jesuits*, pp. 67–8, and on the Theatines, ibid., p. 307.

9. Ibid., pp. 299–300.

10. Ibid., p. 51. On Ignatius and female support, see chapter 15 below, pp. 640–5.

11. O'Malley, *First Jesuits*, pp. 159–62; and chapter 7 below, p. 325; and chapter 9, pp. 414–17.

12. T. M. McCoog, 'Ignatius Loyola and Reginald Pole: a reconsideration', *JEH* 47 (1996), 257–73, at 267.

13. O'Malley, *First Jesuits*, pp. 202–5, 211–12, 274. On Jesuit fund-raising, chapter 16 below, pp. 640–5.

14. B. J. Spruyt, '"En bruit d'estre bonne luteriene": Mary of Hungary (1505–58) and religious reform', *EHR* 109 (1994), 275–307.

15. J. Estes, 'Melanchthon's confrontation with the "Erasmian" *via media* in politics: the *De officio principum* of 1539', in J. Loehr (ed.), *Dona Melanchthoniana* (Stuttgart, 2001), pp. 83–101, at pp. 93–5.

16. MacCulloch, *Cranmer*, p. 65.

17. C. S. Meyer, 'Melanchthon, theologian of ecumenism', *JEH* 17 (1966), 185–207, at 195–6.

18. J. K. Cameron, 'The Cologne Reformation and the Church of Scotland', *JEH* 30 (1979), 39–64.

19. L. von Ranke, *Sämmtliche Werke*, 3rd edn. 37, *Die Römischen Päpste in den letzten vier Jahrhunderten* I, p. 107, quote in B. Hall, 'The colloquies between Catholics and Protestants, 1539–41', in G. J. Cuming and D. Baker (eds), *Councils and Assemblies (SCH* 7, 1971), pp. 235–66, at p. 235.

20. D. C. Steinmetz, *Reformers in the Wings* (2nd edn. Oxford, 2001), pp. 25–7, has a useful discussion of Gropper's views.

21. Hall, 'Colloquies', pp. 246, 254.

22. G. W. Searle, *The Counter-Reformation* (London, 1973), p. 78.

23. On the religious links between Colonna and Michelangelo see B. Collett, *A Long and Troubled Pilgrimage: the correspondence of Marguerite D'Angoulême and Vittoria Colonna 1540–1545 (Studies in Reformed Theology and History* new ser. 6, 2001), pp. 87, 89–92. On Venice and Manelfi, Williams, *Radical Reformation*, pp. 559–65.

24. M. A. L. Overell, 'Edwardian court humanism and *Il Beneficio di Cristo*, 1547–1553', in J. Woolfson (ed.), *Reassessing Tudor Humanism* (Basingstoke, 2002), pp. 151–73. Pole's biographer Thomas Mayer makes out a rather hazy case for Pole's direct involvement in preparing the *Beneficio*: T. F. Mayer, *Reginald Pole: prince and prophet* (Cambridge, 2000), pp. 119–21.

25. T. Freudenberger, *Die Fürstbischofe von Würzburg und das Konzil von Trient* (Münster, 1989).

26. T. F. Mayer, 'Marco Mantova: a bronze age conciliarist', *Annuarium Historiae Conciliorum* 14 (1984), 392n, 406.

27. Mayer, *Pole*, p. 150.

28. A. Tallon, *La France et le Concile de Trent (1518–1563)* (Rome, 1997), pp. 167–8, 754–70. For the text of the decrees, see H. J. Schroeder (ed.), *Canons and Decrees of the Council of Trent* (London, 1941).

29. D. Fenlon, *Heresy and Obedience in Tridentine Italy: Cardinal Pole and the Counter Reformation* (Cambridge, 1972), pp. 135–6.

30. H. Jedin, 'The blind "Doctor Scotus"', *JEH* 1 (1950), 76–84, at 81–3.

31. For detailed accounts of this crucial moment, see T. F. Mayer, *Cardinal Pole in European context: a via media in the Reformation* (Aldershot, 2000), sections IV and V.

32. W. G. Naphy, 'Baptisms, church riots and social unrest in Calvin's Geneva', *SCJ* 26 (1995), 87–97.

33. J. Wilkinson, *The Medical History of the Reformers* (Edinburgh, 2001), p. 62.

34. G. R. Potter and M. Greengrass (eds), *John Calvin: Documents of Modern History* (London, 1983), p. 101.

35. G. B. Graybill, 'The evolution of Philipp Melanchthon's thought on free will', Oxford University D.Phil. thesis, 2002, pp. 157–8, 168, 211, 226.

36. Calvin, ed. McNeill and Battles, *Institutes*, p. 920 [*Institutes* III.xxi.1].

37. Ibid., p. 929 [*Institutes* III.xxi.6.].

38. H. Davies, *The vigilant God: providence in the thought of Augustine, Aquinas, Calvin and Barth* (New York, 1992), pp. 37–8. Cf. Calvin, ed. McNeill and Battles, *Institutes*, p. 955 [*Institutes* III.xxiii. 7.]; for Luther's similar but less often-quoted remarks accepting the 'offence' of double predestination, see J. I. Packer and O. R. Johnston (eds), *Martin Luther: the Bondage of the Will* (London, 1957), p. 217; *WA*, xviii, p. 719.

39. For the proportions, see respectively Calvin, ed. McNeill and Battles, *Institutes*, pp. 47, 61, 868 [*Institutes* I.iv.1; I.v.8; III.xx.14]; ibid., p. 979 [III.xxiv.12]; Naphy, *Documents* p. 53.

40. E. Cameron, 'Philipp Melanchthon: image and substance', *JEH* 48 (1997), 705–22, at 711–12; cf. Calvin, ed. McNeill and Battles, *Institutes*, p. 201 [*Institutes* I.xvi.3]. On Calvin's relations with Melanchthon, see Graybill, 'Melanchthon and free will', pp. 218–21.

41. *Apologia of Alphonsus Lyncurius*, quoted by M. A. Overell, 'The exploitation of Francesco Spiera', *SCJ* 26 (1995), 619–37, at 631. Williams, *Radical Reformation*, pp. 623–4n, provides a strong case for fixing authorship of this tract on the Italian legist Matteo Gribaldi, who also openly defended Servetus.

42. H. R. Guggisberg, 'Tolerance and intolerance in sixteenth-century Basel', in Grell and Scribner (eds), *Tolerance in the Reformation*, pp. 145–63, at pp. 150–61.

43. Pettegree (ed.), *Early Reformation*, p. 225.

44. Cottret, *Calvin*, p. 199.

45. T. H. L. Parker, *Calvin's Preaching* (Edinburgh, 1992), Ch. 8.

46. T. H. L. Parker, *John Calvin* (Berkhamsted, 1975), p. 109.

47. Calvin, ed. McNeill and Battles, *Institutes*, p. 1367 [*Institutes* IV.xvii.7]. For his 1550s comment, Cottret, *Calvin*, p. 66.

48. *Short treatise on the Lord's Supper* (1541), quoted in P. Rorem, 'Calvin and Bullinger on the Lord's Supper', *Lutheran Quarterly* 2 (1988), 155–84 and 357–89, at 156.

49. Cottret, *Calvin*, p. 345. The image is derived from Mt. 23.37, but is still a remarkable adaptation.

50. *Calvin's Theological Treatises*, vol. 1, pp. 118–20; this is Calvin's riposte to 25 Articles put out on 10 March 1542 by the doctors of theology in the University of Paris. On Luther: W. Tappolet with A. Ebneter, *Das Marienlob der Reformatoren: Martin Luther, Johannes Calvin, Huldrych Zwingli,*

Heinrich Bullinger (Tübingen, 1962), p. 126, and on Zürich, G. W. Locher, *Zwingli's Thought: New Perspectives* (Leiden, 1981), p. 60.

51. *Commentary on Isaiah* (published 1551), p. 211, quoted by Potter and Greengrass (eds), *Calvin*, p. 36. On ubiquity, Calvin, ed. McNeill and Battles, *Institutes*, ii, pp. 1379-1403 [*Institutes* IV.xvii. 16-31].

52. Ibid., p. 1277 [*Institutes* IV.xiv.1].

53. The key discussion here is the 1559 version of the *Institutes*, IV xvii, pp. 16-34.

54. Useful discussion, with many quotations of the *Consensus*, in Rorem, 'Calvin and Bullinger on the Lord's Supper', 367-73. For an English text, see e.g. H. Beveridge (ed.), *Calvin's Tracts and Treatises* (3 vols, Edinburgh, 1849), ii, pp. 212-20.

55. O. P. Grell, 'Exile and tolerance', in Grell and Scribner (eds), *Tolerance in the Reformation*, pp. 167-72.

56. For the abusive origin of these labels, see Cottret, *Calvin*, pp. 236n, 239.

57. H. E. Janssen, *Gräfin Anna von Ostfriesland: eine hochadelige Frau der späten Reformationszeit (1540/42-1575)* (Münster, 1988).

58. On Łaski's haircut, see H. P. Jürgens, 'Auctoritas Dei und auctoritas principis. A Lasco in Ostfriesland' in C. Strohm (ed.), *Johannes à Lasco: Polnischer Baron, Humanist und europäischer Reformator* (Tübingen, 2000), pp. 219-44, at pp. 223-4. Much of my comment on Łaski reflects discussion in various essays in the Strohm volume.

59. C. Haigh, *English Reformations* (Oxford, 1993), pp. 161-2, and R. Rex, *Henry VIII and the English Reformation* (Basingstoke, 1993), pp. 169-70, claim that Henry did not know or care about the religious opinions of his son's tutors. The best evidence that he was well aware of the implications of his appointments comes from a New Year's gift to the King from one of Edward's tutors during these years – a cautiously but explicitly evangelical introduction to a classical text: J. F. McDiarmid, 'John Cheke's Preface to *De Superstitione*', *JEH* 48 (1997), 100-20.

60. A. Ryrie, 'The strange death of Lutheran England', *JEH* 53 (2002), 64-92.

61. M. Merriman, 'James Henrisoun and "Great Britain": British Union and the Scottish Commonweal', in R. Mason (ed.), *Scotland and England 1286-1815* (Edinburgh, 1987), pp. 85-112.

62. MacCulloch, *Tudor Church Militant*, pp. 43-8.

63. MacCulloch, *Cranmer*, pp. 539-40. Cf. also Cranmer's warm words in March 1552 for the prominent Philippist cleric in Wittenberg, Georg Major: J. E. Cox (ed.), *Works of Archbishop Cranmer* (2 vols., PS, 1844-46), ii, p. 433.

64. MacCulloch, *Tudor Church Militant*, pp. 173–4, 176; A. Pettegree, 'Printing and the Reformation: the English exception', in Marshall and Ryrie (eds), *Beginnings of English Protestantism*, pp. 157–79, at p. 172.

65. A. Müller (ed.), *Reformation zwischen Ost und West. Valentin Wagners griechischer Katechismus (Kronstadt 1550)* (Cologne, 2000), esp. p. xxiv. For summary discussion of Hungarian-speaking theologians, see Pettegree (ed.), *Early Reformation*, pp. 64–6.

66. Pettegree (ed.), *Early Reformation*, pp. 66–7.

67. Williams, *Radical Reformation*, pp. 545–59.

68. Quoted in Murdock, *Calvinism on the Frontier*, p. 110. See discussion, ibid., pp. 15–16, 19–20.

69. Cf. comments in Murdock, *Calvinism on the Frontier*, pp. 111, 113, 122–3.

70. T. F. Mayer, ' "Heretics be not in all things heretics": Cardinal Pole, his circle, and the potential for toleration', in J. C. Laursen and C. J. Nederman (eds), *Beyond the Persecuting Society: religious toleration before the Enlightenment* (Philadelphia, 1998), pp. 107–24, at pp. 110–11.

71. Michalski, *Reformation and Visual Arts*, pp. 130–1, 135.

72. Davies, *God's Playground*, pp. 167, 183.

73. U. Borkowska, 'The funeral ceremonies of the Polish kings from the fourteenth to the eighteenth centuries', *JEH* 36 (1985), 513–34, at 519.

74. Kłoczowski, *Polish Christianity*, p. 101.

75. Williams, *Radical Reformation*, pp. 622–4, 647–8.

76. E. Read, *Catherine Duchess of Suffolk: a Portrait* (London, 1962), pp. 121–9.

77. Michalski, *Reformation and Visual Arts*, pp. 106–8; another useful summary account is Chadwick, *Early Reformation*, pp. 311–14.

78. F. M. Higman, *Piety and the People: religious printing in French, 1511–1551* (Aldershot, 1996), pp. 5, 17.

79. J. Wright, 'Marian exiles and the legitimacy of flight from persecution', *JEH* 52 (2001), 220–43.

80. K. J. Lualdi, 'A body of beliefs and believers: sacramental confession and parish worship in Reformation France', in Lualdi and Thayer (eds), *Penitence*, pp. 134–51, at p. 148.

6 Reunion Scorned, 1547-70

1. W. Eberhard, in Pettegree (ed.), *Early Reformation*, pp. 34-6, 42-3, 47.

2. V. H. Drecoll, *Der Passauer Vertrag (1552). Einleitung und Edition* (Berlin, 2000). On Passau's connection with the 1629 Edict of Restitution, see below, chapter 11, p. 497.

3. MacCulloch, *Cranmer*, pp. 500-503, 518-20.

4. H. O. Evenett, 'The manuscripts of the Vargas-Granvelle correspondence', *JEH* 11 (1960), 219-24.

5. B. McClung Hallman, *Italian cardinals, Reform, and the Church as Property* (Berkeley, 1985), pp. 153-4.

6. J. Tazbir, *A State Without Stakes: Polish Religious Toleration in the Sixteenth and Seventeenth Centuries* (New York, 1973), p. 119.

7. C. Black, 'Perugia and post-Tridentine church reform', *JEH* 35 (1984), 429-51, at 450.

8. Bireley, *Refashioning*, p. 52.

9. D. Fenlon, 'The origins of modern Catholicism', *JEH* 43 (1992), 102-9, at 104.

10. D. A. Bellenger and S. Fletcher, *Princes of the Church: A History of the English Cardinals* (Stroud, 2001), p. 81.

11. MacCulloch, *Cranmer*, pp. 597-605.

12. T. M. McCoog, 'Ignatius Loyola and Reginald Pole: a reconsideration', *JEH* 47 (1996), 257-73.

13. See the provisions in G. Bray (ed.), *The Anglican Canons 1529-1947* (Church of England Record Society 6, 1998), pp. 68-162, at 91, 95, 127-9.

14. London, Lambeth Palace MS 751, p. 142: sessions of Convocation 16, 20 Dec. 1555.

15. Brian Murdoch, *Cornish Literature* (Cambridge, 1993), Ch. 6. I am indebted to Dr J. P. D. Cooper for pointing me to this reference.

16. W. Wizeman, 'Recalled to life: the theology and spirituality of Mary Tudor's Church', unpublished Oxford D. Phil. thesis, 2002, pp. 281 92; E. Duffy, *The Stripping of the Altars* (New Haven and London, 1992), Ch. 16.

17. J. C. Gray, 'The origins of the word Huguenot', *SCJ* 14 (1983), 349-59.

18. The best account is D. Starkey, *Elizabeth* (London, 2001).

19. K. Sharpe, 'Representations and negotiations: texts, images and authority in early modern England', *HJ* 42 (1999), 853-81, at 870.

20. J. M. Richards, 'The English accession of James VI: "National" identity, gender and the personal monarchy of England', *EHR* 118 (2002), 513-35, at 533.

21. N. Jones, *Faith by Statute: Parliament and the Settlement of Religion 1559* (London, 1982), Ch. 5.

22. MacCulloch, *Tudor Church Militant*, pp. 191–2.

23. Ibid., pp. 185–91.

24. D. Crankshaw, 'Preparations for the Canterbury Provincial Convocation of 1562–63: a question of attribution', in S. Wabuda and C. Litzenberger (eds), *Belief and Practice in Reformation England* (Aldershot, 1998), pp. 60–93; G. R. Elton, *The Parliament of England 1559–1581* (Cambridge, 1986), pp. 199–214.

25. The best account, though not a biography, is now R. A. Mason (ed.), *John Knox and the British Reformations* (Aldershot, 1998).

26. J. E. A. Dawson, 'The two John Knoxes: England, Scotland and the 1558 tracts', *JEH* 42 (1991), 555–76, at 557.

27. MacCulloch, *Cranmer*, p. 622; D. MacCulloch, 'The importance of Jan Łaski in the English Reformation' in C. Strohm (ed.), *Johannes à Lasco: Polnischer Baron, Humanist und europäischer Reformator* (Tübingen, 2000) pp. 325–46, at 342–3.

28. Chadwick, *Early Reformation*, p. 144.

29. Z. V. David, 'The strange fate of Czech Utraquism: the second century, 1517–1621', *JEH* 46 (1995), 641–68, at 654–5. On the Archduke Ferdinand and the Tyrol, I am indebted to discussions with Mr Michael Chisholm: we await his forthcoming Oxford doctoral thesis 'Tyrol and the origins of the Habsburg Counter-Reformation, 1550–1565'.

30. E. Rummel, *The Confessionalization of Humanism in Reformation Germany* (Oxford, 2000), pp. 144–9.

31. H. Louthan, *The Quest for Compromise: peacemakers in Counter-Reformation Vienna* (Cambridge, 1997).

32. R. Taylor, 'Architecture and magic: considerations of the *Idea* of the Escorial', in D. Fraser, H. Hibbard and M. J. Levine (eds), *Essays in the History of Architecture presented to Rudolf Wittkower* (London, 1967), pp. 81–109, at 89–97.

33. A. G. Kinder in Pettegree (ed.), *Early Reformation*, pp. 225–9, 234.

34. R. W. Truman (ed.), *Felipe de la Torre: Institucíon de un rey christiano (Antwerp 1556)* (Exeter, 1979).

35. H. E. Rawlings, 'The secularisation of Castilian episcopal office under the Habsburgs, c. 1516–1700', *JEH* 38 (1987), 53–79, at 64.

36. E. García Hernán, *Francisco de Borja, grande de Espāna* (Valencia, 1999), esp. pp. 165–75, 179–81.

37. P. Salazar de Mendoza, *Vida y sucesos prosperos y adversos de don Fr. B. de Carranza y Miranda, arzobispo de Toledo* (Madrid, 1788), sig. A 4rv.

On the Borromeo comparison, J. I. Tellechea Idigoras, *Bartolomé Carranza de Miranda, Comentarios sobre el Catechismo christiano* (2 vols, Madrid, 1972), i, p. 31. I am indebted to Dr R. W. Truman for pointing me to these sources. On Borromeo, see chapter, 9, pp. 410-14.

38. Naphy (ed.), *Documents*, p. 128.

39. T. Wanegffelen, *Ni Rome ni Genève: des fidèles entre deux chaires en France au XVIe siècle* (Paris, 1997); S. Carroll, 'The compromise of Charles Cardinal de Lorraine: new evidence', *JEH* 54 (2003), 469-83.

40. Naphy (ed.), *Documents*, p. 78.

41. W. MacCaffrey, *The Shaping of the Elizabethan Regime: Elizabethan politics 1558-72* (London, 1969), pp. 78-81.

42. Bireley, *Refashioning*, p. 53.

43. Carroll, 'The compromise of Charles Cardinal de Lorraine'.

44. For contrasting accounts of this incident, see D. Potter (ed.), *The French Wars of Religion* (Basingstoke, 1997), pp. 47-9.

45. S. Broomhall, ' "In my opinion": Charlotte de Minut and female political discussion in print in 16th century France', *SCJ* 31 (2000), 25-45, at 44.

46. R. J. Knecht, *Catherine de' Medici* (London, 1998), pp. 114-15, 121-2, 126-7.

47. I am indebted in this discussion to A. Pettegree, *Huguenot Voices: the book and the communication process during the Protestant Reformation* (Greenville, NC, 1999). See also Pettegree in Pettegree (ed.), *Reformation World*, pp. 120-26.

48. For examples of Catholic violence, see Potter (ed.), *French Wars of Religion*, pp. 53-5, 57, and discussion in N. Davies, *Society and Culture in Early Modern France* (Stanford, 1975), pp. 152-87.

49. Cf. remarks of Alastair Duke, reviewing J. Decavele, *De dageraad van de reformatie in Vlaanderen (1520-1565)*, *JEH* 28 (1977), 422-4.

50. A. Pettegree, 'The exile churches and the Churches "under the Cross": Antwerp and Emden during the Dutch Revolt', *JEH* 38 (1987), 187-209, at 196-7; Pettegree (ed.), *Early Reformation*, p. 147.

51. Naphy, *Documents*, p. 81.

52. Pettegree, 'Antwerp and Emden', 191-3.

53. R. W. Truman and A. Gordon Kinder, 'The pursuit of Spanish heretics in the Low Countries: the activities of Alonso del Canto, 1561-1564', *JEH* 30 (1979), 65-94.

54. *Stadhouder* is not an easy word to translate, and so is usually left as it is. It indicates that an individual has been conceded power by another authority; the word is etymologically the same as 'lieutenant', and might be translated as 'vice-gerent' if that word had kept any currency in English.

55. Pettegree, 'Antwerp and Emden', 200.
56. Cunningham and Grell, *Four Horsemen*, p. 152.

7 The New Europe Defined, 1569–72

1. Cf. R. Peter (ed.), *Bibliotheca Calviniana: les œuvres de Jean Calvin publiées au XVI siècle. 3. Ecrits théologiques, littéraires et juridiques 1565–1600* (Geneva, 2000), pp. 667–8.
2. K. Benda and L. Tardy (eds), *Pierre Lescalopier Utazása Erdélybe [1574]* (Budapest, 1982), p. 64, describing Neustadt, now Cristian in Romania. I am indebted to Maria Crăciun for pointing me to this reference.
3. On one of the chief French dissidents, Jean Morély, see P. Denis and J. Rott (eds), *Jean Morély (ca 1524–ca 1594) et l'utopie d'une démocratie ecclésiastique* (Geneva, 1993).
4. R. Johnston in A. Pettegree (ed.), *The Reformation of the Parishes: the Ministry and the Reformation in Town and Country* (Manchester, 1993), p. 226.
5. Eisenstein, *Printing Revolution*, p. 82. Cf. G. Parker, 'The place of Tudor England in the messianic vision of Philip II of Spain', *TRHS* 6th series 12 (2002), pp. 167–222, at p. 176.
6. J. H. M. Salmon, 'Clovis and Constantine: the uses of history in 16th century Gallicanism', *JEH* 41 (1990), 584–605, at 596.
7. O'Malley, *First Jesuits*, pp. 274–5, 278.
8. O. Grell, A. Cunningham and J. Arrizabalaga (eds), *Health Care and Poor Relief in Counter-Reformation Europe* (London, 1999): see especially the editors' introduction and case studies by J. Henderson, R. Palmer, J. Arrizabalaga and I. Mendes Drumond Braga.
9. D. MacCulloch and P. Hughes, 'A Bailiff's list and Chronicle from Worcester', *Antiquaries Journal* 75 (1995), pp. 235–53, at 248.
10. M. Bent, 'Memento mei: polyphonic music in some 15th century commemorations for the dead', unpublished paper.
11. Illustrated in C. Valone, 'The art of hearing: sermons and images in the chapel of Lucrezia della Rovere', *SCJ* 31 (2000), 753–77, at 764.
12. R. Johnston, 'The implementation of Tridentine reform: the Passau Official and the parish clergy in Lower Austria, 1563–1637', in A. Pettegree (ed.), *The Reformation of the Parishes: the ministry and the Reformation in town and country* (Manchester, 1993), pp. 215–38, at 229.
13. J. Bottin, *Seigneurs et paysans dans l'ouest du pays de Caux, 1540–1640* (Paris, 1983), pp. 269–71.

NOTES TO PAGES 329-46

14. Bireley, *Refashioning*, p. 27.

15. D. Gentilcore, ' "Adapt yourselves to the People's capabilities": missionary strategies, methods and impact in the Kingdom of Naples, 1600–1800', *JEH* 45 (1994), 269–95, at 287–8.

16. Cf. H. Kamen, *The Phoenix and the Flame: Catalonia and the Counter-Reformation* (New Haven and London, 1993), p. 149.

17. J. Craigie (ed.), *The Poems of James VI of Scotland* (2 vols, Scottish Text Society 22, 26, 1948, 1952), i, pp. xlviii–lxii, 197–259, 268–89.

18. J. Wormald, *Court, Kirk and Community: Scotland 1470–1625* (Edinburgh, 1981), pp. 145–6.

19. Personal communication: Owen Chadwick.

20. Pettegree (ed.), *Reformation World*, pp. 264–6, 269–71.

21. O. Grell, 'Exile and Tolerance', in Grell and Scribner (eds), *Tolerance in the Reformation*, pp. 164–81, at pp. 174–9.

22. M. P. Holt, *The French Wars of Religion* (Cambridge, 1995), p. 94.

23. P. Marshall, 'The other Black legend: the Henrician Reformation and the Spanish people', *EHR* 106 (2001), 31–49, at 39.

24. B. B. Diefendorf, *Beneath the Cross: Catholics and Huguenots in 16th century Paris* (New York and Oxford, 1991), p. 91.

25. S. Carroll, 'The compromise of Charles Cardinal de Lorraine: new evidence', *JEH* 54 (2003), 469–83, at 480.

26. S. Carroll, *Noble Power during the French Wars of Religion: the Guise affinity and the Catholic cause in Normandy* (Cambridge, 1998).

27. On names, P. Benedict, *Rouen during the Wars of Religion* (Cambridge, 1981), pp. 104–6, 149–50, 256–60. On wedding customs, P. Benedict, *The Faith and Fortune of France's Huguenots, 1600–85* (Aldershot, 2001), pp. 97–103, and chapter 16, below, p. 661.

28. Davies, *God's Playground*, p. 183.

29. Kłoczowski, *Polish Christianity*, pp. 102, 110; Davies, *God's Playground*, p. 167.

30. Ibid., p. 375.

31. Ibid., p. 183.

32. Williams, *Radical Reformation*, p. 737, slightly altered.

33. Davies, *God's Playground*, pp. 413–25.

34. W. Keatinge Clay (ed.), *Private Prayers put forth by authority during the reign of Queen Elizabeth* (PS, 1851), pp. 463–4.

8 The North: Protestant Heartlands

1. R. W. Scribner, 'Incombustible Luther: the image of the Reformer in early modern Germany', *PP* 110 (Feb. 1986), 38–68, reprinted in Scribner, *Popular culture and Popular Movements in Germany* (London and Ronceverte, 1987), pp. 323–53.

2. E. Wolgast, *Die Wittenberger Luther-Ausgabe: zur überlieferungsgeschichte der Werke Luthers im 16. Jahrhundert* (Nieuwkoop, 1971).

3. R. Kolb, *Martin Luther as Prophet, Teacher, Hero: images of the Reformer 1520–1620* (Grand Rapids, 1999), p. 53, and Ch. 2, passim for further gnesio-Lutheran praise of Luther.

4. P. M. Soergel, 'The afterlives of monstrous infants in Reformation Germany', in Gordon and Marshall (eds), *Place of the Dead*, pp. 288–308, at pp. 292–3.

5. See e.g. Zwingli in 1526 in G. W. Bromiley (ed.), *Zwingli and Bullinger* (Philadelphia, Library of Christian Classics 24, 1953), pp. 218–22. On Calvin, see above, chapter 5, p. 250.

6. K. Jensen, 'Protestant rivalry: metaphysics and rhetoric in Germany c. 1590–1620', *JEH* 41 (1990), 24–43, at 24–5, 30.

7. S. Karant-Nunn, *The Reformation of Ritual: an interpretation of early modern Germany* (London and New York, 1997), pp. 118–24; H. Hotson, 'Irenicism and dogmatics in the Confessional age: Pareus and Comenius in Heidelberg, 1614', *JEH* 46 (1995), 432–56, at 448–9.

8. J. Bossy, 'The German Reformation after Moeller', *JEH* 45 (1994), 673–84, at 679.

9. Examples are given in Chadwick, *Early Reformation*, pp. 168–9.

10. A perceptive account of Friedrich is in Chadwick, *Early Reformation*, pp. 118–19.

11. C. J. Burchill, 'Zacharias Ursinus and the Reformation in Heidelberg', *JEH* 37 (1986), 565–83, at 578–9. For good discussion, see L. D. Bierma, *The doctrine of the sacraments in the Heidelberg Catechism: Melanchthonian, Calvinist, or Zwinglian? (Studies in Reformed Theology and History new series 4, 1999).

12. Murdock, *Calvinism on the Frontier*, p. 48. On Geneva's population decline, Cottret, *Calvin*, p. 160.

13. Burchill, 'Ursinus and the Reformation in Heidelberg', 573–4.

14. T. Johnson, 'Holy fabrications: the catacomb saints and the Counter-Reformation in Bavaria', *JEH* 47 (1996), 274–97, at 285.

15. B. Nischan, 'The Second Reformation in Brandenburg: aims and goals', *SCJ* 14 (1983), 173–87, at 186.

16. Michalski, *Reformation and Visual Arts*, pp. 84–5: and listings of similar incidents from Amberg onwards.

17. Davies, *God's Playground*, pp. 187–8. J. Tazbir, *A State Without Stakes: Polish Religious Toleration in the Sixteenth and Seventeenth Centuries* (New York, 1973), pp. 118–19, describes two other complex cases.

18. Kłoczowski, *Polish Christianity*, p. 123.

19. Naphy, *Documents*, pp. 105–9, for the debates of the Synod of Iwie (now Ivye in Belarus), 1568.

20. G. W. Searle, *The Counter Reformation* (London, 1974), p. 146.

21. Davies, *God's Playground*, p. 168. On this era, see D. Tollet, 'Cohabitation, concurrence et conversion dans la Confédération polono-lithuanienne au tournant ds XVIe et XVIIe siècles', in E. Andor and I. G. Tóth (eds), *Frontiers of Faith: religious exchange and the constitution of religious identities 1400–1750* (Budapest, 2001), pp. 67–78.

22. Davies, *God's Playground*, pp. 170–1; Kłoczowski, *Polish Christianity*, pp. 111–12, 142–9.

23. Kłoczowski, *Polish Christianity*, pp. 111–12.

24. Davies, *God's Playground*, pp. 340–3, 357–60.

25. B. A. Gudziak, *Crisis and Reform: the Kyivan metropolitanate, the patriarchate of Constantinople, and the genesis of the Union of Brest* (Cambridge MA, 1998).

26. Kłoczowski, *Polish Christianity*, pp. 117–18; Davies, *God's Playground*, pp. 172–7.

27. Michalski, *Reformation and Visual Arts*, pp. 81, 133, 146–7.

28. Kłoczowski, *Polish Christianity*, p. 106; Davies, *God's Playground*, p. 162.

29. Michalski, *Reformation and Visual Arts*, pp. 151–2.

30. A. Musteikis, *The Reformation in Lithuania: religious fluctuations in the sixteenth century* (New York, 1988), p. 57.

31. J. Bossy, 'The German Reformation after Moeller', *JEH* 45 (1994), 673–84, at 681.

32. Davies, *God's Playground*, pp. 433–7; Pettegree (ed.), *Reformation World*, pp. 273–4.

33. P. Geyl, *The Revolt of the Netherlands 1555–1609* (London, 2nd edn. 1958), p. 233.

34. Cunningham and Grell, *Four Horsemen*, pp. 205, 243.

35. A. Duke, 'The ambivalent face of Calvinism in the Netherlands 1561–1618', in M. Prestwich (ed.), *International Calvinism 1541–1715* (Oxford,

1985), pp. 109–34, at 127; cf. Geyl, *Revolt of the Netherlands*, pp. 138–9, 171.

36. S. Schama, *The Embarrassment of Riches: an interpretation of Dutch culture in the golden age* (New York, 1987), p. 59.

37. Geyl, *Revolt of the Netherlands*, pp. 203–15.

38. B. J. Kaplan, *Calvinists and Libertines: confession and community in Utrecht, 1578–1620* (Oxford, 1995), pp. 73–5, 157–61, 172–5.

39. C. Kooi, *Liberty and Religion: Church and state in Leiden's Reformation, 1572–1620* (Leiden, 2000), p. 108.

40. Schama, *Embarrassment of Riches*, pp. 60, 115–21.

41. C. H. Parker, 'The moral agency and moral autonomy of church folk in the Dutch Reformed Church of Delft', *JEH* 48 (1997), 44–70, at 59–60.

42. Figures quoted by James D. Tracy, in review of W. Bergsma, *Tussen Gideonsbende en publieke kerk: een studie over gereformeerd Protestantisme in Friesland, 1580–1610* (Hilversum, 1999), in *SCJ* 32 (2001), 892. There have been estimates as high as 20–30 per cent for the northern Netherlands: cf. S. Haude in Pettegree (ed.), *Reformation World*, p. 248.

43. D. Colas, *Civil Society and Fanaticism: conjoined histories* (Stanford, 1997), p. 183.

44. D. C. Steinmetz, *Reformers in the Wings: from Geiler von Kaysersberg to Theodore Beza*, 2nd edn (Oxford, 2001), pp. 117–20.

45. I. Schöffer, *Dirck Volckertszoon Coornhert* (Zutphen, 1989).

46. C. Brandt, *The Life of James Arminius* (London, 1854), pp. 89–94.

47. Ibid., pp. 147–8.

48. A. W. Harrison, *The Beginnings of Arminianism to the Synod of Dort* (London, 1926), p. 110.

49. A. R. Macdonald, 'Ecclesiastical representation in Parliament in post-Reformation Scotland: the two kingdoms theory in practice', *JEH* 50 (1999), 38–61.

50. J. P. Dawson, 'Calvinism and the Gaidhealtached in Scotland', in A. Pettegree, A. Duke and G. Lewis (eds), *Calvinism in Europe, 1540–1620* (Cambridge, 1994), pp. 231–53, esp. p. 240. For the late arrival of a complete Hungarian Bible in Reformed Transylvania (1590), see below, chapter 10, p. 000.

51. M. Dilworth, *The Scots in Franconia: a century of monastic life* (Edinburgh, 1974).

52. K. M. Brown, 'In search of the godly magistrate in Reformation Scotland', *JEH* 40 (1989), 553–81, at 580; T. F. McCoog, 'Tensions: Robert Parsons, William Crichton and the battle for Elizabeth's succession', unpublished paper.

53. On defining Puritanism, see MacCulloch, *Later Reformation*, pp. 69–78.

54. J. Field and T. Wilcox, *An Admonition to the Parliament* (1572): W. H. Frere and C. E. Douglas (eds), *Puritan Manifestos: a study of the origin of the Puritan revolt* (London, 1954), p. 21.

55. On the Queen and preaching, P. McCullough, *Sermons at Court: politics and religion in Elizabethan and Jacobean preaching* (Cambridge, 1998), Ch. 2.

56. P. Collinson, *Archbishop Grindal 1519–83: the Struggle for a Reformed Church* (London, 1983), Chapters 12–15, and see especially pp. 242–5.

57. MacCulloch, *Later Reformation*, pp. 38–40.

58. The best account is P. Collinson, *The Elizabethan Puritan Movement* (London, 1967), especially Part 4.

59. D. MacCulloch, *Suffolk and the Tudors: politics and religion in an English county 1500–1600* (Oxford, 1986), pp. 211–12, 335, 339; Collinson, *Elizabethan Puritan Movement*, p. 278.

60. J. Woodward, *The Theatre of Death: the ritual management of Royal Funerals in Renaissance England, 1570–1625* (Woodbridge, 1997), pp. 74–6.

61. P. Collinson, 'The Elizabethan Exclusion Crisis and the Elizabethan polity', *Proceedings of the British Academy* 84 (1994), 51–92, at 60; Collinson, 'The monarchical republic of Queen Elizabeth I', *Bulletin of the John Rylands Library* 69 (1987), 394–424, reprinted in Collinson, *Elizabethan Essays* (London, 1994), pp. 31–57.

62. S. Doran, 'Juno versus Diana: the treatment of Elizabeth I's marriage in plays and entertainments, 1561–1581', *HJ* 38 (1995), 257–73.

63. *Oh read over D. John Bridges: The Epistle to the terrible priests of the Convocation House* (East Molesey, 1588, *RSTC* 17453), p. 30; *Oh read over D. John Bridges: the epitome* (Fawsley, 1588; *RSTC* 17454), sig. D2rv. The identity of Marprelate remains uncertain: L. H. Carlson, *Martin Marprelate, Gentleman: Master Job Throckmorton Laid Open in his Colors* (San Marino, CA, 1981), seemed to solve the riddle, but now see P. Collinson in J. Guy (ed.), *The Reign of Elizabeth I: court and culture in the last decade* (Cambridge, 1995), pp. 157–8.

64. Collinson, *Elizabethan Puritan Movement*, op. cit., pp. 403–31; A. Walsham, '"Frantick Hacket": prophecy, sorcery, insanity and the Elizabethan puritan movement', *HJ* 41 (1998), 27–66.

65. P. Lake, *Anglicans and Puritans? Presbyterianism and English Conformist Thought from Whitgift to Hooker* (London, 1988), pp. 239–40.

66. Cf. e.g. P. Clark, *English Provincial Society from the Reformation to*

the Revolution: religion, politics and society in Kent 1500–1640 (Hassocks, 1977), pp. 249–68; D. MacCulloch, *Suffolk and the Tudors: politics and religion in an English county 1500–1600* (Oxford, 1986), pp. 217–19, 243–52, 274–82.

67. R. T. Kendall, *Calvin and English Calvinism to 1649* (Oxford, 1979), pp. 52–3.

68. M. H. Prozesky, 'The emergence of Dutch Pietism', *JEH* 28 (1977), 29–37. The historian J. C. Kromsigt seems to have invented the term *nadere Reformatie* in 1904.

69. P. McGrath, *Papists and Puritans under Elizabeth I* (London, 1967), pp. 177n, 255–6; L. McLain, 'Without church, cathedral or shrine: the search for religious space among Catholics in England, 1559–1625', *SCJ* 33 (2002), 381–99, at 393.

70. A. Walsham, *Church Papists: Catholicism, Conformity and Confessional Polemic in Early Modern England* (London, 1993).

71. H. A. Jefferies, 'The early Tudor Reformations in the Irish Pale', *JEH* 52 (2001), 34–62, at 60.

72. G. Williams, *Recovery, Reorientation and Reformation in Wales c.1415–1642* (1987), pp. 328–9. Cf. M. Stoyle, 'English "nationalism", Celtic particularism, and the English Civil War', *HJ* 43 (2000), 1113–28, at 1118; G. Williams, 'William Morgan's Bible and the Cambridge Connection', *Welsh Historical Review* 14 (1988–9), 363–79.

73. T. G. Connors, 'Surviving the Reformation in Ireland (1534–80): Christopher Bodkin, Archbishop of Tuam, and Roland Burke, Bishop of Clonfert', *SCJ* 32 (2001), 335–55, at 352.

74. B. Millett, 'Irish literature in Latin, 1550–1700', in T. W. Moody, F. X. Martin and F. J. Byrne (eds), *A New History of Ireland: 3: Early modern Ireland, 1534–1691*, 2nd edn (Oxford, 1991), pp. 561–86, at 562.

75. B. Bradshaw, 'Revisionism and the Irish Reformation: a rejoinder', *JEH* 51 (2000), 587–91, at 588. P. O. Connell, 'The early-modern Irish College network in Iberia, 1590–1800' and É. Ó Ciosáin, 'A hundred years of Irish migration to France, 1590–1688', in T. O'Connor (ed.), *The Irish in Europe 1580–1815* (Dublin, 2001).

76. Dublin: S. G. Ellis, 'Economic problems of the Church: why the Reformation failed in Ireland', *JEH* 41 (1990), 239–65, at 263n. Kilkenny: A. J. Fletcher, *Drama and the Performing Arts in pre-Cromwellian Ireland: a repertory of sources and documents from the earliest times until c. 1642* (Woodbridge, 2001), pp. 361–5.

77. W. F. Graham, 'The religion of the first Scottish settlers in Ulster', in J. Friedman (ed.), *Regnum, religio et ratio: essays presented to Robert M.*

Kingdon (*Sixteenth Century essays and studies* 8, 1987), pp. 53–68, at pp. 55–6.

78. On the theology of the Church, A. Ford, *The Protestant Reformation in Ireland, 1590–1641* (Dublin, 1997), Ch. 8.

79. B. Ó Cuív, 'The Irish language in the early modern period', in Moody, Martin and Byrne (eds), *Early Modern Ireland, 1534–1691*, pp. 509–45, at p. 511.

80. Ellis, 'Economic problems', op. cit., 261; P. S. Dineen (ed.), *An Irish–English dictionary* (Dublin, 1927), pp. 34, 948.

81. On 1621, cf. review by Helga Robinson-Hammerstein of Ford, *Protestant Reformation in Ireland* (edn. Berne, 1985), *JEH* 37 (1986), 472, and cf. the 1987 Dublin edition of Ford, op. cit., pp. 201–17. On clergy numbers and Jesuits in Dublin, K. Bottigheimer, 'The failure of the Reformation in Ireland: *Une question bien posée*', *JEH* 36 (1985), 196–207, at 198.

9 The South: Catholic Heartlands

1. J. Bergin, 'The Counter-Reformation Church and its bishops', *PP* 165 (Nov. 1999), 30–73, at 41–2. C. Black, 'Perugia and post-Tridentine Church reform', *JEH* 35 (1984), 429–51, at 431, gives a slightly lower figure for Italy of 287 dioceses.

2. Cited by J. S. Cummins, *JEH* 45 (1994), 348.

3. S. Ditchfield, 'Text before trowel: Antonio Bosio's *Roma sotteranea* revisited', in R. N. Swanson (ed.), *The Church Retrospective* (*SCH* 33, 1997), pp. 343–60.

4. T. Johnson, 'Holy fabrications: the catacomb saints and the Counter-Reformation in Bavaria', *JEH* 47 (1996), 274–97, especially at 278–81, and see below, chapter 10, pp. 454–6. Circignani is sometimes confused with his pupil Cristoforo Roncalli, since they both acquired the nickname 'Pomarancio'. Circignani's now-lost frescos at the English College are illustrated in G. B. di Cavallieri, from N. Circignani, *Ecclesiae Anglicanae Trophaea sive Sanctorum Martyrum [...] passiones* (Rome, 1584): See Plates 12, 13.

5. Bireley, *Refashioning*, p. 72.

6. B. McClung Hallman, *Italian Cardinals, Reform, and the Church as Property* (Berkeley, 1985), pp. 9–15. On the drift to France, M. Völkel, *Römische Kardinalshaushalte des 17. Jahrhunderts. Borghese-Barberini-Chigi* (Tübingen, 1993), pp. 376–80.

7. Hallman, *Italian Cardinals*, pp. 2–3, 164–8.

8. G. Fragnito, *La Bibbia al rogo: la censura ecclesiastica e i volgarizzamenti della Scrittura (1471-1605)* (Bologna, 1997), p. 330: 'Non sapete voi come il tanto legger la scrittura guasti la religione Cattolica?'. On the context of the papal conflict with Venice, see below, pp. 408-10.

9. Fragnito, *La Bibbia al rogo*, Ch. 7, and pp. 106-7, 198, 326.

10. Pettegree (ed.), *Early Reformation*, pp. 211-12; A. Pastore, *Nella Valtellina del tardo cinquecento: fede, cultura, società* (Milan, 1975); E. Balmas and G. Zardini (eds), *Denys Bouteroue: Discorso breve delle persecuzioni occorse in questo tempo alle Chiese del Marchesato di Saluzzo (1620)* (Turin, 1978).

11. U. Rozzo, 'Italian literature on the Index', in G. Fragnito (ed.), *Church, Censorship and Culture in Early Modern Italy* (Cambridge, 2001), pp. 194-222.

12. P. Godman, *The Saint as Censor: Robert Bellarmine between Inquisition and Index* (Leiden, 2000); L. Balsamo, 'How to doctor a bibliography: Antonio Possevino's practice', in Fragnito (ed.), *Church, Censorship and Culture*, pp. 50-78.

13. Statistics in M. Laven, 'Sex and celibacy in early modern Venice', *HJ* 44 (2001), 865-88, at 867. R. Mackenney, *Tradesmen and Traders: the world of the guilds in Venice and Europe, c. 1250-c. 1650* (London, 1987).

14. J. Woolfson, *Padua and the Tudors* (Cambridge, 1998), p. 129; for law, see ibid., Ch. 2.

15. Yates, *Rosicrucian Enlightenment*, p. 171.

16. N. Malcolm, *De Dominis (1560-1624): Venetian, Anglican, ecumenist and relapsed heretic* (London, 1984).

17. J. K. Nye, 'Johannes Uhl on penitence: sermons and prayers of the dean of Rottweil, 1579-1602', in Lualdi and Thayer (eds), *Penitence*, pp. 152-68, at p. 156.

18. J. B. Tomaro, 'San Carlo Borromeo and the implementation of the Council of Trent', in J. M. Headley and J. B. Tomaro (eds), *San Carlo Borromeo: Catholic reform and ecclesiastical politics in the second half of the 16th century* (Washington DC, 1988), pp. 67-84, at p. 70.

19. D. Fenlon, 'The origins of modern Catholicism', *JEH* 43 (1992), 102-9, at 103-4. Headley and Tomaro (eds), *San Carlo Borromeo*, provides an excellent set of perspectives on Borromeo in Milan.

20. B. W. Westervelt, 'The Prodigal Son at Santa Justina: the homily in the Borromean reform of pastoral preaching', *SCJ* 32 (2001), 109-25, at 111.

21. For similar later controls on confessors in Naples, see M. Mancino, *Licentia confitendi: selezione e controllo dei confessori a Napoli in età moderna* (Rome, 2000).

22. P. F. Grendler, 'Borromeo and the Schools of Christian Doctrine' in Headley and Tomaro (eds), *San Carlo Borromeo*, pp. 158-71, at p. 165.

23. Nicola M. Sutherland, reviewing Headley and Tomaro (eds), *San Carlo Borromeo, JEH* 40 (1989), 608.

24. E. C. Voelker, 'Borromeo's influence on sacred art and architecture', in Headley and Tomaro (eds), *San Carlo Borromeo*, pp. 172-87, at pp. 178-9, 185.

25. Bergin, 'Counter-Reformation Church and its bishops', op. cit., 46. W. de Boer, 'The politics of the soul: confession in Counter-Reformation Milan' in Lualdi and Thayer (eds), *Penitence*, pp. 124-31, and see also W. de Boer, *The Conquest of the Soul: confession, discipline and social order in Counter-Reformation Milan* (Leiden, 2000).

26. Bireley, *Refashioning*, p. 115, and on Jesuit confraternities, see below, chapter 14, p. 594.

27. S. Ditchfield, 'Sanctity in early modern Italy', *JEH* 47 (1996), 98-112, especially 103-4.

28. R. Copsey, 'Simon Stock and the scapular vision', *JEH* 50 (1999), 652-83. For Iberian inquisitors' equal scepticism about witches, see below, chapter 13, pp. 574-5.

29. Ditchfield, 'Sanctity in early modern Italy', op. cit., 109.

30. Black, 'Perugia and post-Tridentine Church reform', op. cit., 441; D. Gentilcore, '"Adapt yourselves to the People's capabilities": missionary strategies, methods and impact in the Kingdom of Naples, 1600-1800', *JEH* 45 (1994), 269-95, at 282. See also T. Deutscher, 'Seminaries and the education of Novarese parish priests, 1593-1627', *JEH* 32 (1981), 303-20.

31. L. Châtellier, *The Religion of the Poor: rural missions in Europe and the formation of modern Catholicism, c. 1500-1800* (Cambridge, 1997), pp. 40, 42-5.

32. Gentilcore, 'Missionary strategy', op. cit., 278.

33. Quoted in P. Camporesi, *The Fear of Hell: images of damnation and salvation in early modern Europe* (Cambridge, 1991), pp. 69-72.

34. Gentilcore, 'Missionary strategy', op. cit., 278-9, and on Saraco, ibid. 281.

35. G. Parker, *The Grand Strategy of Philip II* (London and New Haven, 1998), pp. 41-2, 277-8.

36. See chapter 6 above, pp. 299-301, and chapter 7, pp. 320-1; on Philip's continued diversion of episcopal energy into royal service, see H. Rawlings, *Church, Religion and Society in Early Modern Spain* (Basingstoke, 2002), p. 67.

37. H. Kamen, *The Phoenix and the Flame: Catalonia and the Counter-*

Reformation (New Haven and London, 1993), p. 67. Cf. above, chapter 2, p. 61, and on nuns and enclosure, below, chapter 16, pp. 642–6.

38. H. E. Rawlings, 'The secularisation of Castilian episcopal office under the Habsburgs, c. 1516–1700', *JEH* 38 (1987), 53–79, at 67.

39. S. T. Nalle, *God in La Mancha: religious reform and the people of Cuenca, 1500–1600* (Baltimore and London, 1992), pp. 118–29. On print, ibid., pp. 114–18, and Kamen, *Phoenix and the Flame*, pp. 140–7, 398, 424–6.

40. Bireley, *Refashioning*, p. 109.

41. E. M. Wilson, 'Spanish and English religious poetry of the seventeenth century', *JEH* 9 (1958), 38–53, at 45–6.

42. J. Contreras, 'The impact of Protestantism in Spain 1520–1600', in S. Haliczer (ed.), *Inquisition and Society in Early Modern Europe* (London, 1987), pp. 47–66, at p. 62.

43. C. Villaseñor Black, 'Love and marriage in the Spanish Empire: depictions of holy matrimony and gender discourses in the 17th century', *SCJ* 32 (2001), 637–67, at 645.

44. M. Flynn, 'Mimesis of the Last Judgement: the Spanish *Auto da fé*', *SCJ* 22 (1991), 281–98; H. Kamen, *The Spanish Inquisition: an historical revision* (London, 1997), p. 98, Ch. 9.

45. Kamen, *Inquisition*, pp. 59–60, 189–90, 203, 301.

46. Kamen, *The Phoenix and the Flame*, pp. 219–21, 347, 403–5.

47. A. K. Harris, 'Forging history: the *Plomos* of the Sacromonte of Granada in Francisco Mermúdez de Pedraza's *Historia Eclesiástica*', *SCJ* 30 (1999), 945–65.

48. C. M. N. Eire, *From Madrid to Purgatory: the art and craft of dying in sixteenth century Spain* (Cambridge, 1995), esp. Ch. 4, pp. 177–88; Kamen, *Phoenix and the Flame*, pp. 11–12, 19–21, 82–3, 127–9, 168–9, 194–5, 432 (quotation); Nalle, *God in La Mancha*, op. cit, pp. 191–25; Rawlings, *Church, Religion and Society in Early Modern Spain*, op. cit., pp. 87–9; Bireley, *Refashioning*, p. 114.

49. J. Bilinkoff, 'Confession, gender, life-writing: some cases (mainly) from Spain', in Lualdi and Thayer (eds), *Penitence*, pp. 169–83, at p. 181.

50. A. Weber, 'Spiritual administration: gender and discernment in the Carmelite Reform', *SCJ* 31 (2000), 123–45, at 124–5.

51. L. Beckett in *Times Literary Supplement*, 28 September 2001, p. 26.

52. V. Lincoln, *Teresa: a woman* (Albany, NY, 1984), p. 75, quoted in Bilinkoff, 'Confession, gender, life -writing', op. cit., p. 180.

53. R. P. Hardy, *The Life of St John of the Cross: Search for Nothing* (London, 1987), pp. 6–19.

54. *The Spiritual Canticle* 22:4: K. Kavanaugh and O. Rodriguez (eds), *The Collected Works of St John of the Cross* (Washington DC, 1964), p. 497.

55. A. Weber, 'Spiritual administration', op. cit., 143; Hardy, *John of the Cross*, pp. 102–5.

56. J. M. Boyden, 'The worst death becomes a good death: the passion of Don Rodrigo Calderón', in Gordon and Marshall (eds), *Place of the Dead*, pp. 240–65, at p. 264.

57. Bireley, *Refashioning*, p. 147.

58. Cf. e.g. J. A. Licate, *Creation of a Mexican Landscape: territorial organisation and settlement in the Eastern Puebla basin, 1520–1605* (Chicago, 1981).

59. Cf. the remarks of F. Cervantes, reviewing L. N. Rivera, *A Violent Evangelism: the political and religious conquest of the Americas* (Louisville, KY, 1992), *JEH* 45 (1994), 509; see also above, chapter 2, pp. 67–70.

60. C. R. Boxer, *The Church Militant and Iberian expansion, 1440–1770* (Baltimore, 1978), p. 113.

61. R. Ricard, *The Spiritual Conquest of Mexico: an essay on the Apostolate and Evangelising methods of the Mendicant Orders in New Spain, 1523–1572* (Berkeley CA, 1966), pp. 31–6.

62. I. Clendinnen, *Ambivalent Conquests: Maya and Spaniard in Yucatan, 1517–1570* (Cambridge, 1987), pp. 40–1, 72–109; Ricard, *Spiritual Conquest of Mexico*, pp. 264–5.

63. Bireley, *Refashioning*, pp. 153–4, 158.

64. Ricard, *Spiritual Conquest of Mexico*, pp. 122–3.

65. Ibid., pp. 49–50.

66. Ibid., pp. 183–7.

67. K. Burns, *Colonial Habits: convents and the spiritual economy of Cuzco, Peru* (Durham NC, 1999), pp. 2–31, 27–37, 80, 113.

68. D. Brading, *Our Lady of Guadalupe, Image and Tradition 1531–2000* (Cambridge, 2001), pp. 58–70, 361–8.

69. P. K. Thomas, *Christians and Christianity in India* (London, 1954), pp. 51–4.

70. J. Brodrick, *Saint Francis Xavier (1506–1552)* (London, 1952), pp. 239–40.

71. V. Cronin, *A Pearl to India: the life of Roberto de Nobili* (London, 1959).

72. K. S. Latourette, *A History of the Expansion of Christianity* (7 vols, London, 1938–47), iii, pp. 336–66. J. D. Spence, *The Memory Palace of Matteo Ricci* (London, 1984) is illuminating on Ricci's *mentalité*.

73. Latourette, *History of the Expansion of Christianity*, iii, pp. 344, 348.
74. The best single account of the mission is C. R. Boxer, *The Christian Century in Japan, 1549–1650* (Berkeley CA, 1967).
75. G. Schurhammer, *Francis Xavier: his life, his times* (4 vols, Rome, 1973–82), iv, pp. 269, 440, 447, 547, 555.
76. Boxer, *Christian Century in Japan*, pp. 72–83, 89.
77. S. Turnbull, 'Diversity or apostasy? The case of the Japanese "Hidden Christians"', in R. N. Swanson (ed.), *Unity and Diversity in the Church (SCH 32, 1996)*, pp. 441–54.
78. Bireley, *Refashioning*, p. 162; see below, chapter 12, p. 541.
79. Bireley, *Refashioning*, p. 162.
80. R. J. Morgan, 'Jesuit confessors, African slaves and the practice of confession in seventeenth century Cartagena', in Lualdi and Thayer (eds), *Penitence*, pp. 222–39.
81. C. R. Boxer, *Race Relations in the Portuguese Colonial Empire 1415–1825* (Oxford, 1963), pp. 7–9.
82. A. Hastings, *The Church in Africa 1450–1950* (Oxford, 1994), pp. 119–20.
83. B. Sundkler and C. Steed, *A History of the Church in Africa* (Cambridge, 2000), p. 51.
84. J. K. Thornton, *The Kingdom of Kongo: civil war and transition, 1641–1718* (Madison, 1983), especially pp. 63–8.
85. On the Jesuit explorer Pedro Páez Xaramillo SJ, see J. Reverte, *Dios, el Diablo y la Aventura* (Barcelona, 2001).
86. Hastings, *Church in Africa 1450–1950*, pp. 136–60.
87. Boxer, *Church Militant and Iberian expansion*, p. 82; on Canada, cf. e.g. L. Campeau, *La mission des Jésuites chez les Hurons 1634–1650* (Montreal, 1987), Ch. 16, especially pp. 298, 302.
88. Bireley, *Refashioning*, pp. 148–9.

10 Central Europe: Religion Contested

1. Pörtner, *Styria*, p. 120.
2. S. Ozment, *The Reformation in the Cities: the appeal of Protestantism to 16th century Germany and Switzerland* (New Haven and London, 1975), p. 1.
3. Pörtner, *Styria*, pp. 35–40. For a perspective on Tyrol, I am indebted to Michael Chisholm.
4. Ibid., pp. 45, 55–6.

5. U. Köster, *Studien zu den katholischen deutschen Bibelübersetzungen im 16., 17. und 18. Jahrhundert* (Münster, 1995), especially Ch. 5.

6. Pörtner, *Styria*, pp. 99, 182; for further comment, see ibid., pp. 4, 97–8, 187.

7. J. K. Nye, 'Johannes Uhl on penitence: sermons and prayers of the dean of Rottweil, 1579–1602', in Lualdi and Thayer (eds), *Penitence*, pp. 152–68.

8. Bireley, *Refashioning*, pp. 137–9.

9. R. Po-chia Hsia, *Society and Religion in Münster 1535–1618* (New Haven, 1984), pp. 59–60, 151–4, 87, 167–71. On Speyer, M. Forster, *The Counter-Reformation in the Villages: Religion and Reform in the bishopric of Speyer, 1569–1720* (Ithaca and London, 1992), pp. 48, 66–74, 216–17.

10. On Graz, Pörtner, *Styria*, pp. 28–9, 102, and Ingolstadt, A. Seifert, *Weltlicher Staat und Kirchenreform: die Seminarpolitik Bayerns im 16. Jahrhundert* (Münster Westfalen, 1978).

11. G. Parker (ed.), *The Thirty Years War* (New York, 1984), p. 6; Pörtner, *Styria*, pp. 27–31, 71, 81–3.

12. Pörtner, *Styria*, pp. 88, 91–2, 113–14, 181.

13. Ibid., pp. 162–4, 180; Bireley, *Refashioning*, p. 119.

14. Bireley, *Refashioning*, pp. 62–3.

15. Pörtner, *Styria*, pp. 33, 47, 112, 152.

16. Ibid., pp. 198, 203–5, 215–16.

17. T. Johnson, 'Holy fabrications: the catacomb saints and the Counter-Reformation in Bavaria', *JEH* 47 (1996), 274–97, at 277–8.

18. On Benno, Johnson, 'Holy fabrications', 276, and above chapter 3, p. 156.

19. Johnson, 'Holy fabrications', 284.

20. Bireley, *Refashioning*, p. 117.

21. P. Soergel, *Wondrous in his saints: Counter-Reformation propaganda in Bavaria* (Berkeley CA, 1993), pp. 110–30. For another guidebook of 1594 from Loreto, see above, chapter 9, p. 414.

22. Pörtner, *Styria*, pp. 241–3; C. Harline and E. Put, *A Bishop's Tale: Mathias Hovius among his flock in seventeenth-century Flanders* (New Haven and London, 2000), Ch. 6.

23. Bireley, *Refashioning*, p. 144.

24. Murdock, *Calvinism on the Frontier*, p. 25. Graeme Murdock's work is an outstanding contribution to knowledge of this topic, and I owe a great deal to it.

25. Murdock, *Calvinism on the Frontier*, pp. 19–21.

26. Ibid., p. 145.

27. Ibid., p. 65.

28. G. Starr, 'Art and architecture and the Hungarian Reformed Church', in P. C. Finney (ed.), *Seeing beyond the Word: visual arts and the Calvinist tradition* (Grand Rapids, 1999), pp. 301-40, at pp. 303-15; Murdock, *Calvinism on the Frontier*, pp. 153-4.

29. Murdock, *Calvinism on the Frontier*, pp. 18, 41.

30. Ibid., pp. 149-50, 167-9, 172.

31. Ibid., pp. 152-3.

32. Ibid., pp. 194, 206, 254-5.

33. Ibid., especially Ch. 9, and see p. 287.

34. Ibid., pp. 100, 267-9, 285.

35. On Jesuit influence, see A. L. Martin, *Henry III and the Jesuit Politicians* (Geneva, 1973), especially Conclusion.

36. Naphy (ed.), *Documents*, p. 79. On de' Medici, cf. above, chapter 6, p. 306.

37. R. Briggs, 'Finance, religion and the French State', *HJ* 42 (1999), 565-70, at 566.

38. X. Le Person, '"Les larmes du roi": sur l'enregistrement de l'Édit de Nemours le 18 Juillet 1585', *Histoire, économie et société* 17 (1998), 353-76, especially 360.

39. On Navarre's adoption of new military techniques, see T. J. Tucker, 'Eminence over efficacy: social status and cavalry service in 16th century France', *SCJ* 32 (2001), 1057-99, especially at 1081-2.

40. J. H. M. Salmon, 'Clovis and Constantine: the uses of history in 16th century Gallicanism', *JEH* 41 (1990), at 601.

41. D. Reid, 'Carnival in Rouen: a history of the Abbaye des Conards', *SCJ* 32 (2001), 1027-55.

42. D. Potter (ed.), *The French Wars of Religion: selected documents* (London, 1997), p. 208.

43. L. J. Taylor, 'Funeral sermons and orations as religious propaganda in 16th century France', in Gordon and Marshall (eds), *Place of the Dead*, pp. 224-39, at pp. 237-8.

44. Martin, *Henry III and the Jesuit politicians*, p. 129.

45. Taylor, 'Funeral sermons', 237-8.

46. Cunningham and Grell, *Four Horsemen*, pp. 231-4.

47. On the quotation's lack of authenticity, see M. Wolfe, 'The Conversion of Henri IV and the origins of Bourbon absolutism', *Historical reflections/ Réflexions Historiques*, 14 (1987), 287-309, at 287.

48. S. M. Manetsch, *Theodore Beza and the Quest for Peace in France, 1572-1598* (Leiden, 2000), especially pp. 256-61.

49. G. Champeaud, 'The Edict of Poitiers and the Treaty of Nérac, or two steps towards the Edict of Nantes', *SCJ* 32 (2001), 319-33.

50. P. Benedict, *The Faith and Fortunes of France's Huguenots, 1600-85* (Aldershot, 2001), p. 189.

51. P. Benedict, *The Huguenot Population of France, 1600-1685: the Demographic fate and customs of a religious minority* (Philadelphia, 1991, especially pp. 75-77.

52. R. Sauzet, *Contre-Réforme et réforme catholique en Bas-Languedoc: le diocèse de Nîmes au XVIIe siècle* (Louvain, 1979), especially pp. 420, 490.

53. Champeaud, 'Edict of Poitiers and the Treaty of Nérac', 331.

54. J. A. Bergin, *The Making of the French episcopate, 1589-1661* (New Haven and London, 1996), pp. 208-43, 248-9, 251-7.

55. J. A. Bergin, 'The Crown, the papacy and the reform of the old Orders in early 17th century France', *JEH* 33 (1982), 234-55, at 237-8.

56. L. J. Lekai, *The Rise of the Cistercian Strict Observance in seventeenth-century France* (Washington DC, 1968), especially p. 166.

57. V. Harding, 'Whose body? A study of attitudes towards the dead body in early modern Paris', in Gordon and Marshall (eds), *Place of the Dead*, pp. 170-87, at p. 175; Bergin, 'The Crown, the papacy and the reform of the old Orders', 234.

58. R. Kleinman, *François de Sales and the Protestants* (Geneva, 1962), p. 16 (spelling Anglicized). On the encounters with Beza, ibid., p. 90.

59. W. M. Thompson (ed.), *Bérulle and the French School: selected writings* (New York, 1989), p. 183.

60. Thompson (ed.), *Bérulle and the French School*, pp. 125, 170. Useful discussion in W. J. Hankey, 'Augustinian Immediacy and Dionysian Mediation in John Colet, Edmund Spenser, Richard Hooker and the Cardinal de Bérulle', in D. de Courcelles (ed.), *Augustinus in der Neuzeit, Colloque de la Herzog August Bibliothek de Wolfenbüttel, 14-17 octobre, 1996* (Turnhout, 1998), pp. 154-8.

61. E. Duffy, 'The English secular clergy and the Counter-Reformation', *JEH* 34 (1983), 214-30, especially 223-4. For the most extreme - indeed startling - outcome of such attitudes among 'Blackloist' secular clergy in England, see J. R. Collins, 'Thomas Hobbes and the Blackloist conspiracy of 1649', *HJ* (2002), 305-32.

62. Confusingly, there is an elder Cornelius Jansen (1510-76), who as Bishop of Ghent was one of the most distinguished nominees to Philip II's controversial new Netherlands bishoprics in the 1560s.

63. Bireley, *Refashioning*, p. 187.

64. I am grateful to Dr Alexandra Walsham for this point.

65. For a study of this phenomenon, see D. G. Thompson, *A Modern Persecution: Breton Jesuits under the suppression of 1762–1814* (Oxford, 1999).

11 1618–48: Decision and Destruction

1. Cunningham and Grell, *Four Horsemen*, p. 208; G. Parker (ed.), *The Thirty Years War* (New York, 1984), pp. 210–11.

2. Parker (ed.), *Thirty Years War*, p. 84.

3. R. Bireley, *Religion and Politics in the Age of the Counterreformation: Emperor Ferdinand II, William Lamormaini, S. J., and the formation of imperial policy* (Chapel Hill, 1981).

4. Yates, *Rosicrucian Enlightenment*, pp. 49–51.

5. Rummel, *Humanism*, p. 128.

6. Yates, *Rosicrucian Enlightenment*, pp. 1–9.

7. Ibid., pp. 14–23.

8. C. S. Dixon, 'Popular astrology and Lutheran propaganda in Reformation Germany', *History* 84 (1999), 403–18.

9. R. Kolb, *Martin Luther as Prophet, Teacher, Hero: images of the Reformer 1520–1620* (Grand Rapids, 1999), p. 133.

10. Yates, *Rosicrucian Enlightenment*, especially chapter 4.

11. Parker (ed.), *Thirty Years War*, pp. 38–44.

12. Cunningham and Grell, *Four Horsemen*, p. 59.

13. Parker (ed.), *Thirty Years War*, pp. 44–5.

14. Murdock, *Calvinism on the Frontier*, p. 3.

15. Yates, *Rosicrucian Enlightenment*, p. 29.

16. Michalski, *Reformation and Visual Arts*, pp. 84–5.

17. Yates, *Rosicrucian Enlightenment*, pp. 136, 179–81.

18. J. Bepler, 'Vicissitudo temporum: some sidelights on book collecting in the Thirty Years' War', *SCJ* 32 (2001), 953–67, at 955.

19. L. F. Miskovsky, 'The Catholic Counter-Reformation in Bohemia', *Bibliotheca sacra* 57 (1900), 532–52, at 550. I am grateful to Howard Louthan for this reference. See also O. Châline, 'Frontières religieuses: La Bohême après la Montagne Blanche', in E. Andor and I. G. Tóth (eds), *Frontiers of Faith: religious exchange and the constitution of religious identities 1400–1750* (Budapest, 2001), pp. 55–66.

20. Z. V. David, 'The strange fate of Czech Utraquism: the second century, 1517–1621', *JEH* 46 (1995), 641–68, at 646, 657.

21. Pörtner, *Styria*, pp. 138–42.

22. Pettegree (ed.), *Reformation World*, p. 406.

23. Yates, *Rosicrucian Enlightenment*, p. 221.

24. Murdock, *Calvinism on the Frontier*, p. 39.

25. P. Sonnino, 'From D'Avaux to *Dévot*: politics and religion in the Thirty Years War', *History* 87 (2002), 192–203, at 192.

26. Yates, *Rosicrucian Enlightenment*, p. 288.

27. Cf. discussion in K. Scholder, *The Birth of Modern Critical Theology* (London, 1990), pp. 10–11.

12 Coda: a British Legacy, 1600–1700

1. J. Foster (ed.), *Alumni Oxonienses: the members of the University of Oxford 1500–1714* ... (4 vols, Oxford and London, 1891–2), iv, p. 102.

2. For an overview of Hooker's career and his long-term impact, see D. MacCulloch, 'Richard Hooker's Reputation', *EHR* 117 (2002), 773–812.

3. N. Voak, *Richard Hooker and Reformed Theology. A Study of Reason, Will, and Grace* (Oxford, 2003).

4. W. R. Speed Hill et al. (eds) *The Folger Library Edition of the Works of Richard Hooker* (7 vols, Cambridge and Binghamton, 1977–94), n. to vol. ii, p. 343, ll. 6–26. See also B. D. Spinks, *Two Faces of Elizabethan Anglican Theology: sacraments and salvation in the thought of William Perkins and Richard Hooker* (Lanham, 1999).

5. S. Doran, 'Elizabeth I's religion: the evidence of her letters', *JEH* 50 (2000), 699–720; MacCulloch, *Tudor Church Militant*, pp. 185–95.

6. We await the forthcoming ground-breaking biography of Andrewes by Peter McCullough, to whom I am much indebted for this discussion.

7. L. Andrewes, *Ninety-six sermons* ... (5 vols, Oxford, 1841–3) i, pp. 173–4: Sermon 10 'of the Nativity', Christmas Day 1615.

8. *The Works of John Whitgift D. D.* (3 vols, PS 1851), i, p. 184.

9. P. Lake, *Anglicans and Puritans? Presbyterianism and English Conformist Thought from Whitgift to Hooker* (London, 1988).

10. MacCulloch, *Tudor Church Militant*, pp. 169–73, 218–20.

11. P. Lake, 'Lancelot Andrewes, John Buckeridge and avant garde conformity at the court of James I' in L. L. Peck (ed.) *The Mental World of the Jacobean Court* (Cambridge, 1991), pp. 113–33, and see the extensive use of the term in A. Milton, *Catholic and Reformed: the Roman and Protestant Churches in English Protestant thought, 1600–1640* (Cambridge, 1995).

12. J. F. Merritt, 'The cradle of Laudianism? Westminster Abbey, 1558–1630', *JEH* 52 (2001), 623–46.

13. P. Croft, 'The religion of Robert Cecil', *HJ* 34 (1991), 773–96.

14. A. W. Beasley, 'The disability of James VI and I', *Seventeenth Century* 10 (1995), 151–62.

15. W. B. Patterson, *King James I and the reunion of Christendom* (Cambridge, 1997).

16. K. L. Sprunger, *Dutch Puritanism: a history of English and Scottish churches of the Netherlands in the sixteenth and seventeenth centuries* (Leiden, 1982), pp. 285–306.

17. P. McCullough, *Sermons at Court: Politics and Religion in Elizabethan and Jacobean Preaching* (Cambridge, 1997), pp. 194–209.

18. C. Carlton, *Archbishop William Laud* (London and New York, 1987), p. 13.

19. Ibid., pp. 56, 152–3. On the tortoise, ibid., pp. 97, 227.

20. On the proclamation and its effects, N. Tyacke, *Anti-Calvinists: The rise of English Arminianism c. 1590–1640* (Oxford, 1987), pp. 48, 77, 229.

21. Murdock, *Calvinism on the Frontier*, p. 65. On Harsnet, Tyacke, *Anti-Calvinists*, pp. 182–3.

22. C. Hill, *Economic Problems of the Church from Archbishop Whitgift to the Long Parliament* (Oxford, 1956), p. 223.

23. H. R. Trevor-Roper, *Archbishop Laud 1573–1654* (London, 1940), p. 146.

24. MacCulloch, *Tudor Church Militant*, p. 173.

25. J. Gilchrist, *Anglican Church Plate* (London, 1967), pp. 71–6.

26. J. F. Merritt, 'Puritans, Laudians and the phenomenon of church-building in Jacobean London', *HJ* 41 (1998), 935–60. J. Craig, 'Psalms, Groans and Dog-whippers: the soundscape of worship in the English parish church', in W. Coster and A. Spicer (eds.), *Sacred Space* (forthcoming). I am grateful to Dr Craig for alerting me to his findings.

27. C. V. Wedgwood, *The King's Peace, 1637–1641* (London, 1955), pp. 177–8.

28. J. Maltby, *Prayer Book and People in Elizabethan and early Stuart England* (Cambridge, 1998), chapters 3 and 5.

29. H. Simms, 'Violence in County Armagh, 1641', in B. Mac Cuarta (ed.), *Ulster 1641: Aspects of the Rising* (Belfast, 1993), pp. 133–4, and cf. ibid., p. 5.

30. W. Lamont, 'Richard Baxter, "Popery" and the origins of the English Civil War', *History* 87 (2002), 336–52.

31. J. Morrill (ed.), *Oliver Cromwell and the English Revolution* (London, 1990), Ch. 2.

32. The remarkably bitter modern controversy about the existence of the

Ranters is judiciously surveyed in G. E. Aylmer, 'Did the Ranters exist?', *PP* 117 (Nov. 1987), 208-20.

33. D. S. Katz, *Philosemitism and the Readmission of the Jews to England, 1603-1655* (Oxford, 1982), especially pp. 235-8, 241.

34. J. Morrill, 'The Church in England, 1642-9', in J. Morrill (ed.), *Reactions to the English Civil War, 1642-1649* (London and Basingstoke, 1982), pp. 89-114.

35. D. Hirst, 'The failure of godly rule in the English Republic', *PP* 132 (Aug. 1991), 33-66.

36. See especially S. W. P. Hampton, 'Reformed Scholasticism and the battle for orthodoxy in the later Stuart Church', Oxford DPhil thesis, 2003.

37. MacCulloch, 'Hooker's Reputation'; J. Martin, *Walton's Lives: Conformist commemorations and the rise of Biography* (Cambridge, 2001).

38. J. Maltby, ' "The good old way": Prayer book protestantism in the 1640-50s', in R. Swanson (ed.), *The Church and the Book* (SCH 38, 2004), 233-56; L. Gragg, 'The pious and the profane: the religious life of early Barbados planters', *The Historian* 62 (2000), 264-83. I am grateful to Judith Maltby for pointing me to this reference.

39. S. Ahlstrom, *A Religious History of the American People* (New Haven and London, 1972), pp. 136-7.

40. R. T. Handy, *A History of the Churches in the United States and Canada* (Oxford, 1976), p. 20; on north Africa, N. Matar, *Turks, Moors and Englishmen in the Age of Discovery* (New York, 1999), pp. 84-92.

41. F. Bremer, *John Winthrop: America's Forgotten Founding Father* (Oxford, 2003).

42. R. Targoff, *Common Prayer: the language of public devotion in early modern England* (Chicago, 2001), pp. 118-19.

43. A. Zakai, 'The Gospel of Reformation: the origins of the great Puritan migration', *JEH* 37 (1986), 584-602, at 586-7.

44. Ahlstrom, *Religious History of the American People*, pp. 146-7. I am grateful to Francis Bremer for our discussions on this point.

45. B. Wendell, *Cotton Mather: the Puritan Priest* (Cambridge MA, 1926), p. 12. On the origins of 'Congregationalism', L. Ziff (ed.), *John Cotton on the Churches of New England* (Cambridge MA, 1962), p. 2. See also F. J. Bremer, *Congregational Communion: clerical friendship in the Anglo-American Puritan community, 1610-1692* (Boston, 1994).

46. M. Winship, *Making Heretics: militant Protestantism and free grace in Massachusetts, 1636-1641* (Princeton, 2002).

47. Bonomi, *Under the Cope of Heaven*, pp. 20, 23, 34.

48. E. H. Ash, ' "A note and a caveat for the merchant": Mercantile Advisors in Elizabethan England', *SCJ* 33 (2002), 1–31, 27–9.

49. R. W. Cogley, *John Eliot's Mission to the Indians before King Philip's War* (Cambridge, MA, 1999), pp. 5–6, 8, 12–18, 22, 40, 51.

50. Bonomi, *Under the Cope of Heaven*, pp. 119, 252–3.

51. Ibid., p. 23.

52. Ibid., p. 36.

13 Changing Times

1. Cunningham and Grell, *Four Horsemen*, pp. 50–1.

2. Murdock, *Calvinism on the Frontier*, p. 115.

3. G. E. Corrie (ed.), *Sermons and Remains of Hugh Latimer* ... (PS, 1845), p. 20.

4. The doyenne of Joachimite studies is Marjorie Reeves, whose work remains indispensable: cf. especially *The Influence of Prophecy in the Late Middle Ages: a Study in Joachimism* (Oxford, 1969).

5. Cunningham and Grell, *Four Horsemen*, pp. 22–3.

6. Cottret, *Calvin*, p. 103.

7. A fine overall treatment is I. R. Backus, *Reformation Readings of the Apocalypse: Geneva, Zürich and Wittenberg* (Oxford, 2000). For a very similarly changing profile in the fortunes of II Esdras, see A. Hamilton, *The Apocryphal Apocalypse: the reception of the Second Book of Esdras (4 Ezra) from the Renaissance to the Enlightenment* (Oxford, 1999).

8. P. J. Olsen, 'Was John Foxe a millenarian?', *JEH* 45 (1994), 600–24, at 604–6.

9. Cunningham and Grell, *Four Horsemen*, p. 50. On apocalypticism in Scotland, see A. H. Williamson, *Scottish National Consciousness in the Age of James VI: the Apocalypse, the Union and the shaping of Scotland's Public Culture* (Edinburgh, 1979); on England, K. R. Firth, *The Apocalyptic Tradition in Reformation Britain 1530–1645* (Oxford, 1979).

10. W. Johnston, 'The Anglican Apocalypse in Restoration England', *JEH*, forthcoming.

11. P. M. Soergel, 'The afterlives of monstrous infants in Reformation Germany', in Gordon and Marshall (eds), *Place of the Dead*, pp. 288–309.

12. Cunningham and Grell, *Four Horsemen*, p. 84.

13. A. Walsham, *Providence in Early Modern England* (Oxford, 1999), p. 204.

14. Todd, *Protestantism in Scotland*, pp. 388–9, 396–8.

15. A. Walsham, *Providence*, pp. 130-5, 167-8; on herring, cf. also Cunningham and Grell, *Four Horsemen*, p. 86.

16. Walsham, *Providence*, pp. 232-3, 266.

17. Walsham, *Providence*, pp. 137-9, 313; D. Underdown, *Fire from Heaven: the Life of an English Town in the Seventeenth Century* (London, 1992).

18. W. I. P. Hazlett, 'Playing God's card: Knox and fasting, 1565-6', in R. A. Mason (ed.), *John Knox and the British Reformations* (Aldershot, 1998), pp. 176-99; Todd, *Protestantism in Scotland*, pp. 341-52.

19. Walsham, *Providence*, pp. 142-6, 163-6.

20. B. Nischan, 'The Second Reformation in Brandenburg: aims and goals', *SCJ* 14 (1983), 173-87, at 184.

21. Michalski, *Reformation and Visual Arts*, p. 76; Murdock, *Calvinism on the Frontier*, p. 17.

22. For examples, L. E. Whatmore (ed.), *Archdeacon Harpsfield's Visitation, 1557* (Catholic Record Society 45/46, 1950-1), pp. 77, 115, 146, 205, 222, 267; C. Litzenberger, *The English Reformation and the Laity: Gloucestershire, 1540-1580* (Cambridge, 1997), pp. 24, 132; J. E. Foster (ed.), *Churchwardens' Accounts of St Mary the Great Cambridge* (Cambridge, 1905), p. 162.

23. R. Hayden (ed.), *Records of a Church of Christ in Bristol* (Bristol Record Society 27, 1974), pp. 81-5.

24. MacCulloch, *Tudor Church Militant*, pp. 9-10.

25. Murdock, *Calvinism on the Frontier*, pp. 153-4.

26. T. Cooper (ed.), *The Journal of William Dowsing: iconoclasm in East Anglia during the English Civil War* (Woodbridge 2001), especially essay by J. Morrill, pp. 1-28.

27. S. Clark, *Thinking with Demons: the idea of witchcraft in early modern Europe* (Oxford, 1997), p. 594. An edition of the relevant documents in the Hopkins-Stearne trials by Malcolm Gaskill will appear as vol. 3 of J. Sharpe (ed.), *English Witchcraft 1560-1736* (6 vols, London, from 2003), and I am very grateful to Dr Gaskill for telling me of his findings in advance. He is also preparing a study: *Witchfinders: Matthew Hopkins and the Great English Witch-Hunt*.

28. Ronald Hutton, whose help I gratefully acknowledge, first proposed the estimate of deaths for witchcraft: R. Hutton, *The Pagan Religions of the Ancient British Isles: their nature and legacy* (Oxford, 1991), pp. 306, 370. It has now been widely accepted: cf. G. Scarre and J. Callow, *Witchcraft and Magic in sixteenth and seventeenth century Europe* (Basingstoke, 2001), p. 21, and J. Sharpe, *Witchcraft in Early Modern England* (Harlow, 2001),

p. 6. On the heresy comparison, W. Monter, 'Heresy executions in Reformation Europe, 1520–1565', in Grell and Scribner (eds), *Tolerance in the Reformation*, pp. 48–64, at pp. 62–3.

29. A valuable collection of case-studies on Scandinavian witchcraft forms part of B. Ankarloo and G. Henningsen (eds), *Early Modern Witchcraft: centres and peripheries* (Oxford, 1989).

30. Davies, *God's Playground*, pp. 196–7; R. Hutton, *Shamans: Siberian spirituality and the western imagination* (London, 2001), pp. 47–67, 142–6; Ankarloo and Henningsen (eds), *Early Modern Witchcraft*, pp. 266–7.

31. M. Gaskill, *Crime and Mentalities in Early Modern England* (Cambridge, 2000), pp. 48–66, 78. K. Thomas, *Religion and the Decline of Magic* (2nd edn, London, 1973), pp. 660–69, made a formerly much-cited suggestion that witchcraft accusations generally arose from tensions over the breakdown of traditional hospitality obligations to the marginal: this may have some justification, but will not do as a general mode of explanation.

32. C. Harper-Bill (ed.), *The Register of John Morton of Canterbury, 1486–1500, III: Norwich sede vacante, 1499* (Canterbury and York Society, 89, 2000), pp. 215–17.

33. N. L. Brann, *Trithemius and Magical Theology: a chapter in the controversy over occult studies in early modern Europe* (Albany, NY, 1999), pp. 51–7.

34. W. Behringer, 'Witchcraft studies in Austria, Germany and Switzerland', in J. Barry, M. Hester and G. Roberts (eds), *Witchcraft in Early Modern Europe: Studies in Culture and belief* (Cambridge, 1996), pp. 64–95, at pp. 82–3. On Sprenger and the rosary, Ellington, *Mary*, p. 34 and n., 257.

35. *Disquisitionum Magicarum libri sex*: P. G. Maxwell-Stuart (ed.), *Martin Del Rio: Investigations into Magic* (2000), especially p. 8. On publication history of the *Malleus*, Monter, 'Heresy executions', p. 62.

36. M. Summers (ed.), H. Kramer and J. Sprenger, *Malleus Maleficarum* (London, 1928), pp. 41–2.

37. A. Rowlands, 'Witchcraft and old women in early modern Germany', *PP* 173 (Nov. 2001), 50–89, especially 65, 70, 78.

38. Ankarloo and Henningsen (eds), *Early Modern Witchcraft*, p. 290.

39. M. Del Rio, *Disquisitionum Magicarum libri sex* (Lyon, 1612), 'Proloquium', unpaginated: cf. Maxwell-Stuart (ed.), *Martin Del Rio*, pp. 28–9.

40. W. Behringer, *Witchcraft Persecutions in Bavaria: popular Magic, religious zealotry and reason of state in early modern Europe* (Cambridge, 1997), pp. 393, 402–5.

41. J. D. Tracy, *Europe's Reformations 1450–1650* (Lanham, 2000), p. 256.

42. G. Murdock, 'Death, prophecy and judgement in Transylvania', in Gordon and Marshall (eds), *Place of the Dead*, pp. 206–23, at 213–14.

43. W. G. Naphy, *Plagues, Poisons and Potions: Plague-spreading conspiracies in the western Alps c. 1530–1640* (Manchester, 2002), especially pp. 3, 93–4, 197–201. Cf. also Cottret, *Calvin*, pp. 179–81; Clark, *Thinking with Demons*, pp. 522–3.

44. G. Henningsen, *The Witches' Advocate: Basque witchcraft and the Spanish Inquisition (1609–1614)* (Reno, 1980), p. 22. On witchcraft beliefs in the Netherlands, see W. de Blécourt, 'On the continuation of witchcraft', in Barry, Hester and Roberts (eds), *Witchcraft in Early Modern Europe*, pp. 335–52.

45. Chadwick, *Early Reformation*, pp. 408–9; on Hardenberg, see above, chapter 7, p. 317; Clark, *Thinking with Demons*, pp. 198–208.

46. R. B. Evenhuis, *Ook dat was Amsterdam, III: De kerk der hervorming in de tweede helft van der seventiede eeuw: nabloei en inzinking* (Baarn, 1971), Ch. 6, cited in review by C. R. Boxer, *JEH* 25 (1974), 323–6.

47. For examples, J. Wormald, 'The witches, the devil and the King', in T. Brotherstone and D. Ditchburn (eds), *Freedom and Authority: Scotland c. 1050–c. 1650* (Tuckwell, 2000), pp. 165–80, at p. 170.

48. E. J. Cowan, 'The darker vision of the Scottish Renaissance: the Devil and Francis Stewart', in I. B. Cowan and D. Shaw (eds), *The Renaissance and Reformation in Scotland: essays in honour of Gordon Donaldson* (Edinburgh, 1983), pp. 125–40.

49. The extent of James's interest in witches has been questioned by Wormald, 'The witches, the devil and the King': a robust reply is J. Goodare, 'The Scottish witchcraft panic of 1597', in J. Goodare (ed.), *The Scottish Witchhunt in Context* (Edinburgh, 2002), pp. 51–72. The role of Denmark in James's change of mind, previously much emphasized, is questioned in P. Maxwell-Stuart, 'The fear of the King is death: James VI and the witches of East Lothian', *Northern Scotland* 18 (1998), 209–25, at 212–13. The primary sources are presented in L. Normand and G. Roberts (eds), *Witchcraft in Early Modern Scotland* (Exeter, 2000).

50. J. Sharpe, *The bewitching of Anne Gunter: a horrible and true story of football, witchcraft, murder and the king of England* (London, 1999), especially pp. 175–89. See also M. MacDonald (ed.), *Witchcraft and Hysteria in Elizabethan London: Edward Jorden and the Mary Glover case* (London, 1991), introduction, especially pp. xlix–l.

51. I owe this suggestion to Malcolm Gaskill.

52. C. Larner, *Enemies of God: the witch-hunt in Scotland* (London, 1981), especially pp. 63, 107. On similar politically related fluctuations in Scottish

prosecutions for bestiality, see P. G. Maxwell-Stuart, ' "Wilde, filthie, exec-rabill, destestabill and unnatural sin": bestiality in early modern Scotland', in T. Betteridge (ed.), *Sodomy in Early Modern Europe* (Manchester, 2002), pp. 82–93.

53. Behringer, 'Witchcraft studies in Austria, Germany and Switzerland', pp. 86–8.

54. Ibid., pp. 88–9.

55. H. Kamen, *The Spanish Inquisition: an historical revision* (London, 1997), pp. 269–76; Henningsen, *Witches' Advocate*, especially, pp. 387–9.

14 Death, Life and Discipline

1. For a sensible overview, see C. Marsh, ' "Departing well and Christianly": will-making and popular religion in early modern England', in E. J. Carlson (ed.), *Religion and the English People 1500–1640 (16th Century Essays and Studies* 45, 1998), 201–43; for an example of using wills and their preambles, perhaps over-schematically, see C. Litzenberger, 'Local responses to religious changes: evidence from Gloucestershire wills', ibid., 245–70.

2. MacCulloch, *Cranmer*, pp. 508–10.

3. C. Koslofsky, *The Reformation of the Dead: Death and Ritual in Early Modern Germany, 1450–1700* (Basingstoke, 2000), pp. 41–77, 87. On Scotland, Todd, *Protestantism in Scotland*, p. 340, and New England, Bonomi, *Under the Cope of Heaven*, p. 69.

4. Koslofsky, *Reformation of the Dead*, pp. 89–90, 93–5.

5. Ibid., pp. 41–77, 87; R. Houlbrooke, *Death, Religion and the Family in England 1480–1750* (Oxford, 1998), p. 272.

6. J. Ayre (ed.), *The Works of Thomas Becon* (3 vols, PS, 1843–4); on Swiss doubts, Gordon and Marshall (eds), *Place of the Dead*, introduction, p. 13n; on France, L. J. Taylor, 'Funeral sermons and orations as religious propaganda in 16th century France', ibid., pp. 224–39; on England, Houlbrooke, *Death, Religion and the Family in England*, Ch. 10.

7. Murdock, *Calvinism on the Frontier*, pp. 211–12.

8. Houlbrooke, *Death, Religion and the Family in England*, pp. 287–9; D. Levine and K. Wrightson, *The Making of an Industrial Society: Whickham 1560–1765* (Oxford, 1991), pp. 292–4, 341–3.

9. One example, dismantled in the nineteenth century and brusquely recon-structed in the church porch, is the tomb of Sir John Newton, d. 1568, at

East Harptree, Somerset; another survives *in situ* at Elstow, Bedfordshire – Sir Humphrey and Lady Radcliffe, placed about 1590.

10. Todd, *Protestantism in Scotland*, pp. 333–41.

11. For good discussion and some examples of popular scepticism, N. Caciola, 'Spirits seeking bodies: death, possession and communal memory in the Middle Ages', in Gordon and Marshall (eds), *Place of the Dead*, pp. 66–86; cf. also C. S. Watkins, 'Sin, penance and purgatory in the Anglo-Norman realm: the evidence of visions and ghost stories', *PP* 175 (May 2002), 3–33.

12. Koslofsky, *Reformation of the Dead*, p. 48; on purgatory, ibid., pp. 34–9.

13. For an example from Burntisland, Fife, see Todd, *Protestantism in Scotland*, plate 22 (reproduced here as Plate 19b).

14. H. Mayr-Harting, *Perceptions of Angels in History* (Oxford, 1998). Useful discussion in B. Gordon, 'Malevolent ghosts and ministering angels: apparitions and pastoral care in the Swiss Reformation', in Gordon and Marshall (eds), *Place of the Dead*, pp. 87–109.

15. R. W. Scribner, 'Ritual and popular religion in Catholic Germany at the time of the Reformation', *JEH* 35 (1984), 47–77, at 76–7.

16. D. Cressy, *Birth, Marriage and Death: ritual, religion and the life-cycle in Tudor and Stuart England* (Oxford, 1997), Ch. 6.

17. Cf. B. Tolley, *Pastors and Parishioners in Württemberg during the late Reformation 1581–1621* (Stanford, 1995), pp. 64–72; Todd, *Protestantism in Scotland*, pp. 183–226, 358–9; M. Todd, 'Profane pastimes and the Reformed community: the persistence of popular festivities in early modern Scotland', *Journal of British Studies* 39 (2000), 123–56, at 140.

18. R. Hutton, 'The English Reformation and the evidence of folklore', *PP* 148 (Aug. 1995), 89–116, especially at 116.

19. A. McGrath, *Reformation Thought: an introduction* (3rd edn., Oxford, 1999), p. 165.

20. C. Hill, *The English Bible and the seventeenth-century Revolution* (London, 1993), p. 47. On Reformed bibles, F. Higman, ' "Without great effort and with pleasure": sixteenth century Genevan Bibles and reading practices', in O. O'Sullivan (ed.), *The Bible as Book: the Reformation* (London and New Castle DE, 2000), pp. 115–22.

21. A. C. Southern, *Elizabethan Recusant Prose 1559–1603* (London, 1950), p. 233.

22. Todd, *Protestantism in Scotland*, p. 71.

23. For the hour norm, cf. Todd, *Protestantism in Scotland*, pp. 48–9; in

Amsterdam, C. R. Boxer, *JEH* 19 (1968), 254-7, at 256, citing R. B. Evenhuis, *Ook dat was Amsterdam: de kerk der hervorming in de gouden eeuw* (2 vols, Amsterdam, 1965, 1967); in Geneva, O. Fatio and O. Labarthe (eds), *Registres de la Compagnie des Pasteurs de Genève III: 1565-1574* (Geneva, 1969), p. 57.

24. Murdock *Calvinism on the Frontier*, p. 162; on London, M. Morrissey, 'Interdisciplinarity and the study of early modern sermons', *HJ* 42 (1999), 1111-23, at 1112.

25. J. D. Tracy, *Europe's Reformations 1450-1650* (Lanham, 2000), p. 274.

26. Todd, *Protestantism in Scotland*, pp. 29, 40-4, 53-4, 68-9.

27. S. Karant-Nunn, *The Reformation of Ritual: an interpretation of early modern Germany* (London and New York, 1997), p. 161.

28. Todd, *Protestantism in Scotland*, pp. 76, 83, 113. On Germany, I am very grateful to Dr Stefan Ehrenpreis for permission to cite his as yet unpublished paper 'The use of catechisms: production and exchange of texts in 16th and 17th Europe', drawing for its German material on J. M. Reu, *Quellen zur Geschichte des kirchlichen Unterrichts* (9 vols, Leipzig, 1923-35). I. Green, *The Christian's ABC: Catechisms and Catechizing in England c. 1530-1740* (Oxford, 1996), especially table at p. 51.

29. Tolley, *Pastors and Parishioners in Württemberg* (Stanford, 1995), pp. 73-6, 82-5, 116; C. Haigh, 'Success and failure in the English Reformation', *PP* 173 (Nov. 2001), 28-49, at 41-8.

30. On Graz, Pörtner, *Styria*, p. 219; on France, Ehrenpreis, 'Use of catechisms'. On Spain, see above, chapter 10, pp. 419-20.

31. A. Walsham, ' "Domme preachers"? Post-Reformation English Catholicism and the culture of print', *PP* 168 (Aug. 2000), 72-123, especially 104-5; B. S. Gregory, 'The "true and zealouse service of God": Robert Parsons, Edmund Bunny, and *The first booke of the Christian Exercise*', *JEH* 45 (1994), 238-68. Bunny also produced a version of Thomas à Kempis's *Imitation of Christ* made safe for Protestants.

32. K. Konkola, ' "People of the Book": the production of theological texts in early modern England', *Papers of the Bibliographical Soceity of America* 94 (2000), 5-34.

33. P. Benedict, *The Faith and Fortune of France's Huguenots, 1600-85* (Aldershot, 2001), p. 154.

34. Quoted in K. H. Marcus, 'Hymnody and hymnals in Basel, 1526-1606', *SCJ* 32 (2001), 730.

35. M. Rössler, *Bibliographie der deutschen Liedpredigt* (Nieuwkoop, 1976).

36. K. L. Parker, 'Richard Greenham's "Spiritual Physicke": the comfort of

afflicted consciences in Elizabethan pastoral care', in Lualdi and Thayer (eds), *Penitence*, pp. 71–83, at p. 78.

37. Marcus, 'Hymnody in Basel', 735–6.

38. Murdock, *Calvinism on the Frontier*, pp. 18, 167–8.

39. G. R. Potter and M. Greengrass, *John Calvin: Documents of Modern History* (London, 1983), p. 90.

40. G. Strauss, 'The dilemma of popular history', *PP* 132 (Aug. 1991), 130–49, at 133.

41. Cf. P. Burke, *Popular Culture in Early Modern Europe* (London, 1978), Ch. 8, 'The Triumph of Lent'.

42. MacCulloch, *Later Reformation*, pp. 136–7; C. Marsh et al., *Songs of the Seventeenth Century* (Belfast, 1995), pp. 4, 35, 85; J. N. King, *English Reformation Literature: the Tudor origins of the Protestant tradition* (Princeton, 1982), pp. 211, 277–9.

43. R. Hutton, *Stations of the Sun: a History of the ritual year in Britain* (Oxford, 1996), p. 155.

44. M. Maher, 'Confession and consolation: the Society of Jesus and its promotion of the general confession', in Lualdi and Thayer (eds), *Penitence*, pp. 184–200, especially pp. 185–6, 194–5; see above, chapter 8, pp. 412–13.

45. G. Bray (ed.), *Tudor Church Reform: the Henrician Canons of 1535 and the Reformatio Legum Ecclesiasticarum* (Church of England Record Society 8, 2000), especially Introduction.

46. E. Christiansen, reviewing H. Bergan, *Skriftemål og skirftestol: Skriftemålet i den norske kirke fra reformasjonstiden til idag* (Oslo, 1982), in *JEH* 34 (1983), 483. Good discussions of German Lutheran practice are by M. J. Haemig and R. Rittgers in Lualdi and Thayer (eds), *Penitence*, pp. 30–70.

47. C. H. Parker, 'The moral agency and moral autonomy of church folk in the Dutch Reformed Church of Delft', *JEH* 48 (1997), 44–70, at 48.

48. A. Duke, 'The ambivalent face of Calvinism in the Netherlands 1561–1618', in M. Prestwich (ed.), *International Calvinism 1541–1715* (Oxford, 1985), pp. 109–34, at pp. 128–9.

49. Todd, *Protestantism in Scotland*, pp. 96–7.

50. J. Pollmann, 'Off the record: problems in the quantification of Calvinist Church discipline', *SCJ* 33 (2002), 423–37. On France, see R. A. Mentzer, 'Notions of sin and penitence within the French Reformed community', in Lualdi and Thayer (eds), *Penitence*, 84–100, at 87, 92.

51. D. Postles, 'Penance and the market-place: a Reformation dialogue with the medieval church (c. 1250–c. 1600)', *JEH* 54 (2003), 422–40. On what follows, Todd, *Protestantism in Scotland*, Ch. 3.

52. Murdock, *Calvinism on the Frontier*, p. 210.

53. Todd, *Protestantism in Scotland*, pp. 135, 321.

54. Ibid., p. 170.

55. K. M. Brown, 'In search of the godly magistrate in Reformation Scotland', *JEH* 40 (1989), 553–81, at 567. For the Kirk's attitude to parental direction in marriage, see below, chapter 15, p. 619.

56. T. Scott, *Regional Identity and Economic Change: the Upper Rhine, 1450–1660* (Oxford, 1998), pp. 226–8, 234–5.

57. A. Ryrie, 'Counting sheep, counting shepherds: the problem of allegiance', in Marshall and Ryrie (eds), *Beginnings of English Protestantism*, pp. 84–110, at pp. 102–3.

58. D. Cressy, *Bonfires and Bells: National Memory and the Protestant Calendar in Elizabethan and early Stuart England* (London, 1989). Todd, *Protestantism in Scotland*, pp. 225–6.

59. Todd, *Protestantism in Scotland*, Ch. 2.

60. L. E. Schmidt, *Holy Fairs: Scottish communions and American revivals in the early modern period* (Princeton, 1989), pp. 21–6.

61. M. Hill, 'Ulster awakened: the '59 Revival reconsidered', *JEH* 41 (1990), 443–62, at 445.

62. M. J. Westerkamp, *Triumph of the Laity: Scots-Irish piety and the Great Awakening 1625–1760* (Oxford, 1988), p. 15.

63. R. H. Tawney, *Religion and the Rise of Capitalism* (London, 1926), pp. 226–7.

64. Eisenstein, *Printing Revolution*, p. 103.

65. This assertion is at its most explicit in some of the writings of John Bossy: cf. especially J. Bossy, *Christianity in the West 1400–1700* (Oxford, 1985), pp. 140–52, 167–71. It might also be seen as a tendency of the argument in classic English 'revisionist' work on the Reformation such as J. J. Scarisbrick, *The Reformation and the English People* (Oxford, 1983), and E. Duffy, *The Stripping of the Altars: traditional religion in England 1400–1580* (New Haven and London, 1992).

15 Love and Sex: Staying the Same

1. T. Taylor, *The Prehistory of Sex: Four Million Years of Human Sexual Culture* (London, 1996), p. 7.

2. Quoted in J. Boswell, *Christianity, Social Tolerance and Homosexuality* (Chicago, 1980), p. 164.

3. H. J. Schroeder (ed.), *Canons and Decrees of the Council of Trent* (London, 1941), p. 182.

4. Quoted in W. R. Naphy, *Sex Crimes from Renaissance to Enlightenment* (Stroud, 2002), p. 18. For other examples, cf. Ellington, *Mary*, p. 168.

5. I. Maclean, 'The notion of woman in medicine, anatomy and physiology', in R. Hutson (ed.), *Feminism and Renaissance Studies* (Oxford and New York, 1999), pp. 127–35.

6. P. Brown, *The Body and Sexuality: Men, Women and Sexual renunciation in early Christianity* (London, 1989), pp. 396–447, especially at p. 416.

7. A. Fletcher, *Gender, Sex and Subordination in England 1500–1800* (New Haven and London, 1995, especially pt. III.

8. C. Fantazzi (ed.), J. L. Vives, *The Education of a Christian Woman* (Chicago and London, 2000), p. 232.

9. J. Kelly: 'Did women have a Renaissance?', reprinted from R. Bridenthal (ed.), *Becoming Visible: women in European history* (New York, 1977), in Hutson (ed.), *Feminism and Renaissance Studies*, pp. 21–47.

10. M. E. Wiesner, 'Frail, weak and helpless: women's legal position in theory and reality', in J. Friedman (ed.), *Regnum, Religio et Ratio: essays presented to Robert Kingdon* (*SCES* 8, 1987), 161–9; Wiesner, 'The Holy Roman Empire: women and politics beyond liberalism, individual rights and revolutionary theory', in H. L. Smith (ed.), *Women Writers and the Early Modern British Political Tradition* (Cambridge, 1998), pp. 305–23.

11. J. L. Irwin (ed.), A. M. van Schurman, *Whether a Christian woman should be educated and other writings from her intellectual circle* (Chicago and London, 1998), especially p. 5.

12. See my further discussion of this subject in D. MacCulloch, 'Mary and the Protestant Reformers', in R. N. Swanson (ed.), *The Place of Mary in Christian History* (*SCH*, forthcoming, 2005).

13. W. Tappolet with A. Ebneter, *Das Marienlob der Reformatoren: Martin Luther, Johannes Calvin, Huldrych Zwingli, Heinrich Bullinger* (Tübingen, 1962), pp. 245, 280.

14. Naphy (ed.), *Documents*, p. 101.

15. Tappolet with Ebneter, *Marienlob*, p. 246.

16. P. Laslett, *Family Life and Illicit Love in Earlier Generations* (revised edn., Cambridge, 1980), Ch. 1.

17. R. A. Houlbrooke, *The English Family 1450–1700* (London and New York, 1984), pp. 10, 20.

18. D. Cressy, 'Kinship and kin interaction in early modern England', *PP* 113 (Nov. 1986), 38–69, at 67.

19. E. A. Wrigley and R. Schofield, *The Population History of England 1541–1750* (revised edn. Cambridge, 1989), p. 255; cf. E. A. Wrigley, R. S. Davies, J. E. Oeppen and R. S. Schofield, *English Population History from Family Reconstitution 1580–1837* (Cambridge, 1997), p. 135.

20. R. A. Houston, *The Population History of Britain and Ireland 1500–1750* (Basingstoke, 1988), pp. 58–9. Cf. Laslett, *Family Life and Illicit Love*, p. 4.

21. For a case-study from Nuremberg of such reaction to crisis, a time of plague, see M. Beer, 'Private correspondence in Germany in the Reformation era: a forgotten source for the history of the burgher family', *SCJ* 32 (2001), 931–51.

22. Houston, *Population History*, pp. 78–88.

23. Laslett, *Family Life and Illicit Love*, pp. 58, 168.

24. Wrigley and Schofield, *Population History*, pp. 443–50, 528–9.

25. This was a particular fault of the classic exposition of this type of analysis, L. Stone, *The Family, Sex and Marriage in England* (New York, 1977). A representative refutation of Stone's approach is now S. Ozment, *Ancestors: the loving family in old Europe* (Cambridge, MA, 2001). For an assault on Philippe Ariès' influential assertions about medieval children, see N. Orme, *Medieval Children* (New Haven and London, 2001), especially at p. 9.

26. Todd, *Protestantism in Scotland*, p. 266.

27. Houlbrooke, *English Family*, pp. 128, 157; Stone, *Family, Sex and Marriage*, pp. 415–22.

28. Stone, *Family, Sex and Marriage*, pp. 282, 520, 605–7; Laslett, *Family Life and Illicit Love*, p. 111.

29. H. Abelove, 'Some speculations on the history of sexual intercourse during the long eighteenth century in England', *Genders* 6 (1989), 125–30; T. Hitchcock, *English Sexualities, 1700–1800* (New York, 1997), Ch. 3.

30. A. Machard (ed.), T. de Bèze, *Juvenilia* (Paris, 1879), editor's introduction and pp. 234–7, '*De sua in Candidam et Audebertum benevolentia*': '*Sic Bezae cupidus sui Audebertus . . . Sed postquam tamen alterum necesse est / Priores tibi defero, Audeberte: / Quod si Candida forte conqueratur / Quid tum? basiolo tacebit imo.*'

31. N. S. Davidson, 'Sodomy in early modern Venice', in T. Betteridge (ed.), *Sodomy in Early Modern Europe* (Manchester, 2002), pp. 65–81, at pp. 71–4.

32. J. Boswell, *Christianity, Social Tolerance and Homosexuality: gay people in western Europe from the beginning of the Christian era to the fourteenth century* (Chicago and London, 1980); J. Boswell, *The Marriage*

of Likeness: same-sex unions in pre-modern Europe (London, 1995); M. Barber, 'Lepers, Jews and Moslems: the plot to overthrow Christendom in 1321', History 66 (1981), 1−17.

33. A. Bray, Homosexuality in Renaissance England (London, 1981), pp. 21−2.

34. M. Laven, 'Sex and celibacy in early modern Venice', HJ 44 (2001), 865−88, at 865.

35. M. R. Boes, 'On trial for sodomy in early modern Germany', in Betteridge (ed.), Sodomy, pp. 27−45, at p. 27; M. E. Perry, 'The "nefarious sin" in early modern Seville', in K. Gerard and G. Hekma (eds), The Pursuit of Sodomy: male homosexuality in Renaissance and Enlightenment Europe (Binghamton, 1989), pp. 67−89.

36. T. S. Betteridge, 'The place of sodomy in the writings of John Bale and John Foxe', in Betteridge (ed.), Sodomy, pp. 11−26, at p. 14.

37. N. Matar, Turks, Moors and Englishmen in the Age of Discovery (New York, 1999), Ch. 4: on the Jesuit obsession with oriental sodomy, J. D. Spence, The Memory Palace of Matteo Ricci (London, 1984), Ch. 7.

38. C. L. Polecritti, Preaching Peace in Renaissance Italy: Bernardino of Siena and his audience (Washington DC, 2000), pp. 52−3. Cf. M. J. Rocke, 'Sodomites in fifteenth-century Tuscany: the views of Bernardino of Siena', in K. Gerard and G. Hekma (eds), The Pursuit of Sodomy, pp. 7−31.

39. Naphy, Sex Crimes, p. 128; cf. Boes, 'On trial in early modern Germany', p. 42.

40. W. R. Naphy, 'Sodomy in early modern Geneva: various definitions, diverse verdicts', in Betteridge (ed.), Sodomy, pp. 94−111; Naphy, Sex Crimes, pp. 75−6, 120, 156.

41. Bray, Homosexuality in Renaissance England, pp. 68−9. Cf. Davidson, 'Sodomy in early modern Venice', pp. 69−70, and on Bernardino, Rocke, 'Sodomites in fifteenth-century Tuscany', pp. 17−18.

42. Cf. examples cited by Boes, 'On trial in early modern Germany', p. 31. A rare record from Geneva of prosecution of heterosexual group sex in 1569 also reveals that the men participated in hierarchical social order: Naphy, Sex Crimes, pp. 149−50.

43. Bray, Homosexuality in Renaissance England, pp. 52−3.

44. Betteridge (ed.), Sodomy p. 5.

45. D. Clarke, ' "The sovereign's vice begets the subject's error": the Duke of Buckingham, "sodomy" and narratives of Edward II, 1622−28', in Betteridge (ed.), Sodomy, pp. 46−64.

46. Betteridge, 'Sodomy in Bale and Foxe', p. 21.

47. T. Webster, ' "Kiss me with kisses of his mouth": gender inversion and

Canticles in godly spirituality', in Betteridge (ed.), *Sodomy*, 5 op. cit., pp. 148–63. On John of the Cross, see above, chapter 9, p. 526.

48. L. Mott, 'Love's labours lost: five letters from an early seventeenth-century Portuguese sodomite', in Gerard and Hekma (eds), *Pursuit of Sodomy*, pp. 91–101. On Boudin, Boes, 'On trial in early modern Germany', p. 33.

49. R. Norton, *Mother Clap's Molly House: the gay subculture in England 1700–1830* (London, 1992); T. van der Meer, 'The persecutions of sodomites in early eighteenth-century Amsterdam: changing perceptions of sodomy', in Gerard and Hekma (eds), *Pursuit of Sodomy*, pp. 263–309; Hitchcock, *English Sexualities*, Ch. 5.

50. Naphy, *Sex Crimes*, pp. 98–100, 106, 130, 165–70; Hitchcock, *English Sexualities*, Ch. 4.

51. MacCulloch, *Tudor Church Militant*, p. 145.

16 Love and Sex: Moving On

1. M. R. Boes, 'On trial for sodomy in early modern Germany', in T. Betteridge (ed.), *Sodomy in Early Modern Europe* (Manchester, 2002), pp. 27–45, at p. 27; N. S. Davidson, 'Sodomy in early modern Venice', in ibid., pp. 65–81, at p. 75.

2. J. Arrizabalaga, J. Henderson and R. French, *The Great Pox: the French Disease in Renaissance Europe* (New Haven and London, 1997), Chs 7, 8.

3. Cunningham and Grell, *Four Horsemen*, pp. 309, 347–8.

4. M. Honigsbaum, *The Fever Trail: the hunt for the cure for malaria* (Basingstoke, 2001).

5. N. Orme, 'The Reformation and the Red Light', *HT* 37 (March 1987), 36–41.

6. J. S. Cummins, 'Pox and paranoia in Renaissance Europe', *HT* 38 (Aug. 1988), 28–35; S. Andreski, 'The Syphilitic shock', *Encounter* (May 1982), 7–26.

7. Bireley, *Refashioning*, p. 77, and cf. ibid., pp. 181–7.

8. S. Karant-Nunn, in Pettegree (ed.), *Reformation World*, p. 458.

9. W. R. Naphy, *Sex Crimes from Renaissance to Enlightenment* (Stroud, 2002) p. 22; S. Burghartz, *Zeiten der Reinheit – Orte der Unzucht. Ehe und Sexualität in Basel während der frühen Neuzeit* (Paderborn, 1999), pp. 152–63, 287–8, 298; H. Kamen, *The Phoenix and the Flame: Catalonia and the Counter-Reformation* (New Haven and London, 1993), pp. 281–7.

10. M. Ingram, *Church Courts, Sex and Marriage in England, 1570–1642* (Cambridge, 1987), especially Chs. 11, 12.

11. J. Bossy, *The English Catholic Community 1570–1850* (London, 1975), p. 136.

12. Ingram, *Church Courts, Sex and Marriage*, p. 366n.

13. Naphy, *Sex Crimes*, pp. 39, 42.

14. Ingram, *Church Courts, Sex and Marriage*, p. 335; cf. D. Hirst, 'The Failure of Godly Rule in the English Republic', *PP* 132 (August 1991), 33–66.

15. J. M. Ferraro, *Marriage Wars in late Renaissance Venice* (Oxford, 2001), pp. 29, 154–60.

16. C. Villaseñor Black, 'Love and marriage in the Spanish Empire: depictions of holy matrimony and gender discourses in the 17th century', *SCJ* 32 (2001), 637–67, at 663.

17. M. E. Wiesner-Hanks, *Christianity and Sexuality in the Early Modern World: regulating desire, reforming practice* (London and New York, 2000), p. 196.

18. Ellington, *Mary*, is a fine overall study of the subject, but could have brought out more strongly the developing contrast between north and south.

19. O. Hufton, 'Altruism and reciprocity: the early Jesuits and their female patrons', *Renaissance Studies* 15 (2001), 328–53, especially at 336, 340–1, and on Lisbon, cf. B. Telles, *Chronica da Companhia de Iesu, na provincia de Portugal* (2 vols, Lisbon, 1645, 1647), ii, pp. 94–7.

20. Hufton, 'Altruism and reciprocity', 337. On women in processions, J. D. Selwyn, ' "Schools of mortification": theatricality and the role of penitential practice in the Jesuits' popular missions', in Lualdi and Thayer (eds), *Penitence*, pp. 201–21, at pp. 217–18.

21. O. Hufton, 'The widow's mite and other strategies: funding the Catholic Reformation', *TRHS* 6th ser. 8 (1998), 130–72.

22. S. Evangelisti, 'Wives, widows and brides of Christ: marriage and the convent in the historiography of early modern Italy', *HJ* 43 (2000), 233–48, at 241; E. A. Lehfeldt, 'Discipline, vocation, and patronage: Spanish religious women in a Tridentine microclimate', *SCJ* 30 (1999), 1009–29, at 1009, 1022. *L'Invasion mystique (1590–1620)* was the title of vol. 2 of H. Brémond, *Histoire littéraire du sentiment religieux en France depuis la fin des Guerres de Religion jusqu'à nos jours* (12 vols, Paris, 1916–36).

23. J. G. Sperling, *Convents and the Body Politic in Late Renaissance Venice* (Chicago and London, 1999), pp. 3–4.

24. P. R. Baernstein, 'The Counter-Reformation Convent: the Angelics of San Paolo in Milan, 1535–1635' (unpublished Harvard PhD thesis, 1993),

p. 216, quoted in S. Broomhall, ' "In my opinion": Charlotte de Minut and female political discussion in print in 16th century France', *SCJ* 31 (2000), 25–45, at 40.

25. Hufton, 'Altruism and reciprocity', 345–7.

26. M. Wright, *Mary Ward's Institute: the struggle for identity* (Sydney, 1997).

27. Hufton, 'Widow's mite', 134–5.

28. Bireley, *Refashioning*, pp. 40–1.

29. Mère Marie should not be confused with the Discalced Carmelite Barbe Acarie (see above, chapter 10, p. 476), who also took the name Marie de l'Incarnation.

30. E. Rapley, *The Dévotes: women and church in seventeenth century France* (Montreal, 1990), especially Chs 4, 5.

31. For the complicated history of this work, see *CWE*, J. K. Sowards (ed.), *XXV/XXVI: Literary and educational writings*, (1985), pp. 528–9, and for one version of the text, ibid., pp. 129–45.

32. *CWE, XXV/XXVI: Literary and educational writings*, pp. 130, 137.

33. See his response to Clichthove in *CWE*, G. Bedouelle (ed.), *LXXXIII: Controversies* (1998), pp. 115–48, and for an earlier response to a critic, *CWE*, J. K. Sowards (ed.) *LXXI: Controversies* (1993), pp. 85–96.

34. A good summary discussion of clerical marriage is Chadwick, *Early Reformation*, Ch. 7.

35. H. Selderhuis, *Marriage and Divorce in the Thought of Martin Bucer* (Kirksville MO, 1999), pp. 116–17, 121–3.

36. M. Summers (ed.), H. Kramer and J. Sprenger, *Malleus Maleficarum* (London, 1928), p. 44: cf. above, chapter 13, pp. 565–7.

37. Selderhuis, *Marriage and Divorce in Bucer*, pp. 165–80.

38. Ellington, *Mary*, pp. 184–5.

39. E. A. McKee, *Katharina Schütz Zell* (2 vols, Leiden, 1999), i, p. 109.

40. On Cranmer, MacCulloch, *Cranmer*, pp. 361–2, 472; on Hooper. D. MacCulloch, 'Worcester: a cathedral city in the Reformation', in P. Collinson and J. Craig (eds), *The Reformation in English towns, 1500–1640* (Basingstoke, 1998), pp. 94–112, at p. 106.

41. P. Collinson, *The Religion of Protestants: the Church in English society 1559–1642* (Oxford, 1982), p. 142.

42. Bonomi, *Under the Cope of Heaven*, p. 69; Todd, *Protestantism in Scotland*, pp. 73, 272.

43. R. Heber and C. P. Eden (eds), *The Whole Works of the Right Rev. Jeremy Taylor* . . . (12 vols, London, 1847–54), v, pp. 224, 212 (my italics).

44. Quoted in R. Askew, *Muskets and Altars: Jeremy Taylor and the last of the Anglicans* (London, 1997), pp. 57–8. Cf. Taylor's allusion to a Greek

infant enticed off a dangerous precipice by 'his mother's pap': *Works of Taylor*, v, pp. 216-17.

45. MacCulloch, *Cranmer*, p. 481.

46. Selderhuis, *Marriage and Divorce in Bucer*, Ch. 6, pp. 138-43.

47. A. Wabuda, 'Sanctified by the believing spouse: women, men and the marital yoke in the early Reformation', in Marshall and Ryrie (eds), *Beginnings of English Protestantism*, pp. 111-28; Selderhuis, *Marriage and Divorce in Bucer*, pp. 305-6.

48. E. V. Beilin (ed.), *The Examinations of Anne Askew* (Oxford, 1996); P. Collinson, 'John Knox, the Church of England and the women of England', in R. A. Mason (ed.), *John Knox and the British Reformations* (Aldershot, 1998), pp. 74-96. On effeminacy, see above, chapter 15, p. 629.

49. Naphy (ed.), *Documents*, pp. 71-2. It must be pointed out that this story comes from an anti-Calvinist source, Florimond de Raemond, but he does name an eye-witness.

50. J. Christopherson, *An exhortation to all menne to . . . beware of rebellion* (London, 1554, *RSTC* 5207), sig. Sviiiab.

51. C. Garrett, *The Marian Exiles* (London, 1938). The effect is particularly bizarre when one has to find information about Catherine Duchess of Suffolk under the entry for her far less significant husband Richard Bertie.

52. Bossy, *English Catholic Community*, pp. 153-8.

53. McKee, *Katharina Schütz Zell*, i, pp. 461, 194, 209-10.

54. M. J. Haemig, 'Elisabeth Cruciger (1500?-1535): the case of the disappearing hymn writer', *SCJ* 32 (2001), 21-44.

55. Broomhall, 'Charlotte de Minut and female political discussion', op. cit., 28; Naphy (ed.), *Documents*, pp. 51, 64, 103-5.

56. F. L. Rutgers (ed.), *Acta van de Nederlandsche synoden der zestiende eeuw* (Utrecht, 1889), pp. 9-41, at p. 26 (Cap. V no. 10): 'Quibus locis erit etiam mulieres spectata fide ac probitate et aetate provectas ad hoc munus Apostolorum exemplo rectè ascisci posse.' For discussion of the context of this informal 'Synod', see A. Duke at http://dutchrevolt.leidenuniv.nl/English/Sources%20English/1571Wesel.htm.

57. W. Harrison, 'The role of women in Anabaptist thought and practice: the Hutterite experience of the 16th and 17th centuries', *SCJ* 23 (1992), 49-70, at 54.

58. H. Martens, 'Women in the Hutterites' Song Book', in C. A. Snyder and L. A. Huebert Hecht (eds), *Profiles of Anabaptist Women: Sixteenth century Reforming pioneers* (Waterloo, Ontario, 1996), pp. 221-43, at p. 225, and cf. M. Epp, 'Women in the *Chronicle* of the Hutterian Brethren' in ibid., pp. 202-20.

59. Harrison, 'Role of women in Anabaptist thought and practice', 57–8.

60. P. McNair, 'Ochino's Apology: Three Gods or Three Wives?', *History* 60 (1975), 353–73.

61. Cottret, *Calvin*, p. 184.

62. For the divorce provisions, see G. Bray (ed.), *Tudor Church Reform: the Henrician Canons of 1535 and the Reformatio Legum Ecclesiasticarum* (Church of England Record Society 9, 2000), pp. 264–79, and Introduction, pp. xli–lxxvi.

63. *Familie exercise; or, The service of God in families* (Edinburgh, 1641), quoted in Todd, *Protestantism in Scotland*, p. 265.

64. Bossy, *English Catholic Community*, pp. 145–47; cf. above, chapter 7, p. 340.

65. M. Aston, 'Segregation in Church', in W. J. Sheils and D. Wood (eds), *Women in the Church* (SCH 27, 1990), 237–94. D. Hey (ed.) R. Gough, *The History of Myddle* (London, 1981).

66. P. Marshall, 'The company of heaven: identity and sociability in the Enigsh Protestant afterlife c. 1560–1640', *Historical Reflections/Reflexions Historiques* 26 (2000), 311–33, at 331–2.

67. Quoted in S. Wabuda, 'The woman with the rock: the controversy on women and Bible reading', in S. Wabuda and C. Litzenberger (eds), *Belief and Practice in Reformation England* (Cambridge, 1998), pp. 40–59, at p. 40.

68. M. R. G. Spiller, 'A literary "first": the sonnet sequence of Anne Locke (1560)', *Renaissance Studies* 11 (1997), 41–55.

69. Matheson, *Imaginative World*, p. 133.

70. Figures quoted by James D. Tracy, in review of W. Bergsma, *Tussen Gideonsbende en publieke kerk: een studie over gereformeerd Protestantisme in Friesland, 1580–1610* (Hilversum, 1999), in *SCJ* 32 (2001), 893; see also above, chapter 8, p. 373.

71. P. Crawford, *Women and Religion in England, 1500–1720* (London and New York, 1993), p. 143.

72. Bonomi, *Under the Cope of Heaven*, pp. 111–13.

73. Matheson, *Imaginative World*, p. 130.

74. Bonomi, *Under the Cope of Heaven*, p. 113.

75. R. B. Shoemaker, 'The decline of public insult in London 1660–1800', *PP* 169 (Nov. 2000), 97–130, at 128: T. Isaacs, 'The Anglican hierarchy and the reformation of manners 1688–1738', *JEH* 33 (1982), 391–411.

76. Locke, *Second Treatise of Government and a letter concerning Toleration*, quoted in R. A. Houlbrooke, *The English Family 1450–1700* (London and New York, 1984), p. 99.

17 Outcomes

1. A useful perspective is J. F. Bosher, 'The Franco-Catholic danger, 1660–1715', *History* 79 (1994), 5–30.
2. Cunningham and Grell, *Four Horsemen*, p. 95, and see useful discussion of this theme, ibid., Ch. 3.
3. Bosher, 'Franco-Catholic danger', 9.
4. Davies, *God's Playground*, p. 171.
5. P. Cattermole, *Church Bells and Bell-ringing: a Norfolk profile* (Woodbridge, 1990), Ch. 1, especially, pp. 21, 24.
6. Cf. especially R. Fletcher, *The Cross and the Crescent: Christianity and Islam from Muhammad to the Reformation* (London, 2003): in chapter 4 he does offer qualifications to the generally gloomy picture.
7. On medieval discussions of toleration, see C. J. Nederman, *Worlds of Difference: European discourses of toleration c. 1100–c. 1550* (Philadelphia, 2000).
8. Cf. M. Turchetti, 'Religious concord and political tolerance in 16th and 17th century France', *SCJ* 22 (1991), 15–26; M. C. Smith, 'Early French advocates of religious freedom', *SCJ* 25 (1994), 29–51.
9. P. Geyl, *The Revolt of the Netherlands 1555–1609* (London, 2nd edn. 1958), p. 81. For good general discussion of the martyrologists, see B. Gregory: *Salvation at Stake: Christian martyrdom in early modern Europe* (Cambridge, MA, 1999).
10. Murdock, *Calvinism on the Frontier*, pp. 111, 113, 122–3.
11. The phrase is the late Bob Scribner's: 'Preconditions of tolerance and intolerance in sixteenth century Germany', in Grell and Scribner (eds), *Tolerance in the Reformation*, pp. 32–47, at p. 34.
12. J. I. Israel, *The Dutch Republic: its rise, greatness and fall 1477–1806* (Oxford, 1995), pp. 501–5.
13. The calculation is by Brad Gregory: *Salvation at Stake*, p. 6.
14. A. Tallon, *Le Concile de Trente* (Paris, 2000), quoted in review by F. J. Baumgartner, *SCJ* 32 (2001), 1186. On Bugenhagen and Luther, Rummel, *Humanism*, pp. 44, 57.
15. Rummel, *Humanism*, pp. 90–101.
16. D. Stevenson, *The Origins of Freemasonry: Scotland's century, 1590–1710* (Cambridge, 1988), especially p. 76 and Ch. 3.
17. A. Weeks, *Paracelsus: speculative theory and the crisis of the early Reformation* (Albany, NY, 1997), p. 46.
18. K. Biegger, *'De invocatione beatae Mariae Virginis': Paracelsus und die*

Marienverehrung (*Kosmosophie* 6, 1990), especially 26–38, 51, 163, 197, 201, 254–5.

19. C. Webster, *From Paracelsus to Newton: magic and the making of modern science* (Cambridge, 1982), especially, pp. 56–8.

20. H. Hotson, *Johann Heinrich Alsted, 1588–1638: between Renaissance, Reformation and Universal Reform* (Oxford, 2000), especially chapter 5; Hotson, *Paradise Postponed: Johann Heinrich Alsted and the birth of Calvinist millenarianism* (Dordrecht, 2000).

21. Webster, *From Paracelsus to Newton*, pp. 41–2, 68–71; cf. R. S. Westfall, *Never at Rest: a biography of Isaac Newton* (Cambridge, 1980).

22. Yates, *Rosicrucian Enlightenment*, pp. 116–17.

23. Yates, *Rosicrucian Enlightenment*, p. 159; Webster, *From Paracelsus to Newton*, pp. 61–3.

24. M. Peltonen (ed.), *The Cambridge Companion to Bacon* (Cambridge, 1996), pp. 124–5; P. Zagorin, *Francis Bacon* (Princeton, 1998), 91.

25. R. French, *William Harvey's Natural Philosophy* (Cambridge, 1994), pp. 326–7; A. Johns, 'Identity, practice and trust in early modern natural philosophy', *HJ* 42 (1999), 1125–46, at 1130.

26. C. S. Dixon, 'Popular astrology and Lutheran propaganda in Reformation Germany', *History* 84 (1999), 403–18; see also chapter 11, pp. 490–1.

27. Cottret, *Calvin*, pp. 285–6.

28. J. Bossy, *Giordano Bruno and the Embassy Affair* (New Haven and London, 1991), Part II.

29. M. Sharratt, *Galileo: decisive innovator* (Oxford, 1994).

30. T. van Nouhuys, 'Netherlandish heterodoxy in the United Provinces of the early seventeenth century', unpublished paper.

31. On Sephardic Jews at the Collège de Guyenne, see chapter 4, p. 198.

32. I. A. Rashkow, 'Hebrew Bible Translation and the fear of Judaization', *SCJ* 21 (1990), 217–33, especially at 217, 219–20. Cf. H. O. Oberman, 'Discovery of Hebrew and Discrimination against the Jews: the *Veritas Hebraica* as Double-Edged Sword in Renaissance and Reformation', in A. C. Fix and S. Karant-Nunn (eds), *Germania Illustrata: essays on early modern Germany presented to Gerald Strauss* (*SCES* 18, 1992), 19–34, at 23–4.

33. C. Augustijn, *Erasmus: his life, works, and influence* (Toronto, 1992), p. 111.

34. *CWE*, R. A. B. Mynors, D. F. S. Thomson et al. (eds) *Correspondence*, v, p. 347 (punctuation altered), and P. S. Allen, H. M. Allen and H. W. Garrod (eds), *Opus Epistolarum Des. Erasmi Roterodami . . .*, (12 vols,

Oxford 1906–58), iii, no. 798; cf. no. 597, p. 6; no. 629, p. 52. H. M. Pabel, 'Erasmus of Rotterdam and Judaism: a re-evaluation in the light of new evidence', *ARG* 87 (1996), 9–37.

35. R. Marius, *Martin Luther: the Christian between God and death* (Cambridge, MA, and London, 1999), Ch. 22. The texts are *WA*, xi, pp. 314–36 (1523); *WA*, liii, pp. 417–552, 573–648 (1543).

36. R. Po-chia Hsia, *The Myth of Ritual Murder: Jews and magic in Reformation Germany* (New Haven and London, 1988), pp. 136–43.

37. W. Nijenhuis, 'A remarkable historical argumentation in Bucer's "Judenratschlag"'; 'Bucer and the Jews' in Nijenhuis, *Ecclesia Reformata: studies on the Reformation* (2 vols, Leiden, 1972, 1994), i, pp. 23–72: 'so ist der Päpstler und Juden glaube und Religion eben ein ding': ibid., i., p. 48, and cf. p. 52.

38. P. L. Avis, 'Moses and the Magistrate: a study in the rise of Protestant legalism', *JEH* 26 (1975), 149–72, at 163–5.

39. D. S. Katz, *Philosemitism and the Readmission of the Jews to England, 1603–1655* (Oxford, 1982), pp. 212, 220.

40. Murdock, *Calvinism on the Frontier*, p. 113.

41. Z. David, 'Hájek, Dubravius and the Jews: a contrast in sixteenth-century Czech historiography', *SCJ* 27 (1996), 997–1013, at 998, 1009.

42. J. Friedman, 'Unitarians and New Christians in sixteenth-century Europe', *ARG* 81 (1996), 9–37.

43. A. del Col, J. and A. Tedeschi (trans.), *Domenico Scandella known as Menocchio: his trials before the Inquisition (1583–1599)* (Binghamton NY, 1996): the case is vividly though not entirely helpfully analysed in C. Ginzburg, J. and A. Tedeschi (trans.) *The Cheese and the Worms* (London, 1980).

44. J. Edwards, 'Religious faith and doubt in late medieval Spain: Soria circa 1450–1500', *PP* 120 (Aug. 1988), 3–25, at 19.

45. J. Edwards, 'Portugal and the expulsion of the Jews from Spain', in *Medievo hispano: estudios in memoriam del Prof. Derek W. Lomax* (Madrid, 1995), pp. 121–39, at p. 137.

46. B. J. Kaplan, '"Remnants of the Papal Yoke": apathy and opposition in the Dutch Reformation', *SCJ* 25 (1994), 653–68.

47. D. M. Swetschinski, *Reluctant Cosmopolitans: the Portuguese Jews of seventeenth-century Amsterdam* (London, 2000).

48. J. I. Israel, *Radical Enlightenment: philosophy and the making of modernity 1650–1750* (Oxford, 2001), pp. 159–74.

49. J. Overhoff, 'The theology of Thomas Hobbes's *Leviathan*', *JEH* 51 (2000), 527–55.

50. Israel, *Radical Enlightenment*, pp. 695–700.

51. R. H. Popkin, *Isaac la Peyrère (1596–1676): his life, work and influence* (Leiden, 1987).

52. Katz, *Philosemitism and the Readmission of the Jews to England*.

53. D. Berman, *A History of Atheism in Britain from Hobbes to Russell* (London, 1988), pp. 35–7.

54. A. C. Fix, 'Radical religion and the age of reason', in Fix and Karant-Nunn (eds), *Germania Illustrata*, 35–55, at 54; Fix, *Prophecy and Reason: the Dutch Collegiants in the early Enlightenment* (Princeton, 1991).

55. H. D. Rack, *Reasonable Enthusiast: John Wesley and the rise of Methodism* (London, 1989).

56. A masterly gathering of all these strands is W. R. Ward, *The Protestant Evangelical Awakening* (Cambridge, 1992).

57. Currently reliable sources of recent statistics apart from those compiled (generally with integrity) by mainstream Churches and denominations are P. Briereley (ed.), *The World churches handbook: based on the Operation world database by Patrick Johnstone, WEC International, 1993* (London, 1997); P. Brierley and H. Wraight (eds), *Atlas of world Christianity: 2000 years* (Alresford, 1998).

58. C. Allen, *The Buddha and the Sahibs: the men who discovered India's lost religion* (London, 2002).

59. H. Küng, *Judaism* (London, 1992), p. 24.

60. Matheson, *Imaginative World*, p. 81.

61. Herbert McCabe made this observation to me late in an evening of wine, whiskey and argument.

62. Arthur Golding's preface to *Beneficio di Cristo*, 1573: quoted in M. A. Overell, *Notes and Queries* new series 25 (Oct 1978), 425.

Further Reading

This section is designed to provide general introductory reading or classic works on various themes and areas of the Reformation and Counter-Reformation. Detailed reading on particular topics is cited in the endnotes relating to each chapter, often in works in languages other than English, and those references are not necessarily repeated here; the same applies to books listed in the table of abbreviations. User-friendly introductory works are marked with an *asterisk.

GENERAL

E. Cameron, *The European Reformation* (Oxford, 1991)

*O. Chadwick, *The Reformation* (London, 1964)

O. Chadwick, *The Early Reformation on the Continent* (Oxford, 2001)

F. L. Cross and E. A. Livingstone (eds), *The Oxford Dictionary of the Christian Church* (3rd revised edition, Oxford, 1995)

E. Eisenstein, *The Printing Revolution in early modern Europe* (Cambridge, 1983)

M. Greengrass (ed.), *Conquest and Coalescence: the shaping of the state in early modern Europe* (London, 1991) [contains local case studies]

H. J. Hillerbrand (ed.), *The Oxford Encyclopaedia of the Reformation* (4 vols, Oxford, 1996)

C. Lindberg (ed.), *The European Reformations Sourcebook* (Oxford, 2000) [documents]

*A. E. McGrath, *Reformation Thought. An Introduction* (3rd edn, Oxford, 1999)

W. R. Naphy (ed.), *Documents on the Continental Reformation* (Basingstoke, 1996) [documents]

*A. Pettegree (ed.), *The Early Reformation in Europe* (Cambridge, 1992) [contains local case studies]

*A. Pettegree (ed.), *The Reformation World* (London, 2000) [contains local case studies]

*B. Scribner, R. Porter and M. Teich (eds), *The Reformation in National Context* (Cambridge, 1994) [contains local case studies]

*D. C. Steinmetz, *Reformers in the Wings: from Geiler von Kayserberg to Theodore Beza* (2nd edn, Oxford, 2001) [contains case studies]

*J. D. Tracy, *Europe's Reformations 1450–1650* (Lanham and New York, 2000)

The medieval background

*J. Bossy, *Christianity in the West 1400–1700* (Oxford, 1985)

E. Duffy, *The Stripping of the Altars: traditional religion in England 1400–1580* (New Haven and London, 1992)

B. Hamilton, *Religion in the medieval West* (London, 1986)

R. I. Moore, *The Formation of a Persecuting Society: power and deviance in Western Europe 950–1250* (Oxford, 1987)

Humanism and Erasmus

*P. Burke, *The Renaissance* (Basingstoke, 1987)

*J. Huizinga, *Erasmus of Rotterdam* (London, 1952)

*J. K. McConica, *Erasmus* (Oxford, 1991)

*R. Porter and M. Teich (eds), *The Renaissance in National Context* (Cambridge, 1992) [contains local case studies]

Luther

*A. G. Dickens, *Martin Luther and the Reformation* (London, 1967)

B. Lohse, *Martin Luther: an introduction to his life and work* (Edinburgh, 1986)

R. Marius, *Martin Luther: the Christian between God and death* (Cambridge, MA, 1999)

Zürich, Calvin and the Reformed Tradition

B. Cottret, *Calvin: a biography* (Grand Rapids and Edinburgh, 2000)

*U. Gäbler, *Huldrych Zwingli: his life and work* (Edinburgh, 1986)

*A. Pettegree, A. Duke and G. Lewis (eds), *Calvinism in Europe, 1540–1620* (Cambridge, 1994) [contains local case studies]

G. R. Potter, *Zwingli* (Cambridge, 1976)

*M. Prestwich (ed.), *International Calvinism 1548–1715* (Oxford, 1985) [contains local case studies]

F. Wendel, *Calvin: the origins and development of his religious thought* (London, 1963)

Counter-Reformation

*R. Bireley, *The Refashioning of Catholicism, 1450–1700* (Basingstoke, 1999)

*M. Greengrass, *The French Reformation* (Oxford, 1987)

*M. D. W. Jones, *The Counter Reformation: religion and society in early modern Europe* (Cambridge, 1995)

J. W. O'Malley, *The First Jesuits* (Cambridge, MA, 1993)

*M. A. Mullett, *The Catholic Reformation* (London, 1999)

R. Po-Chia Hsia, *The World of Catholic Renewal, 1540–1770* (Cambridge, 1998)

Radical religion

*H-J. Goertz, *The Anabaptists* (London, 1996)

H-J. Goertz (ed.), *Profiles of Radical Reformers: biographical sketches from Thomas Muntzer to Paracelsus* (Ann Arbor, MI, 1982)

*M. Mullett, *Radical Religious Movements in Early Modern Europe* (London, 1980)

G. H. Williams, *The Radical Reformation* (3rd edn, Kirksville, MO, 1992)

World expansion

*P. Bonomi, *Under the Cope of Heaven: religion, society and politics in Colonial America* (New York and Oxford, 1986)

G. V. Scammell, *The First Imperial Age: European Overseas Expansion c. 1400–1715* (London, 1989)

A. D. Wright, *The Counter-Reformation: Catholic Europe and the non-Catholic World* (London, 1982)

PARTICULAR REGIONS

(see also above for local case studies)

Central Europe (the Habsburg lands)

K. Maag (ed.), *The Reformation in Eastern and Central Europe* (Aldershot, 1997)

P. S. Wandycz, *The Price of Freedom: a history of east central Europe from the Middle Ages to the present* (London, 1992) [also useful for Poland]

England and Wales

*S. Doran and C. Durston, *Princes, pastors and people: the Church and religion in England, 1500–1700* (revised edn, London, 2002)

D. Cressy and L. A. Ferrell (eds), *Religion and Society in Early Modern England: a sourcebook* (London, 1996) [documents]

*D. MacCulloch, *The Later Reformation in England 1547–1603* (2nd edn, Basingstoke, 2000)

*J. Spurr, *The Restoration Church of England, 1646–1689* (New Haven and London, 1991)

France

J. Garrison, *A History of sixteenth-century France, 1438–1589* (Basingstoke, 1995)

*M. Greengrass, *The French Reformation* (Oxford, 1987)

H. Phillips, *Church and Culture in 17th century France* (Cambridge, 1997)

Germany

*C. S. Dixon, *The Reformation in Germany* (Oxford, 2002)

*P. H. Wilson, *The Holy Roman Empire, 1495–1806* (Basingstoke, 1999)

*R. W. Scribner, *The German Reformation* (Basingstoke, 1986)

Iberia

*J. Edwards, *The Spanish Inquisition* (Stroud, 1999)

H. Kamen, *Inquisition and Society in Spain: in the Sixteenth and Seventeenth Centuries* (London, 1985)

*H. Rawlings, *Church, Religion and Society in Early Modern Spain* (Basingstoke, 2002)

Ireland

A. Ford, *The Protestant Reformation in Ireland, 1590–1641* (2nd edn, Dublin, 1997)

R. Gillespie, *Devoted People: belief and religion in early modern Ireland* (Dublin, 1997)

Italy

*C. F. Black, *Early Modern Italy: a social history* (London, 2001)

S. Caponetto, *The Protestant Reformation in sixteenth century Italy* (SCES 43, 1998)

*D. Hay and J. Law, *Italy in the Age of the Renaissance, 1380–1530* (London, 1989)

Netherlands

*G. Darby (ed.), *The Origins and Development of the Dutch Revolt* (London and New York, 2001)

J. Israel, *The Dutch Republic: its rise, greatness and fall, 1477–1806* (Oxford, 1995)

Poland-Lithuania

N. Davies, *God's Playground: a History of Poland. 1: the origins to 1795* (Oxford, 1981)

*J. Kłoczowski, *A History of Polish Christianity* (Cambridge, 2000)

Scandinavia

O. P. Grell (ed.), *The Scandinavian Reformation: from evangelical movement to institutionalisation of reform* (Cambridge, 1994)

S. P. Oakley, *War and Peace in the Baltic 1560–1790* (London, 1992)

Scotland

*I. B. Cowan, *The Scottish Reformation: church and society in 16th century Scotland* (London, 1982)
M. Todd, *The Culture of Protestantism in Early Modern Scotland* (New Haven and London, 2002)

South-east Europe

J. McCarthy, *The Ottoman Turks: an introductory history to 1923* (London, 1997)
G. Murdock, *Calvinism on the Frontier 1600–1660: international Calvinism and the Reformed Church in Hungary and Transylvania* (Oxford, 2000)

PARTICULAR THEMES

Art and architecture

*J. Dillenberger, *Style and Content in Christian Art* (New York, 1965)
*A. Graham-Dixon, *Renaissance* (London, 1999)
C. Harbison, *The Mirror of the Artist: Northern Renaissance Art in its Historical Context* (New York, 1995)
J. F. White, *Protestant Worship and Church Architecture* (New York and Oxford, 1964)

Iconoclasm

M. Aston, *England's Iconoclasts I. Laws against images* (Oxford, 1988)
C. M. N. Eire, *War against the Idols: the reformation of worship from Erasmus to Calvin* (Cambridge, 1986)
S. Michalski, *The Reformation and the Visual Arts: the Protestant image question in western and eastern Europe* (London, 1993)

Judaism

*J. Edwards, *The Jews in Christian Europe, 1400–1700* (London and New York, 1991)

J. Israel, *European Jewry in the age of mercantilism, 1550–1750* (3rd edn, Oxford, 1998)

N. Roth, *Conversos, inquisition and the expulsion of the Jews from Spain* (Madison, WI, 1995)

Mentalities and society

A. Cunningham and O. P. Grell, *The Four Horsemen of the Apocalypse: religion, war, famine and death in Reformation Europe* (Cambridge, 2000)

*H. Kamen, *European Society 1500–1700* (London, 1985)

P. Spierenburg, *The Broken Spell: a cultural and anthropological history of Pre-Industrial Europe* (Basingstoke, 1991)

Science and natural philosophy

J. Hedley Brooke, *Science and Religion: some historical perspectives* (Cambridge, 1991)

*J. Henry, *The Scientific Revolution and the Origins of Modern Science* (2nd edn, Basingstoke, 2002)

D. C. Lindberg and R. S. Westman (eds), *Reappraisals of the Scientific Revolution* (Cambridge, 1990)

Sexuality and the family

S. Ozment, *Ancestors: the loving family in old Europe* (Cambridge, MA, 2001)

*W. R. Naphy, *Sex Crimes from Renaissance to Enlightenment* (Stroud, 2002)

M. Wiesner-Hanks, *Christianity and Sexuality in the Early Modern World: regulating desire, reforming practice* (London, 2000)

Tolerance and persecution

B. S. Gregory, *Salvation at Stake: Christian martyrdom in early modern Europe* (Cambridge, MA, 1999)

O. Grell and B. Scribner (eds), *Tolerance and Intolerance in the European Reformation* (Cambridge, 1996)

P. Zagorin, *Ways of Lying: dissimulation, persecution and conformity in early modern Europe* (Cambridge, MA, 1990)

Witchcraft

J. Barry, M. Hester and G. Roberts (eds), *Witchcraft in Early Modern Europe: studies in culture and belief* (Cambridge, 1996)

L. Roper, *Oedipus and the Devil: witchcraft, sexuality and religion in early modern Europe* (London, 1994)

*G. Scarre, *Witchcraft and Magic in 16th and 17th century Europe* (Basingstoke, 1987)

Worship

*C. Jones et al. (eds), *The Study of Liturgy* (revised edn, London, 1992)

S. Karant-Nunn, *The Reformation of Ritual: an interpretation of early modern Germany* (London, 1997)

E. Muir, *Ritual in Early Modern Europe* (Cambridge, 1997)

Index

Popes are cross-referenced from their entry under their birth-name to their papal name, s.v. Rome; monarchs are gathered under their principal territory. Monarchs and Popes have their birth-date followed by the date of their accession to the throne, followed by their date of death. Members of European nobility are indexed under their surnames. Those who have been declared saints by one or other Christian Church are indexed either under their first names or their surnames. Dates are CE unless otherwise stated.

INDEX

Reformed Protestantism – cont.
590, 595–7, 658, 664–6, 697; in
Moldavia 266–7; in North America
176, 378, 390–91, 533–45, 590, 604,
664–6; in Poland-Lithuania 263–6,
340–44, 355, 670; in Scandinavia
366–7; in Scotland 291–5, 319–20,
356, 373, 378–82, 398, 459–60,
514–15, 521–4, 557–8, 571–3, 577,
584, 586–7, 590, 596–606, 636; in
Switzerland 136–50, 155, 157, 159,
166, 174–9, 196, 208, 242, 244, 249,
251, 253, 255, 261, 273, 302, 354–5,
384, 448, 460, 502, 590; and witchcraft
562, 568–75
  see also Belgic Confession; Bucer, Martin;
  Bullinger, Heinrich; Calvin, John;
  Calvinism; consistories; discipline;
  England; iconoclasm; Geneva;
  Germany; Heidelberg; Huguenots;
  Hungary; Łaski, Jan; metrical psalms;
  Poland-Lithuania; Puritanism; Scotland;
  Second Reformation; Strassburg;
  Switzerland; Transylvania; Vermigli,
  Peter Martyr; Zürich
Regalism, Polish 362
Regensburg (Ratisbon) 271, 489; Our Lady
  of 19, 142; Colloquy of 230–31,
  270
registers, parish 211, 636
Reichsverweser 489
Reims 585
relics 18–19, 102, 117, 329, 454–5
Remonstrants, Dutch 377–8, 485, 495, 514
  see also Arminianism
Renaissance 76–9, 490, 612, 621, 679–80,
  688–9
  see also humanism
repentance: see penance
Requesens, Luis de Zuniga y (d. 1576) 411
resistance, right of 240, 295, 453, 469, 482,
  673
Restitution, Edict of (1629) 497–8, 737
Reuchlin, Johannes (1454/5–1522) 85–6,
  91, 104, 689
reunion of Churches 296–7, 313, 354–5,
  363–6, 489, 682
  see also Augsburg; Brest; Poissy;
  Regensburg

revival 416, 603–4; Evangelical 511, 544–5,
  562, 586, 603–4, 700
  see also Great Awakening; 'holy fairs'
Rhaetian Republic: see Graubünden
Rhegius, Urbanus (Urban Rieger;
  1489–1541) 211
rhetoric 77, 507
Rhine, River 97, 179
Rhineland 179, 600
Rhode Island 539, 541–42
Rhodes 54, 330
Ribadaneira, Pedro de (1526–1611) 642
Ricci, Matteo (1552–1610) 434
Richelieu, Armand Jean du Plessis
  (1585–1642) 472, 482, 499–500
Ridley, Nicholas (c. 1500–55) 10, 24, 26,
  629
Ridolfi, Roberto (1531–1612) 333–4
Riedemann, Peter (1506–56) 659
Rieger, Urban: see Rhegius
Riga 155, 361, 658
Rinck, Melchior (d. 1493) 160
Robespierre, Maximilien (1758–94) 698
Rochefoucauld, François La (1558–1645)
  475
Rocco, Antonio (1576–1653) 621, 625
Roger, Pierre: see Rome, Popes: Clement VI
Rogers, Richard (?1550–1618) 536
Rogerus, Servatius 98, 102, 723
Roman Catholicism 38, 213–26, 318–46,
  336, 483, 507–8, 510, 518, 522–4,
  527, 530–32, 534–5, 542–3, 556,
  571–5, 603, 656, 658, 661, 668–9,
  673–5, 677, 679, 689–91, 701–2, 706;
  and Bible 406, 447, 482, 584–5, 689
  see also Counter-Reformation; Old
  Catholic Church; Uniate Churches
Rome 17, 28, 35, 77, 79, 91, 93, 115–16,
  217, 219, 222, 231, 279, 300–301,
  331, 401, 404–5, 443, 451, 480, 565,
  631–2, 635, 639, 686, 721; Collegium
  Germanicum 448; English College 404,
  Plates 12, 13; Sack (1527) 173, 213;
  Gregorian University 641; St Peter's
  Basilica 42, 120–21, 322, 401, Plate 11;
  Scots College 381; Sistine Chapel 278;
  Vatican 322, 334, 408, 496, Plate 11
  Empire and Emperors 106–7, 672, 694,
  703

822